V.D. Novikov
L.L. Pogrebnaya
V.M. Borsch

Dictionary of Physics

Wörterbuch Physik

V.D. Novikov
L.L. Pogrebnaya
V.M. Borsch

Dictionary of Physics

English • German • French • Russian

Wörterbuch Physik

Englisch • Deutsch • Französisch • Russisch

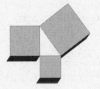

1995
Verlag Harri Deutsch
Thun und Frankfurt am Main

V. D. Novikov
L. L. Pogrebnaya
V. M. Borsch

Dictionary of Physics
Wörterbuch Physik

Erhältlich als Hardcover-Ausgabe (ISBN 3-8171-1450-8)
und als kartonierte Studentenausgabe (ISBN 3-8171-1449-4)

Ответственный за выпуск
ЗАХАРОВА Г.В.

Ведущий редактор
ПАНКИН А.В.

Редакторы
ВАСИЛЬЕВА А.Ю.
ГВОЗДЕВА Т.Ф.
КОЛПАКОВА Г.М.
МОКИНА Н.Р.
УРВАНЦЕВА А.И.

Оригинал-макет
НЕЧИПОРЕНКО К.А.
МИТРОВИЧ В.Л.

ISBN 3-8171-1450-8 (geb.)
ISBN 3-8171-1449-4 (kart.)

1995
© Copyright by RUSSO
© Copyright by NAUKA
Alleinvertriebsrecht Verlag Harri Deutsch, Thun und Frankfurt am Main
Druck: Fuldaer Verlagsanstalt GmbH
Printed in Germany

PUBLISHER'S PREFACE

The Dictionary of Physics (English-German-French-Russian) is published by the "Russo Ltd" firm with support of the "Nauka" Exhibition Complex of the Russian Exhibition Center.

The purpose of this Dictionary is to help both specialists and non-specialists interested in modern physics to read and translate physical texts or to find an equivalent term in one of the four languages named above. The Dictionary contains 10 943 terms.

In compiling the Dictionary the authors used a wide range of encyclopedias, reference books, monographs and periodicals published in the USA, Great Britain, Germany, France and Russia.

With a little time spent, the user is able to find the needed equivalent in one of the four languages in the German, French and Russian indexes which are placed at the end of the book.

The authors and the "Russo Ltd" firm would be glad to receive any possible remarks and suggestions from the readers. These should be sent to the "Russo Ltd" firm, Leninski Prospect 15, office No. 325, Moscow 117922, Russia.

Verlag Harri Deutsch
Gräfstraße 47/51
60486 Frankfurt am Main
Fax: 0 69-7 07 37 39
E-mail (Internet): verlag@harri-deutsch.de

FOREWORD

Physics is a science studying the simplest and at the same time the most general laws of natural phenomena, properties and structure of matter and its motion. Therefore physical ideas are the basis of all natural sciences.

This Dictionary includes terms of all branches of physics-both classical and modern ones, such as theoretical physics, solid state and semiconductor physics, optics, spectroscopy, holography, laser physics, radiophysics and electronics, acoustics and ultrasonics, plasma physics and fluid dynamics, nuclear and high-energy physics, high-temperature physics and thermodynamics, astrophysics, cosmology and space research, solar-terrestrial physics, physical instruments, units and measurements. Taking into account comparatively small volume of the Dictionary (the comprehensive dictionary of contemporary physics can include more than 100.000 terms) authors tried to choose the most important terms.

The borders between physics and the other natural sciences often cannot be drawn exactly. Methods of physical research play the leading part in all natural sciences and determine their achievements in many cases. Not without reason a number of related sciences was formed, such as biophysics, geophysics, physical chemistry and chemical physics, atmospheric physics, physics of the ocean and so on. Terminology of these sciences as well as some general scientific terms are also included to a greater or lesser extent.

Physics is an exact science; it studies quantitative relations formulated in mathematical expressions. Therefore some mathematical terms are included.

A wide range of readers will find this Dictionary useful: scientists, engineers, professors, teachers and students, science editors, translators and interpreters. It can be used as a reference or a supplementary book in universities, colleges and schools by students studying English scientific language because English at present is widely used at physical conferences, symposia, schools and exhibitions all over the world. Thus the Dictionary will help personal contacts between the scientists living and working in different countries.

Physics is a foundation of new technologies. The application of physical principles serves as a practically inexhaustible source of new ideas for electrical and power engineering, radio engineering, electronics, communication methods, material processing, medicine and so on. The achievements of physics were a decisive factor of progress in semiconductor industry, microelectronics, computer hardware, nuclear power engineering and nuclear weapons, space research, military technologies. Physics was the first science which became one of the elements of national prestige. The state of physical investigations, their scale and rate of progress belong to the signs determining the nation power. Therefore the Dictionary can be used by specialists, managers and administrators in industry and government, politicians, businessmen, science publishers, journalists and simply by people with an inquisitive mind.

Work at the Dictionary was initiated by Nobel Prize winner, academician A.Prokhorov. The author, Dr. V.Novikov worked more than 25 years in Lebedev Physical Institute, Institute of General Physics and Department of General Physics and Astronomy of the Russian Academy of Sciences and was the coordinator of national programs on laser physics and nonlinear optics, radiophysics, electronics, holography. The list of his scientific works includes papers in microwave electronics, sea wave dynamics, hyperacoustics, laser physics, plasma physics, radiophysics and solar-terrestrial physics. That gave him the possibility to approach the material selection from extensive positions.

The book is prepared under the sponsorship of the "Nauka" Exhibition Complex (Science) which is a part of the Russian Exhibition Center. By a happy accident (but possibly it was God's will) the director of the "Nauka" Exhibition Complex Mr. E.Ostrovski is also the physicist who graduated from the Moscow Physical and Technical Institute, the best physical university in Russia. The "Nauka" Exhibition Complex is engaged not only in organizing scientific exhibitions in Russia and in the other countries. A broad approach to the exhibition activity as an important channel of information exchange and human contacts is typical for the Complex. With this book the Complex starts the program of publishing dictionaries to expand and facilitate contacts between the specialists of various countries.

G. Mesyats
Academician, Vice President
of the Russian Academy of Sciences

HOW TO USE THE DICTIONARY

All leading English terms are arranged in the dictionary in alphabetical order, compound terms being regarded as one word, e.g.:

> strange attractor
> strangeness
> strange particles.

Each entry of the dictionary consists of the English, German, French and Russian terms arranged in a column. References from one term to another are made with reference words *see*. All German, French and Russian terms are supplied with the indication of their gender (*m* for the masculine, *f* for the feminine, *n* for the neuter) and, when necessary, with the mark *pl* (for the plural). All the leading English terms are numbered within each letter of the alphabet to enable the user to find the necessary English, German, French or Russian equivalent by using the indexes. Thus, a dictionary entry looks as this:

N106 *e* neutron capture
   d Neutroneneinfang *m*
   f capture *f* des neutrons
   r захват *m* нейтронов

Different meanings of terms are divided by figures, variants of close meaning — by semi-colons, and synonymous meanings — by commas.

Explanations are put in parentheses and typed in italics.

To find the equivalents for German, French or Russian terms, the user should refer to the indexes at the end of the dictionary, where each term is supplied with an indication (letter and figures), corresponding to that of the leading English term.

Personal names have been widely used for designating physical theories and phenomena, so a sufficient number of name entries have been included. The use of apostrophes and possessive case inflections in such entries has been avoided for simplification, e. g.:

> Newton law (not Newton's law)

A

A1
  e Abbe refractometer
  d Abbe-Refraktometer *n*, Abbesches Refraktometer *n*
  f réfractomètre *m* d'Abbe
  r рефрактометр *m* Аббе

A2
  e aberration
  d Aberration *f*; Abbildungsfehler *m*
  f 1. aberration *f* 2. défaut *m* de l'image
  r 1. аберрация *f* 2. искажение *n*

A3
  e aberration of light
  d Lichtaberration *f*, Aberration *f* des Fixsternlichts
  f aberration *f* de la lumière
  r аберрация *f* света

A4
  e aberrations of electron lenses
  d Aberrationen *f pl* der Elektronenlinsen
  f aberrations *f pl* des lentilles électroniques
  r аберрации *f pl* электронных линз, электронно-оптические аберрации *f pl*

A5
  e aberrations of optical systems
  d Aberrationsfehler *m pl* der optischen Systeme
  f aberrations *f pl* des systèmes optiques
  r аберрации *f pl* оптических систем

A6
  e ablation
  d Ablation *f*
  f ablation *f*
  r абляция *f*

A7
  e abnormal dispersion *see* anomalous dispersion

A8
  e abrasion
  d Abrieb *m*
  f abrasion *f*
  r истирание *n*

A9
  e abrasive
  d Schleifmittel *n*
  f abrasif *m*
  r абразив *m*, абразивный материал *m*

A10
  e abrasive wear
  d Verschleiß *m*; Gleitverschleiß *m*
  f usure *f* abrasive
  r абразивный износ *m*

A11
  e Abrikosov lattice
  d Abrikosov-Gitter *n*
  f réseau *m* d'Abrikossov
  r решётка *f* вихрей Абрикосова

A12
  e abscissa
  d Abszisse *f*
  f abscisse *f*
  r абсцисса *f*

A13
  e absolute error
  d absoluter Fehler *m*
  f erreur *f* absolue
  r абсолютная погрешность *f*

A14
  e absolute humidity
  d absolute Feuchtigkeit *f*
  f humidité *f* absolue
  r абсолютная влажность *f*

A15
  e absolute instability
  d absolute Instabilität *f*, absolute Labilität *f*
  f instabilité *f* absolue
  r абсолютная неустойчивость *f*

A16
  e absolute instability criterion
  d absolutes Instabilitätskriterium *n*, absolutes Labilitätskriterium *n*
  f critère *m* d'instabilité absolue
  r критерий *m* абсолютной неустойчивости

A17
  e absolute measurement
  d absolute Messung *f*
  f mesure *f* absolue
  r абсолютное измерение *n*

A18
  e absolute permeability
  d absolute Permeabilität *f*
  f perméabilité *f* absolue
  r абсолютная магнитная проницаемость *f*

A19
  e absolute permittivity
  d absolute Dielektrizitätskonstante *f*, Permittivität *f* des Vakuums, Permittivität *f*
  f permittivité *f* absolue
  r абсолютная диэлектрическая проницаемость *f*

A20
  e absolute radiator
  d absoluter Strahler *m*
  f radiateur *m* absolu
  r абсолютный излучатель *m*

A21
  e absolute stellar magnitude

d absolute Helligkeit *f*, absolute Größenklasse *f (von Sternen)*
f magnitude *f* stellaire absolue
r абсолютная звёздная величина *f*

A22 *e* absolute temperature
d absolute Temperatur *f*
f température *f* absolue
r абсолютная температура *f*

A23 *e* absolute time
d absolute Zeit *f*
f temps *m* absolu
r абсолютное время *n*

A24 *e* absolute units
d absolute Einheiten *f pl*
f unités *f pl* absolues
r абсолютные единицы *f pl*

A25 *e* absolute value
d Absolutwert *m*, Absolutbetrag *m*
f valeur *f* réelle, valeur *f* absolue
r абсолютная величина *f*, модуль *m*

A26 *e* absolute zero (*of temperature*)
d absoluter Nullpunkt *m*, absoluter Temperaturnullpunkt *m*
f zéro *m* absolu (*de la température*)
r абсолютный нуль *m* температуры

A27 *e* absorbance
d dekadischer Logarithmus *m* des Absorptionsvermögens
f absorbance *f*
r логарифм *m* коэффициента поглощения

A28 *e* absorbate
d Absorbat *n*, absorbierter Stoff *m*
f absorbat *m*
r абсорбат *m*, абсорбируемое вещество *n*

A29 *e* absorbed dose
d absorbierte Dosis *f*
f dose *f* absorbée
r поглощённая доза *f*

A30 *e* absorbed electron image
d Abbildung *f* in absorbierten Elektronen
f image *f* en électrons absorbés
r изображение *n* в поглощённых электронах

A31 *e* absorbed quantum
d absorbiertes Quant *n*
f quantum *m* absorbé
r поглощённый квант *m*

A32 *e* absorbed radiation
d absorbierte Strahlung *f*
f radiation *f* absorbée, rayonnement *m* absorbé
r поглощённое излучение *n*

A33 *e* absorbent
d Absorbens *n*, Absorptionsmittel *n*, absorbierender Stoff *m*
f absorbant *m*
r поглотитель *m*, абсорбент *m*

A34 *e* absorber
d Absorber *m*, Absorptionsapparat *m*
f absorbeur *m*
r поглотитель *m*, абсорбер *m*

A35 *e* absorbing ability
d Absorptionsvermögen *n*
f pouvoir *m* absorbant
r поглощательная способность *f*

A36 *e* absorptance
d Absorptionszahl *f*, Absorptionsgrad *m*, Absorptionskoeffizient *m*
f facteur *m* d'absorption, indice *m* d'absorption
r коэффициент *m* поглощения

A37 *e* absorptiometer
d Absorptiometer *n*
f absorptiomètre *m*
r абсорбциометр *m*, измеритель *m* поглощающей способности

A38 *e* absorption
d Absorption *f*
f absorption *f*
r абсорбция *f*; поглощение *n*

A39 *e* absorption analysis
d Absorptionsspektralanalyse *f*, Absorptionsanalyse *f*
f analyse *f* spectrale absorptive
r абсорбционный анализ *m*

A40 *e* absorption band
d Absorptionsbande *f*
f bande *f* d'absorption
r полоса *f* поглощения

A41 *e* absorption cell
d Absorptionszelle *f*
f cellule *f* d'absorption
r поглощающая ячейка *f*

A42 *e* absorption coefficient *see* absorptance

A43 *e* absorption cross-section
d Absorptionsquerschnitt *m*
f section *f* d'absorption
r сечение *n* поглощения

A44 *e* absorption curve
d Absorptionskurve *f*
f courbe *f* d'absorption
r кривая *f* поглощения

A45 *e* absorption edge
d Absorptionskante *f*
f bord *m* d'absorption
r край *m* полосы поглощения

A46 *e* absorption factor *see* absorptance

A47   *e*   **absorption intensity**
  d   Absorptionsintensität *f*, Intensität *f* der Absorption
  f   intensité *f* d'absorption
  r   интенсивность *f* поглощения

A48   *e*   **absorption jump**
  d   Absorptionssprung *m*
  f   discontinuité *f* d'absorption
  r   скачок *m* поглощения

A49   *e*   **absorption length**
  d   Absorptionslänge *f*
  f   longueur *f* d'absorption
  r   длина *f* поглощения

A50   *e*   **absorption line**
  d   Absorptionslinie *f*
  f   raie *f* d'absorption
  r   линия *f* поглощения (*в спектре*)

A51   *e*   **absorption loss, absorption losses**
  d   Absorptionsverluste *m pl*
  f   pertes *f pl* par absorption
  r   потери *f pl* на поглощение

A52   *e*   **absorption measurement**
  d   Absorptionsmessung *f*
  f   mesure *f* de l'absorption
  r   измерение *n* поглощения

A53   *e*   **absorption meter** *see* **absorptiometer**

A54   *e*   **absorption spectrophotometry**
  d   Absorptions-Spektralphotometrie *f*
  f   spectrophotométrie *f* d'absorption
  r   абсорбционная спектрофотометрия *f*

A55   *e*   **absorption spectroscopy**
  d   Absorptionsspektroskopie *f*
  f   spectroscopie *f* d'absorption
  r   абсорбционная спектроскопия *f*

A56   *e*   **absorption spectrum**
  d   Absorptionsspektrum *n*
  f   spectre *m* d'absorption
  r   спектр *m* поглощения, абсорбционный спектр *m*

A57   *e*   **absorptive power**
  d   Absorptionsvermögen *n*
  f   pouvoir *m* absorbant
  r   поглощательная способность *f*

A58   *e*   **absorptivity**
  d   Absorptionsvermögen *n*
  f   absorptivité *f*
  r   удельный коэффициент *m* поглощения, коэффициент *m* поглощения, поглощательная способность *f*

A59   *e*   **abundance of isotopes**
  d   Häufigkeit *f* von Isotopen
  f   teneur *f* des éléments isotopiques
  r   распространённость *f* изотопов

A60   *e*   **a. c.** *see* **alternating current**

A61   *e*   **accelerated motion**
  d   beschleunigte Bewegung *f*
  f   mouvement *m* accéléré
  r   ускоренное движение *n*

A62   *e*   **accelerating field**
  d   Beschleunigungsfeld *n*, beschleunigendes Feld *n*
  f   champ *m* d'accélération
  r   ускоряющее поле *n*

A63   *e*   **accelerating-storage complex**
  d   Beschleunigungsspeicherkomplex *m*
  f   ensemble *m* accélérateur-accumulateur
  r   ускорительно-накопительный комплекс *m*

A64   *e*   **accelerating tube**
  d   Beschleunigungsrohr *n*
  f   tube *m* d'accélération
  r   ускоряющая трубка *f*

A65   *e*   **accelerating voltage**
  d   Beschleunigungsspannung *f*
  f   tension *f* accélératrice, tension *f* d'accélération
  r   ускоряющее напряжение *n*

A66   *e*   **acceleration**
  d   Beschleunigung *f*
  f   accélération *f*
  r   ускорение *n*

A67   *e*   **acceleration mechanism**
  d   Beschleunigungsmechanismus *m*
  f   mécanisme *m* d'accélération
  r   механизм *m* ускорения

A68   *e*   **acceleration of free fall, acceleration of gravity**
  d   Fallbeschleunigung *f*, Erdbeschleunigung *f*
  f   accélération *f* de la pesanteur
  r   ускорение *n* свободного падения

A69   *e*   **accelerator**
  d   Beschleuniger *m*, Teilchenbeschleuniger *m*
  f   accélérateur *m*, accélérateur *m* de particules
  r   ускоритель *m*, ускоритель *m* заряженных частиц

A70   *e*   **accelerator channel**
  d   Beschleunigungskanal *m*
  f   canal *m* accélérateur
  r   ускорительный канал *m*

A71   *e*   **accelerator target**
  d   Beschleunigertarget *n*
  f   cible *f* d'accélérateur
  r   мишень *f* ускорителя

A72   *e*   **accelerometer**
  d   Beschleunigungsmesser *m*

    f accéléromètre *m*
    r акселерометр *m*

A73 *e* acceptor
    d Akzeptor *m*; Akzeptorverunreinigung *f*
    f accepteur *m*
    r акцептор *m*; акцепторная примесь *f*

A74 *e* acceptor atom
    d Akzeptoratom *n*
    f atome *m* accepteur
    r примесный атом *m*,
       атом-акцептор *m*

A75 *e* acceptor center
    d Akzeptorzentrum *n*
    f centre *m* accepteur
    r акцепторный центр *m*

A76 *e* acceptor level
    d Akzeptorniveau *n*, Akzeptorterm *m*
    f niveau *m* accepteur
    r акцепторный уровень *m*

A77 *e* accidental count
    d Zufallszählung *f*
    f coup *m* accidentel
    r случайный отсчёт *m*

A78 *e* accident dose
    d Havariedosis *f*
    f dose *f* d'avarie
    r аварийная доза *f*

A79 *e* accommodation
    d Akkommodation *f*
    f accommodation *f*
    r аккомодация *f*

A80 *e* accommodation coefficient
    d Akkommodationskoeffizient *m*
    f coefficient *m* d'accommodation
    r коэффициент *m* аккомодации

A81 *e* accommodation of the eye
    d Akkommodation *f* des Auges
    f accommodation *f* de l'œil
    r аккомодация *f* глаза

A82 *e* accreting white dwarf
    d akkrezierender weißer Zwerg *m*
    f naine *f* blanche à accrétion
    r аккреционный белый карлик *m*

A83 *e* accretion
    d Akkretion *f*, Zunahme *f*, Zuwachs *m*;
       Wachsen *n*
    f accrétion *f*
    r аккреция *f*

A84 *e* accretion disk
    d Akkretionsscheibe *f*
    f disque *m* d'accrétion
    r аккреционный диск *m*

A85 *e* accumulation
    d Akkumulation *f*; Anhäufung *f*

    f accumulation *f*
    r накопление *n*; аккумулирование *n*

A86 *e* accumulator
    d Akkumulator *m*; Speicher *m*
    f accumulateur *m*
    r аккумулятор; накопитель *m*

A87 *e* accuracy class
    d Genauigkeitsklasse *f*
    f classe *f* de précision
    r класс *m* точности

A88 *e* accuracy of measurement
    d Meßgenauigkeit *f*
    f précision *f* de la mesure
    r точность *f* измерения

A89 *e* accurate measurement
    d genaue Messung *f*
    f mesure *f* précise
    r точное измерение *n*

A90 *e* achromat *see* achromatic lens

A91 *e* achromatic color
    d unbunte Farbe *f*, achromatische Farbe
       f
    f couleur *f* achromatique
    r ахроматический цвет *m*

A92 *e* achromatic lens
    d achromatische Linse *f*, Achromat *m*
    f lentille *f* achromatique
    r ахромат *m*, ахроматическая линза *f*

A93 *e* achromatization of lens systems
    d Achromatisierung *f* eines
       Linsensystems
    f achromatisation *f* des systèmes de
       lentilles
    r ахроматизация *f* линзовых систем

A94 *e* acoustic absorber
    d Schallschluckstoff *m*,
       schallschluckender Stoff *m*,
       schallschluckendes Material *n*,
       Schallschlucker *m*
    f absorbeur *m* acoustique
    r звукопоглотитель *m*

A95 *e* acoustical waves
    d akustische Wellen *f pl*,
       Schallwellen *f pl*
    f ondes *f pl* acoustiques
    r акустические волны *f pl*, звуковые
       волны *f pl*

A96 *e* acoustic breakdown
    d akustischer Durchschlag *m*
    f rupture *f* acoustique
    r акустический пробой *m*

A97 *e* acoustic cavitation
    d Ultraschallkavitation *f*
    f cavitation *f* ultrasonique
    r акустическая кавитация *f*

A98　e　acoustic coagulation
　　　d　akustische Koagulation *f*
　　　f　coagulation *f* acoustique
　　　r　акустическая коагуляция *f*

A99　e　acoustic concentrator
　　　d　Schallkonzentrator *m*, akustischer
　　　　　Konzentrator *m*
　　　f　concentrateur *m* acoustique
　　　r　акустический концентратор *m*

A100　e　acoustic conductance
　　　d　akustische Leitfähigkeit *f*
　　　f　conductance *f* acoustique
　　　r　акустическая проводимость *f*

A101　e　acoustic delay
　　　d　akustische Verzögerung *f*
　　　f　retard *m* acoustique
　　　r　акустическая задержка *f*

A102　e　acoustic delay line
　　　d　akustische Verzögerungsleitung *f*
　　　f　ligne *f* à retard acoustique
　　　r　акустическая линия *f* задержки

A103　e　acoustic detector
　　　d　Schallempfänger *m*
　　　f　récepteur *m* acoustique
　　　r　приёмник *m* звука, акустический
　　　　　детектор *m*

A104　e　acoustic dipole
　　　d　akustischer Dipol *m*
　　　f　dipôle *m* acoustique
　　　r　акустический диполь *m*

A105　e　acoustic energy
　　　d　Schallenergie *f*
　　　f　énergie *f* acoustique, énergie *f* sonore
　　　r　звуковая энергия *f*

A106　e　acoustic field *see* sound field

A107　e　acoustic filter
　　　d　akustisches Filter *n*
　　　f　filtre *m* acoustique
　　　r　акустический фильтр *m*

A108　e　acoustic flow
　　　d　akustische Strömung *f*
　　　f　écoulement *m* acoustique
　　　r　акустическое течение *n*

A109　e　acoustic grating
　　　d　akustisches Gitter *n*
　　　f　réseau *m* à diffraction acoustique
　　　r　акустическая дифракционная
　　　　　решётка *f*

A110　e　acoustic holography
　　　d　akustische Holographie *f*
　　　f　holographie *f* acoustique
　　　r　акустическая голография *f*

A111　e　acoustic image
　　　d　Schallbild *n*, akustisches Bild *n*,
　　　　　akustische Abbildung *f*
　　　f　image *f* acoustique
　　　r　акустическое изображение *n*,
　　　　　звуковое изображение *n*

A112　e　acoustic imaging
　　　d　akustische Bilderzeugung *f*
　　　f　formation *f* acoustique des images
　　　r　звуковидение *n*

A113　e　acoustic impedance
　　　d　akustische Impedanz *f*
　　　f　impédance *f* acoustique
　　　r　акустический импеданс *m*

A114　e　acoustic interference
　　　d　akustische Interferenz *f*,
　　　　　Schallwelleninterferenz *f*
　　　f　interférence *f* acoustique
　　　r　интерференция *f* акустических волн

A115　e　acoustic interferometer
　　　d　akustisches Interferometer *n*
　　　f　interféromètre *m* acoustique
　　　r　акустический интерферометр *m*

A116　e　acoustic lens
　　　d　akustische Linse *f*
　　　f　lentille *f* acoustique
　　　r　акустическая линза *f*

A117　e　acoustic measurements
　　　d　akustische Messung *f*, akustische
　　　　　Messungen *f pl*
　　　f　mesures *f pl* acoustiques
　　　r　акустические измерения *n pl*

A118　e　acoustic microscope
　　　d　akustisches Mikroskop *n*
　　　f　microscope *m* acoustique
　　　r　акустический микроскоп *n*

A119　e　acoustic mirror
　　　d　akustischer Spiegel *m*
　　　f　miroir *m* acoustique
　　　r　акустическое зеркало *n*

A120　e　acoustic noise
　　　d　akustisches Rauschen *n*
　　　f　bruit *m* acoustique
　　　r　акустический шум *m*

A121　e　acoustic nonlinearity
　　　d　akustische Nichtlinearität *f*
　　　f　non-linéarité *f* acoustique
　　　r　акустическая нелинейность *f*

A122　e　acoustic nuclear magnetic resonance
　　　d　akustische magnetische Kernresonanz
　　　　　f, akustische NMR *f*
　　　f　résonance *f* acoustique nucléaire
　　　　　magnétique
　　　r　акустический ядерный магнитный
　　　　　резонанс *m*

A123　e　acoustic oscillation, acoustic
　　　　　oscillations *see* acoustic vibration

A124   *e*   acoustic paramagnetic resonance
      d   akustische paramagnetische Resonanz *f*, akustische magnetische Resonanz *f*
      f   résonance *f* paramagnétique acoustique
      r   акустический парамагнитный резонанс *m*

A125   *e*   acoustic power
      d   Schalleistung *f*
      f   puissance *f* acoustique
      r   акустическая мощность *f*, мощность звука *f*

A126   *e*   acoustic pressure
      d   Schalldruck *m*
      f   pression *f* sonore
      r   звуковое давление *n*, давление *n* звукового излучения

A127   *e*   acoustic probe
      d   Schallsonde *f*
      f   sonde *f* acoustique
      r   акустический зонд *m*

A128   *e*   acoustic pulse
      d   akustischer Impuls *m*
      f   impulsion *f* acoustique
      r   акустический импульс *m*, звуковой импульс *m*

A129   *e*   acoustic quadrupole
      d   akustischer Quadrupol *m*
      f   quadripôle *m* acoustique
      r   акустический квадруполь *m*

A130   *e*   acoustic radiator
      d   akustischer Strahler *m*, Schallstrahler *m*
      f   radiateur *m* acoustique
      r   излучатель *m* звука, акустический излучатель *m*

A131   *e*   acoustic radiometer
      d   Schallstrahlungsdruckmesser *m*, Schallwaage *m*
      f   radiomètre *m* acoustique
      r   акустический радиометр *m*

A132   *e*   acoustic reflection *see* sound reflection

A133   *e*   acoustic reflector
      d   akustischer Reflektor *m*
      f   réflecteur *m* acoustique
      r   акустический рефлектор *m*

A134   *e*   acoustic relaxation
      d   akustische Relaxation *f*
      f   relaxation *f* acoustique
      r   акустическая релаксация *f*

A135   *e*   acoustic resistance
      d   akustischer Widerstand *m*, Schallwellenwiderstand *m*
      f   résistance *f* acoustique
      r   акустическое сопротивление *n*

A136   *e*   acoustic resonator
      d   akustischer Resonator *m*
      f   résonateur *m* acoustique
      r   акустический резонатор *m*

A137   *e*   acoustics
      d   Akustik *f*
      f   acoustique *f*
      r   акустика *f*

A138   *e*   acoustics of moving media
      d   Akustik *f* der bewegten Medien
      f   acoustique *f* des milieux en mouvement
      r   акустика *f* движущихся сред

A139   *e*   acoustic sounder
      d   Tonlot *n*, Tonecholot *n*, akustisches Echolot *n*
      f   localisateur *m* acoustique
      r   акустический локатор *m*

A140   *e*   acoustic spectroscopy
      d   Schallspektroskopie *f*
      f   spectroscopie *f* acoustique
      r   акустическая спектроскопия *f*

A141   *e*   acoustic vibration, acoustic vibrations
      d   akustische Schwingungen *f pl*
      f   oscillations *f pl* acoustiques
      r   акустические колебания *n pl*, звуковые колебания *n pl*

A142   *e*   acoustic wave
      d   Schallwelle *f*
      f   onde *f* acoustique
      r   акустическая волна *f*, звуковая волна *f*

A143   *e*   acoustic waveguide
      d   akustischer Wellenleiter *m*
      f   guide *m* d'ondes acoustiques
      r   акустический волновод *m*

A144   *e*   acoustic wave momentum
      d   Schallwellenimpuls *m*
      f   impulsion *f* de l'onde acoustique
      r   импульс *m* звуковой волны

A145   *e*   acoustic wind
      d   akustischer Wind *m*
      f   vent *m* acoustique
      r   акустический ветер *m*, звуковой ветер *m*

A146   *e*   acoustoelectric domain
      d   akustoelektrische Domäne *f*
      f   domaine *m* acousto-électrique
      r   акустоэлектрический домен *m*

A147   *e*   acoustoelectric effect
      d   akustoelektrischer Effekt *m*
      f   effet *m* acousto-électrique
      r   акустоэлектрический эффект *m*

A148   *e*   acoustoelectric interaction
      d   akustoelektrische Wechselwirkung *f*

	f	interaction f acousto-électrique
	r	акустоэлектронное взаимодействие n
A149	e	acoustoelectronics
	d	Akustoelektronik f
	f	acousto-électronique f
	r	акустоэлектроника f
A150	e	acousto-optical deflector
	d	akustooptischer Deflektor m, akustooptischer Ablenker m
	f	déflecteur m acousto-optique
	r	акустооптический дефлектор m
A151	e	acousto-optical interaction
	d	akustooptische Wechselwirkung f
	f	interaction f acousto-optique
	r	акустооптическое взаимодействие n
A152	e	acousto-optic correlator
	d	akustooptischer Korrelator m
	f	corrélateur m acousto-optique
	r	акустооптический коррелятор m
A153	e	acousto-optic effect
	d	akustooptischer Effekt m
	f	effet m acousto-optique
	r	акустооптический эффект m
A154	e	acousto-optic modulation
	d	akustooptische Modulation f
	f	modulation f acousto-optique
	r	акустооптическая модуляция f
A155	e	acousto-optic modulator
	d	akustooptischer Modulator m
	f	modulateur m acousto-optique
	r	акустооптический модулятор m
A156	e	acousto-optic quality
	d	akustooptische Qualität f
	f	qualité f acousto-optique
	r	акустооптическое качество n (материала)
A157	e	acousto-optics
	d	Akustooptik f
	f	acousto-optique f
	r	акустооптика f
A158	e	acousto-optic spectroscopy
	d	akustooptische Spektroskopie f
	f	spectroscopie f acousto-optique
	r	акустооптическая спектроскопия f
A159	e	actinic light
	d	aktinisches Licht n
	f	lumière f actinique
	r	актиничный свет m
A160	e	actinide element see actinoide
A161	e	actinism
	d	Aktinität f
	f	actinisme m, actinité f
	r	актиничность f

A162	e	actinium, Ac
	d	Actinium n, Aktinium n
	f	actinium m
	r	актиний m
A163	e	actinoid
	d	Aktinoid n, Actinoid n, Aktinid n
	f	actinide m
	r	актиноид m, актинид m
A164	e	actinometer
	d	Aktinometer n
	f	actinomètre m
	r	актинометр m
A165	e	actinometry
	d	Aktinometrie f
	f	actinométrie f
	r	актинометрия f
A166	e	action
	d	Eingriff m, Einwirkung f, Wirkung f
	f	action f; effet m
	r	действие n, воздействие n
A167	e	action at a distance
	d	Fernwirkung f
	f	action f à distance
	r	действие n на расстоянии, дальнодействие n
A168	e	action integral
	d	Wirkungsintegral n
	f	intégrale f d'action
	r	интеграл m действия
A169	e	activated cathode
	d	aktivierte Katode f, aktive Katode f
	f	cathode f activée
	r	активированный катод m
A170	e	activating agent see activator
A171	e	activation
	d	Aktivierung f
	f	activation f
	r	активация f
A172	e	activation analysis
	d	Aktivierungsanalyse f
	f	analyse f par activation
	r	активационный анализ m
A173	e	activation energy
	d	Aktivierungsenergie f
	f	énergie f d'activation
	r	энергия f активации
A174	e	activation method
	d	Aktivierungsmethode f
	f	méthode f d'activation
	r	активационный метод m (измерения ионизирующих излучений)
A175	e	activator
	d	Aktivator m, Aktivierungsmittel n

	f	activateur *m*
	r	активатор *m*
A176	e	**active current**
	d	Wirkstrom *m*
	f	courant *m* actif
	r	активный ток *m*
A177	e	**active days**
	d	aktive Tage *m pl*
	f	jours *m pl* actifs
	r	активные дни *m pl*, возмущённые дни *m pl*
A178	e	**active dipole**
	d	aktiver Dipol *m*
	f	dipôle *m* actif
	r	активный диполь *m*
A179	e	**active medium**
	d	aktives Medium *n*
	f	milieu *m* actif
	r	активная среда *f*
A180	e	**active mirror** *see* **adaptive mirror**
A181	e	**active mode locking**
	d	aktive Modenkopplung *f*
	f	synchronisation *f* active des modes
	r	активная синхронизация *f* мод
A182	e	**active power**
	d	Wirkleistung *f*
	f	puissance *f* active
	r	активная мощность *f*
A183	e	**active Q-switching**
	d	aktive Güteschaltung *f*
	f	commutation *f* active en Q
	r	активная модуляция *f* добротности
A184	e	**active region**
	d	Aktivitätsgebiet *n*
	f	région *f* active
	r	активная область *f*
A185	e	**active substance**
	d	aktiver Stoff *m*, aktive Substanz *f*
	f	substance *f* active
	r	активное вещество *n*
A186	e	**active voltage**
	d	Wirkspannung *f*
	f	tension *f* active
	r	активное напряжение *n*
A187	e	**activity**
	d	Aktivität *f*
	f	activité *f*
	r	активность *f*
A188	e	**acuity**
	d	Sehschärfe *f*; Gehörschärfe *f*
	f	acuité *f* visuelle; acuité *f* auditive
	r	острота *f* зрения; острота *f* слуха
A189	e	**a. c. voltage**
	d	Wechselspannung *f*
	f	tension *f* alternative
	r	переменное напряжение *n*
A190	e	**adaptation**
	d	Adaptation *f*; Anpassung *f*
	f	adaptation *f*
	r	адаптация *f*
A191	e	**adaptive compensation**
	d	adaptive Kompensation *f*
	f	compensation *f* adaptive
	r	адаптивная компенсация *f*
A192	e	**adaptive mirror**
	d	adaptiver Spiegel *m*
	f	miroir *m* adaptif
	r	адаптивное зеркало *n*, активное зеркало *n*
A193	e	**adaptive optics**
	d	adaptive Optik *f*
	f	optique *f* adaptive
	r	адаптивная оптика *f*
A194	e	**adaptive system**
	d	adaptives System *n*
	f	système *m* adaptif
	r	адаптивная система *f*
A195	e	**adaptometer**
	d	Adaptometer *n*
	f	adaptomètre *m*
	r	адаптометр *m*
A196	e	**adding interferometer**
	d	Summierinterferometer *n*
	f	interféromètre *m* totalisateur
	r	суммирующий интерферометр *m*, двухэлементный интерферометр *m*
A197	e	**additive quantum number**
	d	additive Quantenzahl *f*
	f	nombre *m* quantique additif
	r	аддитивное квантовое число *n*
A198	e	**additivity**
	d	Additivität *f*
	f	additivité *f*
	r	аддитивность *f*
A199	e	**adhesion**
	d	Adhäsion *f*; Anhalten *n*
	f	adhésion *f*
	r	адгезия *f*; прилипание *n*
A200	e	**adhesion contact**
	d	Adhäsionskontakt *m*
	f	contact *m* d'adhésion
	r	адгезионный контакт *m*
A201	e	**adiabat**
	d	Adiabate *f*
	f	adiabatique *f*, courbe *f* adiabatique
	r	адиабата *f*
A202	e	**adiabatic approximation**

d adiabatische Näherung *f*
f approximation *f* adiabatique
r адиабатическое приближение *n*

A203 *e* adiabatic calorimeter
d adiabatisches Kalorimeter *n*,
Kalorimeter *n* mit veränderlicher
Temperatur
f calorimètre *m* adiabatique
r адиабатический калориметр *m*

A204 *e* adiabatic change
d adiabatische Änderung *f*
f transformation *f* adiabatique
r адиабатическое изменение *n*

A205 *e* adiabatic curve *see* adiabat

A206 *e* adiabatic demagnetization
d adiabatische Entmagnetisierung *f*
f désaimantation *f* adiabatique
r адиабатическое размагничивание *n*

A207 *e* adiabatic fluctuations
d adiabatische Fluktuationen *f pl*
f fluctuations *f pl* adiabatiques
r адиабатические флуктуации *f pl*

A208 *e* adiabatic heating
d adiabatische Erwärmung *f*
f chauffage *m* adiabatique
r адиабатический нагрев *m*

A209 *e* adiabatic insulation
d adiabatische Isolierung *f*,
adiabatisches Isolieren *n*
f isolation *f* adiabatique
r адиабатическая изоляция *f*

A210 *e* adiabatic invariant
d adiabatische Invariante *f*
f invariant *m* adiabatique
r адиабатический инвариант *m*

A211 *e* adiabatic invariant method
d adiabatische Invariantenmethode *f*
f méthode *f* d'invariants adiabatiques
r метод *m* адиабатических
инвариантов

A212 *e* adiabatic perturbation
d adiabatische Störung *f*
f perturbation *f* adiabatique
r адиабатическое возмущение *n*

A213 *e* adiabatic process
d adiabatischer Prozeß *m*
f procédé *m* adiabatique
r адиабатический процесс *m*

A214 *e* adiabatic shell
d adiabatische Hülle *f*
f enveloppe *f* adiabatique
r адиабатная оболочка *f*

A215 *e* adiabatic trap
d adiabatische Falle *f*

f piège *m* adiabatique
r адиабатическая ловушка *f*

A216 *e* adjusting mechanism
d Justierungsmechanismus *m*
f mécanisme *m* de compensation
r механизм *m* юстировки

A217 *e* adjustment
d Einstellung *f*; Justierung *f*;
Einregelung *f*
f ajustement *m*, ajustage *m*
r настройка *f*; юстировка *f*;
регулировка *f*

A218 *e* admittance
d Admittanz *f*, Scheinleitwert *m*
f admittance *f*
r полная проводимость *f*,
адмиттанс *m*

A219 *e* ADP *see* ammonium dihydrogen
phosphate

A220 *e* adsorbate
d Adsorbat *n*, Adsorptiv *n*, adsorbierter
Stoff *m*
f substance *f* adsorbée, adsorbat *m*
r адсорбат *m*

A221 *e* adsorbent
d Adsorbens *n*, Adsorptionsmittel *n*,
adsorbierender Stoff *m*
f substance *f* adsorbante, adsorbant *m*
r адсорбент *m*

A222 *e* adsorption
d Adsorption *f*
f adsorption *f*
r адсорбция *f*

A223 *e* adsorption catalysis
d Adsorptionskatalyse *f*
f catalyse *f* d'adsorption
r адсорбционный катализ *m*

A224 *e* adsorption chromatography
d Adsorptionschromatographie *f*
f chromatographie *f* par adsorption
r адсорбционная хроматография *f*

A225 *e* adsorption equilibrium
d Adsorptionsgleichgewicht *n*
f équilibre *m* d'adsorption
r адсорбционное равновесие *n*

A226 *e* adsorption indicator
d Adsorptionsindikator *m*
f indicateur *m* d'adsorption
r адсорбционный индикатор *m*

A227 *e* adsorption isostere
d Adsorptionsisostere *f*
f isostère *f* d'adsorption
r изостера *f* адсорбции

A228 *e* adsorption isotherm

    d Adsorptionsisotherme *f*
    f   isotherme *f* d'adsorption
    r изотерма *f* адсорбции

A229 *e* adsorption kinetics
    d Adsorptionskinetik *f*
    f   cinétique *f* d'adsorption
    r кинетика *f* адсорбции

A230 *e* adsorption pump
    d Adsorptionspumpe *f*
    f   pompe *f* d'adsorption
    r адсорбционный насос *m*

A231 *e* advanced potential
    d avanciertes Potential *n*
    f   potentiel *m* avancé
    r опережающий потенциал *m*

A232 *e* advection
    d Advektion *f*
    f   advection *f*
    r адвекция *f*

A233 *e* Aeolian harp
    d Äolsharfe *f*
    f   harpe *f* éolienne
    r эолова арфа *f*

A234 *e* aerial
    d Antenne *f*
    f   antenne *f*
    r антенна *f*

A235 *e* aerial array
    d Antennengitter *n*, Antennengruppe *f*
    f   réseau *m* d'antennes
    r антенная решётка *f*

A236 *e* aerial gain *see* antenna gain

A237 *e* aerial noise
    d Antennenrauschen *n*
    f   bruit *m* d'antenne
    r антенный шум *m*

A238 *e* aerial temperature
    d Antennentemperatur *f*
    f   température *f* d'antenne
    r температура *f* антенны

A239 *e* aerodynamic center
    d aerodynamischer Neutralpunkt *m*
    f   centre *m* aérodynamique
    r аэродинамический фокус *m*

A240 *e* aerodynamic characteristic
    d aerodynamische Eigenschaft *f*
    f   finesse *f* aérodynamique
    r аэродинамическое качество *n*

A241 *e* aerodynamic coefficients
    d aerodynamische Beiwerte *m pl*
    f   coefficients *m pl* aérodynamiques
    r аэродинамические коэффициенты *m pl*

A242 *e* aerodynamic force
    d Luftkraft *f*, aerodynamische Kraft *f*
    f   force *f* aérodynamique
    r аэродинамическая сила *f*

A243 *e* aerodynamic heating
    d aerodynamische Erwärmung *f*
    f   échauffement *m* aérodynamique
    r аэродинамический нагрев *m*

A244 *e* aerodynamic lift
    d Auftrieb *m*
    f   portance *f* aérodynamique
    r аэродинамическая подъёмная сила *f*

A245 *e* aerodynamic measurements
    d aerodynamische Messungen *f pl*
    f   mesures *f pl* aérodynamiques
    r аэродинамические измерения *n pl*

A246 *e* aerodynamic moment
    d aerodynamisches Moment *n*
    f   moment *m* aérodynamique
    r аэродинамический момент *m*

A247 *e* aerodynamic noise
    d aerodynamisches Rauschen *n*
    f   bruit *m* aérodynamique
    r аэродинамический шум *m*

A248 *e* aerodynamic resistance
    d Strömungswiderstand *m*, aerodynamischer Widerstand *m*
    f   traînée *f* aérodynamique
    r аэродинамическое сопротивление *n*

A249 *e* aerodynamics
    d Aerodynamik *f*
    f   aérodynamique *f*
    r аэродинамика *f*

A250 *e* aerodynamic trail
    d Nachlauf *m*, Nachstrom *m*
    f   sillage *m* aérodynamique
    r аэродинамический след *m*

A251 *e* aerodynamic tunnel *see* wind tunnel

A252 *e* aeroelasticity
    d Aeroelastizität *f*
    f   aéro-élasticité *f*
    r аэроупругость *f*

A253 *e* aerology
    d Aerologie *f*
    f   aérologie *f*
    r аэрология *f*

A254 *e* aeronomy
    d Aeronomie *f*
    f   aéronomie *f*
    r аэрономия *f*

A255 *e* aerosol
    d Aerosol *n*
    f   aérosol *m*
    r аэрозоль *m*

A256   e   aerosol coagulation
       d   Aerosolkoagulation f
       f   coagulation f des aérosols
       r   коагуляция f аэрозолей

A257   e   aerostatics
       d   Aerostatik f
       f   aérostatique f
       r   аэростатика f

A258   e   affine space
       d   affiner Raum m
       f   espace m affin
       r   аффинное пространство n

A259   e   affinity
       d   Affinität f
       f   affinité f
       r   сродство n

A260   e   after-effect
       d   Nachwirkung f, Nachwirkungseffekt m
       f   persistance f, rémanence f
       r   последействие n

A261   e   afterglow
       d   Nachleuchten n
       f   postluminescence f
       r   послесвечение n

A262   e   afterimage
       d   Nachbild n
       f   postimage f
       r   послеизображение n

A263   e   age determination
       d   Altersbestimmung f, Datierung f
           (durch Radioaktivität)
       f   détermination f de l'âge (par
           radioactivité)
       r   определение n возраста (по
           радиоактивности)

A264   e   age hardening
       d   Ausscheidungshärtung f
       f   raidissement m dû à l'âge
       r   дисперсионное твердение n

A265   e   ageing
       d   Alterung f (von magnetischen
           Werkstoffen)
       f   durcissement m (des matériaux
           magnétiques)
       r   старение n (магнитных
           материалов)

A266   e   age of the Universe
       d   Alter n des Universums
       f   âge m de l'Univers
       r   возраст m Вселенной

A267   e   agglomeration
       d   Agglomerieren n; Sintern n
       f   agglomération f
       r   агломерация f; спекание n

A268   e   agglutination
       d   Agglutination f; Verklebung f
       f   agglutination f
       r   агглютинация f; склеивание n

A269   e   aggregate
       d   Aggregat n
       f   agrégat m
       r   агрегат m (совокупность частиц)

A270   e   aggregation
       d   Aggregation f
       f   agrégation f
       r   агрегация f, агрегирование n

A271   e   Aharonov-Bohm effect
       d   Effekt m von Aharonov und Bohm
       f   effet m de Aharonov-Bohm
       r   эффект m Ааронова - Бома

A272   e   air
       d   Luft f
       f   air m
       r   воздух m

A273   e   air conditioning
       d   Klimatisierung f
       f   climatisation f
       r   кондиционирование n воздуха

A274   e   air gap
       d   Luftspalt m
       f   espace m d'air
       r   воздушный зазор m

A275   e   airglow
       d   Nachthimmelleuchten n
       f   luminosité f de l'air
       r   свечение n ночного
           неба

A276   e   air humidity
       d   Luftfeuchtigkeit f
       f   humidité f d'air
       r   влажность f воздуха

A277   e   air pollution
       d   Atmosphärenverschmutzung f,
           Verunreinigung f der Luft
       f   pollution f atmosphérique, pollution f
           de l'air
       r   загрязнение n атмосферы,
           загрязнение n воздуха

A278   e   air pollution monitoring
       d   Luftverunreinigungskontrolle f,
           Luftverunreinigungsüberwachung f
       f   contrôle m de la pollution
           atmosphérique, contrôle m de la
           pollution de l'air
       r   контроль m загрязнений
           атмосферы

A279   e   air shower
       d   Luftschauer m
       f   gerbe f atmosphérique
       r   атмосферный ливень m

A280   *e*   Airy integral
      d   Airysches Regenbogenintegral *n*,
         Regenbogenintegral *n* von Airy,
         Airysches Integral *n*
      f   intégrale *f* d'Airy
      r   интеграл *m* Эйри

A281   *e*   albedo
      d   Albedo *n*, Rückstrahlvermögen *n*
      f   albédo *m*
      r   альбедо *n*

A282   *e*   alexandrite
      d   Alexandrit *m*
      f   alexandrite *f*
      r   александрит *m*

A283   *e*   Alfvén waves
      d   Alfvén-Wellen *f pl*,
         Alfvénsche Wellen *f pl*
      f   ondes *f pl* d'Alfvén
      r   альвеновские волны *f pl*

A284   *e*   algebra
      d   Algebra *f*
      f   algèbre *f*
      r   алгебра *f*

A285   *e*   alidade
      d   Alhidade *f*
      f   alidade *f*
      r   алидада *f*

A286   *e*   alignment
      d   1. Orientierung *f*, Ausrichtung *f*
         2. Justierung *f*
      f   1. orientation *f*, alignement *m*
         2. accord *m* secondaire
      r   1. выстраивание *n*, ориентация *f*
         2. юстировка *f*

A287   *e*   alkali metal
      d   Alkalimetall *n*
      f   métal *m* alcalin
      r   щелочной металл *m*

A288   *e*   all-fiber components
      d   Allfaserkomponenten *f pl*
      f   composants *m pl* toute-fibre
      r   чисто волоконные компоненты *m pl*

A289   *e*   allobar
      d   Allobar *n*
      f   allobar *m*
      r   аллобар *m*

A290   *e*   all-optical components
      d   voll optische Komponenten *f pl*
      f   composants *m pl* optiques purs
      r   чисто оптические компоненты *m pl*

A291   *e*   allotropic modification
      d   allotrope Modifikation *f*, allotrope
         Kristallmodifikation *f*
      f   modification *f* allotropique
      r   аллотропная модификация *f*
         (кристалла)

A292   *e*   allotropy
      d   Allotropie *f*
      f   allotropie *f*
      r   аллотропия *f*

A293   *e*   allowed band
      d   erlaubter Energiebereich *m*, erlaubtes
         Band *n*
      f   zone *f* permise
      r   разрешённая зона *f*

A294   *e*   allowed line
      d   erlaubte Linie *f*
      f   raie *f* permise
      r   разрешённая линия *f*

A295   *e*   allowed transition
      d   erlaubter Übergang *m*
      f   transition *f* permise
      r   разрешённый переход *m*

A296   *e*   alloy
      d   Legierung *f*
      f   alliage *m*
      r   сплав *m*

A297   *e*   alpha-active isotope
      d   alpha-aktives Isotop *n*, alpha-
         strahlendes Isotop *n*
      f   isotope *m* émetteur de rayons alpha
      r   альфа-активный изотоп *m*

A298   *e*   alpha decay
      d   Alphazerfall *m*, Alphaumwandlung *f*
      f   désintégration *f* alpha
      r   альфа-распад *m*

A299   *e*   alpha particle
      d   Alphateilchen *n*
      f   particule *f* alpha
      r   альфа-частица *f*

A300   *e*   alpha-particle emission
      d   Alphastrahlung *f*,
         Alphateilchenemission *f*
      f   émission *f* des particules alpha
      r   испускание *n* альфа-частиц

A301   *e*   alpha radiation
      d   Alphastrahlung *f*
      f   rayonnement *m* alpha, radiation *f*
         alpha
      r   альфа-излучение *n*,
         альфа-лучи *m pl*

A302   *e*   alpha-ray isotope *see* alpha-active
         isotope

A303   *e*   alpha-rays
      d   Alphastrahlen *pl*
      f   rayons *pl* alpha
      r   альфа-лучи *pl*

A304   *e*   alpha-ray source
      d   Alphastrahlungsquelle *f*, Alphaquelle *f*
      f   source *f* des rayons alpha
      r   источник *m* альфа-излучения

A305 *e* **alpha-ray spectrometer**
     d Alphaspektrometer *n*
     f spectromètre *m* alpha
     r альфа-спектрометр *m*

A306 *e* **alpha-ray spectroscopy**
     d Alphaspektroskopie *f*
     f spectroscopie *f* alpha
     r альфа-спектроскопия *f*

A307 *e* **alpha-stable isotope**
     d alpha-stabiles Isotop *n*
     f isotope *m* alpha stable
     r альфа-стабильный изотоп *m*

A308 *e* **altazimuth mounting**
     d azimutale Montierung *f*
     f montage *m* d'altazimut
     r азимутальная монтировка *f*
        (*телескопа*)

A309 *e* **alternating current**
     d Wechselstrom *m*
     f courant *m* alternatif
     r переменный ток *m*

A310 *e* **alternating motion** *see* **reciprocating motion**

A311 *e* **alternative energy sources**
     d alternative Energiequellen *f pl*
     f sources *f pl* d'énergie alternatives
     r альтернативные источники *m pl* энергии

A312 *e* **altimeter**
     d Höhenmesser *m*
     f altimètre *m*
     r альтиметр *m*, высотомер *m*

A313 *e* **altimetry**
     d Flughöhenmessung *f*
     f altimétrie *f*, hypsométrie *f*, mesure *f* altimétrique
     r измерение *n* высоты (*полета*), альтиметрия *f*

A314 *e* **altitude**
     d Höhe *f*
     f altitude *f*
     r высота *f*

A315 *e* **aluminium, Al**
     d Aluminium *n*
     f aluminium *m*
     r алюминий *m*

A316 *e* **alychne**
     d Alychne *f*
     f alychne *f*
     r алихна *f*

A317 *e* **AM** *see* **amplitude modulation**

A318 *e* **ambient temperature**
     d Umgebungstemperatur *f*
     f température *f* ambiante
     r температура *f* окружающей среды

A319 *e* **ambiguity**
     d Mehrdeutigkeit *f*, Zweideutigkeit *f*
     f ambiguïté *f*
     r неоднозначность *f*; неопределённость *f*

A320 *e* **ambipolar diffusion**
     d ambipolare Diffusion *f*
     f diffusion *f* ambipolaire
     r амбиполярная диффузия *f*

A321 *e* **ambipolar diffusion coefficient**
     d ambipolarer Diffussionskoeffizient *m*, Koeffizient *m* der ambipolaren Diffusion
     f coefficient *m* de diffusion ambipolaire
     r коэффициент *m* амбиполярной диффузии

A322 *e* **americium, Am**
     d Americium *n*, Amerizium *n*
     f américium *m*
     r америций *m*

A323 *e* **Amici prism**
     d Amici-Prisma *n*
     f prisme *m* d'Amici
     r призма *f* Амичи

A324 *e* **ammeter**
     d Ampermeter *n*, Strommesser *m*
     f ampèremètre *m*
     r амперметр *m*

A325 *e* **amino acid**
     d Aminosäure *f*
     f acide *m* aminé
     r аминокислота *f*

A326 *e* **ammonia maser**
     d Ammoniakmaser *m*
     f maser *m* à ammoniac
     r аммиачный мазер *m*

A327 *e* **ammonium dihydrogen phosphate**
     d Ammoniumdihydrogenorthophosphat *n*, Ammoniumdihydrogenphosphat *n*
     f dihydrogène-orthophosphate *m* d'ammonium
     r дигидрофосфат *m* аммония (*нелинейный кристалл*), ADP

A328 *e* **amorphizing addition**
     d destrukturierende Zugabe *f*
     f addition *f* mettant en état amorphe
     r аморфизирующая добавка *f*

A329 *e* **amorphous cluster**
     d amorpher Cluster *m*, amorpher Schwarm *m*
     f cluster *m* amorphe
     r аморфный кластер *m*

A330 *e* **amorphous condensate**

	d	amorphes Kondensat n
	f	condensat m amorphe
	r	аморфный конденсат m

A331 e **amorphous magnet**
    d amorphes Magnetikum n
    f magnétique m amorphe
    r аморфный магнетик m

A332 e **amorphous material**
    d amorphes Material n
    f matériau m amorphe
    r аморфный материал m

A333 e **amorphous metal**
    d amorphes Metall n
    f métal m amorphe
    r аморфный металл m

A334 e **amorphous silicon**
    d amorphes Silicium n
    f silicium m amorphe
    r аморфный кремний m

A335 e **amorphous state**
    d amorpher Zustand m
    f état m amorphe
    r аморфное состояние n

A336 e •**amorphous substance**
    d amorphe Substanz f,
       amorpher Stoff m
    f substance f amorphe
    r аморфное вещество n

A337 e **ampere, A**
    d Ampere n
    f ampère m
    r ампер m, A

A338 e **ampere balance** see **current balance**

A339 e **Ampere's law**
    d Amperesches Gesetz n
    f théorème m d'Ampère
    r закон m Ампера

A340 e **ampere turns**
    d Amperwindungen f pl
    f ampère-tours m pl
    r ампер-витки m pl

A341 e **ampholyt** see **amphoteric electrolyte**

A342 e **amphoteric electrolyte**
    d Ampholyt m, amphoteres Elektrolyt m
    f ampholyte m, électrolyte m
       amphotérique
    r амфотерный электролит m

A343 e **amplification**
    d Verstärkung f
    f amplification f
    r усиление n

A344 e **amplification coefficient** see
      amplification factor

A345 e **amplification factor**
    d Verstärkungsfaktor m,
       Verstärkungskoeffizient m
    f facteur m d'amplification, coefficient
       m d'amplification
    r коэффициент m усиления

A346 e **amplification stage**
    d Verstärkerstufe f, Verstärkungsstufe f
    f étage m d'amplification
    r усилительный каскад m

A347 e **amplified emission**
    d verstärkte Emission f
    f rayonnement m amplifié
    r усиленное излучение n

A348 e **amplifier**
    d Verstärker m
    f amplificateur m
    r усилитель m

A349 e **amplifier klystron**
    d Verstärkerklystron n
    f klystron m d'amplificateur
    r усилительный клистрон m

A350 e **amplifying stage** see **amplification
      stage**

A351 e **amplitude**
    d Amplitude f, Schwingungsweite f
    f amplitude f
    r амплитуда f

A352 e **amplitude characteristic**
    d Amplitudenkennlinie f,
       Amplitudencharakteristik f
    f caractéristique f amplitude-amplitude,
       réponse f amplitude-amplitude
    r амплитудная характеристика f

A353 e **amplitude detection**
    d Amplitudendetektion f,
       Amplitudendetektierung f
    f détection f d'amplitude
    r амплитудное детектирование n

A354 e **amplitude detector**
    d Amplitudendemodulator m, AM-
       Demodulator m
    f détecteur m d'amplitude
    r амплитудный детектор m

A355 e **amplitude discriminator**
    d Amplitudendiskriminator m
    f discriminateur m d'amplitude
    r амплитудный дискриминатор m

A356 e **amplitude distortion**
    d Amplitudenverzerrung f
    f distorsion f d'amplitude
    r амплитудные искажения n pl

A357 e **amplitude division**
    d Amplitudenteilung f
    f division f de l'amplitude
    r деление n амплитуды

A358   *e*   **amplitude-frequency characteristic**
        see frequency response

A359   *e*   **amplitude hologram**
        d   Amplitudenhologramm *n*
        f   hologramme *m* par amplitude
        r   амплитудная голограмма *f*

A360   *e*   **amplitude limiter**
        d   Amplitudenbegrenzer *m*
        f   limiteur *m* d'amplitude
        r   амплитудный ограничитель *m*

A361   *e*   **amplitude-modulated oscillation**
        d   amplitudenmodulierte
           Schwingungen *f pl*
        f   oscillations *f pl* modulées en amplitude
        r   амплитудно-модулированные
           колебания *n pl*

A362   *e*   **amplitude modulation**
        d   Amplitudenmodulation *f*, AM
        f   modulation *f* d'amplitude, M. A.
        r   амплитудная модуляция *f*, AM

A363   *e*   **a.m.u.** *see* atomic mass unit

A364   *e*   **analog filter**
        d   Analogfilter *n*
        f   filtre *m* analogique
        r   аналоговый фильтр *m*

A365   *e*   **analog-to-digital converter**
        d   Analog-Digital-Umsetzer *m*, A/D-
           Umsetzer *m*
        f   convertisseur *m* analogique-digital
        r   аналого-цифровой преобразователь
           m, АЦП *m*

A366   *e*   **analogy**
        d   Analogie *f*
        f   analogie *f*
        r   аналогия *f*

A367   *e*   **analysis**
        d   1. Analyse *f* 2. Analysis *f*
           (*Mathematik*)
        f   analyse *f*
        r   анализ *m*

A368   *e*   **analytical balance**
        d   Analysenwaage *f*, Feinwaage *f*
        f   balance *f* d'analyse
        r   аналитические весы *pl*

A369   *e*   **analytical dependence**
        d   analytische Abhängigkeit *f*
        f   dépendance *f* analytique
        r   аналитическая зависимость *f*

A370   *e*   **analytical extension**
        d   analytische Fortsetzung *f*
        f   suite *f* analytique
        r   аналитическое продолжение *n*

A371   *e*   **analytical function**
        d   analytische Funktion *f*

        f   fonction *f* analytique
        r   аналитическая функция *f*

A372   *e*   **analytical mass spectrometer**
        d   analytisches Massenspektrometer *n*
        f   spectromètre *m* de masse analytique
        r   аналитический масс-спектрометр *m*

A373   *e*   **analytical method**
        d   analytische Methode *f*
        f   méthode *f* analytique
        r   аналитический метод *m*

A374   *e*   **analytical signal**
        d   analytisches Signal *n*
        f   signal *m* analytique
        r   аналитический сигнал *m*

A375   *e*   **analyzer**
        d   Analysator *m*
        f   analyseur *m*
        r   анализатор *m*

A376   *e*   **anamorphotic adapter**
        d   anamorphotischer Objektivvorsatz *m*,
           Anamorphotvorsatz *m*
        f   adapteur *m* anamorphotique
        r   анаморфотная насадка *f*

A377   *e*   **anamorphotic lens**
        d   anamorphotische Linse *f*
        f   lentille *f* anamorphotique
        r   анаморфот *m*

A378   *e*   **anastigmat, anastigmatic lens**
        d   Anastigmat *m*
        f   anastigmat *m*, anastigmatique *m*
        r   анастигмат *m*, анастигматическая
           линза *f*

A379   *e*   **Anderson localization**
        d   Anderson-Lokalisierung *f*
        f   localisation *f* d'Anderson
        r   андерсоновская локализация *f*

A380   *e*   **anechoic chamber**
        d   schalltoter Raum *m*, reflexionsfreier
           Raum *m*
        f   chambre *f* anéchoïde, chambre *f* sans
           échos
        r   безэховая камера *f*, заглушённая
           камера *f*

A381   *e*   **anechoic room** *see* anechoic
           chamber

A382   *e*   **anelasticity**
        d   Inelastizität *f*
        f   non-élasticité *f*
        r   неупругость *f*

A383   *e*   **anemometer**
        d   Anemometer *n*, Windmesser *m*
        f   anémomètre *m*
        r   анемометр *m*

A384   *e*   **aneroid barometer**

d Aneroidbarometer *n*
f baromètre *m* anéroïde
r барометр-анероид *m*

A385 e angle
d Winkel *m*
f angle *m*
r угол *m*

A386 e angle of attack
d Anstellwinkel *m*, Anströmwinkel *m*
f angle *m* d'attaque
r угол *m* атаки

A387 e angle of friction
d Reibungswinkel *m*
f angle *m* de frottement
r угол *m* трения

A388 e angle of incidence
d Einfallswinkel *m*
f angle *m* d'incidence
r 1. угол *m* падения 2. угол *m* атаки

A389 e angle of phase synchronism
d Phasensynchronismuswinkel *m*
f angle *m* adapté à la phase
r угол *m* фазового синхронизма

A390 e angle of reflection
d Reflexionswinkel *m*
f angle *m* de réflexion
r угол *m* отражения

A391 e angle of refraction
d Brechungswinkel *m*,
    Refraktionswinkel *m*
f angle *m* de réfraction
r угол *m* преломления

A392 e angle of view
d Sehwinkel *m*, Gesichtswinkel *m*
f angle *m* visuel
r угол *m* зрения

A393 e Angström, A
d Angström-Einheit *f*, Angström *n*
f unité *f* Angström, angstrœm *m*
r ангстрем *m*

A394 e angular acceleration
d Winkelbeschleunigung *f*
f accélération *f* angulaire
r угловое ускорение *n*

A395 e angular aperture
d Öffnungswinkel *m*, Aperturwinkel *m*
f ouverture *f* angulaire
r угловая апертура *f*

A396 e angular correlation
d Winkelkorrelation *f*,
    Richtungskorrelation *f*
f corrélation *f* angulaire
r угловая корреляция *f*

A397 e angular dependence

d Winkelabhängigkeit *f*
f dépendance *f* angulaire
r угловая зависимость *f*

A398 e angular distribution
d Winkelverteilung *f*,
    Richtungsverteilung *f*
f distribution *f* angulaire, répartition *f* angulaire
r угловое распределение *n*

A399 e angular distribution isotropy
d Winkelverteilungsisotropie *f*
f isotropie *f* de distribution angulaire
r изотропия *f* углового распределения

A400 e angular frequency
d Winkelfrequenz *f*
f fréquence *f* angulaire, fréquence *f* de rotation
r угловая частота *f*, круговая частота *f*

A401 e angular measurements
d Winkelmessungen *f pl*
f mesures *f pl* angulaires
r угловые измерения *n pl*

A402 e angular momentum
d Drehimpuls *m*
f moment *m* angulaire
r момент *m* импульса, кинетический момент *m*, момент *m* количества движения, угловой момент *m*

A403 e angular motion
d Winkelbewegung *f*
f mouvement *m* circulaire
r круговое движение *n*, движение *n* по окружности

A404 e angular quantum number *see* orbital quantum number

A405 e angular resolution
d Winkelauflösung *f*
f résolution *f* angulaire
r угловое разрешение *n*

A406 e angular velocity
d Winkelgeschwindigkeit *f*
f vitesse *f* angulaire
r угловая скорость *f*

A407 e angular width
d Winkelbreite *f*; Strahldivergenz *f*
f largeur *f* angulaire; divergence *f* du faisceau
r угловая ширина *f*

A408 e anharmonicity
d Anharmonizität *f*
f anharmonicité *f*
r ангармонизм *m*

A409 e anharmonic molecule
d anharmonisches Molekül *n*

f molécule *f* anharmonique
r ангармоническая молекула *f*

A410 *e* **anharmonic oscillation, anharmonic oscillations**
d anharmonische Oszillation *f*
f oscillations *f pl* anharmoniques
r ангармонические колебания *n pl*

A411 *e* **anharmonic oscillator**
d anharmonischer Oszillator *m*, unharmonischer Oszillator *m*
f oscillateur *m* anharmonique
r ангармонический осциллятор *m*

A412 *e* **anion**
d Anion *n*
f anion *m*
r анион *m*

A413 *e* **anisotropic crystal**
d anisotroper Kristall *m*
f cristal *m* anisotrópe
r анизотропный кристалл *m*

A414 *e* **anisotropic emission**
d anisotrope Strahlung *f*
f rayonnement *m* anisotrope, radiation *f* anisotrope
r анизотропное излучение *n*

A415 *e* **anisotropic medium**
d anisotropes Medium *n*
f milieu *m* anisotropique
r анизотропная среда *f*

A416 *e* **anisotropic model**
d anisotropes Modell *n (des Universums)*
f modèle *m* anisotropique *(de l'Univers)*
r анизотропная модель *f* Вселенной, модель *f* анизотропной Вселенной

A417 *e* **anisotropic scattering**
d anisotrope Streuung *f*
f diffusion *f* anisotrope
r анизотропное рассеяние *n*

A418 *e* **anisotropic substance**
d anisotrope Substanz *f*
f substance *f* anisotropique
r анизотропное вещество *n*

A419 *e* **anisotropy**
d Anisotropie *f*
f anisotropie *f*
r анизотропия *f*

A420 *e* **anisotropy energy**
d Anisotropieenergie *f*, kristallographische Anisotropieenergie *f*
f énergie *f* d'anisotropie
r энергия *f* анизотропии

A421 *e* **anisotropy of elastic properties**
d Anisotropie *f* von elastischen Eigenschaften, elastische Anisotropie *f*

f anisotropie *f* des propriétés élastiques, anisotropie *f* élastique
r анизотропия *f* упругих свойств

A422 *e* **anisotropy of magnetic properties**
d Anisotropie *f* von magnetischen Eigenschaften
f anisotropie *f* des propriétés magnétiques
r анизотропия *f* магнитных свойств

A423 *e* **annealing**
d Glühen *n*, Tempern *n*
f recuit *m*
r отжиг *m*

A424 *e* **annealing curve**
d Entspannungskurve *f*
f courbe *f* de recuit
r кривая *f* отжига

A425 *e* **annihilation**
d Annihilation *f*, Vernichtung *f*
f annihilation *f*
r аннигиляция *f*

A426 *e* **annihilation losses**
d Annihilationsverluste *m pl*
f pertes *f pl* par annihilation
r аннигиляционные потери *f pl*

A427 *e* **annihilation of electron-positron pairs**
d Vernichtung *f* von Elektron-Positron-Paaren
f annihilation *f* de paires électron-positron
r аннигиляция *f* электронно-позитронных пар

A428 *e* **annihilation radiation**
d Annihilationsstrahlung *f*, Vernichtungsstrahlung *f*
f rayonnement *m* d'annihilation
r аннигиляционное излучение *n*

A429 *e* **annual aberration**
d jährliche Aberration *f*
f aberration *f* annuelle
r годичная аберрация *f*

A430 *e* **annual variation**
d jährliche Änderung *f (des geomagnetischen Feldes)*
f variation *f* annuelle *(de champ géomagnétique)*
r годичные вариации *f pl (геомагнитного поля)*

A431 *e* **anode**
d Anode *f*
f anode *f*
r анод *m*

A432 *e* **anode characteristic**
d Anodencharakteristik *f*

25

f caractéristique f de plaque
r анодная характеристика f

A433 e anode current
d Anodenstrom m
f courant m anodique
r анодный ток m

A434 e anode dark space
d Anodendunkelraum m
f espace m sombre anodique
r анодное тёмное пространство n

A435 e anode detection
d Anodendetektion f,
Anodendetektierung f
f détection f par anode
r анодное детектирование n

A436 e anode drop see anode fall

A437 e anode fall
d Anodenfall m
f chute f anodique
r анодное падение n

A438 e anode glow
d Anodenglimmlicht n
f lueur f anodique
r анодное свечение n

A439 e anode region
d Anodengebiet n, Anodenraum m
f région f anodique
r анодная область f (тлеющего разряда)

A440 e anode voltage
d Anodenspannung f
f tension f anodique
r анодное напряжение n

A441 e anodizing
d Anodisieren n, anodische Behandlung f
f anodisation f
r анодирование n

A442 e anomalon
d Anomalon n
f anomalon m
r аномалон m

A443 e anomalous dispersion
d anomale Dispersion f
f dispersion f anormale
r аномальная дисперсия f

A444 e anomalous magnetic moment
d anomales magnetisches Moment n
f moment m magnétique anormal
r аномальный магнитный момент m

A445 e anomalous radiation
d anomale Strahlung f
f rayonnement m anormal
r аномальное излучение n

A446 e anomalous refraction
d anomale Refraktion f, anomale Brechung f
f réfraction f anormale
r аномальная рефракция f

A447 e anomalous viscosity
d anomale Viskosität f
f viscosité f anormale
r аномальная вязкость f

A448 e anomalous Zeeman effect
d anomaler Zeeman-Effekt m, zusammengesetzer Zeeman-Effekt m
f effet m Zeeman anormal
r аномальный эффект m Зеемана, сложный эффект m Зеемана

A449 e anomaly
d Anomalie f
f anomalie f
r аномалия f

A450 e anorthic system see triclinic system

A451 e antenna see aerial

A452 e antenna effective length
d effektive Antennenlänge f, wirksame Antennenlänge f, Antennenwirklänge f
f longueur f efficace d'antenne
r действующая длина f антенны

A453 e antenna feeder
d Antennenspeiseleitung f, Antennenzuleitung f
f alimentateur m d'antenne, feeder m d'antenne
r антенный фидер m

A454 e antenna gain
d Antennenverstärkung f, Antennengewinn m
f gain m d'antenne
r усиление n антенны

A455 e antenna noise see aerial noise

A456 e anthropic principle
d anthropisches Prinzip n (in der Kosmologie)
f principe m anthropique (dans la cosmologie)
r антропный принцип m (в космологии)

A457 e antibaryon
d Antibaryon n
f antibaryon m
r антибарион m

A458 e anticathode
d Antikatode f
f anticathode f
r антикатод m

A459 e anticoincidence circuit

d Antikoinzidenzschaltung *f*
f circuit *m* à anticoïncidences
r схема *f* антисовпадений

A460 e **anticoincidence counter**
d Antikoinzidenzzähler *m*
f compteur *m* à anticoïncidences
r счётчик *m* антисовпадений

A461 e **anticoincidence technique**
d Antikoinzidenzverfahren *n*
f méthode *f* à anticoïncidences
r метод *m* антисовпадений

A462 e **anticommutator**
d Antikommutator *m*
f anticommutateur *m*
r антикоммутатор *m*

A463 e **anticorrosive material**
d Korrosionsschutzstoff *m*
f matériau *m* anticorrosif
r антикоррозионный материал *m*

A464 e **anticyclone**
d Antizyklon *m*
f anticyclone *m*
r антициклон *m*

A465 e **antiferroelectric**
d Antiferroelektrikum *n*,
antiferroelektrischer Stoff *m*
f antiferroélectrique *m*
r антисегнетоэлектрик *m*

A466 e **antiferromagnet**
d Antiferromagnetikum *n*,
antiferromagnetischer Stoff *m*
f antiferromagnétique *m*
r антиферромагнетик *m*

A467 e **antiferromagnetic domain**
d antiferromagnetische Domäne *f*,
antiferroelektrischer Bezirk *m*
f domaine *m* antiferromagnétique
r антиферромагнитный домен *m*

A468 e **antiferromagnetic ordering**
d antiferromagnetische Ordnung *f*
f ordonnancement *m*
antiferromagnétique
r антиферромагнитное
упорядочение *n*

A469 e **antiferromagnetic resonance**
d antiferromagnetische Resonanz *f*
f résonance *f* antiferromagnétique
r антиферромагнитный резонанс *m*

A470 e **antiferromagnetism**
d Antiferromagnetismus *m*
f antiferromagnétisme *m*
r антиферромагнетизм *m*

A471 e **antimatter**
d Antimaterie *f*
f antimatière *f*
r антивещество *n*, антиматерия *f*

A472 e **antimony, Sb**
d Antimon *n*
f antimoine *m*
r сурьма *f*

A473 e **antineutrino**
d Antineutrino *n*
f antineutrino *m*
r антинейтрино *n*

A474 e **antineutron**
d Antineutron *n*
f antineutron *m*
r антинейтрон *m*

A475 e **antinode**
d Schwingungsbauch *m*; Wellenbauch
m, Bauch *m* der stehender Welle
f antinœud *m*
r пучность *f* (колебания)

A476 e **antinucleon**
d Antinukleon *n*
f antinucléon *m*
r антинуклон *m*

A477 e **antiparallel injection**
d entgegengerichtete Injektion *f*,
antiparallele Injektion *f*
f injection *f* à contre-courant
r встречная инжекция *f*

A478 e **antiparticle**
d Antiteilchen *n*
f antiparticule *f*
r античастица *f*

A479 e **antiproton**
d Antiproton *n*
f antiproton *m*
r антипротон *m*

A480 e **antiquark**
d Antiquark *n*
f antiquark *m*
r антикварк *m*

A481 e **antireflection coating**
d 1. Vergütung *f* 2. reflexmindernde
Schicht *f*, Antireflexbelag *m*,
T-Belag *m*
f 1. bleutage *m* d'optique 2. couche *f*
antiréfléchissante
r 1. просветление *n* оптики 2.
просветляющее покрытие *n*

A482 e **anti-Stokes component**
d antistokessche Komponente *f*, Anti-
Stokes-Komponente *f*
f composante *f* antistokes
r антистоксова компонента *f*

A483 e **anti-Stokes line**
d Anti-Stokes-Linie *f*, antistokessche
Linie *f*, anti-Stokessche Linie *f*

f raie *f* antistokes
r антистоксова линия *f*

A484 *e* antisymmetry
d Antisymmetrie *f*
f antisymétrie *f*
r антисимметрия *f*

A485 *e* aperiodic circuit
d aperiodischer Kreis *m*
f circuit *m* apériodique
r апериодический контур *m*

A486 *e* aperiodicity
d Aperiodizität *f*
f apériodicité *f*
r апериодичность *f*,
непериодичность *f*

A487 *e* aperiodic motion
d aperiodische Bewegung *f*
f mouvement *m* apériodique
r апериодическое движение *n*

A488 *e* aperiodic oscillation, aperiodic
oscillations
d aperiodische Schwingungen *f pl*
f oscillations *f pl* apériodiques
r апериодические колебания *n pl*

A489 *e* aperture
d 1. Apertur *f*, Blende *f*,
Blendenöffnung *f* 2. Öffnungsweite *f*
f ouverture *f*
r 1. апертура *f* 2. отверстие *n*

A490 *e* aperture diaphragm
d Öffnungsblende *f*, Aperturblende *f*
f diaphragme *m* d'ouverture
r апертурная диафрагма *f*,
действующая диафрагма *f*

A491 *e* aperture distortion
d Aperturverzerrungen *f pl*
f aberrations *f pl* d'ouverture
r апертурные искажения *n pl*

A492 *e* aperture integrator
d Aperturintegrator *m*
f intégrateur *m* d'ouverture
r апертурный интегратор *m*

A493 *e* aperture ratio
d Öffnungsverhältnis *n*,
relative Öffnung *f*
f ouverture *f* relative
r относительное отверстие *n*

A494 *e* aperture stop *see* aperture
diaphragm

A495 *e* aperture synthesis
d Apertur-Synthese *f*
f synthèse *f* d'ouverture
r апертурный синтез *m*

A496 *e* apex

d Apex *m*
f apex *m*
r апекс *m*

A497 *e* aphelion
d Sonnenferne *f*
f aphélie *f*
r афелий *m*

A498 *e* aplanat *see* aplanatic lens

A499 *e* aplanatic lens
d Aplanat *m*, aplanatisches Objektiv *n*;
aplanatische Linse *f*
f aplanétique *m*, aplanat *m*
r апланат *m*, апланатическая линза *f*

A500 *e* apochromat *see* apochromatic lens

A501 *e* apochromatic lens
d Apochromat *m*, apochromatisches
Objektiv *n*; apochromatische Linse *f*
f apochromat *m*, apochromatique *m*
r апохромат *m*, апохроматическая
линза *f*

A502 *e* apodization
d Apodization *f*
f apodisation *f*
r аподизация *f*

A503 *e* apogee
d Apogäum *n*
f apogée *m*
r апогей *m*

A504 *e* applied optics
d angewandte Optik *f*
f optique *f* appliquée
r прикладная оптика *f*

A505 *e* applied physics
d angewandte Physik *f*
f physique *f* appliquée
r прикладная физика *f*

A506 *e* applied research
d angewandte Forschung *f*
f recherche *f* appliquée
r прикладные исследования *n pl*

A507 *e* approximate method
d Näherungsmethode *f*,
Näherungsverfahren *n*
f méthode *f* approximative
r приближённый метод *m*

A508 *e* approximate value
d Näherungswert *m*
f valeur *f* approximative
r приближённое значение *n*

A509 *e* approximation
d Annäherung *f*, Approximation *f*,
Approximierung *f*
f approximation *f*
r аппроксимация *f*, приближение *n*

A510
e aquadag
d Aquadag *n*
f aquadag *m*
r аквадаг *m*

A511
e arbitrary units
d willkürliche Einheiten *f pl*
f unités *f pl* arbitraires
r произвольные единицы *f pl*;
внесистемные единицы *f pl*

A512
e arbitrary value
d willkürlicher Wert *m*
f valeur *f* arbitraire
r произвольное значение *n*

A513
e arc
d Bogen *m*
f arc *m*
r дуга *f*

A514
e arc discharge
d Lichtbogenentladung *f*,
Bogenentladung *f*
f décharge *f* par arc, décharge *f* en arc
r дуговой разряд *m*

A515
e Archimedes principle
d Archimedisches Gesetz *n*, Prinzip *n*
von Archimedes
f principe *m* d'Archimède, théorème *m*
d'Archimède
r закон *m* Архимеда

A516
e Archimedian force *see* buoyancy
force

A517
e architectural acoustics
d Raumakustik *f*, Raum- und
Bauakustik *f*
f acoustique *f* architecturale
r архитектурная акустика *f*

A518
e arc lamp
d Bogenlampe *f*
f lampe *f* à arc
r дуговая лампа *f*

A519
e arc spectrum
d Lichtbogenspektrum *n*
f spectre *m* d'arc
r дуговой спектр *m*

A520
e area
d 1. Fläche *f*, Gebiet *n*, Bereich *m*,
Zone *f* 2. Flächeninhalt *m*;
Grundfläche *f*
f aire *f*
r 1. область *f*, зона *f* 2. площадь *f*

A521
e areometer
d Aräometer *n*
f aréomètre *m*
r ареометр *m*, плотномер *m*,
денсиметр *m*

A522
e argentum, Ag
d Silber *n*
f argent *m*
r серебро *n*

A523
e argon, Ar
d Argon *n*
f argon *m*
r аргон *m*

A524
e argon laser
d Argonlaser *m*, Ar-Laser *m*
f laser *m* à argon
r аргоновый лазер *m*, Ar-лазер *m*

A525
e Argonne National Laboratory
d ANL-Laboratorium *n* (USA)
f laboratoire *m* ANL (USA)
r Аргоннская Национальная
лаборатория *f* (США)

A526
e arm
d 1. Arm *m* 2. Hebel *m* 3. Zeiger *m*
f 1. bras *m* 2. levier *m* 3. aiguille *f*
r 1. плечо *n* 2. рычаг *m* 3. стрелка *f*
(прибора)

A527
e arm of couple
d Kraftarm *m*
f bras *m* de levier du couple
r плечо *n* пары сил, плечо *n* пары

A528
e armature
d Anker *m*
f induit *m*
r якорь *m* (электрической машины)

A529
e armco, armco iron
d Armco-Eisen *n*
f fer *m* armco
r армко-железо *n*

A530
e arsenic, As
d Arsen *n*
f arsenic *m*
r мышьяк *m*

A531
e artificial horizon
d künstlicher Horizont *m*,
Kreiselhorizont *m*
f horizon *m* artificiel
r искусственный горизонт *m*

A532
e artificial intelligence
d künstliche Intelligenz *f*, KI
f intelligence *f* artificielle
r искусственный интеллект *m*

A533
e artificial radioactivity
d künstliche Radioaktivität *f*
f radioactivité *f* artificielle
r искусственная радиоактивность *f*

A534
e artificial satellite
d künstlicher Satellit *m*
f satellite *m* artificiel
r искусственный спутник *m* (напр.
Земли)

A535   *e* **ascending node**
       d aufsteigender Knoten *m*
       f nœud *m* ascendant
       r восходящий узел *m*

A536   *e* **asdic** *see* sonar

A537   *e* **asperity**
       d Oberflächenunebenheit *f*, Rauheit *f*
       f aspérité *f*, rugosité *f*
       r шероховатость *f*, неровность *f*

A538   *e* **aspherical optics**
       d asphärische Optik *f*
       f optique *f* asphérique
       r асферическая оптика *f*

A539   *e* **assembly**
       d 1. Anordnung *f* 2. Zusammenbau *m*,
          Montage *f* 3. Baugruppe *f*
       f 1. assemblage *m* 2. assemblage *m*,
          montage *m* 3. ensemble *m*
       r 1. сборка *f* (*в ядерном реакторе*)
          2. сборка *f*, монтаж *m* 3. узел *m*

A540   *e* **associated Legendre functions**
       d zugeordnete Legendre-Funktionen *f pl*
       f fonctions *f pl* associées de Legendre
       r присоединённые функции *f pl*
          Лежандра

A541   *e* **associated production**
       d assoziierte Paarerzeugung *f*
       f création *f* associée (*des paires de
          particules*)
       r совместное рождение *n* (*пар
          частиц*)

A542   *e* **associative ionization**
       d assoziative Ionisation *f*
       f ionisation *f* associative
       r ассоциативная ионизация *f*

A543   *e* **associative recombination**
       d assoziative Recombination *f*
       f recombination *f* associative
       r ассоциативная рекомбинация *f*

A544   *e* **associativity**
       d Assoziativität *f*
       f associativité *f*
       r ассоциативность *f*

A545   *e* **assumption**
       d Voraussetzung *f*; Annahme *f*
       f supposition *f*
       r допущение *n*

A546   *e* **astatine, At**
       d Astat *n*
       f astate *m*
       r астат *m*

A547   *e* **asterism**
       d Asterismus *m*
       f astérisme *m*
       r астеризм *m*

A548   *e* **asteroid**
       d Asteroid *m*, Planetoid *m*
       f astéroïde *m*
       r астероид *m*

A549   *e* **astigmatism**
       d Astigmatismus *m*
       f astigmatisme *m*
       r астигматизм *m*

A550   *e* **astigmatism correction**
       d Astigmatismuskorrektion *f*,
          Astigmatismusberichtigung *f*
       f correction *f* de l'astigmatisme
       r коррекция *f* астигматизма

A551   *e* **astigmatism of eye**
       d Astigmatismus *m* des Auges
       f astigmatisme *m* de l'œil
       r астигматизм *m* глаза

A552   *e* **Aston dark space**
       d Astonscher Dunkelraum *m*
       f espace *m* sombre d'Aston
       r астоново тёмное пространство *n*

A553   *e* **astrobiology**
       d Astrobiologie *f*
       f astrobiologie *f*
       r астробиология *f*

A554   *e* **astroclimate**
       d Astroklima *n*
       f astroclimat *m*
       r астроклимат *m*

A555   *e* **astrograph** *see* astrographic camera

A556   *e* **astrographic camera**
       d Astrograph *m*, photographischer
          Refraktor *m*, Astrokamera *f*
       f astrographe *m*, caméra *f*
          astrographique
       r астрограф *m*, астрографическая
          камера *f*

A557   *e* **astrographic telescope** *see*
          astrographic camera

A558   *e* **astrolabe**
       d Astrolabium *n*
       f astrolabe *m*
       r астролябия *f*

A559   *e* **astrometry**
       d Astrometrie *f*
       f astrométrie *f*
       r астрометрия *f*

A560   *e* **astronomical calendar**
       d astronomischer Kalender *m*
       f calendrier *m* astronomique
       r астрономический календарь *m*

A561   *e* **astronomical colorimetry**
       d astronomische Kolorimetrie *f*
       f colorimétrie *f* astronomique
       r астрономическая колориметрия *f*

A562 e **astronomical instruments**
　　　d astronomische Instrumente *n pl*
　　　f instruments *m pl* astronomiques
　　　r астрономические инструменты *m pl*

A563 e **astronomical observatory**
　　　d astronomisches Observatorium *n*
　　　f observatoire *m* astronomique
　　　r астрономическая обсерватория *f*

A564 e **astronomical photometry**
　　　d Astrophotometrie *f*, Sternphotometrie *f*
　　　f astrophotométrie *f*
　　　r астрофотометрия *f*

A565 e **astronomical spectroscopy**
　　　d Astrospektrometrie *f*,
　　　　 Sternspektroskopie *f*
　　　f astrospectroscopie *f*
　　　r астроспектроскопия *f*

A566 e **astronomical telescope**
　　　d astronomisches Fernrohr *n*
　　　f télescope *m* astronomique
　　　r астрономический телескоп *m*

A567 e **astronomical unit**
　　　d astronomische Einheit *f*, AE
　　　f unité *f* astronomique, U.A.
　　　r астрономическая единица *f (1 а.e. =*
　　　　 4959787.10⁸ км)

A568 e **astronomy**
　　　d Astronomie *f*
　　　f astronomie *f*
　　　r астрономия *f*

A569 e **astrophysics**
　　　d Astrophysik *f*
　　　f astrophysique *f*
　　　r астрофизика *f*

A570 e **asymmetric molecule**
　　　d asymmetrisches Molekül *n*
　　　f molécule *f* asymétrique
　　　r асимметричная молекула *f*

A571 e **asymmetric top molecule**
　　　d Molekül *n* vom Typ des
　　　　 unsymmetrischen Kreisels
　　　f molécule *f* du type toupie asymétrique
　　　r молекула *f* типа асимметричного
　　　　 волчка

A572 e **asymmetry**
　　　d Asymmetrie *f*, Unsymmetrie *f*
　　　f asymétrie *f*
　　　r асимметрия *f*

A573 e **asymptote**
　　　d Asymptote *f*
　　　f asymptote *f*
　　　r асимптота *f*

A574 e **asymptotic dependence**

　　　d asymptotische Abhängigkeit *f*
　　　f dépendance *f* asymptotique
　　　r асимптотическая зависимость *f*

A575 e **asymptotic expansion**
　　　d asymptotische Entwicklung *f*
　　　f développement *m* asymptotique
　　　r асимптотическое разложение *n*

A576 e **asymptotic freedom**
　　　d asymptotische Freiheit *f*
　　　f liberté *f* asymptotique
　　　r асимптотическая свобода *f*

A577 e **asymptotic series**
　　　d asymptotische Reihe *f*
　　　f série *f* asymptotique
　　　r асимптотический ряд *m*

A578 e **atmosphere**
　　　d Atmosphäre *f*, Lufthülle *f*
　　　f atmosphère *f*
　　　r атмосфера *f*

A579 e **atmosphere dynamics**
　　　d atmosphärische Dynamik *f*
　　　f dynamique *f* de l'atmosphère
　　　r динамика *f* атмосферы

A580 e **atmospheric absorption**
　　　d atmosphärische Absorption *f*
　　　f absorption *f* atmosphérique
　　　r атмосферное поглощение *n*,
　　　　 поглощение *n* в атмосфере

A581 e **atmospheric attenuation**
　　　d atmosphärische Dämpfung *f*
　　　f affaiblissement *m* dans l'atmosphère
　　　r затухание *n* радиоволн в атмосфере

A582 e **atmospheric circulation**
　　　d atmosphärische Zirkulation *f*,
　　　　 Luftkreislauf *m*
　　　f circulation *f* atmosphérique
　　　r циркуляция *f* атмосферы,
　　　　 атмосферная циркуляция *f*

A583 e **atmospheric convection**
　　　d Luftkonvektion *f*, atmosphärische
　　　　 Konvektion *f*
　　　f convection *f* atmosphérique
　　　r атмосферная конвекция *f*

A584 e **atmospheric diffraction**
　　　d atmosphärische Beugung *f*
　　　f diffraction *f* atmosphérique
　　　r атмосферная дифракция *f*,
　　　　 дифракция *f* в атмосфере

A585 e **atmospheric diffusion**
　　　d atmosphärische Diffusion *f*
　　　f diffusion *f* atmosphérique
　　　r атмосферная диффузия *f*,
　　　　 диффузия *f* в атмосфере

A586 e **atmospheric electricity**
　　　d Luftelektrizität *f*

f électricité f atmosphérique
r атмосферное электричество n

A587 e atmospheric ionization
d Luftionisation f, Luftionisierung f, atmosphärische Ionisation f, Ionisation f der Atmosphäre
f ionisation f de l'atmosphère
r атмосферная ионизация f

A588 e atmospheric irregularity
d atmosphärische Inhomogenität f
f irrégularité f atmosphérique
r атмосферная неоднородность f

A589 e atmospheric opacity
d Lufttrübung f
f opacité f atmosphérique
r непрозрачность f атмосферы

A590 e atmospheric optics
d atmosphärische Optik f, Optik f der Atmosphäre
f optique f atmosphérique
r атмосферная оптика f

A591 e atmospheric ozone
d atmosphärisches Ozon n
f ozone m atmosphérique
r атмосферный озон m

A592 e atmospheric pollution see air pollution

A593 e atmospheric pressure
d atmosphärischer Druck m, barometrischer Druck m
f pression f atmosphérique; pression f barométrique
r атмосферное давление n; барометрическое давление n

A594 e atmospheric radiation
d Luftstrahlung f, atmosphärische Strahlung f
f rayonnement m atmosphérique
r атмосферное излучение n, излучение n атмосферы

A595 e atmospheric refraction
d atmosphärische Refraktion f, atmosphärische Strahlenbrechung f
f réfraction f atmosphérique
r атмосферная рефракция f; рефракция f в атмосфере

A596 e atmospherics
d Atmospherics pl, atmosphärische Störungen f pl
f atmosphériques m pl
r атмосферики m pl

A597 e atmospheric scattering
d atmosphärische Streuung f
f diffusion f atmosphérique
r атмосферное рассеяние n, рассеяние n в атмосфере

A598 e atmospheric tides
d atmosphärische Gezeiten pl
f marées f pl atmosphériques
r атмосферные приливы m pl, приливы m pl в атмосфере

A599 e atmospheric transparency window
d Fenster n der Atmosphäre
f fenêtre f de transparence atmosphérique, fenêtre f atmosphérique
r окно n прозрачности атмосферы

A600 e atmospheric turbulence
d atmosphärische Turbulenz f
f turbulence f atmosphérique
r атмосферная турбулентность f

A601 e atmospheric waveguide
d atmosphärischer Wellenleiter m, Dukt m, Duct m
f guide m d'ondes atmosphérique
r атмосферный волновод m

A602 e atmospheric waves
d Raumwellen f pl
f ondes f pl atmosphériques
r атмосферные волны f pl

A603 e atom
d Atom n
f atome m
r атом m

A604 e atom core see atomic core

A605 e atomic absorption
d atomare Absorption f
f absorption f atomique
r атомное поглощение n

A606 e atomic and molecular spectroscopy
d Atom- und Molekülspektroskopie f
f spectroscopie f atomique et moléculaire
r спектроскопия f атомов и молекул

A607 e atomic beam
d Atomstrahl m
f faisceau m atomique
r атомный пучок m

A608 e atomic beam frequency standard
d Atomstrahlfrequenzstandard m
f standard m de fréquence de faisceau atomique
r атомный стандарт m частоты, атомно-лучевой стандарт m частоты, атомный эталон m частоты

A609 e atomic beam source
d Atomstrahlquelle f
f source f du faisceau atomique
r источник m атомного пучка

A610 e atomic bomb see nuclear bomb

A611   *e*   **atomic clock**
     d   Atomuhr *f*
     f   horloge *f* atomique
     r   атомные часы *pl*; атомный стандарт *m* времени

A612   *e*   **atomic collisions**
     d   Atomstöße *m pl*, Zusammenstöße *m pl* von Atomen
     f   collisions *f pl* atomiques
     r   атомные столкновения *n pl*

A613   *e*   **atomic core**
     d   Atomrumpf *m*
     f   cœur *m* d'un atome
     r   атомный остов *m (атом без валентных электронов)*

A614   *e*   **atomic crystal**
     d   Atomkristall *m*, Atomgitterkristall *m*
     f   cristal *m* atomique
     r   атомный кристалл *m*

A615   *e*   **atomic detection**
     d   Atomdetektion *f*, Atomdetektierung *f*
     f   détection *f* des atomes
     r   детектирование *n* атомов

A616   *e*   **atomic energy** *see* **nuclear energy**

A617   *e*   **atomic energy levels**
     d   Energieniveaus *n pl* des Atoms, Atomniveaus *n pl*
     f   niveaux *m pl* d'énergie de l'atome
     r   уровни *m pl* энергии атома

A618   *e*   **atomic form factor**
     d   Atomformfaktor *m*
     f   facteur *m* de forme atomique, facteur *m* atomique
     r   атомный фактор *m*, атомный форм-фактор *m*

A619   *e*   **atomic frequency standard** *see* **atom beam frequency standard**

A620   *e*   **atomic interferometer**
     d   Atominterferometer *n*
     f   interféromètre *m* atomique
     r   атомный интерферометр *m*

A621   *e*   **atomic ion**
     d   Atomion *n*
     f   ion *m* atomique
     r   атомный ион *m*, атомарный ион *m*; ионизированный атом *m*

A622   *e*   **atomic Landé factor**
     d   Landéscher g-Faktor *m*, Atom-g-Faktor *m*
     f   facteur *m* de Landé
     r   атомный множитель *m* Ланде, атомный g-фактор *m*

A623   *e*   **atomic magnetic moment**
     d   magnetisches Moment *n* des Atoms
     f   moment *m* magnétique atomique, moment *m* magnétique de l'atome
     r   магнитный момент *m* атома

A624   *e*   **atomic mass**
     d   Atommasse *f*, relative Atommasse *f*
     f   masse *f* atomique
     r   атомная масса *f*, масса *f* атома

A625   *e*   **atomic mass unit**
     d   atomare Masseneinheit *f*, amu
     f   unité *f* de masse atomique, u.m.a.
     r   атомная единица *f* массы

A626   *e*   **atomic nucleus**
     d   Atomkern *m*, Kern *m (des Atoms)*
     f   noyau *m* atomique
     r   атомное ядро *n*

A627   *e*   **atomic number**
     d   Atomnummer *f*; Kernladungszahl *f*
     f   nombre *m* atomique
     r   атомный номер *m*; порядковый номер *m (элемента в периодической таблице Менделеева)*

A628   *e*   **atomic orbital**
     d   Atomorbital *n*, AO
     f   orbitale *f* atomique
     r   атомная орбиталь *f*

A629   *e*   **atomic physics**
     d   Atomphysik *f*
     f   physique *f* atomique
     r   атомная физика *f*

A630   *e*   **atomic polarizability**
     d   Atompolarisierbarkeit *f*, atomare Polarisierbarkeit *f*
     f   polarisabilité *f* atomique
     r   поляризуемость *f* атомов

A631   *e*   **atomic polarization**
     d   Atompolarisation *f*
     f   polarisation *f* atomique
     r   атомная поляризация *f*

A632   *e*   **atomic probe**
     d   Atomsonde *f*
     f   sonde *f* atomique
     r   атомный зонд *m*

A633   *e*   **atomic radius**
     d   Atomradius *m*
     f   rayon *m* atomique
     r   атомный радиус *m*

A634   *e*   **atomic scale**
     d   Atommaßstab *m*
     f   échelle *f* atomique
     r   атомный масштаб *m*

A635   *e*   **atomic scattering factor** *see* **atomic form factor**

A636   *e*   **atomic spectra**
     d   Atomspektren *n pl*
     f   spectres *m pl* atomiques
     r   атомные спектры *m pl*

A637   e   atomic spectroscopy
      d   Atomspektroskopie *f*
      f   spectroscopie *f* atomique
      r   атомная спектроскопия *f*,
        спектроскопия *f* атомов

A638   e   atomic standard
      d   Atomstandard *m*
      f   étalon *m* atomique
      r   атомный стандарт *m* *(частоты,*
        времени)

A639   e   atomic structure
      d   Atombau *m*
      f   structure *f* atomique, structure *f* de
        l'atome
      r   строение *n* атома

A640   e   atomic time
      d   Atomzeit *f*
      f   temps *m* atomique
      r   атомное время *n*

A641   e   atomic time standard
      d   Atomzeitstandard *m*
      f   étalon *m* atomique de temps
      r   атомный стандарт *m* времени,
        атомный эталон *m* времени

A642   e   atomic weight
      d   Atomgewicht *n*, Atommasse *f*, relative
        Atommasse *f*
      f   poids *m* atomique, masse *f* atomique,
        masse *f* atomique relative
      r   атомный вес *m*, атомная масса *f*

A643   e   atomization
      d   Zerstäubung *f*
      f   atomisation *f*
      r   распыление *n*

A644   e   atom site *(in a lattice)*
      d   Gitterplatz *m*, Gitterstelle *f*
      f   site *m* dans le réseau, place *f* de
        l'atome *(en réseau)*
      r   место *n* атома *(в решетке)*; узел *m*
        кристаллической решётки

A645   e   attachment, attachment of electrons
      d   Anlagerung *f*, Anlagerung *f* von
        Elektronen, Attachment *n*;
        Anschluß *m*
      f   attachement *m*, attachement *m*
        d'électrons
      r   прилипание *n*, прилипание *n*
        электронов; присоединение *n*

A646   e   attenuation
      d   1. Schwächung *f* 2. Dämpfung *f*
      f   1. atténuation *f*; affaiblissement *m*
        2. affaiblissement *m*; amortissement *m*
      r   1. ослабление *n* 2. затухание *n*

A647   e   attenuation coefficient
      d   1. Schwächungskoeffizient *m*,
        Schwächungsfaktor *m*
        2. Dämpfungsfaktor *m*
      f   1. facteur *m* d'affaiblissement
        2. coefficient *m* d'amortissement
      r   1. коэффициент *m* ослабления
        2. коэффициент *m* затухания

A648   e   attenuation constant *see* attenuation
        coefficient

A649   e   attenuation factor *see* attenuation
        coefficient

A650   e   attenuation length *(of cosmic rays)*
      d   Schwächungslänge *f* *(der kosmischen*
        Strahlung)
      f   longueur *f* d'affaiblissement *(des*
        ondes cosmiques)
      r   длина *f* ослабления *(космических*
        лучей)

A651   e   attenuator
      d   Abschwächer *m*; Dämpfungsglied *n*
      f   atténuateur *m*, affaiblisseur *m*
      r   аттенюатор *m*, ослабитель *m*

A652   e   attraction
      d   Anziehung *f*, Attraktion *f*
      f   attraction *f*
      r   притяжение *n*

A653   e   attractor
      d   Attraktor *m*
      f   attracteur *m*
      r   аттрактор *m*

A654   e   audibility
      d   Hörbarkeit *f*
      f   audibilité *f*
      r   слышимость *f*

A655   e   audio-band *see* audio-frequency
        band

A656   e   audiofrequencies
      d   Tonfrequenzen *f pl*,
        Hörfrequenzen *f pl*
      f   audiofréquences *f pl*, fréquences *f pl*
        audibles, fréquences *f pl* acoustiques
      r   звуковые частоты *f pl*

A657   e   audio-frequency band
      d   Tonfrequenzband *n*,
        Hörfrequenzband *n*
      f   gamme *f* de fréquences acoustiques
      r   диапазон *m* звуковых частот

A658   e   audio masking
      d   Tonmaskierung *f*
      f   camouflage *m* aural
      r   маскировка *f* звука

A659   e   audiometer
      d   Audiometer *n*, Hörschwellenmeßgerät
        n, Hörschärfemesser *m*
      f   audiomètre *m*
      r   аудиометр *m*

A660   *e*   Auger effect
       d   Auger-Effekt *m*
       f   effet *m* Auger
       r   оже-эффект *m*, эффект *m* Оже

A661   *e*   Auger-electron image
       d   Auger-Elektronenabbildung *f*, Auger-Elektronenbild *n*
       f   image *f* en électrons Auger
       r   изображение *n* в оже-электронах, оже-изображение *n*

A662   *e*   Auger electrons
       d   Auger-Elektronen *n pl*
       f   électrons *m pl* Auger
       r   оже-электроны *m pl*

A663   *e*   Auger spectroscopy
       d   Auger-Spektroskopie *f*
       f   spectroscopie *f* Auger
       r   оже-спектроскопия *f*

A664   *e*   augmented plane wave method
       d   erweiterte Methode *f* der ebenen Wellen
       f   méthode *f* augmentée des ondes planes
       r   метод *m* присоединённых плоских волн

A665   *e*   aureole
       d   Aureole *f*, Kranzerscheinung *f*
       f   auréole *f*
       r   ореол *m*

A666   *e*   aurora
       d   Polarlicht *n*
       f   aurore *f* polaire
       r   полярное сияние *n*

A667   *e*   aurora australis
       d   südliches Polarlicht *n*, Südlicht *n*
       f   aurore *f* australe
       r   южное сияние *n*

A668   *e*   aurora borealis
       d   nördliches Polarlicht *n*, Nordlicht *n*
       f   aurore *f* boréale
       r   северное сияние *n*

A669   *e*   auroral arc
       d   Aurorabogen *m*
       f   arc *m* auroral
       r   авроральная дуга *f*

A670   *e*   auroral ionization
       d   Auroraionisation *f*, Auroraionisierung *f*
       f   ionisation *f* aurorale
       r   авроральная ионизация *f*

A671   *e*   auroral ionosphere
       d   Polarlichtionosphäre *f*
       f   ionosphère *f* aurorale
       r   авроральная ионосфера *f*

A672   *e*   auroral line
       d   Auroralinie *f*, Auroraspektrallinie *f*
       f   raie *f* aurorale
       r   авроральная линия *f*

A673   *e*   auroral oval
       d   Polarlichtoval *n*; Nordlichtoval *n*; Südlichtoval *n*
       f   ovale *m* d'aurore
       r   авроральный овал *m*

A674   *e*   auroral reflections
       d   Polarradioreflexionen *f pl*
       f   réflexions *f pl* aurores
       r   авроральные радиоотражения *n pl*, полярные радиоотражения *n pl*

A675   *e*   auroral X-rays
       d   Polarlicht-Röntgenstrahlung *f*
       f   radiation *f* X aurorale
       r   авроральное рентгеновское излучение *n*

A676   *e*   auroral zones
       d   Polarlichtzonen *f pl*, Zonen *f pl* der Polarlichter
       f   zones *f pl* aurorales
       r   авроральные зоны *f pl*

A677   *e*   austenite
       d   Austenit *m*
       f   austénite *f*
       r   аустенит *m*

A678   *e*   austenitic grain
       d   Austenitkorn *n*
       f   grain *m* austénitique
       r   аустенитное зерно *n*

A679   *e*   autocatalysis
       d   Autokatalyse *f*
       f   autocatalyse *f*
       r   автокатализ *m*

A680   *e*   autoclave
       d   Autoklav *m*
       f   autoclave *m*
       r   автоклав *m*

A681   *e*   autocollimation
       d   Autokollimation *f*
       f   autocollimation *f*
       r   автоколлимация *f*

A682   *e*   autocollimator
       d   Autokollimationsfernrohr *n*
       f   autocollimateur *m*
       r   автоколлиматор *m*

A683   *e*   autocorrelation
       d   Autokorrelation *f*
       f   autocorrélation *f*
       r   автокорреляция *f*

A684   *e*   autocorrelation function
       d   Autokorrelationsfunktion *f*
       f   fonction *f* d'autocorrélation
       r   автокорреляционная функция *f*

A685   *e*   autoelectronic emission *see* field emission

A686   *e*   autoionization
     d   Autoionisation *f*, Selbstionisation *f*
     f   auto-ionisation *f*
     r   автоионизация *f*

A687   *e*   automatic tuning
     d   automatische Abstimmung *f*
     f   accord *m* automatique
     r   автоматическая настройка *f*

A688   *e*   autoradiography
     d   Autoradiographie *f*
     f   autoradiographie *f*
     r   авторадиография *f*

A689   *e*   avalanche
     d   Lawine *f*
     f   avalanche *f*
     r   лавина *f*

A690   *e*   avalanche breakdown
     d   Lawinendurchbruch *m*
     f   claquage *m* en avalanche
     r   лавинный пробой *m*

A691   *e*   avalanche chamber
     d   Lawinenkammer *f*
     f   chambre *f* à avalanche
     r   лавинная камера *f*

A692   *e*   avalanche discharge
     d   Lawinenentladung *f*
     f   décharge *f* en avalanche
     r   лавинный разряд *m*

A693   *e*   avalanche ionization
     d   Lawinenionisation *f*
     f   ionisation *f* par avalanche
     r   лавинная ионизация *f*

A694   *e*   avalanche transit-time diode
     d   Lawinenlaufzeitdiode *f*
     f   diode *f* à avalanche à temps de transit
     r   лавинно-пролётный диод *m*, ЛПД

A695   *e*   average life *see* mean life

A696   *e*   average, average value
     d   Mittelwert *m*, Mittel *n*
     f   valeur *f* moyenne, moyenne *f*
     r   среднее значение *n*

A697   *e*   averaging
     d   Mittelung *f*, Mitteln *n*, Mittelwertbildung *f*
     f   moyennage *m*, prise *f* de moyen
     r   усреднение *n*

A698   *e*   Avogadro constant *see* Avogadro number

A699   *e*   Avogadro number
     d   Avogadro-Konstante *f*; Avogadro-Zahl *f*
     f   constante *f* d'Avogadro; nombre *m* d'Avogadro
     r   постоянная *f* Авогадро; число *n* Авогадро

A700   *e*   axial channeling
     d   axiale Kanalierung *f*
     f   canalisation *f* axiale
     r   аксиальное каналирование *n*

A701   *e*   axial current
     d   Axialstrom *m*
     f   courant *m* axial
     r   аксиальный ток *m*

A702   *e*   axial deformation
     d   axiale Deformation *f*, axiale Verformung *f*
     f   déformation *f* axiale
     r   аксиальная деформация *f (ядер)*

A703   *e*   axial gage
     d   axiale Eichung *f*
     f   calibrage *m* axial
     r   аксиальная калибровка *f*

A704   *e*   axial hologram
     d   axiales Hologramm *n*
     f   hologramme *m* axial
     r   осевая голограмма *f*

A705   *e*   axially symmetric field
     d   axialsymmetrisches Feld *n*
     f   champ *m* symétrique axial
     r   аксиально-симметричное поле *n*

A706   *e*   axial quadrupole
     d   axialer Quadrupol *m*
     f   quadripôle *m* axial
     r   аксиальный квадруполь *m*

A707   *e*   axial vector
     d   axialer Vektor *m*
     f   vecteur *m* axial
     r   аксиальный вектор *m*

A708   *e*   axiom
     d   Axiom *n*
     f   axiome *m*
     r   аксиома *f*

A709   *e*   axiomatic method
     d   axiomatische Methode *f*
     f   méthode *f* axiomatique
     r   аксиоматический метод *m*

A710   *e*   axiomatic quantum field theory
     d   axiomatische Quantenfeldtheorie *f*
     f   théorie *f* des champs quantique axiomatique
     r   аксиоматическая квантовая теория *f* поля

A711   *e*   axion
     d   Axion *n*

	f	axion *m*
	r	аксион *m*

A712 *e* axis
    d Achse *f*
    f axe *m*
    r ось *f*

A713 *e* **axis of easy magnetization**
    d Richtung *f* der leichtesten Magnetisierbarkeit
    f axe *m* d'aimantation facile
    r ось *f* лёгкого намагничивания

A714 *e* **axis of inertia**
    d Trägheitsachse *f*
    f axe *m* d'inertie
    r ось *f* инерции

A715 *e* **axis of rotation**
    d Drehachse *f*
    f axe *m* de rotation
    r ось *f* вращения

A716 *e* **axis of strain**
    d Dehnungsachse *f*
    f axe *m* de déformation
    r ось *f* деформации

A717 *e* **axis of symmetry**
    d Symmetrieachse *f*
    f axe *m* de symétrie
    r ось *f* симметрии

A718 *e* **axoid**
    d Axoid *n*, Achsenfläche *f*
    f surface *f* axoïde
    r аксоид *m*

A719 *e* **Azbel-Kaner effect**
    d Azbel-Kaner-Effekt *m*
    f effet *m* d'Azbel-Kaner
    r эффект *m* Азбеля - Канера

A720 *e* **azimuth**
    d Azimut *m, n*
    f azimut *m*
    r азимут *m*

A721 *e* **azimuthal quantum number**
    d azimutale Quantenzahl *f*, Nebenquantenzahl *f*
    f nombre *m* quantique azimutal
    r азимутальное квантовое число *n*

B

B1 *e* **Babinet principle**
    d Babinet-Prinzip *n*
    f principe *m* de Babinet
    r теорема *f* Бабине

B2 *e* **back-and-forth motion** *see* reciprocating motion

B3 *e* **back focus**
    d Bildbrennpunkt *m*, bildseitiger Brennpunkt *m*, hinterer Brennpunkt *m*
    f foyer *m* secondaire
    r задний фокус *m*, второй фокус *m*

B4 *e* **background**
    d 1. Hintergrund *m* 2. Untergrund *m*
    f fond *m*
    r фон *m*

B5 *e* **background contamination**
    d Untergrundkontamination *f*
    f contamination *f* de fond
    r фоновое загрязнение *n*

B6 *e* **background intensity**
    d Untergrundintensität *f*
    f intensité *f* du fond
    r фоновая интенсивность *f*

B7 *e* **background light** *see* background radiation

B8 *e* **background radiation**
    d Untergrundstrahlung *f*
    f radiation *f* ambiante
    r фоновое излучение *n*

B9 *e* **back-reflection method**
    d Laue-Methode *f*, Rückstrahl-Laue-Methode *f (Röntgenstrukturanalyse)*
    f méthode *f* de rétroréflexion *(en diffraction des rayons X)*, méthode *f* de Laue en retour *(analyse radiocristallographique)*
    r метод *m* обратного отражения *(в рентгеноструктурном анализе)*

B10 *e* **back scatter**
    d Rückstreuung *f*
    f diffusion *f* inverse, diffusion *f* rétrograde
    r обратное рассеяние *n*

B11 *e* **backscattered electron image**
    d Abbildung *f* in rückgestreuten Elektronen
    f image *f* en électrons réfléchis
    r изображение *n* в отражённых электронах

B12 *e* **back scattering** *see* back scatter

B13 *e* **back scatter ionospheric sounding**
    d Rückstreuungs-Ionosphärensondierung *f*
    f sondage *m* ionosphérique par diffusion en retour
    r возвратно-наклонное зондирование *n* ионосферы

B14 *e* **back voltage**
    d Rückspannung *f*, Gegenspannung *f*; Sperrspannung *f*

f   tension *f* inverse
r   обратное напряжение *n*

B15 e   backward direction
d   Gegenrichtung *f*; Sperrichtung *f*
f   sens *m* d'arrêt, sens *m* de blocage
r   обратное направление *n*,
противоположное направление *n*

B16 e   backward wave
d   Rückwärtswelle *f*, rücklaufende
Welle *f*
f   onde *f* inverse, onde *f* de retour
r   обратная волна *f*

B17 e   backward wave tube
d   Rückwärtswellenröhre *f*, Carcinotron
n, Karzinotron *n*
f   tube *m* à onde régressive
r   лампа *f* обратной волны, ЛОВ,
карцинотрон *m*

B18 e   baffle
d   Prallplatte *f*
f   chicane *f*
r   перегородка *f*; отражатель *m*

B19 e   bag model
d   Beutelmodell *n*
f   modèle *m* de sac
r   модель *f* мешка

B20 e   balance
d   1. Balance *f*; Gleichgewicht *n* 2.
Waage *f*
f   1. bilan *m*; équilibre *m* 2. balance *f*
r   1. баланс *m*; равновесие *n*
2. весы *pl*

B21 e   balanced amplifier
d   Gegentaktverstärker *m*
f   amplificateur *m* compensé
r   балансный усилитель *m*

B22 e   balanced load
d   symmetrische Belastung *f*
f   charge *f* compensée
r   симметрическая нагрузка *f*

B23 e   ball
d   Ball *m*; Kugel *f*
f   bille *f*
r   шар *m*; шарик *m*

B24 e   ballistic curve
d   ballistische Kurve *f*
f   courbe *f* balistique
r   баллистическая кривая *f*

B25 e   ballistic galvanometer
d   ballistisches Galvanometer *n*
f   galvanomètre *m* balistique
r   баллистический гальванометр *m*

B26 e   ballistic phonon
d   ballistisches Phonon *n*
f   phonon *m* balistique
r   баллистический фонон *m*

B27 e   ballistics
d   Ballistik *f*
f   balistique *f*
r   баллистика *f*

B28 e   ball lightning
d   Kugelblitz *m*
f   foudre *f* globulaire
r   шаровая молния *f*

B29 e   balloon
d   Ballon *m*, Luftballon *m*
f   ballon *m*
r   баллон *m* (*воздушный шар*)

B30 e   balloon astronomy
d   Ballonastronomie *f*
f   astronomie *f* stratosphérique
r   баллонная астрономия *f*

B31 e   ballooning instability
d   Balloninstabilität *f*
f   instabilité *f* due au ballon
r   баллонная неустойчивость *f*

B32 e   Balmer discontinuity
d   Balmer-Sprung *m*
f   discontinuité *f* de Balmer
r   бальмеровский скачок *m*

B33 e   Balmer series
d   Balmer-Serie *f*
f   série *f* de Balmer
r   серия *f* Бальмера

B34 e   Banach space
d   Banach-Raum *m*
f   espace *m* de Banach
r   банахово пространство *n*

B35 e   band
d   1. Band *n*, Frequenzband *n* 2. Band *n*,
Bereich *m* 3. Zone *f*, Energieband *n*,
Energiebereich *m*
f   bande *f*
r   1. полоса *f* (частот) 2. диапазон *m*
3. зона *f*

B36 e   band bottom
d   Bandunterkante *f*
f   fond *m* de la bande
r   дно *n* зоны

B37 e   band intensity
d   Bandenintensität *f*
f   intensité *f* de la bande
r   интенсивность *f* полосы

B38 e   band magnetism
d   Zonenmagnetismus *m*
f   magnétisme *m* des bandes
r   зонный магнетизм *m*

B39 e   band model
d   Bändermodell *n*,
Energiebändermodell *n*

f modèle *m* des bandes
r зонная модель *f*

B40 *e* **band-pass filter**
d Bandfilter *n*; Bandpaß *m*
f filtre *m* passe-bande
r полосовой фильтр *m*

B41 *e* **band spectra**
d Bandenspektren *n pl*
f spectres *m pl* de bande
r полосатые спектры *m pl*

B42 *e* **band structure**
d Bänderstruktur *f*
f structure *f* en bande
r зонная структура *f*

B43 *e* **band theory**
d Bändertheorie *f (der Festkörper)*
f théorie *f* des bandes *(du solide)*
r зонная теория *f (твердого тела)*

B44 *e* **bandwidth**
d Bandbreite *f*
f largeur *f* de la bande
r ширина *f* полосы *(частот, пропускания)*

B45 *e* **bandwidth measurement**
d Bandbreitenmessung *f*
f mesure *f* de la bande passante *(p. ex. de guide d'ondes optiqie)*
r измерение *n* полосы пропускания *(напр. световода)*

B46 *e* **bar**
d 1. Bar *n* 2. Stab *m*; Barren *m*
f 1. bar *m* 2. barre *f*
r 1. бар *m (единица давления)* 2. стержень *m*, слиток *m*

B47 *e* **Bardeen-Cooper-Schrieffer model**
d Bardeen-Cooper-Schrieffer-Modell *n*
f modèle *m* de Bardeen-Cooper-Schrieffer, modèle *m* B.C.S.
r модель *f* Бардина - Купера - Шриффера, модель *f* БКШ

B48 *e* **bare core**
d nackter Kern *m*
f noyau *m* nu
r «голое» ядро *n*

B49 *e* **bare particle**
d nacktes Teilchen *n*, mathematisches Teilchen *n*
f particule *f* nue
r «голая» частица *f*

B50 *e* **bare source**
d offene Radionuklidquelle *f*
f source *f* de radionucléides ouverte
r открытый радионуклидный источник *m*, открытый источник *m*

B51 *e* **barium, Ba**

d Barium *n*
f baryum *m*
r барий *m*

B52 *e* **Barkhausen effect**
d Barkhausen-Effekt *m*
f effet *m* Barkhausen
r эффект *m* Баркгаузена

B53 *e* **Barkhausen-Kurz oscillator**
d Barkhausen-Kurz-Generator *m*
f oscillateur *m* de Barkhausen-Kurz
r генератор *m* Баркгаузена - Курца

B54 *e* **barn, barn unit**
d Barn *n*
f barn *m*
r барн *m*

B55 *e* **Barnett effect**
d Barnett-Effekt *m*
f effet *m* Barnett
r эффект *m* Барнетта

B56 *e* **barograph**
d Barograph *m*
f barographe *m*
r барограф *m*

B57 *e* **barometer**
d Barometer *n*
f baromètre *m*
r барометр *m*

B58 *e* **barometric height formula**
d barometrische Höhenformel *f*, Barometerformel *f*
f formule *f* de hauteur barométrique
r барометрическая формула *f*

B59 *e* **barometric pressure** *see* atmospheric pressure

A60 *e* **barotropic phenomenon**
d barotropes Phänomen *n*, barotropisches Phänomen *n*
f phénomène *m* barotrope
r баротропное явление *n*

B61 *e* **barrel distortion, barrel-shaped distortion**
d tonnenförmige Verzeichnung *f*, tonnenförmige negative Verzeichnung *f*, Tonnenverzeichnung *f*, Tonnenverzerrung *f*
f distorsion *f* en barillet
r бочкообразная дисторсия *f*, отрицательная дисторсия *f*

B62 *e* **barretter**
d Barretter *m*
f barretter *m*
r бареттер *m*

B63 *e* **barrier**
d Schranke *f*, Barriere *f*; Sperre *f*
f barrière *f*
r барьер *m*

B64   *e*   **barrier height**
     d   Höhe *f* des Potentialwalls
     f   hauteur *f* de la barrière de potentiel
     r   высота *f* потенциального барьера

B65   *e*   **barrier layer**
     d   Sperrschicht *f*
     f   couche *f* d'arrêt
     r   запирающий слой *m*

B66   *e*   **barrier-layer capacitance**
     d   Sperrschichtkapazität *f*,
       Grenzschichtkapazität *f*
     f   capacité *f* de la couche d'arrêt
     r   барьерная ёмкость *f*

B67   *e*   **barrier-layer rectification**
     d   Sperrschichtgleichrichtung *f*
     f   redressement *m* par couche d'arrêt
     r   выпрямление *n* на запирающем
       слое

B68   *e*   **barrier penetrability** *see* **barrier transparency**

B69   *e*   **barrier transparency**
     d   Durchlässigkeit *f* des Potentialwalls
     f   transparence *f* de la barrière de potentiel
     r   прозрачность *f* потенциального барьера, проницаемость *f* потенциального барьера

B70   *e*   **baryon**
     d   Baryon *n*
     f   baryon *m*
     r   барион *m*

B71   *e*   **baryon asymmetry of the Universe**
     d   Baryonenasymmetrie *f* des Weltalls
     f   asymétrie *f* baryonique de l'Univers
     r   барионная асимметрия *f* Вселенной

B72   *e*   **baryon charge**
     d   Baryonenladung *f*, Baryonenzahl *f*
     f   charge *f* baryonique, nombre *m* baryonique
     r   барионный заряд *m*, барионное число *n*

B73   *e*   **baryon decuplet**
     d   Baryonendekuplett *n*
     f   decuplet *m* baryonique
     r   барионный декуплет *m*

B74   *e*   **baryonic charge** *see* **baryon charge**

B75   *e*   **baryonium**
     d   Baryonium *n*
     f   baryonium *m*
     r   барионий *m*

B76   *e*   **baryon number** *see* **baryon charge**

B77   *e*   **baryon number conservation**
     d   Erhaltung *f* der Baryonenzahl
     f   conservation *f* du nombre baryonique
     r   сохранение *n* барионного числа

B78   *e*   **basal plane**
     d   Basisfläche *f*, Grundfläche *(Kristall)*
     f   plan *m* de base *(du cristal)*
     r   базисная плоскость *f (кристалла)*

B79   *e*   **base**
     d   1. Base *f* 2. Basis *f* 3. Grundlage *f*
     f   base *f*
     r   1. основание *n (химическое соединение)* 2. база *f (напр. биполярного транзистора)* 3. основа *f* 4. базис *m*

B80   *e*   **basic interaction**
     d   Fundamentalwechselwirkung *f*
     f   interaction *f* fondamentale
     r   фундаментальное взаимодействие *n*

B81   *e*   **basic research**
     d   Grundlagenforschung *f*
     f   recherches *f pl* fondamentales
     r   фундаментальные исследования *n pl*

B82   *e*   **basis**
     d   Basis *f*; Grundlage *f*
     f   base *f*
     r   базис *m*; основа *f*, основание *n*

B83   *e*   **battery**
     d   Batterie *f*
     f   batterie *f*
     r   батарея *f*

B84   *e*   **Bauschinger effect**
     d   Bauschinger-Effekt *m*
     f   effet *m* Bauschinger
     r   эффект *m* Баушингера

B85   *e*   **BCS model** *see* **Bardeen-Cooper-Schrieffer model**

B86   *e*   **beacon**
     d   1. Leuchtfeuer *n* 2. Funkbake *f*
     f   1. balise *f* 2. radiobalise *f*
     r   1. маяк *m* 2. радиомаяк *m*

B87   *e*   **bead lightning**
     d   Perlschnurblitz *m*
     f   foudre *f* perlée
     r   чёточная молния *f*

B88   *e*   **beam**
     d   1. Bündel *n* 2. Strahl *m* 3. Balken *m*; Träger *m* 4. Waagebalken *m*
     f   1. faisceau *m* 2. rayon *m* 3. poutre *f* 4. fléau *m*
     r   1. пучок *m* 2. луч *m* 3. балка *f* 4. коромысло *n (весов)*

B89   *e*   **beam channel**
     d   Strahlenkanal *m*
     f   canal *m* de faisceau
     r   канал *m* пучка

B90   *e*   **beam chopper**
     d   Chopper *m*, Strahlunterbrecher *m*
     f   interrupteur *m* du faisceau,
       obturateur *m*
     r   прерыватель *m* пучка; обтюратор
       m; модулятор *m* света

B91   *e*   **beam collimator**
     d   Strahlkollimator *m*
     f   collimateur *m* du faisceau
     r   коллиматор *m* пучка

B92   *e*   **beam cooling**
     d   Strahlenkühlung *f*
     f   refroidissement *m* des faisceaux
     r   охлаждение *n* пучков (*заряженных
       частиц*)

B93   *e*   **beam crossover**
     d   Strahlencrossover *n*,
       Strahlenkreuzungspunkt *m*
     f   point *m* de croisement du faisceau
     r   кроссовер *m* пучка

B94   *e*   **beam cross-section**
     d   Strahlquerschnitt *m*
     f   section *f* transversale du faisceau,
       section *f* du faisceau
     r   сечение *n* пучка

B95   *e*   **beam deflector**
     d   Strahlendeflektor *m*,
       Strahlenablenker *m*
     f   déflecteur *m* du faisceau
     r   дефлектор *m* пучка

B96   *e*   **beam defocusing**
     d   Strahlentbündelung *f*,
       Strahldefokussierung *f*
     f   défocalisation du faisceau
     r   дефокусировка *f* пучка

B97   *e*   **beam diaphragming**
     d   Strahlausblendung *f*,
       Strahlbegrenzung *f*
     f   diaphragmation *f* du faisceau
     r   диафрагмирование *n* пучка

B98   *e*   **beam divergence**
     d   Strahldivergenz *f*
     f   divergence *f* du faisceau
     r   расходимость *f* пучка

B99   *e*   **beam divider**
     d   Strahlteiler *m*
     f   dédoubleur *m* du faisceau
     r   делитель *m* пучка, расщепитель *m*
       пучка

B100   *e*   **beam extraction**
     d   Auslenken *n* des Strahls,
       Strahlejektion *f*
     f   extraction *f* du faisceau
     r   вывод *m* пучка (*из ускорителя*)

B101   *e*   **beam extractor**
     d   Strahlauslenkvorrichtung *f*
     f   extracteur *m* du faisceau
     r   устройство *n* вывода пучка, система
       f вывода пучка

B102   *e*   **beam focusing**
     d   Strahlenbündelung *f*,
       Strahlenfokussierung *f*
     f   focalisation *f* du faisceau
     r   фокусировка *f* пучка

B103   *e*   **beam forming**
     d   Bündelerzeugung *f*, Strahlformung *f*
     f   formation *f* du faisceau
     r   формирование *n* пучка

B104   *e*   **beam impedance**
     d   Strahlimpedanz *f*
     f   impédance *f* du faisceau
     r   импеданс *m* пучка

B105   *e*   **beam injection**
     d   Strahlinjektion *f*, Injektion *f* des
       Strahls
     f   injection *f* du faisceau
     r   инжекция *f* пучка

B106   *e*   **beam injector**
     d   Strahlinjektor *m*,
       Strahlinjektionsvorrichtung *f*
     f   injecteur *m* du faisceau
     r   инжектор *m* пучка

B107   *e*   **beam instability**
     d   Strahlinstabilität *f*
     f   instabilité *f* du faisceau
     r   пучковая неустойчивость *f*,
       неустойчивость *f* пучка

B108   *e*   **beam intensity**
     d   Strahlstärke *f*, Strahlintensität *f*
     f   intensité *f* du faisceau
     r   интенсивность *f* пучка

B109   *e*   **beam modulation**
     d   Strahlmodulation *f*
     f   modulation *f* du faisceau
     r   модуляция *f* пучка; модуляция *f*
       луча

B110   *e*   **beam-plasma discharge**
     d   Strahl-Plasma-Entladung *f*
     f   décharge *f* à faisceau de plasma
     r   плазменно-пучковый разряд *m*

B111   *e*   **beam position indicator**
     d   Strahlsensor *m*
     f   indicateur *m* de position du faisceau
     r   индикатор *m* положения пучка

B112   *e*   **beam position monitor**
     d   Monitor *m* der Strahlposition,
       Strahlpositionsmonitor *m*
     f   moniteur *m* de position du faisceau
     r   монитор *m* положения пучка

B113   *e* **beam position monitoring**
    d Strahlüberwachung *f*, Strahlkontrolle *f*
    f contrôle *m* de position du faisceau
    r контроль *m* положения пучка

B114   *e* **beam scanning**
    d Strahlscanning *n*
    f balayage *m* du faisceau
    r сканирование *n* луча

B115   *e* **beam-shaping channel**
    d Strahlformungskanal *m*
    f canal *m* de formation du faisceau
    r канал *m* формирования пучка

B116   *e* **beam splitter**
    d Strahlteiler *m*, Strahlenteiler *m*
    f dédoubleur *m* du faisceau
    r расщепитель *m* пучка *или* луча; светоделитель *m*

B117   *e* **beam splitting**
    d Strahlteilung *f*, Strahlspaltung *f*, Strahlenteilung *f*, Strahlenspaltung *f*
    f division *f* du faisceau
    r деление *n* пучка

B118   *e* **beam splitting cube**
    d Strahlenteilungswürfel *m*
    f cube *m* de division du faisceau
    r светоделительный куб *m*, светоделительный кубик *m*

B119   *e* **beam spread**
    d Strahlstreuung *f*
    f dispersion *f* du faisceau
    r размытие *n* пучка, рассеяние *n* пучка

B120   *e* **beam swinging**
    d Strahlschwenkung *f*
    f balayage *m* du faisceau
    r качание *n* луча *(антенны)*

B121   *e* **beam transport channel**
    d Strahltransportkanal *m*
    f canal *m* de transport du faisceau
    r канал *m* транспортировки пучка

B122   *e* **bearing**
    d 1. Stütze *f* 2. Lager *n*
    f palier *m*
    r 1. опора *f* 2. подшипник *m*

B123   *e* **beat envelope**
    d Schwebungseinhüllende *f*
    f enveloppe *f* des battements
    r огибающая *f* биений

B124   *e* **beat frequency**
    d Schwebungsfrequenz *f*
    f fréquence *f* des battements
    r частота *f* биений

B125   *e* **beats**
    d Schwebungen *f pl*
    f battements *m pl*
    r биения *n pl*

B126   *e* **beautiful meson**
    d Beauty-Meson *n*, schönes Meson *n*
    f beau méson *m*
    r «красивый» мезон *m*

B127   *e* **beautiful quark**
    d Beauty-Quark *n*
    f beau quark *m*
    r «красивый» кварк *m*, «прелестный» кварк *m*

B128   *e* **beauty**
    d Beauty *f (Begriff der Kernphysik)*
    f beauté *f (physique nucléaire)*
    r «красота» *f*, «прелесть» *f (в ядерной физике)*

B129   *e* **becquerel, Bq**
    d Becquerel *n*
    f becquerel *m*
    r беккерель *m*, Бк

B130   *e* **bel, B**
    d Bel *n*
    f bel *m*
    r бел *m*, Б

B131   *e* **bending**
    d Biegung *f*; Krümmung *f*
    f courbure *f*; flexion *f*
    r изгиб *m*

B132   *e* **bending deformation**
    d Biegungsdeformation *f*, Biegedeformation *f*, Biegeverformung *f*
    f déformation *f* de flexion
    r изгибная деформация *f*, деформация *f* изгиба

B133   *e* **bending moment**
    d Biegemoment *n*
    f moment *m* de flexion, moment *m* fléchissant
    r изгибающий момент *m*

B134   *e* **bending of a beam**
    d Balkenbiegung *f*
    f flexion *f* de la poutre
    r изгиб *m* бруса

B135   *e* **bending of a plate**
    d Plattenbiegung *f*
    f flexion *f* de la plaque
    r изгиб *m* пластинки

B136   *e* **bending of energy band**
    d Bandverbiegung *f*
    f flexion *f* de la bande
    r изгиб *m* зоны

B137   *e* **bending stiffness**
    d Biegesteifigkeit *f*
    f rigidité *f* à la flexion
    r жёсткость *f* при изгибе

B138 *e* bending stress
d Biegebeanspruchung *f*,
Biegespannung *f*
f effort *m* de flexion
r напряжение *n* при изгибе

B139 *e* bending torsion
d Biegeverdrehung *f*, Biegetorsion *f*
f torsion *f* de flexion
r изгибное кручение *n*

B140 *e* bending vibration
d Biegeschwingungen *f pl*
f oscillations *f pl* de flexion
r изгибные колебания *n pl*

B141 *e* bend test
d Biegeversuch *m*
f essai *m* de flexion
r испытание *n* на изгиб

B142 *e* berkelium, Bk
d Berkelium *n*
f berkélium *m*
r берклий *m*

B143 *e* Bernoulli equation
d Bernoullische Differentialgleichung *f*
f équation *f* différentielle de Bernoulli,
équation *f* de Bernoulli
r уравнение *n* Бернулли

B144 *e* Bernstein mode
d Bernsteinsche Mode *f*
f mode *m* de Bernstein
r мода *f* Бернштейна

B145 *e* beryllium, Be
d Beryllium *n*
f béryllium *m*
r бериллий *m*

B146 *e* beryllium ceramics
d Berylliumkeramik *f*
f céramique *f* à béryllium
r бериллиевая керамика *f*

B147 *e* Bessel functions
d Besselfunktionen *f pl*
f fonctions *f pl* de Bessel
r функции *f pl* Бесселя

B148 *e* beta-absorption gage *see* beta gage

B149 *e* beta-active isotope
d betaaktives Isotop *n*
f isotope *m* émetteur des rayons bêta
r бета-активный изотоп *m*

B150 *e* beta-decay
d Betazerfall *m*, Betaumwandlung *f*
f désintégration *f* bêta
r бета-распад *m*

B151 *e* beta emitter
d Beta-Strahler *m*
f radiateur *m* bêta, émetteur *m* bêta
r бета-излучатель *m*

B152 *e* beta gage
d Beta-Dickenmesser *m*
f jauge *f* bêta
r бета-толщиномер *m*

B153 *e* beta-particle
d Betateilchen *n*
f particule *f* bêta
r бета-частица *f*

B154 *e* beta phase
d Betaphase *f* (*von Legierungen*)
f phase *f* bêta (*des alliages*)
r бета-фаза *f* (*сплавов*)

B155 *e* beta radiation *see* beta-rays

B156 *e* beta-ray detector
d Betastrahlendetektor *m*
f détecteur *m* de rayons bêta
r бета-детектор *m*

B157 *e* beta-ray isotope *see* beta-active
isotope

B158 *e* beta-rays
d Betastrahlung *f*, Betastrahlen *pl*
f rayonnement *m* bêta, rayons *pl* bêta
r бета-излучение *n*, бета-лучи *pl*

B159 *e* beta-ray source
d Beta-Quelle *f*, Beta-Strahlungsquelle *f*
f source *f* de rayons bêta, radiateur *m*
bêta
r источник *m* бета-излучения

B160 *e* beta-ray spectrometer
d Beta-Spektrometer *n*
f spectromètre *m* bêta, spectromètre *m*
à rayons bêta
r бета-спектрометр *m*

B161 *e* beta-ray spectroscopy
d Beta-Spektroskopie *f*
f spectroscopie *f* bêta
r бета-спектроскопия *f*

B162 *e* beta-ray spectrum
d Beta-Spektrum *n*
f spectre *m* bêta
r бета-спектр *m*

B163 *e* beta-ray therapy
d Betastrahlentherapie *f*
f thérapie *f* bêta
r бета-лучевая терапия *f*

B164 *e* beta source *see* beta-ray source

B165 *e* beta spectroscopy *see* beta-ray
spectroscopy

B166 *e* beta-stable isotope
d betastabiles Isotop *n*
f isotope *m* bêta stable
r бетастабильный изотоп *m*

B167   *e*   betatron
       d   Betatron *n*
       f   bêtatron *m*
       r   бетатрон *m*

B168   *e*   betatron condition
       d   Wideröe-Bedingung *f*,
          Betatronbedingung *f*
       f   condition *f* bêtatron
       r   бетатронное условие *n*, условие *n*
          Видероэ

B169   *e*   betatron emission *see* betatron
          radiation

B170   *e*   betatronic acceleration mechanism
       d   Betatronbeschleunigungsmechanismus
          m
       f   mécanisme *m* d'accélération bêtatron
       r   бетатронный механизм *m* ускорения

B171   *e*   betatron oscillation, betatron
          oscillations
       d   Betatronschwingungen *f pl*
       f   oscillations *f pl* de bêtatron
       r   бетатронные колебания *n pl*

B172   *e*   betatron radiation
       d   Betatronstrahlung *f*
       f   rayonnement *m* de bêtatron
       r   бетатронное излучение *n*

B173   *e*   Bethe-Salpeter equation
       d   Bethe-Salpeter-Gleichung *f*, Salpeter-
          Bethe-Zweinukleonengleichung *f*
       f   équation *f* de Bethe-Salpeter
       r   уравнение *n* Бете - Солпитера

B174   *e*   bias
       d   1. Vormagnetisierung *f*
          2. Vorspannung *f*
       f   1. préaimantation *f*, prémagnétisation
          f; polarisation *f* 2. polarisation *f*
       r   1. подмагничивание *n* (постоянным
          током), смещение *n* 2. смещение *n*
          (*в полупроводниковых приборах с*
          p—n-переходом)

B175   *e*   bias voltage
       d   1. Vormagnetisierungsspannung *f*
          2. Vorspannung *f*
       f   tension *f* de polarisation
       r   напряжение *n* смещения

B176   *e*   biaxial crystal
       d   zweiachsiger Kristall *m*
       f   cristal *m* biaxial
       r   двухосный кристалл *m*

B177   *e*   bichromatic pyrometer
       d   bichromatisches Pyrometer *n*
       f   pyromètre *m* bichromatique
       r   двухцветный пирометр *m*, цветовой
          пирометр *m*

B178   *e*   biconcave lens

B179   *d*   Bikonkavlinse *f*
       f   lentille *f* biconcave
       r   двояковогнутая линза *f*

B179   *e*   biconvex lens
       d   Bikonvexlinse *f*
       f   lentille *f* biconvexe
       r   двояковыпуклая линза *f*

B180   *e*   biexciton
       d   Biexciton *n*
       f   biexciton *m*
       r   биэкситон *m*

B181   *e*   bifilar winding
       d   Bifilarwicklung *f*
       f   enroulement *m* bifilaire
       r   бифилярная намотка *f*

B182   *e*   bifurcation
       d   Gabelung *f*, Bifurkation *f*
       f   bifurcation *f*
       r   бифуркация *f*

B183   *e*   bifurcation diagram
       d   Bifurkationsdiagramm *n*
       f   diagramme *m* de bifurcation
       r   бифуркационная диаграмма *f*

B184   *e*   big bang
       d   Urknall *m*
       f   big bang *m*
       r   Большой взрыв *m* (*начальный этап*
          развития расширяющейся
          Вселенной)

B185   *e*   big bang nucleosynthesis *see*
          cosmological nucleosynthesis

B186   *e*   bimetallic strip
       d   Bimetallstreifen *m*
       f   lame *f* bimétallique, bilame *m*
       r   биметаллическая пластинка *f*

B187   *e*   binary pulsar
       d   Binär-Pulsar *m*
       f   pulsar *m* binaire
       r   двойной пульсар *m*

B188   *e*   binary star *see* double star

B189   *e*   binary system
       d   Doppelsystem *n*
       f   système *m* binaire
       r   двойная система *f*,
          двухкомпонентная система *f*

B190   *e*   binaural effect
       d   Binauraleffekt *m*
       f   effet *m* binaural
       r   бинауральный эффект *m*

B191   *e*   binder
       d   Bindemittel *n*
       f   liant *m*
       r   связующее вещество *n*,
          связующее *n*

B192　*e*　binding energy
　　　d　Bindungsenergie *f*
　　　f　énergie *f* de liaison
　　　r　энергия *f* связи

B193　*e*　binoculars
　　　d　Fernglas *n*
　　　f　jumelle(s) *f (pl)*
　　　r　бинокль *m*

B194　*e*　binocular vision
　　　d　binokulares Sehen *n*, zweiäugiges Sehen *n*
　　　f　vision *f* binoculaire
　　　r　бинокулярное зрение *n*

B195　*e*　binomial coefficient
　　　d　Binomialkoeffizient *m*, Binomialzahl *f*
　　　f　coefficient *m* binomial
　　　r　биномиальный коэффициент *m*

B196　*e*　binomial distribution
　　　d　Binomialverteilung *f*
　　　f　distribution *f* binomial
　　　r　биномиальное распределение *n*

B197　*e*　binormal
　　　d　Binormale *f*
　　　f　binormale *f*
　　　r　бинормаль *f*

B198　*e*　bioacoustics
　　　d　Bioakustik *f*
　　　f　bioacoustique *f*
　　　r　биологическая акустика *f*, биоакустика *f*

B199　*e*　biochemistry
　　　d　Biochemie *f*
　　　f　biochimie *f*
　　　r　биохимия *f*

B200　*e*　bioelectricity
　　　d　Bioelektrizität *f*
　　　f　bioélectricité *f*
　　　r　биоэлектричество *n*

B201　*e*　bioelectric potentials
　　　d　bioelektrische Potentiale *n pl*
　　　f　potentiels *m pl* bioélectriques
　　　r　биоэлектрические потенциалы *m pl*

B202　*e*　biological crystals
　　　d　biologische Kristalle *m pl*
　　　f　cristaux *m pl* biologiques
　　　r　биологические кристаллы *m pl*

B203　*e*　biological effects of radiation
　　　d　biologische Wirkung *f* der Strahlung, biologische Strahlenwirkung *f*, biologischer Strahlungseffekt *m*
　　　f　actions *f pl* biologiques de la radiation
　　　r　биологические действия *n pl* излучения

B204　*e*　biological shielding
　　　d　biologische Abschirmung *f*, biologischer Schild *m*

　　　f　protection *f* biologique
　　　r　биологическая защита *f*

B205　*e*　bioluminescence
　　　d　Biolumineszenz *f*
　　　f　bioluminescence *f*
　　　r　биолюминесценция *f*

B206　*e*　biophysics
　　　d　Biophysik *f*
　　　f　biophysique *f*
　　　r　биофизика *f*

B207　*e*　Biot-Savart law
　　　d　Biot-Savartsches Gesetz *n*
　　　f　loi *f* de Biot et Savart
　　　r　закон *m* Био - Савара

B208　*e*　biprism
　　　d　Biprisma *n*, Doppelprisma *n*
　　　f　biprisme *m*
　　　r　бипризма *f*

B209　*e*　birefringence
　　　d　Doppelbrechung *f*
　　　f　biréfringence *f*
　　　r　двойное лучепреломление *n*, двулучепреломление *n*

B210　*e*　bisectrix
　　　d　Winkelhalbierende *f*
　　　f　bissectrice *f*
　　　r　биссектриса *f*

B211　*e*　bismuth, Bi
　　　d　Wismut *n*
　　　f　bismuth *m*
　　　r　висмут *m*

B212　*e*　bistability
　　　d　Bistabilität *f*
　　　f　bistabilité *f*
　　　r　бистабильность *f*

B213　*e*　bistable interferometer
　　　d　bistabiles Interferometer *n*
　　　f　interféromètre *m* bistable
　　　r　бистабильный интерферометр *m*

B214　*e*　bit
　　　d　Bit *n*
　　　f　bit *m*
　　　r　бит *m*

B215　*e*　Bitter figures *see* magnetic powder patterns

B216　*e*　black body
　　　d　schwarzer Körper *m*, schwarzer Strahler *m*
　　　f　corps *m* noir
　　　r　чёрное тело *n*, абсолютно чёрное тело *n*

B217　*e*　black body radiation
　　　d　Hohlraumstrahlung *f*, Schwarzkörperstrahlung *f*

f rayonnement *m* du corps noir
r излучение *n* чёрного тела

B218 e blackening
      d Schwärzung *f*
      f noircissement *m*
      r почернение *n*

B219 e blackening density *see* photographic
         density

B220 e black hole
      d schwarzes Loch *n*
      f trou *m* noir
      r чёрная дыра *f*

B221 e blanket
      d Brutmantel *m*, Blanket *n*
      f enveloppe *f* fertile
      r бланкет *m* (*термоядерного
         реактора*)

B222 e blast
      d Explosion *f*; Detonation *f*
      f explosion *f*; détonation *f*
      r взрыв *m*

B223 e blast wave
      d Druckwelle *f*; Detonationswelle *f*
      f onde *f* de détente, onde *f* expansive;
         onde *f* de détonation
      r взрывная волна *f*

B224 e bleaching
      d 1. Ausbleichen *n*, Bleichen *n* 2.
         Ausbleichen *n*, Entfärbung *f*
      f blanchiment *m*
      r 1. отбеливание *n* 2. обесцвечивание
         n (*кристалла*)

B225 e bleaching dye
      d ausbleichbarer Farbstoff *m*
      f colorant *m* blanchissable
      r просветляющийся краситель *m*

B226 e Bleustein-Gulyaev waves
      d Bleustein-Gulyaev-Wellen *f pl*
      f ondes *f pl* de Bleustein-Gulyaev
      r волны *f pl* Гуляева - Блюстейна

B227 e Bloch curve
      d Blochsche Kurve *f*, Bloch-Kurve *f*
      f courbe *f* de Bloch
      r блоховская кривая *f*

B228 e Bloch functions
      d Blochsche Funktionen *f pl*
      f fonctions *f pl* de Bloch
      r функции *f pl* Блоха, блоховские
         функции *f pl*

B229 e Bloch law
      d Blochsches Gesetz *n*
      f loi *f* de Bloch
      r закон *m* Блоха

B230 e Bloch line

B231 e Bloch theorem
      d Blochsches Theorem *n*
      f théorème *m* de Bloch
      r теорема *f* Блоха

d Blochsche Linie *f*, Bloch-Linie *f*
f raie *f* de Bloch
r блоховская линия *f*

B232 e Bloch wall
      d Bloch-Wand *f*, Domänengrenzfläche *f*
      f cloison *f* de Bloch, paroi *f* de Bloch
      r блоховская стенка *f*, доменная
         стенка *f*

B233 e block diagram
      d Blockschema *n*, Blockdiagramm *n*,
         Blockschaltbild *n*
      f diagramme *m* synoptique
      r блок-схема *f*

B234 e blocking oscillator
      d Sperrschwinger *m*
      f oscillateur *m* à blocage
      r блокинг-генератор *m*

B235 e blue sky catastrophe
      d Blauhimmelkatastrophe *f*
      f catastrophe *f* du ciel bleu
      r катастрофа *f* голубого неба

B236 e bluff body
      d Körper *m* mit hohem
         Strömungswiderstand
      f corps *m* obtus
      r плохо обтекаемое тело *n*

B237 e body
      d Körper *n*
      f corps *m*
      r тело *n*

B238 e body-centered cube
      d raumzentrierter Würfel *m*
      f cube *m* centré
      r объёмноцентрированный куб *m*

B239 e body-centered cubic crystal
      d raumzentrierter kubischer Kristall *m*
      f cristal *m* cubique centré
      r объёмноцентрированный
         кубический кристалл *m*

B240 e body-centered lattice
      d raumzentriertes Gitter *n*
      f réseau *m* centré
      r объёмноцентрированная решётка *f*

B241 e body kinematics
      d Körperkinematik *f*
      f cinématique *f* du corps
      r кинематика *f* тела

B242 e Bohr atom model
      d Bohrsches Atommodell *n*
      f modèle *m* atomique de Bohr
      r боровская модель *f* атома

B243   *e*   **Bohr magneton**
      d   Bohrsches Magneton *n*
      f   magnéton *m* de Bohr
      r   магнетон *m* Бора

B244   *e*   **Bohr orbit**
      d   Bohrsche Bahn *f*
      f   orbite *f* de Bohr, trajectoire *f* de Bohr
      r   боровская орбита *f*

B245   *e*   **Bohr radius**
      d   Bohrscher Radius *m*, Radius *m* der ersten Bohrschen Bahn
      f   rayon *m* de Bohr
      r   радиус *m* Бора

B246   *e*   **boiling**
      d   Sieden *n*
      f   ébullition *f*
      r   кипение *n*

B247   *e*   **boiling crisis**
      d   Siedekrise *f*
      f   crise *f* d'ébullition
      r   кризис *m* кипения

B248   *e*   **boiling liquid**
      d   siedende Flüssigkeit *f*
      f   liquide *m* bouillant
      r   кипящая жидкость *f*

B249   *e*   **boiling point**
      d   Siedepunkt *m*, Siedetemperatur *f*
      f   température *f* d'ébullition, point *m* d'ébullition
      r   температура *f* кипения, точка *f* кипения

B250   *e*   **boiling temperature** *see* **boiling point**

B251   *e*   **bolide**
      d   Feuerkugel *f*, Bolid *m*
      f   bolide *m*
      r   болид *m*

B252   *e*   **bolometer**
      d   Bolometer *n*
      f   bolomètre *m*
      r   болометр *m*

B253   *e*   **bolometric correction**
      d   bolometrische Korrektion *f*
      f   correction *f* bolométrique
      r   болометрическая поправка *f*

B254   *e*   **bolometric magnitude**
      d   bolometrische Helligkeit *f*
      f   magnitude *f* bolométrique, magnitude *f* stellaire bolométrique
      r   болометрическая звёздная величина *f*

B255   *e*   **Boltzmann constant**
      d   Boltzmann-Konstante *f*
      f   constante *f* de Boltzmann
      r   постоянная *f* Больцмана

B256   *e*   **Boltzmann distribution**
      d   Boltzmann-Verteilung *f*, Boltzmannsche Verteilung *f*
      f   distribution *f* de Boltzmann
      r   распределение *n* Больцмана

B257   *e*   **Boltzmann statistics**
      d   Boltzmann-Statistik *f*
      f   statistique *f* de Boltzmann
      r   статистика *f* Больцмана

B258   *e*   **bombardment**
      d   Beschuß *m*, Beschießung *f*
      f   bombardement *m*
      r   бомбардировка *f*

B259   *e*   **bomb calorimeter**
      d   kalorimetrische Bombe *f*, Bombenkalorimeter *n*
      f   bombe *f* calorimétrique
      r   калориметрическая бомба *f*

B260   *e*   **bond**
      d   Bindung *f*
      f   liaison *f*
      r   связь *f*

B261   *e*   **bond energy**
      d   Bindungsenergie *f*
      f   énergie *f* de liaison
      r   энергия *f* связи

B262   *e*   **bonding**
      d   1. Bindung *f* 2. Verbindung *f*
      f   1. liaison *f* 2. liant *m*
      r   1. связь *f* 2. соединение *n*

B263   *e*   **bonding force**
      d   Bindungskraft *f*
      f   force *f* de liaison
      r   сила *f* связи

B264   *e*   **bonding orbitals**
      d   Bindungsorbitale *n pl*
      f   orbitales *f pl* de liaison
      r   связывающие орбитали *f pl*

B265   *e*   **bond length**
      d   Bindungslänge *f*, Bindungsabstand *m*, Valenzabstand *m*
      f   longueur *f* de liaison
      r   длина *f* связи *(в молекуле)*

B266   *e*   **bond order**
      d   Bindungsordnung *f*, Ordnung *f* der Bindung
      f   ordre *m* de liaison, indice *m* de liaison
      r   кратность *f* связи

B267   *e*   **bond saturation**
      d   Bindungssättigung *f*
      f   saturation *f* de la liaison
      r   насыщение *n* связи

B268   *e*   **bond strength** *see* **bond energy**

B269   *e*   **Boolean algebra**
      d   Boolesche Algebra *f*
      f   algèbre *f* de Boole
      r   булева алгебра *f*, алгебра *f* логики

B270   *e*   **booster**
      d   Booster *m*
      f   booster *m*
      r   бустер *m (промежуточный ускоритель)*

B271   *e*   **bootstrap**
      d   Bootstrap *m*
      f   bootstrap *m*
      r   шнуровка *f*, бутстрап *m*

B272   *e*   **Born approximation**
      d   Bornsche Näherung *f*
      f   approximation *f* de Born
      r   борновское приближение *n*

B273   *e*   **boron, B**
      d   Bor *n*
      f   bore *m*
      r   бор *m*

B274   *e*   **boron carbide**
      d   Borkarbid *n*
      f   carbure *m* de bore
      r   карбид *m* бора

B275   *e*   **Bose condensate** *see* **Bose-Einstein condensate**

B276   *e*   **Bose condensation** *see* **Bose-Einstein condensation**

B277   *e*   **Bose-Einstein condensate**
      d   Bose-Einstein-Kondensat *n*, Bose-Kondensat *n*
      f   condensat *m* de Bose-Einstein, condensat *m* de Bose
      r   бозе-конденсат *m*

B278   *e*   **Bose-Einstein condensation**
      d   Bose-Einstein-Kondensation *f*, Bose-Kondensation *f*
      f   condensation *f* de Bose-Einstein, condensation *f* de Bose
      r   бозе-конденсация *f*, конденсация *f* Бозе - Эйнштейна

B279   *e*   **Bose-Einstein liquid**
      d   Bose-Flüssigkeit *f*
      f   liquide *m* de Bose
      r   бозе-жидкость *f*

B280   *e*   **Bose-Einstein statistics**
      d   Bose-Einstein-Statistik *f*, BE-Statistik *f*
      f   statistique *f* de Bose
      r   статистика *f* Бозе - Эйнштейна

B281   *e*   **Bose gas**
      d   Bose-Gas *n*
      f   gaz *m* de Bose
      r   бозе-газ *m*

B282   *e*   **Bose particle** *see* **boson**

B283   *e*   **boson**
      d   Boson *n*, Bose-Teilchen *n*
      f   boson *m*, particule *f* Bose
      r   бозон *m*, бозе-частица *f*

B284   *e*   **bottom of energy band**
      d   Unterkante *f* des Energiebandes
      f   fond *m* de la bande énergétique
      r   дно *n* энергетической зоны

B285   *e*   **bottom quark**
      d   b-Quark *n*
      f   b-quark *m*
      r   нижний кварк *m*, b-кварк *m*

B286   *e*   **Bouguer-Lambert-Beer law**
      d   Bouguer-Lambert-Beer-Gesetz *n*
      f   loi *f* de Bouguer-Lambert-Beer
      r   закон *m* Бугера - Ламберта - Бера

B287   *e*   **boundary**
      d   Grenze *f*
      f   limite *f*
      r   граница *f*

B288   *e*   **boundary conditions**
      d   Grenzbedingungen *f pl*
      f   conditions *f pl* limites
      r   граничные условия *n pl*

B289   *e*   **boundary layer**
      d   Grenzschicht *f*
      f   couche *f* limite
      r   пограничный слой *m*

B290   *e*   **boundary value**
      d   Randwert *m*
      f   valeur *f* frontière
      r   граничное значение *n*

B291   *e*   **boundary-value problem**
      d   Randwertaufgabe *f*, Randwertproblem *n*
      f   problème *m* aux limites
      r   краевая задача *f*, граничная задача *f*

B292   *e*   **bound-bound transition**
      d   Gebunden-Gebunden-Übergang *m*
      f   transition *f* liée-liée
      r   связанно-связанный переход *m*

B293   *e*   **bound charge**
      d   Polarisationsladung *f*, gebundene Ladung *f*
      f   charge *f* de polarisation, charge *f* liée
      r   связанный заряд *m*

B294   *e*   **bound electron**
      d   gebundenes Elektron *n*
      f   électron *m* lié
      r   связанный электрон *m*

B295   *e*   **bound energy**
      d   gebundene Energie *f*

	f	énergie *f* liée
	r	связанная энергия *f*
B296	*e*	**bound state**
	d	gebundener Zustand *m*
	f	état *m* lié
	r	связанное состояние *n*
B297	*e*	**bound vortex**
	d	gebundener Wirbel *m*
	f	tourbillon *m* asservi
	r	присоединённый вихрь *m*
B298	*e*	**bow shock, bow-shock wave**
	d	Kopfwelle *f*
	f	onde *f* de tête
	r	головная ударная волна *f*
B299	*e*	**bow wave**
	d	Bugwelle *f*
	f	onde *f* de choc frontale
	r	носовая волна *f*
B300	*e*	**Boyle law**
	d	Boyle-Mariottesches Gesetz *n*, Boylesches Gesetz *n*
	f	loi *f* de Boyle-Mariotte, loi *f* de Boyle
	r	закон *m* Бойля - Мариотта
B301	*e*	**brachistochrone**
	d	Brachistochrone *f*, Brachystochrone *f*
	f	brachystochrone *f*
	r	брахистохрона *f*
B302	*e*	**Brackett series**
	d	Brackett-Serie *f*
	f	série *f* de Brackett
	r	спектральная серия *f* Брэкета, серия *f* Брэкета
B303	*e*	**Bragg angle**
	d	Bragg-Winkel *m*, Braggscher Winkel *m*
	f	angle *m* de Bragg
	r	угол *m* Брэгга, брэгговский угол *m*
B304	*e*	**Bragg diffraction**
	d	Braggsche Beugung *f*
	f	diffraction *f* de Bragg
	r	брэгговская дифракция *f*
B305	*e*	**Bragg equation**
	d	Bragg-Gleichung *f*, Braggsche Gleichung *f*, Reflexionsbedingung *f* von Bragg
	f	condition *f* de Bragg
	r	условие *n* Брэгга - Вульфа
B306	*e*	**Bragg law** *see* **Bragg equation**
B307	*e*	**Bragg reflection**
	d	Bragg-Reflexion *f*, Braggsche Reflexion *f*
	f	réflexion *f* de Bragg
	r	брэгговское отражение *n*
B308	*e*	**braking radiation** *see* **bremsstrahlung**
B309	*e*	**branch**
	d	Abzweigung *f*; Zweig *m*
	f	branche *f*
	r	ветвь *f*
B310	*e*	**branching**
	d	Verzweigung *f*
	f	branchement *m*; ramification *f*
	r	ветвление *n*
B311	*e*	**branch point**
	d	Verzweigungsstelle *f*
	f	point *m* de bifurcation
	r	точка *f* ветвления
B312	*e*	**brass**
	d	Messing *n*
	f	laiton *m*
	r	латунь *f*
B313	*e*	**Bravais lattice**
	d	Bravais-Gitter *n*
	f	réseau *m* de Bravais
	r	решётка *f* Браве
B314	*e*	**breakdown**
	d	1. Durchschlag *m* 2. Zusammenbruch *m*
	f	1. rupture *f*, claquage *m* 2. destruction *f*
	r	1. пробой *m* 2. разрушение *n*
B315	*e*	**breakdown mechanism**
	d	Durchschlagmechanismus *m*
	f	mécanisme *m* de claquage
	r	механизм *m* пробоя
B316	*e*	**breakdown test**
	d	elektrische Festigkeitsprüfung *f*
	f	essai *m* de rigidité diélectrique
	r	испытания *n pl* на электрическую прочность
B317	*e*	**breakdown voltage**
	d	Durchschlagspannung *f*
	f	tension *f* de claquage
	r	пробивное напряжение *n*, напряжение *n* пробоя
B318	*e*	**breaking strain**
	d	Bruchverformung *f*
	f	déformation *f* destructive
	r	разрушающая деформация *f*
B319	*e*	**breaking strength**
	d	Bruchfestigkeit *f*
	f	puissance *f* de rupture
	r	сопротивление *n* разрушению; предел *m* прочности на разрыв
B320	*e*	**breaking stress**
	d	Bruchspannung *f*
	f	contrainte *f* de rupture
	r	разрушающее напряжение *n*, предел *m* прочности на растяжение
B321	*e*	**breeder, breeder reactor**

    d Brutreaktor *m*, Brüter *m*
    f réacteur *m* régénérateur, breeder *m*
    r реактор-размножитель *m*, бридер *m*

B322 *e* breeding
    d Brüten *n (von Spaltmaterial)*
    f régénération *f* des matériaux de fission
    r расширенное воспроизводство *n* ядерного топлива

B323 *e* breeding factor *see* breeding ratio

B324 *e* breeding gain
    d Brutgewinn *m*
    f gain *m* de régénération
    r избыточный коэффициент *m* воспроизводства *(ядерного топлива)*

B325 *e* breeding ratio
    d Brutrate *f*, Brutverhältnis *n*, Brutfaktor *m*
    f coefficient *m* de régénération
    r коэффициент *m* воспроизводства *(ядерного топлива)*

B326 *e* Breit-Wigner formula
    d Breit-Wigner-Formel *f*, Dispersionsformel *f* für isoliertes Resonanzniveau
    f formule *f* de Breit et Wigner
    r формула *f* Брейта - Вигнера

B327 *e* bremsstrahlung
    d Bremsstrahlung *f*
    f bremsstrahlung *m*, rayonnement *m* de freinage
    r тормозное излучение *n*

B328 *e* Brewster angle
    d Brewsterscher Winkel *m*
    f angle *m* de Brewster
    r угол *m* Брюстера

B329 *e* Brewster angle window
    d Brewster-Fenster *n*
    f fenêtre *f* d'angle de Brewster
    r окно *n* Брюстера; окно *n*, расположенное под углом Брюстера

B330 *e* Brewster law
    d Brewstersches Gesetz *n*
    f loi *f* de Brewster
    r закон *m* Брюстера

B331 *e* bridge
    d Brücke *f*, Meßbrücke *f*
    f pont *m*
    r мост *m*, измерительный мост *m*

B332 *e* Bridgman method
    d Bridgman-Methode *f*
    f méthode *f* de Bridgman
    r метод *m* Бриджмена

B333 *e* brightness

    d Helligkeit *f*; Leuchtdichte *f*
    f brillance *f*, luminance *f* visuelle
    r яркость *f*

B334 *e* brightness temperature
    d schwarze Temperatur *f*, Luminanztemperatur *f*
    f température *f* de luminance
    r яркостная температура *f*

B335 *e* brilliance
    d 1. Helligkeit *f*, Sternhelligkeit *f* 2. Helligkeit *f*
    f 1. éclat *m* apparent 2. brillance *f*, luminance *f* visuelle
    r 1. блеск *m (звезды)* 2. яркость *f*

B336 *e* Brillouin scattering
    d Brillouin-Streuung *f*
    f diffusion *f* Brillouin, diffusion *f* de Brillouin
    r рассеяние *n* Мандельштама - Бриллюэна

B337 *e* Brillouin zone
    d Brillouinsche Zone *f*, Brillouin-Zone *f*
    f zone *f* de Brillouin
    r зона *f* Бриллюэна

B338 *e* Brinell hardness
    d Brinell-Härte *f*
    f dureté *f* à la bille
    r твёрдость *f* по Бринеллю

B339 *e* brittle-ductile transition
    d Umwandlung *f* spröde-duktil
    f transition *f* fragile/ductile
    r переход *m* хрупкость - пластичность

B340 *e* brittle fracture
    d Sprödbruch *m*, spröder Bruch *m*
    f fracture *f* fragile
    r хрупкий излом *m*

B341 *e* brittleness
    d Sprödigkeit *f*
    f fragilité *f*
    r хрупкость *f*

B342 *e* broadband aerial
    d Breitbandantenne *f*
    f antenne *f* à large bande
    r широкополосная антенна *f*

B343 *e* broadband amplifier
    d Breitbandverstärker *m*
    f amplificateur *m* à large bande
    r широкополосный усилитель *m*

B344 *e* broadband radiation
    d Breitbandstrahlung *f*
    f rayonnement *m* à large bande
    r широкополосное излучение *n*

B345 *e* broadened line
    d verbreiterte Linie *f*

	f	raie *f* élargie
	r	уширенная линия *f*
B346	*e*	**broadening of spectral lines**
	d	Spektrallinienverbreiterung *f*
	f	élargissement *m* des raies spectrales
	r	уширение *n* спектральных линий
B347	*e*	**broken symmetry**
	d	gebrochene Symmetrie *f*
	f	symétrie *f* dérangée
	r	нарушенная симметрия *f*
B348	*e*	**bromine, Br**
	d	Brom *n*
	f	brome *m*
	r	бром *m*
B349	*e*	**bronze**
	d	Bronze *f*
	f	bronze *m*
	r	бронза *f*
B350	*e*	**Brownian motion**
	d	Brownsche Bewegung *f*, Brownsche Molekularbewegung *f*
	f	mouvement *m* brownien, mouvement *m* Brown
	r	броуновское движение *n*
B351	*e*	**brush discharge**
	d	Büschelentladung *f*
	f	décharge *f* en aigrette
	r	кистевой разряд *m*
B352	*e*	**bubble**
	d	1. Blase *f* 2. Blase *f*, Blasendomäne *f*
	f	1. bulle *f* 2. domaine *m* en bulle
	r	1. пузырёк *m* 2. цилиндрический магнитный домен *m*, ЦМД
B353	*e*	**bubble cavitation**
	d	Blasenkavitation *f*
	f	cavitation *f* à bulles
	r	пузырьковая кавитация *f*
B354	*e*	**bubble chamber**
	d	Blasenkammer *f*
	f	chambre *f* à bulles
	r	пузырьковая камера *f*
B355	*e*	**bubble formation**
	d	Blasenbildung *f*
	f	formation *f* de bulles
	r	образование *n* пузырьков *(при кипении)*
B356	*e*	**buckling**
	d	Knickung *f*
	f	flambage *m*
	r	продольный изгиб *m*
B357	*e*	**Budker ring**
	d	Budkerscher Ring *m*
	f	anneau *m* de Budker
	r	будкеровское кольцо *n*

B358	*e*	**buffer action**
	d	Pufferwirkung *f*
	f	action *f* tampon, pouvoir *m* tampon
	r	буферное действие *n*
B359	*e*	**buffer solution**
	d	Pufferlösung *f*
	f	solution *f* tampon
	r	буферный раствор *m*
B360	*e*	**buffer stage**
	d	1. Zwischenstufe *f* 2. Pufferstufe *f*
	f	étage *m* intermédiaire
	r	1. промежуточная ступень *f* 2. буферный каскад *m*
B361	*e*	**bulk boiling**
	d	Blasenverdampfung *f*, Blasensieden *n*, Bläschensieden *n*
	f	bouillonnement *m* au sein de liquide
	r	объёмное кипение *n*
B362	*e*	**bulk elasticity**
	d	Volumenelastizität *f*
	f	élasticité *f* de volume
	r	объёмная упругость *f*
B363	*e*	**bulk modulus**
	d	1. Volumenelastizitätsmodul *m* 2. Kompressionsmodul *m*
	f	1. module *m* d'élasticité de volume 2. module *m* de compressibilité volumique
	r	1. модуль *m* объёмной упругости 2. модуль *m* всестороннего сжатия
B364	*e*	**bulk velocity** *see* volume velocity
B365	*e*	**bunch**
	d	Paket *n*; Ballung *f*, Zusammenballung *f*
	f	groupe *m*
	r	сгусток *m (частиц)*
B366	*e*	**buncher**
	d	Buncher *m*
	f	groupeur *m*
	r	банчер *m*, группирователь *m*
B367	*e*	**bunching**
	d	Bündelung *f*
	f	rassemblement *m*, groupage *m*
	r	группирование *n*
B368	*e*	**bundle**
	d	Bündel *n*
	f	faisceau *m*
	r	пучок *m*; жгут *m*
B369	*e*	**bundle of rays**
	d	Strahlenbündel *n*
	f	faisceau *m* de rayons
	r	пучок *m* лучей
B370	*e*	**Bunsen burner**
	d	Bunsen-Brenner *m*
	f	brûleur *m* Bunsen
	r	горелка *f* Бунзена

B371   *e*   Bunsen photometer
     d   Bunsen-Photometer *n*
     f   photomètre *m* de Bunsen
     r   фотометр *m* Бунзена

B372   *e*   buoyancy
     d   Auftrieb *m*; hydrostatischer
        Auftrieb *m*
     f   flottabilité *f*
     r   1. плавучесть *f* 2. выталкивающая
        сила *f*, архимедова сила *f*

B373   *e*   buoyancy force
     d   Auftrieb *m*, Auftriebskraft *f*
     f   force *f* d'Archimède
     r   выталкивающая сила *f*, архимедова
        сила *f*

B374   *e*   burette
     d   Bürette *f*
     f   burette *f*
     r   бюретка *f*

B375   *e*   Burgers dislocation *see* screw
        dislocation

B376   *e*   Burgers vector
     d   Burgers-Vektor *m*
     f   vecteur *m* de Burgers, vecteur *m* de
        glissement de Burgers
     r   вектор *m* Бюргерса

B377   *e*   burial of radioactive waste
     d   Endlagerung *f* radioaktiver Abfälle
     f   stockage *m* des déchets radioactifs
     r   захоронение *n* радиоактивных
        отходов

B378   *e*   burning
     d   1. Brennen *n*; Abbrand *m* 2. Brennen
        n, Brand *m*
     f   1. brûlage *m*; combustion *f*
        2. cuisson *f*
     r   1. горение *n*; выгорание *n* 2. обжиг
        m (напр. керамики)

B379   *e*   burning velocity of flames
     d   Flammenfortpflanzungsgeschwindigkeit
        f
     f   vitesse *f* de calcination par les flammes
     r   скорость *f* распространения
        пламени

B380   *e*   burst
     d   Burst *m*, Ausbruch *m*
     f   burst *m*
     r   всплеск *m (излучения)*; вспышка *f*

B381   *e*   burster
     d   Burster *m*
     f   burster *m*
     r   барстер *m*

B382   *e*   bus
     d   Sammelschiene *f*; Bus *m*
     f   barre *f*; bus *m*
     r   шина *f*

B383   *e*   button
     d   Taste *f*; Knopf *m*, Druckknopf *m*
     f   bouton *m*
     r   кнопка *f*

C

C1   *e*   Cabibbo angle
     d   Cabibbo-Winkel *m*
     f   angle *m* de Cabibbo
     r   угол *m* Кабиббо

C2   *e*   cable
     d   Kabel *n*, Leitungskabel *n*
     f   câble *m*
     r   кабель *m*

C3   *e*   cadmium, Cd
     d   Cadmium *n*, Kadmium *n*
     f   cadmium *m*
     r   кадмий *m*

C4   *e*   cadmium cutoff
     d   Cadmiumgrenze *f*, Einfanggrenze *f* im
        Cadmium
     f   limite *f* de capture pour le cadmium
     r   граница *f* поглощения в кадмии

C5   *e*   caesium, Cs
     d   Caesium *n*, Zäsium *n*
     f   césium *m*, cæsium *m*
     r   цезий *m*

C6   *e*   caesium frequency standard
     d   Caesiumfrequenznormal *n*
     f   étalon *m* de fréquence à césuim
     r   цезиевый стандарт *m* частоты,
        цезиевый эталон *m* частоты

C7   *e*   calcium, Ca
     d   Calcium *n*, Kalzium *n*
     f   calcium *m*
     r   кальций *m*

C8   *e*   calculation
     d   Berechnung *f*
     f   calcul *m*
     r   вычисление *n*, расчёт *m*

C9   *e*   calculus
     d   Kalkül *m*; Differential- und
        Integralrechnung *f*
     f   calcul *m*; calcul *m* différentiel et
        intégral
     r   исчисление *n*; дифференциальное и
        интегральное исчисление *n*

C10   *e*   calculus of variations
     d   Variationsrechnung *f*
     f   calcul *m* des variations
     r   вариационное исчисление *n*

C11   *e*   calibration
     d   Eichung *f*; Kalibrierung *f*
     f   calibrage *m*
     r   1. градуировка *f* 2. калибровка *f*
        (прибора)

C12   *e*   calibration curve
     d   Eichkurve *f*
     f   courbe *f* de calibrage
     r   калибровочная кривая *f*,
        градуировочная кривая *f*

C13   *e*   calibration source
     d   Kalibrierungsquelle *f*, Kalibrierquelle
        f, Eichquelle *f*
     f   source *f* de calibrage
     r   калибровочный источник *m*,
        градуировочный источник *m*

C14   *e*   californium, Cf
     d   Californium *n*, Kalifornium *n*
     f   californium *m*
     r   калифорний *m*

C15   *e*   calm days *see* quiet days

C16   *e*   calorescence
     d   Kaloreszenz *f*
     f   calorescence *f*
     r   калоресценция *f*

C17   *e*   caloric power *see* calorific value

C18   *e*   calorie, cal
     d   Kalorie *f*
     f   calorie *f*, cal
     r   калория *f*, кал

C19   *e*   calorific value
     d   Heizwert *m*; Brennwert *m*
     f   pouvoir *m* calorifique
     r   теплотворная способность *f*

C20   *e*   calorimeter
     d   Kalorimeter *n*, Wärmemengenmesser
        m, Wärmemesser *m*
     f   calorimètre *m*
     r   калориметр *m*

C21   *e*   calorimetry
     d   Kalorimetrie *f*, Wärmemessung *f*
     f   calorimétrie *f*
     r   калориметрия *f*

C22   *e*   calutron
     d   Calutron *n*
     f   calutron *m*
     r   калютрон *m*

C23   *e*   CAMAC (Computer Application for
        Measurement and Control)
     d   CAMAC-System *n*
     f   système *m* CAMAC
     r   КАМАК

C24   *e*   camera
     d   1. Kammer *f*, Aufnahmekammer *f*
        (*Fotogrammetrie*) 2. Kamera *f*,
        Fotoapparat *m*
     f   caméra *f*
     r   1. камера *f* 2. фотокамера *f*

C25   *e*   camera obscura
     d   Camera *f* obscura, Lichtkamera *f*
     f   chambre *f* obscure
     r   камера-обскура *f*

C26   *e*   Canada balsam
     d   Kanadabalsam *m*
     f   baume *m* du Canada
     r   канадский бальзам *m*

C27   *e*   canal rays
     d   Kanalstrahlen *pl*
     f   rayons *pl* canaux
     r   каналовые лучи *pl*

C28   *e*   candela, Cd
     d   Candela *f*
     f   candela *f*
     r   кандела *f*, кд

C29   *e*   canonical assembly *see* canonical
        ensemble

C30   *e*   canonical distribution
     d   kanonische Verteilung *f*, Gibbs-
        Verteilung *f*
     f   distribution *f* canonique, répartition *f*
        canonique
     r   каноническое распределение *n*

C31   *e*   canonical ensemble
     d   kanonische Gesamtheit *f*
     f   ensemble *m* canonique
     r   канонический ансамбль *m*

C32   *e*   canonical equations of motion
     d   kanonische Bewegungsgleichungen *f*
        pl, Hamiltonsche Gleichungen *f pl* der
        Dynamik
     f   équations *f pl* canoniques du
        mouvement
     r   канонические уравнения *n pl*
        механики

C33   *e*   canonical momentum
     d   kanonischer Impuls *m*
     f   impulsion *f* canonique
     r   канонический импульс *m*

C34   *e*   canonical transformation
     d   kanonische Transformation *f*,
        kanonische Abbildung *f*
     f   transformation *f* canonique,
        changement *m* canonique
     r   каноническое преобразование *n*

C35   *e*   cantilever
     d   Konsole *f*; Kragträger *m*
     f   porte-à-faux *m*, encorbellement *m*;
        console *f*
     r   консоль *f*; кронштейн *m*

C36 *e* capacitance
     d 1. Kapazität *f*, elektrische Kapazität *f*
          2. kapazitiver Widerstand *m*
     f 1. capacité *f* 2. capacitance *f*
     r 1. ёмкость *f* 2. ёмкостное
          сопротивление *n*

C37 *e* capacitance meter
     d Kapazitätsmesser *m*
     f faradmètre *m*, capacimètre *m*
     r фарадметр *m*, измеритель *m*
          ёмкости

C38 *e* capacitive coupling
     d kapazitive Kopplung *f*
     f couplage *m* capacitif
     r ёмкостная связь *f*

C39 *e* capacitive diaphragm
     d kapazitive Blende *f*
     f diaphragme *m* capacitif
     r ёмкостная *f* диафрагма

C40 *e* capacitive load
     d kapazitive Belastung *f*
     f charge *f* capacitive
     r ёмкостная нагрузка *f*

C41 *ê* capacitive sensor
     d kapazitiver Geber *m*; kapazitiver
          Sensor *m*
     f capteur *m* capacitif
     r ёмкостный датчик *m*

C42 *e* capacitive storage
     d kapazitiver Speicher *m*
     f accumulateur *m* capacitif
     r ёмкостный накопитель *m*

C43 *e* capacitometer *see* capacitance meter

C44 *e* capacitor
     d Kondensator *m*; Kapazität *f*
     f condensateur *m*
     r конденсатор *m*

C45 *e* capacitor charge
     d Kondensatorladung *f*
     f charge *f* du condensateur
     r заряд *m* конденсатора

C46 *e* capacitor plate
     d Kondensatorbelag *m*
     f armature *f* du condensateur
     r обкладка *f* конденсатора

C47 *e* capacity *see* capacitance 1.

C48 *e* capacity manometer
     d Kapazitätsmanometer *n*
     f manomètre *m* capacitif
     r ёмкостный манометр *m*

C49 *e* capillary
     d Kapillare *f*, Kapillarröhre *f*,
          Kapillarröhrchen *n*
     f capillaire *m*
     r капилляр *m*

C50 *e* capillary condensation
     d Kapillarkondensation *f*
     f condensation *f* capillaire
     r капиллярная конденсация *f*

C51 *e* capillary convection
     d Kapillarkonvektion *f*
     f convection *f* capillaire
     r капиллярная конвекция *f*

C52 *e* capillary forces
     d Kapillarkräfte *pl*
     f forces *pl* capillaires
     r капиллярные силы *pl*

C53 *e* capillary phenomena
     d Kapillarerscheinungen *f pl*,
          Kapillarphänomene *n pl*
     f phénomènes *m pl* de capillarité
     r капиллярные явления *n pl*

C54 *e* capillary pressure
     d Kapillardruck *m*
     f pression *f* capillaire
     r капиллярное давление *n*

C55 *e* capillary waves
     d Kapillarwellen *f pl*, Kräuselwellen *f pl*,
          Rippelwellen *f pl*
     f ondes *f pl* capillaires
     r капиллярные волны *f pl*

C56 *e* capsule
     d Kapsel *f*
     f capsule *f*
     r капсула *f*

C57 *e* capture *see* trapping

C58 *e* capture cross-section
     d Einfangquerschnitt *m*,
          Wirkungsquerschnitt *m* des Einfangs
     f section *f* efficace de capture
     r сечение *n* захвата

C59 *e* capture of charged particles
     d Einfang *m* von geladenen Teilchen
     f capture *f* des particules chargées
     r захват *m* заряженных частиц

C60 *e* capture of electron by a nucleus
     d Elektroneneinfang *m* durch den Kern
     f capture *f* de l'électron par un noyau
     r захват *m* электрона ядром

C61 *e* carat
     d Karat *n*, metrisches Karat *n*
     f carat *m*
     r карат *m*

C62 *e* Carathéodory principle
     d Carathéodorysches
          Unerreichbarkeitsaxiom *n*,
          Carathéodorysches Prinzip *n* der
          adiabatischen Unerreichbarkeit

f principe *m* de Carathéodory
r принцип *m* Каратеодори

C63 *e* carbon, C
d Kohlenstoff *m*
f carbone *m*
r углерод *m*

C64 *e* carbonado
d Karbonado *m*
f carbonado *m*
r карбонадо *m*

C65 *e* carbon arc
d Kohlenbogen *m*
f arc *m* au charbon
r угольная дуга *f*

C66 *e* carbon dioxide
d Kohlendioxid *n*
f dioxyde *m* de carbone
r углекислый газ *m*, диоксид *m* углерода

C67 *e* carbon-nitrogen cycle
d Kohlenstoff-Stickstoffzyklus *m*, Kohlenstoffzyklus *m*
f cycle *m* carbone-azote
r углеродно-азотный цикл *m*

C68 *e* carbon steel
d Kohlenstoffstahl *m*
f acier *m* au carbone
r углеродистая сталь *f*

C69 *e* carcinotron
d Carcinotron *n*, Karzinotron *n*, Rückwärtswellenröhre *f*
f carcinotron *m*
r карцинотрон *m*, лампа *f* обратной волны, ЛОВ

C70 *e* cardinal points
d Kardinalpunkte *m pl*, Grundpunkte *m pl*
f points *m pl* cardinaux *(d'une lentille)*
r кардинальные точки *f pl (оптической системы)*

C71 *e* cardioid condenser
d Kardioidkondensor *m*
f condenseur *m* cardioïde
r кардиоид-конденсор *m*

C72 *e* carmatron
d Karmatron *n*, Rückwärtswellenmagnetron *n*
f carmatron *m*
r карматрон *m*

C73 *e* Carnot cycle
d Carnotscher Kreisprozeß *m*, Carnot-Prozeß *m*
f cycle *m* de Carnot
r цикл *m* Карно

C74 *e* Carnot principle
d Carnotsches Prinzip *n*, Carnotsches Theorem *n*
f principe *m* de Carnot
r теорема *f* Карно

C75 *e* carrier
d 1. Träger *m*, Ladungsträger *m* 2. Träger *m*, Trägerfrequenz *f*
f porteur *m*
r 1. носитель *m*, носитель *m* заряда 2. несущая *f*, несущая частота *f*

C76 *e* carrier concentration, carrier density
d Ladungsträgerkonzentration *f*, Ladungsträgerdichte *f*
f concentration *f* des porteurs
r концентрация *f* носителей заряда

C77 *e* carrier drift
d Ladungsträgerdrift *f*
f dérive *f* des porteurs
r дрейф *m* носителей заряда

C78 *e* carrier freezing-out
d Ladungsträgerausfrierung *f*
f séparation *f* des porteurs par congélation
r вымораживание *n* носителей заряда

C79 *e* carrier frequency *see* carrier 2.

C80 *e* carrier injection
d Ladungsträgerinjektion *f*
f injection *f* des porteurs
r инжекция *f* носителей заряда

C81 *e* carrier mobility
d Ladungsträgerbeweglichkeit *f*
f mobilité *f* des porteurs
r подвижность *f* носителей заряда

C82 *e* carrier trapping
d Trägerhaftung *f*, Ladungsträgereinfang *m*
f capture *f* des porteurs
r захват *m* носителей заряда

C83 *e* CARS technique *see* coherent anti-Stokes Raman scattering

C84 *e* Cartesian coordinates
d kartesische Koordinaten *f pl*
f coordonnées *f pl* cartésiennes
r декартовы координаты *f pl*, прямоугольные координаты *f pl*

C85 *e* cascade
d 1. Kaskade *f* 2. Trennkaskade *f*, Gasdiffusionstrennkaskade *f*
f cascade *f*
r каскад *m*

C86 *e* cascade connection
d Kaskadenschaltung *f*
f couplage *m* en cascade
r каскадное соединение *n*, каскадное включение *n*

C87   *e* cascade generator
      d Kaskadengenerator *m*
      f générateur *m* en cascade
      r каскадный генератор *m*

C88   *e* cascade liquefaction
      d Kaskadenverflüssigung *f*
      f liquéfaction *f* en cascade
      r каскадное ожижение *n*

C89   *e* cascade of bifurcations
      d Kaskade *f* von Bifurkationen
      f cascade *f* de bifurcations
      r каскад *m* бифуркаций

C90   *e* cascade particle
      d Kaskadenteilchen *n*
      f particule *f* en cascade
      r каскадная частица *f*

C91   *e* cascade shower
      d Kaskadenschauer *m*
      f gerbe *f* en cascade
      r каскадный ливень *m*

C92   *e* Cassegrain telescope
      d Cassegrain-Reflektor *m*
      f télescope *m* de Cassegrain
      r система *f* Кассегрена

C93   *e* casting
      d Gießen *n*
      f coulage *m*
      r литьё *n*

C94   *e* cast iron
      d Gußeisen *n*
      f fonte *f*
      r чугун *m*

C95   *e* catadioptric lens
      d katadioptrisches Objektiv *n*
      f objectif *m* catadioptrique
      r зеркально-линзовый объектив *m*

C96   *e* catalysis
      d Katalyse *f*
      f catalyse *f*
      r катализ *m*

C97   *e* catalyst
      d Katalysator *m*, Kontaktstoff *m*
      f catalyseur *m*
      r катализатор *m*

C98   *e* catalytic agent *see* catalyst

C99   *e* cataphoresis
      d Kataphorese *f*
      f cataphorèse *f*
      r катафорез *m*

C100 *e* catastrophe
      d Katastrophe *f*
      f catastrophe *f*
      r катастрофа *f*

C101 *e* cathode
      d Katode *f*
      f cathode *f*
      r катод *m*

C102 *e* cathode crater
      d Katodenkrater *m*
      f cratère *m* cathodique
      r катодный кратер *m*

C103 *e* cathode dark space
      d Katodendunkelraum *m*
      f espace *m* sombre cathodique
      r катодное тёмное пространство *n*

C104 *e* cathode drop *see* cathode fall

C105 *e* cathode fall
      d Katodenfall *m*,
          Katodenspannungsabfall *m*
      f chute *f* cathodique
      r катодное падение *n*

C106 *e* cathode follower
      d Katodenverstärker *m*,
          Katodenfolgeschaltung *f*,
          Katodenfolger *m*
      f amplificateur *m* cathodique
      r катодный повторитель *m*

C107 *e* cathode glow
      d Katodenglimmlicht *n*, Katodenlicht *n*
      f lueur *f* de cathode, lueur *f* cathodique
      r катодное свечение *n*

C108 *e* cathode-ray oscilloscope
      d Elektronenstrahloszillograph *m*
      f oscillographe *m* à rayons cathodiques
      r электронно-лучевой осциллограф *m*

C109 *e* cathode rays
      d Katodenstrahlen *pl*
      f rayons *pl* cathodiques
      r катодные лучи *pl*

C110 *e* cathode-ray tube
      d Elektronenstrahlröhre *f*
      f tube *m* cathodique
      r электронно-лучевая трубка *f*;
          осциллографическая трубка *f*

C111 *e* cathode region
      d Katodengebiet *n*, Katodenraum *m*
      f compartiment *m* cathodique, zone *f*
          cathodique
      r катодная область *f* (*тлеющего*
          разряда)

C112 *e* cathode spot
      d Katodenfleck *m*, Brennfleck *m*
      f spot *m* cathodique
      r катодное пятно *n*

C113 *e* cathode sputtering
      d Katodenzerstäubung *f*
      f désagrégation *f* de cathode,
          pulvérisation *f* cathodique
      r катодное распыление *n*

C114   *e*   **cathodoluminescence**
     d   Katodolumineszenz *f*
     f   cathodoluminescence *f*
     r   катодолюминесценция *f*

C115   *e*   **cathodoluminescence source**
     d   Katodolumineszenz-Lichtquelle *f*
     f   source *f* cathodoluminescente
     r   катодолюминесцентный источник *m* света, катодолюминесцентный источник *m*

C116   *e*   **cathodophosphor**
     d   Katodoluminophor *m*, Katodenluminophor *m*
     f   cathodoluminophore *m*
     r   катодолюминофор *m*

C117   *e*   **cation**
     d   Kation *n*
     f   cation *m*
     r   катион *m*

C118   *e*   **catoptrics**
     d   Katoptrik *f*
     f   catoptrique *f*
     r   катоптрика *f*

C119   *e*   **Cauchy theorem**
     d   Cauchyscher Integralsatz *m*, Integralsatz *m* von Cauchy
     f   théorème *m* fondamental de Cauchy
     r   теорема *f* Коши

C120   *e*   **causality**
     d   Kausalität *f*
     f   causalité *f*
     r   причинность *f*

C121   *e*   **caustic, caustic surface**
     d   Kaustikfläche *f*, kaustische Fläche *f*
     f   caustique *f*, surface *f* caustique
     r   каустика *f*, каустическая поверхность *f*

C122   *e*   **cave**
     d   Zelle *f*
     f   cellule *f*, enceinte *f* étanche
     r   экранированная *(от радиоактивных излучений)* камера *f*

C123   *e*   **Cavendish experiment**
     d   Cavendish-Versuch *m*
     f   expérience *f* de Cavendish
     r   опыт *m* Кавендиша

C124   *e*   **cavitation**
     d   Kavitation *f*
     f   cavitation *f*
     r   кавитация *f*

C125   *e*   **cavitation bubble**
     d   Kavitationsblase *f*
     f   bulle *f* de cavitation
     r   кавитационный пузырёк *m*

C126   *e*   **cavitation cavity**
     d   Kavitationshohlraum *m*
     f   cavité *f* de cavitation
     r   кавитационная каверна *f*

C127   *e*   **cavitation number** *see* **cavitation parameter**

C128   *e*   **cavitation parameter**
     d   Kavitationsparameter *m*
     f   paramètre *m* de cavitation
     r   число *n* кавитации

C129   *e*   **cavitation pressure**
     d   Kavitationsdruck *m*
     f   pression *f* de cavitation
     r   давление *n* при кавитации

C130   *e*   **cavitation wear**
     d   Verschleiß *m* durch Auswaschung, Sogverschleiß *m*
     f   usure *f* par cavitation
     r   кавитационный износ *m*

C131   *e*   **caviton**
     d   Kaviton *n*
     f   caviton *m*
     r   кавитон *m*

C132   *e*   **cavity**
     d   1. Hohlraumresonator *m* 2. Hohlraum *m*
     f   cavité *f*
     r   1. резонатор *m*, полый резонатор *m*, объёмный резонатор *m* 2. полость *f*

C133   *e*   **cavity magnetron**
     d   Hohlraummagnetron *n*
     f   magnétron *m* à cavités
     r   многорезонаторный магнетрон *m*

C134   *e*   **cavity Q factor**
     d   Gütefaktor *m* des Hohlraumresonators
     f   facteur *m* Q de la cavité
     r   добротность *f* объёмного резонатора

C135   *e*   **cavity radiation**
     d   Hohlraumstrahlung *f*, schwarze Strahlung *f*
     f   rayonnement *m* du corps noir
     r   излучение *n* чёрного тела

C136   *e*   **cavity resonator**
     d   Hohlraumresonator *m*
     f   résonateur *m* à cavité
     r   объёмный резонатор *m*, полый резонатор *m*

C137   *e*   **CCD** *see* **charge-coupled device**

C138   *e*   **CCD matrix** *see* **charge-coupled device matrix**

C139   *e*   **celestial coordinates**
     d   astronomische Koordinaten *f pl*

    f coordonnées *f pl* célestes
    r небесные координаты *f pl*

C140 *e* celestial equator
    d Himmelsäquator *m*
    f équateur *m* céleste
    r небесный экватор *m*

C141 *e* celestial mechanics
    d Himmelsmechanik *f*
    f mécanique *f* céleste
    r небесная механика *f*

C142 *e* celestial meridian
    d Himmelsmeridian *m*
    f méridien *m* céleste
    r небесный меридиан *m*

C143 *e* celestial sphere
    d Himmelskugel *f*
    f sphère *f* céleste
    r небесная сфера *f*

C144 *e* cell
    d 1. Zelle *f* 2. galvanische Zelle *f*;
       galvanisches Element *n*;
       Akkumulatorzelle *f* 3. Zelle *f*
       (Biologie) 4. Küvette *f*
    f cellule *f*
    r 1. ячейка *f* 2. элемент *m* 3. клетка *f*
       4. кювета *f*

C145 *e* Celsius scale
    d Celsius-Skala *f*
    f échelle *f* Celsius
    r шкала *f* Цельсия

C146 *e* center
    d Zentrum *n*, Mitte *f*, Mittelpunkt *m*
    f centre *m*
    r центр *m*

C147 *e* center of crystallization
    d Kristallisationskeim *m*;
       Kristallisationszentrum *n*
    f centre *m* de cristallisation
    r центр *m* кристаллизации

C148 *e* center of gravity
    d Schwerpunkt *m*
    f centre *m* de gravité
    r центр *m* тяжести

C149 *e* center of inertia *see* center of mass

C150 *e* center-of-inertia system
    d Schwerpunktsystem *n*
    f système *m* de centre d'inertie
    r система *f* центра инерции

C151 *e* center of mass
    d Massenmittelpunkt *m*
    f centre *m* de masse
    r центр *m* масс, центр *m* инерции

C152 *e* center-of-mass motion

    d Massenmittelpunktbewegung *f*,
       Trägheitsmittelpunktbewegung *f*
    f mouvement *m* de centre de masse
    r движение *n* центра масс

C153 *e* center-of-mass system
    d Massenmittelpunktsystem *n*
    f système *m* de centre de masse
    r система *f* центра масс

C154 *e* center of oscillation
    d Schwingungsmittelpunkt *m (Pendel)*
    f centre *m* d'oscillation *(d'un pendule)*
    r центр *m* качания *(маятника)*

C155 *e* center of parallel forces
    d Zentrum *n* der parallelen Kräfte
    f centre *m* des forces parallèles
    r центр *m* параллельных сил

C156 *e* center of percussion
    d Stoßzentrum *n*
    f centre *m* de percussion
    r центр *m* удара

C157 *e* center of pressure
    d Druckmittelpunkt *m*, Druckzentrum *n*,
       Druckpunkt *m*
    f centre *m* de compression
    r центр *m* давления

C158 *e* center of rotation
    d Drehpol *m*, Drehpunkt *m*,
       Drehzentrum *n*, Rotationszentrum *n*
    f centre *m* de rotation
    r центр *m* вращения

C159 *e* center of symmetry
    d Symmetriezentrum *n*
    f centre *m* de symétrie
    r центр *m* симметрии

C160 *e* centimeter, cm
    d Zentimeter *n*
    f centimètre *m*
    r сантиметр *m*, см

C161 *e* centimeter waves
    d Zentimeterwellen *f pl*
    f ondes *f pl* centimétriques
    r сантиметровые волны *f pl*

C162 *e* central forces
    d Zentralkräfte *f pl*
    f forces *f pl* centrales
    r центральные силы *f pl*

C163 *e* centre *see* center

C164 *e* centrifugal acceleration
    d Zentrifugalbeschleunigung *f*
    f accélération *f* centrifuge
    r центробежное ускорение *n*

C165 *e* centrifugal force
    d Zentrifugalkraft *f*, Fliehkraft *f*,
       Schleuderkraft *f*

	f	force *f* centrifuge
	r	центробежная сила *f*
C166	*e*	**centrifuge**
	d	Zentrifuge *f*, Trennschleuder *f*
	f	centrifugeuse *f*
	r	центрифуга *f*
C167	*e*	**centripetal acceleration**
	d	Zentripetalbeschleunigung *f*
	f	accélération *f* centripète
	r	центростремительное ускорение *n*
C168	*e*	**centripetal force**
	d	Zentripetalkraft *f*
	f	force *f* centripète
	r	центростремительная сила *f*
C169	*e*	**centroide**
	d	Zentroide *f*, Polhodie *f*
	f	centroïde *f*, polhodie *f*
	r	центроида *f*, полодия *f*
C170	*e*	**centrosymmetrical crystal**
	d	zentralsymmetrischer Kristall *m*
	f	cristal *m* centro-symétrique
	r	центросимметричный кристалл *m*
C171	*e*	**cepheides, cepheid variables**
	d	Cepheiden *m pl*
	f	céphéides *f pl*
	r	цефеиды *f pl*
C172	*e*	**cepstrum**
	d	Cepstrum *n*
	f	cepstrum *m*
	r	кепстр *m*
C173	*e*	**ceramic metal**
	d	Sinterwerkstoff *m*
	f	céramique *f* à métal, céramet *m*
	r	металлокерамика *f*
C174	*e*	**ceramics**
	d	Keramik *f*
	f	céramique *f*
	r	керамика *f*
C175	*e*	**Čerenkov...** *see* **Cherenkov...**
C176	*e*	**cerium, Ce**
	d	Zer *n*
	f	cérium *m*
	r	церий *m*
C177	*e*	**cermet** *see* **ceramic metal**
C178	*e*	**CGS units**
	d	CGS-Einheiten *f pl*
	f	unités *f pl* C.G.S.
	r	единицы *f pl* СГС
C179	*e*	**chain**
	d	Kette *f*
	f	chaîne *f*
	r	цепь *f*
C180	*e*	**chain reaction**

	d	Kettenreaktion *f*
	f	réaction *f* en chaîne, processus *m* en chaîne
	r	цепная реакция *f*
C181	*e*	**chamber**
	d	Kammer *f*, Raum *m*
	f	chambre *f*
	r	камера *f*
C182	*e*	**change of state**
	d	Zustandsänderung *f*; Aggregatzustandsänderung *f*
	f	changement *m* de l'état
	r	изменение *n* состояния, фазовый переход *m*
C183	*e*	**change of variables**
	d	Variablentransformation *f*
	f	changement *m* des variables
	r	замена *f* переменных
C184	*e*	**channel**
	d	Kanal *m*
	f	canal *m*
	r	канал *m*
C185	*e*	**channeling in single crystals**
	d	Kanalierung *f* im Einkristall
	f	canalisation *f* dans les monocristaux
	r	каналирование *n* в монокристаллах
C186	*e*	**channeling of charged particles**
	d	Kanalierung *f* geladener Teilchen
	f	canalisation *f* des particules chargées
	r	каналирование *n* заряженных частиц
C187	*e*	**chaos**
	d	Chaos *n*
	f	chaos *m*
	r	хаос *m*
C188	*e*	**chaotic state**
	d	chaotischer Zustand *m*
	f	état *m* chaotique
	r	хаотическое состояние *n*
C189	*e*	**characteristic**
	d	Kennlinie *f*, Charakteristik *f*
	f	caractéristique *f*
	r	характеристика *f*
C190	*e*	**characteristic curve**
	d	Kennlinie *f*
	f	courbe *f* caractéristique
	r	характеристическая кривая *f*
C191	*e*	**characteristic equation**
	d	charakteristische Gleichung *f*
	f	équation *f* caractéristique
	r	характеристическое уравнение *n*
C192	*e*	**characteristic function**
	d	charakteristische Funktion *f*
	f	fonction *f* caractéristique
	r	характеристическая функция *f*

C193　e　characteristic impedance
　　　d　Kennimpedanz *f*, Wellenwiderstand *m*
　　　f　impédance *f* caractéristique
　　　r　характеристический импеданс *m*,
　　　　волновой импеданс *m*

C194　e　characteristic radiation
　　　d　Eigenstrahlung *f*, charakteristische
　　　　Strahlung *f*
　　　f　rayonnement *m* caractéristique
　　　r　характеристическое излучение *n*

C195　e　characteristic spectrum
　　　d　charakteristisches Spektrum *n*
　　　f　spectre *m* caractéristique
　　　r　характеристический спектр *m*

C196　e　charge
　　　d　Ladung *f*, elektrische Ladung *f*
　　　f　charge *f*
　　　r　заряд *m*

C197　e　charge capture
　　　d　Ladungseinfang *m*
　　　f　captage *m* de la charge
　　　r　захват *m* заряда (*напр. дефектами*)

C198　e　charge carrier diffusion
　　　d　Ladungsträgerdiffusion *f*
　　　f　diffusion *f* des porteurs de charge
　　　r　диффузия *f* носителей заряда

C199　e　charge carriers
　　　d　Ladungsträger *m pl*
　　　f　porteurs *m pl* de charge
　　　r　носители *m pl* заряда

C200　e　charge cloud
　　　d　Ladungswolke *f*
　　　f　nuage *m* d'électricité; nuage *m*
　　　　d'électrons
　　　r　облако *n* заряда, облако *n*
　　　　пространственного заряда;
　　　　электронное облако *n*

C201　e　charge conjugation
　　　d　Ladungskonjugation *f*
　　　f　conjugaison *f* de charge
　　　r　зарядовое сопряжение *n*

C202　e　charge conservation law
　　　d　Ladungserhaltungssatz *m*, Satz *m* von
　　　　der Erhaltung der Ladung
　　　f　loi *f* de la conservation de la charge
　　　r　закон *m* сохранения заряда

C203　e　charge-coupled device
　　　d　CCD-Bauelement *n*,
　　　　ladungsgekoppeltes
　　　　Halbleiterbauelement *n*
　　　f　élément *m* CCD, dispositif *m* à
　　　　couplage de charge
　　　r　прибор *m* с зарядовой связью,
　　　　ПЗС

C204　e　charge-coupled device matrix

　　　d　CCD-Array *n*, CCD-Matrix *f*
　　　f　matrice *f* CCD, réseau *m* à couplage
　　　　de charge
　　　r　ПЗС-матрица *f*, матрица *f* приборов
　　　　с зарядовой связью

C205　e　charged component
　　　d　geladene Komponente *f*
　　　f　composante *f* chargée
　　　r　заряженная компонента *f*

C206　e　charged current
　　　d　geladener Strom *m*
　　　f　courant *m* chargé
　　　r　заряженный ток *m*

C207　e　charge density
　　　d　Ladungsdichte *f*
　　　f　densité *f* de charge
　　　r　плотность *f* заряда

C208　e　charge density wave
　　　d　Ladungsdichtewelle *f*
　　　f　onde *f* à densité de charge
　　　r　волна *f* зарядовой плотности

C209　e　charge discreteness
　　　d　Ladungsdiskretheit *f*
　　　f　discrèteté *f* de la charge
　　　r　дискретность *f* заряда

C210　e　charge distribution
　　　d　Ladungsverteilung *f*
　　　f　distribution *f* de la charge
　　　r　распределение *n* заряда

C211　e　charged kaon, charged K-meson
　　　d　geladenes Kaon *n*, geladenes
　　　　K-Meson *n*
　　　f　K-méson *m* chargé
　　　r　заряженный каон *m*, заряженный
　　　　K-мезон *m*

C212　e　charged lepton
　　　d　geladenes Lepton *n*
　　　f　lepton *m* chargé
　　　r　заряженный лептон *m*

C213　e　charged meson
　　　d　geladenes Meson *n*
　　　f　méson *m* chargé
　　　r　заряженный мезон *m*

C214　e　charged particle
　　　d　geladenes Teilchen *n*,
　　　　Ladungsteilchen *n*
　　　f　particule *f* chargée
　　　r　заряженная частица *f*

C215　e　charged particle accelerator
　　　d　Teilchenbeschleuniger *m*,
　　　　Beschleuniger *m*
　　　f　accélérateur *m* des particules chargées
　　　r　ускоритель *m* заряженных частиц

C216　e　charged particle capture *see* charged
　　　　particle trapping

C217   *e*   charged particle concentration
      d   Ladungsteilchenkonzentration *f*,
         Ladungsteilchendichte *f*,
         Konzentration *f* der geladenen
         Teilchen
      f   concentration *f* des particules chargées
      r   концентрация *f* заряженных частиц

C218   *e*   charged particle confinement
      d   Einschließung *f* von geladenen
         Teilchen *(im Feld)*
      f   confinement *m* des particules chargées
         (dans un champ)
      r   удержание *n* заряженных частиц *(в*
         поле)

C219   *e*   charged particle density *see* charged
         particle concentration

C220   *e*   charged particle drift
      d   Ladungsteilchendrift *f*, Drift *f* von
         geladenen Teilchen
      f   dérive *f* des particules chargées
      r   дрейф *m* заряженных частиц

C221   *e*   charged particle focusing
      d   Fokussierung *f* von geladenen
         Teilchen
      f   focalisation *f* des particules chargées
      r   фокусировка *f* заряженных частиц

C222   *e*   charged particle injection
      d   Injektion *f* von geladenen Teilchen
      f   injection *f* des particules chargées
      r   инжекция *f* заряженных частиц

C223   *e*   charged particle trapping
      d   Einfang *m* von geladenen Teilchen
      f   capture *f* des particules chargées
      r   захват *m* заряженных частиц

C224   *e*   charge exchange
      d   Ladungsaustausch *m*
      f   échange *m* de charge
      r   перезарядка *f*

C225   *e*   charge invariance
      d   Ladungsinvarianz *f*
      f   invariance *f* de la charge
      r   зарядовая инвариантность *f*

C226   *e*   charge migration
      d   Ladungswanderung *f*
      f   migration *f* des charges
      r   миграция *f* зарядов

C227   *e*   charge neutralization
      d   Ladungsneutralisation *f*
      f   neutralisation *f* de la charge
      r   зарядовая нейтрализация *f*,
         нейтрализация *f* заряда

C228   *e*   charge nonconservation
      d   Ladungsnichterhaltung *f*
      f   non-conservation *f* de la charge
      r   несохранение *n* заряда

C229   *e*   charge parity
      d   Ladungsparität *f*
      f   parité *f* de charge
      r   зарядовая чётность *f*

C230   *e*   charge transfer
      d   Ladungstransfer *m*,
         Ladungstransport *m*
      f   transfert *m* de la charge
      r   перенос *m* заряда

C231   *e*   **Charles law**
      d   **Charlessches Gesetz** *n*
      f   loi *f* de Charles
      r   закон *m* Шарля

C232   *e*   **charm**
      d   Charme *m*, Charmezahl *f*
      f   charme *m*
      r   очарование *n*, чарм *m*
         (характеристика элементарных
         частиц)

C233   *e*   **charmed particles**
      d   Charm-Teilchen *n pl*, Teilchen *n pl*
         mit Charm
      f   particules *f pl* charmées
      r   очарованные частицы *f pl*

C234   *e*   **charmed quark**
      d   Charm-Quark *n*
      f   quark *m* charmé
      r   очарованный кварк *m*

C235   *e*   **charmonium**
      d   Charmonium *n*
      f   charmonium *m*
      r   чармоний *m*

C236   *e*   **chart** *see* diagram

C237   *e*   **chemical affinity**
      d   chemische Affinität *f*
      f   affinité *f* chimique
      r   химическое сродство *n*

C238   *e*   **chemical bond**
      d   chemische Bindung *f*
      f   liaison *f* chimique
      r   химическая связь *f*

C239   *e*   **chemical chain reaction**
      d   chemische Kettenreaktion *f*
      f   réaction *f* chimique en chaîne
      r   химическая цепная реакция *f*

C240   *e*   **chemical dissociation**
      d   chemische Dissoziation *f*
      f   dissociation *f* chimique
      r   химическая диссоциация *f*

C241   *e*   **chemical elements**
      d   chemische Elemente *n pl*
      f   éléments *m pl* chimiques
      r   химические элементы *m pl*

C242   *e*   **chemical formula**

    d chemische Formel *f*
    f formule *f* chimique
    r химическая формула *f*

C243 *e* chemical inertness
    d chemische Trägheit *f*, chemische Inaktivität *f*
    f inertie *f* chimique
    r химическая инертность *f*

C244 *e* chemical isomer
    d chemisches Isomer *n*
    f isomère *m* chimique
    r химический изомер *m*

C245 *e* chemical isomerism
    d chemische Isomerie *f*
    f isomérie *f* chimique
    r химическая изомерия *f*

C246 *e* chemical kinetics
    d chemische Kinetik *f*
    f cinétique *f* chimique
    r химическая кинетика *f*

C247 *e* chemical laser
    d chemischer Laser *m*
    f laser *m* chimique
    r химический лазер *m*

C248 *e* chemical physics
    d chemische Physik *f*
    f physique *f* chimique
    r химическая физика *f*

C249 *e* chemical potential
    d chemisches Potential *n*
    f potentiel *m* chimique
    r химический потенциал *m*

C250 *e* chemical reaction
    d chemische Reaktion *f*
    f réaction *f* chimique
    r химическая реакция *f*

C251 *e* chemical reaction rate, chemical reaction velocity
    d Geschwindigkeit *f* der chemischen Reaktion
    f taux *m* de réaction chimique, vélocité *f* de réaction chimique
    r скорость *f* химической реакции

C252 *e* chemiluminescence
    d Chemilumineszenz *f*
    f chimiluminescence *f*
    r хемилюминесценция *f*

C253 *e* chemisorption
    d Chemisorption *f*, Chemosorption *f*, chemische Adsorption *f*
    f chimisorption *f*
    r хемосорбция *f*

C254 *e* chemistry
    d Chemie *f*

    f chimie *f*
    r химия *f*

C255 *e* Cherenkov cone
    d Tscherenkov-Kegel *m*
    f cône *m* de Cherenkov
    r черенковский конус *m*

C256 *e* Cherenkov counter
    d Tscherenkov-Zähler *m*
    f compteur *m* de Cherenkov
    r черенковский счётчик *m*

C257 *e* Cherenkov detector
    d Tscherenkov-Detektor *m*
    f détecteur *m* de Cherenkov
    r черенковский детектор *m*

C258 *e* Cherenkov effect
    d Tscherenkov-Effekt *m*
    f effet *m* Cherenkov
    r эффект *m* Вавилова - Черенкова

C259 *e* Cherenkov radiation
    d Tscherenkov-Strahlung *f*
    f rayonnement *m* de Cherenkov
    r черенковское излучение *n*, излучение *n* Вавилова - Черенкова

C260 *e* Cherenkov radiator
    d Tscherenkov-Strahler *m*
    f radiateur *m* de Cherenkov
    r черенковский излучатель *m*

C261 *e* chip
    d Chip *m*
    f chip *m*
    r кристалл *m* интегральной микросхемы; интегральная микросхема *f*

C262 *e* chiral field
    d chirales Feld *n*
    f champ *m* chiral
    r киральное поле *n*

C263 *e* chiral invariance
    d chirale Invarianz *f*
    f invariance *f* chirale
    r киральная инвариантность *f*

C264 *e* chirality
    d Chiralität *f*
    f chiralité *f*
    r киральность *f*, хиральность *f*

C265 *e* chiral symmetry
    d chirale Symmetrie *f*
    f symétrie *f* chirale
    r киральная симметрия *f*, хиральная симметрия *f*

C266 *e* chirped pulse, chirp pulse
    d linearer FM-Impuls *m*, linearer frequenzmodulierter Impuls *m*
    f impulsion *f* à modulation linéaire de fréquence
    r импульс *m* с линейной частотной модуляцией, ЛЧМ-импульс *m*

C267   *e* **chi-squared distribution**
      d Chi-Quadrat-Verteilung *f*
      f distribution *f* de chi-carré
      r хи-квадрат распределение *n*

C268   *e* **Chladni figures**
      d Chladnische Klangfiguren *f pl*,
          Schwingungsfiguren *f pl*
      f figures *f pl* de Chladni
      r фигуры *f pl* Хладни

C269   *e* **chlorine, Cl**
      d Chlor *n*
      f chlore *m*
      r хлор *m*

C270   *e* **choke groove**
      d Choke-Nut *f*
      f rainure *f* de bobine de choc
      r дроссельная канавка *f (в*
          волноводе)

C271   *e* **cholesteric liquid crystal**
      d cholesterischer Flüssigkristall *m*
      f cristal *m* liquide cholestérique
      r холестерический жидкий
          кристалл *m*

C272   *e* **chopper**
      d Zerhacker *m*; Modulator *m*
      f interrupteur *m*; modulateur *m*
      r прерыватель *m*; модулятор *m*

C273   *e* **chord**
      d Profilsehne *f*, Sehne *f*
      f corde *f*
      r хорда *f*

C274   *e* **Christoffel symbols**
      d Christoffelsche Symbole *n pl*
      f symboles *m pl* de Christoffel
      r символы *m pl* Кристоффеля

C275   *e* **chromatic aberration**
      d chromatische Aberration *f*
      f aberration *f* chromatique
      r хроматическая аберрация *f*

C276   *e* **chromaticity**
      d Farbart *f*, Farbmaßzahl; Farbton *m*
      f chromaticité *f*
      r цветность *f*

C277   *e* **chromaticity coordinates**
      d Farbwertanteile *m pl*
      f coordonnées *f pl* de chromaticité
      r координаты *f pl* цветности

C278   *e* **chromaticity diagram**
      d Farbtafel *f*, Farbdreieck *n*
      f triangle *m* des couleurs
      r диаграмма *f* цветностей, цветовой
          треугольник *m*, цветовой график *m*

C279   *e* **chromatic polarization**
      d chromatische Polarisation *f*
      f polarisation *f* chromatique
      r хроматическая поляризация *f*

C280   *e* **chromatic sensation**
      d Farbempfindung *f*
      f sensation *f* chromatique
      r цветовое восприятие *n*, цветовое
          ощущение *n*

C281   *e* **chromatograph**
      d Chromatograph *m*
      f chromatographe *m*
      r хроматограф *m*

C282   *e* **chromatography**
      d Chromatographie *f*
      f chromatographie *f*
      r хроматография *f*

C283   *e* **chromium, Cr**
      d Chrom *n*
      f chrome *m*
      r хром *m*

C284   *e* **chromizing**
      d Verchromung *f*
      f chromisation *f*
      r хромирование *n*

C285   *e* **chromodynamics**
      d Chromodynamik *f*
      f chromodynamique *f*
      r хромодинамика *f*

C286   *e* **chromosphere**
      d Chromosphäre *f*
      f chromosphère *f*
      r хромосфера *f*

C287   *e* **chromospheric flare**
      d chromosphärische Eruption *f*
      f éruption *f* chromosphérique
      r хромосферная вспышка *f*

C288   *e* **chronograph**
      d Chronograph *m*
      f chronographe *m*
      r хронограф *m*

C289   *e* **chronometry**
      d Chronometrie *f*, Zeitmessung *f*
      f chronométrie *f*
      r хронометрия *f*

C290   *e* **CI** *see* color index

C291   *e* **CIE standard source**
      d CIE-Normalquelle *f*
      f source *f* standard CIE
      r стандартный источник *m* МКО *(в*
          светотехнике)

C292   *e* **C-invariance**
      d Ladungsinvarianz *f*, C-Invarianz *f*
      f invariance *f* de la charge,
          C-invariance *f*
      r C-инвариантность *f*,
          инвариантность *f* относительно
          зарядового сопряжения

C293 *e* circle
  d Kreis *m*; Kreislinie *f*
  f cercle *m*; circonférence *f*
  r круг *m*; окружность *f*

C294 *e* circle diagram
  d Kreisdiagramm *n*
  f diagramme *m* circulaire
  r круговая диаграмма *f*

C295 *e* circle of confusion
  d Unschärfekreis *m*, Streuungskreis *m*,
     Streukreis *m*
  f cercle *m* de confusion
  r кружок *m* рассеяния

C296 *e* circuit
  d Stromkreis *m*, Kreis *m*, Schaltung *f*
  f circuit *m*
  r цепь *f*, схема *f*, контур *m*

C297 *e* circular accelerator
  d Kreisbeschleuniger *m*,
     Ringbeschleuniger *m*
  f accélérateur *m* circulaire
  r кольцевой ускоритель *m*

C298 *e* circular dichroism
  d zirkularer Dichroismus *m*,
     Rotationsdichroismus *m*,
     Cotton-Effekt *m*
  f dichroïsme *m* circulaire
  r круговой дихроизм *m*,
     циркулярный дихроизм *m*, эффект
     m Коттона

C299 *e* circular frequency *see* angular
     frequency

C300 *e* circular groove
  d Ringnut *f*
  f rainure *f* circulaire
  r кольцевая канавка *f*

C301 *e* circular motion
  d Kreisbewegung *f*, kreisförmige
     Bewegung *f*
  f mouvement *m* circulaire
  r круговое движение *n*, движение *n*
     по окружности

C302 *e* circular orbit
  d Kreisbahn *f*, kreisförmige
     Umlaufbahn *f*
  f trajectoire *f* circulaire, orbite *f*
     circulaire
  r круговая орбита *f*

C303 *e* circular polarization
  d zirkulare Polarisation *f*,
     Zirkularpolarisation *f*
  f polarisation *f* circulaire
  r круговая поляризация *f*,
     циркулярная поляризация *f*

C304 *e* circulation

C305 *e* circulation of a vector field
  d Zirkulation *f* des Vektorfeldes
  f circulation *f* du champ vecteur
  r циркуляция *f* векторного поля

C306 *e* circulator
  d Zirkulator *m*, Mikrowellenzirkulator *m*
  f circulateur *m*
  r циркулятор *m*

C307 *e* cis-trans-isomer
  d cis-trans-Isomer *n*, geometrisches
     Isomer *n*
  f isomère *m* cis-trans, isomère *m*
     géométrique
  r цис-транс-изомер *m*,
     геометрический изомер *m*

C308 *e* cis-trans-isomerism
  d cis-trans-Isomerie *f*, geometrische
     Isomerie *f*
  f isomérie *f* cis-trans, isomérie *f*
     géométrique
  r цис-транс-изомерия *f*,
     геометрическая изомерия *f*

C309 *e* cladding
  d Lichtwellenleiterhülle *f*
  f enveloppe *f* du guide de lumière en
     fibre
  r оболочка *f* волоконного световода

C310 *e* Clapeyron equation
  d Clapeyron-Gleichung *f*,
     Clapeyronsche Gleichung *f*
  f relation *f* de Clapeyron, équation *f* de
     Clapeyron
  r уравнение *n* Клапейрона

C311 *e* classical diffusion
  d klassische Diffusion *f*
  f diffusion *f* classique
  r классическая диффузия *f*

C312 *e* classical dynamics
  d klassische Dynamik *f*, Newtonsche
     Dynamik *f*
  f dynamique *f* classique
  r классическая динамика *f*,
     ньютоновская динамика *f*

C313 *e* classical electrodynamics
  d klassische Elektrodynamik *f*
  f électrodynamique *f* classique
  r классическая электродинамика *f*

C314 *e* classical electron radius
  d klassischer Elektronenradius *m*
  f rayon *m* classique de l'électron
  r классический радиус *m* электрона

C315 *e* classical mechanics

d klassische Mechanik *f*, Newtonsche Mechanik *f*
f mécanique *f* classique, mécanique *f* newtonienne, mécanique *f* de Newton
r классическая механика *f*, механика *f* Ньютона

C316 e **classical model**
d klassisches Model *n*
f modèle *m* classique
r классическая модель *f*

C317 e **classical oscillator**
d klassischer Oszillator *m*
f oscillateur *m* classique
r классический осциллятор *m*

C318 e **classical physics**
d klassische Physik *f*
f physique *f* classique
r классическая физика *f*

C319 e **classical statistics**
d klassische Statistik *f*, Maxwell-Boltzmann-Statistik *f*
f statistique *f* classique
r классическая статистика *f*

C320 e **Clausius theorem**
d Clausius-Gleichung *f*, Clausiussche Gleichung *f*, Satz *m* von Clausius
f théorème *m* de Clausius
r уравнение *n* Клаузиуса

C321 e **clean room**
d staubfreier Raum *m*, Cleanroom *m*
f espace *m* libre de poussière, cleanroom *m*
r чистая комната *f*

C322 e **clearance**
d Zwischenraum *m*, Spiel *n*, Luft *f*, Lose *f*, Spalt *m*
f jeu *m*; interstice *m*
r зазор *m*; просвет *m*

C323 e **cleavage**
d Spaltbarkeit *f*
f clivage *m* (*des cristaux*)
r спайность *f* (*кристаллов*)

C324 e **cleavage fracture**
d Trennungsbruch *m*, Spaltbruch *m*, Spaltung *f*
f rupture *f* par clivage
r излом *m* по плоскости спайности

C325 e **cleavage plane**
d Trennungsfläche *f*, Spaltfläche *f*
f plan *m* de clivage
r плоскость *f* спайности

C326 e **clock**
d Uhr *f*
f horloge *f*
r часы *pl*

C327 e **clock paradox**
d Uhrenparadoxon *n*
f paradoxe *m* de l'horloge
r парадокс *m* времени, парадокс *m* часов, парадокс *m* возврата

C328 e **clock pulse**
d Taktimpuls *m*
f impulsion *f* de minutage
r синхронизирующий импульс *m*, тактовый импульс *m*

C329 e **clockwise polarization** *see* right-hand polarization

C330 e **closed circuit**
d geschlossener Stromkreis *m*, geschlossener Kreis *m*
f circuit *m* fermé
r замкнутый контур *m*

C331 e **closed configuration**
d geschlossene Konfiguration *f*
f configuration *f* fermée
r замкнутая конфигурация *f*

C332 e **closed contour integration**
d Integration *f* nach der geschlossenen Kurve
f intégration *f* en contour fermé
r интегрирование *n* по замкнутому контуру

C333 e **closed curve**
d geschlossene Kurve *f*
f courbe *f* fermée
r замкнутая кривая *f*

C334 e **closed cycle**
d geschlossener Kreislauf *m*
f cycle *m* fermé
r замкнутый цикл *m*

C335 e **closed interval**
d abgeschlossenes Intervall *n*
f intervalle *m* fermé
r замкнутый интервал *m*

C336 e **closed line**
d geschlossene Linie *f*
f ligne *f* fermée
r замкнутая линия *f*

C337 e **closed model**
d geschlossenes Modell *n*
f Univers *m* clos, Univers *m* fermé, modèle *m* clos, modèle *m* fermé
r замкнутая модель *f*, закрытая модель *f* (*Вселенной*), модель *f* закрытой Вселенной

C338 e **closed set**
d abgeschlossene Menge *f*
f ensemble *m* fermé
r замкнутое множество *n*

C339 e **closed shell**

    d abgeschlossene Schale *f*, vollbesetzte
       Schale *f*, besetzte Schale *f*
    f couche *f* pleine, couche *f* saturée,
       couche *f* remplie, couche *f* complète
    r замкнутая оболочка *f*, заполненная
       оболочка *f*

C340 *e* closed system
    d abgeschlossenes System *n*
    f système *m* fermé
    r замкнутая система *f*

C341 *e* close-packed structure
    d dichte Packung *f*, Dichtpackung *f*
    f empilement *m* serré, empilement *m*
       compact; structure *f* serrée, structure *f*
       compacte
    r плотная упаковка *f*;
       плотноупакованная структура *f*

C342 *e* cloud
    d Wolke *f*
    f nuage *m*
    r облако *n*

C343 *e* cloud chamber
    d Nebelkammer *f*, Wilsonsche
       Nebelkammer *f*, Wilson-Kammer *f*
    f chambre *f* à nuage, chambre *f* à
       nuages
    r камера *f* Вильсона

C344 *e* cloudy bag
    d chiraler Beutel *m*
    f sac *m* de chiralité
    r киральный мешок *m*

C345 *e* cluster
    d Cluster *m*
    f cluster *m*
    r кластер *m*

C346 *e* cluster formation *see* clusterization

C347 *e* cluster ion
    d Komplexion *n*, Clusterion *n*
    f ion *m* complexe
    r кластерный ион *m*

C348 *e* clusterization
    d Clusterbildung *f*
    f formation *f* de cluster
    r кластеризация *f*

C349 *e* cluster model
    d Clustermodell *n*
    f modèle *m* «cluster»
    r кластерная модель *f (ядра)*

C350 *e* coagulation
    d Koagulation *f*, Gerinnung *f*
    f coagulation *f*
    r коагуляция *f*

C351 *e* coalescence
    d Koaleszenz *f*, Vereinigung *f*;
       Zusammenfließen *n*; Verschmelzung *f*

    f coalescence *f*
    r коалесценция *f*

C352 *e* coastal refraction
    d Küstenbrechung *f*
    f réfraction *f* côtière
    r береговая рефракция *f*

C353 *e* coated cathode *see* oxide cathode

C354 *e* coaxial cable
    d Koaxialkabel *n*, Koaxkabel *n*
    f câble *m* coaxial
    r коаксиальный кабель *m*

C355 *e* coaxial magnetron
    d Koaxialmagnetron *n*
    f magnétron *m* coaxial
    r коаксиальный магнетрон *m*

C356 *e* cobalt, Co
    d Kobalt *n*
    f cobalt *m*
    r кобальт *m*

C357 *e* coefficient of absorption *see*
       absorptance

C358 *e* coefficient of diffusion *see* diffusion
       coefficient

C359 *e* coefficient of dynamic friction
    d Gleitreibungszahl *f*, Reibungszahl *f*
       der Bewegung, dynamischer
       Reibungskoeffizient *m*
    f coefficient *m* de frottement dynamique
    r коэффициент *m* динамического
       трения

C360 *e* coefficient of elasticity
    d Elastizitätskonstante *f*
    f coefficient *m* d'élasticité
    r коэффициент *m* упругости

C361 *e* coefficient of expansion
    d Ausdehnungskoeffizient *m*
    f coefficient *m* de dilatation
    r коэффициент *m* расширения

C362 *e* coefficient of friction
    d Reibungskoeffizient *m*, Reibungszahl *f*
    f coefficient *m* de frottement
    r коэффициент *m* трения

C363 *e* coefficient of hysteresis losses
    d Hystereseverlustkoeffizient *m*
    f coefficient *m* des pertes par hystérésis
    r коэффициент *m* гистерезисных
       потерь

C364 *e* coefficient of ionization *see*
       ionization coefficient

C365 *e* coefficient of linear expansion
    d linearer Ausdehnungskoeffizient *m*,
       Längeausdehnungskoeffizient *m*
    f coefficient *m* de dilatation linéaire

r коэффициент *m* линейного расширения

C366 *e* **coefficient of proportionality** *see* **proportionality factor**

C367 *e* **coefficient of reflection** *see* **reflection factor**

C368 *e* **coefficient of restitution**
 d Rückkehrkoeffizient *m*, Stoßkoeffizient *m*, Stoßzahl *f*
 f coefficient *m* de restitution
 r коэффициент *m* восстановления (*при ударе*)

C369 *e* **coefficient of thermal expansion**
 d Wärmeausdehnungskoeffizient *m*, Wärmeausdehnungszahl *f*
 f coefficient *m* de dilatation thermique
 r коэффициент *m* теплового расширения

C370 *e* **coefficient of viscosity**
 d Viskositätskoeffizient *m*, Viskosität *f*
 f coefficient *m* de viscosité
 r коэффициент *m* вязкости

C371 *e* **coefficient of volume expansion**
 d kubischer Ausdehnungskoeffizient *m*, Volumausdehnungskoeffizient *m*
 f coefficient *m* de dilatation volumétrique
 r коэффициент *m* объёмного расширения

C372 *e* **coelostat**
 d Coelostat *m*, Zölostat *m*
 f cœlostat *m*
 r целостат *m* (*телескоп*)

C373 *e* **coercimeter**
 d Koerzimeter *n*
 f coercimètre *m*
 r коэрциметр *m*

C374 *e* **coercive force**
 d Koerzitivfeldstärke *f*, Koerzitivkraft *f*
 f force *f* coercitive
 r коэрцитивная сила *f*

C375 *e* **coercivity**
 d Koerzitivkraft *f*, Koerzitivfeldstärke *f*
 f coercibilité *f*
 r коэрцитивность *f*; коэрцитивная сила *f*

C376 *e* **coherence**
 d Kohärenz *f*
 f cohérence *f*
 r когерентность *f*

C377 *e* **coherence area**
 d Kohärenzgebiet *n*
 f domaine *m* de cohérence
 r область *f* когерентности

C378 *e* **coherence length**
 d Kohärenzlänge *f*, Kohärenzabstand *m*
 f longueur *f* de cohérence
 r длина *f* когерентности

C379 *e* **coherence matrix**
 d Kohärenzmatrix *f*
 f matrice *f* de cohérence
 r матрица *f* когерентности

C380 *e* **coherence of light**
 d Lichtkohärenz *f*
 f cohérence *f* de la lumière
 r когерентность *f* света

C381 *e* **coherence time**
 d Kohärenzzeit *f*
 f temps *m* de cohérence
 r время *n* когерентности

C382 *e* **coherence volume**
 d Kohärenzvolumen *n*
 f volume *m* de cohérence
 r объём *m* когерентности

C383 *e* **coherent anti-Stokes Raman scattering**
 d kohärente anti-Stokessche Raman-Streuung *f*
 f diffusion *f* cohérente anti-Stokes Raman
 r метод *m* КАРС, метод *m* когерентного антистоксова комбинационного рассеяния света

C384 *e* **coherent anti-Stokes Raman spectroscopy**
 d kohärente anti-Stokessche Raman-Spektroskopie *f*
 f spectroscopie *f* cohérente anti-Stokes Raman
 r спектроскопия *f* когерентного антистоксова комбинационного рассеяния света, спектроскопия *f* КАРС

C385 *e* **coherent detection**
 d Kohärentgleichrichtung *f*
 f détection *f* cohérente
 r когерентное детектирование *n*

C386 *e* **coherent emission** *see* **coherent radiation**

C387 *e* **coherent emitter** *see* **coherent radiator**

C388 *e* **coherent frequency technique** *see* **dispersion interferometer technique**

C389 *e* **coherent oscillation, coherent oscillations**
 d kohärente Schwingungen *f pl*
 f oscillations *f pl* cohérentes
 r когерентные колебания *n pl*

C390 *e* **coherent pulse**

  d kohärenter Impuls *m*
  f impulsion *f* cohérente
  r когерентный импульс *m*

C391 e coherent radiation
  d kohärente Strahlung *f*
  f radiation *f* cohérente, rayonnement *m* cohérent
  r когерентное излучение *n*

C392 e coherent radiator
  d kohärenter Strahler *m*
  f radiateur *m* cohérent
  r когерентный излучатель *m*

C393 e coherent scattering
  d kohärente Streuung *f*
  f diffusion *f* cohérente
  r когерентное рассеяние *n*

C394 e coherent source
  d kohärente Lichtquelle *f*
  f source *f* cohérente
  r когерентный источник *m*

C395 e coherent spectroscopy
  d kohärente Spektroskopie *f*
  f spectroscopie *f* cohérente
  r когерентная спектроскопия *f*

C396 e coherent states
  d kohärente Zustände *m pl*
  f états *m pl* cohérents
  r когерентные состояния *n pl*

C397 e cohesion
  d Kohäsion *f*
  f cohésion *f*
  r когезия *f*

C398 e coil
  d Spule *f*
  f bobine *f*
  r катушка *f*; обмотка *f*

C399 e coincidence circuit
  d Koinzidenzschaltung *f*
  f circuit *m* de coïncidences
  r схема *f* совпадений

C400 e coincidence counter
  d Koinzidenzzähler *m*
  f compteur *m* de coïncidences, compteur *m* à coïncidences
  r счётчик *m* совпадений

C401 e coincidence technique
  d Koinzidenzmethode *f*
  f technique *f* de coïncidences
  r метод *m* совпадений

C402 e CO laser
  d Kohlenmonoxidlaser *m*, CO-Laser *m*
  f laser *m* à oxyde de carbone, laser *m* CO
  r CO-лазер *m*, лазер *m* на оксиде углерода

C403 e CO_2 laser
  d Kohlendioxidlaser *m*, CO_2-Laser *m*
  f laser *m* à gas carbonique, laser *m* CO_2
  r CO_2-лазер *m*, лазер *m* на углекислом газе

C404 e cold carriers
  d kalte Träger *m pl*
  f porteurs *m pl* froids
  r холодные носители *m pl*

C405 e cold cathode
  d Kaltkatode *f*, kalte Katode *f*
  f cathode *f* froide
  r холодный катод *m*

C406 e cold container
  d Kaltcontainer *m*
  f conteneur *m* froid
  r холодный контейнер *m*

C407 e cold crucible technique
  d Kalttiegelverfahren *n*
  f technique *f* de creuset froid
  r метод *m* холодного тигля

C408 e cold emission *see* field emission

C409 e cold neutrons
  d kalte Neutronen *n pl*
  f neutrons *m pl* froids
  r холодные нейтроны *m pl*

C410 e collapse
  d Zusammensturz *m*, Kollaps *m*; Zusammenbruch *m*
  f collapsus *m*
  r 1. коллапс *m* 2. схлопывание *n* (пузырьков жидкости)

C411 e collecting lens
  d 1. Feldlinse *f*, Kollektivlinse *f* 2. Sammellinse *f*
  f 1. lentille *f* de champ 2. lentille *f* collectrice
  r 1. коллектив *m*, коллективная линза *f* 2. собирающая линза *f*

C412 e collecting mirror
  d Sammelspiegel *m*
  f miroir *m* collecteur
  r собирающее зеркало *n*

C413 e collective acceleration
  d Kollektivbeschleunigung *f*
  f accélération *f* collective
  r коллективное ускорение *n*

C414 e collective electrons
  d kollektive Elektronen *n pl*
  f électrons *m pl* itinérants
  r коллективизированные электроны *m pl*

C415 e collective interaction
  d kollektive Wechselwirkung *f*

f interaction f collective
r коллективное взаимодействие n

C416 e **collective method**
d kollektive Methode f *(der Beschleunigung)*
f méthode f collective *(d'accélération)*
r коллективный метод m *(ускорения)*

C417 e **collective paramagnetism** *see* **superparamagnetism**

C418 e **collective phenomena**
d kollektive Phänomene n pl *(im Plasma)*
f phénomènes m pl collectifs *(au plasma)*
r коллективные явления n pl *(в плазме)*

C419 e **collective radiation**
d kollektive Strahlung f
f radiation f collective, rayonnement m collectif
r коллективное излучение n

C420 e **collector**
d Kollektorelektrode f, Kollektor m
f collecteur m
r коллектор m

C421 e **collider**
d Collider m
f collisionneur m
r коллайдер m

C422 e **colliding beams**
d kollidierende Strahlen *pl*, gegeneinanderlaufende Strahlen *pl*, gegeneinandergeführte Strahlen *pl*
f faisceaux *pl* de sens contraires
r встречные пучки *pl*

C423 e **colliding beam technique**
d Methode f der kollidierenden Strahlen, Methode f der gegeneinandergeführten Strahlen
f technique f des faisceaux de sens contraires
r метод m встречных пучков

C424 e **colliding pulses**
d kollidierende Impulse m pl, zusammenstoßende Impulse m pl
f impulsions f pl entrechoquantes
r сталкивающиеся импульсы m pl

C425 e **collimated radiation**
d kollimierte Strahlung f
f radiation f collimatée, rayonnement m collimaté
r коллимированное излучение n

C426 e **collimation**
d Kollimation f
f collimation f
r коллимация f

C427 e **collimator**
d Kollimator m
f collimateur m
r коллиматор m

C428 e **collinearity**
d Kollinearität f
f collinéarité f
r коллинеарность f

C429 e **collision**
d Zusammenstoß m, Kollision f, Stoß m, Zusammenprall m
f collision f
r соударение n, столкновение n

C430 e **collisional broadening, collision broadening**
d Stoßverbreiterung f, Linienverbreiterung f durch Stoßdämpfung
f élargissement m dû aux collisions, élargissement m dû aux chocs
r столкновительное уширение n

C431 e **collision cross-section**
d Stoßwirkungsquerschnitt m
f section f efficace de collision
r сечение n столкновения

C432 e **collision diffusion**
d Stoßdiffusion f, Diffusion f durch Stoß
f diffusion f par collision
r столкновительная диффузия f

C433 e **collision frequency**
d Stoßfrequenz f
f fréquence f de collisions
r частота f столкновений

C434 e **collision integral**
d Stoßintegral n
f intégrale f de collision
r интеграл m столкновений

C435 e **collision ionization**
d Stoßionisation f
f ionisation f par choc
r столкновительная ионизация f, ударная ионизация f

C436 e **collisionless damping**
d stoßfreie Dämpfung f, Landau-Dämpfung f
f amortissement m non collisionnel
r бесстолкновительное затухание n, затухание n Ландау

C437 e **collisionless dissociation**
d stoßfreie Dissoziation f
f dissociation f non collisionnelle
r бесстолкновительная диссоциация f

C438 e **collisionless shock waves**
d Stoßwellen f pl im stoßfreien Plasma, stoßfreie Stoßwellen f pl

f ondes f pl de choc non collisionnelles
r бесстолкновительные ударные
волны f pl

C439 e collision loss
d Stoßverlust m
f pertes f pl par suite de collisions
r потери f pl при столкновениях

C440 e collision of the first kind
d Stoß m erster Art
f choc m de première espèce
r соударение n первого рода

C441 e collision of the second kind
d Stoß m zweiter Art
f choc m de deuxième espèce
r соударение n второго рода

C442 e collision probability
d Stoßwahrscheinlichkeit f
f probabilité f de collision
r вероятность f столкновения

C443 e colloid
d Kolloid n
f colloïde m
r коллоид m

C444 e color
d Farbe f
f couleur f
r цвет m

C445 e color atlas
d Farbatlas m, Farbenkarte f
f atlas m des couleurs
r атлас m цветов

C446 e color blindness
d Farbblindheit f, Farbenblindheit f
f daltonisme m
r дальтонизм m, цветовая слепота f

C447 e color center
d Farbzentrum n, F-Zentrum n
f centre m de couleur
r центр m окраски

C448 e color-center laser
d Farbzentrenlaser m, F-Zentrenlaser m
f laser m à centres de couleur
r лазер m на центрах окраски

C449 e color charge
d Farbladung f
f charge f de couleur
r цветовой заряд m

C450 e color confinement
d Farbeinschließung f
f confinement m de couleur
r удержание n цвета

C451 e color contrast
d Farbkontrast m

f contraste m des couleurs
r цветовой контраст m

C452 e color excess
d Farbexzeß m, Farbenexzeß m
f excès m de couleur
r колор-эксцесс m; избыток m цвета

C453 e color filter
d Farbfilter n
f filtre m coloré
r цветной фильтр m

C454 e color image
d Farbbild n
f image f de couleur
r цветное изображение n

C455 e colorimeter
d Kolorimeter n
f colorimètre m
r колориметр m

C456 e colorimetric measurements
d Kolorimetrie f
f mesure f colorimétrique, colorimétrie f
r цветовые измерения n pl,
колориметрия f

C457 e colorimetry
d Kolorimetrie f
f colorimétrie f
r колориметрия f

C458 e color index
d Farbenindex m
f indice m de couleur
r колор-индекс m; показатель m
цвета

C459 e color photography
d Farbphotographie f
f photographie f en couleurs
r цветная фотография f

C460 e color picture see color image

C461 e color pyrometer
d Farbpyrometer n
f pyromètre m en couleurs
r цветовой пирометр m

C462 e color quark
d Color-Quark n, farbiges Quark n,
Quark n mit Farbquantenzahl
f quark m de couleur
r цветной кварк m

C463 e color rendering
d Farbenwiedergabe f
f reproduction f des couleurs, rendu m
des couleurs
r цветопередача f

C464 e color symmetry
d Farbsymmetrie f
f symétrie f de couleurs
r цветная симметрия f, цветовая
симметрия f

C465   *e*   color temperature
       d   Farbtemperatur *f*
       f   température *f* de couleur
       r   цветовая температура *f*

C466   *e*   color triangle *see* chromaticity diagram

C467   *e*   color vision
       d   Farbensehen *n*, Farbwahrnehmung *f*
       f   vision *f* des couleurs
       r   цветовое зрение *n*

C468   *e*   colour *see* color

C469   *e*   coma
       d   Koma *f*, Asymmetriefehler *m*
       f   coma *f*
       r   кома *f*

C470   *e*   combination
       d   Kombination *f*; Verknüpfung *f*
       f   combinaison *f*
       r   комбинация *f*

C471   *e*   combination frequency
       d   Kombinationsfrequenz *f*
       f   fréquence *f* de combinaison
       r   комбинационная частота *f*

C472   *e*   combination tones
       d   Kombinationstöne *m pl*
       f   sons *m pl* de combinaison
       r   комбинационные тона *m pl*

C473   *e*   combined inversion
       d   kombinierte Inversion *f*
       f   inversion *f* combinée
       r   комбинированная инверсия *f*

C474   *e*   combined parity
       d   kombinierte Parität *f*
       f   parité *f* combinée
       r   комбинированная чётность *f*

C475   *e*   combined parity violation
       d   Nichterhaltung *f* der kombinierten Parität, Verletzung *f* der kombinierten Parität, CP-Paritätsverletzung *f*
       f   violation *f* de la parité combinée
       r   нарушение *n* комбинированной чётности

C476   *e*   combined resonance
       d   kombinierte Resonanz *f*
       f   résonance *f* combinée
       r   комбинированный резонанс *m*

C477   *e*   combustion
       d   Brennen *n*, Verbrennen *n*
       f   combustion *f*
       r   горение *n*, сгорание *n*

C478   *e*   combustion chamber
       d   Verbrennungskammer *f*, Verbrennungsraum *m*; Brennkammer *f*
       f   chambre *f* de combustion
       r   камера *f* сгорания

C479   *e*   comet
       d   Komet *m*
       f   comète *f*
       r   комета *f*

C480   *e*   cometary nucleus
       d   Kern *m* des Kometen, Kometenkern *m*
       f   noyau *m* cométaire, noyau *m* de la comète
       r   ядро *n* кометы

C481   *e*   comet tail
       d   Kometenschweif *m*
       f   queue *f* de la comète
       r   хвост *m* кометы

C482   *e*   commensurate phase
       d   kommensurable Phase *f*
       f   phase *f* commensurable
       r   соизмеримая фаза *f*

C483   *e*   common factor
       d   gemeinsamer Faktor *m*
       f   facteur *m* commun
       r   общий множитель *m*

C484   *e*   communicating vessels
       d   kommunizierende Röhren *f pl*, kommunizierende Gefäße *m pl*
       f   vases *m pl* communicants
       r   сообщающиеся сосуды *m pl*

C485   *e*   communication channel
       d   Nachrichtenkanal *m*, Nachrichtenübertragungskanal *m*, Übertragungskanal *m*
       f   voie *f* de communication
       r   канал *m* связи

C486   *e*   communication line
       d   Fernmeldeleitung *f*; Kommunikationsleitung *f*
       f   ligne *f* de communication
       r   линия *f* связи

C487   *e*   commutation
       d   1. Kommutation *f*; Kommutierung *f* 2. Vertauschung *f*
       f   commutation *f*
       r   1. коммутация *f*, переключение *n* 2. перестановка *f*

C488   *e*   commutation relations
       d   Vertauschungsrelationen *f pl*
       f   relations *f pl* de commutation
       r   перестановочные соотношения *n pl*; коммутационные соотношения *n pl*

C489   *e*   commutator
       d   Kommutator *m*
       f   commutateur *m*
       r   коммутатор *m*

C490   *e*   comparator
       d   Komparator *m*

	f	comparateur *m*
	r	компаратор *m*
C491	*e*	comparison lamp
	d	Vergleichslampe *f*
	f	lampe *f* tare
	r	лампа *f* сравнения
C492	*e*	comparison test
	d	Vergleichstest *m*
	f	essai *m* comparatif
	r	сравнительные испытания *n pl*
C493	*e*	comparison voltage *see* reference voltage
C494	*e*	compatibility
	d	Kompatibilität *f*
	f	compatibilité *f*
	r	совместимость *f*; совместность *f*
C495	*e*	compensated semiconductor
	d	Kompensationshalbleiter *m*
	f	semi-conducteur *m* compensé
	r	компенсированный полупроводник *m*
C496	*e*	compensation
	d	Kompensation *f*, Ausgleich *m*
	f	compensation *f*
	r	компенсация *f*
C497	*e*	compensator
	d	Kompensator *m*
	f	compensateur *m*
	r	компенсатор *m*
C498	*e*	competing modes
	d	konkurrierende Moden *f pl*, Konkurrenzmoden *f pl*
	f	modes *m pl* de compétition
	r	конкурирующие моды *f pl*
C499	*e*	complementarity
	d	Komplementarität *f* (*Quantenmechanik*)
	f	complémentarité *f*
	r	дополнительность *f* (*в квантовой механике*)
C500	*e*	complementarity principle
	d	Komplementaritätsprinzip *n*
	f	principe *m* de complémentarité
	r	принцип *m* дополнительности
C501	*e*	complementary colors
	d	Komplementärfarben *f*, Ergänzungsfarben *f pl*
	f	couleurs *f pl* complémentaires
	r	дополнительные цвета *m pl*
C502	*e*	complete radiator
	d	schwarzer Strahler *m*, Hohlraumstrahler *m*
	f	radiateur *m* noir
	r	полный излучатель *m*, чёрное тело *n*, абсолютно чёрное тело *n*
C503	*e*	complete set of eigenstates
	d	vollständiges System *n* von Eigenzuständen
	f	système *m* complet des états propres
	r	полный набор *m* собственных состояний
C504	*e*	complete set of quantum numbers
	d	vollständiges System *n* von Quantenzahlen
	f	système *m* complet des nombres quantiques
	r	полный набор *m* квантовых чисел
C505	*e*	complex
	d	Komplex *m*
	f	complexe *m*
	r	комплекс *m*
C506	*e*	complex conjugation
	d	komplexe Konjugation *f*
	f	conjugaison *f* complexe
	r	комплексное сопряжение *n*
C507	*e*	complexones
	d	Komplexone *n pl*
	f	complexons *m pl*
	r	комплексоны *m pl*
C508	*e*	compliance
	d	Nachgiebigkeit *f*
	f	déformabilité *f*
	r	податливость *f*
C509	*e*	component of a vector
	d	Vektorkomponente *f*
	f	composante *f* d'un vecteur
	r	компонента *f* вектора
C510	*e*	composite, composite material
	d	Verbundstoff *m*, Verbundwerkstoff *m*
	f	composite *m*
	r	композит *m*, композиционный материал *m*
C511	*e*	composition
	d	Zusammensetzung *f*
	f	composition *f*
	r	1. состав *m*; структура *f* 2. сложение *n* (*напр. векторов*)
C512	*e*	composition of forces
	d	Kräftezusammensetzung *f*, Kräfteaddition *f*
	f	composition *f* des forces
	r	сложение *n* сил
C513	*e*	composition of velocities
	d	Addition *f* von Geschwindigkeiten
	f	composition *f* des vitesses
	r	сложение *n* скоростей
C514	*e*	compound
	d	Verbindung *f*
	f	composé *m*
	r	соединение *n*, химическое соединение *n*

C515   *e*   compound nucleus
     d   Verbundkern *m*, Compoundkern *m*, Zwischenkern *m*
     f   noyau *m* composé
     r   составное ядро *n*

C516   *e*   compound pendulum *see* physical pendulum

C517   *e*   compressed pulse
     d   komprimierter Impuls *m*
     f   impulsion *f* comprimée
     r   сжатый импульс *m*

C518   *e*   compressibility
     d   Kompressibilität *f*
     f   compressibilité *f*
     r   сжимаемость *f*

C519   *e*   compressible fluid
     d   kompressible Flüssigkeit *f*
     f   fluide *m* compressible
     r   сжимаемая жидкость *f*

C520   *e*   compressible fluid dynamics
     d   Dynamik *f* kompressibler Flüssigkeiten
     f   dynamique *f* du fluide compressible
     r   динамика *f* сжимаемой жидкости

C521   *e*   compressible liquid *see* compressible fluid

C522   *e*   compression
     d   Kompression *f*, Zusammendrücken *n*
     f   compression *f*
     r   сжатие *n*

C523   *e*   compressional deformation
     d   Druckverformung *f*
     f   déformation *f* de compression
     r   деформация *f* сжатия

C524   *e*   compression curve
     d   Verdichtungskurve *f*
     f   courbe *f* de compression
     r   кривая *f* сжатия

C525   *e*   compression fracture
     d   Kompressionsbruch *m*
     f   fracture *f* par compression
     r   излом *m* при сжатии

C526   *e*   compression modulus *see* bulk modulus

C527   *e*   compression shock
     d   Verdichtungsstoß *m*
     f   choc *m* de compression
     r   ударная волна *f*, скачок *m* уплотнения

C528   *e*   compression stress
     d   Druckbelastung *f*, Druckbeanspruchung *f*
     f   contrainte *f* de compression
     r   сжимающее напряжение *n*, напряжение *n* сжатия

C529   *e*   compression wave
     d   Kompressionswelle *f*
     f   onde *f* de compression
     r   волна *f* сжатия

C530   *e*   compressive strength
     d   Druckfestigkeit *f*
     f   résistance *f* à la compression
     r   предел *m* прочности на сжатие; прочность *f* сжатия

C531   *e*   compressor
     d   Kompressor *m*, Verdichter *m*
     f   compresseur *m*
     r   компрессор *m*

C532   *e*   Compton effect
     d   Compton-Effekt *m*
     f   effet *m* Compton
     r   эффект *m* Комптона, комптон-эффект *m*, комптоновское рассеяние

C533   *e*   Compton electron
     d   Compton-Elektron *n*
     f   électron *m* Compton
     r   комптоновский электрон *m*

C534   *e*   Compton laser
     d   Compton-Laser *m*
     f   laser *m* Compton
     r   комптоновский лазер *m*

C535   *e*   Compton scatter, Compton scattering
     d   Compton-Streuung *f*
     f   diffusion *f* Compton
     r   комптоновское рассеяние *n*

C536   *e*   Compton wavelength
     d   Compton-Wellenlänge *f*
     f   longueur *f* d'onde de Compton
     r   комптоновская длина *f* волны

C537   *e*   computed tomography
     d   rechnergestützte Tomographie *f*
     f   tomographie *f* par voie d'ordinateur
     r   компьютерная томография *f*

C538   *e*   computer
     d   Computer *m*, Rechner *m*
     f   ordinateur *m*
     r   компьютер *m*, вычислительная машина *f*

C539   *e*   concave diffraction grating
     d   konkaves Beugungsgitter *n*
     f   grille *f* de diffraction concave
     r   вогнутая дифракционная решётка *f*

C540   *e*   concave mirror
     d   Konkavspiegel *m*, Hohlspiegel *m*
     f   miroir *m* concave
     r   вогнутое зеркало *n*

C541   *e*   concentrated load *see* lumped load

C542　*e*　concentration
　　　d　Konzentration *f*
　　　f　concentration *f*
　　　r　концентрация *f*

C543　*e*　concentration quenching
　　　d　1. Selbstauslöschung *f*,
　　　　　Konzentrationsauslöschung *f*
　　　　　2. Konzentrationsabschreckung *f*
　　　f　1. extinction *f* par concentration
　　　　　2. trempe *f* de concentration (*des particules*)
　　　r　1. концентрационное тушение *n*
　　　　　(*люминесценции*) 2. закалка *f*
　　　　　концентрации (*частиц*)

C545　*e*　concentrator
　　　d　Konzentrator *m*
　　　f　concentrateur *m*
　　　r　концентратор *m*

C546　*e*　concentric rings
　　　d　konzentrische Ringe *m pl*
　　　f　anneaux *m pl* concentriques
　　　r　концентрические кольца *n pl*

C547　*e*　condensate
　　　d　Kondensat *n*
　　　f　condensat *m*, liquide *m* de condensation
　　　r　конденсат *m*

C548　*e*　condensation
　　　d　Kondensation *f*
　　　f　condensation *f*
　　　r　конденсация *f*

C549　*e*　condensation coefficient
　　　d　Kondensationskoeffizient *m*
　　　f　coefficient *m* de condensation
　　　r　коэффициент *m* конденсации

C550　*e*　condensation kinetics
　　　d　Kondensationskinetik *f*
　　　f　cinétique *f* de condensation
　　　r　кинетика *f* конденсации

C551　*e*　condensation nucleus
　　　d　Kondensationskern *m*
　　　f　noyau *m* de condensation
　　　r　зародыш *m* конденсации

C552　*e*　condensation shock
　　　d　Kondensationsstoß *m*
　　　f　choc *m* de condensation
　　　r　скачок *m* конденсации

C553　*e*　condensed matter
　　　d　kondensierte Materie *f*
　　　f　matière *f* condensée
　　　r　конденсированное вещество *n*

C554　*e*　condensed medium
　　　d　kondensiertes Medium *n*
　　　f　milieu *m* condensé
　　　r　конденсированная среда *f*

C555　*e*　condensed phase
　　　d　kondensierte Phase *f*
　　　f　phase *f* condensée
　　　r　конденсированная фаза *f*

C556　*e*　condensed state
　　　d　kondensierter Zustand *m*
　　　f　état *m* condensé
　　　r　конденсированное состояние *n*

C557　*e*　condenser
　　　d　1. Kondensor *m* (*Optik*)
　　　　　2. Kondensator *m*
　　　f　1. condenseur *m* 2. condensateur *m*
　　　r　1. конденсор *m* (*в оптике*)
　　　　　2. конденсатор *m*

C558　*e*　condition
　　　d　Bedingung *f*; Voraussetzung *f*
　　　f　condition *f*
　　　r　условие *n*

C559　*e*　conductance
　　　d　Wirkleitwert *m*, Konduktanz *f*
　　　f　conductance *f*
　　　r　проводимость *f*, активная проводимость *f*

C560　*e*　conducting channel *see* conductive channel

C561　*e*　conduction
　　　d　Leitung *f*
　　　f　conduction *f*
　　　r　проводимость *f*

C562　*e*　conduction band
　　　d　Leitungsband *n*
　　　f　bande *f* de conduction
　　　r　зона *f* проводимости

C563　*e*　conduction band valley
　　　d　Leitungsbandtal *n*
　　　f　vallée *f* de la bande de conduction
　　　r　долина *f* зоны проводимости

C564　*e*　conduction current
　　　d　Leitungsstrom *m*
　　　f　courant *m* de conduction
　　　r　ток *m* проводимости

C565　*e*　conduction electron
　　　d　Leitungselektron *n*
　　　f　électron *m* de conduction
　　　r　электрон *m* проводимости

C566　*e*　conductive channel
　　　d　leitender Kanal *m*
　　　f　canal *m* conducteur
　　　r　проводящий канал *m*

C567　*e*　conductivity
　　　d　spezifischer Leitwert *m*, spezifische Leitfähigkeit *f*
　　　f　conductivité *f*
　　　r　удельная проводимость *f*, удельная электропроводность *f*

C568   e   conductivity band *see* conduction band

C569   e   conductivity ellipsoid
       d   Leitfähigkeitsellipsoid *n*
       f   ellipsoïde *m* de conductivité
       r   эллипсоид *m* проводимости

C570   e   conductor
       d   Leiter *m*
       f   conducteur *m*
       r   проводник *m*

C571   e   cone
       d   Kegel *m*, Konus *m*
       f   cône *m*
       r   конус *m*

C572   e   cone flow
       d   kegelförmige Strömung *f*, konische Strömung *f*
       f   écoulement *m* conique
       r   коническое течение *n*

C573   e   cone of friction
       d   Reibungskegel *m*
       f   cône *m* de frottement
       r   конус *m* трения

C574   e   cone of silence
       d   Schweigekegel *m*
       f   cône *m* de silence
       r   конус *m* молчания

C575   e   cones
       d   Zäpfchen *n pl (lichtempfindliche Zellen im Auge)*
       f   cônes *m pl (de l'œil)*
       r   колбочки *f pl (глаза)*

C576   e   confidence
       d   Konfidenz *f*
       f   confiance *f*; fiabilité *f*
       r   достоверность *f (в теории вероятности)*

C577   e   confidence interval
       d   Vertrauensbereich *m*, Konfidenzintervall *n*
       f   intervalle *m* de confiance
       r   доверительный интервал *m*

C578   e   configuration
       d   Konfiguration *f*; Gestalt *f*, Bauform *f*; räumliche Anordnung *f*
       f   configuration *f*
       r   конфигурация *f*; форма *f*; расположение *n*

C579   e   configurational representation
       d   Konfigurationsdarstellung *f*
       f   représentation *f* configurationnelle
       r   конфигурационное представление *n*, координатное представление *n*

C580   e   configurational space
       d   Konfigurationsraum *m*, Lagenraum *m*

       f   espace *m* configurationnel
       r   конфигурационное пространство *n*

C581   e   configuration integral
       d   Konfigurationsintegral *n*
       f   intégrale *f* de configuration
       r   конфигурационный интеграл *m*

C582   e   configuration interaction
       d   Konfigurationswechselwirkung *f*
       f   interaction *f* de configuration, interaction *f* configurationnelle
       r   конфигурационное взаимодействие *n*

C583   e   configuration space *see* configurational space

C584   e   confinement
       d   Einschließung *f*; Confinement *n*
       f   confinement *m*
       r   удержание *n*; конфайнмент *m*

C585   e   confocal resonator
       d   konfokaler Resonator *m*
       f   résonateur *m* confocal
       r   конфокальный резонатор *m*

C586   e   conformal invariance
       d   konforme Invarianz *f*
       f   invariance *f* conforme
       r   конформная инвариантность *f*

C587   e   conformal mapping, conformal representation
       d   konforme Abbildung *f*
       f   représentation *f* conforme
       r   конформное отображение *n*

C588   e   conformal transformation
       d   konforme Transformation *f*
       f   transformation *f* conforme
       r   конформное преобразование *n*

C589   e   conformation
       d   Konformation *f*, Konstellation *f*
       f   conformation *f (d'une molécule)*
       r   конформация *f (молекулы)*

C590   e   conformation isomer *see* conformer

C591   e   conformation isomerism
       d   Konformationsisomerie *f*, Rotationsisomerie *f*
       f   isomérie *f* de conformation
       r   конформационная изомерия *f*

C592   e   conformer
       d   Konformer *n*, Konformationsisomer *n*, Rotamer *n*, Rotationsisomer *n*
       f   conformère *m*, isomère *m* rotationnel, isomère *m* de conformation, isomère *m* de rotation, rotamère *m*
       r   конформер *m*, конформационный изомер *m*

C593   e   confuser

d   Konfusor *m*
f   convergent *m*
r   конфузор *m*

C594   *e*   congruence
d   Kongruenz *f*
f   congruence *f*
r   конгруэнтность *f*

C595   *e*   conic
d   Kegelschnitt *m*
f   conique *f*, section *f* conique
r   коническое сечение *n*

C596   *e*   conical flow *see* cone flow

C597   *e*   conical indenter
d   Eindringkegel *m*
f   pénétrateur *m* conique
r   конический индентор *m*

C598   *e*   conical pendulum
d   Kegelpendel *n*, konisches Pendel *n*
f   pendule *m* conique
r   конический маятник *m*

C599   *e*   conical refraction
d   konische Refraktion *f*
f   réfraction *f* conique
r   коническая рефракция *f*

C600   *e*   conic section *see* conic

C601   *e*   conjugate double bonds
d   konjugierte Doppelbindungen *f pl*
f   doubles liaisons *f pl* conjuguées
r   сопряжённые двойные связи *f pl*

C602   *e*   conjugate foci
d   konjugierte Brennpunkte *m pl*
f   foyers *m pl* conjugués
r   сопряжённые фокусы *m pl*

C603   *e*   conjugate images
d   konjugierte Bilder *n pl*
f   images *f pl* conjuguées
r   сопряжённые изображения *n pl*

C604   *e*   conjugate points
d   konjugierte Punkte *m pl*
f   points *m pl* conjugués
r   сопряжённые точки *f pl*

C605   *e*   conjugation
d   Konjugation *f*
f   conjugaison *f*
r   сопряжение *n*

C606   *e*   connection
d   Verbindung *f*
f   connexion *f*
r   соединение *n*

C607   *e*   conoscopic figures
d   konoskopische Figuren *f pl*
f   figures *f pl* conoscopiques
r   коноскопические фигуры *f pl*

C608   *e*   conoscopy
d   Konoskopie *f*, Kristallachsenmessung *f*
f   conoscopie *f*
r   коноскопия *f*

C609   *e*   conservation laws
d   Erhaltungssätze *m pl*
f   lois *f pl* de conservation
r   законы *m pl* сохранения

C610   *e*   conservation of angular momentum
d   Erhaltung *f* des Drehimpulses, Drehimpulserhaltung *f*
f   conservation *f* du moment cinétique
r   сохранение *n* момента количества движения

C611   *e*   conservation of charge
d   Ladungserhaltung *f*
f   conservation *f* de la charge
r   сохранение *n* заряда

C612   *e*   conservation of energy
d   Energieerhaltung *f*
f   conservation *f* de l'énergie
r   сохранение *n* энергии

C613   *e*   conservation of linear momentum
d   Erhaltung *f* des Impulses, Impulserhaltung *f*
f   conservation *f* de l'impulsion, conservation *f* de la quantité de mouvement
r   сохранение *n* количества движения

C614   *e*   conservation of mass
d   Erhaltung *f* der Masse, Masseerhaltung *f*
f   conservation *f* de la masse
r   сохранение *n* массы

C615   *e*   conservation of vector current
d   Erhaltung *f* des Vektorstroms
f   conservation *f* du courant de vecteur
r   сохранение *n* векторного тока

C616   *e*   conservatism
d   Konservatismus *m*
f   conservatisme *m*
r   консервативность *f*

C617   *e*   conservative force
d   konservative Kraft *f*
f   force *f* conservative
r   консервативная сила *f*

C618   *e*   conservative system
d   konservatives System *n*
f   système *m* conservatif
r   консервативная система *f*

C619   *e*   conserved mass
d   Erhaltungsmasse *f*
f   masse *f* obéissant à la loi de conservation
r   сохраняющаяся масса *f*

C620 e consonance
d Konsonanz f, Gleichklang m
f consonance f
r консонанс m, созвучие n

C621 e constant
d Konstante f, konstante Größe f
f constante f
r константа f, постоянная f

C622 e constituent quark
d konstituentes Quark n
f quark m constituant
r конституэнтный кварк m

C623 e constitution diagram
d Zustandsdiagramm n
f diagramme m d'état, diagramme m de phase
r диаграмма f состояния, фазовая диаграмма f

C624 e constrained motion see forced motion

C625 e constraint
d Bindung f, Zwang m; Einschränkung f
f contrainte f, liaison f
r связь f, ограничение n

C626 e constraint reactions
d Zwangskräfte f pl
f réactions f pl des contraintes
r реакции f pl связей

C627 e constringence
d Abbesche Zahl f (Kernwert der relativen Dispersion)
f constringence f
r обратное значение n относительной дисперсии, число n Аббе, коэффициент m дисперсии

C628 e constructive interference
d konstruktive Interferenz f
f interférence f constructive
r конструктивная интерференция f

C629 e contact
d Kontakt m
f contact m
r контакт m

C630 e contact lens
d Kontaktschale f, Kontaktglas n, Haftschale f, Haftglas n
f lentille f de contact
r контактная линза f

C631 e contactless diagnostics
d kontaktlose Plasmadiagnostik f
f diagnostic m sans contact
r бесконтактная диагностика f (плазмы)

C632 e contact potential difference
d Kontaktpotentialdifferenz f, Kontaktspannung f

f différence f de potentiel de contact
r контактная разность f потенциалов

C633 e contact stress
d Berührungsspannung f
f contrainte f de contact
r контактное напряжение n (в механике)

C634 e contact voltage
d Kontaktspannung f, Kontaktpotentialdifferenz f
f tension f de contact
r контактное напряжение n, контактная разность f потенциалов

C635 e container
d Container m, Behälter m
f conteneur m
r контейнер m

C636 e containment
d Einschließung f
f confinement m
r удержание n

C637 e contaminated area
d Zone f der radioaktiven Verseuchung
f zone f contaminée
r зона f радиоактивного заражения

C638 e contamination
d 1. Verunreinigung f, Verschmutzung f 2. Verseuchung f, radioaktive Verseuchung f
f contamination f
r 1. загрязнение n 2. заражение n, радиоактивное заражение n

C639 e continental drift
d Kontinentaldrift f
f dérive f des continents
r дрейф m континентов

C640 e continental shelf
d Festlandsockel m, Kontinentalschelf m
f terrasse f continentale
r континентальный шельф m

C641 e continual integral
d Kontinuitätsintegral n, kontinuelles Integral n
f intégrale f continue
r континуальный интеграл m

C642 e continual integration
d Kontinuitätsintegration f; kontinuelle Integration f
f intégration f continue
r континуальное интегрирование n

C643 e continuity
d Kontinuität f; Beständigkeit f; Stetigkeit f
f continuité f
r непрерывность f, неразрывность f

C644 e **continuity equation**
    d Kontinuitätsgleichung *f*
    f équation *f* de continuité
    r уравнение *n* непрерывности,
      уравнение *n* неразрывности

C645 e **continuous absorption**
    d kontinuierliche Absorption *f*
    f absorption *f* continue
    r непрерывное поглощение *n*,
      сплошное поглощение *n*

C646 e **continuous current** *see* **direct current**

C647 e **continuous dependence**
    d stetige Abhängigkeit *f*
    f dépendance *f* continue
    r непрерывная зависимость *f*

C648 e **continuous emission** *see* **continuous radiation**

C649 e **continuous evacuation chamber**
    d Kammer *f* für kontinuierliche Evakuierung
    f chambre *f* d'évacution continue
    r камера *f* непрерывной откачки

C650 e **continuous flow**
    d Kontinuum-Strömung *f*
    f écoulement *m* continu
    r неразрывное течение *n*

C651 e **continuous function**
    d stetige Funktion *f*
    f fonction *f* continue
    r непрерывная функция *f*

C652 e **continuous medium**
    d kontinuales Medium *n*, Kontinuum *n*
    f milieu *m* continu
    r непрерывная среда *f*, сплошная среда *f*, континуум *m*

C653 e **continuous oscillations**
    d ungedämpfte Schwingungen *f pl*, kontinuierliche Schwingungen *f pl*
    f oscillations *f pl* continues
    r незатухающие колебания *n pl*, непрерывные колебания *n pl*

C654 e **continuous radiation**
    d kontinuierliche Strahlung *f*, Dauerstrahlung *f*
    f radiation *f* continue, rayonnement *m* continu, émission *f* continue
    r непрерывное излучение *n*

C655 e **continuous spectrum**
    d kontinuierliches Spektrum *n*
    f spectre *m* continu
    r непрерывный спектр *m*, сплошной спектр *m*

C656 e **continuous wave**
    d ungedämpfte Welle *f*

C657 e **continuous wave laser**
    d Dauerstrichlaser *m*
    f laser *m* continu
    r непрерывный лазер *m*

C658 e **continuum**
    d 1. Kontinuum *n* 2. kontinuierliches Spektrum *n*, Kontinuum *n*
    f 1. continuum *m* 2. spectre *m* continu
    r 1. континуум *m* 2. непрерывный спектр *m*

C659 e **continuum intensity**
    d Kontinuumintensität *f*
    f intensité *f* du spectre continu
    r интенсивность *f* непрерывного спектра

C660 e **contour integral**
    d Umlaufintegral *n*
    f intégrale *f* circulatoire
    r контурный интеграл *m*

C661 e **contour integration**
    d Umlaufintegration *f*
    f intégration *f* de contour
    r контурное интегрирование *n*, интегрирование *n* по контуру

C662 e **contracted discharge**
    d kontrahierte Ladung *f*
    f décharge *f* contractée
    r контрагированный разряд *m*

C663 e **contraction**
    d Kontraktion *f*, Zusammenziehung *f*; Einschnürung *f*
    f contraction *f*
    r 1. контракция *f* 2. сжатие *n*

C664 e **contrast**
    d Kontrast *m*
    f contraste *m*
    r контраст *m*

C665 e **contrast image**
    d kontrastreiches Bild *n*
    f image *f* contraste
    r контрастное изображение *n*

C666 e **contrast photometer**
    d Kontrastphotometer *n*
    f photomètre *m* à contraste
    r контрастный фотометр *m*

C667 e **contravariance**
    d Kontravarianz *f*
    f contravariance *f*
    r контрвариантность *f*

C668 e **control**
    d Regelung *f*; Steuerung *f*; Überwachung *f*

_f_ commande _f_; contrôle _m_
_r_ управление _n_; контроль _m_

C669 _e_ controlled fusion research
_d_ Forschungen _f pl_ auf dem Gebiet der gesteuerten Kernfusion
_f_ recherches _f pl_ sur la fusion thermonucléaire ménagée
_r_ исследования _n pl_ по управляемому термоядерному синтезу

C670 _e_ controlled thermonuclear fusion
_d_ gesteuerte thermonukleare Fusion _f_
_f_ fusion _f_ thermonucléaire ménagée, fusion _f_ thermonucléaire contrôlée
_r_ управляемый термоядерный синтез _m_

C671 _e_ controlled thermonuclear reactions
_d_ gesteuerte Kernfusionsreaktionen _f pl_
_f_ réactions _f pl_ thermonucléaires contrôlées
_r_ управляемые термоядерные реакции _f pl_

C672 _e_ convection
_d_ Konvektion _f_
_f_ convection _f_
_r_ конвекция _f_

C673 _e_ convection core
_d_ Konvektionskern _m (Stern)_
_f_ noyau _m_ convectif _(d'une étoile)_
_r_ конвективное ядро _n (звезды)_

C674 _e_ convection current
_d_ Konvektionsstrom _m_
_f_ courant _m_ de convection
_r_ конвекционный ток _m_

C675 _e_ convection zone _see_ convective zone

C676 _e_ convective equilibrium
_d_ konvektives Gleichgewicht _n_, Konvektionsgleichgewicht _n_
_f_ équilibre _m_ convectif
_r_ конвективное равновесие _n_

C677 _e_ convective heat exchange
_d_ Wärmeübertragung _f_ durch Konvektion, konvektivier Wärmeaustausch _m_
_f_ échange _m_ thermique convectif
_r_ конвективный теплообмен _m_

C678 _e_ convective heating
_d_ Konvektionsheizung _f_
_f_ chauffage _m_ par convection
_r_ конвективный нагрев _m_

C679 _e_ convective heat transfer
_d_ konvektiver Wärmeübergang _m_
_f_ transfert _m_ de chaleur convectif
_r_ конвективная теплоотдача _f_

C680 _e_ convective instability
_d_ konvektive Instabilität _f_

_f_ instabilité _f_ convective
_r_ конвективная неустойчивость _f_

C681 _e_ convective instability criterion
_d_ Kriterium _n_ der konvektiven Instabilität
_f_ critère _m_ d'instabilité convective
_r_ критерий _m_ конвективной неустойчивости

C682 _e_ convective motion
_d_ konvektive Bewegung _f_
_f_ mouvement _m_ convectif
_r_ конвекционное движение _n_

C683 _e_ convective zone
_d_ Konvektionszone _f (Stern)_
_f_ zone _f_ convective _(d'une étoile)_
_r_ конвективная зона _f (звезды)_

C684 _e_ convergence
_d_ Konvergenz _f_
_f_ convergence _f_
_r_ конвергенция _f_; сходимость _f_

C685 _e_ convergence limit
_d_ Konvergenzgrenze _f_
_f_ limite _f_ de convergence
_r_ предел _m_ сходимости

C686 _e_ convergent beam
_d_ konvergentes Strahlbündel _m_
_f_ faisceau _m_ convergent
_r_ сходящийся пучок _m_

C687 _e_ convergent lens
_d_ Sammellinse _f_
_f_ lentille _f_ convergente
_r_ собирающая линза _f_

C688 _e_ converging beam _see_ convergent beam

C689 _e_ conversion
_d_ Konversion _f_, Umwandlung _f_; Konvertierung _f_
_f_ conversion _f_
_r_ 1. конверсия _f_ 2. перевод _m_; преобразование _n_

C690 _e_ conversion coefficient
_d_ Umwandlungskoeffizient _m_, Konversionskoeffizient _m_
_f_ coefficient _m_ de conversion
_r_ коэффициент _m_ конверсии

C691 _e_ conversion electrons
_d_ Konversionselektronen _n pl_
_f_ électrons _m pl_ de conversion
_r_ конверсионные электроны _m pl_

C692 _e_ conversion factor
_d_ Umrechnungsfaktor _m_
_f_ facteur _m_ de conversion
_r_ переводной множитель _m_, переводной коэффициент _m_

C693 _e_ converter

d Wandler *m*, Konverter *m*
f convertisseur *m*
r преобразователь *m*

C694 e convex mirror
d Konvexspiegel *m*
f miroir *m* convexe
r выпуклое зеркало *n*

C695 e convex plane lens
d plankonvexe Linse *f*,
Plankonvexlinse *f*
f lentille *f* plan-convexe
r плосковыпуклая линза *f*

C696 e convolution
d Faltung *f*
f convolution *f*
r свёртка *f*

C697 e convolver
d Konvolver *m*
f convolver *m*
r конвольвер *m*

C698 e cooling
d Abkühlen *n*, Abkühlung *f*; Kühlung *f*
f refroidissement *m*
r охлаждение *n*

C699 e cooling by adiabatic
demagnetization
d Kühlung *f* durch adiabatische
Entmagnetisierung
f refroidissement *m* par désaimantation
adiabatique
r магнитное охлаждение *n*,
охлаждение *n* путём
адиабатического размагничивания

C700 e cooling liquid
d Kühlflüssigkeit *f*
f liquide *m* de refroidissement
r охлаждающая жидкость *f*

C701 e cooperative emission
d kooperative Strahlung *f*
f émission *f* coopérative
r кооперативное излучение *n*

C702 e cooperative luminescence
d kooperative Lumineszenz *f*
f luminescence *f* coopérative
r кооперативная люминесценция *f*

C703 e cooperative method *see* collective
method

C704 e cooperative phenomena
d kooperative Erscheinungen *f pl*
f phénomènes *m pl* coopératifs
r кооперативные явления *n pl*

C705 e Cooper pair
d Cooper-Paar *n*
f paire *f* de Cooper
r куперовская пара *f*

C706 e coordinate
d Koordinate *f*
f coordonnée *f*
r координата *f*

C707 e coordinate representation *see*
configurational representation

C708 e coordinate system
d Koordinatensystem *n*
f système *m* de coordonnées
r система *f* координат

C709 e coordination bond
d koordinative Bindung *f*,
Koordinationsbindung *f*
f liaison *f* coordonnée, coordinance *f*
r координационная связь *f*

C710 e coordination chemistry
d Koordinationschemie *f*
f chimie *f* de coordination
r координационная химия *f*

C711 e coordination number
d Koordinationszahl *f*,
Koordinationsziffer *f*
f nombre *m* de coordination
r координационное число *n*

C712 e coordination polyhedron
d Koordinationspolyeder *n*
f polyèdre *m* de coordination
r координационный многогранник *m*

C713 e Copernican system
d Kopernikanisches System *n*
f système *m* de Copernic
r система *f* Коперника

C714 e copper, Cu
d Kupfer *n*
f cuivre *m*
r медь *f*

C715 e copper-oxide rectifier
d Kuproxgleichrichter *m*, Kupfer(I)-
oxidgleichrichter *m*
f redresseur *m* à oxyde de cuivre
r купроксный выпрямитель *m*,
меднозакисный выпрямитель *m*

C716 e copper vapor laser
d Kupferdampflaser *m*
f laser *m* à vapeur de cuivre
r лазер *m* на парáх меди

C717 e Corbino disk
d Corbino-Scheibe *f*
f disque *m* de Corbino
r диск *m* Корбино

C718 e cord
d Schnur *f*; Verbindungsschnur *f*;
Leitung *f*
f corde *f*; câble *m*
r шнур *m*, провод *m*

C719　e　core
　　　d　1. Kern *m* 2. Kern *m*, Eisenkern *m* 3.
　　　　　Spaltzone *f*, aktive Zone *f*
　　　f　noyau *m*; cœur *m*
　　　r　1. ядро *n*, сердцевина *f* 2.
　　　　　сердечник *m* 3. активная зона *f*
　　　　　(*ядерного реактора*)

C720　e　core charge
　　　d　Spaltzonenbeladung *f*; Kerneinsatz *m*,
　　　　　Kernladung *f*
　　　f　chargement *m* du cœur
　　　r　загрузка *f* активной зоны (*ядерного
　　　　　реактора*)

C721　e　Coriolis acceleration
　　　d　Coriolis-Beschleunigung *f*
　　　f　accélération *f* de Coriolis
　　　r　ускорение *n* Кориолиса,
　　　　　кориолисово ускорение *n*

C722　e　Coriolis force
　　　d　Coriolis-Kraft *f*
　　　f　force *f* de Coriolis
　　　r　сила *f* Кориолиса

C723　e　corkscrew rule
　　　d　Uhrzeigerregel *f*, Korkenzieherregel *f*
　　　f　règle *f* de tire-bouchon, règle *f*
　　　　　d'Ampère
　　　r　правило *n* буравчика, правило *n*
　　　　　Ампера

C724　e　corner reflector
　　　d　Winkelreflektor *m*, Winkelspiegel *m*
　　　f　réflecteur *m* en coin
　　　r　уголковый отражатель *m*

C725　e　Cornu prism
　　　d　Cornu-Prisma *n*, Cornusches Prisma *n*
　　　f　prisme *m* de Cornu
　　　r　призма *f* Корню

C726　e　Cornu spiral
　　　d　Cornu-Spirale *f*, Cornusche Spirale *f*
　　　f　spirale *f* de Cornu
　　　r　спираль *f* Корню

C727　e　corona
　　　d　Korona *f*
　　　f　couronne *f*
　　　r　корона *f*

C728　e　corona discharge
　　　d　Koronaentladung *f*
　　　f　décharge *f* en couronne
　　　r　коронный разряд *m*

C729　e　coronagraph
　　　d　Koronograph *m*
　　　f　coronographe *m*
　　　r　коронограф *m*

C730　e　coronal condensation
　　　d　koronale Kondensation *f*

C731　e　coronal hole
　　　d　Koronaloch *n*
　　　f　trou *m* coronal
　　　r　корональная дыра *f*

C732　e　coronal ray
　　　d　Koronastrahl *m*
　　　f　jet *m* coronal
　　　r　корональный луч *m*

C733　e　corpuscle
　　　d　Korpuskel *n*, Materieteilchen *n*;
　　　　　Teilchen *n*
　　　f　corpuscule *m*
　　　r　корпускула *f*; частица *f*

C734　e　corpuscle-wave duality *see* wave-
　　　　　corpuscle duality

C735　e　corpuscular emission *see*
　　　　　corpuscular radiation

C736　e　corpuscular optics
　　　d　Korpuskularoptik *f*
　　　f　optique *f* corpusculaire
　　　r　корпускулярная оптика *f*

C737　e　corpuscular radiation
　　　d　Korpuskularstrahlung *f*,
　　　　　Teilchenstrahlung *f*
　　　f　rayonnement *m* corpusculaire
　　　r　корпускулярное излучение *n*

C738　e　corpuscular theory of light
　　　d　Korpuskulartheorie *f* des Lichtes
　　　f　théorie *f* corpusculaire de la lumière
　　　r　корпускулярная теория *f* света

C739　e　correcting coil
　　　d　Korrekturspule *f*, Korrektionsspule *f*
　　　f　bobine *f* de compensation, bobine *f* de
　　　　　correction
　　　r　корректирующая катушка *f*

C740　e　correcting lens
　　　d　Korrektionslinse *f*
　　　f　lentille *f* de correction
　　　r　корректирующая линза *f*,
　　　　　корригирующая линза *f*

C741　e　correction of atmospheric distortion
　　　d　Korrektion *f* der atmosphärischen
　　　　　Verzerrung
　　　f　correction *f* des distorsions
　　　　　atmosphériques
　　　r　коррекция *f* атмосферных
　　　　　искажений

C742　e　corrector
　　　d　Korrektor *m*, Korrektureinrichtung *f*
　　　f　correcteur *m*
　　　r　корректор *m*

C743　e　correlation
　　　d　Korrelation *f*

    f corrélation *f*
    r корреляция *f*

C744 *e* correlation coefficient
    d Korrelationskoeffizient *m*
    f coefficient *m* de corrélation
    r коэффициент *m* корреляции

C745 *e* correlation energy
    d Korrelationsenergie *f*
    f énergie *f* de corrélation
    r корреляционная энергия *f*

C746 *e* correlation factor *see* correlation coefficient

C747 *e* correlation function
    d Korrelationsfunktion *f*
    f fonction *f* de corrélation
    r корреляционная функция *f*

C748 *e* correlation length
    d Korrelationslänge *f*
    f longueur *f* de corrélation
    r длина *f* корреляции, корреляционная длина *f*

C749 *e* correlation radius
    d Korrelationsradius *m*
    f rayon *m* de corrélation
    r корреляционный радиус *m*

C750 *e* correlator
    d Korrelator *m*, Korrelationsanalysator *m*; Korrelationsmesser *m*
    f corrélateur *m*
    r коррелятор *m*; коррелометр *m*

C751 *e* correlometer
    d Korrelationsmesser *m*
    f corrélomètre *m*
    r коррелометр *m*

C752 *e* correspondence principle
    d Korrespondenzprinzip *n*, Bohrsches Korrespondenzprinzip *n*
    f principe *m* de correspondance
    r принцип *m* соответствия

C753 *e* corresponding states
    d übereinstimmende Zustände *m pl*, korrespondierende Zustände *m pl*
    f états *m pl* correspondants
    r соответственные состояния *n pl*

C754 *e* corrosion
    d Korrosion *f*
    f corrosion *f*
    r коррозия *f*

C755 *e* corrosion fatigue
    d Korrosionsermüdung *f*
    f fatigue *f* due à la corrosion
    r коррозионная усталость *f*

C756 *e* corrosion inhibitor
    d Korrosionsschutzmittel *n*, Korrosionshemmstoff *m*, Korrosionsverzögerer *m*
    f inhibiteur *m* de corrosion
    r ингибитор *m* коррозии

C757 *e* corrosion protection
    d Korrosionsschutz *m*
    f protection *f* contre la corrosion
    r защита *f* от коррозии

C758 *e* corrosion-resistant material
    d korrosionsbeständiger Stoff *m*, korrosionsfester Stoff *m*
    f matériau *m* résistant à la corrosion
    r коррозионностойкий материал *m*

C759 *e* corrosion wear
    d korrosiver Verschleiß *m*, Korrosionsabnutzung *f*
    f usure *f* par corrosion, usure *f* corrosive
    r коррозионное изнашивание *n*

C760 *e* corrugated waveguide
    d Runzelleiter *m*, gefalteter Hohlleiter *m*
    f guide *m* d'ondes ondulé
    r гофрированный волновод *m*

C761 *e* cosine, cos
    d Kosinus *m*, Cosinus *m*
    f cosinus *m*
    r косинус *m*

C762 *e* cosmic abundance
    d kosmische Häufigkeit *f* eines Elementes, relative Elementenhäufigkeit *f* im Kosmos
    f abondance *f* cosmique *(d'un élément)*
    r распространённость *f* элемента в космосе

C763 *e* cosmic background
    d kosmische Untergrundstrahlung *f*; Reliktstrahlung *f*, kosmische Urstrahlung *f*
    f rayonnement *m* cosmologique, rayonnement *m* à relique
    r фоновое излучение *n* Вселенной; реликтовое излучение *n*

C764 *e* cosmic body
    d kosmischer Körper *m*
    f corps *m* cosmique
    r космическое тело *n*

C765 *e* cosmic muons
    d kosmische Myonen *n pl*, Myonen *n pl* der kosmischen Strahlung
    f muons *m pl* cosmiques
    r мюоны *m pl* космических лучей

C766 *e* cosmic radiation *see* cosmic rays

C767 *e* cosmic radio source
    d kosmische Radioquelle *f*

f radiosource f cosmique
r источник m космического радиоизлучения

C768 e cosmic-ray albedo
d Albedo f der kosmischen Strahlung
f albédo m des rayons cosmiques
r альбедо n космических лучей

C769 e cosmic-ray cascade
d Schauer m, Schauer m der kosmischen Strahlung
f cascade f des rayons cosmiques
r каскад m космических лучей, ливень m космических лучей

C770 e cosmic-ray intensity
d Intensität f der kosmischen Strahlung, Höhenstrahlungsintensität f
f intensité f de rayonnement cosmique
r интенсивность f космического излучения

C771 e cosmic-ray isotropization
d Isotropisation f der kosmischen Strahlung
f isotropisation f des rayons cosmiques
r изотропизация f космических лучей

C772 e cosmic rays
d kosmische Strahlen pl, Höhenstrahlen pl, kosmische Strahlung f, Höhenstrahlung f
f rayons pl cosmiques, rayonnement m cosmique
r космические лучи pl, космическое излучение n

C773 e cosmic-ray shower
d Schauer m, Schauer m der kosmischen Strahlung, Höhenstrahlungsschauer m
f gerbe f cosmique, gerbe f des rayons cosmiques
r космический ливень m, ливень m космических лучей

C774 e cosmic-ray source
d kosmische Strahlungsquelle f
f source f des rayons cosmiques
r источник m космического излучения

C775 e cosmic-ray variations
d Höhenstrahlungsvariationen f pl
f variations f pl de rayons cosmiques
r вариации f pl космических лучей

C776 e cosmic source
d kosmische Quelle f
f source f cosmique
r космический источник m

C777 e cosmic X-ray source
d kosmische Röntgenstrahlungsquelle f, kosmische Röntgenquelle f

f source f des rayons X cosmiques
r источник m космического рентгеновского излучения

C778 e cosmochronology
d Kosmochronologie f
f chronologie f cosmique
r космохронология f

C779 e cosmogony
d Kosmogonie f
f cosmogonie f
r космогония f

C780 e cosmological baryon excess
d kosmologischer Baryonenüberschuß m
f excès m de baryons cosmologique
r космологический избыток m барионов

C781 e cosmological constant
d kosmologische Konstante f
f constante f cosmologique
r космологическая постоянная f

C782 e cosmological model
d kosmologisches Modell n
f modèle m cosmologique
r космологическая модель f

C783 e cosmological nucleosynthesis
d kosmologische Nukleosynthese f
f synthèse f nucléaire cosmologique
r космологический нуклеосинтез m

C784 e cosmological radiation
d kosmologische Strahlung f
f rayonnement m cosmologique
r космологическое излучение n

C785 e cosmology
d Kosmologie f
f cosmologie f
r космология f

C786 e cosmos
d Kosmos m, Weltraum m, Raum m, All n
f cosmos m, espace m
r космос m

C787 e Cotton effect see circular dichroism

C788 e Cotton-Mouton effect
d Cotton-Mouton-Effekt m
f effet m Cotton-Mouton
r эффект m Коттона - Мутона

C789 e Cottrell cluster
d Cottrell-Wolke f, Cottrellsche Versetzungswolke f
f nuage m de Cottrell
r облако n Котрелла

C790 e Couette-Taylor flow
d Couette-Taylor-Strömung f

f écoulement *m* de Couette-Taylor
r течение *n* Куэтта - Тейлора

C791 e coulomb, C
d Coulomb *n*
f coulomb *m*
r кулон *m*, K

C792 e Coulomb barrier
d Coulombscher Potentialwall *m*,
Coulomb-Barriere *f*
f barrière *f* de Coulomb
r кулоновский барьер *m*

C793 e Coulomb collision integral
d Coulombsches Stoßintegral *n*
f intégrale *f* coulombienne de collision
r кулоновский интеграл *m*
столкновений

C794 e Coulomb excitation *(of nucleus)*
d Coulomb-Anregung *f*
f excitation *f* de Coulomb *(du noyau)*
r кулоновское возбуждение *n* *(ядра)*

C795 e Coulomb fission *(of nucleus)*
d Coulomb-Spaltung *f*
f fission *f* de Coulomb *(du noyau)*
r кулоновское деление *n* *(ядра)*

C796 e Coulomb force
d Coulomb-Kraft *f*
f force *f* de Coulomb
r кулоновская сила *f*

C797 e Coulomb interaction
d Coulombsche Wechselwirkung *f*,
Coulomb-Wechselwirkung *f*
f interaction *f* de Coulomb
r кулоновское взаимодействие *n*

C798 e Coulomb law
d Coulombsches Gesetz *n*
f loi *f* de Coulomb
r закон *m* Кулона

C799 e Coulomb logarithm
d Coulombscher Logarithmus *m*,
Coulomb-Logarithmus *m*
f logarithme *m* coulombien, logarithme
m de Coulomb
r кулоновский логарифм *m*

C800 e Coulomb loss
d Coulomb-Verluste *m pl*
f pertes *f pl* de Coulomb
r кулоновские потери *f pl*

C801 e Coulomb scattering
d Coulomb-Streuung *f*
f diffusion *f* coulombienne
r кулоновское рассеяние *n*

C802 e count
d Zählen *n*
f lecture *f*; compte *m*
r отсчёт *m*; счёт *m*

C803 e counter
d 1. Zähler *m*; Zählwerk *n* 2. Zählrohr
n, Zähler *n*
f compteur *m*
r счётчик *m*

C804 e counter-clockwise polarization
d Linkspolarisation *f*
f polarisation *f* rotatoire gauche
r левая поляризация *f*

C805 e counter telescope
d Zählerteleskop *n*; Zählrohrteleskop *n*
f télescope *m* à compteurs
r телескоп *m* счётчиков

C806 e counting
d Zählen *n*
f compte *m*; comptage *m*
r счёт *m*; подсчёт *m*

C807 e counting rate
d Zählrate *f*, Impulsrate *f*,
Impulsdichte *f*
f cadence *f* de comptage, vitesse *f* de
comptage, taux *m* d'impulsions
r скорость *f* счёта

C808 e counting-rate meter
d Zählratenmesser *m*,
Impulsdichtemesser *m*, Ratemeter *n*
f ictomètre *m*, mesureur *m* de vitesse de
comptage
r измеритель *m* скорости счёта

C809 e couple
d Kräftepaar *n*
f couple *m*, couple *m* de forces
r пара *f* сил

C810 e coupled circuits
d gekoppelte Kreise *m pl*
f circuits *m pl* couplés
r связанные контуры *m pl*

C811 e coupled modes
d gekoppelte Moden *f pl*
f modes *m pl* couplés
r связанные моды *f pl*

C812 e coupled oscillations
d gekoppelte Schwingungen *f pl*
f oscillations *f pl* couplées
r связанные колебания *n pl*

C813 e coupled systems
d gekoppelte Systeme *n pl*
f systèmes *m pl* couplés
r связанные системы *f pl*

C814 e coupler
d Kopplungsglied *n*, Koppelelement *n*
f coupleur *m*
r ответвитель *m*

C815 e coupling
d Kopplung *f*

f liaison *f*, couplage *m*
r связь *f*, взаимодействие *n*

C816 *e* coupling coefficient
d Kopplungsfaktor *m*
f coefficient *m* de couplage
r коэффициент *m* связи

C817 *e* coupling constant
d Kopplungskonstante *f*
f constante *f* de couplage
r константа *f* связи, константа *f* взаимодействия

C818 *e* covalence
d Kovalenz *f*
f covalence *f*
r ковалентность *f*

C819 *e* covalent bond
d kovalente Bindung *f*, Elektronenpaarbindung *f*, Atombindung *f*
f liaison *f* covalente
r ковалентная связь *f*, гомеополярная связь *f*

C820 *e* covalent crystal
d kovalenter Kristall *m*, Atomkristall *m*
f cristal *m* covalent
r ковалентный кристалл *m*

C821 *e* covalent radius
d kovalenter Radius *m*
f rayon *m* covalent
r ковалентный радиус *m*

C822 *e* covariance
d Kovarianz *f*
f covariance *f*
r ковариантность *f*

C823 *e* covariant derivation
d kovariante Ableitung *f*
f dérivée *f* covariante
r ковариантная производная *f*

C824 *e* covector
d Kovektor *m*
f covecteur *m*
r ковектор *m*

C825 *e* CP-invariance
d CP-Invarianz *f*
f invariance *f* CP
r CP-инвариантность *f*, инвариантность *f* относительно комбинированной чётности

C826 *e* CPT-invariance
d CPT-Invarianz *f*
f invariance *f* CPT
r CPT-инвариантность *f* (*инвариантность относительно зарядового сопряжения пространственной инверсии и обращения времени*)

C827 *e* CPT-theorem
d CPT-Theorem *n*
f théorème *m* CPT
r теорема *f* CPT, CPT-теорема *f*

C828 *e* CP violation *see* combined parity violation

C829 *e* c-quark *see* charmed quark

C830 *e* Crab nebula
d Krabbennebel *m*
f nébuleuse *f* du Crabe
r Крабовидная туманность *f*

C831 *e* crack formation *see* cracking

C832 *e* cracking
d Rißbildung *f*
f fissuration *f*
r образование *n* трещин, трещинообразование *n*

C833 *e* crack nucleus
d Rißkeim *m*
f noyau *m* de fissure
r зародыш *m* трещины

C834 *e* crack tip
d Rißspitze *f*, Rißende *n*
f extrémité *f* de fissure, fin *f* de fissure
r кончик *m* трещины

C835 *e* crater
d Krater *m*
f cratère *m*
r кратер *m*

C836 *e* creation operator
d Erzeugungsoperator *m*
f opérateur *m* de création
r оператор *m* рождения частиц, оператор *m* рождения

C837 *e* creep
d Kriechen *n*
f fluage *m*
r ползучесть *f* (*материалов*)

C838 *e* crest value
d Spitzenwert *m*, Amplitudenwert *m*
f valeur *f* de crête
r пиковое значение *n*, амплитуда *f*

C839 *e* crisis of attractor
d Attraktorkrise *f*
f crise *f* de l'attracteur
r кризис *m* аттрактора

C840 *e* criterion
d Kriterium *m*
f critère *m*
r критерий *m*

C841 *e* critical angle
d Grenzwinkel *m*

   f angle *m* critique
   r критический угол *m*

C842 *e* critical assembly *(of fissile material)*
   d kritische Anordnung *f*
   f assemblage *m* critique
   r критическая сборка *f (ядерного топлива)*

C843 *e* critical charge
   d kritische Beladung *f*
   f charge *f* critique
   r критическая загрузка *f (ядерного реактора)*

C844 *e* critical current
   d kritische Stromstärke *f (von Supraleitern)*
   f courant *m* critique *(aux supraconducteurs)*
   r критический ток *m (в сверхпроводниках)*

C845 *e* critical damping
   d kritische Dämpfung *f*
   f amortissement *m* critique
   r критическое затухание *n*

C846 *e* critical density
   d kritische Dichte *f*
   f densité *f* critique
   r критическая плотность *f*

C847 *e* critical dynamics
   d kritische Dynamik *f*
   f dynamique *f* critique
   r критическая динамика *f*

C848 *e* critical frequency *(of the ionosphere)*
   d kritische Frequenz *f (höchste Frequenz, die von einer Ionosphärenschicht reflektiert wird)*
   f fréquence *f* critique *(de l'ionosphère)*
   r критическая частота *f (ионосферы)*

C849 *e* critical indices
   d kritische Indizes *m pl*
   f indices *m pl* critiques
   r критические индексы *m pl*, критические показатели *m pl (в термодинамике)*

C850 *e* criticality
   d Kritikalität *f*; Kritizität *f*, kritischer Zustand *m (Kernreaktor)*
   f criticité *f (du réacteur nucléaire)*
   r критичность *f (ядерного реактора)*

C851 *e* critical luminosity
   d kritische Leuchtkraft *f*, Eddingtonsche Leuchtkraft *f (Astronomie)*
   f luminosité *f* critique
   r критическая светимость *f*, эддингтоновская светимость *f*

C852 *e* critical magnetic field *(in superconductors)*

   d kritische magnetische Feldstärke *f (von Supraleitern)*
   f champ *m* magnétique critique *(aux supraconducteurs)*
   r критическое магнитное поле *n (в сверхпроводниках)*

C853 *e* critical mass
   d kritische Masse *f*
   f masse *f* critique
   r критическая масса *f*

C854 *e* critical opalescence
   d kritische Opaleszenz *f*
   f opalescence *f* critique
   r критическая опалесценция *f*

C855 *e* critical phenomena
   d kritische Phänomene *n pl*, kritische Erscheinungen *f pl*
   f phénomènes *m pl* critiques
   r критические явления *n pl*

C856 *e* critical point
   d kritischer Punkt *m*
   f point *m* critique
   r критическая точка *f*

C857 *e* critical pressure
   d kritischer Druck *m*
   f pression *f* critique
   r критическое давление *n*

C858 *e* critical radius
   d kritischer Radius *m*
   f rayon *m* critique
   r критический радиус *m*

C859 *e* critical size
   d kritische Größe *f (des Kernreaktors)*
   f taille *f* critique *(du réacteur nucléaire)*
   r критические размеры *m pl (ядерного реактора)*

C860 *e* critical state
   d kritischer Zustand *m*
   f état *m* critique
   r критическое состояние *n*

C861 *e* critical temperature
   d kritische Temperatur *f*
   f température *f* critique
   r критическая температура *f*

C862 *e* critical velocity
   d kritische Geschwindigkeit *f*
   f vitesse *f* critique
   r критическая скорость *f*

C863 *e* critical volume
   d kritisches Volumen *n*
   f volume *m* critique
   r критический объём *m*

C864 *e* Crookes dark space

   d Crookesscher Dunkelraum *m*,
Katodendunkelraum *m*, zweiter
Katodendunkelraum *m*
   f espace *m* sombre de Crookes
   r круксово тёмное пространство *n*,
катодное тёмное пространство *n*

C865 *e* **cross correlation**
   d Kreuzkorrelation *f*, gegenseitige
Korrelation *f*
   f corrélation *f* mutuelle,
intercorrélation *f*
   r кросс-корреляция *f*

C866 *e* **crossed fields**
   d gekreuzte Felder *n pl*
   f champs *m pl* croisés
   r скрещённые поля *n pl*

C867 *e* **crossing beams** *see* **colliding beams**

C868 *e* **cross modulation**
   d Kreuzmodulation *f*
   f modulation *f* croisée
   r перекрёстная модуляция *f*,
Люксембург-Горьковский эффект *m*

C869 *e* **crossover**
   d Überkreuzungspunkt *m*,
Strahlkreuzungspunkt *m*
   f cross-over *m*, crossover *m*, point *m* de
croisement
   r кроссовер *m*

C870 *e* **cross relaxation**
   d Kreuzrelaxation *f*, Crossrelaxation *f*
   f cross-relaxation *f*, relaxation *f* croisée
   r кросс-релаксация *f*

C871 *e* **cross-section**
   d Querschnitt *m*
   f section *f* efficace
   r сечение *n*; поперечное сечение *n*

C872 *e* **cross-section for absorption**
   d Absorptionswirkungsquerschnitt *m*,
Wirkungsquerschnitt *m* für Absorption
   f section *f* d'absorption
   r сечение *n* поглощения

C873 *e* **cross-section for capture**
   d Einfangquerschnitt *m*,
Wirkungsquerschnitt *m* für Einfang
   f section *f* de capture
   r сечение *n* захвата

C874 *e* **cross-section for charge exchange**
   d Umladungsquerschnitt *m*,
Umladungswirkungsquerschnitt *m*
   f section *f* d'échange de charge
   r сечение *n* перезарядки

C875 *e* **cross-section for collision**
   d Stoßquerschnitt *m*,
Wirkungsquerschnitt *m* für Stoß
   f section *f* de collision
   r сечение *n* столкновения

C876 *e* **cross-section for recombination**
   d Rekombinationsquerschnitt *m*
   f section *f* de recombinaison
   r сечение *n* рекомбинации

C877 *e* **cross-section for scattering**
   d Streuquerschnitt *m*,
Wirkungsquerschnitt *m* für Streuung
   f section *f* de diffusion
   r сечение *n* рассеяния

C878 *e* **cross talk**
   d Nebensprechen *n*
   f distorsion *f* d'intermodulation
   r перекрёстные искажения *n pl*

C879 *e* **cross-type interferometer**
   d Kreuzinterferometer *n*
   f radio-interféromètre *m* en croix;
interféromètre *m* en croix
   r крестообразный
радиоинтерферометр *m*,
крестообразный интерферометр *m*

C880 *e* **crowdion**
   d Crowdion *n*
   f crowdion *m*
   r краудион *m*

C881 *e* **crucibleless method**
   d tiegelfreies Verfahren *n*, tiegelfreies
Züchtungsverfahren *n*
   f méthode *f* sans creuset
   r бестигельный метод *m*
(*выращивания кристаллов*)

C882 *e* **cryoelectronics, cryogenic electronics**
   d Kryoelektronik *f*
   f cryo-électronique *f*, électronique *f*
cryogénique
   r криоэлектроника *f*, криогенная
электроника *f*

C883 *e* **cryogenic liquid**
   d kryogene Flüssigkeit *f*
   f liquide *m* cryogénique
   r криогенная жидкость *f*

C884 *e* **cryogenics**
   d Kryogenik *f*
   f cryogénique *f*
   r криогеника *f*

C885 *e* **cryoliquid**
   d Kryoflüssigkeit *f*
   f cryoliquide *m*
   r криожидкость *f*

C886 *e* **cryophysics**
   d Kryophysik *f*
   f cryophysique *f*
   r криофизика *f*

C887 *e* **cryostat**
   d Kryostat *m*,
Tieftemperaturthermostat *m*

    f cryostat *m*
    r криостат *m*

C888 *e* cryotron
    d Kryotron *n*,
        Tieftemperaturschaltelement *n*
    f cryotron *m*
    r криотрон *m*

C889 *e* crystal
    d Kristall *m*
    f cristal *m*
    r кристалл *m*

C890 *e* crystal acoustics
    d Kristallakustik *f*
    f cristallo-acoustique *f*
    r кристаллоакустика *f*

C891 *e* crystal analysis
    d Kristallstrukturanalyse *f*
    f analyse *f* cristallographique
    r кристаллографический анализ *m*

C892 *e* crystal anisotropy
    d Kristallanisotropie *f*
    f anisotropie *f* cristalline
    r кристаллическая анизотропия *f*

C893 *e* crystal bending
    d Kristallbiegung *f*
    f flexion *f* du cristal
    r изгиб *m* кристалла

C894 *e* crystal bleaching
    d Ausbleichen *n* von Kristallen
    f blanchiment *m* du cristal
    r обесцвечивание *n* кристалла

C895 *e* crystal calibrator
    d Quarzeichoszillator *m*, Quarzeicher *m*
    f calibrateur *m* piézo-électrique
    r кварцевый калибратор *m*

C896 *e* crystal chemistry
    d Kristallchemie *f*
    f chimie *f* des cristaux, cristallochimie *f*
    r кристаллохимия *f*

C897 *e* crystal classes
    d Kristallklassen *f pl*
    f classes *f pl* de cristaux, classes *f pl* cristallographiques
    r классы *m pl* кристаллов, кристаллографические классы *m pl*, точечные группы *f pl* симметрии

C898 *e* crystal counter
    d Kristallzähler *m*
    f compteur *m* à cristal
    r кристаллический счётчик *m*

C899 *e* crystal defect
    d Kristallbaufehler *m*, Kristallstörstelle *f*
    f imperfection *f* cristalline, imperfection *f* du cristal, perturbation *f* cristalline, perturbation *f* du cristal
    r дефект *m* кристалла

C900 *e* crystal field *see* cristalline field

C901 *e* crystal growth
    d Kristallzüchtung *f*; Kristallwachstum *n*
    f croissance *f* de cristaux
    r выращивание *n* кристаллов; рост *m* кристаллов

C902 *e* crystal holder
    d Kristallhalterung *f*
    f support *m* de cristal
    r кристаллодержатель *m*

C903 *e* crystal imperfection
    d Kristallbaufehler *m*, Kristalldefekt *m*; Kristallunvollkommenheit *f*
    f imperfection *f* du cristal
    r несовершенство *n* кристалла

C904 *e* crystal indices
    d kristallographische Indizes *m pl*
    f indices *m pl* cristallographiques
    r кристаллографические индексы *m pl*

C905 *e* crystal laser
    d Kristallaser *m*
    f laser *m* à cristal
    r лазер *m* на кристалле

C906 *e* crystal lattice
    d Kristallgitter *n*
    f réseau *m* cristallin
    r кристаллическая решётка *f*

C907 *e* crystal lattice basis
    d Kristallgitterbasis *f*
    f base *f* du réseau cristallin
    r базис *m* кристаллической решётки

C908 *e* crystal lattice dynamics
    d Kristallgitterdynamik *f*
    f dynamique *f* du réseau cristallin
    r динамика *f* кристаллической решётки

C909 *e* crystal lattice parameter
    d Kristallgitterparameter *m*, Gitterparameter *m*
    f constante *f* du réseau cristallin
    r параметр *m* кристаллической решётки

C910 *e* crystal lattice vibration
    d Kristallgittervibration *f*
    f vibration *f* du réseau cristallin
    r колебания *n pl* кристаллической решётки

C911 *e* crystalline field
    d Kristallfeld *n*
    f champ *m* cristallin
    r внутрикристаллическое поле *n*

C912 *e* crystalline state

d kristalliner Zustand *m*
f état *m* cristallin
r кристаллическое состояние *n*

C913 e crystalline substance
d kristalliner Stoff *m*
f substance *f* cristalline
r кристаллическое вещество *n*

C914 e crystallite
d Kristallit *m*
f cristallite *m*
r кристаллит *m*

C915 e crystallization
d Kristallisation *f*, Kristallisieren *n*,
Kristallbildung *f*
f cristallisation *f*, formation *f* des
cristaux
r кристаллизация *f*

C916 e crystallization from melt
d Kristallisation *f* aus der Schmelze
f cristallisation *f* de fonte
r кристаллизация *f* из расплава

C917 e crystallization from solution
d Kristallisation *f* aus der Lösung
f cristallisation *f* de solution
r кристаллизация *f* из раствора

C918 e crystallization from vapor *see*
crystallisation from vapor phase

C919 e crystallization from vapor phase
d Kristallisation *f* aus der Dampfphase
f cristallisation *f* de phase gazeuse,
cristallisation *f* de phase vapeuse
r кристаллизация *f* из газовой фазы

C920 e crystallization front curvature
d Kristallisationsfrontkrümmung *f*
f courbure *f* du front de cristallisation
r кривизна *f* фронта кристаллизации

C921 e crystallization isotherm
d Kristallisationsisotherme *f*
f isotherme *f* de cristallisation
r изотерма *f* кристаллизации

C922 e crystallization kinetics
d Kristallisationskinetik *f*
f cinétique *f* de cristallisation
r кинетика *f* кристаллизации

C923 e crystallization waves
d Kristallisationswellen *f pl*
f ondes *f pl* de cristallisation
r кристаллизационные волны *f pl*

C924 e crystallographic axis
d Kristallachse *f*, kristallographische
Achse *f*
f axe *m* cristallographique
r кристаллографическая ось *f*

C925 e crystallographic direction

d kristallographische Richtung *f*,
Kristallrichtung *f*
f direction *f* cristallographique
r кристаллографическое
направление *n*

C926 e crystallographic index
d kristallographischer Index *m*
f indice *m* cristallographique
r кристаллографический индекс *m*

C927 e crystallography
d Kristallographie *f*, Kristallkunde *f*
f cristallographie *f*
r кристаллография *f*

C928 e crystalloid
d Kristalloid *n*
f cristalloïde *m*
r кристаллоид *m*

C929 e crystal optics
d Kristalloptik *f*
f optique *f* cristalline
r кристаллооптика *f*

C930 e crystal oscillator
d Quarzoszillator *m*
f oscillateur *m* à quarz
r кварцевый генератор *m*

C931 e crystal parameter *see* crystal lattice
parameter

C932 e crystal phosphor
d Kristallphosphor *m*
f phosphore *m* cristallin
r кристаллофосфóр *m*

C933 e crystal physics
d Kristallphysik *f*
f physique *f* des cristaux
r физика *f* кристаллов,
кристаллофизика *f*

C934 e crystal pick-up *see* piezoelectric pick-
up

C935 e crystal plane
d Kristallebene *f*
f plan *m* cristallographique
r кристаллографическая плоскость *f*

C936 e crystal spectroscopy
d Kristallspektroskopie *f*
f spectroscopie *f* des cristaux
r спектроскопия *f* кристаллов

C937 e crystal structure
d Kristallstruktur *f*, Kristallgefüge *n*
f structure *f* cristalline
r кристаллическая структура *f*,
структура *f* кристалла

C938 e crystal symmetry
d Kristallsymmetrie *f*

f symétrie f cristallographique, symétrie
f des cristaux
r симметрия f кристаллов

C939 e crystal symmetry groups
d Kristallsymmetriegruppen f pl
f groupes m pl de symétrie
cristallographique
r кристаллографические группы f pl
симметрии, группы f pl симметрии
кристаллов

C940 e crystal system
d Kristallsystem n, Syngonie f
f système m cristallin
r сингония f, кристаллографическая
система f

C941 e crystal water
d Kristallwasser n
f eau f de cristallisation
r кристаллизационная вода f

C942 e crystal whiskers
d Whiskers m pl, Haarkristalle m pl
f cristaux m pl filamenteux
r нитевидные кристаллы m pl

C943 e cube
d Würfel m
f cube m
r куб m

C944 e cubic close packing
d kubisch dichte Kugelpackung f,
kubisch dichteste Kugelpackung f
f empilement m cubique compact
r кубическая плотная упаковка f

C945 e cubic crystal
d kubischer Kristall m
f cristal m cubique
r кубический кристалл m

C946 e cubic equation
d kubische Gleichung f
f équation f cubique
r кубическое уравнение n

C947 e cubic meter, m³
d Kubikmeter n
f mètre m cube
r кубический метр m, м³

C948 e cubic nonlinearity
d kubische Nichtlinearität f
f non-linéarité f cubique
r кубическая нелинейность f

C949 e cubic structure
d kubische Struktur f
f structure f cubique
r кубическая структура f

C950 e cubic system
d kubisches Kristallsystem n,
regelmäßiges Kristallsystem n

f système m cubique
r кубическая сингония f, кубическая
кристаллографическая система f

C951 e culmination
d Kulmination f
f culmination f
r кульминация f

C952 e cumulation
d Kumulation f, kumulativer Prozeß m
f cumulation f, processus m cumulatif
r кумуляция f

C953 e cumulative charge
d kumulative Ladung f
f charge f creuse
r кумулятивный заряд m

C954 e cumulative effect
d kumulative Wirkung f
f effet m cumulatif
r кумулятивный эффект m

C955 e cup anemometer
d Schalenkreuzanemometer n
f anémomètre m à coquilles
r чашечный анемометр m

C956 e Curie, Ci
d Curie n
f curie m
r кюри n, Ки

C957 e Curie point, Curie temperature
d Curie-Punkt m, Curie-Temperatur f
f point m de Curie
r точка f Кюри

C958 e Curie-Weiss law
d Curie-Weisssches Gesetz n
f loi f de Curie-Weiss
r закон m Кюри - Вейса

C959 e Curium, Cm
d Curium n
f curium m
r кюрий m

C960 e curl
d 1. Rotation f (Mathematik)
2. Wirbel m
f 1. rotationnel m (mathématique)
2. tourbillon m
r 1. ротор m (в математике)
2. вихрь m

C961 e current
d 1. Strom m, elektrischer Strom m;
Stromstärke f 2. Strömung f; Fluß m
f courant m
r 1. ток m; сила f тока 2. течение n;
поток m

C962 e current algebra
d Stromalgebra f

	f	algèbre *f* des courants
	r	алгебра *f* токов
C963	*e*	**current balance**
	d	Stromwaage *f*
	f	balance *f* d'Ampère, balance *f* électrométrique
	r	ампер-весы *pl*, токовые весы *pl*
C964	*e*	**current carriers**
	d	Ladungsträger *m pl*
	f	porteurs *m pl* de charge
	r	носители *m pl* заряда
C965	*e*	**current channel**
	d	Stromkanal *m*
	f	canal *m* de courant
	r	токовый канал *m*
C966	*e*	**current density**
	d	Stromdichte *f*
	f	densité *f* de courant
	r	плотность *f* тока
C967	*e*	**current injection**
	d	Strominjektion *f*
	f	injection *f* de courant
	r	инжекция *f* тока
C968	*e*	**current instability**
	d	Strominstabilität *f*
	f	instabilité *f* du courant
	r	токовая неустойчивость *f*
C969	*e*	**current line**
	d	Stromlinie *f*
	f	ligne *f* de courant
	r	линия *f* тока
C970	*e*	**current node**
	d	Stromknoten *m*
	f	nœud *m* de courant
	r	узел *m* тока
C971	*e*	**current quark**
	d	Stromquark *n*
	f	quark *m* de courant
	r	токовый кварк *m*
C972	*e*	**current sheet**
	d	Stromblatt *n*, Stromfläche *f*
	f	couche *f* de courant, surface *f* de courant
	r	токовый слой *m*
C973	*e*	**current source**
	d	Stromquelle *f*
	f	source *f* de courant
	r	источник *m* тока
C974	*e*	**current stabilization**
	d	Stromstabilisierung *f*, Stromkonstanthaltung *f*
	f	stabilisation *f* de courant
	r	стабилизация *f* тока
C975	*e*	**current standing-wave ratio**
	d	Strom-Stehwellenverhältnis *n*, SSWV

	f	taux *m* d'ondes stationnaires en courant, T.O.S.C.
	r	коэффициент *m* стоячей волны по току, КСВТ
C976	*e*	**current transformer**
	d	Stromtransformator *m*
	f	transformateur *m* de courant
	r	трансформатор *m* тока
C977	*e*	**current turn deformation**
	d	Stromwindungsdeformation *f*
	f	déformation *f* de la spire de courant
	r	деформация *f* витка с током
C978	*e*	**curvature**
	d	Krümmung *f*
	f	courbure *f*
	r	кривизна *f*
C979	*e*	**curve**
	d	Kurve *f*; Kennlinie *f*
	f	courbe *f*
	r	кривая *f*
C980	*e*	**curved space**
	d	gekrümmter Raum *m*
	f	espace *m* courbe
	r	искривлённое пространство *n*
C981	*e*	**curvilinear coordinates**
	d	krummlinige Koordinaten *f pl*
	f	coordonnées *f pl* curvilignes
	r	криволинейные координаты *f pl*
C982	*e*	**curvilinear motion**
	d	krummlinige Bewegung *f*
	f	mouvement *m* curviligne
	r	криволинейное движение *n*
C983	*e*	**cusp**
	d	Rückkehrpunkt *m*, Kuspidalpunkt *m*, Kehrpunkt *m*, Spitze *f*
	f	point *m* de rebroussement
	r	касп *m*
C984	*e*	**cut** *(of a crystal)*
	d	Schnitt *m (Kristall)*
	f	taille *f (du cristal)*
	r	срез *m (кристалла)*
C985	*e*	**cutoff frequency**
	d	Grenzfrequenz *f*
	f	fréquence *f* critique
	r	критическая частота *f*, частота *f* отсечки
C986	*e*	**cutoff mode**
	d	kritische Mode *f*
	f	mode *m* de coupure
	r	критическая мода *f*
C987	*e*	**cutout**
	d	Schalter *m*
	f	interrupteur *m*
	r	выключатель *m*

C988   *e*   CW laser *see* continuous wave laser

C989   *e*   cybernetics
    d   Kybernetik *f*
    f   cybernétique *f*
    r   кибернетика *f*

C990   *e*   cycle
    d   Zyklus *m*; Periode *f*
    f   cycle *m*
    r   цикл *m*; период *m*

C991   *e*   cycle per second, cps, Hz
    d   Hertz *n*, Hz
    f   période *f* par seconde, cycle *m* par seconde, hertz *m*, p.p.s., c.p.s., Hz
    r   герц *m*, Гц

C992   *e*   cyclic accelerator
    d   zyklischer Beschleuniger *m*, Mehrfachbeschleuniger *m*
    f   accélérateur *m* cyclique
    r   циклический ускоритель *m*

C993   *e*   cyclic demagnetization
    d   zyklische Entmagnetisierung *f*
    f   démagnétisation *f* cyclique
    r   циклическое перемагничивание *n*

C994   *e*   cyclic stressing
    d   Schwingbeanspruchung *f*
    f   charge *f* cyclique
    r   циклическое нагружение *n*

C995   *e*   cyclogram
    d   Zyklogramm *n*
    f   cyclogramme *m*
    r   циклограмма *f*

C996   *e*   cyclograph
    d   Zyklograph *m*, Zykloskop *n*
    f   cyclographe *m*, cycloscope *m*
    r   циклограф *m*

C997   *e*   cycloid
    d   Zykloide *f*, Zykloidenkurve *f*, Radlinie *f*, Radkurve *f*
    f   cycloïde *f*
    r   циклоида *f*

C998   *e*   cyclone
    d   Tiefdruckgebiet *n*, Zyklone *f*
    f   cyclone *m*
    r   циклон *m*

C999   *e*   cyclotron
    d   Zyklotron *n*
    f   cyclotron *m*
    r   циклотрон *m*

C1000   *e*   cyclotron frequency
    d   Zyklotronresonanzfrequenz *f*, Zyklotronfrequenz *f*
    f   fréquence *f* cyclotron, fréquence *f* cyclotronique
    r   циклотронная частота *f*, гиромагнитная частота *f*

C1001   *e*   cyclotron oscillation
    d   Zyklotronschwingungen *f pl*
    f   oscillations *f pl* cyclotroniques
    r   циклотронные колебания *n pl*

C1002   *e*   cyclotron radiation
    d   Zyklotronstrahlung *f*
    f   rayonnement *m* cyclotron, radiation *f* cyclotron
    r   циклотронное излучение *n*

C1003   *e*   cyclotron resonance
    d   Zyklotronresonanz *f*
    f   résonance *f* cyclotron
    r   циклотронный резонанс *m*

C1004   *e*   cyclotron-resonance maser
    d   Zyklotronresonanzmaser *m*
    f   maser *m* à résonance cyclotronique
    r   мазер *m* на циклотронном резонансе

C1005   *e*   cylinder
    d   Zylinder *m*
    f   cylindre *m*
    r   цилиндр *m*

C1006   *e*   cylinder lens
    d   zylindrische Linse *f*
    f   lentille *f* cylindrique
    r   цилиндрическая линза *f*

C1007   *e*   cylindrical coordinates
    d   zylindrische Koordinaten *f pl*
    f   coordonnées *f pl* cylindriques
    r   цилиндрические координаты *f pl*

C1008   *e*   cylindrical function
    d   zylindrische Funktion *f*
    f   fonction *f* cylindrique
    r   цилиндрическая функция *f*

C1009   *e*   cylindrical magnetic domain
    d   Magnetblase *f*
    f   bulle *f*
    r   цилиндрический магнитный домен *m*, ЦМД

C1010   *e*   cylindrical wave
    d   Zylinderwelle *f*. Kreiszylinderwelle *f*
    f   onde *f* cylindrique
    r   цилиндрическая волна *f*

C1011   *e*   cylindrical waveguide
    d   zylindrischer Hohlleiter *m*
    f   guide *m* d'ondes cylindrique
    r   цилиндрический волновод *m*

C1012   *e*   Czochralski method
    d   Czochralski-Methode *f*, Kristallzüchtung *f* nach dem Czochralski-Verfahren
    f   méthode *f* Czochralski
    r   метод *m* Чохральского (*метод выращивания кристаллов по Чохральскому*)

D

D1
e daily variation (of geomagnetic field)
d Tagesgang m, Tagesvariation f (des geomagnetischen Feldes)
f variation f diurne (du champ géomagnétique)
r суточная вариация f (геомагнитного поля)

D2
e d'Alembertian operator
d d'Alembertscher Operator m
f opérateur m de d'Alembert
r оператор m Д'Аламбера

D3
e d'Alembert principle
d d'Alembertsches Prinzip n
f principe m de d'Alembert
r принцип m Д'Аламбера

D4
e daltonism
d Daltonismus m
f daltonisme m
r дальтонизм m

D5
e Dalton law (of partial pressures)
d Daltonsches Gesetz n, Gesetz n der Partialdrücke
f loi f de Dalton (pour les pressions partielles)
r закон m Дальтона (для парциальных давлений)

D6
e damage star
d Durchschlagsstern m
f étoile f de claquage
r звезда f пробоя

D7
e damped oscillation, damped oscillations
d gedämpfte Schwingungen f pl, abklingende Schwingungen f pl
f oscillations f pl décroissantes, oscillations f pl amorties
r затухающие колебания n pl

D8
e damper
d Dämpfer m, Dämpfungsvorrichtung f
f damper m, amortisseur m
r демпфер m; успокоитель m

D9
e damping
d Dämpfung f, Abklingen n
f amortissement m; affaiblissement m
r 1. затухание n, ослабление n 2. успокоение n, демпфирование n

D10
e damping coefficient, damping factor
d Dämpfungskoeffizient m, Dämpfungszahl f; Abklingkonstante f
f coefficient m d'amortissement
r коэффициент m затухания; декремент m затухания

D11
e dampness see humidity

D12
e Darcy law
d Darcysches Gesetz n
f loi f de Darcy
r формула f Дарси

D13
e Darcy-Weisbach formula
d Darcy-Weisbachsche Formel f
f formule f de Darcy-Weisbach
r формула f Дарси - Вейсбаха

D14
e dark adaptation
d Dunkeladaptation f
f adaptation f à l'obscurité
r темновая адаптация f

D15
e dark conduction
d Dunkelleitfähigkeit f
f conduction f d'obscurité
r темновая проводимость f, темновая электропроводность f

D16
e dark current
d Dunkelstrom m
f courant m d'obscurité
r темновой ток m

D17
e darkening (at the limb)
d Randverdunkelung f
f assombrissement m au bord solaire
r потемнение n к краю солнечного диска

D18
e dark-field method
d Dunkelfeldverfahren n
f méthode f à fond noir
r метод m затемнённого поля, метод m тёмного поля

D19
e dark matter
d unsichtbare Materie f, dunkle Materie f
f matière f invisible
r невидимая материя f

D20
e dark space
d Dunkelraum m
f espace m sombre
r тёмное пространство n (в газовом разряде)

D21
e Darwin-Fowler method
d Darwin-Fowler-Methode f, Darwin-Fowlersche Methode f
f méthode f de Darwin-Fowler
r метод m Дарвина - Фаулера

D22
e data
d Daten pl
f données pl
r данные pl; информация f

D23
e data processing
d Datenverarbeitung f
f traitement m des données
r обработка f данных

D24 e dating by radioactivity
     d radiometrische Altersbestimmung f
     f détermination f de l'âge par radio-
        isotopes
     r радиоизотопное датирование n,
        радиоизотопное определение n
        возраста

D25 e daughter atom
     d Folgeatom n, Tochteratom n
     f atome m produit, atome m fils
     r дочерний атом m

D26 e Dauphiné twin
     d Dauphinéer Zwilling m
     f jumeau m dauphinéen, macle f
        dauphinéenne
     r дофинейский двойник m

D27 e Davisson-Germer experiment
     d Davisson-Germer-Versuch m
     f expérience f de Davisson-Germer
     r опыт m Дэвиссона - Джермера

D28 e Davydov splitting
     d Dawydow-Aufspaltung f
     f subdivision f Davydov, dédoublement
        m Davydov
     r давыдовское расщепление n

D29 e day
     d Tag m
     f jour m
     r 1. сутки pl 2. день m

D30 e daylight lamp
     d Tageslichtlampe f
     f lampe f à lumière du jour
     r лампа f дневного света

D31 e dc amplifier
     d Gleichstromverstärker m
     f amplificateur m à courant continu
     r усилитель m постоянного тока

D32 e dc magnetization
     d Gleichstrommagnetisierung f
     f magnétisation f par courant continu
     r постоянная намагниченность f

D33 e dc voltage
     d Gleichspannung f
     f tension f continue
     r постоянное напряжение n

D34 e deactivation
     d Deaktivierung f, Desaktivierung f
     f désactivation f, décontamination f
     r дезактивация f

D35 e deactivator
     d Deaktivator m, Desaktivator m
     f désactivateur m
     r дезактиватор m

D36 e dead time
     d Totzeit f

D37 e dead zone
     d tote Zone f, neutrale Zone f, Totzone
        f, Unempfindlichkeitsbereich m
     f zone f morte
     r мёртвая зона f

D38 e de Broglie wavelength
     d de-Broglie-Wellenlänge f
     f longeur f d'onde de De Broglie
     r де-бройлевская длина f волны

D39 e de Broglie waves
     d de-Broglie-Wellen f pl,
        Materiewellen f pl
     f ondes f pl brogliennes
     r волны f pl де Бройля, волны f pl
        материи

D40 e debuncher
     d Bündelzerstreuer m,
        Phasenentbündeler m, Debuncher m
     f debuncher m
     r дебанчер m, разгруппирователь m

D41 e debunching
     d Bündelzerstreuung f, Debunching n
     f dégroupement m
     r разгруппирование n (пучка)

D42 e Debye, D
     d Debye n, Debye-Einheit f
     f debye m
     r дебай m, Д (внесистемная единица
        электрического дипольного
        момента)

D43 e Debye frequency
     d Debye-Frequenz f, Debyesche
        Frequenz f
     f fréquence f de Debye
     r частота f Дебая

D44 e Debye length
     d Debye-Länge f
     f longueur f de Debye
     r дебаевская длина f, дебаевский
        радиус m (экранирования)

D45 e Debye-Scherrer method
     d Debye-Scherrer-Verfahren n
     f méthode f de Debye-Scherrer
     r метод m Дебая - Шеррера

D46 e Debye-Scherrer powder photograph
     d Debye-Scherrer-Aufnahme f, Debye-
        Scherrer-Diagramm n,
        Pulverbeugungsaufnahme f
     f diagramme m Debye-Scherrer,
        diagramme m de Debye-Scherrer,
        cristallogramme m à poudre
     r дебаеграмма f, порошковая
        рентгенограмма f

D47   *e* Debye temperature
     d Debye-Temperatur *f*
     f température *f* de Debye
     r температура *f* Дебая

D48   *e* Debye theory of solids
     d Debyesche Festkörpertheorie *f*
     f théorie *f* du corps solide de Debye
     r теория *f* твёрдого тела Дебая, теория *f* Дебая

D49   *e* Debye unit *see* Debye

D50   *e* Debye-Waller factor
     d Debye-Wallerscher Temperaturfaktor *m*, Debye-Wallerscher Faktor *m*, Debye-Waller-Faktor *m*
     f facteur *m* de Debye-Waller
     r фактор *m* Дебая - Уоллера

D51   *e* decay
     d 1. Zerfall *m* 2. Abklingen *n*, Abfall *m*
     f 1. désintégration *f* 2. déclin *m*, évanouissement *m*
     r 1. распад *m* 2. затухание *n*, ослабление *n*

D52   *e* decay constant
     d Zerfallskonstante *f*, radioaktive Zerfallskonstante *f*
     f constante *f* de désintégration
     r постоянная *f* распада

D53   *e* decay curve
     d 1. Abklingkurve *f* 2. Zerfallskurve *f*
     f 1. courbe *f* de déclin 2. courbe *f* de désintégration
     r 1. кривая *f* затухания 2. кривая *f* распада

D54   *e* decay instability
     d Zerfallsinstabilität *f*
     f instabilité *f* de désintégration
     r распадная неустойчивость *f*

D55   *e* decay kinematics
     d Zerfallskinematik *f*
     f cinématique *f* de désintégration
     r кинематика *f* распада

D56   *e* decay period
     d Halbwertzeit *f*
     f période *f* de demi-valeur
     r период *m* полураспада

D57   *e* decay time
     d 1. Zerfallszeit *f*, Abklingzeit *f* (*Lumineszenz*) 2. Zerfallszeit *f* 3. Abklingzeit *f*
     f 1. durée *f* d'émission, durée *f* d'émission (*du phosphore*) 2. période *f* de désintégration 3. temps *m* de décroissance
     r 1. время *n* высвечивания (*люминофора*) 2. время *n* распада 3. время *n* спада

D58   *e* decelerated motion
     d verzögerte Bewegung *f*
     f mouvement *m* décéléré
     r замедленное движение *n*

D59   *e* decelerating voltage
     d Verzögerungsspannung *f*, retardierende Spannung *f*
     f tension *f* de décélération
     r замедляющее напряжение *n*, тормозящее напряжение *n*

D60   *e* deceleration
     d Verzögerung *f*
     f décélération *f*
     r замедление *n*, торможение *n*

D61   *e* dechanneling
     d Dekanalierung *f*, Dekanalierungseffekt *m*, Dechanneling *n*
     f décanalisation *f*
     r деканалирование *n*

D62   *e* dechanneling by defects
     d Defekt-Dekanalierung *f*
     f décanalisation *f* aux défauts
     r деканалирование *n* на дефектах

D63   *e* decibel, dB
     d Dezibel *n*
     f décibel *m*
     r децибел *m*, дБ

D64   *e* decimal logarithm, lg
     d Briggscher Logarithmus *m*, dekadischer Logarithmus *m*, Zehnerlogarithmus *m*
     f logarithme *m* décimal, logarithme *m* de Brigg
     r десятичный логарифм *m*

D65   *e* decimetric waves
     d Dezimeterwellen *f pl*
     f ondes *f pl* décimétriques
     r дециметровые волны *f pl*

D66   *e* declination
     d Deklination *f*
     f déclinaison *f*
     r склонение *n*

D67   *e* decoder
     d Dekoder *m*, Dekodierer *m*
     f décodeur *m*
     r декодер *m*

D68   *e* decontamination chamber
     d Dekontaminationszelle *f*
     f chambre *f* de décontamination
     r дезактивационная камера *f*

D69   *e* decoration
     d Dekorieren *n*
     f décoration *f*
     r декорирование *n*

D70   *e* decoration technique

    d Dekorierverfahren *n*
    f méthode *f* de décoration
    r метод *m* декорирования

D71 *e* **decrement**
    d Dämpfungsdekrement *n*,
       Schwingungsdekrement *n*,
       Dämpfungsverhältnis *n*, Dekrement *n*
    f décrément *m*
    r декремент *m*

D72 *e* **decrystallization**
    d Entkristallisation *f*
    f décristallisation *f*
    r декристаллизация *f*

D73 *e* **dee**
    d Duant *m*, D-Elektrode *f*, Dee *n*
    f dé *m*
    r дуант *m*

D74 *e* **deenergizing**
    d Abschalten *n*, Stromlosmachen *n*
    f désexcitation *f*
    r обесточивание *n*

D75 *e* **deep inelastic process, deeply inelastic
      process**
    d tiefinelastischer Prozeß *m*,
       tiefunelastischer Prozeß *m*
    f processus *m* profondément inélastique
    r глубоко неупругий процесс *m*

D76 *e* **deep inelastic scattering, deeply
      inelastic scattering**
    d tiefinelastische Streuung *f*,
       tiefunelastische Streuung *f*
    f diffusion *f* profondément inélastique
    r глубоко неупругое рассеяние *n*

D77 *e* **deep trap**
    d tiefe Haftstelle *f*, tiefliegende
       Haftstelle *f*
    f piège *m* profond
    r глубокая ловушка *f*

D78 *e* **deexcitation**
    d Aberregung *f*; Relaxation *f*
    f désexcitation *f*; relaxation *f*
    r снятие *n* возбуждения; релаксация
       f; переход *m* в невозбуждённое
       состояние

D79 *e* **defect**
    d Defekt *m*, Fehler *m*; Störstelle *f*
    f défaut *m*
    r дефект *m*

D80 *e* **defect concentration**
    d Störstellendichte *f*,
       Verunreinigungskonzentration *f*
    f concentration *f* des défauts
    r концентрация *f* дефектов

D81 *e* **defect delocalization**
    d Defektdelokalisierung *f*

    f délocalisation *f* des défauts
    r делокализация *f* дефектов

D82 *e* **defect formation**
    d Fehlstellenerzeugung *f*,
       Defektbildung *f*
    f formation *f* des défauts
    r образование *n* дефектов,
       дефектообразование *n*

D83 *e* **defect migration**
    d Fehlstellenwanderung *f*
    f migration *f* de défauts
    r миграция *f* дефектов

D84 *e* **defecton**
    d Defekton *n (Quasiteilchen)*
    f defecton *m (quasi-particule)*
    r дефектон *m (квазичастица)*

D85 *e* **definite integral**
    d bestimmtes Integral *n*
    f intégrale *f* définie
    r определённый интеграл *m*

D86 *e* **deflagration**
    d Deflagration *f*, Verpuffung *f*,
       Abbrennen *n*
    f déflagration *f*
    r дефлаграция *f (режим
       распространения пламени)*

D87 *e* **deflected beam**
    d abgelenkter Strahl *m*, abgelenktes
       Strahlenbündel *n*
    f faisceau *m* dévié, rayon *m* dévié
    r отклонённый пучок *m*,
       отклонённый луч *m*

D88 *e* **deflecting coil**
    d ablenkende Spule *f*, Ablenkspule *f*,
       Auslenkspule *f*
    f bobine *f* de déviation
    r отклоняющая катушка *f*

D89 *e* **deflecting plates**
    d Ablenkplatten *f pl*
    f plaques *f pl* de déviation
    r отклоняющие пластины *f pl*

D90 *e* **deflecting voltage**
    d Ablenkspannung *f*
    f tension *f* de déviation
    r отклоняющее напряжение *n*

D91 *e* **deflection**
    d Ablenkung *f*; Deviation *f*
    f déflexion *f*; déviation *f*
    r отклонение *n*

D92 *e* **deflection angle**
    d Ablenkungswinkel *m*
    f angle *m* de déviation
    r угол *m* отклонения

D93 *e* **deflector**
    d Deflektor *m*, Auslenkvorrichtung *f*

f déflecteur *m*
r дефлектор *m*

D94 *e* **defocusing**
d Defokussierung *f*
f défocalisation *f*
r дефокусировка *f*

D95 *e* **deformability**
d Deformierbarkeit *f*,
Formänderungsfähigkeit *f*,
Formänderungsvermögen *n*
f déformabilité *f*
r деформируемость *f*

D96 *e* **deformable medium kinematics**
d Kinematik *f* des deformierbaren
Mediums
f cinématique *f* du milieu déformable
r кинематика *f* деформируемой среды

D97 *e* **deformation**
d 1. Deformation *f*, Deformierung *f*,
Verformung *f* 2. Verzerrung *f*,
Verbiegung *f*
f 1. déformation *f* 2. changement *m* de
forme
r 1. деформация *f* 2. искажение *n*

D98 *e* **deformation of band**
d Deformation *f* des Energiebereiches,
Energiebanddeformation *f*
f déformation *f* de la bande
r деформация *f* зоны, деформация *f*
энергетической зоны

D99 *e* **deformation potential**
d Deformationspotential *n*
f potentiel *m* de déformation
r деформационный потенциал *m*

D100 *e* **deformation vibrations** (*of a molecule*)
d Deformationsschwingungen *f pl*
f oscillations *f pl* de déformation (*d'une
molécule*)
r деформационные колебания *n pl*
(*молекулы*)

D101 *e* **deformed nucleus**
d deformierter Kern *m*, nichtaxialer
Kern *m*
f noyau *m* déformé
r деформированное ядро *n*,
несимметричное ядро *n*

D102 *e* **degassing**
d Entgasung *f*, Gasaustreibung *f*
f dégazage *m*, dégazation *f*
r обезгаживание *n*

D103 *e* **degeneracy**
d Entartung *f*
f dégénérescence *f*
r вырождение *n*

D104 *e* **degeneracy multiplicity** *see*
degeneracy order

D105 *e* **degeneracy of energy levels**
d Entartung *f* des Energieniveaus
f dégénérescence *f* des niveaux
énergétiques
r вырождение *n* уровней энергии

D106 *e* **degeneracy of vacuum**
d Vakuumentartung *f*
f dégénérescence *f* du vide
r вырождение *n* вакуума

D107 *e* **degeneracy order**
d Grad *m* der Entartung,
Entartungsgrad *m*
f multiplicité *f* de dégénérescence,
multiplicité *f* de dégénération
r кратность *f* вырождения

D108 *e* **degeneracy temperature**
d Entartungstemperatur *f*
f température *f* de dégénérescence
r температура *f* вырождения

D109 *e* **degenerate band**
d entartete Zone *f*
f zone *f* dégénérée
r вырожденная зона *f*

D110 *e* **degenerate gas**
d entartetes Gas *n*
f gaz *m* dégénéré
r вырожденный газ *m*

D111 *e* **degenerate helium dwarf**
d entarteter Heliumzwerg *m*
f naine *f* à hélium dégénérée
r вырожденный гелиевый карлик *m*

D112 *e* **degenerate mode**
d entartete Mode *f*
f mode *m* dégénéré
r вырожденная мода *f*, вырожденный
тип *m* колебаний

D113 *e* **degenerate oscillation**
d entartete Schwingungen *f pl*
f oscillations *f pl* dégénérées
r вырожденные колебания *n pl*

D114 *e* **degenerate semiconductor**
d entarteter Halbleiter *m*
f semi-conducteur *m* dégénéré
r вырожденный полупроводник *m*

D115 *e* **degenerate state**
d entarteter Zustand *m*
f état *m* dégénéré
r вырожденное состояние *n*

D116 *e* **degenerate state interference**
d Interferenz *f* der entarteten Zustände
f interférence *f* des états dégénérés
r интерференция *f* вырожденных
состояний

D117 *e* **degradation of energy**
d Energiedegradation *f*

f dégradation f d'énergie
r деградация f энергии

D118 e degree
      d Grad m
      f degré m
      r 1. градус m (угловой или
        температурный) 2. степень f

D119 e degree of coherence
      d Kohärenzgrad m
      f degré m de cohérence
      r степень f когерентности

D120 e degree of freedom
      d Freiheitsgrad m
      f degré m de liberté
      r степень f свободы

D121 e degree of ionization
      d Ionisierungsgrad m, Ionisationsgrad m
      f degré m d'ionisation
      r степень f ионизации

D122 e De Haas-van Alphen effect
      d De-Haas-Van-Alphen-Effekt m
      f effet m de Haas-van Alphen
      r эффект m де-Хааза - ван Альфена

D123 e deionization
      d Entionisierung f, Deionisierung f
      f déionisation f
      r деионизация f

D124 e deionization time
      d Entionisierungszeit f
      f temps m de déionisation
      r время n деионизации

D125 e dekatron
      d Dekatron n, Dekadenzählröhre f,
        dekadische Zählröhre f
      f décatron m
      r декатрон m

D126 e delay
      d Verzögerung f; Verzug m
      f retard m
      r задержка f; запаздывание n

D127 e delay coefficient
      d Verzögerungsfaktor m
      f coefficient m de retard
      r коэффициент m замедления

D128 e delayed action
      d verzögerte Wirkung f
      f action f retardée
      r замедленное действие n

D129 e delayed neutrons
      d verzögerte Neutronen n pl
      f neutrons m pl différés
      r запаздывающие нейтроны m pl

D130 e delay lens
      d Phasenverzögerungslinse f

f lentille f ralentisseuse
r замедляющая линза f

D131 e delay line
      d Verzögerungsleitung f
      f ligne f à retard
      r линия f задержки

D132 e delay time
      d Verzögerungszeit f; Verzugszeit f
      f temps m de retard, période f de
        retard, durée f de retard
      r время n задержки; время n
        запаздывания

D133 e Delbrück scattering
      d Delbrück-Streuung f
      f diffusion f de Delbrück
      r дельбрюковское рассеяние n

D134 e delocalized defect
      d delokalisierter Defekt m
      f défaut m délocalisé
      r делокализованный дефект m

D135 e delta electron
      d Deltaelektron n
      f électron m delta
      r дельта-электрон m

D136 e delta function
      d Deltafunktion f, Dirac-Funktion f,
        δ-Funktion f, Diracsche δ-Funktion f
      f fonction f de Dirac
      r дельта-функция f, δ-функция f

D137 e delta rays
      d Deltastrahlen pl
      f rayons pl delta
      r дельта-лучи pl

D138 e demagnetization
      d Entmagnetisierung f
      f désaimantation f
      r размагничивание n

D139 e demagnetization coefficient see
        demagnetization factor

D140 e demagnetization curve
      d Entmagnetisierungskurve f
      f courbe f de désaimantation
      r кривая f размагничивания

D141 e demagnetization factor
      d Entmagnetisierungsfaktor m
      f facteur m de désaimantation
      r размагничивающий фактор m,
        коэффициент m размагничивания

D142 e demagnetizing see demagnetization

D143 e demagnetizing field
      d Entmagnetisierungsfeld n,
        entmagnetisierendes Feld n
      f champ m de démagnétisation
      r размагничивающее поле n

D144 e Dember effect
      d Dember-Effekt *m*
      f effet *m* Dember
      r эффект *m* Дембера

D145 e demodulation
      d Demodulation *f*
      f démodulation *f*
      r демодуляция *f*; детектирование *n*

D146 e demodulator
      d Demodulator *m*
      f démodulateur *m*; détecteur *m*
      r демодулятор *m*; детектор *m*

D147 e demultiplexer
      d Demultiplexer *m*
      f démultiplexeur *m*
      r демультиплексор *m*

D148 e dendrite
      d Dendrit *m*
      f dendrite *f*
      r дендрит *m*

D149 e dendritic crystal
      d dendritischer Kristall *m*,
         Baumkristall *m*
      f squelette *m* de cristal
      r дендритный кристалл *m*,
         древовидный кристалл *m*

D150 e densimeter
      d Dichtemesser *n*; Aräometer *n*
      f densitomètre *m*
      r плотномер *m*; денсиметр *m*,
         ареометр *m*

D151 e densimetry
      d Densimetrie *f*, Dichtemessung *f*,
         Dichtebestimmung *f*
      f densimétrie *f*
      r денсиметрия *f*

D152 e densitometer
      d Densitometer *n*, Schwärzungsmesser *m*
      f densitomètre *m*
      r денситометр *m*

D153 e densitometry
      d Densitometrie *f*,
         Schwärzungsmessung *f*
      f densitométrie *f*
      r денситометрия *f*

D154 e density
      d 1. Dichte *f* 2. Konzentration *f*
         3. optische Dichte *f*,
         Schwärzungsdichte *f*
      f 1. densité *f* 2. concentration *f*
         3. densité *f* optique
      r 1. плотность *f* 2. концентрация *f*
         3. оптическая плотность *f*

D155 e density inversion
      d Dichteinversion *f*

      f inversion *f* de densité
      r инверсия *f* плотности

D156 e density matrix
      d Dichtematrix *f*; Dichteoperator *m*
      f matrice *f* de densité
      r матрица *f* плотности

D157 e density of saturated vapor
      d Sättigungsdichte *f*
      f densité *f* de la vapeur saturée
      r плотность *f* насыщенного пара

D158 e density of states
      d Zustandsdichte *f*
      f densité *f* des états
      r плотность *f* состояний

D159 e density range
      d Schwärzungsumfang *m*,
         Schwärzungsbereich *m*,
         Dichteumfang *m*
      f intervalle *m* des densités
      r интервал *m* плотностей

D160 e density waves
      d Dichtewellen *f pl*
      f ondes *f pl* de densité
      r волны *f pl* плотности

D161 e deoxyribonucleic acid, DNA
      d Desoxyribonukleinsäure *f*, DNS
      f acide *m* désoxyribonucléique, ADN
      r дезоксирибонуклеиновая кислота *f*,
         ДНК *f*

D162 e dependence
      d Abhängigkeit *f*
      f dépendance *f*, relation *f*
      r зависимость *f*

D163 e dependence of viscosity on
         temperature
      d Temperaturabhängigkeit *f* der
         Viskosität
      f relation *f* viscosité/température
      r зависимость *f* вязкости от
         температуры

D164 e dephasing
      d Außer-Phase-Bringen *n*,
         Phasenverschiebung *f*
      f déphasage *m*
      r дефазировка *f*

D165 e depinning
      d Depinning *n*
      f dépiégeage *m*
      r депиннинг *m*

D166 e depletion
      d Entleerung *f (des Energieniveaus)*;
         Verarmung *f*; Erschöpfung *f*
      f épuisement *m*; appauvrissement *m*
      r опустошение *n (энергетического
         уровня)*; обеднение *n*, истощение *n*

D167   *e*   depletion layer
      d   Verarmungsschicht *f*
      f   couche *f* épuisée
      r   обеднённый слой *m*

D168   *e*   depletion-layer contact
      d   Verarmungsschichtkontakt *m*
      f   contact *m* avec la couche épuisée
      r   контакт *m* с обеднённым слоем

D169   *e*   depletion of pump wave
      d   Pumpwellenverarmung *f*
      f   épuisement *m* de l'onde de pompage
      r   истощение *n* волны накачки

D170   *e*   depletion region
      d   Verarmungsgebiet *n*,
         Verarmungsbereich *m*
      f   région *f* d'épuisement, couche *f*
         d'épuisement
      r   обеднённая область *f*

D171   *e*   depolarization of light
      d   Lichtdepolarisation *f*
      f   dépolarisation *f* de lumière
      r   деполяризация *f* света

D172   *e*   depolarizer
      d   Depolarisator *m*
      f   dépolarisant *m*
      r   деполяризатор *m*

D173   *e*   depopulation
      d   Entleeren *n (des Energieniveaus)*
      f   dépopulation *f*
      r   опустошение *n*, уменьшение *n*
         населённости

D174   *e*   deposition
      d   Auftragen *n*; Aufdampfen *n*;
         Abscheiden *n*, Abscheidung *f*
      f   déposition *f*
      r   нанесение *n*; напыление *n*;
         осаждение *n*

D175   *e*   depression
      d   Depression *f*
      f   dépression *f*
      r   1. понижение *n*; снижение *n*
         2. подавление *n* 3. зона *f*
         пониженного давления

D176   *e*   depression of freezing point
      d   Gefrierpunkterniedrigung *f*
      f   abaissement *m* du point de
         congélation
      r   понижение *n* точки замерзания

D177   *e*   depth
      d   Tiefe *f*; Stärke *f*
      f   profondeur *f*; épaisseur *f*
      r   глубина *f*; толщина *f*

D178   *e*   depth of field *see* depth of focus

D179   *e*   depth of focus
      d   Schärfentiefe *f*, Tiefenschärfe *f*,
         Abbildungstiefe *f*

      f   profondeur *f* de champ, profondeur *f*
         de foyer
      r   глубина *f* резкости

D180   *e*   depth of modulation
      d   Aussteuerungstiefe *f*,
         Aussteuerungsgrad *m*
      f   profondeur *f* de modulation
      r   глубина *f* модуляции; коэффициент
         m модуляции

D181   *e*   depth of penetration
      d   Eindringtiefe *f*
      f   profondeur *f* de pénétration
      r   глубина *f* проникновения

D182   *e*   derivation
      d   1. Herleiten *n (Formel)*
         2. Differenzierung *f*
      f   1. déduction *f (formule)*
         2. différentiation *f*
      r   1. вывод *m (формулы)*
         2. дифференцирование *n*

D183   *e*   derivative
      d   Ableitung *f*
      f   dérivée *f*
      r   производная *f*

D184   *e*   derived unit
      d   abgeleitete Einheit *f*
      f   unité *f* dérivée
      r   производная единица *f*

D185   *e*   desaccommodation
      d   Desakkommodation *f*
      f   désaccommodation *f*
      r   дезаккомодация *f*

D186   *e*   descending node
      d   absteigender Knoten *m*
      f   nœud *m* descendant
      r   нисходящий узел *m*

D187   *e*   description
      d   Beschreibung *f*
      f   description *f*
      r   описание *n*

D188   *e*   desensitization
      d   Desensibilisierung *f*
      f   désensibilisation *f*
      r   десенсибилизация *f*

D189   *e*   desensitizer
      d   Desensibilisator *m*
      f   désensibilisateur *m*
      r   десенсибилизатор *m*

D190   *e*   de Sitter space-time
      d   de-Sittersche Raum-Zeit *f*
      f   espace-temps *m* de De Sitter
      r   пространство-время *n* де Ситтера

D191   *e*   de Sitter universe
      d   de-Sitter-Welt *f*

f Univers *m* de De Sitter
r Вселенная *f* де Ситтера

D192 e desorption
d Desorption *f*
f désorption *f*
r десорбция *f*

D193 e desorption kinetics
d Desorptionskinetik *f*
f cinétique *f* de désorption
r кинетика *f* десорбции

D194 e destruction
d 1. Destruktion *f*; Abbau *m*
2. Zerstörung *f*
f destruction *f*
r 1. деструкция *f* (полимеров)
2. разрушение *n*

D195 e destruction operator
d Vernichtungsoperator *m*
f opérateur *m* de destruction
r оператор *m* уничтожения

D196 e destruction test
d Zerstörungsprüfung *f*, zerstörende
Werkstoffprüfung *f*
f essai *m* destructif
r испытание *n* с разрушением
образца

D197 e destructive interference
d Auslöschung *f*
f interférence *f* destructive
r деструктивная интерференция *f*

D198 e desublimation
d Desublimation *f*
f desublimation *f*
r десублимация *f*

D199 e detached flow
d abgelöste Strömung *f*
f écoulement *m* décollé
r отрывное течение *n*

D200 e detachment of electrons
d Ablösung *f* der Elektronen
f décollement *m* des électrons
r отлипание *n* электронов

D201 e detailed balancing principle
d Prinzip *n* des detaillierten
Gleichgewichtes
f principe *m* d'équilibre détaillé
r принцип *m* детального равновесия

D202 e detection
d 1. Gleichrichtung *f*; Demodulation *f*
2. Nachweis *m*, Detektion *f*
f détection *f*
r 1. детектирование *n*, выпрямление
n 2. обнаружение *n*, регистрация *f*

D203 e detection of single atoms
d Auffinden *n* von Einzelatomen
f détection *f* des atomes uniques

r детектирование *n* единичных
атомов

D204 e detection of single molecules
d Auffinden *n* von Einzelmolekülen
f détection *f* des molécules uniques
r детектирование *n* единичных
молекул

D205 e detector
d Detektor *m*
f détecteur *m*
r детектор *m*

D206 e determinant
d Determinante *f*, Bestimmungsgröße *f*
f déterminant *m*
r детерминант *m*

D207 e determination of crystal structure
d Kristallstrukturbestimmung *f*
f détermination *f* de la structure des
cristaux
r определение *n* структуры
кристаллов

D208 e determinism
d Determinismus *m*
f déterminisme *m*
r детерминизм *m*

D209 e detonation
d Detonation *f*
f détonation *f*
r детонация *f*

D210 e detonation wave
d Detonationswelle *f*
f onde *f* de détonation
r детонационная волна *f*

D211 e deuterides
d Deuteride *n pl*
f hydrures *m pl* lourds
r дейтериды *m pl*

D212 e deuterium, D, 2H
d Deuterium *n*, schwerer Wasserstoff *m*
f deutérium *m*, hydrogène *m* lourd
r дейтерий *m*

D213 e deuterium target
d Deuteriumtarget *n*
f cible *f* de deutérium
r дейтериевая мишень *f*

D214 e deuteron
d Deuteron *n*, Deuton *n*,
Deuteriumkern *m*
f deutéron *m*, deuton *m*
r дейтрон *m*

D215 e development
d Entwicklung *f*
f développement *m*
r 1. проявление *n* (фотографический
процесс) 2. развитие *n*

D216 *e* deviation
      d 1. Ablenkung *f* 2. Abweichung *f*,
         Deviation *f*
      f déviation *f*
      r 1. отклонение *n* 2. девиация *f*

D217 *e* deviator
      d Deviator *m*
      f déviateur *m*
      r девиатор *m*

D218 *e* device
      d Gerät *n*
      f instrument *m*, appareil *m*
      r прибор *m*

D219 *e* dew
      d Tau *m*
      f rosée *f*
      r роса *f*

D220 *e* **Dewar, Dewar vessel**
      d Dewar-Gefäß *n*
      f dewar *m*, vase *m* Dewar
      r дьюар *m*, сосуд *m* Дьюара

D221 *e* **dew point**
      d *Taupunkt *m*
      f point *m* de rosée
      r точка *f* росы

D222 *e* diagnostics
      d Diagnose *f*
      f diagnostic *m*
      r диагностика *f*

D223 *e* diagonal
      d Diagonale *f*
      f diagonale *f*
      r диагональ *f*

D224 *e* diagram
      d Diagramm *n*, graphische Darstellung *f*
      f diagramme *m*
      r диаграмма *f*, схема *f*

D225 *e* **diagram technique of Feynman**
      d Feynman-Graph *m*, Feynman-Diagramm *n*
      f technique *f* de diagrammes de Feynman
      r метод *m* диаграмм Фейнмана

D226 *e* dial
      d Skale *f*
      f cadran *m*; échelle *f*
      r шкала *f*

D227 *e* dialysis
      d Dialyse *f*
      f dialyse *f*
      r диализ *m*

D228 *e* **diamagnet** see **diamagnetic substance**

D229 *e* **diamagnetic substance**
      d Diamagnetikum *n*, diamagnetischer Stoff *m*
      f diamagnétique *m*
      r диамагнетик *m*

D230 *e* **diamagnetic susceptibility**
      d diamagnetische Suszeptibilität *f*
      f susceptibilité *f* diamagnétique
      r диамагнитная восприимчивость *f*

D231 *e* **diamagnetism**
      d Diamagnetismus *m*
      f diamagnétisme *m*
      r диамагнетизм *m*

D232 *e* **diameter**
      d Durchmesser *m*
      f diamètre *m*
      r диаметр *m*

D233 *e* **diamond**
      d Diamant *m*
      f diamant *m*
      r алмаз *m*

D234 *e* **diamond anvil**
      d Diamantamboß *m*
      f enclume *f* de diamant
      r алмазная наковальня *f*

D235 *e* **diamond detector**
      d Diamantdetektor *m*
      f détecteur *m* à diamant
      r алмазный детектор *m*

D236 *e* **diamond indenter**
      d Diamanteindringkörper *m*
      f pénétrateur *m* à diamant
      r алмазный индентор *m*

D237 *e* **diamond-lattice crystal**
      d Diamantgitterkristall *m*
      f cristal *m* à structure type diamant
      r кристалл *m* с алмазной решёткой

D238 *e* **diamond structure**
      d Diamantgitter *n*, Diamantstruktur *f*
      f structure *f* du diamant
      r структура *f* алмаза

D239 *e* **diaphragm**
      d 1. Diaphragma *n*, Blende *f* 2. Membran *f*
      f 1. diaphragme *m* 2. membrane *f*
      r 1. диафрагма *f* 2. мембрана *f*

D240 *e* **diastereoisomer**
      d Diastereomer *n*, Diastereoisomer *n*
      f diastéréoisomère *m*, diamère *m*
      r диастереомер *m*, диастереоизомер *m*

D241 *e* **diathermy**
      d Diathermie *f*
      f diathermie *f*
      r диатермия *f*

D242   e   diatomic molecule
      d   zweiatomiges Molekül *n*
      f   molécule *f* diatomique
      r   двухатомная молекула *f*

D243   e   dibaryon
      d   Dibaryon *n*
      f   dibaryon *m*
      r   дибарион *m*

D244   e   dichroic mirror
      d   dichroitischer Spiegel *m*
      f   miroir *m* dichroïque
      r   дихроичное зеркало *n*

D245   e   dichroism
      d   Dichroismus *m*
      f   dichroïsme *m*
      r   дихроизм *m*

D246   e   dichromated gelatin
      d   Bichromatgelatine *f*
      f   gélatine *f* bichromateé
      r   бихромированная желатина *f*

D247   e   dielectric
      d   Dielektrikum *n*; Nichtleiter *m*;
         Isolator *m*
      f   diélectrique *m*
      r   диэлектрик *m*

D248   e   dielectric absorption
      d   dielektrische Absorption *f*
      f   absorption *f* diélectrique
      r   поглощение *n* в диэлектрике

D249   e   dielectric aerial, dielectric antenna
      d   dielektrische Antenne *f*
      f   antenne *f* à barreau diélectrique
      r   диэлектрическая антенна *f*

D250   e   dielectric breakdown
      d   dielektrischer Durchschlag *m*
      f   rupture *f* diélectrique
      r   пробой *m* диэлектрика

D251   e   dielectric constant *see* permittivity

D252   e   dielectric hysteresis
      d   dielektrische Hysterese *f*
      f   hystérésis *f* diélectrique
      r   диэлектрический гистерезис *m*

D253   e   dielectric loss
      d   dielektrische Verluste *m pl*
      f   pertes *f pl* diélectriques
      r   диэлектрические потери *f pl*

D254   e   dielectric loss angle
      d   dielektrischer Verlustwinkel *m*
      f   angle *m* de pertes diélectriques
      r   угол *m* диэлектрических потерь

D255   e   dielectric loss factor
      d   Verlustfaktor *m*
      f   facteur *m* de pertes, coefficient *m* de
         pertes, facteur *m* de pertes

         diélectriques, coefficient *m* de pertes
         diélectriques
      r   коэффициент *m* диэлектрических
         потерь

D256   e   dielectric-metal transition
      d   Dielektrikum-Metall-Übergang *m*
      f   transition *f* diélectruqie - métal
      r   переход *m* диэлектрик - металл

D257   e   dielectric mirror
      d   dielektrischer Spiegel *m*
      f   miroir *m* diélectrique
      r   диэлектрическое зеркало *n*

D258   e   dielectric polarization
      d   dielektrische Polarisation *f*, elektrische
         Polarisation *f* des Dielektrikums
      f   polarisation *f* diélectrique
      r   поляризация *f* диэлектрика

D259   e   dielectric strength
      d   Durchschlagsfestigkeit *f*
      f   rigidité *f* diélectrique
      r   электрическая прочность *f*,
         пробивная напряжённость *f*

D260   e   dielectric susceptibility
      d   dielektrische Suszeptibilität *f*
      f   susceptibilité *f* diélectrique
      r   диэлектрическая восприимчивость *f*

D261   e   dielectric waveguide
      d   dielektrischer Wellenleiter *m*
      f   guide *m* d'ondes diélectrique
      r   диэлектрический волновод *m*

D262   e   dielectronic recombination
      d   dielektronische Rekombination *f*,
         Zweielektronenrekombination *f*
      f   recombinaison *f* à deux électrons
      r   диэлектронная рекомбинация *f*

D263   e   Diesel cycle
      d   Dieselscher Kreisprozeß *m*, Diesel-
         Prozeß *m*
      f   cycle *m* de Diesel
      r   цикл *m* Дизеля

D264   e   difference tones
      d   Differenztöne *m pl*
      f   sons *m pl* différentiels
      r   разностные тона *m pl*

D265   e   differential
      d   Differential *n*
      f   différentiel *m*
      r   дифференциал *m*

D266   e   differential analyzer
      d   Differentialanalysator *m*
      f   analyseur *m* différentiel
      r   дифференциальный анализатор *m*

D267   e   differential cross-section
      d   differentieller Wirkungsquerschnitt *m*,
         Differentialquerschnitt *m*

f section f efficace différentielle
r дифференциальное сечение n рассеяния, дифференциальное сечение n

D268 e differential equation
d Differentialgleichung f
f équation f différentielle
r дифференциальное уравнение n

D269 e differential manometer
d Differentialmanometer n
f manomètre m différentiel
r дифференциальный манометр m, дифманометр m

D270 e differential operator
d Differentialoperator m
f opérateur m différentiel
r дифференциальный оператор m

D271 e differentiating circuit
d Differenzierschaltung f
f circuit m de différentiation
r дифференцирующая цепь f

D272 e differentiation
d Differentiation f
f différentiation f
r дифференцирование n

D273 e diffracted beam
d gebeugter Strahl m
f rayon m diffracté
r дифрагированный луч m

D274 e diffracted radiation
d gebeugte Strahlung f
f rayonnement m diffracté
r дифрагированное излучение n

D275 e diffraction
d Beugung f, Diffraktion f
f diffraction f
r дифракция f

D276 e diffraction analysis
d Beugungsanalyse f, Beugungsuntersuchung f
f analyse f par diffraction, diffractométrie f
r структурный анализ m

D277 e diffraction by circular aperture
d Beugung f an einer runden Blende, Beugung f an kreisrundem Loch
f diffraction f par une ouverture circulaire
r дифракция f на круглом отверстии

D278 e diffraction by crystals
d Kristallbeugung f, Beugung f am Kristall
f diffraction f cristalline
r дифракция f в кристаллах

D279 e diffraction by slit

d Beugung f am Spalt, Beugung f an einer Spaltblende
f diffraction f par une fente
r дифракция f на щели

D280 e diffraction coupler
d Beugungskoppler m
f coupleur m de diffraction
r дифракционный ответвитель m

D281 e diffraction dissociation
d Beugungsdissoziation f
f dissociation f de diffraction
r дифракционная диссоциация f

D282 e diffraction divergence
d Beugungsdivergenz f
f divergence f naturelle
r дифракционная расходимость f

D283 e diffraction fringes
d Beugungsstreifen m pl
f franges f pl de diffraction
r дифракционные полосы f pl

D284 e diffraction grating
d Beugungsgitter n
f réseau m de diffraction
r дифракционная решётка f

D285 e diffraction image
d Beugungsbild n
f figure f de diffraction, image f de diffraction
r дифракционное изображение n

D286 e diffraction-limited laser
d beugungsbegrenzter Laser m
f laser m à divergence naturelle du faisceau
r лазер m с дифракционной расходимостью пучка

D287 e diffraction maximum
d Beugungsmaximum n
f maximum m de diffraction
r дифракционный максимум m

D288 e diffraction method
d Diffraktionsmethode f
f méthode f de diffraction
r дифракционный метод m

D289 e diffraction minimum
d Beugungsminimum n
f minimum m de diffraction
r дифракционный минимум m

D290 e diffraction of atoms and molecules
d Beugung f von Atomen und Molekülen
f diffraction f des atomes et molécules
r дифракция f атомов и молекул

D291 e diffraction of electrons see electron diffraction

D292 e diffraction of electrons by solids, diffraction of electrons in solids

	d	Elektronenbeugung *f* in Festkörpern
	f	diffraction *f* des électrons dans les corps solides
	r	дифракция *f* электронов в твёрдых телах

D293 e **diffraction of light**
 d Lichtbeugung *f*
 f diffraction *f* de la lumière
 r дифракция *f* света

D294 e **diffraction of light by ultrasonics**
 d Lichtbeugung *f* an den Ultraschallwellen
 f diffraction *f* de la lumière par ultrason
 r дифракция *f* света на ультразвуке

D295 e **diffraction of neutrons** *see* **neutron diffraction**

D296 e **diffraction of partially coherent fields**
 d Diffraktion *f* der teilweise kohärenten Felder
 f diffraction *f* des champs partiellement cohérents
 r дифракция *f* частично когерентных полей

D297 e **diffraction of radio waves**
 d Funkwellendiffraktion *f*
 f diffraction *f* des ondes radio, diffraction *f* des ondes radio-électroniques
 r дифракция *f* радиоволн

D298 e **diffraction of sound**
 d Schalldiffraktion *f*
 f diffraction *f* du son
 r дифракция *f* звука

D299 e **diffraction of X-rays** *see* **X-ray diffraction**

D300 e **diffraction pattern**
 d Beugungsfigur *f*, Beugungsbild *n*, Beugungsdiagramm *m*
 f figure *f* de diffraction, image *f* de diffraction; diffractogramme *m*
 r дифракционная картина *f*; дифрактограмма *f*

D301 e **diffraction peak** *see* **diffraction maximum**

D302 e **diffraction ring**
 d Beugungsring *m*
 f anneau *m* de diffraction
 r дифракционное кольцо *n*

D303 e **diffraction scattering**
 d Diffraktionsstreuung *f*, Beugungsstreuung *f*
 f diffusion *f* par diffraction
 r дифракционное рассеяние *n*

D304 e **diffractogram**

	d	Beugungsdiagramm *n*
	f	diagramme *m* de diffraction, diffractogramme *m*
	r	дифрактограмма *f*

D305 e **diffractometer**
 d Beugungsgerät *n*, Diffraktometer *n*
 f diffractomètre *m*
 r дифрактометр *m*

D306 e **diffuse discharge**
 d diffuse Entladung *f*
 f décharge *f* par diffusion
 r диффузный разряд *m*

D307 e **diffused mesa**
 d diffuse Mesastruktur *f*
 f structure *f* mesa diffusée
 r диффузионная мезаструктура *f*

D308 e **diffuse edge**
 d Randauflockerung *f*, Randverschmierung *f*
 f bord *m* diffusé
 r размытый край *m*

D309 e **diffuse image**
 d verschwommenes Bild *n*; unscharfes Bild *n*
 f image *f* floue
 r размытое изображение *n*

D310 e **diffuser**
 d Lichtdiffusor *m*, Streukörper *m*, Diffusor *m*
 f diffuseur *m*
 r диффузор *m*

D311 e **diffuse radiation**
 d Streustrahlung *f*, diffuse Strahlung *f*
 f rayonnement *m* diffus
 r диффузное излучение *n*

D312 e **diffuse reflection**
 d diffuse Reflexion *f*
 f réflexion *f* diffuse
 r диффузное отражение *n*

D313 e **diffuse scattering**
 d diffuse Streuung *f*
 f dispersion *f* diffuse
 r диффузное рассеяние *n*

D314 e **diffuse source**
 d diffuse Quelle *f*, Streustrahlungsquelle *f*
 f source *f* diffuse
 r диффузный источник *m*

D315 e **diffusion**
 d Diffusion *f*
 f diffusion *f*
 r диффузия *f*

D316 e **diffusion capacity**
 d Diffusionskapazität *f*
 f capacité *f* de diffusion
 r диффузионная ёмкость *f*

DIFFUSION

D317   *e*   **diffusion chamber**
       d   Diffusionsnebelkammer *f*
       f   chambre *f* à diffusion
       r   диффузионная камера *f*

D318   *e*   **diffusion coefficient**
       d   Streukoeffizient *m*
       f   coefficient *m* de diffusion
       r   коэффициент *m* диффузии

D319   *e*   **diffusion current**
       d   Diffusionsstrom *m*
       f   courant *m* de diffusion
       r   диффузионный ток *m*

D320   *e*   **diffusion distance** *see* diffusion
            length

D321   *e*   **diffusion equation**
       d   Diffusionsgleichung *f*
       f   équation *f* de diffusion
       r   уравнение *n* диффузии

D322   *e*   **diffusion flow**
       d   Diffusionsstrom *m*
       f   courant *m* de diffusion
       r   диффузионный поток *m*

D323   *e*   **diffusion in gases**
       d   Diffusion *f* in Gasen
       f   diffusion *f* en gaz
       r   диффузия *f* в газах

D324   *e*   **diffusion in liquids**
       d   Diffusion *f* in Flüssigkeiten
       f   diffusion *f* en liquides
       r   диффузия *f* в жидкостях

D325   *e*   **diffusion in solids**
       d   Diffusion *f* in Festkörpern
       f   diffusion *f* dans les corps solides
       r   диффузия *f* в твёрдых телах

D326   *e*   **diffusion length**
       d   Diffusionslänge *f*
       f   longueur *f* de diffusion
       r   длина *f* диффузии, диффузионная
          длина *f*

D327   *e*   **diffusion mean free path**
       d   mittlere freie Diffusionsweglänge *f*
       f   parcours *m* libre moyen pour diffusion
       r   средний свободный пробег *m* для
          диффузии

D328   *e*   **diffusion of minority**
       d   Diffusion *f* der
          Minoritätsladungsträger
       f   diffusion *f* des porteurs minoritaires
       r   диффузия *f* неосновных носителей

D329   *e*   **diffusion of neutrons**
       d   Neutronendiffusion *f*
       f   diffusion *f* des neutrons
       r   диффузия *f* нейтронов

D330   *e*   **diffusion potential**
       d   Diffusionspotential *n*
       f   potentiel *m* de diffusion
       r   диффузионный потенциал *m*

D331   *e*   **diffusion pump**
       d   Diffusionspumpe *f*
       f   pompe *f* à diffusion
       r   диффузионный насос *m*

D332   *e*   **diffusion zone**
       d   Diffusionszone *f*
       f   zone *f* de diffusion
       r   зона *f* диффузии, диффузионная
          зона *f*

D333   *e*   **diffusivity**
       d   1. Diffusionsfaktor *m*
          2. Temperaturleitfähigkeit *f*,
          Temperaturleitzahl *f*
       f   1. coefficient *m* de diffusion
          2. coefficient *m* de conductibilité
          thermique
       r   1. коэффициент *m* диффузии
          2. коэффициент *m*
          температуропроводности

D334   *e*   **digital holography**
       d   digitale Holographie *f*; Computer-
          Holographie *f*
       f   holographie *f* digitale
       r   цифровая голография *f*

D335   *e*   **digital image**
       d   Digitaldarstellung *f*
       f   image *f* digitale
       r   цифровое изображение *n*

D336   *e*   **digital instruments**
       d   digitale Elektromeßgeräte *n pl*,
          elektrische Digitalmeßgeräte *n pl*
       f   instruments *m pl* digitaux
       r   цифровые электроизмерительные
          приборы *m pl*

D337   *e*   **digital measurements**
       d   Digitalmessungen *f pl*
       f   mesures *f pl* digitales
       r   цифровые измерения *n pl*

D338   *e*   **digital oscilloscope**
       d   Digitaloszilloskop *n*
       f   oscilloscope *m* digital
       r   цифровой осциллограф *m*

D339   *e*   **digital-to-analog converter**
       d   Digital-Analog-Umsetzer *m*, D/A-
          Umsetzer *m*
       f   convertisseur *m* digital-analogique
       r   цифро-аналоговый
          преобразователь *m*

D340   *e*   **digitizer**
       d   Digitaldarstellungsgerät *n*,
          Digitalisiergerät *n*
       f   échantillonneur *m*
       r   дискретизатор *m*

D341　e　dilatation
　　　d　Dilatation f
　　　f　dilatation f
　　　r　1. расширение n 2. всестороннее
　　　　　растяжение n

D342　e　dilatometer
　　　d　Dilatometer n
　　　f　dilatomètre m
　　　r　дилатометр m

D343　e　dilatometry
　　　d　Dilatometrie f
　　　f　dilatométrie f
　　　r　дилатометрия f

D344　e　dilepton
　　　d　Dilepton n
　　　f　dilepton m
　　　r　дилептон m

D345　e　dilution
　　　d　Verdünnung f
　　　f　dilution f
　　　r　разведение n, разбавление n

D346　e　dimension
　　　d　1. Abmessung f, Größe f, Größenart f
　　　　　2. Abmessung f; Dimension f
　　　f　dimension f
　　　r　1. размер m 2. размерность f,
　　　　　измерение n

D347　e　dimensional analysis
　　　d　Dimensionsanalyse f
　　　f　analyse f de dimensions
　　　r　анализ m размерностей

D348　e　dimensional quantization
　　　d　dimensionelle Quantisierung f
　　　f　quantisation f dimensionnelle
　　　r　размерное квантование n

D349　e　dimensionless constant
　　　d　dimensionslose Konstante f
　　　f　constante f non dimensionnelle
　　　r　безразмерная константа f

D350　e　dimensionless coordinates
　　　d　dimensionslose Koordinaten f pl
　　　f　coordonnées f pl non dimensionnelles
　　　r　безразмерные координаты f pl

D351　e　dimensionless factor
　　　d　dimensionsloser Faktor m
　　　f　facteur m non dimensionnel
　　　r　безразмерный множитель m

D352　e　dimensionless quantity
　　　d　Dimensionslose f, dimensionslose
　　　　　Größe f
　　　f　valeur f non dimensionnelle, valeur f
　　　　　adimensionnée
　　　r　безразмерная величина f

D353　e　dimer
　　　d　Dimer n, Dimeres n
　　　f　dimère m
　　　r　димер m

D354　e　dimerization
　　　d　Dimerisation f
　　　f　dimérisation f
　　　r　димеризация f

D355　e　dimorphism
　　　d　Dimorphie f
　　　f　dimorphisme m
　　　r　диморфизм m

D356　e　diocotron effect
　　　d　Diocotroneffekt m
　　　f　effet m diocotron
　　　r　диокотронный эффект m

D357　e　diode
　　　d　Diode f
　　　f　diode f
　　　r　диод m

D358　e　diode detection
　　　d　Diodendemodulation f
　　　f　détection f par diode
　　　r　диодное детектирование n

D359　e　diode laser
　　　d　Diodenlaser m
　　　f　laser m à diode
　　　r　диодный лазер m

D360　e　diode pumping
　　　d　Diodenpumpen n
　　　f　pompage m par diode
　　　r　диодная накачка f

D361　e　diopter, D
　　　d　Dioptrie f, dpt
　　　f　dioptrie f, dpt, dptr
　　　r　диоптрия f, дп

D362　e　dioptrics
　　　d　Dioptrik f
　　　f　dioptrique f
　　　r　диоптрика f

D363　e　dip
　　　d　1. Tauchen n 2. Neigung f
　　　f　1. immersion f 2. inclinaison f
　　　r　1. погружение n 2. наклон m,
　　　　　наклонение n

D364　e　dipole
　　　d　1. Dipol m 2. Dipol m,
　　　　　Dipolantenne f
　　　f　dipôle m
　　　r　1. диполь m 2. вибратор m
　　　　　(антенна)

D365　e　dipole antenna
　　　d　Dipolantenne f
　　　f　antenne f dipôle
　　　r　симметричный вибратор m,
　　　　　вибраторная антенна f

D366 e dipole-dipole interaction
    d Dipol-Dipol-Wechselwirkung *f*
    f interaction *f* dipôle-dipôle
    r диполь-дипольное взаимодействие *n*

D367 e dipole moment
    d Dipolmoment *n*
    f moment *m* du dipôle
    r дипольный момент *m*

D368 e dipole radiation
    d Dipolstrahlung *f*
    f rayonnement *m* dipolaire
    r дипольное излучение *n*

D369 e dipole radiator
    d Dipolstrahler *m*
    f radiateur *m* dipolaire
    r дипольный излучатель *m*

D370 e Dirac delta function
    d Diracsche Deltafunktion *f*, Dirac-
       Funktion *f*
    f fonction *f* de Dirac
    r дельта-функция *f* Дирака

D371 e Dirac equation
    d Dirac-Gleichung *f*
    f équation *f* de Dirac
    r уравнение *n* Дирака

D372 e Dirac field
    d Dirac-Feld *n*
    f champ *m* de Dirac
    r поле *n* Дирака

D373 e Dirac matrix
    d Diracsche Spinmatrix *f*, Diracsche
       Matrix *f*
    f matrice *f* de Dirac
    r матрица *f* Дирака

D374 e Dirac monopole
    d magnetischer Monopol *m*, Diracscher
       Monopol *m*
    f monopôle *m* de Dirac
    r монополь *m* Дирака

D375 e Dirac quantization
    d Dirac-Quantisierung *f*, Dirac-
       Quantelung *f*
    f quantification *f* de Dirac
    r квантование *n* Дирака

D376 e direct conversion of heat to
       electricity
    d Direktumwandlung *f* der
       Wärmeenergie in die elektrische
       Energie
    f conversion *f* directe chaleur/électricité
    r прямое преобразование *n* тепловой
       энергии в электрическую

D377 e direct current
    d Gleichstrom *m*
    f courant *m* continu
    r постоянный ток *m*

D378 e direct-current amplifier
    d Gleichstromverstärker *m*
    f amplificateur *m* à courant continu
    r усилитель *m* постоянного тока

D379 e direct heating
    d direkte Heizung *f*
    f chauffage *m* direct
    r прямой нагрев *m*

D380 e direction
    d Richtung *f*; Sinn *m*
    f direction *f*, sens *m*
    r направление *n*

D381 e directional coupler
    d Richtkoppler *m*
    f coupleur *m* directionnel, coupleur *m*
       directif
    r направленный ответвитель *m*

D382 e directionality *see* directivity

D383 e directional pattern
    d Richtdiagramm *n*
    f diagramme *m* directionnel
    r диаграмма *f* направленности
       (антенны)

D384 e directional radiation
    d Richtstrahlung *f*, gerichtete
       Strahlung *f*
    f radiation *f* directive, radiation *f*
       guidée
    r направленное излучение *n*

D385 e direction cosines
    d Richtungscosinusse *m pl*
    f cosinus *m pl* directeurs
    r направляющие косинусы *m pl*

D386 e direction of easy magnetization
    d Richtung *f* der leichtesten
       Magnetisierbarkeit, magnetische
       Vorzugsrichtung *f*
    f direction *f* d'aimantation facile, axe *m*
       d'aimantation facile
    r направление *n* лёгкого
       намагничивания

D387 e direction of propagation
    d Fortpflanzungsrichtung *f*,
       Ausbreitungsrichtung *f*
    f direction *f* de propagation
    r направление *n* распространения

D388 e directive gain *see* directivity

D389 e directive pattern *see* directional
       pattern

D390 e directive radiator
    d Richtstrahler *m*
    f émetteur *m* directif
    r направленный излучатель *m*

D391   *e*   **directivity**
      d   Richtfähigkeit *f*, Richtvermögen *n*;
          Richtfaktor *m*, Richtverhältnis *n*
      f   facteur *m* de directivité, coefficient *m*
          de directivité; directivité *f*
      r   коэффициент *m* направленного
          действия *(антенны)*, КНД

D392   *e*   **directly heated cathode**
      d   direktgeheizte Katode *f*
      f   cathode *f* à chauffage direct
      r   катод *m* прямого накала

D393   *e*   **direct nuclear reaction**
      d   direkte Kernreaktion *f*
      f   réaction *f* nucléaire directe
      r   прямая ядерная реакция *f*

D394   *e*   **director**
      d   Direktor *m*, Wellenrichter *m*
      f   directeur *m*
      r   директор *m (антенны)*

D395   *e*   **direct transitions**
      d   direkte Übergänge *m pl*
      f   transitions *f pl* directes
      r   прямые переходы *m pl*

D396   *e*   **Dirichlet problem**
      d   Dirichletsches Problem *n*,
          Dirichletproblem *n*
      f   problème *m* de Dirichlet
      r   задача *f* Дирихле

D397   *e*   **disc** *see* **disk**

D398   *e*   **discharge**
      d   Entladung *f*
      f   décharge *f*
      r   разряд *m*

D399   *e*   **discharge channel**
      d   Entladekanal *m*, Entladungskanal *m*
      f   canal *m* de décharge
      r   канал *m* разряда

D400   *e*   **discharge firing** *see* **discharge**
          ignition

D401   *e*   **discharge ignition**
      d   Entladungszündung *f*
      f   ignition *f* de la décharge
      r   зажигание *n* разряда

D402   *e*   **discharge initiation**
      d   Entladungsinitiierung *f*
      f   initiation *f* de la décharge
      r   инициирование *n* разряда

D403   *e*   **discharge lamp**
      d   Gasentladungslampe *f*
      f   lampe *f* à décharge gazeuse
      r   газоразрядная лампа *f*

D404   *e*   **discharge tube**
      d   Gasentladungsröhre *f*
      f   tube *m* à décharge gazeuse

      r   **1.** газоразрядная лампа *f*
          2. газоразрядная трубка *f*

D405   *e*   **disclination**
      d   Disklination *f*
      f   disclinaison *f*
      r   дисклинация *f*

D406   *e*   **discontinuity**
      d   Diskontinuität *f*, Unstetigkeit *f*
      f   discontinuité *f*
      r   **1.** разрыв *m (непрерывности)*
          2. скачок *m* **3.** неоднородность *f*

D407   *e*   **discontinuity line**
      d   Unstetigkeitslinie *f*,
          Diskontinuitätslinie *f*
      f   ligne *f* de discontinuité
      r   линия *f* разрыва

D408   *e*   **discontinuity point**
      d   Unstetigkeitsstelle *f*
      f   point *m* de discontinuité
      r   точка *f* разрыва, точка *f* разрыва
          непрерывности

D409   *e*   **discontinuous flow**
      d   Nichtkontinuum-Strömung *f*
      f   écoulement *m* discontinu
      r   разрывное течение *n*

D410   *e*   **discontinuous function**
      d   unstetige Funktion *f*
      f   fonction *f* discontinue
      r   разрывная функция *f*

D411   *e*   **discontinuous vibration**
      d   diskontinuierliche Schwingungen *f pl*
      f   oscillations *f pl* discontinues
      r   разрывные колебания *n pl*

D412   *e*   **discrete filter**
      d   Diskretfilter *n*, diskretes Filter *n*
      f   filtre *m* discret
      r   дискретный фильтр *m*

D413   *e*   **discrete source**
      d   diskrete Radioquelle *f*, Punktquelle *f*
      f   source *f* ponctuelle
      r   дискретный источник *m*, точечный
          источник *m*

D414   *e*   **discrete spectrum**
      d   diskretes Spektrum *n*
      f   spectre *m* discret
      r   дискретный спектр *m*

D415   *e*   **discretization**
      d   Diskretisierung *f*
      f   échantillonnage *m*
      r   дискретизация *f*

D416   *e*   **discriminator**
      d   Diskriminator *m*
      f   discriminateur *m*
      r   дискриминатор *m*

DISINTEGRATION

D417   *e*   disintegration
      d   Zerfall *m*
      f   désintégration *f*
      r   распад *m*; разложение *n*,
        расщепление *n*

D418   *e*   disintegration constant
      d   Zerfallskonstante *f*, radioaktive
        Zerfallskonstante *f*
      f   constante *f* de désintégration
      r   постоянная *f* распада

D419   *e*   disintegration rate
      d   Zerfallsrate *f*
      f   vitesse *f* de désintégration
      r   скорость *f* распада

D420   *e*   disjoining pressure
      d   Spreizdruck *m*
      f   pression *f* de coinçage
      r   расклинивающее давление *n*

D421   *e*   disk
      d   Disk *f*; Scheibe *f*
      f   disque *m*; cercle *m*
      r   диск *m*; круг *m*, кружок *m*

D422   *e*   disk of least confusion
      d   Zerstreuungskreis *m*,
        Unschärfekreis *m*
      f   cercle *m* de moindre diffusion, cercle
        m de diffusion, cercle *m* de confusion
      r   кружок *m* наименьшего рассеяния

D423   *e*   dislocation
      d   Versetzung *f (im Kristall)*
      f   dislocation *f*
      r   дислокация *f*

D424   *e*   dislocation concentration
      d   Versetzungskonzentration *f*
      f   concentration *f* des dislocations
      r   концентрация *f* дислокаций

D425   *e*   dislocation dynamics
      d   Versetzungsdynamik *f*
      f   dynamique *f* des dislocations
      r   динамика *f* дислокаций

D426   *e*   dislocation-free crystal
      d   versetzungsfreier Kristall *m*
      f   cristal *m* sans dislocations
      r   бездислокационный кристалл *m*

D427   *e*   dislocation-free single crystal
      d   versetzungsfreier Einkristall *m*
      f   monocristal *m* sans dislocations
      r   бездислокационный
        монокристалл *m*

D428   *e*   dislocation nucleation
      d   Versetzungskeimbildung *f*,
        Versetzungseinsetzung *f*
      f   germination *f* des dislocations
      r   зарождение *n* дислокаций

D429   *e*   dislocation source

---

      d   Versetzungsquelle *f*
      f   source *f* de dislocations
      r   источник *m* дислокаций

D430   *e*   dislocation wall
      d   Versetzungswand *f*
      f   paroi *f* de dislocation
      r   дислокационная стенка *f*

D431   *e*   disorder
      d   Unordnung *f*, Regellosigkeit *f*;
        Fehlordnung *f*
      f   désordre *m*
      r   беспорядок *m*

D432   *e*   disordered crystal
      d   fehlgeordneter Kristall *m*
      f   cristal *m* désordonné
      r   неупорядоченный кристалл *m*,
        разупорядоченный кристалл *m*

D433   *e*   disordered magnet
      d   ungeordneter magnetischer
        Werkstoff *m*
      f   aimant *m* désordonné
      r   разупорядоченный магнетик *m*

D434   *e*   disordered system
      d   ungeordnetes System *n*
      f   système *m* désordonné
      r   неупорядоченная система *f*

D435   *e*   disordering
      d   1. Fehlordnung *f* 2. ungeordneter
        Zustand *m*
      f   1. mise *f* en désordre 2. désordre *m*
      r   разупорядочение *n*

D436   *e*   disorder-order transformation *see*
       order-disorder transformation

D437   *e*   dispergator, disperser, dispersing
       agent
      d   Dispergiermittel *n*,
        Dispergierungsmittel *n*,
        Dispersionsmittel *n*
      f   dispersant *m*, dispersif *m*, agent *m* de
        dispersion
      r   диспергатор *m*

D438   *e*   dispersing prism
      d   Dispersionsprisma *n*
      f   prisme *m* dispersant
      r   дисперсионная призма *f*,
        спектральная призма *f*

D439   *e*   dispersion
      d   1. Dispersion *f* 2. Zerstreuung *f*
        3. Dispergierung *f*
      f   dispersion *f*
      r   1. дисперсия *f* 2. рассеяние *n*
        3. диспергирование *n*

D440   *e*   dispersion analysis
      d   Dispersionsanalyse *f*
      f   analyse *f* dispersive
      r   дисперсионный анализ *m*

D441　*e*　dispersion curve
　　　d　Dispersionskurve *f*
　　　f　courbe *f* de dispersion
　　　r　дисперсионная кривая *f*

D442　*e*　dispersion equation
　　　d　Dispersionsgleichung *f*
　　　f　équation *f* de dispersion
　　　r　дисперсионное уравнение *n*

D443　*e*　dispersion interferometer
　　　d　Dispersionsinterferometer *n*
　　　f　interféromètre *m* à dispersion
　　　r　дисперсионный интерферометр *m*

D444　*e*　dispersion interferometer technique
　　　d　Dispersionsinterferometerverfahren *n*
　　　f　technique *f* de l'interféromètre à dispersion
　　　r　метод *m* дисперсионного интерферометра

D445　*e*　dispersion law
　　　d　Dispersionsgesetz *n*
　　　f　loi *f* de dispersion
　　　r　закон *m* дисперсии

D446　*e*　dispersion of an instrument
　　　d　Dispersion *f* eines Instrumenten
　　　f　dispersion *f* d'un instrument
　　　r　дисперсия *f* прибора

D447　*e*　dispersion of light *see* optical dispersion

D448　*e*　dispersion of optical rotation *see* optical rotary dispersion

D449　*e*　dispersion of refractive index
　　　d　Brechzahldispersion *f*, Brechungsindexdispersion *f*
　　　f　dispersion *f* de l'indice de réfraction
　　　r　дисперсия *f* показателя преломления

D450　*e*　dispersion relations
　　　d　Dispersionsbeziehungen *f pl*
　　　f　relations *f pl* de dispersion
　　　r　дисперсионные соотношения *n pl*

D451　*e*　dispersity
　　　d　Dispersität *f*
　　　f　dispersité *f*
　　　r　дисперсность *f*

D452　*e*　dispersive delay line
　　　d　Dispersionsverzögerungsleitung *f*
　　　f　ligne *f* à retard dispersive
　　　r　дисперсионная линия *f* задержки

D453　*e*　dispersive medium
　　　d　Dispergiermittel *n*
　　　f　milieu *m* dispersif
　　　r　диспергирующая среда *f*

D454　*e*　dispersive power
　　　d　relative Dispersion *f*
　　　f　dispersion *f* relative
　　　r　относительная дисперсия *f*

D455　*e*　dispersive resonator
　　　d　dispersiver Resonator *m*
　　　f　résonateur *m* dispersif
　　　r　дисперсионный резонатор *m*

D456　*e*　dispersivity, dispersivity quotient
　　　d　Materialdispersion *f*
　　　f　dispersivité *f*
　　　r　дисперсия *f* показателя преломления

D457　*e*　displaced liquid
　　　d　verdrängte Flüssigkeit *f*
　　　f　liquide *m* déplacé
　　　r　вытесненная жидкость *f*

D458　*e*　displacement
　　　d　1. Verschiebung *f* 2. Substitution *f* 3. elektrische Verschiebung *f*
　　　f　1. décalage *m* 2. substitution *f* 3. déplacement *m*
　　　r　1. смещение *n*, сдвиг *m* 2. замещение *n* 3. электрическое смещение *n*

D459　*e*　displacement current
　　　d　Verschiebungsstrom *m*
　　　f　courant *m* de déplacement
　　　r　ток *m* смещения

D460　*e*　displacement pickup
　　　d　Verschiebungsgeber *m*
　　　f　capteur *m* de déplacement
　　　r　датчик *m* смещения, датчик *m* перемещения

D461　*e*　display
　　　d　Display *n*
　　　f　display *m*, afficheur *m* visuel
　　　r　дисплей *m*; устройство *n* отображения

D462　*e*　disposal of radioactive effluent
　　　d　Endlagerung *f* von radioaktiven Abfällen
　　　f　décharge *f* terrestre des déchets radio-actifs
　　　r　захоронение *n* радиоактивных отходов

D463　*e*　disruptive electric strength *see* dielectric strength

D464　*e*　dissector
　　　d　Dissektor *m*
　　　f　dissecteur *m*
　　　r　диссектор *m*

D465　*e*　dissipation
　　　d　Dissipation *f*, Zerstreuung *f*
　　　f　dissipation *f*
　　　r　диссипация *f*; рассеяние *n*

D466 e dissipation of energy
d Energiedissipation f
f dissipation f de l'énergie
r диссипация f энергии

D467 e dissipative acceleration mechanism
d dissipativer Beschleunigungsmechanismus m
f mécanisme m d'accélération dissipatif
r диссипативный механизм m ускорения

D468 e dissipative forces
d dissipative Kräfte f pl
f forces f pl dissipatives
r диссипативные силы f pl

D469 e dissipative function
d Dissipationsfunktion f
f fonction f de dissipation
r диссипативная функция f

D470 e dissipative instability
d dissipative Instabilität f
f instabilité f dissipative
r диссипативная неустойчивость f

D471 e dissipative medium
d dissipatives Medium n
f milieu m dissipatif
r диссипативная среда f

D472 e dissipative system
d dissipatives System n
f système m dissipatif
r диссипативная система f

D473 e dissociation
d Dissoziation f
f dissociation f
r диссоциация f

D474 e dissociation channel
d Dissoziationskanal m
f canal m de dissociation
r канал m диссоциации

D475 e dissociation constant
d Dissoziationskonstante f
f constante f de dissociation
r константа f диссоциации

D476 e dissociation energy
d Dissoziationsenergie f
f énergie f de dissociation
r энергия f диссоциации

D477 e dissociation equilibrium
d Dissoziationsgleichgewicht n
f équilibre m de dissociation
r диссоциативное равновесие n

D478 e dissociation laser
d Dissoziationslaser m
f laser m à dissociation
r диссоциационный лазер m

D479 e dissociative ionization
d dissoziative Ionisation f
f ionisation f dissociative
r диссоциативная ионизация f

D480 e dissociative recombination
d dissoziative Rekombination f
f recombinaison f dissociative
r диссоциативная рекомбинация f

D481 e dissolution
d Auflösung f
f dissolution f
r растворение n

D482 e dissolution chamber
d Auflösungskammer f
f chambre f de dissolution
r камера f растворения (в криостате)

D483 e dissonance
d Dissonanz f
f dissonance f
r диссонанс m

D484 e distance
d 1. Abstand m, Entfernung f; Strecke f 2. Reichweite f
f distance f
r 1. расстояние n 2. дальность f

D485 e distance measurement
d Entfernungsmessung f, Streckenmessung f
f mesure f de distance
r измерение n дальности, измерение n расстояния

D486 e distance meter see rangefinder

D487 e distant object
d entferntes Objekt n, ferner Gegenstand m
f objet m éloigné, objet m distant
r удалённый объект m

D488 e distillation
d Destillation f
f distillation f
r дистилляция f, перегонка f

D489 e distilled water
d destilliertes Wasser n
f eau f distillée
r дистиллированная вода f

D490 e distorted image
d verzerrtes Bild n, verzeichnetes Bild n
f image f distordue
r искажённое изображение n

D491 e distorted wave method
d Störwellenmethode f
f méthode f à ondes distordues
r метод m искажённых волн

D492 *e* distortion
      d 1. Verzeichnung *f*, Distorsion *f*
          2. Verzerrung *f*
      f distorsion *f*
      r 1. дисторсия *f* 2. искажение *n*

D493 *e* distortion factor
      d Klirrfaktor *m*
      f taux *m* de distorsion harmonique
      r коэффициент *m* нелинейных
          искажений, коэффициент *m*
          гармоник

D494 *e* distortion meter
      d Klirrfaktormesser *m*
      f mesureur *m* des distorsions non
          linéaires
      r измеритель *m* нелинейных
          искажений

D495 *e* distortion of optical images
      d Verzerrung *f* von optischen Bildern
      f distorsion *f* des images optiques
      r искажение *n* оптических
          изображений

D496 *e* distributed Bragg reflector laser
      d DBR-Laser *m*
      f laser *m* à réflecteur réparti de Bragg
      r лазер *m* с распределённым
          брэгговским отражателем

D497 *e* distributed charge
      d verteilte Ladung *f*
      f charge *f* répartie
      r распределённый заряд *m*

D498 *e* distributed-feedback laser
      d DFB-Laser *m*
      f laser *m* à réaction distribuée, laser *m*
          à réaction répartie
      r лазер *m* с распределённой обратной
          связью, РОС-лазер *m*

D499 *e* distributed inductance
      d verteilte Induktivität *f*
      f inductance *f* répartie
      r распределённая индуктивность *f*

D500 *e* distributed load
      d verteilte Last *f*, verteilte Belastung *f*
      f charge *f* répartie, charge *f* distribuée
      r распределённая нагрузка *f*

D501 *e* distributed-parameter system
      d System *n* mit verteilten Parametern
      f système *m* à paramètres répartis
      r система *f* с распределёнными
          параметрами

D502 *e* distributed reflector
      d verteilter Reflektor *m*
      f réflecteur *m* distribué, réflecteur *m*
          réparti
      r распределённый отражатель *m*

D503 *e* distributed source
      d verteilte Quelle *f*
      f source *f* étendue
      r протяжённый источник *m*,
          распределённый источник *m*

D504 *e* distributed system
      d verteiltes System *n*
      f système *m* à paramètres répartis
      r распределённая система *f*

D505 *e* distribution
      d Verteilung *f*
      f distribution *f*
      r распределение *n*

D506 *e* distribution coefficient
      d Verteilungskoeffizient *m*
      f coefficient *m* de distribution
      r коэффициент *m* распределения

D507 *e* distribution curve
      d Verteilungskurve *f*
      f fonction *f* de répartition
      r кривая *f* распределения

D508 *e* distribution function
      d Verteilungsfunktion *f*
      f fonction *f* de distribution, fonction *f*
          de répartition
      r функция *f* распределения

D509 *e* distribution of energy in spectrum
      d Energieverteilung *f* im Spektrum
      f répartition *f* de l'énergie par spectre
      r распределение *n* энергии по
          спектру

D510 *e* disturbance
      d Störung *f*; Perturbation *f*
      f perturbation *f*
      r возмущение *n*; нарушение *n*

D511 *e* disturbed day
      d gestörter Tag *m*
      f jour *m* perturbé
      r возмущённый день *m*

D512 *e* disturbed ionosphere
      d gestörte Ionosphäre *f*
      f ionosphère *f* perturbée
      r возмущённая ионосфера *f*

D513 *e* disturbed region
      d gestörtes Gebiet *n*
      f région *f* perturbée
      r возмущённая область *f*

D514 *e* diurnal variations
      d Tagesvariationen *f pl*,
          Tagesschwankungen *f pl*
      f variations *f pl* diurnes
      r суточные вариации *f pl*
          (геомагнитного поля)

D515   *e*   divergence
      d   Divergenz *f*
      f   divergence *f*
      r   1. расходимость *f* 2. дивергенция *f*

D516   *e*   divergence of axial current
      d   Axialstromdivergenz *f*
      f   divergence *f* du courant axial
      r   дивергенция *f* аксиального тока

D517   *e*   divergence of vector
      d   Vektordivergenz *f*
      f   divergence *f* du vecteur
      r   дивергенция *f* вектора

D518   *e*   divergent beam
      d   divergentes Strahlenbündel *n*,
         divergenter Strahl *m*
      f   rayon *m* divergent; faisceau *m*
         divergent
      r   расходящийся луч *m*,
         расходящийся пучок *m*

D519   *e*   divergent lens
      d   Zerstreuungslinse *f*, Streulinse *f*
      f   lentille *f* divergente
      r   рассеивғющая линза *f*

D520   *e*   diverging lens *see* divergent lens

D521   *e*   divertor
      d   Divertor *m*
      f   divertisseur *m*
      r   дивертор *m (в ядерном реакторе)*

D522   *e*   dividing head
      d   Teilkopf *m*
      f   poupée *f* à diviser, diviseur *m*
      r   делительная головка *f*

D523   *e*   division
      d   1. Teilung *f*, Skalenteilung *f*
         2. Division *f*, Dividieren *n*
      f   division *f*
      r   1. деление *n (шкалы)* 2. деление *n*
         (в математике)

D524   *e*   DNA laser modification
      d   DNS-Lasermodifikation *f*
      f   modification *f* laser DNA
      r   лазерная модификация *f* ДНК

D525   *e*   domain
      d   Domäne *f*
      f   domaine *m*
      r   домен *m*

D526   *e*   domain boundary
      d   Domänengrenze *f*, Domänenwand *f*
      f   limite *f* du domaine; paroi *f* du
         domaine
      r   доменная граница *f*; доменная
         стенка *f*

D527   *e*   domain energy
      d   Domänenenergie *f*
      f   énergie *f* du domaine
      r   энергия *f* домена

D528   *e*   domain magnetization
      d   Domänenmagnetisierung *f*
      f   aimantation *f* des domaines
      r   доменная намагниченность *f*

D529   *e*   domain of attraction
      d   Anziehungsbereich *m*,
         Attraktionsdomäne *f*
      f   domaine *m* d'attraction
      r   область *f* притяжения аттрактора

D530   *e*   domain of definition
      d   Definitionsbereich *m*
      f   domaine *m* de définition
      r   область *f* определения

D531   *e*   domain of existence
      d   Existenzbereich *m*
      f   domaine *m* d'existence
      r   область *f* существования

D532   *e*   domain wall
      d   Domänenwand *f*; Domänengrenze *f*
      f   paroi *f* du domaine; limite *f* du
         domaine
      r   доменная стенка *f*; доменная
         граница *f*

D533   *e*   domain wall bending
      d   Domänenwandbiegung *f*
      f   flexion *f* de la paroi du domaine
      r   изгиб *m* доменной границы

D534   *e*   domain wall motion
      d   Domänenwandbewegung *f*
      f   mouvement *m* des parois de domaines
      r   движение *n* доменных стенок

D535   *e*   donor
      d   Donator *m*
      f   donneur *m*
      r   донор *m*

D536   *e*   donor center
      d   Donatorzentrum *n*
      f   centre *m* donneur, centre *m* donateur
      r   донорный центр *m*

D537   *e*   donor impurity
      d   Donatorstörstelle *f*
      f   impureté *f* donatrice
      r   донорная примесь *f*

D538   *e*   donor level
      d   Donatorniveau *n*, Donatorterm *m*
      f   niveau *m* donneur
      r   донорный уровень *m*

D539   *e*   doped crystal
      d   dotierter Kristall *m*
      f   cristal *m* dopé
      r   легированный кристалл *m*

D540   *e*   doped semiconductor
      d   dotierter Halbleiter *m*

f semi-conducteur *m* dopé
r легированный полупроводник *m*

D541 e doped silicon
    d dotiertes Silizium *n*
    f silicium *m* dopé
    r легированный кремний *m*

D542 e doping
    d Dotierung *f (von Halbleitern)*
    f dopage *m (des semi-conducteurs)*
    r легирование *n (полупроводников)*

D543 e doping concentration
    d Dotierungskonzentration *f*
    f concentration *f* de dopage
    r концентрация *f* легирующей примеси

D544 e doping material
    d Dotierstoff *m*, Dotierungsstoff *m*, Dotant *m*
    f matière *f* de dopage
    r легирующее вещество *n*

D545 e Doppler broadening
    d Doppler-Verbreiterung *f*
    f élargissement *m* par effet Doppler, élargissement *m* Doppler
    r доплеровское уширение *n*

D546 e Doppler effect
    d Doppler-Effekt *m*
    f effet *m* Doppler
    r эффект *m* Доплера

D547 e Doppler line
    d Doppler-Linie *f*
    f ligne *f* Doppler
    r доплеровская линия *f*

D548 e doppleron
    d Doppleron *n*
    f doppleron *m*
    r доплерон *m*

D549 e Doppler profile
    d Doppler-Profil *n (der Spektrallinie)*
    f profil *m* Doppler *(de la raie spectrale)*
    r доплеровский контур *m (спектральной линии)*

D550 e Doppler shift
    d Doppler-Verschiebung *f*
    f déplacement *m* Doppler
    r доплеровское смещение *n*, доплеровский сдвиг *m*

D551 e Doppler sounding
    d Doppler-Sondierung *f*
    f sondage *m* Doppler
    r доплеровское зондирование *n*

D552 e Doppler technique
    d Doppler-Verfahren *n*
    f technique *f* Doppler
    r доплеровский метод *m*

D553 e dose
    d Dosis *f*
    f dose *f*
    r доза *f*

D554 e dose equivalent
    d Dosisäquivalent *n*
    f dose *f* équivalente
    r эквивалентная доза *f*

D555 e dosemeter *see* dosimeter

D556 e dose rate
    d Dosisleistung *f*
    f taux *m* de dose
    r мощность *f* дозы *(облучения)*

D557 e dose-rate meter, dosimeter
    d Dosimeter *n*, Dosismeßgerät *n*
    f dosimètre *m*
    r дозиметр *m*

D558 e dosimetry
    d Dosimetrie *f*, Dosismessung *f*
    f dosimétrie *f*, mesure *f* de dose
    r дозиметрия *f*

D559 e double beta-ray decay
    d doppelter Beta-Zerfall *m*
    f double bêta désintégration *f*
    r двойной бета-распад *m*

D560 e double bond
    d Doppelbindung *f*
    f double liaison *f*
    r двойная связь *f*

D561 e double calorimeter
    d Zwillingskalorimeter *n*
    f double calorimètre *m*
    r двойной калориметр *m*

D562 e double-cavity klystron
    d Zweikammerklystron *n*, Zweikreisklystron *n*
    f klystron *m* à deux cavités
    r двухрезонаторный клистрон *m*

D563 e double electrical layer
    d elektrische Doppelschicht *f*
    f couche *f* bipolaire
    r двойной электрический слой *m*

D564 e double electric probe
    d elektrische Doppelsonde *f*
    f sonde *f* électrique double
    r двойной электрический зонд *m*

D565 e double electron excitation
    d Doppelelektronenanregung *f*
    f excitation *f* à deux électrons
    r двухэлектронное возбуждение *n*

D566 e double-frequency interferometer
    d Zweifrequenzinterferometer *n*

    f interféromètre *m* à double fréquence
    r двухчастотный интерферометр *m*

D567 *e* **double image**
    d Doppelbild *n*
    f double image *f*
    r двойное изображение *n*

D568 *e* **double injection**
    d Doppelinjektion *f*
    f injection *f* double
    r биполярная инжекция *f*, двойная
       инжекция *f*

D569 *e* **double interferometer**
    d Doppelinterferometer *n*
    f interféromètre *m* double
    r двойной интерферометр *m*

D570 *e* **double magnetic resonance**
    d magnetische Doppelresonanz *f*
    f résonance *f* magnétique double
    r двойной магнитный резонанс *m*

D571 *e* **double monochromator**
    d Doppelmonochromator *m*,
       Doppelspiegelmonochromator *m*
    f monochromateur *m* double
    r двойной монохроматор *m*

D572 *e* **double quantum transition**
    d Doppelquantenübergang *m*
    f transition *f* quantique double
    r двухквантовый переход *m*

D573 *e* **double refraction**
    d Doppelbrechung *f*
    f biréfringence *f*
    r двойное лучепреломление *n*,
       двулучепреломление *n*

D574 *e* **double resonance**
    d Doppelresonanz *f*
    f double résonance *f*
    r двойной резонанс *m*

D575 *e* **double star**
    d Doppelstern *m*
    f étoile *f* double, étoile *f* binaire
    r двойная звезда *f*

D576 *e* **doublet**
    d Dublett *n*
    f doublet *m*
    r дублет *m*

D577 *e* **doublet lens**
    d zweiteiliges Objektiv *n*
    f doublet *m*, objectif *m* à deux lentilles
    r двухлинзовый объектив *m*

D578 *e* **doubly ionized atom**
    d doppeltionisiertes Atom *n*
    f atome *m* deux fois ionisé
    r дважды ионизованный атом *m*,
       двукратно ионизованный атом *m*

D579 *e* **down quark**
    d d-Quark *n*, Down-Quark *n*
    f down-quark *m*, d-quark *m*
    r нижний кварк *m*, d-кварк *m*

D580 *e* **drag**
    d 1. Ziehen *n*; Mitreißen *n*,
       Mitschleppen *n* 2. Widerstand *m*;
       Hemmung *f*, Bremsung *f*
    f 1. traction *f* 2. résistance *f*; traînée *f*
    r 1. увлечение *n* 2. сопротивление *n*;
       торможение *n*

D581 *e* **drag coefficient**
    d Mitführungskoeffizient *m*
    f coefficient *m* d'entraînement
    r коэффициент *m* увлечения

D582 *e* **drag of a sphere**
    d Widerstand *m* gegen die
       Kugelbewegung
    f résistance *f* au mouvement de la
       sphère
    r сопротивление *n* движению шара *(в*
       среде)

D583 *e* **drain**
    d Drain *m*, Senke *f*
    f drain *m*
    r сток *m*

D584 *e* **D-region**
    d D-Gebiet *n* *(Ionosphäre)*
    f région *f* D *(d'ionosphère)*
    r область *f* D *(ионосферы)*

D585 *e* **drift**
    d Drift *f*
    f dérive *f*
    r дрейф *m*

D586 *e* **drift chamber**
    d Driftkammer *f*
    f chambre *f* de dérive
    r дрейфовая камера *f*

D587 *e* **drift current**
    d Driftstrom *m*
    f courant *m* de dérive
    r дрейфовый ток *m*

D588 *e* **drift instability**
    d Driftinstabilität *f*, Instabilität *f* durch
       Anregung von Driftwellen
    f instabilité *f* de dérive
    r дрейфовая неустойчивость *f*

D589 *e* **drift klystron**
    d Triftröhre *f*
    f klystron *m* de glissement, klystron *m*
       à temps de transit, klystron *m* à
       transit
    r пролётный клистрон *m*

D590 *e* **drift motion**
    d Driftbewegung *f*

f mouvement *m* de dérive
r дрейфовое движение *n*

D591 *e* drift tube
d Driftröhre *f*
f tube *m* de dérive
r дрейфовая трубка *f*

D592 *e* drift velocity
d Driftgeschwindigkeit *f*
f vitesse *f* de dérive
r дрейфовая скорость *f*, скорость *f* дрейфа

D593 *e* drift waves
d Driftwellen *f pl*
f ondes *f pl* de dérive
r дрейфовые волны *f pl*

D594 *e* drop, droplet
d Tropfen *m*
f goutte *f*
r капля *f*

D595 *e* drop in free fall
d Tropfen *m* im freien Fall
f goutte *f* en chute libre
r падающая капля *f*

D596 *e* drop nuclear model
d Tröpfchenkernmodell *n*
f modèle *m* de la goutte
r капельная модель *f* ядра

D597 *e* dropping characteristic *see* falling characteristic

D598 *e* dropwise condensation
d Tropfenkondensation *f*
f condensation *f* sous forme de gouttes
r капельная конденсация *f*

D599 *e* Drude equation
d Drudesche Gleichung *f*, Drudesches Gesetz *n*
f équation *f* de Drude
r формула *f* Друде

D600 *e* dual beam oscilloscope
d Zweistrahloszilloskop *n*
f oscilloscope *m* à deux faisceaux
r двухлучевой осциллограф *m*

D601 *e* dualism
d Dualismus *m*
f dualisme *m*
r дуализм *m*

D602 *e* duality
d 1. Dualität *f* 2. Dualismus *m*
f dualité *f*
r 1. дуальность *f* 2. дуализм *m*

D603 *e* duality interval
d Dualitätsintervall *n*
f intervalle *m* de dualité
r интервал *m* дуальности

D604 *e* duality principle
d Dualitätsprinzip *n*
f principe *m* de dualité
r принцип *m* двойственности, принцип *m* дуальности

D605 *e* ductile metal
d streckbares Metall *n*, schmiedbares Metall *n*
f métal *m* ductile
r пластичный металл *m*, ковкий металл *m*

D606 *e* ductility
d Duktilität *f*
f ductilité *f*
r ковкость *f*, пластичность *f* (металла)

D607 *e* Dulong and Petit law
d Dulong-Petitsches Gesetz *n*
f loi *f* de Dulong et Petit
r закон *m* Дюлонга и Пти

D608 *e* duoplasmatron
d Duoplasmatronquelle *f*
f duoplasmatron *m*
r дуоплазматрон *m*

D609 *e* duration
d Dauer *f*, Zeitdauer *f*
f durée *f*
r длительность *f*, продолжительность *f*

D610 *e* dust
d Staub *m*
f poussière *f*
r пыль *f*

D611 *e* dust cloud
d Staubwolke *f*
f nuage *m* de poussière
r пылевое облако *n* (*в астрофизике*)

D612 *e* dwarf, dwarf star
d Zwerg *m*
f étoile *f* naine, naine *f*
r карлик *m*, звезда-карлик *m*

D613 *e* dye
d Farbstoff *m* (*Lasertechnik*)
f colorant *m* (*pour lasers*)
r краситель *m* (*для лазеров*)

D614 *e* dye cell
d Farbstoffküvette *f*
f cuvette *f* de colorant
r кювета *f* с красителем

D615 *e* dye laser
d Farbstofflaser *m*
f laser *m* à colorant
r лазер *m* на красителе, лазер *m* на красителях

D616 *e* dynamic equilibrium

d dynamisches Gleichgewicht n
f équilibre m dynamique
r динамическое равновесие n

D617 e dynamic head *see* dynamic pressure

D618 e dynamic holography
d dynamische Holographie f
f holographie f dynamique
r динамическая голография f

D619 e dynamic hysteresis *see* elastic hysteresis

D620 e dynamic inductance
d dynamische Induktivität f
f inductance f dynamique
r динамическая индуктивность f

D621 e dynamic instability
d dynamische Instabilität f
f instabilité f dynamique
r динамическая неустойчивость f

D622 e dynamic load
d dynamische Belastung f; dynamischer Lastwert m
f charge f dynamique
r динамическая нагрузка f

D623 e dynamic polarization
d dynamische Polarisation f
f polarisation f dynamique
r динамическая поляризация f

D624 e dynamic pressure
d Staudruck m
f pression f dynamique
r динамическое давление n, скоростной напор m

D625 e dynamic range
d Lautstärkeumfang m, Dynamikbereich m, Dynamikumfang m
f étendue f de dynamique
r динамический диапазон m

D626 e dynamics
d Dynamik f
f dynamique f
r динамика f

D627 e dynamics of deformable solids
d Dynamik f der deformierbaren Festkörper
f dynamique f des corps solides déformables
r динамика f деформируемого тела

D628 e dynamics of rarefied gases
d Supraaerodynamik f, Superaerodynamik f, Dynamik f der stark verdünnten Gase
f dynamique f des gaz raréfiés
r динамика f разрежённых газов

D629 e dynamics of rigid bodies
d Dynamik f starrer Körper
f dynamique f des corps solides
r динамика f твёрдого тела

D630 e dynamic stability
d Bewegungsstabilität f
f stabilité f dynamique
r динамическая устойчивость f, устойчивость f движения

D631 e dynamic stress
d dynamische Spannung f
f tension f dynamique, effort m dynamique
r динамическое напряжение n

D632 e dynamic symmetry
d dynamische Symmetrie f
f symétrie f dynamique
r динамическая симметрия f

D633 e dynamic system
d dynamisches System n
f système m dynamique
r динамическая система f

D634 e dynamic viscosity
d dynamische Viskosität f, dynamische Zähigkeit f
f viscosité f dynamique
r динамическая вязкость f

D635 e dynamo
d Dynamo m (*Bildungsmechanismus von Magnetfeldern der Himmelskörper*)
f dynamo f (*mécanisme de formation des champs magnétique des corps célestes*)
r динамо n (*механизм образования магнитных полей небесных тел*)

D636 e dynamometer
d Dynamometer n, Kraftmesser m
f dynamomètre m
r динамометр m

D637 e dyne
d Dyn n
f dyne f
r дина f

D638 e dynode
d Dynode f
f dynode f
r динод m

D639 e dysprosium, Dy
d Dysprosium n
f dysprosium m
r диспрозий m

E

E1
e early Universe cosmology
d Kosmologie f der Frühphase des Weltalls
f cosmologie f de l'Univers primitif
r космология f ранней Вселенной

E2
e earth
d Erde f, Masse f, Erdschluß m
f terre f, mise f à la terre
r земля f, заземление n

E3
e Earth
d Erde f
f terre f, Terre f
r Земля f (планета)

E4
e earth currents
d Erdströme pl
f courants pl de terre
r земные токи pl, теллурические токи pl

E5
e earthquake
d Erdbeben n
f tremblement m de terre
r землетрясение n

E6
e easy glide
d Einfachgleitung f
f glissement m facile
r лёгкое скольжение n

E7
e easy magnetic axis
d Richtung f der leichtesten Magnetisierbarkeit, magnetische Vorzugsrichtung f
f axe m d'aimantation facile, direction f d'aimantation facile
r ось f лёгкого намагничивания

E8
e ebullioscopy
d Ebullioskopie f
f ébullioscopie f
r эбуллиоскопия f

E9
e eccentricity
d Exzentrizität f
f excentricité f
r эксцентриситет m

E10
e echelette, echelette grating
d Echelettegitter n
f réseau m échelette
r эшелетт m

E11
e echelle, echelle grating
d Echellegitter n
f réseau m échelle
r эшелле n

E12
e echelon
d Stufengitter n, Echelon n, Michelson-Gitter n
f réseau m échelon
r эшелон m

E13
e echo
d Echo n; Echosignal n
f écho m
r эхо n

E14
e echo sounding
d Echolotung f
f sondage m acoustique
r эхо-локация f

E15
e eclipse
d Finsternis f, Verfinsterung f
f éclipse f
r затмение n

E16
e eclipse of the Moon see lunar eclipse

E17
e eclipse of the Sun see solar eclipse

E18
e eclipsing binary, eclipsing binary star see eclipsing variable

E19
e eclipsing variable, eclipsing variable star
d Bedeckungsveränderliche(r) m
f variable f à éclipse
r затменная переменная f, затменная переменная звезда f

E20
e ecliptic
d Ekliptik f
f écliptique f
r эклиптика f

E21
e Eddington luminosity
d Eddington-Grenze f
f luminosité f d'Eddington
r критическая светимость f, эддингтоновская светимость f

E22
e eddy
d Wirbel m
f tourbillon m
r вихрь m

E23
e eddy currents
d Wirbelströme pl
f courants pl tourbillonnaires
r вихревые токи pl, токи pl Фуко

E24
e edge dislocation
d Stufenversetzung f
f dislocation f du type coin, dislocation f coin
r краевая дислокация f

E25
e edge focusing
d Kantenfokussierung f, Randfokussierung f
f focalisation f par arête
r краевая фокусировка f

E26
e effect

    d 1. Effekt *m* 2. Wirkung *f*; Einfluß *m*,
Einwirkung *f*
    f 1. effet *m* 2. action *f*; influence *f*
    r 1. эффект *m* 2. действие *n*;
влияние *n*

E27   *e*   effective charge
    d effektive Ladung *f*
    f charge *f* effective
    r эффективный заряд *m*

E28   *e*   effective cross-section
    d effektiver Wirkungsquerschnitt *m*
    f section *f* efficace
    r эффективное сечение *n*

E29   *e*   effective height
    d wirksame Antennenhöhe *f*, effektive
Antennenhöhe *f*
    f hauteur *m* efficace *(d'antenne)*
    r действующая высота *f* *(антенны)*

E30   *e*   effective mass
    d effektive Masse *f*, wirksame Masse *f*
    f masse *f* effective
    r эффективная масса *f*

E31   *e*   effective temperature
    d effektive Temperatur *f*
    f température *f* effective
    r эффективная температура *f*

E32   *e*   effective value
    d 1. Effektivwert *m*, effektiver Wert *m*,
wirksamer Wert *m* 2. quadratischer
Mittelwert *m*, mittlerer quadratischer
Wert *m*
    f valeur *f* effective
    r 1. эффективное значение *n*,
действующее значение *n*
2. среднеквадратичное значение *n*

E33   *e*   effective voltage
    d effektive Spannung *f*,
Effektivspannung *f*
    f tension *f* efficace
    r действующее напряжение *n*

E34   *e*   efficiency
    d Wirkungsgrad *m*; Nutzeffekt *m*;
Effektivität *f*, Wirksamkeit *f*
    f rendement *m*; efficience *f*
    r коэффициент *m* полезного
действия, кпд *m*; эффективность *f*

E35   *e*   effusion
    d Effusion *f*
    f effusion *f*
    r эффузия *f*

E36   *e*   eigenfunction
    d Eigenfunktion *f*
    f fonction *f* propre
    r собственная функция *f*

E37   *e*   eigenfunction expansion method

    d Entwicklungsmethode *f* nach
Eigenfunktionen
    f méthode *f* d'expansion aux fonctions
propres
    r метод *m* разложения по
собственным функциям

E38   *e*   eigenfunction problem
    d Eigenfunktionsaufgabe *f*
    f problème *m* de fonctions propres
    r задача *f* на собственные функции

E39   *e*   eigenmode expansion method
    d Entwicklung *f* nach Eigenmoden
    f méthode *f* d'expansion aux modes
propres
    r метод *m* разложения по
собственным модам

E40   *e*   eigenmodes
    d Normalschwingungsmoden *f pl*,
Eigenschwingungsmoden *f pl*,
Eigenmoden *f pl*
    f oscillations *f pl* propres, modes *m pl*
propres
    r собственные колебания *n pl*,
собственные моды *f pl*

E41   *e*   eigenvalue
    d Eigenwert *m*
    f valeur *f* propre
    r собственное значение *n*

E42   *e*   eigenvalue problem
    d Eigenwertproblem *n*,
Eigenwertaufgabe *f*
    f problème *m* de valeurs propres
    r задача *f* на собственные значения

E43   *e*   eigenvector
    d Eigenvektor *m*
    f vecteur *m* propre
    r собственный вектор *m*

E44   *e*   eikonal
    d Eikonal *n*
    f iconal *m*
    r эйконал *m*

E45   *e*   Einstein coefficients
    d Einstein-Koeffizienten *m pl*
    f coefficients *m pl* d'Einstein
    r коэффициенты *m pl* Эйнштейна

E46   *e*   Einstein-de Haas effect
    d Einstein-de-Haas-Effekt *m*
    f effet *m* Einstein-de Haas
    r эффект *m* Эйнштейна - де Хааза

E47   *e*   einsteinium, Es
    d Einsteinium *n*
    f einsteinium *m*
    r эйнштейний *m*

E48   *e*   ejector
    d Ejektor *m*

f éjecteur *m*
r эжектор *m*

E49
e elastic aftereffect
d elastische Nachwirkung *f*
f posteffet *m* élastique
r упругое последействие *n*

E50
e elastic anisotropy
d elastische Anisotropie *f*
f anisotropie *f* élastique
r анизотропия *f* упругих свойств

E51
e elastic bending
d elastische Biegung *f*
f flexion *f* élastique
r упругий изгиб *m*

E52
e elastic channel
d Kanal *m* der elastischen Streuung
f canal *m* de diffusion élastique
r упругий канал *m*, канал *m* упругого
рассеяния

E53
e elastic collisions
d elastische Stöße *m pl*
f collisions *f pl* élastiques
r упругие столкновения *n pl*

E54
e elastic constant
d Elastizitätskonstante *f*
f constante *f* élastique, constante *f*
d'élasticité
r упругая константа *f*

E55
e elastic cross-section *see* elastic
scattering cross-section

E56
e elastic deformation
d elastische Verformung *f*, elastische
Deformation *f*
f déformation *f* élastique
r упругая деформация *f*

E57
e elastic hysteresis
d elastische Hysterese *f*
f hystérésis *f* élastique
r упругий гистерезис *m*

E58
e elasticity
d Elastizität *f*
f élasticité *f*
r упругость *f*

E59
e elastic limit
d Elastizitätsgrenze *f*
f limite *f* élastique
r предел *m* упругости

E60
e elastic liquid
d elastische Flüssigkeit *f*
f liquide *m* élastique
r упругая жидкость *f*

E61
e elastic material
d elastischer Stoff *m*, elastischer
Werkstoff *m*

f matériau *m* élastique
r упругий материал *m*

E62
e elastic modulus
d Elastizitätsmodul *m*
f module *m* d'élasticité
r модуль *m* упругости

E63
e elastic region *see* elastic scattering
region

E64
e elastic scattering
d elastische Streuung *f*
f diffusion *f* élastique
r упругое рассеяние *n*

E65
e elastic scattering cross-section
d Wirkungsquerschnitt *m* für elastische
Streuung
f section *f* efficace de diffusion élastique
r сечение *n* упругого рассеяния

E66
e elastic scattering region
d Gebiet *n* der elastischen Streuung,
Bereich *m* der elastischen Streuung
f région *f* de diffusion élastique
r область *f* упругого рассеяния

E67
e elastic vibration
d elastische Schwingungen *f pl*
f oscillations *f pl* élastiques
r упругие колебания *n pl*

E68
e elastic waves
d elastische Wellen *f pl*
f ondes *f pl* élastiques
r упругие волны *f pl*

E69
e elastomer
d Elastomer *n*
f élastomère *m*
r эластомер *m*

E70
e elastoplastic bending
d elastoplastische Biegung *f*
f flexion *f* élastico-plastique
r упругопластический изгиб *m*

E71
e elastoplastic material
d elastoplastischer Stoff *m*
f matériau *m* élastico-plastique
r упругопластический материал *m*

E72
e elastoplastic wave
d elastoplastische Welle *f*
f onde *f* élasto-plastique
r упругопластическая волна *f*

E73
e elastoviscous liquid *see* viscoelastic
liquid

E74
e E-layer
d E-Schicht *f* (*der Ionosphäre*)
f couche *f* E (*d'ionosphère*)
r слой *m* E (*ионосферы*)

E75
e electret

ELECTRICAL

d   Elektret *n*
f   électret *m*
r   электрет *m*

E76   e   electrical breakdown
d   elektrischer Durchschlag *m*
f   claquage *m* électrique
r   электрический пробой *m*

E77   e   electrical circuit
d   Stromkreis *m*, elektrischer Stromkreis *m*
f   circuit *m* électrique
r   электрическая цепь *f*

E78   e   electrical circuit analysis
d   Netzwerktheorie *f*
f   théorie *f* des circuits électriques
r   теория *f* электрических цепей

E79   e   electrical conduction *see* electrical conductivity

E80   e   electrical conductivity
d   Leitfähigkeit *f*, elektrische Leitfähigkeit *f*
f   conductibilité *f* électrique
r   электрическая проводимость *f*, электропроводность *f*

E81   e   electrical connection
d   elektrische Verbindung *f*
f   connexion *f* électrique
r   электрическое соединение *n*

E82   e   electrical contact
d   elektrischer Kontakt *m*
f   contact *m* électrique
r   электрический контакт *m*

E83   e   electrical displacement
d   elektrische Verschiebung *f*, elektrische Flußdichte *f*
f   déplacement *m* électrique
r   электрическое смещение *n*

E84   e   electrical displacement current
d   Verschiebungsstrom *m*
f   courant *m* de déplacement électrique
r   ток *m* электрического смещения

E85   e   electrical double layer
d   elektrische Doppelschicht *f*
f   couche *f* bipolaire
r   двойной электрический слой *m*

E86   e   electrical instrument
d   elektrisches Meßgerät *n*
f   appareil *m* mesureur électrique
r   электроизмерительный прибор *m*

E87   e   electrical insulation
d   elektrische Isolation *f*
f   isolement *m* électrique
r   электрическая изоляция *f*

E88   e   electrical load

d   elektrische Belastung *f*
f   charge *f* électrique
r   электрическая нагрузка *f*

E89   e   electrical measurements
d   elektrische Messungen *f pl*
f   mesures *f pl* électriques
r   электрические измерения *n pl*

E90   e   electrical measurements of non-electrical quantities
d   elektrische Messungen *f pl* von nichtelektrischen Größen
f   mesures *f pl* électriques des grandeurs non électriques
r   электрические измерения *n pl* неэлектрических величин

E91   e   electrical network
d   elektrische Schaltung *f*; Netzwerk *n*
f   circuit *m* électrique
r   электрическая цепь *f*

E92   e   electrical potential
d   elektrisches Potential *n*
f   potentiel *m* électrique
r   электрический потенциал *m*

E93   e   electrical resistance
d   elektrischer Widerstand *m*
f   résistance *f* électrique
r   электрическое сопротивление *n*

E94   e   electrical signal
d   elektrisches Signal *n*
f   signal *m* électrique
r   электрический сигнал *m*

E95   e   electric arc
d   Lichtbogen *m*
f   arc *m* électrique
r   электрическая дуга *f*

E96   e   electric charge
d   elektrische Ladung *f*
f   charge *f* électrique
r   электрический заряд *m*

E97   e   electric current
d   elektrischer Strom *m*
f   courant *m* électrique
r   электрический ток *m*

E98   e   electric dipole
d   elektrischer Dipol *m*
f   dipôle *m* électrique
r   электрический диполь *m*

E99   e   electric discharge
d   elektrische Entladung *f*
f   décharge *f* électrique
r   электрический разряд *m*

E100   e   electric discharge chamber
d   Entladungskammer *f*, Entladekammer *f*
f   chambre *f* à décharge électrique
r   электроразрядная камера *f*

E101   *e*   electric discharge initiation
     d   Initiierung *f* mit elektrischer Entladung
     f   initiation *f* par décharge électrique
     r   инициирование *n* электрическим разрядом

E102   *e*   electric discharge laser
     d   Entladungslaser *m*
     f   laser *m* à décharge électrique
     r   электроразрядный лазер *m*

E103   *e*   electric displacement *see* electrical displacement

E104   *e*   electric drift
     d   elektrische Drift *f*
     f   dérive *f* électrique
     r   электрический дрейф *m*

E105   *e*   electric energy
     d   elektrische Energie *f*, Elektroenergie *f*
     f   énergie *f* électrique
     r   электрическая энергия *f*

E106   *e*   electric field
     d   elektrisches Feld *n*
     f   champ *m* électrique
     r   электрическое поле *n*

E107   *e*   electric field strength
     d   elektrische Feldstärke *f*
     f   intensité *f* de champ électrique
     r   напряжённость *f* электрического поля

E108   *e*   electric flux density *see* electrical displacement

E109   *e*   electric induction
     d   elektrische Flußdichte *f*, elektrische Verschiebung *f*
     f   induction *f* électrique, déplacement *m* électrique
     r   электрическая индукция *f*, электрическое смещение *n*

E110   *e*   electric instability
     d   elektrische Instabilität *f*
     f   instabilité *f* électrique
     r   электрическая неустойчивость *f*

E111   *e*   electricity
     d   Elektrizität *f*
     f   électricité *f*
     r   электричество *n*

E112   *e*   electric line of force
     d   elektrische Kraftlinie *f*
     f   ligne *f* de force électrique
     r   силовая линия *f* электрического поля

E113   *e*   electric moment
     d   elektrisches Moment *n*
     f   moment *m* électrique
     r   электрический момент *m*

E114   *e*   electric power
     d   elektrische Leistung *f*
     f   puissance *f* électrique
     r   электрическая мощность *f*

E115   *e*   electric strength *see* dielectric strength

E116   *e*   electrization
     d   Elektrisierung *f*
     f   électrisation *f*
     r   электризация *f*

E117   *e*   electroacoustical analogy
     d   elektroakustische Analogie *f*
     f   analogie *f* électro-acoustique
     r   электроакустическая аналогия *f*

E118   *e*   electroacoustics
     d   Elektroakustik *f*
     f   électro-acoustique *f*
     r   электроакустика *f*

E119   *e*   electrocaloric effect
     d   elektrokalorischer Effekt *m*
     f   effet *m* électrocalorique
     r   электрокалорический эффект *m*

E120   *e*   electrocardiography
     d   Elektrokardiographie *f*
     f   électrocardiographie *f*
     r   электрокардиография *f*, ЭКГ

E121   *e*   electrochemical cell
     d   galvanisches Element *n*, galvanische Zelle *f*
     f   élément *m* galvanique, pile *f* galvanique
     r   гальванический элемент *m*

E122   *e*   electrochemical equivalent
     d   elektrochemisches Äquivalent *n*
     f   équivalent *m* électrochimique
     r   электрохимический эквивалент *m*

E123   *e*   electrochemical potential
     d   elektrochemisches Potential *n*
     f   potentiel *m* électrochimique
     r   электрохимический потенциал *m*

E124   *e*   electrochemistry
     d   Elektrochemie *f*
     f   électrochimie *f*
     r   электрохимия *f*

E125   *e*   electrode
     d   Elektrode *f*
     f   électrode *f*
     r   электрод *m*

E126   *e*   electrodeless discharge
     d   elektrodenlose Entladung *f*
     f   décharge *f* sans électrodes
     r   безэлектродный разряд *m*

E127   e   electrodynamic instrument *see* electrodynamic meter

E128   e   electrodynamic meter
d   elektrodynamisches Meßinstrument *n*
f   appareil *m* électrodynamique
r   электродинамический измерительный прибор *m*

E129   e   electrodynamics
d   Elektrodynamik *f*
f   électrodynamique *f*
r   электродинамика *f*

E130   e   electrodynamics of moving media
d   Elektrodynamik *f* der bewegten Medien
f   électrodynamique *f* des milieux en mouvement
r   электродинамика *f* движущихся сред

E131   e   electroencephalography
d   Elektroenzephalographie *f*
f   électro-encéphalographie *f*
r   электроэнцефалография *f*

E132   e   electroerosion wear
d   Elektroerosionsverschleiß *m*
f   usure *f* due à l'électro-érosion
r   электроэрозионное изнашивание *n*

E133   e   electrogyration
d   Elektrogyration *f*
f   électrogiration *f*
r   электрогирация *f*

E134   e   electroinsulation material
d   Elektroisolierstoff *m*, elektrischer Isolierstoff *m*
f   matériau *m* isolant
r   электроизоляционный материал *m*

E135   e   electroionization laser
d   Elektroionisationslaser *m*
f   laser *m* à ionisation électrique
r   электроионизационный лазер *m*

E136   e   electrokinetic phenomena
d   elektrokinetische Erscheinungen *f pl*, elektrokinetische Effekte *m pl*
f   effets *m pl* électrocinétiques
r   электрокинетические явления *n pl*

E137   e   electroluminescence
d   Elektrolumineszenz *f*
f   luminescence *f* électrique
r   электролюминесценция *f*

E138   e   electroluminescent diode *see* light emitting diode

E139   e   electroluminescent source
d   Elektrolumineszenzquelle *f*
f   source *f* d'électroluminescence
r   электролюминесцентный источник *m* света, электролюминесцентный источник *m*

E140   e   electrolysis
d   Elektrolyse *f*
f   électrolyse *f*
r   электролиз *m*

E141   e   electrolyte
d   Elektrolyt *m*
f   électrolyte *m*
r   электролит *m*

E142   e   electromagnet
d   Elektromagnet *m*
f   électro-aimant *m*
r   электромагнит *m*

E143   e   electromagnetic energy
d   elektromagnetische Feldenergie *f*, Energie *f* des elektromagnetischen Feldes
f   énergie *f* électromagnétique
r   энергия *f* электромагнитного поля

E144   e   electromagnetic field
d   elektromagnetisches Feld *n*
f   champ *m* électromagnétique
r   электромагнитное поле *n*

E145   e   electromagnetic field invariants
d   elektromagnetische Feldinvarianten *f pl*
f   invariants *m pl* du champ électromagnétique
r   инварианты *m pl* электромагнитного поля

E146   e   electromagnetic field momentum
d   Impuls *m* des elektromagnetischen Feldes, elektromagnetischer Feldimpuls *m*
f   impulsion *f* du champ électromagnétique
r   импульс *m* электромагнитного поля

E147   e   electromagnetic incompatibility
d   elektromagnetische Inkompatibilität *f*
f   incompatibilité *f* électromagnétique
r   электромагнитная несовместимость *f*

E148   e   electromagnetic induction
d   elektromagnetische Induktion *f*
f   induction *f* électromagnétique
r   электромагнитная индукция *f*

E149   e   electromagnetic induction coefficient
d   elektromagnetischer Induktionsfaktor *m*
f   coefficient *m* d'induction électromagnétique
r   коэффициент *m* электромагнитной индукции

E150   e   electromagnetic interaction
d   elektromagnetische Wechselwirkung *f*
f   interaction *f* électromagnétique
r   электромагнитное взаимодействие *n*

E151　*e*　electromagnetic oscillation
　　　d　elektromagnetische Schwingungen *f pl*
　　　f　oscillations *f pl* électromagnétiques
　　　r　электромагнитные колебания *n pl*

E152　*e*　electromagnetic radiation
　　　d　elektromagnetische Strahlung *f*
　　　f　radiation *f* électromagnétique
　　　r　электромагнитное излучение *n*,
　　　　　электромагнитные волны *f pl*

E153　*e*　electromagnetic wave pressure
　　　d　elektromagnetischer Wellendruck *m*
　　　f　pression *f* de l'onde électromagnétique
　　　r　давление *n* электромагнитной
　　　　　волны

E154　*e*　electromagnetic waves
　　　d　elektromagnetische Wellen *f pl*
　　　f　ondes *f pl* électromagnétiques
　　　r　электромагнитные волны *f pl*

E155　*e*　electromechanical coupling
　　　　　coefficient
　　　d　elektromechanischer
　　　　　Umwandlungsfaktor *m*
　　　f　coefficient *m* de couplage
　　　　　électromécanique
　　　r　коэффициент *m*
　　　　　электромеханической связи

E156　*e*　electrometer
　　　d　Elektrometer *n*
　　　f　électromètre *m*
　　　r　электрометр *m*

E157　*e*　electromotive force
　　　d　elektromotorische Kraft *f*, EMK *f*,
　　　　　Urspannung *f*
　　　f　force *f* électromotrice, f.é.m.
　　　r　электродвижущая сила *f*, эдс *f*

E158　*e*　electron
　　　d　Elektron *n*
　　　f　électron *m*
　　　r　электрон *m*

E159　*e*　electron accelerator
　　　d　Elektronenbeschleuniger *m*
　　　f　accélérateur *m* d'électrons
　　　r　электронный ускоритель *m*

E160　*e*　electron affinity
　　　d　Elektronenaffinität *f*
　　　f　affinité *f* électronique
　　　r　сродство *n* к электрону

E161　*e*　electron attachment
　　　d　Elektronenanlagerung *f*
　　　f　adhérence *f* de l'électron
　　　r　прилипание *n* электрона *(к атому)*

E162　*e*　electron avalanche
　　　d　Elektronenlawine *f*
　　　f　avalanche *f* électronique
　　　r　электронная лавина *f*

E163　*e*　electron beam
　　　d　Elektronenbündel *n*,
　　　　　Elektronenstrahl *m*
　　　f　faisceau *m* électronique, rayon *m*
　　　　　électronique
　　　r　электронный пучок *m*, электронный
　　　　　луч *m*

E164　*e*　electron-beam deposition
　　　d　Elektronenstrahlaufdampfen *n*
　　　f　déposition *f* par faisceau électronique
　　　r　электронно-лучевое напыление *n*

E165　*e*　electron-beam devices
　　　d　Elektronenstrahlgeräte *n pl*
　　　f　appareils *m pl* à faisceau
　　　　　électronique
　　　r　электронно-лучевые приборы *m pl*

E166　*e*　electron-beam evaporation
　　　d　Elektronenstrahlverdampfung *f*
　　　f　évaporation *f* par faisceau électronique
　　　r　электронно-лучевое испарение *n*

E167　*e*　electron-beam heating
　　　d　Elektronenstrahlerwärmung *f*,
　　　　　Elektronenstrahlerhitzung *f*
　　　f　chauffage *m* par faisceau électronique
　　　r　нагрев *m* электронным пучком

E168　*e*　electron-beam initiation
　　　d　Elektronenstrahlinitiierung *f*
　　　f　initiation *f* par faisceau électronique
　　　r　инициирование *n* электронным
　　　　　пучком

E169　*e*　electron-beam interference
　　　d　Elektronenstrahlinterferenz *f*
　　　f　interférence *f* des faisceaux
　　　　　électroniques
　　　r　интерференция *f* электронных
　　　　　пучков

E170　*e*　electron-beam lithography
　　　d　Elektronenstrahllithographie *f*
　　　f　lithographie *f* à faisceau électronique
　　　r　электронно-лучевая литография *f*

E171　*e*　electron-beam melting
　　　d　Elektronenstrahlschmelzen *n*
　　　f　fusion *f* par faisceau électronique
　　　r　электронно-лучевое плавление *n*

E172　*e*　electron-beam processing
　　　d　Elektronenstrahlbearbeitung *f*
　　　f　traitement *m* par faisceau électronique
　　　r　электронно-лучевая обработка *f*

E173　*e*　electron-beam pumping
　　　d　Elektronenstrahlpumpen *n*
　　　f　pompage *m* par faisceau électronique
　　　r　накачка *f* электронным пучком

E174　*e*　electron-beam recording
　　　d　Elektronenstrahlaufzeichnung *f*

f enregistrement *m* par faisceau
électronique
r запись *f* электронным лучом

E175 *e* electron-beam tube
d Elektronenstrahlröhre *f*,
Katodenstrahlröhre *f*
f tube *m* cathodique
r электронно-лучевая трубка *f*

E176 *e* electron capture
d Elektroneneinfang *m*
f capture *f* électronique
r электронный захват *m*; захват *m*
электрона

E177 *e* electron channeling
d Elektronenkanalierung *f*
f canalisation *f* des électrons
r каналирование *n* электронов

E178 *e* electron charge
d Elektronenladung *f*
f charge *f* d'électron
r заряд *m* электрона

E179 *e* electron cloud
d Elektronenwolke *f*
f nuage *m* d'électrons
r электронное облако *n*

E180 *e* electron collectivization
d Elektronenkollektivierung *f*
f collectivisation *f* des électrons
r коллективизация *f* электронов

E181 *e* electron concentration
d Elektronenkonzentration *f*,
Elektronendichte *f*
f concentration *f* électronique; densité *f*
électronique
r концентрация *f* электронов,
электронная концентрация *f*

E182 *e* electron conduction
d Elektronenleitung *f*
f conduction *f* par électrons
r электронная проводимость *f*

E183 *e* electron conduction of heat
d Elektronen-Wärmeleitung *f*,
Elektronen-Wärmeleitfähigkeit *f*
f conductibilité *f* thermique électronique
r электронная теплопроводность *f*

E184 *e* electron configuration
d Elektronenkonfiguration *f*
f configuration *f* électronique
r электронная конфигурация *f*

E185 *e* electron density
d Elektronendichte *f*,
Elektronenkonzentration *f*
f densité *f* électronique, concentration *f*
électronique
r плотность *f* электронов,
электронная концентрация *f*

E186 *e* electron detachment
d Elektronenablösung *f*
f détachement *m* d'électron
r отрыв *m* электрона (*от
отрицательного иона*)

E187 *e* electron diffraction
d Elektronenbeugung *f*
f diffraction *f* électronique
r дифракция *f* электронов

E188 *e* electron diffraction analysis
d Elektronenbeugungsanalyse *f*
f analyse *f* par diffraction électronique
r электронография *f*,
электронографический анализ *m*

E189 *e* electron diffraction pattern
d Elektronenbeugungsbild *n*,
Elektronenbeugungsaufnahme *f*
f électronogramme *m*
r электронограмма *f*

E190 *e* electron diffraction study
d Elektronenbeugungsuntersuchung *f*
f étude *f* de diffraction électronique
r электронографическое исследование
n, электронография *f*

E191 *e* electron diffractometer
d Elektronenbeugungsgerät *n*
f appareil *m* de diffraction électronique,
diffractomètre *m* électronique
r электронограф *m*

E192 *e* electronegativity
d Elektronegativität *f*
f électronégativité *f*
r электроотрицательность *f*

E193 *e* electron-electron interaction
d Elektron-Elektron-Wechselwirkung *f*
f interaction *f* électron-électron
r электрон-электронное
взаимодействие *n*

E194 *e* electron emission
d Elektronenemission *f*
f émission *f* électronique
r электронная эмиссия *f*

E195 *e* electron energy distribution
d Elektronenenergieverteilung *f*
f distribution *f* d'électrons d'après
l'énergie
r распределение *n* электронов по
энергиям

E196 *e* electron energy level
d Elektronenenergieniveau *n*
f niveau *m* d'énergie d'électrons
r электронный уровень *m* энергии

E197 *e* electron escape
d Durchtunneln *n*, Überwindung *f* der
Potentialschwelle durch das Elektron

f   fuite *f* d'électrons
r   убегание *n* электронов

E198 e **electron gas**
      d Elektronengas *n*
      f gaz *m* électronique
      r электронный газ *m*

E199 e **electron gun**
      d Elektronenkanone *f*,
         Elektronenstrahlerzeuger *m*
      f canon *m* électronique
      r электронная пушка *f*, электронный
         прожектор *m*

E200 e **electron-hole drop, electron-hole**
         droplet
      d Elektronenlochtropfen *m*
      f goutte *f* électron-trou
      r электронно-дырочная капля *f*

E201 e **electron-hole junction**
      d p-n-Übergang *m*, Elektronen-Löcher-
         Übergang *m*
      f jonction *f* p-n
      r электронно-дырочный переход *m*,
         p—n-переход *m*

E202 e **electron-hole liquid**
      d Elektronen-Löcher-Flüssigkeit *f*
      f fluide *m* électron-trou
      r электронно-дырочная жидкость *f*

E203 e **electronic heat capacity**
      d Elektronen-Wärmekapazität *f*
      f capacité *f* thermique électronique
      r электронная теплоёмкость *f*

E204 e **electronic heat conductivity**
      d Elektronen-Wärmeleitung *f*,
         Elektronen-Wärmeleitfähigkeit *f*
      f conductibilité *f* thermique électronique
      r электронная теплопроводность *f*

E205 e **electronic instrument**
      d Elektronenmeßgerät *n*
      f instrument *m* électronique
      r электронный измерительный
         прибор *m*

E206 e **electronic relay**
      d elektronisches Relais *n*
      f relais *m* électronique
      r электронное реле *n*

E207 e **electronics**
      d Elektronik *f*
      f électronique *f*
      r электроника *f*

E208 e **electronic spectra**
      d Elektronenspektren *n pl*
      f spectres *m pl* électroniques
      r электронные спектры *m pl*
         (*молекул*)

E209 e **electronic transition** *see* electron
         transition

E210 e **electronic-vibrational spectra**
      d Elektronen-Schwingungsspektren *n pl*
      f spectres *m pl* électroniques
         vibrationnels
      r электронно-колебательные спектры
         m pl (*молекул*)

E211 e **electron impact**
      d Elektronenstoß *m*
      f choc *m* électronique
      r электронный удар *m*

E212 e **electron injection**
      d Elektroneninjektion *f*
      f injection *f* d'électrons
      r инжекция *f* электронов

E213 e **electron injector**
      d Elektroneninjektor *m*
      f injecteur *m* d'électrons
      r инжектор *m* электронов

E214 e **electron ionization**
      d Elektronenionisation *f*
      f ionisation *f* par électrons
      r ионизация *f* электронами,
         ионизация *f* электронным ударом

E215 e **electron-ion recombination**
      d Elektron-Ion-Rekombination *f*
      f recombinaison *f* électron-ion
      r электронно-ионная рекомбинация *f*

E216 e **electron lens**
      d Elektronenlinse *f*
      f lentille *f* électronique
      r электронная линза *f*

E217 e **electron mass**
      d Elektronenmasse *f*
      f masse *f* d'électron
      r масса *f* электрона

E218 e **electron microscope**
      d Elektronenmikroskop *n*
      f microscope *m* électronique
      r электронный микроскоп *m*

E219 e **electron migration**
      d Elektronenwanderung *f*
      f migration *f* d'électrons
      r миграция *f* электронов

E220 e **electron mirror**
      d Elektronenspiegel *m*
      f miroir *m* électronique
      r электронное зеркало *n*

E221 e **electron mobility**
      d Elektronenbeweglichkeit *f*
      f mobilité *f* des électrons
      r подвижность *f* электронов

E222 e **electron momentum**
      d Elektronenimpuls *m*
      f impulsion *f* d'électron
      r импульс *m* электрона

E223   *e*   **electron-optical aberrations**
      d   elektronenoptische Aberration *f*
      f   aberrations *f pl* électrono-optiques
      r   электронно-оптические аберрации *f pl*, аберрации *f pl* электронных линз

E224   *e*   **electron-optical image converter**
      d   Bildwandler *m*
      f   convertisseur *m* d'image électrono-optique
      r   электронно-оптический преобразователь *m*, ЭОП

E225   *e*   **electron optics**
      d   Elektronenoptik *f*
      f   optique *f* électronique
      r   электронная оптика *f*

E226   *e*   **electron orbit**
      d   Elektronenbahn *f*
      f   orbite *f* d'électron
      r   электронная орбита *f*

E227   *e*   **electron paramagnetic resonance**
      d   paramagnetische Elektronenresonanz *f*
      f   résonance *f* paramagnétique électronique
      r   электронный парамагнитный резонанс *m*, ЭПР *m*

E228   *e*   **electron-phonon interaction**
      d   Elektron-Phonon-Wechselwirkung *f*
      f   interaction *f* électron-phonon
      r   электрон-фононное взаимодействие *n*

E229   *e*   **electron-positron pair**
      d   Elektron-Positron-Paar *n*
      f   paire *f* électron-positron
      r   электрон-позитронная пара *f*

E230   *e*   **electron probe**
      d   Elektronensonde *f*
      f   sonde *f* électronique
      r   электронный зонд *m*

E231   *e*   **electron projector**
      d   Elektronenprojektor *m*
      f   projecteur *m* électronique
      r   электронный проектор *f*

E232   *e*   **electron radiation**
      d   Elektronenstrahlung *f*
      f   radiation *f* électronique
      r   излучение *n* электрона, электронное излучение *n*

E233   *e*   **electron radiography**
      d   Elektronenradiographie *f*
      f   radiographie *f* électronique
      r   электронная радиография *f*

E234   *e*   **electron radius**
      d   Elektronenradius *m*
      f   rayon *m* d'électron
      r   радиус *m* электрона

E235   *e*   **electron recombination** *see* **electron-ion recombination**

E236   *e*   **electron scattering**
      d   Elektronenstreuung *f*
      f   diffusion *f* d'électrons
      r   рассеяние *n* электронов

E237   *e*   **electron shell**
      d   Elektronenschale *f*
      f   couche *f* électronique
      r   электронная оболочка *f (атома)*

E238   *e*   **electron source**
      d   Elektronenquelle *f*
      f   source *f* d'électrons
      r   источник *m* электронов

E239   *e*   **electron spin**
      d   Elektronenspin *m*
      f   spin *m* de l'électron
      r   спин *m* электрона

E240   *e*   **electron spin resonance**
      d   Elektronenspinresonanz *f*
      f   résonance *f* de spin électronique
      r   электронный спиновый резонанс *m*

E241   *e*   **electron temperature**
      d   Elektronentemperatur *f*
      f   température *f* électronique
      r   электронная температура *f*, температура *f* электронов

E242   *e*   **electron theory**
      d   Elektronentheorie *f*
      f   théorie *f* électronique
      r   электронная теория *f*

E243   *e*   **electron transition**
      d   Elektronenübergang *m*
      f   transition *f* électronique
      r   электронный переход *m*

E244   *e*   **electron trap**
      d   Elektronenfalle *f*
      f   piège *m* à électrons
      r   электронная ловушка *f*

E245   *e*   **electron trapping** *see* **electron capture**

E246   *e*   **electron tube**
      d   Elektronenröhre *f*
      f   tube *m* électronique
      r   электронная лампа *f*

E247   *e*   **electron tunneling**
      d   Elektronendurchtunnelung *f*
      f   effet *m* tunnel d'électrons
      r   туннелирование *n* электронов

E248   *e*   **electron valve** *see* **electron tube**

E249   *e*   **electron-volt, eV**
      d   Elektronvolt *n*, Elektronenvolt *n*

    f électron-volt *m*
    r электрон-вольт *m*, эВ

E250 *e* electro-optical coefficient
    d elektrooptischer Koeffizient *m*
    f coefficient *m* électro-optique
    r электрооптический коэффициент *m*

E251 *e* electro-optical effect
    d elektrooptischer Effekt *m*,
        elektrooptischer Kerr-Effekt *m*
    f effet *m* électro-optique
    r электрооптический эффект *m*

E252 *e* electro-optical shutter
    d elektrooptischer Verschluß *m*, Kerr-
        Zellen-Verschluß *m*
    f obturateur *m* électro-optique
    r электрооптический затвор *m*

E253 *e* electro-optic crystal
    d elektrooptischer Kristall *m*
    f cristal *m* électro-optique
    r электрооптический кристалл *m*

E254 *e* electro-optic deflector
    d elektrooptischer Deflektor *m*
    f déflecteur *m* électro-optique
    r электрооптический дефлектор *m*

E255 *e* electro-optic modulator
    d elektrooptischer Modulator *m*
    f modulateur *m* électro-optique
    r электрооптический модулятор *m*

E256 *e* electro-optics
    d Elektrooptik *f*
    f électro-optique *f*
    r электрооптика *f*

E257 *e* electrophoresis
    d Elektrophorese *f*
    f électrophorèse *f*
    r электрофорез *m*

E258 *e* electrophysics
    d Elektrophysik *f*
    f électrophysique *f*
    r электрофизика *f*

E259 *e* electropositivity
    d Elektropositivität *f*
    f électropositivité *f*
    r электроположительность *f*

E260 *e* electroscope
    d Elektroskop *n*
    f électroscope *m*
    r электроскоп *m*

E261 *e* electrostatic field
    d elektrostatisches Feld *n*
    f champ *m* électrostatique
    r электростатическое поле *n*

E262 *e* electrostatic focusing
    d elektrostatische Fokussierung *f*

    f focalisation *f* électrostatique
    r электростатическая фокусировка *f*

E263 *e* electrostatic generator
    d elektrostatischer Generator *m*
    f générateur *m* électrostatique
    r электростатический генератор *m*

E264 *e* electrostatic image
    d elektrostatisches Bild *n*
    f image *f* électrostatique
    r электростатическое изображение *n*

E265 *e* electrostatic induction
    d Influenz *f*, elektrische Influenz *f*,
        elektrostatische Induktion *f*
    f induction *f* électrostatique
    r электростатическая индукция *f*

E266 *e* electrostatic instrument
    d elektrostatisches Meßinstrument *n*
    f appareil *m* mesureur électrostatique
    r электростатический измерительный
        прибор *m*

E267 *e* electrostatic lens
    d elektrostatische Linse *f*, elektrische
        Elektronenlinse *f*
    f lentille *f* électrostatique
    r электростатическая линза *f*

E268 *e* electrostatic potential
    d elektrostatisches Potential *n*
    f potentiel *m* électrostatique
    r электростатический потенциал *m*

E269 *e* electrostatic quadrupole
    d elektrostatischer Quadrupol *m*
    f quadripôle *m* électrostatique
    r электростатический квадруполь *m*

E270 *e* electrostatics
    d Elektrostatik *f*
    f électrostatique *f*
    r электростатика *f*

E271 *e* electrostriction
    d Elektrostriktion *f*
    f électrostriction *f*
    r электрострикция *f*

E272 *e* electroweak interaction
    d elektroschwache Wechselwirkung *f*
    f interaction *f* électrofaible
    r электрослабое взаимодействие *n*

E273 *e* electroweak interference
    d Interferenz *f* der schwachen und der
        elektromagnetischen
        Wechselwirkungen
    f interférence *f* des interactions
        électromagnétique et électrofaible
    r интерференция *f* слабого и
        электромагнитного взаимодействий

E274 *e* electroweak model
    d Modell *n* der elektroschwachen
        Wechselwirkung

f modèle *m* d'interaction électrofaible
r модель *f* электрослабого
взаимодействия

E275 e **element**
d Element *n*
f élément *m*
r элемент *m*

E276 e **elementary charge**
d Elementarladung *f*
f charge *f* élémentaire
r элементарный заряд *m*

E277 e **elementary excitation**
d elementare Anregung *f*
f excitation *f* élémentaire
r элементарное возбуждение *n*

E278 e **elementary length**
d Elementarlänge *f*
f longueur *f* élémentaire
r элементарная длина *f*;
фундаментальная длина *f*

E279 e **elementary particle physics**
d Elementarteilchenphysik *f*
f physique *f* des particules élémentaires
r физика *f* элементарных частиц

E280 e **elementary particles**
d Elementarteilchen *n pl*
f particules *f pl* élémentaires
r элементарные частицы *f pl*

E281 e **element formation**
d Elementenentstehung *f*,
Elementenaufbau *m*,
Elementensynthese *f*, Nukleogenese *f*
f formation *f* des éléments
r образование *n* элементов

E282 e **elevating force**
d Auftrieb *m*
f force *f* portante, portance *f*
r подъёмная сила *f*

E283 e **ellipsometry**
d Ellipsometer *n*
f ellipsomètre *m*
r эллипсометр *m*

E284 e **ellipsometry**
d Ellipsometrie *f*
f ellipsométrie *f*
r эллипсометрия *f*

E285 e **elliptical polarization**
d elliptische Polarisation *f*
f polarisation *f* elliptique
r эллиптическая поляризация *f*

E286 e **elongation**
d Dehnung *f*; Verlängerung *f*
f allongement *m*
r удлинение *n*

E287 e **emission**
d Emission *f*; Ausstrahlung *f*
f émission *f*
r **1.** эмиссия *f*, испускание *n*
2. излучение *n*

E288 e **emission electronics**
d Emissionselektronik *f*
f électronique *f* d'émission
r эмиссионная электроника *f*

E289 e **emission intensity**
d Emissionsintensität *f*
f intensité *f* d'émission
r интенсивность *f* излучения,
интенсивность *f* испускания

E290 e **emission line**
d Emissionslinie *f*
f raie *f* d'émission
r линия *f* испускания, эмиссионная
линия *f*

E291 e **emission measure**
d Emissionsmaß *n*
f mesure *f* d'émission
r мера *f* эмиссии

E292 e **emission microscope**
d Emissionsmikroskop *n*
f microscope *m* à effet de champ
r эмиссионный микроскоп *m*

E293 e **emission spectroscopy**
d Emissionsspektroskopie *f*
f spectroscopie *f* d'émission
r эмиссионная спектроскопия *f*

E294 e **emission spectrum**
d Emissionsspektrum *n*
f spectre *m* d'émission
r спектр *m* испускания, эмиссионный
спектр *m*

E295 e **emissive power**
d Emissionsvermögen *n*
f pouvoir *m* émissif
r излучательная способность *f*

E296 e **emissivity** *see* **emissive power**

E297 e **emittance**
d **1.** spezifische Ausstrahlung *f*,
Emissionsgrad *m* **2.** Emittanz *f*
f émittance *f*
r **1.** излучательность *f*, светимость *f*
2. эмиттанс *m (пучка)*

E298 e **emitted quantum**
d emittiertes Quant *n*
f quantum *m* émis
r испущенный квант *m*

E299 e **emitter**
d **1.** Emitter *m*, Emitterelektrode *f*
2. Strahler *m*
f émetteur *m*
r **1.** эмиттер *m* **2.** излучатель *m*

E300　e　emitter junction
　　　d　Emitterübergang *m*
　　　f　jonction *f* émettrice
　　　r　эмиттерный переход *m*

E301　e　empirical dependence
　　　d　empirische Abhängigkeit *f*
　　　f　dépendance *f* empirique
　　　r　эмпирическая зависимость *f*

E302　e　empirical model
　　　d　empirisches Modell *n*
　　　f　modèle *m* empirique
　　　r　эмпирическая модель *f*

E303　e　empty band
　　　d　unbesetztes Band *n*, unbesetztes
　　　　　Energieband *n*
　　　f　bande *f* vide
　　　r　свободная зона *f*, незаполненная
　　　　　зона *f*

E304　e　emulsifying agent
　　　d　Emulgator *m*
　　　f　agent *m* émulsifiant
　　　r　эмульгатор *m*

E305　e　emulsion
　　　d　Emulsion *f*
　　　f　émulsion *f*
　　　r　эмульсия *f*

E306　e　emulsion chamber
　　　d　Emulsionskammer *f*
　　　f　chambre *f* d'émulsion
　　　r　эмульсионная камера *f*

E307　e　enantiomer
　　　d　Enantiomer *n*, optisches Isomer *n*,
　　　　　Spiegelbildisomer *n*
　　　f　énantiomère *m*, isomère *m* optique
　　　r　энантиомер *m*, оптический
　　　　　изомер *m*

E308　e　enantiomorphism
　　　d　1. Enantiomorphie *f* 2. Chiralität *f*
　　　f　1. énantiomorphisme *m* 2. chiralité *f*
　　　r　1. энантиоморфизм *m* 2.
　　　　　киральность *f*

E309　e　energy
　　　d　Energie *f*
　　　f　énergie *f*
　　　r　энергия *f*

E310　e　energy accumulator
　　　d　Energiespeicher *m*
　　　f　accumulateur *m* d'énergie
　　　r　накопитель *m* энергии

E311　e　energy band
　　　d　Energieband *n*
　　　f　bande *f* énergétique
　　　r　энергетическая зона *f*

E312　e　energy channeling
　　　d　Energiekanalierung *f*
　　　f　canalisation *f* de l'énergie
　　　r　канализация *f* энергии

E313　e　energy conservation law
　　　d　Energieerhaltungssatz *m*
　　　f　loi *f* de la conservation de l'énergie
　　　r　закон *m* сохранения энергии

E314　e　energy conversion
　　　d　Energieumformung *f*
　　　f　conversion *f* d'énergie
　　　r　преобразование *n* энергии

E315　e　energy density
　　　d　Energiedichte *f*
　　　f　densité *f* d'énergie
　　　r　плотность *f* энергии

E316　e　energy dissipation
　　　d　Energiezerstreuung *f*,
　　　　　Energieverlust *m*
　　　f　dissipation *f* de l'énergie
　　　r　диссипация *f* энергии

E317　e　energy distribution
　　　d　Energieverteilung *f*
　　　f　distribution *f* d'énergie
　　　r　распределение *n* энергии

E318　e　energy exchange
　　　d　Energieaustausch *m*
　　　f　échange *m* d'énergie
　　　r　обмен *m* энергией

E319　e　energy flux
　　　d　Energiefluß *m*
　　　f　flux *m* d'énergie
　　　r　поток *m* энергии

E320　e　energy gap
　　　d　Energielücke *f*, verbotene Zone *f*
　　　f　lacune *f* énergétique
　　　r　запрещённая зона *f*, энергетическая
　　　　　щель *f*

E321　e　energy level diagram
　　　d　Energieniveauschema *n*,
　　　　　Termschema *n*
　　　f　diagramme *m* énergétique, diagramme
　　　　　m des niveaux d'énergie
　　　r　диаграмма *f* уровней энергии

E322　e　energy levels
　　　d　Energieniveaus *n pl*
　　　f　niveaux *m pl* énergétiques
　　　r　уровни *m pl* энергии,
　　　　　энергетические уровни *m pl*

E323　e　energy level width
　　　d　Niveaubreite *f*, Breite *f* des
　　　　　Energieniveaus
　　　f　largeur *f* du niveau d'énergie
　　　r　ширина *f* энергетического уровня

E324 *e* **energy loss**
      d Energieverlust *m*
      f pertes *f pl* d'énergie
      r потери *f pl* энергии

E325 *e* **energy measurement**
      d Energiemessung *f*
      f mesure *f* de l'énergie
      r измерение *n* энергии

E326 *e* **energy migration**
      d Energiewanderung *f*
      f migration *f* d'énergie
      r миграция *f* энергии

E327 *e* **energy momentum tensor**
      d Impuls-Energie-Tensor *m*, Energie-Impuls-Tensor *m*
      f tenseur *m* d'impulsion-énergie
      r тензор *m* энергии-импульса

E328 *e* **energy quantization**
      d Energiequantelung *f*, Energiequantisierung *f*
      f quantification *f* de l'énergie
      r квантование *n* энергии

E329 *e* **energy range**
      d Energieintervall *n*, Energiebereich *m*
      f intervalle *m* d'énergie
      r интервал *m* энергий, энергетический интервал *m*, диапазон *m* энергий

E330 *e* **energy region**
      d Energiebereich *m*, Energieintervall *n*
      f région *f* d'énergie
      r область *f* энергий, диапазон *m* энергий

E331 *e* **energy release**
      d Energiefreisetzung *f*, Energieabgabe *f*
      f libération *f* d'énergie
      r освобождение *n* энергии, высвобождение *n* энергии, выделение *n* энергии

E332 *e* **energy source**
      d Energiequelle *f*
      f source *f* d'énergie
      r источник *m* энергии

E333 *e* **energy spectrum**
      d Energiespektrum *n*
      f spectre *m* d'énergie
      r энергетический спектр *m*

E334 *e* **energy states**
      d Energiezustände *m pl*
      f états *m pl* d'énergie
      r энергетические состояния *n pl*

E335 *e* **energy transfer**
      d Energietransport *m*
      f transfert *m* d'énergie
      r перенос *m* энергии

E336 *e* **engine**
      d Motor *m*; Maschine *f*
      f moteur *m*; engin *m*
      r двигатель *m*; машина *f*

E337 *e* **enlarging**
      d Vergrößerung *f*
      f agrandissement *m*
      r увеличение *n (фотографического изображения)*

E338 *e* **enriched isotope**
      d angereichertes Isotop *n*
      f isotope *m* enrichi
      r обогащённый изотоп *m*

E339 *e* **enriched-layer contact**
      d Anreicherungsschichtkontakt *m*
      f contact *m* à couche enrichie
      r контакт *m* с обогащённым слоем

E340 *e* **enriched material**
      d angereichertes Material *n*
      f matériau *m* enrichi
      r обогащённый материал *m*

E341 *e* **enrichment**
      d Anreicherung *f*
      f enrichissement *m*
      r обогащение *n (изотопов)*

E342 *e* **ensemble**
      d Ensemble *n*
      f ensemble *m*
      r ансамбль *m*

E343 *e* **ensemble average**
      d Scharmittel *n*, Scharmittelwert *m*
      f moyenne *f* par ensemble
      r среднее *n* по ансамблю

E344 *e* **ensemble averaging**
      d Scharmittelwertbildung *f*
      f formation *f* de moyennes d'ensemble
      r усреднение *n* по ансамблю

E345 *e* **enthalpy**
      d Enthalpie *f*
      f enthalpie *f*
      r энтальпия *f*

E346 *e* **entrance pupil**
      d Eintrittspupille *f*, Eintrittsöffnung *f*
      f pupille *f* d'entrée
      r входной зрачок *m (оптической системы)*

E347 *e* **entropy**
      d Entropie *f*
      f entropie *f*
      r энтропия *f*

E348 *e* **entropy increase law**
      d Satz *m* über die Entropiezunahme, Satz *m* von der Vermehrung der Entropie
      f loi *f* d'augmentation d'entropie
      r закон *m* возрастания энтропии

E349   *e*   **entropy of the Universe**
     d   Universumsentropie *f*, Entropie *f* des Weltalls
     f   entropie *f* de l'Univers
     r   энтропия *f* Вселенной

E350   *e*   **envelope**
     d   Einhüllende *f*, Enveloppe *f*, Hüllkurve *f*, Umhüllende *f*
     f   enveloppe *f*
     r   огибающая *f*

E351   *e*   **envelope detection**
     d   Hüllkurvengleichrichtung *f*
     f   détection *f* de l'enveloppe
     r   детектирование *n* огибающей

E352   *e*   **environmental pollution**
     d   Umweltverschmutzung *f*
     f   pollution *f* d'environnement, pollution *f* du milieu ambiant
     r   загрязнение *n* окружающей среды

E353   *e*   **environmental protection**
     d   Umweltschutz *m*
     f   protection *f* d'environnement, protection *f* du milieu ambiant
     r   охрана *f* окружающей среды

E354   *e*   **environmental test, environmental testing**
     d   Klimaprüfung *f*
     f   essai *m* climatique
     r   климатические испытания *n pl*

E355   *e*   **eötvös, E**
     d   Eötvös *n*, Eötvös-Einheit *f*
     f   eötvös *m*
     r   этвеш *m*, Э

E356   *e*   **Eötvös torsion balance**
     d   Eötvös-Drehwaage *f*, Eötvössche Drehwaage *f*
     f   balance *f* d'Eötvös
     r   гравитационный вариометр *m* Этвеша

E357   *e*   **ephemeris**
     d   Ephemeride *f*
     f   éphéméride *f*
     r   эфемерида *f*

E358   *e*   **ephemeris time**
     d   Ephemeridenzeit *f*
     f   temps *m* des éphémérides
     r   эфемеридное время *n*

E359   *e*   **epicenter**
     d   Epizentrum *n*
     f   épicentre *m*
     r   эпицентр *m (землетрясения)*

E360   *e*   **epidiascope**
     d   Epidiaskop *n*
     f   épidiascope *m*
     r   эпидиаскоп *m*

E361   *e*   **epitaxial film**
     d   Epitaxialfilm *m*, Epitaxieschicht *f*
     f   film *m* épitaxial
     r   эпитаксиальный слой *m*

E362   *e*   **epitaxial isolation**
     d   Epitaxialisolation *f*, Epitaxieisolation *f*
     f   isolement *m* épitaxial
     r   эпитаксиальная изоляция *f*

E363   *e*   **epitaxial laser**
     d   Epitaxiallaser *m*, Epitaxielaser *m*
     f   laser *m* épitaxial
     r   эпитаксиальный лазер *m*

E364   *e*   **epitaxial technique**
     d   Epitaxialverfahren *n*, Epitaxieverfahren *n*
     f   technique *f* épitaxiale
     r   эпитаксиальный метод *m (выращивания кристаллов)*

E365   *e*   **epitaxy**
     d   Epitaxie *f*
     f   épitaxie *f*
     r   эпитаксия *f*

E366   *e*   **equation of state**
     d   Zustandsgleichung *f*
     f   équation *f* d'état
     r   уравнение *n* состояния

E367   *e*   **equations of telegraphy**
     d   Telegraphengleichungen *f pl*
     f   équations *f pl* des télégraphistes
     r   телеграфные уравнения *n pl*

E368   *e*   **equator**
     d   Äquator *m*
     f   équateur *m*
     r   экватор *m*

E369   *e*   **equatorial ionosphere**
     d   Äquatorialionosphäre *f*
     f   ionosphère *f* équatoriale
     r   экваториальная ионосфера *f*

E370   *e*   **equatorial mounting**
     d   parallaktische Fernrohrmontierung *f*, parallaktische Montierung *f*, äquatoriale Fernrohrmontierung *f*, äquatoriale Montierung *f*
     f   monture *f* équatoriale
     r   экваториальная монтировка *f*, параллактическая монтировка *f (телескопа)*

E371   *e*   **equilibrium**
     d   Gleichgewicht *n*
     f   équilibre *m*
     r   равновесие *n*

E372   *e*   **equilibrium carriers**
     d   Gleichgewichtsträger *m pl*, Gleichgewichtsladungsträger *m pl*

f porteurs *m pl* équilibrés
r равновесные носители *m pl*,
равновесные носители *m pl* заряда

E373 *e* equilibrium concentration
d Gleichgewichtsdichte *f*,
Gleichgewichtskonzentration *f*
f concentration *f* d'équilibre
r равновесная концентрация *f*

E374 *e* equilibrium configuration
d Gleichgewichtskonfiguration *f*
f configuration *f* d'équilibre
r равновесная конфигурация *f*
(*молекул*)

E375 *e* equilibrium curve
d Gleichgewichtskurve *f*
f courbe *f* d'équilibre
r кривая *f* равновесия

E376 *e* equilibrium diagram
d Phasendiagramm *n*,
Zustandsdiagramm *n*
f diagramme *m* d'équilibre, diagramme
m de phase, diagramme *m* d'état
r диаграмма *f* равновесия, фазовая
диаграмма *f*

E377 *e* equilibrium distribution
d Gleichgewichtsverteilung *f*
f distribution *f* équilibrée
r равновесное распределение *n*

E378 *e* equilibrium ionization
d Gleichgewichtsionisation *f*
f ionisation *f* d'équilibre
r равновесная ионизация *f*

E379 *e* equilibrium orbit
d Gleichgewichtsbahn *f*
f orbite *f* d'équilibre
r равновесная орбита *f*

E380 *e* equilibrium phase
d Gleichgewichtsphase *f*
f phase *f* d'équilibre
r равновесная фаза *f*

E381 *e* equilibrium plasma
d Gleichgewichtsplasma *n*
f plasma *m* d'équilibre
r равновесная плазма *f*

E382 *e* equilibrium population
d Gleichgewichtsbesetzung *f*
f population *f* d'équilibre
r равновесная населённость *f*

E383 *e* equilibrium process
d Gleichgewichtsprozeß *m*
f processus *m* d'équilibre
r равновесный процесс *m*

E384 *e* equilibrium radiation
d schwarze Strahlung *f*,
Hohlraumstrahlung *f*,
Schwarzkörperstrahlung *f*

f radiation *f* du corps noir,
rayonnement *m* d'équilibre
r равновесное излучение *n*,
излучение *n* чёрного тела

E385 *e* equilibrium state
d Gleichgewichtszustand *m*
f état *m* d'équilibre
r равновесное состояние *n*, состояние
n равновесия

E386 *e* equinox
d Tagundnachtgleiche *f*, Tag-und-
Nacht-Gleiche *f*
f équinoxe *m*
r равноденствие *n*

E387 *e* equipartition law
d Gleichverteilungssatz *m*,
Energiegleichverteilungssatz *m*
f loi *f* d'équipartition
r закон *m* равнораспределения
(*энергии по степеням свободы*)

E388 *e* equipartition of energy
d Energiegleichverteilung *f*,
Gleichverteilung *f* der Energie
f équipartition *f* de l'énergie,
équipartition *f*
r равнораспределение *n* энергии

E389 *e* equipment
d Ausrüstung *f*; Ausstattung *f*;
Apparatur *f*
f équipement *m*
r оборудование *n*; аппаратура *f*

E390 *e* equipotential *see* equipotential
surface

E391 *e* equipotential contour
d Äquipotentialkreis *m*
f contour *m* équipotentiel
r эквипотенциальный контур *m*

E392 *e* equipotential curve
d Äquipotentialkurve *f*
f courbe *f* équipotentielle
r эквипотенциальная кривая *f*

E393 *e* equipotential surface
d Äquipotentialfläche *f*
f surface *f* équipotentielle
r эквипотенциальная поверхность *f*,
эквипотенциаль *f*

E394 *e* equivalence (*e.g. of heat and
mechanical energy, of mass and
energy*)
d Äquivalenz *f*
f équivalence *f*
r эквивалентность *f* (*напр. тепловой
и механической энергии, массы и
энергии*)

E395 *e* equivalence principle

	d	Äquivalenzprinzip *n*
	f	principe *m* d'équivalence
	r	принцип *m* эквивалентности

E396
e equivalent
d Äquivalent *n*
f équivalent *m*
r эквивалент *m*

E397
e equivalent circuit
d Ersatzschaltbild *n*
f circuit *m* équivalent
r эквивалентная схема *f*

E398
e equivalent dose
d äquivalente Dosis *f*
f dose *f* équivalente
r эквивалентная доза *f*

E399
e erbium, Er
d Erbium *n*
f erbium *m*
r эрбий *m*

E400
e erecting prism
d Umkehrprisma *n*
f prisme *m* de retournement
r оборачивающая призма *f*

E401
e erecting system
d Umkehrsystem *n*
f système *m* de retournement
r оборачивающая система *f*

E402
e E-region
d E-Gebiet *n* (*Ionosphäre*)
f région *f* E (*d'ionosphère*)
r область *f* E (*ионосферы*)

E403
e erg
d Erg *n*
f erg *m*
r эрг *m*

E404
e ergodic hypothesis
d Ergodenhypothese *f*
f hypothèse *f* ergodique
r эргодическая гипотеза *f*

E405
e ergodicity
d Ergodizität *f*
f ergodicité *f*
r эргодичность *f*

E406
e error
d Fehler *m*; Abweichung *f*
f erreur *f*
r ошибка *f*, погрешность *f*

E407
e error curve
d Fehlerkurve *f*
f courbe *f* d'erreurs
r кривая *f* ошибок

E408
e error function
d Fehlerfunktion *f*
f fonction *f* des erreurs
r функция *f* ошибок

E409
e error integral
d Fehlerintegral *n*
f intégrale *f* des erreurs
r интеграл *m* вероятности ошибок

E410
e escape
d 1. Austritt *m* 2. Runaway-Effekt *m* (*der Elektronen*)
f 1. fuite *f* 2. effet *m* des électrons découplés
r 1. вылет *m* (*частицы*) 2. убегание *n* (*электронов*)

E411
e escape direction
d Austrittsrichtung *f*
f direction *f* de la fuite
r направление *n* вылета (*частицы*)

E412
e escape velocity
d zweite kosmische Geschwindigkeit *f*, Entweichungsgeschwindigkeit *f*
f vitesse *f* de libération
r вторая космическая скорость *f*

E413
e escaping electrons
d Runaway-Elektronen *n pl*
f électrons *m pl* découplés
r убегающие электроны *m pl*

E414
e etalon
d Etalon *m*, Eichmaß *n*, Normal *n*, Normalmaß *n*
f étalon *m*
r эталон *m*

E415
e etch groove
d Ätzgraben *m*
f rainure *f* de décapage
r канавка *f* травления

E416
e etching
d Ätzen *n*, Ätzung *f*
f décapage *m*
r травление *n*

E417
e etch pits
d Ätzgruben *f pl*
f fosses *f pl* de décapage
r ямки *f pl* травления

E418
e etch pitting technique
d Ätzgrubenverfahren *n*
f technique *f* de fosses de décapage
r метод *m* ямок травления

E419
e ether
d Äther *m*, Weltäther *m*
f éther *m*
r эфир *m*

E420
e ether wind
d Ätherwind *m*
f vent *m* d'éther
r эфирный ветер *m*

E421   *e* **Ettingshausen effect**
     d Ettingshausen-Effekt *m*
     f effet *m* d'Ettingshausen
     r эффект *m* Эттингсгаузена

E422   *e* **Euclidean geometry**
     d euklidische Geometrie *f*
     f géométrie *f* euclidienne
     r геометрия *f* Евклида

E423   *e* **Euclidean space**
     d euklidischer Raum *m*
     f espace *m* euclidien
     r евклидово пространство *n*

E424   *e* **Euler equations**
     d Eulersche Gleichungen *f pl*
     f équations *f pl* d'Euler
     r уравнения *n pl* Эйлера

E425   *e* **European Organization for Nuclear Research**
     d Europäische Organisation *f* für Kernforschung, CERN
     f Conseil *m* Européen pour Recherche Nucléaire, CERN
     r Европейская организация *f* ядерных исследований, ЦЕРН

E426   *e* **europium, Eu**
     d Europium *n*
     f europium *m*
     r европий *m*

E427   *e* **eutectic**
     d Eutektik *f*
     f eutectique *f*
     r эвтектика *f*

E428   *e* **evacuation**
     d Evakuierung *f*, Evakuieren *n*, Abpumpen *n*
     f évacuation *f*
     r откачка *f*

E429   *e* **evacuation chamber**
     d Evakuierungskammer *f*
     f chambre *f* d'évacuation
     r камера *f* откачки *(в криостате)*

E430   *e* **evaporation**
     d Verdampfung *f*
     f évaporation *f*, vaporisation *f*
     r испарение *n*; парообразование *n*

E431   *e* **evaporation chamber**
     d Verdampfungskammer *f*
     f chambre *f* d'évaporation
     r камера *f* испарения

E432   *e* **«evaporation» of black holes**
     d «Verdampfung» *f* von schwarzen Löchern
     f «évaporation» *f* des trous noirs
     r «испарение» *n* чёрных дыр

E433   *e* **evaporation rate**
     d Verdampfungsgeschwindigkeit *f*, Verdampfungsrate *f*
     f vitesse *f* de vaporisation, vitesse *f* d'évaporation
     r интенсивность *f* испарения

E434   *e* **evaporimeter**
     d Evaporimeter *n*
     f évaporimètre *m*
     r эвапориметр *m*

E435   *e* **even-even nucleus**
     d gg-Kern *m*, Gerade-gerade-Kern *m*, doppelt gerader Kern *m*
     f noyau *m* pair-pair
     r чётно-чётное ядро *n*

E436   *e* **even-odd nucleus**
     d gu-Kern *m*, Gerade-ungerade-Kern *m*
     f noyau *m* pair-impair
     r чётно-нечётное ядро *n*

E437   *e* **event**
     d Ereignis *n*
     f événement *m*
     r событие *n*

E438   *e* **event horizon**
     d Ereignishorizont *m*
     f horizon *m* d'événements
     r горизонт *m* событий

E439   *e* **evolution**
     d Entwicklung *f*
     f évolution *f*
     r эволюция *f*

E440   *e* **evolutionary model**
     d Entwicklungsmodell *n*
     f modèle *m* évolutif
     r эволюционная модель *f*

E441   *e* **excess concentration**
     d Konzentrationsüberschuß *m*, Überschußkonzentration *f*
     f concentration *f* excessive
     r избыточная концентрация *f*

E442   *e* **excess of energy**
     d Energieüberschuß *m*
     f excès *m* d'énergie
     r избыток *m* энергии

E443   *e* **excess population**
     d Überschußbesetzung *f*
     f population *f* d'excès
     r избыточная населённость *f* *(уровней энергии)*

E444   *e* **exchange**
     d Austausch *m*; Wechsel *m*
     f échange *m*
     r обмен *m*

E445   *e* **exchange constant**
     d Austauschkonstante *f*
     f constante *f* d'échange
     r обменная константа *f*

E446	*e*	exchange degeneracy
	d	Austauschentartung *f*
	f	dégénérence *f* par échange
	r	обменное вырождение *n*

E447	*e*	exchange forces
	d	Austauschkräfte *pl*
	f	forces *pl* d'échange
	r	обменные силы *pl*

E448	*e*	exchange integral
	d	Austauschintegral *n*
	f	intégrale *f* d'échange
	r	обменный интеграл *m*

E449	*e*	exchange interaction
	d	Austauschwechselwirkung *f*
	f	interaction *f* d'échange
	r	обменное взаимодействие *n*

E450	*e*	exchange mode
	d	Austauschmode *f*
	f	mode *m* d'échange
	r	обменная мода *f*

E451	*e*	exchange model
	d	Austauschmodell *n*
	f	modèle *m* d'échange
	r	обменная модель *f*

E452	*e*	excimer laser
	d	Excimerlaser *m*
	f	laser *m* à excimère
	r	эксимерный лазер *m*

E453	*e*	excitation
	d	Anregung *f*; Erregung *f*
	f	excitation *f*
	r	возбуждение *n*

E454	*e*	excitation channel
	d	Anregungskanal *m*
	f	canal *m* d'excitation
	r	канал *m* возбуждения

E455	*e*	excitation cross-section
	d	Anregungsquerschnitt *m*, Wirkungsquerschnitt *m* für Anregung
	f	section *f* d'excitation
	r	сечение *n* возбуждения

E456	*e*	excitation curve
	d	Anregungskurve *f*
	f	courbe *f* d'excitation
	r	кривая *f* возбуждения

E457	*e*	excitation energy
	d	Anregungsenergie *f*
	f	énergie *f* d'excitation
	r	энергия *f* возбуждения

E458	*e*	excitation kinetics
	d	Anregungskinetik *f*
	f	cinétique *f* d'excitation
	r	кинетика *f* возбуждения

E459	*e*	excitation method
	d	Anregungsmethode *f*
	f	méthode *f* d'excitation
	r	метод *m* возбуждения

E460	*e*	excitation pulse
	d	Anregungsimpuls *m*
	f	impulsion *f* d'excitation
	r	возбуждающий импульс *m*

E461	*e*	excitation source
	d	Anregungsquelle *f*
	f	source *f* d'excitation
	r	источник *m* возбуждения

E462	*e*	excited atom
	d	angeregtes Atom *n*
	f	atome *m* excité
	r	возбуждённый атом *m*

E463	*e*	excited ion
	d	angeregtes Ion *n*
	f	ion *m* excité
	r	возбуждённый ион *m*

E464	*e*	excited molecule
	d	angeregtes Molekül *n*
	f	molécule *f* excitée
	r	возбуждённая молекула *f*

E465	*e*	excited state
	d	angeregter Zustand *m*
	f	état *m* excité
	r	возбуждённое состояние *n*

E466	*e*	exciting pulse *see* excitation pulse

E467	*e*	exciton
	d	Exciton *n*, Exziton *n*
	f	exciton *m*
	r	экситон *m*

E468	*e*	exciton condensation
	d	Excitonenkondensation *f*
	f	condensation *f* d'excitons
	r	конденсация *f* экситонов

E469	*e*	exciton drop
	d	Excitontropfen *m*
	f	goutte *f* excitoniqie
	r	экситонная капля *f*

E470	*e*	excitonic molecule
	d	Excitonmolekül *n*
	f	molécule *f* excitonique
	r	экситонная молекула *f*

E471	*e*	exciton liquid
	d	Excitonflüssigkeit *f*
	f	liquide *m* excitonique
	r	экситонная жидкость *f*

E472	*e*	exciton migration
	d	Excitonenwanderung *f*
	f	migration *f* des excitons
	r	миграция *f* экситонов

E473   *e*   exciton-phonon interaction
       d   Exciton-Phonon-Wechselwirkung *f*
       f   interaction *f* exciton-phonon
       r   экситон-фононное
          взаимодействие *n*

E474   *e*   exciton spectroscopy
       d   Excitonspektroskopie *f*
       f   spectroscopie *f* excitonique
       r   экситонная спектроскопия *f*

E475   *e*   exclusion principle
       d   Pauli-Prinzip *n*, Pauli-Verbot *n*
       f   principe *m* d'exclusion de Pauli
       r   принцип *m* запрета, принцип *m*
          Паули

E476   *e*   exhaustion of hydrogen
       d   Wasserstoffbrennen *n*, Ausbrennen *n*
          des Wasserstoffs, Verbrennen *n* des
          Wasserstoffs
       f   épuisement *m* de l'hydrogène
       r   исчерпание *n* водорода *(в звезде)*

E477   *e*   existence proof
       d   Existenzbeweis *m*
       f   preuve *f* d'existence
       r   доказательство *n* существования

E478   *e*   exit mirror
       d   Austrittsspiegel *m*
       f   miroir *m* de sortie
       r   выходное зеркало *n (лазера)*

E479   *e*   exit pupil
       d   Austrittsöffnung *f*, Austrittspupille *f*
       f   pupille *f* de sortie
       r   выходной зрачок *m (оптической
          системы)*

E480   *e*   exoelectron
       d   Exoelektron *n*
       f   exo-électron *m*
       r   экзоэлектрон *m*

E481   *e*   exoelectron emission
       d   Exoelektronenemission *f*
       f   émission *f* exo-électronique
       r   экзоэлектронная эмиссия *f*

E482   *e*   exosphere
       d   Exosphäre *f*, äußere Atmosphäre *f*
       f   exosphère *f*
       r   экзосфера *f*

E483   *e*   exothermic reaction
       d   exotherme Reaktion *f*
       f   réaction *f* exothermique
       r   экзотермическая реакция *f*

E484   *e*   expander *see* expansion machine

E485   *e*   expanding model
       d   Modell *n* des expandierenden Weltalls
       f   modèle *m* d'expansion, modèle *m*
          d'Univers expansif
       r   модель *f* расширяющейся
          Вселенной

E486   *e*   expanding Universe
       d   expandierendes Weltall *n*
       f   Univers *m* expansif, Univers *m* en
          expansion
       r   расширяющаяся Вселенная *f*

E487   *e*   expansion
       d   1. Ausdehnung *f*, Expansion *f* 2.
          Entwicklung *f*, Reihenentwicklung *f*
       f   1. dilatation *f* 2. développement *m* en
          série
       r   1. расширение *n* 2. разложение *n*,
          разложение *n* в ряд

E488   *e*   expansion chamber
       d   Nebelkammer *f*,
          Expansionsnebelkammer *f*
       f   chambre *f* d'expansion, chambre *f* de
          Wilson
       r   камера *f* Вильсона

E489   *e*   expansion coefficient
       d   Ausdehnungskoeffizient *m*,
          Ausdehnungszahl *f*
       f   coefficient *m* d'expansion, coefficient
          m de dilatation
       r   коэффициент *m* расширения

E490   *e*   expansion curve
       d   Ausdehnungskurve *f*
       f   courbe *f* de dilatation
       r   кривая *f* расширения

E491   *e*   expansion machine
       d   Expansionsmaschine *f*, Detander *m*
       f   machine *f* à expansion
       r   детандер *m*

E492   *e*   expansion wave
       d   Expansionswelle *f*
       f   onde *f* d'expansion
       r   волна *f* разрежения

E493   *e*   experiment
       d   Experiment *n*, Versuch *m*
       f   expérience *f*
       r   эксперимент *m*

E494   *e*   experimental channel
       d   Experimentierkanal *m*,
          Versuchskanal *m*
       f   canal *m* expérimental
       r   экспериментальный канал *m*

E495   *e*   experimental curve
       d   Versuchskurve *f*
       f   courbe *f* expérimentale
       r   экспериментальная кривая *f*

E496   *e*   experimental data
       d   Versuchsdaten *pl*
       f   données *pl* expérimentales
       r   экспериментальные данные *pl*

E497   *e*   experimental dependence
       d   experimentelle Abhängigkeit *f*

	f	dépendance *f* expérimentale
	r	экспериментальная зависимость *f*
E498	*e*	**experimental hole** *see* experimental channel
E499	*e*	**experimental investigation**
	d	experimentelle Untersuchung *f*, experimentelle Erforschung *f*
	f	étude *f* expérimentale
	r	экспериментальное исследование *n*
E500	*e*	**experimental physics**
	d	Experimentalphysik *f*
	f	physique *f* expérimentale
	r	экспериментальная физика *f*
E501	*e*	**explicit dependence**
	d	explizite Abhängigkeit *f*
	f	dépendance *f* explicite
	r	явная зависимость *f*
E502	*e*	**exploding wires**
	d	explodierende Drähte *m pl*
	f	cordes *f pl* explosives
	r	взрывающиеся проволочки *f pl*
E503	*e*	**explosion**
	d	Explosion *f*
	f	explosion *f*
	r	взрыв *m*
E504	*e*	**explosive boiling**
	d	Explosionssieden *n*
	f	bouillonnement *m* explosif
	r	взрывное кипение *n*
E505	*e*	**explosive electron emission**
	d	Explosionselektronenemission *f*
	f	émission *f* électronique explosive
	r	взрывная электронная эмиссия *f*
E506	*e*	**explosive evaporation**
	d	Explosionsverdampfung *f*
	f	évaporation *f* explosive
	r	взрывное испарение *n*
E507	*e*	**explosive instability**
	d	Explosionsinstabilität *f*
	f	instabilité *f* explosive
	r	взрывная неустойчивость *f*
E508	*e*	**explosive nucleosynthesis**
	d	Explosionsnukleosynthese *f*
	f	synthèse *f* nucléaire explosive
	r	взрывной нуклеосинтез *m*
E509	*e*	**explosive wave**
	d	Explosionswelle *f*
	f	onde *f* explosive
	r	взрывная волна *f*
E510	*e*	**exponential curve**
	d	Exponentialkurve *f*
	f	courbe *f* exponentielle
	r	экспоненциальная кривая *f*

E511	*e*	**exponential damping** *see* exponential decay
E512	*e*	**exponential decay**
	d	exponentieller Abfall *m*
	f	décroissance *f* exponentielle, diminution *f* exponentielle
	r	экспоненциальное затухание *n*
E513	*e*	**exponential dependence**
	d	exponentielle Abhängigkeit *f*
	f	dépendance *f* exponentielle
	r	экспоненциальная зависимость *f*
E514	*e*	**exponential function**
	d	Exponentialfunktion *f*
	f	fonction *f* exponentielle
	r	экспоненциальная функция *f*, экспонента *f*
E515	*e*	**exponential law**
	d	Exponentialgesetz *n*
	f	loi *f* exponentielle
	r	экспоненциальный закон *m*
E516	*e*	**exposure**
	d	Exponierung *f*; Exposition *f*; Bestrahlung *f*; Belichtung *f*
	f	exposition *f*
	r	экспозиция *f*; облучение *n*
E517	*e*	**exposure dose**
	d	Strahlenbelastung *f*, Exposition *f*
	f	dose *f* d'irradiation
	r	доза *f* облучения, экспозиционная доза *f*
E518	*e*	**extended source**
	d	ausgedehnte Quelle *f*
	f	source *f* étendue
	r	протяжённый источник *m*
E519	*e*	**extension**
	d	1. Ausdehnung *f*; Dehnung *f* 2. Erweiterung *f* 3. Verallgemeinerung *f* 4. Fortsetzung *f*
	f	1. extension *f* 2. centralisation *f* 3. suite *f*
	r	1. расширение *n*; растяжение *n*; удлинение *n* 2. обобщение *n* 3. продолжение *n*
E520	*e*	**extensive parameters, extensive variables**
	d	extensive Zustandsgrößen *f pl*, extensive Größen *f pl*
	f	paramètres *m pl* extensifs
	r	экстенсивные параметры *m pl*
E521	*e*	**external forces**
	d	äußere Kräfte *f pl*
	f	forces *f pl* externes
	r	внешние силы *f pl*
E522	*e*	**external friction**
	d	äußere Reibung *f*

f frottement *m* externe
r внешнее трение *n*

E523 *e* **external photoelectric effect**
d äußerer photoelektrischer Effekt *m*,
äußerer lichtelektrischer Effekt *m*,
äußerer Photoeffekt *m*,
Photoemissionseffekt *m*
f effet *m* photo-électrique externe
r внешний фотоэффект *m*

E524 *e* **external triggering**
d Außentriggerung *f*
f déclenchement *m* extérieur
r внешний запуск *m*

E525 *e* **extinction**
d 1. Extinktion *f*
(Strahlungsschwächung, insbesondere
Lichtschwächung durch Absorption
und Streuung in einem Medium; Maß
einer solchen Schwächung) 2.
Löschung *f*, Auslöschung *f*
f extinction *f*
r экстинкция *f*

E526 *e* **extraction**
d 1. Extraktion *f*, Herausziehen *n*,
Herauslösen *n* 2. Herausführung *f*
f extraction *f*
r 1. экстракция *f*; извлечение *n* 2.
вывод *m (напр. пучка из*
ускорителя)

E527 *e* **extraction channel**
d Extraktionskanal *m*, Ausführungskanal
m, Ausschleusungskanal *m*
f canal *m* d'extraction
r канал *m* вывода *(пучка из*
ускорителя)

E528 *e* **extragalactic radiation**
d extragalaktische Strahlung *f*
f radiation *f* extragalactique
r внегалактическое излучение *n*

E529 *e* **extragalactic source**
d extragalaktische Quelle *f*
f source *f* extragalactique
r внегалактический источник *m*

E530 *e* **extraordinary ray**
d außerordentlicher Strahl *m*
f rayon *m* extraordinaire
r необыкновенный луч *m*

E531 *e* **extraordinary wave**
d außerordentliche Welle *f*
f onde *f* extraordinaire
r необыкновенная волна *f*

E532 *e* **extrapolation**
d Extrapolation *f*
f extrapolation *f*
r экстраполяция *f*

E533 *e* **extraterrestrial astronomy**
d extraterrestrische Astronomie *f*
f astronomie *f* extraterrestre
r внеатмосферная астрономия *f*

E534 *e* **extraterrestrial civilizations**
d extraterrestrische Zivilisationen *f pl*
f civilisations *f pl* extraterrestres
r внеземные цивилизации *f pl*

E535 *e* **extraterrestrial radiation**
d extraterrestrische Strahlung *f*
f rayonnement *m* extraterrestre
r внеземное излучение *n*

E536 *e* **extreme value**
d Extremwert *m*, Extremum *n*
f valeur *f* extrême
r экстремальное значение *n*

E537 *e* **extrinsic semiconductor**
d Störstellenhalbleiter *m*
f semi-conducteur *m* extrinsèque
r примесный полупроводник *m*

E538 *e* **extrusion**
d Extrusion *f*; Strangpressen *n*
f extrusion *f*
r экструзия *f*

E539 *e* **eye**
d Auge *n*
f œil *m*
r глаз *m*

E540 *e* **eye optics**
d Augenoptik *f*
f optique *f* de l'œil
r оптика *f* глаза

E541 *e* **eyepiece**
d Okular *n*
f oculaire *m*
r окуляр *m*

E542 *e* **eye's aberrations**
d Augenabbildungsfehler *m pl*,
Aberrationen *f pl* des Auges
f aberrations *f pl* de l'œil
r аберрации *f pl* глаза

F

F1 *e* **Fabry-Perot etalon**
d Fabry-Perot-Etalon *m*
f étalon *m* de Fabry-Perot
r эталон *m* Фабри - Перо

F2 *e* **Fabry-Perot interferometer**
d Fabry-Perot-Interferometer *n*
f interféromètre *m* de Fabry-Perot

	r	интерферометр *m* Фабри — Перо
F3	e	face-centered cube
	d	flächenzentrierter Würfel *m*
	f	cube *m* à faces centrées
	r	гранецентрированный куб *m*
F4	e	face-centered cubic crystal
	d	kubisch-flächenzentrierter Kristall *m*
	f	cristal *m* cubique à faces centrées
	r	гранецентрированный кубический кристалл *m*
F5	e	face-centered lattice
	d	flächenzentriertes Gitter *n*
	f	réseau *m* à faces centrées
	r	гранецентрированная решётка *f*
F6	e	faceted crystal
	d	Facettenkristall *m*
	f	cristal *m* à facettes
	r	огранённый кристалл *m*
F7	e	faceting
	d	Facettieren *n*
	f	formation *f* de facettes
	r	огранка *f* (*кристалла*)
F8	e	factor
	d	Koeffizient *m*; Beiwert *m*; Faktor *m*
	f	facteur *m*
	r	множитель *m*; фактор *m*; коэффициент *m*
F9	e	factorial
	d	Fakultät *f*
	f	factorielle *f*
	r	факториал *m*
F10	e	factorization method
	d	Faktorisierungsmethode *f*
	f	méthode *f* de factorisation
	r	метод *m* факторизации
F11	e	fading
	d	Schwund *m*, Fading *n*
	f	évanouissement *m*, fading *m*
	r	замирание *n* (*сигнала*)
F12	e	Fahrenheit scale *see* Fahrenheit temperature scale
F13	e	Fahrenheit temperature scale
	d	Fahrenheit-Skala *f*
	f	échelle *f* de Fahrenheit
	r	температурная шкала *f* Фаренгейта, шкала *f* Фаренгейта
F14	e	failure
	d	Versagen *n*; Ausfall *m*
	f	défaillance *f*
	r	отказ *m* (*аппаратуры*)
F15	e	fall
	d	Fall *m*
	f	chute *f*
	r	падение *n* (*тел, капель и т. п.*)

F16	e	falling characteristic
	d	fallende Kennlinie *f*
	f	caractéristique *f* décroissante
	r	падающая характеристика *f*
F17	e	farad, F
	d	Farad *n*
	f	farad *m*
	r	фарада *f*, Ф
F18	e	faraday
	d	Faraday *n*, Faraday-Konstante *f*, Faraday-Zahl *f*
	f	faraday *m*
	r	фарадей *m* (*единица заряда*)
F19	e	Faraday cage
	d	Faraday-Käfig *m*, Faradayscher Käfig *m*
	f	cage *f* de Faraday
	r	клетка *f* Фарадея
F20	e	Faraday dark spaced
	d	Faradayscher Dunkelraum *m*, zweiter Katodendunkelraum *m*
	f	espace *m* sombre de Faraday
	r	фарадеево тёмное пространство *n*
F21	e	Faraday effect
	d	Faraday-Effekt *m*, Magnetorotation *f*
	f	effet *m* de Faraday
	r	эффект *m* Фарадея, фарадеевское вращение *n* (*плоскости поляризации*)
F22	e	Faraday induction law *see* Faraday law of induction
F23	e	Faraday law of induction
	d	Induktionsgesetz *n*, Induktionsgesetz *n* von Faraday, Faradaysches Induktionsgesetz *n*
	f	loi *f* d'induction de Faraday
	r	закон *m* индукции Фарадея
F24	e	Faraday rotation *see* Faraday effect
F25	e	far-field zone
	d	Fernfeldzone *f*
	f	champ *m* éloigné
	r	дальняя зона *f*
F26	e	far-infrared radiation
	d	ferne Infrarotstrahlung *f*
	f	rayonnement *m* infrarouge lointain
	r	далёкое инфракрасное излучение *n*
F27	e	far-infrared region
	d	fernes Infrarot *n*
	f	région *f* infrarouge lointaine
	r	далёкая инфракрасная область *f* (*спектра*)
F28	e	far IR radiation *see* far-infrared radiation
F29	e	fast Fourier transform method

d Methode *f* der schnellen Fourier-Transformation
f méthode *f* de transformation rapide de Fourier
r метод *m* быстрого преобразования Фурье

F30 *e* fast-neutron reactor
d schneller Reaktor *m*
f réacteur *m* à neutrons rapides
r реактор *m* на быстрых нейтронах

F31 *e* fast neutrons
d schnelle Neutronen *n pl*
f neutrons *m pl* rapides
r быстрые нейтроны *m pl*

F32 *e* fast subsystem
d schnelles Untersystem *n*
f sous-système *m* rapide
r быстрая подсистема *f*

F33 *e* fatigue
d Ermüdung *f*
f fatigue *f*
r усталость *f* (*материалов*)

F34 *e* fatigue deformation
d Ermüdungsdeformation *f*
f déformation *f* de fatigue
r усталостная деформация *f*

F35 *e* fatigue fracture
d Ermüdungsbruch *m*, Dauerschwingungsbruch *m*
f rupture *f* par fatigue, fracture *f* par fatigue
r усталостный излом *m*

F36 *e* fatigue limit
d Dauerschwingfestigkeit *f*
f limite *f* de fatigue
r усталостная прочность *f*; предел *m* выносливости

F37 *e* fatigue strength
d Ermüdungsfestigkeit *f*
f résistance *f* à la fatigue
r усталостная прочность *f*

F38 *e* fatigue strength coefficient
d Dauerschwingfestigkeitskoeffizient *m*
f coefficient *m* de résistance à la fatigue
r коэффициент *m* усталостной прочности

F39 *e* fatigue test
d Ermüdungsversuch *m*, Dauerschwingversuch *m*
f essai *m* de fatigue
r испытание *n* на усталость

F40 *e* fatigue wear
d Ermüdungsverschleiß *m*
f usure *f* par fatigue
r усталостное изнашивание *n*

F41 *e* F-center
d F-Zentrum *n*
f centre *m* F
r F-центр *m*

F42 *e* F-center laser
d F-Zentrumlaser *m*
f laser *m* à centres F
r лазер *m* на F-центрах

F43 *e* Fedorov groups
d Fjodorow-Gruppen *f pl*
f groupes *m pl* de Fédorov
r фёдоровские группы *f pl*, фёдоровские группы *f pl* симметрии

F44 *e* feedback
d Rückkopplung *f*
f réaction *f*
r обратная связь *f*

F45 *e* feedback factor
d Rückkopplungsfaktor *m*
f facteur *m* de réaction, coefficient *m* de réaction
r коэффициент *m* обратной связи

F46 *e* feeder
d Speiseleitung *f*, Feeder *m*
f feeder *m*
r фидер *m*, фидерная линия *f*

F47 *e* feed line *see* feeder

F48 *e* femtosecond
d Femtosekunde *f*
f femtoseconde *f*
r фемтосекунда *f*

F49 *e* femtosecond laser
d Femtosekundenlaser *m*
f laser *m* à femtosecondes
r фемтосекундный лазер *m*

F50 *e* femtosecond pulse
d Femtosekundenimpuls *m*
f impulsion *f* à femtosecondes
r фемтосекундный импульс *m*

F51 *e* Fermat principle
d Fermatsches Prinzip *n*, Prinzip *n* des kürzesten Weges
f principe *m* de Fermat
r принцип *m* Ферма

F52 *e* Fermi acceleration
d Fermi-Beschleunigung *f*
f accélération *f* de Fermi
r ускорение *n* Ферми

F53 *e* Fermi age
d Fermi-Alter *n*
f âge *m* de Fermi
r фермиевский возраст *m*

F54   *e*   **Fermi-Dirac statistics**
      d   Fermi-Dirac-Statistik *f*
      f   statistique *f* de Fermi et Dirac
      r   статистика *f* Ферми - Дирака

F55   *e*   **Fermi energy**
      d   Fermi-Energie *f*, Fermische Energie *f*
      f   énergie *f* de Fermi
      r   энергия *f* Ферми

F56   *e*   **Fermi gas**
      d   Fermi-Gas *n*
      f   gaz *m* de Fermi
      r   ферми-газ *m*

F57   *e*   **Fermi level**
      d   Fermi-Niveau *n*
      f   niveau *m* de Fermi
      r   уровень *m* Ферми

F58   *e*   **Fermi liquid**
      d   Fermi-Flüssigkeit *f*
      f   liquide *m* de Fermi
      r   ферми-жидкость *f*

F59   *e*   **fermion**
      d   Fermion *n*, Fermi-Teilchen *n*
      f   fermion *m*
      r   фермион *m*

F60   *e*   **Fermi particle** *see* **fermion**

F61   *e*   **Fermi surface**
      d   Fermi-Fläche *f*, Fermi-Oberfläche *f*
      f   surface *f* de Fermi
      r   поверхность *f* Ферми

F62   *e*   **fermium, Fm**
      d   Fermium *n*
      f   fermium *m*
      r   фермий *m*

F63   *e*   **ferrimagnet**
      d   Ferrimagnetikum *n*, ferrimagnetischer Stoff *m*
      f   ferrimagnétique *m*
      r   ферримагнетик *m*

F64   *e*   **ferrimagnetic resonance**
      d   ferrimagnetische Resonanz *f*
      f   résonance *f* ferrimagnétique
      r   ферримагнитный резонанс *m*

F65   *e*   **ferrimagnetism**
      d   Ferrimagnetismus *m*
      f   ferrimagnétisme *m*
      r   ферримагнетизм *m*

F66   *e*   **ferrite**
      d   Ferrit *n*
      f   ferrite *f*
      r   феррит *m*

F67   *e*   **ferrite circulator**
      d   Ferritzirkulator *m*
      f   circulateur *m* à ferrite
      r   ферритовый циркулятор *m*

F68   *e*   **ferrite-cored coil**
      d   Ferritkernspule *f*
      f   bobine *f* à noyau en ferrite
      r   катушка *f* с ферритовым сердечником

F69   *e*   **ferrite ring**
      d   Ferritring *m*
      f   anneau *m* en ferrite
      r   ферритовое кольцо *n*

F70   *e*   **ferroelastic**
      d   Seignetteelastikum *n*
      f   ferroélastique *m*
      r   сегнетоэластик *m*

F71   *e*   **ferroelasticity**
      d   Seignetteelastizität *f*
      f   ferroélasticité *f*
      r   сегнетоупругость *f*

F72   *e*   **ferroelectric**
      d   Ferroelektrikum *n*
      f   ferroélectrique *m*
      r   сегнетоэлектрик *m*

F73   *e*   **ferroelectric crystal**
      d   ferroelektrischer Kristall *m*, seignetteelektrischer Kristall *m*
      f   cristal *m* ferroélectrique
      r   сегнетоэлектрический кристалл *m*

F74   *e*   **ferroelectric domain**
      d   ferroelektrischer Bezirk *m*, seignetteelektrischer Bezirk *m*
      f   domaine *m* ferroélectrique
      r   сегнетоэлектрический домен *m*

F75   *e*   **ferroelectric hysteresis**
      d   ferroelektrische Hysteresis *f*
      f   hysterérésis *f* ferroélectrique
      r   сегнетоэлектрический гистерезис *m*

F76   *e*   **ferroelectricity**
      d   Ferroelektrizität *f*, Seignetteelektrizität *f*
      f   ferroélectricité *f*
      r   сегнетоэлектричество *n*

F77   *e*   **ferrofluid**
      d   ferromagnetische Flüssigkeit *f*
      f   fluide *m* ferromagnétique
      r   ферромагнитная жидкость *f*

F78   *e*   **ferrohydrodynamics**
      d   Ferrohydrodynamik *f*
      f   ferrohydrodynamique *f*
      r   феррогидродинамика *f*

F79   *e*   **ferromagnet**
      d   Ferromagnetikum *n*, ferromagnetischer Stoff *m*
      f   ferromagnétique *m*
      r   ферромагнетик *m*

F80   *e*   **ferromagnetic crystal**
      d   ferromagnetischer Kristall *m*

f cristal m ferromagnétique
r ферромагнитный кристалл m

F81 e ferromagnetic domain
d ferromagnetischer Bezirk m, Weißscher Bezirk m
f domaine m ferromagnétique
r ферромагнитный домен m

F82 e ferromagnetic resonance
d ferromagnetische Resonanz f
f résonance f ferromagnétique
r ферромагнитный резонанс m

F83 e ferromagnetism
d Ferromagnetismus m
f ferromagnétisme m
r ферромагнетизм m

F84 e ferrometer
d Ferrometer n
f ferromètre m
r феррометр m

F85 e Feynman diagram
d Feynman-Graph m, Feynman-Diagramm n
f diagramme m de Feynman, graphe m de Feynman
r диаграмма f Фейнмана, фейнмановская диаграмма f

F86 e Feynman gauge
d Feynman-Eichung f
f jaugeage m de Feynman
r фейнмановская калибровка f

F87 e fiber
d Faser f
f fibre f
r волокно n

F88 e fiber composite
d Faserverbundstoff m
f composition f en fibres
r волокнистый композит m

F89 e fiber laser
d faseroptischer Laser m
f laser m à fibres
r волоконный лазер m

F90 e fiber-optic cable
d Lichtleitfaserkabel n, faseroptisches Kabel n
f câble m de fibres optiques.
r волоконно-оптический кабель m

F91 e fiber-optic communication channel
d faseroptischer Nachrichtenkanal m
f canal m de communication à fibres optiques
r волоконно-оптический канал m связи

F92 e fiber-optic interferometer
d faseroptisches Interferometer n

f interféromètre m à fibres optiques
r волоконно-оптический интерферометр m

F93 e fiber optics
d Glasfaseroptik f, Faseroptik f
f optique f des fibres
r волоконная оптика f

F94 e fidelity
d Wiedergabetreue f, Wiedergabegüte f
f fidélité f
r верность f воспроизведения, верность f воспроизведения звука

F95 e field
d Feld n
f champ m
r поле n

F96 e field components
d Feldkomponenten f pl
f composants m pl du champ
r компоненты f pl поля

F97 e field curvature
d Feldkrümmung f
f courbure f de champ
r кривизна f поля

F98 e field desorption
d Felddesorption f
f désorption f du champ
r десорбция f полем, полевая десорбция f

F99 e field emission
d Feldemission f
f émission f de champ, émission f par effet de champ
r автоэлектронная эмиссия f, холодная эмиссия f, полевая эмиссия f

F100 e field intensity see field strength

F101 e field invariants
d Feldinvarianten f pl
f invariants m pl du champ
r инварианты m pl поля

F102 e field ionization
d Feldionisierung f, Feldionisation f
f ionisation f par champ électrique
r полевая ионизация f, ионизация f полем

F103 e field Lagrangian
d Feld-Lagrangian n, Feld-Lagrange-Funktion f
f lagrangien m de champ
r лагранжиан m поля

F104 e field of application
d Anwendungsbereich m
f domaine m d'application
r область f применения

F105   *e*   field of force *see* force field

F106   *e*   field of view
     d   Sehfeld *n*, Gesichtsfeld *n*
     f   champ *m* de vision
     r   поле *n* зрения

F107   *e*   field quantization
     d   Feldquantelung *f*, Feldquantisierung *f*
     f   quantification *f* du champ
     r   квантование *n* поля

F108   *e*   field stop
     d   Bildfeldblende *f*, Sehfeldblende *f*,
        Gesichtsfeldblende *f*
     f   diaphragme *m* de champ visuel,
        diaphragme *m* de champ
     r   полевая диафрагма *f*

F109   *e*   field strength
     d   Feldstärke *f*
     f   intensité *f* de champ
     r   напряжённость *f* поля

F110   *e*   field theory
     d   Feldtheorie *f*
     f   théorie *f* du champ
     r   теория *f* поля

F111   *e*   field transistor
     d   Feldeffekttransistor *m*
     f   transistor *m* à effet de champ
     r   полевой транзистор *m*

F112   *e*   figure of Earth
     d   Form *f* der Erde
     f   figure *f* de la Terre, forme *f* de la
        Terre
     r   фигура *f* Земли

F113   *e*   figure of merit
     d   Güte *f*, Gütezahl *f*
     f   Q-facteur *m*
     r   добротность *f*

F114   *e*   filament
     d   1. Faden *m* 2. Heizfaden *m*;
        Glühfaden *m* 3. Plasmastrahl *m*
     f   filament *m*
     r   1. волокно *n*; нить *f* 2. нить *f*
        накала 3. пучок *m* (*плазмы*)

F115   *e*   filament channel
     d   Filamentkanal *m*
     f   canal *m* des filaments
     r   канал *m* волокон (*на Солнце*)

F116   *e*   filled band
     d   besetztes Energieband *n*, besetztes
        Band *n*
     f   bande *f* occupée
     r   заполненная зона *f*

F117   *e*   filled shell
     d   vollbesetzte Schale *f*
     f   couche *f* remplie, couche *f* saturée
     r   заполненная оболочка *f*

F118   *e*   filling of a level
     d   Niveaubesetzung *f*
     f   remplissage *m* d'un niveau
     r   заселение *n* уровня

F119   *e*   film
     d   Film *m*; Schicht *f*, dünne Schicht *f*
     f   film *m*, pellicule *f*
     r   плёнка *f*

F120   *e*   film boiling
     d   Filmsieden *n*, Filmverdampfung *f*
     f   bouillonnement *m* en film,
        bouillonnement *m* en pellicule
     r   плёночное кипение *n*

F121   *e*   film cathode
     d   Metallfilmkatode *f*
     f   cathode *f* à couche rapportée
     r   плёночный катод *m*

F122   *e*   film condensation, filmwise
        condensation
     d   Filmkondensation *f*
     f   condensation *f* en film
     r   плёночная конденсация *f*

F123   *e*   film deposition
     d   Schichtaufdampfen *n*, Beschichtung *f*
     f   déposition *f* des films
     r   напыление *n* плёнок

F124   *e*   film evaporation *see* film deposition

F125   *e*   film transducer
     d   Folienwandler *m*
     f   convertisseur *m* à film
     r   плёночный преобразователь *m*

F126   *e*   filter
     d   Filter *n*
     f   filtre *m*
     r   фильтр *m*

F127   *e*   filter discrimination
     d   Selektivität *m* des Filters,
        Trennschärfe *m* des Filters
     f   discrimination *f* du filtre
     r   избирательность *f* фильтра

F128   *e*   filtering *see* filtration

F129   *e*   filtration
     d   Filtration *f*, Filtrierung *f*
     f   filtration *f*
     r   фильтрация *f*

F130   *e*   final stage
     d   Endstufe *f*
     f   étage *m* final
     r   оконечный каскад *m*

F131   *e*   fine mechanics
     d   Feinmechanik *f*
     f   mécanique *f* exacte
     r   точная механика *f*

F132   *e*   **finess, finess value** *see* **figure of merit**

F133   *e*   **fine structure**
     d   Feinstruktur *f*
     f   structure *f* fine
     r   тонкая структура *f*

F134   *e*   **fine-structure constant**
     d   Feinstrukturkonstante *f*
     f   constante *f* de structure fine
     r   постоянная *f* тонкой структуры

F135   *e*   **finite deformation**
     d   endliche Deformation *f*
     f   déformation *f* finale
     r   конечная деформация *f*

F136   *e*   **finite element method**
     d   Finit-Element-Methode *f*
     f   méthode *f* des éléments finis
     r   метод *m* конечных элементов

F137   *e*   **finite interval**
     d   endliches Intervall *n*
     f   intervalle *m* final
     r   конечный интервал *m*

F138   *e*   **finite motion**
     d   endliche Bewegung *f*, gebundene Bewegung *f*
     f   mouvement *m* fini
     r   финитное движение *n*

F139   *e*   **finiteness of the Universe**
     d   Endlichkeit *f* des Universums
     f   finitude *f* de l'Univers
     r   конечность *f* Вселенной

F140   *e*   **fire**
     d   Feuer *n*
     f   feu *m*
     r   огонь *m*

F141   *e*   **fireball**
     d   Feuerball *m*
     f   boule *f* de feu
     r   файербол *m*

F142   *e*   **firing**
     d   1. Anzünden *n*, Entzünden *n* 2. Zündung *f* (*der Rakete*) 3. Sinterung *f*
     f   1. mise *f* à feu 2. allumage *m* 3. cuisson *f*
     r   1. зажигание *n* 2. запуск *m* 3. обжиг *m*

F143   *e*   **firing potential** *see* **ignition potential**

F144   *e*   **first law of thermodynamics**
     d   erster Hauptsatz *m* der Thermodynamik
     f   premier principe *m* de la thermodynamique
     r   первое начало *n* термодинамики

F145   *e*   **first-order effect**
     d   Effekt *m* erster Ordnung
     f   effet *m* de premier ordre
     r   эффект *m* первого порядка

F146   *e*   **first sound** (*in helium II*)
     d   erster Schall *m* (*im Helium II*)
     f   premier son *m* (*en hélium II*)
     r   первый звук *m* (*в гелии II*)

F147   *e*   **first-wall configuration**
     d   Konfiguration *f* der ersten Wand
     f   configuration *f* de la première paroi
     r   конфигурация *f* первой стенки

F148   *e*   **fissile core** *see* **reactor core**

F149   *e*   **fissile material** *see* **fissionable material**

F150   *e*   **fission**
     d   Spaltung *f*, Aufspaltung *f*; Kernspaltung *f*
     f   fission *f*, fission *f* nucléaire
     r   деление *n*; расщепление *n*

F151   *e*   **fissionable material**
     d   spaltbares Material *n*
     f   matière *f* fissile
     r   делящийся материал *m*

F152   *e*   **fissionable nucleus**
     d   spaltfähiger Kern *m*
     f   noyau *m* fissile
     r   делящееся ядро *n*

F153   *e*   **fission barrier**
     d   Spaltbarriere *f*, Spaltungsbarriere *f*
     f   barrière *f* de fission
     r   барьер *m* деления

F154   *e*   **fission chamber**
     d   Spaltkammer *f*, Spaltungskammer *f*
     f   chambre *f* à fission
     r   камера *f* деления

F155   *e*   **fission cross-section**
     d   Spaltquerschnitt *m*, Spaltungsquerschnitt *m*
     f   section *f* efficace de fission
     r   сечение *n* деления

F156   *e*   **fission factor**
     d   Multiplikationsfaktor *m*, Vermehrungsfaktor *m*, Reproduktionsfaktor *m*
     f   coefficient *m* de multiplication
     r   коэффициент *m* размножения нейтронов, коэффициент *m* размножения

F157   *e*   **fission fragments**
     d   Spaltbruchstücke *n pl*, Spaltfragmente *n pl*
     f   fragments *m pl* de fission
     r   осколки *m pl* деления

F158   *e*   **fissioning isomer** *see* **fission isomer**

F159   *e*   fission isomer
      d   spaltendes Isomer *n*
      f   isomère *m* fissile
      r   делящийся изомер *m*

F160   *e*   fission isomerism
      d   Spaltungsisomerie *f*
      f   isomérie *f* de fission
      r   делительная изомерия *f*

F161   *e*   fission neutrons
      d   Spaltneutronen *n pl*
      f   neutrons *m pl* de fission
      r   нейтроны *m pl* деления

F162   *e*   fission probability
      d   Spaltwahrscheinlichkeit *f*
      f   probabilité *f* de fission
      r   вероятность *f* деления

F163   *e*   fission-product contamination
      d   Spaltproduktkontamination *f*
      f   contamination *f* par les produits de fission
      r   загрязнение *n* продуктами деления

F164   *e*   fission threshold
      d   Spaltschwelle *f*, Spaltungsschwelle *f*
      f   seuil *m* de fission
      r   порог *m* деления

F165   *e*   five-minute oscillations *(in solar atmosphere)*
      d   5-Minuten-Schwingungen *f pl* *(in der Sonnenatmosphäre)*
      f   oscillations *f pl* à cinq minutes *(en atmosphère solaire)*
      r   пятиминутные колебания *n pl* *(в атмосфере Солнца)*

F166   *e*   fixed coil
      d   Festspule *f*, feststehende Spule *f*
      f   bobine *f* fixe
      r   неподвижная катушка *f*

F167   *e*   fixed target
      d   unbewegliches Target *n*, festes Target *n*, stationäres Target *n*
      f   cible *f* fixe
      r   неподвижная мишень *f*

F168   *e*   Fizeau experiment
      d   Fizeauscher Interferenzversuch *m*, Fizeauscher Versuch *m*
      f   expérience *f* de Fizeau
      r   опыт *m* Физо

F169   *e*   flame
      d   Flamme *f*
      f   flamme *f*
      r   пламя *n*

F170   *e*   flame front
      d   Flammenfront *f*
      f   front *m* de flamme
      r   фронт *m* пламени

F171   *e*   flame photometry
      d   Flammenphotometrie *f*
      f   photométrie *f* de flamme
      r   пламенная фотометрия *f*, фотометрия *f* пламени

F172   *e*   flame spectrum
      d   Flammenspektrum *n*
      f   spectre *m* de flamme
      r   спектр *m* пламени

F173   *e*   flare
      d   1. Aufflackern *n* 2. Eruption *f*, Sonneneruption *f*
      f   1. éruption *f* 2. éruption *f* solaire
      r   1. вспышка *f* 2. солнечная вспышка *f*

F174   *e*   flare class
      d   Sonneneruptionsklasse *f*
      f   classe *f* d'éruption solaire
      r   класс *m* солнечной вспышки, класс *m* вспышки

F175   *e*   flare discharge *see* torch discharge

F176   *e*   flare star
      d   Flackerstern *m*, UV Ceti-Stern *m*, UV Ceti-Veränderlicher *m*
      f   variable *f* à flare, variable *f* du type UV Ceti
      r   вспыхивающая звезда *f*

F177   *e*   flash *see* flare

F178   *e*   flash lamp
      d   Blitzlampe *f*
      f   lampe-éclair *f*
      r   лампа-вспышка *f*, импульсная лампа *f*

F179   *e*   flashlamp pumping
      d   Impulsröhrenpumpen *n*
      f   pompage *m* par lampes-éclairs
      r   накачка *f* импульсными лампами

F180   *e*   flash photolysis
      d   Blitzlichtphotolyse *f*
      f   photolyse *f* par éclair
      r   импульсный фотолиз *m*

F181   *e*   flash photolysis initiation
      d   Blitzlichtphotolyse-Initiierung *f*
      f   initiation *f* de la photolyse par éclair
      r   импульсное фотолитическое инициирование *n*

F182   *e*   flat mirror *see* plane mirror

F183   *e*   flatness
      d   Ebenheit *f*
      f   planéité *f*; régularité *f*
      r   плоскостность *f*; равномерность *f*

F184   *e*   flavor
      d   Flavor *n* *(Quantenzahl)*
      f   flavor *m* *(nombre quantique)*
      r   аромат *m* *(квантовое число)*

F185 *e* flaw
      d 1. Fehler *m*, Defekt *m* 2. Riß *m*
      f 1. défaut *m* 2. fissure *f*
      r 1. дефект *m* 2. трещина *f*

F186 *e* flaw detection
      d Defektoskopie *f*
      f détection *f* des défauts,
         défectoscopie *f*
      r дефектоскопия *f*

F187 *e* flaw detector
      d Defektoskop *n*, Risseprüfer *m*
      f défectoscope *m*, détecteur *m* des
         défauts
      r дефектоскоп *m*

F188 *e* F-layer
      d F-Schicht *f* (*der Ionosphäre*)
      f couche *f* F (*d'ionosphère*)
      r слой *m* F (*ионосферы*)

F189 *e* flexibility
      d Flexibilität *f*
      f flexibilité *f*
      r гибкость *f*

F190 *e* flexible mirror
      d biegsamer Spiegel *m*
      f miroir *m* flexible
      r гибкое зеркало *n*

F191 *e* flexural centre
      d Schubmittelpunkt *m*,
         Querkraftmittelpunkt *m*
      f centre *m* de flexion
      r центр *m* изгиба

F192 *e* flexural deformation *see* bending
         deformation

F193 *e* flexural rigidity
      d Biegungsfestigkeit *f*, Biegesteifigkeit *f*
      f rigidité *f* à la flexion
      r изгибная жёсткость *f*, жёсткость *f*
         на изгиб

F194 *e* flexural vibration
      d Biegeschwingungen *f pl*
      f vibrations *f pl* de flexion
      r изгибные колебания *n pl*

F195 *e* flexural wave
      d Biegungswelle *f*, Biegewelle *f*
      f onde *f* de flexion
      r изгибная волна *f*

F196 *e* flicker effect
      d Funkeleffekt *m*, Flickereffekt *m*;
         Flackereffekt *m*
      f effet *m* flicker
      r фликкер-эффект *m*

F197 *e* flicker photometer
      d Flimmerphotometer *n*,
         Flackerphotometer *n*
      f photomètre *m* à papillotement,
         photomètre *m* à vacillation
      r мигающий фотометр *m*

F198 *e* flip
      d Umkippen *n*
      f culbutage *m*
      r опрокидывание *n*, переворот *m*

F199 *e* floating
      d Schwimmen *n*
      f flottement *m*
      r плавание *n*, плавание *n* тел

F200 *e* floating potential
      d inneres Kontaktpotential *n*
      f potentiel *m* flottant
      r плавающий потенциал *m*;
         свободный потенциал *m*

F201 *e* floating zone method
      d tiegelfreies Zonenschmelzen *n*
      f méthode *f* de la zone fondue
      r метод *m* зонной плавки

F202 *e* flocculi
      d Flocculi *m pl*, Flocken *f pl*
      f flocculi *m pl*
      r флоккулы *f pl* (*на Солнце*)

F203 *e* flotation
      d Flotation *f*
      f flottation *f*
      r флотация *f*

F204 *e* flow
      d Fluß *f*; Fließen *n*; Strömen *n*
      f flux *m*; écoulement *m*
      r поток *m*; течение *n*

F205 *e* flow around a body
      d Umströmen *n*, Umströmung *f*
      f écoulement *m* autour d'un corps
      r обтекание *n* тела

F206 *e* flow continuity
      d Strömungskontinuität *f*
      f continuité *f* du courant
      r неразрывность *f* потока

F207 *e* flow diagram
      d Strömungsdiagramm *n*,
         Strömungsbild *n*
      f diagramme *m* d'écoulement
      r диаграмма *f* течения

F208 *e* flow dynamics *see* fluid dynamics

F209 *e* flowmeter
      d Mengenmeßgerät *n*,
         Verbrauchsmesser *m*
      f débitmètre *m*
      r расходомер *m*

F210 *e* flow pattern
      d Strömungsbild *n*, Stromlinienbild *n*
      f image *f* de l'écoulement
      r картина *f* течения

F211   *e*   **flow visualization**
      d   Sichtbarmachung *f* der Strömung
      f   visualisation *f* de l'écoulement
      r   визуализация *f* потока

F212   *e*   **fluctuation correlation**
      d   Schwankungskorrelation *f*, Korrelation *f* von Fluktuationen
      f   corrélation *f* des fluctuations
      r   корреляция *f* флуктуаций

F213   *e*   **fluctuations**
      d   Fluktuationen *f pl*, Schwankungen *f pl*
      f   fluctuations *f pl*
      r   флуктуации *f pl*

F214   *e*   **fluctuon**
      d   Fluktuon *n*, Phason *n*
      f   fluctuon *m*, phason *m*
      r   флуктон *m*, флуктуон *m*

F215   *e*   **fluence**
      d   Fluenz *f*
      f   fluence *f*
      r   плотность *f* потока

F216   *e*   **fluid**
      d   Fluid *n*
      f   fluide *m*
      r   жидкость *f*, текучая среда *f*

F217   *e*   **fluid dynamics**
      d   Strömungsdynamik *f*, Aerohydrodynamik *f*
      f   dynamique *f* des fluides
      r   динамика *f* жидкостей и газов

F218   *e*   **fluid flow**
      d   Fluidströmung *f*
      f   écoulement *m* de fluide
      r   поток *m* жидкости, поток *m* текучей среды

F219   *e*   **fluidity**
      d   Fluidität *f*, Flüssigkeitscharakter *m*
      f   fluidité *f*
      r   текучесть *f*

F220   *e*   **fluid mechanics**
      d   Strömungsmechanik *f*, Mechanik *f* der Flüssigkeiten und Gase
      f   mécanique *f* des fluides
      r   механика *f* жидкостей и газов

F221   *e*   **fluid pressure**
      d   hydrostatischer Druck *m*
      f   pression *f* du liquide
      r   давление *n* жидкости

F222   *e*   **fluorescence**
      d   Fluoreszenz *f*
      f   fluorescence *f*
      r   флуоресценция *f*

F223   *e*   **fluorescence yield**
      d   Fluoreszenzausbeute *f*
      f   sortie *f* de fluorescence
      r   выход *m* флуоресценции

F224   *e*   **fluorescent light source**
      d   Fluoreszenzlichtquelle *f*
      f   source *f* de lumière fluorescente
      r   люминесцентный источник *m* света

F225   *e*   **fluorescent radiation**
      d   Fluoreszenzstrahlung *f*
      f   rayonnement *m* de fluorescence
      r   флуоресцентное излучение *n*

F226   *e*   **fluorimeter**
      d   Fluorometer *n*, Fluorimeter *n*
      f   fluorimètre *m*
      r   флуориметр *m*, флуорометр *m*

F227   *e*   **fluorimetric analysis**
      d   Fluoreszenzanalyse *f*
      f   analyse *m* par fluorescence
      r   флуоресцентный анализ *m*

F228   *e*   **fluorimetry**
      d   Fluorometrie *f*
      f   fluorimétrie *f*
      r   флуориметрия *f*, флуорометрия *f*

F229   *e*   **fluorine, F**
      d   Fluor *n*
      f   fluor *m*
      r   фтор *m*

F230   *e*   **fluorography**
      d   Schirmbildaufnahme *f*, Röntgenschirmbildphotographie *f*
      f   fluorographie *f*
      r   флюорография *f*

F231   *e*   **fluorometer** *see* **fluorimeter**

F232   *e*   **flute instability**
      d   Rinneninstabilität *f*
      f   instabilité *f* à cannelures
      r   желобковая неустойчивость *f*

F233   *e*   **flutter**
      d   1. Flattern *n* 2. Vibration *f*
      f   1. flutter *m* 2. flottement *m*
      r   1. флаттер *m* 2. дрожание *n*

F234   *e*   **flux**
      d   Fluß *m*; Strom *m*
      f   flux *m*
      r   поток *m*

F235   *e*   **flux density**
      d   Flußdichte *f*
      f   densité *f* du flux
      r   плотность *f* потока

F236   *e*   **flux gate**
      d   Saturationskernsonde *f*, SK-Sonde *f*
      f   ferrosonde *f*
      r   феррозонд *m*

F237   *e*   **flux gate magnetometer**

	d	Kernsättigungsmagnetometer n, SK-Magnetometer n
	f	magnétomètre m à ferrosonde
	r	феррозондовый магнитометр m

F238
e flux meter, fluxmeter
d Fluxmeter n, Flußmesser m
f fluxmètre m
r флюксметр m, веберметр m

F239
e fluxoid
d Fluxoid n
f fluxoïde m
r флюксоид m, вихрь m магнитного потока

F240
e fluxoid quantization
d Fluxoidquantisierung f
f quantification f des fluxoïdes
r квантование n вихрей магнитного потока

F241
e flux quantization
d Flußquantisierung f
f quantification f du flux
r квантование n потока

F242
e flux quantum
d Flußquant n, magnetisches Flußquant n
f quantum m de flux, quantum m de flux magnétique
r квант m потока

F243
e flux tube
d Stromröhre f, Stromrohr n
f tube m de courant
r трубка f потока

F244
e flywheel
d Schwungrad n
f volant m
r маховик m

F245
e f-number
d Blendenzahl f
f nombre f d'ouverture
r обратная величина f относительного отверстия объектива

F246
e foam
d Schaum m
f mousse f
r пена f

F247
e focal distance
d Brennweite f
f distance f focale
r фокусное расстояние n

F248
e focal length see focal distance

F249
e focal plane
d Brennebene f, Fokalebene f
f plan m focal
r фокальная плоскость f

F250
e focal power
d Brechkraft f, Brechwert m
f pouvoir m convergent
r оптическая сила f (линзы)

F251
e focal region
d Fokalgebiet n
f région f focale
r фокальная область f

F252
e focal surface
d Brennfläche f, Fokalfläche f
f surface f focale
r фокальная поверхность f

F253
e Fock space
d Fock-Raum m
f espace m de Fock
r пространство n Фока

F254
e focon
d Fokalkonus m, Fokon n
f cône m focalisateur
r фокон m

F255
e focus
d Brennpunkt m, Fokus m
f foyer m
r фокус m

F256
e focusator
d Fokussator m
f focusateur m
r фокусатор m

F257
e focus coil see focusing coil

F258
e focused radiation
d fokussierte Strahlung f, gebündelte Strahlung f
f rayonnement m focalisé
r сфокусированное излучение n

F259
e focused ray
d gebündelter Strahl m
f rayon m focalisé
r сфокусированный луч m

F260
e focusing
d Fokussierung f
f focalisation f
r фокусировка f

F261
e focusing action
d Fokussierung f, Bündelung f
f réglage m de foyer
r фокусирующее действие n

F262
e focusing coil
d Fokussierspule f, Fokussierungsspule f
f bobine f de focalisation
r фокусирующая катушка f

F263
e focusing length
d Fokussierungslänge f
f longueur f de focalisation
r длина f фокусировки

F264   *e* focusing lens
     d Fokussierlinse *f*; Einstellobjektiv *f*
     f lentille *f* de focalisation
     r фокусирующая линза *f*

F265   *e* focusing quadrupole
     d Fokussierungsquadrupol *m*
     f quadripôle *m* de focalisation
     r фокусирующий квадруполь *m*

F266   *e* focusing voltage
     d Fokussierspannung *f*
     f tension *f* de focalisation
     r фокусирующее напряжение *n*

F267   *e* focuson
     d Fokuson *n*
     f focuson *m*
     r фокусон *m* *(квазичастица)*

F268   *e* fog
     d 1. Nebel *m* 2. Schleier *m*,
        photographischer Schleier *m*
     f 1. brouillard *m* 2. voile *m*, voile *m*
        photographique
     r 1. туман *m* 2. вуаль *f* *(в
        фотографии)*

F269   *e* foil
     d Folie *f*
     f feuille *f*
     r фольга *f*

F270   *e* foil target
     d Folientarget *n*
     f cible *f* à feuille
     r фольговая мишень *f*

F271   *e* foot
     d Fuß *m* *(Längeneinheit)*
     f pied *m* *(unité de longueur)*
     r фут *m* *(единица длины)*

F272   *e* forbidden band
     d verbotenes Band *n*, verbotener
        Energiebereich *m*, verbotene Zone *f*
     f bande *f* interdite
     r запрещённая зона *f*

F273   *e* forbidden line
     d verbotene Linie *f* *(im Spektrum)*
     f raie *f* interdite *(en spectre)*
     r запрещённая линия *f* *(в спектре)*

F274   *e* forbidden mode
     d verbotene Mode *f*
     f mode *m* interdit
     r запрещённая мода *f*

F275   *e* forbidden zone *see* forbidden band

F276   *e* Forbush decrease
     d Forbush-Abfall *m*
     f décroissance *f* de Forbush
     r Форбуш-понижение *n*

F277   *e* force
     d Kraft *f*
     f force *f*
     r сила *f*, усилие *n*

F278   *e* forced convection
     d erzwungene Konvektion *f*
     f convection *f* forcée
     r вынужденная конвекция *f*

F279   *e* forced motion
     d erzwungene Bewegung *f*
     f mouvement *m* forcé
     r вынужденное движение *n*

F280   *e* forced oscillation
     d erzwungene Schwingungen *f pl*
     f oscillations *f pl* forcées
     r вынужденные колебания *n pl*

F281   *e* forced vibrations
     d erzwungene Schwingungen *f pl*
     f oscillations *f pl* forcées
     r вынужденные колебания *n pl*

F282   *e* force field
     d Kraftfeld *n*, Kraftlinienfeld *n*
     f champ *m* de forces
     r силовое поле *n*

F283   *e* forgeability
     d Schmiedbarkeit *f*
     f malléabilité *f*, ductilité *f*
     r ковкость *f*

F284   *e* forging
     d Schmieden *n*; Gesenkschmieden *n*
     f forgeage *m*; estampage *m*
     r ковка *f*; штамповка *f*

F285   *e* form
     d Form *f*
     f forme *f*
     r форма *f*

F286   *e* formal axiomatic method
     d formale axiomatische Methode *f*
     f méthode *f* axiomatique formelle
     r формальный аксиоматический
        метод *m*

F287   *e* formalism
     d Formalismus *m*
     f formalisme *m*
     r формализм *m*

F288   *e* form anisotropy
     d Formanisotropie *f*, Gestaltanisotropie *f*
     f anisotrópie *f* de forme
     r анизотропия *f* формы

F289   *e* formant
     d Formant *m*
     f formant *m*
     r форманта *f* *(в акустике)*

F290   *e* formation
     d 1. Formierung *f*; Formung *f* 2.
        Bildung *f*; Erzeugung *f*

| | f | formation f |
| | r | 1. формирование n 2. образование n |

F291 | e | formation of the Solar system
| | d | Sonnensystementwicklung f
| | f | formation f du système solaire
| | r | образование n Солнечной системы

F292 | e | form drag
| | d | Formwiderstand m
| | f | résistance f de forme
| | r | сопротивление n формы

F293 | e | form factor
| | d | Formfaktor m
| | f | facteur m de forme
| | r | форм-фактор m

F294 | e | forming
| | d | Formierung f
| | f | formation f
| | r | формирование n

F295 | e | formula
| | d | Formel f
| | f | formule f
| | r | формула f

F296 | e | forward scatter, forward scattering
| | d | Vorwärtsstreuung f
| | f | diffusion f en avant
| | r | рассеяние n вперёд

F297 | e | Foucault currents
| | d | Foucault-Ströme pl, Wirbelströme pl
| | f | courants pl de Foucault
| | r | токи pl Фуко

F298 | e | Foucault pendulum
| | d | Foucaultsches Pendel n
| | f | pendule m de Foucault
| | r | маятник m Фуко

F299 | e | fountain effect
| | d | Springbrunneneffekt m
| | f | effet m de fontaine
| | r | фонтанный эффект m

F300 | e | four-dimensional interval
| | d | vierdimensionales Intervall n
| | f | intervalle m quadridimensionnel
| | r | четырёхмерный интервал m

F301 | e | four-dimensional momentum
| | d | vierdimensionaler Drehimpuls m
| | f | quadri-impulsion f
| | r | четырёхмерный импульс m

F302 | e | four-dimensional potential
| | d | vierdimensionales Potential n
| | f | potentiel m quadridimensionnel
| | r | четырёхмерный потенциал m

F303 | e | four-dimensional vector
| | d | vierdimensionaler Vektor m
| | f | vecteur m quadridimensionnel
| | r | четырёхмерный вектор m

F304 | e | four-dimensional velocity
| | d | vierdimensionale Geschwindigkeit f
| | f | vitesse f quadridimensionnelle
| | r | четырёхмерная скорость f

F305 | e | four-fermion interaction
| | d | Vierfermionenwechselwirkung f
| | f | interaction f à quatre fermions
| | r | четырёхфермионное взаимодействие n

F306 | e | Fourier coefficient
| | d | Fourier-Koeffizient m
| | f | coefficient m de Fourier
| | r | коэффициент m Фурье

F307 | e | Fourier component
| | d | Fourier-Komponente f
| | f | composante f de Fourier
| | r | Фурье-компонента f, компонента f Фурье

F308 | e | Fourier integral
| | d | Fourier-Integral n, Fouriersches Integral n
| | f | intégrale f de Fourier
| | r | интеграл m Фурье

F309 | e | Fourier series
| | d | Fourier-Reihe f, Fouriersche Reihe f
| | f | série f de Fourier
| | r | ряд m Фурье

F310 | e | Fourier spectrometer
| | d | Fourier-Spektrometer n
| | f | spectromètre m de Fourier
| | r | Фурье-спектрометр m

F311 | e | Fourier spectroscopy
| | d | Fourier-Spektroskopie f
| | f | spectroscopie f de Fourier
| | r | Фурье-спектроскопия f

F312 | e | Fourier transform
| | d | Fourier-Transformation f
| | f | transformation f de Fourier
| | r | преобразование n Фурье

F313 | e | four-level laser
| | d | Vierniveaulaser m
| | f | laser m à quatre niveaux
| | r | четырёхуровневый лазер m

F314 | e | fourth sound
| | d | vierter Schall m (im Helium)
| | f | quatrième son m (en hélium)
| | r | четвёртый звук (в гелии)

F315 | e | four-velocity see four-dimensional velocity

F316 | e | FP interferometer see Fabry-Perot interferometer

F317 | e | fractal
| | d | Fraktal n

f fractal *m*
r фрактал *m*

F318 e **fractal cluster**
d Fraktalcluster *m*
f cluster *m* de fractales
r кластер *m* фракталов, фрактальный кластер *m*

F319 e **fraction**
d Fraktion *f*
f fraction *f*
r доля *f*; фракция *f*

F320 e **fracture**
d 1. Zerstörung *f*, Bruch *m* 2. Bruch *m*; Bruchfläche *f*
f 1. destruction *f* 2. cassure *f*, fracture *f*, rupture *f*
r 1. разрушение *n* 2. излом *m*

F321 e **fracture criterion**
d Bruchkriterium *n*
f critère *m* de rupture
r критерий *m* разрушения

F322 e **fracture mechanism**
d Bruchmechanismus *m*
f mécanisme *m* de rupture
r механизм *m* разрушения

F323 e **fragility**
d Sprödigkeit *f*, Brüchigkeit *f*, Zerbrechlichkeit *f*
f fragilité *f*
r ломкость *f*; хрупкость *f*

F324 e **fragment**
d Fragment *n*, Bruchstück *n*
f fragment *m*
r осколок *m* (*напр. молекулы или ядра*); фрагмент *m*

F325 e **fragmentation**
d Fragmentierung *f*; Zertrümmerung *f*
f fragmentation *f*; désintégration *f*
r фрагментация *f*; расщепление *n*

F326 e **frame**
d 1. Bezugssystem *n* 2. Rahmen *m* 3. Bild *n*
f 1. système *m* de référence 2. cadre *m* 3. image *f*
r 1. система *f* отсчёта 2. рамка *f* 3. кадр *m*

F327 e **frame aerial**
d Rahmenantenne *f*
f antenne *f* à cadre
r рамочная антенна *f*

F328 e **frame of reference**
d Bezugssystem *n*
f système *m* de référence
r система *f* отсчёта

F329 e **francium, Fr**

d Francium *n*, Franzium *n*, Frankium *n*
f francium *m*
r франций *m*

F330 e **Franck-Condon principle**
d Franck-Condon-Prinzip *n*
f principe *m* de Franck et Condon
r принцип *m* Франца - Кондона

F331 e **Franck-Hertz experiment**
d Franck-Hertz-Versuch *m*
f expérience *f* de Franck-Hertz
r опыт *m* Франца - Герца

F332 e **Franz-Keldysh effect**
d Franz-Keldysh-Effekt *m*
f effet *m* de Franz-Keldysh
r эффект *m* Франца - Келдыша

F333 e **Fraunhofer diffraction**
d Fraunhofersche Beugung *f*
f diffraction *f* de Fraunhofer
r дифракция *f* Фраунгофера

F334 e **Fraunhofer diffraction pattern**
d Fraunhofersche Beugungsfigur *f*, Fraunhofersches Beugungsbild *n*
f phénomènes *m pl* de diffraction de Fraunhofer
r картина *f* дифракции Фраунгофера

F335 e **Fraunhofer lines**
d Fraunhofer-Linien *f pl*, Fraunhofersche Linien *f pl*
f raies *f pl* de Fraunhofer
r фраунгоферовы линии *f pl*

F336 e **Fredholm equation**
d Fredholmsche Gleichung *f*
f équation *f* de Fredholm
r уравнение *n* Фредгольма

F337 e **free carrier concentration**
d Konzentration *f* freier Ladungsträger
f concentration *f* des porteurs libres
r концентрация *f* свободных носителей заряда

F338 e **free carriers**
d freie Träger *m pl*, freie Ladungsträger *m pl*
f porteurs *m pl* libres
r свободные носители *m pl*, свободные носители *m pl* заряда

F339 e **free charge**
d freie Ladung *f*
f charge *f* libre
r свободный заряд *m*

F340 e **free convection**
d freie Konvektion *f*, natürliche Konvektion *f*
f convection *f* libre, convection *f* naturelle
r свободная конвекция *f*, естественная конвекция *f*

F341   *e*   free electron
      d   freies Elektron *n*, frei bewegliches
         Elektron *n*
      f   électron *m* libre
      r   свободный электрон *m*

F342   *e*   free electron laser
      d   Freielektronenlaser *m*
      f   laser *m* à électrons libres
      r   лазер *m* на свободных электронах

F343   *e*   free energy
      d   freie Energie *f*
      f   énergie *f* libre
      r   свободная энергия *f*

F344   *e*   free fall
      d   freier Fall *m*
      f   chute *f* libre
      r   свободное падение *n*

F345   *e*   free fall acceleration
      d   Fallbeschleunigung *f*,
         Schwerebeschleunigung *f*,
         Erdbeschleunigung *f*
      f   accélération *f* de la pesanteur
      r   ускорение *n* свободного падения,
         ускорение *n* силы тяжести

F346   *e*   free Lagrangian
      d   freies Lagrangian *n*
      f   lagrangien *m* libre
      r   свободный лагранжиан *m*

F347   *e*   free motion
      d   freie Bewegung *f*
      f   mouvement *m* libre
      r   свободное движение *n*

F348   *e*   free oscillation, free oscillations
      d   freie Schwingungen *f pl*,
         Eigenschwingungen *f pl*
      f   oscillations *f pl* libres
      r   свободные колебания *n pl*,
         собственные колебания *n pl*

F349   *e*   free path (*of a particle*)
      d   freie Weglänge *f*
      f   libre parcours *m* (*d'une particule*)
      r   длина *f* пробега (*частицы*)

F350   *e*   free pendulum
      d   freies Pendel *n*
      f   pendule *m* libre
      r   свободный маятник *m*

F351   *e*   free radical
      d   freies Radikal *n*
      f   radical *m* libre
      r   свободный радикал *m*

F352   *e*   free-running laser
      d   eigenerregter Laser *m*, selbsterregter
         Laser *m*
      f   laser *m* à auto-excitation
      r   лазер *m*, работающий в режиме
         свободной генерации

F353   *e*   free space
      d   freier Raum *m*
      f   espace *m* libre
      r   свободное пространство *n*

F354   *e*   free-space attenuation
      d   Freiraumdämpfung *f*
      f   atténuation *f* dans l'espace libre
      r   затухание *n* в свободном
         пространстве

F355   *e*   free-space wavelength
      d   Freiraumwellenlänge *f*
      f   longueur *f* d'onde dans l'espace libre
      r   длина *f* волны в свободном
         пространстве

F356   *e*   freezing
      d   Einfrieren *n*, Gefrieren *n*
      f   gel *m*, congélation *f*
      r   замерзание *n*

F357   *e*   freezing-in
      d   Einfrieren *n*
      f   gel *m*
      r   вмороженность *f* (*магнитного
         поля*)

F358   *e*   freezing point
      d   Gefrierpunkt *m*
      f   point *m* de congélation
      r   точка *f* замерзания, температура *f*
         замерзания

F359   *e*   F-region
      d   F-Gebiet *n* (*der Ionosphäre*)
      f   région *f* F (*d'ionosphère*)
      r   F-область *f* (*ионосферы*)

F360   *e*   Frenkel defects
      d   Frenkel-Defekte *m pl*, Frenkel-
         Fehlstellen *f pl*, Frenkel-
         Fehlordnungen *f pl*
      f   défauts *m pl* de Frenkel
      r   дефекты *m pl* Френкеля

F361   *e*   freon
      d   Freon *n*, Frigen *n*
      f   fréon *m*
      r   фреон *m*

F362   *e*   frequency
      d   Frequenz *f*
      f   fréquence *f*
      r   частота *f*

F363   *e*   frequency band
      d   Frequenzband *n*, Frequenzbereich *m*
      f   bande *f* de fréquences
      r   полоса *f* частот, диапазон *m* частот

F364   *e*   frequency conversion
      d   Frequenzumsetzung *f*
      f   conversion *f* de la fréquence
      r   преобразование *n* частоты

F365   *e*   frequency dependence

    d Frequenzabhängigkeit f
    f dépendance f fréquentielle
    r частотная зависимость f,
       зависимость f от частоты

F366 e **frequency detection**
    d Frequenzdemodulation f
    f détection f de fréquence
    r частотное детектирование n

F367 e **frequency deviation**
    d Frequenzdeviation f,
       Frequenzabweichung f
    f déviation f de fréquence
    r девиация f частоты

F368 e **frequency distortion**
    d Frequenzverzerrung f
    f distorsions f pl de fréquence
    r частотные искажения n pl

F369 e **frequency divider**
    d Frequenzteiler m
    f diviseur m de fréquence
    r делитель m частоты

F370 e **frequency division**
    d Frequenzteilung f
    f division f de fréquence
    r деление n частоты

F371 e **frequency drift**
    d Frequenzdrift f,
       Frequenzabwanderung f
    f dérive f de fréquence
    r дрейф m частоты, частотный
       дрейф m

F372 e **frequency instability**
    d Frequenzinstabilität f
    f instabilité f de la fréquence
    r нестабильность f частоты

F373 e **frequency jitter**
    d Frequenzzittern n, Frequenzjitter m, n
    f sautillement m de fréquence
    r дрожание n частоты

F374 e **frequency locking**
    d Frequenzmitnahme f
    f entraînement m de fréquence
    r захватывание n частоты

F375 e **frequency measurement**
    d Frequenzmessung f
    f mesure f de fréquence
    r измерение n частоты

F376 e **frequency meter**
    d Frequenzmesser m
    f fréquencemètre m
    r частотомер m, волномер m

F377 e **frequency-modulated oscillation**
    d frequenzmodulierte Schwingungen f pl
    f oscillations f pl modulées en fréquence
    r частотно-модулированные
       колебания n pl

F378 e **frequency modulation, FM**
    d Frequenzmodulation f, FM
    f modulation f en fréquence, M.F.
    r частотная модуляция f, ЧМ

F379 e **frequency multiplication**
    d Frequenzverfielfachung f
    f multiplication f de fréquence
    r умножение n частоты

F380 e **frequency multiplicity (in accelerators)**
    d Frequenzmultiplizität f (in Beschleunigern)
    f multiplicité f de fréquence (dans les accélérateurs)
    r кратность f частоты (в ускорителях)

F381 e **frequency multiplier**
    d Frequenzvervielfacher m
    f multiplicateur m de fréquence
    r умножитель m частоты

F382 e **frequency pulling**
    d Frequenzmitziehen n,
       Frequenzmitnahme f
    f entraînement m de fréquence
    r затягивание n частоты

F383 e **frequency range**
    d Frequenzbereich m, Frequenzband n
    f gamme f de fréquences, bande f de
       fréquences
    r область f частот, диапазон m частот

F384 e **frequency response**
    d Amplitudenfrequenz-Kennlinie f,
       Amplitudenfrequenzcharakteristik f
    f caractéristique f amplitude-fréquence
    r амплитудно-частотная
       характеристика f

F385 e **frequency selectivity**
    d Frequenzselektivität f,
       Frequenztrennschärfe f
    f sélectivité f fréquentielle
    r избирательность f по частоте

F386 e **frequency spectrum**
    d Frequenzspektrum n
    f spectre m de fréquences
    r частотный спектр m, спектр m
       частот

F387 e **frequency stability**
    d Frequenzstabilität f
    f stabilité f de la fréquence
    r стабильность f частоты

F388 e **frequency stabilization**
    d Frequenzstabilisierung f
    f stabilisation f de fréquence
    r стабилизация f частоты

F389 e **frequency standard**
    d Frequenznormal n

f standard *m* de fréquence, étalon *m* de fréquence
r стандарт *m* частоты; эталон *m* частоты

F390 *e* frequency sweep
d Frequenzhub *m*, Frequenzwobbelung *f*
f balayage *m* de fréquence
r качание *n* частоты

F391 *e* frequency transformation
d Frequenzumformung *f*, Frequenztransformation *f*
f transformation *f* de fréquence
r преобразование *n* частоты

F392 *e* frequency-tuned laser
d abstimmbarer Laser *m*
f laser *m* accordable
r перестраиваемый лазер *m*, лазер *m*, перестраиваемый по частоте

F393 *e* Fresnel biprism
d Fresnelsches Doppelprisma *n*
f biprisme *m* de Fresnel
r бипризма *f* Френеля

F394 *e* Fresnel diffraction
d Fresnelsche Beugung *f*
f diffraction *f* de Fresnel
r дифракция *f* Френеля

F395 *e* Fresnel ellipsoid
d Fresnelsches Ellipsoid *n*
f ellipsoïde *m* de Fresnel
r эллипсоид *m* Френеля

F396 *e* Fresnel integral
d Fresnelsches Integral *n*
f intégrale *f* de Fresnel
r интеграл *m* Френеля

F397 *e* Fresnel lens
d Fresnel-Linse *f*, Fresnelsche Linse *f*
f lentille *f* de Fresnel
r линза *f* Френеля

F398 *e* Fresnel mirrors
d Fresnelsche Spiegel *m pl*
f mirroirs *m pl* de Fresnel
r зеркала *n pl* Френеля

F399 *e* Fresnel zone
d Fresnel-Bereich *m*, Fresnelsche Beugungszone *f*
f zone *f* de Fresnel
r зона *f* Френеля

F400 *e* friction
d Reibung *f*
f friction *f*, frottement *m*
r трение *n*

F401 *e* frictional electricity
d Reibungselektrizität *f*
f tribo-électricité *f*
r трибоэлектричество *n*

F402 *e* frictional electrification
d Reibungselektrisierung *f*
f électrisation *f* par frottement
r электризация *f* трением, электризация *f* при трении

F403 *e* friction coefficient
d Reibungszahl *f*
f coefficient *m* de frottement
r коэффициент *m* трения

F404 *e* friction damping
d Friktionsdämpfung *f*
f amortissement *m* à friction
r фрикционное демпфирование *n*

F405 *e* friction factor *see* friction coefficient

F406 *e* friction loss, friction losses
d Reibungsverluste *m pl*
f pertes *f pl* dues au frottement
r потери *f pl* на трение

F407 *e* friction machine
d Reibungsprobemaschine *f*
f machine *f* d'essai de friction
r машина *f* трения, машина *f* для испытаний на трение

F408 *e* Friedman model
d Friedman-Modell *n*
f modèle *m* de Friedman
r фридмановская модель *f* Вселенной, модель *f* Фридмана

F409 *e* fringe
d Streifen *m*, Interferenzstreifen *m*
f frange *f*, frange *f* d'interférence
r полоса *f*, интерференционная полоса *f*

F410 *e* front
d Flanke *f* (*Impuls*)
f front *m* (*d'impulsion*)
r фронт *f* (*волны или импульса*)

F411 *e* frost point
d Reifpunkt *m*, Reifbildungstemperatur *f*
f point *m* de givre
r точка *f* образования инея (*температура равновесия твердой и газообразной фаз*)

F412 *e* Froude number
d Froude-Zahl *f*, Froudesche Zahl *f*
f nombre *m* de Froude
r число *n* Фруда

F413 *e* Froude pendulum
d Froudesches Pendel *n*, Reibungspendel *n*
f pendule *m* à friction, pendule *m* de Froude
r маятник *m* Фруда, фрикционный маятник *m*

F414 *e* frustrated total internal reflection

d gestörte Totalreflexion *f*, verhinderte
Totalreflexion *f*
f réflexion *f* totale interne frustrée
r нарушенное полное внутреннее
отражение *n*

F415 e **fuel cell**
d Brennstoffelement *n*
f pile *m* à combustible
r топливный элемент *m*

F416 e **fuel element**
d Brennelement *n*
f cartouche *f* de combustible
r тепловыделяющий элемент *m*
(*ядерного реактора*)

F417 e **fugacity**
d Flüchtigkeit *f*
f fugacité *f*
r летучесть *f*

F418 e **fullerenes**
d Fullerene *n pl*
f fullerenes *m pl*, cristaux *m pl* de
fullerenes
r фуллерены *m pl*

F419 e **full radiator**
d schwarzer Körper *m*, schwarzer
Strahler *m*
f corps *m* noir, radiateur *m* intégral
r чёрное тело *n*, абсолютно чёрное
тело *n*

F420 e **full-scale model**
d Modell *n* in natürlicher Größe
f modèle *m* au naturel
r натурная модель *f*

F421 e **full-wave rectifier**
d Zweiweggleichrichter *m*,
Doppelweggleichrichter *m*
f redresseur *m* diphasé
r двухполупериодный выпрямитель *m*

F422 e **fully ionized atom**
d vollständig ionisiertes Atom *n*
f atome *m* totalement ionisé
r полностью ионизированный атом *m*

F423 e **function**
d Funktion *f*
f fonction *f*
r функция *f*

F424 e **functional**
d Funktional *n*
f fonctionnelle *f*
r функционал *m*

F425 e **functional integration**
d Funktionalintegration *f*
f intégration *f* fonctionelle
r функциональное интегрирование *n*

F426 e **functional relationschip**

d funktionale Abhängigkeit *f*,
funktionaler Zusammenhang *m*
f dépendance *f* fonctionelle
r функциональная зависимость *f*

F427 e **fundamental**
d Grundschwingung *f*,
Fundamentalschwingung *f*,
Fundamentale *f*
f fondamentale *f*
r основное колебание *n*, основная
гармоника *f*

F428 e **fundamental catalog**
d Fundamentalkatalog *m*
f catalogue *m* fondamental
r фундаментальный каталог *m*

F429 e **fundamental length**
d Fundamentallänge *f*
f longueur *f* fondamentale
r фундаментальная длина *f*

F430 e **fundamental mode**
d Grundschwingungstyp *m*,
Grundwelle *f*
f mode *m* fondamental
r основная мода *f*

F431 e **fundamental particles**
d Elementarteilchen *n pl*
f particules *f pl* élémentaires
r элементарные частицы *f pl*

F432 e **fundamental physical constants**
d Fundamentalkonstanten *f pl*
f constantes *f pl* physiques
fondamentales
r фундаментальные физические
постоянные *f pl*

F433 e **fundamental research**
d Grundlagenforschung *f*
f recherche *f* fondamentale
r фундаментальные исследования *n pl*

F434 e **funnel**
d Trichter *m*
f entonnoir *m*
r воронка *f*

F435 e **furnace**
d Ofen *m*
f four *m*
r печь *f*

F436 e **fuse**
d 1. Schmelzsicherung *f* 2. Keim *m*,
Kristallkeim *m*
f 1. fusible *m* 2. amorce *f*
r 1. плавкий предохранитель *m* 2.
затравка *f* (*при выращивании
кристаллов*)

F437 e **fusible plug**
d Schmelzstöpsel *m*

f   coup-circuit *m* à fusible
r   пробка *f (плавкий предохранитель)*

F438   e   **fusion**
d   1. Fusion *f* 2. Schmelzen *n*
f   1. fusion *f* 2. fonte *f*
r   1. ядерный синтез *m* 2. плавление *n*

G

G1   e   **Ga-As laser**
d   GaAs-Laser *m*, Galliumarsenidlaser *m*
f   laser *m* à arséniure de gallium
r   лазер *m* на арсениде галлия

G2   e   **gadolinium, Gd**
d   Gadolinium *n*
f   gadolinium *m*
r   гадолиний *m*

G3   e   **gage**
d   1. Eichung *f* 2. Meßgerät *n*, Meßinstrument *n*
f   1. jauge *f* 2. instrument *m*
r   1. калибровка *f* 2. измерительный прибор *m*

G4   e   **gage boson**
d   Eichboson *n*
f   boson *m* jauge
r   калибровочный бозон *m*

G5   e   **gage factor**
d   Eichfaktor *m*
f   facteur *m* d'étallonnage
r   калибровочный множитель *m*

G6   e   **gage fields**
d   Eichfelder *n pl*
f   champs *m pl* de jauge
r   калибровочные поля *n pl*

G7   e   **gage invariance**
d   Eichinvarianz *f*
f   invariance *f* de jauge
r   калибровочная инвариантность *f*

G8   e   **gage invariant**
d   Eichinvariante *f*
f   invariant *m* de jauge
r   калибровочный инвариант *m*

G9   e   **gage symmetry**
d   Eichsymmetrie *f*
f   symétrie *f* de jauge
r   калибровочная симметрия *f*

G10   e   **gage theories**
d   Eichfeldtheorien *f pl*
f   théories *f pl* de jauge
r   калибровочные теории *f pl*

G11   e   **gage transformation**
d   Eichtransformation *f*
f   transformation *f* de jauge
r   калибровочное преобразование *n*

G12   e   **gain**
d   1. Verstärkung *f* 2. Verstärkungskoeffizient *m*, Verstärkungsfaktor *m*
f   1. gain *m* 2. coefficient *m* d'amplification, facteur *m* d'amplification
r   1. усиление *n* 2. коэффициент *m* усиления

G13   e   **gain increment**
d   Verstärkungsinkrement *n*
f   incrément *m* d'amplification
r   инкремент *m* усиления

G14   e   **gain saturation**
d   Verstärkungssättigung *f*
f   saturation *f* d'amplification
r   насыщение *n* усиления

G15   e   **galactic center**
d   galaktisches Zentrum *n*
f   centre *m* galactique
r   галактический центр *m*, центр *m* галактики

G16   e   **galactic cluster**
d   galaktischer Haufen *m*, galaktischer Sternhaufen *m*
f   amas *m* galactique, amas *m* de galaxies
r   скопление *n* галактик

G17   e   **galactic cosmic rays**
d   galaktische kosmische Strahlen *pl*
f   rayons *pl* cosmiques galactiques
r   галактические космические лучи *pl*

G18   e   **galactic disk**
d   galaktische Scheibe *f*
f   disque *m* galactique
r   галактический диск *m*, диск *m* галактики

G19   e   **galactic halo**
d   Halo *m*, galaktischer Halo *m*
f   halo *m* galactique
r   галактическое гало *n*

G20   e   **galactic maser**
d   galaktischer Maser *m*
f   maser *m* galactique
r   галактический мазер *m*

G21   e   **galactic nucleus**
d   galaktischer Kern *m*
f   noyau *m* galactique
r   ядро *n* галактики

G22   e   **galactic radiation**
d   galaktische Strahlung *f*

	f	rayonnement *m* galactique
	r	галактическое излучение *n*

G23 *e* **galactic rotation**
d galaktische Rotation *f*
f rotation *f* galactique
r вращение *n* галактики

G24 *e* **galactic source**
d galaktische Quelle *f*
f source *f* galactique
r галактический источник *m*

G25 *e* **galaxy**
d Galaxie *f*, Sternsystem *n*
f galaxie *f*
r галактика *f*

G26 *e* **Galilean telescope**
d Galileisches Fernrohr *n*, Galilei-Fernrohr *n*
f lunette *f* de Galilée
r телескоп *m* Галилея

G27 *e* **Galilean transformations**
d Galilei-Transformationen *f pl*
f transformations *f pl* de Galilée
r преобразования *n pl* Галилея

G28 *e* **Galileo relativity principle**
d Galileisches Relativitätsprinzip *n*
f principe *m* de relativité de Galilée
r принцип *m* относительности Галилея

G29 *e* **gallium, Ga**
d Gallium *n*
f gallium *m*
r галлий *m*

G30 *e* **gallon**
d Gallone *f*
f gallon *m*
r галлон *m*

G31 *e* **Galton whistle**
d Galtonsche Pfeife *f*
f sifflet *m* de Galton
r свисток *m* Гальтона

G32 *e* **galvanoluminescence**
d Galvanolumineszenz *f*
f galvanoluminescence *f*
r гальванолюминесценция *f*

G33 *e* **galvanomagnetic effects**
d galvanomagnetische Effekte *m pl*
f effets *m pl* galvanomagnétiques
r гальваномагнитные явления *n pl*

G34 *e* **galvanometer**
d Galvanometer *n*
f galvanomètre *m*
r гальванометр *m*

G35 *e* **gamma**
d Gamma *n*
f gamma *m*
r гамма *f*

G36 *e* **gamma quantum**
d Gamma-Quant *n*
f quantum *m* gamma
r гамма-квант *m*

G37 *e* **gamma radiation** *see* **gamma rays**

G38 *e* **gamma-ray astronomy**
d Gamma-Astronomie *f*, Gamma-Strahlenastronomie *f*
f astronomie *f* au rayonnement gamma
r гамма-астрономия *f*

G39 *e* **gamma-ray burst detector**
d Gammastrahlenausbruchdetektor *m*
f détecteur *m* des sursauts de rayons gamma
r детектор *m* гамма-всплесков

G40 *e* **gamma-ray bursts**
d Gamma-Ausbrüche *m pl*
f sursauts *m pl* gamma, sursauts *m pl* de rayons gamma
r гамма-всплески *m pl*

G41 *e* **gamma-ray burst source**
d Gammastrahlenausbruchquelle *f*
f source *f* de sursauts de rayons gamma
r источник *m* гамма-всплесков

G42 *e* **gamma-ray flaw detection**
d Gamma-Defektoskopie *f*
f gammaradiographie *f*, contrôle *m* par rayons gamma
r гамма-дефектоскопия *f*

G43 *e* **gamma-ray laser**
d Gammastrahlenlaser *m*
f laser *m* gamma
r гамма-лазер *m*

G44 *e* **gamma rays**
d Gamma-Strahlung *f*, Gamma-Strahlen *pl*
f rayons *pl* gamma
r гамма-лучи *pl*, гамма-излучение *n*

G45 *e* **gamma-ray source**
d Gammastrahlenquelle *f*, Gammaquelle *f*
f source *f* de rayons gamma
r источник *m* гамма-излучения

G46 *e* **gamma-ray spectrometer**
d Gamma-Spektrometer *n*
f spectromètre *m* gamma
r гамма-спектрометр *m*

G47 *e* **gamma-ray spectroscopy**
d Gamma-Spektroskopie *f*
f spectroscopie *f* gamma
r гамма-спектроскопия *f*

G48 *e* **gamma-ray spectrum**

    d Gamma-Spektrum *n*, Gamma-
        Strahlenspektrum *n*
    f spectre *m* du rayonnement gamma
    r спектр *m* гамма-излучения

G49 *e* **Gantmakher effect**
    d Gantmakher-Effekt *m*
    f effet *m* Gantmakher
    r эффект *m* Гантмахера
        (*радиочастотный размерный
        эффект*)

G50 *e* **gap**
    d Lücke *f*; Zwischenraum *m*; Spalt *m*;
        Schlitz *m*; Abstand *m*
    f écartement *m*; fente *f*; interstice *m*
    r зазор *m*; щель *f*; промежуток *m*

G51 *e* **garnet**
    d Granat *m*
    f grenat *m*
    r гранат *m*

G52 *e* **gas**
    d Gas *n*
    f gaz *m*
    r газ *m*

G53 *e* **gas amplification**
    d Gasverstärkung *f*
    f amplification *f* gazeuse
    r газовое усиление *n*, ионное
        усиление *n*

G54 *e* **gas analysis**
    d Gasanalyse *f*
    f analyse *f* de gaz
    r газовый анализ *m*

G55 *e* **gas analyzer**
    d Gasanalysator *m*
    f analyseur *m* de gaz
    r газоанализатор *m*

G56 *e* **gas constant**
    d Gaskonstante *f*
    f constante *f* de gaz
    r газовая постоянная *f*

G57 *e* **gas discharge**
    d Gasentladung *f*
    f décharge *f* gazeuse, décharge *f* dans
        un gaz
    r газовый разряд *m*

G58 *e* **gas-discharge chamber**
    d Gasentladungskammer *f*
    f chambre *f* de décharge, chambre *f* de
        décharge gazeuse
    r газоразрядная камера *f*

G59 *e* **gas-discharge contraction**
    d Gasentladungskontraktion *f*
    f contraction *f* de la décharge gazeuse
    r контракция *f* газового разряда

G60 *e* **gas-discharge device**

    d Gasentladungsgerät *n*
    f appareil *m* à décharge gazeuse
    r газоразрядный прибор *m*

G61 *e* **gas-discharge laser**
    d Gasentladungslaser *m*
    f laser *m* à décharge gazeuse
    r газоразрядный лазер *m*

G62 *e* **gas-discharge plasma**
    d Gasentladungsplasma *n*
    f plasma *m* de décharge gazeuse
    r газоразрядная плазма *f*

G63 *e* **gas-discharge source**
    d Gasentladungsquelle *f*,
        Gasentladungslichtquelle *f*
    f source *f* à décharge gazeuse
    r газоразрядный источник *m*,
        газоразрядный источник *m* света

G64 *e* **gas-dynamic laser**
    d dynamischer Gaslaser *m*
    f laser *m* gazodynamique
    r газодинамический лазер *m*

G65 *e* **gas dynamics**
    d Gasdynamik *f*
    f dynamique *f* des gaz
    r газовая динамика *f*, газодинамика *f*

G66 *e* **gaseous mixture**
    d Gasgemisch *n*
    f mélange *m* des gaz
    r газовая смесь *f*

G67 *e* **gaseous nebula**
    d Gasnebel *m*
    f nébuleuse *f* gazeuse
    r газовая туманность *f*

G68 *e* **gaseous phase**
    d Gasphase *f*; gasförmiger Zustand *m*
    f phase *f* gazeuse
    r газовая фаза *f*; газообразное
        состояние *n* вещества

G69 *e* **gaseous substance**
    d gasförmiger Stoff *m*
    f substance *f* gazeuse
    r газообразное вещество *n*

G70 *e* **gas-filled diode**
    d Gasdiode *f*, gasgefüllte Diode *f*
    f diode *f* ionique à gaz
    r газотрон *m*

G71 *e* **gas flow**
    d Gasströmung *f*
    f flux *m* de gaz
    r газовый поток *m*, течение *n* газа

G72 *e* **gas jet**
    d Gasstrahl *m*
    f jet *m* de gaz
    r газовая струя *f*

G73 e gas laser
     d Gaslaser *m*
     f laser *m* à gaz
     r газовый лазер *m*

G74 e gas permeability
     d Gasdurchlässigkeit *f*
     f perméabilité *f* aux gaz
     r газопроницаемость *f*

G75 e gas phase *see* gaseous phase

G76 e gas-phase chromatography
     d Gaschromatographie *f*
     f chromatographie *f* en phase gazeuse
     r газовая хроматография *f*

G77 e gas purification
     d Gasreinigung *f*
     f épuration *f* des gaz
     r очистка *f* газов

G78 e gas thermometer
     d Gasthermometer *n*
     f thermomètre *m* à gaz
     r газовый термометр *m*

G79 e gas turbine
     d Gasturbine *f*
     f turbine *f* à gaz
     r газовая турбина *f*

G80 e gate
     d 1. Gate *n*, Tor *n*, Gateelektrode *f*
        2. logisches Element *n*
        3. Selektorimpuls *m*
     f 1. gate *m* 2. élément *m* porte
        3. impulsion *f* sélectrice
     r 1. затвор *m* 2. логический элемент
        m 3. селекторный импульс *m*

G81 e gate pulse *see* gating pulse

G82 e gating pulse
     d Öffnungsimpuls *m*
     f impulsion *f* de déblocage
     r отпирающий импульс *m*

G83 e gauge *see* gage

G84 e gauss, Gs
     d Gauß *n*
     f gauss *m*
     r гаусс *m*, Гс

G85 e Gaussian distribution
     d Gauß-Verteilung *f*, Normalverteilung *f*
     f distribution *f* gaussienne
     r распределение *n* Гаусса,
        нормальное распределение *n*

G86 e Gaussian units
     d Gaußsches Einheitensystem *n*
     f système *m* d'unités de Gauss
     r гауссова система *f* единиц

G87 e Gauss meter

     d Gaußmeter *n*
     f gaussmètre *m*
     r измеритель *m* магнитной индукции

G88 e Gauss principle (*of least constraint*)
     d Gaußsches Prinzip *n* (*des kleinsten Zwanges*)
     f principe *m* de Gauss (*le principe de la moindre contrainte*)
     r принцип *m* Гаусса (*принцип наименьшего принуждения*)

G89 e Gauss profile
     d Gauß-Profil *n* (*einer Spektrallinie*)
     f profil *m* de Gauss
     r гауссов контур *m* (*спектральной линии*)

G90 e Gauss theorem
     d Gaußscher Satz *m*
     f théorème *m* de Gauss
     r теорема *f* Гаусса

G91 e Gay-Lussac law
     d Gay-Lussacsches Gesetz *n*, Gay-Lussac-Gesetz *n*
     f loi *f* de Gay-Lussac
     r закон *m* Гей-Люссака

G92 e Geiger-Müller counter
     d Geiger-Müller-Zählrohr *n*
     f compteur *m* de Geiger-Müller
     r счётчик *m* Гейгера, счётчик *m* Гейгера - Мюллера

G93 e Geiger-Nuttall rule
     d Geiger-Nuttall-Regel *f*
     f règle *f* de Geiger-Nuttall
     r закон *m* Гейгера - Неттолла

G94 e gel
     d Gel *n*
     f gel *m*
     r гель *m*

G95 e Gell-Mann matrices
     d Gell-Mann-Matrizen *f pl*
     f matrices *f pl* de Gell-Mann
     r матрицы *f pl* Гелл-Мана

G96 e Gell-Mann-Nishijima formula
     d Gell-Mann-Nishijima-Formel *f*
     f formule *f* de Gell-Mann-Nishijima
     r формула *f* Гелл-Мана - Нишиджимы

G97 e General Conference of Weights and Measures
     d Generalkonferenz *f* für Maß und Gewicht
     f Conférence *f* Générale des Poids et Mesures, CGPM
     r Генеральная конференция *f* по мерам и весам

G98 e generalized coordinates

d verallgemeinerte Koordinaten *f pl*
f coordonnées *f pl* généralisées
r обобщённые координаты *f pl*

G99 e **generalized force**
d verallgemeinerte Kraft *f*
f force *f* généralisée
r обобщённая сила *f*

G100 e **generalized function**
d verallgemeinerte Funktion *f*
f fonction *f* généralisée
r обобщённая функция *f*

G101 e **generalized law**
d verallgemeinertes Gesetz *n*
f loi *f* généralisée
r обобщённый закон *m*

G102 e **generalized model**
d verallgemeinertes Modell *n*
f modèle *m* généralisé
r обобщённая модель *f (напр. ядра)*

G103 e **generalized momentum**
d verallgemeinerter Impuls *m*
f impulsion *f* généralisée
r обобщённый импульс *m*

G104 e **generalized susceptibility**
d verallgemeinerte Suszeptibilität *f*
f susceptibilité *f* généralisée
r обобщённая восприимчивость *f*

G105 e **generalized symmetry**
d verallgemeinerte Symmetrie *f*
f symétrie *f* généralisée
r обобщённая симметрия *f*

G106 e **generalized velocity**
d verallgemeinerte Geschwindigkeit *f*
f vitesse *f* généralisée
r обобщённая скорость *f*

G107 e **general relativity theory**
d allgemeine Relativitätstheorie *f*
f théorie *f* de la relativité générale,
relativité *f* générale
r общая теория *f* относительности

G108 e **generation**
d 1. Generierung *f*, Erzeugung *f*
2. Entstehung *f* 3. Generation *f*
f 1. génération *f* 2. formation *f*
3. génération *f*
r 1. генерация *f*, генерирование *n*
2. образование *n*, рождение *n*
3. поколение *n*

G109 e **generation channel**
d Generierungskanal *m*
f canal *m* de génération
r канал *m* генерации *(лазера)*

G110 e **generation-recombination noise**
d Generations-Rekombinations-
Rauschen *n*

f bruit *m* de génération-recombinaison
r генерационно-рекомбинационный
шум *m*

G111 e **generator**
d Generator *m*
f générateur *m*
r генератор *m*

G112 e **genetically significant dose**
d genetisch bedeutsame Dosis *f*
f dose *f* génétiquement significative
r генетически значимая доза *f*

G113 e **geoacoustics**
d Geoakustik *f*
f géoacoustique *f*
r геоакустика *f*

G114 e **geochronology**
d Geochronologie *f*
f géochronologie *f*
r геохронология *f*

G115 e **geodesic**
d geodätische Linie *f*, Geodätische *f*
f ligne *f* géodésique
r геодезическая линия *f*

G116 e **geodesy**
d Geodäsie *f*
f géodésie *f*
r геодезия *f*

G117 e **geographical coordinates**
d geographische Koordinaten *f pl*
f coordonnées *f pl* géographiques
r географические координаты *f pl*

G118 e **geoid**
d Geoid *n*
f géoïde *m*
r геоид *m*

G119 e **geomagnetic coordinates**
d geomagnetische Koordinaten *f pl*
f coordonnées *f pl* géomagnétiques
r геомагнитные координаты *f pl*

G120 e **geomagnetic field**
d geomagnetisches Feld *n*
f champ *m* géomagnétique
r геомагнитное поле *n*

G121 e **geomagnetic latitude**
d geomagnetische Breite *f*
f latitude *f* géomagnétique
r геомагнитная широта *f*

G122 e **geomagnetic longitude**
d geomagnetische Länge *f*
f longitude *f* géomagnétique
r геомагнитная долгота *f*

G123 e **geomagnetic meridian**
d geomagnetischer Meridian *m*

f méridien *m* géomagnétique
r геомагнитный меридиан *m*

G124 e **geomagnetic pole**
d geomagnetischer Pol *m*
f pôle *m* géomagnétique
r геомагнитный полюс *m*

G125 e **geomagnetic storm**
d erdmagnetischer Sturm *m*,
magnetischer Sturm *m*
f orage *m* géomagnétique
r геомагнитная буря *f*

G126 e **geomagnetic trap**
d geomagnetische Falle *f*
f piège *m* géomagnétique
r геомагнитная ловушка *f*

G127 e **geomagnetic variations**
d erdmagnetische Variationen *f pl*
f variations *f pl* géomagnétiques
r геомагнитные вариации *f pl*

G128 e **geomagnetism**
d Erdmagnetismus *m*,
Geomagnetismus *m*
f géomagnétisme *m*
r земной магнетизм *m*,
геомагнетизм *m*

G129 e **geometrical acoustics**
d geometrische Akustik *f*,
Strahlenakustik *f*
f acoustique *f* géométrique
r геометрическая акустика *f*, лучевая
акустика *f*

G130 e **geometrical cross-section**
d geometrischer Querschnitt *m*
f section *f* efficace géométrique
r геометрическое поперечное
сечение *n*

G131 e **geometrical crystallography**
d geometrische Kristallographie *f*
f cristallographie *f* géométrique
r геометрическая кристаллография *f*

G132 e **geometrical isomer**
d geometrisches Isomer *n*, cis-trans-
Isomer *n*
f isomère *m* géométrique, isomère *m*
cis-trans
r геометрический изомер *m*, цис-
транс-изомер *m*

G133 e **geometrical isomerism**
d geometrische Isomerie *f*, cis-trans-
Isomerie *f*
f isomérie *f* géométrique, isomérie *f* cis-
trans
r геометрическая изомерия *f*, цис-
транс-изомерия *f*

G134 e **geometrical optics**

d geometrische Optik *f*, Strahlenoptik *f*
f optique *f* géométrique
r геометрическая оптика *f*, лучевая
оптика *f*

G135 e **geometrical oscillations**
d geometrische Oszillationen *f pl*
f oscillations *f pl* géométriques
r геометрические осцилляции *f pl*

G136 e **geometric cross-section** *see*
geometrical cross-section

G137 e **geometric factor**
d geometrischer Faktor *m*
f facteur *m* géométrique
r геометрический фактор *m*

G138 e **geometric interference**
d geometrische Interferenz *f*
f interférence *f* géométrique
r геометрическая интерференция *f*

G139 e **geometry**
d 1. Geometrie *f* 2. geometrische
Anordnung *f*, geometrische
Gestaltung *f*
f 1. géométrie *f* 2. configuration *f*
r 1. геометрия *f* 2. форма *f*,
конфигурация *f*

G140 e **geophone**
d Geophon *n*
f géophone *m*
r геофон *m*

G141 e **geophysics**
d Geophysik *f*
f géophysique *f*
r геофизика *f*

G142 e **geostationary orbit**
d geostationäre Bahn *f*
f orbite *f* géostationnaire
r геостационарная орбита *f*
(*искусственного спутника Земли*)

G143 e **geothermal energy**
d geothermische Energie *f*
f énergie *f* géothermique
r геотермическая энергия *f*

G144 e **geothermal gradient**
d geothermischer Gradient *m*
f gradient *m* géothermique
r геотермический градиент *m*

G145 e **geothermy**
d Geothermie *f*
f géothermie *f*
r геотермика *f*, геотермия *f*

G146 e **germanium, Ge**
d Germanium *n*
f germanium *m*
r германий *m*

G147　e　getter
　　　d　Getter m
　　　f　getter m
　　　r　геттер m; газопоглотитель m

G148　e　getter pump
　　　d　Getterpumpe f
　　　f　pompe f à getter
　　　r　геттерный насос m

G149　e　g-factor
　　　d　g-Faktor m, Landescher g-Faktor m
　　　f　facteur m de Landé, facteur m g
　　　r　g-фактор m, множитель m Ланде

G150　e　ghosts
　　　d　Geister m pl, Gittergeister m pl,
　　　　　falsche Linien f pl (im Spektrum)
　　　f　raies f pl fantômes (dans le spectre)
　　　r　дỳхи m pl (в спектре)

G151　e　giant optical nonlinearity
　　　d　optische Riesennichtlinearität f
　　　f　non-linéarité f optique géante
　　　r　гигантская оптическая
　　　　　нелинейность f

G152　e　giant oscillations
　　　d　Riesenoszillationen f pl
　　　f　oscillations f pl géantes
　　　r　гигантские осцилляции f pl

G153　e　giant pulse (in laser)
　　　d　Riesenimpuls m (Laser)
　　　f　impulsion f géante (au laser)
　　　r　гигантский импульс m (в лазере)

G154　e　giant-pulse laser
　　　d　Riesenimpulslaser m
　　　f　laser m à impulsions géantes
　　　r　лазер m, работающий в режиме
　　　　　гигантских импульсов

G155　e　giant resonance
　　　d　Riesenresonanz f
　　　f　résonance f géante
　　　r　гигантский резонанс m

G156　e　giant star
　　　d　Riesenstern m, Riese m, Gigant m
　　　f　étoile f géante
　　　r　звезда-гигант m, гигант m

G157　e　Gibbs distribution
　　　d　Gibbssche Verteilung f, Gibbs-
　　　　　Verteilung f
　　　f　distribution f de Gibbs
　　　r　распределение n Гиббса

G158　e　Gibbs-Duhem equation
　　　d　Gibbs-Duhemsche Gleichung f
　　　f　équation f de Gibbs-Duhem
　　　r　уравнение n Гиббса - Дюгема

G159　e　Gibbs free energy
　　　d　Gibbssche freie Energie f, freie
　　　　　Enthalpie f

　　　f　énergie f libre de Gibbs
　　　r　энергия f Гиббса

G160　e　Gibbs-Helmholtz relations
　　　d　Gibbs-Helmholtzsche Gleichungen f pl
　　　f　relations f pl de Gibbs-Helmholtz
　　　r　уравнения n pl Гиббса -
　　　　　Гельмгольца

G161　e　Gibbs paradox
　　　d　Gibbssches Paradoxon n
　　　f　paradoxe m de Gibbs
　　　r　парадокс m Гиббса

G162　e　Gibbs phase rule
　　　d　Gibbssche Phasenregel f
　　　f　règle f des phases, règle f des phases
　　　　　de Gibbs
　　　r　правило n фаз, правило n фаз
　　　　　Гиббса

G163　e　Gibbs statistical assembly
　　　d　Gibbssche Gesamtheit f
　　　f　ensemble m statistique de Gibbs
　　　r　статистический ансамбль m Гиббса

G164　e　Gibbs thermodynamic potential
　　　d　Gibbssches thermodynamisches
　　　　　Potential n
　　　f　potentiel m thermodynamique de
　　　　　Gibbs, potentiel m de Gibbs
　　　r　термодинамический потенциал m
　　　　　Гиббса

G165　e　gilbert, Gb
　　　d　Gilbert n
　　　f　gilbert m, Gb
　　　r　гильберт m, Гб

G166　e　Ginsburg-Landau theory
　　　d　Ginsburg-Landausche Theorie f
　　　f　théorie f de Ginsburg-Landau
　　　r　теория f сверхпроводимости
　　　　　Гинзбурга - Ландау, теория f
　　　　　Гинзбурга - Ландау

G167　e　Glan-Thompson prism
　　　d　Glan-Thompson-Prisma n
　　　f　prisme m de Glan-Thompson
　　　r　поляризационная призма f Глана -
　　　　　Томсона

G168　e　glare
　　　d　Blendung f
　　　f　éblouissement m
　　　r　блескость f

G169　e　glass
　　　d　Glas n
　　　f　verre m
　　　r　стекло n

G170　e　glass fiber
　　　d　Glasfaser f
　　　f　fibre f de verre
　　　r　стеклянное волокно n,
　　　　　стекловолокно n

G171　e　glass laser
　　　d　Glaslaser *m*
　　　f　laser *m* à verre
　　　r　лазер *m* на стекле

G172　e　glass-like semiconductors *see* glassy
　　　　　semiconductors

G173　e　glassy semiconductors
　　　d　Glashalbleiter *m pl*, glasartiger
　　　　　Halbleiter *m pl*
　　　f　semi-conducteurs *m pl* vitreux
　　　r　стеклообразные
　　　　　полупроводники *m pl*

G174　e　glassy state
　　　d　Glaszustand *m*, glasartiger Zustand *m*
　　　f　état *m* vitreux
　　　r　стеклообразное состояние *n*

G175　e　Glauber corrections
　　　d　Glauber-Korrektionen *f pl*
　　　f　corrections *f pl* de Glauber
　　　r　глауберовские поправки *f pl* (в
　　　　　квантовой теории поля)

G176　e　glide
　　　d　Gleiten *n*
　　　f　glissement *m*
　　　r　скольжение *n*; проскальзывание *n*

G177　e　glide plane
　　　d　Gleitebene *f*
　　　f　plan *m* de glissement
　　　r　плоскость *f* скольжения

G178　e　glitter
　　　d　Glänzen *n*
　　　f　éclat *m*
　　　r　блеск *m*

G179　e　global duality
　　　d　globale Dualität *f*
　　　f　dualité *f* globale
　　　r　глобальная дуальность *f*

G180　e　global instability
　　　d　globale Instabilität *f*
　　　f　instabilité *f* globale
　　　r　глобальная неустойчивость *f*

G181　e　global invariance
　　　d　Globalinvarianz *f*
　　　f　invariance *f* globale
　　　r　глобальная инвариантность *f*

G182　e　global symmetry
　　　d　Globalsymmetrie *f*
　　　f　symétrie *f* globale
　　　r　глобальная симметрия *f*

G183　e　globular star cluster
　　　d　Kugelsternhaufen *m*
　　　f　amas *m* globulaire
　　　r　шаровое звёздное скопление *n*

G184　e　glow

G185　e　glow discharge
　　　d　Glimmentladung *f*
　　　f　décharge *f* à lueur, décharge *f*
　　　　　incandescente
　　　r　тлеющий разряд *m*

G186　e　glow-discharge lamp
　　　d　Glimmlampe *f*
　　　f　lampe *f* à décharge incandescente
　　　r　лампа *f* тлеющего разряда

G187　e　glueball
　　　d　Glueball *m*
　　　f　glueball *m*
　　　r　глюбол *m*

G188　e　gluino
　　　d　Gluino *n*
　　　f　gluino *m*
　　　r　глюино *n*

G189　e　gluon
　　　d　Gluon *n*
　　　f　gluon *m*
　　　r　глюон *m*

G190　e　gluon bag
　　　d　Gluonsack *m*, Gluonbag *m*
　　　f　poche *f* de gluon
　　　r　глюонный мешок *m*

G191　e　gold, Au
　　　d　Gold *n*
　　　f　or *m*
　　　r　золото *n*

G192　e　Goldberger-Treiman relation
　　　d　Goldberger-Treimansche Beziehung *f*
　　　f　relation *f* de Goldberger-Treiman
　　　r　соотношение *n* Голдбергера -
　　　　　Тримена

G193　e　Goldstone boson
　　　d　Goldstonesches Boson *n*, Goldstone-
　　　　　Boson *n*
　　　f　boson *m* de Goldstone
　　　r　голдстоуновский бозон *m*

G194　e　Goldstone fermion
　　　d　Goldstone-Fermion *n*
　　　f　fermion *m* de Goldstone
　　　r　голдстоуновский фермион *m*

G195　e　Goldstone modes
　　　d　Goldstone-Moden *f pl*
　　　f　modes *m pl* de Goldstone
　　　r　голдстоуновские моды *f pl*

G196　e　goniometer
　　　d　Goniometer *n*
　　　f　goniomètre *m*
　　　r　гониометр *m*

d　Glimmen *n*
f　lueur *f*
r　свечение *n*

G197   *e*   goniometry
       d   Goniometrie *f*
       f   goniométrie *f*
       r   гониометрия *f*

G198   *e*   gradation
       d   Gradation *f*, Stufe *f*
       f   gradation *f*
       r   градация *f*

G199   *e*   graded index fiber
       d   Gradientenfaser *f*
       f   fibre *f* à variation régulière de l'indice de réfraction
       r   градиентное волокно *n*, волокно *n* с плавным изменением показателя преломления

G200   *e*   gradient
       d   Gradient *m*
       f   gradient *m*
       r   градиент *m*

G201   *e*   gradient drift
       d   Gradientendrift *f*
       f   dérive *f* de gradient
       r   градиентный дрейф *m*

G202   *e*   gradient invariance
       d   Gradienteninvarianz *f*
       f   invariance *f* de gradient
       r   градиентная инвариантность *f*

G203   *e*   gradiometer
       d   Gradiometer *n*
       f   gradiomètre *m*
       r   градиометр *m*, градиентометр *m*

G204   *e*   graduation
       d   Eichung *f*
       f   graduation *f*
       r   градуировка *f*

G205   *e*   grain
       d   Korn *n*, Kristallkorn *n*
       f   grain *m*
       r   зерно *n*

G206   *e*   grain boundary
       d   Korngrenze *f*
       f   joint *m* de grains
       r   межзёренная граница *f*; граница *f* зерна

G207   *e*   graininess
       d   Kornstruktur *f*, Korngefüge *n*
       f   granulosité *f*
       r   зернистость *f*, зернистая структура *f*

G208   *e*   gram, g
       d   Gramm *n*
       f   gramme *m*
       r   грамм *m*

G209   *e*   gram-atom
       d   Grammatom *n*

       f   gramme-atome *m*
       r   грамм-атом *m*

G210   *e*   gram-molecule
       d   Grammolekül *n*, Mol *n*
       f   gramme-molécule *m*
       r   грамм-молекула *f*

G211   *e*   grand unification
       d   große Unifikation *f*
       f   grande unification *f*
       r   великое объединение *n*

G212   *e*   grand unified model
       d   Modell *n* der großen Unifikation
       f   modèle *m* de grande unification
       r   модель *f* великого объединения

G213   *e*   granularity
       d   Körnigkeit *f*
       f   granulosité *f*
       r   зернистость *f* (*напр. фотоэмульсии*)

G214   *e*   granulation
       d   Granulierung *f*, Granulation *f*
       f   granulation *f*
       r   грануляция *f*

G215   *e*   graph
       d   1. Grafik *f*, Diagramm *n* 2. Graph *m*
       f   1. abaque *m*, diagramme *m* 2. graphe *m*
       r   1. график *m*, диаграмма *f* 2. граф *m*

G216   *e*   graphical integration
       d   graphische Integration *f*
       f   intégration *f* graphique
       r   графическое интегрирование *n*

G217   *e*   graphical representation
       d   grafische Darstellung *f*
       f   représentation *f* graphique
       r   графическое представление *n*

G218   *e*   graphite
       d   Graphit *m*
       f   graphite *m*
       r   графит *m*

G219   *e*   graphite-moderated reactor
       d   graphitmoderierter Reaktor *m*, Graphitreaktor *m*
       f   réacteur *m* modéré au graphite, réacteur *m* à graphite
       r   графитовый реактор *m*

G220   *e*   graphite moderator
       d   Graphitmoderator *m*
       f   modérateur *m* au graphite
       r   графитовый замедлитель *m*

G221   *e*   graphite stacking
       d   Graphitkonstruktion *f*, Graphitstapel *m*, Graphitstruktur *f*
       f   empilement *m* de graphite
       r   графитовая кладка *f* (*ядерного реактора*)

G222   *e*   **Grashof number**
      d   Grashof-Zahl *f*, Grashofsche Kennzahl *f*
      f   nombre *m* de Grashof
      r   число *n* Грасгофа

G223   *e*   **Grassmann algebra**
      d   Grassmann-Algebra *f*, Grassmannsche Algebra *f*
      f   algèbre *f* de Grassemann
      r   алгебра *f* Грассмана

G224   *e*   **grating**
      d   1. Beugungsgitter *n* 2. Gitter *n*
      f   1. réseau *m* de diffraction 2. réseau *m*
      r   1. дифракционная решётка *f* 2. решётка *f*

G225   *e*   **grating compressor** (*of laser pulses*)
      d   Gitterkompressor *m* (*von Laserimpulsen*)
      f   compresseur *m* à réseau (*d'impulsions laser*)
      r   решёточный компрессор *m* (*лазерных импульсов*)

G226   *e*   **grating constant**
      d   Gitterkonstante *f*
      f   constante *f* de réseau
      r   период *m* дифракционной решётки

G227   *e*   **grating deflector**
      d   Beugungsgitterablenker *m*
      f   déflecteur *m* à réseau
      r   решёточный дефлектор *m*, дефлектор *m* на дифракционной решётке

G228   *e*   **grating interferometer**
      d   Gitterinterferometer *n*
      f   interféromètre *m* à réseau
      r   дифракционный интерферометр *m*

G229   *e*   **grating spectrometer**
      d   Beugungsgitterspektrometer *n*
      f   spectromètre *m* à réseau
      r   дифракционный спектрометр *m*, спектрометр *m* с дифракционной решёткой

G230   *e*   **gravimeter**
      d   Gravimeter *n*
      f   gravimètre *m*
      r   гравиметр *m*

G231   *e*   **gravimetry**
      d   Gravimetrie *f*
      f   gravimétrie *f*
      r   гравиметрия *f*

G232   *e*   **gravitating mass**
      d   schwere Masse *f*
      f   masse *f* lourde, masse *f* pesante, masse *f* gravitationnelle
      r   гравитационная масса *f*, тяжёлая масса *f*

G233   *e*   **gravitation**
      d   Gravitation *f*, Massenanziehung *f*
      f   gravitation *f*
      r   тяготение *n*, гравитация *f*

G234   *e*   **gravitational acceleration**
      d   Gravitationsbeschleunigung *f*, Schwerebeschleunigung *f*, Fallbeschleunigung *f*, Erdbeschleunigung *f*
      f   accélération *f* de la pesanteur
      r   ускорение *n* силы тяжести, ускорение *n* свободного падения

G235   *e*   **gravitational capture**
      d   Gravitationseinfang *m*
      f   capture *f* par gravitation
      r   гравитационный захват *m*

G236   *e*   **gravitational collapse**
      d   Gravitationskollaps *m*
      f   collapsus *m* gravitationnel
      r   гравитационный коллапс *m*

G237   *e*   **gravitational constant**
      d   Gravitationskonstante *f*
      f   constante *f* de gravitation
      r   гравитационная постоянная *f*

G238   *e*   **gravitational field**
      d   Gravitationsfeld *n*, Schwerefeld *n*
      f   champ *m* gravitationnel
      r   гравитационное поле *n*, поле *n* тяготения

G239   *e*   **gravitational focusing**
      d   Gravitationsfokussierung *f*
      f   focalisation *f* gravitationnelle
      r   гравитационная фокусировка *f*

G240   *e*   **gravitational instability**
      d   Gravitationsinstabilität *f*
      f   instabilité *f* gravitationnelle
      r   гравитационная неустойчивость *f*

G241   *e*   **gravitational instanton**
      d   Gravitationsinstanton *n*
      f   instanton *m* gravitationnel
      r   гравитационный инстантон *m*

G242   *e*   **gravitational interaction**
      d   Gravitationswechselwirkung *f*, gravitative Wechselwirkung *f*
      f   interaction *f* gravitationnelle
      r   гравитационное взаимодействие *n*

G243   *e*   **gravitational mass defect**
      d   Gravitationsmassendefekt *m*
      f   défaut *m* de masse gravitationnel
      r   гравитационный дефект *m* массы

G244   *e*   **gravitational paradox**
      d   Gravitationsparadoxon *n*
      f   paradoxe *m* de gravitation
      r   гравитационный парадокс *m*

G245   *e*   **gravitational radiation**

d Gravitationsstrahlung *f*
f rayonnement *m* gravitationnel
r гравитационное излучение *n*

G246 e **gravitational radius**
d Gravitationsradius *m*
f rayon *m* gravitationnel
r гравитационный радиус *m*

G247 e **gravitational shift**
d Gravitationsverschiebung *f*
f déplacement *m* gravitationel
r гравитационное смещение *n*

G248 e **gravitational wave detection**
d Gravitationswellendetektion *f*
f détection *f* des ondes gravitationnelles
r детектирование *n* гравитационных
волн

G249 e **gravitational waves**
d Gravitationswellen *f pl*
f ondes *f pl* gravitationelles
r гравитационные волны *f pl*

G250 e **gravitino**
d Gravitino *n*
f gravitino *m*
r гравитино *n*

G251 e **graviton**
d Graviton *n*, Gravitationsquant *n*
f graviton *m*
r гравитон *m*

G252 e **gravity**
d Schwerkraft *f*, Schwere *f*
f force *f* de pesanteur; gravité *f*
r сила *f* тяжести; тяготение *n*

G253 e **gravity anomalies**
d Schwereanomalien *f pl*
f anomalies *f pl* de la force de
pesanteur, anomalies *f pl* de
pesanteur, anomalies *f pl* de gravité
r аномалии *f pl* силы тяжести

G254 e **gravity waves**
d Gravitationswellen *f pl*
f ondes *f pl* gravitationelles, ondes *f pl*
de gravité
r гравитационные волны *f pl*

G255 e **Gray, Gy**
d Gray *n*
f gray *m*
r грэй *m*, Гр

G256 e **grazing angular momentum**
d Drehimpuls *m* bei streifendem Einfall,
«grazing»-Drehimpuls *m*
f moment *m* angulaire à l'incidence
rasante
r импульс *m* при скользящем
падении

G257 e **grazing incidence**

d streifender Einfall *m*
f incidence *f* rasante
r скользящее падение *n* (*падение
пучка частиц или излучения под
малым углом к поверхности*)

G258 e **grease**
d Schmierstoff *m*
f graisse *f*, lubrifiant *m*
r смазка *f*, смазочный материал *m*

G259 e **Green functions**
d Greensche Funktionen *f pl*
f fonctions *f pl* de Green
r функции *f pl* Грина

G260 e **greenhouse effect**
d Glashauseffekt *m*, Treibhauseffekt *m*
f effet *m* de serre
r парниковый эффект *m*,
оранжерейный эффект *m*

G261 e **Green-Kubo formulae**
d Green-Kubosche Formeln *f pl*
f formules *f pl* de Green-Kubo
r формулы *f pl* Грина - Кубо

G262 e **grey body**
d grauer Körper *m*, grauer Strahler *m*,
Graustrahler *m*
f corps *m* gris
r серое тело *n*

G263 e **grey body radiation**
d Graustrahlung *f*, graue Strahlung *f*
f rayonnement *m* du corps gris
r излучение *n* серого тела, серое
излучение *n*

G264 e **grey radiation**
d Graustrahlung *f*, graue Strahlung *f*
f rayonnement *m* gris
r серое излучение *n*

G265 e **grid**
d Gitter *n*
f réseau *m*
r 1. сетка *f* 2. решётка *f*

G266 e **grid bias**
d Gittervorspannung *f*
f tension *f* de grille
r сеточное смещение *n*

G267 e **grid detection**
d Gittergleichrichtung *f*
f détection *f* à grille
r сеточное детектирование *n*

G268 e **grid focusing**
d Gitterfokussierung *f*
f focalisation *f* par grille
r сеточная фокусировка *f*

G269 e **grid modulation**
d Gittermodulation *f*

f modulation *f* à grille
r сеточная модуляция *f*

G270 *e* groove
 d 1. Furche *f*, Rille *f* 2. Furche *f*,
  Gitterfurche *f*, Strich *m*,
  Gitterstrich *m*
 f rainure *f*
 r 1. канавка *f* 2. штрих *m*
  дифракционной решётки

G271 *e* ground
 d Erde *f*, Erdschluß *m*, Masse *f*
 f mise *f* à la terre, terre *f*
 r заземление *n*, земля *f*

G272 *e* ground connection
 d Erdung *f*
 f mise *f* à la terre
 r заземление *n*

G273 *e* ground level
 d Grundniveau *n*
 f niveau *m* fondamental
 r основной уровень *m*

G274 *e* ground state
 d Grundzustand *m*, Normalzustand *m*
 f état *m* fondamental
 r основное состояние *n* (*напр.
  атома*)

G275 *e* ground wave
 d Bodenwelle *f*
 f onde *f* superficielle
 r земная волна *f*; поверхностная
  волна *f*

G276 *e* group
 d Gruppe *f*
 f groupe *m*
 r группа *f*

G277 *e* group delay
 d Gruppenlaufzeit *f*,
  Gruppenverzögerung *f*
 f retard *m* de groupe
 r групповая задержка *f*, групповое
  запаздывание *n*

G278 *e* group generator
 d Gruppengenerator *m*
 f générateur *m* de groupe
 r генератор *m* группы

G279 *e* group synchronism
 d Gruppensynchronismus *m*
 f synchronisme *m* de groupe
 r групповой синхронизм *m*

G280 *e* **group-theoretical method**
 d gruppentheoretische Methode *f*
 f méthode *f* de théorie des groupes
 r теоретико-групповой метод *m*

G281 *e* **group velocity**

G282 *e* **group velocity dispersion**
 d Gruppengeschwindigkeitsdispersion *f*
 f dispersion *f* de la vitesse de groupe
 r дисперсия *f* групповой скорости

G283 *e* **group velocity modulation**
 d Gruppengeschwindigkeitsmodulation *f*
 f modulation *f* de la vitesse de groupe
 r модуляция *f* групповой скорости

G284 *e* **growing**
 d Züchten *n*, Züchtung *f* (*Kristallen*)
 f croissance *f* (*des cristaux*)
 r выращивание *n* (*кристаллов*)

G285 *e* **growth**
 d Wachstum *n*
 f croissance *f*
 r 1. рост *m* (*кристаллов*) 2.
  выращивание *n* (*кристаллов*)

G286 *e* **growth curve**
 d 1. Wachstumskurve *f*, Zunahmekurve *f*
  2. Nachbildungskurve *f*, Anstiegskurve
  f (*Kernphysik*)
 f courbe *f* de croissance
 r 1. кривая *f* роста 2. кривая *f*
  накопления (*изотопа*)

G287 *e* **growth kinetics**
 d Wachstumskinetik *f* (*Kristall*)
 f cinétique *f* de croissance (*de cristal*)
 r кинетика *f* роста (*кристалла*)

G288 *e* **growth pyramid**
 d Wachstumspyramide *f*
 f pyramide *f* de croissance
 r пирамида *f* роста

G289 *e* **Grüneisen constant**
 d Grüneisen-Konstante *f*
 f constante *f* de Grüneisen
 r параметр *m* Грюнайзена

G290 *e* **Grüneisen law**
 d Grüneisensche Regel *f*
 f loi *f* de Grüneisen, deuxième règle *f*
  de Grüneisen
 r закон *m* Грюнайзена

G291 *e* **guide**
 d Wellenleiter *m*, Hohlleiter *m*
 f guide *m* d'ondes
 r волновод *n*

G292 *e* **guide wavelength**
 d Wellenlänge *f* im Hohlleiter
 f longueur *f* d'onde dans le guide
  d'ondes
 r длина *f* волны в волноводе

G293 *e* **guided mode**
 d Hohlleitermode *f*

d Gruppengeschwindigkeit *f*
f vitesse *f* de groupe
r групповая скорость *f*

f mode *m* de guide d'ondes
r волноводная мода *f*, волноводная волна *f*

G294 *e* guided wave
d Hohlleiterwelle *f*
f onde *f* de guide d'ondes
r волноводная волна *f*

G295 *e* guiding center
d Führungszentrum *n*
f centre *m* guide, centre *m* de guidance
r ведущий центр *m*

G296 *e* guiding magnetic field
d magnetisches Führungsfeld *n*
f champ *m* magnétique guide
r ведущее магнитное поле *n*

G297 *e* gun
d Elektronenkanone *f*; Elektronenstrahlerzeuger *m*
f canon *m* électronique
r электронная пушка *f*; электронный прожектор *m*

G298 *e* Gunn diode
d Gunn-Diode *f*
f diode *f* Gunn, diode *f* à effet Gunn
r диод *m* Ганна

G299 *e* Gunn domain
d Gunn-Domäne *f*
f domaine *m* de Gunn
r домен *m* Ганна

G300 *e* Gunn effect
d Gunn-Effekt *m*
f effet *m* Gunn
r эффект *m* Ганна

G301 *e* Gunn oscillator
d Gunn-Oszillator *m*
f oscillateur *m* de Gunn
r генератор *m* Ганна

G302 *e* gyration
d Gyration *f*
f gyration *f*
r вращение *n*

G303 *e* gyrator
d Gyrator *m*
f gyrateur *m*
r гиратор *m*

G304 *e* gyromagnetic effects
d gyromagnetische Effekte *m pl*
f effets *m pl* gyromagnétiques
r гиромагнитные явления *n pl*, магнитомеханические явления *n pl*

G305 *e* gyromagnetic frequency
d gyromagnetische Frequenz *f*
f fréquence *f* gyromagnétique
r гиромагнитная частота *f*

G306 *e* gyromagnetic ratio
d gyromagnetisches Verhältnis *n*
f rapport *m* gyromagnétique
r гиромагнитное отношение *n*

G307 *e* gyroscope
d Kreisel *m*
f gyroscope *m*
r гироскоп *m*

G308 *e* gyroscopic forces
d Kreiselkräfte *f pl*, gyroskopische Kräfte *f pl*
f forces *f pl* gyroscopiques
r гироскопические силы *f pl*

G309 *e* gyroscopic inertia
d Kreiselträgheit *f*
f inertie *f* de gyroscope
r инерция *f* гироскопа

G310 *e* gyroscopic moment *see* gyroscopic torque

G311 *e* gyroscopic torque
d Kreiselmoment *n*, Gyralmoment *n*
f moment *m* gyroscopique
r гироскопический момент *m*

G312 *e* gyrostabilizer
d Stabilisierungskreisel *m*
f gyrostabilisateur *m*
r гиростабилизатор *m*

G313 *e* gyrotron
d Gyrotron *n*
f gyrotron *m*
r гиротрон *m*

G314 *e* gyrotropic crystal
d gyrotroper Kristall *m*
f cristal *m* gyrotrope
r гиротропный кристалл *m*

G315 *e* gyrotropic medium
d gyrotropes Medium *n*
f milieu *m* gyrotrope
r гиротропная среда *f*

G316 *e* gyrotropy
d Gyrotropie *f*
f gyrotropie *f*
r гиротропия *f*

H

H1 *e* habit
d Habitus *m*, Kristallhabitus *m*
f faciès *m*
r форма *f* кристалла, габитус *m*

H2	e	hadrodynamics
	d	Hadrondynamik f
	f	dynamique f d'hadrons
	r	адродинамика f, динамика f адронов

H3	e	hadron
	d	Hadron n
	f	hadron m
	r	адрон m

H4	e	hadron collider
	d	Hadroncollider m
	f	collisionneur m hadronique
	r	адронный коллайдер m

H5	e	hadron current
	d	Hadronstrom m
	f	courant m hadronique
	r	адронный ток m

H6	e	hadronic atom
	d	hadronisches Atom n, Hadronatom n
	f	atome m hadronique
	r	адронный атом m

H7	e	hadronic bag
	d	Hadronensack m
	f	sac m hadronique
	r	адронный мешок m

H8	e	hadronic boiling
	d	hadronisches Sieden n
	f	bouillonnement m hadronique
	r	адронное кипение n

H9	e	hadronic calorimeter
	d	hadronisches Kalorimeter n
	f	calorimètre m hadronique
	r	адронный калориметр m

H10	e	hadronic charge
	d	Hadronenladung f
	f	charge f hadronique
	r	адронный заряд m

H11	e	hadronic decay
	d	hadronischer Zerfall m
	f	désintégration f hadronique
	r	адронный распад m

H12	e	hadronic fluid
	d	Hadronenflüssigkeit f
	f	fluide m hadronique
	r	адронная жидкость f

H13	e	half-amplitude duration
	d	Halbamplitudendauer f
	f	durée f à demi-amplitude
	r	длительность f импульса на уровне 0,5, длительность f импульса на полувысоте, длительность f импульса на уровне половинной амплитуды

H14	e	half-breadth (of a spectral line)
	d	Halbwertsbreite f (Spektrallinie)

	f	demi-largeur f (de raie spectrale)
	r	полуширина f (спектральной линии)

H15	e	half-life
	d	Halbwertszeit f
	f	période f de demi-vie
	r	период m полураспада

H16	e	half-plane
	d	Halbebene f
	f	demi-plan m
	r	полуплоскость f

H17	e	half-shadow
	d	Halbschatten m
	f	pénombre f
	r	полутень f

H18	e	half-shadow device
	d	Halbschattengerät n
	f	appareil m à pénombre
	r	полутеневой прибор m

H19	e	half-wave dipole
	d	Halbwellendipol m
	f	dipôle m à demi-onde
	r	полуволновой вибратор m

H20	e	half-wave line
	d	Halbwellenlinie f
	f	ligne f demi-onde
	r	полуволновая линия f

H21	e	half-wave plate
	d	Halbwellenplättchen n
	f	plaque f demi-onde
	r	полуволновая пластинка f

H22	e	half-wave rectifier
	d	Halbwellengleichrichter m, Einweggleichrichter m
	f	redresseur m à une alternance
	r	однополупериодный выпрямитель m

H23	e	half-width see half-breadth

H24	e	Hall coefficient
	d	Hall-Koeffizient m
	f	coefficient m de Hall
	r	коэффициент m Холла

H25	e	Hall effect
	d	Hall-Effekt m
	f	effet m Hall
	r	эффект m Холла

H26	e	Hall mobility
	d	Hall-Beweglichkeit f
	f	mobilité f de Hall
	r	холловская подвижность f

H27	e	Hall resistance quantization
	d	Hall-Widerstandsquantisierung f
	f	quantification f de la résistance de Hall
	r	квантование n холловского сопротивления

H28 *e* **Hall voltage**
    d Hall-Spannung *f*, Hall-Urspannung *f*
    f tension *f* d'effet Hall
    r холловское напряжение *n*,
       холловская эдс *f*

H29 *e* **halo**
    d Halo *m*
    f halo *m*
    r ореол *m*; гало *n*

H30 *e* **halogens**
    d Halogene *n pl*
    f halogènes *m pl*
    r галогены *m pl*

H31 *e* **Hamilton gage**
    d Hamilton-Eichung *f*
    f jauge *f* de Hamilton
    r гамильтонова калибровка *f*

H32 *e* **Hamiltonian**
    d Hamilton-Operator *m*, Hamiltonscher
       Operator *m*
    f hamiltonien *m*, opérateur *m* de
       Hamilton
    r гамильтониан *m*, оператор *m*
       Гамильтона

H33 *e* **Hamiltonian formalism**
    d Hamilton-Formalismus *m*,
       Hamiltonscher Formalismus *m*
    f formalisme *m* de Hamilton
    r гамильтонов формализм *m*

H34 *e* **Hamiltonian function**
    d Hamilton-Funktion *f*, Hamiltonsche
       Funktion *f*
    f fonction *f* de Hamilton
    r функция *f* Гамильтона

H35 *e* **Hamiltonian system**
    d Hamiltonsches System *n*
    f système *m* de Hamilton
    r гамильтонова система *f*

H36 *e* **Hamilton-Jacobi equation**
    d Hamilton-Jacobi-Gleichung *f*,
       Hamilton-Jacobische
       Differentialgleichung *f*
    f équation *f* de Hamilton-Jacobi
    r уравнение *n* Гамильтона - Якоби

H37 *e* **Hamilton principle**
    d Hamilton-Prinzip *n*, Hamiltonsches
       Prinzip *n*
    f principe *m* de Hamilton
    r принцип *m* Гамильтона

H38 *e* **Hankel functions**
    d Hankelsche Funktionen *f pl*, Hankel-
       Funktionen *f pl*
    f fonctions *f pl* de Hankel
    r функции *f pl* Ханкеля

H39 *e* **Hanle effect**

H39 *d* Hanle-Effekt *m*
    f effet *m* Hanle
    r эффект *m* Ханле

H40 *e* **Hanle magnetometer**
    d Hanle-Magnetometer *n*, Hanlesches
       Magnetometer *n*
    f magnétomètre *m* de Hanle
    r магнетометр *m* Ханле

H41 *e* **hard component**
    d harte Komponente *f*, durchdringende
       Komponente *f*
    f composante *f* dure
    r жёсткая компонента *f*

H42 *e* **hardening**
    d 1. Härten *n*, Härtung *f* 2.
       Verfestigung *f*
    f durcissement *m*
    r 1. закалка *f* 2. упрочнение *n*

H43 *e* **hard magnetic material**
    d hartmagnetischer Werkstoff *m*,
       Dauermagnetwerkstoff *m*
    f matériau *m* dur magnétique
    r магнитно-твёрдый материал *m*,
       магнитно-жёсткий материал *m*,
       жёсткий магнитный материал *m*

H44 *e* **hardness**
    d 1. Härte *f* 2.
       Durchdringungsvermögen *n*
    f dureté *f*
    r 1. твёрдость *f* 2. жёсткость *f*

H45 *e* **hardness test**
    d Härteprüfung *f*, Härtemessung *f*
    f essai *m* de dureté
    r испытание *n* на твёрдость

H46 *e* **hard quantum**
    d hartes Quant *n*
    f quantum *m* dur
    r жёсткий квант *m*

H47 *e* **hard radiation**
    d harte Strahlung *f*, durchdringende
       Strahlung *f*
    f rayonnement *m* dur
    r жёсткое излучение *n*

H48 *e* **harmonic**
    d Harmonische *f*; Oberwelle *f*,
       Oberschwingung *f*
    f harmonique *m*
    r гармоника *f*

H49 *e* **harmonic analyser**
    d harmonischer Analysator *m*
    f analyseur *m* harmonique
    r анализатор *m* гармоник

H50 *e* **harmonic analysis**
    d harmonische Analyse *f*, Fourier-
       Analyse *f*

f analyse *f* harmonique
r гармонический анализ *m*

H51 *e* **harmonic distortion**
   d harmonische Verzerrungen *f pl*, nichtlineare Verzerrungen *f pl*
   f distorsion *f* harmonique
   r нелинейные искажения *n pl*

H52 *e* **harmonic function**
   d harmonische Funktion *f*
   f fonction *f* harmonique
   r гармоническая функция *f*

H53 *e* **harmonic generation**
   d Oberwellenerzeugung *f*
   f génération *f* d'harmoniques
   r генерация *f* гармоник

H54 *e* **harmonic generator**
   d Oberwellengenerator *m*
   f générateur *m* d'harmoniques
   r генератор *m* гармоник

H55 *e* **harmonic motion**
   d harmonische Bewegung *f*, harmonische Schwingung *f*
   f mouvement *m* harmonique
   r гармоническое движение *n*, гармонические колебания *n pl*

H56 *e* **harmonic oscillation**
   d harmonische Schwingungen *f pl*
   f oscillation *f* harmonique
   r гармонические колебания *n pl*

H57 *e* **harmonic oscillator**
   d harmonischer Oszillator *m*
   f oscillateur *m* harmonique
   r гармонический осциллятор *m*

H58 *e* **harmonic series**
   d harmonische Reihe *f*
   f série *f* harmonique
   r гармонический ряд *m*

H59 *e* **harmonic vibration** *see* **harmonic oscillation**

H60 *e* **Hartmann diaphragm**
   d Hartmann-Blende *f*
   f diaphragme *m* de Hartmann
   r диафрагма *f* Гартмана, гартмановская диафрагма *f*

H61 *e* **Hartmann flow**
   d Hartmann-Strömung *f*
   f écoulement *m* de Hartmann
   r гартмановское течение *n*

H62 *e* **Hartmann number**
   d Hartmann-Zahl *f*, Hartmannsche Kennzahl *f*, Hartmannsche Ähnlichkeitszahl *f*
   f nombre *m* de Hartmann
   r число *n* Гартмана

H63 *e* **Hartmann oscillator**
   d Hartmann-Generator *m*, Gasstromgenerator *m*, Hartmannsche Pfeife *f*
   f oscillateur *m* de Hartmann
   r генератор *m* Гартмана, газоструйный излучатель *m*

H64 *e* **Hartree-Fock method**
   d Hartree-Focksche Methode *f*
   f méthode *f* de Hartree-Fock
   r метод *m* Хартри - Фока, метод *m* самосогласованного поля

H65 *e* **haze**
   d leichter Nebel *m*; Dunst *m*
   f brume *f*
   r дымка *f*

H66 *e* **head**
   d 1. Druckhöhe *f*; Staudruck *m* 2. Kopf *m*; Aufsatz *m*
   f 1. pression *f* 2. tête *f*
   r 1. напор *m* 2. головка *f*, насадка *f*

H67 *e* **head-on collision**
   d 1. zentraler Stoß *m*, Zentralstoß *m*, gerader Stoß *m* 2. Frontalzusammenstoß *m*
   f 1. collision *f* centrale 2. collision *f* frontale
   r 1. центральное соударение *n* 2. лобовое столкновение *n*

H68 *e* **head wave**
   d Kopfwelle *f*
   f onde *f* de choc de tête
   r головная ударная волна *f*

H69 *e* **healing of defects**
   d Ausheilen *n* von Defekten
   f élimination *f* des défauts
   r залечивание *n* дефектов (*структуры*)

H70 *e* **hearing**
   d Gehör *n*
   f ouïe *f*
   r слух *m*

H71 *e* **hearing threshold**
   d Hörschwelle *f*
   f seuil *m* d'audibilité
   r порог *m* слышимости

H72 *e* **heat**
   d Wärme *f*
   f chaleur *f*
   r теплота *f*

H73 *e* **heat balance**
   d Wärmebilanz *f*
   f bilan *m* de la chaleur
   r тепловой баланс *m*

H74 *e* **heat capacity**

	d	Wärmekapazität *f*
	f	capacité *f* thermique
	r	теплоёмкость *f*

H75 *e* heat conduction
d Wärmeleitung *f*
f conductibilité *f* thermique
r теплопроводность *f*

H76 *e* heat conduction mechanism
d Wärmeleitungsmechanismus *m*
f mécanisme *m* de conductibilité thermique
r механизм *m* теплопроводности

H77 *e* heat conductivity
d Wärmeleitfähigkeit *f*, Wärmeleitzahl *f*
f coefficient *m* de conduction de chaleur
r коэффициент *m* теплопроводности, теплопроводность *f*

H78 *e* heat conductor
d Wärmeleiter *m*
f conducteur *m* de la chaleur
r проводник *m* тепла

H79 *e* heat content
d Enthalpie *f*
f enthalpie *f*
r энтальпия *f*, теплосодержание *n*

H80 *e* heat emission *see* heat radiation

H81 *e* heat engine
d Wärmekraftmaschine *f*
f moteur *m* thermique
r тепловой двигатель *m*

H82 *e* heater
d 1. Heizkörper *m*; Heizelement *n*
2. Katodenheizer *m*
f 1. réchauffeur *m*; élément *m* chauffant 2. réchauffeur *m* de cathode
r 1. нагреватель *m* 2. подогреватель *m*, подогреватель *m* катода

H83 *e* heat exchange
d Wärmetausch *m*, Wärmeaustausch *m*
f échange *m* de chaleur
r теплообмен *m*

H84 *e* heat exchanger
d Wärmetauscher *m*, Wärmeaustauscher *m*
f échangeur *m* de chaleur
r теплообменник *m*

H85 *e* heat flow, heat flow rate
d 1. Wärmedurchgang *m*
2. Wärmestrom *m*
f 1. transfert *m* thermique 2. flux *m* thermique
r 1. теплопередача *f* 2. тепловой поток *m*

H86 *e* heat flux
d Wärmestromdichte *f*
f densité *f* de flux thermique
r плотность *f* теплового потока

H87 *e* heating
d Heizen *n*, Heizung *f*; Erhitzen *n*, Erwärmung *f*
f chauffage *m*
r нагрев *m*, нагревание *n*

H88 *e* heat-insulating material
d Wärmedämmstoff *m*, Wärmeisolierstoff *m*
f isolant *m* thermique, calorifuge *m*
r теплоизоляционный материал *m*

H89 *e* heat insulation
d Wärmedämmung *f*, Wärmeschutzisolierung *f*
f calorifugeage *m*, isolation *f* calorifuge, isolation *f* thermique
r теплоизоляция *f*, тепловая изоляция *f*

H90 *e* heat of combustion
d Verbrennungswärme *f*
f chaleur *f* de combustion
r теплота *f* сгорания

H91 *e* heat of condensation
d Kondensationswärme *f*
f chaleur *f* de condensation
r теплота *f* конденсации

H92 *e* heat of evaporation *see* heat of vaporization

H93 *e* heat of melting
d Schmelzwärme *f*
f chaleur *f* de fusion
r теплота *f* плавления

H94 *e* heat of phase transition
d Umwandlungswärme *f*
f chaleur *f* de changement de phase
r теплота *f* фазового перехода

H95 *e* heat of vaporization
d Verdampfungswärme *f*, Verdunstungswärme *f*
f chaleur *f* de vaporisation, chaleur *f* d'évaporation
r теплота *f* испарения, теплота *f* парообразования

H96 *e* heat pipe
d Wärmerohr *n*
f tuyau *m* calorique, tube *m* calorique
r тепловая труба *f*

H97 *e* heat pump
d Wärmepumpe *f*
f pompe *f* à chaleur
r тепловой насос *m*

H98 *e* heat radiation

d Wärmestrahlung *f*, thermische
Strahlung *f*, Temperaturstrahlung *f*
f rayonnement *m* thermique, radiation *f*
thermique
r тепловое излучение *n*

H99 e **heat reservoir**
d Wärmebehälter *m*
f réservoir *m* thermique
r тепловой резервуар *m*

H100 e **heat shield**
d Wärmeschutzschirm *m*,
Wärmeschutzabschirmung *f*
f écran *m* thermique; calorifugeage *m*
r тепловой экран *m*, теплозащита *f*

H101 e **heat source**
d Wärmequelle *f*
f source *f* de chaleur
r источник *m* теплоты, источник *m*
тепла, тепловой источник *m*

H102 e **heat transfer**
d Wärmeübertragung *f*,
Wärmetransport *m*
f transfert *m* de la chaleur, transport *m*
de la chaleur
r теплообмен *m*, перенос *m* тепла

H103 e **heat-transfer agent**
d Wärmeträger *m*,
Wärmeübertragungsmittel *n*
f agent *m* de transfert de la chaleur,
agent *m* d'échange thermique
r теплоноситель *m*

H104 e **heat transmission**
d Wärmedurchgang *m*
f transfert *m* thermique
r теплопередача *f*

H105 e **heavy isotope**
d schweres Isotop *n*
f isotope *m* lourd
r тяжёлый изотоп *m*

H106 e **heavy lepton**
d schweres Lepton *n*
f lepton *m* lourd
r тяжёлый лептон *m*

H107 e **heavy meson**
d schweres Meson *n*
f méson *m* lourd
r тяжёлый мезон *m*

H108 e **heavy particle**
d schweres Teilchen *n*
f particule *f* lourde
r тяжёлая частица *f*

H109 e **heavy quark**
d schweres Quark *n*
f quark *m* lourd
r тяжёлый кварк *m*

H110 e **heavy water**
d Schwerwasser *n*, schweres Wasser *n*
f eau *f* lourde
r тяжёлая вода *f*

H111 e **heavy-water moderator**
d Schwerwasser-Moderator *m*
f modérateur *m* en eau lourde
r замедлитель *m* на тяжёлой воде

H112 e **hectopascal, hPa**
d Hektopaskal *n*
f hectopascal *m*, hPa
r гектопаскаль *m*, гПа

H113 e **HEED method** *see* **high-energy
electron diffraction method**

H114 e **height**
d Höhe *f*
f hauteur *f*
r высота *f*

H115 e **height above sea level**
d Höhe *f* über dem Meeresspiegel
f hauteur *f* au-dessus du niveau de la
mer
r высота *f* над уровнем моря

H116 e **Heisenberg indeterminacy principle**
see **Heisenberg uncertainty principle**

H117 e **Heisenberg model**
d Heisenberg-Modell *n*
f modèle *m* de Heisenberg
r модель *f* Гейзенберга,
гейзенберговская модель *f*

H118 e **Heisenberg uncertainty principle**
d Heisenbergsches
Unbestimmtheitsprinzip *n*
f principe *m* d'incertitude de
Heisenberg
r принцип *m* неопределённости
Гейзенберга

H119 e **Heisenberg uncertainty relation**
d Heisenberg's
Unbestimmtheitsrelation *f*
f relation *f* d'incertitude de Heisenberg
r соотношение *n* неопределённостей
Гейзенберга

H120 e **helical aerial, helical antenna**
d Wendelantenne *f*
f antenne *f* hélicoïdale
r спиральная антенна *f*

H121 e **helical motion**
d Schraubenbewegung *f*
f mouvement *m* hélicoïdal
r винтовое движение *n*, движение *n*
по спирали

H122 e **helical structure**
d Spiralstruktur *f*, Helikalstruktur *f*

    f structure *f* hélicoïdale
    r геликоидальная структура *f*

H123 *e* **helicity**
    d Helizität *f*, Schraubensinn *m*
    f hélicité *f*
    r спиральность *f*

H124 *e* **helicon**
    d Helicon *n*, Helikon *n*, Helikonwelle *f*
    f hélicon *m*
    r геликон *m*

H125 *e* **heliocentric coordinates**
    d heliozentrische Koordinaten *f pl*
    f coordonnées *f pl* héliocentriques
    r гелиоцентрические координаты *f pl*

H126 *e* **heliograph**
    d Heliograph *m*
    f héliographe *m*
    r гелиограф *m*

H127 *e* **heliostat**
    d Heliostat *m*
    f héliostat *m*
    r гелиостат *m*

H128 *e* **helium, He**
    d Helium *n*
    f hélium *m*
    r гелий *m*

H129 *e* **helium cryostat**
    d Heliumkryostat *m*
    f cryostat *m* à hélium
    r гелиевый криостат *m*

H130 *e* **helium expansion machine**
    d Heliumexpansionsmaschine *f*
    f détendeur *m* d'hélium
    r гелиевый детандер *m*

H131 *e* **helium flare**
    d Heliumeruption *f*, Heliumausbruch *m*
    f éclair *m* d'hélium
    r гелиевая вспышка *f*

H132 *e* **helium magnetometer**
    d Heliummagnetometer *n*
    f magnétomètre *m* à hélium
    r гелиевый магнитометр *m*

H133 *e* **helium-neon laser**
    d Helium-Neon-Laser *m*,
        He-Ne-Laser *m*
    f laser *m* hélium-néon
    r гелий-неоновый лазер *m*, He-Ne-
        лазер *m*

H134 *e* **helix**
    d Spirale *f*
    f spirale *f*
    r спираль *f*

H135 *e* **Helmholtz coils**
    d Helmholtzsche Spulen *f pl*,
        Helmholtz-Spulen *f pl*

    f bobines *f pl* de Helmholtz
    r катушки *f pl* Гельмгольца

H136 *e* **Helmholtz free energy**
    d Helmholtzsche freie Energie *f*, freie
        Energie *f*
    f énergie *f* libre de Helmholtz, énergie *f*
        libre
    r энергия *f* Гельмгольца, свободная
        энергия *f*

H137 *e* **Helmholtz resonator**
    d Helmholtz-Resonator *m*,
        Helmholtzscher Resonator *m*
    f résonateur *m* de Helmholtz
    r резонатор *m* Гельмгольца

H138 *e* **He-Ne. laser** *see* **helium-neon laser**

H139 *e* **henry, H**
    d Henry *n*
    f henry *m*
    r генри *m*, Гн

H140 *e* **Henry law**
    d Henrysches Gesetz *n*
    f loi *f* de Henry
    r закон *m* Генри

H141 *e* **heptode**
    d Heptode *f*, Siebenpolröhre *f*
    f heptode *f*
    r гептод *m*

H142 *e* **Hermitian matrices**
    d Hermitesche Matrizen *f pl*
    f matrices *f pl* hermitiennes
    r эрмитовы матрицы *f pl*

H143 *e* **Hermitian operator**
    d hermitescher Operator *m*
    f opérateur *m* hermitien
    r эрмитов оператор *m*

H144 *e* **Hermitian polynomials**
    d hermitesche Polynome *n pl*
    f polynômes *m pl* hermitiens
    r многочлены *m pl* Эрмита

H145 *e* **hermiticity**
    d Hermitezität *f*
    f hermiticité *f*
    r эрмитовость *f*

H146 *e* **herpolhode**
    d Herpolhodie *f*, Rastpolkurve *f*
    f herpolodie *f*
    r герполодия *f*

H147 *e* **hertz, Hz**
    d Hertz *n*
    f hertz *m*
    r герц *m*, Гц

H148 *e* **Hertzian dipole**
    d Hertzscher Oszillator *m*, Hertzscher
        Dipol *m*

	f	dipôle *m* de Hertz
	r	вибратор *m* Герца, диполь *m* Герца
H149	e	**Hertzian vector**
	d	Hertzscher Vektor *m*
	f	vecteur *m* de Hertz
	r	вектор *m* Герца
H150	e	**Hertzsprung-Russel diagram**
	d	Hertzsprung-Russel-Diagramm *n*
	f	diagramme *m* d'Hertzsprung-Russel
	r	диаграмма *f* Герцшпрунга - Рассела
H151	e	**heterochromatic photometry**
	d	heterochrome Photometrie *f*,
		heterochromatische Photometrie *f*
	f	photométrie *f* hétérochrome
	r	гетерохромная фотометрия *f*
H152	e	**heterodyne**
	d	Überlagerer *m*,
		Überlagerungsoszillator *m*
	f	hétérodyne *f*
	r	гетеродин *m*
H153	e	**heterodyning of light**
	d	Lichtüberlagerung *f*
	f	hétérodynage *m* de la lumière
	r	гетеродинирование *n* света
H154	e	**heterogeneity**
	d	Heterogenität *f*
	f	hétérogénéité *f*
	r	гетерогенность *f*
H155	e	**heterogeneous catalysis**
	d	heterogene Katalyse *f*
	f	catalyse *f* hétérogène
	r	гетерогенный катализ *m*
H156	e	**heterogeneous condensation**
	d	heterogene Kondensation *f* (*von*
		Aerosolen)
	f	condensation *f* hétérogène (*d'aérosols*)
	r	гетерогенная конденсация *f*
		(*аэрозолей*)
H157	e	**heterogeneous reactor**
	d	heterogener Reaktor *m*,
		Heterogenreaktor *m*
	f	réacteur *m* hétérogène
	r	гетерогенный реактор *m*
H158	e	**heterogeneous system**
	d	heterogenes System *n*
	f	système *m* hétérogène
	r	гетерогенная система *f*
H159	e	**heterojunction**
	d	Heteroübergang *m*
	f	jonction *f* hétérogène
	r	гетеропереход *m*
H160	e	**heterojunction laser** *see* heterolaser
H161	e	**heterolaser**
	d	Laser *m* mit Heteroübergang,
		Heterolaser *m*

	f	hétérolaser *m*
	r	гетеролазер *m*, лазер *m* на
		гетеропереходе
H162	e	**heterophase structure**
	d	heterophasige Struktur *f*
	f	structure *f* hétérophase
	r	гетерофазная структура *f*
H163	e	**heteropolar bond**
	d	heteropolare Bindung *f*
	f	liaison *f* hétéropolaire
	r	гетерополярная связь *f*
H164	e	**heterostructure**
	d	Heterostruktur *f*
	f	hétérostructure *f*
	r	гетероструктура *f*
H165	e	**heterostructure laser** *see* heterolaser
H166	e	**heterovalent isomorphism**
	d	heterovalente Isomorphie *f*
	f	isomorphisme *m* hétérovalent
	r	гетеровалентный изоморфизм *m*
H167	e	**heuristic model**
	d	heuristisches Modell *n*
	f	modèle *m* heuristique
	r	эвристическая модель *f*
H168	e	**hexagon**
	d	Sechseck *n*
	f	hexagone *m*
	r	шестиугольник *m*
H169	e	**hexagonal close-packed structure**
	d	hexagonal dichteste Kugelpackung *f*,
		hexagonale Kugelpackung *f*
	f	structure *f* hexagonale compacte
	r	гексагональная плотноупакованная
		структура *f*
H170	e	**hexagonal crystal**
	d	hexagonaler Kristall *m*
	f	cristal *m* hexagonal
	r	гексагональный кристалл *m*
H171	e	**hexagonal system**
	d	hexagonales System *n*
	f	système *m* hexagonal
	r	гексагональная сингония *f*,
		гексагональная система *f*
H172	e	**hexahedron**
	d	Hexaeder *n*, Sechsflächner *m*
	f	hexaèdre *m*
	r	шестигранник *m*
H173	e	**hexode**
	d	Hexode *f*, Sechspolröhre *f*
	f	hexode *f*
	r	гексод *m*
H174	e	**HF** *see* **high frequencies**
H175	e	**HF heating in cold container**

d Hochfrequenzerwärmung *f* im
Kaltcontainer
f chauffage *m* à haute fréquence dans
le conteneur froid
r метод *m* высокочастотного нагрева в
холодном контейнере

H176 e **hidden mass**
d verdeckte Masse *f*
f masse *f* cacheé
r скрытая масса *f* (*в астрофизике*)

H177 e **hierarchy**
d Hierarchie *f*
f hiérarchie *f*
r иерархия *f*

H178 e **Higgs boson**
d Higgssches Boson *n*
f boson *m* de Higgs
r хиггсовский бозон *m*

H179 e **high-current accelerator**
d Hochstrombeschleuniger *m*
f accélérateur *m* à courant d'intensité
élevée
r сильноточный ускоритель *m*

H180 e **high-current electronics**
d Hochstromelektronik *m*
f électronique *f* de courant d'intensité
élevée
r сильноточная электроника *f*

H181 e **high-current implanter**
d Hochstromimplantationsanlage *f*
f implanteur *m* à courant d'intensité
élevée
r сильноточный имплантер *m*

H182 e **high-current source**
d Hochstromquelle *f*
f source *f* de courant d'intensité élevée
r сильноточный источник *m*

H183 e **high-energy electron diffraction**
d Hochenergie-Elektronenbeugung *f*
f diffraction *f* des électrons de haute
énergie
r дифракция *f* быстрых электронов,
дифракция *f* электронов высоких
энергий

H184 e **high-energy electron diffraction
method**
d Hochenergie-
Elektronendiffraktionsmethode *f*,
HEED-Methode *f*
f méthode *f* de diffraction des électrons
de haute énergie
r метод *m* дифракции электронов
высоких энергий, метод *m* HEED

H185 e **high-energy ion implantation**
d Implantation *f* von Hochenergieionen
f implantation *f* des ions de haute
énergie
r имплантация *f* ионов высокой
энергии

H186 e **high-energy physics**
d Hochenergiephysik *f*
f physique *f* des hautes énergies
r физика *f* высоких энергий

H187 e **high-energy region**
d Bereich *m* hoher Energien,
Hochenergiegebiet *n*
f région *f* des hautes énergies
r область *f* высоких энергий

H188 e **higher harmonics**
d höhere Harmonische *f pl*
f harmoniques *m pl* supérieurs
r высшие гармоники *f pl*

H189 e **higher levels**
d höhere Niveaus *n pl*
f niveaux *m pl* supérieurs
r высшие уровни *m pl*

H190 e **higher order curve**
d Kurve *f* höherer Ordnung
f courbe *f* d'ordre supérieur
r кривая *f* высшего порядка

H191 e **higher order modes**
d Moden *f pl* höherer Ordnung
f modes *m pl* d'ordre supérieur
r моды *f pl* высшего порядка

H192 e **higher order moment**
d Moment *n* höherer Ordnung
f moment *m* d'ordre supérieur
r момент *m* высшего порядка

H193 e **high fidelity**
d hohe Wiedergabetreue *f*
f haute fidélité *f*
r высокая верность *f* воспроизведения

H194 e **high frequencies**
d Hochfrequenzen *f pl*
f hautes fréquences *f pl*
r высокие частоты *f pl*

H195 e **high-frequency band**
d Hochfrequenzband *n*
f bande *f* haute fréquence, gamme *f*
haute fréquence
r высокочастотный диапазон *m*,
диапазон *m* высоких частот

H196 e **high-frequency conduction**
d Hochfrequenzleitfähigkeit *f*, HF-
Leitfähigkeit *f*
f conduction *f* à haute fréquence
r высокочастотная проводимость *f*

H197 e **high-frequency discharge**
d Hochfrequenzentladung *f*
f décharge *f* à haute fréquence
r высокочастотный разряд *m*

H198   *e*   **high-frequency oscillation**
       d   Hochfrequenzschwingungen *f pl*
       f   oscillation *f* à haute fréquence
       r   высокочастотные колебания *n pl*

H199   *e*   **highly excited state**
       d   hochangeregter Zustand *m*
       f   état *m* hautement excité
       r   высоковозбуждённое состояние *n*

H200   *e*   **high-pass filter**
       d   Hochpaßfilter *n*, Hochpaß *m*
       f   filtre *m* passe-haut
       r   фильтр *m* верхних частот

H201   *e*   **high-power electronics**
       d   Leistungselektronik *f*
       f   électronique *f* de puissance
       r   электроника *f* больших мощностей

H202   *e*   **high-power radiation**
       d   energiereiche Strahlung *f*
       f   rayonnement *m* de haute puissance
       r   мощное излучение *n*

H203   *e*   **high pressure**
       d   Hochdruck *m*, hoher Druck *m*
       f   haute pression *f*
       r   высокое давление *n*

H204   *e*   **high-pressure chamber**
       d   Hochdruckkammer *f*
       f   chambre *f* à haute pression
       r   камера *f* высокого давления

H205   *e*   **high-pressure physics**
       d   Hochdruckphysik *f*, Physik *f* der hohen Drücke
       f   physique *f* des hautes pressions
       r   физика *f* высоких давлений

H206   *e*   **high resolution**
       d   hohe Auflösung *f*
       f   haute résolution *f*
       r   высокое разрешение *n*

H207   *e*   **high-resolution interferometry**
       d   Interferometrie *f* hoher Auflösung
       f   interférométrie *f* à haute résolution
       r   интерферометрия *f* высокого разрешения

H208   *e*   **high-speed photography**
       d   Hochgeschwindigkeitsfotografie *f*
       f   photographie *f* ultra-rapide
       r   высокоскоростная фотография *f*

H209   *e*   **high-speed process**
       d   Hochgeschwindigkeitsprozeß *m*
       f   processus *m* à déroulement rapide
       r   быстропротекающий процесс *m*

H210   *e*   **high-spin state**
       d   Hochspinzustand *m*
       f   état *m* à haut spin
       r   высокоспиновое состояние *n*

H211   *e*   **high-symmetry crystal**
       d   hochsymmetrischer Kristall *m*
       f   cristal *m* de haut ordre de symétrie
       r   кристалл *m* высокой симметрии

H212   *e*   **high-temperature calorimetry**
       d   Hochtemperaturkalorimetrie *f*
       f   calorimétrie *f* à haute température
       r   высокотемпературная калориметрия *f*

H213   *e*   **high-temperature plasma**
       d   Hochtemperaturplasma *n*
       f   plasma *m* à haute température
       r   высокотемпературная плазма *f*, горячая плазма *f*

H214   *e*   **high temperatures**
       d   Hochtemperaturen *f pl*, hohe Temperaturen *f pl*
       f   hautes températures *f pl*
       r   высокие температуры *f pl*

H215   *e*   **high voltage**
       d   Hochspannung *f*
       f   haute tension *f*
       r   высокое напряжение *n*

H216   *e*   **high-voltage accelerator**
       d   Hochspannungsbeschleuniger *m*, Hochvoltbeschleuniger *m*
       f   accélérateur *m* de haut voltage
       r   высоковольтный ускоритель *n*

H217   *e*   **high-voltage cable**
       d   Hochspannungskabel *n*
       f   câble *m* à haute tension
       r   высоковольтный кабель *m*

H218   *e*   **high-voltage discharge**
       d   Hochspannungsentladung *f*
       f   décharge *f* à haute tension
       r   высоковольтный разряд *m*

H219   *e*   **high-voltage pulse**
       d   Hochspannungsimpuls *m*
       f   impulsion *f* à haute tension, impulsion *f* de haute tension
       r   высоковольтный импульс *m*

H220   *e*   **high-voltage source**
       d   Hochspannungsquelle *f*
       f   source *f* de haute voltage
       r   источник *m* высокого напряжения

H221   *e*   **Hilbert space**
       d   Hilbert-Raum *m*
       f   espace *m* de Hilbert
       r   гильбертово пространство *n*

H222   *e*   **Hilbert transform**
       d   Hilbert-Transformation *f*
       f   transformation *f* de Hilbert
       r   преобразование *n* Гильберта

H223   *e*   **histogram**
       d   Histogramm *n*

f histogramme *m*
r гистограмма *f*

H224 e **hodograph**
    d Hodograph *m*, Hodographenkurve *f*
    f hodographe *m*
    r годограф *m*

H225 e **hodograph method**
    d Hodographenmethode *f*
    f méthode *f* de l'hodographe
    r метод *m* годографа

H226 e **hodoscope**
    d Hodoskop *n*
    f hodoscope *m*
    r годоскоп *m*

H227 e **hole**
    d Loch *n*
    f trou *m*
    r дырка *f*

H228 e **hole burning**
    d Lochbrennen *n*
    f brûlage *m* des trous
    r выжигание *n* провала, выгорание *n* провала (*в линии излучения*)

H229 e **hole capture**
    d Locheinfang *m*
    f capture *f* du trou
    r захват *m* дырки

H230 e **hole concentration**
    d Löcherkonzentration *f*
    f concentration *f* des trous
    r концентрация *f* дырок

H231 e **hole conduction**
    d Löcherleitung *f*, Löcherleitfähigkeit *f*
    f conduction *f* par trous
    r дырочная проводимость *f*

H232 e **hole injection**
    d Löcherinjektion *f*
    f injection *f* des trous
    r инжекция *f* дырок

H233 e **hole injector**
    d Löcherinjektor *m*
    f injecteur *m* des trous
    r инжектор *m* дырок

H234 e **hole migration**
    d Löcherwanderung *f*
    f migration *f* des trous
    r миграция *f* дырок

H235 e **hole mobility**
    d Löcherbeweglichkeit *f*
    f mobilité *f* des trous
    r подвижность *f* дырок

H236 e **hole trapping** *see* **hole capture**

H237 e **hollow cathode**

    d Hohlkatode *f*
    f cathode *f* creuse
    r полый катод *m*

H238 e **hollow cathode discharge**
    d Hohlkatodenentladung *f*
    f décharge *f* de cathode creuse
    r разряд *m* с полым катодом

H239 e **Holmium, Ho**
    d Holmium *n*
    f holmium *m*
    r гольмий *m*

H240 e **hologram**
    d Hologramm *n*
    f hologramme *m*
    r голограмма *f*

H241 e **hologram degradation**
    d Hologrammdegradation *f*
    f dégradation *f* d'hologramme
    r деградация *f* голограммы

H242 e **hologram synthesis**
    d Hologrammsynthese *f*
    f synthèse *f* des hologrammes; synthèse *f* d'hologramme
    r синтез *m* голограмм, синтез *m* голограммы

H243 e **holographic diagnostics**
    d holographische Diagnostik *f*
    f diagnostic *m* holographique
    r голографическая диагностика *f*

H244 e **holographic image**
    d holographische Darstellung *f*, holographisches Bild *n*
    f image *f* holographique
    r голографическое изображение *n*

H245 e **holographic image recognition**
    d holographische Mustererkennung *f*
    f reconnaissance *f* holographique des images
    r голографическое распознавание *n* образов

H246 e **holographic interferogram**
    d holographisches Interferogramm *n*
    f interférogramme *m* holographique
    r голографическая интерферограмма *f*

H247 e **holographic interferometer**
    d holographisches Interferometer *n*
    f interféromètre *m* holographique
    r голографический интерферометр *m*

H248 e **holographic interferometry**
    d holographische Interferometrie *f*, Hologramminterferometrie *f*
    f interférométrie *f* holographique
    r голографическая интерферометрия *f*

H249 e **holographic recording**

    d holographische Aufzeichnung *f*
    f enregistrement *m* holographique
    r голографическая запись *f*

H250 *e* **holographic storage**
    d holographischer Speicher *m*
    f mémoire *f* holographique
    r голографическое запоминающее
       устройство *n*, голографическое ЗУ *n*

H251 *e* **holography**
    d Holographie *f*
    f holographie *f*
    r голография *f*

H252 *e* **holomorphic function**
    d holomorphe Funktion *f*
    f fonction *f* holomorphique
    r голоморфная функция *f*,
       аналитическая функция *f*

H253 *e* **holonomic system**
    d holonomes System *n*
    f système *m* holonome
    r голономная система *f*

H254 *e* **homocentric beam**
    d homozentrisches Bündel *n*
    f faisceau *m* homocentrique
    r гомоцентрический пучок *m*

H255 *e* **homogeneity**
    d Homogenität *f*
    f homogénéité *f*
    r однородность *f*

H256 *e* **homogeneity of the Universe**
    d Homogenität *f* des Universums
    f homogénéité *f* de l'Univers
    r однородность *f* Вселенной

H257 *e* **homogeneous catalysis**
    d homogene Katalyse *f*
    f catalyse *f* homogène
    r гомогенный катализ *m*

H258 *e* **homogeneous condensation**
    d homogene Kondensation *f* (*von*
       Aerosolen)
    f condensation *f* homogène (*d'aérosols*)
    r гомогенная конденсация *f*
       (*аэрозолей*)

H259 *e* **homogeneous function**
    d homogene Funktion *f*
    f fonction *f* homogène
    r однородная функция *f*

H260 *e* **homogeneous medium**
    d homogenes Medium *n*
    f milieu *m* homogène
    r однородная среда *f*

H261 *e* **homogeneous model**
    d homogenes Modell *n*
    f modèle *m* homogène
    r однородная модель *f* (*Вселенной*),
       модель *f* однородной Вселенной

H262 *e* **homogeneous reactor**
    d homogener Reaktor *m*,
       Homogenreaktor *m*
    f réacteur *m* homogène
    r гомогенный реактор *m*

H263 *e* **homogeneous system**
    d homogenes System *n*,
       Einphasensystem *n*
    f système *m* homogène
    r гомогенная система *f*; однородная
       система *f*

H264 *e* **homojunction**
    d Homoübergang *m*
    f jonction *f* homogène
    r гомопереход *m*

H265 *e* **homologous series**
    d homologe Reihe *f*
    f série *f* homologue
    r гомологический ряд *m*

H266 *e* **homology class**
    d Homologieklasse *f*
    f classe *f* d'homologies
    r класс *m* гомологий

H267 *e* **homopolar bond**
    d homöopolare Bindung *f*
    f liaison *f* homopolaire
    r гомополярная связь *f*

H268 *e* **Hooke law**
    d Hookesches Gesetz *n*
    f loi *f* de Hooke
    r закон *m* Гука

H269 *e* **horizon**
    d Horizont *m*
    f horizon *m*
    r горизонт *m*

H270 *e* **horizontally polarized radiation**
    d horizontal polarisierte Strahlung *f*
    f rayonnement *m* à polarisation
       horizontale
    r горизонтально-поляризованное
       излучение *n*

H271 *e* **horn**
    d 1. Schalltrichter *m*, Trichter *m* 2.
       Horn *n*, Hornstrahler *m*, Hornantenne
       f, Trichterantenne *f*
    f 1. pavillon *m* 2. antenne *f* à cornet
    r 1. рупор *m* 2. рупорная антенна *f*

H272 *e* **horn aerial, horn antenna**
    d Hornantenne *f*, Trichterantenne *f*
    f antenne *f* à cornet
    r рупорная антенна *f*

H273 *e* **horse power**
    d Pferdestärke *f*
    f cheval-vapeur *m*, ch
    r лошадиная сила *f*, л.с.

H274   e   host crystal
        d   Wirtskristall *m*
        f   cristal *m* fondamental
        r   кристалл-хозяин *m*, основной
          кристалл *m*

H275   e   hot carriers
        d   heiße Träger *m pl*, heiße
          Ladungsträger *m pl*
        f   porteurs *m pl* chauds
        r   горячие носители *m pl*, горячие
          носители *m pl* заряда

H276   e   hot cathode
        d   Thermokatode *f*
        f   cathode *f* thermo-électronique
        r   термокатод *m*

H277   e   hot channel
        d   Heißkanal *m*, heißer Kanal *m*
        f   canal *m* chaud
        r   горячий канал *m*, рабочий канал *m*

H278   e   hot electrons
        d   heiße Elektronen *n pl*,
          Heißelektronen *n pl*
        f   électrons *m pl* chauds
        r   горячие электроны *m pl*

H279   e   hot-hole maser
        d   Heißlöchermaser *m*
        f   maser *m* à trous chauds
        r   мазер *m* на горячих дырках

H280   e   hot holes
        d   heiße Löcher *n pl*
        f   trous *m pl* chauds
        r   горячие дырки *f pl*

H281   e   hot laboratory
        d   heißes Labor *n*
        f   laboratoire *m* chaud
        r   горячая лаборатория *f*

H282   e   hot luminescence
        d   Heißlumineszenz *f*
        f   luminescence *f* chaude
        r   горячая люминесценция *f*

H283   e   hot plasma
        d   heißes Plasma *n*
        f   plasma *m* chaud
        r   горячая плазма *f*,
          высокотемпературная плазма *f*

H284   e   hot plasma diagnostics
        d   Diagnostik *f* des heißen Plasmas
        f   diagnostic *m* du plasma chaud
        r   диагностика *f* горячей плазмы

H285   e   hot Universe
        d   heißes Universum *n*
        f   Univers *m* chaud
        r   горячая Вселенная *f*

H286   e   hot-wire anemometer
        d   Hitzdrahtanemometer *n*,
          Hitzdrahtwindmesser *m*
        f   anémomètre *m* à fil chaud
        r   термоанемометр *m*

H287   e   hour
        d   Stunde *f*
        f   heure *f*
        r   час *m*

H288   e   hour angle
        d   Stundenwinkel *m*
        f   angle *m* horaire
        r   часовой угол *m*

H289   e   h-quark *see* heavy quark

H290   e   Hubble constant
        d   Hubble-Konstante *f*, Hubblesche
          Konstante *f*
        f   constante *f* de Hubble
        r   постоянная *f* Хаббла

I

I1   e   ice
     d   Eis *n*
     f   glace *f*
     r   лёд *m*

I2   e   ice modifications
     d   Eismodifikationen *f pl*
     f   modifications *f pl* de glace
     r   модификации *f pl* льда

I3   e   ice point
     d   Eispunkt *m*
     f   point *m* de congélation d'eau
     r   точка *f* замерзания воды,
       температура *f* замерзания воды

I4   e   iconoscope
     d   Ikonoskop *n*, Bildspeicherröhre *f*
     f   iconoscope *m*
     r   иконоскоп *m*

I5   e   icosahedron
     d   Ikosaeder *n*, Zwanzigflächner *m*
     f   icosaèdre *m*
     r   икосаэдр *m*

I6   e   ideal fluid
     d   ideale Flüssigkeit *f*
     f   fluide *m* parfait
     r   идеальная жидкость *f*

I7   e   ideal gas
     d   ideales Gas *n*
     f   gaz *m* parfait
     r   идеальный газ *m*

I8   e   idealization
     d   Idealisierung *f*

f idéalisation f
r идеализация f

I9 e idealized problem
d idealisiertes Problem n
f problème m idéalisé
r идеализированная задача f

I10 e identification
d Identifizierung f, Erkennung f
f identification f
r идентификация f, распознавание n

I11 e identity
d Identität f
f identité f
r идентичность f, тождественность f;
тождество n

I12 e idiomorphism
d Idiomorphie f
f idiomorphisme m
r идиоморфизм m

I13 e idle component
d Blindanteil m
f composante f réactive
r реактивная составляющая f

I14 e idle current
d Blindstrom m
f courant m réactif
r реактивный ток m

I15 e idler wave
d Leerlaufwelle f
f onde f idling
r холостая волна f

I16 e ignition
d Zündung f
f allumage m, amorçage m
r зажигание n

I17 e ignition criterion
d Zündkriterium n
f critère m d'allumage
r критерий m зажигания

I18 e ignition potential
d Zündspannung f, Zündpotential n
f tension f d'amorçage
r потенциал m зажигания

I19 e ignitron
d Ignitron n
f ignitron m
r игнитрон m

I20 e ill-posed problem
d inkorrekte Aufgabenstellung f
f problème m incorrectement posé,
problème m incorrectement formulé
r некорректная задача f

I21 e illuminance
d Beleuchtungsstärke f

f éclairement m, éclairement m
lumineux
r освещённость f

I22 e illumination
d 1. Beleuchtung f; Beleuchtungsstärke f
2. Einstrahlung f
f 1. éclairage m 2. irradiation f
r 1. освещение n; освещённость f
2. облучение n

I23 e image
d Bild n, Abbildung f; Abbild n
f image f
r изображение n; отображение n;
образ m

I24 e image converter
d Bildwandler m
f convertisseur m d'image électrono-
optique
r электронно-оптический
преобразователь m, ЭОП;
преобразователь m изображения

I25 e image converter camera
d Bildwandlerkamera f
f caméra f électronique optique
r электронно-оптическая камера f

I26 e image correction
d Abbildungsfehlerkorrektur f
f correction f d'image
r коррекция f изображения

I27 e image distortion
d Bildverzeichnung f
f défaut m de l'image, déformation f
d'image
r искажение n изображения

I28 e image iconoscope
d Superikonoskop n
f supericonoscope m
r супериконоскоп m

I29 e image intensifier
d Bildverstärker m
f renforçateur m d'image
r усилитель m яркости изображения

I30 e image jitter
d Bildschwankung f
f tremblement m d'image, sautillement
m d'image
r дрожание n изображения

I31 e image method
d Methode f der Bilder, Bildermethode f
f méthode f des images, principe m des
images
r метод m изображений

I32 e image orthicon
d Superorthikon n

f image-orthicon *m*
r суперортикон *m*

I33 e image space
d Bildraum *m*
f espace *m* d'images
r пространство *n* изображений

I34 e image theory
d Abbildungstheorie *f*
f théorie *f* de l'image
r теория *f* изображения

I35 e imaginary number
d imaginäre Zahl *f*
f nombre *m* imaginaire
r мнимое число *n*

I36 e imaging
d Abbilden *n*; Bilderzeugung *f*
f formation *f* d'images
r формирование *n* изображений

I37 e immersion
d Immersion *f*
f immersion *f*
r 1. иммерсия *f* 2. погружение *n*

I38 e immersion lens
d Immersionslinse *f*
f lentille *f* à immersion
r иммерсионная линза *f*

I39 e immersion liquid
d Immersionsflüssigkeit *f*
f liquide *m* à immersion
r иммерсионная жидкость *f*

I40 e immersion method
d Immersionsmethode *f*
f méthode *f* d'essai à immersion
r иммерсионный метод *m*

I41 e impact
d Stoß *m*, Zusammenstoß *m*, Kollision *f*
f impact *m*
r удар *m*, соударение *n*;
   столкновение *n*

I42 e impact broadening
d Stoßverbreiterung *f*
f élargissement *m* par collisions
r ударное уширение *n*

I43 e impact grinding
d Schlagmahlen *n*
f broyage *m* par chocs
r ударное измельчение *n*

I44 e impact ionization
d Stoßionisation *f*, Stoßionisierung *f*
f ionisation *f* par choc, ionisation *f* par impact
r ударная ионизация *f*

I45 e impact load
d schlagartige Beanspruchung *f*,
   Schlagbeanspruchung *f*;
   Stoßbeanspruchung *f*
f charge *f* de choc
r ударная нагрузка *f*

I46 e impact momentum
d Schlagimpuls *m*, Stoßimpuls *m*
f choc *m*, percussion *f*
r ударный импульс *m*

I47 e impact parameter
d Stoßparameter *m*
f paramètre *m* d'impact
r прицельный параметр *m*, параметр *m* удара

I48 e impact parameter method
d Stoßparametermethode *f*
f méthode *f* du paramètre d'impact
r метод *m* прицельного параметра

I49 e impact strength
d Schlagzähigkeit *f*
f résilience *f*
r ударная вязкость *f*

I50 e impact tests
d Schlagversuche *m pl*
f essais *m pl* de choc
r ударные испытания *n pl*

I51 e impedance
d Impedanz *f*, Scheinwiderstand *m*
f impédance *f*
r полное сопротивление *n*,
   импеданс *m*

I52 e imperfect crystal
d Realkristall *m*, nichtidealer Kristall *m*
f cristal *m* imparfait
r неидеальный кристалл *m*, реальный
   кристалл *m*, несовершенный
   кристалл *m*

I53 e imperfect gas
d nichtideales Gas *n*, Realgas *n*
f gaz *m* réel
r неидеальный газ *m*, реальный газ *m*

I54 e imperfection
d Unvollkommenheit *f*; Fehler *m*
f imperfection *f*; défaut *m*
r несовершенство *n*; дефект *m*

I55 e implantation
d Implantation *f*
f implantation *f*
r имплантация *f*; внедрение *n*

I56 e implanted ion
d implantiertes Ion *n*
f ion *m* implanté
r имплантированный ион *m*

I57 e implanter
d Implanter *m*, Implantationsanlage *f*

	f	implanteur *m*
	r	имплантер *m*
I58	*e*	**implicit dependence**
	d	implizite Abhängigkeit *f*
	f	dépendance *f* implicite
	r	неявная зависимость *f*
I59	*e*	**importance**
	d	Bedeutung *f*
	f	importance *f*
	r	1. значимость *f* 2. балл *m* (*солнечной вспышки*)
I60	*e*	**imposition of boundary conditions**
	d	Überlagerung *f* von Grenzbedingungen
	f	imposition *f* des conditions limites
	r	наложение *n* граничных условий
I61	*e*	**impregnation**
	d	Tränkung *f*
	f	imprégnation *f*
	r	пропитка *f*
I62	*e*	**imprisonment**
	d	Einfang *m*
	f	capture *f*
	r	пленение *n (излучения)*
I63	*e*	**improper integral**
	d	uneigentliches Integral *n*
	f	intégrale *f* impropre
	r	несобственный интеграл *m*
I64	*e*	**impulse**
	d	Impuls *m*
	f	impulsion *f*
	r	импульс *m*
I65	*e*	**impulse approximation**
	d	Impulsnäherung *f*
	f	approximation *f* des impulsions
	r	импульсное приближение *n*
I66	*e*	**impulse generator**
	d	Impulsgenerator *m*
	f	générateur *m* d'impulsions
	r	импульсный генератор *m*, генератор *m* импульсов
I67	*e*	**impulse of force**
	d	Kraftimpuls *m*
	f	impulsion *f*
	r	импульс *m* силы
I68	*e*	**impulse photometry**
	d	Impulsphotometrie *f*
	f	photométrie *f* impulsionnelle
	r	импульсная фотометрия *f*
I69	*e*	**impulse representation**
	d	Impulsdarstellung *f*
	f	représentation *f* impulsionnelle
	r	импульсное представление *n*
I70	*e*	**impulse space**

	d	Impulsraum *m*
	f	espace *m* de la quantité de mouvement
	r	импульсное пространство *n*
I71	*e*	**impurity**
	d	Verunreinigung *f*; Beimengung *f*; Störstelle *f*
	f	impureté *f*
	r	примесь *f*
I72	*e*	**impurity atom**
	d	Fremdatom *n*, Störstellenatom *n*, Störatom *n*
	f	atome *m* d'impureté
	r	примесный атом *m*
I73	*e*	**impurity band**
	d	Störstellenband *n*
	f	bande *f* d'impureté, zone *f* d'impureté
	r	примесная зона *f*
I74	*e*	**impurity capture**
	d	Störstelleneinfang *m*
	f	capture *f* d'impureté
	r	захват *m* примеси
I75	*e*	**impurity center**
	d	Störstellenzentrum *n*, Störzentrum *n*
	f	centre *m* d'impureté
	r	примесный центр *m*
I76	*e*	**impurity concentration**
	d	Störstellenkonzentration *f*, Störstellendichte *f*
	f	concentration *f* des impuretés
	r	концентрация *f* примесей
I77	*e*	**impurity conduction**
	d	Störstellenleitung *f*
	f	conduction *f* d'impureté
	r	примесная проводимость *f*
I78	*e*	**impurity ion**
	d	Störion *n*, Fremdion *n*
	f	ion *m* d'impureté
	r	примесный ион *m*
I79	*e*	**impurity level**
	d	Storstellenniveau *n*, Störniveau *n*
	f	niveau *m* d'impureté
	r	примесный уровень *m*
I80	*e*	**impurity migration**
	d	Störstellenwanderung *f*
	f	migration *f* des impuretés
	r	миграция *f* примесей
I81	*e*	**impurity region**
	d	Störstellengebiet *n*
	f	région *f* d'impureté
	r	примесная область *f*
I82	*e*	**impurity trapping** *see* **impurity capture**
I83	*e*	**incandescent lamp**

    d Glühlampe *f*
    f lampe *f* à incandescence
    r лампа *f* накаливания

I84   *e* inch
    d Zoll *n*
    f pouce *m*
    r дюйм *m*

I85   *e* incidence
    d Einfall *m*
    f incidence *f*
    r падение *n*

I86   *e* incident beam
    d einfallender Strahl *m*
    f faisceau *m* incident
    r падающий пучок *m*

I87   *e* incident radiation
    d einfallende Strahlung *f*
    f rayonnement *m* incident
    r падающее излучение *n*

I88   *e* incident ray
    d einfallender Strahl *m*
    f rayon *m* incident
    r падающий луч *m*

I89   *e* incident wave
    d einlaufende Welle *f*,
        einfallende Welle *f*
    f onde *f* incidente
    r падающая волна *f*

I90   *e* inclination
    d 1. Neigung *f*, Gefälle *n*, Steigung *f* 2.
        Inklination *f* 3. Bahnneigung *f*,
        Bahnebenenneigung *f*
    f inclinaison *f*
    r 1. наклон *m* 2. наклонение *n*

I91   *e* inclinator
    d Inklinator *m*
    f boussole *f* d'inclinaison
    r инклинатор *m*

I92   *e* inclined beam
    d Schrägstrahl *m*
    f faisceau *m* incliné
    r наклонный пучок *m*

I93   *e* inclined plane
    d schiefe Ebene *f*
    f plan *m* incliné
    r наклонная плоскость *f*

I94   *e* inclusion
    d Inklusion *f*, Einschluß *m*
    f inclusion *f*
    r 1. инклюзия *f* 2. включение *n*,
        примесь *f*

I95   *e* inclusive cross-section
    d inklusiver Querschnitt *m*
    f section *f* d'inclusion
    r инклюзивное сечение *n*

I96   *e* inclusive process
    d inklusiver Prozeß *m*
    f processus *m* d'inclusion
    r инклюзивный процесс *m*

I97   *e* incoherence
    d Inkohärenz *f*, Nichtkohärenz *f*
    f incohérence *f*
    r некогерентность *f*

I98   *e* incoherent emission *see* incoherent
        radiation

I99   *e* incoherent oscillation, incoherent
        oscillations
    d inkohärente Schwingungen *f pl*
    f oscillations *f pl* incohérentes
    r некогерёнтные колебания *n pl*

I100 *e* incoherent radiation
    d inkohärente Strahlung *f*
    f rayonnement *m* incohérent
    r некогерентное излучение *n*

I101 *e* incoherent scattering
    d inkohärente Streuung *f*
    f diffusion *f* incohérente
    r некогерентное рассеяние *n*
        (*радиоволн в ионосфере*)

I102 *e* incoherent scatter technique
    d inkohärentes Streuverfahren *n*
    f méthode *f* de diffusion incohérente
    r метод *m* некогерентного рассеяния

I103 *e* incoherent source
    d inkohärente Quelle *f*
    f source *f* incohérente
    r некогерентный источник *m*

I104 *e* incommensurability
    d Inkommensurabilität *f*
    f incommensurabilité *f*
    r несоизмеримость *f*,
        несоразмерность *f*

I105 *e* incommensurate phases
    d inkommensurable Phasen *f pl*
    f phases *f pl* incommensurables
    r несоразмерные фазы *f pl*

I106 *e* incommensurate structure
    d inkommensurable Struktur *f*
    f structure *f* incommensurable
    r несоразмерная структура *f*

I107 *e* incompatibility
    d Inkompatibilität *f*
    f incompatibilité *f*
    r несовместимость *f*

I108 *e* incompressibility
    d Inkompressibilität *f*
    f incompressibilité *f*
    r несжимаемость *f*

I109 *e* incompressible flow

    d inkompressible Strömung *f*
    f flux *m* du milieu incompressible
    r поток *m* несжимаемой среды

I110 *e* **incompressible fluid**
    d inkompressible Flüssigkeit *f*
    f fluide *m* incompressible
    r несжимаемая жидкость *f*

I111 *e* **incompressible fluid dynamics**
    d Dynamik *f* der inkompressiblen
       Flüssigkeit
    f dynamique *f* du fluide incompressible
    r динамика *f* несжимаемой жидкости

I112 *e* **incorrectly formulated problem** *see*
       ill-posed problem

I113 *e* **increment**
    d Inkrement *n*
    f incrément *m*
    r инкремент *m*; приращение *n*

I114 *e* **indefinite integral**
    d unbestimmtes Integral *n*
    f intégrale *f* indéfinie
    r неопределённый интеграл *m*

I115 *e* **indefinite metric**
    d indefinite Metrik *f*
    f métrique *f* indéfinie
    r индефинитная метрика *f*

I116 *e* **indentation**
    d 1. Eindrücken *n*, Eindringen *n* 2.
       Eindringstelle *f*
    f 1. pénétration *f* 2. empreinte *f*
    r 1. вдавливание *n* 2. вмятина *f*,
       ямка *f*, лунка *f*

I117 *e* **indenter**
    d Eindringkörper *m*
    f pénétrateur *m*
    r индентор *m*

I118 *e* **independence**
    d Unabhängigkeit *f*
    f indépendance *f*
    r независимость *f*

I119 *e* **independent variable**
    d unabhängige Variable *f*
    f variable *f* indépendante
    r независимая переменная *f*

I120 *e* **indeterminacy principle**
    d Unbestimmtheitsprinzip *n*
    f principe *m* d'incertitude, principe *m*
       d'indétermination
    r принцип *m* неопределённости

I121 *e* **indeterminism**
    d Indeterminismus *m*
    f indéterminisme *m*
    r индетерминизм *m*

I122 *e* **index**

    d 1. Index *m*; Kennziffer *f*
       2. Beiwert *m*, Faktor *m*
    f indice *m*
    r 1. индекс *m* 2. коэффициент *m*
       3. показатель *m*

I123 *e* **index of Feynman diagram**
    d Feynman-Diagrammindex *m*,
       Feynman-Graphindex *m*
    f indice *m* du diagramme de Feynman
    r индекс *m* диаграммы Фейнмана

I124 *e* **indicator**
    d Anzeiger *m*
    f indicateur *m*
    r индикатор *m*; указатель *m*

I125 *e* **indicatrix of diffusion**
    d Streuindikatrix *f*
    f indicatrice *f* de diffusion
    r индикатриса *f* диффузии

I126 *e* **indirect heating**
    d indirekte Heizung *f*
    f chauffage *m* indirect
    r косвенный накал *m*

I127 *e* **indirectly heated cathode**
    d indirekt geheizte Katode *f*
    f cathode *f* à chauffage indirect
    r катод *m* косвенного накала

I128 *e* **indirect transitions**
    d indirekte Übergänge *m pl*
    f transitions *f pl* indirectes
    r непрямые переходы *m pl*

I129 *e* **indium, In**
    d Indium *m*
    f indium *m*
    r индий *m*

I130 *e* **induced activity**
    d induzierte Aktivität *f*
    f activité *f* induite
    r наведённая активность *f*

I131 *e* **induced anisotropy**
    d induzierte Anisotropie *f*
    f anisotropie *f* induite
    r наведённая анизотропия *f*

I132 *e* **induced birefringence**
    d induzierte Doppelbrechung *f*
    f biréfringence *f* induite
    r наведённое двулучепреломление *n*,
       индуцированное
       двулучепреломление *n*

I133 *e* **induced charge**
    d Influenzladung *f*, influenzierte
       Ladung *f*
    f charge *f* induite
    r наведённый заряд *m*,
       индуцированный заряд *m*

I134 *e* **induced current**

d induzierter Strom *m*
f courant *m* induit
r наведённый ток *m*,
индуцированный ток *m*

I135 e induced dispersion
d induzierte Dispersion *f*
f dispersion *f* induite
r индуцированная дисперсия *f*

I136 e induced e.m.f.
d induzierte EMK *f*
f f.é.m. *f* induite
r наведённая эдс *f*

I137 e induced emission
d induzierte Emission *f*
f émission *f* induite
r вынужденное излучение *n*,
индуцированное излучение *n*,
стимулированное излучение *n*

I138 e induced field
d induziertes Feld *n*
f champ *m* induit
r наведённое поле *n*

I139 e induced oscillation, induced
oscillations
d erzwungene Schwingungen *f pl*
f oscillations *f pl* induites
r вынужденные колебания *n pl*

I140 e induced population change
d induzierte Besetzungsdichteänderung
f, induzierte Besetzungsänderung *f*
f changement *m* induit de la population
r наведённое изменение *n*
населённости

I141 e induced quantum
d induziertes Quant *n*
f quantum *m* induit
r индуцированный квант *m*,
стимулированный квант *m*

I142 e induced radiation *see* induced
emission

I143 e induced radioactivity
d induzierte Radioaktivität *f*
f radioactivité *f* induite
r искусственная радиоактивность *f*

I144 e induced refractive index change
d erzwungene Brechzahländerung *f*
f changement *m* induit de l'indice de
réfraction
r наведённое изменение *n* показателя
преломления

I145 e inductance
d Induktivität *f*
f inductance *f*
r индуктивность *f*

I146 e inductance coil

d Induktivitätsspule *f*, Induktivität *f*
f bobine *f* d'inductance
r катушка *f* индуктивности,
индуктивность *f*

I147 e induction
d Induktion *f*
f induction *f*
r индукция *f*

I148 e induction accelerator
d Induktionsbeschleuniger *m*
f accélérateur *m* à induction
r индукционный ускоритель *m*

I149 e induction coil
d Induktionsspule *f*
f bobine *f* d'induction
r индукционная катушка *f*

I150 e induction heating
d Induktionsheizung *f*,
Induktionserwärmung *f*
f chauffage *m* par induction
r индукционный нагрев *m*

I151 e inductive coupling
d induktive Kopplung *f*
f couplage *m* inductif
r индуктивная связь *f*;
трансформаторная связь *f*

I152 e inductive diaphragm
d induktive Blende *f*
f diaphragme *m* inductif
r индуктивная диафрагма *f*

I153 e inductive load
d induktive Belastung *f*
f charge *f* inductive
r индуктивная нагрузка *f*

I154 e inductive sensor
d induktiver Geber *m*; induktiver
Sensor *m*
f capteur *m* à induction
r индуктивный датчик *m*

I155 e inductive storage
d Induktionsspeicher *m*
f accumulateur *m* inductif
r индуктивный накопитель *m*

I156 e inductive transducer
d induktiver Wandler *m*
f convertisseur *m* inductif
r индуктивный преобразователь *m*

I157 e inductor *see* inductance coil

I158 e inelastic bending, inelastic buckling
d unelastische Biegung *f*
f flexion *f* inélastique
r неупругий изгиб *m*

I159 e inelastic channel
d Kanal *m* der unelastischen Streuung

f canal *m* inélastique
r неупругий канал *m*, канал *m* неупругого рассеяния

I160 *e* inelastic collisions
d unelastische Stöße *m pl*, inelastische Stöße *m pl*
f collisions *f pl* inélastiques
r неупругие столкновения *n pl*

I161 *e* inelastic deformation
d unelastische Deformation *f*, unelastische Verformung *f*
f déformation *f* inélastique
r неупругая деформация *f*

I162 *e* inelastic region *see* inelastic scattering region

I163 *e* inelastic scattering
d unelastische Streuung *f*
f diffusion *f* inélastique
r неупругое рассеяние *n*

I164 *e* inelastic scattering region
d Gebiet *n* der unelastischen Streuung
f région *f* de diffusion inélastique
r область *f* неупругого рассеяния

I165 *e* inequality
d Ungleichung *f*; Ungleichheit *f*
f inégalité *f*
r неравенство *n*

I166 *e* inert gas
d Inertgas *n*; Edelgas *n*
f gaz *m* inerte; gaz *m* noble
r инертный газ *m*; благородный газ *m*

I167 *e* inertia
d Trägheit *f*, Beharrung *f*, Beharrungsvermögen *n*
f inertie *f*
r инерция *f*, инертность *f*; инерционность *f*

I168 *e* inertia ellipsoid
d Trägheitsellipsoid *n*
f ellipsoïde *m* d'inertie
r эллипсоид *m* инерции

I169 *e* inertial confinement
d Trägheitserhaltung *f*, Inertialeinschluß *m*
f confinement *m* inertiel
r инерциальное удержание *n* (*плазмы*)

I170 *e* inertial forces
d Trägheitskräfte *f pl*
f forces *f pl* d'inertie
r силы *f pl* инерции, инерционные силы *f pl*

I171 *e* inertial frame of reference
d Inertialsystem *n*, inertiales Koordinatensystem *n*

f système *m* de référence d'inertie
r инерциальная система *f* отсчёта

I172 *e* inertial guidance
d Trägheitsnavigation *f*
f navigation *f* à inertie
r инерциальная навигация *f*

I173 *e* inertial mass
d träge Masse *f*, Inertialmasse *f*
f masse *f* inerte
r инертная масса *f*, инерциальная масса *f*

I174 *e* inertial motion
d Trägheitsbewegung *f*
f mouvement *m* d'inertie
r инерциальное движение *n*, движение *n* по инерции

I175 *e* inert mass *see* inertial mass

I176 *e* inertness
d 1. Trägheit *f*, Beharrungsvermögen *n*; Massenwiderstand *m* 2. Reaktionsträgheit *f*, Inaktivität *f*
f inertie *f*
r инертность *f*

I177 *e* inferior planets
d sonnennahe Planeten *m pl*
f planètes *f pl* telluriques, planètes *f pl* terrestres
r планеты *f pl* земной группы

I178 *e* infinite interval
d unendliches Intervall *n*
f intervalle *m* infini
r бесконечный интервал *m*

I179 *e* infinite series
d unendliche Reihe *f*
f série *f* infinie
r бесконечный ряд *m*

I180 *e* infinitesimal change
d infinitesimale Änderung *f*, unendlich kleine Änderung *f*
f changement *m* infinitésimal
r бесконечно малое изменение *n*

I181 *e* infinitesimal deformation
d infinitesimale Deformation *f*, infinitesimale Verformung *f*
f déformation *f* infinitésimale
r бесконечно малая деформация *f*

I182 *e* infinity
d Unendlichkeit *f*
f infini *m*, infinité *f*
r бесконечность *f*

I183 *e* inflation (*in cosmology*)
d Inflation *f* (*in der Kosmologie*)
f inflation *f* (*en cosmologie*)
r инфляция *f* (*в космологии*)

I184
e inflationary cosmology
d Inflationskosmologie f
f cosmologie f d'inflation
r инфляционная космология f

I185
e inflation model
d inflationäres Model n
f modèle m à inflation
r инфляционная модель f, модель f раздувающейся Вселенной

I186
e inflector
d Inflektor m
f inflecteur m
r инфлектор m

I187
e influence
d Einfluß m, Beeinfussung f, Einwirkung f
f influence f
r влияние n, воздействие n, действие n

I188
e in-focus image
d fokussierte Abbildung f, scharfe Abbildung f
f image f focalisée
r сфокусированное изображение n

I189
e informatics
d Informatik f, Informationswissenschaft f
f informatique f
r информатика f

I190
e information
d Information f
f information f
r информация f

I191
e information channel
d Informationskanal m
f voie f d'information
r информационный канал m

I192
e information coding
d Informationskodierung f
f codage m de l'information
r кодирование n информации

I193
e information sciences see informatics

I194
e information theory
d Informationstheorie f
f théorie f de l'information
r теория f информации

I195
e infrared astronomy
d Infrarotastronomie f
f astronomie f infrarouge
r инфракрасная астрономия f

I196
e infrared catastrophe
d Infrarotkatastrophe f, IR-Katastrophe f
f catastrophe f infrarouge
r инфракрасная катастрофа f

I197
e infrared divergence
d Infrarotdivergenz f, IR-Divergenz f
f divergence f infrarouge
r инфракрасная расходимость f

I198
e infrared emission see infrared radiation

I199
e infrared multiphoton dissociation
d Infrarot-Multiphotonendissoziation f
f dissociation f infrarouge multiphotonique
r инфракрасная многофотонная диссоциация f

I200
e infrared radiation
d Infrarotstrahlung f, infrarote Strahlung f, IR-Strahlung f
f radiation f infrarouge, rayonnement m infrarouge
r инфракрасное излучение n, ИК-излучение n

I201
e infrared region
d Infrarotbereich m, Infrarotgebiet n
f région f infrarouge
r инфракрасная область f спектра

I202
e infrared source
d Infrarotstrahlungsquelle f, IR-Quelle f
f source f d'infrarouge
r источник m инфракрасного излучения

I203
e infrared spectroscopy
d Infrarotspektroskopie f
f spectroscopie f infrarouge
r инфракрасная спектроскопия f

I204
e infrared waves
d Infrarotwellen f pl
f ondes f pl infrarouges
r инфракрасные волны f pl

I205
e infrasonic vibration, infrasonic vibrations
d Infraschallschwingungen f pl
f vibration f infrasonore
r инфразвуковые колебания n pl

I206
e infrasonic waves
d Infraschallwellen f pl
f ondes f pl infrasonores
r инфразвуковые волны f pl

I207
e infrasound
d Infraschall m
f infra-son m
r инфразвук m

I208
e inhomogeneity
d Inhomogenität f
f inhomogénéité f
r неоднородность f

I209
e inhomogeneously broadened line
d inhomogen verbreitete Linie f

f raie f à élargissement inhomogène
r неоднородно уширенная линия f (в спектре)

I210 e inhomogeneous medium
d inhomogenes Medium n
f milieu m inhomogène
r неоднородная среда f

I211 e initial conditions
d Anfangsbedingungen f pl
f conditions f pl initiales
r начальные условия n pl

I212 e initiating pulse
d Auslöseimpuls m, Startimpuls m
f impulsion f initiale
r запускающий импульс m, возбуждающий импульс m, инициирующий импульс m

I213 e initiation
d Initiierung f, Anregung f, Auslösung f
f initiation f
r инициирование n

I214 e initiation of the reaction
d Reaktionsstart m, Reaktionsbeginn m
f entraînement m de la réaction
r инициирование n реакции

I215 e injection
d Injektion f; Einschuß m
f injection f
r инжекция f

I216 e injection laser
d Injektionslaser m
f laser m à injection
r инжекционный лазер m

I217 e injector
d Injektor m
f injecteur m
r инжектор m

I218 e inner magnetosphere
d innere Magnetosphäre f
f magnétosphère f interne
r внутренняя магнитосфера f

I219 e inner problem
d inneres Problem n (Elektrodynamik)
f problème m interne (électrodynamique)
r внутренняя задача f (в электродинамике)

I220 e inner radiation belt
d innerer Strahlungsgürtel m
f ceinture f de radiation intérieure
r внутренний радиационный пояс m

I221 e inner shell
d Innenschale f (Atom)
f couche f interne (de l'atome)
r внутренняя оболочка f (атома)

I222 e inner shell ionization
d Innenschalenionisation f
f ionisation f des électrons internes
r ионизация f внутренней оболочки (атома)

I223 e input circuit
d Eingangsstromkreis m, Eingangskreis m
f circuit m d'entrée
r входной контур m

I224 e input impedance
d Eingangsimpedanz f
f impédance f d'entrée
r входной импеданс m

I225 e input power
d Eingangsleistung f
f puissance f d'entrée
r входная мощность f

I226 e input stage
d Eingangsstufe f
f étage m d'entrée
r входной каскад m

I227 e input terminals
d Eingangsklemmen f pl
f bornes f pl d'entrée
r входные зажимы m pl

I228 e input voltage
d Eingangsspannung f
f tension f d'entrée
r входное напряжение n

I229 e insertion loss
d Einfügungsverlust m, Einfügungsdämpfung f
f pertes f pl d'insertion; amortissement m apporté
r вносимые потери f pl, вносимое затухание n

I230 e in situ measurement
d In-Situ-Messung f
f mesure f in situ
r измерение n in situ, измерение n в месте нахождения

I231 e insolation
d Insolation f, Sonneneinstrahlung f, Sonnenbestrahlung f
f insolation f
r инсоляция f

I232 e insolubility
d Unlöslichkeit f
f insolubilité f
r нерастворимость f

I233 e instability
d Instabilität f, Labilität f, Unbeständigkeit f

    f instabilité *f*
    r неустойчивость *f*; нестабильность *f*

I234 *e* instability criterion
    d Instabilitätskriterium *n*
    f critère *m* d'instabilité
    r критерий *m* неустойчивости

I235 *e* instability increment
    d Instabilitätsinkrement *n*
    f incrément *m* d'instabilité
    r инкремент *m* неустойчивости

I236 *e* instantaneous center
    d Momentanpol *m*
    f centre *m* instantané
    r мгновенный центр *m*

I237 *e* instantaneous value
    d Augenblickswert *m*, Momentanwert *m*
    f valeur *f* instantanée
    r мгновенное значение *n*

I238 *e* instantaneous velocity
    d Momentangeschwindigkeit *f*
    f vitesse *f* instantanée
    r мгновенная скорость *f*

I239 *e* instantaneous voltage
    d Augenblicksspannung *f*, Momentanspannung *f*
    f tension *f* instantanée
    r мгновенное напряжение *n*

I240 *e* instant center *see* instantaneous center

I241 *e* instanton
    d Instanton *n*
    f instanton *m*
    r инстантон *m*

I242 *e* instrument
    d 1. Meßinstrument *n*; Meßgerät *n* 2. Instrument *n*, Gerät *n*, Apparat *m*
    f instrument *m*
    r измерительный прибор *m*; инструмент *m*

I243 *e* instrumental distortion
    d Instrumentenverzerrung *f*, Geräteverzerrung *f*
    f distorsion *f* instrumentale
    r инструментальные искажения *n pl*

I244 *e* instrumental errors
    d Instrumentenfehler *m pl*, Gerätefehler *m pl*
    f erreurs *f pl* instrumentales
    r погрешности *f pl* прибора, инструментальные погрешности *f pl*

I245 *e* insulation
    d Isolation *f*; Isolierung *f*
    f isolement *m*; isolation *f*
    r изоляция *f*

I246 *e* insulator
    d 1. Isolator *m*, Isolierkörper *m* 2. Dielektrikum *n*, Isolator *m*, Nichtleiter *m*
    f 1. isolant *m* 2. diélectrique *m*
    r 1. изолятор *m* 2. диэлектрик *m*

I247 *e* integer
    d ganze Zahl *f*
    f nombre *m* entier
    r целое число *n*

I248 *e* integral
    d Integral *n*
    f intégrale *f*
    r интеграл *m*

I249 *e* integral equation
    d Integralgleichung *f*
    f équation *f* intégrale
    r интегральное уравнение *n*

I250 *e* integral intensity
    d Gesamtintensität *f*
    f intensité *f* intégrale
    r интегральная интенсивность *f*, полная интенсивность *f*

I251 *e* integral of motion
    d Bewegungsintegral *n*
    f intégrale *f* de mouvement
    r интеграл *m* движения

I252 *e* integral over the optical path
    d Strahlengangintegral *n*
    f intégrale *f* du chemin optique
    r интеграл *m* по оптическому пути

I253 *e* integral transform
    d Integraltransformation *f*
    f transformation *f* intégrale
    r интегральное преобразование *n*

I254 *e* integrated circuit
    d integrierter Schaltkreis *m*
    f circuit *m* intégré
    r интегральная микросхема *f*, интегральная схема *f*

I255 *e* integrated intensity *see* integral intensity

I256 *e* integrated optics
    d integrierte Optik *f*
    f optique *f* intégrée
    r интегральная оптика *f*

I257 *e* integrating circuit
    d Integrierschaltung *f*, Integrierkreis *m*
    f circuit *m* intégrateur
    r интегрирующая цепь *f*

I258 *e* integrating ionization chamber
    d integrierende Ionisationskammer *f*
    f chambre *f* d'ionisation à intégration
    r интегрирующая ионизационная камера *f*

I259   *e* integrating photometer
      d Integralphotometer *n*
      f photomètre *m* intégrateur
      r интегрирующий фотометр *m*

I260   *e* integration
      d Integration *f*
      f intégration *f*
      r 1. интеграция *f (в микроэлектронике)*
         2. интегрирование *n*

I261   *e* intense radiation
      d intensive Strahlung *f*
      f rayonnement *m* intense
      r интенсивное излучение *n*, мощное излучение *n*

I262   *e* intensity
      d Intensität *f*, Stärke *f*
      f intensité *f*
      r 1. интенсивность *f*
         2. напряжённость *f (поля)*

I263   *e* intensity interferometer
      d Intensitätsinterferometer *n*
      f interféromètre *m* de l'intensité
      r интерферометр *m* интенсивности

I264   *e* intensity interferometry
      d Intensitätsinterferometrie *f*
      f interférométrie *f* de l'intensité
      r интерферометрия *f* интенсивности

I265   *e* intensity modulation
      d Helligkeitsmodulation *f*, Intensitätsmodulation *f*
      f modulation *f* de brillance
      r модуляция *f* яркости

I266   *e* intensity of a spectral line
      d Spektrallinienintensität *f*
      f intensité *f* d'une raie spectrale
      r интенсивность *f* спектральной линии

I267   *e* intensive parameters, intensive variables
      d intensive Zustandsgrößen *f pl*, intensive Größen *f pl*
      f paramètres *m pl* intensifs
      r интенсивные параметры *m pl*

I268   *e* interaction
      d Wechselwirkung *f*
      f interaction *f*
      r взаимодействие *n*

I269   *e* interaction area
      d Wechselwirkungsgebiet *n*
      f aire *f* d'interaction, région *f* d'interaction
      r область *f* взаимодействия

I270   *e* interaction constant
      d Wechselwirkungskonstante *f*
      f constante *f* d'interaction
      r константа *f* взаимодействия, константа *f* связи

I271   *e* interaction energy
      d Wechselwirkungsenergie *f*
      f énergie *f* d'interaction
      r энергия *f* взаимодействия

I272   *e* interaction factor
      d Wechselwirkungsfaktor *m*
      f facteur *m* d'interaction
      r коэффициент *m* взаимодействия

I273   *e* interaction Lagrangian
      d Wechselwirkungs-Lagrange-Dichte *f*
      f lagrangien *m* d'interaction
      r лагранжиан *m* взаимодействия

I274   *e* interaction locality
      d Wechselwirkungslokalität *f*
      f localité *f* d'interaction
      r локальность *f* взаимодействия

I275   *e* interaction operator
      d Wechselwirkungsoperator *m*
      f opérateur *m* d'interaction
      r оператор *m* взаимодействия

I276   *e* interaction region *see* interaction area

I277   *e* interatomic distance
      d interatomarer Abstand *m*, Atomabstand *m*
      f distance *f* interatomique
      r межатомное расстояние *n*

I278   *e* interatomic interaction
      d interatomare Wechselwirkung *f*
      f interaction *f* interatomique
      r межатомное взаимодействие *n*

I279   *e* interband transitions
      d Band-Band-Übergänge *m pl*, Interbandübergänge *m pl*
      f transitions *f pl* interbandes
      r межзонные переходы *m pl*

I280   *e* interband tunneling
      d Zwischenbandtunnelung *f*
      f effet *m* tunnel interbande
      r межзонное туннелирование *n*

I281   *e* intercalated compounds
      d schichtförmig ausgebildete Einlagerungsverbindungen *f pl*, lamellare Verbindungen *f pl*
      f composés *m pl* lamellaires
      r интеркалированные соединения *n pl*

I282   *e* interchange
      d Austausch *m*; Platzwechsel *m*
      f permutation *f*; échange *m* de places
      r перестановка *f*; обмен *m* местами

I283   *e* interchanging instability

d   Austauschinstabilität f
f   instabilité f commutative
r   перестановочная неустойчивость f

I284   e   intercombination lines
d   Interkombinationslinien f pl
f   raies f pl d'intercombinaison
r   интеркомбинационные линии f pl

I285   e   intercombination transitions
d   Interkombinationsübergänge m pl
f   transitions f pl d'intercombinaison
r   интеркомбинационные
переходы m pl

I286   e   intercrystalline failure
d   interkristalliner Bruch m,
Korngrenzenbruch m
f   rupture f intercristalline
r   излом m по границам зёрен

I287   e   interdiffusion
d   Interdiffusion f
f   interdiffusion f
r   взаимная диффузия f

I288   e   interdiffusion coefficient
d   Interdiffusionskoeffizient m
f   coefficient m d'interdiffusion
r   коэффициент m взаимной
диффузии

I289   e   interelectrode capacitance
d   Zwischenelektrodenkapazität f
f   capacité f interélectrode
r   межэлектродная ёмкость f

I290   e   interface
d   1. Interface n, Schnittstelle f 2.
Grenzfläche f, Phasengrenzfläche f;
Grenzschicht f
f   1. interface f 2. surface f limite,
surface f de séparation
r   1. интерфейс m 2. граница f
раздела

I291   e   interface region
d   Grenzschichtgebiet n,
Grenzschichtbereich m
f   zone f de couche limite, région f de
couche limite
r   граничная область f (двух сред)

I292   e   interference
d   1. Interferenz f, Überlagerung f 2.
Störung f, störende Beeinflussung f
f   1. interférence f 2. parasites m pl
r   1. интерференция f 2. помехи f pl

I293   e   interference colors
d   Interferenzfarben f pl
f   couleurs f pl d'interférence
r   интерференционные цвета m pl

I294   e   interference comparator
d   Interferenzkomparator m

f   comparateur m d'interférence
r   интерференционный компаратор m

I295   e   interference figures
d   Interferenzfiguren f pl
f   images f pl d'interférence
r   интерференционные фигуры f pl

I296   e   interference filter
d   Interferenzfilter n
f   filtre m interférentiel
r   интерференционный фильтр m

I297   e   interference fringes
d   Interferenzstreifen m pl
f   franges f pl d'interférence
r   интерференционные полосы f pl

I298   e   interference of light
d   Interferenz f des Lichtes
f   interférence f de la lumière
r   интерференция f света, оптическая
интерференция f

I299   e   interference of states
d   Zustandsinterferenz f
f   interférence f des états
r   интерференция f состояний

I300   e   interference pattern
d   Interferenzbild n, Interferenzfigur f
f   image f d'interférences
r   интерференционная картина f,
интерферограмма f

I301   e   interference rings
d   Interferenzringe m pl
f   anneaux m pl d'interférence
r   интерференционные кольца n pl

I302   e   interference source
d   Störquelle f
f   source f d'interférence
r   источник m помех

I303   e   interferogram see interference
pattern

I304   e   interferometer
d   Interferometer n
f   interféromètre m
r   интерферометр m

I305   e   interferometer base
d   Interferometerbasis f
f   base f de l'interféromètre
r   база f интерферометра

I306   e   interferometric compensator
d   interferometrischer Kompensator m
f   compensateur m interférométrique
r   интерферометрический
компенсатор m

I307   e   interferometric measurements
d   interferometrische Messungen f pl
f   mesures f pl interférométriques

r интерферометрические
измерения *n pl*

I308 e interferometry
d Interferometrie *f*
f interférométrie *f*
r интерферометрия *f*

I309 e intergalactic gas
d intergalaktisches Gas *n*
f gaz *m* intergalactique
r межгалактический газ *m*

I310 e intermediate boson
d intermediäres Boson *n*
f boson *m* intermédiaire
r промежуточный бозон *m*

I311 e intermediate-energy region
d Mittelenergiebereich *m*
f région *f* d'énergies intermédiaires
r область *f* промежуточных энергий

I312 e intermediate frequency
d Zwischenfrequenz *f*
f fréquence *f* intermédiaire
r промежуточная частота *f*

I313 e intermediate neutrons
d mittelschnelle Neutronen *n pl*
f neutrons *m pl* intermédiaires
r промежуточные нейтроны *m pl*

I314 e intermediate state
d Zwischenzustand *m*
f état *m* intermédiaire
r промежуточное состояние *n*

I315 e intermediate vector boson
d intermediäres Vektorboson *n*
f boson *m* vecteur intermédiaire
r промежуточный векторный бозон *m*

I316 e intermetallic compounds
d intermetallische Verbindungen *f pl*
f composés *m pl* intermétalliques
r интерметаллические соединения *n pl*, металлиды *m pl*

I317 e intermodal interference
d Zwischenmodeninterferenz *f*
f interférence *f* intermode
r межмодовая интерференция *f*

I318 e intermode conversion
d Zwischenmodenkonversion *f*
f conversion *f* intermode
r межмодовая конверсия *f*

I319 e intermode dispersion
d Zwischenmodendispersion *f*
f dispersion *f* intermode
r межмодовая дисперсия *f*

I320 e intermolecular interaction
d intermolekulare Wechselwirkung *f*, zwischenmolekulare Wechselwirkung *f*

f interaction *f* intermoléculaire
r межмолекулярное взаимодействие *n*

I321 e internal conversion
d innere Konversion *f*, innere Umwandlung *f*
f conversion *f* interne
r внутренняя конверсия *f*

I322 e internal energy
d innere Energie *f*
f énergie *f* interne
r внутренняя энергия *f*

I323 e internal friction
d Eigenreibung *f*, innere Reibung *f*
f frottement *m* interne
r внутреннее трение *n*

I324 e internal gravitational waves
d innere Gravitationswellen *f pl*
f ondes *f pl* de gravité internes
r внутренние гравитационные волны *f pl*

I325 e internal photoelectric effect
d innerer Photoeffekt *m*, innerer photoelektrischer Effekt *m*, innerer lichtelektrischer Effekt *m*
f effet *m* photo-électrique interne
r внутренний фотоэффект *m*

I326 e internal quantum number
d innere Quantenzahl *f*
f nombre *m* quantique interne
r внутреннее квантовое число *n*

I327 e internal reflection
d innere Reflexion *f*
f réflexion *f* interne
r внутреннее отражение *n*

I328 e internal rotation
d innere Rotation *f*
f rotation *f* interne
r внутреннее вращение *n*

I329 e internal symmetry
d innere Symmetrie *f*
f symétrie *f* interne
r внутренняя симметрия *f*

I330 e International System of Units
d internationales Einheitensystem *n*, SI-System *n*, SI
f système *m* international d'unités, SI
r Международная система *f* единиц, СИ

I331 e interplanetary matter
d interplanetare Materie *f*
f matière *f* interplanétaire
r межпланетное вещество *n*, межпланетная среда *f*

I332 e interplanetary space
d interplanetarer Raum *m*

f espace *m* interplanétaire
r межпланетное пространство *n*

I333 *e* interpolation
d Interpolation *f*, Interpolierung *f*
f interpolation *f*
r интерполяция *f*,
интерполирование *n*

I334 *e* interpretation
d Interpretieren *n*, Interpretation *f*,
Auslegung *f*
f interprétation *f*
r интерпретация *f*, истолкование *n*

I335 *e* interpretation of diffraction patterns
d Beugungsbilderinterpretation *f*
f interprétation *f* des images de
diffraction
r интерпретация *f* дифракционных
картин

I336 *e* interpretation of spectra
d Interpretation *f* der Spektren
f interprétation *f* de spectres
r интерпретация *f* спектров

I337 *e* intersection
d Schneiden *n*; Schnitt *m*
f intersection *f*
r пересечение *n*

I338 *e* interstellar absorption
d interstellare Absorption *f*
f absorption *f* interstellaire
r межзвёздное поглощение *n (света)*

I339 *e* interstellar dust
d interstellarer Staub *m*
f poussière *f* interstellaire
r межзвёздная пыль *f*

I340 *e* interstellar emission
d interstellare Strahlung *f*
f émission *f* interstellaire
r межзвёздное излучение *n*

I341 *e* interstellar gas
d interstellares Gas *n*
f gaz *m* interstellaire
r межзвёздный газ *m*

I342 *e* interstellar hydrogen
d interstellarer Wasserstoff *m*
f hydrogène *m* interstellaire
r межзвёздный водород *m*

I343 *e* interstellar matter
d interstellare Materie *f*
f matière *f* interstellaire
r межзвёздное вещество *n*,
межзвёздная среда *f*

I344 *e* interstellar space
d interstellarer Raum *m*
f espace *m* interstellaire
r межзвёздное пространство *n*

I345 *e* interstitial atom
d Zwischengitteratom *n*, Atom *n* auf
Zwischengitterplatz
f atome *m* interstitiel
r межузельный атом *m*, атом *m*
внедрения

I346 *e* interstitial defect
d Zwischengitterfehlstelle *f*,
Zwischengitterdefekt *m*
f défaut *m* interstitiel
r дефект *m* внедрения, межузельный
дефект *m*

I347 *e* interstitial position *see* interstitial
site

I348 *e* interstitial site
d Zwischengitterplatz *m*
f position *f* interstitielle
r междоузлие *n*

I349 *e* interval
d Intervall *n*; Zwischenraum *m*,
Abstand *m*
f intervalle *m*
r интервал *m*; промежуток *m*

I350 *e* intervalley transitions
d Intervalley-Übergänge *m pl*
f transitions *f pl* intervalées
r междолинные переходы *m pl*

I351 *e* intraband transition
d Intrabandübergang *m*
f transition *f* intrabande
r внутризонный переход *m*

I352 *e* intrabeam scattering
d Intrastrahlstreuung *f*
f diffusion *f* au faisceau
r внутрипучковое рассеяние *n*

I353 *e* intracavity laser spectroscopy
d Intracavity-Laserspektroskopie *f*
f spectroscopie *f* d'intracavité laser
r внутрирезонаторная лазерная
спектроскопия *f*

I354 *e* intramode dispersion
d Intramodendispersion *f*
f dispersion *f* intramode
r внутримодовая дисперсия *f*

I355 *e* intramolecular bonds
d innermolekulare Bindungen *f pl*
f liaisons *f pl* intramoléculaires
r внутримолекулярные связи *f pl*

I356 *e* intramolecular interaction
d innermolekulare Wechselwirkung *f*
f interaction *f* intramoléculaire
r внутримолекулярное
взаимодействие *n*

I357 *e* intrinsic conduction
d Eigenleitung *f*

f conduction *f* intrinsèque
r собственная проводимость *f*

I358 *e* intrinsic energy *see* internal energy

I359 *e* intrinsic parity
d innere Parität *f*
f parité *f* intrinsèque
r внутренняя чётность *f*

I360 *e* intrinsic semiconductor
d Eigenhalbleiter *m*, Intrinsic-Halbleiter *m*
f semi-conducteur *m* intrinsèque
r собственный полупроводник *m*

I361 *e* invar
d Invar *n*
f invar *m*
r инвар *m*

I362 *e* invariance
d Invarianz *f*
f invariance *f*
r инвариантность *f*

I363 *e* invariance violation
d Invarianzverletzung *f*
f violation *f* de l'invariance
r нарушение *n* инвариантности

I364 *e* invariant
d 1. Invariante *f* 2. Skalar *m*
f invariant *m*
r инвариант *m*

I365 *e* invariant charge
d invariante Ladung *f*
f charge *f* d'invariant
r инвариантный заряд *m*

I366 *e* invariant method
d Invariantenmethode *f*
f méthode *f* des invariants
r метод *m* инвариантов

I367 *e* inverse Fourier transformation
d inverse Fourier-Transformation *f*, Fourier-Rücktransformation *f*
f transformation *f* de Fourier inverse
r обратное преобразование *n* Фурье

I368 *e* inverse population
d inverse Besetzung *f*
f population *f* inverse
r инверсная населённость *f*

I369 *e* inverse problem
d inverses Problem *n*
f problème *m* inverse
r обратная задача *f*

I370 *e* inverse relationship
d inverse Abhängigkeit *f*
f rapport *m* inverse
r обратная зависимость *f*

I371 *e* inverse scattering problem
d inverses Streuungsproblem *n*
f problème *m* de diffusion inverse
r обратная задача *f* рассеяния

I372 *e* inverse voltage
d Rückspannung *f*
f tension *f* inverse
r обратное напряжение *n*

I373 *e* inversion
d Inversion *f*; Umwandlung *f*
f inversion *f*
r инверсия *f*; обращение *n*

I374 *e* inversion curve
d Inversionskurve *f*
f courbe *f* d'inversion
r кривая *f* инверсии

I375 *e* inversion layer
d Inversionsschicht *f*
f couche *f* d'inversion
r инверсионный слой *m*

I376 *e* inversion temperature
d Inversionstemperatur *f*
f température *f* d'inversion
r температура *f* инверсии

I377 *e* inverter
d Inverter *m*
f inverteur *m*
r инвертор *m*

I378 *e* invisible radiation
d unsichtbare Strahlung *f*
f rayonnement *m* invisible
r невидимое излучение *n*

I379 *e* invited paper, invited report
d eingeladener Bericht *m*
f rapport *m* invité
r приглашённый доклад *m*

I380 *e* iodine, I
d Iod *n*
f iode *m*
r иод *m*

I381 *e* ion
d Ion *n*
f ion *m*
r ион *m*

I382 *e* ion accelerator
d Ionenbeschleuniger *m*
f accélérateur *m* d'ions
r ускоритель *m* ионов

I383 *e* ion-acoustic instability
d Ionenschallinstabilität *f*
f instabilité *f* acoustique ionique
r ионно-звуковая неустойчивость *f*

I384 *e* ion-acoustic oscillation
d Ionenschall *m*, Ionenschallschwingungen *f pl*

f oscillations *f pl* acoustiques ioniques
r ионно-звуковые колебания *n pl*

I385 *e* ion beam
d Ionenstrahl *m*
f faisceau *m* ionique
r ионный пучок *m*

I386 *e* ion-beam implantation
d Ionenimplantation *f*
f implantation *f* à faisceau ionique
r ионная имплантация *f*

I387 *e* ion-beam lithography
d Ionenstrahllithographie *f*
f lithographie *f* à faisceau ionique
r ионно-лучевая литография *f*

I388 *e* ion-beam modification
d Ionenstrahlmodifikation *f*
f modification *f* de faisceau ionique
r ионно-лучевая модификация *f*

I389 *e* ion bombardment
d Ionenbeschuß *m*
f bombardement *m* ionique
r ионная бомбардировка *f*

I390 *e* ion channeling
d Ionenkanalierung *f*
f canalisation *f* d'ions
r каналирование *n* ионов

I391 *e* ion charge
d Ionenladung *f*
f charge *f* de l'ion
r заряд *m* иона, ионный заряд *m*

I392 *e* ion cluster
d Ionencluster *m*, Ionenschwarm *m*
f groupe *m* d'ions
r ионный кластер *m*

I393 *e* ion concentration
d Ionenkonzentration *f*
f concentration *f* d'ions
r концентрация *f* ионов, ионная концентрация *f*

I394 *e* ion dechanneling
d Ionendekanalierung *f*
f décanalisation *f* d'ions
r деканалирование *n* ионов

I395 *e* ion density *see* ion concentration

I396 *e* ion-electron emission
d Ion-Elektron-Emission *f*
f émission ion-électron *f*
r ионно-электронная эмиссия *f*

I397 *e* ion-electron recombination
d Ion-Elektron-Rekombination *f*
f recombinaison *f* ion-électron
r ионно-электронная рекомбинация *f*

I398 *e* ion emission

d Ionenemission *f*
f émission *f* ionique
r ионная эмиссия *f*

I399 *e* ion-exchange catalysis
d Ionenaustauschkatalyse *f*
f catalyse *f* à échange d'ions
r ионообменный катализ *m*

I400 *e* ion-exchange chromatography
d Ionenaustauschchromatographie *f*
f chromatographie *f* par échange d'ions
r ионообменная хроматография *f*

I401 *e* ion gun
d Ionenkanone *f*
f canon *m* ionique
r ионный прожектор *m*, ионная пушка *f*

I402 *e* ionic bond
d Ionenbindung *f*; heteropolare Bindung *f*
f liaison *f* ionique
r ионная связь *f*; гетерополярная связь *f*

I403 *e* ionic conduction
d Ionenleitung *f*
f conduction *f* ionique
r ионная проводимость *f*, ионная электропроводность *f*

I404 *e* ionic crystal
d Ionenkristall *m*
f cristal *m* ionique
r ионный кристалл *m*

I405 *e* ionic devices
d Ionengeräte *n pl*
f appareils *m pl* ioniques
r ионные приборы *m pl*

I406 *e* ionic etching
d Ionenätzung *f*
f attaque *f* ionique
r ионное травление *n*

I407 *e* ionic radius
d Ionenradius *m*
f rayon *m* ionique
r ионный радиус *m*

I408 *e* ionic sputtering
d Ionensputtering *n*, Ionensputtern *n*, Ionenzerstäubung *f*
f pulvérisation *f* ionique
r ионное распыление *n*

I409 *e* ion implantation *see* ion-beam implantation

I410 *e* ion implantation chamber
d Ionenimplantationskammer *f*
f chambre *f* à implantation d'ions
r камера *f* для ионной имплантации

I411 e ion-implantation doping
      d Ionendotierung f
      f implantation f d'ions
      r ионное легирование n

I412 e ion-ion emission
      d Ion-Ion-Emission f
      f émission f ion-ion
      r ионно-ионная эмиссия f

I413 e ionization
      d Ionisation f, Ionisierung f
      f ionisation f
      r ионизация f

I414 e ionization by collision
      d Stoßionisation f, Stoßionisierung f
      f ionisation f par collision
      r столкновительная ионизация f

I415 e ionization by electron impact
      d Elektronenstoßionisation f
      f ionisation f par choc électronique
      r ионизация f электронным ударом

I416 e ionization calorimeter
      d Ionisationskalorimeter n
      f calorimètre m d'ionisation
      r ионизационный калориметр m

I417 e ionization chamber
      d Ionisationskammer f
      f chambre f d'ionisation
      r ионизационная камера f

I418 e ionization channel
      d Ionisationskanal m
      f canal m d'ionisation
      r канал m ионизации

I419 e ionization coefficient
      d Ionisationskoeffizient m
      f coefficient m d'ionisation
      r коэффициент m ионизации

I420 e ionization continuum
      d Ionisationskontinuum n
      f continuum m d'ionisation
      r ионизационный континуум m

I421 e ionization cross-section
      d Ionisationsquerschnitt m
      f section f d'ionisation, section f efficace
         d'ionisation
      r сечение n ионизации

I422 e ionization curve
      d Ionisationskurve f
      f courbe f d'ionisation
      r ионизационная кривая f

I423 e ionization energy
      d Ionisierungsenergie f,
         Ionisationsenergie f
      f énergie f d'ionisation
      r энергия ионизации f

I424 e ionization equilibrium
      d Ionisationsgleichgewicht n,
         Ionisierungsgleichgewicht n
      f équilibre m d'ionisation
      r ионизационное равновесие n

I425 e ionization gage
      d Ionisationsmanometer n,
         Ionisationsvakuummesser m
      f manomètre m à ionisation, jauge f à
         ionisation
      r ионизационный манометр m

I426 e ionization instability
      d Ionisationsinstabilität f
      f instabilité f d'ionisation
      r ионизационная неустойчивость f

I427 e ionization losses
      d Ionisationsverluste m pl
      f pertes f pl d'ionisation
      r ионизационные потери f pl

I428 e ionization of atmosphere
      d Luftionisation f, atmosphärische
         Ionisation f
      f ionisation f atmosphérique
      r атмосферная ионизация f

I429 e ionization potential
      d Ionisierungsspannung f,
         Ionisationsspannung f
      f potentiel m d'ionisation
      r потенциал m ионизации,
         ионизационный потенциал m

I430 e ionization rate
      d Ionisierungsgeschwindigkeit f,
         Ionisationsgeschwindigkeit f
      f taux m d'ionisation
      r скорость f ионизации

I431 e ionization source
      d Ionisationsquelle f,
         Ionisierungsquelle f
      f source f d'ionisation, source f
         ionisante
      r источник m ионизации

I432 e ionization state
      d Ionisierungszustand m
      f état m d'ionisation
      r ионизованное состояние n,
         ионизированное состояние n

I433 e ionization temperature
      d Ionisationstemperatur f
      f température f d'ionisation
      r температура f ионизации

I434 e ionization vacuum gage
      d Ionisationsvakuummeter n
      f jauge f du vide à ionisation
      r ионизационный вакуумметр m

I435 e ionization waves

    d Ionisationswellen *f pl*
    f ondes *f pl* d'ionisation
    r ионизационные волны *f pl*, волны *f*
      pl ионизации

I436 *e* **ionized atom**
    d ionisiertes Atom *n*
    f atome *m* ionisé
    r ионизованный атом *m*

I437 *e* **ionized gas**
    d ionisiertes Gas *n*
    f gaz *m* ionisé
    r ионизированный газ *m*,
      ионизованный газ *m*

I438 *e* **ionized molecule**
    d ionisiertes Molekül *n*
    f molécule *f* ionisée
    r ионизованная молекула *f*

I439 *e* **ionizer**
    d Ionisator *m*
    f ioniseur *m*
    r ионизатор *m*

I440 *e* **ionizing radiation**
    d ionisierende Strahlung *f*
    f rayonnement *m* ionisant
    r ионизирующее излучение *n*

I441 *e* **ionizing radiation source**
    d ionisierende Strahlungsquelle *f*
    f source *f* de rayonnement ionisant
    r источник *m* ионизирующего
      излучения

I442 *e* **ion laser**
    d Ionenlaser *m*
    f laser *m* à ions
    r ионный лазер *m*

I443 *e* **ion microscope**
    d Ionenmikroskop *n*
    f microscope *m* ionique
    r ионный микроскоп *m*

I444 *e* **ionogram**
    d Ionogramm *n*,
      Ionosphärendurchdrehaufnahme *f*
    f ionogramme *m*
    r ионограмма *f*

I445 *e* **ionoluminescence**
    d Ionolumineszenz *f*
    f ionoluminescence *f*
    r ионолюминесценция *f*

I446 *e* **ionosonde**
    d Ionosonde *f*
    f ionosonde *f*
    r ионозонд *m*

I447 *e* **ionosphere**
    d Ionosphäre *f*
    f ionosphère *f*
    r ионосфера *f*

I448 *e* **ionospheric channel**
    d Ionosphärenkanal *m*
    f canal *m* ionosphérique
    r ионосферный канал *m*

I449 *e* **ionospheric data**
    d ionosphärische Daten *pl*
    f données *pl* ionosphériques
    r ионосферные данные *pl*

I450 *e* **ionospheric disturbances**
    d ionosphärische Störungen *f pl*,
      Ionosphärenstörungen *f pl*
    f perturbations *f pl* ionosphériques
    r ионосферные возмущения *n pl*

I451 *e* **ionospheric dynamo**
    d Ionosphärendynamoeffekt *m*
    f effet *m* dynamo ionosphérique
    r ионосферное динамо *n*

I452 *e* **ionospheric irregularity**
    d ionosphärische Ungleichheit *f*
    f irrégularité *f* ionosphérique
    r ионосферная неоднородность *f*

I453 *e* **ionospheric region**
    d Ionosphärengebiet *n*
    f région *f* ionosphérique
    r область *f* ионосферы

I454 *e* **ionospheric scintillation**
    d ionosphärische Szintillation *f*,
      ionosphärisches Flimmern *n*
    f scintillations *f pl* ionosphériques
    r ионосферные мерцания *n pl*

I455 *e* **ionospheric sounding**
    d Ionosphärensondierung *f*
    f sondage *m* ionosphérique
    r зондирование *n* ионосферы

I456 *e* **ionospheric waveguide**
    d Ionosphärenwellenleiter *m*
    f guide *m* d'ondes ionosphérique
    r ионосферный волновод *m*

I457 *e* **ion projector**
    d Ionenprojektor *m*
    f projecteur *m* ionique
    r ионный проектор *m*

I458 *e* **ion sound**
    d Ionenschall *m*,
      Ionenschallschwingung *f*
    f son *m* ionique
    r ионный звук *m (в плазме)*

I459 *e* **ion-sound oscillation** *see* **ion-acoustic oscillation**

I460 *e* **ion source**
    d Ionenquelle *f*
    f source *f* d'ions
    r ионный источник *m*, источник *m*
      ионов

I461　e　ion temperature
　　　 d　Ionentemperatur *f*
　　　 f　température *f* ionique
　　　 r　ионная температура *f*, температура *f* ионов

I462　e　ion thermonuclear fusion
　　　 d　Ionenfusion *f*
　　　 f　fusion *f* thermonucléaire ionique
　　　 r　ионный термоядерный синтез *m*

I463　e　iridium, Ir
　　　 d　Iridium *n*
　　　 f　iridium *m*
　　　 r　иридий *m*

I464　e　iris *see* iris diaphragm

I465　e　iris diaphragm
　　　 d　Irisblende *f*
　　　 f　diaphragme *m* iris
　　　 r　ирисовая диафрагма *f*

I466　e　iron, Fe
　　　 d　Eisen *n*
　　　 f　fer *m*
　　　 r　железо *n*

I467　e　iron-core coil
　　　 d　Eisenkernspule *f*, Eisenkerndrossel *f*, Eisendrossel *f*
　　　 f　bobine *f* à noyau de fer
　　　 r　катушка *f* с железным сердечником

I468　e　iron losses
　　　 d　Eisenkernverluste *m pl*
　　　 f　pertes *f pl* au fer
　　　 r　потери *f pl* в железе; потери *f pl* в сердечнике

I469　e　irradiance
　　　 d　Bestrahlungsstärke *f*
　　　 f　irradiance *f*
　　　 r　облучённость *f*

I470　e　irradiation
　　　 d　1. Bestrahlung *f* 2. Irradiation *f*
　　　 f　irradiation *f*
　　　 r　1. облучение *n* 2. иррадиация *f*

I471　e　IR radiation *see* infrared radiation

I472　e　irradiator
　　　 d　Strahler *m*, Strahlungsquelle *f*
　　　 f　irradiateur *m*
　　　 r　облучатель *m*

I473　e　irrecoverable deformation *see* irreversible deformation

I474　e　irreducible diagram
　　　 d　irreduzibles Diagramm *n*
　　　 f　diagramme *m* irréductible
　　　 r　неприводимая диаграмма *f*

I475　e　irreducible representation
　　　 d　irreduzible Darstellung *f (einer Gruppe)*

　　　 f　représentation *f* irréductible *(d'un groupe)*
　　　 r　неприводимое представление *n* *(группы)*

I476　e　irregularity
　　　 d　Irregularität *f*; Ungleichheit *f*; Inhomogenität *f*
　　　 f　irrégularité *f*
　　　 r　нерегулярность *f*; неоднородность *f*; неравномерность *f*

I477　e　irregular motion
　　　 d　ungeordnete Bewegung *f*, regellose Bewegung *f*
　　　 f　mouvement *m* irrégulier
　　　 r　неравномерное движение *n*

I478　e　irreversibility
　　　 d　Irreversibilität *f*, Nichtumkehrbarkeit *f*
　　　 f　irréversibilité *f*
　　　 r　необратимость *f*

I479　e　irreversible deformation
　　　 d　bleibende Formänderung *f*
　　　 f　déformation *f* irréversible
　　　 r　необратимая деформация *f*

I480　e　irreversible process
　　　 d　irreversibler Prozeß *m*, nichtumkehrbarer Prozeß *m*
　　　 f　processus *m* irréversible
　　　 r　необратимый процесс *m*

I481　e　irreversible thermodynamics
　　　 d　irreversible Thermodynamik *f*, Thermodynamik *f* irreversibler Prozesse
　　　 f　thermodynamique *f* des processus irréversibles
　　　 r　термодинамика *f* необратимых процессов

I482　e　irreversible transformation
　　　 d　irreversible Umwandlung *f*
　　　 f　transformation *f* irréversible
　　　 r　необратимое превращение *n*

I483　e　irrotational flow
　　　 d　wirbelfreie Strömung *f*, Potentialströmung *f*
　　　 f　écoulement *m* sans tourbillon, écoulement *m* potentiel
　　　 r　безвихревое течение *n*, потенциальное течение *n*

I484　e　IR source *see* infrared source

I485　e　isallobar
　　　 d　Isallobare *f*
　　　 f　isallobare *f*
　　　 r　изаллобара *f*

I486　e　isallotherm
　　　 d　Isallotherme *f*

f isallotherme *f*
r изаллотерма *f*

I487   *e* **isanemone**
     d Isanemone *f*
     f isanémone *f*
     r изанемона *f*

I488   *e* **isanomal line, isanomalous line**
     d Isanomale *f*
     f isanomale *f*, ligne *f* isanomale
     r изаномала *f*

I489   *e* **isenthalpic process**
     d isenthalpischer Prozeß *m*,
       isenthalpische Zustandsänderung *f*
     f processus *m* isenthalpique
     r изоэнтальпийный процесс *m*

I490   *e* **isentropic process**
     d isentropischer Prozeß *m*, isentropische
       Zustandsänderung *f*
     f processus *m* isentropique
     r изоэнтропийный процесс *m*

I491   *e* **Ising model**
     d Ising-Modell *n*
     f modèle *m* d'Ising
     r модель *f* Изинга, изинговская
       модель *f*

I492   *e* **isobar**
     d 1. Isobare *f*, Isobarenlinie *f* 2. Isobar
       n, Kernisobar *n*
     f 1. isobare *f* 2. noyau *m* isobare
     r 1. изобара *f* 2. изобар *m*

I493   *e* **isobaric line** *see* isobar 1.

I494   *e* **isobaric process**
     d isobarer Prozeß *m*, Isobarenprozeß *m*
     f processus *m* isobarique
     r изобарный процесс *m*

I495   *e* **isobaric spin**
     d Isobarenspin *m*, isobarer Spin *m*,
       Isospin *m*
     f spin *m* isobarique
     r изобарический спин *m*

I496   *e* **isocandela curve, isocandela line**
     d Isokandelakurve *f*, Linie *f* gleicher
       Lichtstärke
     f courbe *f* isocandela
     r кривая *f* равной силы света,
       изокандела *f*

I497   *e* **isochasm**
     d Isochasme *f*
     f isochasme *f*
     r изохазма *f*

I498   *e* **isochore**
     d Isochore *f*
     f isochore *f*
     r изохора *f*

I499   *e* **isochoric process**

d isochorer Prozeß *m*
f processus *m* isochore
r изохорный процесс *m*

I500   *e* **isochromatic curve, isochromatic**
       line
     d Isochromate *f*, isochromatische
       Kurve *f*
     f ligne *f* isochromatique, courbe *f*
       isochromatique
     r изохрома *f*

I501   *e* **isochrone**
     d Isochrone *f*
     f isochrone *f*
     r изохрона *f*

I502   *e* **isochrone pendulum**
     d Isochronenpendel *n*
     f pendule *m* isochrone
     r изохронный маятник *m*

I503   *e* **isochronism**
     d Isochronie *f*, Isochronismus *m*
     f isochronisme *m*
     r изохронность *f*

I504   *e* **isochronism of oscillation**
     d Schwingungsisochronismus *m*
     f isochronisme *m* des oscillations
     r изохронность *f* колебаний

I505   *e* **isochronism of pendulum**
     d Pendelisochronie *f*
     f isochronisme *m* du pendule
     r изохронность *f* маятника

I506   *e* **isochronous cyclotron**
     d Isochronzyklotron *n*
     f cyclotron *m* isochrone
     r изохронный циклотрон *m*

I507   *e* **isochronous motion**
     d isochrone Bewegung *f*
     f mouvement *m* isochrone
     r изохронное движение *n*

I508   *e* **isochronous vibration, isochronous**
       vibrations
     d isochrone Schwingungen *f pl*
     f oscillations *f pl* isochrones
     r изохронные колебания *n pl*

I509   *e* **isoclinic line**
     d Isokline *f*
     f isocline *f*
     r изоклина *f*

I510   *e* **isodence**
     d Isodense *f*
     f isodense *f*
     r изоденса *f*

I511   *e* **isodose**
     d Isodosenkurve *f*, Isodosis *f*
     f isodose *f*
     r изодоза *f*

I512   *e*   **isodynamic line**
     d   Isodyname *f*
     f   ligne *f* isodynamique
     r   изодинама *f*

I513   *e*   **isoelectronic sequence**
     d   isoelektronische Reihe *f*
     f   séquence *f* isoélectronique, série *f* isoélectronique
     r   изоэлектронный ряд *m*

I514   *e*   **isogon** *see* **isogonic line**

I515   *e*   **isogonic line**
     d   Isogone *f*
     f   ligne *f* isogonique, isogone *f*
     r   изогона *f*

I516   *e*   **isogroup**
     d   Isogruppe *f*
     f   isogroupe *m*
     r   изогруппа *f*

I517   *e*   **isokinetic**
     d   Isokinetik *f*
     f   isocinétique *f*
     r   изокинета *f*

I518   *e*   **isolated dislocation**
     d   Einzelversetzung *f*, isolierte Dislokation *f*
     f   dislocation *f* isolée
     r   изолированная дислокация *f*, одиночная дислокация *f*

I519   *e*   **isolated system**
     d   isoliertes System *n*
     f   système *m* isolé
     r   изолированная система *f*, замкнутая система *f*

I520   *e*   **isolation**
     d   1. Isolierung *f*, Isolation *f* 2. Entkopplung *f*; Trennung *f*
     f   1. isolation *f* 2. séparation *f*
     r   1. изоляция *f* 2. развязка *f*

I521   *e*   **isoline**
     d   Isolinie *f*
     f   isoligne *f*
     r   изолиния *f*

I522   *e*   **isoluminance curve**
     d   Kurve *f* gleicher Leuchtdichte
     f   courbe *f* isophote de luminance
     r   кривая *f* равной яркости

I523   *e*   **isolux curve**
     d   Isoluxe *f*, Isoluxkurve *f*
     f   courbe *f* isoluxe
     r   кривая *f* равной освещённости, изолюкс *m*

I524   *e*   **isomer**
     d   Isomer *n*, Isomeres *n*
     f   isomère *m*
     r   изомер *m*

I525   *e*   **isomerism**
     d   Isomerie *f*
     f   isomérie *f*
     r   изомерия *f*

I526   *e*   **isomerization**
     d   Isomerisation *f*
     f   isomérisation *f*
     r   изомеризация *f*

I527   *e*   **isomorphism**
     d   Isomorphie *f*; Isomorphismus *m*
     f   isomorphisme *m*
     r   изоморфизм *m*

I528   *e*   **isomultiplet**
     d   Isomultiplett *n*, Isotopenmultiplett *n*
     f   isomultiplet *m*
     r   изомультиплет *m*, изотопический мультиплет *m*

I529   *e*   **isophasal line**
     d   Isophase *f* (*der Sonnenfinsternis*)
     f   isophase *f* (*de l'éclipse solaire*)
     r   изофаза *f* (*солнечного затмения*)

I530   *e*   **isophot curve**
     d   Isophote *f*
     f   isophote *f*
     r   изофот *m*

I531   *e*   **isoplanatism**
     d   Isoplanasie *f*
     f   isoplanatisme *m*
     r   изопланатизм *m*

I532   *e*   **isopycnic, isopycnic line**
     d   Isopykne *f*
     f   isopycne *f*
     r   изопикна *f*

I533   *e*   **isoscalar**
     d   Isoskalar *m*
     f   isoscalaire *m*
     r   изоскаляр *m*

I534   *e*   **isosinglet**
     d   Isosingulett *n*, Isotopensingulett *n*
     f   isosinglet *m*
     r   изосинглет *m*

I535   *e*   **isospace**
     d   Isospinraum *m*, Iso-Raum *m*
     f   espace *m* isobarique
     r   изопространство *n*

I536   *e*   **isospin**
     d   Isospin *m*, Isotopenspin *m*
     f   isospin *m*
     r   изоспин *m*, изотопический спин *m*

I537   *e*   **isospin doublet**
     d   Isospindublett *n*, Isotopenspindublett *n*, Isodublett *n*
     f   isodoublet *m*
     r   изоспиновый дублет *m*, изотопический дублет *m*

I538
- *e* isospin multiplet
- *d* Isospinmultiplett *n*, Isotopenspinmultiplett *n*, Isomultiplett *n*
- *f* isomultiplet *m*
- *r* изоспиновый мультиплет *m*, изотопический мультиплет *m*

I539
- *e* isospin triplet
- *d* Isospintriplett *n*, Isotopenspintriplett *n*, Isotriplett *n*
- *f* isotriplet *m*
- *r* изоспиновый триплет *m*, изотопический триплет *m*

I540
- *e* isostere
- *d* Isostere *f*, isostere Kurve *f*
- *f* isostère *f*
- *r* изостера *f*

I541
- *e* isostructurality
- *d* Isostrukturalität *f*
- *f* isotypie *f*
- *r* изоструктурность *f*

I542
- *e* isosymmetry
- *d* Isosymmetrie *f*
- *f* isosymétrie *f*
- *r* изосимметрия *f*

I543
- *e* isotensor
- *d* Isotensor *m*
- *f* isotenseur *m*
- *r* изотензор *m*

I544
- *e* isotherm
- *d* Isotherme *f*
- *f* isotherme *f*
- *r* изотерма *f*

I545
- *e* isothermal expansion
- *d* isotherme Ausdehnung *f*
- *f* expansion *f* isotherme
- *r* изотермическое расширение *n*

I546
- *e* isothermal process
- *d* isothermer Prozeß *m*, isotherme Zustandsänderung *f*
- *f* processus *m* isotherme
- *r* изотермический процесс *m*

I547
- *e* isotone
- *d* Isoton *n*
- *f* isotone *m*
- *r* изотон *m*

I548
- *e* isotope
- *d* Isotop *n*
- *f* isotope *m*
- *r* изотоп *m*

I549
- *e* isotope chronology
- *d* Altersbestimmung *f* mit Radionukliden
- *f* chronologie *f* isotopique
- *r* изотопная хронология *f*; изотопная датировка *f*

I550
- *e* isotope dilution method
- *d* Isotopenverdünnungsmethode *f*, Isotopenverdünnungsanalyse *f*
- *f* méthode *f* de dilution isotopique
- *r* метод *m* изотопного разведения

I551
- *e* isotope effect
- *d* Isotopeneffekt *m*, Isotopieeffekt *m*
- *f* effet *m* isotopique
- *r* изотопический эффект *m*

I552
- *e* isotope separation
- *d* Isotopentrennung *f*
- *f* séparation *f* des isotopes
- *r* разделение *n* изотопов

I553
- *e* isotope shift
- *d* Isotopieverschiebung *f*
- *f* écart *m* isotopique
- *r* изотопический сдвиг *m*

I554
- *e* isotope source
- *d* Isotopenquelle *f*
- *f* source *f* d'isotopes
- *r* изотопный источник *m*

I555
- *e* isotopic abundance
- *d* Isotopenhäufigkeit *f*
- *f* abondance *f* isotopique
- *r* распространённость *f* изотопов

I556
- *e* isotopically selective dissociation
- *d* isotopenselektive Dissoziation *f*
- *f* dissociation *f* sélective d'isotopes
- *r* изотопически селективная диссоциация *f*

I557
- *e* isotopic doublet
- *d* Isotopendublett *n*, Isodublett *n*
- *f* doublet *m* isotopique
- *r* изотопический дублет *m*

I558
- *e* isotopic index
- *d* Isotopieindex *m*, isotopischer Index *m*
- *f* indice *m* isotopique
- *r* изотопический индекс *m*

I559
- *e* isotopic invariance
- *d* Isotopieinvarianz *f*, isotopische Invarianz *f*
- *f* invariance *f* isotopique
- *r* изотопическая инвариантность *f*

I560
- *e* isotopic invariant
- *d* isotopische Invariante *f*
- *f* invariant *m* isotopique
- *r* изотопический инвариант *m*

I561
- *e* isotopic method
- *d* Isotopenmethode *f*
- *f* méthode *f* des atomes marqués
- *r* изотопный метод *m*

I562
- *e* isotopic multiplet
- *d* Isotopenmultiplett *n*, Isomultiplett *n*
- *f* multiplet *m* isotopique
- *r* изотопический мультиплет *m*

I563　e　isotopic ratio
　　　d　Isotopenverhältnis *n*
　　　f　rapport *m* isotopique
　　　r　изотопное отношение *n*

I564　e　isotopic space
　　　d　Isospinraum *m*, Iso-Raum *m*
　　　f　espace *m* isotopique
　　　r　изотопическое пространство *n*

I565　e　isotopic spin *see* isospin

I566　e　isotopic tag
　　　d　Markierungsisotop *n*
　　　f　marque *f* isotopique
　　　r　изотопная метка *f*

I567　e　isotopic tracer
　　　d　Isotopenindikator *m*
　　　f　traceur *m* isotopique
　　　r　изотопный индикатор *m*

I568　e　isotriplet
　　　d　Isotopentriplett *n*, Isotriplett *n*
　　　f　isotriplet *m*
　　　r　изотриплет *m*

I569　e　isotropic emission *see* isotropic
　　　　radiation

I570　e　isotropic material
　　　d　isotropes Material *n*
　　　f　matériau *m* isotrope
　　　r　изотропный материал *m*

I571　e　isotropic medium
　　　d　isotropes Medium *n*
　　　f　milieu *m* isotropique
　　　r　изотропная среда *f*

I572　e　isotropic model
　　　d　isotropes Modell *n*
　　　f　modèle *m* isotrope
　　　r　изотропная модель *f (Вселенной)*

I573　e　isotropic radiation
　　　d　Isotropstrahlung *f*, isotrope
　　　　Strahlung *f*
　　　f　rayonnement *m* isotrope, radiation *f*
　　　　isotrope
　　　r　изотропное излучение *n*

I574　e　isotropic radiator
　　　d　isotroper Strahler *m*; Kugelstrahler *m*
　　　f　radiateur *m* isotrope
　　　r　изотропный излучатель *m*

I575　e　isotropic substance
　　　d　isotrope Substanz *f*
　　　f　corps *m* isotrope
　　　r　изотропное вещество *n*

I576　e　isotropization
　　　d　Isotropisierung *f*
　　　f　isotropisation *f*
　　　r　изотропизация *f*

I577　e　isotropy
　　　d　Isotropie *f*
　　　f　isotropie *f*
　　　r　изотропия *f*

I578　e　isotropy of Universe
　　　d　Isotropie *f* des Weltalls
　　　f　isotropie *f* de l'Univers
　　　r　изотропия *f* Вселенной

I579　e　isovalent isomorphism
　　　d　isovalenter Isomorhismus *m*
　　　f　isomorphisme *m* isovalent
　　　r　изовалентный изоморфизм *m*

I580　e　isovector
　　　d　Isovektor *m*
　　　f　isovecteur *m*
　　　r　изовектор *m*

I581　e　ISWR *see* current standing wave
　　　　ratio

I582　e　iteration
　　　d　Iteration *f*
　　　f　itération *f*
　　　r　итерация *f*

I583　e　iteration technique
　　　d　Iterationsverfahren *n*
　　　f　méthode *f* d'itération
　　　r　метод *m* итераций

J

J1　e　jacobian
　　d　Jacobische Determinante *f*
　　f　jacobien *m*
　　r　якобиан *m*

J2　e　Jacobi ellipsoid
　　d　Jacobisches Ellipsoid *n*, Jacobi-
　　　Ellipsoid *n*
　　f　ellipsoïde *m* de Jacobi
　　r　эллипсоид *m* Якоби

J3　e　Jahn-Teller effect
　　d　Jahn-Teller-Effekt *m*
　　f　effet *m* de Jahn-Teller
　　r　эффект *m* Яна - Теллера

J4　e　Jamin interferometer
　　d　Jamin-Interferometer *n*, Jaminscher
　　　Interferometer *n*
　　f　interféromètre *m* de Jamin
　　r　интерферометр *m* Жамена

J5　e　Jansky, Jy
　　d　Jansky *n*
　　f　jansky *m*
　　r　янский *m*, Ян *(внесистемная
　　　единица спектральной плотности*

потока космического
радиоизлучения)

J6　　e　Jaynes-Cummings model
　　　d　Jaynes-Cummings-Modell n
　　　f　modèle m de Jaynes-Cummings
　　　r　модель f Джейниса - Каммингса

J7　　e　Jeans criterion
　　　d　Jeans-Kriterium n
　　　f　critère m de Jeans
　　　r　критерий m Джинса

J8　　e　jet
　　　d　Strahl m; Schubstrahl m
　　　f　jet m
　　　r　струя m

J9　　e　jet-edge generator
　　　d　Hartmann-Generator m
　　　f　générateur m de Hartmann,
　　　　　oscillateur m de Hartmann
　　　r　газоструйный излучатель m,
　　　　　генератор m Гартмана

J10　　e　jet engine
　　　d　Strahltriebwerk n
　　　f　réacteur m
　　　r　реактивный двигатель m

J11　　e　jet propulsion
　　　d　1. Rückstoßbewegung f 2.
　　　　　Strahlantrieb m
　　　f　propulsion f à réaction
　　　r　1. реактивное движение n 2.
　　　　　реактивная тяга f

J12　　e　jitter
　　　d　Jitter m
　　　f　tremblement, m
　　　r　дрожание n (напр. частоты)

J13　　e　Jones matrix method
　　　d　Jonessches Matrixverfahren n
　　　f　méthode f de matrice de Jones
　　　r　матричный метод m Джонса

J14　　e　Josephson contact
　　　d　Josephson-Kontakt m
　　　f　contact m de Josephson, contact m
　　　　　Josephson
　　　r　джозефсоновский контакт m

J15　　e　Josephson effect
　　　d　Josephson-Effekt m
　　　f　effet m Josephson
　　　r　эффект m Джозефсона

J16　　e　Josephson oscillation
　　　d　Josephson-Oszillation f
　　　f　oscillation f de Josephson
　　　r　джозефсоновские колебания n pl

J17　　e　Joule, J
　　　d　Joule n
　　　f　joule m, J
　　　r　джоуль m, Дж

J18　　e　Joule equivalent see mechanical
　　　　　equivalent of heat

J19　　e　Joule heating
　　　d　Joulesche Aufheizung f, Joule-Effekt-
　　　　　Aufheizung f
　　　f　chauffage m de Joule
　　　r　джоулев нагрев m, омический
　　　　　нагрев m

J20　　e　Joule law (in thermodynamics)
　　　d　Joulesches Gesetz n, Joulesches
　　　　　Gesetz n der Thermodynamik
　　　f　loi f de Joule (en thermodynamique)
　　　r　закон m Джоуля (в
　　　　　термодинамике)

J21　　e　Joule law (of electrical heating)
　　　d　Joulesches Gesetz n
　　　f　loi f de Joule (de chauffage
　　　　　électrique)
　　　r　закон m Джоуля - Ленца

J22　　e　Joule loss, Joule losses
　　　d　Joulesche Verluste m pl
　　　f　pertes f pl de Joule
　　　r　джоулевы потери f pl

J23　　e　Joule-Thomson effect
　　　d　Joule-Thomson-Effekt m
　　　f　effet m Joule-Thomson
　　　r　эффект m Джоуля - Томсона

J24　　e　jump
　　　d　Sprung m
　　　f　saut m
　　　r　скачок m

J25　　e　junction
　　　d　1. Übergang m 2. Verbindung f;
　　　　　Anschluß m
　　　f　jonction f
　　　r　1. переход m 2. контакт m,
　　　　　соединение n

J26　　e　junction region
　　　d　Übergangszone f
　　　f　zone f de jonction, zone f de
　　　　　transition
　　　r　область f перехода (в
　　　　　полупроводнике)

J27　　e　Jupiter
　　　d　Jupiter m
　　　f　Jupiter m
　　　r　Юпитер m

K

K1　　e　kaon
　　　d　Kaon n, K-Meson n

    f méson *m* K
    r каон *m*, К-мезон *m*

K2 *e* **Kapitza law**
    d Kapitzasches Gesetz *n*
    f loi *f* de Kapitza
    r закон *m* Капицы

K3 *e* **Kapitza temperature jump**
    d Kapitzascher Temperatursprung *m*
    f saut *m* de température de Kapitza
    r температурный скачок *m* Капицы

K4 *e* **Karman vortex street**
    d Karmansche Wirbelstraße *f*
    f chemin *m* de tourbillons de Karman
    r вихревая дорожка *f* Кармана

K5 *e* **K-capture**
    d K-Einfang *m*
    f capture *f* K
    r К-захват *m*

K6 *e* **Keldysh approximation**
    d Keldysh-Approximation *f*
    f approximation *f* de Keldych
    r приближение *n* Келдыша

K7 *e* **Kelvin, K**
    d Kelvin *n*
    f kelvin *m*
    r кельвин *m*, K

K8 *e* **Kelvin double bridge**
    d Thomson-Brücke *f*, Thomsonsche Doppelbrücke *f*
    f pont *m* double de Kelvin
    r двойной мост *m* Кельвина

K9 *e* **Kelvin temperature scale**
    d Kelvin-Skala *f*
    f échelle *f* de Kelvin
    r шкала *f* Кельвина

K10 *e* **Kennelly-Heaviside layer**
    d Heaviside-Kennelly-Schicht *f*, E-Schicht *f*
    f couche *f* de Kennelly-Heaviside
    r слой *m* Кеннели - Хевисайда, слой *m* E *(ионосферы)*

K11 *e* **kenotron**
    d Kenotron *n*, Hochvakuumgleichrichterröhre *f*
    f kénotron *m*
    r кенотрон *m*

K12 *e* **Kepler law**
    d Keplersches Gesetz *n*
    f loi *f* de Kepler
    r закон *m* Кеплера

K13 *e* **kerma**
    d Kerma *f*
    f kerma *m*
    r керма *f*

K14 *e* **kerma rate**
    d Kermaleistung *f*
    f débit *m* de kerma
    r мощность *f* кермы

K15 *e* **kernel**
    d Kern *m*
    f noyau *m*
    r ядро *m*; сердцевина *f*

K16 *e* **Kerr cell**
    d Kerr-Zelle *f*
    f cellule *f* de Kerr
    r ячейка *f* Керра

K17 *e* **Kerr effect**
    d Kerr-Effekt *m*
    f effet *m* Kerr
    r эффект *m* Керра

K18 *e* **Kerr space-time**
    d Kerrsche Raumzeit *f*
    f espace-temps *m* de Kerr
    r пространство-время *n* Керра

K19 *e* **ket vector**
    d ket-Vektor *m*, ket *n*
    f vecteur *m* ket
    r кет-вектор *n*

K20 *e* **key**
    d 1. Schlüssel *m* 2. Taste *f*, Drucktaste *f*
    f 1. clé *f* 2. touche *f*
    r 1. ключ *m* 2. клавиша *f*

K21 *e* **keyboard**
    d Tastatur *f*
    f clavier *m*
    r клавиатура *f*

K22 *e* **Kikoin-Noskov effect**
    d Kikoin-Noskov-Effekt *m*
    f effet *m* de Kikoin-Noskov
    r эффект *m* Кикоина - Носкова

K23 *e* **killer**
    d Lumineszenzgift *n*, Lumineszenzkiller *m*
    f destructeur *m* de luminescence, poison *m* de luminescence
    r тушитель *m* *(люминесценции)*

K24 *e* **kiloelectron-volt, keV**
    d Kiloelektronenvolt *n*
    f kiloélectron-volt *m*
    r килоэлектрон-вольт *m*, кэВ

K25 *e* **kilogram, kg**
    d Kilogramm *n*
    f kilogramme *m*
    r килограмм *m* , кг

K26 *e* **kilogram-force**
    d Kilopond *n*, kp
    f kilogramme-force *m*, kgf
    r килограмм-сила *f*, кгс

K27　*e*　kilogram-meter per second
　　　d　Kilopond *n* je Sekunde, kp/s
　　　f　kilogrammètre *m* par seconde, kg·m/s
　　　r　килограмм-метр *m* в секунду, кг·м/с

K28　*e*　kiloparsec
　　　d　Kiloparsek *n*, Kiloparsec *n*
　　　f　kiloparsec *m*
　　　r　килопарсек *m*

K29　*e*　kinematic invariant
　　　d　kinematische Invariante *f*
　　　f　invariant *m* cinématique
　　　r　кинематический инвариант *m*

K30　*e*　kinematics
　　　d　Kinematik *f*, Bewegungslehre *f*
　　　f　cinématique *f*
　　　r　кинематика *f*

K31　*e*　kinematic screw
　　　d　kinematische Schraube *f*
　　　f　vis *f* cinématique
　　　r　кинематический винт *m*

K32　*e*　kinematics of a point
　　　d　Kinematik *f* eines Massepunktes
　　　f　cinématique *f* du point
　　　r　кинематика *f* точки

K33　*e*　kinematics of fluids
　　　d　Kinematik *f* der Flüssigkeiten und Gase, Strömungskinematik *f*
　　　f　cinématique *f* des fluides
　　　r　кинематика *f* жидкостей и газов

K34　*e*　kinematics of liquids
　　　d　Kinematik *f* der Flüssigkeiten
　　　f　cinématique *f* des liquides
　　　r　кинематика *f* жидкостей

K35　*e*　kinematics of rigid body
　　　d　Kinematik *f* des starren Körpers
　　　f　cinématique *f* du solide
　　　r　кинематика *f* твёрдого тела

K36　*e*　kinematic viscosity
　　　d　kinematische Viskosität *f*
　　　f　viscosité *f* cinématique
　　　r　кинематическая вязкость *f*

K37　*e*　kinescope
　　　d　Bildwiedergaberöhre *f*, Bildröhre *f*, Kineskop *n*
　　　f　kinescope *m*, cinescope *m*
　　　r　кинескоп *m*

K38　*e*　kinetic coefficient
　　　d　kinetischer Koeffizient *m*
　　　f　coefficient *m* cinétique
　　　r　кинетический коэффициент *m*

K39　*e*　kinetic energy
　　　d　kinetische Energie *f*
　　　f　énergie *f* cinétique
　　　r　кинетическая энергия

K40　*e*　kinetic equation
　　　d　kinetische Gleichung *f*
　　　f　équation *f* cinétique
　　　r　кинетическое уравнение *n*

K41　*e*　kinetic momentum
　　　d　Impulsmoment *n*, Drehimpuls *m*
　　　f　moment *m* cinétique
　　　r　кинетический момент *m*, момент *m* количества движения

K42　*e*　kinetic potential
　　　d　kinetisches Potential *n*, Lagrangesche Funktion *f*, Lagrange-Funktion *f*
　　　f　potentiel *m* cinétique
　　　r　кинетический потенциал *m*, функция *f* Лагранжа

K43　*e*　kinetics
　　　d　Kinetik *f*
　　　f　cinétique *f*
　　　r　кинетика *f*

K44　*e*　kinetics of chemical reactions
　　　d　Reaktionskinetik *f*
　　　f　cinétique *f* des réactions chimiques
　　　r　кинетика *f* химических реакций

K45　*e*　kinetics of evaporation
　　　d　Evaporationskinetik *f*
　　　f　cinétique *f* de l'évaporation
　　　r　кинетика *f* испарения

K46　*e*　kinetics of fluids
　　　d　Kinetik *f* der Flüssigkeiten und Gase
　　　f　cinétique *f* des fluides
　　　r　кинетика *f* жидкостей и газов

K47　*e*　kinetics of level population
　　　d　Besetzungskinetik *f*
　　　f　cinétique *f* de la population des niveaux
　　　r　кинетика *f* заселения уровней

K48　*e*　kinetics of magnetic phenomena
　　　d　Kinetik *f* der magnetischen Phänomene
　　　f　cinétique *f* des phénomènes magnétiques
　　　r　кинетика *f* магнитных явлений

K49　*e*　kinetics of nuclear reactor
　　　d　Kinetik *f* des Kernreaktors
　　　f　cinétique *f* du réacteur nucléaire
　　　r　кинетика *f* ядерного реактора

K50　*e*　kinetics of recrystallization
　　　d　Kinetik *f* der Rekristallisation, Rekristallisationskinetik *f*
　　　f　cinétique *f* de la recristallisation
　　　r　кинетика *f* рекристаллизации

K51　*e*　kinetic theory of gases
　　　d　kinetische Gastheorie *f*

     f théorie *f* cinétique des gaz
     r кинетическая теория *f* газов

K52 *e* **kinetostatics**
     d Kinetostatik *f*
     f cinétostatique *f*
     r кинетостатика *f*

K53 *e* **kink**
     d Knick *m*, Abknickung *f*; Knickstelle *f*
     f coude *m*
     r **1.** излом *m*, перегиб *m* **2.** кинк *m*

K54 *e* **kink instability**
     d Instabilität *f* gegen Knickung, Knickinstabilität *f*, «Kink»-Instabilität *f*
     f instabilité *f* à coques
     r шланговая неустойчивость *f*, винтовая неустойчивость *f* (*плазмы*)

K55 *e* **kinoform**
     d Kinoform *m*
     f kinoform *f*
     r киноформ *m*

K56 *e* **Kirchhoff law**
     d Kirchhoffsches Gesetz *n*
     f loi *f* de Kirchhoff
     r закон *m* Кирхгоффа

K57 *e* **Kirchhoff method**
     d Kirchhoffsche Methode *f*
     f méthode *f* de Kirchhoff
     r метод *m* Кирхгофа

K58 *e* **Klebsch-Gordon coefficients**
     d Klebsch-Gordon-Koeffizienten *m pl*
     f coefficients *m pl* de Klebsch-Gordon
     r коэффициенты *m pl* Клебша - Гордона

K59 *e* **Klein-Gordon equation**
     d Klein-Gordon-Gleichung *f*
     f équation *f* de Klein-Gordon
     r уравнение *n* Клейна - Гордона

K60 *e* **Klein-Nishina formula**
     d Klein-Nishina-Formel *f*
     f formule *f* de Klein-Nishina
     r формула *f* Клейна - Нишины

K61 *e* **klystron**
     d Klystron *n*
     f klystron *m*
     r клистрон *m*

K62 *e* **K-meson**
     d K-Meson *n*, Kaon *n*
     f méson *m* K
     r K-мезон *m*, каон *m*

K63 *e* **Knudsen flow**
     d Knudsen-Strömung *f*, Knudsensche Strömung *f*

     f flux *m* de Knudsen
     r поток *m* Кнудсена

K64 *e* **Knudsen number**
     d Knudsen-Zahl *f*
     f nombre *m* de Knudsen
     r число *n* Кнудсена

K65 *e* **Kondo effect**
     d Kondo-Effekt *m*
     f effet *m* Kondo
     r эффект *m* Кондо

K66 *e* **Kondo lattice**
     d Kondo-Gitter *n*
     f réseau *m* de Kondo
     r кондо-решётка *f*

K67 *e* **Korteweg-de Vries equation**
     d Korteweg-de Vries-Gleichung *f*
     f équation *f* de Korteweg-de Vries
     r уравнение *n* Кортевега - де Фриса

K68 *e* **Kramers-Kronig relation**
     d Kramers-Kronigsche Relation *f*, Kronig-Kramersche Beziehung *f*
     f relation *f* de Kramers-Kronig
     r соотношение *n* Крамерса - Кронига

K69 *e* **Kramers theorem**
     d Kramers-Theorem *n*
     f théorème *m* de Kramers
     r теорема *f* Крамерса

K70 *e* **Kroneker symbols**
     d Kroneker-Symbole *n pl*
     f symboles *m pl* de Kroneker
     r символы *m pl* Кронекера

K71 *e* **Kruskal-Shafranov criterion**
     d Kruskal-Schafranow-Bedingung *f*, Kruskal-Bedingung *f*
     f critère *m* de Kruskal-Schafranov
     r критерий *m* Крускала - Шафранова

K72 *e* **krypton, Kr**
     d Krypton *n*
     f krypton *m*
     r криптон *m*

K73 *e* **kurchatovium, Ku**
     d Kurtschatovium *n*
     f kourtchatovium *m*, kurtchatovium *m*
     r курчатовий *m*

L

L1   *e* **label**
     d **1.** Markierung *f* **2.** Etikett *n*
     f label *m*
     r **1.** метка *f* **2.** этикетка *f*

209

L2 e labelled atom
    d markiertes Atom *n*, Indikatoratom *n*,
       Traceratom *n*
    f atome *m* marqué
    r меченый атом *m*

L3 e laboratory
    d Laboratorium *n*, Labor *n*
    f laboratoire *m*
    r лаборатория *f*

L4 e laboratory system of coordinates
    d Laborkoordinatensystem *n*,
       Laborsystem *n*
    f système *m* de référence du
       laboratoire, coordonnées *f pl* du
       laboratoire
    r лабораторная система *f* координат

L5 e laboratory test
    d Laboruntersuchung *f*, Laborversuch
       m, Laborprüfung *f*
    f essai *m* de laboratoire
    r лабораторные испытания *n pl*

L6 e lag
    d Nacheilung *f*; Verzögerung *f*;
       Zurückbleiben *n*; Verspätung *f*
    f retard *m*, délai *m*
    r отставание *n*, запаздывание *n*,
       задержка *f*, замедление *n*

L7 e Lagrange coordinates
    d Lagrangesche Koordinaten *f pl*,
       verallgemeinerte Koordinaten *f pl*
    f coordonnées *f pl* de Lagrange,
       coordonnées *f pl* généralisées
    r лагранжевы координаты *f pl*,
       обобщённые координаты *f pl*

L8 e Lagrange equation
    d Lagrange-Gleichungen *f pl*,
       Lagrangesche Gleichungen *f pl*
    f équations *f pl* de Lagrange
    r уравнения *n pl* Лагранжа

L9 e Lagrangian
    d Lagrange-Funktion *f*
    f lagrangien *m*
    r лагранжиан *m*; оператор *m*
       Лагранжа

L10 e Lagrangian coordinates *see*
       Lagrange coordinates

L11 e Lagrangian formalism
    d Lagrange-Formalismus *m*,
       Lagrangescher Formalismus *m*
    f formalisme *m* de Lagrange
    r лагранжев формализм *m*

L12 e Lagrangian function
    d Lagrange-Funktion *f*, kinetisches
       Potential *n*
    f fonction *f* de Lagrange
    r функция *f* Лагранжа, кинетический
       потенциал *m*

L13 e lambda doubling
    d Lambda-Aufspaltung *f*, Lambda-Typ-
       Aufspaltung *f*
    f duplication *f* lambda
    r лямбда-удвоение *n* (*уровней
       энергии*)

L14 e lambda hyperon, lambda particle
    d *λ*-Hyperon *n*, Lambda-Hyperon *n*
    f hypéron *m* lambda
    r лямбда-гиперон *m*, *λ*-гиперон *m*

L15 e lambda point
    d Lambda-Punkt *m*
    f point *m* lambda
    r лямбда-точка *f*

L16 e Lamb dip
    d Lamb-Dip *m*
    f chute *f* de Lamb
    r провал *m* Лэмба, лэмбовский
       провал *m*

L17 e lambert, Lb
    d Lambert *n*
    f lambert *m*
    r ламберт *m*, Лб

L18 e Lambert law
    d Lambertsches Gesetz *n*
    f loi *f* de Lambert
    r закон *m* Ламберта

L19 e Lamb-Rutherford shift *see* Lamb
       shift

L20 e Lamb shift
    d Lamb-Verschiebung *f*, Lamb-
       Rutherford-Verschiebung *f*, Lamb-
       Shift *m*
    f déplacement *m* de Lamb
    r лэмбовский сдвиг *m*

L21 e Lamb waves
    d Lamb-Wellen *f pl*
    f ondes *f pl* de Lamb
    r волны *f pl* Лэмба

L22 e Lamé constants
    d Lamésche Konstanten *f pl*
    f constantes *f pl* de Lamé
    r постоянные *f pl* Ламе

L23 e laminar flow
    d laminare Strömung *f*,
       Laminarströmung *f*
    f écoulement *m* laminaire
    r ламинарное течение *n*

L24 e laminarity
    d Laminarität *f*
    f laminarité *f*
    r ламинарность *f*

L25 e lamp
    d Lampe *f*

f lampe *f*
r лампа *f*

L26 *e* **lamp pumping**
d Pumpen *n* mittels Lampenlicht
f pompage *m* par lampe
r ламповая накачка *f*

L27 *e* **Landau collision integral**
d Landau-Stoßintegral *n*
f intégrale *f* de collision de Landau
r интеграл *m* столкновений Ландау

L28 *e* **Landau criterion**
d Landau-Kriterium *n*
f critère *m* de Landau
r критерий *m* Ландау

L29 *e* **Landau damping**
d Landau-Dämpfung *f*
f amortissement *m* de Landau
r затухание *n* Ландау,
бесстолкновительное затухание *n*

L30 *e* **Landau damping coefficient**
d Landau-Dämpfungskoeffizient *m*
f coefficient *m* d'amortissement de
Landau
r коэффициент *m* затухания Ландау

L31 *e* **Landau diamagnetism**
d Landauscher Diamagnetismus *m*
f diamagnétisme *m* de Landau
r диамагнетизм *m* Ландау

L32 *e* **Landau levels**
d Landau-Niveaus *n pl*
f niveaux *m pl* de Landau
r уровни *m pl* Ландау

L33 *e* **Landau theory of phase transitions**
d Landau-Theorie *f* der
Phasenumwandlungen
f théorie *f* de transitions de phase de
Landau
r теория *f* фазовых переходов Ландау

L34 *e* **Landé splitting factor**
d Landé-Faktor *m*, Landéscher
Faktor *m*
f facteur *m* de Landé
r множитель *m* Ланде, фактор *m*
магнитного расщепления,
g-фактор *m*

L35 *e* **Langmuir-Blodgett technique**
d Langmuir-Blodgett-Verfahren *n*
f technique *f* de Langmuir-Blodgett
r метод *m* Ленгмюра - Блоджетта
(*метод выращивания тонких
плёнок*)

L36 *e* **Langmuir collapse**
d Langmuir-Kollaps *m*
f collapsus *m* de Langmuir
r ленгмюровский коллапс *m*

L37 *e* **Langmuir frequency**
d Langmuir-Frequenz *f*
f fréquence *f* de Langmuir
r ленгмюровская частота *f*

L38 *e* **Langmuir oscillations**
d Langmuir-Schwingungen *f pl*
f oscillations *f pl* de Langmuir
r плазменные колебания *n pl*,
ленгмюровские колебания *n pl*

L39 *e* **Langmuir probe**
d Langmuir-Sonde *f*
f sonde *f* de Langmuir
r ленгмюровский зонд *m*

L40 *e* **Langmuir-Saha equation**
d Langmuir-Saha-Gleichung *f*
f équation *f* de Langmuir-Saha
r уравнение *n* Ленгмюра - Сáха

L41 *e* **Langmuir waves**
d Langmuir-Wellen *f pl*
f ondes *f pl* de Langmuir
r ленгмюровские волны *f pl*

L42 *e* **lanthanides**
d Lanthanide *n pl*
f lanthanides *m pl*
r лантаноиды *m pl*, лантаниды *m pl*

L43 *e* **lanthanum, La**
d Lanthan *n*
f lanthane *m*
r лантан *m*

L44 *e* **Laplace equation**
d Laplacesche Differentialgleichung *f*
f équation *f* de Laplace
r уравнение *n* Лапласа

L45 *e* **Laplace operator** *see* **Laplacian**

L46 *e* **Laplace transform**
d Laplace-Transformation *f*,
Laplacesche Transformation *f*
f transformation *f* de Laplace
r преобразование *n* Лапласа

L47 *e* **Laplacian**
d Laplace-Operator *m*
f laplacien *m*, opérateur *m* laplacien
r лапласиан *m*, оператор *m* Лапласа

L48 *e* **large canonical distribution**
d große kanonische Verteilung *f*
f large distribution *f* canonique
r большое каноническое
распределение *n*

L49 *e* **large kinematic invariant**
d große kinematische Invariante *f*
f large invariant *m* cinématique
r большой кинематический
инвариант *m*

L50 *e* **large-scale irregularity**

    d weiträumige Irregularität *f*
    f irrégularité *f* à large échelle
    r крупномасштабная неоднородность *f*

L51 *e* large-scale model
    d großmaßstäbliches Modell *n*
    f modèle *m* à large échelle
    r крупномасштабная модель *f*

L52 *e* Larmor frequency
    d Larmor-Frequenz *f*
    f fréquence *f* de Larmor
    r ларморовская частота *f*

L53 *e* Larmor precession
    d Larmor-Präzession *f*, Larmorsche Präzession *f*
    f précession *f* de Larmor
    r прецессия *f* Лармора, ларморовская прецессия *f*

L54 *e* laser
    d Laser *m*
    f laser *m*
    r лазер *m*; оптический квантовый генератор *m*

L55 *e* laser anemometer
    d Laseranemometer *n*
    f anémomètre *m* laser
    r лазерный анемометр *m*

L56 *e* laser annealing
    d Laserausheilung *f*
    f recuit *m* à laser *(des semi-conducteurs)*
    r лазерный отжиг *m* *(полупроводников)*

L57 *e* laser beacon
    d Laserbake *f*
    f balise *f* laser
    r лазерный маяк *m*

L58 *e* laser beam
    d Laserstrahl *m*
    f faisceau *m* laser
    r лазерный пучок *m*, лазерный луч *m*

L59 *e* laser beam defocusing
    d Laserstrahldefokussierung *f*
    f défocalisation *f* du faisceau laser
    r дефокусировка *f* лазерного пучка

L60 *e* laser cell
    d Laserzelle *f*
    f cellule *f* laser
    r лазерная кювета *f*

L61 *e* laser chemistry
    d Laserchemie *f*
    f chimie *f* de laser
    r лазерная химия *f*

L62 *e* laser crystal
    d Laserkristall *m*
    f cristal *m* pour laser
    r лазерный кристалл *m*

L63 *e* laser cutting
    d Laserschneiden *n*
    f coupe *f* laser
    r лазерная резка *f*

L64 *e* laser deposition
    d Laserbeschichtung *f*, Laseraufdampfung *f*
    f déposition *f* par laser
    r лазерное осаждение *n* *(плёнок)*, лазерное напыление *n*

L65 *e* laser desorption
    d Laserdesorption *f*
    f désorption *f* par laser
    r лазерная десорбция *f*

L66 *e* laser desorption mass spectrometry
    d Laser-Desorptions-Massenspektrometrie *f*
    f spectrométrie *f* de masse à désorption par laser
    r лазерная десорбционная масс-спектрометрия *f*

L67 *e* laser detection
    d Laserdetektion *f*, Laserdetektierung *f*
    f détection *f* par laser
    r лазерное детектирование *n*

L68 *e* laser diagnostics
    d Laserdiagnostik *f*
    f diagnostic *m* laser
    r лазерная диагностика *f*

L69 *e* laser diode
    d Laserdiode *f*
    f diode *f* laser
    r лазерный диод *m*, диодный лазер *m*

L70 *e* laser emission
    d Laseremission *f*
    f émission *f* laser
    r лазерное излучение *n*

L71 *e* laser evaporation
    d Laserverdampfung *f*
    f évaporation *f* laser
    r лазерное испарение *n*; лазерное напыление *n*

L72 *e* laser focus
    d Laserfokus *m*
    f foyer *m* laser
    r лазерный фокус *m*

L73 *e* laser gate *see* laser shutter

L74 *e* laser glasses
    d Lasergläser *n pl*
    f verres *m pl* laser
    r лазерные стёкла *n pl*

L75 *e* laser guidance

d Laserlenkung *f*
f guidage *m* laser
r лазерное наведение *n*

L76 e **laser gyroscope**
d Lasergyroskop *n*
f gyroscope *m* à laser
r лазерный гироскоп *m*

L77 e **laser hardening**
d Laserhärtung *f*
f trempe *f* au laser
r лазерная закалка *f*

L78 e **laser heterodyning**
d Laserheterodynierung *f*
f hétérodynage *m* laser
r лазерное гетеродинирование *n*

L79 e **laser-induced phase transition**
d laserinduzierte Phasenumwandlung *f*
f transition *f* de phase induite par laser
r лазерно-индуцированный
   переход *m*

L80 e **laser-induced spark** *see* **laser spark**

L81 e **laser initiation**
d Laseranregung *f*
f initiation *f* de laser
r инициирование *n* лазера

L82 e **laser interferometer**
d Laserinterferometer *n*
f interféromètre *m* laser
r лазерный интерферометр *m*

L83 e **laser interferometry**
d Laserinterferometrie *f*
f interférométrie *f* laser
r лазерная интерферометрия *f*

L84 e **laser iridectomy**
d Laseriridektomie *f*
f iridectomie *f* laser
r лазерная иридэктомия *f*

L85 e **laser isotope separation**
d Laserisotopentrennung *f*
f séparation *f* des isotopes par laser
r лазерное разделение *n* изотопов

L86 e **laser labeling**
d Lasermarkierung *f*
f marquage *m* laser
r лазерная маркировка *f* (*атомов и*
   молекул)

L87 e **laser medicine**
d Lasermedizin *f*
f médecine *f* laser
r лазерная медицина *f*

L88 e **laser microsurgery**
d Lasermikrochirurgie *f*
f microchirurgie *f* laser
r лазерная микрохирургия *f*

L89 e **laser mirror**
d Laserspiegel *m*
f miroir *m* laser
r лазерное зеркало *n*

L90 e **laser ophthalmology**
d Laserophthalmologie *f*
f ophthalmologie *f* laser
r лазерная офтальмология *f*

L91 e **laser photochemistry**
d Laserphotochemie *f*
f photochimie *f* laser
r лазерная фотохимия *f*

L92 e **laser photoionization spectroscopy**
d Laser-Photoionisationsspektroskopie *f*
f spectroscopie *f* à photo-ionisation laser
r лазерная фотоионизационная
   спектроскопия *f*

L93 e **laser pick-up**
d Laserabtaster *m*
f pick-up *m* laser
r лазерный звукосниматель *m*

L94 e **laser plasma**
d Laserplasma *n*
f plasma *m* laser
r лазерная плазма *f*

L95 e **laser plasma heating**
d Lasererhitzung *f* des Plasmas
f chauffage *m* laser du plasma
r лазерный нагрев *m* плазмы

L96 e **laser processing**
d Laserbehandlung *f*
f traitement *m* laser
r лазерная обработка *f*

L97 e **laser projection microscope**
d Laserprojektionsmikroskopie *f*
f microscope *m* laser de projection
r лазерный проекционный
   микроскоп *m*

L98 e **laser pulse**
d Laserimpuls *m*
f impulsion *f* laser
r лазерный импульс *m*

L99 e **laser pulse compression**
d Laserimpulskompression *f*
f compression *f* des impulsions laser
r сжатие *n* лазерных импульсов

L100 e **laser pumping**
d Laserpumpen *n*
f pompage *m* par laser
r лазерная накачка *f*

L101 e **laser radar**
d Laserradar *n*
f radar *m* laser
r лазерный локатор *m*

L102   *e*   laser radiation *see* laser emission

L103   *e*   laser range finder
      d   Laserentfernungsmesser *m*
      f   télémètre *m* laser
      r   лазерный дальномер *m*

L104   *e*   laser ranging
      d   Laserortung *f*
      f   localisation *f* laser
      r   лазерная локация *f*

L105   *e*   laser selective detection
      d   selektive Laserdetektion *f*
      f   détection *f* laser sélective
      r   лазерное селективное
          детектирование *n (атомов и молекул)*

L106   *e*   laser shot *see* laser pulse

L107   *e*   laser shutter
      d   Laserunterbrecher *m*
      f   obturateur *m* de laser
      r   лазерный затвор *m*

L108   *e*   laser sounding
      d   Lasersondierung *f*
      f   sondage *m* laser
      r   лазерное зондирование *n*

L109   *e*   laser source
      d   Laserquelle *f*
      f   source *f* laser
      r   лазерный источник *m*

L110   *e*   laser spark
      d   Laserfunken *m*
      f   étincelle *f* laser
      r   лазерная искра *f*

L111   *e*   laser spectroscopy
      d   Laserspektroskopie *f*
      f   spectroscopie *f* laser
      r   лазерная спектроскопия *f*

L112   *e*   laser surgery
      d   Laserchirurgie *f*
      f   chirurgie *f* laser
      r   лазерная хирургия *f*

L113   *e*   laser switch *see* laser shutter

L114   *e*   laser target
      d   Lasertarget *n*
      f   cible *f* laser
      r   лазерная мишень *f*

L115   *e*   laser technology
      d   Lasertechnik *f*
      f   technologie *f* laser
      r   лазерная технология *f*

L116   *e*   laser therapy
      d   Lasertherapie *f*
      f   thérapie *f* laser
      r   лазерная терапия *f*

L117   *e*   laser thermochemistry
      d   Laserthermochemie *f*
      f   thermochimie *f* laser
      r   лазерная термохимия *f*

L118   *e*   laser thermonuclear fusion, laser thermonuclear synthesis
      d   Laserfusion *f*
      f   fusion *f* thermonucléaire par laser
      r   лазерный термоядерный синтез *m*

L119   *e*   laser transition
      d   Laserübergang *m*
      f   transition *f* laser
      r   лазерный переход *m*

L120   *e*   laser velocimeter *see* laser anemometer

L121   *e*   laser weapon
      d   Laserwaffen *f pl*
      f   arme *f* laser, arme *f* à laser
      r   лазерное оружие *n*

L122   *e*   laser welding
      d   Laserschweißung *f*
      f   soudage *m* laser
      r   лазерная сварка *f*

L123   *e*   lasing line
      d   Laserlinie *f*
      f   raie *f* lasante
      r   линия *f* генерации лазера

L124   *e*   latent heat
      d   Umwandlungswärme *f*
      f   chaleur *f* spécifique
      r   удельная теплота *f*, скрытая теплота *f*, теплота *f* фазового перехода

L125   *e*   latent image
      d   latentes Bild *n*
      f   image *f* latente
      r   скрытое изображение *n*

L126   *e*   lateral bending
      d   Querbiegung *f*
      f   flexion *f* transversale
      r   поперечный изгиб *m*

L127   *e*   lateral coherence
      d   Querkohärenz *f*
      f   cohérence *f* transversale
      r   поперечная когерентность *f*

L128   *e*   lateral mode *see* transverse mode

L129   *e*   lateral vibration, lateral vibrations
      d   transversale Schwingungen *f pl*, Transversalschwingungen *f pl*
      f   oscillations *f pl* transversales
      r   поперечные колебания *n pl*

L130   *e*   latitude
      d   Breite *f*, geographische Breite *f*
      f   latitude *f*
      r   широта *f*

L131　e　lattice
　　　d　Gitter n, Kristallgitter n
　　　f　réseau m, réseau m cristallin
　　　r　решётка f, кристаллическая
　　　　　решётка f

L132　e　lattice cell
　　　d　Gitterbaustein m
　　　f　cellule f de réseau
　　　r　элементарная ячейка f

L133　e　lattice conduction of heat
　　　d　Gitterwärmeleitfähigkeit f,
　　　　　Gitterleitfähigkeit f
　　　f　conductibilité f thermique due au
　　　　　réseau, conductibilité f du réseau
　　　r　решёточная теплопроводность f

L134　e　lattice constants
　　　d　Gitterkonstanten f pl
　　　f　constantes f pl du réseau
　　　r　постоянные f pl решётки,
　　　　　параметры m pl решётки

L135　e　lattice defect
　　　d　Gitterbaufehler m, Gitterfehler m,
　　　　　Gitterstörstelle f, Gitterdefekt m
　　　f　défaut m du réseau
　　　r　дефект m решётки

L136　e　lattice deformation
　　　d　Gitterdeformation f
　　　f　déformation f du réseau
　　　r　деформация f решётки

L137　e　lattice energy
　　　d　Gitterenergie f
　　　f　énergie f du réseau
　　　r　энергия f кристаллической решётки

L138　e　lattice heat capacity
　　　d　Gitterwärmekapazität f
　　　f　capacité f thermique du réseau
　　　r　решёточная теплоёмкость f

L139　e　lattice imperfection
　　　d　Gitterbaufehler m, Gitterfehlordnung
　　　　　f, Gitterunregelmäßigkeit f
　　　f　imperfection f du réseau, imperfection
　　　　　f du réseau cristallin
　　　r　несовершенство n кристаллической
　　　　　решётки

L140　e　lattice mode
　　　d　Gittermode f
　　　f　mode m de réseau
　　　r　решёточная мода f

L141　e　lattice parameters see lattice
　　　　　constants

L142　e　lattice site
　　　d　Gitterplatz m
　　　f　site m (dans le réseau)
　　　r　узел m кристаллической решётки

L143　e　lattice vibration, lattice vibrations

　　　d　Gitterschwingungen f pl
　　　f　vibrations f pl du réseau
　　　r　колебания n pl решётки

L144　e　**Laue method**
　　　d　Laue-Verfahren n, Laue-Methode f
　　　f　méthode f de Laue
　　　r　метод m Лауэ

L145　e　**Laue pattern**
　　　d　Laue-Diagramm n, Laue-Aufnahme f
　　　f　diagramme m de Laue
　　　r　лауэграмма f

L146　e　**launching mass**
　　　d　Startmasse f
　　　f　masse f de lancement
　　　r　стартовая масса f (космического
　　　　　аппарата)

L147　e　**Laurent series**
　　　d　Laurent-Reihe f, Laurentsche Reihe f
　　　f　série f de Laurent
　　　r　ряд m Лорана

L148　e　**Laval nozzle**
　　　d　Laval-Düse f
　　　f　tuyère f de Laval
　　　r　сопло n Лаваля

L149　e　**Laves phases**
　　　d　Laves-Phasen f pl
　　　f　phases f pl de Laves
　　　r　фазы f pl Лавеса

L150　e　**law**
　　　d　Gesetz n; Prinzip n; Satz m
　　　f　loi f
　　　r　закон m, правило n

L151　e　**law of action and reaction**
　　　d　Wechselwirkungsgesetz n
　　　f　loi f de l'action et de la réaction
　　　r　закон m действия и
　　　　　противодействия

L152　e　**law of chemical equilibrium**
　　　d　Gesetz n des chemischen
　　　　　Gleichgewichts
　　　f　loi f de l'équilibre chimique
　　　r　закон m химического равновесия

L153　e　**law of conservation of momentum**
　　　d　Impulserhaltungssatz m, Prinzip n von
　　　　　der Erhaltung der Bewegungsgröße
　　　f　loi f de la conservation du moment
　　　r　закон m сохранения количества
　　　　　движения

L154　e　**law of mass action**
　　　d　Massenwirkungsgesetz n
　　　f　loi f d'action de masse
　　　r　закон m действующих масс

L155　e　**Lawrence Livermore Laboratory**
　　　　　(USA)
　　　d　Lawrence-Livermore-Laboratorium n
　　　f　laboratoire m Lawrence à Livermore

r Ливерморская лаборатория *f* им. Лоуренса *(США)*

L156 e **Lawrencium, Lr**
d Lawrencium *n*
f lawrencium *m*
r лоуренсий *m*

L157 e **Lawson criterion**
d Lawson-Kriterium *n*
f critère *m* de Lawson
r критерий *m* Лоусона

L158 e **layer**
d Schicht *f*; Lage *f*
f couche *f*
r слой *m*

L159 e **LCAO method** *see* **method of linear combination of atomic orbitals**

L160 e **lead, Pb**
d Blei *n*
f plomb *m*
r свинец *m*

L161 e **leader**
d Leader *m*
f leader *m*
r лидер *m (в газовом разряде)*

L162 e **leading edge**
d 1. Vorderflanke *f* 2. Vorderkante *f*, Anströmseite *f*
f 1. flanc *m* avant *(d'impulsion)* 2. bord *m* d'attaque
r 1. фронт *m* импульса 2. передняя кромка *f*; ребро обтекания

L163 e **leak**
d Leck *n*, Leckstelle *f*; Undichtigkeit *f*, Undichtigkeitstelle *f*
f fuite *f*
r утечка *f*; течь *f*

L164 e **leak detector**
d Lecksucher *m*, Leckprüfer *m*
f chercheur *m* de fuites
r течеискатель *m*

L165 e **leakage** *see* **leak**

L166 e **leakage current**
d Irrstrom *m*; Leckstrom *m*
f courant *m* de fuite
r ток *m* утечки

L167 e **least action**
d kleinste Wirkung *f*
f moindre action *f*
r наименьшее действие *n*

L168 e **Le Chatelier principle**
d Le Chatelier-Prinzip *n*
f principe *m* de Le Chatelier
r принцип *m* Ле-Шателье

L169 e **LEED method** *see* **low-energy electron diffraction method**

L170 e **left-hand rule**
d Linke-Hand-Regel *f*
f règle *f* de la main gauche, règle *f* des trois doigts de la main gauche
r правило *n* левой руки

L171 e **left quark**
d Left-Quark *n*
f quark *m* gauche
r левый кварк *m*

L172 e **Legendre functions**
d Legendresche Funktionen *f pl*
f fonctions *f pl* de Legendre
r функции *f pl* Лежандра

L173 e **Legendre polinomials**
d Legendresche Polynome *n pl*
f polynômes *m pl* de Legendre
r полиномы *m pl* Лежандра

L174 e **length**
d Länge *f*
f longueur *f*
r длина *f*

L175 e **lens**
d 1. Linse *f* 2. Objektiv *n* 3. Brillenglas *n*; Lupe *f*
f 1.lentille *f* 2. objectif *m* 3. loupe *f*
r 1. линза *f* 2. объектив *m* 3. лупа *f*

L176 e **lens aerial, lens antenna**
d Linsenantenne *f*
f antenne *f* à lentille
r линзовая антенна *f*

L177 e **lens radiator, lens-type radiator**
d Linsenstrahler *m*
f radiateur *m* à lentille
r линзовый излучатель *m*

L178 e **lens waveguide**
d Linsenwellenleiter *m*
f guide *m* d'ondes à lentille
r линзовый волновод *m*

L179 e **Lenz law**
d Lenzsche Regel *f*, Lenzsches Gesetz *n*
f loi *f* de Lenz
r правило *n* Ленца

L180 e **Leontowitch bounding conditions**
d Leontowitsch-Grenzbedingungen *f pl*
f conditions *f pl* aux limites approximatives de Leontowitch
r граничные условия *n pl* Леонтовича

L181 e **lepton**
d Lepton *n*
f lepton *m*
r лептон *m*

L182 e **lepton current**

	d	Leptonenstrom m
	f	courant m leptonique
	r	лептонный ток m

L183 e leptonic charge
  d Leptonenladung f
  f charge f leptonique
  r лептонный заряд m

L184 e leptonic decay
  d leptonischer Zerfall m, Leptonenzerfall m
  f désintégration f leptonique
  r лептонный распад m

L185 e leptoquark
  d Leptoquark n
  f leptoquark m
  r лептокварк m

L186 e level
  d Niveau n
  f niveau m
  r уровень m

L187 e level crossing
  d Niveaukreuzung f
  f croisement m des niveaux
  r пересечение n уровней энергии

L188 e level filling see level occupation

L189 e level gage
  d Füllstandmesser m, Standhöhenmesser m
  f jauge f de niveau
  r уровнемер m

L190 e level occupation
  d Niveaubesetzung f
  f remplissage m des niveaux
  r заполнение n уровней

L191 e level population
  d Niveaubesetzung f
  f population f du niveau
  r населённость f уровня

L192 e level shift
  d Niveauverschiebung f
  f déplacement m des niveaux
  r сдвиг m уровней

L193 e Levi-Civita symbol
  d Levi-Civita-Symbol n
  f symbole m de Levi-Civita
  r символ m Леви - Чивиты

L194 e levitation
  d Schweben n, Levitation f
  f lévitation f
  r левитация f

L195 e libration of the Moon
  d Mondlibration f
  f libration f de la Lune
  r либрация f Луны

L196 e libron
  d Libron n (Quasiteilchen)
  f libron m (quasi-particule)
  r либрон m (квазичастица)

L197 e Lichtenberg figures
  d Lichtenberg-Figuren f pl
  f figures f pl de Lichtenberg
  r фигуры f pl Лихтенберга

L198 e lidar
  d Lidar m
  f lidar m, radar m optique
  r лидар m

L199 e Lie algebra
  d Lie-Algebra f
  f algèbre f de Lie
  r алгебра f Ли

L200 e life test
  d Lebensdauerprüfung f
  f essais m pl de durée de vie
  r испытания n pl на срок службы, ресурсные испытания n pl

L201 e life time
  d Lebensdauer f
  f 1. vie f 2. durée f de vie
  r 1. время n жизни 2. срок m службы

L202 e lift
  d Auftrieb m
  f force f ascensionelle, portance f
  r подъёмная сила f

L203 e ligands
  d Ligande m pl
  f ligands m pl
  r лиганды m pl

L204 e light
  d Licht n
  f lumière f
  r свет m

L205 e light absorption
  d Lichtabsorption f
  f absorption f de la lumière
  r поглощение n света

L206 e light adaptation
  d Helladaption f
  f adaptation f à la lumière
  r световая адаптация f

L207 e light amplification
  d Lichtverstärkung f
  f amplification f de la lumière
  r усиление n света

L208 e light attenuation coefficient
  d Lichtschwächungskoeffizient m
  f coefficient m d'atténuation de la lumière
  r коэффициент m ослабления света

L209　e　light beam
　　　d　Lichtbündel *n*; Lichtstrahl *m*
　　　f　faisceau *m* lumineux
　　　r　световой пучок *m*, световой луч *m*

L210　e　light-beam oscillograph
　　　d　Lichtstrahloszillograph *m*
　　　f　oscillographe *m* à cadre, oscillographe *m* à boucle
　　　r　светолучевой осциллограф *m*

L211　e　light chopper
　　　d　1. Lichtmodulator *m* 2. Blende *f*
　　　f　1. modulateur *m* de lumière 2. obturateur *m*
　　　r　1. модулятор *m* света
　　　　　2. обтюратор *m*

L212　e　light cone
　　　d　Lichtkegel *m*, Strahlenkegel *m*
　　　f　cône *m* de lumière
　　　r　световой конус *m*

L213　e　light curve
　　　d　Lichtkurve *f*
　　　f　courbe *f* de lumière
　　　r　кривая *f* блеска *(переменной звезды)*

L214　e　light detection
　　　d　Lichtempfang *m*, Lichtdetektierung *f*
　　　f　détection *f* de lumière
　　　r　детектирование *n* света

L215　e　light diffraction
　　　d　Lichtdiffraktion *f*
　　　f　diffraction *f* de lumière
　　　r　дифракция *f* света

L216　e　light emission
　　　d　Lichtemission *f*, Lichtstrahlung *f*
　　　f　émission *f* de lumière, émission *f* optique
　　　r　световое излучение *n*, оптическое излучение *n*

L217　e　light emitter
　　　d　Lichtstrahler *m*
　　　f　émetteur *m* de lumière
　　　r　излучатель *m* света

L218　e　light emitting diode
　　　d　Lichtemissionsdiode *f*, Lumineszenzdiode *f*, Leuchtdiode *f*
　　　f　diode *f* émettrice de lumière
　　　r　светодиод *m*, светоизлучающий диод *m*

L219　e　light field
　　　d　Lichtfeld *n*
　　　f　champ *m* lumineux
　　　r　световое поле *n*

L220　e　light filter
　　　d　Lichtfilter *n*
　　　f　filtre *m* de lumière
　　　r　светофильтр *m*

L221　e　light guide
　　　d　Lichtleiter *m*
　　　f　guide *m* de lumière, guide *m* d'ondes optiques
　　　r　световод *m*; оптический волновод *m*

L222　e　light-induced diffusion
　　　d　lichtinduzierte Diffusion *f*
　　　f　diffusion *f* induite par la lumière
　　　r　светоиндуцированная диффузия *f*

L223　e　light-induced drift
　　　d　lichtinduzierte Drift *f*, lichtinduzierte Driftbewegung *f*
　　　f　dérive *f* induite par la lumière
　　　r　светоиндуцированный дрейф *m*

L224　e　light-induced phase transition
　　　d　lichtinduzierte Phasenumwandlung *f*
　　　f　transition *f* de phase induite par la lumière
　　　r　светоиндуцированный фазовый переход *m*

L225　e　lighting
　　　d　Beleuchtung *f*
　　　f　éclairage *m*
　　　r　освещение *n*

L226　e　light intensity
　　　d　Lichtintensität *f*
　　　f　intensité *f* lumineuse
　　　r　интенсивность *f* света

L227　e　light microscope *see* optical microscope

L228　e　light modulation
　　　d　Lichtmodulation *f*
　　　f　modulation *f* de lumière
　　　r　модуляция *f* света

L229　e　light modulator *see* optical modulator

L230　e　lightning
　　　d　Blitz *m*
　　　f　éclair *m*
　　　r　молния *f*

L231　e　lightning arrester
　　　d　Überspannungsableiter *m*
　　　f　parafoudre *m*
　　　r　грозоразрядник *m*

L232　e　lightning channel
　　　d　Blitzkanal *m*
　　　f　canal *m* d'éclair
　　　r　канал *m* молнии, канал *m* разряда молнии

L233　e　lightning conductor
　　　d　1. Ableitung *f* 2. Blitzableiter *m*
　　　f　paratonnerre *m*
　　　r　1. токоотводящий спуск *m* *(молниеотвода)* 2. молниеотвод *m*

L234   *e*   **lightning discharge**
      d   Blitzentladung *f*
      f   décharge *f* orageuse
      r   грозовой разряд *m*

L235   *e*   **lightning rod**
      d   Blitzableiter *m*
      f   paratonnerre *m*
      r   молниеотвод *m*, стержневой
         молниеотвод *m*

L236   *e*   **lightning stroke**
      d   Blitzeinschlag *m*
      f   coup *m* de foudre
      r   удар *m* молнии

L237   *e*   **light pressure**
      d   Lichtdruck *m*
      f   pression *f* de la lumière
      r   давление *n* света, световое
         давление *n*

L238   *e*   **light pulse**
      d   Lichtimpuls *m*
      f   impulsion *f* lumineuse
      r   световой импульс *m*

L239   *e*   **light quantum** *see* **photon**

L240   *e*   **light ray** *see* **light beam**

L241   *e*   **light scattering**
      d   Lichtstreuung *f*
      f   diffusion *f* de la lumière
      r   рассеяние *n* света

L242   *e*   **light-sensitive material**
      d   lichtempfindliches Material *n*
      f   matériel *m* photosensible
      r   светочувствительный материал *m*

L243   *e*   **light source**
      d   Lichtquelle *f*
      f   source *f* de lumière
      r   источник *m* света, источник *m*
         оптического излучения

L244   *e*   **light variation**
      d   Lichtwechsel *m* (*Veränderung der
         scheinbaren Sternhelligkeit*)
      f   variation *f* lumineuse (*d'une étoile*)
      r   изменение *n* блеска (*звезды*)

L245   *e*   **light waves**
      d   Lichtwellen *f pl*
      f   ondes *f pl* lumineuses
      r   световые волны *f pl*

L246   *e*   **light year**
      d   Lichtjahr *n*
      f   année-lumière *f*
      r   световой год *m*

L247   *e*   **limb**
      d   Teilkreis *m*
      f   limbe *m*
      r   лимб *m*

L248   *e*   **limit cycle**
      d   Grenzzyklus *m*
      f   cycle *m* limite
      r   предельный цикл *m*

L249   *e*   **limiter**
      d   1. Begrenzer *m* 2. Plasmabegrenzer
         m, Limiter *m*
      f   limiteur *m*
      r   1. ограничитель *m* 2. диафрагма *f*
         (*в токамаке*)

L250   *e*   **line**
      d   Linie *f*
      f   ligne *f*
      r   линия *f*

L251   *e*   **linear accelerator**
      d   Linearbeschleuniger *m*
      f   accélérateur *m* linéaire
      r   линейный ускоритель *m*

L252   *e*   **linear amplifier**
      d   Linearverstärker *m*
      f   amplificateur *m* linéaire
      r   линейный усилитель *m*

L253   *e*   **linear combination**
      d   lineare Kombination *f*
      f   combinaison *f* linéaire
      r   линейная комбинация *f*

L254   *e*   **linear defects**
      d   lineare Defekte *m pl*
      f   défauts *m pl* linéaires
      r   линейные дефекты *m pl*

L255   *e*   **linear deformation**
      d   lineare Deformation *f*
      f   déformation *f* linéaire
      r   линейная деформация *f*

L256   *e*   **linear dependence**
      d   lineare Abhängigkeit *f*
      f   relation *f* linéaire, rapport *m* linéaire
      r   линейная зависимость *f*

L257   *e*   **linear detection**
      d   lineare Demodulation *f*
      f   détection *f* linéaire
      r   линейное детектирование *n*

L258   *e*   **linear differential equations**
      d   lineare Differentialgleichungen *f pl*
      f   équations *f pl* différentielles linéaires
      r   линейные дифференциальные
         уравнения *n pl*

L259   *e*   **linear expansion**
      d   lineare Ausdehnung *f*,
         Längenausdehnung *f*
      f   expansion *f* linéaire
      r   линейное расширение *n*

L260   *e*   **linear law**
      d   lineares Gesetz *n*

      f loi *f* linéaire
      r линейный закон *m*

L261 *e* **linearly polarized radiation**
      d linear polarisierte Strahlung *f*
      f radiation *f* linéairement polarisée
      r линейно-поляризованное излучение *n*

L262 *e* **linear measurements**
      d Längenmessungen *f pl*; Streckenmessungen *f pl*
      f mesures *f pl* de longueur
      r линейные измерения *n pl*

L263 *e* **linear molecule**
      d Fadenmolekül *n*, Linearmolekül *n*
      f molécule *f* linéaire
      r линейная молекула *f*

L264 *e* **linear motion**
      d geradlinige Bewegung *f*
      f mouvement *m* rectiligne
      r линейное движение *n*, прямолинейное движение *n*

L265 *e* **linear polarization**
      d lineare Polarisation *f*, Linearpolarisation *f*
      f polarisation *f* linéaire
      r линейная поляризация *f*

L266 *e* **linear problem**
      d lineares Problem *n*
      f problème *m* linéaire
      r линейная задача *f*

L267 *e* **linear system**
      d lineares System *n*
      f système *m* linéaire
      r линейная система *f*

L268 *e* **linear transformation**
      d lineare Transformation *f*
      f transformation *f* linéaire
      r линейное преобразование *n*

L269 *e* **line broadening**
      d Linienverbreiterung *f*
      f élargissement *m* de raie
      r уширение *n* линии

L270 *e* **line dislocation**
      d Stufenversetzung *f*
      f dislocation *f* en coins, dislocation *f* coin
      r краевая дислокация *f*, линейная дислокация *f*

L271 *e* **line intensity**
      d Linienintensität *f*, Spektrallinienintensität *f*
      f intensité *f* de la raie
      r интенсивность *f* линии

L272 *e* **line of action**
      d Angriffslinie *f*, Kraftangriffslinie *f*, Wirkungslinie *f*

L273 *e* **line of force**
      f ligne *f* d'action
      r линия *f* действия

L273 *e* **line of force**
      d Kraftlinie *f*, Feldstärkelinie *f*
      f ligne *f* de force
      r силовая линия *f*

L274 *e* **liner**
      d Liner *m*
      f liner *m*
      r лайнер *m*

L275 *e* **line saturation**
      d Liniensättigung *f*
      f saturation *f* de la ligne
      r насыщение *n* линии

L276 *e* **line spectrum**
      d Linienspektrum *n*
      f spectre *m* de raies
      r линейчатый спектр *m*

L277 *e* **line width**
      d Spektrallinienbreite *f*
      f largeur *f* de la raie
      r ширина *f* спектральной линии

L278 *e* **link**
      d 1. Verbindungsleitung *f* 2. Verbindung *f*
      f 1. ligne *f* de liaison 2. liaison *f*
      r 1. линия *f* связи 2. связь *f*

L279 *e* **Liouville theorem**
      d Liouvillescher Satz *m*
      f théorème *m* de Liouville
      r теорема *f* Лиувилля

L280 *e* **liquefaction of gases**
      d Gasverflüssigung *f*
      f liquéfaction *f* des gaz
      r ожижение *n* газов, сжижение *n* газов

L281 *e* **liquid**
      d Flüssigkeit *f*
      f liquide *m*, fluide *m*
      r жидкость *f*

L282 *e* **liquid calorimeter**
      d Flüssigkeitskalorimeter *n*
      f calorimètre *m* à liquide
      r жидкостный калориметр *m*

L283 *e* **liquid crystal**
      d flüssiger Kristall *m*, Flüssigkristall *m*
      f cristal *m* liquide
      r жидкий кристалл *m*

L284 *e* **liquid dielectric**
      d flüssiges Dielektrikum *n*
      f diélectrique *m* liquide
      r жидкий диэлектрик *m*

L285 *e* **liquid-drop model**
      d Flüssigkeitströpfchenmodell *n*, Tröpfchenmodell *n*

f modèle *m* de la goutte liquide *(du noyau)*
r жидкокапельная модель *f (ядра)*

L286 *e* liquid-filled thermometer
d Flüssigkeitsthermometer *n*
f thermomètre *m* à liquide
r жидкостный термометр *m*

L287 *e* liquid helium
d flüssiges Helium *n*
f hélium *m* liquide
r жидкий гелий *m*

L288 *e* liquid-hydrogen bubble chamber
d Wasserstoffblasenkammer *f*
f chambre *f* à bulles de l'hydrogène liquide
r жидководородная пузырьковая камера *f*

L289 *e* liquid laser
d Flüssigkeitslaser *m*
f laser *m* à fluide
r жидкостный лазер *m*

L290 *e* liquid metal
d Metallschmelze *f*, Flüssigmetall *n*
f métal *m* liquide
r жидкий металл *m*

L291 *e* liquid nitrogen
d Flüssigstickstoff *m*
f azote *m* liquide
r жидкий азот *m*

L292 *e* liquid nitrogen cryostat
d Flüssigstickstoffkryostat *m*
f cryostat *m* à azote liquide
r азотный криостат *m*

L293 *e* liquid outflow through a hole
d Flüssigkeitsausfluß *m* aus einem Loch
f écoulement *m* du liquide d'un trou
r истечение *n* жидкости из отверстия

L294 *e* liquid oxygen
d Flüssigsauerstoff *m*
f oxygène *m* liquide
r жидкий кислород *m*

L295 *e* liquid semiconductor
d Flüssighalbleiter *m*, flüssiger Halbleiter *m*
f semi-conducteur *m* liquide
r жидкий полупроводник *m*

L296 *e* liquid state
d flüssiger Zustand *m*
f état *m* liquide
r жидкое состояние *n*

L297 *e* liquid substance
d flüssige Substanz *f*
f substance *f* liquide
r жидкое вещество *n*

L298 *e* liquidus, liquidus line
d Liquiduslinie *f*, Liquiduskurve *f*
f courbe *f* liquidus
r ликвидус *m*

L299 *e* Lissajous figures
d Lissajous-Figuren *f pl*
f figures *f pl* de Lissajous
r фигуры *f pl* Лиссажу

L300 *e* lithium, Li
d Lithium *n*
f lithium *m*
r литий *m*

L301 *e* lithography
d Lithografie *f*
f lithographie *f*
r литография *f*

L302 *e* litre, l
d Liter *n*
f litre *m*
r литр *m*, л

L303 *e* load
d Belastung *f*, Last *f*
f charge *f*
r нагрузка *f*

L304 *e* loaded line
d Lastlinie *f*
f ligne *f* de charge
r нагруженная линия *f*

L305 *e* loaded Q factor
d belasteter Gütewert *m*, Gütefaktor *m* bei Belastung
f facteur *m* Q à pleine charge
r нагруженная добротность *f*

L306 *e* load impedance
d Lastimpedanz *f*
f impédance *f* de charge
r импеданс *m* нагрузки

L307 *e* loading
d 1. Belastung *f*; Beanspruchung *f* 2. Beschickung *f*
f 1. chargement *m* 2. empilement *m*
r 1. нагружение *n* 2. загрузка *f* *(ядерного реактора)*

L308 *e* lobe
d Lappen *m*, Keule *f*, Strahlungslappen *m*, Strahlungszipfel *m*
f lobe *m*
r лепесток *m (диаграммы направленности антенны)*

L309 *e* local concentration
d lokale Konzentration *f*
f concentration *f* locale
r локальная концентрация *f*

L310 *e* local density *see* local concentration

L311   e   local duality
       d   lokale Dualität *f*
       f   dualité *f* locale
       r   локальная дуальность *f*

L312   e   local field
       d   lokales Feld *n*, Lokalfeld *n*
       f   champ *m* local
       r   локальное поле *n*

L313   e   local gage invariance
       d   lokale Eichinvarianz *f*
       f   invariance *f* locale de jauge
       r   локальная калибровочная
          инвариантность *f*

L314   e   local interaction
       d   lokale Wechselwirkung *f*
       f   interaction *f* locale
       r   локальное взаимодействие *n*

L315   e   local ion implantation
       d   lokale Ionenimplantation *f*
       f   implantation *f* ionique locale
       r   локальная ионная имплантация *f*

L316   e   locality
       d   Lokalität *f*, Mikrokausalität *f*,
          Einstein-Kausalität *f*
       f   localité *f*, microcausalité *f*
       r   локальность *f*, микропричинность *f*

L317   e   localization
       d   Lokalisierung *f*
       f   localisation *f*
       r   локализация *f*

L318   e   localized charge
       d   lokalisierte Ladung *f*
       f   charge *f* localisée
       r   локализованный заряд *m*

L319   e   local observable
       d   lokale Observable *f*
       f   observable *f* locale
       r   локальная наблюдаемая *f*

L320   e   local operator
       d   Lokaloperator *m*
       f   opérateur *m* local
       r   локальный оператор *m*

L321   e   local symmetry
       d   lokale Symmetrie *f*, Lokalsymmetrie *f*
       f   symétrie *f* locale
       r   локальная симметрия *f*

L322   e   local thermodynamic equilibrium
       d   lokales thermodynamisches
          Gleichgewicht *n*
       f   équilibre *m* thermodynamique local
       r   локальное термодинамическое
          равновесие *n*

L323   e   local time
       d   Ortszeit *f*

       f   temps *m* local
       r   местное время *n*

L324   e   locked-in detection *see* synchronous
          detection

L325   e   locking
       d   1. Synchronisation *f*, Synchronisierung
          f 2. Blockierung *f* 3.
          Frequenzmitnahme *f*
       f   1. synchronisation *f* 2. blocage *m* 3.
          accrochage *m* des fréquences
       r   1. синхронизация *f* 2. блокировка *f*
          3. захватывание *n* частоты

L326   e   locus
       d   Ort *m*, geometrischer Ort *m*
       f   lieu *m*, lieu *m* géométrique
       r   геометрическое место *n* (*точек*)

L327   e   logarithm
       d   Logarithmus *m*
       f   logarithme *m*
       r   логарифм *m*

L328   e   logarithmic decrement
       d   logarithmisches Dekrement *n*
       f   décrément *m* logarithmique
       r   логарифмический декремент *m*,
          логарифмический декремент *m*
          затухания

L329   e   logarithmic increment
       d   logarithmisches Inkrement *n*
       f   incrément *m* logarithmique
       r   логарифмический инкремент *m*

L330   e   logarithmic law
       d   logarithmisches Gesetz *n*
       f   loi *f* logarithmique
       r   логарифмический закон *m*

L331   e   logarithmic scale
       d   logarithmischer Maßstab *m*
       f   échelle *f* logarithmique
       r   логарифмический масштаб *m*

L332   e   logic circuit
       d   Logikschaltung *f*, logische Schaltung *f*
       f   circuit *m* logique
       r   логическая схема *f*

L333   e   Londons equation
       d   London-Gleichung *f*, Londonsche
          Gleichung *f*
       f   équation *f* des Londons
       r   уравнение *n* Лондонов, уравнение *n*
          Ф. и Г. Лондонов

L334   e   long-base interferometer
       d   Langbasisinterferometer *n*
       f   interféromètre *m* à longue base
       r   радиоинтерферометр *m* с длинной
          базой

L335   e   longitude
       d   Länge *f*, geographische Länge *f*

f longitude *f*
r долгота *f*

L336 *e* **longitudinal adiabatic invariant**
d longitudinale adiabatische Invariante *f*
f invariant *m* longitudinal adiabatique
r продольный адиабатический
инвариант *m*

L337 *e* **longitudinal coherence**
d longitudinale Kohärenz *f*
f cohérence *f* longitudinale
r продольная когерентность *f*

L338 *e* **longitudinal deformation**
d Längsverformung *f*
f déformation *f* longitudinale
r продольная деформация *f*

L339 *e* **longitudinal mode**
d longitudinale Mode *f*, longitudinaler
Schwingungstyp *m*
f mode *m* longitudinal
r продольная мода *f*

L340 *e* **longitudinal vibration, longitudinal
vibrations**
d Längsschwingung *f*,
Dehnungsschwingung *f*,
Longitudinalschwingung *f*
f vibration *f* longitudinale
r продольные колебания *n pl*

L341 *e* **longitudinal waves**
d Longitudinalwellen *f pl*,
Längswellen *f pl*
f ondes *f pl* longitudinales
r продольные волны *f pl*

L342 *e* **long line**
d 1. lange Linie *f* 2. lange Leitung *f*
f longue ligne *f*
r длинная линия *f*

L343 *e* **long-lived component**
d langlebige Komponente *f*
f composante *f* à longue période
r долгоживущая компонента *f*

L344 *e* **long-lived isotope**
d langlebiges Isotop *n*
f isotope *m* à longue période
r долгоживущий изотоп *m*

L345 *e* **long-period oscillation**
d langperiodische Schwingungen *f pl*
f oscillations *f pl* à longue période
r длиннопериодные колебания *n pl*

L346 *e* **long-range component**
d fernwirkende Komponente *f*
f composante *f* à grand rayon d'action
r дальнодействующая компонента *f*

L347 *e* **long-range interaction**
d Fernwirkung *f*
f interaction *f* à longue distance
r дальнодействие *n*

L348 *e* **long-range order**
d Fernordnung *f*
f ordre *m* à longue distance
r дальний порядок *m*

L349 *e* **long sight**
d Weitsichtigkeit *f*
f hypermétropie *f*
r дальнозоркость *f*

L350 *e* **long-term instability**
d Langzeitinstabilität *f*
f instabilité *f* à long terme
r долговременная нестабильность *f*

L351 *e* **long-term stability**
d Langzeitstabilität *f*
f stabilité *f* à long terme
r долговременная стабильность *f*

L352 *e* **long-wavelength continuum**
d langwelliges Kontinuum *n*
f continuum *m* à ondes longues
r длинноволновый континуум *m*

L353 *e* **long-wave radiation**
d langwellige Strahlung *f*,
Langwellenstrahlung *f*
f rayonnement *m* à ondes longues,
radiation *f* à ondes longues
r длинноволновое излучение *n*

L354 *e* **long-wave range**
d Langwellenbereich *m*
f ondes *f pl* longues
r длинноволновый диапазон *m*

L355 *e* **long-wave region**
d Langwellengebiet *n*
f domaine *m* à ondes longues
r длинноволновая область *f*
(спектра)

L356 *e* **long waves**
d lange Wellen *f pl*
f ondes *f pl* longues
r длинные волны *f pl*

L357 *e* **loop**
d 1. Schleife *f* 2. Rahmen *m* 3. Kreis *m*,
geschlossener Kreis *m*
f 1. boucle *f* 2. cadre *m* 3. circuit *m*
r 1. петля *f* 2. рамка *f* 3. контур *m*,
замкнутый контур *m*

L358 *e* **loop antenna**
d Rahmenantenne *f*
f antenne *f* à cadre, antenne *f* en cadre
r рамочная антенна *f*

L359 *e* **Lorentz force**
d Lorentz-Kraft *f*
f force *f* de Lorentz
r сила *f* Лоренца

L360 *e* **Lorentz-Dirac equation**
d Lorentz-Dirac-Gleichung *f*

    f équation *f* de Lorentz-Dirac
    r уравнение *n* Лоренца - Дирака

L361 *e* **Lorentz gage**
    d Lorentz-Konvention *f*, Lorentz-
      Eichung *f*
    f condition *f* de Lorentz
    r калибровка *f* Лоренца

L362 *e* **Lorentz group**
    d Lorentz-Gruppe *f*
    f groupe *m* de Lorentz
    r группа *f* Лоренца

L363 *e* **Lorentz invariance**
    d Lorentz-Invarianz *f*, relativistische
      Invarianz *f*
    f invariance *f* de Lorentz
    r лоренц-инвариантность *f*,
      релятивистская инвариантность *f*

L364 *e* **Lorentz-invariant**
    d Lorentz-Invariante *f*
    f invariant *m* de Lorentz
    r лоренц-инвариант *m*

L365 *e* **Lorentz lemma**
    d Lorentz-Lemma *n*
    f lemme *m* de Lorentz
    r лемма *f* Лоренца

L366 *e* **Lorentz line**
    d Lorentz-Linie *f*
    f ligne *f* de Lorentz
    r лоренцева линия *f*

L367 *e* **Lorentz-Lorenz formula**
    d Lorentz-Lorenzsche Formel *f*
    f formule *f* de Lorentz-Lorenz
    r формула *f* Лоренца - Лоренца

L368 *e* **Lorentz profile**
    d Lorentz-Profil *n*
    f profil *m* lorentzien
    r лоренцевский контур *m*
      (спектральной линии)

L369 *e* **Lorentz system**
    d Lorentz-System *n*
    f système *m* de Lorentz
    r система *f* Лоренца

L370 *e* **Lorentz transformation**
    d Lorentz-Transformation *f*
    f transformation *f* de Lorentz
    r преобразование *n* Лоренца

L371 *e* **Loschmidt number**
    d Loschmidt-Konstante *f*
    f nombre *m* de Loschmidt
    r постоянная *f* Лошмидта

L372 *e* **loss**
    d 1. Verluste *m pl*; Verlust *m*
      2. Dämpfung *f*
    f 1. pertes *f pl*, perte *f*
      2. amortissement *m*

    r 1. потери *f pl*; потеря *f*
      2. затухание *n*

L373 *e* **loss angle**
    d dielektrischer Verlustwinkel *m*
    f angle *m* de pertes
    r угол *m* потерь

L374 *e* **loss cone**
    d Verlustkegel *m*
    f cône *m* de perte
    r конус *m* потерь

L375 *e* **loss cone instability**
    d Verlustkegelinstabilität *f*
    f instabilité *f* conique
    r конусная неустойчивость *f*

L376 *e* **loss factor**
    d dielektrischer Verlustfaktor *m*
    f facteur *m* de pertes
    r коэффициент *m* потерь

L377 *e* **loss-free dielectric**
    d verlustfreies Dielektrikum *n*, idealer
      Isolierstoff *m*
    f diélectrique *m* sans pertes
    r диэлектрик *m* без потерь

L378 *e* **loss of strength**
    d Entfestigung *f*
    f déconsolidation *f*
    r разупрочнение *n*

L379 *e* **losses** *see* **loss**

L380 *e* **loudness**
    d Lautstärke *f*
    f volume *m* de son, intensité *f* sonore
    r громкость *f*

L381 *e* **loudspeaker**
    d Lautsprecher *m*
    f haut-parleur *m*
    r громкоговоритель *m*

L382 *e* **Love wave**
    d Love-Welle *f*, Lovesche Welle *f*
    f onde *f* de Love
    r волна *f* Лява

L383 *e* **low-angle scattering**
    d Kleinwinkelstreuung *f*
    f diffusion *f* à angle réduit
    r малоугловое рассеяние *n*

L384 *e* **low-dimensional magnetic**
    d niederdimensionales Magnetikum *n*
    f magnétique *m* de faible encombrement
    r низкоразмерный магнетик *m*

L385 *e* **low energy electron diffraction**
    d Niederenergie-Elektronenbeugung *f*
    f diffraction *f* d'électrons lents
    r дифракция *f* медленных
      электронов, дифракция *f*
      электронов низких энергий

L386　e　low energy electron diffraction
method
　　d　LEED-Verfahren n
　　f　méthode f de diffraction des électrons
lents
　　r　метод m дифракции электронов
низких энергий, метод m LEED

L387　e　low energy region
　　d　Niederenergiegebiet n
　　f　région f de faibles énergies
　　r　область f малых энергий

L388　e　lower band
　　d　unteres Band n
　　f　zone f inférieure, bande f inférieure
　　r　нижняя зона f

L389　e　lower ionosphere
　　d　niedere Ionosphäre f, tiefe
Ionosphäre f
　　f　ionosphère f inférieure
　　r　нижняя ионосфера f

L390　e　lower sublevel
　　d　unteres Subniveau n
　　f　sous-niveau m inférieur
　　r　нижний подуровень m

L391　e　lower yield point
　　d　untere Streckgrenze f
　　f　limite f inférieure d'élasticité
　　r　нижний предел m текучести

L392　e　low frequencies
　　d　Niederfrequenzen f pl
　　f　basses fréquences f pl
　　r　низкие частоты f pl

L393　e　low-frequency band
　　d　Niederfrequenzband n
　　f　gamme f de basses fréquences
　　r　низкочастотный диапазон m,
диапазон m низких частот

L394　e　low-frequency oscillation
　　d　Niederfrequenzschwingungen f pl
　　f　oscillations f pl à basse fréquence
　　r　низкочастотные колебания n pl

L395　e　low-frequency radiation
　　d　Niederfrequenzstrahlung f
　　f　rayonnement m à basse fréquence,
radiation f à basse fréquence
　　r　низкочастотное излучение n,
длинноволновое излучение n

L396　e　low-frequency region
　　d　Niederfrequenzbereich m
　　f　domaine m de basses fréquences
　　r　область f низких частот,
низкочастотная область f

L397　e　low-noise amplifier
　　d　rauscharmer Verstärker m

　　f　amplificateur m à faible bruit
　　r　малошумящий усилитель m

L398　e　low-pass filter
　　d　Tiefpaßfilter n, Tiefpaß m
　　f　filtre m passe-bas
　　r　фильтр m нижних частот

L399　e　low temperature
　　d　tiefe Temperatur f, niedrige
Temperatur f, Tieftemperatur f
　　f　basse température f
　　r　низкая температура f

L400　e　low-temperature calorimetry
　　d　Tieftemperaturkalorimetrie f
　　f　calorimétrie f à basse température
　　r　низкотемпературная калориметрия f

L401　e　low-temperature chamber
　　d　Tieftemperaturkammer f
　　f　chambre f à basse température
　　r　низкотемпературная камера f

L402　e　low-temperature container
　　d　Tieftemperaturcontainer m
　　f　conteneur m à basse température
　　r　низкотемпературный контейнер m

L403　e　low-temperature physics
　　d　Kryophysik f, Tieftemperaturphysik f
　　f　physique f de basses températures
　　r　физика f низких температур

L404　e　low-temperature plasma
　　d　Niedertemperaturplasma n
　　f　plasma m à basse température
　　r　низкотемпературная плазма f

L405　e　low-voltage arc
　　d　Niedervoltbogen m,
Niederspannungsbogen m
　　f　arc m à basse tension
　　r　низковольтная дуга f

L406　e　LS-coupling see Russell-Saunders
coupling

L407　e　lubrication
　　d　Schmieren n, Schmierung f
　　f　graissage m, lubrification f
　　r　смазывание n, смазка f

L408　e　Lüders lines
　　d　Lüderssche Linien f pl, Gleitlinien f pl
　　f　lignes f pl de Lüders
　　r　линии f pl Людерса - Чернова,
линии f pl скольжения

L409　e　lumen, lm
　　d　Lumen n
　　f　lumen m
　　r　люмен m, лм

L410　e　lumen second, lm·s
　　d　Lumensekunde f

　　　f lumen-seconde
　　　r люмен-секунда *f*, лм·с

L411　*e* **luminance**
　　　d Leuchtdichte *f*
　　　f luminance *f*
　　　r яркость *f*

L412　*e* **luminance contrast**
　　　d Leuchtdichtekontrast *m*
　　　f contraste *m* de luminance
　　　r яркостный контраст *m*

L413　*e* **luminance factor**
　　　d Remissionsgrad *m*; Hellbezugswert *m* (*Farbmetrik*)
　　　f facteur *m* de luminance
　　　r коэффициент *m* яркости

L414　*e* **luminance temperature**
　　　d schwarze Temperatur *f*
　　　f température *f* de luminance
　　　r яркостная температура *f*

L415　*e* **luminescence**
　　　d Lumineszenz *f*
　　　f luminescence *f*
　　　r люминесценция *f*

L416　*e* **luminescence center**
　　　d Lumineszenzzentrum *n*
　　　f centre *m* luminogène
　　　r центр *m* люминесценции

L417　*e* **luminescence decay**
　　　d Lumineszenzabklingen *n*, Abklingen *n* der Lumineszenz
　　　f déclin *m* de la luminescence
　　　r затухание *n* люминесценции

L418　*e* **luminescence decay time**
　　　d Lumineszenzabklingzeit *f*
　　　f temps *m* de déclin de la luminescence
　　　r время *n* затухания люминесценции

L419　*e* **luminescence depolarization**
　　　d Lumineszenzdepolarisation *f*
　　　f dépolarisation *f* de la luminescence
　　　r деполяризация *f* люминесценции

L420　*e* **luminescence intensity**
　　　d Lumineszenzintensität *f*, Lumineszenzstärke *f*
　　　f intensité *f* de luminescence
　　　r интенсивность *f* люминесценции

L421　*e* **luminescence quenching**
　　　d Lumineszenzlöschen *n*
　　　f extinction *f* de la luminescence
　　　r тушение *n* люминесценции

L422　*e* **luminescence yield**
　　　d Lumineszenzausbeute *f*
　　　f rendement *m* de luminescence
　　　r выход *m* люминесценции

L423　*e* **luminescent analysis**

　　　d Lumineszenzanalyse *f*
　　　f analyse *f* par luminescence
　　　r люминесцентный анализ *m*

L424　*e* **luminescent image**
　　　d Leuchtbild *n*, Lumineszenzbild *n*
　　　f image *f* luminescente
　　　r люминесцентное изображение *n*

L425　*e* **luminescent material**
　　　d Lumineszenzstoff *m*
　　　f substance *f* luminescente, matière *f* luminescente
　　　r люминесцентное вещество *n*

L426　*e* **luminophor**
　　　d Leuchtstoff *m*
　　　f luminophore *m*
　　　r люминофор *m*

L427　*e* **luminosity**
　　　d Leuchtkraft *f* (*Stern*)
　　　f luminosité *f* (*d'une étoile*)
　　　r светимость *f* (*звезды*)

L428　*e* **luminosity class**
　　　d Leuchtkraftklasse *f*
　　　f classe *f* de luminosité
　　　r класс *m* светимости (*звёзд*)

L429　*e* **luminous efficacy**
　　　d 1. photometrisches Strahlungsäquivalent *n* der Gesamtstrahlung 2. Lichtausbeute *f*; Wirtschaftlichkeit *f* der Lichtquelle
　　　f efficacité *f* lumineuse
　　　r 1. световая эффективность *f* потока, световая эффективность *f* (*излучения*) 2. световая отдача *f* (*источника света*)

L430　*e* **luminous efficiency**
　　　d visueller Wirkungsgrad *m*, visueller Nutzeffekt *m*
　　　f efficacité *f* lumineuse relative
　　　r спектральная чувствительность *f* (*глаза*), относительная световая эффективность *f*

L431　*e* **luminous emittance, luminous exitance**
　　　d spezifische Lichtausstrahlung *f*
　　　f émittance *f* lumineuse
　　　r светимость *f*

L432　*e* **luminous energy**
　　　d Lichtenergie *f*
　　　f énergie *f* lumineuse
　　　r световая энергия *f*

L433　*e* **luminous exitance** *see* **luminous emittance**

L434　*e* **luminous flux**
　　　d Lichtstrom *m*

f flux *m* lumineux
r световой поток *m*

L435 *e* luminous intensity
   d Lichtstärke *f*
   f intensité *f* lumineuse
   r сила *f* света

L436 *e* Lummer-Brodhune cube
   d Lummer-Brodhune-Würfel *m*,
     Photometerwürfel *m*
   f cube *m* photométrique
   r кубик *m* Люммера - Бродхуна,
     фотометрический кубик *m*

L437 *e* lumped load
   d konzentrierte Belastung *f*,
     konzentrierte Last *f*
   f charge *f* concentrée
   r сосредоточенная нагрузка *f*

L438 *e* lumped-parameter system
   d System *n* mit konzentrierten
     Parametern
   f système *m* à paramètres concentrés
   r система *f* с сосредоточенными
     параметрами

L439 *e* lunar eclipse
   d Mondfinsternis *f*
   f éclipse *f* de la Lune
   r лунное затмение *n*

L440 *e* lunar laser ranging
   d Laserortung *f* des Mondes
   f localisation *f* laser de la Lune
   r лазерная локация *f* Луны

L441 *e* lunokhod
   d Mondfahrzeug *n*, Mondauto *n*
   f lunakhode *m*
   r луноход *m*

L442 *e* lutecium, Lu
   d Lutetium *n*
   f lutécium *m*
   r лютеций *m*

L443 *e* lux, lx
   d Lux *n*
   f lux *m*
   r люкс *m*, лк

L444 *e* Luxemburg effect
   d Luxemburg-Effekt *m*
   f effet *m* Luxemburg
   r Люксембург-Горьковский эффект *m*

L445 *e* luxmeter
   d Luxmeter *n*,
     Beleuchtungsstärkemesser *m*
   f luxmètre *m*
   r люксметр *m*

L446 *e* Lyman series
   d Lyman-Serie *f*

f série *f* de Lyman
r серия *f* Лаймана

L447 *e* lyophily
   d Lyophilie *f*
   f lyophilie *f*
   r лиофильность *f*

L448 *e* lyophoby
   d Lyophobie *f*
   f lyophobie *f*
   r лиофобность *f*

L449 *e* lyotropy
   d Lyotropie *f*
   f lyotropie *f*
   r лиотропия *f*

M

M1 *e* Mach angle
   d Machscher Winkel *m*, Mach-Winkel *m*
   f angle *m* de Mach
   r угол *m* Маха

M2 *e* Mach cone
   d Machscher Kegel *m*
   f cône *m* de Mach, cône *m* de
     perturbation, front *m* de Mach
   r конус *m* Маха

M3 *e* Mach number
   d Mach-Zahl *f*, Machsche Zahl *f*
   f nombre *m* de Mach
   r число *n* Маха

M4 *e* Mach-Zehnder interferometer
   d Mach-Zehnder-Interferometer *n*
   f interféromètre *m* de Mach-Zehnder
   r интерферометр *m* Маха - Цендера

M5 *e* Maclaurin series
   d Maclaurinsche Reihe *f*
   f série *f* de Maclaurin
   r ряд *m* Маклорена

M6 *e* macrocosm
   d Makrokosmos *m*
   f macrocosmos *m*
   r макромир *m*

M7 *e* macrokinetics
   d Makrokinetik *f*
   f macrocinétique *f*
   r макрокинетика *f*

M8 *e* macromolecule
   d Makromolekül *n*
   f macromolécule *f*
   r макромолекула *f*

M9 *e* macroparticle

    d Makroteilchen *n*
    f macroparticule *f*
    r макрочастица *f*

M10 *e* **macroscopic chemical kinetics**
    d makroskopische chemische Kinetik *f*
    f cinétique *f* chimique macroscopique
    r макроскопическая химическая
       кинетика *f*

M11 *e* **macroscopic electromagnetic field**
    d makroskopisches elektromagnetisches
       Feld *n*
    f champ *m* électromagnétique
       macroscopique
    r макроскопическое
       электромагнитное поле *n*

M12 *e* **macroscopic quantum effects**
    d makroskopische Quanteneffekte *m pl*
    f effets *m pl* macroscopiques quantiques
    r макроскопические квантовые
       эффекты *m pl*

M13 *e* **macrostructure**
    d Makrogefüge *n*, Makrostruktur *f*
    f macrostructure *f*
    r макроструктура *f*

M14 *e* **macrouniverse** *see* macrocosm

M15 *e* **Maggi-Righi-Leduc effect**
    d Maggi-Righi-Leduc-Effekt *m*
    f effet *m* Maggi-Righi-Leduc
    r эффект *m* Маджи - Риги - Ледюка

M16 *e* **magic nuclei**
    d magische Kerne *m pl*
    f noyaux *m pl* à nombre magique
    r магические ядра *n pl*

M17 *e* **magnesium, Mg**
    d Magnesium *n*
    f magnésium *m*
    r магний *m*

M18 *e* **magnet**
    d **1.** Magnet *m* **2.** Magnetikum *n*
    f **1.** aimant *m* **2.** magnétique *m*
    r **1.** магнит *m* **2.** магнетик *m*

M19 *e* **magnetic accommodation**
    d magnetische Akkommodation *f*
    f accommodation *f* magnétique
    r магнитная аккомодация *f*

M20 *e* **magnetic after-effect**
    d magnetische Nachwirkung *f*
    f traînage *m* magnétique
    r магнитное последействие *n*

M21 *e* **magnetic aging**
    d magnetische Alterung *f*
    f vieillissement *m* magnétique
    r магнитное старение *n*

M22 *e* **magnetic alloys**

    d magnetische Legierungen *f pl*
    f alliages *m pl* magnétiques
    r магнитные сплавы *m pl*

M23 *e* **magnetic amplifier**
    d Magnetverstärker *m*
    f amplificateur *m* magnétique
    r магнитный усилитель *m*

M24 *e* **magnetic anisotropy**
    d magnetische Anisotropie *f*
    f anisotropie *f* magnétique
    r магнитная анизотропия *f*

M25 *e* **magnetic anomaly**
    d magnetische Anomalie *f*,
       Magnetanomalie *f*
    f anomalie *f* magnétique
    r магнитная аномалия *f*

M26 *e* **magnetic atomic structure**
    d magnetische Atomstruktur *f*
    f structure *f* atomique magnétique
    r магнитная атомная структура *f*

M27 *e* **magnetic balance**
    d Feldwaage *f*, magnetische Feldwaage *f*
    f balance *f* magnétique
    r магнитные весы *pl*

M28 *e* **magnetic breakdown**
    d magnetischer Durchbruch *m*
    f rupture *f* magnétique
    r магнитный пробой *m*

M29 *e* **magnetic cation**
    d magnetisches Kation *n*
    f cation *m* magnétique
    r магнитный катион *m*

M30 *e* **magnetic cell**
    d magnetische Zelle *f*
    f cellule *f* magnétique
    r магнитная ячейка *f*

M31 *e* **magnetic charge**
    d magnetische Ladung *f*
    f charge *f* magnétique
    r магнитный заряд *m*

M32 *e* **magnetic circuit**
    d magnetischer Kreis *m*, Magnetkreis *m*
    f circuit *m* magnétique
    r магнитная цепь *f*

M33 *e* **magnetic circular dichroism**
    d magnetischer Rotationsdichroismus *m*,
       magnetischer zirkularer
       Dichroismus *m*
    f dichroïsme *m* circulaire magnétique
    r магнитный круговой дихроизм *m*

M34 *e* **magnetic cluster**
    d magnetischer Cluster *m*
    f cluster *m* magnétique
    r магнитный кластер *m*

M35   *e* **magnetic coil**
      d Magnetspule *f*
      f bobine *f* magnétique
      r магнитная катушка *f*

M36   *e* **magnetic conductance**
      d magnetischer Leitwert *m*, magnetische Leitfähigkeit *f*
      f conductivité *f* magnétique
      r магнитная проводимость *f*

M37   *e* **magnetic configuration**
      d Magnetkonfiguration *f*
      f configuration *f* magnétique
      r магнитная конфигурация *f*

M38   *e* **magnetic confinement**
      d magnetische Einschließung *f*
      f confinement *m* magnétique
      r магнитное удержание *n*

M39   *e* **magnetic cooling**
      d magnetische Kühlung *f*
      f refroidissement *m* magnétique
      r магнитное охлаждение *n*

M40   *e* **magnetic crochets**
      d erdmagnetische Crochets *n pl*
      f crochets *m pl* magnétiques
      r магнитные кроше *n pl*

M41   *e* **magnetic declination**
      d magnetische Deklination *f*
      f déclinaison *f* magnétique
      r магнитное склонение *n*

M42   *e* **magnetic deflector**
      d Magnetdeflektor *m*, Magnetablenker *m*
      f déflecteur *m* magnétique
      r магнитный дефлектор *m*; магнитная отклоняющая система *f*

M43   *e* **magnetic defocusing**
      d magnetische Defokussierung *f*
      f défocalisation *f* magnétique
      r магнитная дефокусировка *f*

M44   *e* **magnetic deviation**
      d Deviation *f*, Magnetkompaßdeviation *f*
      f déviation *f* du compas
      r девиация *f* компаса

M45   *e* **magnetic dielectric**
      d magnetisches Dielektrikum *n*
      f diélectrique *m* magnétique
      r магнитный диэлектрик *m*

M46   *e* **magnetic dip** *see* **magnetic inclination**

M47   *e* **magnetic dipole**
      d magnetischer Dipol *m*
      f dipôle *m* magnétique
      r магнитный диполь *m*

M48   *e* **magnetic dipole moment**
      d magnetisches Dipolmoment *n*
      f moment *m* du dipôle magnétique
      r дипольный магнитный момент *m*

M49   *e* **magnetic dipole radiation**
      d magnetische Dipolstrahlung *f*
      f radiation *f* dipolaire magnétique
      r магнитное дипольное излучение *n*

M50   *e* **magnetic domain**
      d magnetische Domäne *f*, Weißscher Bezirk *m*
      f domaine *m* magnétique
      r магнитный домен *m*

M51   *e* **magnetic domain structure**
      d magnetische Domänenstruktur *f*
      f structure *f* magnétique de domaines
      r магнитная доменная структура *f*

M52   *e* **magnetic drift**
      d magnetische Drift *f*
      f dérive *f* magnétique
      r магнитный дрейф *m*

M53   *e* **magnetic energy**
      d magnetische Energie *f*, Energie *f* des magnetischen Feldes
      f énergie *f* magnétique
      r магнитная энергия *f*

M54   *e* **magnetic equator**
      d magnetischer Äquator *m*, erdmagnetischer Äquator *m*
      f équateur *m* magnétique, équateur *m* géomagnétique
      r магнитный экватор *m*

M55   *e* **magnetic field**
      d Magnetfeld *n*, magnetisches Feld *n*
      f champ *m* magnétique
      r магнитное поле *n*

M56   *e* **magnetic field configuration**
      d Magnetfeldkonfiguration *f*
      f configuration *f* du champ magnétique
      r конфигурация *f* магнитного поля

M57   *e* **magnetic field gradient**
      d magnetischer Feldgradient *m*
      f gradient *m* du champ magnétique
      r градиент *m* магнитного поля

M58   *e* **magnetic field-induced surface levels** *see* **magnetic surface levels**

M59   *e* **magnetic field line** *see* **magnetic line of force**

M60   *e* **magnetic field line reconnection**
      d Neuverbinden *n* von magnetischen Feldstärkelinien
      f reconnexion *f* de lignes de force magnétiques
      r пересоединение *n* магнитных силовых линий

M61　*e*　**magnetic field nonuniformity**
　　d　Magnetfeldinhomogenität *f*
　　f　non-uniformité *f* du champ
　　　　magnétique
　　r　неоднородность *f* магнитного поля

M62　*e*　**magnetic field pattern**
　　d　Magnetfeld-Linienbild *n*
　　f　lignes *f* du champ magnétique
　　r　картина *f* силовых линий
　　　　магнитного поля

M63　*e*　**magnetic field pressure**
　　d　Magnetfelddruck *m*
　　f　pression *f* du champ magnétique
　　r　давление *n* магнитного поля

M64　*e*　**magnetic field strength**
　　d　magnetische Feldstärke *f*,
　　　　Magnetfeldstärke *f*
　　f　intensité *f* du champ magnétique
　　r　напряжённость *f* магнитного поля

M65　*e*　**magnetic film**
　　d　Magnetschicht *f*
　　f　film *m* magnétique
　　r　магнитная плёнка *f*

M66　*e*　**magnetic flux**
　　d　magnetischer Fluß *m*
　　f　flux *m* magnétique
　　r　магнитный поток *m*

M67　*e*　**magnetic flux density** *see* **magnetic induction**

M68　*e*　**magnetic flux quantization**
　　d　Magnetflußquantisierung *f*
　　f　quantification *f* du flux magnétique
　　r　квантование *n* магнитного потока

M69　*e*　**magnetic flux quantum**
　　d　magnetisches Flußquant *n*
　　f　quantum *m* du flux magnétique
　　r　квант *m* магнитного потока

M70　*e*　**magnetic focusing**
　　d　magnetische Fokussierung *f*
　　f　focalisation *f* magnétique
　　r　магнитная фокусировка *f*

M71　*e*　**magnetic form factor**
　　d　magnetischer Formfaktor *m*
　　f　facteur *m* de forme magnétique
　　r　магнитный форм-фактор *m*

M72　*e*　**magnetic hardness**
　　d　magnetische Härte *f*
　　f　dureté *f* magnétique
　　r　магнитная жёсткость *f*

M73　*e*　**magnetic hydrodynamics**
　　d　Magnetohydrodynamik *f*
　　f　hydrodynamique *f* magnétique
　　r　магнитная гидродинамика *f*,
　　　　магнитогидродинамика *f*

M74　*e*　**magnetic hyperfine structure**
　　d　magnetische Hyperfeinstruktur *f*
　　f　structure *f* magnétique hyperfine
　　r　сверхтонкая магнитная структура *f*

M75　*e*　**magnetic hysteresis**
　　d　magnetische Hysterese *f*, magnetische
　　　　Hysteresis *f*
　　f　hystérésis *f* magnétique
　　r　магнитный гистерезис *m*

M76　*e*　**magnetic image**
　　d　magnetisches Bild *n*
　　f　image *f* magnétique
　　r　магнитное изображение *n*

M77　*e*　**magnetic inclination**
　　d　Inklination *f*, magnetische Inklination *f*
　　f　inclinaison *f*, inclinaison *f* magnétique
　　r　магнитное наклонение *n*

M78　*e*　**magnetic induction**
　　d　magnetische Flußdichte *f*, magnetische
　　　　Induktion *f*
　　f　induction *f* magnétique, densité *f* de
　　　　flux magnétique
　　r　магнитная индукция *f*

M79　*e*　**magnetic inflector**
　　d　magnetischer Inflektor *m*
　　f　inflecteur *m* magnétique
　　r　магнитный инфлектор *m*

M80　*e*　**magnetic insulation**
　　d　magnetische Isolierung *f*,
　　　　Magnetfeldisolierung *f*
　　f　isolation *f* magnétique
　　r　магнитная изоляция *f*

M81　*e*　**magnetic intensity** *see* **magnetic field strength**

M82　*e*　**magnetic interaction**
　　d　magnetische Wechselwirkung *f*
　　f　interaction *f* magnétique
　　r　магнитное взаимодействие *n*

M83　*e*　**magnetic latitude**
　　d　magnetische Breite *f*
　　f　latitude *f* magnétique
　　r　магнитная широта *f*

M84　*e*　**magnetic lens**
　　d　magnetische Linse *f*
　　f　lentille *f* magnétique
　　r　магнитная линза *f*

M85　*e*　**magnetic line of force**
　　d　magnetische Feldstärkelinie *f*,
　　　　magnetische Kraftlinie *f*
　　f　ligne *f* de force magnétique
　　r　магнитная силовая линия *f*

M86　*e*　**magnetic liquid**
　　d　magnetische Flüssigkeit *f*
　　f　fluide *m* magnétique
　　r　магнитная жидкость *f*

M87 *e* **magnetic long-range order**
  d magnetische Fernordnung *f*
  f ordre *m* magnétique à grande distance
  r дальний магнитный порядок *m*

M88 *e* **magnetic loss**
  d Magnetisierungsverluste *m pl*
  f pertes *f pl* magnétiques
  r магнитные потери *f pl*

M89 *e* **magnetic loss factor**
  d Magnetisierungsverlustfaktor *m*
  f coefficient *m* de pertes magnétiques
  r коэффициент *m* магнитных потерь

M90 *e* **magnetic material**
  d magnetischer Werkstoff *m*,
    Magnetwerkstoff *m*
  f matériau *m* magnétique
  r магнитный материал *m*

M91 *e* **magnetic measurements**
  d magnetische Messungen *f pl*
  f mesures *f pl* magnétiques
  r магнитные измерения *n pl*

M92 *e* **magnetic meridian**
  d magnetischer Meridian *m*
  f méridien *m* magnétique
  r магнитный меридиан *m*

M93 *e* **magnetic mirror**
  d magnetischer Spiegel *m*
  f miroir *m* magnétique
  r магнитное зеркало *n*

M94 *e* **magnetic moment**
  d magnetisches Moment *n*
  f moment *m* magnétique
  r магнитный момент *m*

M95 *e* **magnetic monopole**
  d magnetischer Monopol *m*
  f monopôle *m* magnétique
  r магнитный монополь *m*

M96 *e* **magnetic neutron diffraction
    analysis**
  d magnetische Neutronendiffraktometrie
    f, magnetische
    Neutronenbeugungsuntersuchung *f*,
    magnetische Neutronographie *f*
  f analyse *f* par diffraction neutronique
    magnétique
  r магнитная нейтронография *f*

M97 *e* **magnetic neutron scattering**
  d magnetische Neutronenstreuung *f*
  f diffusion *f* magnétique des neutrons
  r магнитное рассеяние *n* нейтронов

M98 *e* **magnetic nondestructive testing**
  d magnetische Werkstoffprüfung *f*,
    nichtzerstörende Werkstoffprüfung *f*
  f contrôle *m* magnétoscopique non
    destructif
  r магнитная дефектоскопия *f*

M99 *e* **magnetic order**
  d magnetische Ordnung *f*
  f ordre *m* magnétique
  r магнитный порядок *m*

M100 *e* **magnetic ordering**
  d magnetische Ordnung *f*
  f ordonnancement *m* magnétique
  r магнитное упорядочение *n*

M101 *e* **magnetic permeability**
  d Permeabilität *f*
  f perméabilité *f* magnétique
  r магнитная проницаемость *f*

M102 *e* **magnetic phase**
  d magnetische Phase *f*
  f phase *f* magnétique
  r магнитная фаза *f*

M103 *e* **magnetic phase transitions**
  d magnetische Phasenübergänge *m pl*
  f transitions *f pl* de phase magnétiques
  r магнитные фазовые переходы *m pl*

M104 *e* **magnetic polarity**
  d magnetische Polarität *f*
  f polarité *f* magnétique
  r магнитная полярность *f*

M105 *e* **magnetic pole**
  d magnetischer Pol *m*
  f pôle *m* magnétique
  r магнитный полюс *m*

M106 *e* **magnetic potential**
  d magnetisches Potential *n*
  f potentiel *m* magnétique
  r магнитный потенциал *m*

M107 *e* **magnetic powder patterns**
  d Magnetpulverfiguren *f pl*
  f figures *f pl* à poudre magnétique
  r порошковые фигуры *f pl*

M108 *e* **magnetic quadrupole**
  d magnetischer Quadrupol *m*
  f quadripôle *m* magnétique
  r магнитный квадруполь *m*

M109 *e* **magnetic quadrupole moment**
  d magnetisches Quadrupolmoment *n*
  f moment *m* quadripolaire magnétique
  r магнитный квадрупольный
    момент *m*

M110 *e* **magnetic quantum number**
  d magnetische Quantenzahl *f*
  f nombre *m* quantique magnétique
  r магнитное квантовое число *n*

M111 *e* **magnetic radiation**
  d magnetische Strahlung *f*
  f radiation *f* magnétique
  r магнитное излучение *n*

M112   *e*   **magnetic recording**
     d   magnetische Aufzeichnung *f*
     f   enregistrement *m* magnétique
     r   магнитная запись *f*

M113   *e*   **magnetic relaxation**
     d   magnetische Nachwirkung *f*,
        magnetische Relaxation *f*
     f   relaxation *f* magnétique
     r   магнитная релаксация *f*

M114   *e*   **magnetic reluctance**
     d   magnetischer Widerstand *m*,
        Reluktanz *f*
     f   résistance *f* magnétique
     r   магнитное сопротивление *n*

M115   *e*   **magnetic resonance**
     d   magnetische Resonanz *f*
     f   résonance *f* magnétique
     r   магнитный резонанс *m*

M116   *e*   **magnetic rigidity** *see* **magnetic hardness**

M117   *e*   **magnetic rotation**
     d   Magnetorotation *f*, Faraday-Effekt *m*
     f   rotation *f* magnétique, rotation *f*
        magnétique du plan de polarisation
     r   фарадеевское вращение *n*, эффект
        m Фарадея

M118   *e*   **magnetic saturation**
     d   magnetische Sättigung *f*
     f   saturation *f* magnétique
     r   магнитное насыщение *n*

M119   *e*   **magnetic screen**
     d   magnetischer Schirm *m*, magnetische
        Abschirmung *f*
     f   écran *m* magnétique
     r   магнитный экран *m*

M120   *e*   **magnetic screening**
     d   magnetische Abschirmung *f*
     f   blindage *m* magnétique
     r   магнитное экранирование *n*

M121   *e*   **magnetic semiconductors**
     d   magnetische Halbleiter *m pl*
     f   semi-conducteurs *m pl* magnétiques
     r   магнитные полупроводники *m pl*

M122   *e*   **magnetic shielding** *see* **magnetic screening**

M123   *e*   **magnetic spark chamber**
     d   magnetische Funkenkammer *f*
     f   chambre *f* à étincelles magnétique
     r   магнитная искровая камера *f*

M124   *e*   **magnetic spectrometer**
     d   Magnetspektrometer *n*
     f   spectromètre *m* magnétique
     r   магнитный спектрометр *m*

M125   *e*   **magnetic star**
     d   magnetischer Stern *m*
     f   étoile *f* magnétique
     r   магнитная звезда *f*

M126   *e*   **magnetic storm**
     d   magnetischer Sturm *m*,
        erdmagnetischer Sturm *m*
     f   orage *m* magnétique, orage *m*
        géomagnétique
     r   магнитная буря *f*

M127   *e*   **magnetic structure**
     d   magnetische Struktur *f*
     f   structure *f* magnétique
     r   магнитная структура *f*

M128   *e*   **magnetic sublattice**
     d   magnetisches Untergitter *n*
     f   sous-réseau *m* magnétique
     r   магнитная подрешётка *f*

M129   *e*   **magnetic substorm**
     d   Substurm *m*, Baystörung *f*,
        buchtähnliche magnetische Störung *f*
     f   sous-orage *m* magnétique, sous-orage
        m géomagnétique
     r   магнитная суббуря *f*

M130   *e*   **magnetic superconductors**
     d   magnetische Supraleiter *m pl*
     f   supraconducteurs *m pl* magnétiques
     r   магнитные сверхпроводники *m pl*

M131   *e*   **magnetic surface levels**
     d   magnetische Oberflächenniveaus *n pl*
     f   niveaux *m pl* superficiels magnétiques
     r   магнитные поверхностные
        уровни *m pl*

M132   *e*   **magnetic susceptibility**
     d   magnetische Suszeptibilität *f*
     f   susceptibilité *f* magnétique
     r   магнитная восприимчивость *f*

M133   *e*   **magnetic symmetry**
     d   magnetische Symmetrie *f*
     f   symétrie *f* magnétique
     r   магнитная симметрия *f*

M134   *e*   **magnetic texture**
     d   magnetische Textur *f*
     f   texture *f* magnétique
     r   магнитная текстура *f*

M135   *e*   **magnetic trap**
     d   magnetische Falle *f*
     f   piège *m* magnétique
     r   магнитная ловушка *f*

M136   *e*   **magnetic variations**
     d   magnetische Variationen *f pl*
     f   variations *f pl* magnétiques
     r   магнитные вариации *f pl*

M137   *e*   **magnetic variometer**
     d   Magnetvariometer *n*, magnetisches
        Variometer *n*

f variomètre *m* magnétique
r магнитный вариометр *m*

M138 *e* **magnetic viscosity**
d magnetische Viskosität *f*
f viscosité *f* magnétique
r магнитная вязкость *f*

M139 *e* **magnetism**
d Magnetismus *m*
f magnétisme *m*
r магнетизм *m*

M140 *e* **magnetization**
d Magnetisierung *f*
f aimantation *f*
r **1.** намагниченность *f*
2. намагничивание *n*

M141 *e* **magnetization by rotation**
d Barnett-Effekt *m*
f aimantation *f* par rotation, effet *m* Barnett
r эффект *m* Барнетта, намагничивание *n* при вращении

M142 *e* **magnetization curve**
d Magnetisierungskurve *f*
f courbe *f* d'aimantation
r кривая *f* намагничивания

M143 *e* **magnetization reversal**
d Ummagnetisierung *f*
f inversion *f* d'aimantation
r перемагничивание *n*

M144 *e* **magnetization vector**
d Magnetisierungsvektor *m*
f vecteur *m* de l'aimantation
r вектор *m* намагниченности

M145 *e* **magnetized area**
d magnetisiertes Gebiet *n*
f domaine *m* aimanté
r намагниченная область *f*

M146 *e* **magnetized body**
d magnetisierter Körper *m*
f corps *m* aimanté
r намагниченное тело *n*

M147 *e* **magnetized plasma**
d Magnetoplasma *n*, magnetisches Plasma *n*
f plasma *m* magnétisé
r замагниченная плазма *f*

M148 *e* **magnetoacoustic effect**
d magnetoakustischer Effekt *m*
f effet *m* magnéto-acoustique
r магнитоакустический эффект *m*

M149 *e* **magnetoacoustic resonance**
d magnetoakustische Resonanz *f*
f résonance *f* magnéto-acoustique
r магнитоакустический резонанс *m*

M150 *e* **magnetoacoustics**
d Magnetoakustik *f*
f magnéto-acoustique *f*
r магнитоакустика *f*

M151 *e* **magnetoacoustic waves**
d magnetoakustische Wellen *f pl*
f ondes *f pl* magnéto-acoustiques
r магнитозвуковые волны *f pl*

M152 *e* **magneto-bremsstrahlung**
d magnetische Bremsstrahlung *f*, Magnetobremsstrahlung *f*
f rayonnement *m* de freinage magnétique
r магнитотормозное излучение *n*

M153 *e* **magnetocaloric effect**
d magnetokalorischer Effekt *m*
f effet *m* magnétocalorique
r магнитокалорический эффект *m*

M154 *e* **magnetochemistry**
d Magnetochemie *f*
f magnétochimie *f*
r магнитохимия *f*

M155 *e* **magnetodielectric**
d Magnetodielektrikum *n*
f magnétodiélectrique *m*
r магнитодиэлектрик *m*

M156 *e* **magnetoelastic interaction**
d magnetoelastische Wechselwirkung *f*
f interaction *f* magnéto-élastique
r магнитоупругое взаимодействие *n*

M157 *e* **magnetoelastic waves**
d magnetoelastische Wellen *f pl*
f ondes *f pl* magnéto-élastiques
r магнитоупругие волны *f pl*

M158 *e* **magnetoelectric effect**
d magnetoelektrischer Effekt *m*
f effet *m* magnéto-électrique
r магнитоэлектрический эффект *m*

M159 *e* **magnetograph**
d Magnetograph *m*
f magnétographe *m*
r магнитограф *m*

M160 *e* **magnetohydrodynamic generator**
d magnetohydrodynamischer Generator *m*, MHD-Generator *m*
f générateur *m* magnétohydrodynamique, générateur *m* MHD
r магнитогидродинамический генератор *m*, МГД-генератор *m*

M161 *e* **magnetohydrodynamic instability**
d magnetohydrodynamische Instabilität *f*, MHD-Instabilität *f*
f instabilité *f* magnétohydrodynamique
r магнитогидродинамическая

неустойчивость *f*,
МГД-неустойчивость *f*

M162 *e* **magnetohydrodynamic oscillation**
    d magnetohydrodynamische
       Schwingungen *f pl*
    f oscillations *f pl*
       magnétohydrodynamiques
    r магнитогидродинамические
       колебания *n pl*,
       МГД-колебания *n pl*

M163 *e* **magnetohydrodynamics**
    d Magnetohydrodynamik *f*
    f magnétohydrodynamique *f*
    r магнитная гидродинамика *f*

M164 *e* **magnetohydrodynamic waves**
    d magnetohydrodynamische Wellen *f pl*,
       MHD-Wellen *f pl*
    f ondes *f pl* magnétohydrodynamiques
    r магнитогидродинамические волны *f*
       pl, МГД-волны *f pl*

M165 *e* **magnetoionic theory**
    d magnetoionische Theorie *f*
    f théorie *f* magnéto-ionique
    r магнитоионная теория *f*
       (*распространения радиоволн*)

M166 *e* **magnetomechanical effects**
    d magnetomechanische Effekte *m pl*
    f effets *m pl* magnétomécaniques
    r магнитомеханические явления *n pl*

M167 *e* **magnetomechanic ratio**
    d magnetomechanisches Verhältnis *n*
    f rapport *m* magnétomécanique
    r магнитомеханическое отношение *n*

M168 *e* **magnetometer**
    d Magnetometer *n*
    f magnétomètre *m*
    r магнитометр *m*

M169 *e* **magnetomotive force**
    d magnetische Spannung *f*,
       magnetomotorische Kraft *f*
    f force *f* magnétomotrice
    r магнитодвижущая сила *f*,
       намагничивающая сила *f*

M170 *e* **magneton**
    d Magneton *n*
    f magnéton *m*
    r магнетон *m*

M171 *e* **magnetooptical deflector**
    d magnetooptischer Deflektor *m*
    f déflecteur *m* magnéto-optique
    r магнитооптический дефлектор *m*

M172 *e* **magnetooptical Kerr effect**
    d magnetooptischer Kerr-Effekt *m*
    f effet *m* magnéto-optique de Kerr
    r магнитооптический эффект *m*
       Керра

M173 *e* **magnetooptics**
    d Magnetooptik *f*
    f magnéto-optique *f*
    r магнитооптика *f*

M174 *e* **magnetopause**
    d Magnetopause *f*
    f magnétopause *f*
    r магнитопауза *f*

M175 *e* **magnetophonon resonance**
    d Magnetophononenresonanz *f*
    f résonance *f* magnétophononique
    r магнитофононный резонанс *m*

M176 *e* **magnetoplasma**
    d Magnetoplasma *n*
    f plasma *m* magnétique
    r магнитоплазма *f*

M177 *e* **magnetoplasma compressor**
    d Magnetoplasmakompressor *m*
    f compresseur *m* à plasma magnétique
    r магнитоплазменный компрессор *m*

M178 *e* **magnetoresistance**
    d Magnetowiderstand *m*
    f magnétorésistance *f*
    r магнетосопротивление *n*

M179 *e* **magnetoresistor**
    d Feldplatte *f*
    f magnétorésistance *f*
    r магниторезистор *m*

M180 *e* **magnetosheath**
    d magnetische Trennschicht *f*
    f couche *f* intermédiaire magnétique
    r магнитослой *m*, магнитный
       переходный слой *m*
       (*магнитосферы Земли*)

M181 *e* **magnetosonic wave** *see*
      magnetoacoustic wave

M182 *e* **magnetosphere**
    d Magnetosphäre *f*
    f magnétosphère *f*
    r магнитосфера *f*

M183 *e* **magnetospheric convection**
    d magnetosphärische Konvektion *f*
    f convection *f* magnétosphérique
    r магнитосферная конвекция *f*

M184 *e* **magnetospheric disturbances**
    d magnetosphärische Störungen *f pl*
    f perturbations *f pl* magnétosphériques
    r магнитосферные возмущения *n pl*

M185 *e* **magnetospheric tail**
    d Magnetosphärenschweif *m*
    f queue *f* de magnétosphère
    r хвост *m* магнитосферы

M186 *e* **magnetostatic energy**
    d magnetostatische Energie *f*

	f	énergie *f* magnétostatique
	r	магнитостатическая энергия *f*
M187	*e*	**magnetostatics**
	d	Magnetostatik *f*
	f	magnétostatique *f*
	r	магнитостатика *f*
M188	*e*	**magnetostatic waves**
	d	magnetostatische Wellen *f pl*
	f	ondes *f pl* magnétostatiques
	r	магнитостатические волны *f pl*
M189	*e*	**magnetostriction**
	d	Magnetostriktion *f*
	f	magnétostriction *f*
	r	магнитострикция *f*
M190	*e*	**magnetostriction transducer**
	d	Magnetostriktionswandler *m*
	f	transducteur *m* magnétostrictif
	r	магнитострикционный преобразователь *m*
M191	*e*	**magnetothermoelectric power**
	d	magnetothermoelektrische Spannung *f*, Magnetothermo-EMK *f*
	f	puissance *f* magnétothermoélectrique
	r	магнитотермоэдс *f*
M192	*e*	**magnetron**
	d	Magnetron *n*
	f	magnétron *m*
	r	магнетрон *m*
M193	*e*	**magnetron arcing**
	d	Funkenbildung *f* im Magnetron, Magnetronfunkenbildung *f*
	f	formation *f* d'arc au magnétron
	r	искрение *n* в магнетроне
M194	*e*	**magnetron target**
	d	Magnetrontarget *n*
	f	cible *f* à magnétron
	r	магнетронная мишень *f*
M195	*e*	**magnification**
	d	Vergrößerung *f*
	f	pouvoir *m* amplificateur, pouvoir *m* grandissant
	r	увеличение *n*
M196	*e*	**magnified image**
	d	vergrößertes Bild *n*
	f	image *f* amplifiée
	r	увеличенное изображение *n*
M197	*e*	**magnifying glass**
	d	Vergrößerungsglas *n*, Lupe *f*
	f	loupe *f*
	r	лупа *f*
M198	*e*	**magnitude**
	d	1. Betrag *m*, Absolutwert *m* 2. Größe *f* 3. Amplitude *f*, Scheitelwert *m*
	f	1. module *m* 2. magnitude *f* 3. amplitude *f*
	r	1. модуль *m*, абсолютная величина *f* 2. величина *f*, размер *m* 3. амплитуда *f*
M199	*e*	**magnon**
	d	Magnon *n*
	f	magnon *m*
	r	магнон *m* (*квантовый аналог спиновой волны в магнитоупорядоченных средах*)
M200	*e*	**Magnus effect**
	d	Magnus-Effekt *m*
	f	effet *m* Magnus
	r	эффект *m* Магнуса
M201	*e*	**Magnus expansion**
	d	Magnus-Entwicklung *f*
	f	décomposition *f* de Magnus
	r	разложение *n* Магнуса
M202	*e*	main mirror *see* primary mirror
M203	*e*	**main-sequence star**
	d	Hauptreihenstern *m*
	f	étoile *f* de la série principale
	r	звезда *f* главной последовательности
M204	*e*	**Majorana neutrino**
	d	Majorana-Neutrino *n*
	f	neutrino *m* de Majorana
	r	майорановское нейтрино *n*
M205	*e*	**Majorana neutrino mass**
	d	Majorana-Neutrinomasse *f*
	f	masse *f* de Majorana du neutrino
	r	майорановская масса *f* нейтрино
M206	*e*	**Majorana particle**
	d	Majorana-Teilchen *n*
	f	particule *f* de Majorana
	r	майорановская частица *f*
M207	*e*	**majority carrier**
	d	Majoritätsträger *m*, Majoritätsladungsträger *m*
	f	porteur *m* majoritaire
	r	основной носитель *m*, основной носитель *m* заряда
M208	*e*	**major maximum**
	d	Hauptmaximum *n*
	f	maximum *m* principal
	r	главный максимум *m*
M209	*e*	**majoron**
	d	Majoron *n*
	f	majoron *m*
	r	майорон *m* (*гипотетическая частица*)
M210	*e*	**Malus law**
	d	Malusscher Satz *m*, Satz *m* von Malus
	f	loi *f* de Malus
	r	закон *m* Малюса
M211	*e*	**Mandelstam representation**

    d Mandelstam-Darstellung *f*
    f représentation *f* de Mandelstam
    r представление *n* Манделстама

M212 *e* **manganese, Mn**
    d Mangan *n*
    f manganèse *m*
    r марганец *m*

M213 *e* **manifold**
    d Mannigfaltigkeit *f*
    f variété *f*, multiplicité *f*
    r многообразие *n*

M214 *e* **manipulator**
    d Manipulator *m*
    f manipulateur *m*
    r манипулятор *m*

M215 *e* **Manley-Rowe relations**
    d Manley-Rowe-Gleichungen *f pl*
    f relations *f pl* de Manley-Rowe,
       formules *f pl* de Manley-Rowe
    r соотношения *n pl* Мэнли - Роу

M216 *e* **manometer**
    d Manometer *n*, Druckmesser *m*
    f manomètre *m*
    r манометр *m*

M217 *e* **mantle**
    d Mantel *m*
    f manteau *m*
    r мантия *f*

M218 *e* **manual tuning**
    d Handeinstellung *f*, manuelle
       Einstellung *f*
    f accord *m* manuel
    r ручная *f* настройка

M219 *e* **many-body interaction** *see* **many-particle interaction**

M220 *e* **many-body problem**
    d Mehrkörperproblem *n*,
       Vielkörperproblem *n*
    f problème *m* de plusieurs corps
    r задача *f* многих тел

M221 *e* **many-particle interaction**
    d Mehrteilchenwechselwirkung *f*
    f interaction *f* entre plusieurs particules
    r многочастичное взаимодействие *n*

M222 *e* **map, mapping**
    d Abbildung *f*
    f application *f*, transformation *f*;
       représentation *f*
    r отображение *n*

M223 *e* **margin of safety** *see* **safety factor**

M224 *e* **mark**
    d Marke *f*, Markierung *f*
    f marque *f*, repère *m*
    r метка *f*

M225 *e* **Markov chains**
    d Markowsche Ketten *f pl*
    f châines *f pl* de Markov
    r цепи *f pl* Маркова

M226 *e* **Markovian process, Markov process**
    d Markowscher Prozeß *m*
    f processus *m* de Markov, processus *m* markovien
    r марковский процесс *m*

M227 *e* **Mars**
    d Mars *m*
    f Mars *m*
    r Марс *m*

M228 *e* **martensite**
    d Martensit *m*
    f martensite *f*
    r мартенсит *m*

M229 *e* **martensitic transformations**
    d Martensitumwandlungen *f pl*
    f transformations *f pl* martensitiques
    r мартенситные превращения *n pl*

M230 *e* **maser**
    d Maser *m*
    f maser *m*
    r мазер *m*

M231 *e* **maser effect**
    d Masereffekt *m*, interstellarer
       Maserprozeß *m*
    f effet *m* maser (*à l'espace*)
    r мазерный эффект *m* (*в космосе*)

M232 *e* **maser emission**
    d Maserstrahlung *f*
    f émission *f* maser
    r мазерное излучение *n*

M233 *e* **maser radiation** *see* **maser emission**

M234 *e* **mask**
    d Maske *f*
    f cache *m*, masque *m*
    r маска *f*

M235 *e* **mass**
    d Masse *f*
    f masse *f*
    r масса *f*

M236 *e* **mass absorption coefficient**
    d Massenabsorptionskoeffizient *m*
    f coefficient *m* d'absorption de masse
    r массовый коэффициент *m* поглощения

M237 *e* **mass action law** *see* **law of mass action**

M238 *e* **mass analyzer**
    d Massenanalysator *m*
    f analyseur *m* de masse
    r масс-анализатор *m*

M239	*e*	**mass at rest**
	d	Ruhemasse *f*, Ruhmasse *f*
	f	masse *f* au repos
	r	масса *f* покоя

M240	*e*	**mass defect**
	d	Massendefekt *m*, Massenschwund *m*
	f	défaut *m* de masse
	r	дефект *m* массы

M241	*e*	**mass-energy equivalence**
	d	Masse-Energie-Äquivalenz *f*
	f	équivalence *f* masse-énergie
	r	эквивалентность *f* массы и энергии

M242	*e*	**mass force**
	d	Massenkraft *f*; Volumenkraft *f*
	f	force *f* des masses; force *f* volumique
	r	массовая сила *f*; объёмная сила *f*

M243	*e*	**massless quark**
	d	masseloses Quark *n*
	f	quark *m* sans masse
	r	безмассовый кварк *m*

M244	*e*	**mass-luminosity relation**
	d	Masse-Leuchtkraft-Beziehung *f*, Masse-Helligkeits-Beziehung *f*
	f	relation *f* masse-luminosité
	r	зависимость *f* масса - светимость (*зависимость абсолютной светимости звезд от их массы*)

M245	*e*	**mass number**
	d	Massenzahl *f*
	f	nombre *m* de masse
	r	массовое число *n*

M246	*e*	**mass of a particle**
	d	Teilchenmasse *f*
	f	masse *f* d'une particule
	r	масса *f* частицы

M247	*e*	**mass operator**
	d	Massenoperator *m*
	f	opérateur *m* de masse
	r	массовый оператор *m*

M248	*e*	**mass separator**
	d	Massenseparator *m*
	f	séparateur *m* de masses
	r	масс-сепаратор *m*

M249	*e*	**mass spectrograph**
	d	Massenspektrograph *m*
	f	spectrographe *m* de masse
	r	масс-спектрограф *m*

M250	*e*	**mass spectrometer**
	d	Massenspektrometer *n*
	f	spectromètre *m* de masse
	r	масс-спектрометр *m*

M251	*e*	**mass spectrometry**
	d	Massenspektrometrie *f*
	f	spectrométrie *f* de masse
	r	масс-спектрометрия *f*

M252	*e*	**mass spectroscopy**
	d	Massenspektroskopie *f*
	f	spectroscopie *f* de masse
	r	масс-спектроскопия *f*

M253	*e*	**mass spectrum**
	d	Massenspektrum *n*
	f	spectre *m* de masse
	r	масс-спектр *m*

M254	*e*	**mass transfer, mass transport**
	d	Massentransport *m*
	f	transfert *m* de masse
	r	массоперенос *m*, массопередача *f*, перенос *m* массы

M255	*e*	**master oscillator**
	d	Steueroszillator *m*, Steuergenerator *m*
	f	oscillateur *m* pilote
	r	задающий генератор *m*

M256	*e*	**matched filter**
	d	angepaßtes Filter *n*
	f	filtre *m* adapté
	r	согласованный фильтр *m*

M257	*e*	**matched load**
	d	angepaßte Last *f*
	f	charge *f* adaptée
	r	согласованная нагрузка *f*

M258	*e*	**matching diaphragm**
	d	Anpassungsblende *f*
	f	diaphragme *m* d'adaptation
	r	согласующая диафрагма *f*

M259	*e*	**matching factor**
	d	Anpassungsgrad *m*
	f	coefficient *m* d'adaptation
	r	коэффициент *m* согласования

M260	*e*	**material**
	d	Stoff *m*, Material *n*
	f	matériau *m*
	r	материал *m*

M261	*e*	**material dispersion**
	d	Materialdispersion *f*
	f	dispersion *f* du matériau
	r	дисперсия *f* материала; материальная дисперсия *f*

M262	*e*	**material modification by charged particle beams**
	d	Stoffmodifikation *f* durch Strahlen geladener Teilchen
	f	modification *f* des matériaux par les faisceaux des particules chargées
	r	модификация *f* материалов пучками заряженных частиц

M263	*e*	**material particle**
	d	1. Massenpunkt *m* 2. Materieteilchen *n*
	f	1. point *m* matériel 2. particule *f* de matière

r 1. материальная точка *f* 2. частица
f вещества

M264 e **material point**
d Massenpunkt *m*
f point *m* matériel
r материальная точка *f*

M265 e **material world**
d materielle Welt *f*
f monde *m* matériel
r материальный мир *m*

M266 e **mathematical pendulum**
d mathematisches Pendel *n*
f pendule *m* mathématique
r математический маятник *m*

M267 e **mathematical physics**
d mathematische Physik *f*
f physique *f* mathématique
r математическая физика *f*

M268 e **Mathieu equation**
d Mathieusche Gleichung *f*
f équation *f* de Mathieu
r уравнение *n* Матьё

M269 e **Mathieu function**
d Mathieusche Funktion *f*
f fonction *f* de Mathieu
r функция *f* Матьё

M270 e **matrix**
d Matrix *f*
f matrice *f*
r матрица *f*

M271 e **matrix deformation**
d Matrixdeformation *f*
f déformation *f* de matrice
r деформация *f* матрицы

M272 e **matrix element**
d Matrixelement *n*
f élément *m* de matrice
r матричный элемент *m*

M273 e **matrix mechanics**
d Matrizenmechanik *f*
f mécanique *f* matrice
r матричная механика *f*

M274 e **matter**
d Materie *f*; Stoff *m*
f matière *f*
r материя *f*; вещество *n*

M275 e **matter effluence**
d Massenabströmung *f* (*aus dem Stern*)
f écoulement *m* du matériau (*de l'étoile*)
r истечение *n* вещества (*из звезды*)

M276 e **Matthiessen rule**
d Matthießensche Regel *f*

f règle *f* de Matthiessen
r правило *n* Маттисена

M277 e **matt surface**
d matte Oberfläche *f*
f surface *f* mate
r матовая поверхность *f*

M278 e **maximon**
d Maximon *n*
f maximon *m*
r максимон *m* (*гипотетическая частица*)

M279 e **maximum**
d Maximum *n*
f maximum *m*
r максимум *m*

M280 e **maximum likelihood method**
d Maximum-Likelihood-Methode *f*, Methode *f* der maximalen Stichprobenwahrscheinlichkeit
f méthode *f* du maximum de vraisemblance
r метод *m* максимального правдоподобия

M281 e **maximum modulus theorem**
d Maximalmodulprinzip *n*, Satz *m* vom Maximum des Moduls
f principe *m* de maximum de module
r принцип *m* максимума модуля

M282 e **maximum work** (*in thermodynamics*)
d maximale Arbeit *f* (*in der Thermodynamik*)
f travail *m* maximum (*en thermodynamique*)
r максимальная работа *f* (*в термодинамике*)

M283 e **maxwell, Mx**
d Maxwell *n*
f maxwell *m*
r максвелл *m*, Мкс

M284 e **Maxwell-Boltzmann distribution**
d Maxwell-Boltzmann-Verteilung *f*
f distribution *f* de Maxwell-Boltzmann
r распределение *n* Максвелла - Больцмана

M285 e **Maxwell bridge**
d Maxwell-Brücke *f*, Maxwellsche Brücke *f*
f pont *m* de Maxwell
r мост *m* Максвелла

M286 e **Maxwell color triangle**
d Maxwell-Helmholtzsches Farbendreieck *n*, Maxwellsches Dreieck *n*
f triangle *m* de couleurs de Maxwell
r треугольник *m* Максвелла

M287   e   **Maxwell demon**
     d   Maxwellscher Dämon *m*, Dämon *m*
       von Maxwell
     f   démon *m* de Maxwell
     r   демон *m* Максвелла

M288   e   **Maxwell distribution**
     d   Maxwell-Verteilung *f*, Maxwellsche
       Verteilung *f*, Maxwellsche
       Geschwindigkeitsverteilung *f*
     f   distribution *f* de Maxwell
     r   максвелловское распределение *n*

M289   e   **Maxwell equations**
     d   Maxwellsche Gleichungen *f pl*
     f   équations *f pl* de Maxwell
     r   уравнения *n pl* Максвелла

M290   e   **Maxwellian distribution** *see* **Maxwell**
       distribution

M291   e   **Maxwellian stress tensor**
     d   Maxwellscher Spannungstensor *m*
     f   tenseur *m* de contrainte de Maxwell
     r   тензор *m* напряжений Максвелла

M292   e   **Maxwell relations**
     d   Maxwellsche Beziehungen *f pl*
     f   relations *f pl* de Maxwell
     r   соотношения *n pl* Максвелла

M293   e   **Mayer diagrams**
     d   Mayer-Diagramme *n pl*
     f   diagrammes *m pl* de Mayer
     r   диаграммы *f pl* Майера

M294   e   **Mayer equation**
     d   Mayersche Beziehung *f*, Gleichung *f*
       von J. R. Mayer
     f   équation *f* de Mayer
     r   уравнение *n* Майера

M295   e   **mean free path**
     d   mittlere freie Weglänge *f*
     f   libre parcours *m* moyen
     r   средняя длина *f* свободного пробега

M296   e   **mean life, mean lifetime**
     d   mittlere Lebensdauer *f*
     f   vie *f* moyenne
     r   среднее время *n* жизни

M297   e   **mean value** *see* **average value**

M298   e   **measure**
     d   Maß *n*
     f   mesure *f*
     r   мера *f*

M299   e   **measurement**
     d   Messung *f*
     f   mesurage *m*, mesure *f*
     r   измерение *n*

M300   e   **measurement errors**
     d   Meßfehler *m pl*

     f   erreurs *f pl* de mesure
     r   погрешности *f pl* измерения

M301   e   **measurement of atmospheric**
       pressure
     d   Luftdruckmessung *f*, Barometrie *f*
     f   mesure *f* de la pression atmosphérique
     r   измерение *n* атмосферного
       давления

M302   e   **measurement of radiation dose**
     d   Strahlendosismessung *f*
     f   mesure *f* de la dose de radiation
     r   измерение *n* дозы излучения

M303   e   **measure of dispersion**
     d   Streuungsmaß *n*
     f   mesure *f* de dispersion
     r   мера *f* дисперсии

M304   e   **measuring** *see* **measurement**

M305   e   **measuring microscope**
     d   Meßmikroskop *n*; Feinmeßmikroskop *n*
     f   microscope *m* de mesure
     r   измерительный микроскоп *m*

M306   e   **mechanical constraints**
     d   mechanische Bindungen *f pl*
     f   liaisons *f pl* mécaniques
     r   механические связи *f pl*

M307   e   **mechanical deformation**
     d   mechanische Deformation *f*,
       mechanische Verformung *f*
     f   déformation *f* mécanique
     r   механическая деформация *f*

M308   e   **mechanical determinism**
     d   mechanischer Determinismus *m*
     f   déterminisme *m* mécanique
     r   механический детерминизм *m*

M309   e   **mechanical efficiency**
     d   mechanischer Wirkungsgrad *m*
     f   rendement *m* mécanique
     r   механический кпд *m*

M310   e   **mechanical equilibrium**
     d   mechanisches Gleichgewicht *n*
     f   équilibre *m* mécanique
     r   равновесие *n* механической
       системы

M311   e   **mechanical equivalent of heat**
     d   mechanisches Wärmeäquivalent *n*
     f   équivalent *m* mécanique de la chaleur
     r   механический эквивалент *m*
       теплоты

M312   e   **mechanical equivalent of light**
     d   mechanisches Lichtäquivalent *n*
     f   équivalent *m* mécanique de la lumière
     r   механический эквивалент *m* света

M313   e   **mechanical hysteresis**
     d   mechanische Hysterese *f*

    f hystérésis *f* mécanique
    r механический гистерезис *m*

M314 *e* **mechanical inertia**
    d Massenträgheit *f*
    f inertie *f* mécanique
    r механическая инерция *f*

M315 *e* **mechanical motion**
    d mechanische Bewegung *f*
    f mouvement *m* mécanique
    r механическое движение *n*

M316 *e* **mechanical properties**
    d mechanische Eigenschaften *f pl*
    f propriétés *f pl* mécaniques
    r механические свойства *n pl*

M317 *e* **mechanical stress**
    d mechanische Beanspruchung *f*
    f contrainte *f* mécanique
    r механическое напряжение *n*

M318 *e* **mechanical testing**
    d mechanische Prüfung *f*
    f contrôle *m* mécanique
    r механические испытания *n pl*

M319 *e* **mechanical vibration, mechanical**
        vibrations
    d mechanische Schwingungen *f pl*
    f oscillations *f pl* mécaniques
    r механические колебания *n pl*

M320 *e* **mechanics**
    d Mechanik *f*
    f mécanique *f*
    r механика *f*

M321 *e* **mechanics of continua**
    d Kontinuumsmechanik *f*, Mechanik *f*
        der Kontinua
    f mécanique *f* des milieux continus
    r механика *f* сплошных сред

M322 *e* **mechanics of rigid bodies**
    d Festkörpermechanik *f*, Mechanik *f* der
        festen Körper
    f mécanique *f* des solides
    r механика *f* твёрдого тела

M323 *e* **mechanism of heat transfer**
    d Mechanismus *m* der
        Wärmeübertragung
    f mécanisme *m* de transmission de la
        chaleur
    r механизм *m* теплопередачи

M324 *e* **mechanocaloric effect**
    d mechanokalorischer Effekt *m*
    f effet *m* mécanocalorique
    r механокалорический эффект *m*

M325 *e* **mechanostriction**
    d Mechanostriktion *f*
    f mécanostriction *f*
    r механострикция *f*

M326 *e* **median**
    d Mediane *f*
    f médiane *f*
    r медиана *f*

M327 *e* **medical physics**
    d medizinische Physik *f*
    f physique *f* médicale
    r медицинская физика *f*

M328 *e* **medium frequencies**
    d mittlere Frequenzen *f pl*,
        Mittelfrequenzen *f pl*
    f fréquences *f pl* d'ondes moyennes
    r средние частоты *f pl*

M329 *e* **medium waves**
    d Mittelwellen *f pl*
    f ondes *f pl* moyennes
    r средние волны *f pl*

M330 *e* **megacycle per second** *see* **megahertz**

M331 *e* **megaelectron-volt, MeV**
    d Megaelektronvolt *n*
    f méga-électron-volt *m*
    r мегаэлектронвольт *m*, МэВ

M332 *e* **megahertz, MHz**
    d Megahertz *n*
    f mégahertz *m*
    r мегагерц *m*, МГц

M333 *e* **megawatt, MW**
    d Megawatt *n*
    f mégawatt *m*
    r мегаватт *m*, МВт

M334 *e* **Meissner effect**
    d Meißner-Effekt *m*
    f effet *m* Meissner
    r эффект *m* Мейснера

M335 *e* **Mellin transform**
    d Mellin-Transformation *f*, Mellinsche
        Transformation *f*
    f transformation *f* de Mellin
    r преобразование *n* Меллина

M336 *e* **melting**
    d Schmelzen *n*, Schmelzung *f*
    f fusion *f*
    r плавление *n*

M337 *e* **melting curve**
    d Schmelzkurve *f*
    f courbe *f* des points de fusion
    r линия *f* плавления, кривая *f*
        плавления

M338 *e* **melting point**
    d Schmelzpunkt *m*
    f température *f* de fusion, point *m* de
        fusion
    r температура *f* плавления

M339 *e* **membrane**

    d 1. Membran *f* 2. Scheidewand *f*,
       Trennwand *f*
    f membrane *f*
    r 1. мембрана *f* 2. перегородка *f*

M340 *e* **mendelevium, Md**
    d Mendelevium *n*
    f mendélévium *m*
    r менделевий *m*

M341 *e* **meniscus**
    d Meniskus *m*
    f ménisque *m*
    r мениск *m*

M342 *e* **meniscus telescope**
    d Meniskusteleskop *n*
    f télescope *m* à ménisque
    r менисковый телескоп *m*, телескоп
       m Максутова

M343 *e* **mercury, Hg**
    d Quecksilber *n*
    f mercure *m*
    r ртуть *f*

M344 *e* **Mercury**
    d Merkur *m*
    f Mercure *m*
    r Меркурий *m*

M345 *e* **mercury barometer**
    d Quecksilberbarometer *n*
    f baromètre *m* à mercure
    r ртутный барометр *m*

M346 *e* **mercury lamp**
    d Quecksilberdampflampe *f*
    f lampe *f* à vapeur de mercure
    r ртутная лампа *f*

M347 *e* **mercury thermometer**
    d Quecksilberthermometer *n*
    f thermomètre *m* à mercure
    r ртутный термометр *m*

M348 *e* **meridian**
    d Meridian *m*
    f méridien *m*
    r меридиан *m*

M349 *e* **Mermin-Wagner theorem**
    d Mermin-Wagner-Theorem *n*
    f théorème *m* de Mermin-Wagner
    r теорема *f* Мёрмина - Вагнера

M350 *e* **meromorphic function**
    d meromorphe Funktion *f*
    f fonction *f* méromorphique
    r мероморфная функция *f*

M351 *e* **mesa, mesa structure**
    d Mesastruktur *f*
    f structure *f* mesa
    r мезаструктура *f*

M352 *e* **mesic charge**

M352 (cont.)
    d Mesonenladung *f*, mesonische Ladung
       f, mesische Ladung *f*
    f charge *f* mésonique
    r мезонный заряд *m*

M353 *e* **mesoatom**
    d Mesonenatom *n*, mesonisches Atom *n*,
       Mesoatom *n*, mesisches Atom *n*
    f atome *m* mésonique, atome *m* mésique
    r мезоатом *m*

M354 *e* **mesodynamics**
    d Mesodynamik *f*
    f mésodynamique *f*
    r мезодинамика *f*

M355 *e* **mesomolecule**
    d Mesomolekül *n*
    f molécule *f* mésonique, molécule *f*
       mésique
    r мезомолекула *f*

M356 *e* **mesomorphic state**
    d mesomorpher Zustand *m*
    f état *m* mésomorphique
    r мезоморфное состояние *n*

M357 *e* **mesomorphism**
    d Mesomorphie *f*
    f mésomorphie *f*
    r мезоморфизм *m*

M358 *e* **meson**
    d Meson *n*
    f méson *m*
    r мезон *m*

M359 *e* **meson chemistry**
    d Mesonenchemie *f*
    f chimie *f* mésonique
    r мезонная химия *f*

M360 *e* **meson facility**
    d Mesonenfabrik *f*
    f fabrique *f* de mésons
    r мезонная фабрика *f*

M361 *e* **mesonic atom** *see* **mesoatom**

M362 *e* **mesonic dynamics** *see*
      mesodynamics

M363 *e* **mesonic molecule** *see* **mesomolecule**

M364 *e* **mesonium**
    d Mesonium *n*
    f mésonium *m*
    r мезоний *m*

M365 *e* **mesopause**
    d Mesopause *f*
    f mésopause *f*
    r мезопауза *f*

M366 *e* **mesophase**
    d Mesophase *f*

    f mésophase *f*
    r мезофаза *f*

M367 *e* mesoscopics
    d Mesoskopik *f*
    f mésoscopique *f*
    r мезоскопика *f*

M368 *e* mesosphere
    d Mesosphäre *f*
    f mésosphère *f*
    r мезосфера *f*

M369 *e* metacenter
    d Metazentrum *n*
    f métacentre *m*
    r метацентр *m*

M370 *e* metacentric height
    d metazentrische Höhe *f*,
       Metazentrumhöhe *f*
    f hauteur *f* métacentrique
    r метацентрическая высота *f*

M371 *e* metacolor
    d Metafarbe *f*
    f métacouleur *f*
    r метацвет *m (квантовое число)*

M372 *e* metagalactic cosmic rays
    d metagalaktische Höhenstrahlung *f*
    f rayons *pl* cosmiques métagalactiques
    r метагалактические космические
       лучи *pl*

M373 *e* metagalaxy
    d Metagalaxis *f*
    f métagalaxie *f*
    r метагалактика *f*

M374 *e* metal
    d Metall *n*
    f métal *m*
    r металл *m*

M375 *e* metal ceramics
    d Metallkeramik *f*
    f métallocéramique *f*
    r металлокерамика *f*

M376 *e* metal crystal
    d metallischer Kristall *m*
    f cristal *m* métallique
    r металлический кристалл *m*

M377 *e* metal-insulator-semiconductor
       structure
    d MIS-Struktur *f*
    f structure *f* métal-diélectrique-semi-
       conducteur
    r МДП-структура *f*, структура *f*
       металл - диэлектрик -
       полупроводник

M378 *e* metallic bond
    d metallische Bindung *f*

    f liaison *f* métallique
    r металлическая связь *f*

M379 *e* metallic glass
    d metallisches Glas *n*, Glasmetall *n*
    f verre *m* métallique
    r металлическое стекло *n*, метглас *m*

M380 *e* metallic hydrogen
    d metallischer Wasserstoff *m*
    f hydrogène *m* métallique
    r металлический водород *m*

M381 *e* metallic line stars
    d Metalliniensterne *m pl*
    f étoiles *f pl* à raies métalliques
    r металлические звёзды *f pl*

M382 *e* metallic state
    d metallischer Zustand *m*
    f état *m* métallique
    r металлическое состояние *n*

M383 *e* metallization
    d Metallisierung *f*
    f métallisation *f*
    r металлизация *f*

M384 *e* metallography
    d Metallographie *f*
    f métallographie *f*
    r металлография *f*

M385 *e* metalloid
    d Nichtmetall *n*
    f métalloïde *m*
    r неметалл *m*

M386 *e* metallurgical microscope
    d Metallmikroskop *n*
    f microscope *m* métallographique
    r металлографический микроскоп *m*

M387 *e* metal optics
    d Metalloptik *f*
    f métallo-optique *f*
    r металлоптика *f*

M388 *e* metal-oxide-semiconductor structure
    d MOS-Struktur *f*
    f structure *f* métal-oxyde-semi-
       conducteur
    r МОП-структура *f*, структура *f*
       металл - оксид - полупроводник

M389 *e* metal-semiconductor contact
    d Halbleiter-Metall-Kontakt *m*
    f contact *m* métal - semi-conducteur
    r контакт *m* металл - полупроводник

M390 *e* metal vapor laser
    d Metalldampflaser *m*
    f laser *m* à vapeur métallique
    r лазер *m* на парáх металлов

M391 *e* metamagnetism
    d Metamagnetismus *m*

f métamagnétisme *m*
r метамагнетизм *m*

M392　*e* **metamerism**
　　d Metamerie *f*
　　f métamérie *f*
　　r метамерия *f*

M393　*e* **metamorphism**
　　d Metamorphie *f*, Metamorphismus *m*
　　f métamorphisme *m*
　　r метаморфизм *m*

M394　*e* **metastability**
　　d Metastabilität *f*
　　f métastabilité *f*
　　r метастабильность *f*

M395　*e* **metastable luminescence**
　　d metastabile Lumineszenz *f*
　　f luminescence *f* métastable
　　r метастабильная люминесценция *f*

M396　*e* **metastable state**
　　d metastabiler Zustand *m*
　　f état *m* métastable
　　r метастабильное состояние *n*

M397　*e* **meteor**
　　d Meteor *n*
　　f météore *m*
　　r метеор *m*

M398　*e* **meteor communication**
　　d Meteorkommunikation *f*
　　f communication *f* météorique
　　r метеорная радиосвязь *f*

M399　*e* **meteorite**
　　d Meteorit *m*
　　f météorite *f*
　　r метеорит *m*

M400　*e* **meteor shower**
　　d Meteorfall *m*, Sternschnuppenfall *m*
　　f pluie *f* météorique, pluie *f* d'étoiles filantes, averse *f* météorique
　　r метеорный дождь *m*, звёздный дождь *m*

M401　*e* **meter**
　　d 1. Meßgerät *n*, Meßinstrument *n*, Messer *m* 2. Meter *n*
　　f 1. appareil *m* de mesure 2. mètre *m*
　　r 1. измерительный прибор *m*; счётчик *m* 2. метр *m*

M402　*e* **meter waves**
　　d Meterwellen *f pl*
　　f ondes *f pl* métriques
　　r метровые волны *f pl*

M403　*e* **method**
　　d Methode *f*; Verfahren *n*; Technik *f*
　　f méthode *f*
　　r метод *m*, способ *m*

M404　*e* **method of characteristics**
　　d Methode *f* der charakteristischen Kurven
　　f méthode *f* de caractéristiques
　　r метод *m* характеристик

M405　*e* **method of finite differences**
　　d Differenzenverfahren *n*
　　f méthode *f* de différences finies
　　r метод *m* конечных разностей

M406　*e* **method of least squares**
　　d Methode *f* der kleinsten Quadrate, Fehlerquadratmethode *f*
　　f méthode *f* des moindres carrés
　　r метод *m* наименьших квадратов

M407　*e* **method of linear combinations of atomic orbitals**
　　d LCAO-Methode *f*
　　f méthode *f* des combinations linéaires des orbitales atomiques
　　r метод *m* ЛКАО, метод *m* линейных комбинаций атомных орбиталей

M408　*e* **method of molecular replacement**
　　d Molekularaustauschmethode *f*
　　f méthode *f* de remplacement moléculaire
　　r метод *m* молекулярного замещения

M409　*e* **method of sequential approximations** *see* method of successive approximations

M410　*e* **method of small perturbations**
　　d Störungsmethode *f*
　　f méthode *f* perturbationnelle
　　r метод *m* малых возмущений

M411　*e* **method of steepest descent**
　　d Methode *f* des steilsten Abstiegs
　　f méthode *f* de la plus rapide descente
　　r метод *m* наибыстрейшего спуска

M412　*e* **method of successive approximations**
　　d Methode *f* der sukzessiven Approximationen
　　f méthode *f* des approximations successives
　　r метод *m* последовательных приближений

M413　*e* **metric**
　　d Metrik *f*
　　f métrique *f*
　　r метрика *f*

M414　*e* **metrical tensor**
　　d metrischer Tensor *m*, Meßtensor *m*
　　f tenseur *m* métrique
　　r метрический тензор *m*

M415　*e* **metric space**
　　d metrischer Raum *m*

	f	espace *m* métrique
	r	метрическое пространство *n*
M416	e	**metric system of units**
	d	metrisches System *n*, metrisches Einheitensystem *n*
	f	système *m* métrique
	r	метрическая система *f* мер
M417	e	**metric tensor** *see* **metrical tensor**
M418	e	**metrology**
	d	Metrologie *f*
	f	métrologie *f*
	r	метрология *f*
M419	e	**MHD generator**
	d	MHD-Generator *m*, magnetohydrodynamischer Generator *m*
	f	générateur *m* MHD, générateur *m* magnétohydrodynamique
	r	МГД-генератор *m*
M420	e	**MHD oscillation** *see* **magneto-hydrodynamic oscillation**
M421	e	**mica**
	d	Glimmer *m*
	f	mica *m*
	r	слюда *f*
M422	e	**Michelson echelon**
	d	Stufengitter *n*, Michelsonsches Stufengitter *n*, Echelon *n*
	f	réseau *m* échelon, échelon *m* de Michelson
	r	эшелон *m* Майкельсона
M423	e	**Michelson interferometer**
	d	Michelson-Interferometer *n*
	f	interféromètre *m* de Michelson
	r	интерферометр *m* Майкельсона
M424	e	**Michelson-Morley experiment**
	d	Interferenzversuch *m* von Michelson und Morley, Michelson-Morley-Versuch *m*
	f	expérience *f* de Michelson-Morley
	r	опыт *m* Майкельсона - Морли
M425	e	**microanalysis**
	d	Mikroanalyse *f*
	f	micro-analyse *f*
	r	микроанализ *m*
M426	e	**microanalyzer**
	d	Mikroanalysator *m*
	f	micro-analyseur *m*
	r	микроанализатор *m*
M427	e	**microbarograph**
	d	Mikrobarograph *m*
	f	microbarographe *m*
	r	микробарограф *m*
M428	e	**microbend, microbending**

	d	Mikrobiegung *f*
	f	microflexion *f*
	r	микроизгиб *m* (*оптического волокна*)
M429	e	**microcanonical assembly**
	d	mikrokanonische Gesamtheit *f*
	f	ensemble *m* microcanonique
	r	микроканонический ансамбль *m*
M430	e	**microcanonical distribution**
	d	mikrokanonische Verteilung *f*
	f	distribution *f* microcanonique
	r	микроканоническое распределение *n*
M431	e	**microcausality**
	d	Mikrokausalität *f*
	f	microcausalité *f*
	r	микропричинность *f*, локальность *f*
M432	e	**microcosm, microcosmos** *see* **microworld**
M433	e	**microcrack**
	d	Mikroriß *m*
	f	microfissure *f*
	r	микротрещина *f*
M434	e	**microdensitometer**
	d	Mikrodensitometer *n*, Mikroschwärzungsmesser *m*
	f	microdensitomètre *m*
	r	микроденситометр *m*
M435	e	**microdiffraction**
	d	Mikrodiffraktion *f*
	f	microdiffraction *f*
	r	микродифракция *f*
M436	e	**microdosimetry**
	d	Mikrodosimetrie *f*
	f	microdosimétrie *f*
	r	микродозиметрия *f*
M437	e	**microelectronics**
	d	Mikroelektronik *f*
	f	micro-électronique *f*
	r	микроэлектроника *f*
M438	e	**microexplosion**
	d	Mikroexplosion *f*
	f	micro-explosion *f*
	r	микровзрыв *m*
M439	e	**microfield**
	d	Mikrofeld *n*
	f	microchamp *m*
	r	микрополе *n*
M440	e	**microhardness**
	d	Mikrohärte *f*
	f	microdureté *f*
	r	микротвёрдость *f*
M441	e	**microhardness test**
	d	Mikrohärteprüfung *f*

    f essai *m* de microdureté
    r испытание *n* на микротвёрдость

M442 *e* **microinclusion**
    d Mikroinklusion *f*
    f micro-inclusion *f*
    r микровключение *n*

M443 *e* **microinhomogeneity**
    d Mikroinhomogenität *f*
    f micro-inhomogénéité *f*
    r микронеоднородность *f*

M444 *e* **microinstability**
    d Mikroinstabilität *f*
    f micro-instabilité *f*
    r микронеустойчивость *f (плазмы)*

M445 *e* **microlens**
    d Mikroobjektiv *n*; Mikrolinse *f*
    f micro-objectif *m*
    r микрообъектив *m*; микролинза *f*

M446 *e* **microlithography**
    d Mikrolithographie *f*
    f microlithographie *f*
    r микролитография *f*

M447 *e* **micromagnetism**
    d Mikromagnetismus *m*
    f micromagnétisme *m*
    r микромагнетизм *m*

M448 *e* **micrometer**
    d Mikrometer *n*
    f micromètre *m*
    r 1. микрóметр *m (инструмент для точных измерений)* 2. микрóметр *m, уст.* микрон *m (единица измерения)*

M449 *e* **micrometer microscope**
    d Meßmikroskop *n*
    f microscope *m* de mesure
    r измерительный микроскоп *m*

M450 *e* **micron**
    d Mikron *n*, Mikrometer *n*
    f micron *m*, micromètre *m*
    r микрон *m*, микрóметр *m*

M451 *e* **microparticle**
    d Mikroteilchen *n*
    f microparticule *f*
    r микрочастица *f*

M452 *e* **microparticle magnetism**
    d Mikroteilchenmagnetismus *m*
    f magnétisme *m* des microparticules
    r магнетизм *m* микрочастиц

M453 *e* **microphone**
    d Mikrophon *n*
    f microphone *m*
    r микрофон *m*

M454 *e* **microphotography**

    d Mikrophotographie *f*
    f microphotographie *f*
    r микрофотография *f*

M455 *e* **microphotometer**
    d Mikrophotometer *n*
    f microphotomètre *m*
    r микрофотометр *m*

M456 *e* **micropinch**
    d Mikropinch *m*
    f micropincement *m*
    r микропинч *m*

M457 *e* **microplasma**
    d Mikroplasma *n*
    f microplasma *m*
    r микроплазма *f*

M458 *e* **microprobe**
    d Mikrosonde *f*
    f microsonde *f*
    r микрозонд *m*

M459 *e* **microprocessor**
    d Mikroprozessor *m*
    f microprocesseur *m*
    r микропроцессор *m*

M460 *e* **microprojection**
    d Mikroprojektion *f*
    f microprojection *f*
    r микропроекция *f*

M461 *e* **micropulsation**
    d Mikropulsation *f*
    f micropulsation *f*
    r микропульсации *f pl*

M462 *e* **microrelief**
    d Mikrorelief *n*
    f microrelief *m*
    r микрорельеф *m (поверхности)*

M463 *e* **microscope**
    d Mikroskop *n*
    f microscope *m*
    r микроскоп *m*

M464 *e* **microscopy**
    d Mikroskopie *f*
    f microscopie *f*
    r микроскопия *f*

M465 *e* **microseism**
    d seismische Unruhe *f*, Mikrobeben *n*, mikroseismische Erschütterungen *f pl*
    f microséisme *m*
    r микросейсм *m*

M466 *e* **microspectrophotometer**
    d Mikrospektrophotometer *n*
    f microspectrophotomètre *m*
    r микроспектрофотометр *m*

M467 *e* **microstress**
    d Mikrospannung *f*

f microtension *f*
r микронапряжение *n*

M468 *e* **microstructure**
    d Mikrostruktur *f*
    f microstructure *f*
    r микроструктура *f*

M469 *e* **microtarget**
    d Mikrotarget *n*
    f microcible *f*
    r микромишень *f*

M470 *e* **microtron**
    d Mikrotron *n*
    f microtron *m*
    r микротрон *m*

M471 *e* **microturbulence**
    d Mikroturbulenz *f*
    f turbulence *f* microscopique
    r микротурбулентность *f*

M472 *e* **microviscosity**
    d Mikroviskosität *f*
    f microviscosité *f*
    r микровязкость *f*

M473 *e* **microwave background radiation**
    d Mikrowellen-Untergrundstrahlung *f*
    f radiation *f* ambiante de micro-ondes
    r микроволновое фоновое излучение *n*

M474 *e* **microwave diagnostics**
    d Mikrowellendiagnostik *f*
    f diagnostic *m* à hyperfréquence, diagnostic *m* à micro-ondes
    r СВЧ-диагностика *f*, микроволновая диагностика *f*

M475 *e* **microwave discharge**
    d Mikrowellenentladung *f*
    f décharge *f* en micro-ondes
    r сверхвысокочастотный разряд *m*, СВЧ-разряд *m*

M476 *e* **microwave electronics**
    d Mikrowellenelektronik *f*
    f électronique *f* de micro-ondes, électronique *f* d'hyperfréquence
    r микроволновая электроника *f*, электроника *f* СВЧ

M477 *e* **microwave frequencies**
    d Mikrowellenfrequenz *f*, Höchstfrequenzen *f pl*
    f ultra-hautes fréquences *f pl*
    r сверхвысокие частоты *f pl*, СВЧ

M478 *e* **microwave measurements**
    d Mikrowellenmessungen *f pl*
    f mesures *f pl* d'hyperfréquence
    r сверхвысокочастотные измерения *n pl*

M479 *e* **microwave oscillation**

d Höchstfrequenzschwingungen *f pl*
f oscillations *f pl* à hyperfréquence
r СВЧ-колебания *n pl*

M480 *e* **microwave pulse**
    d Höchstfrequenzimpuls *m*
    f impulsion *f* à hyperfréquence
    r СВЧ-импульс *m*

M481 *e* **microwave radiation**
    d Mikrowellenstrahlung *f*
    f radiation *f* à hyperfréquence
    r микроволновое излучение *n*, СВЧ-излучение *n*

M482 *e* **microwave range**
    d Höchstfrequenzbereich *m*
    f gamme *f* à hyperfréquence
    r микроволновый диапазон *m*, диапазон *m* сверхвысоких частот, диапазон *m* СВЧ

M483 *e* **microwaves**
    d Mikrowellen *f pl*, Höchstfrequenzwellen *f pl*
    f micro-ondes *f pl*
    r микроволны *f pl*

M484 *e* **microwave spectroscopy**
    d Mikrowellenspektroskopie *f*
    f spectroscopie *f* en micro-ondes
    r микроволновая спектроскопия *f*

M485 *e* **microworld**
    d Mikrowelt *f*
    f microcosmos *m*, micro-univers *m*
    r микромир *m*

M486 *e* **mictomagnetism**
    d Miktomagnetismus *m*
    f mictomagnétisme *m*
    r миктомагнетизм *m*

M487 *e* **Mie theory**
    d Miesche Theorie *f*, Miesche Theorie *f* der Streustrahlung, Miesche Beugungstheorie *f*
    f théorie *f* de Mie
    r теория *f* Ми

M488 *e* **migration**
    d Wanderung *f*, Migration *f*
    f migration *f*
    r миграция *f*; перенос *m*

M489 *e* **Milky way**
    d Milchstraße *f*
    f Voie *f* lactée
    r Млечный путь *m*

M490 *e* **Miller indices**
    d Millersche Indizes *m pl*, Miller-Indizes *m pl*
    f indices *m pl* de Miller
    r миллеровские индексы *m pl*

M491 *e* **Millikan experiment, Millikan oil-drop experiment**

    d Millikan-Versuch *m*, Millikanscher
       Öltröpfchenversuch *m*
    f expérience *f* de Millikan
    r опыт *m* Милликена

M492 *e* **millimeter, mm**
    d Millimeter *n*
    f millimètre *m*, mm
    r миллиметр *m*, мм

M493 *e* **millimeter of mercury**
    d Millimeter *n* Quecksilbersäule
    f millimètre *m* de mercure
    r миллиметр *m* ртутного столба

M494 *e* **millimeter of water column**
    d Millimeter *n* Wassersäule
    f millimètre *m* de colonne d'eau,
       millimètre *m* d'eau
    r миллиметр *m* водяного столба

M495 *e* **millimeter waves**
    d Millimeterwellen *f pl*
    f ondes *f pl* millimétriques
    r миллиметровые волны *f pl*

M496 *e* **Mills cross**
    d Mills-Kreuz *n*, Mills-Kreuzantenne *f*
    f croix *f* de Mills
    r крест *m* Миллса

M497 *e* **minimum**
    d Minimum *n*
    f minimum *m*
    r минимум *m*

M498 *e* **minitron**
    d Minitron *n*
    f minitron *m*
    r минитрон *m*

M499 *e* **Minkowski space-time**
    d Minkowskisches Raum-Zeit-
       Kontinuum *n*
    f espace-temps *m* de Minkowski
    r пространство-время *n* Минковского

M500 *e* **minority carrier injection**
    d Minoritätsträgerinjektion *f*
    f injection *f* de porteurs minoritaires
    r инжекция *f* неосновных носителей

M501 *e* **minority carriers**
    d Minoritätsträger *m pl*,
       Minoritätsladungsträger *m pl*
    f porteurs *m pl* minoritaires
    r неосновные носители *m pl*,
       неосновные носители *m pl* заряда

M502 *e* **minor planet**
    d Planetoid *n*, Asteroid *n*,
       Kleinplanet *m*
    f petite planète *f*, astéroïde *m*
    r малая планета *f*, астероид *m*

M503 *e* **minute**
    d Minute *f*

    f minute *f*
    r минута *f*

M504 *e* **mirage**
    d Luftspiegelung *f*
    f mirage *m*
    r мираж *m*

M505 *e* **mirror**
    d Spiegel *m*
    f miroir *m*
    r зеркало *n*

M506 *e* **mirror aerial** *see* **reflector aerial**

M507 *e* **mirror image**
    d Spiegelbild *n*
    f image *f* reflétée
    r зеркальное изображение *n*

M508 *e* **mirror isobar**
    d Spiegelisobar *n*
    f isobare *f* reflétée
    r зеркальный изобар *m*

M509 *e* **mirror isomer**
    d Spiegelisomer *n*
    f isomère *m* reflété
    r зеркальный изомер *m*

M510 *e* **mirror loss, mirror losses**
    d Spiegelverluste *m pl*
    f pertes *f pl* au miroir
    r потери *f pl* на зеркале *(лазера)*,
       потери *f pl* на отражение

M511 *e* **mirror nuclei**
    d Spiegelkerne *m pl*
    f noyaux *m pl* miroirs
    r зеркальные ядра *n pl*

M512 *e* **mirror plane**
    d Spiegelebene *f*
    f plan *m* réflecteur
    r зеркальная плоскость *f* симметрии

M513 *e* **mirror reflexion**
    d Spiegelung *f*
    f réflexion *f* spéculaire
    r зеркальное отражение *n*

M514 *e* **mirror symmetry**
    d Spiegelsymmetrie *f*
    f symétrie *f* par réflexion
    r зеркальная симметрия *f*

M515 *e* **mirror trap**
    d Spiegelfalle *f*
    f piège *m* à miroir
    r зеркальная магнитная ловушка *f*

M516 *e* **mitron**
    d Mitron *n*
    f mitron *m*
    r митрон *m*

M517 *e* **mixed dislocation**

    d gemischte Versetzung *f*
    f dislocation *f* mixte
    r смешанная дислокация *f*

M518 *e* **mixed state**
    d gemischter Zustand *m*
    f état *m* mixte
    r смешанное состояние *n*

M519 *e* **mixer**
    d Mischer *m*, Mischapparat *m*
    f mélangeur *m*
    r смеситель *m*

M520 *e* **mixing**
    d Mischen *n*, Mischung *f*; Vermischen *n*
    f mélange *m*
    r смешение *n*; смешивание *n*,
       перемешивание *n*

M521 *e* **mixing chamber**
    d Mischkammer *f*
    f chambre *f* de mélange
    r смесительная камера *f*
       (*химического лазера*)

M522 *e* **mixing length**
    d Mischungsweg *m*, Mischungslänge *f*
    f longueur *f* de mélange
    r длина *f* перемешивания

M523 *e* **MKSA system of units**
    d MKSA-System *n*
    f système *m* MKSA
    r система *f* единиц МКСА

M524 *e* **mobility**
    d Beweglichkeit *f*
    f mobilité *f*
    r подвижность *f*

M525 *e* **modal dispersion**
    d Modendispersion *f*
    f dispersion *f* de mode
    r модовая дисперсия *f*

M526 *e* **mode**
    d 1. Mode *f*, Schwingungsmodus *m*
       2. Betriebsart *f*
    f mode *m*
    r 1. мода *f*, вид *m* колебаний
       2. режим *m*

M527 *e* **mode competition**
    d Modenkonkurrenz *f*
    f compétition *f* de mode
    r конкуренция *f* мод, конкуренция *f*
       колебаний

M528 *e* **mode conversion**
    d Modenumwandlung *f*,
       Modenkonversion *f*
    f conversion *f* des modes
    r преобразование *n* мод

M529 *e* **mode converter**
    d Modenumwandler *m*,
       Modenkonverter *m*

    f convertisseur *m* des modes
    r преобразователь *m* мод

M530 *e* **model**
    d Modell *n*
    f modèle *m*
    r модель *f*

M531 *e* **modeling**
    d Simulation *f*
    f simulation *f*
    r моделирование *n*

M532 *e* **mode-locked laser**
    d modengekoppelter Laser *m*
    f laser *m* à verrouillage des modes
    r лазер *m* с синхронизацией мод

M533 *e* **mode locking**
    d Modenkopplung *f*, Mode-Locking *n*,
       Modensynchronisation *f*
    f verrouillage *m* des modes
    r синхронизация *f* мод

M534 *e* **mode mixing**
    d Modenmischung *f*
    f mélange *m* des modes
    r смешение *n* мод

M535 *e* **moderated neutrons**
    d abgebremste Neutronen *n pl*,
       Bremsneutronen *n pl*
    f neutrons *m pl* modérés
    r замедленные нейтроны *m pl*

M536 *e* **moderation of neutrons**
    d Neutronenbremsung *f*
    f modération *f* des neutrons,
       ralentissement *m* des neutrons
    r замедление *n* нейтронов

M537 *e* **moderator**
    d Moderator *m*, Bremsmittel *n*,
       Bremsstoff *m*
    f modérateur *m*
    r замедлитель *m*

M538 *e* **moderator method**
    d Moderator-Methode *f*
    f méthode *f* de modérateur
    r метод *m* замедлителя

M539 *e* **mode selection**
    d Modenselektion *f*, Modenauswahl *f*
    f sélection *f* des modes
    r селекция *f* мод

M540 *e* **mode structure**
    d Modenstruktur *f*
    f structure *f* de modes
    r модовая структура *f*

M541 *e* **mode suppression**
    d Modenunterdrückung *f*
    f suppression *f* de modes
    r подавление *n* мод

M542   e   modification
      d   Modifikation *f*, Modifizierung *f*
      f   modification *f*
      r   модификация *f*

M543   e   modulated oscillation
      d   modulierte Schwingungen *f pl*
      f   oscillations *f pl* modulées
      r   модулированные колебания *n pl*

M544   e   modulated radiation
      d   modulierte Strahlung *f*
      f   radiation *f* modulée
      r   модулированное излучение *n*

M545   e   modulated voltage
      d   modulierte Spannung *f*
      f   tension *f* modulée
      r   модулированное напряжение *n*

M546   e   modulation
      d   Modulation *f*
      f   modulation *f*
      r   модуляция *f*

M547   e   modulation depth *see* depth of modulation

M548   e   modulation factor *see* modulation index

M549   e   modulation index
      d   Modulationsgrad *m*
      f   indice *m* de modulation
      r   коэффициент *m* модуляции

M550   e   modulation instability
      d   Modulationinstabilität *f*
      f   instabilité *f* de modulation
      r   модуляционная неустойчивость *f*

M551   e   modulator
      d   Modulator *m*
      f   modulateur *m*
      r   модулятор *m*

M552   e   module
      d   Modul *m*; Modulbaustein *m*, Modulbauelement *n*
      f   module *m*
      r   модуль *m*; блок *m*; узел *m*

M553   e   modulus
      d   Modul *m*
      f   module *m*
      r   модуль *m*

M554   e   modulus of dilatation
      d   Kompressionsmodul *m*
      f   module *m* d'élasticité volumique
      r   модуль *m* всестороннего сжатия, модуль *m* объёмного сжатия

M555   e   modulus of elasticity
      d   Elastizitätsmodul *m*, E-Modul *m*
      f   module *m* d'élasticité
      r   модуль *m* упругости

M556   e   modulus of elongation
      d   linearer Elastizitätsmodul *m*, Youngscher Modul *m*
      f   module *m* d'élasticité, module *m* d'Young
      r   модуль *m* продольной упругости, модуль *m* Юнга

M557   e   modulus of rigidity
      d   Schubmodul *m*, Scherungsmodul *m*
      f   module *m* de cisaillement
      r   модуль *m* сдвига

M558   e   moiré
      d   Moiré *f*
      f   moirage *m*, moirure *f*
      r   муар *m*

M559   e   moiré fringes
      d   Moiréeffekt *m*, Moiréstreifen *m pl*, Moirémuster *n*, Moiréinterferenzmuster *n*
      f   franges *f pl* moirées
      r   муаровые узоры *m pl*, муаровые интерференционные полосы *f pl*

M560   e   moiré pattern
      d   Moiréeffekt *m*, Moirémuster *n*
      f   image *f* moirée
      r   муаровая картина *f*; муаровые узоры *m pl*

M561   e   moisture
      d   Feuchte *f*, Feuchtigkeit *f*
      f   humidité *f*
      r   влага *f*; влажность *f*

M562   e   mol *see* mole

M563   e   molality
      d   Molalität *f*
      f   molalité *f*
      r   моляльность *f*

M564   e   molarity
      d   Molarität *f*, molare Konzentration *f*, Stoffmengenkonzentration *f*
      f   molarité *f*
      r   мольность *f*, молярность *f*

M565   e   MO LCAO approximation
      d   LCAO-MO-Näherung *f*
      f   approximation *f* MO LCAO
      r   метод *m* МО ЛКАО (*приближение молекулярных орбиталей в форме линейной комбинации атомных орбиталей*)

M566   e   MO LCAO method *see* MO LCAO approximation

M567   e   mole
      d   Mol *n*
      f   mole *f*
      r   моль *m*

M568   e   molecular acoustics

d Molekularakustik *f*
f acoustique *f* moléculaire
r молекулярная акустика *f*

M569 e **molecular beam**
d Molekularstrahl *m*,
Molekularstrahlenbündel *n*
f faisceau *m* moléculaire
r молекулярный пучок *m*

M570 e **molecular-beam epitaxy**
d Molekularstrahlepitaxie *f*
f épitaxie *f* à faisceau moléculaire
r молекулярная эпитаксия *f*,
молекулярно-пучковая эпитаксия *f*

M571 e **molecular-beam source**
d Molekularstrahlquelle *f*
f source *f* de faisceau moléculaire
r источник *m* молекулярного пучка

M572 e **molecular collisions**
d Zusammenstöße *m pl* der Moleküle
f collisions *f pl* des molécules
r столкновения молекул *n pl*

M573 e **molecular concentration**
d molekulare Konzentration *f*,
Molekularkonzentration *f*
f concentration *f* moléculaire
r концентрация *f* молекул

M574 e **molecular configuration**
d Molekülkonfiguration *f*
f configuration *f* des molécules;
configuration *f* de molécule
r конфигурация *f* молекул;
конфигурация *f* молекулы

M575 e **molecular conformation**
d Molekülkonformation *f*
f conformation *f* des molécules
r конформация *f* молекул

M576 e **molecular crystal**
d Molekülkristall *m*, molekularer
Kristall *m*
f cristal *m* moléculaire
r молекулярный кристалл *m*

M577 e **molecular diffusion**
d Molekulardiffusion *f*
f diffusion *f* moléculaire
r молекулярная диффузия *f*

M578 e **molecular dissociation**
d Moleküldissoziation *f*, molekulare
Dissoziation *f*
f dissociation *f* des molécules;
dissociation *f* de molécule
r диссоциация *f* молекул;
диссоциация *f* молекулы

M579 e **molecular dynamics**
d Molekulardynamik *f*
f dynamique *f* moléculaire
r молекулярная динамика *f*

M580 e **molecular energy levels**
d molekulare Energieniveaus *n pl*
f niveaux *m pl* énergétiques
moléculaires
r энергетические уровни *m pl*
молекулы, уровни *m pl* энергии
молекулы

M581 e **molecular exciton**
d Molekularexciton *n*
f exciton *m* moléculaire
r молекулярный экситон *m*

M582 e **molecular field**
d Molekularfeld *n*
f champ *m* moléculaire
r молекулярное поле *n*

M583 e **molecular flow**
d Molekularströmung *f*, molekulare
Strömung *f*
f écoulement *m* moléculaire
r молекулярное течение *n*

M584 e **molecular integral**
d Molekularintegral *n*
f intégrale *f* moléculaire
r молекулярный интеграл *m*

M585 e **molecular ion**
d Molekülion *n*
f ion *m* moléculaire
r молекулярный ион *m*

M586 e **molecular isomerism**
d molekulare Isomerie *f*
f isomérie *f* moléculaire
r изомерия *f* молекул

M587 e **molecular laser**
d Molekularlaser *m*
f laser *m* moléculaire
r молекулярный лазер *m*

M588 e **molecular maser**
d Molekularmaser *m*
f maser *m* moléculaire
r молекулярный мазер *m*,
молекулярный генератор *m*

M589 e **molecular mass**
d Molekülmasse *f*
f masse *f* moléculaire
r молекулярная масса *f*

M590 e **molecular motion**
d Molekularbewegung *f*
f agitation *f* moléculaire
r движение *n* молекул

M591 e **molecular orbital**
d Molekülorbital *n*, molekulares
Orbital *n*
f orbitale *f* moléculaire
r молекулярная орбиталь *f*

M592　e　molecular orbital approximation
　　　d　Molekülorbitalnäherung f
　　　f　méthode f des orbitales moléculaires
　　　r　метод m молекулярных орбиталей

M593　e　molecular physics
　　　d　Molekularphysik f, Molekülphysik f
　　　f　physique f moléculaire
　　　r　молекулярная физика f

M594　e　molecular polarizability
　　　d　molekulare Polarisierbarkeit f,
　　　　　Molekularpolarisation f
　　　f　polarisabilité f moléculaire
　　　r　поляризуемость f молекул

M595　e　molecular pump
　　　d　Molekularpumpe f,
　　　　　molekularkinetische Vakuumpumpe f
　　　f　pompe f moléculaire
　　　r　молекулярный насос m

M596　e　molecular refraction
　　　d　Molekularrefraktion f, Molrefraktion f
　　　f　réfraction f moléculaire
　　　r　молекулярная рефракция f

M597　e　molecular replacement
　　　d　Molekularaustausch m,
　　　　　Molekularsubstitution f
　　　f　substitution f moléculaire,
　　　　　remplacement m moléculaire
　　　r　молекулярное замещение n

M598　e　molecular rotation
　　　d　Molekülrotation f
　　　f　rotation f moléculaire
　　　r　молекулярное вращение n

M599　e　molecular spectroscopy
　　　d　Molekülspektroskopie f
　　　f　spectroscopie f moléculaire
　　　r　спектроскопия f молекул,
　　　　　молекулярная спектроскопия f

M600　e　molecular spectrum
　　　d　Molekülspektrum n
　　　f　spectre m moléculaire
　　　r　молекулярный спектр m

M601　e　molecular structure
　　　d　molekulare Struktur f,
　　　　　Molekularstruktur f
　　　f　structure f moléculaire; structure f de
　　　　　molécule
　　　r　структура f молекул; структура f
　　　　　молекулы

M602　e　molecular substitution see molecular
　　　　　replacement

M603　e　molecular symmetry
　　　d　Molekülsymmetrie f
　　　f　symétrie f des molécules
　　　r　симметрия f молекул

M604　e　molecular vibration, molecular
　　　　　vibrations
　　　d　Molekülschwingungen f pl
　　　f　vibration f moléculaire, vibration f des
　　　　　molécules
　　　r　колебания n pl молекул,
　　　　　молекулярные колебания n pl

M605　e　molecule
　　　d　Molekül n
　　　f　molécule f
　　　r　молекула f

M606　e　Møller scattering
　　　d　Møller-Streuung f, Elektron-Elektron-
　　　　　Streuung f
　　　f　diffusion f de Møller
　　　r　мёллеровское рассеяние n

M607　e　molybdenum, Mo
　　　d　Molybdän n
　　　f　molybdène m
　　　r　молибден m

M608　e　moment
　　　d　Moment n
　　　f　moment m
　　　r　момент m

M609　e　moment of couple
　　　d　Moment n des Kräftepaares
　　　f　moment m d'un couple
　　　r　момент m пары

M610　e　moment of force
　　　d　Kraftmoment n
　　　f　moment m de force
　　　r　момент m силы

M611　e　moment of inertia
　　　d　Trägheitsmoment n
　　　f　moment m d'inertie
　　　r　момент m инерции

M612　e　moment of momentum
　　　d　Impulsmoment n, Drehimpuls m
　　　f　moment m angulaire, moment m
　　　　　cinétique
　　　r　момент m импульса, момент m
　　　　　количества движения,
　　　　　кинетический момент m

M613　e　momentum
　　　d　Impuls m, Bewegungsgröße f
　　　f　impulsion f, quantité f de mouvement
　　　r　импульс m, количество n движения

M614　e　momentum component
　　　d　Impulskomponente f
　　　f　composante f d'une impulsion
　　　r　компонента f импульса

M615　e　momentum conservation
　　　d　Impulserhaltung f
　　　f　conservation f de l'impulsion,
　　　　　conservation f de la quantité de
　　　　　mouvement
　　　r　сохранение n импульса, сохранение
　　　　　n количества движения

M616 *e* **momentum flux**
    d Impulsfluß *m*
    f flux *m* de la quantité de mouvement
    r поток *m* импульса, поток *m* количества импульса

M617 *e* **momentum quantization**
    d Impulsquantisierung *f*, Impulsquantelung *f*
    f quantification *f* d'une impulsion
    r квантование *n* импульса

M618 *e* **momentum space**
    d Impulsraum *m*
    f espace *m* des impulsions
    r пространство *n* импульсов

M619 *e* **momentum transfer**
    d Impulstransport *m*, Impulsübertragung *f*
    f transfert *m* de la quantité de mouvement
    r передача *f* импульса

M620 *e* **monitoring**
    d 1. Monitoring *m*, Überwachung *f* 2. Strahlenüberwachung *f*
    f 1. monitoring *m*, surveillance *f* 2. surveillance *f*, surveillance *f* des rayonnements
    r 1. мониторинг *m* 2. радиационный контроль *m*; дозиметрический контроль *m*

M621 *e* **monochromaticity**
    d Monochromasie *f*
    f monochromatisme *m*
    r монохроматичность *f*

M622 *e* **monochromatic light**
    d monochromatisches Licht *n*
    f lumière *f* monochromatique
    r монохроматический свет *m*

M623 *e* **monochromatic radiation**
    d monochromatische Strahlung *f*
    f radiation *f* monochromatique
    r монохроматическое излучение *n*

M624 *e* **monochromatic source**
    d monochromatische Lichtquelle *f*
    f source *f* d'émission monochromatique
    r монохроматический источник *m*

M625 *e* **monochromatic waves**
    d monochromatische Wellen *f pl*
    f ondes *f pl* monochromatiques
    r монохроматические волны *f pl*

M626 *e* **monochromator**
    d Monochromator *m*
    f monochromateur *m*
    r монохроматор *m*

M627 *e* **monoclinic system**

M628 *e* **mono crystal**
    d monoklines System *n*
    f système *m* monoclinique
    r моноклинная сингония *f*, моноклинная система *f*

M628 *e* **mono crystal**
    d Einkristall *m*
    f monocristal *m*
    r монокристалл *m*

M629 *e* **monolayer**
    d Monoschicht *f*; monomolekulare Schicht *f*
    f monocouche *f*
    r монослой *m* (*напр. молекул на поверхности*)

M630 *e* **monomode fiber**
    d Einmodenfaser *f*, Monomode-Faser *f*
    f fibre *f* monomode
    r одномодовое волокно *n*

M631 *e* **monomolecular layer** *see* **monolayer**

M632 *e* **monopole**
    d Monopol *m*
    f monopôle *m*
    r монополь *m*

M633 *e* **monostable multivibrator** *see* **single-shot multivibrator**

M634 *e* **monotonic function**
    d monotone Funktion *f*
    f fonction *f* monotone
    r монотонная функция *f*

M635 *e* **Monte Carlo method**
    d Monte-Carlo-Methode *f*
    f méthode *f* de Monte-Carlo
    r метод *m* Монте-Карло, метод *m* статистических испытаний

M636 *e* **Monte Carlo study**
    d Monte-Carlo-Methode *f*, Anwendung *f* der Monte-Carlo-Methode
    f technique *f* de Monte-Carlo
    r исследование *n* методом Монте-Карло, исследование *n* методом статистических испытаний

M637 *e* **month**
    d Monat *m*
    f mois *m*
    r месяц *m*

M638 *e* **Moon**
    d Mond *m*
    f Lune *f*
    r Луна *f*

M639 *e* **Morin point**
    d Morin-Punkt *m*
    f point *m* de Morin
    r точка *f* Морина

M640 *e* **Morin transition**

     d Morin-Übergang *m*
     f transition *f* de Morin
     r переход *m* Морина

M641 *e* **morphology**
     d Morphologie *f*
     f morphologie *f*
     r морфология *f*

M642 *e* **mosaic crystal**
     d Mosaikkristall *m*
     f cristal *m* mosaïque
     r мозаичный кристалл *m*

M643 *e* **mosaic structure**
     d Mosaikstruktur *f*, Mosaiktextur *f* (*Kristall*)
     f structure *f* mosaïque (*des cristaux*)
     r мозаичность *f* (*кристаллов*)

M644 *e* **Moseley law**
     d Moseleysches Gesetz *n*
     f loi *f* de Moseley
     r закон *m* Мозли

M645 *e* **Mössbauer effect**
     d Mößbauer-Effekt *m*
     f effet *m* Mössbauer
     r эффект *m* Мёссбауэра

M646 *e* **Mössbauer factor**
     d Mößbauer-Faktor *m*
     f facteur *m* Mössbauer
     r фактор *m* Мёссбауэра

M647 *e* **Mössbauer line**
     d Mößbauer-Linie *f*
     f ligne *f* Mössbauer
     r мёссбауэровская линия *f*

M648 *e* **Mössbauer spectrometer**
     d Mößbauer-Spektrometer *n*
     f spectromètre *m* Mössbauer
     r мёссбауэровский спектрометр *m*

M649 *e* **Mössbauer spectroscopy**
     d Mößbauer-Spektroskopie *f*
     f spectroscopie *f* Mössbauer
     r мёссбауэровская спектроскопия *f*

M650 *e* **Mössbauer spectrum**
     d Mößbauer-Spektrum *n*
     f spectre *m* Mössbauer
     r мёссбауэровский спектр *m*

M651 *e* **motion**
     d Bewegung *f*
     f mouvement *m*
     r движение *n*

M652 *e* **motion about fixed point**
     d Bewegung *f* um einen Fixpunkt
     f mouvement *m* autour d'un point fixe
     r движение *n* вокруг неподвижной точки

M653 *e* **motion of charged particles in crossed fields**
     d Bewegung *f* der geladenen Teilchen in gekreuzten Feldern
     f mouvement *m* des particules chargées dans les champs croisés
     r движение *n* заряженных частиц в скрещённых полях

M654 *e* **motion of rigid body**
     d Starrkörperbewegung *f*
     f mouvement *m* du corps solide
     r движение *n* твёрдого тела

M655 *e* **motion stability**
     d Bewegungsstabilität *f*
     f stabilité *f* du mouvement
     r устойчивость *f* движения

M656 *e* **motion under a force**
     d Bewegung *f* unter Krafteinwirkung
     f mouvement *m* sous l'effet d'une force
     r движение *n* под действием силы

M657 *e* **Mott detector**
     d Mott-Detektor *m*
     f détecteur *m* de Mott
     r детектор *m* Мотта

M658 *e* **Mott dielectrics**
     d Mottsche Dielektrika *n pl*
     f diélectriques *m pl* de Mott
     r моттовские диэлектрики *m pl*

M659 *e* **Mott scattering**
     d Mottsche Streuung *f*
     f diffusion *f* de Mott
     r моттовское рассеяние *n*

M660 *e* **Mott transition**
     d Mottscher Übergang *m*
     f transition *f* de Mott
     r переход *m* Мотта

M661 *e* **mounting**
     d 1. Montierung *f* 2. Montage *f*
     f 1. monture *f* 2. montage *m*
     r 1. монтировка *f* (*телескопа*) 2. монтаж *m*

M662 *e* **movement**
     d 1. Bewegung *f*, Verschiebung *f* 2. Meßwerk *n*
     f 1. mouvement *m*, déplacement *m* 2. équipage *m* mobile
     r 1. движение *n*, перемещение *n* 2. механизм *m* (*измерительного прибора*)

M663 *e* **moving charge**
     d Bewegtladung *f*
     f charge *f* mobile
     r движущийся заряд *m*

M664 *e* **moving coil**
     d bewegliche Spule *f*; Drehspule *f*; Tauchspule *f*

	f	bobine f mobile
	r	подвижная катушка f
M665	e	moving coil movement
	d	magnetelektrisches Drehspulmeßwerk n, magnetelektrisches Meßwerk n, Drehspulmeßwerk n
	f	équipage m à bobine mobile
	r	магнитоэлектрический механизм m (измерительного прибора)
M666	e	moving image
	d	bewegtes Bild n, Bewegtbild n
	f	image f mobile, image f dynamique
	r	движущееся изображение n; динамическое изображение n
M667	e	moving-iron movement
	d	Dreheisenmeßwerk n
	f	équipage m électromagnétique
	r	электромагнитный механизм m (измерительного прибора)
M668	e	moving-target selection
	d	Bewegtzielselektion f
	f	sélection f d'un objectif en mouvement
	r	селекция f движущейся цели
M669	e	moving-target simulator
	d	Bewegtzielsimulator m
	f	simulateur m d'un objectif mobile
	r	имитатор m движущейся цели
M670	e	Müller matrix
	d	Müller-Matrix f, Müllersche Matrix f
	f	matrice f de Müller
	r	матрица f Мюллера
M671	e	multibody state see multiparticle state
M672	e	multicavity magnetron
	d	Mehrkammermagnetron n
	f	magnétron m à cavités multiples
	r	многорезонаторный магнетрон m
M673	e	multichannel discriminator
	d	Vielkanaldiskriminator m, Mehrkanaldiskriminator m
	f	discriminateur m multicanal
	r	многоканальный дискриминатор m
M674	e	multicomponent order parameter
	d	mehrkomponentiger Ordnungsparameter m
	f	paramètre m d'ordre multicomposant
	r	многокомпонентный параметр m порядка
M675	e	multicomponent plasma
	d	Mehrkomponentenplasma n
	f	plasma m à plusieurs composants
	r	многокомпонентная плазма f
M676	e	multicomponent system
	d	Mehrkomponentensystem n

	f	système m multiple
	r	многокомпонентная система f
M677	e	multidimensional space
	d	mehrdimensionaler Raum m
	f	espace m multidimensionnel
	r	многомерное пространство n
M678	e	multielement interferometer
	d	Vielfachinterferometer n
	f	interféromètre m à éléments multiples
	r	многоэлементный интерферометр m
M679	e	multielement mirror
	d	Mehrelementspiegel m
	f	miroir m à plusieurs éléments
	r	многоэлементное зеркало n
M680	e	multilayer film
	d	Mehrschichtfilm m
	f	film m à plusieurs couches
	r	многослойная плёнка f
M681	e	multimode fiber
	d	Multimode-Faser f
	f	fibre f multimode
	r	многомодовое волокно n
M682	e	multimode laser
	d	Multimode-Laser m
	f	laser m multimode
	r	многомодовый лазер m
M683	e	multimode property
	d	Multimodenbildung f
	f	propriété f multimode
	r	многомодовость f
M684	e	multimode radiation
	d	Multimodenstrahlung f, Vielmodenstrahlung f
	f	radiation f multimode
	r	многомодовое излучение n
M685	e	multiparticle correlator
	d	Vielteilchenkorrelator m
	f	corrélateur m multiparticule
	r	многочастичный коррелятор m
M686	e	multiparticle dynamics
	d	Vielteilchendynamik f
	f	dynamique f multiparticule
	r	многочастичная динамика f
M687	e	multiparticle interaction
	d	Mehrteilchenwechselwirkung f
	f	interaction f multiparticule
	r	многочастичное взаимодействие n
M688	e	multiparticle production
	d	Mehrteilchenerzeugung f
	f	production f multiparticule
	r	множественное рождение n частиц
M689	e	multiparticle state
	d	Mehrteilchenzustand m
	f	état m multiparticule
	r	многочастичное состояние n

M690 e **multipath interference** *see* **multiple-beam interference**

M691 e **multipath propagation**
    d Mehrwegeausbreitung *f*, Mehrfachwegeeffekt *m*
    f propagation *f (d'ondes radio)* sur trajets multiples
    r многолучевое распространение *n* (*радиоволн*)

M692 e **multiperipheral interaction**
    d multiperiphere Wechselwirkung *f*
    f interaction *f* multipériphérique
    r мультипериферическое взаимодействие *n*

M693 e **multiphase flow**
    d Mehrphasenströmung *f*
    f écoulement *m* multiphase
    r многофазное течение *n*

M694 e **multiphonon process**
    d Mehrphononenprozeß *m*
    f processus *m* multiphononique
    r многофононный процесс *m*

M695 e **multiphoton absorption**
    d Mehrphotonenabsorption *f*
    f absorption *f* multiphotonique
    r многофотонное поглощение *n*

M696 e **multiphoton dissociation**
    d Mehrphotonendissoziation *f*
    f dissociation *f* multiphotonique
    r многофотонная диссоциация *f*

M697 e **multiphoton excitation**
    d Mehrphotonenanregung *f*
    f excitation *f* multiphotonique
    r многофотонное возбуждение *n*

M698 e **multiphoton ionization**
    d Mehrphotonenionisation *f*
    f ionisation *f* multiphotonique
    r многофотонная ионизация *f*

M699 e **multiphoton isomerization**
    d Mehrphotonenisomerisation *f*
    f isomérisation *f* multiphotonique
    r многофотонная изомеризация *f*

M700 e **multiphoton photoelectric effect**
    d Mehrphotonen-Photoeffekt *m*
    f effet *m* photo-électrique à photons multiples
    r многофотонный фотоэффект *m*

M701 e **multiphoton process**
    d Mehrphotonenprozeß *m*
    f processus *m* multiphotonique
    r многофотонный процесс *m*

M702 e **multiphoton spectroscopy**
    d Mehrphotonenspektroskopie *f*
    f spectroscopie *f* multiphotonique
    r многофотонная спектроскопия *f*

M703 e **multiphoton transition**
    d Mehrphotonenübergang *m*
    f transition *f* multiphotonique
    r многофотонный переход *m*

M704 e **multiple-beam interference**
    d Mehrstrahlinterferenz *f*, Mehrfachinterferenz *f*
    f interférence *f* à faisceaux multiples, interférence *f* multiple
    r многолучевая интерференция *f*

M705 e **multiple-beam interferometer**
    d Mehrstrahlinterferometer *n*, Vielstrahlinterferometer *n*
    f interféromètre *m* à faisceaux multiples, interféromètre *m* multiple
    r многолучевой интерферометр *m*

M706 e **multiple-cavity klystron**
    d Mehrkammerklystron *n*, Vielkammerklystron *n*
    f klystron *m* multicavité, klystron *m* à multicavités
    r многорезонаторный клистрон *m*

M707 e **multiple interaction**
    d Mehrfachwechselwirkung *f*
    f interaction *f* multiple
    r многократное взаимодействие *n*

M708 e **multiple ionization**
    d Mehrfachionisation *f*, Vielfachionisierung *f*
    f ionisation *f* multiple
    r многократная ионизация *f*

M709 e **multiple process**
    d Vielfachprozeß *m*, Mehrfachprozeß *m*
    f processus *m* multiple
    r множественный процесс *m*

M710 e **multiple production** *see* **multiparticle production**

M711 e **multiple scattering**
    d Vielfachstreuung *f*
    f diffusion *f* multiple
    r многократное рассеяние *n*

M712 e **multiplet**
    d Multiplett *n*
    f multiplet *m*
    r мультиплет *m*

M713 e **multiple units**
    d Mehrfacheinheiten *f pl*
    f unités *f pl* multiples
    r кратные единицы *f pl*

M714 e **multiplexer**
    d Multiplexer *m*
    f multiplexeur *m*
    r мультиплексор *m*

M715 e **multiplex holography**
    d Multiplex-Holographie *f*

    f holographie *f* multiplex
    r мультиплексная голография *f*

M716 *e* **multiplication**
    d 1. Multiplikation *f* 2. Vervielfältigung *f*
    f multiplication *f*
    r 1. умножение *n* 2. размножение *n*

M717 *e* **multiplication constant** *see* **multiplication factor**

M718 *e* **multiplication factor**
    d Multiplikationsfaktor *m*, Vermehrungsfaktor *m*
    f facteur *m* de multiplication
    r коэффициент *m* размножения (*нейтронов*)

M719 *e* **multiplicative quantum number**
    d multiplikative Quantenzahl *f*
    f nombre *m* quantique multiplicatif
    r мультипликативное квантовое число *n*

M720 *e* **multiplicity**
    d Multiplizität *f*
    f multiplicité *f*
    r 1. множественность *f* (*частиц*) 2. мультипликативность *f*

M721 *e* **multiplier**
    d Vervielfacher *m*
    f multiplicateur *m*
    r умножитель *m*

M722 *e* **multiply charged ion**
    d mehrfach geladenes Ion *n*
    f ion *m* plusieurs fois chargé
    r многозарядный ион *m*

M723 *e* **multiply connected contour**
    d mehrfach gekoppelter Kreis *m*
    f circuit *m* à connexion multiple
    r многосвязный контур *m*

M724 *e* **multiply connected region**
    d mehrfach zusammenhängendes Gebiet *n*
    f région *f* à connexion multiple
    r многосвязная область *f*

M725 *e* **multipolarity**
    d Multipolordnung *f*, Multipolarität *f*
    f multipolarité *f*
    r мультипольность *f*

M726 *e* **multipole**
    d Multipol *m*
    f multipôle *m*
    r мультиполь *m*

M727 *e* **multipole moment**
    d Multipolmoment *n*
    f moment *m* multipôle
    r мультипольный момент *m*

M728 *e* **multipole radiation**

M729 *e* **multiquark state**
    d Mehrquarkzustand *m*
    f état *m* multiquark
    r многокварковое состояние *n*

M730 *e* **multiresonator magnetron** *see* **multicavity magnetron**

M731 *e* **multistability**
    d Multistabilität *f*
    f multistabilité *f*
    r мультистабильность *f*

M732 *e* **multistage ionization**
    d mehrstufige Ionisation *f*, Mehrstufenionisation *f*
    f ionisation *f* à plusieurs étages
    r многоступенчатая ионизация *f*

M733 *e* **multistage rocket**
    d mehrstufige Rakete *f*
    f fusée *f* à plusieurs étages
    r многоступенчатая ракета *f*

M734 *e* **multiturn injection**
    d Injektion *f* über mehrere Umläufe
    f injection *f* à plusieurs tours
    r многооборотная инжекция *f* (*в ускорителе*)

M735 *e* **multivalued function**
    d mehrwertige Funktion *f*
    f fonction *f* multiforme
    r многозначная функция *f*

M736 *e* **multivibrator**
    d Multivibrator *m*
    f multivibrateur *m*
    r мультивибратор *m*

M737 *e* **mu meson** *see* **muon**

M738 *e* **muon**
    d Myon *n*, Müon *n*
    f muon *m*
    r мюон *m*, мю-мезон *m*, μ-мезон *m*

M739 *e* **muonic atom**
    d myonisches Atom *n*, Myonatom *n*, Müonatom *n*
    f atome *m* muonique
    r мюонный атом *m*

M740 *e* **muonic catalysis**
    d Myonkatalyse *f*, Myonenkatalyse *f*
    f catalyse *f* muonique
    r мюонный катализ *m*

M741 *e* **muonic molecule**
    d Myonmolekül *n*, Myonenmolekül *n*
    f molécule *f* muonique
    r мюонная молекула *f*

M728 *e* **multipole radiation**
    d Multipolstrahlung *f*
    f rayonnement *m* multipolaire, radiation *f* multipolaire
    r мультипольное излучение *n*

M742   *e* muonic neutrino
      d Myonneutrino *n*, Müonneutrino *n*
      f neutrino *m* muonique
      r мюонное нейтрино *n*

M743   *e* muonic number
      d Myonenzahl *f*
      f nombre *m* muonique
      r мюонное число *n*

M744   *e* muonium
      d Myonium *n*, Müonium *n*
      f muonium *m*
      r мюоний *m*

M745   *e* muon spin relaxation
      d Myonspinrelaxation *f*
      f relaxation *f* spin-muon
      r мюонная спиновая релаксация *f*

M746   *e* musical acoustics
      d Musikakustik *f*
      f acoustique *f* musicale
      r музыкальная акустика *f*

M747   *e* mutual coherence
      d gegenseitige Kohärenz *f*
      f cohérence *f* mutuelle
      r взаимная когерентность *f*

M748   *e* mutual coherence function
      d gegenseitige Kohärenzfunktion *f*
      f fonction *f* de cohérence mutuelle
      r функция *f* взаимной когерентности

M749   *e* mutual correlation
      d Kreuzkorrelation *f*
      f corrélation *f* mutuelle
      r взаимная корреляция *f*

M750   *e* mutual inductance
      d Gegeninduktivität *f*
      f inductance *f* mutuelle
      r взаимная индуктивность *f*

M751   *e* mutual induction
      d Gegeninduktion *f*
      f induction *f* mutuelle
      r взаимная индукция *f*

M752   *e* myopia
      d Kurzsichtigkeit *f*, Myopie *f*
      f myopie *f*
      r миопия *f*, близорукость *f*

N

N1   *e* nabla
     d Nablaoperator *m*, Hamiltonoperator *m*
     f nabla *m*
     r набла *m*, набла-оператор *m*,
        оператор *m* Гамильтона

N2   *e* nadir
     d Nadir *m*, Nadirpunkt *m*
     f nadir *m*
     r надир *m*

N3   *e* naked-eye object
     d mit bloßem Auge sichtbares Objekt *n*
     f objet *m* visible à l'œil
     r объект *m*, видимый невооружённым
        глазом

N4   *e* nanodiffraction
     d Nanodiffraktion *f*, Nanobeugung *f*
     f nanodiffraction *f*
     r нанодифракция *f*

N5   *e* nanolithography
     d Nanolithographie *f*
     f nanolithographie *f*
     r нанолитография *f*

N6   *e* nanosecond pulse
     d Nanosekundenimpuls *m*
     f impulsion *f* nanoseconde
     r наносекундный импульс *m*

N7   *e* narrow-band filter
     d Schmalbandfilter *n*
     f filtre *m* à bande passante étroite
     r узкополосный фильтр *m*

N8   *e* narrow-band radiation
     d Schmalbandstrahlung *f*
     f radiation *f* à bande étroite,
        rayonnement *m* à bande étroite
     r узкополосное излучение *n*

N9   *e* narrow-band semiconductor
     d Schmalbandhalbleiter *m*
     f semi-conducteur *m* à bande étroite
     r узкозонный полупроводник *m*

N10   *e* narrow beam
      d schmales Bündel *n*
      f faisceau *m* étroit
      r узкий пучок *m*

N11   *e* narrow peak
      d schmale Spitze *f*
      f sommet *m* étroit
      r узкий пик *m*

N12   *e* narrow resonance
      d schmale Resonanz *f*
      f résonance *f* étroite
      r узкий резонанс *m*

N13   *e* NASA *see* National Aeronautics and
         Space Administration

N14   *e* National Aeronautics and Space
         Administration
      d NASA *f* (*Weltraumbehörde der USA*)
      f NASA *f* (*office national d'études et de
        recherches aérospatiales, USA*)
      r Национальное управление *n* по
        аэронавтике и космонавтике
        (*США*)

N15 *e* **natural breadth of spectral line**
  d natürliche Spektrallinienbreite *f*
  f largeur *f* naturelle de la raie spectrale
  r естественная ширина *f* спектральной линии

N16 *e* **natural convection**
  d freie Konvektion *f*, natürliche Konvektion *f*
  f convection *f* naturelle
  r свободная конвекция *f*, естественная конвекция *f*

N17 *e* **natural frequency**
  d Eigenfrequenz *f*
  f fréquence *f* propre
  r собственная частота *f*

N18 *e* **natural isotope**
  d natürliches Isotop *n*
  f isotope *m* naturel
  r природный изотоп *m*

N19 *e* **natural isotope abundance**
  d natürliche Häufigkeit *f*, natürliche Isotopenhäufigkeit *f*
  f abondance *f* naturelle
  r распространённость *f* изотопов в природе

N20 *e* **natural light**
  d natürliches Licht *n*
  f lumière *f* naturelle
  r естественный свет *m*

N21 *e* **natural logarithm, ln**
  d natürlicher Logarithmus *m*, Neperscher Logarithmus *m*
  f logarithme *m* naturel
  r натуральный логарифм *m*

N22 *e* **natural mode** *see* **normal mode**

N23 *e* **natural system of units**
  d natürliches Einheitensystem *n*
  f système *m* d'unités naturel
  r естественная система единиц *f*

N24 *e* **Navier-Stokes equation**
  d Navier-Stokessche Gleichung *f*
  f équation *f* de Navier-Stokes
  r уравнение *n* Навье - Стокса

N25 *e* **navigation system**
  d Navigationssystem *n*
  f système *m* de navigation
  r навигационная система *f*

N26 *e* **Nd-glass laser** *see* **neodymium-glass laser**

N27 *e* **Nd laser**
  d Neodymlaser *m*
  f laser *m* au néodyme
  r неодимовый лазер *m*

N28 *e* **near-electrode phenomena**
  d elektrodennahe Erscheinungen *f pl*
  f phénomènes *m pl* voisins de l'électrode
  r приэлектродные явления *n pl*

N29 *e* **near field**
  d Nahfeld *n*
  f champ *m* proche
  r поле *n* в ближней зоне

N30 *e* **near-field microscope**
  d Nahfeldmikroskop *n*
  f microscope *m* de champ proche
  r микроскоп *m* ближнего поля

N31 *e* **near-field zone**
  d Nahzone *f*, Nahwirkungsgebiet *n*
  f zone *f* proche
  r ближняя зона *f*

N32 *e* **near-infrared radiation**
  d Infrarot-Hellstrahlung *f*, nahe Infrarotstrahlung *f*
  f rayonnement *m* infrarouge proche
  r ближнее инфракрасное излучение *n*

N33 *e* **near-infrared region**
  d nahes Infrarotgebiet *n*, nahes Infrarot *n*
  f région *f* infrarouge proche (*du spectre*)
  r ближняя инфракрасная область *f* (*спектра*)

N34 *e* **near IR radiation** *see* **near-infrared radiation**

N35 *e* **nearsightedness** *see* **myopia**

N36 *e* **near space**
  d naher Kosmos *m*
  f espace *m* proche
  r ближний космос *m*

N37 *e* **nearultraviolet region**
  d nahes Ultraviolettgebiet *n*, nahes Ultraviolett *n*
  f région *f* ultraviolette proche (*du spectre*)
  r ближняя ультрафиолетовая область *f* (*спектра*)

N38 *e* **nebula**
  d Nebel *m*
  f nébuleuse *f*
  r туманность *f*

N39 *e* **Néel point, Néel temperature**
  d Néel-Punkt *m*, Néel-Temperatur *f*
  f point *m* de Néel
  r точка *f* Нееля

N40 *e* **Néel wall**
  d Néel-Wand *f*
  f paroi *f* de Néel
  r стенка *f* Нееля

N41   e **negative absorption**
       d negative Absorption *n*
       f absorption *f* négative
       r отрицательное поглощение *n*

N42   e **negative charge**
       d negative Ladung *f*
       f charge *f* négative
       r отрицательный заряд *m*

N43   e **negative crystal**
       d negativer Kristall *m*
       f cristal *m* négatif
       r отрицательный кристалл *m*

N44   e **negative curvature**
       d negative Krümmung *f*
       f courbure *f* négative
       r отрицательная кривизна *f*

N45   e **negative differential resistance**
       d negativer Differentialwiderstand *m*
       f résistance *f* différentielle négative
       r отрицательное дифференциальное сопротивление *n*

N46   e **negative dispersion**
       d negative Dispersion *f*; normale Dispersion *f*
       f dispersion *f* négative; dispersion *f* normale
       r отрицательная дисперсия *f*; нормальная дисперсия *f*

N47   e **negative entropy** *see* **negentropy**

N48   e **negative feedback**
       d Gegenkopplung *f*
       f réaction *f* négative
       r отрицательная обратная связь *f*

N49   e **negative image**
       d Negativ *n*, photographisches Negativ *n*; Negativbild *n*
       f négatif *m*; image *f* négative
       r негативное изображение *n*

N50   e **negative ion**
       d negatives Ion *n*, negativgeladenes Ion *n*
       f ion *m* négatif
       r отрицательный ион *m*

N51   e **negative luminescence**
       d negative Lumineszenz *f*
       f luminescence *f* négative
       r отрицательная люминесценция *f*

N52   e **negative picture** *see* **negative image**

N53   e **negative resistance**
       d negativer Widerstand *m*
       f résistance *f* négative
       r отрицательное сопротивление *n*

N54   e **negative temperature**
       d negative Temperatur *f* (*in der Themodynamik*)
       f température *f* négative (*en thermodynamique*)
       r отрицательная температура *f* (*в термодинамике*)

N55   e **negentropy**
       d Negentropie *f*, negative Entropie *f*
       f néguentropie *f*, entropie *f* négative
       r негэнтропия *f*

N56   e **neighboring level**
       d Nachbarniveau *n*
       f niveau *m* voisin
       r соседний уровень *m*

N57   e **nematic** *see* **nematic liquid crystal**

N58   e **nematic liquid crysral**
       d nematischer flüssiger Kristall *m*
       f cristal *m* liquide nématique
       r нематический жидкий кристалл *m*

N59   e **nematic-smectic phase**
       d Phasenumwandlung *f* «nematisch-smektisch»
       f transition *f* de phase «nématique-smectique»
       r фазовый переход *m* нематик - смектик

N60   e **neoclassical diffusion**
       d neoklassische Diffusion *f*
       f diffusion *f* néoclassique
       r неоклассическая диффузия *f*

N61   e **neoclassic transport**
       d neoklassischer Transport *m* (*im Plasma*)
       f transfert *m* néoclassique (*au plasma*)
       r неоклассический перенос *m* (*в плазме*)

N62   e **neodymium, Nd**
       d Neodym *n*
       f néodyme *m*
       r неодим *m*

N63   e **neodymuim-glass laser**
       d Neodymglaslaser *m*
       f laser *m* à verre dopé au néodyme
       r лазер *m* на неодимовом стекле

N64   e **neon, Ne**
       d Neon *n*
       f néon *m*
       r неон *m*

N65   e **neper, Np**
       d Neper *n*
       f néper *m*
       r непер *m*, Нп

N66   e **nephelometer**
       d Nephelometer *n*, Trübungsmesser *m*
       f néphélomètre *m*
       r нефелометр *m*

N67   *e* nephelometry
       d Nephelometrie *f*, Trübungsmessung *f*
       f néphélométrie *f*
       r нефелометрия *f*

N68   *e* **Neptune**
       d Neptun *m*
       f Neptune *m*
       r Нептун *m*

N69   *e* neptunium, Np
       d Neptunium *n*
       f neptunium *m*
       r нептуний *m*

N70   *e* **Nernst effect**
       d Nernst-Effekt *m*
       f effet *m* Nernst
       r эффект *m* Нернста

N71   *e* **Nernst-Ettingshausen effect**
       d Nernst-Ettingshausen-Effekt *m*
       f effet *m* Nernst-Ettingshausen
       r эффект *m* Нернста -
          Эттингсгаузена

N72   *e* **Nernst heat theorem**
       d Nernstscher Wärmesatz *m*, dritter
          Hauptsatz *m* der Thermodynamik
       f troisième principe *m* de la
          thermodynamique, théorème *m* de
          Nernst, principe *m* de Nernst
       r теорема *f* Нернста, третье начало *n*
          термодинамики

N73   *e* **nerve cell**
       d Nervenzelle *f*
       f cellule *f* nerveuse
       r нервная клетка *f*

N74   *e* **nerve impulse**
       d Nervenimpuls *m*
       f impulsion *f* nerveuse
       r нервный импульс *m*

N75   *e* **net charge**
       d Nettoladung *f*
       f charge *f* nette
       r результирующий заряд *m*

N76   *e* **network analysis**
       d 1. Netzwerktheorie *f* 2.
          Schaltungsanalyse *f*
       f 1. théorie *f* des réseaux 2. analyse *f*
          de connexions
       r 1. теория *f* цепей 2. схемный
          анализ *m*

N77   *e* **Neumann function**
       d Neumann-Funktion *f*
       f fonction *f* de Neumann
       r функция *f* Неймана

N78   *e* **Neumann principle**
       d Neumannsches Prinzip *n*

       f principe *m* de Neumann
       r принцип *m* Неймана

N79   *e* **Neumann problem**
       d Neumannsches Problem *n*, Neumann-
          Problem *n*
       f problème *m* de Neumann
       r задача *f* Неймана

N80   *e* **Neumann-Seeliger paradox**
       d Neumann-Seeliger-Paradoxon *n*,
          Gravitationsparadoxon *n*
       f paradoxe *m* de Neumann-Seeliger,
          paradoxe *m* de gravitation
       r парадокс *m* Неймана - Зеелигера,
          гравитационный парадокс *m*

N81   *e* **neuron**
       d Neuron *n*
       f neurone *m*
       r нейрон *m*

N82   *e* **neutral axis**
       d neutrale Achse *f*
       f axe *m* neutre
       r нейтральная ось *f*

N83   *e* **neutral component**
       d neutrale Komponente *f*
       f composante *f* neutre
       r нейтральная компонента *f*

N84   *e* **neutral current**
       d Neutralstrom *m*, neutraler Strom *m*
       f courant *m* neutre
       r нейтральный ток *m*

N85   *e* **neutral current sheet**
       d Neutralstromschicht *f*
       f couche *f* de courant neutre
       r нейтральный токовый слой *m*

N86   *e* **neutral density filter**
       d Neutralfilter *n*, Graufilter *n*
       f filtre *m* neutre
       r нейтральный светофильтр *m*

N87   *e* **neutral injection**
       d Neutralteilcheneinschuß *m*
       f injection *f* de neutres, injection *f* de
          particules neutres
       r инжекция *f* нейтральных частиц

N88   *e* **neutralization**
       d Neutralisation *f*
       f neutralisation *f*
       r нейтрализация *f*

N89   *e* **neutral kaon, neutral K-meson**
       d neutrales Kaon *n*, neutrales
          K-Meson *n*
       f méson *m* K neutre
       r нейтральный каон *m*, нейтральный
          К-мезон *m*

N90   *e* **neutral particle**
       d neutrales Teilchen *n*

　　　　f　particule *f* neutre
　　　　r　нейтральная частица *f*

N91　*e*　**neutral pion**
　　　　d　neutrales Pion *n*
　　　　f　pion *m* neutre
　　　　r　нейтральный пион *m*

N92　*e*　**neutral point**
　　　　d　Nullpunkt *m*
　　　　f　point *m* neutre
　　　　r　нейтральная точка *f*, нейтраль *f*

N93　*e*　**neutral vector meson**
　　　　d　neutrales Vektormeson *n*
　　　　f　méson *m* vectoriel neutre
　　　　r　нейтральный векторный мезон *m*

N94　*e*　**neutral wedge**
　　　　d　Graukeil *m*, Neutralkeil *m*
　　　　f　coin *m* gris, coin *m* neutre
　　　　r　нейтральный клин *m*

N95　*e*　**neutrino**
　　　　d　Neutrino *n*
　　　　f　neutrino *m*
　　　　r　нейтрино *n*

N96　*e*　**neutrino astronomy**
　　　　d　Neutrinoastronomie *f*
　　　　f　astronomie *f* de neutrino, astronomie *f* neutrinique
　　　　r　нейтринная астрономия *f*

N97　*e*　**neutrino astrophysics**
　　　　d　Neutrinoastrophysik *f*
　　　　f　astrophysique *f* de neutrino
　　　　r　нейтринная астрофизика *f*

N98　*e*　**neutrino oscillation, neutrino oscillations**
　　　　d　Neutrinooszillationen *f pl*
　　　　f　oscillations *f pl* de neutrinos
　　　　r　осцилляции *f pl* нейтрино, нейтринные осцилляции *f pl*

N99　*e*　**neutrino radiation**
　　　　d　Neutrinostrahlung *f*
　　　　f　rayonnement *m* à neutrino
　　　　r　нейтринное излучение *n*

N100　*e*　**neutrino telescope**
　　　　d　Neutrinoteleskop *n*
　　　　f　télescope *m* à neutrino
　　　　r　нейтринный телескоп *m*

N101　*e*　**neutron**
　　　　d　Neutron *n*
　　　　f　neutron *m*
　　　　r　нейтрон *m*

N102　*e*　**neutron absorption**
　　　　d　Neutronenabsorption *f*
　　　　f　absorption *f* de neutrons
　　　　r　поглощение *n* нейтронов

N103　*e*　**neutron age**

　　　　d　Neutronenalter *n*
　　　　f　âge *m* des neutrons
　　　　r　возраст *m* нейтронов

N104　*e*　**neutron albedo**
　　　　d　Neutronenalbedo *f*
　　　　f　albédo *m* neutronique
　　　　r　альбедо *n* нейтронов, нейтронное альбедо *n*

N105　*e*　**neutron beam**
　　　　d　Neutronenstrahl *m*; Neutronenbündel *n*
　　　　f　faisceau *m* de neutrons
　　　　r　нейтронный пучок *m*

N106　*e*　**neutron capture**
　　　　d　Neutroneneinfang *m*
　　　　f　capture *f* des neutrons
　　　　r　захват *m* нейтронов

N107　*e*　**neutron channel**
　　　　d　Neutronenkanal *m*
　　　　f　canal *m* neutronique
　　　　r　нейтронный канал *m*

N108　*e*　**neutron charge**
　　　　d　Neutronenladung *f*
　　　　f　charge *f* du neutron
　　　　r　заряд *m* нейтрона

N109　*e*　**neutron cross-section**
　　　　d　Neutronenquerschnitt *m*
　　　　f　section *f* neutronique
　　　　r　нейтронное сечение *n*

N110　*e*　**neutron cycle**
　　　　d　Neutronenzyklus *m*
　　　　f　cycle *m* neutronique
　　　　r　нейтронный цикл *m*

N111　*e*　**neutron decay**
　　　　d　Neutronenzerfall *m*
　　　　f　désintégration *f* du neutron
　　　　r　распад *m* нейтрона

N112　*e*　**neutron deficit**
　　　　d　Neutronendefizit *n*, Neutronenmangel *m*
　　　　f　manque *m* de neutrons, déficit *m* neutronique
　　　　r　дефицит *m* нейтронов

N113　*e*　**neutron-deficit isotope**
　　　　d　neutronendefizites Isotop *n*, Neutronenmangelisotop *n*
　　　　f　isotope *m* déficient en neutrons
　　　　r　нейтронно-дефицитный изотоп *m*

N114　*e*　**neutron-deficit nuclei**
　　　　d　neutronendefizite Kerne *m pl*, Neutronenmangelkerne *m pl*
　　　　f　noyaux *m pl* déficients en neutrons
　　　　r　нейтронно-дефицитные ядра *n pl*

N115　*e*　**neutron density**
　　　　d　Neutronendichte *f*,

Neutronenzahldichte *f*,
Neutronenkonzentration *f*
f densité *f* de neutrons
r концентрация *f* нейтронов

N116 *e* **neutron detection**
d Neutronendetektion *f*,
Neutronennachweis *m*
f détection *f* de neutrons
r детектирование *n* нейтронов

N117 *e* **neutron detector**
d Neutronendetektor *m*
f détecteur *m* de neutrons
r нейтронный детектор *m*

N118 *e* **neutron diffraction**
d Neutronenbeugung *f*,
Neutronenstrahlbeugung *f*,
Neurtonendiffraktion *f*
f diffraction *f* de neutrons
r дифракция *f* нейтронов

N119 *e* **neutron diffraction analysis**
d Neutronenbeugungsanalyse *f*,
Neutronenbeugungsuntersuchung *f*
f diffractométrie *f* neutronique
r нейтронография *f*,
нейтронографический анализ *m*

N120 *e* **neutron diffraction pattern**
d Neutronenbeugungsbild *n*,
Neurtonenbeugungsdiagramm *n*
f neutronogramme *m*
r нейтронограмма *f*

N121 *e* **neutron diffraction study**
d Neutronenbeugungsuntersuchung *f*
f diffractométrie *f* neutronique
r нейтронографическое
исследование *n*

N122 *e* **neutron diffractometer**
d Neutronendiffraktometer *n*
f diffractomètre *m* neutronique
r нейтронограф *m*, нейтронный
дифрактометр *m*

N123 *e* **neutron diffusion**
d Neutronendiffusion *f*
f diffusion *f* des neutrons
r диффузия *f* нейтронов

N124 *e* **neutron-excess isotope**
d Neutronenüberschußisotop *n*
f isotope *m* à excès de neutrons
r нейтронно-избыточный изотоп *m*

N125 *e* **neutron-excess nuclei**
d Neutronenüberschußkerne *m pl*
f noyaux *m pl* à excès de neutrons
r нейтронно-избыточные ядра *n pl*

N126 *e* **neutron flux**
d Neutronenfluß *m*

f flux *m* de neutrons
r поток *m* нейтронов

N127 *e* **neutron form-factor**
d Neutronenformfaktor *m*
f facteur *m* de forme de neutron
r форм-фактор *m* нейтрона

N128 *e* **neutron generator**
d Neutronengenerator *m*,
Neutronenerzeuger *m*
f générateur *m* de neutrons
r нейтронный генератор *m*

N129 *e* **neutron guide**
d Neutronenleiter *m*
f guide *m* de neutrons, conduit *m* de
neutrons
r нейтроновод *m*

N130 *e* **neutron-impoverished isotope**
d neutronenarmes Isotop *n*
f isotope *m* pauvre en neutrons
r нейтронно-обеднённый изотоп *m*

N131 *e* **neutron interferometer**
d Neutroneninterferometer *n*
f interféromètre *m* neutronique
r нейтронный интерферометр *m*

N132 *e* **neutron interferometry**
d Neutroneninterferometrie *f*
f interférométrie *f* neutronique
r нейтронная интерферометрия *f*

N133 *e* **neutronization**
d Neutronisation *f*
f neutronisation *f*
r нейтронизация *f*

N134 *e* **neutronization threshold**
d Neutronisationsschwelle *f*
f seuil *m* de neutronisation
r порог *m* нейтронизации

N135 *e* **neutron lens**
d Neutronenlinse *f*
f lentille *f* neutronique
r нейтронная линза *f*

N136 *e* **neutron magnetic moment**
d magnetisches Neutronenmoment *n*
f moment *m* magnétique du neutron
r магнитный момент *m* нейтрона

N137 *e* **neutron moderation**
d Neutronenbremsung *f*
f ralentissement *m* des neutrons
r замедление *n* нейтронов

N138 *e* **neutron moderator**
d Neutronenmoderator *m*,
Neutronenbremsmittel *n*
f ralentisseur *m* de neutrons
r замедлитель *m* нейтронов

N139   *e*   **neutron monitor**
    d   Neutronenmonitor *m*
    f   moniteur *m* à neutrons
    r   нейтронный монитор *m*

N140   *e*   **neutron monochromator**
    d   Neutronenmonochromator *m*
    f   monochromateur *m* neutronique
    r   нейтронный монохроматор *m*

N141   *e*   **neutron multiplication**
    d   Neutronenmultiplikation *f*,
        Neutronenvermehrung *f*
    f   multiplication *f* des neutrons
    r   размножение *n* нейтронов

N142   *e*   **neutron optics**
    d   Neutronenoptik *f*
    f   optique *f* neutronique
    r   нейтронная оптика *f*

N143   *e*   **neutron physics**
    d   Neutronenphysik *f*
    f   physique *f* neutronique
    r   нейтронная физика *f*

N144   *e*   **neutron polarization**
    d   Neutronenpolarisation *f*
    f   polarisation *f* de neutrons
    r   поляризация *f* нейтронов

N145   *e*   **neutron powder diffractometer**
    d   Pulver-Neutronendiffraktometer *n*
    f   diffractomètre *m* neutronique à
        poudre
    r   порошковый нейтронограф *m*

N146   *e*   **neutron prism**
    d   Neutronenprisma *n*
    f   prisme *m* neutronique
    r   нейтронная призма *f*

N147   *e*   **neutron radiation**
    d   Neutronenstrahlung *f*
    f   rayonnement *m* à neutrons,
        rayonnement *m* neutronique
    r   нейтронное излучение *n*

N148   *e*   **neutron radiography**
    d   Neutronenradiographie *f*
    f   radiographie *f* neutronique
    r   нейтронная радиография *f*

N149   *e*   **neutron resonance**
    d   Neutronenresonanz *f*
    f   résonance *f* neutronique
    r   нейтронный резонанс *m*

N150   *e*   **neutron-rich isotope**
    d   neutronenreiches Isotop *n*,
        Neutronenüberschußisotop *n*
    f   isotope *m* riche en neutrons
    r   нейтронно-обогащённый изотоп *m*

N151   *e*   **neutron-rich nuclei** *see* **neutron-excess nuclei**

N152   *e*   **neutron scattering**
    d   Neutronenstreuung *f*
    f   diffusion *f* neutronique
    r   рассеяние *n* нейтронов

N153   *e*   **neutron source**
    d   Neutronenquelle *f*
    f   source *f* de neutron
    r   источник *m* нейтронов, нейтронный
        источник *m*

N154   *e*   **neutron spectrometer**
    d   Neutronenspektrometer *n*
    f   spectromètre *m* neutronique
    r   нейтронный спектрометр *m*

N155   *e*   **neutron spectrometry**
    d   Neutronenspektrometrie *f*
    f   spectrométrie *f* neutronique
    r   нейтронная спектрометрия *f*

N156   *e*   **neutron spin**
    d   Neutronenspin *m*
    f   spin *m* du neutron
    r   спин *m* нейтрона

N157   *e*   **neutron star**
    d   Neutronenstern *m*
    f   étoile *f* à neutrons, étoile *f*
        neutronique
    r   нейтронная звезда *f*

N158   *e*   **neutron structure**
    d   Neutronenstruktur *f*
    f   structure *f* du neutron
    r   структура *f* нейтрона

N159   *e*   **neutron temperature**
    d   Neutronentemperatur *f*
    f   température *f* de neutrons
    r   температура *f* нейтронов

N160   *e*   **neutron velocity distribution**
    d   Neutronengeschwindigkeitsverteilung *f*
    f   distribution *f* des neutrons d'après la
        vitesse
    r   распределение *n* нейтронов по
        скоростям

N161   *e*   **neutron wave**
    d   Neutronenwelle *f*
    f   onde *f* neutronique
    r   нейтронная волна *f*

N162   *e*   **neutron width**
    d   Neutronenbreite *f*
    f   largeur *f* neutronique
    r   нейтронная ширина *f*, нейтронная
        ширина *f* резонанса

N163   *e*   **neutron yield**
    d   Neutronenausbeute *f*
    f   rendement *m* de neutrons
    r   выход *m* нейтронов

N164   *e*   **newton, N**
    d   Newton *n*

    f newton *m*
    r ньютон *m*, H

N165 *e* **Newtonian liquid**
    d Newtonsche Flüssigkeit *f*
    f fluide *m* newtonien
    r ньютоновская жидкость *f*

N166 *e* **Newtonian mechanics** *see* **classical mechanics**

N167 *e* **Newton law of gravitation**
    d Newtonsches Gravitationsgesetz *n*
    f loi *f* de l'attraction universelle de Newton
    r закон *m* всемирного тяготения Ньютона

N168 *e* **Newton laws of motion**
    d Newtonsche Axiome *n pl*, Newtonsche Gesetze *n pl* der Mechanik
    f lois *f pl* de Newton
    r законы *m pl* механики Ньютона

N169 *e* **Newton rings**
    d Newtonsche Ringe *m pl*, Newton-Ringe *m pl*
    f anneaux *m pl* de Newton, cercles *m pl* de Newton, halos *m pl* de Newton
    r кольца *n pl* Ньютона

N170 *e* **nickel, Ni**
    d Nickel *n*
    f nickel *m*
    r никель *m*

N171 *e* **Nicol prism**
    d Nicol-Prisma *n*, Nicolsches Prisma *n*
    f prisme *m* de Nicol
    r призма *f* Николя

N172 *e* **nilpotent group**
    d nilpotente Gruppe *f*
    f groupe *m* nilpotent
    r нильпотентная группа *f*

N173 *e* **nilsbohrium, Ns**
    d Nilsbohrium *n*
    f nilsbohrium *m*
    r нильсборий *m*

N174 *e* **niobium, Nb**
    d Niob *n*
    f niobium *m*
    r ниобий *m*

N175 *e* **nit, nt**
    d Nit *n*
    f nit *m*
    r нит *m*, нт *(устаревшее наименование единицы яркости)*

N176 *e* **nitrogen, N**
    d Stickstoff *m*
    f nitrogène *m*
    r азот *m*

N177 *e* **NMR magnetometer** *see* **nuclear magnetic resonance magnetometer**

N178 *e* **nobelium, No**
    d Nobelium *n*
    f nobélium *m*
    r нобелий *m*

N179 *e* **noble gas**
    d Edelgas *n*
    f gaz *m* inerte
    r инертный газ *m*, благородный газ *m*

N180 *e* **noble metals**
    d Edelmetalle *n pl*
    f métaux *m pl* nobles
    r благородные металлы *m pl*

N181 *e* **nodal plane**
    d Knotenebene *f*
    f plan *m* nodal
    r узловая плоскость *f*

N182 *e* **node**
    d Knoten *m*
    f nœud *m*
    r узел *m*

N183 *e* **Noether theorem**
    d Noetherscher Satz *m*, Noethersches Theorem *n*
    f théorème *m* de Noether
    r теорема *f* Нётер

N184 *e* **noise**
    d Lärm *m*; Rauschen *n*; Geräusch *n*
    f bruit *m*
    r шум *m*, шумы *m pl*

N185 *e* **noise factor**
    d Rauschfaktor *m*, Rauschzahl *f*
    f facteur *m* de bruit, coefficient *m* de bruit
    r шум-фактор *m*, коэффициент *m* шума

N186 *e* **noise figure** *see* **noise factor**

N187 *e* **noise generator**
    d Rauschgenerator *m*, Rauscherzeuger *m*
    f générateur *m* de bruit, générateur *m* de bruits
    r шумовой генератор *m*, генератор *m* шума

N188 *e* **noise immunity**
    d Störfestigkeit *f*
    f insensibilité *f* aux parasites, immunité *f* contre les brouillages
    r помехозащищённость *f*, помехоустойчивость *f*

N189 *e* **noise level**
    d Störpegel *m*; Rauschpegel *m*
    f niveau *m* de bruit
    r уровень *m* шумов, уровень *m* помех

N190 e noise measurement
      d Rauschmessung f
      f mesure f de bruit
      r измерение n шумов

N191 e noise power
      d Rauschleistung f
      f puissance f du bruit, puissance f de
         bruit
      r мощность f шума

N192 e noise source
      d Rauschquelle f
      f source f de brouillages
      r источник m шума

N193 e noise spectrum
      d Rauschspektrum n
      f spectre m de bruits
      r спектр m шумов

N194 e noise temperature
      d Rauschtemperatur f
      f température f de bruit
      r шумовая температура f

N195 e nomogram
      d Nomogramm n, Kurventafel f
      f nomogramme m, abaque m
      r номограмма f

N196 e non-Abelian gage field
      d nichtabelsches Eichfeld n
      f champ m de jauge non abélien
      r неабелево калибровочное поле n

N197 e nonadiabatic transition
      d nichtadiabatischer Übergang m
      f transition f non adiabatique
      r неадиабатический переход m

N198 e noncentral force
      d nichtzentrale Kraft f
      f force f non centrale
      r нецентральная сила f

N199 e noncharged particle
      d nicht geladenes Teilchen n
      f particule f non chargée
      r незаряженная частица f

N200 e noncoherence
      d Inkohärenz f
      f incohérence f
      r некогерентность f

N201 e noncoherent emission see
         noncoherent radiation

N202 e noncoherent emitters see
         noncoherent radiators

N203 e noncoherent radiation
      d nichtkohärente Strahlung f
      f radiation f non cohérente,
         rayonnement m non cohérent
      r некогерентное излучение n

N204 e noncoherent radiators
      d nichtkohärente Strahler m pl
      f radiateurs m pl non cohérents
      r некогерентные излучатели m pl

N205 e noncommuting operators
      d nicht kommutierende Operatoren m pl
      f opérateurs m pl non commutatifs
      r некоммутирующие операторы m pl

N206 e nonconservation
      d Nichterhaltung f
      f non-conservation f
      r несохранение n

N207 e nonconservative force
      d nichtkonservative Kraft f
      f force f non conservative
      r неконсервативная сила f

N208 e nonconservative system
      d nichtkonservatives System n
      f système m non conservatif
      r неконсервативная система f

N209 e nondegenerate oscillation
      d nichtentartete Schwingungen f pl
      f oscillations f pl non dégénérées
      r невырожденные колебания n pl

N210 e nondestructive technique
      d zerstörungsfreie Methode f
      f méthode f de contrôle non destructif
      r неразрушающий метод m

N211 e nondestructive test, nondestructive
         testing
      d zerstörungsfreie Werkstoffprüfung f
      f essai m non destructif
      r 1. дефектоскопия f 2.
         неразрушающие испытания n pl,
         неразрушающий контроль m

N212 e nondissipative nonlinearity
      d nichtdissipative Nichtlinearität f
      f non-linéarité f non dissipative
      r недиссипативная нелинейность f

N213 e nonelastic cross-section
      d Querschnitt m der nichtelastischen
         Streuung
      f section f de diffusion non élastique
      r сечение n неупругого рассеяния

N214 e nonelastic interaction
      d nichtelastische Wechselwirkung f
      f interaction f non élastique
      r неупругое взаимодействие n

N215 e nonequilibrium carriers
      d Nichtgleichgewichtsträger m pl,
         Nichtgleichgewichtsladungsträger m pl
      f porteurs m pl non équilibrés
      r неравновесные носители m pl,
         неравновесные носители m pl
         заряда

N216   *e*   **nonequilibrium concentration**
     d   Nichtgleichgewichtsdichte *f*,
       Nichtgleichgewichtskonzentration *f*
     f   concentration *f* non équilibrée
     r   неравновесная концентрация *f*
       (носителей заряда)

N217   *e*   **nonequilibrium flow**
     d   Nichtgleichgewichtsströmung *f*
     f   flux *m* non équilibré
     r   неравновесное течение *n*

N218   *e*   **nonequilibrium phase transitions**
     d   Nichtgleichgewichtsphasenübergänge
       m pl
     f   transitions *f pl* de phase non
       équilibrées
     r   неравновесные фазовые
       переходы *m pl*

N219   *e*   **nonequilibrium plasma**
     d   Nichtgleichgewichtsplasma *n*
     f   plasma *m* hors d'équilibre
     r   неравновесная плазма *f*

N220   *e*   **nonequilibrium population**
     d   Nichtgleichgewichtsbesetzung *f*
     f   population *f* non équilibrée
     r   неравновесная населённость *f*

N221   *e*   **nonequilibrium-process kinetics**
     d   Nichtgleichgewichtskinetik *f*, Kinetik *f*
       nichtstatischer Prozesse
     f   cinétique *f* de non-équilibre
     r   кинетика *f* неравновесных
       процессов

N222   *e*   **nonequilibrium state**
     d   Nichtgleichgewichtszustand *m*
     f   état *m* non équilibré
     r   неравновесное состояние *n*

N223   *e*   **nonet**
     d   Nonett *n*
     f   nonet *m*
     r   нонет *m*

N224   *e*   **non-Euclidian geometry**
     d   nichteuklidische Geometrie *f*
     f   géométrie *f* non euclidienne
     r   неевклидова геометрия *f*

N225   *e*   **nonexcited atom**
     d   nichtangeregtes Atom *n*
     f   atome *m* non excité
     r   невозбуждённый атом *m*

N226   *e*   **nonholonomic system**
     d   nichtholonomes System *n*
     f   système *m* non holonomique
     r   неголономная система *f*

N227   *e*   **nonhomogeneous medium**
     d   inhomogenes Medium *n*
     f   milieu *m* hétérogène
     r   неоднородная среда *f*

N228   *e*   **nonideal gas** *see* **real gas**

N229   *e*   **nonideal plasma**
     d   nichtideales Plasma *n*
     f   plasma *m* non idéal
     r   неидеальная плазма *f*

N230   *e*   **noninertial frame**
     d   nichtinertiales Trägheitssystem *n*
     f   système *m* de référence non inertiel
     r   неинерциальная система *f* отсчёта

N231   *e*   **noninteracting particle**
     d   nichtwechselwirkendes Teilchen *n*
     f   particule *f* de non-interaction
     r   невзаимодействующая частица *f*

N232   *e*   **nonleptonic process**
     d   nichtleptonischer Prozeß *m*
     f   processus *m* non leptonique
     r   нелептонный процесс *m*

N233   *e*   **nonlinear absorption**
     d   nichtlineare Absorption *f*
     f   absorption *f* non linéaire
     r   нелинейное поглощение *n*

N234   *e*   **nonlinear acoustics**
     d   nichtlineare Akustik *f*
     f   acoustique *f* non linéaire
     r   нелинейная акустика *f*

N235   *e*   **nonlinear capacitance**
     d   nichtlineare Kapazität *f*
     f   capacité *f* non linéaire
     r   нелинейная ёмкость *f*

N236   *e*   **nonlinear compression**
     d   nichtlineare Impulsverdichtung *f*
     f   compression *f* non linéaire
     r   нелинейное сжатие *n* (импульса)

N237   *e*   **nonlinear dependence**
     d   nichtlineare Abhängigkeit *f*
     f   relation *f* non linéaire, rapport *m* non
       linéaire
     r   нелинейная зависимость *f*

N238   *e*   **nonlinear detection**
     d   nichtlineare Demodulation *f*
     f   détection *f* non linéaire
     r   нелинейное детектирование *n*

N239   *e*   **nonlinear dispersion**
     d   nichtlineare Dispersion *f*
     f   dispersion *f* non linéaire
     r   нелинейная дисперсия *f*

N240   *e*   **nonlinear distortion**
     d   nichtlineare Verzerrungen *f pl*,
       Klirrverzerrungen *f pl*
     f   distorsions *f pl* non linéaires
     r   нелинейные искажения *n pl*

N241   *e*   **nonlinear dynamics**
     d   nichtlineare Dynamik *f*

f dynamique *f* non linéaire
r нелинейная динамика *f*

N242 *e* **nonlinear effects**
d nichtlineare Effekte *m pl*
f effets *m pl* non linéaires
r нелинейные эффекты *m pl*

N243 *e* **nonlinear equation**
d nichtlineare Gleichung *f*
f équation *f* non linéaire
r нелинейное уравнение *n*

N244 *e* **nonlinear filtering**
d nichtlineare Filtration *f*
f filtration *f* non linéaire
r нелинейная фильтрация *f*

N245 *e* **nonlinear inductance**
d nichtlineare Induktivität *f*
f inductance *f* non linéaire
r нелинейная индуктивность *f*

N246 *e* **nonlinear interaction**
d nichtlineare Wechselwirkung *f*
f interaction *f* non linéaire
r нелинейное взаимодействие *n*

N247 *e* **nonlinearity**
d Nichtlinearität *f*
f non-linéairité *f*
r нелинейность *f*

N248 *e* **nonlinear Landau damping**
d nichtlineare Landau-Dämpfung *f*
f amortissement *m* non linéaire de Landau
r нелинейное затухание *n* Ландау

N249 *e* **nonlinear materials**
d nichtlineare Werkstoffe *m pl*
f matériaux *m pl* non linéaires
r нелинейные материалы *m pl*

N250 *e* **nonlinear mechanics**
d nichtlineare Mechanik *f*
f mécanique *f* non linéaire
r нелинейная механика *f*

N251 *e* **nonlinear medium**
d nichtlineares Medium *n*
f milieu *m* non linéaire
r нелинейная среда *f*

N252 *e* **nonlinear optical absorption**
d nichtlineare optische Absorption *f*
f absorption *f* optique non linéaire
r нелинейное оптическое поглощение *n*

N253 *e* **nonlinear optical activity**
d nichtlineare optische Aktivität *f*
f activité *f* optique non linéaire
r нелинейная оптическая активность *f*

N254 *e* **nonlinear optical crystal**

d nichtlinear-optischer Kristall *m*
f cristal *m* optique non linéaire
r нелинейно-оптический кристалл *m*

N255 *e* **nonlinear optical phase conjugation**
d Lichtwellenfrontkonjugation *f* im nichtlinearen Medium
f conjugaison *f* du front d'onde du rayonnement optique en milieu non linéaire
r обращение *n* волнового фронта оптического излучения в нелинейной среде

N256 *e* **nonlinear optics**
d nichtlineare Optik *f*
f optique *f* non linéaire
r нелинейная оптика *f*

N257 *e* **nonlinear oscillation**
d nichtlineare Schwingungen *f pl*
f oscillations *f pl* non linéaires
r нелинейные колебания *n pl*

N258 *e* **nonlinear phase conjugation** *see* **nonlinear optical phase conjugation**

N259 *e* **nonlinear phenomena** (*in plasma*)
d nichtlineare Erscheinungen *f pl (im Plasma)*
f phénomènes *m pl* non linéaires (*au plasma*)
r нелинейные явления *n pl (в плазме)*

N260 *e* **nonlinear polarization**
d nichtlineare Polarisation *f*
f polarisation *f* non linéaire
r нелинейная поляризация *f*

N261 *e* **nonlinear quantum field theory**
d nichtlineare Quantenfeldtheorie *f*
f théorie *f* quantique du champ non linéaire
r нелинейная квантовая теория *f* поля

N262 *e* **nonlinear response**
d nichtlineare Antwort *f*
f réponse *f* non linéaire
r нелинейный отклик *m*

N263 *e* **nonlinear spectroscopy**
d nichtlineare Spektroskopie *f*
f spectroscopie *f* non linéaire
r нелинейная спектроскопия *f*

N264 *e* **nonlinear susceptibility**
d nichtlineare Suszeptibilität *f*
f susceptibilité *f* non linéaire
r нелинейная восприимчивость *f*

N265 *e* **nonlinear system**
d nichtlineares System *n*
f système *m* non linéaire
r нелинейная система *f*

N266 *e* **nonlinear transformation**

    d nichtlineare Transformation *f*
    f transformation *f* non linéaire
    r нелинейное преобразование *n*

N267 *e* **nonlinear vibration** *see* nonlinear oscillation

N268 *e* **nonlinear waves**
    d nichtlineare Wellen *f pl*
    f ondes *f pl* non linéaires
    r нелинейные волны *f pl*

N269 *e* **nonlocal interaction**
    d nichtlokale Wechselwirkung *f*
    f interaction *f* non locale
    r нелокальное взаимодействие *n*

N270 *e* **nonlocality**
    d Nichtlokalität *f*
    f non-localité *f*
    r нелокальность *f*

N271 *e* **nonlocal quantum field theory**
    d nichtlokale Quantenfeldtheorie *f*
    f théorie *f* quantique du champ non locale
    r нелокальная квантовая теория *f* поля

N272 *e* **nonmetal**
    d Nichtmetall *n*
    f non-métal *m*
    r неметалл *m*

N273 *e* **nonmonochromaticity**
    d Nichtmonochromasie *f*
    f non-monochromatisme *m*
    r немонохроматичность *f*

N274 *e* **non-Newtonian liquid**
    d nichtnewtonsche Flüssigkeit *f*
    f liquide *m* non newtonien
    r неньютоновская жидкость *f*

N275 *e* **nonparametric method**
    d nichtparametrisches Verfahren *n*
    f méthode *f* non paramétrique
    r непараметрический метод *m*

N276 *e* **nonperiodic oscillation, nonperiodic oscillations**
    d aperiodische Schwingungen *f pl*
    f oscillations *f pl* apériodiques
    r непериодические колебания *n pl*

N277 *e* **nonperiodic process**
    d aperiodischer Prozeß *m*
    f processus *m* apériodique
    r непериодический процесс *m*

N278 *e* **nonpolar molecules**
    d nichtpolare Moleküle *n pl*
    f molécules *f pl* non polaires
    r неполярные молекулы *f pl*

N279 *e* **nonpolynomial quantum field theory**
    d nichtpolynomiale Quantenfeldtheorie *f*
    f théorie *f* du champ quantique non polynomiale
    r неполиномиальная квантовая теория *f* поля

N280 *e* **nonpotentiality**
    d Wirbelfreiheit *f (Feld)*
    f non-potentialité *f*
    r непотенциальность *f (поля)*

N281 *e* **nonproliferation of nuclear weapon**
    d Nichtweiterverbreitung *f* von Kernwaffen
    f non-prolifération *f* des armes nucléaires
    r нераспространение *n* ядерного оружия

N282 *e* **nonradiative recombination**
    d strahlungslose Rekombination *f*
    f recombinaison *f* non radiative
    r безызлучательная рекомбинация *f*

N283 *e* **nonradiative transfer**
    d strahlungslose Übertragung *f*
    f transfert *m* non radiatif
    r безызлучательный перенос *m*

N284 *e* **nonradiative transition**
    d strahlungsloser Übergang *m*
    f transition *f* non radiative
    r безызлучательный переход *m*

N285 *e* **nonreciprocal element**
    d nichtumkehrbares Element *n*
    f élément *m* non réciproque
    r невзаимный элемент *m*

N286 *e* **nonreciprocal phase shifter**
    d nichtreziproker Phasenschieber *m*
    f déphaseur *m* non réciproque
    r невзаимный фазовращатель *m*

N287 *e* **nonreciprocity**
    d Nichtreziprozität *f*
    f non-réciprocité *f*
    r невзаимность *f*

N288 *e* **nonreducible representation**
    d irreduzible Darstellung *f*
    f représentation *f* irréductible
    r неприводимое представление *n*

N289 *e* **nonrelativistic mechanics**
    d nichtrelativistische Mechanik *f*, Newtonsche Mechanik *f*
    f mécanique *f* non relativiste, mécanique *f* newtonienne
    r нерелятивистская механика *f*, механика *f* Ньютона

N290 *e* **nonrelativistic momentum**
    d nichtrelativistischer Impuls *m*
    f moment *m* non relativiste
    r нерелятивистский импульс *m*

N291 *e* **nonrelativistic motion**

d nichtrelativistische Bewegung *f*
f mouvement *m* non relativiste
r нерелятивистское движение *n*

N292 e nonrelativistic particle radiation
d nichtrelativistische Teilchenstrahlung *f*
f radiation *f* des particules non relativistes
r излучение *n* нерелятивистских частиц

N293 e nonrenormalizability
d Nichtrenormierbarkeit *f*
f non-rénormalisabilité *f*
r неперенормируемость *f*

N294 e nonrenormalizable quantum field theory
d nichtrenormierbare Quantenfeldtheorie *f*
f théorie *f* de champ quantique non rénormalisable
r неперенормируемая квантовая теория *f* поля

N295 e nonresonant scattering
d Nichtresonanzstreuung *f*
f diffusion *f* non résonnante
r нерезонансное рассеяние *n*

N296 e nonreversible change
d irreversible Änderung *f*
f changement *m* irréversible
r необратимое изменение *n*

N297 e nonselective receiver
d nichtselektiver Empfänger *m*
f récepteur *m* non sélectif
r неселективный приёмник *m*

N298 e nonselfsustaining discharge
d unselbständige Entladung *f*
f décharge *f* semi-autonome
r несамостоятельный разряд *m*

N299 e nonsphericity
d Nichtkugelförmigkeit *f (Kern)*
f non-sphéricité *f (noyau)*
r несферичность *f (ядра)*

N300 e nonstationary flow
d nichtstationäre Strömung *f*
f écoulement *m* non stationnaire
r нестационарное течение *n*, неустановившееся течение *n*

N301 e nonstationary interference
d nichtstationäre Interferenz *f*
f interférence *f* non stationnaire, interférence *f* non permanente
r нестационарная интерференция *f*

N302 e nonstationary motion
d nichtstationäre Bewegung *f*
f mouvement *m* non stationnaire, mouvement *m* non permanent

r нестационарное движение *n*, неустановившееся движение *n*

N303 e nonstationary problem
d nichtstationäres Problem *n*
f problème *m* non stationnaire
r нестационарная задача *f*

N304 e nonstationary process
d nichtstationärer Prozeß *m*
f processus *m* non stationnaire
r нестационарный процесс *m*, неустановившийся процесс *m*

N305 e nonstationary self-focusing
d nichtstationäre Selbstfokussierung *f*
f autofocalisation *f* non stationnaire
r нестационарная самофокусировка *f*

N306 e nonsymmetrical junction
d nichtsymmetrischer Übergang *m*
f jonction *f* asymétrique
r несимметричный переход *m*

N307 e nonuniform broadening
d ungleichmäßige Verbreiterung *f*
f élargissement *m* non uniforme
r неоднородное уширение *n*

N308 e nonuniformity
d Ungleichförmigkeit *f*; Ungleichmäßigkeit *f*
f non-uniformité *f*
r 1. неоднородность *f* 2. неравномерность *f*

N309 e nonuniform motion
d ungleichförmige Bewegung *f*
f mouvement *m* irrégulier
r неравномерное движение *n*

N310 e nonvanishing mass *see* nonzero mass

N311 e nonvertical transition
d indirekter Übergang *m*
f transition *f* indirecte
r непрямой переход *m*

N312 e nonvisible radiation
d unsichtbare Strahlung *f*
f radiation *f* invisible
r невидимое излучение *n*

N313 e nonzero mass
d von Null verschiedene Masse *f*
f masse *f* autre que nulle
r ненулевая масса *f*

N314 e normal
d Senkrechte *f*, Lot *n*, Normale *f*
f normale *f*
r нормаль *f*, перпендикуляр *m*

N315 e normal acceleration
d Normalbeschleunigung *f*
f accélération *f* normale, accélération *f* centripète

r нормальное ускорение *n*,
центростремительное ускорение *n*

N316 e **normal dispersion** *see* **negative**
dispersion

N317 e **normal distribution**
d Normalverteilung *f*, Gaußsche
Verteilung *f*
f distribution *f* normale, distribution *f*
de Gauss
r нормальное распределение *n*,
распределение *n* Гаусса

N318 e **normal incidence**
d senkrechter Einfall *m*, normaler
Einfall *m*, Normaleinfall *m*
f incidence *f* normale
r нормальное падение *n*

N319 e **normalization**
d Normierung *f*
f normalisation *f*
r нормировка *f*

N320 e **normalized amplitude**
d normierte Amplitude *f*
f amplitude *f* normalisée
r нормированная амплитуда *f*

N321 e **normalized distribution**
d normierte Verteilung *f*
f distribution *f* normalisée
r нормированное распределение *n*

N322 e **normalizing**
d Normalglühen, Normalisierung *f*
f normalisation *f* (*traitement thermique*
du métal)
r нормализация *f* (*металла*)

N323 e **normalizing factor**
d Normierungsfaktor *m*
f facteur *m* de normalisation
r нормирующий множитель *m*

N324 e **normal mode**
d Normalschwingung *f*, normale Mode *f*,
Normalmode *f*
f mode *m* normal
r нормальная мода *f*, собственная
мода *f*

N325 e **normal oscillation, normal**
oscillations
d normale Schwingungen *f pl*
f oscillations *f pl* normales
r нормальные колебания *n pl*

N326 e **normal product**
d Normalprodukt *n*
f produit *m* normal
r нормальное произведение *n*
(*операторов*)

N327 e **normal temperature and pressure**
d Normalbedingungen *f pl*

f conditions *f pl* normales
r нормальные условия *n pl*

N328 e **normal tone**
d Normalton *m*
f ton *m* normal
r нормальный тон *m*

N329 e **normal vibration, normal vibrations**
d Normalschwingungen *f pl*
f oscillations *f pl* normales
r нормальные колебания *n pl*

N330 e **normal waves**
d Normalwellen *f pl*
f ondes *f pl* normales
r нормальные волны *f pl*, собственные
волны *f pl*

N331 e **normal Zeeman effect**
d normaler Zeeman-Effekt *m*
f effet *m* normal de Zeeman
r нормальный эффект *m* Зеемана

N332 e **notation**
d Notation *f*
f notation *f*
r система *f* обозначений
(*спектральных термов*)

N333 e **notch**
d Kerbe *f*, Einschnitt *m*
f entaille *f*
r надрез *m*

N334 e **Nöther theorem** *see* **Noether**
theorem

N335 e **Nottingham effect**
d Nottingham-Effekt *m*
f effet *m* de Nottingham
r эффект *m* Ноттингема

N336 e **nova**
d Nova *f*
f nova *f*, étoile *f* nouvelle
r новая *f*, новая звезда *f*

N337 e **nozzle**
d Düse *f*
f tuyère *f*
r сопло *n*

N338 e **n-photon absorption**
d n-Photonen-Absorption *f*
f absorption *f* de n-photons
r *n*-фотонное поглощение *n*

N339 e **n-region**
d n-Gebiet *n*, n-leitende Zone *f*
f région *f* n
r *n*-область *f*, область *f* электронной
проводимости

N340 e **N.T.P.** *see* **normal temperature and**
pressure

N341　e　n-type semiconductor
　　　d　n-Halbleiter *m*,
　　　　　Überschußhalbleiter *m*
　　　f　semi-conducteur *m* de n-type
　　　r　электронный полупроводник *m*,
　　　　　полупроводник *m* n-типа

N342　e　nuclear acoustic resonance
　　　d　akustische Kernresonanz *f*
　　　f　résonance *f* acoustique nucléaire
　　　r　ядерный акустический резонанс *m*

N343　e　nuclear adiabatic demagnetization
　　　d　adiabatische Kernentmagnetisierung *f*
　　　f　démagnétisation *f* nucléaire
　　　　　adiabatique
　　　r　ядерное адиабатическое
　　　　　размагничивание *n*

N344　e　nuclear astrophysics
　　　d　Astrokernphysik *f*
　　　f　astrophysique *f* nucléaire
　　　r　ядерная астрофизика *f*

N345　e　nuclear bomb
　　　d　Atombombe *f*, Kernbombe *f*,
　　　　　Kernspaltungsbombe *f*
　　　f　bombe *f* nucléaire
　　　r　атомная бомба *f*, ядерная бомба *f*

N346　e　nuclear cascade
　　　d　Kernkaskade *f*
　　　f　cascade *f* nucléaire
　　　r　ядерный каскад *m*

N347　e　nuclear chain reaction
　　　d　Kernkettenreaktion *f*
　　　f　réaction *f* en chaîne nucléaire
　　　r　ядерная цепная реакция *f*

N348　e　nuclear charge
　　　d　Kernladung *f*
　　　f　charge *f* du noyau, charge *f* nucléaire
　　　r　заряд *m* ядра

N349　e　nuclear chemistry
　　　d　Kernchemie *f*
　　　f　chimie *f* nucléaire
　　　r　ядерная химия *f*

N350　e　nuclear decay
　　　d　Kernzerfall *m*
　　　f　désintégration *f* nucléaire
　　　r　ядерный распад *m*

N351　e　nuclear deformation
　　　d　Kerndeformation *f*
　　　f　déformation *f* nucléaire
　　　r　деформация *f* ядра

N352　e　nuclear demagnetization cryostat
　　　d　Kernentmagnetisierungskryostat *m*
　　　f　cryostat *m* de démagnétisation
　　　　　nucléaire
　　　r　криостат *m* ядерного
　　　　　размагничивания

N353　e　nuclear density
　　　d　Dichte *f* der Kernmaterie,
　　　　　Kerndichte *f*
　　　f　densité *f* nucléaire
　　　r　ядерная плотность *f*

N354　e　nuclear disintegration *see* nuclear
　　　　　decay

N355　e　nuclear electronics
　　　d　Kernelektronik *f*
　　　f　électronique *f* nucléaire
　　　r　ядерная электроника *f*

N356　e　nuclear emulsion
　　　d　Kernemulsion *f*, Kernspuremulsion *f*
　　　f　émulsion *f* nucléaire
　　　r　ядерная эмульсия *f*

N357　e　nuclear energy
　　　d　Kernenergie *f*, Atomkernenergie *f*
　　　f　énergie *f* nucléaire
　　　r　атомная энергия *f*, ядерная
　　　　　энергия *f*

N358　e　nuclear energy level
　　　d　Kernniveau *n*, Kernenergieniveau *n*
　　　f　terme *m* nucléaire, niveau *m* nucléaire
　　　r　ядерный энергетический уровень *m*

N359　e　nuclear explosion
　　　d　Kernexplosion *f*
　　　f　explosion *f* nucléaire
　　　r　ядерный взрыв *m*

N360　e　nuclear ferromagnetism
　　　d　Kernferromagnetismus *m*
　　　f　ferromagnétisme *m* nucléaire
　　　r　ядерный ферромагнетизм *m*

N361　e　nuclear fission
　　　d　Kernspaltung *f*
　　　f　fission *f* nucléaire
　　　r　деление *n* атомного ядра

N362　e　nuclear forces
　　　d　Kernkräfte *pl*, Kernfeldkräfte *pl*
　　　f　forces *pl* nucléaires
　　　r　ядерные силы *pl*

N363　e　nuclear fuel
　　　d　Kernbrennstoff *m*
　　　f　combustible *m* nucléaire
　　　r　ядерное топливо *n*

N364　e　nuclear fuel conversion
　　　d　Konversion *f* von Kernbrennstoff
　　　f　conversion *f* du combustible nucléaire
　　　r　воспроизводство *n* ядерного топлива

N365　e　nuclear fusion
　　　d　Kernfusion *f*, Fusion *f*
　　　f　fusion *f* nucléaire
　　　r　ядерный синтез *m*

N366　e　nuclear gyroscope
　　　d　Kerngyroskop *n*, Kernspingyroskop *n*

f gyroscope m nucléaire
r ядерный гироскоп m

N367 e nuclear isobar
d Kernisobar n
f isobare f nucléaire
r ядерный изобар m

N368 e nuclear isomer
d Kernisomer n
f isomère m nucléaire
r ядерный изомер m

N369 e nuclear isomerism
d Kernisomerie f
f isomérie f nucléaire
r ядерная изомерия f, изомерия f
атомных ядер

N370 e nuclear isospin
d Kernisospin m
f isospin m nucléaire
r изоспин m ядра

N371 e nuclear magnetic moment
d magnetisches Kernmoment n
f moment m magnétique nucléaire
r магнитный момент m ядра,
ядерный магнитный момент m

N372 e nuclear magnetic resonance
d magnetische Kernresonanz f
f résonance f magnétique nucléaire
r ядерный магнитный резонанс m,
ЯМР

N373 e nuclear magnetic resonance
magnetometer
d NMR-Magnetometer n, magnetisches
Kernresonanzmagnetometer n
f magnétomètre m à résonance
nucléaire magnétique
r ЯМР-магнитометр m, магнитометр
m ядерного магнитного резонанса

N374 e nuclear magnetism
d Kernmagnetismus m, Magnetismus m
des Atomkerns
f magnétisme m nucléaire
r ядерный магнетизм m

N375 e nuclear magneton
d Kernmagneton n
f magnéton m nucléaire
r ядерный магнетон m

N376 e nuclear matter
d Kernmaterie f
f matière f nucléaire
r ядерная материя f

N377 e nuclear models
d Kernmodelle n pl
f modèles m pl nucléaires
r модели f pl ядра, ядерные
модели f pl

N378 e nuclear moment
d Kernmoment n, Moment n des
Atomkerns
f moment m nucléaire
r ядерный момент m

N379 e nuclear orientation
d Kernorientierung f, Kernausrichtung f
f orientation f nucléaire
r ориентация f ядер

N380 e nuclear paramagnetism
d Kernparamagnetismus m,
Paramagnetismus m des Atomkerns
f paramagnétisme m nucléaire
r ядерный парамагнетизм m

N381 e nuclear photoelectric effect
d Kernphotoeffekt m
f effet m photo-électrique nucléaire
r ядерный фотоэффект m

N382 e nuclear physics
d Kernphysik f
f physique f nucléaire
r ядерная физика f

N383 e nuclear polarizability
d Kernpolarisierbarkeit f
f polarisabilité f nucléaire
r поляризуемость f ядер

N384 e nuclear polarization
d Kernpolarisation f
f polarisation f nucléaire
r поляризация f ядер

N385 e nuclear potential
d Kernpotential n
f potentiel m nucléaire
r ядерный потенциал m

N386 e nuclear power
d 1. Kernenergie f, Kernkraft f 2.
Kernenergetik f
f 1. énergie f nucléaire 2. énergétique f
nucléaire
r 1. ядерная энергия f 2. ядерная
энергетика f

N387 e nuclear precession
d Kernpräzession f
f précession f nucléaire
r ядерная прецессия f

N388 e nuclear pumping
d nukleares Pumpen n
f pompage m nucléaire
r ядерная накачка f

N389 e nuclear quadrupole resonance
d Kernquadrupolresonanz f
f résonance f quadripolaire nucléaire
r ядерный квадрупольный резонанс
m, ЯКР

N390 e nuclear radiation

d Kernstrahlung *f*
f radiation *f* nucléaire, rayonnement *m* nucléaire
r ядерное излучение *n*

N391 e **nuclear radius**
d Kernradius *m*
f rayon *m* du noyau, rayon *m* nucléaire
r радиус *m* атомного ядра

N392 e **nuclear reaction**
d Kernreaktion *f*
f réaction *f* nucléaire
r ядерная реакция *f*

N393 e **nuclear reaction channel**
d Kernreaktionskanal *m*
f canal *m* de réaction nucléaire
r канал *m* ядерной реакции

N394 e **nuclear reaction cross-section**
d Reaktionsquerschnitt *m*, Wirkungsquerschnitt *m* für eine Kernreaktion
f section *f* de réaction nucléaire
r сечение *n* ядерной реакции

N395 e **nuclear reactor**
d Kernreaktor *m*, Reaktor *m*
f réacteur *m* nucléaire, réacteur *m*
r ядерный реактор *m*

N396 e **nuclear refraction**
d Kernrefraktion *f*
f réfraction *f* nucléaire
r ядерная рефракция *f*

N397 e **nuclear relaxation**
d Kernrelaxation *f*
f relaxation *f* nucléaire
r ядерная релаксация *f*

N398 e **nuclear saturation** *see* **saturation of nuclear forces**

N399 e **nuclear shell**
d Kernschale *f*
f couche *f* nucléaire
r ядерная оболочка *f*

N400 e **nuclear spectroscopy**
d Kernspektroskopie *f*
f spectroscopie *f* nucléaire
r ядерная спектроскопия *f*

N401 e **nuclear spin**
d Kernspin *m*, Kerndrehimpuls *m*
f spin *m* nucléaire
r ядерный спин *m*, спин *m* ядра

N402 e **nuclear spin alignment**
d Kernspinausrichtung *f*
f alignement *m* des spins nucléaires
r выстраивание *n* ядерных спинов

N403 e **nuclear sublattice**
d Kernuntergitter *n*

f sous-réseau *m* nucléaire
r ядерная подрешётка *f*

N404 e **nuclear target**
d Target *n*
f cible *f* nucléaire
r ядерная мишень *f*

N405 e **nuclear weapon**
d Kernwaffe *f*
f arme *f* nucléaire
r ядерное оружие *n*

N406 e **nucleate boiling**
d Blasensieden *n*, Blasenverdampfung *f*, Bläschensieden *n*
f ébullition *f* de bulles
r пузырьковое кипение *n*

N407 e **nucleation**
d Keimbildung *f*
f nucléation *f*
r 1. зародышеобразование *n* 2. нуклеация *f (зарождение аэрозольной частицы)* 3. зарождение *n*

N408 e **nucleation center**
d Kristallisationskeim *m*
f germe *m*
r зародыш *m* кристаллизации, зародыш *m*

N409 e **nucleon**
d Nukleon *n*
f nucléon *m*
r нуклон *m*

N410 e **nucleon association**
d Nukleonenassoziation *f*
f association *f* nucléonique
r нуклонная ассоциация *f*

N411 e **nucleon bag**
d Sack-Nukleon *n*
f poche-nucléon *f*
r мешок-нуклон *m*

N412 e **nucleon charge**
d Nukleonenladung *f*
f charge *f* de nucléon
r заряд *m* нуклона, нуклонный заряд *m*

N413 e **nucleonic cluster**
d Nukleonencluster *m*
f cluster *m* à nucléons
r нуклонный кластер *m*

N414 e **nucleon pairing**
d Nukleonenpaarung *f*, Nukleonenpaarbildung *f*
f création *f* des paires de nucléons
r спаривание *n* нуклонов

N415 e **nucleosynthesis**
d Nukleosynthese *f*

f synthèse f nucléon
r нуклеосинтез m

N416 e nucleus
d 1. Kern m, Atomkern m
2. Keim m
f 1. noyau m 2. germe m
r 1. ядро n 2. зародыш m
(кристалла)

N417 e nucleus coagulation
d Keimkoagulation f
f coagulation f des germes
r коагуляция f зародышей

N418 e nuclide
d Nuklid n
f nucléide m
r нуклид m

N419 e null charge
d Nulladung f
f charge f nulle
r нуль-заряд m

N420 e null indicator
d Nullanzeiger m, Nullindikator m
f indicateur m de zéro
r нуль-индикатор m

N421 e number
d 1. Zahl f 2. Nummer f
f nombre m
r 1. число n 2. номер m

N422 e number of degrees of freedom
d Anzahl f der Freiheitsgrade, Zahl f
der Freiheitsgrade
f nombre m de degrés de liberté
r число n степеней свободы

N423 e numerical aperture
d numerische Apertur f
f ouverture f numérique
r числовая апертура f

N424 e numerical integration
d numerische Integration f
f intégration f numérique
r численное интегрирование n

N425 e Nusselt number
d Nußelt-Zahl f, Nußeltsche Zahl f
f nombre m de Nusselt
r число n Нуссельта

N426 e nutation
d Nutation f
f nutation f
r нутация f

N427 e Nyquist formula
d Nyquist-Formel f
f formule f de Nyquist
r формула f Найквиста

O

O1 e object beam
d Objektbündel n
f faisceau m d'objet
r предметный пучок m, объектный
пучок m (в голографии)

O2 e objective
d Objektiv n
f objectif m
r объектив m

O3 e object space
d Objektraum m, Dingraum m,
Gegenstandsraum m
f espace m d'objets
r пространство n предметов

O4 e object wave
d Objektwelle f
f onde f d'objets
r предметная волна f, объектная
волна f

O5 e oblateness
d Abplattung f
f aplatissement m
r сплющенность f, сплюснутость f

O6 e oblique incidence
d Schrägeinfall m , schräger Einfall m
f incidence f oblique
r наклонное падение n

O7 e obliquity (of the ecliptic)
d Schiefe f der Ekliptik
f obliquité f (d'ecliptique)
r наклон m (эклиптики)

O8 e observable
d Observable f, beobachtbare Größe f
f observable f, m, grandeur f
observable
r наблюдаемая f (в квантовой
механике)

O9 e observations
d Beobachtungen f pl
f observations f pl
r наблюдения f pl

O10 e observatory
d Observatorium n
f observatoire m
r обсерватория f

O11 e observed data
d Beobachtungsdaten pl
f données pl d'observation
r данные pl наблюдений

O12 e obstacle

d Hindernis *n*
f obstacle *m*
r препятствие *n*; помеха *f*

O13 e occlusion
d Okklusion *f*
f occlusion *f*
r окклюзия *f*

O14 e occultation
d Bedeckung *f*
f occultation *f*
r покрытие *n* (*в астрономии*)

O15 e occupancy of states
d Auffüllung *f* von Zuständen, Besetzung *f* von Zuständen
f remplissage *m* des états
r заполнение *n* состояний

O16 e occupation
d Besetzung *f*
f occupation *f*
r заполнение *n*, заполненность *f*; населённость *f*, заселённость *f*

O17 e occupied band
d besetztes Band *n*
f bande *f* occupée, bande *f* pleine
r заполненная зона *f*

O18 e occupied level
d besetztes Niveau *n*, besetztes Energieniveau *n*
f niveau *m* occupé
r занятый уровень *m*, заполненный уровень *m*

O19 e occurrence
d 1. Ereignis *n*; Fall *m*; Erscheinung *f*, Erscheinen *n* 2. Häufigkeit *f*
f 1. événement *m* 2. abondance *f*
r 1. событие *n*, случай *m*, появление *n* 2. распространённость *f*

O20 e oceanology
d Meeresforschung *f*, Ozeanologie *f*
f océanologie *f*
r океанология *f*

O21 e octahedron
d Oktaeder *n*, Achtflach *n*, Achtflächner *m*
f octaèdre *m*
r октаэдр *m*

O22 e octave
d Oktave *f*
f octave *f*
r октава *f*

O23 e octet
d Oktett *n*
f octet *m*
r октет *m*

O24 e octupole

d Oktupol *m*, Oktopol *m*
f octopôle *m*
r октуполь *m*

O25 e octupole moment
d Oktupolmoment *n*
f moment *m* octupolaire
r октупольный момент *m*

O26 e ocular *see* eyepiece

O27 e odd states
d ungerade Zustände *m pl*
f états *m pl* impairs
r нечётные состояния *n pl*

O28 e oersted, Oe
d Oersted *n*
f œrsted *m*
r эрстед *m*, Э

O29 e off-axis beam
d außeraxialer Strahl *m*
f faisceau *m* hors d'axe
r внеосевой пучок *m*

O30 e off-axis hologram
d achsenentferntes Hologramm *n*
f hologramme *m* hors d'axe
r внеосевая голограмма *f*

O31 e off-resonance state
d Off-Resonanz-Zustand *m*; resonanzferner Zustand *m*
f état *m* d'absence de résonance; état *m* hors de résonance
r нерезонансное состояние *n*; состояние *n*, далёкое от резонанса

O32 e offset
d Offset *m*
f décalage *m*; déplacement *m*
r смещение *n*, сдвиг *m*

O33 e offset beam
d Offsetstrahl *m*
f faisceau *m* décalé
r смещённый пучок *m*

O34 e ohm, Ω
d Ohm *n*
f ohm *m*
r ом *m*, Ом

O35 e ohmic contact
d ohmscher Kontakt *m*
f contact *m* ohmique
r омический контакт *m*

O36 e ohmic heating *see* Joule heating

O37 e ohmic loss
d ohmscher Verlust *m*
f pertes *f pl* ohmiques
r омические потери *f pl*, джоулевы потери *f pl*

O38　e　**Ohm law**
　　　d　ohmsches Gesetz *n*
　　　f　loi *f* d'Ohm
　　　r　закон *m* Ома

O39　e　**ohmmeter**
　　　d　Ohmmeter *n*
　　　f　ohmmètre *m*
　　　r　омметр *m*

O40　e　**oil pump**
　　　d　Ölpumpe *f*
　　　f　pompe *f* à huile
　　　r　масляный насос *m*

O41　e　**omega particles**
　　　d　Omegateilchen *n pl*, *ω*-Teilchen *n pl*
　　　f　particules *f pl* oméga
　　　r　омега-частицы *f pl*

O42　e　**omegatron**
　　　d　Omegatron *n*
　　　f　omégatron *m*
　　　r　омегатрон *m*

O43　e　**omnidirectional aerial**
　　　d　Rundstrahlantenne *f*
　　　f　antenne *f* omnidirectionnelle
　　　r　всенаправленная антенна *f*, ненаправленная антенна *f*

O44　e　**omnidirectional radiation**
　　　d　ungerichtete Strahlung *f*, Rundstrahlung *f*
　　　f　radiation *f* omnidirectionnelle
　　　r　всенаправленное излучение *n*

O45　e　**omnidirectional radiator**
　　　d　Rundstrahler *m*
　　　f　radiateur *m* omnidirectionnel
　　　r　всенаправленный излучатель *m*

O46　e　**one-body model** *see* **one-particle model**

O47　e　**one-dimensional model**
　　　d　eindimensionales Modell *n*
　　　f　modèle *m* unidimensionnel
　　　r　одномерная модель *f*

O48　e　**one-dimensional motion**
　　　d　eindimensionale Bewegung *f*
　　　f　mouvement *m* unidimensionnel
　　　r　одномерное движение *n*

O49　e　**one-electron approximation**
　　　d　Einelektronenannäherung *f*
　　　f　approximation *f* à électron unique
　　　r　одноэлектронное приближение *n*

O50　e　**one-loop Feynman diagram**
　　　d　Einschleifen-Feynman-Diagramm *n*
　　　f　diagramme *m* à boucle unique de Feynman
　　　r　однопетлевая диаграмма *f* Фейнмана

O51　e　**one-parameter representation**
　　　d　einparametrige Darstellung *f*
　　　f　représentation *f* à paramètre unique
　　　r　однопараметрическое представление *n*

O52　e　**one-particle approximation**
　　　d　Einteilchenannäherung *f*
　　　f　approximation *f* à particule unique
　　　r　одночастичное приближение *n*

O53　e　**one-particle model** (*of atomic nucleus*)
　　　d　Einteilchenmodell *n*
　　　f　modèle *m* à particule unique (*de noyau atomique*)
　　　r　одночастичная модель *f* (*атомного ядра*)

O54　e　**one-photon absorption**
　　　d　Einzelphotonenabsorption *f*
　　　f　absorption *f* à photon unique
　　　r　однофотонное поглощение *n*

O55　e　**Onsager reciprocity relations**
　　　d　Onsagersche Reziprozitätsbedingungen *f pl*
　　　f　relations *f pl* d'Onsager
　　　r　соотношения *n pl* взаимности Онсагера

O56　e　**Onsager theorem**
　　　d　Onsagerscher Reziprozitätssatz *m*
　　　f　théorème *m* d'Onsager
　　　r　теорема *f* Онсагера

O57　e　**opacity**
　　　d　Lichtundurchlässigkeit *f*
　　　f　opacité *f*
　　　r　непрозрачность *f*

O58　e　**opalescence**
　　　d　Opaleszenz *f*
　　　f　opalescence *f*
　　　r　опалесценция *f*

O59　e　**opaque plasma**
　　　d　undurchlässiges Plasma *n*
　　　f　plasma *m* opaque
　　　r　непрозрачная плазма *f*

O60　e　**open-circuit voltage**
　　　d　Leerlaufspannung *f*
　　　f　tension *f* en circuit ouvert, f.é.m. *f* en circuit ouvert
　　　r　напряжение *n* холостого хода

O61　e　**open cluster**
　　　d　offener Sternhaufen *m*
　　　f　amas *m* ouvert
　　　r　рассеянное скопление *n* (*звёзд*)

O62　e　**open configuration**
　　　d　offene Konfiguration *f*
　　　f　configuration *f* ouverte
　　　r　открытая конфигурация *f*

O63　e　**open curve**

d offene Kurve *f*
f courbe *f* ouverte
r незамкнутая кривая *f*

O64 *e* open cycle
d offener Zyklus *m*
f cycle *m* ouvert
r незамкнутый цикл *m*

O65 *e* opening
d Öffnung *f*; Loch *n*
f orifice *m* ; trou *m*
r отверстие *n*

O66 *e* open model
d offenes Weltmodell *n*, offene Welt *f*
f Univers *m* ouvert, modèle *m* ouvert
r открытая модель (*Вселенной*), модель *f* открытой Вселенной

O67 *e* open resonator
d offener Resonator *m*
f résonateur *m* ouvert
r открытый резонатор *m*

O68 *e* open system (*in thermodynamics*)
d offenes System *n* (*in der Thermodynamik*)
f système *m* ouvert (*en thermodynamique*)
r открытая система *f* (*в термодинамике*)

O69 *e* open trap
d offene Falle *f*
f piège *m* ouvert
r открытая ловушка *f*

O70 *e* operation
d Operation *f*
f opération *f*
r операция *f*

O71 *e* operational amplifier
d Operationsverstärker *m*
f amplificateur *m* opérationnel
r операционный усилитель *m*

O72 *e* operational calculus
d Operatorenrechnung *f*
f calcul *m* opérationnel
r операционное исчисление *n*

O73 *e* operator
d Operator *m*
f opérateur *m*
r оператор *m*

O74 *e* operator expansion
d Operatorentwicklung *f*
f expansion *f* d'opérateurs
r операторное разложение *n*

O75 *e* operator field
d Operatorfeld *n*
f champ *m* d'opérateurs
r операторное поле *n*

O76 *e* operator isometry
d Operatorenisometrie *f*
f isométrie *f* d'opérateurs
r изометрия *f* операторов

O77 *e* **Oppenheimer-Phillips process**
d Oppenheimer-Phillips-Prozeß *m*
f processus *m* d'Oppenheimer-Phillips
r процесс *m* Оппенгеймера - Филлипса

O78 *e* opposite direction *see* backward direction

O79 *e* opposition (*of a celestial body*)
d Opposition *f*, Gegenschein *m*
f opposition *f* (*du corps céleste*)
r противостояние *n* (*небесного тела*)

O80 *e* optic-acoustic receiver
d optisch-akustischer Empfänger *m*
f récepteur *m* optique-acoustique
r оптико-акустический приёмник *m*

O81 *e* optical absorption
d optische Absorption *f*
f absorption *f* optique
r оптическое поглощение *n*

O82 *e* optical absorption edge
d optischer Absorptionsrand *m*
f bord *m* d'absorption optique
r край *m* оптического поглощения

O83 *e* optical activator
d optischer Aktivator *m*
f activateur *m* optique
r активатор *m* люминофора

O84 *e* optical activity
d optische Aktivität *f*, optisches Drehvermögen *n*
f activité *f* optique
r оптическая активность *f*

O85 *e* optical amplifier
d optischer Verstärker *m*
f amplificateur *m* optique
r оптический усилитель *m*

O86 *e* optical anisotropy
d optische Anisotropie *f*
f anisotropie *f* optique
r оптическая анизотропия *f*

O87 *e* optical antipodes
d optische Antipoden *m pl*
f antipodes *m pl* optiques
r оптические антиподы *m pl*

O88 *e* optical axis
d optische Achse *f*
f axe *m* optique
r оптическая ось *f* (*линзы*)

O89 *e* optical bench
d optische Bank *f*

	f	banc *m* optique
	r	оптическая скамья *f*
O90	e	**optical bistability**
	d	optische Bistabilität *f*
	f	bistabilité *f* optique
	r	оптическая бистабильность *f*
O91	e	**optical breakdown**
	d	optischer Durchschlag *m*
	f	rupture *f* optique
	r	оптический пробой *m*
O92	e	**optical capture** (*of atoms*)
	d	optischer Einfang *m*, optischer Atomeinfang *m*
	f	capture *f* optique (*d'atomes*)
	r	оптический захват *m* (*атомов*)
O93	e	**optical cavity** *see* **optical resonator**
O94	e	**optical channel**
	d	optischer Nachrichtenkanal *m*
	f	canal *m* optique
	r	оптический канал *m*, оптический канал *m* связи
O95	e	**optical chopper** *see* **light chopper**
O96	e	**optical clock**
	d	optische Uhr *f*
	f	horloge *f* optique
	r	оптические часы *pl*
O97	e	**optical communication**
	d	optische Nachrichtenübermittlung *f*, optische Kommunikation *f*
	f	communication *f* optique
	r	оптическая связь *f*
O98	e	**optical comparator**
	d	optischer Komparator *m*
	f	comparateur *m* optique
	r	оптический компаратор *m*
O99	e	**optical compensator**
	d	optischer Kompensator *m*
	f	compensateur *m* optique
	r	оптический компенсатор *m*
O100	e	**optical compressor**
	d	optischer Verdichter *m*
	f	compresseur *m* optique
	r	оптический компрессор *m*
O101	e	**optical computer**
	d	lichtoptische Rechenanlage *f*
	f	ordinateur *m* optique
	r	оптический компьютер *m*, оптическая ЭВМ *f*
O102	e	**optical constant**
	d	optische Konstante *f*
	f	constante *f* optique
	r	оптическая постоянная *f*
O103	e	**optical contact**

	d	optischer Kontakt *m*
	f	contact *m* optique
	r	оптический контакт *m*
O104	e	**optical contrast**
	d	optischer Kontrast *m*
	f	contraste *m* optique
	r	оптический контраст *m*
O105	e	**optical cooling**
	d	optische Abkühlung *f* (*von Atomkernen*)
	f	refroidissement *m* optique (*de noyaux*)
	r	оптическое охлаждение *n* (*ядер*)
O106	e	**optical correlator**
	d	optischer Korrelator *m*
	f	corrélateur *m* optique
	r	оптический коррелятор *m*
O107	e	**optical cryostat**
	d	optischer Kryostat *m*
	f	cryostat *m* optique
	r	оптический криостат *m*
O108	e	**optical data processing**
	d	optische Informationsverarbeitung *f*
	f	traitement *m* optique de l'information
	r	оптическая обработка *f* информации
O109	e	**optical density**
	d	optische Dichte *f*
	f	densité *f* optique
	r	оптическая плотность *f*
O110	e	**optical depth**
	d	1. optische Dicke *f* 2. optische Tiefe *f*
	f	1. épaisseur *f* optique 2. profondeur *f* optique
	r	1. оптическая толщина *f*, оптическая толща *f* 2. оптическая глубина *f*
O111	e	**optical detection**
	d	optische Detektion *f*
	f	détection *f* optique
	r	оптическое детектирование *n*, детектирование *n* света
O112	e	**optical detectors**
	d	optische Empfänger *m pl*; Lichtempfänger *m pl*, Lichtdetektoren *m pl*
	f	détecteurs *m pl* optiques
	r	приёмники *m pl* оптического излучения; фотоприёмники *m pl*
O113	e	**optical diffraction** *see* **light diffraction**
O114	e	**optical discharge**
	d	optische Entladung *f*
	f	décharge *f* optique
	r	оптический разряд *m*

O115   *e*   optical dispersion
     d   Lichtdispersion *f*, Lichtzerlegung *f*
     f   dispersion *f* de lumière
     r   дисперсия *f* света

O116   *e*   optical extinction
     d   optische Extinktion *f*
     f   extinction *f* optique
     r   оптическая экстинция *f*

O117   *e*   optical fiber
     d   Lichtleitfaser *f*
     f   fibre *m* optique
     r   оптическое волокно *n*, световод *m*

O118   *e*   optical fiber communication line
     d   faseroptische Nachrichtenstrecke *f*
     f   ligne *f* de communication à fibre optique
     r   волоконно-оптическая линия *f* связи

O119   *e*   optical filter
     d   Lichtfilter *n*
     f   filtre *m* optique
     r   оптический фильтр *m*

O120   *e*   optical fluorescence
     d   optische Fluoreszenz *f*
     f   fluorescence *f* optique
     r   оптическая флуоресценция *f*

O121   *e*   optical frequency converter
     d   optischer Frequenzwandler *m*
     f   convertisseur *m* de fréquence optique
     r   оптический преобразователь *m* частоты

O122   *e*   optical frequency multiplier
     d   optischer Frequenzvervielfacher *m*
     f   multiplicateur *m* de fréquence optique
     r   оптический умножитель *m* частоты

O123   *e*   optical frequency standard
     d   optischer Frequenzstandard *m*, optisches Frequenznormal *n*
     f   étalon *m* de fréquence optique
     r   оптический стандарт *m* частоты

O124   *e*   optical gain
     d   optische Verstärkung *f*
     f   amplification *f* optique
     r   оптическое усиление *n*

O125   *e*   optical gate *see* optical shutter

O126   *e*   optical glass
     d   optisches Glas *n*, Linsenglas *n*
     f   verre *m* optique
     r   оптическое стекло *n*

O127   *e*   optical gyroscope
     d   optischer Kreisel *m*; Laserkreisel *m*
     f   gyroscope *m* optique; gyroscope *m* laser
     r   оптический гироскоп *m*; лазерный гироскоп *m*

O128   *e*   optical harmonics
     d   optische Harmonischen *f pl*
     f   harmoniques *m pl* optiques
     r   оптические гармоники *f pl*

O129   *e*   optical homogeneity
     d   optische Homogenität *f*
     f   homogénéité *f* optique
     r   оптическая однородность *f*

O130   *e*   optical hysteresis
     d   optische Hysterese *f*
     f   hystérésis *f* optique
     r   оптический гистерезис *m*

O131   *e*   optical illusions
     d   optische Täuschungen *f pl*
     f   illusions *f pl* optiques
     r   оптические иллюзии *f pl*, зрительные иллюзии *f pl*

O132   *e*   optical image
     d   optisches Bild *n*
     f   image *f* optique
     r   оптическое изображение *n*

O133   *e*   optical indicatrix
     d   Indikatrix *f*, Indexellipsoid *n*
     f   indicatrice *f* optique
     r   оптическая индикатриса *f*

O134   *e*   optical information
     d   optische Information *f*
     f   information *f* optique
     r   оптическая информация *f*

O135   *e*   optical information processing *see* optical data processing

O136   *e*   optical inhomogeneity
     d   optische Inhomogenität *f*
     f   inhomogénéité *f* optique
     r   оптическая неоднородность *f*

O137   *e*   optical interference
     d   optische Interferenz *f*, Lichtinterferenz *f*
     f   interférence *f* optique, interférence *f* de lumière
     r   оптическая интерференция *f*, интерференция *f* света

O138   *e*   optical interferometer
     d   optisches Interferometer *n*
     f   interféromètre *m* optique
     r   оптический интерферометр *m*

O139   *e*   optical isomer
     d   optisches Isomer *n*, Spiegelbildisomer *n*
     f   isomère *m* optique
     r   оптический изомер *m*

O140   *e*   optical isomerism
     d   optische Isomerie *f*, Spiegelbildisomerie *f*

    f isomérie *f* optique
    r оптическая изомерия *f*

O141 *e* **optical isotropy**
    d optische Isotropie *f*
    f isotropie *f* optique
    r оптическая изотропия *f*

O142 *e* **optical Kerr effect**
    d optischer Kerr-Effekt *m*
    f effet *m* optique de Kerr
    r оптический эффект *m* Керра

O143 *e* **optical Kerr shutter**
    d Kerr-Zellen-Verschluß *m*
    f obturateur *m* à cellule de Kerr
    r оптический затвор *m* на ячейке Керра

O144 *e* **optical klystron**
    d optisches Klystron *n*
    f klystron *m* optique
    r оптический клистрон *m*

O145 *e* **optical length** *see* **optical path**

O146 *e* **optical levitation**
    d optisches Schweben *n*, optische Levitation *f*
    f lévitation *f* optique
    r оптическая левитация *f*

O147 *e* **optical logic unit**
    d optische Logikeinheit *f*
    f unité *f* logique optique
    r оптическое логическое устройство *n*

O148 *e* **optically active substance**
    d optisch aktive Substanz *f*
    f substance *f* optiquement active
    r оптически активное вещество *n*

O149 *e* **optically thick media**
    d optisch dicke Medien *n pl*
    f milieux *m pl* optiquement épais
    r оптически толстые среды *f pl*

O150 *e* **optically thick plasma radiation**
    d Strahlung *f* des optisch dicken Plasmas
    f radiation *f* du plasma optiquement épais
    r излучение *n* оптически толстой плазмы

O151 *e* **optically thin media**
    d optisch dünne Medien *n pl*
    f milieux *m pl* optiquement minces
    r оптически тонкие среды *n pl*

O152 *e* **optically thin plasma radiation**
    d Strahlung *f* des optisch dünnen Plasmas
    f radiation *f* du plasma optiquement mince
    r излучение *n* оптически тонкой плазмы

O153 *e* **optical magnification**
    d optische Vergrößerung *f*
    f grossissement *m* optique
    r оптическое увеличение *n*

O154 *e* **optical measurements**
    d optische Messungen *f pl*
    f mesures *f pl* optiques
    r оптические измерения *n pl*

O155 *e* **optical memory**
    d optischer Speicher *m*
    f mémoire *f* optique
    r оптическая память *f*, оптическое запоминающее устройство *n*

O156 *e* **optical microscope**
    d Lichtmikroskop *n*, optisches Mikroskop *n*
    f microscope *m* optique
    r оптический микроскоп *m*

O157 *e* **optical mixing**
    d optische Mischung *f*
    f mélange *m* optique
    r оптическое смещение *n*

O158 *e* **optical model** (*of nucleus*)
    d optisches Modell *n*, optisches Kernmodell *n*
    f modèle *m* optique, modèle *m* optique du noyau
    r оптическая модель *f* (*ядра*)

O159 *e* **optical modulator**
    d Lichtmodulator *m*
    f modulateur *m* optique, modulateur *m* de lumière
    r оптический модулятор *m*, модулятор *m* света

O160 *e* **optical monochromator**
    d optischer Monochromator *m*
    f monochromateur *m* optique
    r оптический монохроматор *m*

O161 *e* **optical multiplication**
    d optische Vervielfachung *f*
    f multiplication *f* optique
    r оптическое увеличение *n*

O162 *e* **optical multistability**
    d optische Multistabilität *f*
    f multistabilité *f* optique
    r оптическая мультистабильность *f*

O163 *e* **optical nonlinearity**
    d optische Nichtlinearität *f*
    f non-linéarité *f* optique
    r оптическая нелинейность *f*

O164 *e* **optical nutation**
    d optische Nutation *f*
    f nutation *f* optique
    r оптическая нутация *f*

O165 *e* **optical orientation**

d optische Orientierung f
f orientation f optique
r оптическая ориентация f

O166 e optical path
d optische Weglänge f
f chemin m optique, trajet m optique
r оптическая длина f пути;
оптический путь m

O167 e optical phase conjugation
d optische Phasenkonjugation f
f conjugaison f du front d'onde optique
r обращение n волнового фронта
оптического излучения

O168 e optical phonon
d optisches Phonon n
f phonon m optique
r оптический фонон m

O169 e optical plasmatron
d optisches Plasmatron n
f plasmatron m optique
r оптический плазматрон m

O170 e optical potential
d optisches Potential n
f potentiel m optique
r оптический потенциал m

O171 e optical power
d Brechwert m, Brechkraft f
f puissance f (p. e. d'une lentille)
r оптическая сила f (напр. линзы)

O172 e optical probe technique
d Lichtsondenmethode f
f méthode f de sonde optique
r метод m оптического зонда

O173 e optical processor
d optischer Prozessor m
f processeur m optique
r оптический процессор m

O174 e optical propagation
d Lichtwellenausbreitung f
f propagation f d'ondes lumineuses
r распространение n световых волн

O175 e optical properties
d optische Eigenschaften f pl
f propriétés f pl optiques
r оптические свойства n pl

O176 e optical pulse
d optischer Impuls m
f impulsion f optique
r оптический импульс m

O177 e optical pumping
d optisches Pumpen n
f pompage m optique
r оптическая накачка f

O178 e optical pyrometer
d optisches Pyrometer n
f pyromètre m optique
r оптический пирометр m

O179 e optical pyrometry
d optische Pyrometrie f
f pyrométrie f optique
r оптическая пирометрия f

O180 e optical radar
d optisches Radar n, Laserradar n,
Lidar n
f radar m optique, lidar m
r оптический локатор m

O181 e optical radiation
d Strahlung f im optischen
Spektralbereich; optische Strahlung f,
sichtbare Strahlung f
f radiation f optique, rayonnement m
optique
r оптическое излучение n

O182 e optical rangefinder
d optischer Entfernungsmesser m
f télémètre m optique
r оптический дальномер m,
светодальномер m

O183 e optical recording
d optische Aufzeichnung f
f enregistrement m optique
r оптическая запись f

O184 e optical rectification see optical
detection

O185 e optical reflection see reflection of
light

O186 e optical registration
d Lichtregistrierung f,
Lichtstrahlregistrierung f
f enregistrement m optique
r оптическая регистрация f

O187 e optical resonator
d optischer Resonator m
f résonateur m optique
r оптический резонатор m

O188 e optical rotary dispersion
d Rotationsdispersion f
f dispersion f rotatoire
r дисперсия f оптического вращения

O189 e optical rotation
d optische Drehung f
f rotation f du plan de polarisation de
lumière
r вращение n плоскости поляризации
света

O190 e optical shutter
d Lichtverschluß m
f obturateur m optique
r оптический затвор m

O191   *e* **optical soliton**
     d optisches Soliton *n*
     f soliton *m* optique
     r оптический солитон *m*

O192   *e* **optical source**
     d optische Strahlungsquelle *f*
     f source *f* optique
     r источник *m* света, источник *m* оптического излучения

O193   *e* **optical spectrometer**
     d optisches Spektrometer *n*
     f spectromètre *m* optique
     r оптический спектрометр *m*

O194   *e* **optical spectroscopy**
     d Spektroskopie *f* im Sichtbaren
     f spectroscopie *f* optique
     r оптическая спектроскопия

O195   *e* **optical spectrum**
     d Lichtspektrum *n*, optisches Spektrum *n*
     f spectre *m* optique
     r оптический спектр *m*

O196   *e* **optical Stark effect**
     d optischer Stark-Effekt *m*
     f effet *m* optique de Stark
     r оптический эффект *m* Штарка

O197   *e* **optical strength**
     d Lichtstrahlfestigkeit *f*
     f résistance *f* du rayon lumineux
     r лучевая прочность *f*

O198   *e* **optical surface**
     d optische Oberfläche *f*
     f surface *f* optique
     r оптическая поверхность *f*

O199   *e* **optical switch**
     d Lichtschalter *m*
     f commutateur *m* optique
     r оптический переключатель *m*

O200   *e* **optical switching**
     d optische Kommutation *f*, optische Schaltung *f*
     f commutation *f* optique
     r оптическая коммутация *f*, оптическое переключение *n*

O201   *e* **optical system**
     d optisches System *n*
     f système *m* optique
     r оптическая система *f*

O202   *e* **optical telescope**
     d optisches Fernrohr *n*
     f télescope *m* optique
     r оптический телескоп *m*

O203   *e* **optical theorem** (*in quantum theory*)
     d optischer Satz *m*, optisches Theorem *n* (*Quantentheorie*)
     f théorème *m* optique (*en théorie quantique*)
     r оптическая теорема *f* (*в квантовой теории*)

O204   *e* **optical thickness** *see* **optical depth 1.**

O205   *e* **optical transducer**
     d optischer Meßumformer *m*
     f convertisseur *m* optique
     r оптический преобразователь *m*

O206   *e* **optical transistor**
     d Optotransistor *m*
     f optotransistor *m*
     r оптический транзистор *m*, оптотранзистор *m*

O207   *e* **optical transition**
     d optischer Übergang *m*
     f transition *f* optique
     r оптический переход *m*

O208   *e* **optical trigger**
     d optischer Trigger *m*
     f trigger *m* optique
     r оптический триггер *m*

O209   *e* **optical waves**
     d optische Wellen *f pl*, Lichtwellen *f pl*
     f ondes *f pl* optiques, ondes *f pl* de lumière
     r оптические волны *f pl*, световые волны *f pl*

O210   *e* **optical wedge**
     d Keil *m*, optischer Keil *m*
     f coin *m* optique
     r оптический клин *m*

O211   *e* **optic axis**
     d optische Achse *f* (*Kristall*)
     f axe *m* optique (*du cristal*)
     r оптическая ось (*кристалла*)

O212   *e* **optics**
     d Optik *f*
     f optique *f*
     r оптика *f*

O213   *e* **optics of inhomogeneous media**
     d Optik *f* inhomogener Medien
     f optique *f* des milieux inhomogènes
     r оптика *f* неоднородных сред

O214   *e* **optics of moving media**
     d Optik *f* bewegter Medien
     f optique *f* des milieux mouvants
     r оптика *f* движущихся сред

O215   *e* **optics of thin layers**
     d Dünnschichtoptik *f*, Optik *f* dünner Schichten
     f optique *f* des couches minces
     r оптика *f* тонких слоёв

O216   *e* **opto-acoustic effect**
     d optoakustischer Effekt *m*

      f effet *m* opto-acoustique
      r оптоакустический эффект *m*

O217 *e* **opto-acoustic spectroscopy**
      d optoakustische Spektroskopie *f*
      f spectroscopie *f* opto-acoustique
      r оптоакустическая спектроскопия *f*

O218 *e* **optoelectronic devices**
      d optoelektronische Geräte *n pl*
      f instruments *m pl* opto-électroniques
      r оптоэлектронные приборы *m pl*

O219 *e* **optoelectronics**
      d Optoelektronik *f*
      f opto-électronique *f*
      r оптоэлектроника *f*

O220 *e* **optron**
      d Optokoppler *m*, Optron *n*
      f optron *m*
      r оптрон *m*

O221 *e* **orbit**
      d Umlaufbahn *f*, Orbit *m*
      f orbite *f*
      r орбита *f*

O222 *e* **orbital**
      d Orbital *n*
      f orbitale *f*
      r орбиталь *f*

O223 *e* **orbital angular momentum**
      d Bahndrehimpuls *m*
      f moment *m* cinétique orbital
      r орбитальный момент *m* количества
         движения

O224 *e* **orbital flight**
      d Orbitalflug *m*
      f vol *m* orbital
      r орбитальный полёт *m*

O225 *e* **orbital moment**
      d Bahnmoment *n*
      f moment *m* orbital
      r орбитальный момент *m*

O226 *e* **orbital moment quenching**
      d Quenchen *n* von Bahnmomenten
      f congélation *f* des moments orbitaux
      r замораживание *n* орбитальных
         моментов

O227 *e* **orbital motion**
      d Orbitalbewegung *f*; Bahnbewegung *f*
      f mouvement *m* orbital
      r орбитальное движение *n*

O228 *e* **orbital quantum number**
      d Bahndrehimpuls-Quantenzahl *f*,
         azimutale Quantenzahl *f*
      f nombre *m* quantique orbital
      r орбитальное квантовое число *n*

O229 *e* **orbital velocity**

      d Bahngeschwindigkeit *f*
      f vitesse *f* orbitale
      r орбитальная скорость *f*; первая
         космическая скорость *f*

O230 *e* **orbit diameter**
      d Bahndurchmesser *m*
      f diamètre *m* de l'orbite
      r диаметр *m* орбиты

O231 *e* **orbit parameter**
      d Bahnparameter *m*
      f paramètre *m* de l'orbite
      r параметр *m* орбиты

O232 *e* **orbit plane**
      d Bahnebene *f*
      f plan *m* de l'orbite
      r плоскость *f* орбиты

O233 *e* **orbit quantization**
      d Bahnenquantelung *f*
      f quantification *f* des orbites
      r квантование *n* орбит

O234 *e* **order**
      d Ordnung *f*
      f ordre *m*
      r порядок *m*

O235 *e* **order-disorder transformation,**
        order-disorder transition
      d Ordnungs-Unordnungs-Umwandlung
         f, Ordnungs-Unordnungs-Übergang *m*
      f transformation *f* ordre-désordre
      r переход *m* порядок - беспорядок

O236 *e* **ordered phase**
      d geordnete Phase *f*
      f phase *f* ordonnée
      r упорядоченная фаза *f*

O237 *e* **ordering**
      d Ordnen *n*, Ordnung *f*
      f ordonnancement *m*
      r упорядочение *n*

O238 *e* **order of interference**
      d Ordnung *f* der Interferenz,
         Ordnungszahl *f* der Interferenz
      f ordre *m* d'interférence
      r порядок *m* интерференции

O239 *e* **order of magnitude**
      d Größenordnung *f*
      f ordre *m* de grandeur
      r порядок *m* величины

O240 *e* **order of reflection**
      d Reflexionsordnung *f*
      f ordre *m* de réflexion
      r порядок *m* отражения

O241 *e* **order of spectrum**
      d Ordnung *f* des Spektrums,
         Ordnungszahl *f* des Spektrums

f ordre *m* de spectre
r порядок *m* спектра

O242 e order parameter
d Ordnungsparameter *n*
f paramètre *m* d'ordre
r параметр *m* порядка

O243 e ordinary ray
d ordentlicher Strahl *m*
f rayon *m* ordinaire
r обыкновенный луч *m*

O244 e ordinary wave
d ordentliche Welle *f*
f onde *f* ordinaire
r обыкновенная волна *f*

O245 e ordinate
d Ordinate *f*
f ordonnée *f*
r ордината *f*

O246 e organic conductors
d organische Leiter *m pl*
f conducteurs *m pl* organiques
r органические проводники *m pl*

O247 e organic crystal
d organischer Kristall *m*
f cristal *m* organique
r органический кристалл *m*

O248 e organic semiconductors
d organische Halbleiter *m pl*
f semi-conducteurs *m pl* organiques
r органические полупроводники *m pl*

O249 e organic superconductors
d organische Supraleiter *m pl*
f supraconducteurs *m pl* organiques
r органические сверхпроводники *m pl*

O250 e orientation
d Orientierung *f*
f orientation *f*
r ориентация *f*; ориентирование *n*

O251 e orientation phase transitions
d Orientierungsphasenübergänge *m pl*
f transitions *f pl* de phase d'orientation
r ориентационные фазовые переходы *m pl*

O252 e origin
d 1. Koordinatenursprung *m*
2. Ursprung *m*
f origine *f*
r 1. начало *n* координат
2. происхождение *n*

O253 e Ornstein-Uhlenbeck statistics
d Ornstein-Uhlenbeck-Statistik *f*
f statistique *f* d'Ornstein-Uhlenbeck
r статистика *f* Орнштейна - Уленбека

O254 e Ornstein-Zernike formula

d Ornstein-Zernike-Formel *f*
f formule *f* d'Ornstein-Zernike
r формула *f* Орнштейна - Цернике

O255 e orthicon
d Orthikon *n*
f orthicon *m*
r ортикон *m*

O256 e orthogonal basis
d orthogonale Basis *f*
f base *f* orthogonale
r ортогональный базис *m*

O257 e orthogonal functions
d Orthogonalfunktionen *f pl*
f fonctions *f pl* orthogonales
r ортогональные функции *f pl*

O258 e orthogonality
d Orthogonalität *f*
f orthogonalité *f*
r ортогональность *f*

O259 e orthogonalization
d Orthogonalisation *f*
f orthogonalisation *f*
r ортогонализация *f*

O260 e orthogonal modes
d orthogonale Moden *f pl*
f modes *m pl* orthogonaux
r ортогональные моды *f pl*

O261 e orthogonal polynomials
d orthogonale Polynome *n pl*
f polynômes *m pl* orthogonaux
r ортогональные полиномы *m pl*

O262 e orthogonal states
d Orthogonalzustände *m pl*
f états *m pl* orthogonaux
r ортогональные состояния *n pl*

O263 e orthohelium
d Orthohelium *n*
f orthohélium *m*
r ортогелий *m*

O264 e orthohydrogen
d Orthowasserstoff *m*
f orthohydrogène *m*
r ортоводород *m*

O265 e orthonormal system
d Orthonormalsystem *n*, normiertes Orthogonalsystem *n*
f système *m* orthonormal
r ортонормированная система *f*

O266 e orthopositronium
d Orthopositronium *n*
f orthopositronium *m*
r ортопозитроний *m*

O267 e orthorhombic system
d rhombisches Kristallsystem *n*

f système m romboïdal
r ромбическая система f

O268 e orthostate
d Orthozustand m
f ortho-état m
r ортосостояние n

O269 e oscillating particle
d oszillierendes Teilchen n
f particule f oscillante
r осциллирующая частица f

O270 e oscillating tube
d Generatorröhre f, Oszillatorröhre f
f tube m oscillateur
r генераторная лампа f

O271 e oscillation
d 1. Schwingungen f pl 2. Oszillation f,
   Oszillationen f pl
f oscillations f pl
r 1. колебания n pl
   2. осцилляции f pl

O272 e oscillation amplitude
d Schwingungsamplitude f
f amplitude f d'oscillations
r амплитуда f колебаний

O273 e oscillation damping
d Schwingungsdämpfung f
f évanouissement m des oscillations
r демпфирование n колебаний;
   затухание n колебаний

O274 e oscillation depth
d Oszillationstiefe f
f profondeur f d'oscillations
r глубина f осцилляций

O275 e oscillation frequency
d Schwingungsfrequenz f
f fréquence f d'oscillations
r частота f колебаний

O276 e oscillation length
d Oszillationslänge f
f longueur f d'oscillations
r длина f осцилляций

O277 e oscillation period
d Schwingungsperiode f,
   Schwingungsdauer f
f période f d'oscillations
r период m колебаний; период m
   осцилляций

O278 e oscillation phase
d Schwingungsphase f
f phase f d'oscillation
r фаза f колебания

O279 e oscillations
d Oszillationen f pl
f oscillations f pl
r осцилляции f pl

O280 e oscillation stability
d Schwingungsstabilität f
f stabilité f d'oscillations
r устойчивость f колебаний

O281 e oscillation threshold
d Generationsschwelle f
f seuil m d'oscillation
r порог m генерации

O282 e oscillator
d Oszillator m; Generator m
f oscillateur m
r 1. осциллятор m 2. генератор m

O283 e oscillator strength
d Oszillatorstärke f
f force f d'oscillateur
r сила f осциллятора

O284 e oscillatory circuit
d Schwingkreis m, Resonanzkreis m
f circuit m oscillant
r колебательный контур m

O285 e oscillatory motion see vibrational
   motion

O286 e oscillistor
d Oszillistor m
f oscillistor m
r осциллистор m

O287 e oscillogram
d Oszillogramm n
f oscillogramme m
r осциллограмма f

O288 e oscillograph see oscilloscope

O289 e oscilloscope
d Oszilloskop n, Oszillograph m
f oscilloscope m, oscillographe m
r осциллограф m

O290 e osmium, Os
d Osmium
f osmium m
r осмий m

O291 e osmometer
d Osmometer n
f osmomètre m
r осмометр m

O292 e osmosis
d Osmose f
f osmose f
r осмос m

O293 e osmotic pressure
d osmotischer Druck m
f pression f osmotique
r осмотическое давление n

O294 e Otto cycle
d Ottoscher Kreisprozeß m

f cycle *m* d'Otto
r цикл *m* Отто

O295 *e* outbursts (*of solar radio emission*)
d solare Radiofrequenzstrahlungsausbrüche *m pl*
f sursauts *m pl* solaires, sursauts *m pl* radio-solaires
r всплески *m pl* (*солнечного радиоизлучения*), радиовсплески *m pl*

O296 *e* outer magnetosphere
d äußere Magnetosphäre *f*
f magnétosphère *f* externe
r внешняя магнитосфера *f*

O297 *e* outer planets
d äußere Planeten *m pl* (*von Jupiter bis Pluto*)
f planètes *f pl* extérieures
r планеты *f pl* группы Юпитера, внешние планеты *f pl*

O298 *e* outer problem
d äußeres Problem *n* (*Elektrodynamik*)
f problème *m* externe (*en électrodynamique*)
r внешняя задача *f* (*в электродинамике*)

O299 *e* outer radiation belt
d äußerer Strahlungsgürtel *m*
f ceinture *f* de radiation extérieure
r внешний радиационный пояс *m*

O300 *e* outer shell
d Außenschale *f*
f couche *f* externe, couche *f* périphérique
r внешняя оболочка *f* (*атома*)

O301 *e* outer shell ionization
d Ionisation *f* äußerer Schale, Außenschalenionisation *f*
f ionisation *f* de la couche périphérique
r ионизация *f* внешней оболочки (*атома*)

O302 *e* outgassing *see* degassing

O303 *e* output circuit
d Ausgangskreis *m*, Ausgangsstromkreis *m*
f circuit *m* de sortie
r выходной контур *m*

O304 *e* output power
d Ausgangsleistung *f*
f puissance *f* de sortie
r выходная мощность *f*

O305 *e* output stage
d Endstufe *f*
f étage *m* de sortie
r выходной каскад *m*

O306 *e* output terminals
d Ausgangsklemmen *f pl*
f bornes *f pl* de sortie
r выходные зажимы *m pl*

O307 *e* output voltage
d Ausgangsspannung *f*
f tension *f* de sortie
r выходное напряжение *n*

O308 *e* overcooling
d Unterkühlung *f*
f sous-refroidissement *m*
r переохлаждение *n*

O309 *e* overexcitation
d Übererregung *f*
f surexcitation *f*
r перевозбуждение *n*

O310 *e* Overhauser effect
d Overhauser-Effekt *m*
f effet *m* Overhauser
r эффект *m* Оверхаузера

O311 *e* overheating
d Überhitzung *f*
f surchauffage *m*, surchauffe *f*
r перегрев *m*

O312 *e* overlap
d Überlappung *f*
f recouvrement *m*
r перекрытие *n*; наложение *n*

O313 *e* overlap integral
d Überlappungsintegral *n*
f intégrale *f* de recouvrement
r интеграл *m* перекрытия

O314 *e* overlapping *see* overlap

O315 *e* overlapping bands
d überlappende Energiebänder *n pl*
f bandes *f pl* de recouvrement
r перекрывающиеся зоны *f pl*

O316 *e* overlapping fields
d überlappende Felder *n pl*
f champs *m pl* de recouvrement
r перекрывающиеся поля *n pl*

O317 *e* overload indicator
d Überlastungsanzeiger *m*
f indicateur *m* de surcharge
r индикатор *m* перегрузки

O318 *e* over-the-horizon propagation
d Über-Horizont-Ausbreitung *f*
f propagation *f* transhorizon
r загоризонтное распространение *n* (*радиоволн*)

O319 *e* overtone

d Oberton *m*, Oberschwingung *f*
f son *m* harmonique
r обертон *m*

O320 e overvoltage
d Überspannung *f*
f surtension *f*
r перенапряжение *n*

O321 e Ovshinsky effect
d Ovshinsky-Effekt *m*
f effet *m* d'Ovshinsky
r эффект *m* Овшинского

O322 e oxidation
d Oxidation *f*, Oxydation *f*
f oxydation *f*
r окисление *n*

O323 e oxide
d Oxid *n*
f oxyde *m*
r оксид *m*; окисел *m*

O324 e oxide cathode
d Oxidkatode *f*
f cathode *f* à oxyde
r оксидный катод *m*

O325 e oxide high-temperature superconductors
d Hochtemperatur-Oxidsupraleiter *m pl*
f supraconducteurs *m pl* à oxyde à haute température
r оксидные высокотемпературные сверхпроводники *m pl*

O326 e oxygen, O
d Sauerstoff *m*
f oxygène *m*
r кислород *m*

O327 e ozone, Oz
d Ozon *n*
f ozone *m*
r озон *m*

O328 e ozone absorption
d Ozonabsorption *f*
f absorption *f* par ozone
r поглощение *n* озоном, поглощение *n* в озоновом слое

O329 e ozone layer
d Ozonschicht *f*
f couche *f* d'ozone
r озоновый слой *n*

O330 e ozonizer
d Ozonisator *m*
f ozoniseur *m*
r озонатор *m*; генератор *m* озона

P

P1 e packet blooming
d Paketverbreiterung *f*
f flou *m* du packet
r расплывание *n* пакета

P2 e packing coefficient
d Packungskoeffizient *m*
f facteur *m* de tassement
r коэффициент *m* упаковки

P3 e Padé approximation
d Padé-Approximation *f*
f approximation *f* de Padé
r аппроксимация *f* Паде

P4 e Painlevé equations
d Painlevé-Gleichungen *f pl*
f équations *f pl* de Painlevé
r уравнения *n pl* Пенлеве

P5 e Painlevé functions
d Painlevé-Funktionen *f pl*
f fonctions *f pl* de Painlevé
r функции *f pl* Пенлеве

P6 e pair collision
d Paarkollision *f*
f collision *f* de paire
r парное столкновение *n*

P7 e pair conversion
d Paarkonversion *f*, Paarumwandlung *f*
f conversion *f* de paire
r парная конверсия *f*

P8 e pair correlation
d Paarkorrelation *f*
f corrélation *f* des paires
r парная корреляция *f*

P9 e pair-correlation function
d Paarkorrelationsfunktion *f*
f fonction *f* de corrélation des paires
r парная корреляционная функция *f*

P10 e pair creation
d Paarbildung *f*, Paarerzeugung *f*
f création *f* de paires, formation *f* de paires
r рождение *n* пар, образование *n* пар

P11 e pairing
d Paarung *f*, Elektronenpaarung *f*
f pairage *m* (*des électrons*)
r спаривание *n* (*электронов*)

P12 e pair production *see* pair creation

P13 e pair spectrometer
d Paarspektrometer *n*
f spectromètre *m* à paires
r парный спектромет

PALEOMAGNETISM

P14
 e paleomagnetism
 d Paläomagnetismus *m*
 f paléomagnétisme *m*
 r палеомагнетизм *m*

P15
 e palladium, Pd
 d Palladium *n*
 f palladium *m*
 r палладий *m*

P16
 e paper chromatography
 d Papierchromatographie *f*
 f chromatographie *f* sur papier
 r бумажная хроматография *f*

P17
 e parabola
 d Parabel *f*
 f parabole *f*
 r парабола *f*

P18
 e parabolic aerial, parabolic antenna
 d Parabolantenne *f*
 f antenne *f* parabolique
 r параболическая антенна *f*

P19
 e parabolic cylinder functions
 d Funktionen *f pl* des parabolischen Zylinders, parabolische Zylinderfunktionen *f pl*
 f fonctions *f pl* du cylindre parabolique
 r функции *f pl* параболического цилиндра

P20
 e parabolic equation
 d parabolische Differentialgleichung *f*
 f équation *f* parabolique
 r параболическое уравнение *n*

P21
 e parabolic mirror, parabolic reflector
 d Parabolspiegel *m*
 f miroir *m* parabolique
 r параболическое зеркало *n*

P22
 e parabolic velocity
 d parabolische Geschwindigkeit *f*
 f vitesse *f* parabolique; vitesse *f* d'évasion, vitesse *f* de libération
 r параболическая скорость *f*; вторая космическая скорость *f*

P23
 e paraboloid
 d Paraboloid *n*
 f paraboloïde *m*
 r параболоид *m*

P24
 e para-Bose statistics
 d Para-Bose-Statistik *f*
 f parastatistique *f* de Bose
 r парабозе-статистика *f*

P25
 e paracommutation relations
 d Paravertauschungsrelationen *f pl*
 f relations *f pl* de paracommutation
 r паракоммутационные соотношения *n pl*

P26
 e paraconductivity

P27
 d Paraleitfähigkeit *f*
 f paraconductibilité *f*
 r парапроводимость *f*

P27
 e paradox
 d Paradoxon *n*
 f paradoxe *m*
 r парадокс *m*

P28
 e paraelectric
 d Paraelektrikum *n*
 f para-électrique *m*
 r параэлектрик *m*

P29
 e paraelectric resonance
 d paraelektrische Resonanz *f*
 f résonance *f* para-électrique
 r параэлектрический резонанс *m*

P30
 e para-Fermi statistics
 d Para-Fermi-Statistik *f*
 f parastatistique *f* de Fermi
 r параферми-статистика *f*

P31
 e parafields
 d Parafelder *n pl*
 f parachamps *m pl*
 r параполя *n pl*

P32
 e parahydrogen
 d Parawasserstoff *m*
 f parahydrogène *m*
 r параводород *m*

P33
 e parallactic angle
 d parallaktischer Winkel *m*, Parallaxenwinkel *m*
 f angle *m* parallactique
 r параллактический угол *m*

P34
 e parallax
 d Parallaxe *f*
 f parallaxe *f*
 r параллакс *m*

P35
 e parallel
 d Parallele *f*
 f parallèle *f*
 r параллель *f*

P36
 e parallel circuit
 d Parallelkreis *m*
 f circuit *m* parallèle
 r параллельный контур *m*

P37
 e parallel connection
 d Parallelschaltung *f*
 f couplage *m* en parallèle
 r параллельное соединение *n* (в электрической цепи)

P38
 e parallel data transfer
 d parallele Datenübertragung *f*
 f transfert *m* parallèle des données
 r параллельная передача *f* данных

P39
 e parallel injection

    d Parallelinjektion *f*
    f injection *f* parallèle
    r параллельная инжекция *f*

P40 *e* **parallelogram of forces**
    d Parallelogramm *n* der Kräfte,
       Kräfteparallelogramm *n*
    f parallélogramme *m* des forces
    r параллелограмм *m* сил

P41 *e* **parallel resonance**
    d Parallelresonanz *f*, Stromresonanz *f*
    f résonance *f* parallèle, résonance *f* des
       courants
    r параллельный резонанс *m*, резонанс
       m токов

P42 *e* **parallel transfer**
    d Parallelübertragung *f*
    f transfert *m* parallèle
    r параллельная передача *f*

P43 *e* **paramagnet**
    d Paramagnetikum *n*, paramagnetischer
       Stoff *m*
    f paramagnétique *m*
    r парамагнетик *m*

P44 *e* **paramagnetic crystal**
    d paramagnetischer Kristall *m*
    f cristal *m* paramagnétique
    r парамагнитный кристалл *m*

P45 *e* **paramagnetic ion**
    d paramagnetisches Ion *n*
    f ion *m* paramagnétique
    r парамагнитный ион *m*

P46 *e* **paramagnetic materials**
    d Paramagnetika *n pl*, paramagnetische
       Stoffe *m pl*
    f paramagnétiques *m pl*, matériaux *m*
       pl paramagnétiques
    r парамагнетики *m pl*,
       парамагнитные материалы *m pl*

P47 *e* **paramagnetic relaxation**
    d paramagnetische Relaxation *f*
    f relaxation *f* paramagnétique
    r парамагнитная релаксация *f*

P48 *e* **paramagnetic resonance**
    d paramagnetische Resonanz *f*
    f résonance *f* paramagnétique
    r парамагнитный резонанс *m*

P49 *e* **paramagnetic susceptibility**
    d paramagnetische Suszeptibilität *f*
    f susceptibilité *f* paramagnétique
    r парамагнитная восприимчивость *f*

P50 *e* **paramagnetism**
    d Paramagnetismus *m*
    f paramagnétisme *m*
    r парамагнетизм *m*

P51 *e* **parameter**

    d Parameter *m*
    f paramètre *m*
    r параметр *m*

P52 *e* **parametric amplification**
    d parametrische Verstärkung *f*
    f amplification *f* paramétrique
    r параметрическое усиление *n*

P53 *e* **parametric amplifier**
    d parametrischer Verstärker *m*
    f amplificateur *m* paramétrique
    r параметрический усилитель *m*

P54 *e* **parametric conversion**
    d parametrische Umwandlung *f*
    f conversion *f* paramétrique
    r параметрическое преобразование *n*

P55 *e* **parametric converter**
    d parametrischer Wandler *m*
    f convertisseur *m* paramétrique
    r параметрический
       преобразователь *m*

P56 *e* **parametric coupling**
    d parametrische Kopplung *f*
    f liaison *f* paramétrique
    r параметрическая связь *f*

P57 *e* **parametric emission**
    d parametrische Strahlung *f*
    f émission *f* paramétrique
    r параметрическое излучение *n*

P58 *e* **parametric emitter**
    d parametrischer Strahler *m*
    f émetteur *m* paramétrique
    r параметрический излучатель *m*

P59 *e* **parametric excitation**
    d parametrische Erregung *f*
    f excitation *f* paramétrique
    r параметрическое возбуждение *n*

P60 *e* **parametric fluorescense**
    d parametrische Fluoreszenz *f*
    f fluorescence *f* paramétrique
    r параметрическая флуоресценция *f*

P61 *e* **parametric four-wave mixing**
    d parametrische Vierwellenmischung *f*
    f mélange *m* paramétrique de quatre
       ondes
    r параметрическое четырёхволновое
       смешение *n*

P62 *e* **parametric generation**
    d parametrische Generation *f*
    f génération *f* paramétrique
    r параметрическая генерация *f*

P63 *e* **parametric instability**
    d parametrische Instabilität *f*
    f instabilité *f* paramétrique
    r параметрическая неустойчивость *f*

P64　*e*　**parametric interaction**
　　d　parametrische Wechselwirkung *f*
　　f　interaction *f* paramétrique
　　r　параметрическое взаимодействие *n*

P65　*e*　**parametric light oscillator**
　　d　parametrischer optischer Oszillator *m*
　　f　oscillateur *m* de lumière paramétrique
　　r　параметрический генератор *m* света

P66　*e*　**parametric luminescence**
　　d　parametrische Lumineszenz *f*
　　f　luminescence *f* paramétrique
　　r　параметрическая люминесценция *f*

P67　*e*　**parametric mixing**
　　d　parametrische Mischung *f*
　　f　mélange *m* paramétrique
　　r　параметрическое смешение *n*

P68　*e*　**parametric oscillation, parametric oscillations**
　　d　parametrische Schwingungen *f pl*
　　f　oscillations *f pl* paramétriques
　　r　параметрические колебания *n pl*

P69　*e*　**parametric oscillator**
　　d　parametrischer Oszillator *m*
　　f　oscillateur *m* paramétrique
　　r　параметрический генератор *m*

P70　*e*　**parametric pumping**
　　d　parametrisches Pumpen *n*
　　f　pompage *m* paramétrique
　　r　параметрическая накачка *f*

P71　*e*　**parametric radiation** *see* **parametric emission**

P72　*e*　**parametric receiver**
　　d　parametrischer Empfänger *m*
　　f　récepteur *m* paramétrique
　　r　параметрический приёмник *m*

P73　*e*　**parametric resonance**
　　d　parametrische Resonanz *f*
　　f　résonance *f* paramétrique
　　r　параметрический резонанс *m*

P74　*e*　**parametric scattering**
　　d　parametrische Streuung *f*, parametrische Lichtstreuung *f*
　　f　diffusion *f* paramétrique *(de la lumière)*
　　r　параметрическое рассеяние *n* *(света)*

P75　*e*　**parametric soliton**
　　d　parametrisches Soliton *n*
　　f　soliton *m* paramétrique
　　r　параметрический солитон *m*

P76　*e*　**parametric superfluorescence**
　　d　parametrische Superfluoreszenz *f*
　　f　superfluorescence *f* paramétrique
　　r　параметрическая суперфлуоресценция *f*

P77　*e*　**parametrization**
　　d　Parametrisierung *f*
　　f　paramétrisation *f*
　　r　параметризация *f*

P78　*e*　**parametron**
　　d　Parametron *n*
　　f　paramétron *m*
　　r　параметрон *m*

P79　*e*　**parapositronium**
　　d　Parapositronium *n*
　　f　parapositronium *m*
　　r　парапозитроний *m*

P80　*e*　**paraprocess**
　　d　Paraprozeß *m*, wahre Magnetisierung *f*
　　f　aimantation *f* vraie
　　r　парапроцесс *m* *(истинное намагничивание)*

P81　*e*　**parasitic capacitance** *see* **stray capacitance**

P82　*e*　**parastate**
　　d　Parazustand *m*
　　f　para-état *m*
　　r　парасостояние *n*

P83　*e*　**parastatistic parameter**
　　d　Parastatistikparameter *m*
　　f　paramètre *m* de parastatistique
　　r　параметр *m* парастатистики

P84　*e*　**parastatistics**
　　d　Parastatistik *f*
　　f　parastatistique *f*
　　r　парастатистика *f*

P85　*e*　**paraxial beam**
　　d　paraxiales Bündel *n*, Paraxialbündel *n*
　　f　faisceau *m* paraxial
　　r　параксиальный пучок *m*

P86　*e*　**paraxial image**
　　d　paraxiales Bild *n*
　　f　image *f* paraxiale
　　r　параксиальное изображение *n*

P87　*e*　**paraxial ray**
　　d　paraxialer Strahl *m*, Paraxialstrahl *m*
　　f　rayon *m* paraxial
　　r　параксиальный луч *m*

P88　*e*　**parent particle**
　　d　Ausgangsteilchen *n*, Mutterteilchen *n*
　　f　particule *f* père, particule *f* parent
　　r　материнская частица *f*

P89　*e*　**parhelium**
　　d　Parhelium *n*, Parahelium *n*
　　f　parahélium *m*
　　r　парагелий *m*

P90　*e*　**parity**
　　d　Parität *f*

	f	parité *f*
	r	чётность *f*
P91	*e*	parity-even interaction
	d	«Parität + 1»-Wechselwirkung *f*
	f	interaction *f* à parité paire, interaction *f* à parité positive
	r	чётное взаимодействие *n*
P92	*e*	parity-forbidden transition
	d	paritätsverbotener Übergang *m*
	f	transition *f* interdite par parité
	r	переход *m*, запрещённый по чётности
P93	*e*	parity nonconservation
	d	Nichterhaltung *f* der Parität
	f	non-conservation *f* de la parité
	r	несохранение *n* чётности
P94	*e*	parity-odd interaction
	d	«Parität - 1»-Wechselwirkung *f*
	f	interaction *f* à parité impaire, interaction *f* à parité négative
	r	нечётное взаимодействие *n*
P95	*e*	parity violation
	d	Paritätsverletzung *f*
	f	violation *f* de la parité
	r	нарушение *n* чётности
P96	*e*	parsec
	d	Parsec *n*, Parsek *n*, Parallaxensekunde *f*
	f	parsec *m*
	r	парсек *m*
P97	*e*	partial coherence
	d	partielle Kohärenz *f*
	f	cohérence *f* partielle
	r	частичная когерентность *f*
P98	*e*	partial conservation of axial current
	d	partielle Erhaltung *f* des Axialstromes
	f	conservation *f* partielle du courant axial
	r	частичное сохранение *n* аксиального тока
P99	*e*	partial cross-section
	d	partieller Wirkungsquerschnitt *m*
	f	section *f* partielle
	r	парциальное сечение *n*
P100	*e*	partial differential equations
	d	partielle Differentialgleichungen *f pl*
	f	équations *f pl* différentielles partielles
	r	дифференциальные уравнения *n pl* в частных производных
P101	*e*	partial entropy
	d	Partialentropie *f*
	f	entropie *f* partielle
	r	парциальная энтропия *f*
P102	*e*	partial filling
	d	teilweise Besetzung *f*

	f	remplissage *m* partiel
	r	частичное заполнение *n* (зоны)
P103	*e*	partial inversion
	d	Teilinversion *f*, teilweise Inversion *f*
	f	inversion *f* partielle
	r	частичная инверсия *f*
P104	*e*	partially polarized light
	d	teilweise polarisiertes Licht *n*
	f	lumière *f* partiellement polarisée
	r	частично поляризованный свет *m*
P105	*e*	partial polarization
	d	Teilpolarisation *f*, teilweise Polarisation *f*
	f	polarisation *f* partielle
	r	частичная поляризация *f*
P106	*e*	partial pressure
	d	Partialdruck *m*
	f	pression *f* partielle
	r	парциальное давление *n*
P107	*e*	partial reflection technique
	d	Teilreflexionverfahren *n*
	f	méthode *f* de réflexions partielles
	r	метод *m* частичных отражений
P108	*e*	partial solution
	d	partielle Lösung *f*
	f	solution *f* partielle
	r	частное решение *n*
P109	*e*	partial wave
	d	Teilwelle *f*, Partialwelle *f*
	f	onde *f* partielle
	r	парциальная волна *f*
P110	*e*	partial width
	d	Partialbreite *f*
	f	largeur *f* partielle
	r	парциальная ширина *f*
P111	*e*	particle
	d	Teilchen *n*, Partikel *f*
	f	particule *f*
	r	частица *f*
P112	*e*	particle acceleration
	d	Teilchenbeschleunigung *f*
	f	accélération *f* de particules
	r	ускорение *n* частиц
P113	*e*	particle accelerator
	d	Teilchenbeschleuniger *m*
	f	accélérateur *m* des particules chargées
	r	ускоритель *m* заряженных частиц
P114	*e*	particle-antiparticle pair
	d	Teilchen-Antiteilchen-Paar *n*
	f	paire *f* particule-antiparticule
	r	пара *f* частица - античастица
P115	*e*	particle beam
	d	Teilchenstrahl *m*

f faisceau *m* de particules
r пучок *m* частиц

P116 e particle classification
d Teilchenklassifizierung *f*
f classification *f* des particules
r классификация *f* частиц

P117 e particle collision
d Teilchenkollision *f*,
Teilchenzusammenstoß *m*
f collision *f* de particules
r столкновение *n* частиц

P118 e particle concentration
d Teilchenkonzentration *f*,
Teilchendichte *f*
f concentration *f* des particules
r концентрация *f* частиц

P119 e particle counter
d Teilchenzähler *m*
f compteur *m* de particules
r счётчик *m* частиц

P120 e particle deflection
d Teilchenablenkung *f*
f déflexion *f* de particules
r отклонение *n* частиц

P121 e particle density *see* particle
concentration

P122 e particle detector
d Teilchendetektor *m*
f détecteur *m* de particules
r детектор *m* частиц

P123 e particle diffraction
d Teilchenbeugung *f*, Beugung *f* von
Teilchen
f diffraction *f* de particules
r дифракция *f* частиц

P124 e particle dynamics
d Teilchendynamik *f*, Dynamik *f* der
Teilchen
f dynamique *f* des particules
r динамика *f* материальной точки;
динамика *f* частицы

P125 e particle emission
d Partikelstrahlung *f*, Teilchenstrahlung
f, Korpuskularstrahlung *f*
f émission *f* des particules
r испускание *n* частиц;
корпускулярное излучение *n*

P126 e particle flare
d Teilchenausbruch *m*
f éruption *f* des particules
r вспышка *f* частиц

P127 e particle fluence
d Teilchenfluenz *f*
f fluence *f* des particules
r интегральная плотность *f* потока
частиц

P128 e particle flux density
d Teilchenflußdichte *f*
f densité *f* du flux des particules
r плотность *f* потока частиц

P129 e particle focusing
d Teilchenbündelung *f*
f focalisation *f* des particules
r фокусировка *f* частиц (*в
ускорителе*)

P130 e particle identification
d Teilchenidentifizierung *f*
f identification *f* des particules
r идентификация *f* частиц

P131 e particle injection
d Teilcheninjektion *f*
f injection *f* des particules
r инжекция *f* частиц

P132 e particle injector
d Teilcheninjektor *m*
f injecteur *m* des particules
r инжектор *m* частиц

P133 e particle kinematics
d Massenpunktkinematik *f*
f cinématique *f* du point matériel
r кинематика *f* материальной точки

P134 e particle mechanics
d Mechanik *f* der Massenpunkte,
Punktmechanik *f*
f mécanique *f* du point matériel
r механика *f* материальной точки

P135 e particle momentum
d Teilchenimpuls *m*
f impulsion *f* de la particule
r импульс *m* частицы

P136 e particle motion
d Bewegung *f* des freien Massenpunktes
f mouvement *m* du point matériel
r движение *n* материальной точки

P137 e particle optics
d Korpuskularoptik *f*
f optique *f* corpusculaire
r оптика *f* частиц, корпускулярная
оптика *f*

P138 e particle orbit
d Teilchenbahn *f*
f orbite *f* de la particule
r орбита *f* частицы

P139 e particle path *see* particle trajectory

P140 e particle phase
d Teilchenphase *f*, Phase *f* eines
Teilchens
f phase *f* de la particule
r фаза *f* частицы (*в ускорителе*)

P141 e particle precipitation

    d Teilchenpräzipitation *f*
    f précipitation *f* de particules
    r высыпание *n* частиц *(в магнитосфере)*

P142 e particle production
    d Teilchenerzeugung *f*
    f production *f* de particules
    r рождение *n* частиц

P143 e particle radiation
    d Partikelstrahlung *f*, Teilchenstrahlung *f*, Korpuskularstrahlung *f*
    f radiation *f* des particules, émission *f* des particules
    r излучение *f* частиц, испускание *n* частиц; испускание *n* частицы

P144 e particle range
    d Teilchenweg *m*
    f parcours *m* d'une particule
    r пробег *m* частицы

P145 e particle scattering
    d Teilchenstreuung *f*
    f diffusion *f* des particules
    r рассеяние *n* частиц

P146 e particle trajectory
    d Teilchenbewegungsbahn *f*
    f trajectoire *f* d'une particule
    r траектория *f* частицы

P147 e particle-wave dualism *see* wave-corpuscle duality

P148 e partition chromatography
    d Verteilungschromatographie *f*
    f chromatographie *f* de partage
    r распределительная хроматография *f*

P149 e partition function
    d Verteilungsfunktion *f*
    f fonction *f* de répartition
    r функция *f* распределения

P150 e parton
    d Parton *n*
    f parton *m*
    r партон *m*

P151 e part per million, ppm
    d Teil *m* pro Million
    f part *f* par million
    r миллионная доля *f*

P152 e pascal, Pa
    d Paskal *n*
    f pascal *m*
    r паскаль *m*, Па

P153 e Pascal law
    d Pascal-Gesetz *n*
    f principe *m* de Pascal
    r закон *m* Паскаля

P154 e Paschen-Back effect

    d Paschen-Back-Effekt *m*
    f effet *m* Paschen-Back
    r эффект *m* Пашена - Бака

P155 e Paschen law
    d Paschensches Gesetz *n*
    f loi *f* de Paschen
    r закон *m* Пашена

P156 e Paschen series
    d Paschen-Serie *f*
    f série *f* de Paschen
    r серия *f* Пашена

P157 e passage
    d Durchgang *m*
    f passage *m*
    r прохождение *n*

P158 e pass band
    d Durchlässigkeitsbereich *m*, Durchlässigkeitsband *n*
    f bande *f* passante
    r полоса *f* пропускания

P159 e passive parton
    d passives Parton *n*
    f parton *m* passif
    r пассивный партон *m*

P160 e passive Q-switching
    d passive Gütemodulation *f*
    f commutation *f* passive en Q
    r пассивная модуляция *f* добротности

P161 e passive quantum frequency standard
    d passiver Quantenfrequenzstandard *m*
    f étalon *m* de fréquence quantique passif
    r пассивный квантовый стандарт *m* частоты

P162 e passive resistance
    d passiver Widerstand *m*
    f résistance *f* passive
    r пассивное сопротивление *n*

P163 e passive shutter
    d passiver Lichtverschluß *m*
    f obturateur *m* optique passif
    r пассивный оптический затвор *m*, пассивный затвор *m*

P164 e path
    d Weg *m*; Bahn *f*
    f trajectoire *f*; chemin *m*
    r траектория *f*; путь *m*

P165 e path difference
    d Gangunterschied *m*
    f différence *f* de marche
    r разность *f* хода *(лучей)*

P166 e path integral
    d Bahnintegral *n*
    f intégrale *f* de trajectoire
    r интеграл *m* по траектории

P167 *e* path length
      d 1. Weglänge *f* 2. Bahnlänge *f*,
         Bahnumfang *m*
      f 1. longueur *f* de la voie 2. parcours
         m, longueur *f* de parcours
      r 1. длина *f* пути 2. длина *f* пробега

P168 *e* pattern
      d 1. Bild *n*, Muster *n* 2. Diagramm *n* 3.
         Struktur *f*
      f 1. image *f* 2. diagramme *m* 3.
         structure *f*
      r 1. картина *f* 2. диаграмма *f* 3.
         структура *f*

P169 *e* Patterson function
      d Pattersonsche Funktion *f*, Patterson-
         Funktion *f*
      f fonction *f* de Patterson
      r функция *f* Паттерсона

P170 *e* Pauli equation
      d Pauli-Gleichung *f*
      f équation *f* de Pauli
      r уравнение *n* Паули

P171 *e* Pauli exclusion principle
      d Pauli-Verbot *n*, Paulisches
         Ausschließungsprinzip *n*
      f principe *m* d'exclusion de Pauli,
         principe *m* de Pauli
      r принцип *m* Паули, принцип *m*
         запрета

P172 *e* Pauli paramagnetism
      d Pauli-Paramagnetismus *m*, Paulischer
         Paramagnetismus *m*
      f paramagnétisme *m* de Pauli
      r парамагнетизм *m* Паули

P173 *e* Pauli spin matrix
      d Paulische Spinmatrix *f*
      f matrice *f* de spin de Pauli
      r спиновая матрица *f* Паули

P174 *e* Pauli theorem
      d Pauli-Theorem *n*
      f théorème *m* de Pauli
      r теорема *f* Паули

P175 *e* peaceful use of atomic energy
      d friedliche Nutzung *f* der Kernenergie,
         Anwendung *f* der Kernenergie für
         friedliche Zwecke
      f utilisation *f* pacifique de l'énergie
         atomique
      r использование *n* атомной энергии в
         мирных целях

P176 *e* peak
      d Peak *m*, Maximum *n*, Spitze *f*
      f pic *m*, maximum *m*
      r пик *m*, максимум *m*

P177 *e* peak power
      d Spitzenleistung *f*
      f puissance *f* de crête
      r пиковая мощность *f*; импульсная
         мощность *f*

P178 *e* peak value
      d Spitzenwert *m*, Scheitelwert *m*,
         Amplitude *f*
      f valeur *f* de crête
      r максимальное значение *n*,
         амплитуда *f*

P179 *e* pearlite
      d Perlit *m*
      f perlite *f*
      r перлит *m*

P180 *e* Péclet number
      d Péclet-Zahl *f*, Pécletsche Kennzahl *f*
      f nombre *m* de Péclet
      r число *n* Пекле

P181 *e* peculiarity
      d Besonderheit *f*
      f particularité *f*
      r особенность *f*

P182 *e* peculiar star
      d Pekuliarstern *m*
      f étoile *f* particulière
      r пекулярная звезда *f*; необычная
         звезда *f*

P183 *e* Pedersen conductivity
      d Pedersen-Leitfähigkeit *f*
      f conductivité *f* de Pedersen
      r проводимость *f* Педерсена

P184 *e* Pedersen current
      d Pedersen-Strom *m*
      f courant *m* de Pedersen
      r ток *m* Педерсена

P185 *e* Pedersen ray
      d Pedersen-Strahl *m*
      f rayon *m* de Pedersen
      r луч *m* Педерсена

P186 *e* pedestal
      d Schulter *f*
      f piédestal *m*
      r пьедестал *m* (*импульса*)

P187 *e* pedestal method
      d Pjedestal-Verfahren *n*
      f méthode *f* de piédestal
      r метод *m* пьедестала (*выращивания*
         кристаллов)

P188 *e* Peierls dielectric
      d Peierls-Dielektrikum *n*, Peierlssches
         Dielektrikum *n*
      f diélectrique *m* de Peierls
      r пайерлсовский диэлектрик *m*

P189 *e* Peierls theorem

d Peierlsscher Satz *m*
f théorème *m* de Peierls
r теорема *f* Пайерлса

P190 e **Peierls transition**
d Peierls-Übergang *m*
f transition *f* de Peierls
r переход *m* Пайерлса

P191 e **pellet injection**
d Tabletteninjektion *f*,
Kernbrennstofftabletteninjektion *f*
f injection *f* des pellets
r инжекция *f* таблеток

P192 e **pellet injector**
d Tabletteninjektor *m*
f injecteur *m* des pellets
r инжектор *m* таблеток

P193 e **Peltier coefficient**
d Peltier-Koeffizient *m*
f coefficient *m* de Peltier
r коэффициент *m* Пельтье

P194 e **Peltier effect**
d Peltier-Effekt *m*
f effet *m* Peltier
r эффект *m* Пельтье

P195 e **Peltier heat**
d Peltier-Wärme *f*
f chaleur *f* de Peltier
r теплота *f* Пельтье

P196 e **pencil**
d schmaler Lichtstrahl *m*
f faisceau *m* étroit de lumière
r узкий пучок *m* *(света)*

P197 e **pencil-beam pattern**
d Supercharakteristik *f*
f diagramme *m* de directivité en crayon
r игольчатая диаграмма *f* направленности *(антенны)*

P198 e **pendulum**
d Pendel *n*
f pendule *n*
r маятник *m*

P199 e **penetrability**
d Durchdringungsfähigkeit *f*;
Durchdringbarkeit *f*; Durchlässigkeit *f*
f pénétrabilité *f*
r проницаемость *f*

P200 e **penetrating radiation**
d durchdringende Strahlung *f*; harte Strahlung *f*
f rayonnement *m* pénétrant, rayonnement *m* dur
r проникающее излучение *n*; жёсткое излучение *n*

P201 e **penetration**
d Durchdringung *f*

f pénétration *f*
r проникновение *n*

P202 e **penetration depth**
d Eindringtiefe *f*
f profondeur *f* de pénétration
r глубина *f* проникновения

P203 e **penguin diagram**
d Pinguindiagramm *n*
f diagramme *m* pingouin
r пингвинная диаграмма *f*

P204 e **Penning discharge**
d Penning-Entladung *f*
f décharge *f* de Penning
r разряд *m* Пеннинга

P205 e **Penning effect**
d Penning-Effekt *m*
f effet *m* Penning
r эффект *m* Пеннинга

P206 e **Penrose tiling**
d Penrose-Tiling *n (in der nichtlinearen Dynamik)*
f «tiling» *m* de Penrose *(en dynamique nonlinéaire)*
r паркет *m* Пенроуза *(в нелинейной динамике)*

P207 e **pentagonal prism** *see* **pentaprism**

P208 e **pentaprism**
d Pentaprisma *n*, Fünfseitenprisma *n*
f pentaprisme *m*
r пентапризма *f*

P209 e **pentode**
d Pentode *f*
f penthode *f*
r пентод *m*

P210 e **penumbra**
d Halbschatten *m*
f demi-ombre *f*
r полутень *f*

P211 e **percentage test**
d Stichprobenprüfung *f*
f essai *m* pourcentuel
r выборочные испытания *n pl*

P212 e **percolation**
d Perkolation *f*
f percolation *f*
r перколяция *f*; протекание *n*, просачивание *n*

P213 e **percolation transition**
d Perkolationsübergang *m*
f transition *f* de percolation
r перколяционный переход *m*

P214 e **Percus-Yevick equation**
d Percus-Yevick-Gleichung *f*

f équation f de Percus-Yevick
r уравнение n Перкуса - Йевика

P215　e　perfect crystal
　　　d　Idealkristall m, idealer Kristall m,
　　　　　ungestörter Kristall m
　　　f　cristal m idéal, cristal m parfait
　　　r　идеальный кристалл m,
　　　　　совершенный кристалл m

P216　e　perfect dielectric
　　　d　ideales Dielektrikum n
　　　f　diélectrique m parfait
　　　r　идеальный диэлектрик m

P217　e　perfect gas
　　　d　ideales Gas n, vollkommenes Gas n
　　　f　gaz m idéal, gaz m parfait
　　　r　идеальный газ m

P218　e　perfect gas laws
　　　d　Zustandsgleichung f der idealen Gase
　　　f　lois f pl de gaz parfait
　　　r　законы m pl для идеального газа

P219　e　perfection
　　　d　Vollkommenheit f
　　　f　perfection f
　　　r　совершенство n

P220　e　perfect liquid
　　　d　ideale Flüssigkeit f
　　　f　liquide m parfait
　　　r　идеальная жидкость f

P221　e　perfect optical system
　　　d　ideales optisches System n
　　　f　système m optique parfait
　　　r　идеальная оптическая система f

P222　e　perfect plasma
　　　d　ideales Plasma n
　　　f　plasma m parfait
　　　r　идеальная плазма f

P223　e　perfect plasticity
　　　d　vollkommene Plastizität f
　　　f　plasticité f parfaite
　　　r　идеальная пластичность f

P224　e　perfect radiator
　　　d　idealer Temperaturstrahler m
　　　f　radiateur m parfait
　　　r　полный излучатель m, чёрное тело
　　　　　n, излучатель m Планка

P225　e　perfect vacuum
　　　d　absolutes Vakuum n
　　　f　vide m parfait
　　　r　абсолютный вакуум m

P226　e　periastron
　　　d　Periastron n, Sternnähe f
　　　f　périastre m
　　　r　периастр m

P227　e　perigee
　　　d　Perigäum n, Erdnähe f

f périgée m
r перигей m

P228　e　perihelion
　　　d　Perihel n, Perihelium n,
　　　　　Sonnennähe f
　　　f　périhélie m
　　　r　перигелий m

P229　e　period
　　　d　Periode f; Periodendauer f
　　　f　période f
　　　r　период m

P230　e　periodicity
　　　d　Periodizität f
　　　f　périodicité f
　　　r　периодичность f

P231　e　periodic motion
　　　d　periodische Bewegung f
　　　f　mouvement m périodique
　　　r　периодическое движение n

P232　e　periodic oscillation, periodic
　　　　　oscillations
　　　d　periodische Schwingungen f pl
　　　f　oscillations f pl périodiques
　　　r　периодические колебания n pl

P233　e　periodic system of the elements
　　　d　Periodensystem n der Elemente
　　　f　classification f périodique des éléments
　　　r　периодическая система f элементов

P234　e　periodic table of the elements see
　　　　　periodic system of the elements

P235　e　period-luminosity law
　　　d　Periode-Leuchtkraft-Beziehung f,
　　　　　Perioden-Leuchtkraft-Beziehung f
　　　f　relation f période-luminosité (pour les
　　　　　céphéides)
　　　r　зависимость f период - светимость
　　　　　(для цефеид)

P236　e　period measurement
　　　d　Periodenmessung f,
　　　　　Periodendauermessung f
　　　f　mesure f de la période
　　　r　измерение n периода

P237　e　peripheral interaction
　　　d　periphere Wechselwirkung f
　　　f　interaction f périphérique
　　　r　периферическое взаимодействие n

P238　e　periphery
　　　d　Peripherie f
　　　f　périphérie f
　　　r　периферия f

P239　e　periscope
　　　d　Periskop n
　　　f　périscope m
　　　r　перископ m

P240   e   peritectic
      d   Peritektikum *m*
      f   péritectique *f*
      r   перитектика *f*

P241   e   permalloy
      d   Permalloy *n*
      f   permalloy *m*
      r   пермаллой *m*

P242   e   **permanent deformation** *see* **residual deformation**

P243   e   permanent magnet
      d   Permanentmagnet *m*, Dauermagnet *m*
      f   aimant *m* permanent
      r   постоянный магнит *m*

P244   e   permeability
      d   1. magnetische Permeabilität *f*, magnetische Durchlässigkeit *f*
        2. Permeabilität *f*, Durchlässigkeit *f*
      f   perméabilité *f*
      r   1. магнитная проницаемость *f*
        2. проницаемость *f*

P245   e   permeability of free space
      d   magnetische Feldkonstante *f*, Permeabilität *f* des leeren Raumes, Permeabilität *f* des Vakuums
      f   perméabilité *f* du vide
      r   магнитная проницаемость *f* вакуума, магнитная постоянная *f*

P246   e   permeameter
      d   Permeabilitätsmesser *m*, Permeameter *n*
      f   perméamètre *m*
      r   пермеаметр *m*

P247   e   permeance
      d   magnetischer Leitwert *f*; magnetische Leitfähigkeit *f*
      f   perméance *f*
      r   магнитная проводимость *f*

P248   e   permissible dose
      d   Toleranzdosis *f*, zulässige Dosis *f*, zulässige Strahlungsdosis *f*
      f   dose *f* admissible *(de la radiation ionisante)*
      r   допустимая доза *f (ионизирующего излучения)*

P249   e   permissible overload
      d   zulässige Überlastung *f*
      f   surcharge *f* admissible
      r   допустимая перегрузка *f*

P250   e   permitted band
      d   erlaubte Zone *f*, erlaubtes Band *m*
      f   bande *f* permise
      r   разрешённая зона *f*

P251   e   permitted transition
      d   erlaubter Übergang *m*

      f   transition *f* permise
      r   разрешённый переход *m*

P252   e   permittivity
      d   Dielektrizitätskonstante *f*
      f   permittivité *f*
      r   диэлектрическая проницаемость *f*, диэлектрическая постоянная *f*

P253   e   permittivity of free space
      d   elektrische Feldkonstante *f*
      f   permittivité *f* du vide
      r   диэлектрическая проницаемость *f* вакуума, электрическая постоянная *f*

P254   e   permutation
      d   Permutation *f*
      f   permutation *f*
      r   перестановка *f*

P255   e   permutation functions
      d   Permutationsfunktionen *f pl*
      f   fonctions *f pl* de la permutation
      r   перестановочные функции *f pl*

P256   e   permutation group
      d   Permutationsgruppe *f*
      f   groupe *m* de permutations
      r   группа *f* перестановок

P257   e   permutation relations
      d   Permutationsbeziehungen *f pl*
      f   relations *f pl* de permutation
      r   перестановочные соотношения *n pl*

P258   e   perovskite
      d   Perowskit *m*
      f   perowskite *f*
      r   перовскит *m*

P259   e   perovskite structure
      d   Perowskitstruktur *f*
      f   structure *f* du type perowskite
      r   структура *f* типа перовскита

P260   e   perpetual motion
      d   Perpetuum *n* mobile
      f   perpetuum *m* mobile
      r   вечный двигатель *m*

P261   e   perpetual motion of the first kind
      d   Perpetuum *n* mobile erster Art
      f   perpetuum *m* mobile de la première sorte, perpetuum *m* mobile de première espèce
      r   вечный двигатель *m* первого рода

P262   e   perpetual motion of the second kind
      d   Perpetuum *n* mobile zweiter Art
      f   perpetuum *m* mobile de la deuxième sorte, perpetuum *m* mobile de seconde espèce
      r   вечный двигатель *m* второго рода

P263   e   **perpetuum mobile** *see* **perpetual motion**

P264　e　persistence
　　　　d　Nachleuchten n
　　　　f　postluminescence f
　　　　r　послесвечение n

P265　e　persistence of vision
　　　　d　Trägheit f der Sehempfindung,
　　　　　　Augenträgheit f, Visionspersistenz f
　　　　f　persistance f de vision
　　　　r　инерционность f зрительного
　　　　　　восприятия

P266　e　personal dosimeter
　　　　d　Personendosimeter n,
　　　　　　Individualdosimeter n
　　　　f　dosimètre m individuel
　　　　r　индивидуальный дозиметр m

P267　e　perturbation
　　　　d　1. Störung f 2. Perturbation f
　　　　　　(Astronomie)
　　　　f　perturbation f
　　　　r　возмущение n

P268　e　perturbation theory
　　　　d　Störungstheorie f
　　　　f　théorie f des perturbations
　　　　r　теория f возмущений

P269　e　perturbed motion
　　　　d　gestörte Bewegung f
　　　　f　mouvement m perturbé
　　　　r　возмущённое движение n

P270　e　perturbed problem
　　　　d　gestörtes Problem n
　　　　f　problème m perturbé
　　　　r　возмущённая задача f

P271　e　perturbing force
　　　　d　störende Kraft f, Störkraft f
　　　　f　force f perturbante
　　　　r　возмущающая сила f

P272　e　perveance
　　　　d　Raumladungskonstante f, Perveanz f
　　　　f　pervéance f
　　　　r　первеанс m

P273　e　Petschek mechanism
　　　　d　Petschek-Mechanismus m
　　　　f　méchanisme m de Petschek
　　　　r　механизм m Петчека

P274　e　Petzval surface
　　　　d　Petzval-Fläche f
　　　　f　surface f de Petzval
　　　　r　поверхность f Петцваля

P275　e　Pfund series
　　　　d　Pfund-Serie f
　　　　f　série f de Pfund
　　　　r　серия f Пфунда

P276　e　pH
　　　　d　pH-Wert m

f　valeur f pH
r　водородный показатель m, pH

P277　e　phantastron
　　　　d　Phantastron n
　　　　f　phantastron m, circuit m phantastron
　　　　r　фантастрон m

P278　e　phantom
　　　　d　Phantom n
　　　　f　fantôme m
　　　　r　фантом m (устройство,
　　　　　　заменяющее облучаемый объект)

P279　e　phase
　　　　d　Phase f
　　　　f　phase f
　　　　r　фаза f

P280　e　phase aberrations see phase
　　　　　　distortion

P281　e　phase analysis
　　　　d　Phasenanalyse f
　　　　f　analyse f de phases
　　　　r　фазовый анализ m

P282　e　phase angle
　　　　d　Phasenwinkel m
　　　　f　angle m de phase
　　　　r　фазовый угол m

P283　e　phase boundary
　　　　d　Phasengrenze f
　　　　f　interface f
　　　　r　граница f раздела фаз

P284　e　phase change see phase transition

P285　e　phase characteristic
　　　　d　Phasengang m
　　　　f　caractéristique f phase-fréquence
　　　　r　фазовая характеристика f,
　　　　　　фазочастотная характеристика f

P286　e　phase coherence
　　　　d　Phasenkohärenz f
　　　　f　cohérence f de phase-cohérence f en
　　　　　　phase
　　　　r　фазовая когерентность f

P287　e　phase comparator
　　　　d　Phasenvergleicher m,
　　　　　　Phasenkomparator m
　　　　f　comparateur m de phase
　　　　r　фазовый компаратор m

P288　e　phase-conjugate Brillouin mirror
　　　　d　SBS-Umkehrspiegel m
　　　　f　miroir m Brillouin à conjugaison des
　　　　　　phases
　　　　r　обращающее ВРМБ-зеркало n

P289　e　phase-conjugate mirror
　　　　d　Umkehrspiegel m
　　　　f　miroir m à conjugaison des phases
　　　　r　обращающее зеркало n, ОВФ-
　　　　　　зеркало n

P290   *e*   **phase-conjugate wave**
     d   phasenkonjugierte Welle *f*
     f   onde *f* conjuguée en phase
     r   обращённая волна *f*

P291   *e*   **phase conjugation**
     d   Umkehrung *f* der Wellenfront
     f   conjugaison *f* du front d'onde
     r   обращение *n* волнового фронта

P292   *e*   **phase constant**
     d   Phasenkonstante *f*
     f   constante *f* de phase
     r   фазовая постоянная *f*

P293   *e*   **phase contrast**
     d   Phasenkontrast *m*
     f   contraste *m* de phase
     r   фазовый контраст *m*

P294   *e*   **phase-contrast microscope**
     d   Phasenkontrastmikroskop *n*
     f   microscope *m* à contraste de phase
     r   фазово-контрастный микроскоп *m*

P295   *e*   **phase corrector**
     d   Phasenentzerrer *m*
     f   correcteur *m* de phase
     r   фазовый корректор *m*

P296   *e*   **phase correlation**
     d   Phasenkorrelation *f*
     f   corrélation *f* par la phase
     r   фазовая корреляция *f*

P297   *e*   **phased array**
     d   phasiertes Antennengitter *n*
     f   réseau *m* d'antennes phasé
     r   фазированная антенная решётка *f*

P298   *e*   **phase delay**
     d   Phasenverzögerung *f*
     f   retard *m* de phase
     r   запаздывание *n* по фазе

P299   *e*   **phase detection**
     d   Phasendemodulation *f*
     f   détection *f* de phase
     r   фазовое детектирование *n*

P300   *e*   **phase deviation**
     d   Phasenhub *m*
     f   déviation *f* de phase
     r   фазовый сдвиг *m*

P301   *e*   **phase diagram**
     d   Phasendiagramm *n*,
        Zustandsdiagramm *n*
     f   diagramme *m* de phase, diagramme *m* de phases
     r   фазовая диаграмма *f*; диаграмма *f* состояния, диаграмма *f* равновесия

P302   *e*   **phase difference**
     d   Phasenunterschied *m*, Phasendifferenz *f*
     f   différence *f* des phases
     r   разность *f* фаз

P303   *e*   **phase distortion**
     d   Phasenverzerrung *f*
     f   distorsion *f* de phase
     r   фазовые искажения *n pl*

P304   *e*   **phase equation**
     d   Phasengleichung *f*
     f   équation *f* de phase
     r   фазовое уравнение *n*

P305   *e*   **phase equilibrium**
     d   Phasengleichgewicht *n*
     f   équilibre *m* des phases
     r   фазовое равновесие *n*

P306   *e*   **phase equilibrium curve**
     d   Phasengleichgewichtskurve *f*
     f   courbe *f* d'équilibre des phases
     r   кривая *f* фазового равновесия

P307   *e*   **phase extent**
     d   Phasenausdehnung *f*
     f   extension *f* de phase
     r   фазовая протяжённость *f (сгустка частиц)*

P308   *e*   **phase fluctuations**
     d   Phasenschwankungen *f pl*
     f   fluctuations *f pl* de phase
     r   фазовые флуктуации *f pl*, флуктуации фазы *f pl*

P309   *e*   **phase focusing**
     d   Phasenfokussierung *f*
     f   focalisation *f* de phase
     r   фазовая фокусировка *f*

P310   *e*   **phase front**
     d   Phasenfront *f*
     f   front *m* de phase
     r   фазовый фронт *m*

P311   *e*   **phase integral**
     d   Phasenintegral *n*
     f   intégrale *f* de phase
     r   фазовый интеграл *m*

P312   *e*   **phase inverter**
     d   Phaseninverter *m*
     f   inverseur *m* de phase
     r   фазоинвертор *m*

P313   *e*   **phase lag** *see* **phase delay**

P314   *e*   **phase locking**
     d   Phasenfrequenznachstimmung *f*
     f   commande *f* automatique de la fréquence par la phase
     r   фазовая автоподстройка *f* частоты

P315   *e*   **phase matching** *see* **phase synchronism**

P316   *e*   **phase-matching direction**

d Phasenanpassungsrichtung f
f direction f de concordance des phases
r направление n фазового
синхронизма

P317 e phase memory
d Phasenspeicher m
f mémoire f de phase
r фазовая память f (в оптике)

P318 e phase meter
d Phasenmesser m, Phasenmeßgerät n
f phasemètre m
r фазометр m

P319 e phase modulation
d Phasenmodulation f
f modulation f de phase
r фазовая модуляция f

P320 e phase oscillation
d Phasenschwingungen f pl
f oscillations f pl de phase
r фазовые колебания n pl

P321 e phase path
d Phasenweg m
f trajectoire f de phase
r фазовая траектория f, фазовый путь
f, фазовая длина f пути

P322 e phase plane
d Phasenebene f
f plan m de phase
r фазовая плоскость f

P323 e phase plate
d Phasenplatte f
f lame f de phase, plaque f de phase
r фазовая пластинка f

P324 e phase polar
d Phasenpolare f
f polaire f de phase
r фазовая поляра f

P325 e phase portrait
d Phasenbild n
f portrait m de phase
r фазовый портрет m

P326 e phase ring
d Phasenring m
f anneau m de phase
r фазовое кольцо n

P327 e phase rule
d Gibbssche Phasenregel f
f règle f des phases
r правило n фаз

P328 e phase self-modulation
d Phasenselbstmodulation f
f automodulation f de phase
r фазовая автомодуляция f

P329 e phase shift

d Phasenverschiebung f
f déphasage m
r фазовый сдвиг m

P330 e phase-shift bridge
d Phasenschieberbrücke f
f pont m déphaseur
r фазосдвигающий мост m

P331 e phase shifter
d Phasenschieber m
f déphaseur m, variateur m de phase
r фазовращатель m

P332 e phase-shifting plate
d Phasenschieberplatte f
f plaque f de déphasage
r фазосдвигающая пластинка f

P333 e phase space
d Phasenraum m
f espace m de phase
r фазовое пространство n

P334 e phase-space cell
d Phasenraumzelle f
f cellule f d'espace de phase
r клетка f фазового пространства

P335 e phase-space coordinates
d Phasenraumkoordinaten f pl
f coordonnées f pl d'espace de phase
r координаты f pl в фазовом
пространстве

P336 e phase-space volume
d Phasenvolumen n
f volume m d'extension en phase
r фазовый объём m

P337 e phase stability
d 1. Phasenstabilität f, Autophasierung
f, automatische Phasenstabilisierung f
2. Phasenstabilität f
f 1. autophasage m 2. stabilité f de
phase
r 1. автофазировка f (в ускорителях)
2. стабильность f фазы

P338 e phase state
d Phasenzustand m
f état m de phase
r фазовое состояние n

P339 e phase structure function
d Phasenstrukturfunktion f
f fonction f de structure de phase
r структурная функция f фазы

P340 e phase synchronism
d Phasensynchronismus m
f synchronisme m des phases
r фазовый синхронизм m

P341 e phase-switched interferometer
d Phasenschaltinterferometer n
f interféromètre m à commutation de
phase

r   интерферометр *m* с переключением
     фазы

P342 *e* **phase trajectory**
     d Phasenbahn *f*
     f trajectoire *f* de phase
     r фазовая траектория *f*

P343 *e* **phase transformation heat**
     d Phasenübergangswärme *f*
     f chaleur *f* de la transformation de
     phases
     r теплота *f* фазового превращения

P344 *e* **phase transformations**
     d Phasenumwandlungen *f pl*,
     Phasenübergänge *m pl*
     f transformations *f pl* de phases
     r фазовые переходы *m pl*, фазовые
     превращения *n pl*

P345 *e* **phase transition**
     d Phasenübergang *m*
     f transition *f* de phase
     r фазовый переход *m*

P346 *e* **phase transition kinetics**
     d Phasenübergangskinetik *f*
     f cinétique *f* des transitions de phase
     r кинетика *f* фазовых переходов

P347 *e* **phase transition model**
     d Phasenübergangsmodell *n*
     f modèle *m* de transition de phase
     r модель *f* фазового перехода

P348 *e* **phase transition of the first order**
     d Phasenübergang *m* 1. Art,
     diskontinuierlicher Phasenübergang *m*
     f transition *f* de phase du premier ordre
     r фазовый переход *m* первого рода

P349 *e* **phase transition of the second order**
     d Phasenübergang *m* 2. Art,
     kontinuierlicher Phasenübergang *m*
     f transition *f* de phase du deuxième
     ordre
     r фазовый переход *m* второго рода

P350 *e* **phase velocity**
     d Phasengeschwindigkeit *f*
     f vitesse *f* de phase, vitesse *f* de
     propagation de phase
     r фазовая скорость *f*

P351 *e* **phase volume**
     d Phasenvolumen *n*
     f volume *m* de phase
     r фазовый объём *m*

P352 *e* **phasing**
     d 1. Phaseneinstellung *f*, In-Phase-
     Bringen *n* 2. Phasensynchronisation *f*
     f 1. phasage *m* 2. synchronisation *f* en
     phase
     r 1. фазирование *n*
     2. синхронизация *f*

P353 *e* **phasitron**
     d Phasitron *n*
     f phasitron *m*
     r фазитрон *m*

P354 *e* **phason**
     d Phason *n (Quasiteilchen)*
     f phason *m (quasi-particule)*
     r фазон *m (квазичастица)*

P355 *e* **phasotron**
     d Phasotron *n*
     f phasotron *m*
     r фазотрон *m*

P356 *e* **phenomenological model**
     d phänomenologisches Modell *n*
     f modèle *m* phénoménologique
     r феноменологическая модель *f*

P357 *e* **phenomenological theory**
     d phänomenologische Theorie *f*
     f théorie *f* phénoménologique
     r феноменологическая теория *f*

P358 *e* **phenomenon**
     d Erscheinung *f*, Phänomen *n*
     f phénomène *m*
     r явление *n*

P359 *e* **phon**
     d Phon *n*
     f phone *m*
     r фон *m (единица громкости)*

P360 *e* **phonon**
     d Phonon *n*, Schallquant *n*
     f phonon *m*
     r фонон *m*

P361 *e* **phonon decay**
     d Phononzerfall *m*
     f désintégration *f* du phonon
     r распад *m* фонона

P362 *e* **phonon distribution function**
     d Phononenverteilungsfunktion *f*
     f fonction *f* de distribution des phonons
     r функция *f* распределения фононов

P363 *e* **phonon drag**
     d Phononen-Drag *m*,
     Phononenmitreißen *n*
     f entraînement *m (des électrons)* par
     les phonons
     r увлечение *n (электронов)*
     фононами

P364 *e* **phonon drag effect**
     d Phononen-Drageffekt *m*, Effekt *m* des
     Phononmitreißens, Effekt *m* des
     Mitreißens der Elektrone durch die
     Phononen
     f effet *m* d'entraînement *(des électrons)*
     par les phonons
     r эффект *m* увлечения электронов
     фононами

P365　e　phonon energy
　　　d　Phononenergie *f*
　　　f　énergie *f* de phonon
　　　r　энергия *f* фонона

P366　e　phonon focusing
　　　d　Phononenbündelung *f*
　　　f　focalisation *f* de phonon
　　　r　фононная фокусировка *f*

P367　e　phonon free path
　　　d　freie Weglänge *f* von Phononen
　　　f　longueur *f* du parcours libre des phonons
　　　r　длина *f* свободного пробега фононов

P368　e　phonon gas
　　　d　Phononengas *n*
　　　f　gaz *m* de phonons
　　　r　фононный газ *m*

P369　e　phononless line
　　　d　phononenlose Linie *f*
　　　f　ligne *f* sans phonons
　　　r　бесфононная линия *f*

P370　e　phonon mode
　　　d　Phononenmode *f*
　　　f　mode *m* phononique
　　　r　фононная мода *f*

P371　e　phonon momentum
　　　d　Phononimpuls *m*
　　　f　impulsion *f* du phonon
　　　r　импульс *m* фонона

P372　e　phonon-phonon collisions
　　　d　Phonon-Phonon-Zusammenstöße *m pl*
　　　f　collisions *f pl* phonon-phonon
　　　r　фонон-фононные столкновения *n pl*

P373　e　phonon-phonon interaction
　　　d　Phonon-Phonon-Wechselwirkung *f*
　　　f　interaction *f* phonon-phonon
　　　r　фонон-фононное взаимодействие *n*

P374　e　phonon quasi-momentum
　　　d　Phonon-Quasiimpuls *m*
　　　f　quasi-impulsion *f* du phonon
　　　r　квазиимпульс *m* фонона

P375　e　phonon scattering
　　　d　Phononenstreuung *f*
　　　f　diffusion *f* de phonons
　　　r　рассеяние *n* фононов

P376　e　phonon spectrum
　　　d　Phononenspektrum *n*
　　　f　spectre *m* de phonons, spectre *m* phononique
　　　r　фононный спектр *m*

P377　e　phosphate glass laser
　　　d　Phosphatglaslaser *m*
　　　f　laser *m* à verre de phosphate
　　　r　лазер *m* на фосфатном стекле

P378　e　phosphor
　　　d　Leuchtstoff *m*
　　　f　luminophore *m*
　　　r　люминофор *m*

P379　e　phosphor activator
　　　d　Leuchtstoffaktivator *m*
　　　f　activateur *m* de luminophore
　　　r　активатор *m* люминофора

P380　e　phosphorescence
　　　d　Phosphoreszenz *f*
　　　f　phosphorescence *f*
　　　r　фосфоресценция *f*

P381　e　phosphoroscope
　　　d　Phosphoroskop *n*
　　　f　phosphoroscope *m*
　　　r　фосфороскоп *m*

P382　e　phosphor persistence
　　　d　Nachleuchten *n* des Leuchtstoffs
　　　f　persistance *f* de luminophore
　　　r　послесвечение *n* люминофора

P383　e　phosphorus, P
　　　d　Phosphor *m*
　　　f　phosphore *m*
　　　r　фосфор *m*

P384　e　phot
　　　d　Phot *n*
　　　f　phot *m*
　　　r　фот *m*

P385　e　photoabsorption *see* photoelectric absorption

P386　e　photoacoustical effects
　　　d　photoakustische Effekte *m pl*
　　　f　effets *m pl* photo-acoustiques
　　　r　фотоакустические явления *n pl*

P387　e　photocatalysis
　　　d　Photokatalyse *f*, photochemische Katalyse *f*
　　　f　photocatalyse *f*
　　　r　фотокатализ *m*

P388　e　photocathode
　　　d　Photokatode *f*
　　　f　photocathode *f*
　　　r　фотокатод *m*

P389　e　photocell
　　　d　Photoelement *n*; Photozelle *f*
　　　f　cellule *f* photo-électrique
　　　r　фотоэлемент *m*; фотоприёмник *m*

P390　e　photochemical dissociation
　　　d　Photodissoziation *f*, photochemische Dissoziation *f*
　　　f　dissociation *f* photochimique, photodissociation *f*
　　　r　фотохимическая диссоциация *f*, фотодиссоциация *f*

P391　*e*　**photochemical equivalence**
　　　d　photochemische Äquivalenz *f*
　　　f　équivalence *f* photochimique
　　　r　фотохимическая эквивалентность *f*

P392　*e*　**photochemical process**
　　　d　photochemischer Vorgang *m*
　　　f　processus *m* photochimique
　　　r　фотохимический процесс *m*

P393　*e*　**photochemistry**
　　　d　Photochemie *f*
　　　f　photochimie *f*
　　　r　фотохимия *f*

P394　*e*　**photochromic material**
　　　d　photochromer Stoff *m*
　　　f　matière *f* photochrome
　　　r　фотохромный материал *m*

P395　*e*　**photochromism**
　　　d　Photochromie *f*
　　　f　photochromisme *m*
　　　r　фотохромизм *m*

P396　*e*　**photocolorimeter**
　　　d　Photokolorimeter *n*
　　　f　photocolorimètre *m*
　　　r　фотоколориметр *m*

P397　*e*　**photoconduction**
　　　d　Photoleitung *f*; Photoleitfähigkeit *f*
　　　f　photoconduction *f*
　　　r　фотопроводимость *f*

P398　*e*　**photoconductive cell**
　　　d　Widerstandsphotozelle *f*,
　　　　　Widerstandszelle *f*
　　　f　cellule *f* photoconductrice
　　　r　фотоэлемент *m* с внутренним
　　　　　фотоэффектом

P399　*e*　**photoconductivity** *see*
　　　　　photoconduction

P400　*e*　**photoconductor**
　　　d　Photoleiter *m*
　　　f　photoconducteur *m*
　　　r　фоторезистор *m*

P401　*e*　**photocurrent**
　　　d　Photostrom *m*, photoelektrischer
　　　　　Strom *m*
　　　f　courant *m* photo-électrique
　　　r　фототок *m*

P402　*e*　**photodesorption** *see* **photostimulated**
　　　　　desorption

P403　*e*　**photodetachment**
　　　d　Photoablösung *f* (*von Elektronen*)
　　　f　photodétachement *m* (*d'électrons*)
　　　r　фотоотлипание *n* (*электронов*),
　　　　　фотоотрыв *m*

P404　*e*　**photodetector**
　　　d　Photodetektor *m*, lichtelektrischer
　　　　　Strahlungsempfänger *m*

　　　f　photodétecteur *m*, détecteur *m* de
　　　　　lumière
　　　r　фотоприёмник *m*; фотодетектор *m*

P405　*e*　**photodetector array**
　　　d　Photodetektormatrix *f*
　　　f　matrice *f* de photodétecteurs
　　　r　матрица *f* фотоприёмников

P406　*e*　**photodielectric effect**
　　　d　photodielektrischer Effekt *m*
　　　f　effet *m* photodiélectrique
　　　r　фотодиэлектрический эффект *m*

P407　*e*　**photodiffusion effect**
　　　d　Photodiffusionseffekt *m*, Dember-
　　　　　Effekt *m*, Kristall-Photoeffekt *m*
　　　f　effet *m* Dember
　　　r　эффект *m* Дембера

P408　*e*　**photodiode**
　　　d　Photodiode *f*
　　　f　photodiode *f*
　　　r　фотодиод *m*

P409　*e*　**photodisintegration**
　　　d　Kernphotoeffekt *m*, Photozerfall *m*,
　　　　　Photokernreaktion *f*
　　　f　photodésintégration *f*
　　　r　фотоделение *n*, фоторасщепление *n*
　　　　　(*ядра*)

P410　*e*　**photodissociation**
　　　d　Photodissoziation *f*, photochemische
　　　　　Dissoziation *f*
　　　f　photodissociation *f*
　　　r　фотодиссоциация *f*

P411　*e*　**photodissociation laser**
　　　d　Photodissoziationslaser *m*
　　　f　laser *m* à photodissociation
　　　r　фотодиссоциационный лазер *m*

P412　*e*　**photodynamic effect**
　　　d　photodynamischer Effekt *m*
　　　f　effet *m* photodynamique
　　　r　фотодинамический эффект *m*

P413　*e*　**photoeffect** *see* **photoelectric effect**

P414　*e*　**photoelasticity**
　　　d　Photoelastizität *f*
　　　f　photo-élasticité *f*
　　　r　фотоупругость *f*

P415　*e*　**photoelectret**
　　　d　Photoelektret *n*
　　　f　photo-électret *m*
　　　r　фотоэлектрет *m*

P416　*e*　**photoelectric absorption**
　　　d　Photoabsorption *f*, photoelektrische
　　　　　Absorption *f*, lichtelektrische
　　　　　Absorption *f*
　　　f　photo-absorption *f*, absorption *f*
　　　　　photo-électrique

r фотоэлектрическое поглощение n,
фотопоглощение n

P417 e photoelectric cell see photocell

P418 e photoelectric current see
photocurrent

P419 e photoelectric effect
d Photoeffekt m, lichtelektrischer
Effekt m
f effet m photo-électrique
r фотоэффект m

P420 e photoelectric electron emission see
photoemission

P421 e photoelectric photometry
d lichtelektrische Photometrie f
f photométrie f photo-électrique
r фотоэлектрическая фотометрия f

P422 e photoelectric pyrometer
d Photoelementpyrometer n
f pyromètre m photo-électrique
r фотоэлектрический пирометр m

P423 e photoelectric spectroscopy
d lichtelektrische Spektroskopie f,
photoelektrische Spektroskopie f
f spectroscopie f photo-électrique
r фотоэлектрическая спектроскопия f

P424 e photoelectric threshold
d Photoschwelle f, Grenzenergie f des
äußeren Photoeffekts, photoelektrische
Schwellenenergie f
f seuil m photo-électrique, seuil m
d'énergie photo-électrique
r порог m фотоэффекта

P425 e photoelectromotive force
d Photo-EMK f, photoelektromotorische
Kraft f, Photospannung f
f force f photo-électromotrice
r фотоэдс f

P426 e photoelectron
d Photoelektron n
f photo-électron m
r фотоэлектрон m

P427 e photoelectron detector
d Photoelektronendetektor m
f détecteur m photo-électronique
r фотоэлектронный детектор m

P428 e photoelectron image
d photoelektronisches Bild n,
Photoemissionsbild n
f image f photo-électronique
r изображение n в фотоэлектронах

P429 e photoelectron microscope
d Photoelektronenmikroskop n
f microscope m à photo-électrons
r фотоэлектронный микроскоп m

P430 e photoelectron spectroscopy
d Photoelektronenspektroskopie f
f spectroscopie f de photo-électrons
r фотоэлектронная спектроскопия f

P431 e photoemission
d Photoemission f; äußerer Photoeffekt
m, äußerer lichtelektrischer Effekt m
f émission f photo-électrique; effet m
photo-électrique externe
r фотоэлектронная эмиссия f;
внешний фотоэффект m

P432 e photoemissive cell
d Photozelle f
f cellule f photo-émissive
r фотоэлемент m с внешним
фотоэффектом

P433 e photoemissive detector
d Emissionsphotozelle f;
Photoemissionsdetektor m
f cellule f photo-émissive;
photodétecteur m à effet photo-
électrique externe
r фотоэлектронный приёмник m,
фотоприёмник m на внешнем
фотоэффекте

P434 e photoemissive effect
d äußerer Photoeffekt m, äußerer
lichtelektrischer Effekt m
f effet m photo-émetteur
r внешний фотоэффект m

P435 e photoemissive sensor see
photoemissive detector

P436 e photoexcitation
d Photoanregung f
f photo-excitation f, photo-amorçage m
r фотовозбуждение n

P437 e photofission
d Photospaltung f
f photodésintégration f
r фотоделение n

P438 e photogalvanic effect
d Sperrschichtphotoeffekt m
f effet m photovoltaïque
r фотогальванический эффект m,
фотовольтаический эффект m,
вентильный фотоэффект m

P439 e photogalvanomagnetic effects
d photoelektromagnetische Effekte m pl,
photogalvanomagnetische Effekte m pl
f effets m pl photo-électromagnétiques
r фотогальваномагнитные
явления n pl

P440 e photogrammetry
d Photogrammetrie f
f photogrammétrie f
r фотограмметрия f

P441   e   **photographic density**
     d   Schwärzung *f*
     f   densité *f* photographique
     r   плотность *f* почернения,
       фотографическая плотность *f*

P442   e   **photographic development**
     d   photographische Entwicklung *f*
     f   développement *m* photographique
     r   фотографическое проявление *n*

P443   e   **photographic emulsion**
     d   Photoemulsion *f*, photographische
       Emulsion *f*, lichtempfindliche
       Emulsion *f*
     f   émulsion *f* photographique
     r   фотографическая эмульсия *f*;
       фотоэмульсия *f*

P444   e   **photographic exposure**
     d   Photobelichtung *f*
     f   exposition *f* photographique
     r   фотографическая экспозиция *f*

P445   e   **photographic image**
     d   photographisches Bild *n*
     f   image *f* photographique
     r   фотографическое изображение *n*

P446   e   **photographic magnitude** *(of a star)*
     d   photographische Helligkeit *f (Gestirn)*
     f   magnitude *f* stellaire photographique
     r   фотографическая звёздная
       величина *f*

P447   e   **photographic photometry**
     d   photographische Photometrie *f*
     f   photométrie *f* photographique
     r   фотографическая фотометрия *f*

P448   e   **photographic sensitometry**
     d   photographische Sensitometrie *f*
     f   sensitométrie *f* photographique
     r   фотографическая сенситометрия *f*

P449   e   **photographic spectrometry**
     d   photographische Spektrometrie *f*
     f   spectrométrie *f* photographique
     r   фотографическая спектрометрия *f*

P450   e   **photography**
     d   Photographie *f*
     f   photographie *f*
     r   фотография *f*

P451   e   **photoinduced drift**
     d   photoinduzierte Drift *f*
     f   photodérive *f*
     r   светоиндуцированный дрейф *m*,
       СИД

P452   e   **photoinduced Friedericksz**
       transition
     d   photoinduzierter Friedericksz-
       Übergang *m*
     f   transition *f* photo-induite de
       Friedericksz

     r   светоиндуцированный переход *m*
       Фредерикса

P453   e   **photoinduced isomerization**
     d   photoinduzierte Isomerisation *f*,
       Photoisomerisation *f*
     f   photo-isomérisation *f*
     r   фотоиндуцированная
       изомеризация *f*

P454   e   **photoinduced light absorption**
     d   photoinduzierte Lichtabsorption *f*
     f   absorption *f* de lumière photo-induite
     r   фотоиндуцированное поглощение *n*
       света

P455   e   **photoionization**
     d   Photoionisation *f*, lichtelektrische
       Ionisation *f*, photoelektrische
       Ionisation *f*
     f   photo-ionisation *f*
     r   фотоионизация *f*

P456   e   **photoionization chamber**
     d   Photoionisationskammer *f*
     f   chambre *f* à photo-ionisation
     r   фотоионизационная камера *f*

P457   e   **photoionization detection**
     d   Photoionisationsdetektierung *f*
     f   détection *f* par photo-ionisation
     r   фотоионизационное детектирование
       n (атомов и молекул)

P458   e   **photoionization rate**
     d   Photoionisationsrate *f*
     f   vitesse *f* de photo-ionisation
     r   скорость *f* фотоионизации

P459   e   **photoionization spectroscopy**
     d   Photoionisationsspektroskopie *f*
     f   spectroscopie *f* par photo-ionisation
     r   фотоионизационная
       спектроскопия *f*

P460   e   **photoion microscope**
     d   Photoionenmikroskop *n*
     f   microscope *m* à photo-ions
     r   фотоионный микроскоп *m*

P461   e   **photolithography**
     d   Photolitographie *f*
     f   photolithographie *f*
     r   фотолитография *f*

P462   e   **photoluminescence**
     d   Photolumineszenz *f*
     f   photoluminescence *f*
     r   фотолюминесценция *f*

P463   e   **photolysis**
     d   Photolyse *f*
     f   photolyse *f*
     r   фотолиз *m*

P464   e   **photolytical dissociation**
     d   photolytische Dissoziation *f*

    f dissociation *f* photolytique
    r фотолитическая диссоциация *f*

P465 *e* **photolytic initiation**
    d photolytische Initiierung *f*
    f initiation *f* photolytique
    r фотолитическое инициирование *n*

P466 *e* **photomagnetic effect**
    d photomagnetischer Effekt *m*
    f effet *m* photomagnétique
    r фотомагнитный эффект *m*

P467 *e* **photomagnetoelectric effect**
    d photomagnetoelektrischer Effekt *m*
    f effet *m* photomagnéto-électrique
    r фотомагнитоэлектрический эффект *m*, эффект *m* Кикоина - Носкова

P468 *e* **photomeson**
    d Photomeson *n*
    f photoméson *m*
    r фотомезон *m*

P469 *e* **photometer**
    d Photometer *n*
    f photomètre *m*
    r фотометр *m*

P470 *e* **photometer bench**
    d Photometerbank *f*
    f banc *m* photométrique
    r фотометрическая скамья *f*

P471 *e* **photometer head**
    d Photometerkopf *m*
    f tête *f* photométrique
    r фотометрическая головка *f*

P472 *e* **photometric cube**
    d Photometerwürfel *m*
    f cube *m* photométrique
    r фотометрический кубик *m*, кубик *m* Люммера - Бродхуна

P473 *e* **photometric measurements**
    d photometrische Messungen *f pl*, Lichtmessungen *f pl*
    f mesures *f pl* photométriques
    r фотометрические измерения *n pl*

P474 *e* **photometric paradox**
    d photometrisches Paradoxon *n*
    f paradoxe *m* photométrique
    r фотометрический парадокс *m*

P475 *e* **photometric parallax**
    d photometrische Parallaxe *f*
    f parallaxe *f* photométrique
    r фотометрический параллакс *m*

P476 *e* **photometric studies**
    d photometrische Untersuchungen *f pl*
    f études *f pl* photométriques
    r фотометрические исследования *n pl*

P477 *e* **photometric units**

    d photometrische Einheiten *f pl*
    f unités *f pl* photométriques
    r фотометрические единицы *f pl*

P478 *e* **photometric wedge**
    d photometrischer Keil *m*
    f coin *m* photométrique, coin *m* optique
    r фотометрический клин *m*

P479 *e* **photometry**
    d Photometrie *f*
    f photométrie *f*
    r фотометрия *f*

P480 *e* **photomultiplication factor**
    d Photovervielfachungskoeffizient *m*, Photomultiplikationsfaktor *m*
    f facteur *m* de photomultiplication
    r коэффициент *m* фотоумножения

P481 *e* **photomultiplier**
    d Photovervielfacher *m*
    f photomultiplicateur *m*
    r фотоумножитель *m*

P482 *e* **photon**
    d Photon *n*; Lichtquant *n*
    f photon *m*; quantum *m* de lumière
    r фотон *m*; квант *m* света

P483 *e* **photon antibunching**
    d Photon-Antibunching *n*
    f «antibunching» *m* des photons
    r антигруппировка *f* фотонов

P484 *e* **photon bunching**
    d Photonbunching *n*
    f «bunching» *m* des photons
    r группировка *f* фотонов

P485 *e* **photon drag**
    d Photonen-Drag *m*, Photonenmitreißen *n*
    f entraînement *m (d'électrons)* par les photons
    r увлечение *n (электронов)* фотонами

P486 *e* **photon echo**
    d Photonenecho *n*
    f écho *m* photonique
    r фотонное эхо *n*

P487 *e* **photon emission**
    d Photonenemission *f*
    f rayonnement *m* photonique
    r испускание *n* фотонов

P488 *e* **photon engine**
    d Photonenantrieb *m*
    f propulseur *m* photonique
    r фотонный двигатель *m*

P489 *e* **photoneutrino**
    d Photoneutrino *n*
    f photoneutrino *m*
    r фотонейтрино *n*

P490   e   photoneutron
       d   Photoneutron n
       f   photoneutron m
       r   фотонейтрон m

P491   e   photon gas
       d   Photonengas n
       f   gaz m photonique
       r   фотонный газ m

P492   e   photon momentum
       d   Photonenimpuls m
       f   impulsion f du photon
       r   импульс m фотона

P493   e   photon-photon interactions
       d   Photon-Photon-Wechselwirkungen f pl
       f   interactions f pl photon-photon
       r   фотон-фотонные
         взаимодействия n pl

P494   e   photon propagator
       d   Photonenpropagator m
       f   propagateur m à photons
       r   фотонный пропагатор m

P495   e   photon radiation
       d   Photonenstrahlung f
       f   rayonnement m photonique
       r   фотонное излучение n

P496   e   photon scattering
       d   Photonenstreuung f
       f   diffusion f des photons
       r   рассеяние n фотонов

P497   e   photon source
       d   Photonenquelle f
       f   source f de photons
       r   источник m фотонов

P498   e   photon statistics
       d   Photonenstatistik f
       f   statistique f de photons
       r   статистика f фотонов

P499   e   photonuclear reactions
       d   photonukleare Reaktionen f pl
       f   réactions f pl photonucléaires
       r   фотоядерные реакции f pl

P500   e   photophoresis
       d   Photophorese f
       f   photophorèse f
       r   фотофорез m

P501   e   photophysical process
       d   photophysikalischer Prozeß m
       f   processus m photophysique
       r   фотофизический процесс m

P502   e   photopiezoelectric effect
       d   photopiezoelektrischer Effekt m
       f   effet m photopiézo-électrique
       r   фотопьезоэлектрический эффект m

P503   e   photopolymerization

P   d   Photopolymerisation f
       f   photopolymérisation f
       r   фотополимеризация f

P504   e   photoproduction of particles
       d   Photoerzeugung f von Teilchen
       f   photoproduction f de particules
       r   фоторождение n частиц

P505   e   photorecombination
       d   Photorekombination f
       f   photorecombinaison f
       r   фоторекомбинация f

P506   e   photorecombination radiation
       d   Photorekombinationsstrahlung f
       f   rayonnement m de
         photorecombinaison
       r   фоторекомбинационное
         излучение n

P507   e   photoresist
       d   Photoresist n, Photolack m
       f   photorésist m
       r   фоторезист m

P508   e   photoresistive cell see
         photoconductive cell

P509   e   photoresistor
       d   Photowiderstand m
       f   photorésistance f
       r   фоторезистор m

P510   e   photoresonance plasma
       d   Photoresonanzplasma n
       f   plasma m à photorésonance
       r   фоторезонансная плазма f

P511   e   photosensitive material
       d   lichtempfindlicher Stoff m
       f   matière f photosensible
       r   фоточувствительный материал m

P512   e   photosensitization
       d   Photosensibilisierung f
       f   photosensibilisation f
       r   фотосенсибилизация f

P513   e   photosphere
       d   Photosphäre f
       f   photosphère f
       r   фотосфера f (Солнца, звезды)

P514   e   photospheric faculae
       d   photosphärische Fackeln f pl
       f   facules f pl photosphériques
       r   фотосферные факелы m pl

P515   e   photospheric granulation
       d   Granulation f der Photosphäre
       f   granulation f photosphérique
       r   фотосферная грануляция f

P516   e   photospheric oscillations
       d   photosphärische Oszillationen f pl
       f   oscillations f pl photosphériques
       r   фотосферные осцилляции f pl

P517 e **photospheric radiation**
     d photosphärische Strahlung *f*,
        Photosphärenstrahlung *f*
     f rayonnement *m* photosphérique
     r излучение *n* фотосферы *(Солнца)*

P518 e **photospheric supergranulation**
     d Supergranulation *f* der Photosphäre
     f supergranulation *f* photosphérique
     r фотосферная супергрануляция *f*

P519 e **photostimulated desorption**
     d photoinduzierte Desorption *f*
     f désorption *f* photostimulée
     r фотостимулированная десорбция *f*,
        фотодесорбция *f*

P520 e **photostimulated light absorption** *see*
       photoinduced light absorption

P521 e **photosynthesis**
     d Photosynthese *f*
     f photosynthèse *f*
     r фотосинтез *m*

P522 e **photothyristor**
     d Photothyristor *m*
     f photothyristor *m*
     r фототиристор *m*

P523 e **phototransistor**
     d Phototransistor *m*
     f phototransistor *m*
     r фототранзистор *m*

P524 e **phototropy** *see* **photochromism**

P525 e **phototube**
     d Vakuumphotozelle *f*
     f cellule *f* photo-électrique à vide
     r вакуумный фотоэлемент *m*

P526 e **photovoltaic effect**
     d Sperrschichtphotoeffekt *m*
     f effet *m* photovoltaïque
     r фотогальванический эффект *m*,
        фотовольтаический эффект *m*,
        вентильный фотоэффект *m*

P527 e **physical chemistry**
     d physikalische Chemie *f*
     f chimie *f* physique
     r физическая химия *f*

P528 e **physical constants**
     d physikalische Konstanten *f pl*
     f constantes *f pl* physiques
     r физические константы *m pl*,
        физические постоянные *f pl*

P529 e **physical instruments**
     d physikalische Geräte *n pl*
     f instruments *m pl* physiques
     r физические приборы *m pl*

P530 e **physical kinetics**
     d physikalische Kinetik *f*
     f cinétique *f* physique
     r физическая кинетика *f*

P531 e **physical laboratory**
     d physikalisches Laboratorium *n*
     f laboratoire *m* physique
     r физическая лаборатория *f*

P532 e **physical measurements**
     d physikalische Messungen *f pl*
     f mesures *f pl* physiques
     r физические измерения *n pl*

P533 e **physical oceanography**
     d physikalische Ozeanograpie *f*
     f océanographie *f* physique
     r физическая океанография *f*

P534 e **physical optics**
     d physikalische Optik *f*
     f optique *f* physique
     r физическая оптика *f*

P535 e **physical pendulum**
     d physikalisches Pendel *n*
     f pendule *m* physique
     r физический маятник *m*

P536 e **physical photometer**
     d physikalisches Photometer *n*
     f photomètre *m* physique
     r физический фотометр *m*

P537 e **physical quantity**
     d physikalische Größe *f*
     f grandeur *f* physique
     r физическая величина *f*

P538 e **physical research**
     d physikalische Forschungen *f pl*
     f recherches *f pl* physiques
     r физические исследования *n pl*

P539 e **physical statistics**
     d physikalische Statistik *f*
     f statistique *f* physique
     r физическая статистика *f*

P540 e **physical units**
     d physikalische Einheiten *f pl*
     f unités *f pl* physiques
     r единицы *f pl* физических величин

P541 e **physics**
     d Physik *f*
     f physique *f*
     r физика *f*

P542 e **physics of high-speed phenomena**
     d Physik *f* der kurzzeitigen Prozesse
     f physique *f* des phénomènes ultra-
        rapides
     r физика *f* быстропротекающих
        процессов

P543   *e*   physics of metals
       d   Metallphysik *f*
       f   physique *f* des métaux
       r   физика *f* металлов,
         металлофизика *f*

P544   *e*   physiological acoustics
       d   physiologische Akustik *f*
       f   acoustique *f* physiologique
       r   физиологическая акустика *f*

P545   *e*   physiological optics
       d   physiologische Optik *f*
       f   optique *f* physiologique
       r   физиологическая оптика *f*

P546   *e*   pickup
       d   1. Sensor *m* 2. Tonabnehmer *m*
       f   1. capteur *m* 2. phonocapteur *m*
       r   1. датчик *m* 2. звукосниматель *m*

P547   *e*   picosecond laser
       d   Pikosekundenlaser *m*
       f   laser *m* picoseconde
       r   пикосекундный лазер *m*

P548   *e*   picosecond pulse
       d   Pikosekundenimpuls *m*
       f   impulsion *f* picoseconde
       r   пикосекундный импульс *m*

P549   *e*   picosecond spectroscopy
       d   Pikosekundenspektroskopie *f*
       f   spectroscopie *f* picoseconde
       r   пикосекундная спектроскопия *f*

P550   *e*   picture
       d   1. Abbildung *f*; Bild *n* 2. Aufnahme *f*,
         Bild *n*
       f   image *f*
       r   1. изображение *n* 2. снимок *m*

P551   *e*   piecewise-smooth dependence
       d   stückweise glatte Abhängigkeit *f*
       f   dépendance *f* lisse par morceaux
       r   кусочно-гладкая зависимость *f*

P552   *e*   pi electron
       d   pi-Elektron *n*
       f   électron *m* pi
       r   пи-электрон *m*

P553   *e*   Pierce gun
       d   Pierce-Kanone *f*
       f   canon *m* de Pierce
       r   пушка *f* Пирса

P554   *e*   piezoceramics *see* piezoelectric
         ceramics

P555   *e*   piezocrystal
       d   Piezokristall *m*, piezoelektrischer
         Kristall *m*
       f   piézocristal *m*, cristal *m* piézo-
         électrique
       r   пьезокристалл *m*,
         пьезоэлектрический кристалл *m*

P556   *e*   piezoeffect *see* piezoelectric effect

P557   *e*   piezoelectric
       d   Piezoelektrikum *n*, piezoelektrischer
         Stoff *m*
       f   piézo-électrique *m*
       r   пьезоэлектрик *m*

P558   *e*   piezoelectric cell
       d   Piezoelement *n*, piezoelektrisches
         Element *n*
       f   cellule *f* piézo-électrique
       r   пьезоэлемент *m*

P559   *e*   piezoelectric ceramics
       d   piezoelektrische Keramik *f*,
         Piezokeramik *f*
       f   céramique *f* piézo-électrique
       r   пьезокерамика *f*,
         пьезоэлектрическая керамика *f*

P560   *e*   piezoelectric coupling coefficient *see*
         electromechanical coupling
         coefficient

P561   *e*   piezoelectric crystal *see* piezocrystal

P562   *e*   piezoelectric deflector
       d   piezoelektrischer Deflektor *m*
       f   déflecteur *m* piézo-électrique
       r   пьезоэлектрический дефлектор *m*

P563   *e*   piezoelectric effect
       d   piezoelektrischer Effekt *m*,
         Piezoeffekt *m*
       f   effet *m* piézo-électrique
       r   пьезоэффект *m*

P564   *e*   piezoelectric film
       d   piezoelektrische Schicht *f*
       f   film *m* piézo-électrique
       r   пьезоэлектрическая плёнка *f*

P565   *e*   piezoelectricity
       d   Piezoelektrizität *f*
       f   piézo-électricité *f*
       r   пьезоэлектричество *n*

P566   *e*   piezoelectric materials
       d   piezoelektrische Stoffe *m pl*,
         Piezoelektrika *n pl*
       f   matériaux *m pl* piézo-électriques
       r   пьезоэлектрические материалы *m*
         pl, пьезоэлектрики *m pl*

P567   *e*   piezoelectric mirror
       d   piezoelektrischer Spiegel *m*
       f   miroir *m* piézo-électrique
       r   пьезоэлектрическое зеркало *n*

P568   *e*   piezoelectric pickup
       d   piezoelektrischer Tonabnehmer *m*,
         Kristalltonabnehmer *m*
       f   lecteure *m* piézo-électrique
       r   пьезоэлектрический
         звукосниматель *m*

P569   *e*   **piezoelectric polarization**
     d   piezoelektrische Polarisation *f*
     f   polarisation *f* piézo-électrique
     r   пьезоэлектрическая поляризация *f*

P570   *e*   **piezoelectric pressure gage**
     d   piezoelektrisches Manometer *n*
     f   manomètre *m* piézo-électrique
     r   пьезоэлектрический манометр *m*

P571   *e*   **piezoelectric resonator**
     d   piezoelektrischer Resonator *m*
     f   résonateur *m* piézo-électrique
     r   пьезоэлектрический резонатор *m*

P572   *e*   **piezoelectric semiconductor**
     d   Piezohalbleiter *m*, piezoelektrischer Halbleiter *m*
     f   semi-conducteur *m* piézo-électrique
     r   пьезополупроводник *m*

P573   *e*   **piezoelectric sensor**
     d   piezoelektrischer Geber *m*, Piezogeber *m*; piezoelektrischer Sensor *m*
     f   capteur *m* piézo-électrique
     r   пьезоэлектрический датчик *m*

P574   *e*   **piezoelectric substrate**
     d   piezoelektrisches Substrat *n*
     f   substrat *m* piézo-électrique
     r   пьезоэлектрическая подложка *f*

P575   *e*   **piezoelectric tensor**
     d   piezoelektrischer Tensor *m*
     f   tenseur *m* piézo-électrique
     r   пьезоэлектрический тензор *m*

P576   *e*   **piezoelectric transducer**
     d   piezoelektrischer Wandler *m*; piezoelektrischer Umformer *m*
     f   convertisseur *m* piézo-électrique
     r   пьезоэлектрический преобразователь *m*

P577   *e*   **piezomagnetic crystal**
     d   piezomagnetischer Kristall *m*
     f   cristal *m* piézomagnétique
     r   пьезомагнитный кристалл *m*

P578   *e*   **piezomagnetic effect**
     d   piezomagnetischer Effekt *m*
     f   effet *m* piézomagnétique
     r   пьезомагнитный эффект *m*

P579   *e*   **piezomagnetism**
     d   Piezomagnetismus *m*
     f   piézomagnétisme *m*
     r   пьезомагнетизм *m*

P580   *e*   **piezometer**
     d   Piezometer *n*
     f   piézomètre *m*
     r   пьезометр *m*

P581   *e*   **piezooptic effect**
     d   piezooptischer Effekt *m*
     f   effet *m* piézo-optique
     r   пьезооптический эффект *m*

P582   *e*   **piezoquartz**
     d   Schwingquarz *m*
     f   quartz *m* piézo-électrique
     r   пьезокварц *m*

P583   *e*   **pilot plant**
     d   Versuchsbetrieb *m*, Versuchsanlage *f*
     f   usine *f* pilote
     r   опытный завод *m*; СКБ (специальное конструкторское бюро)

P584   *e*   **pi meson, π meson**
     d   pi-Meson *n*, Pion *n*
     f   méson *m* π, méson *m* pi, pion *m*
     r   пи-мезон *m*, π-мезон *m*, пион *m*

P585   *e*   **pi mode**
     d   pi-Mode *f*
     f   mode *m* pi
     r   пи-вид *m* (колебаний в магнетроне), π-вид *m*

P586   *e*   **pinacoid**
     d   Pinakoid *n*
     f   pinacoïde *m*
     r   пинакоид *m*

P587   *e*   **pinch, pinch discharge**
     d   Pinchentladung *f*, Pinch *m*
     f   décharge *f* à autostriction
     r   самостягивающийся разряд *m*, пинч *m*

P588   *e*   **pinch effect**
     d   Pincheffekt *m*, Einschnüreffekt *m*
     f   effet *m* de pincement
     r   пинч-эффект *m*

P589   *e*   **pincushion distorsion**
     d   kissenförmige Verzeichnung *f*, Kissenverzeichnung *f*
     f   distorsion *f* en coussinet
     r   подушкообразная дисторсия *f*, положительная дисторсия *f*

P590   *e*   **pin diode, p-i-n diode**
     d   pin-Diode *f*
     f   diode *f* pin
     r   *pin*-диод *m*

P591   *e*   **pinning**
     d   Pinning *n*, Flußverankerung *f*
     f   piégeage *m*
     r   пиннинг *m*, зацепление *n*

P592   *e*   **pion**
     d   Pion *n*, pi-Meson *n*
     f   pion *m*, méson *m* pi
     r   пион *m*, пи-мезон *m*

P593   *e*   **pionic atom**
     d   Pionatom *n*, Pionenatom *n*, pi-mesisches Atom *n*, pi-mesonisches Atom *n*

f atome *m* pionique, atome *m* pi-mésonique
r пионный атом *m*

P594 *e* pionic decay
d Pionzerfall *m*
f désintégration *f* du pion
r распад *m* пиона

P595 *e* pionic pole
d Pionenpol *m*
f pôle *m* de pion
r пионный полюс *m*, пи-мезонный полюс *m*

P596 *e* pionic production *see* pion production

P597 *e* pionium
d Pionium *n*, pi-Mesonium *n*
f pionium *n*
r пионий *m*

P598 *e* pion photoproduction
d Pionenphotoerzeugung *f*
f photocréation *f* de pions
r фоторождение *n* пионов

P599 *e* pion production
d Pionenerzeugung *f*
f création *f* de pions
r образование *n* пионов

P600 *e* pipe
d 1. Rohr *n* 2. Wellenleiter *m*
f 1. tube *m* 2. guide *m* d'ondes
r 1. труба *f* 2. волновод *m*

P601 *e* Pippard equation
d Pippard-Gleichung *f*
f équation *f* de Pippard
r уравнение *n* Пиппарда

P602 *e* pi pulse
d pi-Impuls *m*
f impulsion *f* pi
r пи-импульс *m*, π-импульс *m*

P603 *e* Pirani pressure gage
d Pirani-Manometer *n*
f manomètre *m* de Pirani
r манометр *m* Пирани

P604 *e* Pirson criterion
d Pirson-Kriterium *n*
f critère *m* de Pirson
r критерий *m* Пирсона

P605 *e* piston attenuator
d Kolbendämpfungsglied *n*
f atténuateur *m* à piston
r поршневой аттенюатор *m*

P606 *e* pitch angle
d Pitchwinkel *m*, Steigungswinkel *m*
f inclinaison *f*
r питч-угол *m* (*угол вхождения частицы в магнитное поле*)

P607 *e* pitch-angle diffusion
d Pitchwinkeldiffusion *f*
f diffusion *f* à inclinaison
r питч-угловая диффузия *f*

P608 *e* pitch-angle distribution
d Pitchwinkelverteilung *f*
f distribution *f* à inclinaison
r питч-угловое распределение *n*

P609 *e* pitch-angle instability
d Pitchwinkelinstabilität *f*
f instabilité *f* à inclinaison
r питч-угловая неустойчивость *f*

P610 *e* pitch-angle scattering
d Pitchwinkelstreuung *f*
f diffusion *f* à inclinaison
r питч-угловое рассеяние *n*

P611 *e* pitch of a screw
d Ganghöhe *f*
f pas *m* de vis
r шаг *m* винта

P612 *e* pitch of sound
d Tonhöhe *f*
f hauteur *f* du son
r высота *f* звука

P613 *e* Pitot tube
d Pitot-Rohr *n*, Pitotsches Rohr *n*
f tube *m* de Pitot
r трубка *f* Пито

P614 *e* plages
d Fackeln *f pl*, chromosphärische Fackeln *f pl*, Chromosphärenfackeln *f pl*
f plages *f pl* faculaires, facules *f pl* chromosphériques
r флоккулы *f pl* (*в хромосфере Солнца*)

P615 *e* planar channel
d Planarkanal *m*
f canal *m* plan
r плоскостной канал *m*

P616 *e* planar channeling
d Planarkanalierung *f*
f canalisation *f* plane
r плоскостное каналирование *n*

P617 *e* planar epitaxial device
d Epiplanargerät *n*, Epitaxial-Planargerät *n*
f dispositif *m* planaire épitaxial
r планарный эпитаксиальный прибор *m*

P618 *e* Planck constant
d Planck-Konstante *f*, Plancksche Konstante *f*, Plancksches Wirkungsquantum *n*
f constante *f* de Planck

	r	постоянная *f* Планка, квант *m* действия

P619 e Planck length
d Planck-Länge *f*
f longueur *f* de Planck
r планковская длина *f*

P620 e Planck mass
d Planck-Masse *f*
f masse *f* de Planck
r планковская масса *f*

P621 e Planck radiation formula
d Plancksches Strahlungsgesetz *n*; Plancksche Strahlungsformel *f*
f loi *f* de Planck; formule *f* de Planck, formule *f* du rayonnement de Planck
r закон *m* излучения Планка, формула *f* Планка

P622 e Planck time interval
d Plancksches Zeitintervall *n*
f intervalle *m* de temps de Planck
r планковский промежуток *m* времени

P623 e plane
d Ebene *f*
f plan *m*
r плоскость *f*

P624 e plane mirror
d Planspiegel *m*, Flachspiegel *m*
f miroir *m* plan
r плоское зеркало *n*

P625 e plane of polarization
d Polarisationsebene *f*
f plan *m* de polarisation
r плоскость *f* поляризации

P626 e plane of symmetry
d Symmetrieebene *f*
f plan *m* de symétrie
r плоскость *f* симметрии

P627 e plane-parallel motion
d planparallele Bewegung *f*
f mouvement *m* plan, mouvement *m* à deux dimensions
r плоскопараллельное движение *n*

P628 e plane-parallel plate
d planparallele Platte *f*
f plaque *f* à faces parallèles
r плоскопараллельная пластинка *f*

P629 e plane-polarized radiation
d planpolarisierte Strahlung *f*
f rayonnement *m* plan-polarisé
r плоскополяризованное излучение *n*

P630 e plane-stratified medium
d planargeschichtetes Medium *n*

f milieu *m* plan-stratifié
r плоско-слоистая среда *f*

P631 e planet
d Planet *m*
f planète *f*
r планета *f*

P632 e planetary atmosphere
d Planetenatmosphäre *f*
f atmosphère *f* planétaire
r планетная атмосфера *f*

P633 e planetary model
d Planetenmodell *n*, Rutherfordsches Atommodell *n*
f modèle *m* planétaire, modèle *m* planétaire d'atome
r планетарная модель *f* (*атома*)

P634 e planetary nebula
d planetarischer Nebel *m*
f nébuleuse *f* planétaire
r планетарная туманность *f*

P635 e planetary parallax
d Planetenparallaxe *f*
f parallaxe *f* planétaire
r параллакс *m* планеты

P636 e planetary precession
d Planetenpräzession *f*
f précession *f* planétaire
r планетная прецессия *f*

P637 e plane wave
d ebene Welle *f*, Planwelle *f*
f onde *f* plane
r плоская волна *f*

P638 e plano-concave lens
d plankonkave Linse *f*
f lentille *f* plan-concave
r плоско-вогнутая линза *f*

P639 e plano-convex lens
d plankonvexe Linse *f*
f lentille *f* plan-convexe
r плоско-выпуклая линза *f*

P640 e plasma
d Plasma *n*
f plasma *m*
r плазма *f*

P641 e plasma accelerator
d Plasmabeschleuniger *m*
f accélérateur *m* de plasma
r плазменный ускоритель *m*

P642 e plasma-beam discharge
d Plasmastrahlentladung *f*
f décharge *f* à faisceau de plasma
r плазменно-пучковый разряд *m*

P643 e plasma cathode
d Plasmakatode *f*

  f cathode f à plasma
  r плазменный катод m

P644 e **plasma channel**
  d Plasmakanal m
  f colonne f de plasma, canal m de plasma
  r плазменный канал m

P645 e **plasma-chemical reaction**
  d plasmachemische Reaktion f
  f réaction f plasmochimique
  r плазмохимическая реакция f

P646 e **plasma chemistry**
  d Plasmachemie f
  f plasmochimie f
  r плазмохимия f, химия f плазмы

P647 e **plasma coating**
  d Plasmabeschichtung f
  f revêtement m à plasma
  r плазменное покрытие n

P648 e **plasma conductivity**
  d Plasmaleitfähigkeit f
  f conductibilité f du plasma
  r проводимость f плазмы

P649 e **plasma configuration**
  d Plasmakonfiguration f
  f configuration f à plasma
  r плазменная конфигурация f

P650 e **plasma confinement**
  d Plasmaeinschließung f, Plasmahalterung f
  f confinement m du plasma
  r удержание n плазмы

P651 e **plasma containment** see **plasma confinement**

P652 e **plasma contamination**
  d Plasmaverunreinigung f
  f contamination f du plasma
  r загрязнение n плазмы

P653 e **plasma convection**
  d Plasmakonvektion f
  f convection f du plasma
  r конвекция f плазмы

P654 e **plasma diagnostics**
  d Plasmadiagnostik f
  f diagnostic m du plasma
  r диагностика m плазмы

P655 e **plasma diamagnetism**
  d Plasmadiamagnetismus m
  f diamagnétisme m du plasma
  r диамагнетизм m плазмы

P656 e **plasma dynamics**
  d Plasmadynamik f
  f dynamique f du plasma
  r динамика f плазмы

P657 e **plasma electronics**
  d Plasmaelektronik f
  f électronique f du plasma
  r плазменная электроника f

P658 e **plasma engine**
  d Plasmaantrieb m
  f propulseur m à plasma
  r плазменный двигатель m

P659 e **plasma equilibrium**
  d Plasmagleichgewicht n
  f équilibre m du plasma
  r равновесие n плазмы

P660 e **plasma field**
  d Plasmafeld n
  f champ m de plasma
  r плазменное поле

P661 e **plasma filament**
  d Plasmafaden m, Plasmafilament n
  f filament m de plasma, cordon m de plasma
  r плазменный шнур m, плазменный виток m

P662 e **plasma filament deformation**
  d Plasmafadendeformation f
  f déformation f du filament de plasma, déformation f du cordon de plasma
  r деформация f плазменного шнура

P663 e **plasma focus**
  d Plasmafokus m
  f foyer m du plasma
  r плазменный фокус m

P664 e **plasma frequency**
  d Plasmafrequenz f
  f fréquence f de plasma
  r плазменная частота f

P665 e **plasma generator**
  d Plasmagenerator m
  f générateur m de plasma
  r генератор m плазмы

P666 e **plasma heating**
  d Plasmaaufheizung f
  f chauffage m du plasma
  r нагрев m плазмы

P667 e **plasma hydrodynamics**
  d Hydrodynamik f des Plasmas
  f hydrodynamique f de plasma
  r гидродинамика f плазмы

P668 e **plasma injection**
  d Plasmainjektion f, Plasmaeinschuß m
  f injection f du plasma
  r инжекция f плазмы

P669 e **plasma injector**
  d Plasmainjektor m
  f injecteur m du plasma
  r инжектор m плазмы

P670   e   plasma instability
      d   Plasmainstabilität f
      f   instabilité f du plasma
      r   неустойчивость f плазмы,
        плазменная неустойчивость f

P671   e   plasma kinetics
      d   Plasmakinetik f
      f   cinétique f du plasma
      r   кинетика f плазмы

P672   e   plasma kink
      d   Plasmafadenabknickung f
      f   cassure f du cordon de plasma
      r   излом m плазменного шнура

P673   e   plasma laser
      d   Plasmalaser m
      f   laser m à plasma
      r   плазменный лазер m

P674   e   plasma lens
      d   Plasmalinse f
      f   lentille f à plasma
      r   плазменная линза f

P675   e   plasma mantle
      d   Plasmamantel m (Magnitosphäre)
      f   manteau m de plasma (en
        magnétosphère)
      r   плазменная мантия f (в
        магнитосфере)

P676   e   plasma optics
      d   Plasmaoptik f
      f   optique f de plasma
      r   плазмооптика f

P677   e   plasma oscillation, plasma
        oscillations
      d   Plasmaschwingungen f pl
      f   oscillations f pl de plasma
      r   плазменные колебания n pl,
        ленгмюровские колебания n pl

P678   e   plasmapause
      d   Plasmapause f
      f   plasmopause f
      r   плазмопауза f

P679   e   plasma permittivity
      d   Plasmadielektrizitätskonstante f
      f   permittivité f du plasma
      r   диэлектрическая проницаемость f
        плазмы

P680   e   plasma physics
      d   Plasmaphysik f
      f   physique f du plasma
      r   физика f плазмы

P681   e   plasma pressure
      d   Plasmadruck m
      f   pression f du plasma
      r   давление n плазмы

P682   e   plasma probing

P683   d   Plasmasondierung f
      f   sondage m du plasma
      r   зондирование n плазмы

P683   e   plasma quasi-neutrality
      d   Plasma-Quasineutralität f
      f   quasi-neutralité f du plasma
      r   квазинейтральность f плазмы

P684   e   plasma radiation
      d   Plasmastrahlung f
      f   rayonnement m de plasma
      r   излучение n плазмы

P685   e   plasma resonance
      d   Plasmaresonanz f
      f   résonance f du plasma
      r   плазменный резонанс m

P686   e   plasma source
      d   Plasmaquelle f
      f   source f du plasma
      r   плазменный источник m

P687   e   plasmasphere
      d   Plasmasphäre f
      f   plasmosphère f
      r   плазмосфера f

P688   e   plasma spraying
      d   Plasmaspritzen n
      f   déposition f par pulvérisation du
        plasma
      r   плазменное напыление n

P689   e   plasma stability
      d   Plasmastabilität f
      f   stabilité f du plasma
      r   устойчивость f плазмы

P690   e   plasma target
      d   Plasmatarget n
      f   cible f de plasma
      r   плазменная мишень f

P691   e   plasma technology
      d   Plasmatechnik f, Plasmatechnologie f
      f   technologie f à plasma
      r   плазменная технология f

P692   e   plasma trap
      d   Plasmatrap m
      f   piège m à plasma
      r   плазменная ловушка f

P693   e   plasmatron
      d   Plasmatron n
      f   plasmatron m
      r   плазматрон m

P694   e   plasma turbulence
      d   Plasmaturbulenz f
      f   turbulence f du plasma
      r   турбулентность f плазмы

P695   e   plasma wave
      d   Plasmawelle f

    f onde *f* de plasma
    r плазменная волна *f*

P696 *e* **plasma waveguide**
     d Plasmawellenleiter *m*
     f guide *m* d'ondes à plasma
     r плазменный волновод *m*

P697 *e* **plasmoid**
     d Plasmoid *n*
     f plasmoïde *m*
     r плазмоид *m*

P698 *e* **plasmon**
     d Plasmon *n*
     f plasmon *m*
     r плазмон *m*

P699 *e* **plastic deformation**
     d plastische Verformung *f*, bleibende
       Verformung *f*
     f déformation *f* plastique
     r пластическая деформация *f*

P700 *e* **plastic flow**
     d plastisches Fließen *n*
     f écoulement *m* plastique
     r пластическое течение *n*

P701 *e* **plasticity**
     d Plastizität *f*, Bildsamkeit *f*
     f plasticité *f*
     r пластичность *f*

P702 *e* **plate**
     d 1. Platte *f* 2. Anode *f*
     f 1. plaque *f* 2. anode *f*
     r 1. пластинка *f* 2. анод *m*

P703 *e* **plate bending**
     d Plattenbiegung *f*
     f flexion *f* de la plaque
     r изгиб *m* пластины

P704 *e* **platinotron**
     d Platinotron *n*
     f platinotron *m*
     r платинотрон *m*

P705 *e* **platinum, Pt**
     d Platin *n*
     f platine *m*
     r платина *f*

P706 *e* **playback**
     d Wiedergabe *f*
     f reproduction *f*
     r воспроизведение *n (звукозаписи)*

P707 *e* **pleochroism**
     d Pleochroismus *m*
     f pléochroïsme *m*
     r плеохроизм *m*

P708 *e* **plot**
     d graphische Darstellung *f*; Kurvenbild
       n; Diagramm *n*

    f graphique *m*
    r график *m*; диаграмма *f*

P709 *e* **plumbum, Pb**
     d Blei *n*
     f plomb *m*
     r свинец *m*

P710 *e* **Pluto**
     d Pluto *m*
     f Pluton *m*
     r Плутон *m*

P711 *e* **plutonium, Pu**
     d Plutonium *n*
     f plutonium *m*
     r плутоний *m*

P712 *e* **p-n junction**
     d p-n-Übergang *m*
     f jonction *f* p-n
     r p—n-переход *m*

P713 *e* **Pockels cell**
     d Pockels-Zelle *f*
     f cellule *f* de Pockels
     r ячейка *f* Поккельса

P714 *e* **Pockels effect**
     d Pockels-Effekt *m*, elektrooptischer
       Längseffekt *m*
     f effet *m* Pockels
     r эффект *m* Поккельса

P715 *e* **Poincaré group**
     d Poincaré-Gruppe *f*
     f groupe *m* de Poincaré
     r группа *f* Пуанкаре

P716 *e* **point**
     d Punkt *m*
     f point *m*
     r точка *f*

P717 *e* **point charge**
     d Punktladung *f*, punktförmige Ladung *f*
     f charge *f* ponctuelle
     r точечный заряд *m*

P718 *e* **point contact**
     d Punktkontakt *m*, Spitzenkontakt *m*
     f contact *m* ponctuel
     r точечный контакт *m*

P719 *e* **point defect**
     d Punktdefekt *m*, punktförmige
       Störstelle *f*, Punktfehlstelle *f*
     f défaut *m* ponctuel
     r точечный дефект *m*

P720 *e* **point groups**
     d Punktgruppen *f pl*,
       Punktsymmetriegruppen *f pl*
     f groupes *m pl* ponctuels, groupes *m pl*
       ponctuels de symétrie
     r точечные группы *f pl (симметрии*
       кристаллов)

P721   *e*   point momentum
       d   Punktimpuls *m*
       f   moment *m* d'un point
       r   импульс *m* точки

P722   *e*   point object
       d   Punktobjekt *n*
       f   objet *m* ponctuel
       r   точечный объект *m*

P723   *e*   point source
       d   Punktquelle *f*, punktförmige Quelle *f*
       f   source *f* ponctuelle
       r   точечный источник *m*

P724   *e*   Poise, P
       d   Poise *n*
       f   poise *f*
       r   пуаз *m*, П *(единица вязкости)*

P725   *e*   Poiseuille equation
       d   Hagen-Poiseuillesches Gesetz *n*,
          Hagen-Poiseuillesche Gleichung *f*,
          Poiseuillesches Gesetz *n*,
          Poiseuillesche Gleichung *f*
       f   loi *f* de Poiseuille
       r   закон *m* Пуазейля

P726   *e*   Poiseuille flow
       d   Poiseuille-Strömung *f*, Poiseuillesche
          Rohrströmung *f*
       f   écoulement *m* de Poiseuille
       r   течение *n* Пуазейля

P727   *e*   Poisson distribution
       d   Poisson-Verteilung *f*, Poissonsche
          Verteilung *f*
       f   distribution *f* de Poisson
       r   распределение *n* Пуассона

P728   *e*   Poisson equation
       d   Poisson-Gleichung *f*, Poissonsche
          Gleichung *f*
       f   équation *f* de Poisson
       r   уравнение *n* Пуассона

P729   *e*   Poisson integral
       d   Poissonsches Integral *n*
       f   intégrale *f* de Poisson
       r   интеграл *m* Пуассона

P730   *e*   Poisson ratio
       d   Poisson-Zahl *f*
       f   rapport *m* de Poisson, coefficient *m*
          de Poisson
       r   коэффициент *m* Пуассона

P731   *e*   polar
       d   Polare *f*
       f   polaire *f*
       r   поляра *f*

P732   *e*   polar caps
       d   Polkappen *f pl*
       f   calottes *f pl* polaires
       r   полярные шапки *f pl*

P733   *e*   polar circle
       d   Polarkreis *m*
       f   cercle *m* polaire
       r   полярный круг *m*

P734   *e*   polar coordinates
       d   Polarkoordinaten *f pl*
       f   coordonnées *f pl* polaires
       r   полярные координаты *f pl*

P735   *e*   polar diagram
       d   Polardiagramm *n*
       f   diagramme *m* polaire
       r   полярная диаграмма *f*

P736   *e*   polarimeter
       d   Polarimeter *n*
       f   polarimètre *m*
       r   поляриметр *m*

P737   *e*   polarimetry
       d   Polarimetrie *f*
       f   polarimétrie *f*
       r   поляриметрия *f*

P738   *e*   polar ionosphere
       d   Polarionosphäre *f*
       f   ionosphère *f* polaire
       r   полярная ионосфера *f*

P739   *e*   polariscope
       d   Polariskop *n*
       f   polariscope *m*
       r   полярископ *m*

P740   *e*   polariton
       d   Polariton *n*
       f   polariton *m*
       r   поляритон *m*

P741   *e*   polariton luminescence
       d   Polaritonlumineszenz *f*
       f   luminescence *f* à polariton
       r   поляритонная люминесценция *f*

P742   *e*   polarity
       d   Polarität *f*; Polung *f*
       f   polarité *f*
       r   полярность *f*

P743   *e*   polarizability
       d   Polarisierbarkeit *f*
       f   polarisabilité *f*
       r   поляризуемость *f*

P744   *e*   polarization
       d   Polarisation *f*, Polarisierung *f*
       f   polarisation *f*
       r   поляризация *f*

P745   *e*   polarization compensator
       d   Polarisationskompensator *m*
       f   compensateur *m* à polarisation
       r   поляризационный компенсатор *m*

P746   *e*   polarization measurements
       d   Polarisationsmessungen *f pl*

f mesures *f pl* de polarisation
r поляризационные измерения *n pl*

P747 *e* **polarization microscope**
d Polarisationsmikroskop *n*
f microscope *m* polarisant
r поляризационный микроскоп *m*

P748 *e* **polarization microscopy**
d Polarisationsmikroskopie *f*
f microscopie *f* à polarisation
r поляризационная микроскопия *f*

P749 *e* **polarization of electromagnetic radiation**
d Polarisation *f* der elektromagnetischen Strahlung
f polarisation *f* du rayonnement électromagnétique
r поляризация *f* электромагнитного излучения

P750 *e* **polarization of light**
d Polarisation *f* des Lichtes
f polarisation *f* de la lumière
r поляризация *f* света

P751 *e* **polarization of matter**
d Polarisation *f* des Mediums
f polarisation *f* du milieu
r поляризация *f* среды

P752 *e* **polarization of particles**
d Teilchenpolarisation *f*
f polarisation *f* des particules
r поляризация *f* частиц

P753 *e* **polarization of radio waves**
d Radiowellenpolarisation *f*
f polarisation *f* des ondes radio
r поляризация *f* радиоволн

P754 *e* **polarization of waves**
d Wellenpolarisation *f*
f polarisation *f* des ondes
r поляризация *f* волн

P755 *e* **polarization vector**
d Polarisationsvektor *m*
f vecteur *m* de polarisation
r вектор *m* поляризации

P756 *e* **polarized beam**
d polarisierter Strahl *m*
f faisceau *m* polarisé
r поляризованный пучок *m*, поляризованный луч *m*

P757 *e* **polarized beam interference**
d Interferenz *f* der polarisierten Strahlen
f interférence *f* des rayons polarisés
r интерференция *f* поляризованных лучей

P758 *e* **polarized crystal**
d polarisierter Kristall *m*

f cristal *m* polarisé
r поляризованный кристалл *m*

P759 *e* **polarized dielectric**
d polarisiertes Dielektrikum *n*
f diélectrique *m* polarisé
r поляризованный диэлектрик *m*

P760 *e* **polarized light**
d polarisiertes Licht *n*
f lumière *f* polarisée
r поляризованный свет *m*

P761 *e* **polarized luminescence**
d polarisierte Lumineszenz *f*
f luminescence *f* polarisée
r поляризованная люминесценция *f*

P762 *e* **polarized neutrons**
d polarisierte Neutronen *n pl*
f neutrons *m pl* polarisés
r поляризованные нейтроны *m pl*

P763 *e* **polarized nuclei**
d polarisierte Kerne *m pl*
f noyaux *m pl* polarisés
r поляризованные ядра *n pl*

P764 *e* **polarized radiation**
d polarisierte Strahlung *f*
f rayonnement *m* polarisé
r поляризованное излучение *n*

P765 *e* **polarized target**
d polarisiertes Target *n*
f cible *f* polarisée
r поляризованная мишень *f*

P766 *e* **polarized wave**
d polarisierte Welle *f*
f onde *f* polarisée
r поляризованная волна *f*

P767 *e* **polarizer**
d Polarisator *m*
f polarisateur *m*, polariseur *m*
r поляризатор *m*

P768 *e* **polarizing angle**
d Polarisationswinkel *m*, Brewster-Winkel *m*
f angle *m* de polarisation, angle *m* de Brewster
r угол *m* Брюстера, угол *m* полной поляризации

P769 *e* **polarizing filter**
d Polarisationsfilter *n*
f filtre *m* polarisant
r поляризационный светофильтр *m*; поляроид *m*

P770 *e* **polarizing prism**
d Polarisationsprisma *n*
f prisme *m* polariseur
r поляризационная призма *f*

P771 *e* polar lights *see* aurora

P772 *e* polar molecule
    d polares Molekül *n*
    f molécule *f* polaire
    r полярная молекула *f*

P773 *e* polarogram
    d Polarogramm *n*
    f polarogramme *m*
    r полярограмма *f*

P774 *e* polarograph
    d Polarograph *m*
    f polarographe *m*
    r полярограф *m*

P775 *e* polarography
    d Polarographie *f*
    f polarographie *f*
    r полярография *f*

P776 *e* polaron
    d Polaron *n*
    f polaron *m*
    r полярон *m*

P777 *e* pole
    d Pol *m*
    f pôle *m*
    r полюс *m*

P778 *e* pole piece, pole tip
    d Polschuh *m*
    f pièce *f* polaire
    r полюсный наконечник *m*

P779 *e* polhode
    d Polhodie *f*, Gangpolkurve *f*
    f polhodie *f*
    r полодия *f*

P780 *e* polonium, Po
    d Polonium *n*
    f polonium *m*
    r полоний *m*

P781 *e* polycrystals
    d Polykristalle *m pl*
    f polycristaux *m pl*
    r поликристаллы *m pl*

P782 *e* polygon
    d Polygon *n*, Vieleck *n*
    f polygone *m*
    r многоугольник *m*

P783 *e* polygon of forces
    d Kräftepolygon *n*, Kräftevieleck *n*
    f polygone *m* des forces
    r многоугольник *m* сил

P784 *e* polyhedron
    d Polyeder *n*, Vielflach *n*, Vielflächner *m*
    f polyèdre *m*
    r многогранник *m*

P785 *e* polymer crystal
    d Polymerkristall *m*
    f cristal *m* polymérique
    r полимерный кристалл *m*

P786 *e* polymer destruction
    d Polymerabbau *m*, Abbau *m* von Polymeren
    f destruction *f* des polymères
    r деструкция *f* полимеров

P787 *e* polymerization
    d Polymerisation *f*, Polymerisierung *f*
    f polymérisation *f*
    r полимеризация *f*

P788 *e* polymers
    d Polymere *n pl*
    f polymères *m pl*
    r полимеры *m pl*

P789 *e* polymorphism
    d Polymorphie *f*, Polymorphismus *m*
    f polymorphisme *m*
    r полиморфизм *m*

P790 *e* polynomial
    d Polynom *n*
    f polynôme *m*
    r многочлен *m*, полином *m*

P791 *e* polynomial distribution
    d Polynomialverteilung *f*
    f distribution *f* polynomiale
    r полиномиальное распределение *n*

P792 *e* polytrope
    d Polytrope *f*
    f polytrope *f*
    r политропа *f*

P793 *e* polytropic process
    d polytroper Prozeß *m*, polytropische Zustandsänderung *f*
    f transformation *f* polytropique
    r политропический процесс *m*

P794 *e* polytypism
    d Polytypie *f*
    f polytypisme *m*
    r политипия *f*, политипизм *m*

P795 *e* Pomeranchuk particle *see* pomeron

P796 *e* Pomeranchuk theorem
    d Pomerantschuk-Theorem *n*, Pomerantschuksches Theorem *n*
    f théorème *m* de Pomerantchouk
    r теорема *f* Померанчука

P797 *e* pomeron
    d Pomeron *n*
    f pomeron *m*
    r померон *m*

P798 *e* ponderomotive action
    d ponderomotorische Wirkung *f*

| | f | action f pondéromotrice |
| | r | пондеромоторное действие n |

P799 e ponderomotive force
d ponderomotorische Kraft f
f force f pondéromotrice
r пондеромоторная сила f

P800 e population
d Besetzung f
f population f
r населённость f, заселённость f, заселение n; население n

P801 e population inversion
d Besetzungsinversion f
f inversion f de population
r инверсия f населённостей

P802 e population saturation
d Besetzungssättigung f
f saturation f de population
r насыщение n населённости

P803 e pores
d Poren f pl
f pores m pl
r поры f pl

P804 e porosity
d Porosität f, Porigkeit f
f porosité f
r пористость f

P805 e porous catalyst
d poröser Katalysator m
f catalyseur m poreux
r пористый катализатор m

P806 e position isomerism
d Stellungsisomerie f, Substitutionsisomerie f
f isomérie f de position
r изомерия f положения

P807 e position sensor
d Positionsgeber m
f capteur m de position
r датчик m положения

P808 e positive charge
d positive Ladung f
f charge f positive
r положительный заряд m

P809 e positive column
d positive Säule f
f colonne f positive
r положительный столб m (разряда)

P810 e positive crystal
d positiver Kristall m
f cristal m positif
r положительный кристалл m

P811 e positive curvature
d positive Krümmung f

f courbure f positive
r положительная кривизна f

P812 e positive direction
d positive Richtung f
f direction f positive
r положительное направление n

P813 e positive image
d Positivbild n
f image f positive
r позитивное изображение n

P814 e positive ion
d positives Ion n, positiv geladenes Ion n
f ion m positif
r положительный ион m

P815 e positively definite form
d positiv bestimmte Form f
f forme f positivement définie
r положительно определённая форма f

P816 e positive picture see positive image

P817 e positron
d Positron n
f positron m
r позитрон m

P818 e positron channeling
d Positronenkanalierung f
f canalisation f des positrons
r каналирование n позитронов

P819 e positronium
d Positronium n
f positronium m
r позитроний m

P820 e potassium, K
d Kalium n
f potassium m
r калий m

P821 e potassium dihydrogen phosphate
d Kaliumdihydrophosphat n
f dihydrophosphate m de potassium
r дигидрофосфат m калия (нелинейный кристалл)

P822 e potential
d Potential n
f potentiel m
r потенциал m

P823 e potential barrier
d Potentialwall m, Potentialschwelle f, Potentialbarriere f
f barrière f de potentiel
r потенциальный барьер m

P824 e potential difference
d Potentialdifferenz f, Potentialunterschied m

f différence f des potentiels
r разность f потенциалов

P825 e potential energy
d potentielle Energie f
f énergie f potentielle
r потенциальная энергия f

P826 e potential field
d Potentialfeld n
f champ m potentiel
r потенциальное поле n

P827 e potential flow
d Potentialströmung f
f écoulement m potentiel
r потенциальное течение n

P828 e potential forces
d Potentialkräfte f pl
f forces f pl potentielles
r потенциальные силы f pl

P829 e potential function
d Potentialfunktion f
f fonction f potentielle
r потенциальная функция f

P830 e potential gage
d Potentialeichung f
f calibrage m du potentiel
r калибровка f потенциала

P831 e potential gradient
d Potentialgradient m
f gradient m du potentiel
r градиент m потенциала

P832 e potential motion
d Potentialbewegung f
f mouvement m potentiel
r потенциальное движение n

P833 e potential relief
d Potentialgebirge n
f relief m potentiel
r потенциальный рельеф m

P834 e potential scattering
d Potentialstreuung f (von Teilchen)
f diffusion f potentielle (des particules)
r потенциальное рассеяние n (частиц)

P835 e potential surface
d Potentialfläche f
f surface f potentielle
r потенциальная поверхность f

P836 e potential temperature
d potentielle Temperatur f
f température f potentielle
r потенциальная температура f

P837 e potential well
d Potentialtopf m, Potentialsenke f, Potentialmulde f

f puits m de potentiel
r потенциальная яма f

P838 e potentiometer
d Potentiometer n
f potentiomètre m
r потенциометр m

P839 e powder image
d Pulverbild n
f image f en poudre
r порошковое изображение n

P840 e powder method
d Pulvermethode f, Debye-Scherrer-Methode f, Polykristallmethode f
f méthode f de Debye et Scherrer, méthode f des poudres
r порошковый метод m (рентгеноструктурного анализа), метод m Дебая - Шеррера

P841 e powder X-ray camera
d Pulverröntgenkamera f
f chambre f de diffraction X à poudre
r порошковая рентгеновская камера f

P842 e power
d 1. Leistung f 2. Leistungsvermögen n; Arbeitsvermögen n 3. Potenz f
f puissance f
r 1. мощность f 2. энергия f 3. степень f (в математике)

P843 e power factor
d Leistungsfaktor m
f coefficient m de puissance
r коэффициент m мощности, cos φ

P844 e power law
d Potenzgesetz n
f loi f exponentielle
r степенная зависимость f, степенной закон m

P845 e power source see power supply

P846 e power spectral density
d spektrale Leistungsdichte f
f densité f de puissance spectrale
r спектральная плотность f мощности

P847 e power supply
d Stromversorgung f
f source f d'alimentation
r источник m питания

P848 e Poynting theorem
d Poyntingscher Satz m
f théorème m de Poynting
r теорема f Пойнтинга

P849 e Poynting vector
d Poyntingscher Vektor m
f vecteur m de Poynting
r вектор m Пойнтинга, вектор m Умова - Пойнтинга

P850   e   **Prandtl-Meyer flow**
      d   Prandtl-Meyersche Strömung *f*
      f   écoulement *m* de Prandtl-Meyer
      r   течение *n* Прандтля - Мейера

P851   e   **Prandtl number**
      d   Prandtl-Zahl *f*, Prandtlsche
         Kennzahl *f*
      f   nombre *m* de Prandtl
      r   число *n* Прандтля

P852   e   **praseodymium, Pr**
      d   Praseodym *n*
      f   praséodyme *m*
      r   празеодим *m*

P853   e   **precession**
      d   Präzession *f*
      f   précession *f*
      r   прецессия *f*

P854   e   **precession period**
      d   Präzessionsperiode *f*
      f   période *f* de précession
      r   период *m* прецессии

P855   e   **precipitate**
      d   Niederschlag *m*; Präzipität *n*
      f   précipitation *f*
      r   осадок *m*

P856   e   **precipitating electrons**
      d   Präzipitationselektronen *m pl*
      f   électrons *m pl* de précipitation
      r   высыпающиеся электроны *m pl*

P857   e   **precipitating ions**
      d   Präzipitationsionen *f pl*
      f   ions *m pl* de précipitation
      r   высыпающиеся ионы *m pl*

P858   e   **precipitation**
      d   1. Präzipitation *f* 2. Ausfällung *f*
         3. Niederschlag *m* (*Meteorologie*)
      f   1. précipitation *f* 2. précipitation *f*
         3. précipitations *f pl* (*en météorologie*)
      r   1. высыпание *n* (*частиц в*
         магнитосфере) 2. осаждение *n*,
         выпадение *n* осадка 3. осадки *m pl*
         (*в метеорологии*)

P859   e   **precipitation hardening**
      d   Ausscheidungshärtung *f*
      f   durcissement *m* par précipitation
      r   дисперсионное твердение *n*

P860   e   **precise measurement**
      d   Präzisionsmessung *f*
      f   mesure *f* précise
      r   прецизионное измерение *n*, точное
         измерение *n*

P861   e   **precision**
      d   Genauigkeit *f* (*eines Meßgerätes*)
      f   précision *f* (*d'un instrument de*
         mesure)

      r   точность *f* (*измерительного*
         прибора)

P862   e   **precursor pulse**
      d   Vorimpuls *m*
      f   impulsion *f* prédécesseuse
      r   предшествующий импульс *m*

P863   e   **predissociation**
      d   Prädissoziation *f*
      f   prédissociation *f*
      r   предварительная диссоциация *f*

P864   e   **preferred orientation**
      d   bevorzugte Richtung *f*,
         Vorzugsrichtung *f*, bevorzugte
         Orientation *f*
      f   orientation *f* préférée
      r   преимущественная ориентация *f*,
         предпочтительная ориентация *f*

P865   e   **p-region**
      d   p-Gebiet *n*, p-leitende Zone *f*
      f   région *f* p
      r   *p*-область *f*, дырочная область *f*,
         область *f* дырочной проводимости

P866   e   **preionization**
      d   Präionisierung *f*, Präionisation *f*
      f   préionisation *f*
      r   предварительная ионизация *f*

P867   e   **preliminary data**
      d   vorläufige Werte *m pl*, vorläufige
         Daten *pl*
      f   données *pl* préliminaires
      r   предварительные данные *pl*

P868   e   **pressure**
      d   Druck *m*
      f   pression *f*
      r   давление *n*

P869   e   **pressure broadening**
      d   Druckverbreiterung *f*
      f   élargissement *m* par pression
      r   столкновительное уширение *n*
         (*спектральных линий*)

P870   e   **pressure excess**
      d   Drucküberschuß *m*
      f   excès *m* de pression
      r   избыток *m* давления

P871   e   **pressure gage**
      d   Manometer *n*
      f   manomètre *m*
      r   манометр *m*

P872   e   **pressure gradient**
      d   Druckgefälle *n*, Druckgradient *m*
      f   gradient *m* de pression
      r   градиент *m* давления

P873   e   **pressure head**
      d   Staudruck *m*

  f pression *f* hydrostatique
  r гидростатический напор *m*

P874 *e* **pressure of light**
  d Lichtdruck *m*
  f pression *f* de lumière
  r давление *n* света

P875 *e* **pressure of radiation**
  d Strahlungsdruck *m*
  f pression *f* de rayonnement
  r давление *n* излучения

P876 *e* **pressure of sound**
  d Schalldruck *m*
  f pression *f* acoustique
  r давление *n* звука

P877 *e* **pressure range**
  d Druckbereich *m*
  f gamme *f* de pressions
  r диапазон *m* давлений

P878 *e* **primary colors**
  d Grundfarben *f pl*, Primärfarben *f pl*
  f couleurs *f pl* primaires
  r основные цвета *m pl*

P879 *e* **primary cosmic rays**
  d kosmische Primärstrahlung *f*,
    Primärkomponente *f* der kosmischen
    Strahlung
  f rayons *pl* cosmiques primaires
  r первичные космические лучи *pl*

P880 *e* **primary mirror**
  d Hauptspiegel *m (Fernrohr)*
  f grand miroir *m (du télescope)*
  r главное зеркало *n (телескопа)*

P881 *e* **primary radiation**
  d Primärstrahlung *f*
  f rayonnement *m* primaire
  r первичное излучение *n*

P882 *e* **primary radiator**
  d Primärstrahler *m*
  f radiateur *m* primaire
  r первичный излучатель *m*

P883 *e* **primary standard**
  d Urnormal *n*
  f étalon *m* prototype, étalon *m* primaire
  r первичный эталон *m*

P884 *e* **primary voltage**
  d Primärspannung *f*
  f tension *f* primaire
  r первичное напряжение *n*

P885 *e* **primitive cell**
  d Elementarzelle *f*, Einheitszelle *f*
  f cellule *f* élémentaire
  r примитивная ячейка *f*

P886 *e* **primitive lattice**
  d primitives Gitter *n*

  f réseau *m* primitif
  r примитивная решётка *f*

P887 *e* **principal axis of inertia**
  d Hauptträgheitsachse *f*,
    Trägheitshauptachse *f*
  f axe *m* principal d'inertie
  r главная ось *f* инерции

P888 *e* **principal axis of strain**
  d Hauptdilatationsachse *f*, Hauptachse *f*
    des Verformungszustandes
  f axe *m* principal de déformation
  r главная ось *f* деформации

P889 *e* **principal axis of stress**
  d Hauptspannungsachse *f*, Hauptachse *f*
    des Spannungszustandes
  f axe *m* principal de contrainte
  r главная ось *f* напряжения

P890 *e* **principal direction**
  d Hauptrichtung *f*
  f direction *f* principale
  r главное направление *n*

P891 *e* **principal focus**
  d Hauptbrennpunkt *m*
  f foyer *m* principal
  r главный фокус *m*

P892 *e* **principal maximum**
  d Hauptmaximum *n*
  f maximum *m* primaire
  r главный максимум *m*

P893 *e* **principal mode** *see* **fundamental
    mode**

P894 *e* **principal moment of inertia**
  d Hauptträgheitsmoment *n*
  f moment *m* d'inertie principal
  r главный момент *m* инерции

P895 *e* **principal planes** *(of an optical
    system)*
  d Hauptebenen *f pl (eines optischen
    Systems)*
  f plans *m pl* principaux *(d'un système
    optique)*
  r главные плоскости *f pl (оптической
    системы)*

P896 *e* **principal quantum number**
  d Hauptquantenzahl *f*
  f nombre *m* quantique principal
  r главное квантовое число *n*

P897 *e* **principal series**
  d Hauptserie *f*
  f série *f* principale
  r главная серия *f*, главная
    спектральная серия *f*

P898 *e* **principal stress**
  d Hauptspannung *f*
  f contrainte *f* principale
  r главное напряжение *n*

P899   *e* principle of complementarity
      d Komplementaritätsprinzip *n*
      f principe *m* de complémentarité
      r принцип *m* дополнительности

P900   *e* principle of detailed balancing
      d Prinzip *n* des detaillierten
         Gleichgewichts
      f principe *m* du bilan détaillé
      r принцип *m* детального равновесия

P901   *e* principle of duality
      d Dualitätsprinzip *n*
      f principe *m* de dualité
      r принцип *m* двойственности

P902   *e* principle of equivalence of mass
         and energy
      d Masse-Energie-Äquivalenzprinzip *n*,
         Prinzip *n* der Äquivalenz von Masse
         und Energie
      f principe *m* d'équivalence masse-
         énergie, principe *m* d'équivalence de
         masse et énergie
      r закон *m* эквивалентности массы и
         энергии

P903   *e* principle of least action
      d Prinzip *n* der kleinsten Wirkung
      f principe *m* de la moindre action
      r принцип *m* наименьшего действия

P904   *e* prism
      d Prisma *n*
      f prisme *m*
      r призма *f*

P905   *e* prismatic monochromator
      d Prismenmonochromator *m*
      f monochromateur *m* prismatique
      r призменный монохроматор *m*

P906   *e* prismatic spectrograph
      d Prismenspektrograph *m*
      f spectrographe *m* à prisme,
         spectrographe *m* à prismes
      r призменный спектрограф *m*

P907   *e* probability
      d Wahrscheinlichkeit *f*
      f probabilité *f*
      r вероятность *f*

P908   *e* probability amplitude
      d Wahrscheinlichkeitsamplitude *f*
      f amplitude *f* de probabilité
      r амплитуда *f* вероятности

P909   *e* probability current density
      d Wahrscheinlichkeitsstromdichte *f*
      f densité *f* de courant de probabilité
      r плотность *f* потока вероятности

P910   *e* probability density
      d Wahrscheinlichkeitsdichte *f*

      f densité *f* de probabilité
      r плотность *f* вероятности

P911   *e* probability measure
      d Wahrscheinlichkeitsmaß *n*
      f mesure *f* de probabilité
      r вероятностная мера *f*

P912   *e* probability of collision *see* collision
         probability

P913   *e* probability theory
      d Wahrscheinlichkeitstheorie *f*
      f calcul *m* des probabilités, théorie *f*
         des probabilités
      r теория *f* вероятностей

P914   *e* probability waves
      d Wahrscheinlichkeitswellen *f pl*
      f ondes *f pl* de probabilité
      r волны *f pl* вероятности

P915   *e* probe
      d 1. Sonde *f* 2. Fühler *m*; Taster *m*
      f 1. sonde *f* 2. jauge *f*; essayeur *m*
      r 1. зонд *m* 2. щуп *m*, пробник *m*

P916   *e* probe charge
      d Probeladung *f*
      f charge *f* d'essai
      r пробный заряд *m*

P917   *e* probe diagnostics
      d Sondendiagnostik *f*
      f diagnostic *m* à sonde *(du plasma)*
      r зондовая диагностика *f (плазмы)*

P918   *e* probe measurements
      d Sondenmessungen *f pl*
      f mesures *f pl* à sonde
      r зондовые измерения *n pl*

P919   *e* probe method
      d Sondenmethode *f*
      f méthode *f* de sonde
      r зондовый метод *m*

P920   *e* probe pulse
      d Sondenimpuls *m*, Abtastimpuls *m*
      f impulsion *f* de pilotage
      r зондирующий импульс *m*

P921   *e* probing *see* sounding

P922   *e* problem
      d Problem *n*
      f problème *m*
      r задача *f*; проблема *f*

P923   *e* procedure
      d Verfahren *n*; Technik *f*; Methode *f*;
         Prozedur *f*
      f procédé *m*; méthode *f*
      r методика *f*; процедура *f*; процесс *m*;
         метод *m*

P924   *e* processor
      d Prozessor *m*

f processeur *m*
r процессор *m*

P925 e production channel
d Erzeugungskanal *m*,
Teilchenerzeugungskanal *m*
f canal *m* de production (*des particules*)
r канал *m* рождения (*частиц*)

P926 e production operator
d Erzeugungsoperator *m*,
Teilchenerzeugungsoperator *m*
f opérateur *m* création, créateur *m*
r оператор *m* рождения (*частиц*)

P927 e profiled crystal
d Profilkristall *m*
f cristal *m* profilé
r профилированный кристалл *m*

P928 e profile drag
d Profilwiderstand *m*
f résistance *f* de profil
r профильное сопротивление *n*

P929 e progressive motion
d fortschreitende Bewegung *f*
f mouvement *m* de translation
r поступательное движение *n*

P930 e projectile
d Beschußteilchen *n*; auftreffendes
Teilchen *n*; einfallendes Teilchen *n*
f particule *f* projectile
r налетающая частица *f*

P931 e projectile motion
d Wurfbewegung *f*; Geschoßbewegung *f*
f mouvement *m* du projectile
r движение *n* брошенного тела,
баллистическое движение *n*

P932 e projectile particle *see* projectile

P933 e projection microscope
d Projektionsmikroskop *n*
f microscope *m* de projection,
microscope *m* à projection
r проекционный микроскоп *m*

P934 e projector
d 1. Scheinwerfer *m* 2.Bildwerfer *m*,
Projektor *m*
f projecteur *m*
r 1. прожектор *m* 2. проектор *m*

P935 e prominence
d Protuberanz *f*
f protubérance *f*
r протуберанец *m*

P936 e prompt neutrons
d prompte Neutronen *n pl*,
Promptneutronen *n pl*
f neutrons *m pl* instantanés, neutrons *m*
pl instantanés de fission
r мгновенные нейтроны *m pl* деления

P937 e propagation vector
d Kreiswellenvektor *m*,
Kreiswellenzahlvektor *m*,
Ausbreitungsvektor *m*
f vecteur *m* d'onde circulaire, vecteur
m de nombre d'onde circulaire,
vecteur *m* de propagation
r волновой вектор *m*

P938 e propagator
d Propagator *m*
f propagateur *m*
r пропагатор *m*

P939 e propane bubble chamber
d Propanblasenkammer *f*
f chambre *f* de bulles à propane
r пропановая пузырьковая камера *f*

P940 e proper motion
d Eigenbewegung *f*
f mouvement *m* propre
r собственное движение *n*

P941 e proper time
d Eigenzeit *f*
f temps *m* propre
r собственное время *n* (*для
движущейся частицы*)

P942 e proportional chamber
d Proportionalionisationskammer *f*
f chambre *f* proportionnelle
r пропорциональная камера *f*

P943 e proportional counter
d Proportionalzählrohr *n*,
Proportionalzähler *m*
f compteur *m* proportionnel
r пропорциональный счётчик *m*

P944 e proportionality coefficient,
proportionality factor
d Proportionalitätsfaktor *m*
f coefficient *m* de proportionnalité
r коэффициент *m*
пропорциональности

P945 e proportionality limit
d Proportionalitätsgrenze *f*
f limite *f* de proportionnalité
r предел *m* пропорциональности

P946 e propulsion
d Propulsion *f*; Rückstoßbewegung *f*
f propulsion *f*
r тяга *f*, реактивное движение *n*

P947 e protactinium, Pa
d Protaktinium *n*
f protactinium *m*
r протактиний *m*

P948 e protection
d Schutz *m*

f protection f
r защита f

P949 e protection against ionizing radiation
d Schutz m gegen ionisierende
Strahlung
f protection f contre la radiation
ionisante
r защита f от облучения, защита f от
ионизирующих излучений

P950 e protective action
d Schutzwirkung f, Schutzeffekt m
f action f protective
r защитное действие n

P951 e protein
d Eiweiß n; Protein n
f protéine f
r белок m

P952 e protium
d Protium n
f protium m
r протий m

P953 e protogalaxy
d Protogalaxis f
f protogalaxie f
r протогалактика f

P954 e proton
d Proton n
f proton m
r протон m

P955 e proton accelerator
d Protonenbeschleuniger m
f accélérateur m de protons
r протонный ускоритель m

P956 e proton belt
d Protonengürtel m
f ceinture f de protons
r пояс m протонов

P957 e proton channel
d Protonenkanal m
f canal m à protons
r протонный канал m

P958 e proton channeling
d Protonenkanalierung f
f canalisation f des protons
r каналирование n протонов

P959 e proton flare
d Protonenflash n, Protonenfackel f
f éruption f protonique, flash m
protonique
r протонная вспышка f

P960 e proton magnetometer
d Protonenpräzessionsmagnetometer n
f magnétomètre m à protons
r протонный магнитометр m

P961 e proton-proton chain
d Proton-Proton-Kette f
f chaîne f proton-proton
r протон-протонная цепочка f

P962 e proton radiation
d Protonenstrahlung f
f rayonnement m protonique
r протонное излучение n

P963 e proton radioactivity
d Protonenaktivität f
f radioactivité f protonique
r протонная радиоактивность f

P964 e proton synchrotron
d Protonensynchrotron n
f synchrotron m à protons
r протонный синхротрон m

P965 e protoplanets
d Protoplaneten m pl
f protoplanètes f pl
r протопланеты f pl

P966 e protostars
d Protosterne m pl
f proto-étoiles f pl
r протозвёзды f pl

P967 e pseudo-Euclidean space
d pseudoeuklidischer Raum m
f espace m pseudo-euclidien
r псевдоевклидово пространство n

P968 e pseudoscalar
d Pseudoskalar m, pseudoskalare
Größe f
f pseudo-scalaire f
r псевдоскаляр m

P969 e pseudotensor
d Pseudotensor m
f pseudo-tenseur m
r псевдотензор m

P970 e pseudovector
d Pseudovektor m
f pseudo-vecteur m
r псевдовектор m, аксиальный
вектор m

P971 e psi particle
d Psi-Teilchen n, Psion n
f particule f psi
r пси-частица f

P972 e psychrometer
d Psychrometer n
f psychromètre m
r психрометр m

P973 e p-type semiconductor
d p-Halbleiter m
f semi-conducteur m p
r дырочный полупроводник m,
полупроводник m p-типа

P974   *e*   pulley
      d   Treibscheibe *f*
      f   poulie *f*
      r   шкив *m*

P975   *e*   pulsar
      d   Pulsar *m*
      f   pulsar *m*
      r   пульсар *m*

P976   *e*   pulsar magnetosphere
      d   Pulsarmagnetosphäre *f*
      f   magnétosphère *f* de pulsar
      r   магнитосфера *f* пульсара

P977   *e*   pulsation
      d   Pulsation *f*, Pulsationen *f pl*
      f   pulsation *f*
      r   пульсация *f*, пульсации *f pl*

P978   *e*   pulse
      d   Impuls *m*
      f   impulsion *f*
      r   импульс *m*

P979   *e*   pulse amplifier
      d   Impulsverstärker *m*
      f   amplificateur *m* d'impulsions
      r   импульсный усилитель *m*

P980   *e*   pulse amplitude
      d   Impulsamplitude *f*, Impulshöhe *f*,
         Impulsgröße *f*
      f   amplitude *f* d'impulsion
      r   амплитуда *f* импульса

P981   *e*   pulse-amplitude analyzer *see* pulse-
         height analyzer

P983   *e*   pulse-amplitude modulation
      d   Pulsamplitudenmodulation *f*,
         PAM
      f   modulation *f* d'impulsions en
         amplitude
      r   амплитудно-импульсная
         модуляция *f*

P985   *e*   pulse-code modulation
      d   Pulscodemodulation *f*, PCM
      f   modulation *f* par impulsions
         codées, modulation *f* par codes
         d'impulsions
      r   импульсно-кодовая модуляция *f*

P986   *e*   pulsed discharge
      d   Stoßentladung *f*,
         Impulsentladung *f*
      f   décharge *f* impulsionnelle
      r   импульсный разряд *m*

P987   *e*   pulsed injection
      d   gepulste Injektion *f*
      f   injection *f* impulsionnelle
      r   импульсная инжекция *f*

P988   *e*   pulsed laser

      d   Impulslaser *m*, gepulster Laser *m*,
         pulsierender Laser *m*
      f   laser *m* pulsé
      r   импульсный лазер *m*

P989   *e*   pulsed reactor
      d   Impulsreaktor *m*
      f   réacteur *m* à impulsions
      r   импульсный реактор *m*

P990   *e*   pulsed source
      d   Impulsquelle *f*, pulsierende Quelle *f*
      f   source *f* à impulsions
      r   импульсный источник *m*

P991   *e*   pulse duration
      d   Impulsdauer *f*, Pulsdauer *f*,
         Impulsbreite *f*, Impulslänge *f*
      f   durée *f* d'impulsion
      r   длительность *f* импульса

P992   *e*   pulse-duration modulation
      d   Pulsdauermodulation *f*,
         Pulsbreitenmodulation *f*
      f   modulation *f* de durée
         d'impulsions
      r   широтно-импульсная модуляция *f*

P993   *e*   pulse forming
      d   Impulsformung *f*
      f   formation *f* des impulsions
      r   формирование *n* импульса

P994   *e*   pulse-frequency modulation
      d   Pulsfrequenzmodulation *f*
      f   modulation *f* d'impulsions en
         fréquence
      r   частотно-импульсная модуляция *f*

P995   *e*   pulse generator
      d   Impulsgenerator *m*
      f   générateur *m* d'impulsions
      r   генератор *m* импульсов,
         импульсный генератор *m*

P996   *e*   pulse-height analyzer
      d   Impulshöhenanalysator *m*,
         Amplitudenanalysator *m*
      f   analyseur *m* de la hauteur
         d'impulsions, analyseur *m*
         d'impulsions
      r   амплитудный анализатор *m*
         импульсов

P997   *e*   pulse initiation
      d   Impulsinitiierung *f*
      f   initiation *f* par impulsions
      r   импульсное инициирование *n*

P998   *e*   pulse injector
      d   Impulsinjektor *m*
      f   injecteur *m* des impulsions (*du
         plasma*)
      r   импульсный инжектор *m* (*плазмы*)

P999   *e*   pulse jitter

d   Impulsinstabilität *f*, Jitter *m*
f   tremblement *m* d'impulsion
r   дрожание *n* импульса

P1000   e   pulse modulation
d   Pulsmodulation *f*, Impulsmodulation *f*
f   modulation *f* d'impulsions
r   импульсная модуляция *f*

P1001   e   pulse-periodic laser
d   Impulsperiodenlaser *m*
f   laser *m* à impulsion périodique
r   импульсно-периодический лазер *m*

P1002   e   pulse-phase modulation
d   Pulslagemodulation *f*,
Pulsphasenmodulation *f*
f   modulation *f* d'impulsions en phase,
modulation *f* d'impulsions en position
r   фазово-импульсная модуляция *f*

P1003   e   pulse power
d   Impulsleistung *f*
f   puissance *f* d'impulsion
r   импульсная мощность *f*, мощность *f*
импульса

P1004   e   pulse repetition frequency
d   Impulsfolgefrequenz *f*
f   fréquence *f* de répétition des
impulsions
r   частота *f* повторения импульсов,
частота *f* следования импульсов

P1005   e   pulse rise time
d   Impulsanstiegszeit *f*
f   temps *m* de montée de l'impulsion
r   длительность *f* фронта импульса

P1006   e   pulse separation
d   Impulsabstand *m*, Impulsintervall *n*
f   intervalle *m* d'impulsions
r   интервал *m* между импульсами

P1007   e   pulse series *see* pulse train

P1008   e   pulse sequence
d   Impulsfolge *f*
f   train *m* d'impulsions
r   импульсная последовательность *f*

P1009   e   pulse shape distortion
d   Impulsformverzerrung *f*,
Impulsverformung *f*
f   distorsion *f* de la forme d'impulsion
r   искажения *n pl* формы импульса

P1010   e   pulse shaper
d   Impulsformerschaltung *f*
f   formateur *m* d'impulsions
r   формирователь *m* импульсов

P1011   e   pulse train
d   Impulsreihe *f*; Impulsfolge *f*
f   série *f* d'impulsions; train *m*
d'impulsions
r   серия *f* импульсов; импульсная
последовательность *f*

P1012   e   pulse width *see* pulse duration

P1013   e   pump
d   1. Pumpe *f* 2. Pumpen *n*
f   1. pompe *f* 2. pompage *m*
r   1. насос *m* 2. накачка *f*

P1014   e   pump depletion
d   Pumpentleerung *f*,
Pumpentvölkerung *f*
f   déplétion *f* de pompage
r   истощение *n* накачки

P1015   e   pumping
d   Pumpen *n*
f   pompage *m*
r   накачка *f (лазера)*

P1016   e   pumping intensity *see* pump
intensity

P1017   e   pumping power *see* pump power

P1018   e   pumping pulse *see* pump pulse

P1019   e   pumping source *see* pump source

P1020   e   pumping radiation *see* pump
radiation

P1021   e   pump intensity
d   Pumpintensität *f*
f   intensité *f* de pompage
r   интенсивность *f* накачки

P1022   e   pump lamp
d   Pumplichtquelle *f*, Pumplampe *f*
f   lampe *f* de pompage
r   лампа *f* накачки

P1023   e   pump power
d   Pumpleistung *f*
f   puissance *f* de pompage
r   мощность *f* накачки

P1024   e   pump pulse
d   Pumpimpuls *m*
f   impulsion *f* de pompage
r   импульс *m* накачки

P1025   e   pump radiation
d   Pumpstrahlung *f*
f   rayonnement *m* de pompage
r   излучение *n* накачки

P1026   e   pump saturation
d   Pumpsättigung *f*
f   saturation *f* de pompage
r   насыщение *n* накачки

P1027   e   pump source
d   Pumpquelle *f*
f   source *f* de pompage
r   источник *m* накачки

P1028   e   pure physics *see* theoretical physics

P1029   e   pure substance

d Reinstoff *m*
f substance *f* pure
r чистое вещество *n*

P1030 e **pycnonuclear reactions**
d druckinduzierte Kernreaktionen *f pl*,
pyknonukleare Reaktionen *f pl*
f réactions *f pl* pycnonucléaires
r пикноядерные реакции *f pl*

P1031 e **pycnometer**
d Pyknometer *n*
f pycnomètre *m*
r пикнометр *m*

P1032 e **pyroelectric**
d Pyroelektrikum *n*
f pyro-électrique *m*
r пироэлектрик *m*

P1033 e **pyroelectric constant**
d pyroelektrische Konstante *f*
f constante *f* pyro-électrique
r пироэлектрический коэффициент *m*

P1034 e **pyroelectric effect**
d pyroelektrischer Effekt *m*
f effet *m* pyro-électrique
r пироэлектрический эффект *m*

P1035 e **pyroelectricity**
d Pyroelektrizität *f*
f pyro-électricité *f*
r пироэлектричество *n*

P1036 e **pyrometer**
d Pyrometer *n*
f pyromètre *m*
r пирометр *m*

P1037 e **pyrometry**
d Pyrometrie *f*
f pyrométrie *f*
r пирометрия *f*

Q

Q1 e **Q**
d Gütefaktor *m*, Güte *f*, Q-Faktor *m*
f facteur *m* de qualité, facteur *m* Q
r добротность *f*

Q2 e **Q factor** *see* **Q**

Q3 e **Q factor of oscillatory system**
d Schwingsystemgüte *f*,
Schwingungssystemgüte *f*
f facteur *m* Q du système oscillant
r добротность *f* колебательной
системы

Q4 e **Q meter**

d Gütefaktormesser *m*, Q-Meter *n*
f acuimètre *m*, Q-mètre *m*
r куметр *m*, измеритель *m*
добротности

Q5 e **Q switch**
d Güteschalter *m*, Q-Schalter *m*
f modulateur *m* de Q
r модулятор *m* добротности

Q6 e **Q-switched laser**
d gütegeschalteter Laser *m*
f laser *m* à modulation de Q
r лазер *m* с модулированной
добротностью

Q7 e **Q-switching**
d Gütemodulation *f*
f modulation *f* de qualité, modulation *f*
de facteur Q
r модуляция *f* добротности

Q8 e **quadrant**
d Quadrant *m*
f quadrant *m*
r квадрант *m*

Q9 e **quadratic dependence**
d quadratische Abhängigkeit *f*
f dépendance *f* quadratique
r квадратичная зависимость *f*

Q10 e **quadratic phase corrector**
d quadratischer Phasenentzerrer *m*
f correcteur *m* de phase quadratique
r квадратичный фазовый
корректор *m*

Q11 e **quadrature**
d Quadratur *f*
f quadrature *f*
r квадратура *f*

Q12 e **quadruple**
d Quadrupel *n*
f quadruple *m*
r квадруплет *m*

Q13 e **quadrupole**
d Quadrupol *m*
f quadripôle *m*
r квадруполь *m*

Q14 e **quadrupole focusing**
d Quadrupolfokussierung *f*
f focalisation *f* quadripolaire
r квадрупольная фокусировка *f*

Q15 e **quadrupole interaction**
d Quadrupolwechselwirkung *f*
f interaction *f* quadripolaire
r квадрупольное взаимодействие *n*

Q16 e **quadrupole lens**
d Quadrupollinse *f*
f lentille *f* quadripolaire
r квадрупольная линза *f*

Q17 *e* **quadrupole moment**
  d Quadrupolmoment *n*
  f moment *m* quadripolaire
  r квадрупольный момент *m*

Q18 *e* **quadrupole radiation**
  d Quadrupolstrahlung *f*
  f rayonnement *m* quadripolaire
  r квадрупольное излучение *n*

Q19 *e* **quadrupole radiator**
  d Quadrupolstrahler *m*
  f radiateur *m* quadripolaire
  r квадрупольный излучатель *m*

Q20 *e* **qualitative analysis**
  d qualitative Analyse *f*
  f analyse *f* qualitative
  r качественный анализ *m*

Q21 *e* *qualitative interpretation*
  d qualitative Interpretation *f*
  f interprétation *f* qualitative
  r качественная интерпретация *f*

Q22 *e* **quality**
  d Qualität *f*
  f qualité *f*
  r качество *n*

Q23 *e* **quality factor**
  d Qualitätsfaktor *m*
  f facteur *m* de qualité
  r коэффициент *m* качества
   излучения

Q24 *e* **quantitative analysis**
  d quantitative Analyse *f*
  f analyse *f* quantitative
  r количественный анализ *m*

Q25 *e* *quantitative interpretation*
  d quantitative Interpretation *f*
  f interprétation *f* quantitative
  r количественная интерпретация *f*

Q26 *e* **quantity**
  d 1. Größe *f* 2. Menge *f*, Quantität *f*,
   Anzahl *f*
  f quantité *f*
  r 1. количество *n* 2. величина *f*

Q27 *e* **quantity of electricity**
  d Elektrizitätsmenge *f*; elektrische
   Ladung *f*
  f quantité *f* d'électricité; charge *f*
   électrique
  r количество *n* электричества;
   заряд *m*

Q28 *e* **quantity of heat**
  d Wärmemenge *f*
  f quantité *f* de chaleur
  r количество *n* теплоты

Q29 *e* **quantization**
  d Quantisierung *f*, Quantelung *f*

  f quantification *f*
  r квантование *n*

Q30 *e* **quantization noise**
  d Quantisierungsrauschen *n*
  f bruit *m* de quantification
  r шум *m* квантования

Q31 *e* **quantized vortex**
  d gequantelter Wirbel *m*
  f tourbillon *m* quantifié
  r квантованный вихрь *m*

Q32 *e* **quantometer**
  d Quantometer *n*
  f quantimètre *m*
  r квантометр *m*

Q33 *e* **quantron**
  d Quantron *n*
  f quantron *m*
  r квантрон *m*

Q34 *e* **quantum**
  d Quant *n*
  f quantum *m*
  r квант *m*

Q35 *e* **quantum chemistry**
  d Quantenchemie *f*
  f chimie *f* quantique
  r квантовая химия *f*

Q36 *e* **quantum chromodynamics**
  d Quantenchromodynamik *f*
  f chromodynamique *f* quantique
  r квантовая хромодинамика *f*

Q37 *e* **quantum clock**
  d Quantenuhr *f*
  f horloge *f* quantique
  r квантовые часы *pl*

Q38 *e* **quantum coherence**
  d Quantenkohärenz *f*
  f cohérence *f* quantique
  r квантовая когерентность *f*

Q39 *e* **quantum crystal**
  d Quantenkristall *m*
  f cristal *m* quantique
  r квантовый кристалл *m*

Q40 *e* **quantum defect**
  d Quantendefekt *m*
  f défaut *m* quantique
  r квантовый дефект *m*

Q41 *e* **quantum delocalization**
  d Quantendelokalisierung *f*
  f délocalisation *f* quantique
  r квантовая делокализация *f*

Q42 *e* **quantum diffusion**
  d Quantendiffusion *f*
  f diffusion *f* quantique
  r квантовая диффузия *f*

Q43   *e*   **quantum dimensional effect**
       d   quantendimensioneller Effekt *m*
       f   effet *m* dimensionnel quantique
       r   квантовый размерный эффект *m*

Q44   *e*   **quantum dynamics**
       d   Quantendynamik *f*
       f   dynamique *f* quantique
       r   квантовая динамика *f*

Q45   *e*   **quantum effect**
       d   Quanteneffekt *m*
       f   effet *m* quantique
       r   квантовый эффект *m*

Q46   *e*   **quantum efficiency**
       d   Quantenausbeute *f*,
          Quantenwirkungsgrad *m*
       f   rendement *m* quantique
       r   квантовый КПД *m*, квантовый
          выход *m*

Q47   *e*   **quantum electrodynamics**
       d   Quantenelektrodynamik *f*
       f   électrodynamique *f* quantique
       r   квантовая электродинамика *f*

Q48   *e*   **quantum electronics**
       d   Quantenelektronik *f*
       f   électronique *f* quantique
       r   квантовая электроника *f*

Q49   *e*   **quantum field theory**
       d   Quantenfeldtheorie *f*
       f   théorie *f* des quanta du champ
       r   квантовая теория *f* поля

Q50   *e*   **quantum fluid** *see* **quantum liquid**

Q51   *e*   **quantum frequency standard**
       d   Quantenfrequenzstandard *m*
       f   fréquence *f* standard quantique
       r   квантовый стандарт *m* частоты

Q52   *e*   **quantum gas**
       d   Quantengas *n*
       f   gaz *m* quantique
       r   квантовый газ *m*

Q53   *e*   **quantum interference**
       d   Quanteninterferenz *f*
       f   interférence *f* quantique
       r   квантовая интерференция *f*

Q54   *e*   **quantum interferometer**
       d   Quanteninterferometer *n*
       f   interféromètre *m* quantique
       r   квантовый интерферометр *m*

Q55   *e*   **quantum kinetics**
       d   Quantenkinetik *f*
       f   cinétique *f* quantique
       r   квантовая кинетика *f*

Q56   *e*   **quantum liquid**
       d   Quantenflüssigkeit *f*

       f   liquide *m* quantique
       r   квантовая жидкость *f*

Q57   *e*   **quantum magnetometer**
       d   Quantenmagnetometer *n*
       f   magnétomètre *m* quantique
       r   квантовый магнитометр *m*

Q58   *e*   **quantum mechanics**
       d   Quantenmechanik *f*
       f   mécanique *f* quantique
       r   квантовая механика *f*

Q59   *e*   **quantum metrology**
       d   Quantenmetrologie *f*
       f   métrologie *f* quantique
       r   квантовая метрология *f*

Q60   *e*   **quantum number**
       d   Quantenzahl *f*
       f   nombre *m* quantique
       r   квантовое число *n*

Q61   *e*   **quantum of action** *see* **Planck constant**

Q62   *e*   **quantum optics**
       d   Quantenoptik *f*
       f   optique *f* quantique
       r   квантовая оптика *f*

Q63   *e*   **quantum oscillations** (*in magnetic field*)
       d   Quantenoszillationen *f pl*
       f   oscillations *f pl* quantiques (*dans le champ magnétique*)
       r   квантовые осцилляции *f pl* (*в магнитном поле*)

Q64   *e*   **quantum oscillator**
       d   Quantenoszillator *m*
       f   oscillateur *m* quantique
       r   квантовый осциллятор *m*;
          квантовый генератор *m*

Q65   *e*   **quantum paramagnetic amplifier**
       d   paramagnetischer
          Quantenverstärker *m*
       f   amplificateur *m* paramagnétique quantique
       r   квантовый парамагнитный усилитель *m*

Q66   *e*   **quantum physics**
       d   Quantenphysik *f*
       f   physique *f* quantique
       r   квантовая физика *f*

Q67   *e*   **quantum Poisson brackets**
       d   quantenmechanische Poisson-Klammern *f pl*
       f   parenthèses *f pl* de Poisson en mécanique quantique
       r   квантовые скобки Пуассона *f pl*

Q68   *e*   **quantum radiophysics**
       d   Quantenradiophysik *f*

  f   radiophysique *f* quantique
  r   квантовая радиофизика *f*

Q69   *e*   **quantum state**
  d   Quantenzustand *m*
  f   état *m* quantique
  r   квантовое состояние *n*

Q70   *e*   **quantum statistics**
  d   Quantenstatistik *f*
  f   statistique *f* quantique
  r   квантовая статистика *f*

Q71   *e*   **quantum system**
  d   Quantensystem *n*
  f   système *m* quantique
  r   квантовая система *f*

Q72   *e*   **quantum system radiation**
  d   Quantensystemstrahlung *f*
  f   rayonnement *m* du système quantique
  r   излучение *n* квантовой системы

Q73   *e*   **quantum theory**
  d   Quantentheorie *f*
  f   théorie *f* quantique
  r   квантовая теория *f*

Q74   *e*   **quantum transition**
  d   Quantenübergang *m*,
       quantenmechanischer Übergang *m*
  f   transition *f* quantique
  r   квантовый переход *n*

Q75   *e*   **quantum well**
  d   Quantenwanne *f*, Quantenmulde *f*
  f   puits *m* quantique
  r   квантовая яма *f*

Q76   *e*   **quantum-well laser**
  d   Quantenmuldenlaser *m*,
       Quantenwannenlaser *m*
  f   laser *m* à puits quantique
  r   лазер *m* на квантовой яме

Q77   *e*   **quantum wire**
  d   Quantendraht *m*
  f   fil *m* quantique
  r   квантовая нить *f (одномерная
       квантово-размерная структура)*

Q78   *e*   **quantum yield**
  d   Quantenausbeute *f*
  f   rendement *m* quantique
  r   квантовый выход *m*

Q79   *e*   **quark**
  d   Quark *n*
  f   quark *m*
  r   кварк *m*

Q80   *e*   **quark bag**
  d   Quarkbag *n*, *m*
  f   poche *f* de quark
  r   кварковый мешок *m*

Q81   *e*   **quark classification**
  d   Quarkklassifikation *f*
  f   classification *f* des quarks
  r   классификация кварков *f*

Q82   *e*   **quark combinatorics**
  d   Quarkkombinatorik *f*
  f   calcul *m* combinatoire des quarks
  r   кварковая комбинаторика *f*

Q83   *e*   **quark confinement**
  d   Quark confinement *n*
  f   confinement *m* des quarks
  r   удержание *n* кварков, невылетание
       n кварков, кварковый
       конфайнмент *n*

Q84   *e*   **quark diagram**
  d   Quarkdiagramm *n*
  f   diagramme *m* des quarks
  r   кварковая диаграмма *f*

Q85   *e*   **quark dynamics**
  d   Quarkdynamik *f*
  f   dynamique *f* des quarks
  r   кварковая динамика *f*

Q86   *e*   **quark-hadron duality**
  d   Quark-Hadron-Dualität *f*
  f   dualité *f* quark-hadron
  r   кварк-адронная дуальность *f*

Q87   *e*   **quark model** (*of hadrons*)
  d   Quarkmodell *n*
  f   modèle *m* des quarks (*de hadrons*)
  r   кварковая модель *f* (*адронов*)

Q88   *e*   **quarkonium**
  d   Quarkonium *n*
  f   quarkonium *m*
  r   кварконий *m*

Q89   *e*   **quarter-wave choke**
  d   Viertelwellendrossel *f*
  f   bobine *f* quart d'onde
  r   четвертьволновый дроссель *m*

Q90   *e*   **quarter-wave line**
  d   Viertelwellenleitung *f*
  f   ligne *f* quart d'onde
  r   четвертьволновая линия *f*

Q91   *e*   **quarter-wave plate**
  d   Viertelwellenlängenplättchen *n*
  f   lame *f* quart d'onde
  r   пластинка *f* в четверть длины
       волны

Q92   *e*   **quartet**
  d   Quartett *n*
  f   quartet *m*
  r   квартет *m*

Q93   *e*   **quartz**
  d   Quarz *m*
  f   quartz *m*
  r   кварц *m*

Q94   *e*   **quartz clock**
     d   Quarzuhr *f*
     f   horloge *f* à quartz
     r   кварцевые часы *pl*

Q95   *e*   **quartz crystal**
     d   Quarzkristall *m*
     f   cristal *m* de quartz
     r   кварцевый кристалл *m*

Q96   *e*   **quartz fiber**
     d   Quarzfaser *f*
     f   fibre *f* de quartz
     r   кварцевое волокно *n*

Q97   *e*   **quartz wedge**
     d   Quarzkeil *m*
     f   coin *m* de quartz, coin *m* à quartz
     r   кварцевый клин *m*

Q98   *e*   **quasag** (*quasi-stellar galaxy*)
     d   Quasage *f*, Quasag *m*, quasistellare
        Galaxis *f*
     f   quasag *m*, galaxie *f* quasi stellaire
     r   квазаг *m*, квазизвёздная галактика *f*

Q99   *e*   **quasar** (*quasi-stellar radio source*)
     d   Quasar *m*, quasistellare Radioquelle *f*
     f   quasar *m*, objet *m* quasistellaire
     r   квазар *m*

Q100   *e*   **quasi-classical approximation**
     d   WKB-Näherung *f*, quasiklassische
        Näherung *f*
     f   approximation *f* quasi classique
     r   квазиклассическое приближение *n*,
        метод *m* ВКБ

Q101   *e*   **quasi-closed subsystem**
     d   quasiabgeschlossenes Untersystem *n*
     f   subsystème *m* quasi fermé
     r   квазизамкнутая подсистема *f*

Q102   *e*   **quasi-coordinates**
     d   Quasikoordinaten *f pl*,
        Pseudokoordinaten *f pl*
     f   quasi-coordonnées *f pl*
     r   квазикоординаты *f pl*

Q103   *e*   **quasi-crystal**
     d   Quasikristall *m*
     f   quasi-cristal *m*
     r   квазикристалл *m*

Q104   *e*   **quasi-deuteron**
     d   Quasideuteron *n*
     f   quasi-deutéron *m*
     r   квазидейтрон *m*

Q105   *e*   **quasi-elastic force**
     d   quasielastische Kraft *f*
     f   force *f* quasi élastique
     r   квазиупругая сила *f*

Q106   *e*   **quasi-elastic scattering**
     d   quasielastische Streuung *f*

     f   diffusion *f* quasi élastique
     r   квазиупругое рассеяние *n*

Q107   *e*   **quasi-energy**
     d   Quasienergie *f*
     f   quasi-énergie *f*
     r   квазиэнергия *f*

Q108   *e*   **quasi-equilibrium**
     d   Quasigleichgewicht *n*
     f   quasi-équilibre *m*
     r   квазиравновесие *n*

Q109   *e*   **quasi-ergodic hypothesis**
     d   Quasi-Ergodenhypothese *f*
     f   hypothèse *f* quasi ergodique
     r   квазиэргодическая гипотеза *f*

Q110   *e*   **quasi-Fermi level**
     d   Quasi-Fermi-Niveau *n*
     f   quasi-niveau *m* de Fermi
     r   квазиуровень *m* Ферми

Q111   *e*   **quasi-hole**
     d   Quasiloch *n*
     f   quasi-trou *m*
     r   квазидырка *f*

Q112   *e*   **quasi-level**
     d   Quasiniveau *n*
     f   quasi-niveau *m*
     r   квазиуровень *m*

Q113   *e*   **quasi-linear theory** (*of plasma*)
     d   quasilineare Plasmatheorie *f*
     f   théorie *f* quasi linéaire (*du plasma*)
     r   квазилинейная теория *f* (*плазмы*)

Q114   *e*   **quasi-mode**
     d   Quasimode *f*
     f   quasi-mode *m*
     r   квазимода *f*

Q115   *e*   **quasi-molecule**
     d   Quasimolekül *n*
     f   quasi-molécule *f*
     r   квазимолекула *f*

Q116   *e*   **quasi-momentum**
     d   Quasiimpuls *m*, Pseudoimpuls *m*
     f   quasi-impulsion *f*
     r   квазиимпульс *m*

Q117   *e*   **quasi-neutrality**
     d   Quasineutralität *f*
     f   quasi-neutralité *f*
     r   квазинейтральность *f* (*плазмы*)

Q118   *e*   **quasi-optical line**
     d   quasioptische Linie *f*
     f   ligne *f* quasi optique
     r   квазиоптическая линия *f*

Q119   *e*   **quasi-optics**
     d   Quasioptik *f*
     f   quasi-optique *f*
     r   квазиоптика *f*

Q120   *e* **quasi-particle**
      d Quasiteilchen *n*
      f quasi-particule *f*
      r квазичастица *f*

Q121   *e* **quasi-periodic motion**
      d quasiperiodische Bewegung *f*
      f mouvement *m* quasi périodique
      r квазипериодическое движение *n*

Q122   *e* **quasi-periodic oscillation**
      d quasiperiodische Schwingungen *f pl*
      f oscillations *f pl* quasi périodiques
      r квазипериодические колебания *n pl*

Q123   *e* **quasi-potential**
      d Quasipotential *n*
      f quasi-potentiel *m*
      r квазипотенциал *m*

Q124   *e* **quasi-resonance**
      d Quasiresonanz *f*
      f quasi-résonance *f*
      r квазирезонанс *m*

Q125   *e* **quasi-static process**
      d quasistatischer Prozeß *m*
      f processus *m* quasi statique
      r квазистатический процесс *m*

Q126   *e* **quasi-stationary current**
      d quasistationärer Strom *m*
      f courant *m* quasi stationnaire
      r квазистационарный ток *m*

Q127   *e* **quasi-stationary process**
      d quasistationärer Prozeß *m*
      f processus *m* quasi stationnaire
      r квазистационарный процесс *m*

Q128   *e* **quasi-stellar galaxy** *see* **quasag**

Q129   *e* **quasi-stellar object**
      d quasistellares Objekt *n*, Quasar *m*
      f objet *m* quasi stellaire, quasar *m*
      r квазизвёздный объект *m*, квазар *m*

Q130   *e* **quasi-stellar source**
      d quasistellare Quelle *f*
      f source *f* quasi stellaire
      r квазизвёздный источник *m*

Q131   *e* **quaternion**
      d Quaternion *n*
      f quaternion *m*
      r кватернион *m*

Q132   *e* **quencher**
      d Lumineszenzgift *m*
      f destructeur *m* de luminescence, poison *m* de luminescence
      r тушитель *m*, гаситель *m* (*люминесценции*)

Q133   *e* **quenching**
      d 1. Löschung *f*, Löschen *n* 2. Abschrecken *n* 3. Unterdrückung *f*
      f 1. extinction *f* 2. trempe *f* 3. suppression *f*
      r 1. тушение *n*, гашение *n* 2. закалка *f* 3. подавление *n*

Q134   *e* **quenching agent** *see* **quencher**

Q135   *e* **quenching of luminescence**
      d Löschen *n* der Lumineszenz, Lumineszenzlöschen *n*
      f exctinction *f* de la luminescence
      r тушение *n* люминесценции

Q136   *e* **quiet day**
      d ruhiger Tag *m*
      f jour *m* calme
      r спокойный день *m*

Q137   *e* **quiet ionosphere**
      d ruhige Ionosphäre *f*
      f ionosphère *f* calme
      r невозмущённая ионосфера *f*, спокойная ионосфера *f*

Q138   *e* **quiet Sun**
      d ruhige Sonne *f*
      f Soleil *m* calme
      r спокойное Солнце *n*

Q139   *e* **quintet**
      d Quintett *n*
      f quintet *m*
      r квинтет *m*

Q140   *e* **Q value** *see* **Q**

R

R1   *e* **Rabi frequency**
      d Rabi-Frequenz *f*
      f fréquence *f* de Rabi
      r частота *f* Раби

R2   *e* **Rabi oscillations**
      d Rabi-Oszillationen *f pl*
      f oscillations *f pl* de Rabi
      r осцилляции *f pl* Раби

R3   *e* **Racah coefficients**
      d Racah-Koeffizienten *m pl*
      f coefficients *m pl* de Racah
      r коэффициенты *m pl* Рака

R4   *e* **rad**
      d Rad *n*
      f rad *m*
      r рад *m* (*единица поглощённой дозы ионизирующего излучения*)

R5   *e* **radar**
      d 1. Radar *n* 2. Radargerät *n*
      f radar *m*

	r	1. радиолокация *f*
		2. радиолокатор *m*
R6	*e*	radar astronomy
	d	Radarastronomie *f*
	f	astronomie *f* radar
	r	радиолокационная астрономия *f*
R7	*e*	radial injection
	d	Radialinjektion *f*
	f	injection *f* radiale
	r	радиальная инжекция *f*
R8	*e*	radial quantum number
	d	radiale Quantenzahl *f*, Radialquantenzahl *f*
	f	nombre *m* quantique radial
	r	радиальное квантовое число *n*
R9	*e*	radian
	d	Radiant *m*
	f	radian *m*
	r	радиан *m*
R10	*e*	radiance
	d	Strahldichte *f*
	f	radiance *f*, luminance *f* énergétique
	r	лучистость *f*, энергетическая яркость *f*
R11	*e*	radiance temperature
	d	schwarze Temperatur *f*
	f	température *f* de luminance
	r	яркостная температура *f*
R12	*e*	radiant emittance, radiant exitance
	d	spezifische Ausstrahlung *f*
	f	émittance *f* énergétique, émittance *f* lumineuse
	r	излучательность *f*, энергетическая светимость *f*
R13	*e*	radiant energy
	d	Strahlungsenergie *f*
	f	énergie *f* rayonnante
	r	энергия *f* излучения, лучистая энергия *f*
R14	*e*	radiant exposure
	d	Bestrahlung *f*
	f	exposition *f* énergétique, exposition *f* lumineuse
	r	лучистая экспозиция *f*, энергетическая экспозиция *f*; доза *f*
R15	*e*	radiant flux
	d	Strahlungsfluß *m*
	f	flux *m* rayonnant, flux *m* énergétique
	r	поток *m* излучения, лучистый поток *m*
R16	*e*	radiant flux density
	d	Strahlungsflußdichte *f*
	f	densité *f* de flux rayonnant, densité *f* de flux énergétique
	r	поверхностная плотность *f* потока излучения
R17	*e*	radiant heating
	d	Strahlungsheizung *f*
	f	chauffage *m* par radiation
	r	радиационный нагрев *m*, нагрев *m* излучением
R18	*e*	radiant intensity
	d	Strahlstärke *f*
	f	intensité *f* énergétique de rayonnement
	r	сила *f* излучения
R19	*e*	radiant power *see* radiant flux
R20	*e*	radiated power
	d	Strahlungsleistung *f*
	f	puissance *f* de rayonnement
	r	излучаемая мощность *f*, мощность *f* излучения
R21	*e*	radiating system
	d	Strahlungssystem *n*, strahlendes System *n*
	f	système *m* radiant
	r	излучающая система *f*
R22	*e*	radiation
	d	Strahlung *f*; Ausstrahlung *f*
	f	radiation *f*, rayonnement *m*
	r	1. излучение *n*; лучеиспускание *n* 2. радиация *f*
R23	*e*	radiation background *see* background radiation
R24	*e*	radiation balance
	d	Strahlungsbilanz *f*
	f	bilan *m* de rayonnement
	r	радиационный баланс *m*
R25	*e*	radiation belts
	d	Strahlungsgürtel *m pl*
	f	ceintures *f pl* de radiation
	r	радиационные пояса *m pl*
R26	*e*	radiation-chemical protection
	d	chemischer Strahlenschutz *m*
	f	protection *f* radiochimique
	r	радиационно-химическая защита *f*
R27	*e*	radiation chemistry
	d	Strahlungschemie *f*, Radiochemie *f*
	f	chimie *f* de radiation
	r	радиационная химия *f*
R28	*e*	radiation corrections
	d	Strahlungskorrekturen *f pl*
	f	corrections *f pl* de rayonnement
	r	радиационные поправки *f pl*
R29	*e*	radiation damage
	d	Strahlungsschaden *m*
	f	dommage *m* par rayonnements
	r	радиационное повреждение *n*
R30	*e*	radiation defects
	d	strahleninduzierte Gitterfehlstellen *f pl*

f défauts *m pl* de rayonnement
r радиационные дефекты *m pl*

R31 *e* radiation detector
d Strahlungsempfänger *m*,
Strahlungsdetektor *m*
f détecteur *m* de rayonnement
r детектор *m* излучения; приёмник *m* излучения

R32 *e* radiation diffusion
d Strahlungsdiffusion *f*
f diffusion *f* de rayonnement
r диффузия *f* излучения

R33 *e* radiation directivity
d Strahlungsbündelung *f*
f directivité *f* de rayonnement
r направленность *f* излучения

R34 *e* radiation dose
d Strahlungsdosis *f*
f dose *f* de rayonnement
r доза *f* излучения

R35 *e* radiation effect
d Strahlungswirkung *f*, Strahleneffekt *m*
f effet *m* de rayonnement
r действие *n* излучения

R36 *e* radiation flux *see* radiant flux

R37 *e* radiation hardness
d Strahlungshärte *f*
f dureté *f* de rayonnement
r жёсткость *f* излучения

R38 *e* radiation hazard
d Strahlungsrisiko *n*,
Strahlengefährdung *f*
f dangers *m pl* de rayonnement, risque *m* d'irradiation
r радиационная опасность *f*

R39 *e* radiation imprisonment *see* radiation trapping

R40 *e* radiation-induced defects *see* radiation defects

R41 *e* radiation injury
d biologischer Strahlenschaden *m*,
biologische Strahlenschädigung *f*
f radiolésion *f*, lésion *f* due aux rayonnements ionisants
r радиационное поражение *n*

R42 *e* radiation intensity
d Strahlungsintensität *f*,
Strahlenintensität *f*
f intensité *f* de rayonnement
r интенсивность *f* излучения

R43 *e* radiation isotropy
d Strahlungsisotropie *f*
f isotropie *f* de rayonnement
r изотропия *f* излучения

R44 *e* radiation laws
d Strahlungsgesetze *n pl*
f lois *f pl* de rayonnement
r законы *m pl* излучения

R45 *e* radiation length
d Strahlungslänge *f*
f longueur *f* de radiation
r радиационная длина *f*

R46 *e* radiationless transition
d strahlungsloser Übergang *m*
f transition *f* sans radiation
r безызлучательный переход *m*

R47 *e* radiation loss
d Strahlungsverlust *m*
f pertes *f pl* par rayonnement
r радиационные потери *f pl*, потери *f pl* на излучение

R48 *e* radiation monitoring
d Strahlungskontrolle *f*,
Strahlenüberwachung *f*
f surveillance *f* des rayonnements,
contrôle *m* du niveau de rayonnement
r радиационный контроль *m*,
дозиметрический контроль *m*

R49 *e* radiation pattern *see* directional pattern

R50 *e* radiation pressure
d Strahlungsdruck *m*
f pression *f* de rayonnement, pression *f* de radiation
r давление *n* излучения,
радиационное давление *n*

R51 *e* radiation protection *see* protection against ionizing radiation

R52 *e* radiation pyrometer
d Strahlungspyrometer *n*
f pyromètre *m* optique, pyromètre *m* à radiation
r радиационный пирометр *m*

R53 *e* radiation quantum
d Strahlungsquant *n*
f quantum *m* de rayonnement
r квант *m* излучения

R54 *e* radiation resistance
d 1. Strahlungswiderstand *m* 2.
Strahlungsbeständigkeit *f*
f 1. résistance *f* de rayonnement 2.
résistance *f* au rayonnement
r 1. сопротивление *n* излучения 2.
радиационная стойкость *f*

R55 *e* radiation source
d Strahlungsquelle *f*, Strahlenquelle *f*
f source *f* de rayonnement
r источник *m* излучения

R56 *e* radiation spectrum

d Strahlungsspektrum n
f spectre m de rayonnement
r спектр m излучения

R57 e radiation temperature
d Strahlungstemperatur f
f température f de rayonnement,
température f de radiation
r радиационная температура f

R58 e radiation transfer
d Strahlungsübertragung f
f transfert m du rayonnement
r перенос m излучения

R59 e radiation trapping, radiative capture
d Strahlungseinfang m, strahlender
Einfang m
f capture f radiative
r радиационный захват m

R60 e radiative equilibrium
d Strahlungsgleichgewicht n
f équilibre m radiatif
r лучистое равновесие n

R61 e radiative friction
d Strahlungsreibung f
f frottement m radiatif
r радиационное трение n

R62 e radiative heat exchange
d Wärmeübertragung f durch Strahlung
f échange m de chaleur radiatif
r лучистый теплообмен m

R63 e radiative recombination
d Strahlungsrekombination f
f recombinaison f radiative
r излучательная рекомбинация f

R64 e radiative recombination coefficient
d Strahlungsrekombinationskoeffizient m
f coefficient m de recombinaison
radiative
r коэффициент m излучательной
рекомбинации

R65 e radiative transfer see radiation
transfer

R66 e radiative transition
d Strahlungsübergang m, strahlender
Übergang m
f transition f radiative
r излучательный переход m

R67 e radiator
d 1. Strahler m 2. Radiator m
f radiateur m
r 1. излучатель m 2. радиатор m

R68 e radioactivation analysis
d Aktivierungsanalyse f
f analyse f par activation, analyse f par
radioactivation
r радиоактивационный анализ m,
активационный анализ m

R69 e radioactive ash
d radioaktive Asche f
f cendres f pl radioactives
r радиоактивный пепел m

R70 e radioactive chain see radioactive
series

R71 e radioactive contamination
d radioaktive Kontamination f,
radioaktive Verseuchung f
f contamination f radioactive
r радиоактивное загрязнение n

R72 e radioactive decay, radioactive
disintegration
d radioaktiver Zerfall m
f désintégration f radioactive
r радиоактивный распад m

R73 e radioactive dust
d radioaktiver Staub m
f poussière f radioactive
r радиоактивная пыль f

R74 e radioactive effluent see radioactive
waste

R75 e radioactive fall-out
d Fallout m, radioaktive
Niederschläge m pl
f dépôts m pl radioactifs
r радиоактивные осадки m pl

R76 e radioactive family
d radioaktive Zerfallsfamilie f,
Zerfallsfamilie f
f famille f radioactive
r радиоактивное семейство n

R77 e radioactive half-life
d Halbwertzeit f
f période f de demi-vie
r период m полураспада

R78 e radioactive indicator
d Radioindikator m, radioaktiver
Indikator m, radioaktiver Tracer m
f indicateur m radioactif, traceur m
radioactif
r изотопный индикатор m

R79 e radioactive intensity
d Intensität f der radioaktiven Strahlung
f intensité f de rayonnement radioactif
r интенсивность f радиоактивного
излучения

R80 e radioactive isotope
d radioaktives Isotop n, Radioisotop n
f isotope m radioactif, radio-isotope m
r радиоактивный изотоп m,
радиоизотоп m

R81 e radioactive logging
d radiometrische Bohrlochmessung f

f diagraphie *f* nucléaire
r радиоактивный каротаж *m*

R82 *e* radioactive nuclide
d Radionuklid *n*, radioaktives Nuklid *n*
f radionucléide *m*, nucléide *m* radioactif
r радиоактивный изотоп *m*, радиоизотоп *m*, радионуклид *m*

R83 *e* radioactive radiation
d radioaktive Strahlung *f*
f rayonnement *m* radioactif
r радиоактивное излучение *n*

R84 *e* radioactive series
d radioaktive Zerfallsreihe *f*, Zerfallsreihe *f*
f série *f* radioactive
r радиоактивный ряд *m*

R85 *e* radioactive source
d radioaktive Strahlenquelle *f*, radioaktive Strahlungsquelle *f*, radioaktive Quelle *f*
f source *f* radioactive
r радиоактивный источник *m*

R86 *e* radioactive source isotropism
d Strahlungsquellenisotropie *f*
f isotropie *f* de la source radioactive
r изотропность *f* радиоактивного источника

R87 *e* radioactive substance
d radioaktiver Stoff *m*
f substance *f* radioactive
r радиоактивное вещество *n*

R88 *e* radioactive tracer *see* radioactive indicator

R89 *e* radioactive waste
d radioaktive Abfälle *m pl*
f déchets *m pl* radioactifs
r радиоактивные отходы *m pl*

R90 *e* radioactivity
d Radioaktivität *f*
f radioactivité *f*
r радиоактивность *f*

R91 *e* radio altimeter
d Radiohöhenmesser *m*
f radioaltimètre *m*
r радиовысотомер *m*

R92 *e* radio astronomy, radioastronomy
d Radioastronomie *f*
f radioastronomie *f*
r радиоастрономия *f*

R93 *e* radiobiology
d Radiobiologie *f*
f radiobiologie *f*
r радиобиология *f*

R94 *e* radio burst

d Strahlungsausbruch *m*, Burst *m*
f sursaut *m* radioélectrique
r радиовсплеск *m*, всплеск *m* радиоизлучения

R95 *e* radiocarbon dating
d Radiokohlenstoffdatierung *f*, Kohlenstoffdatierung *f*, Altersbestimmung *f* nach der Kohlenstoffmethode
f datation *f* par le radiocarbone
r радиоуглеродное датирование *n*, датирование *n* по радиоуглероду

R96 *e* radiocarbon method
d Radiokohlenstoffdatierung *f*, Radiokarbonmethode *f*, Kohlenstoffmethode *f*
f méthode *f* du radiocarbone
r радиоуглеродный метод *m* (*определения возраста*)

R97 *e* radiochemical analysis
d radiochemische Analyse *f*
f analyse *f* radiochimique
r радиохимический анализ *m*

R98 *e* radiochemistry
d Radiochemie *f*
f radiochimie *f*
r радиохимия *f*

R99 *e* radio direction finder
d Funkpeiler *m*
f radiogoniomètre *m*
r радиопеленгатор *m*

R100 *e* radio distance finder
d Funkentfernungsmesser *m*
f radiotélémètre *m*
r радиодальномер *m*

R101 *e* radio disturbances
d Funkstörungen *f pl*
f parasites *m pl* radioélectriques
r радиопомехи *f pl*, помехи *f pl* радиоприёму

R102 *e* radio echo
d Funkecho *n*
f écho *m* radioélectrique
r радиоэхо *n*

R103 *e* radio electronics
d Radioelektronik *f*
f radiotechnique *f*
r радиоэлектроника *f*

R104 *e* radio engineering
d Funktechnik *f*
f radio-ingénierie *f*
r радиотехника *f*

R105 *e* radio-frequency band *see* high-frequency band

R106 *e* radio-frequency focusing

    d Hochfrequenzfokussierung *f*
    f focalisation *f* haute fréquence
    r высокочастотная фокусировка *f*

R107 *e* **radio-frequency measurements**
    d radiotechnische Messungen *f pl*
    f mesures *f pl* radioélectriques
    r радиоизмерения *n pl*

R108 *e* **radio-frequency pulse**
    d Hochfrequenzimpuls *m*, HF-Impuls *m*
    f impulsion *f* à haute fréquence
    r радиоимпульс *m*

R109 *e* **radio galaxy**
    d Radiogalaxie *f*
    f radiogalaxie *f*
    r радиогалактика *f*

R110 *e* **radio holography**
    d Radioholographie *f*
    f radioholographie *f*
    r радиоголография *f*

R111 *e* **radio interference**
    d Funkstörung *f*
    f radio-interférence *f*
    r радиопомехи *f pl*

R112 *e* **radio interferometer**
    d Radiointerferometer *n*
    f radio-interféromètre *m*
    r радиоинтерферометр *m*

R113 *e* **radio interferometry**
    d Radiointerferometrie *f*
    f radio-interférométrie *f*
    r радиоинтерферометрия *f*

R114 *e* **radioisotope**
    d Radioisotop *n*, radioaktives Isotop *n*
    f radio-isotope *m*, isotope *m* radioactif
    r радиоизотоп *m*, радиоактивный изотоп *m*

R115 *e* **radioisotope diagnostics**
    d Radioisotopendiagnostik *f*
    f diagnostic *m* radio-isotopique
    r радиоизотопная диагностика *f*

R116 *e* **radiolocation** *see* **radar 1.**

R117 *e* **radiology**
    d Radiologie *f*
    f radiologie *f*
    r радиология *f*

R118 *e* **radioluminescence**
    d Radiolumineszenz *f*
    f radioluminescence *f*
    r радиолюминесценция *f*

R119 *e* **radiolysis**
    d Radiolyse *f*
    f radiolyse *f*
    r радиолиз *m*

R120 *e* **radiometer**
    d Radiometer *n*, Strahlungsmesser *m*
    f radiomètre *m*
    r радиометр *m*

R121 *e* **radiometry**
    d Radiometrie *f*, Strahlungsmessung *f*
    f radiométrie *f*
    r радиометрия *f*

R122 *e* **radio navigation**
    d Funknavigation *f*
    f radionavigation *f*
    r радионавигация *f*

R123 *e* **radionuclide** *see* **radioactive nuclide**

R124 *e* **radiophysics**
    d Radiophysik *f*
    f radiophysique *f*
    r радиофизика *f*

R125 *e* **radio pill**
    d Radiopille *f*
    f endoémetteur *m*
    r радиопилюля *f*

R126 *e* **radio radiation**
    d Radiofrequenzstrahlung *f*, Radiostrahlung *f*
    f rayonnement *m* radioélectrique, émission *f* radioélectrique
    r радиоизлучение *n*, излучение *n* радиоволн

R127 *e* **radio receiver**
    d Funkempfänger *m*; Rundfunkempfänger *m*; Funkempfängsgerät *n*
    f récepteur *m* radio
    r радиоприёмник *m*, радиоприёмное устройство *n*

R128 *e* **radiosensitivity**
    d Strahlungsempfindlichkeit *f*
    f radiosensibilité *f*
    r радиочувствительность *f*

R129 *e* **radio signal**
    d Funksignal *n*; Rundfunksignal *n*
    f radiosignal *m*
    r радиосигнал *m*

R130 *e* **radiosonde**
    d Radiosonde *f*, Funksonde *f*
    f radiosonde *f*
    r радиозонд *m*

R131 *e* **radio source**
    d Radioquelle *f*
    f radiosource *f*
    r источник *m* радиоизлучения

R132 *e* **radio spectroscope**
    d Radiospektroskop *n*
    f radiospectroscope *m*
    r радиоспектроскоп *m*

R133   *e*   radio spectroscopy
       d   Radiospektroskopie *f*
       f   radiospectroscopie *f*
       r   радиоспектроскопия *f*

R134   *e*   radiosurgery
       d   Radiochirurgie *f*
       f   radiochirurgie *f*
       r   радиохирургия *f*

R135   *e*   radio telemetry
       d   Funkfernmessung *f*
       f   radiotélémétrie *f*
       r   радиотелеметрия *f*

R136   *e*   radio telescope
       d   Radioteleskop *n*
       f   radiotélescope *m*
       r   радиотелескоп *m*

R137   *e*   radiotherapy
       d   Radiotherapie *f*, Strahlentherapie *f*
       f   radiothérapie *f*
       r   радиотерапия *f*

R138   *e*   radio transmitter
       d   Sender *m*; Rundfunksender *m*
       f   radiotransmetteur *m*
       r   радиопередатчик *m*,
           радиопередающее устройство *n*

R139   *e*   radio wave attenuation
       d   Funkwellendämpfung *f*,
           Radiowellendämpfung *f*
       f   amortissement *m* des ondes
           radioélectriques
       r   затухание *n* радиоволн

R140   *e*   radio wave diffraction
       d   Radiowellenbeugung *f*
       f   diffraction *f* des ondes
           radioélectriques
       r   дифракция *f* радиоволн

R141   *e*   radio wave interference
       d   Radiowelleninterferenz *f*
       f   interférence *f* des ondes
           radioélectriques
       r   интерференция *f* радиоволн

R142   *e*   radio wave propagation
       d   Funkwellenausbreitung *f*
       f   propagation *f* des ondes
           radioélectriques
       r   распространение *n* радиоволн

R143   *e*   radio waves
       d   Funkwellen *f pl*, Radiowellen *f pl*
       f   ondes *f pl* radioélectriques
       r   радиоволны *f pl*

R144   *e*   radio wave scattering
       d   Funkwellenstreuung *f*,
           Radiowellenstreuung *f*
       f   diffusion *f* des ondes radioélectriques
       r   рассеяние *n* радиоволн

R145   *e*   radium, Ra
       d   Radium *n*
       f   radium *m*
       r   радий *m*

R146   *e*   radius
       d   Radius *m*, Halbmesser *m*
       f   rayon *m*
       r   радиус *m*

R147   *e*   radius of curvature
       d   Krümmungsradius *m*,
           Krümmungshalbmesser *m*
       f   rayon *m* de courbure
       r   радиус *m* кривизны

R148   *e*   radius of gyration *see* radius of
           inertia

R149   *e*   radius of inertia
       d   Trägheitsradius *m*,
           Trägheitshalbmesser *m*
       f   rayon *m* d'inertie
       r   радиус *m* инерции

R150   *e*   radon
       d   Radon *n*
       f   radon *m*
       r   радон *m*

R151   *e*   **Raman amplifier**
       d   Raman-Verstärker *m*
       f   amplificateur *m* de Raman
       r   комбинационный усилитель *m*,
           рамановский усилитель *m*

R152   *e*   **Raman effect**
       d   Raman-Effekt *m*
       f   effet *m* Raman
       r   комбинационное рассеяние *n* света;
           эффект *m* Рамана

R153   *e*   **Raman emission**
       d   Raman-Emission *f*
       f   émission *f* Raman
       r   комбинационное излучение *n*,
           рамановское излучение *n*

R154   *e*   **Raman laser**
       d   Raman-Laser *m*
       f   laser *m* Raman
       r   комбинационный лазер *m*, ВКР-
           лазер *m*, рамановский лазер *m*

R155   *e*   **Raman light scattering**
       d   Raman-Streuung *f*, Ramansche
           Lichtstreuung *f*
       f   diffusion *f* Raman
       r   комбинационное рассеяние *n* света

R156   *e*   **Raman line**
       d   Raman-Linie *f*
       f   raie *f* Raman
       r   линия *f* комбинационного рассеяния
           (*света*)

R157   *e*   **Raman radiation** *see* **Raman**
           emission

R158   *e*   **Raman scattering** *see* **Raman light scattering**

R159   *e*   **Raman spectroscopy**
      d   Raman-Spektroskopie *f*
      f   spectroscopie *f* Raman
      r   спектроскопия *f* комбинационного рассеяния

R160   *e*   **Raman spectrum**
      d   Raman-Spektrum *n*
      f   spectre *m* Raman
      r   спектр *m* комбинационного рассеяния (*света*)

R161   *e*   **Ramsauer effect**
      d   Ramsauer-Effekt *m*
      f   effet *m* Ramsauer
      r   эффект *m* Рамзауэра

R162   *e*   **random dependence**
      d   Zufallsabhängigkeit *f*
      f   dépendance *f* fortuite, dépendance *f* accidentelle
      r   случайная зависимость *f*

R163   *e*   **random error**
      d   zufälliger Fehler *m*
      f   erreur *f* fortuite, erreur *f* accidentelle
      r   случайная погрешность *f*

R164   *e*   **random fluctuations**
      d   zufällige Schwankungen *f pl*
      f   fluctuations *f pl* accidentelles, fluctuations *f pl* aléatoires
      r   случайные флуктуации *f pl*

R165   *e*   **random motion**
      d   ungeordnete Bewegung *f*, chaotische Bewegung *f*
      f   mouvement *m* désordonné
      r   хаотическое движение *n*, беспорядочное движение *n*

R166   *e*   **random oscillation**
      d   Zufallsschwingungen *f pl*
      f   oscillations *f pl* aléatoires
      r   хаотические колебания *n pl*, случайные колебания *n pl*

R167   *e*   **random pulse**
      d   Zufallsimpuls *m*
      f   impulsion *f* aléatoire
      r   случайный импульс *m*

R168   *e*   **random signal detection**
      d   Zufallssignaldemodulation *f*
      f   détection *f* des signaux aléatoires
      r   детектирование *n* случайных сигналов

R169   *e*   **random variable**
      d   Zufallsvariable *f*, Zufallsgröße *f*
      f   variable *f* aléatoire, aléa *m* numérique
      r   случайная величина *f*

R170   *e*   **random variance**
      d   Zufallsvariablendispersion *f*
      f   variance *f* de grandeur aléatoire
      r   дисперсия *f* случайной величины

R171   *e*   **range**
      d   1. Bereich *m*, Gebiet *n*; Intervall *n* 2. Reichweite *f* 3. Schwingungsweite *f*, Amplitude *f* 4. Wertebereich *m*; Wertevorrat *m*
      f   1. gamme *f* 2. portée *f* 3. parcours *m* 4. amplitude *f*, étendue *f* 5. ensemble *m* des valeurs
      r   1. диапазон *m*; интервал *m* 2. дальность *f* 3. пробег *m* 4. размах *m* 5. область *f* значений

R172   *e*   **rangefinder**
      d   Entfernungsmesser *m*, Distanzmesser *m*
      f   télémètre *m*
      r   дальномер *m*

R173   *e*   **range of definition** *see* **domain of definition**

R174   *e*   **range of visibility**
      d   Sichtweite *f*, Sicht *f*
      f   portée *f* de vision
      r   дальность *f* видимости

R175   *e*   **ranger** *see* **rangefinder**

R176   *e*   **Rankine cycle**
      d   Rankinescher Kreißprozeß *m*, Rankine-Prozeß *m*, Rankine-Clausius-Prozeß *m*
      f   cycle *m* de Rankine
      r   цикл *m* Ранкина

R177   *e*   **rank of a matrix**
      d   Rang *m* einer Matrix
      f   rang *m* de la matrice
      r   ранг *m* матрицы

R178   *e*   **rare-earth ion**
      d   Seltenerdion *n*
      f   ion *m* de terre rare
      r   редкоземельный ион *m*

R179   *e*   **rare-earth magnet**
      d   Seltenerdmagnet *m*
      f   aimant *m* de terre rare
      r   редкоземельный магнетик *m*

R180   *e*   **rare-earth metals**
      d   Seltenerdmetalle *n pl*
      f   métaux *m pl* de terres rares
      r   редкоземельные металлы *m pl*

R181   *e*   **rare earths**
      d   seltene Erden *f pl*, Seltenerden *f pl*
      f   terres *f pl* rares
      r   редкоземельные элементы *m pl*, редкие земли *f pl*

R182   *e*   **rarefied gas**
      d   verdünntes Gas *n*

f gaz *m* raréfié
r разрежённый газ *m*

R183 *e* rarefied gas dynamics
d Dynamik *f* der stark verdünnten Gase, Superaerodynamik *f*
f dynamique *f* des gaz raréfiés
r динамика *f* разрежённых газов

R184 *e* raster
d Raster *m*
f trame *f*
r растр *m*

R185 *e* rate
d 1. Geschwindigkeit *f* 2. Häufigkeit *f*; Rate *f*
f 1. vitesse *f* 2. fréquence *f*
r 1. скорость *f* 2. частота *f*

R186 *e* rate meter *see* counting-rate meter

R187 *e* rate of flow
d Durchsatz *m*; Durchflußmenge *f*
f débit *m*
r расход *m*; скорость *f* течения

R188 *e* ratio
d Verhältnis *n*; Verhältniszahl *f*
f rapport *m*
r 1. отношение *n* 2. коэффициент *m*

R189 *e* ray
d Strahl *m*
f rayon *m*
r луч *m*

R190 *e* ray ellipsoid
d Fresnelsches Ellipsoid *n*
f ellipsoïde *m* de Fresnel
r эллипсоид *m* Френеля

R191 *e* Rayleigh criterion
d Rayleigh-Zahl *f*, Rayleighsche Kennzahl *f*
f critère *m* de Rayleigh
r критерий *m* Рэлея

R192 *e* Rayleigh disk
d Rayleigh-Scheibe *f*, Rayleighsche Scheibe *f*
f disque *m* de Rayleigh
r диск *m* Рэлея

R193 *e* Rayleigh interferometer
d Rayleigh-Interferometer *n*
f interféromètre *m* de Rayleigh
r интерферометр *m* Рэлея

R194 *e* Rayleigh-Jeans law
d Rayleigh-Jeanssches Strahlungsgesetz *n*
f principe *m* de Rayleigh-Jeans
r закон *m* излучения Рэлея - Джинса

R195 *e* Rayleigh line
d Rayleigh-Linie *f*

f ligne *f* de Rayleigh
r линия *f* Рэлея

R196 *e* Rayleigh line wing
d Rayleigh-Linienflügel *m*
f aile *f* de ligne de Rayleigh
r крыло *n* линии Рэлея

R197 *e* Rayleigh radiation
d Rayleigh-Strahlung *f*
f rayonnement *m* de Rayleigh
r рэлеевское излучение *n*

R198 *e* Rayleigh scattering
d Rayleigh-Streuung *f*, Rayleighsche Streuung *f*
f diffusion *f* de Rayleigh
r рэлеевское рассеяние *n*

R199 *e* Rayleigh waves
d Rayleigh-Wellen *f pl*, Rayleighsche Wellen *f pl*
f ondes *f pl* de Rayleigh
r волны *f pl* Рэлея

R200 *e* ray optics *see* geometrical optics

R201 *e* ray optics method *see* geometrical optics method

R202 *e* ray velocity
d Strahlengeschwindigkeit *f*
f vitesse *f* de rayon
r лучевая скорость *f*

R203 *e* R-C generator
d RC-Generator *m*
f générateur *m* R.C.
r RC-генератор *m*

R204 *e* reabsorption
d Reabsorption *f*
f réabsorption *f*
r перепоглощение *n*, реабсорбция *f*

R205 *e* reactance
d Blindwiderstand *m*
f réactance *f*
r реактивное сопротивление *n*

R206 *e* reaction
d Reaktion *f*
f réaction *f*
r реакция *f*

R207 *e* reaction channel
d Reaktionskanal *m*, Kanal *m* einer Kernreaktion
f canal *m* de la réaction
r канал *m* реакции

R208 *e* reaction kinematics
d Reaktionskinematik *f*
f cinématique *f* de réaction
r кинематика *f* реакции

R209 *e* reaction kinetics

    d Reaktionskinetik *f*
    f cinétique *f* de réaction
    r кинетика *f* реакции

R210 *e* reaction rate
    d Reaktionsgeschwindigkeit *f*
    f vitesse *f* de réaction
    r скорость *f* реакции

R211 *e* reaction rate constant
    d Reaktionsgeschwindigkeitskonstante *f*
    f constante *f* de la vitesse de réaction
    r константа *f* скорости реакции

R212 *e* reaction threshold
    d Reaktionsschwelle *f*
    f seuil *m* de la réaction
    r порог *m* реакции

R213 *e* reaction yield
    d Reaktionsausbeute *f*
    f rendement *m* de réaction
    r выход *m* реакции

R214 *e* reactive current
    d Blindstrom *m*
    f courant *m* réactif
    r реактивный ток *m*

R215 *e* reactive force
    d Rückwirkungskraft *f*
    f force *f* réactive
    r реактивная сила *f*

R216 *e* reactive load
    d Blindlast *f*, Blindbelastung *f*, reaktive Last *f*
    f charge *f* réactive
    r реактивная нагрузка *f*

R217 *e* reactive power
    d Blindleistung *f*
    f puissance *f* réactive
    r реактивная мощность *f*

R218 *e* reactive voltage
    d Blindspannung *f*
    f tension *f* réactive
    r реактивное напряжение *n*

R219 *e* reactivity of nuclear reactor
    d Kernreaktorreaktivität *f*
    f réactivité *f* du réacteur nucléaire
    r реактивность *f* ядерного реактора

R220 *e* reactor
    d Reaktor *m*
    f réacteur *m*, pile *f*
    r реактор *m*

R221 *e* reactor channel
    d Reaktorkanal *m*, Kanal *m* im Reaktor
    f canal *m* du réacteur
    r канал *m* реактора

R222 *e* reactor charge
    d Brennstoffladung *f*
    f charge *f* du réacteur
    r загрузка *f* реактора

R223 *e* reactor core
    d Spaltzone *f*, aktive Zone *f*, Reaktorkern *m*
    f cœur *m* du réacteur
    r активная зона *f* реактора

R224 *e* reactor dismantling
    d Demontage *f* eines Reaktors
    f désassemblage *m* du réacteur
    r демонтаж *m* реактора

R225 *e* reactor loading *see* reactor charge

R226 *e* reactor vessel
    d Reaktorbehälter *m*
    f cuve *f* du réacteur
    r корпус *m* реактора

R227 *e* real gas
    d reales Gas *n*, Realgas *n*
    f gaz *m* réel
    r реальный газ *m*

R228 *e* real image
    d reelles Bild *n*, wirkliches Bild *n*
    f image *f* réelle
    r действительное изображение *n*

R229 *e* real-time processing
    d Echtzeitdatenverarbeitung *f*
    f traitement *m* des données en temps réel
    r обработка *f* данных в реальном времени

R230 *e* Réaumur scale
    d Réaumur-Skala *f*
    f échelle *f* Réaumur
    r шкала *f* Реомюра

R231 *e* receiving tube
    d Empfangsverstärkerröhre *f*
    f tube *m* amplificateur de réception
    r приёмно-усилительная лампа *f*

R232 *e* reciprocating motion
    d hin- und hergehende Bewegung *f*, Hin- und Herbewegung *f*
    f mouvement *m* alternatif, mouvement *m* de va-et-vient
    r возвратно-поступательное движение *n*

R233 *e* reciprocity
    d Reziprozität *f*, Gegenseitigkeit *f*
    f réciprocité *f*
    r взаимность *f*

R234 *e* reciprocity principle, reciprocity theorem
    d Reziprozitätsprinzip *n*
    f principe *m* de réciprocité
    r принцип *m* взаимности, теорема *f* взаимности

R235   e   recognition
  d   Erkennung *f*; Wiedererkennung *f*;
     Identifizierung *f*
  f   reconnaissance *f*; identification *f*
  r   распознавание *n*, идентификация *f*

R236   e   recoil
  d   Rückstoß *m*, Rückprall *m*,
     Rückschlag *m*
  f   recul *m*
  r   отдача *f*

R237   e   recoil atom
  d   Rückstoßatom *n*
  f   atome *m* de recul
  r   атом *m* отдачи

R238   e   recoil curve
  d   Rückkehrkurve *f*
  f   courbe *f* de recul
  r   кривая *f* возврата

R239   e   recoil ion
  d   Rückstoßion *n*
  f   ion *m* de recul
  r   ион *m* отдачи

R240   e   recoil momentum
  d   Rückstoßimpuls *m*
  f   impulsion *f* de recul
  r   импульс *m* отдачи

R241   e   recoil nucleus
  d   Rückstoßkern *m*
  f   noyau *m* de recul
  r   ядро *n* отдачи

R242   e   recombination
  d   Rekombination *f*
  f   recombinaison *f*
  r   рекомбинация *f*

R243   e   recombination center
  d   Rekombinationszentrum *n*
  f   centre *m* de recombinaison
  r   рекомбинационный центр *m*, центр
     m рекомбинации

R244   e   recombination coefficient
  d   Rekombinationskoeffizient *m*,
     Rekombinationsbeiwert *m*
  f   coefficient *m* de recombinaison
  r   коэффициент *m* рекомбинации

R245   e   recombination cross-section
  d   Rekombinationsquerschnitt *m*
  f   section *f* de recombinaison
  r   сечение *n* рекомбинации

R246   e   recombination luminescence
  d   Rekombinationslumineszenz *f*,
     Rekombinationsleuchten *n*
  f   luminescence *f* de recombinaison
  r   рекомбинационная
     люминесценция *f*

R247   e   recombination of holes and
     electrons
  d   Elektron-Loch-Rekombination *f*
  f   recombinaison *f* électron-trou
  r   электронно-дырочная рекомбинация
     f, рекомбинация *f* электронов и
     дырок

R248   e   recombination radiation
  d   Rekombinationsstrahlung *f*
  f   rayonnement *m* de recombinaison
  r   рекомбинационное излучение *n*

R249   e   recombination transition
  d   Rekombinationsübergang *m*
  f   transition *f* de recombinaison
  r   рекомбинационный переход *m*

R250   e   recombination waves
  d   Rekombinationswellen *f pl*
  f   ondes *f pl* de recombinaison
  r   рекомбинационные волны *f pl*

R251   e   reconnection
  d   Neuschließen *n (von magnetischen*
     Kraftlinien)
  f   reconnexion *f* des lignes de champ
     magnétique
  r   пересоединение *n*, перезамыкание *n*
     (магнитных силовых линий)

R252   e   reconstructed image
  d   rekonstruiertes Bild *n*
  f   image *f* restaurée
  r   восстановленное изображение *n*

R253   e   reconstructing beam
  d   rekonstruierender Strahl *m*
  f   rayon *m* de reconstruction
  r   восстанавливающий луч *m*

R254   e   reconstructing source
  d   rekonstruierende Quelle *f*
  f   source *f* de reconstruction
  r   восстанавливающий источник *m (в*
     голографии)

R255   e   reconstruction of a hologram
  d   Hologrammrekonstruktion *f*
  f   reconstruction *f* de hologramme
  r   реконструкция *f* голограммы

R256   e   reconstruction of an image
  d   Bildrekonstruktion *f*
  f   reconstruction *f* d'image, restauration
     f d'image
  r   восстановление *n* изображения

R257   e   recorded image
  d   aufgezeichnetes Bild *n*, gespeichertes
     Bild *n*
  f   image *f* enregistrée
  r   записанное изображение *n*

R258   e   recoverable deformation *see*
     reversible deformation

R259   e   recovery time
  d   Wiederherstellungszeit *f*,
     Erholungszeit *f*

    f durée *f* de rétablissement
    r время *n* восстановления, время *n* возврата

R260 *e* recrystallization
    d Rekristallisation *f*
    f recristallisation *f*
    r рекристаллизация *f*

R261 *e* rectangular coordinates
    d rechtwinklige Koordinaten *f pl*
    f coordonnées *f pl* rectangulaires
    r прямоугольные координаты *f pl*

R262 *e* rectangular pulse
    d Rechteckimpuls *m*
    f impulsion *f* rectangulaire
    r прямоугольный импульс *m*

R263 *e* rectangular waveguide
    d Rechteckhohlleiter *m*
    f guide *m* d'ondes rectangulaire
    r прямоугольный волновод *m*

R264 *e* rectification
    d Gleichrichtung *f*
    f redressement *m*
    r выпрямление *n* (*электрического тока*)

R265 *e* rectifier
    d Gleichrichter *m*
    f redresseur *m*
    r выпрямитель *m*

R266 *e* rectilinear motion
    d geradlinige Bewegung *f*
    f mouvement *m* rectiligne
    r прямолинейное движение *n*

R267 *e* recuperator
    d Rekuperator *m*
    f récupérateur *m*
    r рекуператор *m*

R268 *e* recurrence phenomena
    d Rekurrenzerscheinungen *f pl*
    f phénomènes *m pl* de récurrence
    r рекуррентные явления *n pl*

R269 *e* red dwarf
    d roter Zwerg *m*
    f naine *f* rouge
    r красный карлик *m*

R270 *e* red giant
    d roter Riese *m*
    f géante *f* rouge
    r красный гигант *m*

R271 *e* red shift
    d Rotverschiebung *f*
    f décalage *m* vers le rouge
    r красное смещение *n*

R272 *e* reduced coordinates
    d reduzierte Koordinaten *f pl*

    f coordonnées *f pl* réduites
    r приведённые координаты *f pl*

R273 *e* reduced equation of state
    d reduzierte Zustandsgleichung *f*
    f équation *f* d'état réduite
    r приведённое уравнение *n* состояния

R274 *e* reduced mass
    d reduzierte Masse *f*
    f masse *f* réduite
    r приведённая масса *f*

R275 *e* reduced momentum
    d reduzierter Impuls *m*
    f impulsion *f* réduite
    r приведённый импульс *m*

R276 *e* reduced temperature
    d reduzierte Temperatur *f*
    f température *f* réduite
    r приведённая температура *f*

R277 *e* reducible diagram
    d reduzibles Diagramm *n*
    f diagramme *m* réductible
    r приводимая диаграмма *f*

R278 *e* reducible representation of a transformation group
    d reduzible Darstellung *f* der Transformationsgruppe
    f représentation *f* réductible du groupe de transformations
    r приводимое представление *n* группы преобразований

R279 *e* reduction
    d 1. Reduktion *f*, Reduzierung *f* 2. (chemische) Reduktion *f*
    f réduction *f*
    r 1. приведение *n* 2. восстановление *n*

R280 *e* reduction of forces
    d Reduktion *f* der Kräfte
    f réduction *f* des forces
    r приведение *n* сил

R281 *e* reference beam
    d Vergleichsstrahl *m*, Referenzstrahl *m*
    f faisceau *m* de référence
    r опорный луч *m*, опорный пучок *m*

R282 *e* reference diode
    d Referenzdiode *f*
    f diode *f* de référence
    r опорный диод *m*

R283 *e* reference source
    d Vergleichsquelle *f*, Standardquelle *f*
    f source *f* de référence
    r опорный источник *m*

R284 *e* reference star
    d Haltestern *m*, Leitstern *m*
    f étoile *f* de référence
    r опорная звезда *f*

R285　*e*　reference voltage
　　　d　Bezugsspannung *f*,
　　　　　Vergleichsspannung *f*
　　　f　tension *f* de référence
　　　r　опорное напряжение *n*

R286　*e*　reference wave
　　　d　Bezugsquelle *f*
　　　f　onde *f* de référence
　　　r　опорная волна *f*

R287　*e*　reflectance *see* reflectivity

R288　*e*　reflected pulse
　　　d　Echoimpuls *m*
　　　f　impulsion *f* réfléchie
　　　r　отражённый импульс *m*, эхо-
　　　　　импульс *m*

R289　*e*　reflected radiation
　　　d　Reflexionsstrahlung *f*, reflektierte
　　　　　Strahlung *f*
　　　f　rayonnement *m* réfléchi
　　　r　отражённое излучение *n*

R290　*e*　reflected ray
　　　d　reflektierter Strahl *m*
　　　f　rayon *m* réfléchi
　　　r　отражённый луч *m*

R291　*e*　reflected wave
　　　d　reflektierte Welle *f*
　　　f　onde *f* réfléchie
　　　r　отражённая волна *f*

R292　*e*　reflecting telescope
　　　d　Spiegelteleskop *n*, Reflektor *m*
　　　f　télescope *m* à miroir, télescope *m*
　　　　　réflecteur, réflecteur *m*
　　　r　зеркальный телескоп *m*, телескоп-
　　　　　рефлектор *m*

R293　*e*　reflection
　　　d　Reflexion *f*, Rückstrahlung *f*
　　　f　réflexion *f*
　　　r　отражение *n*

R294　*e*　reflection coefficient
　　　d　Reflexionskoeffizient *m*,
　　　　　Reflexionsgrad *m*
　　　f　coefficient *m* de réflexion
　　　r　коэффициент *m* отражения

R295　*e*　reflection electron microscope
　　　d　Reflexionsmikroskop *n*,
　　　　　Reflexionselektronenmikroskop *n*
　　　f　microscope *m* électronique à réflexion
　　　r　отражательный электронный
　　　　　микроскоп *m*

R296　*e*　reflection factor *see* reflection
　　　　　coefficient

R297　*e*　reflection high-energy electron
　　　　　diffraction method
　　　d　Hochenergie-
　　　　　Elektronendiffraktionsmethode *f*,
　　　　　RHEED-Methode *f*

　　　f　méthode *f* de diffraction des électrons
　　　　　de haute énergie par réflexion
　　　r　метод *m* дифракции электронов
　　　　　высоких энергий на отражение,
　　　　　метод *m* RHEED

R298　*e*　reflection hologram
　　　d　Reflexionshologramm *n*
　　　f　hologramme *m* par réflexion,
　　　　　hologramme *m* de réflexion
　　　r　отражательная голограмма *f*

R299　*e*　reflection loss
　　　d　Reflexionsverlust *m*
　　　f　pertes *f pl* par réflexion
　　　r　потери *f pl* на отражение

R300　*e*　reflection of light
　　　d　Lichtreflexion *f*
　　　f　réflexion *f* de la lumière
　　　r　отражение *n* света

R301　*e*　reflection of radio waves
　　　d　Radiowellenreflexion *f*
　　　f　réflexion *f* des ondes radioélectriques
　　　r　отражение *n* радиоволн

R302　*e*　reflection prism
　　　d　Reflexionsprisma *n*
　　　f　prisme *m* de réflexion
　　　r　отражательная призма *f*

R303　*e*　reflection spectrum
　　　d　Reflexionsspektrum *n*
　　　f　spectre *m* de réflexion
　　　r　спектр *m* отражения

R304　*e*　reflective coating
　　　d　Reflexionsschicht *f*
　　　f　revêtement *m* réflecteur
　　　r　отражающее покрытие *n*

R305　*e*　reflectivity
　　　d　Reflexionsgrad *m*,
　　　　　Reflexionskoeffizient *m*
　　　f　réflexibilité *f*
　　　r　отражательная способность *f*,
　　　　　коэффициент *m* отражения

R306　*e*　reflector
　　　d　Reflektor *m*; Rückstrahler *m*;
　　　　　Spiegel *m*
　　　f　réflecteur *m*
　　　r　1. отражатель *m* 2. зеркало *n* 3.
　　　　　рефлектор *m*

R307　*e*　reflector aerial, reflector antenna
　　　d　Spiegelantenne *f*
　　　f　antenne *f* à réflecteur
　　　r　зеркальная антенна *f*

R308　*e*　reflector voltage
　　　d　Reflektorspannung *f*
　　　f　tension *f* de réflecteur
　　　r　напряжение *n* отражателя
　　　　　(*клистрона*)

R309   *e*   reflex klystron
      d   Reflexklystron *n*, Spiegelklystron *n*
      f   klystron *m* à réflexion
      r   отражательный клистрон *m*

R310   *e*   refracted beam *see* refracted ray

R311   *e*   refracted ray
      d   gebrochener Strahl *m*
      f   rayon *m* réfracté
      r   преломлённый луч *m*

R312   *e*   refracted wave
      d   gebrochene Welle *f*
      f   onde *f* réfractée
      r   преломлённая волна *f*

R313   *e*   refracting telescope
      d   Refraktor *m*
      f   réfracteur *m*, lunette *f*
      r   телескоп-рефрактор *m*, линзовый
         телескоп *m*

R314   *e*   refraction
      d   Brechung *f*; Refraktion *f*
      f   réfraction *f*
      r   1. преломление *n* 2. рефракция *f*

R315   *e*   refraction index *see* refractive index

R316   *e*   refraction of light
      d   Lichtbrechung *f*, Refraktion *f* des
         Lichtes
      f   réfraction *f* de la lumière
      r   преломление *n* света; рефракция *f*
         света

R317   *e*   refraction of radio waves
      d   Funkwellenbrechung *f*,
         Radiowellenbrechung *f*
      f   réfraction *f* des ondes radioélectriques
      r   рефракция *f* радиоволн;
         преломление *n* радиоволн

R318   *e*   refraction of sound
      d   Schallbrechung *f*
      f   réfraction *f* du son
      r   рефракция *f* звука

R319   *e*   refractive index
      d   Brechungsindex *m*, Brechzahl *f*
      f   indice *m* de réfraction
      r   показатель *m* преломления

R320   *e*   refractive index irregularity
      d   Irregularität *f* der Brechzahl
      f   irrégularité *f* de l'indice de réfraction
      r   неоднородность *f* показателя
         преломления

R321   *e*   refractometer
      d   Refraktometer *n*, Brechzahlmesser *m*
      f   réfractomètre *m*
      r   рефрактометр *m*

R322   *e*   refractometry
      d   Refraktometrie *f*,
         Brechzahlbestimmung *f*

      f   réfractométrie *f*
      r   рефрактометрия *f*

R323   *e*   refractor *see* refracting telescope

R324   *e*   refrigeration
      d   1. Kühlung *f*, Abkühlung *f* 2.
         Gefrieren *n*
      f   1. refroidissement *m* 2. réfrigération *f*
      r   1. охлаждение *n*
         2. замораживание *n*

R325   *e*   refringence
      d   Brechung *f*, Strahlenbrechung *f*,
         Refraktion *f*
      f   réfraction *f*
      r   лучепреломление *n*

R326   *e*   regeneration
      d   Regeneration *f*, Regenerierung *f*
      f   régénération *f*
      r   1. регенерация *f*; воспроизводство *n*
         2. восстановление *n*

R327   *e*   regeneration reception
      d   Regenerativempfang *m*,
         Rückkopplungsempfang *m*
      f   réception *f* par réaction
      r   регенеративный приём *m*

R328   *e*   Regge diagram
      d   Regge-Diagramm *n*
      f   diagramme *m* de Regge
      r   реджевская диаграмма *f*

R329   *e*   reggeon
      d   Reggeon *n*
      f   reggeon *m*
      r   реджеон *m*

R330   *e*   Regge pole
      d   Regge-Pol *m*
      f   pôle *m* de Regge
      r   полюс *m* Редже

R331   *e*   Regge pole method
      d   Regge-Polenmethode *f*
      f   méthode *f* des pôles de Regge
      r   метод *m* полюсов Редже

R332   *e*   region
      d   Bereich *m*, Gebiet *n*; Zone *f*
      f   région *f*
      r   область *f*; зона *f*

R333   *e*   regression
      d   Regression *f*
      f   régression *f*
      r   регрессия *f*

R334   *e*   regular function *see* analytic
         function

R335   *e*   regularization method
      d   Regularisationsmethode *f*
      f   méthode *f* de régularisation
      r   метод *m* регуляризации, метод *m*
         сглаживания

R336   *e*   regular motion
       d   reguläre Bewegung *f*
       f   mouvement *m* régulier
       r   регулярное движение *n*

R337   *e*   Rehbinder effect
       d   Rehbinder-Effekt *m*
       f   effet *m* Rehbinder
       r   эффект *m* Ребиндера

R338   *e*   reinforcement
       d   1. Verstärkung *f*; Versteifung *f* 2.
          Armierung *f*, Bewehrung *f*
       f   1. renforcement *m* 2. armement *m*
       r   1. усиление *n* 2. укрепление *n*,
          армирование *n*, упрочнение *n*

R339   *e*   relation, relationship
       d   Abhängigkeit *f*, Beziehung *f*;
          Zusammenhang *m*; Verhältnis *n*
       f   relation *f*
       r   зависимость *f*, соотношение *n*

R340   *e*   relative change
       d   relative Änderung *f*
       f   changement *m* relatif
       r   относительное изменение *n*

R341   *e*   relative concentration
       d   relative Konzentration *f*
       f   concentration *f* relative
       r   относительная концентрация *f*

R342   *e*   relative deformation
       d   relative Deformation *f*
       f   déformation *f* relative
       r   относительная деформация *f*

R343   *e*   relative equilibrium
       d   relatives Gleichgewicht *n*
       f   équilibre *m* relatif
       r   относительное равновесие *n*

R344   *e*   relative line intensity
       d   relative Linienintensität *f*
       f   intensité *f* relative de la ligne
       r   относительная интенсивность *f*
          линии

R345   *e*   relative motion
       d   Relativbewegung *f*, relative
          Bewegung *f*
       f   mouvement *m* relatif
       r   относительное движение *n*

R346   *e*   relative permittivity
       d   relative Permeabilität *f*,
          Permeabilitätszahl *f*
       f   permittivité *f* relative
       r   относительная диэлектрическая
          проницаемость *f*

R347   *e*   relativistically invariant gages
       d   relativistisch invariante Eichungen *f pl*
       f   calibrages *m pl* à invariance relativiste
       r   релятивистски инвариантные
          калибровки *f pl*

R348   *e*   relativistic astrophysics
       d   relativistische Astrophysik *f*
       f   astrophysique *f* relativiste
       r   релятивистская астрофизика *f*

R349   *e*   relativistic cosmology
       d   relativistische Kosmologie *f*
       f   cosmologie *f* relativiste
       r   релятивистская космология *f*

R350   *e*   relativistic dynamics
       d   relativistische Dynamik *f*,
          Relativitätsdynamik *f*
       f   dynamique *f* relativiste
       r   релятивистская динамика *f*

R351   *e*   relativistic effects
       d   relativistische Effekte *m pl*
       f   effets *m pl* relativistes
       r   релятивистские эффекты *m pl*

R352   *e*   relativistic electrodynamics
       d   relativistische Elektrodynamik *f*
       f   électrodynamique *f* relativiste
       r   релятивистская электродинамика *f*

R353   *e*   relativistic generalization
       d   relativistische Verallgemeinerung *f*
       f   généralisation *f* relativiste
       r   релятивистское обобщение *n*

R354   *e*   relativistic invariance
       d   relativistische Invarianz *f*, Lorentz-
          Invarianz *f*
       f   invariance *f* relativiste
       r   релятивистская инвариантность *f*,
          лоренц-инвариантность *f*

R355   *e*   relativistic invariant
       d   relativistische Invariante *f*
       f   invariant *m* relativiste
       r   релятивистский инвариант *m*

R356   *e*   relativistic kinematics
       d   relativistische Kinematik *f*,
          Relativitätskinematik *f*
       f   cinématique *f* relativiste
       r   релятивистская кинематика *f*

R357   *e*   relativistic mass
       d   relativistische Masse *f*
       f   masse *f* relativiste
       r   релятивистская масса *f*

R358   *e*   relativistic mass variation
       d   relativistische Massenänderung *f*
       f   variation *f* relativiste de la masse
       r   релятивистское изменение *n* массы

R359   *e*   relativistic mechanics
       d   relativistische Mechanik *f*,
          Relativitätsmechanik *f*
       f   mécanique *f* relativiste
       r   релятивистская механика *f*

R360   *e*   relativistic momentum
       d   relativistischer Impuls *m*

f impulsion f relativiste
r релятивистский импульс m

R361 e relativistic motion
d relativistische Bewegung f
f mouvement m relativiste
r релятивистское движение n

R362 e relativistic particle
d relativistisches Teilchen n
f particule f relativiste
r релятивистская частица f

R363 e relativistic plasma
d relativistisches Plasma n
f plasma m relativiste
r релятивистская плазма f

R364 e relativistic region
d relativistischer Bereich m
f domaine m relativiste
r релятивистская область f

R365 e relativistic thermodynamics
d relativistische Thermodynamik f
f thermodynamique f relativiste
r релятивистская термодинамика f

R366 e relativistic velocity
d relativistische Geschwindigkeit f
f vitesse f relativiste
r релятивистская скорость f

R367 e relativity
d 1. Relativität f 2. Relativitätstheorie f
f relativité f
r 1. относительность f 2. теория f
относительности

R368 e relativity principle
d Relativitätsprinzip n
f principe m de la relativité
r принцип m относительности

R369 e relativity theory
d Relativitätstheorie f
f théorie f de relativité
r теория f относительности

R370 e relaxation
d Relaxation f
f relaxation f
r релаксация f

R371 e relaxation channel
d Relaxationskanal m
f canal m de relaxation
r канал m релаксации

R372 e relaxation curve
d Relaxationskurve f
f courbe f de relaxation
r релаксационная кривая f

R373 e relaxation distance *see* relaxation
length

R374 e relaxation length
d Relaxationslänge f,
Relaxationsweglänge f
f longueur f de relaxation
r длина f релаксации

R375 e relaxation oscillation
d Relaxationsschwingungen f pl,
Kippschwingungen f pl
f oscillations f pl de relaxation
r релаксационные колебания n pl

R376 e relaxation oscillator
d Kippschwingungsgenerator m,
Kippschwinger m,
Relaxationsgenerator m
f oscillateur m de relaxation
r релаксационный генератор m

R377 e relaxation time
d Relaxationszeit f
f temps m de relaxation
r время n релаксации

R378 e relaxation transitions
d Relaxationsübergänge m pl
f transitions f pl à relaxation
r релаксационные переходы m pl

R379 e reliability
d Zuverlässigkeit f
f fiabilité f
r 1. надёжность f 2. надёжность f,
достоверность f (*результатов,
данных*)

R380 e reliability test
d Zuverlässigkeitsprüfung f
f essai m de fiabilité
r испытание n на надёжность

R381 e relict neutrino
d Reliktneutrino n
f neutrino m de relique
r реликтовое нейтрино n

R382 e relict quark
d Reliktquark n
f quark m de relique
r реликтовый кварк m

R383 e relict radiation
d Reliktstrahlung f
f rayonnement m de relique
r реликтовое излучение n

R384 e relict radiation isotropy
d Reliktstrahlungsisotropie f
f isotropie f du rayonnement de relique
r изотропия f реликтового излучения

R385 e reluctance
d magnetischer Widerstand m
f résistance f magnétique
r магнитное сопротивление n

R386 e reluctivity

    d spezifischer magnetischer
        Widerstand *m*
    f résistance *f* magnétique spécifique
    r удельное магнитное
        сопротивление *n*

R387 *e* rem *see* roentgen-equivalent-man

R388 *e* **remanence**
    d Restmagnetisierung *f*, magnetische
        Remanenz *f*
    f induction *f* magnétique rémanente
    r остаточная магнитная индукция *f*

R389 *e* **remanent magnetization**
    d remanente Magnetisierung *f*
    f aimantation *f* rémanente, aimantation *f*
        résiduelle
    r остаточная намагниченность *f*

R390 *e* **remanent polarization**
    d Restpolarisation *f*
    f polarisation *f* rémanente
    r остаточная поляризация *f*

R391 *e* **remote measurement**
    d Fernmessung *f*
    f mesure *f* à distance
    r дистанционное измерение *n*

R392 *e* **remote sensing**
    d Fernsondierung *f*, Fernabtastung *f*
    f sondage *m* à distance
    r дистанционное зондирование *n*

R393 *e* **remote sensor**
    d Ferngeber *m*
    f capteur *m* à distance
    r дистанционный датчик *m*

R394 *e* **renewable source**
    d erneuerbare Quelle *f*
    f source *f* renouvelable
    r возобновляемый источник *m*

R395 *e* **renormalizability**
    d Renormierbarkeit *f*
    f rénormalisabilité *f*
    r перенормируемость *f*

R396 *e* **renormalizable theory**
    d renormierbare Theorie *f*
    f théorie *f* rénormalisable
    r перенормируемая теория *f*

R397 *e* **renormalization**
    d Renormierung *f*
    f rénormalisation *f*
    r перенормировка *f*

R398 *e* **renormalization group**
    d Renormierungsgruppe *f*
    f groupe *m* de rénormalisation
    r ренормализационная группа *f*,
        ренормгруппа *f*

R399 *e* **renormalization invariance**

    d Renormierungsinvarianz *f*
    f invariance *f* de rénormalisation
    r ренормализационная
        инвариантность *f*

R400 *e* **renormalized perturbation theory**
    d renormierbare Störungstheorie *f*
    f théorie *f* des perturbations
        rénormalisée
    r перенормированная теория *f*
        возмущений

R401 *e* **reorientation**
    d Reorientierung *f*
    f réorientation *f*
    r переориентация *f*

R402 *e* **repeatability** *see* reproducibility

R403 *e* **repetition rate**
    d Folgefrequenz *f*
    f fréquence *f* de répétition
    r частота *f* повторения

R404 *e* **replica**
    d Abdruck *m*, Replik *f*
    f réplique *f*
    r реплика *f* (*в электронной
        микроскопии*)

R405 *e* **reprocessing**
    d Wiederaufarbeitung *f* (*von
        abgebranntem Kernbrennstoff*)
    f régénération *f* (*du combustible
        nucléaire*)
    r регенерация *f* (*ядерного топлива*)

R406 *e* **reproducibility**
    d Reproduzierbarkeit *f*
    f reproductibilité *f*
    r воспроизводимость *f*;
        повторяемость *f*

R407 *e* **repulsion**
    d Abstoßung *f*, Repulsion *f*
    f répulsion *f*
    r отталкивание *n*, расталкивание *n*

R408 *e* **research laboratory**
    d Forschungslaboratorium *n*,
        Forschungslabor *n*
    f laboratoire *m* de recherches
    r научно-исследовательская
        лаборатория *f*

R409 *e* **residual activity**
    d Restaktivität *f*
    f radioactivité *f* résiduelle
    r остаточная радиоактивность *f*

R410 *e* **residual deformation**
    d bleibende Verformung *f*,
        Formänderungsrest *m*
    f déformation *f* résiduelle
    r остаточная деформация *f*

R411 *e* **residual magnetization** *see* remanent
        magnetization

R412　*e*　**residual range**
　　d　Restreichweite *f*
　　f　parcours *m* résiduel
　　r　остаточный пробег *m*

R413　*e*　**residual stress**
　　d　Restspannung *f*
　　f　contrainte *f* résiduelle
　　r　остаточное напряжение *n*

R414　*e*　**residue**
　　d　1. Rückstand *m* 2. Rest *m*
　　f　résidu *m*
　　r　1. остаток *m* 2. вычет *m*

R415　*e*　**resistance**
　　d　1. Widerstand *m* 2. Wirkwiderstand *m*
　　f　résistance *f*
　　r　1. сопротивление *n* 2. активное
　　　　сопротивление *n*

R416　*e*　**resistance gage**
　　d　Widerstandsdehnungsmeßstreifen *m*
　　f　jauge *f* de contrainte
　　r　тензорезистор *m*

R417　*e*　**resistance thermometer**
　　d　Widerstandsthermometer *n*
　　f　thermomètre *m* à résistance
　　r　термометр *m* сопротивления

R418　*e*　**resistive load**
　　d　Wirklast *f*, Wirkbelastung *f*
　　f　charge *f* résistive, charge *f* active
　　r　активная нагрузка *f*

R419　*e*　**resistivity**
　　d　spezifischer Widerstand *m*
　　f　résistivité *f*
　　r　удельное сопротивление *n*

R420　*e*　**resistor**
　　d　Widerstand *m*
　　f　résistance *f*
　　r　резистор *m*

R421　*e*　**resolution**
　　d　1. Auflösung *f* 2. Zerlegung *f* (*Vektor*)
　　f　1. résolution *f* 2. partition *f* (*du*
　　　　vecteur)
　　r　1. разрешение *n*, разрешающая
　　　　способность *f* 2. разложение *n*
　　　　(*вектора*)

R422　*e*　**resolved line**
　　d　aufgelöste Linie *f*
　　f　raie *f* résolue
　　r　разрешённая линия *f*

R423　*e*　**resolving power**
　　d　Auflösungsvermögen *n*
　　f　pouvoir *m* de résolution
　　r　разрешающая способность *f*,
　　　　разрешающая сила *f*

R424　*e*　**resonance**
　　d　Resonanz *f*
　　f　résonance *f*
　　r　резонанс *m*

R425　*e*　**resonance absorber**
　　d　Resonanzabsorber *m*
　　f　absorbeur *m* par résonance
　　r　резонансный поглотитель *m*

R426　*e*　**resonance absorption**
　　d　Resonanzabsorption *f*
　　f　absorption *f* par résonance
　　r　резонансное поглощение *n*

R427　*e*　**resonance amplifier**
　　d　Resonanzverstärker *m*
　　f　amplificateur *m* à résonance
　　r　резонансный усилитель *m*

R428　*e*　**resonance broadening**
　　d　Resonanzverbreiterung *f*
　　f　élargissement *m* par résonance
　　r　резонансное уширение *n*

R429　*e*　**resonance capture**
　　d　Resonanzeinfang *m*
　　f　capture *f* de résonance
　　r　резонансный захват *m*

R430　*e*　**resonance channel**
　　d　Resonanzkanal *m*
　　f　canal *m* de résonance
　　r　резонансный канал *m*

R431　*e*　**resonance cross-section**
　　d　Resonanzquerschnitt *m*
　　f　section *f* de résonance
　　r　резонансное сечение *n*

R432　*e*　**resonance curve**
　　d　Resonanzkurve *f*
　　f　courbe *f* de résonance
　　r　резонансная кривая *f*

R433　*e*　**resonance emission** *see* **resonance
　　　　radiation**

R434　*e*　**resonance energy**
　　d　Resonanzenergie *f*
　　f　énergie *f* de résonance
　　r　резонансная энергия *f*

R435　*e*　**resonance escape**
　　d　Resonanzflucht *f*, Vermeiden *n* des
　　　　Resonanzeinfangs
　　f　échappement *m* de résonance
　　r　избежание *n* резонансного захвата

R436　*e*　**resonance fluorescence**
　　d　Resonanzfluoreszenz *f*
　　f　fluorescence *f* de résonance
　　r　резонансная флуоресценция *f*

R437　*e*　**resonance frequency**
　　d　Resonanzfrequenz *f*
　　f　fréquence *f* de résonance
　　r　резонансная частота *f*

R438   e   **resonance level**
d   Resonanzniveau *n*
f   niveau *m* de résonance
r   резонансный уровень *m*

R439   e   **resonance line**
d   Resonanzlinie *f*
f   raie *f* de résonance
r   резонансная линия *f*

R440   e   **resonance luminescence**
d   Resonanzlumineszenz *f*
f   luminescence *f* de résonance
r   резонансная люминесценция *f*

R441   e   **resonance neutrons**
d   Resonanzneutronen *n pl*
f   neutrons *m pl* de résonance
r   резонансные нейтроны *m pl*

R442   e   **resonance oscillation**
d   Resonanzschwingungen *f pl*
f   oscillations *f pl* de résonance
r   резонансные колебания *n pl*

R443   e   **resonance particle**
d   Resonanzteilchen *n*
f   particule *f* de résonance
r   резонанс *m* (*резонансная частица*)

R444   e   **resonance radiation**
d   Resonanzstrahlung *f*
f   rayonnement *m* de résonance,
radiation *f* de résonance
r   резонансное излучение *n*

R445   e   **resonance scattering**
d   Resonanzstreuung *f*
f   diffusion *f* résonnante, diffusion *f* de
résonance
r   резонансное рассеяние *n*

R446   e   **resonance vibration** *see* **resonance
oscillation**

R447   e   **resonant accelerator**
d   Resonanzbeschleuniger *m*
f   accélérateur *m* de résonance
r   резонансный ускоритель *m*

R448   e   **resonant circuit**
d   Resonanzkreis *m*,
Resonanzstromkreis *m*
f   circuit *m* résonnant
r   резонансный контур *m*

R449   e   **resonant frequency** *see* **resonance
frequency**

R450   e   **resonant ionization**
d   Resonanzionisation *f*
f   ionisation *f* de résonance
r   резонансная ионизация *f*

R451   e   **resonant transition**
d   Resonanzübergang *m*;
Resonanzdurchtritt *m*

f   transition *f* de résonance
r   резонансный переход *m*

R452   e   **resonator**
d   Resonator *m*
f   résonateur *m*
r   резонатор *m*

R453   e   **resonator selectivity**
d   Resonatorselektivität *f*
f   sélectivité *f* du résonateur
r   избирательность *f* резонатора

R454   e   **response**
d   1. Antwort *f*, Reaktion *f*; Rückwirkung
f; Ansprechen *n* 2. Kennlinie *f*,
Charakteristik *f*
f   réponse *f*
r   1. отклик *m*, реакция *f*
2. характеристика *f*

R455   e   **response function**
d   Antwortfunktion *f*
f   fonction *f* de réponse
r   функция *f* отклика

R456   e   **response time**
d   Antwortzeit *f*
f   temps *m* de réponse
r   постоянная *f* времени

R457   e   **rest energy**
d   Ruheenergie *f*, Ruhenergie *f*
f   énergie *f* au repos, énergie *f* en repos
r   собственная энергия *f*, энергия *f*
покоя

R458   e   **rest mass** *see* **mass at rest**

R459   e   **restoring couple** *see* **restoring
moment**

R460   e   **restoring moment**
d   Rückstellmoment *n*, Richtmoment *n*,
Rückführmoment *n*
f   moment *m* redresseur
r   возвращающий момент *m*,
восстанавливающий момент *m*

R461   e   **restraint**
d   1. Begrenzung *f* 2. Begrenzer *m*
3. Dämpfer *m*
f   1. limitation *f* 2. limiteur *m*
3. amortisseur *m*
r   1. ограничение *n* 2. ограничитель *m*
3. демпфер *m*

R462   e   **restricted motion**
d   unfreie Bewegung *f*, gebundene
Bewegung *f*, eingeschränkte
Bewegung *f*
f   mouvement *m* restreint
r   ограниченное движение *n*

R463   e   **resultant**
d   Resultierende *f*

f résultante f
r равнодействующая f

R464　e　resultant force
　　　d　resultierende Kraft f, Resultierende f
　　　f　force f résultante
　　　r　равнодействующая сила f,
　　　　результирующая сила f

R465　e　retardation
　　　d　Verzögerung f; Nacheilung f
　　　f　retardation f
　　　r　замедление n, запаздывание n,
　　　　отставание n

R466　e　retarded action
　　　d　verzögerte Wirkung f
　　　f　action f retardée
　　　r　замедленное действие n

R467　e　retarded motion see decelerated
　　　　motion

R468　e　retarded potential
　　　d　retardiertes Potential n
　　　f　potentiel m retardé
　　　r　запаздывающий потенциал m

R469　e　retrograde motion
　　　d　Rückläufigkeit f
　　　f　mouvement m rétrograde (du corps
　　　　céleste)
　　　r　возвратное движение n (небесного
　　　　тела)

R470　e　retroreflector
　　　d　Reflexreflektor m, Rückstrahler m
　　　f　rétroréflecteur m
　　　r　уголковый отражатель m;
　　　　катафот m

R471　e　reverberation
　　　d　Nachhall m
　　　f　réverbération f
　　　r　реверберация f

R472　e　reverberation chamber
　　　d　Hallraum m, Echoraum m,
　　　　Nachhallraum m
　　　f　chambre f de réverbération
　　　r　реверберационная камера f

R473　e　reverberation time
　　　d　Nachhallzeit f, Nachhalldauer f
　　　f　temps m de réverbération
　　　r　время n реверберации

R474　e　reversal
　　　d　Umkehrung f, Richtungsumkehr m
　　　f　inversion f; conjugaison f (du front
　　　　d'onde)
　　　r　изменение n направления на
　　　　обратное; обращение n (волнового
　　　　фронта)

R475　e　reversal of spectral lines
　　　d　Linienumkehr f, Umkehr f der
　　　　Spektrallinien

f　renversement m des raies du spectre,
　inversion f des raies spectrales
r　обращение n спектральных линий

R476　e　reverse direction see backward
　　　　direction

R477　e　reverse voltage see back voltage

R478　e　reversible change
　　　d　reversible Änderung f
　　　f　changement m réversible
　　　r　обратимое изменение n

R479　e　reversible cycle
　　　d　reversibler Zyklus m
　　　f　cycle m réversible
　　　r　обратимый цикл m

R480　e　reversible deformation
　　　d　reversible Deformation f
　　　f　déformation f réversible
　　　r　обратимая деформация f

R481　e　reversible process
　　　d　reversibler Prozeß m. umkehrbarer
　　　　Prozeß m
　　　f　procédé m réversible
　　　r　обратимый процесс m

R482　e　reversible transition
　　　d　reversibler Übergang m
　　　f　transition f réversible
　　　r　обратимый переход m

R483　e　reversing layer
　　　d　umkehrende Schicht f
　　　f　couche f d'inversion
　　　r　обращающий слой m

R484　e　revolutions per second
　　　d　Umdrehungen f pl je Sekunde
　　　f　nombre m de révolutions par seconde
　　　r　обороты m pl в секунду

R485　e　Reynolds number
　　　d　Reynolds-Zahl f, Reynoldssche Zahl f
　　　f　nombre m de Reynolds
　　　r　число n Рейнольдса

R486　e　rf plasma heating
　　　d　Hochfrequenz-Plasmaaufheizung f
　　　f　chauffage m à haute fréquence du
　　　　plasma
　　　r　высокочастотный нагрев m плазмы

R487　e　rf radiation
　　　d　hochfrequente Strahlung f,
　　　　Hochfrequenzstrahlung f,
　　　　HF-Strahlung f
　　　f　rayonnement m à haute fréquence
　　　r　высокочастотное излучение n

R488　e　RHEED method see reflection high-
　　　　energy electron diffraction method

R489　e　rhenium, Re

	d	Rhenium *n*
	f	rhénium *m*
	r	рений *m*
R490	*e*	**rheology**
	d	Rheologie *f*
	f	rhéologie *f*
	r	реология *f*
R491	*e*	**rheostat**
	d	Regelwiderstand *m*, veränderbarer Widerstand *m*
	f	rhéostat *m*
	r	реостат *m*
R492	*e*	**rheostat amplifier**
	d	Widerstandsverstärker *m*
	f	amplificateur *m* à résistances
	r	реостатный усилитель *m*
R493	*e*	**rhodium, Rh**
	d	Rhodium *n*
	f	rhodium *m*
	r	родий *m*
R494	*e*	**rhombic aerial, rhombic antenna**
	d	Rhombusantenne *f*
	f	antenne *f* en losange
	r	ромбическая антенна *f*
R495	*e*	**rhombic crystal**
	d	rhombischer Kristall *m*
	f	cristal *m* rhombique
	r	ромбический кристалл *m*
R496	*e*	**rhombic system**
	d	rhombisches Kristallsystem *n*
	f	système *m* rhomboïdal
	r	ромбическая сингония *f*, ромбическая система *f*
R497	*e*	**rhombohedral system**
	d	rhomboedrisches Kristallsystem *n*
	f	système *m* rhomboédrique
	r	ромбоэдрическая сингония *f*, ромбоэдрическая система *f*, тригональная система *f*
R498	*e*	**Ricci tensor**
	d	Ricci-Tensor *m*
	f	tenseur *m* de Ricci
	r	тензор *m* Риччи
R499	*e*	**Richardson equation**
	d	Richardson-Gleichung *f*, Richardsonsche Gleichung *f*
	f	équation *f* de Richardson
	r	формула *f* Ричардсона
R500	*e*	**Richter scale**
	d	Richter-Skala *f*
	f	échelle *f* de Richter
	r	шкала *f* Рихтера
R501	*e*	**Riemannian space**
	d	Riemannscher Raum *m*

	f	espace *m* de Riemann
	r	риманово пространство *n*
R502	*e*	**Riemann invariant**
	d	Riemannsche Invariante *f*
	f	invariant *m* de Riemann
	r	инвариант *m* Римана
R503	*e*	**Riemann wave**
	d	Riemannsche Welle *f*
	f	onde *f* de Riemann, onde *f* riemannienne
	r	волна *f* Римана, риманова волна *f*
R504	*e*	**Righi-Leduc effect**
	d	Righi-Leduc-Effekt *m*
	f	effet *m* Righi-Leduc
	r	эффект *m* Риги - Ледюка
R505	*e*	**right-hand rule**
	d	Rechte-Hand-Regel *f*, Dreifingerregel *f* der rechten Hand
	f	règle *f* de la main droite
	r	правило *n* правой руки
R506	*e*	**right quark**
	d	rechtes Quark *n*
	f	quark *m* droit
	r	правый кварк *m*
R507	*e*	**rigid body**
	d	starrer Körper *m*
	f	corps *m* rigide
	r	жёсткое тело *n*
R508	*e*	**rigid construction**
	d	starre Konstruktion *f*, Starrkonstruktion *f*, steife Konstruktion *f*
	f	construction *f* rigide
	r	жёсткая конструкция *f*
R509	*e*	**rigid dynamics**
	d	Dynamik *f* starrer Körper
	f	dynamique *f* des corps rigides
	r	динамика *f* неизменяемых систем
R510	*e*	**rigid rotation**
	d	starre Drehung *f*, starre Rotation *f*
	f	rotation *f* rigide
	r	жёсткое вращение *n*, вращение *n* неизменяемой системы
R511	*e*	**rigid rotator**
	d	starrer Rotator *m*
	f	rotateur *m* rigide
	r	жёсткий ротатор *m*
R512	*e*	**ring**
	d	Ring *m*
	f	anneau *m*, bague *f*
	r	кольцо *n*
R513	*e*	**ring accelerator**
	d	Ringbeschleuniger *m*
	f	accélérateur *m* annulaire
	r	кольцевой ускоритель *m*

R514　e　ring interferometer
　　　d　Ringinterferometer n
　　　f　interféromètre m annulaire
　　　r　кольцевой интерферометр m

R515　e　ring laser
　　　d　Ringlaser m
　　　f　laser m annulaire
　　　r　кольцевой лазер m

R516　e　ring resonator
　　　d　Ringresonator m
　　　f　résonateur m annulaire
　　　r　кольцевой резонатор m

R517　e　rise time
　　　d　Anstiegszeit f
　　　f　temps m de montée
　　　r　1. время n нарастания 2.
　　　　　инерционность f

R518　e　r.m.s. value see root-mean-square
　　　　　value

R519　e　Roche limit
　　　d　Rochesche Grenze f
　　　f　limite f de Roche
　　　r　предел m Роша

R520　e　rocket dynamics
　　　d　Raketendynamik f
　　　f　dynamique f de fusées
　　　r　динамика f ракет

R521　e　rocket engine
　　　d　Raketenantrieb m; Raketentriebwerk n
　　　f　moteur-fusée m
　　　r　ракетный двигатель m

R522　e　rocket sounding
　　　d　Raketensondierung f
　　　f　sondage f par fusées
　　　r　ракетное зондирование n

R523　e　Rockwell hardness
　　　d　Rockwell-Härte f
　　　f　dureté f de Rockwell
　　　r　твёрдость f по Роквеллу

R524　e　rod
　　　d　1. Rundstab m, Stange m, Stab m 2.
　　　　　Stäbchen n
　　　f　1. tige f; barre f 2. bâtonnet m
　　　r　1. стержень m, брусок m 2. палочка
　　　　　f (сетчатки глаза)

R525　e　rod deformation
　　　d　Stabdeformation f
　　　f　déformation f d'une tige
　　　r　деформация f стержня

R526　e　rod torsion
　　　d　Stabverdrehung f
　　　f　torsion f des tiges
　　　r　кручение n стержней

R527　e　rod vibration, rod vibrations

　　　d　Stabvibrationen f pl
　　　f　vibrations f pl des tiges
　　　r　колебания n pl стержней

R528　e　roentgen
　　　d　Röntgen n, Röntgeneinheit f
　　　f　rœntgen m, röntgen m
　　　r　рентген m (единица экспозиционной
　　　　　дозы)

R529　e　roentgen-equivalent-man
　　　d　Rem n, Rem-Einheit f, biologisches
　　　　　Röntgenäquivalent n
　　　f　équivalent m biologique du rœntgen,
　　　　　rem
　　　r　биологический эквивалент m
　　　　　рентгена, бэр

R530　e　roentgenoluminescence
　　　d　Röntgenlumineszenz f
　　　f　rœntgenoluminescence f
　　　r　рентгенолюминесценция f

R531　e　rolling friction
　　　d　Wälzreibung f, Rollreibung f
　　　f　frottement m de roulement
　　　r　трение n качения

R532　e　room-temperature laser
　　　d　Raumtemperatur-Laser m,
　　　　　Zimmertemperatur-Laser m
　　　f　laser m émettant à la température
　　　　　ambiante
　　　r　лазер m, работающий при
　　　　　комнатной температуре

R533　e　root-mean-square value
　　　d　quadratischer Mittelwert m
　　　f　valeur f moyenne quadratique, valeur
　　　　　f efficace
　　　r　среднеквадратичное значение n

R534　e　rotamer see rotational isomer

R535　e　rotary dispersion
　　　d　Rotationsdispersion f
　　　f　dispersion f rotatoire
　　　r　вращательная дисперсия f,
　　　　　дисперсия f оптического вращения

R536　e　rotary inertia
　　　d　Rotationsträgheit f
　　　f　inertie f de rotation
　　　r　инерция f вращения

R537　e　rotary motion
　　　d　Drehbewegung f, Rotationsbewegung f
　　　f　mouvement m rotatoire
　　　r　вращательное движение n

R538　e　rotating crystal method
　　　d　Drehkristallmethode f
　　　f　méthode f des cristaux tournants
　　　r　метод m вращения образца
　　　　　(кристалла)

R539　e　rotating dumbbell

	d	rotierende Hantel *f*
	f	haltère *m* rotatif
	r	вращающаяся гантель *f (источник гравитационных волн)*

R540 e rotating stars
d rotierende Sterne *m pl*
f étoiles *f pl* rotatives
r вращающиеся звёзды *f pl*

R541 e rotation
d Rotation *f*, Drehung *f*; Umdrehung *f*
f rotation *f*
r вращение *n*; поворот *m*

R542 e rotation about an axis
d Drehung *f* um eine Achse, Rotation *f* um eine Achse
f rotation *f* autour d'un axe
r вращение *n* вокруг оси, вращательное движение *n* вокруг оси

R543 e rotation about a point
d Drehung *f* um einen Punkt, Rotation *f* um einen Punkt
f rotation *f* autour d'un point
r вращение *n* вокруг точки, вращательное движение *n* вокруг точки

R544 e rotational band
d Rotationsbande *f*
f bande *f* de rotation
r вращательная полоса *f*

R545 e rotational constant
d Rotationskonstante *f*
f constante *f* de rotation
r постоянная *f* вращения, вращательная постоянная *f*

R546 e rotational energy
d Rotationsenergie *f*
f énergie *f* de rotation
r вращательная энергия *f*

R547 e rotational isomer
d Rotationsisomer *n*
f isomère *m* rotationnel
r поворотный изомер *m*

R548 e rotational isomerism
d Rotationsisomerie *f*
f isomérie *f* de rotation
r поворотная изомерия *f*

R549 e rotational level
d Rotationsniveau *n*, Rotationsenergieniveau *n*
f niveau *m* rotationnel
r вращательный уровень *m*

R550 e rotational line
d Rotationslinie *f*
f raie *f* de rotation, raie *f* rotationnelle
r вращательная линия *f*

R551 e rotational motion
d Drehbewegung *f*, Rotationsbewegung *f*
f mouvement *m* rotatif
r вращательное движение *n*, вращение *n*

R552 e rotational quantum
d Rotationsquant *n*, Drehimpulsquant *n*
f quantum *m* de rotation
r вращательный квант *m*

R553 e rotational quantum number
d Rotationsquantenzahl *f*
f nombre *m* quantique de rotation
r вращательное квантовое число *n*

R554 e rotational spectrum
d Rotationsspektrum *n*
f spectre *m* de rotation, spectre *m* rotationnel
r вращательный спектр *m*

R555 e rotational temperature
d Rotationstemperatur *f*
f température *f* rotationnelle, température *f* de rotation
r вращательная температура *f*

R556 e rotational transition
d Rotationsübergang *m*
f transition *f* rotatoinnelle, transition *f* de rotation
r вращательный переход *m*

R557 e rotational wave *see* shear wave

R558 e rotation axis
d Drehachse *f*, Rotationsachse *f*
f axe *m* de rotation
r ось *f* вращения

R559 e rotation by magnetization *see* Einstein-de Haas effect

R560 e rotation group
d Drehgruppe *f*, Drehungsgruppe *f*
f groupe *m* des rotations
r группа *f* вращений

R561 e rotation of the plane of polarization
d Polarisationsdrehung *f*, Drehung *f* der Polarisationsebene
f rotation *f* du plan de polarisation
r вращение *n* плоскости поляризации

R562 e rotator
d Rotator *m*
f rotateur *m*
r ротатор *m*

R563 e rotatory dispersion *see* rotary dispersion

R564 e rotatory polarization

	d	zirkulare Polarisation f, Zirkularpolarisation f
	f	polarisation f rotatoire
	r	круговая поляризация f
R565	e	roton
	d	Roton n
	f	roton m
	r	ротон m (квазичастица)
R566	e	rotor
	d	Läufer m, Rotor m
	f	rotor m
	r	ротор m
R567	e	rough correction
	d	Grobkorrektion f
	f	correction f approximative
	r	грубая корректировка f
R568	e	rubidium, Rb
	d	Rubidium n
	f	rubidium m
	r	рубидий m
R569	e	ruby
	d	Rubin m
	f	rubis m
	r	рубин m
R570	e	ruby crystal
	d	Rubinkristall m
	f	cristal m de rubis
	r	кристалл m рубина
R571	e	ruby laser
	d	Rubinlaser m
	f	laser m à rubis
	r	рубиновый лазер m
R572	e	runaway electrons
	d	Runawayelektronen n pl, Runaway-Elektronen n pl
	f	électrons m pl découplés
	r	убегающие электроны m pl
R573	e	rust protection see corrosion protection
R574	e	ruthenium, Ru
	d	Ruthenium n
	f	ruthénium m
	r	рутений m
R575	e	rutherford
	d	Rutherford n, Rutherford-Einheit f
	f	rutherford m
	r	резерфорд m (единица активности)
R576	e	Rutherford scattering
	d	Rutherford-Streuung f, Rutherfordsche Streuung f
	f	diffusion f de Rutherford
	r	резерфордовское рассеяние n
R577	e	rydberg

	d	Rydberg n
	f	rydberg m, unité f rydberg
	r	ридберг m (единица энергии)
R578	e	Rydberg atom
	d	Rydbergsches Atom n
	f	atome m de Rydberg
	r	атом m Ридберга
R579	e	Rydberg constant
	d	Rydberg-Konstante f
	f	constante f de Rydberg
	r	постоянная f Ридберга
R580	e	Rydberg series
	d	Rydberg-Serie f
	f	série f de Rydberg
	r	серия f Ридберга
R581	e	Rydberg spectrometer
	d	Rydberg-Spektrometer n
	f	spectromètre m de Rydberg
	r	спектрометр m Ридберга

S

S1	e	Sabatier effect
	d	Sabatier-Effekt m
	f	effet m Sabatier
	r	эффект m Сабатье
S2	e	sabin
	d	Sabin n
	f	sabin m
	r	сэбин m (внесистемная единица поглощения звука)
S3	e	saccharimeter
	d	Sacharimeter n, Saccharimeter n
	f	saccharimètre m
	r	сахариметр m
S4	e	saccharimetry
	d	Sacharimetrie f, Saccharimetrie f
	f	saccharimétrie f
	r	сахариметрия f
S5	e	saddle point
	d	Sattelpunkt m
	f	point m du col
	r	точка f перевала, седловая точка f
S6	e	saddle point method
	d	Sattelpunktmethode f
	f	méthode f du col, méthode f des points du col
	r	метод m перевала, метод m седловых точек
S7	e	safe concentration
	d	gefahrlose Konzentration f

	f	concentration f sûre
	r	безопасная концентрация f
S8	e	**safe dose**
	d	Sicherheitsdosis f
	f	dose f de sécurité
	r	безопасная доза f
S9	e	**safety channel**
	d	Sicherheitskanal m
	f	canal m de sécurité
	r	канал m аварийной защиты (ядерного реактора)
S10	e	**safety factor**
	d	Sicherheitsfaktor m, Sicherheitsgrad m
	f	coefficient m de sécurité, facteur m de sécurité
	r	запас m прочности; коэффициент m безопасности
S11	e	**Sagnac experiment**
	d	Sagnacscher Versuch m, Sagnac-Versuch m
	f	expérience f de Sagnac
	r	опыт m Саньяка
S12	e	**Sagnac interferometer**
	d	Sagnac-Interferometer n
	f	interféromètre m de Sagnac
	r	интерферометр m Саньяка
S13	e	**Saha equation**
	d	Saha-Gleichung f
	f	formule f de Saha
	r	формула f Caxa
S14	e	**samarium, Sm**
	d	Samarium n
	f	samarium m
	r	самарий m
S15	e	**sample**
	d	1. Probe f 2. Stichprobe f
	f	échantillon m
	r	1. образец m; проба f 2. выборка f
S16	e	**sampling interval**
	d	Abtastintervall n
	f	intervalle m de discrétisation
	r	интервал m дискретизации
S17	e	**sampling oscilloscope**
	d	Sampling-Oszilloskop n, Abtastoszillosgraph m
	f	oscilloscope m à échantillonnage
	r	стробоскопический осциллограф m
S18	e	**satellite**
	d	1. Satellit m, Trabant m 2. Satellit m
	f	satellite m
	r	1. спутник m (планеты) 2. сателлит m (спектральная линия)
S19	e	**satellite laser ranging**
	d	Satellitenlaserortung f

	f	localisation f à laser des satellites
	r	лазерная локация f искусственных спутников
S20	e	**saturable dye**
	d	sättigungsfähiger Farbstoff m
	f	colorant m saturable
	r	насыщающийся краситель m
S21	e	**saturated solution**
	d	gesättigte Lösung f
	f	solution f saturée
	r	насыщенный раствор m
S22	e	**saturated vapor**
	d	Sattdampf m, gesättigter Dampf m
	f	vapeur f saturée
	r	насыщенный пар m
S23	e	**saturated vapor pressure**
	d	Sättigungsdruck m, Sättigungsdampfdruck m
	f	pression f de vapeur saturée
	r	давление n насыщенного пара
S24	e	**saturation**
	d	Sättigung f
	f	saturation f
	r	насыщение n
S25	e	**saturation curve**
	d	Sättigungskurve f, Sättigungslinie f
	f	courbe f de saturation
	r	кривая f насыщения
S26	e	**saturation magnetization**
	d	Sättigungsmagnetisierung f
	f	aimantation f de saturation
	r	намагниченность f насыщения
S27	e	**saturation of an ionization chamber**
	d	Ionisationskammersättigung f
	f	saturation f de la chambre d'ionisation
	r	насыщение n ионизационной камеры
S28	e	**saturation of a solution**
	d	Lösungssättigung f
	f	saturation f de la solution
	r	насыщенность f раствора
S29	e	**saturation of color**
	d	Farbsättigung f
	f	saturation f de couleur
	r	насыщенность f цвета
S30	e	**saturation of nuclear forces**
	d	Kernkräftesättigung f
	f	saturation f des forces nucléaires
	r	насыщение n ядерных сил
S31	e	**saturation vapor pressure** see **saturated vapor pressure**
S32	e	**Saturn**
	d	Saturn m

f Saturne *m*
r Сатурн *m*

S33 *e* **Savart plate**
   d Savartsche Doppelplatte *f*, Savartsche Platte *f*, Savartsches Polariskop *n*
   f plaque *f* de Savart, biplaque *f* de Savart, polariscope *m* de Savart
   r пластинка *f* Савара

S34 *e* **SAW** *see* **surface acoustic waves**

S35 *e* **sawtooth generator**
   d Sägezahngenerator *m*
   f générateur *m* en dents de scie
   r генератор *m* пилообразного напряжения

S36 *e* **sawtooth voltage**
   d Sägezahnspannung *f*
   f tension *f* en dents de scie
   r пилообразное напряжение *n*

S37 *e* **SBS cell**
   d SBS-Zelle *f*
   f cellule *f* à SBS
   r ВРМБ-кювета *f*

S38 *e* **SBS laser**
   d SBS-Laser *m*
   f laser *m* SBS
   r ВРМБ-лазер *m*

S39 *e* **SBS stimulated** *see* **Brillonin scattering**

S40 *e* **scalar**
   d Skalar *m*, skalare Größe *f*
   f scalaire *m*
   r скаляр *m*

S41 *e* **scalar field**
   d Skalarfeld *n*, skalares Feld *n*
   f champ *m* scalaire
   r скалярное поле *n*

S42 *e* **scalar meson**
   d skalares Meson *n*
   f méson *m* scalaire
   r скалярный мезон *m*

S43 *e* **scalar particle**
   d skalares Teilchen *n*
   f particule *f* scalaire
   r скалярная частица *f*

S44 *e* **scalar photon**
   d skalares Photon *n*
   f photon *m* scalaire
   r скалярный фотон *m*

S45 *e* **scalar potential**
   d skalares Potential *n*, Skalarpotential *n*
   f potentiel *m* scalaire
   r скалярный потенциал *m*

S46 *e* **scalar product**

d Skalarprodukt *n*, skalares Produkt *n*
f produit *m* scalaire
r скалярное произведение *n*

S47 *e* **scale**
   d 1. Maßstab *m* 2. Skala *f*
   f échelle *f*
   r 1. масштаб *m* 2. шкала *f*

S48 *e* **scale division**
   d Skalenteilung *f*, Skalenteilstrichabstand *m*
   f division *f* d'échelle
   r деление *n* шкалы

S49 *e* **scale factor**
   d Maßstabsfaktor *m*
   f facteur *m* de réduction, facteur *m* d'échelle
   r масштабный множитель *m*, масштабный фактор *m*

S50 *e* **scale invariance**
   d Maßstabinvarianz *f*; Scaling *n*
   f invariance *f* d'échelle
   r масштабная инвариантность *f*; скейлинг *m*

S51 *e* **scale of the Universe**
   d Größenmaßstab *m* des Universums
   f échelle *f* de l'Univers
   r масштабы *m pl* Вселенной

S52 *e* **scale of turbulence**
   d Turbulenzlänge *f*, Turbulenzgrad *m*
   f échelle *f* de turbulence, degré *m* de turbulence
   r масштаб *m* турбулентности

S53 *e* **scaling**
   d Scaling *n*; Maßstabinvarianz *f*
   f invariance *f* d'échelle
   r скейлинг *m*; масштабная инвариантность *f*

S54 *e* **scaling law**
   d Maßstabgesetz *n*
   f loi *f* de similitude
   r закон *m* подобия

S55 *e* **scandium, Sc**
   d Skandium *n*
   f scandium *m*
   r скандий *m*

S56 *e* **scanner**
   d Abtaster *m*, Abtastgerät *n*, Scanner *m*
   f dispositif *m* de balayage
   r сканер *m*

S57 *e* **scanning**
   d 1. Abtastung *f* 2. Bildzerlegung *f*
   f 1. exploration *f* 2. balayage *m*
   r 1. сканирование *n* 2. развёртка *f*

S58 *e* **scanning high-energy electron diffraction**

d Raster-Hochenergie-
Elektronendiffraktion *f*,
Rasterdiffraktion *f* hochenergischer
Elektronen
f diffraction *f* à trame des électrons
durs
r растровая дифракция *f* быстрых
электронов

S59 *e* scanning microscope
d Rastermikroskop *n*
f microscope *m* à balayage
r сканирующий микроскоп *m*,
растровый микроскоп *m*

S60 *e* scanning optics
d Abtastoptik *f*
f optique *f* des treillis
r растровая оптика *f*

S61 *e* scatter *see* scattering

S62 *e* scattered neutrons
d Streuneutronen *n pl*, gestreute
Neutronen *n pl*
f neutrons *m pl* diffusés
r рассеянные нейтроны *m pl*

S63 *e* scattered quantum
d Streuquant *n*, gestreutes Quant *n*
f quantum *m* diffusé
r рассеянный квант *m*

S64 *e* scattered radiation
d Streustrahlung *f*, gestreute Strahlung
f, diffuse Strahlung *f*
f rayonnement *m* diffusé
r рассеянное излучение *n*

S65 *e* scattered wave
d Streuwelle *f*, gestreute Welle *f*
f onde *f* diffusée
r рассеянная волна *f*

S66 *e* scattering
d Streuung *f*
f diffusion *f*
r рассеяние *n*

S67 *e* scattering amplitude
d Streuamplitude *f*,
Streuungsamplitude *f*
f amplitude *f* de diffusion
r амплитуда *f* рассеяния

S68 *e* scattering angle
d Streuwinkel *m*
f angle *m* de diffusion
r угол *m* рассеяния

S69 *e* scattering channel
d Streukanal *m*
f voie *f* de diffusion
r канал *m* рассеяния

S70 *e* scattering coefficient
d Streukoeffizient *m*,
Streuungskoeffizient *m*
f coefficient *m* de diffusion
r коэффициент *m* рассеяния

S71 *e* scattering cross-section
d Streuquerschnitt *m*,
Streuungsquerschnitt *m*
f section *f* efficace de diffusion
r сечение *n* рассеяния

S72 *e* scattering diagram
d Streuungsdiagramm *n*
f diagramme *m* de diffusion
r диаграмма *f* рассеяния

S73 *e* scattering factor *see* scattering
coefficient

S74 *e* scattering indicatrix
d Streuindikatrix *f*
f indicatrice *f* de diffusion
r индикатриса *f* рассеяния

S75 *e* scattering integral
d Streuungsintegral *n*
f intégrale *f* de diffusion
r интеграл *m* рассеяния

S76 *e* scattering length
d Streulänge *f*
f longueur *f* de diffusion
r длина *f* рассеяния

S77 *e* scattering matrix
d Streumatrix *f*, S-Matrix *f*
f matrice *f* de diffusion
r матрица *f* рассеянйя

S78 *e* scattering phase
d Streuphase *f*
f phase *f* de diffusion
r фаза *f* рассеяния

S79 *e* schlieren method
d Schlierenmethode *f*
f méthode *f* des stries
r шлирен-метод *m*, метод *m* Тёплера

S80 *e* Schottky barrier
d Schottky-Barriere *f*
f barrière *f* de Schottky
r барьер *m* Шотки

S81 *e* Schottky effect
d Schottky-Effekt *m*
f effet *m* Schottky
r эффект *m* Шотки

S82 *e* Schrödinger equation
d Schrödinger-Gleichung *f*,
Schrödingersche Wellengleichung *f*
f équation *f* de Schrödinger
r уравнение *n* Шрёдингера

S83 *e* Schwartzschild radius
d Schwartzschild-Radius *m*,
Gravitationsradius *m*
f rayon *m* de Schwartzschild

r радиус *m* Шварцшильда, гравитационный радиус *m*

S84 e **scientific research**
d wissenschaftliche Forschung *f*
f recherches *f pl* scientifiques
r научные исследования *n pl*

S85 e **scintillation**
d Szintillation *f*
f scintillation *f*
r сцинтилляция *f*

S86 e **scintillation chamber**
d Szintillationskammer *f*
f caméra *f* à scintillation
r сцинтилляционная камера *f*

S87 e **scintillation counter**
d Szintillationszähler *m*
f compteur *m* à scintillation
r сцинтилляционный счётчик *m*

S88 e **scintillation detector**
d Szintillationsdetektor *m*
f détecteur *m* à scintillation
r сцинтилляционный детектор *m*

S89 e **scintillator**
d Szintillator *m*
f scintillateur *m*
r сцинтиллятор *m*

S90 e **sclerometer**
d Sklerometer *n*, Ritzhärteprüfer *m*
f scléromètre *m*
r склерометр *m*

S91 e **scleroscope** *see* sclerometer

S92 e **screen**
d Schirm *m*; Schutzschirm *m*
f écran *m*
r экран *m*; защита *f*

S93 e **screening**
d Abschirmung *f*
f action *f* d'écran, effet *m* d'écran, blindage *m*
r экранирование *n*, экранировка *f*

S94 e **screening constant**
d Abschirmungskonstante *f*, Abschirmkonstante *f*
f constante *f* d'effet d'écran, constante *f* d'écran
r постоянная *f* экранирования

S95 e **screw axis**
d Schraubenachse *f*
f axe *m* hélicoïdal
r винтовая ось *f*

S96 e **screw dislocation**
d Schraubenversetzung *f*, Burgers-Versetzung *f*
f dislocation *f* vis, dislocation *f* hélicoïdale

r винтовая дислокация *f*, дислокация *f* Бюргера

S97 e **screw instability**
d Schraubeninstabilität *f*
f instabilité *f* hélicoïdale
r винтовая неустойчивость *f*

S98 e **screw motion**
d Schraubenbewegung *f*, schraubenförmige Bewegung *f*
f mouvement *m* hélicoïdal, déplacement *m* hélicoïdal
r винтовое движение *n*

S99 e **sealed source**
d umschlossene Quelle *f*
f source *f* scellée
r закрытый источник *m*, закрытый радионуклидный источник *m*

S100 e **sea level**
d Meeresspiegel *m*
f niveau *m* de la mer
r уровень *m* моря

S101 e **sea quark**
d Seequark *n*
f quark *m* marin
r морской кварк *m*

S102 e **second**
d Sekunde *f*
f seconde *f*
r секунда *f*

S103 e **secondary cosmic rays**
d kosmische Sekundärstrahlung *f*, sekundäre Höhenstrahlung *f*
f rayons *pl* cosmiques secondaires
r вторичные космические лучи *pl*

S104 e **secondary electron emission, secondary emission**
d Sekundärelektronenemission *f*, Sekundäremission *f*
f émission *f* secondaire
r вторичная электронная эмиссия *f*, вторичная эмиссия *f*

S105 e **secondary emission coefficient**
d Sekundäremissionskoeffizient *m*
f coefficient *m* d'émission secondaire
r коэффициент *m* вторичной эмиссии

S106 e **secondary emission image**
d Sekundäremissionsbild *n*
f image *f* en émission secondaire
r изображение *n* во вторичных электронах

S107 e **secondary ion mass spectrometry**
d Sekundärionenmassenspektrometrie *f*, SIMS
f spectrométrie *f* de masse des ions secondaires

r масс-спектрометрия *f* вторичных ионов

S108 e **secondary mirror**
d Sekundärspiegel *m*
f petit miroir *m*, miroir *m* secondaire
r вторичное зеркало *n*, вспомогательное зеркало *n* (*телескопа*)

S109 e **secondary quantization**
d zweite Quantisierung *f*
f quantification *f* secondaire
r вторичное квантование *n*

S110 e **secondary radiation**
d Sekundärstrahlung *f*
f rayonnement *m* secondaire, radiation *f* secondaire
r вторичное излучение *n*

S111 e **secondary radiator**
d Sekundärstrahler *m*
f émetteur *m* secondaire
r вторичный излучатель *m*

S112 e **secondary standard**
d Sekundärnormal *n*
f étalon *m* secondaire
r вторичный эталон *m*

S113 e **secondary voltage**
d Sekundärspannung *f*
f tension *f* secondaire
r вторичное напряжение *n*

S114 e **second law of thermodynamics**
d zweiter Hauptsatz *m* der Thermodynamik, Entropiesatz *m*
f second principe *m* de la thermodynamique
r второе начало *n* термодинамики

S115 e **second-order curve**
d Kurve *f* zweiter Ordnung
f courbe *f* de deuxième ordre
r кривая *f* второго порядка

S116 e **second sound**
d zweiter Schall *m*
f deuxième son *m*, second son *m*
r второй звук *m* (*в гелии*)

S117 e **section**
d 1. Schnitt *m* 2. Abschnitt *m*, Teil *m*
f section *f*
r 1. сечение *n*, разрез *m* 2. участок *m*, отрезок *m*, часть *f*

S118 e **sector velocity**
d Flächengeschwindigkeit *f*
f vitesse *f* aréolaire
r секторная скорость *f*

S119 e **secular parallax**
d säkulare Parallaxe *f*, Säkularparallaxe *f*

f parallaxe *f* séculaire
r вековой параллакс *m*

S120 e **secular variations**
d säkulare Variationen *f pl*, Säkularvariation *f*
f variations *f pl* séculaires
r вековые вариации *f pl*

S121 e **sediment** *see* precipitate

S122 e **sedimentation**
d Sedimentation *f*
f sédimentation *f*
r седиментация *f*; осаждение *n*

S123 e **sedimentation analysis**
d Sedimentationsanalyse *f*
f analyse *f* de sédimentation
r седиментационный анализ *m*, седиментометрический анализ *m*

S124 e **Seeback effect**
d Seeback-Effekt *m*
f effet *m* Seeback
r эффект *m* Зеебека

S125 e **seed**
d Impfkristall *m*, Kristallkeim *m*
f germe *m* (*du cristal*)
r затравка *f* (*кристалла*)

S126 e **Seifert galaxies**
d Seifert-Galaxien *f pl*
f galaxies *f pl* de Seifert
r сейфертовские галактики *f pl*

S127 e **seismicity**
d Seismizität *f*; Erdbebenaktivität *f*
f séismicité *f*
r сейсмичность *f*

S128 e **seismic waves**
d seismische Wellen *f pl*, Erdbebenwellen *f pl*
f ondes *f pl* séismiques
r сейсмические волны *f pl*

S129 e **seismic zone**
d seismische Zone *f*, erdbebenaktive Zone *f*
f région *f* séismique
r сейсмическая зона *f*

S130 e **seismology**
d Seismik *f*, Seismologie *f*
f séismologie *f*
r сейсмология *f*

S131 e **selection**
d 1. Selektion *f*; Auswahl *f* 2. Wahl *f*, Wählen *n*
f sélection *f*
r 1. селекция *f* 2. выделение *n*, выбор *m*

S132 e **selection rules**

	d	Auswahlregeln f pl
	f	règles f pl de sélection
	r	правила n pl отбора
S133	e	selective absorption
	d	selektive Absorption f
	f	absorption f sélective
	r	селективное поглощение n, избирательное поглощение n
S134	e	selective detection
	d	selektive Detektion f, selektive Detektierung f (von Atomen)
	f	détection f sélective (des atomes)
	r	селективное детектирование n (атомов)
S135	e	selective dissociation
	d	selektive Dissoziation f
	f	dissociation f sélective
	r	селективная диссоциация f
S136	e	selective extraction
	d	selektive Extraktion f
	f	extraction f sélective
	r	селективное извлечение n
S137	e	selective ionization
	d	selektive Ionisation f
	f	ionisation f sélective
	r	селективная ионизация f
S138	e	selective mirror
	d	selektiver Spiegel m
	f	miroir m sélectif
	r	селективное зеркало n
S139	e	selective radiator
	d	Selektivstrahler m, selektiver Strahler m
	f	radiateur m sélectif
	r	селективный излучатель m
S140	e	selective transmission
	d	selektive Durchlässigkeit f
	f	transmission f sélective
	r	селективное пропускание n
S141	e	selectivity
	d	Selektivität f
	f	sélectivité f
	r	избирательность f
S142	e	selenium, Se
	d	Selen n
	f	sélénium m
	r	селен m
S143	e	selenium rectifier
	d	Selengleichrichter m
	f	redresseur m au sélénium
	r	селеновый выпрямитель m
S144	e	self-absorption
	d	Selbstabsorption f
	f	auto-absorption f
	r	самопоглощение n
S145	e	self-acceleration
	d	Selbstbeschleunigung f
	f	auto-accélération f
	r	самоускорение n
S146	e	self-action
	d	Selbstwirkung f
	f	auto-action f
	r	самовоздействие n
S147	e	self-annealing ion implantation
	d	Ionenimplantation f mit Selbstausheilung
	f	implantation f ionique à autorecuit
	r	самоотжиговая ионная имплантация f
S148	e	self-channeling
	d	Selbstkanalierung f
	f	self-canalisation f
	r	самоканалирование n
S149	e	self-conjugate operator
	d	selbstkonjugierter Operator m
	f	opérateur m self-conjugué
	r	самосопряжённый оператор m
S150	e	self-consistent field
	d	selbstkonsistentes Feld n
	f	champ m autoconsistant
	r	самосогласованное поле n
S151	e	self-consistent field method
	d	Methode f des selbstkonsistenten Feldes, Hartree-Fock-Methode f
	f	méthode f du champ autoconsistant, méthode f de Hartree-Fock
	r	метод m самосогласованного поля, метод m Хартри - Фока
S152	e	self-contraction
	d	Selbstkontraktion f
	f	autocontraction f
	r	самосжатие n
S153	e	self-defocusing
	d	Selbstdefokussierung f, Eigendefokussierung f
	f	autodéfocalisation f
	r	самодефокусировка f
S154	e	self-diffusion
	d	Selbstdiffusion f, Eigendiffusion f
	f	autodiffusion f
	r	самодиффузия f
S155	e	self-diffusion plasticity
	d	Selbstdiffusionsplastizität f
	f	plasticité f d'autodiffusion
	r	самодиффузионная пластичность f
S156	e	self-discharge
	d	Selbstentladung f
	f	autodécharge f
	r	саморазряд m
S157	e	self-energy

  d Eigenenergie *f*
  f auto-énergie *f*, self-énergie *f*, énergie
   f propre
  r собственная энергия *f*

S158 *e* self-excitation
  d Selbsterregung *f*, Eigenerregung *f*
  f auto-excitation *f*
  r самовозбуждение *n*

S159 *e* self-excited oscillations
  d selbsterregte Schwingungen *f pl*
  f oscillations *f pl* auto-entretenues,
   auto-oscillations *f pl*
  r автоколебания *n pl*

S160 *e* self-focusing
  d Selbstfokussierung *f*
  f autofocalisation *f*
  r самофокусировка *f (света)*

S161 *e* self-focusing ring
  d selbstfokussierender Ring *m*
  f anneau *m* d'autofocalisation
  r самофокусировочное кольцо *n*

S162 *e* self-induced emission
  d selbstinduzierte Strahlung *f*
  f émission *f* auto-induite
  r самоиндуцированное излучение *n*

S163 *e* self-induced transparency
  d selbstinduzierte Transparenz *f*
  f transparence *f* auto-induite
  r самоиндуцированная прозрачность *f*

S164 *e* self-inductance
  d 1. Eigeninduktivität *f*
   2. Selbstinduktivität *f*,
   Selbstinduktionskoeffizient *m*
  f 1. auto-inductance *f* 2. coefficient
   d'auto-induction
  r 1. собственная индуктивность *f*
   2. коэффициент *m* самоиндукции,
   индуктивность *f*

S165 *e* self-induction
  d Selbstinduktion *f*
  f auto-induction *f*
  r самоиндукция *f*

S166 *e* self-maintained discharge *see* self-
   sustaining discharge

S167 *e* self-maintained flow
  d selbstähnliche Strömung *f*
  f écoulement *m* auto-entretenu
  r автомодельное течение *n*

S168 *e* self-mode-locked laser
  d Laser *m* mit
   Modenselbstsynchronisation
  f laser *m* à autosynchronisation des
   modes
  r лазер *m* с самосинхронизацией мод

S169 *e* self-modulation

  d Selbstmodulation *f*
  f automodulation *f*
  r 1. самомодуляция *f (света)*
   2. автомодуляция *f*

S170 *e* self-reversal
  d Selbstumkehrung *f*, Selbstumkehr *f*
  f autorenversement *m*
  r самообращение *n*

S171 *e* self-screening *see* self-shielding

S172 *e* self-shielding
  d Selbstabschirmung *f*
  f autoprotection *f*
  r самоэкранирование *n*

S173 *e* self-similar flow *see* self-maintained
   flow

S174 *e* self-similarity
  d Selbstähnlichkeit *f*
  f autosimilarité *f*
  r автомодельность *f*

S175 *e* self-similar motion
  d selbstähnliche Bewegung *f*
  f mouvement *m* autosemblable
  r автомодельное движение *n*

S176 *e* self-sustained oscillations *see* self-
   excited oscillations

S177 *e* self-sustaining discharge
  d selbständige Entladung *f*
  f décharge *f* autonome, décharge *f*
   auto-entretenue
  r самостоятельный разряд *m*

S178 *e* semiconductor
  d Halbleiter *m*
  f semi-conducteur *m*
  r полупроводник *m*,
   полупроводниковый материал *m*

S179 *e* semiconductor amplifier
  d Halbleiterverstärker *m*
  f amplificateur *m* à semi-conducteur
  r полупроводниковый усилитель *m*

S180 *e* semiconductor bolometer
  d Halbleiterbolometer *n*
  f bolomètre *m* à semi-conducteur
  r полупроводниковый болометр *m*

S181 *e* semiconductor crystal
  d Halbleiterkristall *m*
  f cristal *m* semi-conducteur
  r полупроводниковый кристалл *m*

S182 *e* semiconductor degradation
  d Halbleiterentartung *f*
  f dégradation *f* des semi-conducteurs
  r деградация *f* полупроводников

S183 *e* semiconductor detector
  d Halbleiterdetektor *m*

    f détecteur *m* semi-conducteur
    r полупроводниковый детектор *m*

S184 *e* semiconductor devices
    d Halbleitergeräte *n pl*
    f dispositifs *m pl* à semi-conducteur
    r полупроводниковые приборы *m pl*

S185 *e* semiconductor diode
    d Halbleiterdiode *f*
    f diode *f* à semi-conducteur, diode *f* semi-conductrice
    r полупроводниковый диод *m*

S186 *e* semiconductor doping
    d Halbleiterdotierung *f*
    f dopage *m* des semi-conducteurs
    r легирование *n* полупроводников

S187 *e* semiconductor electronics
    d Halbleiterelektronik *f*
    f électronique *f* des semi-conducteurs
    r полупроводниковая электроника *f*

S188 *e* semiconductor laser
    d Halbleiterlaser *m*
    f laser *m* semi-conducteur
    r полупроводниковый лазер *m*

S189 *e* semiconductor-metal transition
    d Halbleiter-Metall-Übergang *m*
    f jonction *f* semi-conducteur-métal
    r переход *m* полупроводник - металл

S190 *e* semiconductor microelectronics
    d Halbleitermikroelektronik *f*
    f microélectronique *f* des semi-conducteurs
    r полупроводниковая микроэлектроника *f*

S191 *e* semiconductor photodiode
    d Halbleiterphotodiode *f*
    f photodiode *f* à semi-conducteur
    r полупроводниковый фотодиод *m*

S192 *e* semiconductor sensor
    d Halbleitergeber *m*, Halbleitersensor *m*
    f capteur *m* à semi-conducteur
    r полупроводниковый датчик *m*

S193 *e* semileptonic decay
    d semileptonischer Zerfall *m*
    f désintégration *f* semi-leptonique
    r полулептонный распад *m* (*частицы*)

S194 *e* semimetal
    d Halbmetall *n*
    f semi-métal *m*
    r полуметалл *m*

S195 *e* semipermeable membrane
    d halbdurchlässige Membran *f*
    f membrane *f* semi-perméable
    r полупроницаемая мембрана *f*

S196 *e* semireflecting mirror *see* semitransparent mirror

S197 *e* semitransparent mirror
    d halbdurchlässiger Spiegel *m*
    f miroir *m* semi-transparent
    r полупрозрачное зеркало *n*

S198 *e* sensation
    d Empfindung *f*
    f sensation *f*
    r ощущение *n*; восприятие *n*

S199 *e* sense of rotation
    d Drehsinn *m*, Drehrichtung *f*, Rotationsrichtung *f*
    f sens *m* de rotation
    r направление *n* вращения

S200 *e* sensitivity
    d Empfindlichkeit *f*
    f sensibilité *f*
    r чувствительность *f*

S201 *e* sensitization
    d Sensibilisierung *f*
    f sensibilisation *f*
    r сенсибилизация *f*

S202 *e* sensitized luminescence
    d sensibilisierte Lumineszenz *f*
    f luminescence *f* sensibilisée
    r сенсибилизированная люминесценция *f*

S203 *e* sensitometry
    d Sensitometrie *f*
    f sensitométrie *f*
    r сенситометрия *f*

S204 *e* sensor
    d Geber *m*; Fühlglied *n*
    f capteur *m*; élément *m* sensible
    r датчик *m*; чувствительный элемент *m*

S205 *e* separated isotopes
    d getrennte Isotope *n pl*
    f isotopes *m pl* séparés
    r разделённые изотопы *m pl*

S206 *e* separation factor
    d Trennfaktor *m*, Isotopentrennfaktor *m*
    f coefficient *m* de séparation
    r коэффициент *m* разделения (*изотопов*)

S207 *e* series
    d Reihe *f*
    f série *f*
    r ряд *m*; серия *f*

S208 *e* series circuit
    d Serienstromkreis *m*, Serienkreis *m*, Reihenkreis *m*
    f circuit *m* en série
    r последовательный контур *m*

S209   *e*   series connection
     d   Reihenschaltung *f*,
       Hintereinanderschaltung *f*
     f   connexion *f* en série
     r   последовательное соединение *n* (*в*
       электрической цепи)

S210   *e*   series resonance
     d   Reihenresonanz *f*, Serienresonanz *f*
     f   résonance *f* en série
     r   последовательный резонанс *m*,
       резонанс *m* напряжений

S211   *e*   set
     d   1. Satz *m*, Garnitur *f* 2. Reihe *f*, Serie
       f 3. Gerät *n*, Apparat *m*; Aggregat *n*
     f   1. ensemble *m*, jeu *m* 2. système *m* 3.
       dispositif *m*
     r   1. множество *n*; набор *m* 2. серия *f*;
       система *f* 3. установка *f*

S212   *e*   shadow cone
     d   Schattenkegel *m*
     f   cône *m* d'ombre
     r   конус *m* тени

S213   *e*   shadow method
     d   Schattenverfahren *n*,
       Schattenmethode *f*
     f   méthode *f* des ombres
     r   теневой метод *m*

S214   *e*   shadow pattern
     d   Schattenbild *n*
     f   image *f* d'ombre
     r   теневая картина *f*

S215   *e*   shallow trap
     d   flache Haftstelle *f*
     f   piège *m* bas
     r   мелкая ловушка *f*

S216   *e*   shape
     d   Form *f*; Gestalt *f*
     f   forme *f*
     r   форма *f*

S217   *e*   shape anisotropy
     d   Formanisotropie *f*, Gestaltanisotropie *f*
     f   anisotropie *f* de la forme
     r   анизотропия *f* формы

S218   *e*   shape isomer
     d   Formisomer *n*
     f   isomère *m* de forme
     r   изомер *m* формы

S219   *e*   sharp image
     d   scharfes Bild *n*
     f   image *f* nette
     r   резкое изображение *n*, чёткое
       изображение *n*

S220   *e*   sharpness of vision *see* visual acuity

S221   *e*   shear
     d   Scherung *f*; Schub *m*
     f   cisaillement *m*
     r   сдвиг *m* (*вид механической*
       деформации)

S222   *e*   shear deformation
     d   Schubdeformation *f*, Scherdeformation
       f, Schubverformung *f*,
       Scherverformung *f*
     f   déformation *f* de cisaillement
     r   деформация *f* сдвига, сдвиговая
       деформация *f*

S223   *e*   shear fracture
     d   Scherbruch *m*, Schubbruch *m*
     f   fracture *f* de cisaillement
     r   излом *m* при сдвиге

S224   *e*   shear modulus
     d   Schubmodul *m*, Scherungsmodul *m*
     f   module *m* d'élasticité au cisaillement
     r   модуль *m* сдвига

S225   *e*   shear rigidity
     d   Scherungssteifigkeit *f*
     f   rigidité *f* au cisaillement
     r   сдвиговая жёсткость *f*, жёсткость *f*
       при сдвиге

S226   *e*   shear strength
     d   Schubfestigkeit *f*, Scherfestigkeit *f*
     f   résistance *f* au cisaillement
     r   сдвиговая прочность *f*, предел *m*
       прочности при сдвиге

S227   *e*   shear stress
     d   Schubspannung *f*; Scherspannung *f*
     f   tension *f* de cisaillement
     r   напряжение *n* сдвига, сдвиговое
       напряжение *n*

S228   *e*   shear vibration
     d   Scherschwingung *f*,
       Scherungsschwingung *f*
     f   vibration *f* de cisaillement
     r   сдвиговые колебания *n pl*

S229   *e*   shear wave
     d   Scherungswelle *f*, Schubwelle *f*
     f   onde *f* de cisaillement
     r   сдвиговая волна *f*

S230   *e*   sheet
     d   Blatt *n*; Schicht *f*; Platte *f*, Schiebe *f*
     f   feuille *f*; couche *f*
     r   лист *m*; слой *m*

S231   *e*   shell
     d   Schale *f*; Hülle *f*
     f   couche *f*
     r   оболочка *f*

S232   *e*   shell model
     d   Schalenmodell *n* (*Atomkern*)
     f   modèle *m* des couches (*du noyau*),
       modèle *m* à couches, modèle *m* du
       noyau à couches
     r   оболочечная модель *f* (*ядра*)

S233　e　shell target
　　　d　Schalentarget n
　　　f　cible f de couche
　　　r　оболочечная мишень f

S234　e　shield see screen

S235　e　shielded chamber
　　　d　abgeschirmte Kammer f
　　　f　chambre f blindée
　　　r　экранированная камера f

S236　e　shielded coil
　　　d　abgeschirmte Spule f
　　　f　bobine f blindée
　　　r　экранированная катушка f

S237　e　shielding
　　　d　1. Abschirmung f 2. Schutz m
　　　f　1. protection f; blindage m
　　　　　2. protection f
　　　r　1. экранирование n 2. защита f

S238　e　shift
　　　d　Versetzung f; Verschiebung f
　　　f　décalage m
　　　r　сдвиг m, смещение n

S239　e　shock
　　•d　1. Verdichtungsstoß m; Stoßwelle f
　　　　　2. Schlag m, Stoß m
　　　f　choc m
　　　r　1. ударная волна f; скачок m
　　　　　уплотнения 2. удар m

S240　e　shock excitation
　　　d　Stoßanregung f, Stoßerregung f
　　　f　excitation f par choc
　　　r　ударное возбуждение n

S241　e　shock front
　　　d　Stoßfront f, Stoßwellenfront f
　　　f　front m de choc, front m d'onde de
　　　　　choc
　　　r　фронт m ударной волны

S242　e　Shockley diode
　　　d　Shockley-Diode f
　　　f　diode f de Shockley
　　　r　диод m Шокли

S243　e　shock load see impact load

S244　e　shock polar
　　　d　Stoßpolare f
　　　f　polaire f de choc
　　　r　ударная поляра f

S245　e　shock resistance
　　　d　Schlagzähigkeit f
　　　f　résistance f au choc
　　　r　ударная прочность f

S246　e　shock tube, shock tunnel
　　　d　Stoßwellenrohr n
　　　f　tube m de choc
　　　r　ударная труба f

S247　e　shock wave
　　　d　Stoßwelle f
　　　f　onde f de choc
　　　r　ударная волна f

S248　e　short circuit
　　　d　Kurzschluß m
　　　f　court-circuit m
　　　r　короткое замыкание n

S249　e　short-circuited line
　　　d　kurzgeschlossene Leitung f
　　　f　ligne f court-circuitée
　　　r　короткозамкнутая линия f

S250　e　short-circuit voltage
　　　d　Kurzschlußspannung f
　　　f　tension f de court-circuit
　　　r　напряжение n короткого замыкания

S251　e　short-focus lens
　　　d　kurzbrennweitige Linse f,
　　　　　Kurzfokuslinse f
　　　f　lentille f à courte longueur focale
　　　r　короткофокусная линза f,
　　　　　короткофокусный объектив m

S252　e　short-lived component
　　　d　kurzlebige Komponente f
　　　f　composante f à vie courte
　　　r　короткоживущая компонента f

S253　e　short-lived isotope
　　　d　kurzlebiges Isotop n
　　　f　isotope m à vie courte
　　　r　короткоживущий изотоп m

S254　e　short-lived nucleus
　　　d　kurzlebiger Kern m
　　　f　noyau m à vie courte
　　　r　короткоживущее ядро n

S255　e　short-periodic variations
　　　d　kurzperiodische Variationen f pl
　　　f　variations f pl de courte période
　　　r　короткопериодические
　　　　　вариации f pl

S256　e　short pulse
　　　d　kurzzeitiger Impuls m,
　　　　　Kurzzeitimpuls m
　　　f　impulsion f courte
　　　r　короткий импульс m

S257　e　short-range force
　　　d　Nahwirkungskraft f
　　　f　force f à courte distance
　　　r　короткодействующая сила f,
　　　　　близкодействующая сила f

S258　e　short-range interaction
　　　d　Nahwirkung f, kurzreichweitige
　　　　　Wechselwirkung f
　　　f　interaction f à courte distance
　　　r　близкодействие n

S259　e　short-range order

	d	Nahordnung *f*
	f	ordre *m* proche voisin
	r	ближний порядок *m*

S260   e   **short-term instability**
     d   kurzzeitige Instabilität *f*
     f   instabilité *f* de durée réduite
     r   кратковременная нестабильность *f*

S261   e   **short-term stability**
     d   kurzzeitige Stabilität *f*
     f   stabilité *f* de durée réduite
     r   кратковременная стабильность *f*

S262   e   **short-wave radiation**
     d   kurzwellige Strahlung *f*
     f   radiation *f* sur ondes courtes
     r   коротковолновое излучение *n*

S263   e   **short-wave range**
     d   Kurzwellenbereich *m*
     f   gamme *f* des ondes courtes
     r   коротковолновый диапазон *m*

S264   e   **short-wave region**
     d   kurzwelliges Spektrumgebiet *n*
     f   gamme *f* des ondes courtes
     r   коротковолновая область *f*
        (спектра)

S265   e   **short waves**
     d   Kurzwellen *f pl*
     f   ondes *f pl* courtes
     r   короткие волны *f pl*

S266   e   **shot**
     d   Schuß *m*
     f   impulsion *f*
     r   импульс *m (в лазере или токамаке)*

S267   e   **shot noise**
     d   Schrotrauschen *n*, Schroteffekt *m*
     f   effet *m* grenaille, effet *m* de grenaille
     r   дробовой шум *m*

S268   e   **shower**
     d   Schauer *m*
     f   gerbe *f*
     r   ливень *m*

S269   e   **shower chamber**
     d   Schauerkammer *f*
     f   chambre *f* à gerbe
     r   ливневая камера *f*

S270   e   **Shubnikov-de Haas effect**
     d   Schubnikow-de Haas-Effekt *m*
     f   effet *m* Shubnikov-de Haas
     r   эффект *m* Шубникова - де Хааза

S271   e   **shunt**
     d   Nebenschluß *m*, Shunt *m*
     f   shunt *m*
     r   шунт *m*

S272   e   **shutter**
     d   Verschluß *m*; Verschlußblende *f*
     f   obturateur *m*
     r   затвор *m (оптический, фотографический)*, прерыватель *m*

S273   e   **SID** *see* **sudden ionospheric disturbance**

S274   e   **side band**
     d   Seitenband *n*
     f   bande *f* latérale
     r   боковая полоса *f (частот)*

S275   e   **side frequency**
     d   Seitenfrequenz *f*
     f   fréquence *f* latérale
     r   боковая частота *f*

S276   e   **side-mode suppression ratio**
     d   Seitenmodenunterdrückungsverhältnis *n*
     f   coefficient *m* de suppression du mode latéral
     r   коэффициент *m* подавления боковой моды *(в лазере)*

S277   e   **siderial time**
     d   Sternzeit *f*, siderische Zeit *f*
     f   temps *m* sidéral
     r   звёздное время *n*, сидерическое время *n*

S278   e   **siderial year**
     d   Sternjahr *n*, Sternenjahr *n*
     f   année *f* sidérale
     r   звёздный год *m*

S279   e   **siemens, S**
     d   Siemens *n*
     f   siemens *m*
     r   сименс *m*, См *(единица проводимости СИ)*

S280   e   **sievert, Sv**
     d   Sievert *n*
     f   sievert *m*
     r   зиверт *m*, Зв *(единица эквивалентной дозы излучения СИ)*

S281   e   **sight** *see* **viewfinder**

S282   e   **sign**
     d   1. Zeichen *n*; Symbol *m*
        2. Vorzeichen *n*
     f   signe *m*
     r   знак *m*

S283   e   **signal attenuation**
     d   Signalabschwächung *f*, Signaldämpfung *f*
     f   amortissement *m* du signal
     r   затухание *n* сигнала

S284   e   **sign-alternating focusing**
     d   Fokussierung *f* mit alternierenden Feldern

	f	focalisation f par champs alternants
	r	знакопеременная фокусировка f
S285	e	sign-alternating phasing
	d	alternierende Phasierung f
	f	mise f en phase alternée
	r	знакопеременная фазировка f
S286	e	signal-to-noise ratio
	d	Signal-Rausch-Verhältnis n
	f	rapport m signal/bruit
	r	отношение n сигнал/шум
S287	e	signature
	d	Signatur f
	f	signature f
	r	сигнатура f (квантовое число)
S288	e	sign-constant focusing
	d	Fokussierung f mit Gleichfeldern
	f	focalisation f par champs constants
	r	знакопостоянная фокусировка f
S289	e	significance
	d	Signifikanz f
	f	signification f
	r	1. значение n; значимость f 2. достоверность f
S290	e	silent discharge
	d	stille Entladung f
	f	décharge f silencieuse
	r	тихий разряд m
S291	e	silicates
	d	Silikate n pl
	f	silicates m pl
	r	силикаты m pl
S292	e	silicon, Si
	d	Silizium n
	f	silicium m
	r	кремний m
S293	e	similarity
	d	Ähnlichkeit f
	f	similitude f
	r	подобие n
S294	e	similarity criterion
	d	Ähnlichkeitskriterium n
	f	critère m de similitude
	r	критерий m подобия
S295	e	similarity law see scaling law
S296	e	similarity theory
	d	Ähnlichkeitstheorie f
	f	théorie f de la similitude
	r	теория f подобия
S297	e	similitude see similarity
S298	e	simple pendulum see mathematical pendulum
S299	e	simple torsion
	d	einfache Torsion f

	f	torsion f simple, torsion f pure
	r	свободное кручение n, нестеснённое кручение n
S300	e	simulation
	d	1. Modellierung f; Nachbildung f 2. Simulation f
	f	simulation f
	r	1. моделирование n 2. имитация f
S301	e	sine curve
	d	Sinuslinie f, Sinuskurve f, Sinusoide f
	f	sinusoïde f, courbe f sinusoïdale
	r	синусоида f, синусоидальная кривая f
S302	e	sine-Gordon equation
	d	Sinus-Gordon-Gleichung f
	f	équation f de sinus Gordon
	r	уравнение n синус-Гордона
S303	e	sine oscillation see sinusoidal oscillation
S304	e	single crystal
	d	Einkristall m
	f	monocristal m
	r	монокристалл m
S305	e	single crystal diffractometer
	d	Einkristalldiffraktometer n
	f	diffractomètre m à monocristaux
	r	монокристальный дифрактометр m
S306	e	single crystal growing see single crystal growth
S307	e	single crystal growth
	d	Einkristallzüchtung f
	f	croissance f des monocristaux
	r	выращивание n монокристаллов
S308	e	single crystal laser
	d	Einkristall-Laser m
	f	laser m à monocristal
	r	лазер m на монокристалле
S309	e	single dislocation see isolated dislocation
S310	e	single-domain particle
	d	Einbereichsteilchen n
	f	particule f de la dimension du domaine unique, particule f monodomaine
	r	однодомённая частица f
S311	e	single-frequency laser
	d	Einfrequenzlaser m
	f	laser m à fréquence unique
	r	одночастотный лазер m
S312	e	single-mode laser
	d	Einmodenlaser m
	f	laser m monomode
	r	одномодовый лазер m

S313   *e*   single-mode pulse
     d   Einmodenimpuls *m*
     f   impulsion *f* monomode
     r   одномодовый импульс *m*

S314   *e*   single-mode radiation
     d   Einmodenstrahlung *f*
     f   rayonnement *m* monomode
     r   одномодовое излучение *n*

S315   *e*   single-particle motion
     d   Einzelteilchenbewegung *f (Atomkern)*
     f   mouvement *m* de particule unique *(du noyau)*
     r   одночастичное движение *n (ядра)*

S316   *e*   single-particle problem
     d   Einteilchenproblem *n*
     f   problème *m* à une particule
     r   одночастичная задача *f*

S317   *e*   single-photon ionization
     d   Einphotonenionisation *f*
     f   ionisation *f* à photon unique
     r   однофотонная ионизация *f*

S318   *e*   single pulse
     d   Einzelimpuls *m*, diskreter Impuls *m*
     f   impulsion *f* unique
     r   одиночный импульс *m*

S319   *e*   single shot *see* single pulse

S320   *e*   single-shot multivibrator
     d   monostabiler Multivibrator *m*, Univibrator *m*
     f   univibrateur *m*
     r   одновибратор *m*

S321   *e*   singlet
     d   Singulett *n*
     f   singulet *m*
     r   синглет *m*

S322   *e*   singlet state
     d   Singulettzustand *m*
     f   état *m* singulet
     r   синглетное состояние *n*

S323   *e*   single-turn injection
     d   Single-Turn-Injektion *f*
     f   injection *f* en tour unique
     r   однооборотная инжекция *f (в ускорителе заряженных частиц)*

S324   *e*   singly-charged ion
     d   einfach geladenes Ion *n*
     f   ion *m* monochargé
     r   однозарядный ион *m*

S325   *e*   singly-ionized atom
     d   einfach ionisiertes Atom *n*
     f   atome *m* une fois ionisé
     r   однократно ионизованный атом *m*

S326   *e*   singly-ionized molecule
     d   einfach ionisiertes Molekül *n*
     f   molécule *f* une fois ionisée
     r   однократно ионизованная молекула *f*

S327   *e*   singularity
     d   Singularität *f*; singulärer Punkt *m*
     f   singularité *f*
     r   сингулярность *f*; особая точка *f*

S328   *e*   sink
     d   Senke *f*
     f   puits *m*
     r   сток *m*

S329   *e*   sinusoid *see* sine curve

S330   *e*   sinusoidal oscillation
     d   sinusförmige Schwingungen *f pl*, Sinusschwingungen *f pl*
     f   oscillations *f pl* sinusoïdales
     r   синусоидальные колебания *n pl*, гармонические колебания *n pl*

S331   *e*   siren
     d   Sirene *f*
     f   sirène *f*
     r   сирена *f*

S332   *e*   SI units
     d   SI-Einheiten *f pl*
     f   unités *f pl* SI
     r   единицы *f pl* СИ

S333   *e*   size effect
     d   dimensioneller Effekt *m*
     f   effet *m* dimensionnel
     r   размерный эффект *m*

S334   *e*   size quantization
     d   dimensionelle Quantisierung *f*
     f   quantification *f* dimensionnelle
     r   размерное квантование *n*

S335   *e*   skin effect
     d   Skineffekt *m*, Hauteffekt *m*, Stromverdrängungseffekt *m*
     f   effet *m* de peau
     r   скин-эффект *m*

S336   *e*   sky wave
     d   Raumwelle *f*
     f   onde *f* radio ionosphérique
     r   ионосферная радиоволна *f*, ионосферная волна *f*

S337   *e*   sliding friction
     d   Gleitreibung *f*
     f   frottement *m* de glissement
     r   трение *n* скольжения

S338   *e*   slip
     d   Gleiten, Gleitung *f*; Schlupf *m*
     f   glissement *m*
     r   скольжение *n*; проскальзывание *n*

S339   *e*   slip band *see* slip line

S340   *e*   slip line
     d   Gleitlinie *f*, Gleitspur *f*

	f	ligne *f* de glissement
	r	линия *f* скольжения
S341	*e*	slit *see* slot
S342	*e*	slit diaphragm *see* slotted diaphragm
S343	*e*	slope
	d	Neigung *f*; Gefälle *n*; Abfall *m*
	f	pente *f*
	r	наклон *m*; уклон *m*
S344	*e*	slot
	d	Schlitz *m*; Spalt *m*
	f	fente *f*
	r	щель *f*
S345	*e*	slot aerial, slot antenna
	d	Schlitzantenne *f*
	f	antenne *f* à fente
	r	щелевая антенна *f*
S346	*e*	slotted diaphragm
	d	Schlitzblende *f*, Spaltblende *f*
	f	diaphragme *m* à fente
	r	щелевая диафрагма *f*
S347	*e*	slotted line, slotted section
	d	geschlitzte Meßleitung *f*
	f	ligne *f* à fente
	r	измерительная линия *f*; волноводная измерительная линия *f*
S348	*e*	slowing-down *see* deceleration
S349	*e*	slowing structure *see* slow wave structure
S350	*e*	slow neutrons
	d	langsame Neutronen *n pl*
	f	neutrons *m pl* lents
	r	медленные нейтроны *m pl*
S351	*e*	slow-wave structure
	d	Verzögerungssystem *n*
	f	structure *f* décélératrice
	r	замедляющая структура *f*, замедляющая система *f*
S352	*e*	sluggishness
	d	Trägheit *f*
	f	inertie *f*
	r	инерционность *f*, инертность *f*
S353	*e*	small-amplitude oscillation
	d	Schwingungen *f pl* geringer Amplitude
	f	oscillations *f pl* à petite amplitude
	r	колебания *n pl* малой амплитуды
S354	*e*	small-angle scattering
	d	Kleinwinkelstreuung *f*
	f	diffusion *f* à petits angles
	r	малоугловое рассеяние *n*
S355	*e*	small-scale irregularity
	d	kleinmaßstäbliche Inhomogenität *f*
	f	irrégularité *f* en échelle réduite, irrégularité *f* en échelle microscopique
	r	мелкомасштабная неоднородность *f*
S356	*e*	S-matrix *see* scattering matrix
S357	*e*	smectic liquid crystal
	d	smektischer Flüssigkristall *m*
	f	cristal *m* liquide smectique
	r	смектический жидкий кристалл *m*
S358	*e*	smooth curve
	d	glatte Kurve *f*
	f	courbe *f* lisse
	r	гладкая кривая *f*
S359	*e*	Snell law
	d	Snelliussches Brechungsgesetz *n*, Gesetz *n* von Snellius
	f	relation *f* de Descartes-Snell (*de réfraction*)
	r	закон *m* Снеллиуса (*преломления света*)
S360	*e*	sodium, Na
	d	Natrium *n*
	f	sodium *m*
	r	натрий *m*
S361	*e*	soft component
	d	weiche Komponente *f*
	f	composante *f* molle
	r	мягкая компонента *f*
S362	*e*	soft excitation
	d	weiche Erregung *f*
	f	excitation *f* molle
	r	мягкое возбуждение *n*
S363	*e*	soft magnetic material
	d	weichmagnetischer Werkstoff *m*
	f	matériau *m* magnétiquement doux
	r	магнитно-мягкий материал *m*, мягкий магнитный материал *m*
S364	*e*	soft radiation
	d	weiche Strahlung *f*
	f	rayonnement *m* mou, radiation *f* molle
	r	мягкое излучение *n*
S365	*e*	soft X-rays
	d	weiche Röntgenstrahlung *f*
	f	rayons *pl* X mous
	r	мягкое рентгеновское излучение *n*
S366	*e*	sol
	d	Sol *n*
	f	sol *m*
	r	золь *m*
S367	*e*	solar activity
	d	Sonnenaktivität *f*, Sonnentätigkeit *f*
	f	activité *f* solaire
	r	солнечная активность *f*
S368	*e*	solar activity index

d Sonnenaktivitätsindex *m*
f indice *m* d'activité solaire
r индекс *m* солнечной активности

S369 e solar atmosphere
d Sonnenatmosphäre *f*
f atmosphère *f* solaire
r солнечная атмосфера *f*, атмосфера *f* Солнца

S370 e solar battery
d Sonnenbatterie *f*
f batterie *f* solaire
r солнечная батарея *f*

S371 e solar chromosphere
d Sonnenchromosphäre *f*
f chromosphère *f* solaire
r солнечная хромосфера *f*, хромосфера *f* Солнца

S372 e solar concentrator
d Sonnenstrahlungskonzentrator *m*
f concentrateur *m* des rayons solaires
r концентратор *m* солнечного излучения

S373 e solar constant
d Solarkonstante *f*
f constante *f* solaire
r солнечная постоянная *f*

S374 e solar corona
d Sonnenkorona *f*
f couronne *f* solaire
r солнечная корона *f*

S375 e solar cosmic rays
d solare kosmische Strahlung *f*
f rayons *pl* cosmiques du Soleil
r солнечные космические лучи *pl*

S376 e solar cycle
d Zyklus *m* der Sonnenaktivität
f cycle *m* solaire
r солнечный цикл *m*

S377 e solar data
d Sonnendaten *pl*
f données *pl* solaires
r солнечные данные *pl*

S378 e solar day
d Sonnentag *m*
f jour *m* solaire
r солнечные сутки *pl*

S379 e solar eclipse
d Sonnenfinsternis *f*
f éclipse *f* solaire, éclipse *f* du Soleil
r солнечное затмение *n*

S380 e solar eclipse isochrone
d Sonnenfinsternisisochrone *f*
f icochrone *f* d'éclipses solaires
r изохрона *f* солнечных затмений

S381 e solar energy
d Sonnenenergie *f*
f énergie *f* solaire
r солнечная энергия *f*

S382 e solar escape velocity
d dritte kosmische Geschwindigkeit *f*
f vitesse *f* de libération solaire
r третья космическая скорость *f*

S383 e solar flare
d Sonneneruption *f*
f éruption *f* solaire
r солнечная вспышка *f*

S384 e solar flare model
d Sonneneruptionsmodell *n*
f modèle *m* d'éruption solaire
r модель *f* солнечной вспышки

S385 e solar flux
d Sonnenstrahlungsfluß *m*
f flux *m* de rayonnement solaire
r поток *m* солнечного излучения

S386 e solar gamma rays
d solare Gammastrahlung *f*
f rayonnement *m* gamma du Soleil
r солнечное гамма-излучение *n*

S387 e solar granulation
d Sonnengranulation *f*
f granulation *f* solaire
r солнечная грануляция *f*

S388 e solar magnetic field
d Sonnenmagnetfeld *n*
f champ *m* magnétique du Soleil
r солнечное магнитное поле *n*, магнитное поле *n* Солнца

S389 e solar magnetograph
d Sonnenmagnetograph *m*
f magnétographe *m* solaire
r солнечный магнитограф *m*

S390 e solar maximum
d Sonnenaktivitätsmaximum *n*
f maximum *m* solaire, maximum *m* d'activité solaire
r максимум *m* солнечной активности

S391 e solar minimum
d Sonnenaktivitätsminimum *n*
f minimum *m* solaire, minimum *m* d'activité solaire
r минимум *m* солнечной активности

S392 e solar neutrino
d solares Neutrino *n*
f neutrino *m* solaire
r солнечное нейтрино *n*

S393 e solar photosphere
d Sonnenphotosphäre *f*

	f	photosphère *f* solaire
	r	солнечная фотосфера *f*

S394 *e* **solar physics**
d Sonnenphysik *f*
f physique *f* du Soleil
r физика *f* Солнца

S395 *e* **solar plasma**
d Sonnenplasma *n*
f plasma *m* solaire
r солнечная плазма *f*

S396 *e* **solar prominence**
d Sonnenprotuberanz *f*
f protubérance *f* solaire
r солнечный протуберанец *m*

S397 *e* **solar pumping**
d Solarpumpen *n*
f pompage *m* solaire
r накачка *f* солнечным излучением, солнечная накачка *f*

S398 *e* **solar radiation**
d Sonnenstrahlung *f*
f rayonnement *m* solaire, radiation *f* solaire
r солнечное излучение *n*

S399 *e* **solar radio emission, solar radio noise**
d solare Radiostrahlung *f*
f rayonnement *m* radio du Soleil
r радиоизлучение *n* Солнца

S400 *e* **solar spectrum**
d Sonnenspektrum *n*
f spectre *m* solaire
r солнечный спектр *m*

S401 *e* **solar system**
d Sonnensystem *n*
f système *m* solaire
r солнечная система *f*

S402 *e* **solar-terrestrial physics**
d Sonnen-Erden-Physik *f*, solar-terrestrische Physik *f*
f physique *f* solaire-terrestre
r солнечно-земная физика *f*

S403 *e* **solar wind**
d Sonnenwind *m*
f vent *m* solaire
r солнечный ветер *m*

S404 *e* **solar wind pressure**
d Sonnenwinddruck *m*
f pression *f* du vent solaire
r давление *n* солнечного ветра

S405 *e* **solar X-rays**
d Sonnenröntgenstrahlung *f*
f rayons *pl* X du Soleil
r солнечное рентгеновское излучение *n*

S406 *e* **solenoid**
d Solenoid *n*, Solenoidspule *f*
f solénoïde *m*
r соленоид *m*

S407 *e* **solenoidal field**
d solenoidales Feld *n*
f champ *m* solénoïdal
r соленоидальное поле *n*

S408 *e* **sol gel method**
d Sol-Gel-Verfahren *n*
f méthode *f* sol-gel
r золь-гель-метод *m* (*нанесения пленки*)

S409 *e* **solid**
d Festkörper *m*, fester Körper *m*
f corps *m* solide, solide *m*
r твёрдое тело *n*

S410 *e* **solid angle**
d Raumwinkel *m*, räumlicher Winkel *m*
f angle *m* solide
r телесный угол *m*

S411 *e* **solid electrolyte**
d fester Elektrolyt *m*, Festelektrolyt *m*
f électrolyte *m* solide
r твёрдый электролит *m*

S412 *e* **solid helium**
d festes Helium *n*
f hélium *m* solide
r твёрдый гелий *m*

S413 *e* **solidification**
d Erstarrung *f*
f solidification *f*
r затвердевание *n*

S414 *e* **solid solution**
d feste Lösung *f*, Festlösung *f*
f solution *f* solide
r твёрдый раствор *m*

S415 *e* **solid-state laser**
d Festkörperlaser *m*
f laser *m* solide
r твердотельный лазер *m*

S416 *e* **solid-state microelectronics**
d Festkörpermikroelektronik *f*
f microélectronique *f* des corps solides
r твердотельная микроэлектроника *f*

S417 *e* **solid-state physics**
d Festkörperphysik *f*
f physique *f* du corps solide
r физика *f* твёрдого тела

S418 *e* **solid-state plasma**
d Festkörperplasma *n*
f plasma *m* d'état solide
r твердотельная плазма *f*, плазма *f* твёрдого тела

S419　*e*　solid substance
　　　d　Feststoff *m*
　　　f　solide *m*, substance *f* solide, matière *f* solide
　　　r　твёрдое вещество *n*

S420　*e*　solidus, solidus line
　　　d　Soliduslinie *f*, Soliduskurve *f*
　　　f　solidus *m*
　　　r　солидус *m*

S421　*e*　solidus surface
　　　d　Solidusfläche *f*
　　　f　surface *f* de solidus
　　　r　поверхность *f* солидуса

S422　*e*　soliton
　　　d　Soliton *n*
　　　f　soliton *m*
　　　r　солитон *m*; уединённая волна *f*

S423　*e*　soliton laser
　　　d　Solitonlaser *m*
　　　f　laser *m* à soliton
　　　r　солитонный лазер *m*

S424　*e*　solubility
　　　d　Lösbarkeit *f*
　　　f　solubilité *f*
　　　r　растворимость *f*

S425　*e*　solute
　　　d　Gelöstes *n*, aufgelöster Stoff *m*
　　　f　soluté *m*
　　　r　растворённое вещество *n*

S426　*e*　solution
　　　d　Lösung *f*
　　　f　solution *f*
　　　r　1. раствор *m*; растворение *n* 2. решение *n*

S427　*e*　solution concentration
　　　d　Lösungskonzentration *f*, Lösungsstärke *f*
　　　f　concentration *f* de la solution
　　　r　концентрация *f* раствора

S428　*e*　solvatation
　　　d　Solvatation *f*, Solvatisierung *f*
　　　f　solvatation *f*
　　　r　сольватация *f*

S429　*e*　solvent
　　　d　Lösungsmittel *n*
　　　f　solvant *m*
　　　r　растворитель *m*

S430　*e*　Sommerfeld theory of metals
　　　d　Sommerfeldsche Theorie *f*
　　　f　théorie *f* de Sommerfeld
　　　r　теория *f* металлов Зоммерфельда

S431　*e*　sonar
　　　d　Sonar *n*
　　　f　sonage *m* sous-marin; sonar *m*
　　　r　гидролокация *f*; гидролокатор *m*

S432　*e*　sonde
　　　d　Sonde *f*
　　　f　sonde *f*
　　　r　зонд *m*

S433　*e*　sonic barrier
　　　d　Schallmauer *f*
　　　f　barrière *f* du son, mur *m* du son, mur *m* sonique
　　　r　звуковой барьер *m*

S434　*e*　sonic waves *see* acoustic waves

S435　*e*　sonoluminescence
　　　d　Sonolumineszenz *f*
　　　f　sonoluminescence *f*
　　　r　звуколюминесценция *f*

S436　*e*　sorption
　　　d　Sorption *f*
　　　f　sorption *f*
　　　r　сорбция *f*

S437　*e*　sorting chamber
　　　d　Sortierkammer *f*
　　　f　chambre *f* de triage
　　　r　сортирующая камера *f* (*масс-спектрометра*)

S438　*e*　sound
　　　d　1. Schall *m*; Ton *m*; Klang *m* 2. Sonde *f*
　　　f　1. son *m* 2. sonde *f*
　　　r　1. звук *m* 2. зонд *m*

S439　*e*　sound absorber *see* acoustic absorber

S440　*e*　sound-absorbing material
　　　d　Schallschluckstoff *m*, Schallabsorptionsstoff *m*
　　　f　absorbant *m* du son, absorbant *m* acoustique
　　　r　звукопоглощающий материал *m*

S441　*e*　sound absorption
　　　d　Schallabsorption *f*, Schallschluckung *f*
　　　f　absorption *f* du son
　　　r　поглощение *n* звука

S442　*e*　sound analysis
　　　d　Schallanalyse *f*, Klanganalyse *f*; Tonanalyse *f*
　　　f　analyse *f* des sons
　　　r　анализ *m* звука

S443　*e*　sound attenuation
　　　d　Schalldämpfung *f*
　　　f　affaiblissement *m* sonore
　　　r　затухание *n* звука

S444　*e*　sound barrier *see* sonic barrier

S445　*e*　sound diffraction
　　　d　Schalldiffraktion *f*
　　　f　diffraction *f* du son
　　　r　дифракция *f* звука

S446   e   sound energy
     d   Schallenergie f
     f   énergie f sonore
     r   звуковая энергия f

S447   e   sound energy density
     d   Schallenergiedichte f
     f   densité f d'énergie sonore
     r   плотность f звуковой энергии

S448   e   sound energy flux
     d   Schallenergiefluß m
     f   flux m d'énergie sonore
     r   поток m звуковой энергии

S449   e   sound energy flux density see sound intensity

S450   e   sound field
     d   Schallfeld n
     f   champ m acoustique, champ m sonore
     r   звуковое поле n, акустическое поле n

S451   e   sound field visualization
     d   Sichtbarmachung f der Schallfelder
     f   visualisation f des champs acoustiques
     r   визуализация f звуковых полей

S452   e   sound focusing
     d   Schallfokussierung f, Schallbündelung f, Schallkonzentration f
     f   focalisation f du son, concentration f du son
     r   фокусировка f звука

S453   e   sounding
     d   Sondierung f
     f   sondage m
     r   зондирование n

S454   e   sounding pulse
     d   Abtastimpuls m, Sondenimpuls m
     f   impulsion f de sondage
     r   зондирующий импульс m

S455   e   sound-insulating material
     d   Schalldämmstoff m
     f   isolant m acoustique
     r   звукоизоляционный материал m

S456   e   sound insulation
     d   Schalldämmung f, Schallisolierung f
     f   insonorisation f
     r   звуковая изоляция f, звукоизоляция f

S457   e   sound intensity
     d   Schallintensität f, Schallstärke f
     f   intensité f du son
     r   интенсивность f звука, сила f звука

S458   e   sound interference see acoustical interference

S459   e   sound lens see acoustic lens
S460   e   sound level meter

     d   Schallpegelmesser m, Lautstärkemesser m
     f   sonomètre m
     r   шумомер m

S461   e   sound oscillation see sound vibration

S462   e   sound power see acoustic power

S463   e   sound pressure
     d   Schalldruck m
     f   pression f sonore, pression f acoustique
     r   звуковое давление n

S464   e   sound proofing see sound insulation

S465   e   sound propagation
     d   Schallausbreitung f
     f   propagation f du son
     r   распространение n звука

S466   e   sound pulse
     d   Schallimpuls m
     f   impulsion f sonore
     r   звуковой импульс m, акустический импульс m

S467   e   sound radiation
     d   Schallstrahlung f
     f   rayonnement m acoustique
     r   излучение n звука

S468   e   sound rangefinder, sound ranger
     d   akustischer Entfernungsmesser m
     f   télémètre m acoustique
     r   акустический дальномер m

S469   e   sound ranging
     d   Schallortung f, Schallradar n, akustische Ortung f
     f   localisation f sonore
     r   звуколокация f

S470   e   sound reflection
     d   Schallreflexion f
     f   réflexion f acoustique
     r   отражение n звука

S471   e   sound scattering
     d   Schallstreuung f
     f   diffusion f acoustique
     r   рассеяние n звука

S472   e   sound source
     d   Schallquelle f
     f   source f sonore
     r   источник m звука

S473   e   sound spectrum
     d   Schallspektrum n
     f   spectre m sonore, spectre m acoustique
     r   спектр m звука

S474   e   sound velocity dispersion

    d Schallgeschwindigkeitsdispersion *f*
    f dispersion *f* de la vitesse du son
    r дисперсия *f* скорости звука

S475 *e* **sound vibration, sound vibrations**
    d Schallschwingungen *f pl*, akustische
       Schwingungen *f pl*
    f oscillations *f pl* acoustiques, vibrations
       f pl acoustiques
    r звуковые колебания *n pl*,
       акустические колебания *n pl*

S476 *e* **sound waves** *see* **acoustic waves**

S477 *e* **source**
    d **1.** Quelle *f* **2.** Sourceelektrode *f*,
       Quellenelektrode *f*
    f source *f*
    r **1.** источник *m* **2.** исток *m (полевого*
       транзистора)

S478 *e* **source activity**
    d Quellenaktivität *f*
    f activité *f* de la source
    r активность *f* источника

S479 *e* **source power**
    d Quellenleistung *f*
    f puissance *f* de la source
    r мощность *f* источника

S480 *e* **source strength**
    d Quellenstärke *f*
    f intensité *f* de la source
    r интенсивность *f* источника

S481 *e* **space**
    d **1.** Raum *m* **2.** Weltraum *m*,
       kosmischer Raum *m*
    f espace *m*
    r **1.** пространство *n* **2.** космос *m*

S482 *e* **space charge**
    d Raumladung *f*
    f charge *f* d'espace, charge *f* spatiale
    r пространственный заряд *m*;
       объёмный заряд *m*

S483 *e* **space-charge cloud**
    d Raumladungswolke *f*
    f nuage *m* de charge d'espace
    r облако *n* пространственного заряда

S484 *e* **space-charge compensation**
    d Raumladungskompensation *f*
    f compensation *f* de la charge d'espace
    r компенсация *f* пространственного
       заряда

S485 *e* **space-charge density**
    d Raumladungsdichte *f*
    f densité *f* de la charge d'espace
    r плотность *f* пространственного
       заряда

S486 *e* **space charge neutralization**
    d Raumladungsneutralisation *f*

    f neutralisation *f* de la charge d'espace
    r нейтрализация *f* пространственного
       заряда

S487 *e* **space-charge region**
    d Raumladungsgebiet *n*,
       Raumladungszone *f*
    f zone *f* de charge d'espace
    r область *f* пространственного заряда

S488 *e* **space coherence**
    d Raumkohärenz *f*
    f cohérence *f* spatiale
    r пространственная когерентность *f*

S489 *e* **space craft** *see* **space vehicle**

S490 *e* **space curvature**
    d Raumkrümmung *f*
    f courbure *f* de l'espace
    r искривлённость *f* пространства,
       кривизна *f* пространства

S491 *e* **space data**
    d kosmische Daten *pl*
    f données *pl* spatiales
    r космические данные *pl*

S492 *e* **space flight**
    d Raumflug *m*
    f vol *m* spatial
    r космический полёт *m*

S493 *e* **space groups**
    d Raumgruppen *f pl*,
       Raumsymmetriegruppen *f pl*
    f groupes *m pl* spatiaux *(en symétrie*
       cristalline)
    r пространственные группы *f pl*
       (симметрии кристаллов)

S494 *e* **space harmonic**
    d räumliche Harmonische *f*,
       Raumharmonische *f*
    f harmonique *m* spatial
    r пространственная гармоника *f*

S495 *e* **space inversion**
    d räumliche Inversion *f*, Rauminversion
       f, Raumspiegelung *f*
    f inversion *f* d'espace
    r пространственная инверсия *f*

S496 *e* **space lattice**
    d Raumgitter *n*, dreidimensionales
       Gitter *n*
    f réseau *m* spatial
    r пространственная решётка *f*

S497 *e* **space-like interval**
    d raumartiges Intervall *n*
    f intervalle *m* du genre espace
    r пространственноподобный
       интервал *m*

S498 *e* **space-like vector**
    d raumartiger Vektor *m*

    f vecteur *m* du genre espace
    r пространственноподобный вектор *m*

S499 *e* space navigation
    d Raumnavigation *f*,
       Weltraumnavigation *f*
    f navigation *f* spatiale, navigation *f* dans
       l'espace
    r космическая навигация *f*

S500 *e* space quantization
    d räumliche Quantelung *f*,
       Raumquantelung *f*, räumliche
       Quantisierung *f*, Raumquantisierung *f*
    f quantification *f* spatiale
    r пространственное квантование *n*

S501 *e* space research
    d Weltraumforschung *f*,
       Raumforschung *f*
    f recherches *f pl* cosmiques, exploration
       f cosmique, exploration *f* d'espace
    r космические исследования *n pl*

S502 *e* space-time
    d Raumzeit *f*, Raum-Zeit *f*
    f espace-temps *m*
    r пространство-время *n*

S503 *e* space-time correlation
    d zeitlich-räumliche Korrelation *f*,
       räumlich-zeitliche Korrelation *f*,
       Raum-Zeit-Korrelation *f*
    f corrélation *f* espace-temps
    r пространственно-временна́я
       корреляция *f*

S504 *e* space-time curvature
    d Raumzeitkrümmung *f*
    f courbure *f* espace-temps
    r кривизна *f* пространства-времени

S505 *e* space-time isotropy
    d Raum-Zeit-Isotropie *f*
    f isotropie *f* de l'espace-temps
    r изотропия *f* пространства-времени

S506 *e* space-time light modulator
    d Raum-Zeit-Lichtmodulator *m*
    f modulateur *m* de lumière espace-
       temps
    r пространственно-временной
       модулятор *m* света

S507 *e* space-time metric
    d Raum-Zeit-Metrik *f*
    f métrique *f* de l'espace-temps
    r метрика *f* пространства-времени

S508 *e* space-time quantization
    d Raum-Zeit-Quantelung *f*, Raum-Zeit-
       Quantisierung *f*
    f quantification *f* de l'espace-temps
    r квантование *n* пространства-
       времени

S509 *e* space vehicle
    d Raumflugkörper *m*, Raumfahrzeug *n*
    f astronef *m*, véhicule *m* aérospatial,
       véhicule *m* cosmique
    r космический корабль *m*

S510 *e* spark
    d Funke *m*
    f étincelle *f*
    r искра *f*, искровой разряд *m*

S511 *e* spark chamber
    d Funkenkammer *f*
    f chambre *f* à étincelles
    r искровая камера *f*

S512 *e* spark channel
    d Funkenkanal *m*
    f canal *m* d'étincelle
    r канал *m* искры

S513 *e* spark counter
    d Funkenzähler *m*
    f compteur *m* à étincelles
    r искровой счётчик *m*

S514 *e* spark discharge
    d Funkenladung *f*
    f décharge *f* par étincelles, décharge *f* à
       étincelles
    r искровой разряд *m*

S515 *e* spark gap
    d Funkenstrecke *f*
    f éclateur *m*; distance *f* entre électrodes
    r искровой разрядник *m*; искровой
       промежуток *m*

S516 *e* spark photography
    d Funkenphotographie *f*
    f photographie *f* à étincelles
    r искровая фотография *f*

S517 *e* spark source
    d Funkenquelle *f*
    f source *f* d'étincelles
    r искровой источник *m*

S518 *e* spark spectrum
    d Funkenspektrum *n*
    f spectre *m* d'étincelle
    r искровой спектр *m*

S519 *e* spatial coherence *see* space
       coherence

S520 *e* spatial configuration
    d räumliche Konfiguration *f*
    f configuration *f* spatiale
    r пространственная конфигурация *f*

S521 *e* spatial dispersion
    d räumliche Dispersion *f*
    f dispersion *f* spatiale
    r пространственная дисперсия *f*

S522 *e* spatial filtration

d Raumfiltration *f*
f filtration *f* spatiale
r пространственная фильтрация *f*

S523 e spatial frequency
d Raumfrequenz *f*
f fréquence *f* spatiale
r пространственная частота *f*

S524 e spatial homogeneity
d räumliche Homogenität *f*
f homogénéité *f* spatiale
r пространственная однородность *f*

S525 e spatial inhomogeneity
d räumliche Inhomogenität *f*
f inhomogénéité *f* spatiale
r пространственная неоднородность *f*

S526 e spatial inversion *see* space inversion

S527 e spatial period
d räumliche Periode *f*, Raumperiode *f*
f période *f* spatiale
r пространственный период *m*

S528 e spatial quantization *see* space quantization

S529 e spatial-temporal coherence
d räumlich-zeitliche Kohärenz *f*
f cohérence *f* spatiale dans le temps
r пространственно-временнáя когерентность *f*

S530 e special relativity theory, special theory of relativity
d spezielle Relativitätstheorie *f*
f théorie *f* spéciale de la relativité
r специальная теория *f* относительности

S531 e specific concentration
d spezifische Konzentration *f*
f concentration *f* spécifique
r удельная концентрация *f*

S532 e specific conductivity
d spezifische Leitfähigkeit *f*
f conductibilité *f* spécifique
r удельная электропроводность *f*

S533 e specific gravity
d spezifisches Gewicht *n*
f poids *m* spécifique
r удельный вес *m*

S534 e specific heat, specific heat capacity
d spezifische Wärmekapazität *f*
f capacité *f* thermique spécifique
r удельная теплоёмкость *f*

S535 e specific refraction
d spezifische Refraktion *f*
f réfraction *f* spécifique
r удельная рефракция *f*

S536 e specific resistance
d spezifischer Widerstand *m*
f résistance *f* spécifique
r удельное сопротивление *n*

S537 e specific rotation
d spezifische Drehung *f*
f rotation *f* spécifique
r удельное вращение *n*

S538 e specific volume
d spezifisches Volumen *n*
f volume *m* spécifique
r удельный объём *m*

S539 e specimen
d Probe *f*; Probekörper *m*, Prüfkörper *m*
f échantillon *m*
r образец *m* (*напр. для испытаний*)

S540 e speckle interferometry
d Speckle-Interferometrie *f*
f interférométrie *f* tachetée
r спекл-интерферометрия *f*

S541 e spectator
d Spektator *m*
f spectateur *m*
r частица-наблюдатель *m*, частица-спектатор *m* (*в ядерной физике*)

S542 e spectator nucleon
d Spektator-Nukleon *n*
f nucléon *m* spectateur
r нуклон-спектатор *m*, нуклон-наблюдатель *m*

S543 e spectator quark
d Spektator-Quark *n*
f quark *m* spectateur
r кварк-спектатор *m*, спектаторный кварк *m*

S544 e spectral analysis
d Spektralanalyse *f*
f analyse *f* spectrale
r спектральный анализ *m*

S545 e spectral band
d Spektralbande *f*
f bande *f* spectrale
r спектральная полоса *f*

S546 e spectral classes of stars
d Spektralklassen *f pl* der Sterne, Spektraltypen *m pl*
f classes *f pl* spectrales des étoiles
r спектральные классы *m pl* звёзд

S547 e spectral classification
d Spektralklassifikation *f*
f classification *f* spectrale
r спектральная классификация *f*

S548 e spectral correlator
d Spektralkorrelator *m*

　　　f corrélateur *m* spectral
　　　r спектральный коррелятор *m*

S549　*e* spectral density
　　　d Spektraldichte *f*
　　　f densité *f* spectrale
　　　r спектральная плотность *f*
　　　　 (излучения)

S550　*e* spectral distribution
　　　d spektrale Verteilung *f*,
　　　　 Spektralverteilung *f*
　　　f répartition *f* spectrale
　　　r спектральное распределение *n*

S551　*e* spectral doublet
　　　d Spektraldublett *n*
　　　f doublet *m* spectral
　　　r спектральный дублет *m*

S552　*e* spectral ghosts
　　　d Spektralgeister *n pl*
　　　f fantômes *m pl* spectraux, ghosts *m pl*
　　　r спектральные духи *m pl*

S553　*e* spectral index
　　　d Spektralindex *m*
　　　f indice *m* de spectre
　　　r спектральный индекс *m*

S554　*e* spectral intensity
　　　d spektrale Intensität *f*,
　　　　 Spektralintensität *f*
　　　f intensité *f* spectrale
　　　r спектральная интенсивность *f*

S555　*e* spectral line
　　　d Spektrallinie *f*
　　　f raie *f* spectrale
　　　r спектральная линия *f*

S556　*e* spectral line intensity
　　　d Spektrallinienintensität *f*, Intensität *f*
　　　　 der Spektrallinie
　　　f intensité *f* d'une raie spectrale
　　　r интенсивность *f* спектральной
　　　　 линии

S557　*e* spectral line profile
　　　d Spektrallinienprofil, Spektrallinienform
　　　　 f, Spektrallinienkontur *f*
　　　f profil *m* de la raie spectrale
　　　r контур *m* спектральной линии

S558　*e* spectral line Q, spectral line Q-
　　　　 factor
　　　d Spektralliniengüte *f*
　　　f coefficient *m* de qualité de la raie
　　　　 spectrale
　　　r добротность *f* спектральной линии

S559　*e* spectrally limited pulse
　　　d spektralbegrenzter Impuls *m*
　　　f impulsion *f* spectroscopiquement
　　　　 limitée
　　　r спектрально-ограниченный
　　　　 импульс *m*

S560　*e* spectral measurements
　　　d Spektralmessungen *f pl*
　　　f mesures *f pl* spectrales
　　　r спектральные измерения *n pl*

S561　*e* spectral pyrometer *see* optical
　　　　 pyrometer

S562　*e* spectral quartet
　　　d Spektralquartett *n*
　　　f quartet *m* spectral
　　　r спектральный квартет *m*

S563　*e* spectral quintet
　　　d Spektralquintett *n*
　　　f quintet *m* spectral
　　　r спектральный квинтет *m*

S564　*e* spectral radiation
　　　d Spektralstrahlung *f*
　　　f rayonnement *m* spectral
　　　r спектральное излучение *n*

S565　*e* spectral range
　　　d Spektralbereich *m*
　　　f région *f* spectrale, domaine *m* spectral
　　　r спектральный интервал *m*,
　　　　 спектральный диапазон *m*

S566　*e* spectral region
　　　d Spektralbereich *m*, Spektralgebiet *n*
　　　f partie *f* spectrale, région *f* spectrale
　　　r спектральная область *f*

S567　*e* spectral representation
　　　d spektrale Darstellung *f*
　　　f représentation *f* spectrale
　　　r спектральное представление *n*

S568　*e* spectral sensitivity
　　　d spektrale Empfindlichkeit *f*,
　　　　 Spektralempfindlichkeit *f*
　　　f sensibilité *f* spectrale
　　　r спектральная чувствительность *f*

S569　*e* spectral sensitivity curve
　　　d spektrale Empfindlichkeitskurve *f*
　　　f courbe *f* de sensibilité spectrale
　　　r кривая *f* спектральной
　　　　 чувствительности

S570　*e* spectral series
　　　d Spektralserien *f pl*
　　　f séries *f pl* spectrales
　　　r спектральные серии *f pl*

S571　*e* spectral terms
　　　d Spektralterme *m pl*
　　　f termes *m pl* spectraux
　　　r спектральные термы *m pl*

S572　*e* spectrofluorimeter
　　　d Spektrofluorometer *n*
　　　f spectrofluoromètre *m*
　　　r спектрофлуориметр *m*

S573　*e* spectrogram

	d	Spektrogramm n
	f	spectrogramme m
	r	спектрограмма f

S574   e   **spectrograph**
         d   Spektrograph m
         f   spectrographe m
         r   спектрограф m

S575   e   **spectrograph camera**
         d   Spektrographenkammer f
         f   chambre f du spectrographe
         r   камера f спектрографа

S576   e   **spectroheliograph**
         d   Spektroheliograph m
         f   spectrohéliographe m
         r   спектрогелиограф m

S577   e   **spectrometer**
         d   Spektrometer n
         f   spectromètre m
         r   спектрометр m

S578   e   **spectrometric source**
         d   Spektrometerquelle f
         f   source f spectrométrique
         r   спектрометрический источник m

S579   e   **spectrometry**
         d   Spektrometrie f
         f   spectrométrie f
         r   спектрометрия f

S580   e   **spectrophotometer**
         d   Spektralphotometer n
         f   spectrophotomètre m
         r   спектрофотометр m

S581   e   **spectrophotometer curve**
         d   Spektrophotometerkurve f
         f   courbe f spectrophotométrique
         r   спектрофотометрическая кривая f

S582   e   **spectrophotometric analysis**
         d   spektralphotometrische Analyse f
         f   analyse f spectrophotométrique
         r   спектрофотометрический анализ m

S583   e   **spectrophotometry**
         d   Spektralphotometrie f
         f   spectrophotométrie f
         r   спектрофотометрия f

S584   e   **spectropolarimeter**
         d   Spektropolarimeter n
         f   spectropolarimètre m
         r   спектрополяриметр m

S585   e   **spectroradiometer**
         d   Spektroradiometer n
         f   spectroradiomètre m
         r   спектрорадиометр m

S586   e   **spectroscope**
         d   Spektroskop n
         f   spectroscope m
         r   спектроскоп m

S587   e   **spectroscopic analysis** *see* **spectral analysis**

S588   e   **spectroscopic diagnostics**
         d   spektroskopische Diagnostik f, Spektraldiagnostik f
         f   diagnostic m spectroscopique
         r   спектроскопическая диагностика f

S589   e   **spectroscopic parallax**
         d   spektroskopische Parallaxe f
         f   parallaxe f spectroscopique
         r   спектральный параллакс m, спектроскопический параллакс m

S590   e   **spectroscopic prism**
         d   Spektralprisma n
         f   prisme m spectroscopique
         r   спектральная призма f

S591   e   **spectroscopic studies**
         d   Spektralforschungen f pl, spektroskopische Forschungen f pl
         f   études f pl spectroscopiques
         r   спектроскопические исследования n pl

S592   e   **spectroscopy**
         d   Spektroskopie f
         f   spectroscopie f
         r   спектроскопия f

S593   e   **spectrum**
         d   Spektrum n
         f   spectre m
         r   спектр m

S594   e   **spectrum analysis** *see* **spectral analysis**

S595   e   **spectrum analyzer**
         d   Spektralanalysator m
         f   analyseur m des spectres
         r   анализатор m спектра, спектроанализатор m

S596   e   **spectrum line** *see* **spectral line**

S597   e   **spectrum-luminosity diagram** *see* **Hertzsprung-Russel diagram**

S598   e   **specular reflection**
         d   spiegelnde Reflexion f, Spiegelung f, regelmäßige Reflexion f
         f   réflexion f régulière
         r   зеркальное отражение n

S599   e   **speech analyzer**
         d   Sprachanalysator m
         f   analyseur m de voix
         r   анализатор m речи

S600   e   **speed**
         d   Geschwindigkeit f

	f	vitesse *f*
	r	скорость *f*
S601	*e*	**sphere**
	d	Kugel *f*; Sphäre *f*
	f	sphère *f*
	r	сфера *f*; шар *m*
S602	*e*	**spherical aberration**
	d	sphärische Aberration *f*
	f	aberration *f* sphérique
	r	сферическая аберрация *f*
S603	*e*	**spherical coordinates**
	d	Kugelkoordinaten *f pl*, sphärische Koordinaten *f pl*
	f	coordonnées *f pl* sphériques
	r	сферические координаты *f pl*
S604	*e*	**spherical function**
	d	Kugelfunktion *f*
	f	fonction *f* sphérique
	r	сферическая функция *f*
S605	*e*	**spherical harmonic**
	d	Kugelharmonische *f*, sphärische Harmonische *f*
	f	harmonique *m* sphérique
	r	сферическая гармоника *f*
S606	*e*	**spherically symmetric field**
	d	kugelsymmetrisches Feld *n*
	f	champ *m* sphérosymétrique
	r	сферически-симметричное поле *n*
S607	*e*	**spherically symmetric radiation**
	d	sphärosymmetrische Strahlung *f*
	f	rayonnement *m* sphérosymétrique
	r	сферически симметричное излучение *n*
S608	*e*	**spherical mirror**
	d	sphärischer Spiegel *m*, Kugelspiegel *m*
	f	miroir *m* sphérique
	r	сферическое зеркало *n*
S609	*e*	**spherical pendulum**
	d	sphärisches Pendel *n*, Kugelpendel *n*
	f	pendule *m* sphérique
	r	сферический маятник *m*
S610	*e*	**spherical spinor**
	d	Kugelspinor *m*
	f	spineur *m* sphérique
	r	шаровой спинор *m*
S611	*e*	**spherical target**
	d	sphärisches Target *n*
	f	cible *f* sphérique
	r	сферическая мишень *f*
S612	*e*	**spherical wave**
	d	Kugelwelle *f*
	f	onde *f* sphérique
	r	сферическая волна *f*
S613	*e*	**spheroid**

	d	Sphäroid *n*
	f	sphéroïde *m*
	r	сфероид *m*
S614	*e*	**spherometer**
	d	Sphärometer *n*
	f	sphéromètre *m*
	r	сферометр *m*
S615	*e*	**spherulite**
	d	Sphärolith *m*
	f	sphérolite *m*
	r	сферолит *m*
S616	*e*	**spicules**
	d	Spicula *n pl*, Spikulen *f pl*
	f	spicules *f pl*
	r	спикулы *f pl*
S617	*e*	**spike**
	d	Zacken *m*; Spitze *f*; kurzzeitiger Ausschlag *m*
	f	pointe *f*; spike *m*
	r	узкий импульс *m*; выброс *m*; пичок *m (в лазере)*
S618	*e*	**spike cathode**
	d	Haarnadelkatode *f*, Nadelkatode *f*
	f	cathode *f* de spike
	r	игольчатый катод *m*
S619	*e*	**spin**
	d	Spin *m*
	f	spin *m*
	r	спин *m*
S620	*e*	**spin correlation**
	d	Spinkorrelation *f*
	f	corrélation *f* de spin
	r	спиновая корреляция *f*
S621	*e*	**spin diffusion**
	d	Spindiffusion *f*
	f	diffusion *f* de spin
	r	спиновая диффузия *f*
S622	*e*	**spin dynamics**
	d	Spindynamik *f*
	f	dynamique *f* de spin
	r	спиновая динамика *f*
S623	*e*	**spin echo**
	d	Spinecho *n*
	f	écho *m* de spin, spin-écho *m*
	r	спиновое эхо *n*
S624	*e*	**spinel**
	d	Spinell *m*
	f	spinelle *f*
	r	шпинель *m*
S625	*e*	**spin flip**
	d	Umklappen *n* des Spins, Spinumkehr *f*, Spinumkehrung *f*
	f	retournement *m* du spin, basculement *m* du spin
	r	переворот *m* спина

S626　*e*　**spin-flip transition**
　　　d　Spinumkehrübergang *m*
　　　f　transition *f* avec retournement de spin
　　　r　переход *m* с переворотом спина

S627　*e*　**spin flop, spin flop-over**
　　　d　Umorientierung *f* des Spins
　　　f　réorientation *f* du spin
　　　r　переориентация *f* спина

S628　*e*　**spin glasses**
　　　d　Spingläser *n pl*
　　　f　verres *m pl* de spin
　　　r　спиновые стёкла *n pl*

S629　*e*　**spin-lattice interaction**
　　　d　Spin-Gitter-Wechselwirkung *f*
　　　f　interaction *f* spin-réseau
　　　r　спин-решёточное взаимодействие *n*

S630　*e*　**spin-lattice relaxation**
　　　d　Spin-Gitter-Relaxation *f*
　　　f　relaxation *f* spin-réseau
　　　r　спин-решёточная релаксация *f*

S631　*e*　**spinless particle**
　　　d　spinloses Teilchen *n*, Spin-0-Teilchen *n*, Teilchen *n* mit dem Spin 0
　　　f　particule *f* de spin zéro, particule *f* de spin 0, particule *f* sans spin
　　　r　бесспиновая частица *f*

S632　*e*　**spin magnetism**
　　　d　Spinmagnetismus *m*
　　　f　magnétisme *m* de spin
　　　r　спиновый магнетизм *m*

S633　*e*　**spin matrix**
　　　d　Spinmatrix *f*, Paulische Spinmatrix *f*
　　　f　matrice *f* de spin, matrice *f* de spin de Pauli
　　　r　спиновая матрица *f*

S634　*e*　**spin moment**
　　　d　Spinmoment *n*
　　　f　moment *m* de spin
　　　r　спиновый момент *m*

S635　*e*　**spinor**
　　　d　Spinor *m*
　　　f　spineur *m*
　　　r　спинор *m*

S636　*e*　**spin orbital**
　　　d　Spinorbital *n*, Spinwellenfunktion *f*
　　　f　orbitale *f* avec spin, fonction *f* d'onde de spin
　　　r　спин-орбиталь *f*, спиновая волновая функция *f*

S637　*e*　**spin-orbit coupling** *see* **spin-orbit interaction**

S638　*e*　**spin-orbit coupling constant**
　　　d　Konstante *f* der Spin-Bahn-Kopplung, Spin-Bahn-Kopplungskonstante *f*
　　　f　constante *f* de couplage spin-orbite
　　　r　константа *f* спин-орбитальной связи

S639　*e*　**spin-orbit interaction**
　　　d　Spin-Bahn-Wechselwirkung *f*
　　　f　interaction *f* spin-orbite
　　　r　спин-орбитальное взаимодействие *n*

S640　*e*　**spinor electrodynamics**
　　　d　Spinor-Elektrodynamik *f*
　　　f　électrodynamique *f* de spin
　　　r　спинорная электродинамика *f*

S641　*e*　**spinor field**
　　　d　Spinorfeld *n*
　　　f　champ *m* spinoriel
　　　r　спинорное поле *n*

S642　*e*　**spinor particle**
　　　d　Spinorteilchen *n*
　　　f　particule *f* spinorielle
　　　r　спинорная частица *f*

S643　*e*　**spin-phonon coupling** *see* **spin-phonon interaction**

S644　*e*　**spin-phonon interaction**
　　　d　Spin-Phonon-Wechselwirkung *f*
　　　f　interaction *f* spin-phonon
　　　r　спин-фононное взаимодействие *n*

S645　*e*　**spin polarization**
　　　d　Spinpolarisation *f*
　　　f　polarisation *f* de spin
　　　r　спиновая поляризация *f*

S646　*e*　**spin quantization**
　　　d　Spinquantisierung *f*
　　　f　quantification *f* des spins
　　　r　квантование *n* спинов

S647　*e*　**spin quantum number**
　　　d　Spinquantenzahl *f*
　　　f　nombre *m* quantique de spin
　　　r　спиновое квантовое число *n*

S648　*e*　**spin resonance**
　　　d　Spinresonanz *f*
　　　f　résonance *f* de spin
　　　r　спиновый резонанс *m*

S649　*e*　**spin-spin coupling** *see* **spin-spin interaction**

S650　*e*　**spin-spin interaction**
　　　d　Spin-Spin-Wechselwirkung *f*
　　　f　interaction *f* spin-spin
　　　r　спин-спиновое взаимодействие *n*

S651　*e*　**spin temperature**
　　　d　Spintemperatur *f*
　　　f　température *f* de spin
　　　r　спиновая температура *f*

S652　*e*　**spinthariscope**
　　　d　Spinthariskop *n*

	f	spinthariscope *m*
	r	спинтарископ *m*
S653	*e*	**spin transition**
	d	Spinübergang *m*
	f	transition *f* de spin
	r	спиновый переход *m*
S654	*e*	**spin wave**
	d	Spinwelle *f*
	f	onde *f* de spin
	r	спиновая волна *f*
S655	*e*	**spin-wave delay line**
	d	Spinwellen-Verzögerungsleitung *f*
	f	ligne *f* à retard à ondes de spin
	r	линия *f* задержки на спиновых волнах
S656	*e*	**spin wave function** *see* **spin orbital**
S657	*e*	**spiral**
	d	Spirale *f*
	f	spirale *f*
	r	спираль *f*
S658	*e*	**spiral galaxy**
	d	Spiralgalaxie *f*, Spiralnebel *m*
	f	galaxie *f* spirale
	r	спиральная галактика *f*
S659	*e*	**spiral instability** *see* **screw instability**
S660	*e*	**spirality**
	d	Spiralität *f (Quantenzahl)*
	f	hélicisme *m*
	r	спиральность *f (квантовое число)*
S661	*e*	**split lens**
	d	Spaltlinse *f*
	f	lentille *f* fendue
	r	билинза *f*
S662	*e*	**splitting**
	d	Aufspaltung *f*
	f	subdivision *f*; désintégration *f*; fission *f*; dédoublement *m*
	r	расщепление *n*
S663	*e*	**splitting factor**
	d	Aufspaltungsfaktor *m*
	f	facteur *m* de subdivision
	r	коэффициент *m* расщепления; фактор *m* магнитного расщепления
S664	*e*	**spontaneous boiling**
	d	spontanes Sieden *n*
	f	bouillonnement *m* spontané
	r	спонтанное кипение *n*
S665	*e*	**spontaneous breaking of symmetry**
	d	spontane Symmetriebrechung *f*
	f	brisure *f* de symétrie spontanée
	r	спонтанное нарушение *n* симметрии
S666	*e*	**spontaneous dissociation**
	d	spontane Dissoziation *f*
	f	dissociation *f* spontanée
	r	спонтанная диссоциация *f*
S667	*e*	**spontaneous emission**
	d	spontane Emission *f*, Spontanemission *f*
	f	émission *f* spontanée
	r	спонтанное излучение *n*; самопроизвольное излучение *n*
S668	*e*	**spontaneous fission**
	d	spontane Spaltung *f*, Spontanspaltung *f*
	f	fission *f* spontanée
	r	спонтанное деление *n*, самопроизвольное деление *n*
S669	*e*	**spontaneous luminescence**
	d	spontane Lumineszenz *f*, Spontanlumineszenz *f*
	f	luminescence *f* spontanée
	r	спонтанная люминесценция *f*
S670	*e*	**spontaneous magnetization**
	d	spontane Magnetisierung *f*, Spontanmagnetisierung *f*
	f	aimantation *f* spontanée
	r	спонтанная намагниченность *f*, самопроизвольная намагниченность *f*
S671	*e*	**spontaneous polarization**
	d	spontane Polarisation *f*, spontane Polarisierung *f*
	f	polarisation *f* spontanée
	r	спонтанная поляризация *f*
S672	*e*	**spontaneous radiation** *see* **spontaneous emission**
S673	*e*	**spontaneous reconnection**
	d	spontanes Neuverbinden *n*
	f	reconnexion *f* spontanée
	r	спонтанное пересоединение *n* (*магнитных силовых линий*)
S674	*e*	**spontaneous symmetry violation** *see* **spontaneous breaking of symmetry**
S675	*e*	**spontaneous transition**
	d	spontaner Übergang *m*
	f	transition *f* spontanée
	r	спонтанный переход *m*
S676	*e*	**spot**
	d	Fleck *m*
	f	spot *m*
	r	пятно *n*
S677	*e*	**spray discharge**
	d	Sprühentladung *f*
	f	décharge *f* en aigrette
	r	кистевой разряд *m*
S678	*e*	**spraying** *see* **sputtering**

S679   e   spurion
     d   Spurion n (Quasiteilchen)
     f   spurion m (quasi-particule)
     r   шпурион m (квазичастица)

S680   e   spur of a matrix
     d   Matrixspur f
     f   trace f d'une matrice
     r   след m матрицы

S681   e   sputtering
     d   Sputtern n
     f   pulvérisation f ionique; déposition f
        par pulvérisation
     r   напыление n, распыление n

S682   e   square
     d   Quadrat n
     f   carré m
     r   квадрат m

S683   e   square-law detection
     d   quadratische Gleichrichtung f,
        quadratische Demodulation f
     f   détection f quadratique
     r   квадратичное детектирование n

S684   e   square meter, m^2
     d   Quadratmeter n
     f   mètre m carré
     r   квадратный метр m, $м^2$

S685   e   square root
     d   Quadratwurzel f
     f   racine f carrée
     r   квадратный корень m

S686   e   s-quark see strange quark

S687   e   squeezed states
     d   Quetschzustände m pl
     f   états m pl serrés
     r   сжатые состояния n pl (в
        квантовой оптике)

S688   e   squid
     d   Squid n
     f   squid m
     r   сквид m (сверхпроводящий
        квантовый интерференционный
        датчик)

S689   e   SRS radiation
     d   SRS-Strahlung f
     f   rayonnement m SRS
     r   ВКР-излучение n

S690   e   stability
     d   Stabilität f; Beständigkeit f
     f   stabilité f
     r   1. устойчивость f 2. стабильность f

S691   e   stability diagram
     d   Stabilitätsdiagramm n
     f   diagramme m de stabilité
     r   диаграмма f устойчивости

S692   e   stability margin
     d   Stabilitätsreserve f
     f   marge f de stabilité
     r   запас m устойчивости

S693   e   stability of bounding layer
     d   Grenzschichtstabilität f
     f   stabilité f de couche limite
     r   устойчивость f пограничного слоя

S694   e   stability of equilibrium
     d   Gleichgewichtsstabilität f
     f   stabilité f d'équilibre
     r   устойчивость f равновесия

S695   e   stability region
     d   Stabilitätsbereich m, Stabilitätsgebiet n
     f   région f de stabilité
     r   область f устойчивости

S696   e   stabilization
     d   Stabilisierung f, Stabilisation f
     f   stabilisation f
     r   стабилизация f

S697   e   stabilizer
     d   Stabilisator m
     f   stabilisateur m
     r   стабилизатор m

S698   e   stabilizer tube see voltage-reference
        tube

S699   e   stable equilibrium
     d   stabiles Gleichgewicht n
     f   équlilibre m stable
     r   устойчивое равновесие n

S700   e   stable isotope
     d   stabiles Isotop n
     f   isotope m stable
     r   стабильный изотоп m, устойчивый
        изотоп m

S701   e   stable modification
     d   stabile Modifikation f
     f   modification f stable
     r   устойчивая модификация f

S702   e   stable region see stability region

S703   e   stacked optical integration
     d   gestapelte optische Integration f
     f   intégration f à empilement optique
     r   пакетная оптическая интеграция f

S704   e   stacking fault
     d   Stapelfehler m, Stapelfehlordnung f
     f   défaut m d'empilement, faute f
        d'empilement
     r   дефект m упаковки

S705   e   stage
     d   Stufe f
     f   étage m
     r   каскад m, ступснь f

S706
e stagnation point
d Staupunkt m
f point m de stagnation
r точка f застоя

S707
e standard
d 1. Etalon m; Eichmaß n; Normal n 2. Standard m; Norm f
f 1. étalon m 2. standard m
r 1. эталон m 2. стандарт

S708
e standard atmosphere
d Standardatmosphäre f
f atmosphère f standard
r стандартная атмосфера f

S709
e standard colorimetric system
d Normvalenzsystem n, farbmeßtechnisches Normalsystem n
f système m de référence colorimétrique
r стандартная колориметрическая система f

S710
e standard conditions
d Normalbedingungen f pl
f conditions f pl normales
r нормальные условия n pl

S711
e standard deviation
d Standardabweichung f, mittlere quadratische Abweichung f
f écart m quadratique moyen, déviation f standard
r среднеквадратичное отклонение n, стандартное отклонение n

S712
e standard laboratory
d metrologisches Laboratorium n
f laboratoire m de métrologie
r метрологическая лаборатория f

S713
e standard observer
d Normalbeobachter m
f observateur m de référence
r стандартный наблюдатель m

S714
e standard signal generator
d Standardsignalgenerator m, Meßgenerator m, Meßsender m
f générateur m de signaux standard
r генератор m стандартных сигналов, измерительный генератор m

S715
e standard source
d Standardquelle f
f source f étalon
r эталонный источник m, стандартный источник m

S716
e standing wave meter
d Stehwellenmesser m
f détecteur m d'ondes stationnaires
r измеритель m коэффициента стоячей волны, измеритель m КСВ

S717
e standing wave ratio

d Stehwellenverhältnis n
f taux m d'ondes stationnaires, TOS
r коэффициент m стоячей волны, КСВ

S718
e standing waves
d stehende Wellen f pl, Stehwellen f pl
f ondes f pl stationnaires
r стоячие волны f pl

S719
e star
d Stern m
f étoile f
r звезда f

S720
e star association see stellar association

S721
e star catalog, star catalogue
d Sternkatalog m, Sternverzeichnis n
f catalogue m des étoiles
r звёздный каталог m

S722
e star cluster
d Sternhaufen m
f amas m d'étoiles
r звёздное скопление n

S723
e star formation
d Sternentstehung f, Sternbildung f
f formation f des étoiles
r звёздообразование n

S724
e star image
d Sternenbild n
f image f d'étoile
r изображение n звезды

S725
e Stark broadening
d Stark-Verbreiterung f, Stark-Effekt-Verbreiterung f
f élargissement m de Stark
r штарковское уширение n (спектральных линий)

S726
e Stark effect
d Stark-Effekt m
f effet m Stark
r эффект m Штарка

S727
e Stark splitting
d Stark-Aufspaltung f
f désintégration f de Stark, fission f de Stark, dédoublement m de Stark
r штарковское расщепление n (спектральных линий)

S728
e Stark sublevel
d Stark-Unterniveau n, Stark-Teilniveau n
f sous-niveau m de Stark
r штарковский подуровень m

S729
e state
d Zustand m
f état m
r состояние n

S730   *e*   state function
      d   Zustandsfunktion *f*
      f   fonction *f* d'état
      r   функция *f* состояния

S731   *e*   state identification
      d   Zustandsidentifikation *f*, Identifikation *f* der Zustände
      f   identification *f* des états
      r   идентификация *f* состояний

S732   *e*   state matrix
      d   Zustandsmatrix *f*
      f   matrice *f* des états
      r   матрица *f* состояний

S733   *e*   state of aggregation
      d   Aggregatzustand *m*
      f   état *m* d'agrégation
      r   агрегатное состояние *n* (вещества)

S734   *e*   state parameters
      d   Zustandsgrößen *f pl*
      f   paramètres *m pl* d'état
      r   параметры *m pl* состояния

S735   *e*   state probability
      d   Zustandswahrscheinlichkeit *f*
      f   probabilité *f* d'état
      r   вероятность *f* состояния

S736   *e*   state vector
      d   Zustandsvektor *m*
      f   vecteur *m* d'état
      r   вектор *m* состояния

S737   *e*   static charge
      d   statische Ladung *f*
      f   charge *f* statique
      r   статический заряд *m*

S738   *e*   static electricity
      d   statische Elektrizität *f*
      f   électricité *f* statique
      r   статическое электричество *n*

S739   *e*   static friction
      d   Haftreibung *f*
      f   frottement *m* de repos
      r   трение *n* покоя, статическое трение *n*

S740   *e*   static load
      d   statische Belastung *f*
      f   charge *f* statique
      r   статическая нагрузка *f*

S741   *e*   static pressure
      d   statischer Druck *m*, ruhender Druck *m*, Ruhedruck *m*
      f   pression *f* statique
      r   статическое давление *n*

S742   *e*   statics
      d   Statik *f*
      f   statique *f*
      r   статика *f*

S743   *e*   stationary boiling
      d   stationäres Sieden *n*
      f   bouillonnement *m* stationnaire
      r   стационарное кипение *n*

S744   *e*   stationary interference
      d   stationäre Interferenz *f*
      f   interférence *f* stationnaire
      r   стационарная интерференция *f*

S745   *e*   stationary model
      d   stationäres Modell *n*
      f   modèle *m* stationnaire
      r   стационарная модель *f* (Вселенной)

S746   *e*   stationary motion
      d   stationäre Bewegung *f*
      f   mouvement *m* stationnaire, mouvement *m* permanent
      r   стационарное движение *n*, установившееся движение *n*

S747   *e*   stationary oscillation
      d   stationäre Schwingungen *f pl*
      f   oscillations *f pl* stationnaires, oscillations *f pl* permanentes
      r   установившиеся колебания *n pl*, стационарные колебания *n pl*

S748   *e*   stationary process
      d   stationärer Prozeß *m*
      f   processus *m* stationnaire
      r   стационарный процесс *m*

S749   *e*   stationary source
      d   stationäre Quelle *f*
      f   source *f* stationnaire
      r   стационарный источник *m*

S750   *e*   stationary state
      d   stationärer Zustand *m*
      f   état *m* stationnaire
      r   стационарное состояние *n*

S751   *e*   stationary target *see* fixed target

S752   *e*   stationary Universe
      d   stationäres Universum *n*
      f   Univers *m* stationnaire
      r   стационарная Вселенная *f*

S753   *e*   stationary waves *see* standing waves

S754   *e*   statistical bootstrap
      d   statistischer Bootstrap *m*
      f   bootstrap *m* statistique
      r   статистический бутстрап *m* (в квантовой хромодинамике)

S755   *e*   statistical criterion
      d   statistisches Kriterium *n*
      f   critère *m* statistique
      r   статистический критерий *m*

S756   *e*   statistical distribution
      d   statistische Verteilung *f*

	f	distribution f statistique
	r	статистическое распределение n

S757   e statistical ensemble
       d statistische Gesamtheit f
       f ensemble m statistique
       r статистический ансамбль m

S758   e statistical equilibrium
       d statistisches Gleichgewicht n
       f équilibre m statistique
       r статистическое равновесие n

S759   e statistical integral
       d statistisches Integral n
       f intégrale f statistique
       r статистический интеграл m

S760   e statistical interpretation
       d statistische Interpretation f
       f interprétation f statistique
       r статистическая интерпретация f

S761   e statistical mechanics
       d statistische Mechanik f
       f mécanique f statistique
       r статистическая механика f

S762   e statistical model
       d statistisches Modell n
       f modèle m statistique
       r статистическая модель f (ядра)

S763   e statistical optics
       d statistische Optik f
       f optique f statistique
       r статистическая оптика f

S764   e statistical physics
       d statistische Physik f
       f physique f statistique
       r статистическая физика f

S765   e statistical radiophysics
       d statistische Radiophysik f
       f radiophysique f statistique
       r статистическая радиофизика f

S766   e statistical thermodynamics
       d statistische Thermodynamik f
       f thermodynamique f statistique
       r статистическая термодинамика f

S767   e statistical weight
       d statistisches Gewicht n
       f poids m statistique
       r статистический вес m

S768   e statistics
       d Statistik f
       f statistique f
       r статистика f

S769   e steady flow
       d stationäre Strömung f, stationärer Strom m
       f écoulement m stationnaire, écoulement m permanent

       r стационарное течение n, установившееся течение n

S770   e steady motion see stationary motion

S771   e steady state see stationary state

S772   e steady-state current
       d stationärer Strom m
       f courant m stationnaire
       r стационарный ток m, установившийся ток m

S773   e steady-state interference see stationary interference

S774   e steam
       d Wasserdampf m
       f vapeur f d'eau
       r водяной пар m

S775   e steam chamber
       d Dampfkammer f
       f chambre f de vapeur
       r паровая камера f

S776   e steam pressure see vapor pressure

S777   e steepest descent method
       d Methode f des steilsten Abstiegs
       f méthode f de la plus profonde descente
       r метод m быстрейшего спуска, метод m перевала

S778   e steepness
       d Steilheit f
       f raideur f
       r крутизна f

S779   e **Stefan-Boltzmann law**
       d Stefan-Boltzmann-Strahlungsgesetz n
       f loi f de Stefan-Boltzmann
       r закон m излучения Стефана - Больцмана

S780   e stellar aberration
       d Sternaberration f
       f aberration f stellaire
       r звёздная аберрация f

S781   e stellar activity
       d Sternaktivität f
       f activité f stellaire
       r звёздная активность f

S782   e stellar association
       d Sternassoziation f
       f association f stellaire
       r звёздная ассоциация f

S783   e stellar atmosphere
       d Sternatmosphäre f
       f atmosphère f stellaire
       r звёздная атмосфера f

S784   e stellarator
       d Stellarator m

	f	stellarateur m
	r	стелларатор m
S785	e	stellar brightness
	d	Sternhelligkeit f
	f	éclat m stellaire
	r	блеск m звезды
S786	e	stellar distances
	d	Sternabstände m pl
	f	distances f pl stellaires
	r	расстояния n pl звёзд
S787	e	stellar dynamics
	d	Sterndynamik f, Stellardynamik f
	f	dynamique f stellaire
	r	звёздная динамика f
S788	e	stellar evolution
	d	Sternentwicklung f
	f	évolution f stellaire
	r	звёздная эволюция f
S789	e	stellar image see star image
S790	e	stellar interferometer
	d	Sterninterferometer n
	f	interféromètre m stellaire
	r	звёздный интерферометр m
S791	e	stellar interiors
	d	Sterninneres n
	f	intérieur m stellaire
	r	недра pl звёзд
S792	e	stellar luminosity
	d	Leuchtkraft f des Gestirns
	f	luminosité f stellaire
	r	светимость f звезды
S793	e	stellar magnitude
	d	Sterngröße f
	f	magnitude f stellaire
	r	звёздная величина f
S794	e	stellar parallax
	d	Sternparallaxe f
	f	parallaxe f stellaire
	r	параллакс m звезды
S795	e	stellar photometry
	d	Sternphotometrie f
	f	photométrie f stellaire
	r	звёздная фотометрия f
S796	e	stellar population
	d	Sternpopulation f
	f	population f stellaire
	r	звёздное население n
S797	e	stellar radiation
	d	Sternstrahlung f
	f	rayonnement m stellaire
	r	звёздное излучение n
S798	e	stellar rotation
	d	Sternrotation f

	f	rotation f stellaire
	r	вращение n звёзд
S799	e	stellar scintillation
	d	Sternszintillieren n, Sternflimmern n
	f	scintillement m stellaire
	r	мерцание n звёзд
S800	e	stellar spectra
	d	Sternspektren n pl
	f	spectres m pl stellaires
	r	спектры m pl звёзд
S801	e	stellar wind
	d	Sternwind m
	f	vent m stellaire
	r	звёздный ветер m
S802	e	step-by-step excitation
	d	stufenweise Anregung f
	f	excitation f par échelon, excitation f par gradins
	r	ступенчатое возбуждение n
S803	e	step index fiber
	d	Stufenprofilfaser f
	f	fibre f à indice de réfraction variant par gradins
	r	волокно n со ступенчатым изменением показателя преломления
S804	e	step ionization
	d	Stufenionisation f
	f	ionisation f par gradins
	r	ступенчатая ионизация f
S805	e	stepwise transition
	d	abrupter Übergang m
	f	transition f par gradins
	r	ступенчатый переход m
S806	e	steradian
	d	Steradiant m
	f	stéradian m
	r	стерадиан m
S807	e	stereobetatron
	d	Stereobetatron n
	f	stéréobêtatron m
	r	стереобетатрон m
S808	e	stereochemistry
	d	Stereochemie f
	f	stéréochimie f
	r	стереохимия f
S809	e	stereographic projection
	d	stereographische Projektion f
	f	projection f stéréographique
	r	стереографическая проекция f
S810	e	stereoisomerism
	d	Stereoisomerie f, Raumisomerie f
	f	stéréo-isomérie f
	r	пространственная изомерия f, стереоизомерия f

S811　e　stereophony
　　　d　Stereophonie f
　　　f　stéréophonie f
　　　r　стереофония f

S812　e　stereoscopic vision
　　　d　stereoskopisches Sehen n, räumliches
　　　　　Sehen n
　　　f　vision f stéréoscopique
　　　r　стереоскопическое зрение n

S813　e　stereoscopy
　　　d　Stereoskopie f
　　　f　stéréoscopie f
　　　r　стереоскопия f

S814　e　stiffness
　　　d　Steifigkeit f, Steifheit f
　　　f　raideur f, rigidité f
　　　r　жёсткость f

S815　e　stigmatic image
　　　d　stigmatische Abbildung f
　　　f　image f stigmatique
　　　r　стигматическое изображение n

S816　e　stilb, sb
　　　d　Stilb n
　　　f　stilb m
　　　r　стильб m, сб (единица яркости в
　　　　　СГС)

S817　e　stimulated absorption
　　　d　stimulierte Absorption f
　　　f　absorption f stimulée
　　　r　вынужденное поглощение n,
　　　　　индуцированное поглощение n

S818　e　stimulated amplification
　　　d　stimulierte Verstärkung f
　　　f　amplification f stimulée
　　　r　вынужденное усиление n

S819　e　stimulated Brillouin scattering
　　　d　stimulierte Brillouin-Streuung f, SBS
　　　f　diffusion f de Brillouin stimulée
　　　r　вынужденное рассеяние n
　　　　　Мандельштама - Бриллюэна, ВРМБ

S820　e　stimulated Compton scattering
　　　d　stimulierte Compton-Streuung f, SCS
　　　f　diffusion f de Compton stimulée
　　　r　вынужденное комптоновское
　　　　　рассеяние n

S821　e　stimulated desorption
　　　d　stimulierte Desorption f
　　　f　désorption f stimulée
　　　r　вынужденная десорбция f

S822　e　stimulated diffusion
　　　d　stimulierte Diffusion f
　　　f　diffusion f stimulée
　　　r　вынужденная диффузия f

S823　e　stimulated emission
　　　d　induzierte Emission f, erzwungene
　　　　　Emission f, stimulierte Emission f
　　　f　émission f stimulée, émission f induite,
　　　　　émission f forcée
　　　r　вынужденное излучение n,
　　　　　индуцированное излучение n,
　　　　　стимулированное излучение n,
　　　　　вынужденное испускание n

S824　e　stimulated light scattering
　　　d　stimulierte Lichtstreuung f
　　　f　diffusion f stimulée de la lumière
　　　r　вынужденное рассеяние n света

S825　e　stimulated luminescence
　　　d　stimulierte Lumineszenz f
　　　f　luminescence f stimulée
　　　r　вынужденная люминесценция f

S826　e　stimulated oscillation
　　　d　erzwungene Schwingungen f pl
　　　f　oscillations f pl forcées
　　　r　вынужденные колебания n pl

S827　e　stimulated quantum
　　　d　stimuliertes Quant n
　　　f　quantum m stimulé, quantum m induit
　　　r　стимулированный квант m,
　　　　　индуцированный квант m

S828　e　stimulated radiation see stimulated
　　　　　emission

S829　e　stimulated Raman scattering
　　　d　stimulierter Raman-Effekt m,
　　　　　stimulierte Raman-Streuung f
　　　f　effet m Raman stimulé, effet m
　　　　　Raman induit
　　　r　вынужденное комбинационное
　　　　　рассеяние n, ВКР

S830　e　stimulated temperature scattering
　　　d　stimulierte Temperaturstreuung f
　　　f　diffusion f de température stimulée
　　　r　вынужденное температурное
　　　　　рассеяние n

S831　e　stimulated transition
　　　d　induzierter Übergang m, erzwungener
　　　　　Übergang m
　　　f　transition f stimulée
　　　r　вынужденный переход m

S832　e　Stirling cycle
　　　d　Stirlingscher Kreisprozeß m, Stirling-
　　　　　Prozeß m
　　　f　cycle m de Stirling
　　　r　цикл m Стирлинга

S833　e　Stirling formula
　　　d　Stirlingsche Formel f, Stirling-Formel f
　　　f　formule f de Stirling
　　　r　формула f Стирлинга

S834　e　stochastic acceleration
　　　d　stochastische Beschleunigung f
　　　f　accélération f stochastique
　　　r　стохастическое ускорение n

S835   *e*   **stochastic dependence** *see* random
         dependence

S836   *e*   **stochasticity**
         d   Stochastizität *f*
         f   stochasticité *f*
         r   стохастичность *f*

S837   *e*   **stochastic oscillation**
         d   stochastische Schwingungen *f pl*
         f   oscillations *f pl* stochastiques
         r   стохастические колебания *n pl*

S838   *e*   **stochastic process**
         d   stochastischer Prozeß *m*,
            Zufallsprozeß *m*
         f   processus *m* stochastique, processus *m*
            aléatoire
         r   стохастический процесс *m*,
            случайный процесс *m*,
            вероятностный процесс *m*

S839   *e*   **stochastic variable** *see* random
         variable

S840   *e*   **stochastization**
         d   Stochastisierung *f*
         f   stochastisation *f*
         r   стохастизация *f*

S841   *e*   **stoichiometric coefficient**
         d   stöchiometrischer Faktor *m*,
            stöchiometrischer Koeffizient *m*
         f   coefficient *m* stœchiométrique
         r   стехиометрический коэффициент *m*

S842   *e*   **stoichiometric defect**
         d   stöchiometrischer Defekt *m*
         f   défaut *m* stœchiométrique
         r   стехиометрический дефект *m*

S843   *e*   **stoichiometry**
         d   Stöchiometrie *f*
         f   stœchiométrie *f*
         r   стехиометрия *f*

S844   *e*   **stokes, St**
         d   Stokes *n*
         f   stokes *m*
         r   стокс *m*, Ст *(единица*
            кинематической вязкости в СГС)

S845   *e*   **Stokes component**
         d   Stokessche Komponente *f*
         f   composante *f* de Stokes
         r   стоксова компонента *f*

S846   *e*   **Stokes law**
         d   Stokessches Gesetz *n*
         f   loi *f* de Stokes
         r   закон *m* Стокса

S847   *e*   **Stokes line**
         d   Stokessche Linie *f*
         f   raie *f* de Stokes, ligne *f* de Stokes
         r   стоксова линия *f (спектра)*

S848   *e*   **Stokes parameter**
         d   Stokesscher Parameter *m*
         f   paramètre *m* de Stokes
         r   параметр *m* Стокса

S849   *e*   **stop**
         d   Blende *f*
         f   diaphragme *m*
         r   диафрагма *f*

S850   *e*   **stopping power**
         d   Bremsvermögen *n*
         f   pouvoir *m* d'arrêt
         r   тормозная способность *f*
            (вещества)

S851   *e*   **storage**
         d   Speicher *m*
         f   mémoire *f*
         r   1. накопитель *m* 2. память *f*

S852   *e*   **storage oscilloscope**
         d   Speicheroszilloskop *n*
         f   oscilloscope *m* à mémoire
         r   запоминающий осциллограф *m*

S853   *e*   **storage ring**
         d   Speicherring *m*
         f   anneau *m* de stockage
         r   накопитель *m*, накопительное
            кольцо *n (в ускорителе)*

S854   *e*   **straggling**
         d   Streuung *f*
         f   dispersion *f*
         r   разброс *m (параметров)*

S855   *e*   **strain**
         d   1. Spannung *f*, Beanspruchung *f* 2.
            Deformation *f*, Verformung *f*
         f   1. contrainte *f* 2. déformation *f*
         r   1. напряжение *n* 2. деформация *f*

S856   *e*   **strain annealing method**
         d   Streck-Anlaß-Methode *f*
         f   méthode *f* d'allongement-recuit
         r   метод *m* деформационного отжига

S857   *e*   **strain deviator**
         d   Deformationsdeviator *m*, Deviator *m*
            der Streckung
         f   déviateur *m* des déformations
         r   девиатор *m* деформаций

S858   *e*   **strain gage**
         d   Dehnungsmeßgeber *m*,
            Dehnungsmeßstreifen *m*
         f   extensomètre *m*, jauge *f*
            de contrainte
         r   тензодатчик *m*

S859   *e*   **strain hardening**
         d   Kaltverfestigung *f*
         f   durcissement *m* par écrouissage,
            durcissement *m* par déformation
         r   деформационное упрочнение *n*

S860   *e*   strain intensity
       d   Deformationsintensität *f*
       f   intensité *f* de déformation
       r   интенсивность *f* деформации

S861   *e*   strain tensor
       d   Verformungstensor *m*,
          Deformationstensor *m*
       f   tenseur *m* des déformations
       r   тензор *m* деформаций

S862   *e*   strange attractor
       d   seltsamer Attraktor *m*
       f   attracteur *m* étrange
       r   странный аттрактор *m*

S863   *e*   strangeness
       d   Strangeness *f*
       f   étrangeté *f*
       r   странность *f* (квантовое число)

S864   *e*   strangeness oscillation
       d   Strangeness-Oszillationen *f pl*
       f   oscillations *f pl* d'étrangeté
       r   осцилляции *f pl* странности

S865   *e*   strange particles
       d   seltsame Teilchen *n pl*
       f   particules *f pl* étranges
       r   странные частицы *f pl*

S866   *e*   strange quark
       d   s-Quark *n*, Strangeness-Quark *n*
       f   quark *m* étrange
       r   странный кварк *m*

S867   *e*   strapped magnetron
       d   Magnetron *n* mit Kopplungsbügeln
       f   magnétron *m* strappé
       r   магнетрон *m* со связками

S868   *e*   strata
       d   Schichten *f pl*, Strata *n pl*
       f   strates *f pl*
       r   страты *f pl*, слои *m pl*

S869   *e*   stratification
       d   Stratifizierung *f*
       f   stratification *f*
       r   расслоение *n*, стратификация *f*

S870   *e*   stratified atmosphere
       d   geschichtete Atmosphäre *f*
       f   atmosphère *f* stratifiée
       r   слоистая атмосфера *f*

S871   *e*   stratopause
       d   Stratopause *f*
       f   stratopause *f*
       r   стратопауза *f*

S872   *e*   stratosphere
       d   Stratosphäre *f*
       f   stratosphère *f*
       r   стратосфера *f*

S873   *e*   stray capacitance
       d   Streukapazität *f*; Störkapazität *f*
       f   capacité *f* parasite
       r   паразитная ёмкость *f*

S874   *e*   streak camera
       d   Schlierenkammer *f*
       f   chambre *f* strioscopique
       r   электронно-оптическая камера *f*;
          фотохронограф *m*

S875   *e*   stream
       d   Strömung *f*
       f   courant *m*
       r   поток *m*, течение *n*

S876   *e*   streamer
       d   Streamer *m*
       f   streamer *m*
       r   стример *m*

S877   *e*   streamer chamber
       d   Streamerkammer *f*
       f   chambre *f* à streamers
       r   стримерная камера *f*

S878   *e*   streamer channel
       d   Streamerkanal *m*
       f   canal *m* de streamer
       r   стримерный канал *m*

S879   *e*   streamer discharge *see* streamer

S880   *e*   stream function
       d   Stromfunktion *f*, Strömungsfunktion *f*
       f   fonction *f* de courant
       r   функция *f* тока

S881   *e*   streaming *see* stream

S882   *e*   streamline
       d   Stromlinie *f*, Strömungslinie *f*
       f   ligne *f* de courant
       r   линия *f* тока

S883   *e*   streamline flow *see* laminar flow

S884   *e*   strength
       d   1. Intensität *f* 2. Stärke *f*
          3. Festigkeit *f*
       f   1. intensité *f* 2. force *f* 3. résistance *f*
       r   1. напряжённость *f* 2. сила *f* 3.
          прочность *f*

S885   *e*   strength test
       d   Festigkeitsprüfung *f*
       f   essai *m* de résistance
       r   испытание *n* на прочность

S886   *e*   stress
       d   Spannung *f*, mechanische Spannung *f*;
          Beanspruchung *f*
       f   tension *f*; contrainte *f*; effort *m*
       r   напряжение *n*; усилие *n*

S887   *e*   stress concentration
       d   Spannungskonzentration *f*

	f	concentration f des contraintes
	r	концентрация f напряжений
S888	e	**stress corrosion**
	d	Spannungskorrosion f
	f	corrosion f sous tension
	r	коррозия f под напряжением, коррозия f, вызванная напряжением
S889	e	**stress deviator**
	d	Spannungsdeviator m
	f	déviateur m des contraintes
	r	девиатор m напряжений
S890	e	**stress field**
	d	Spannungsfeld n
	f	champ m de tension, champ m des contraintes
	r	поле n напряжений
S891	e	**stress intensity**
	d	Spannungsintensität f
	f	intensité f des efforts, intensité f des tensions
	r	интенсивность f напряжений
S892	e	**stress relaxation**
	d	Spannungsrelaxation f
	f	relaxation f des tensions
	r	релаксация f напряжений
S893	e	**stress-strain curve**
	d	Spannungs-Dehnungs-Kurve f
	f	courbe f tension-déformation
	r	кривая f напряжение - деформация, диаграмма f напряжений
S894	e	**stress-strain diagram**
	d	Spannungs-Dehnungs-Diagramm n
	f	diagramme m tension-déformation
	r	диаграмма f напряжений
S895	e	**stress tensor**
	d	Spannungstensor m
	f	tenseur m des tensions, tenseur m des contraintes
	r	тензор m напряжений
S896	e	**stretching deformation** see tensile deformation
S897	e	**string**
	d	Saite f
	f	corde f
	r	струна f
S898	e	**string model**
	d	Saitenmodell n
	f	modèle m à corde
	r	струнная модель f (адронов)
S899	e	**string polygon**
	d	Seilpolygon n, Seileck n
	f	polygone m funiculaire
	r	верёвочный многоугольник m

S900	e	**string tension**
	d	Saitenspannung f
	f	tension f de corde
	r	натяжение n струны
S901	e	**stringy instanton**
	d	Saiteninstanton n
	f	instanton m à corde
	r	струнный инстантон m
S902	e	**strip line**
	d	Streifenleitung f
	f	ligne f à strip
	r	полосковая линия f
S903	e	**stripping reaction**
	d	Strippingreaktion f, Abstreifreaktion f
	f	réaction f de stripage
	r	реакция f срыва, срыв m
S904	e	**stroboscope**
	d	Stroboskop n
	f	stroboscope m
	r	стробоскоп m
S905	e	**stroboscopic effect**
	d	stroboskopischer Effekt m, Stroboskopeffekt m
	f	effet m stroboscopique
	r	стробоскопический эффект m
S906	e	**strong coupling method**
	d	Methode f der starken Kopplung
	f	méthode f de couplage fort
	r	метод m сильной связи
S907	e	**strong field**
	d	starkes Feld n
	f	champ m fort
	r	сильное поле n
S908	e	**strong focusing**
	d	starke Fokussierung f
	f	forte focalisation f, focalisation f intense
	r	сильная фокусировка f, жёсткая фокусировка f
S909	e	**strong interaction**
	d	starke Wechselwirkung f
	f	interaction f forte
	r	сильное взаимодействие n
S910	e	**strongly nonideal plasma**
	d	stark nichtideales Plasma n
	f	plasma m fortement non idéal
	r	сильно неидеальная плазма f
S911	e	**strontium, Sr**
	d	Strontium n
	f	strontium m
	r	стронций m
S912	e	**structural analysis**
	d	Strukturanalyse f
	f	analyse f structurale
	r	структурный анализ m

S913　e　structural crystallography
　　　d　Kristallstrukturbestimmung *f*
　　　f　cristallographie *f* structurale
　　　r　структурная кристаллография *f*

S914　e　structural defect
　　　d　Strukturfehler *m*; Gefügefehler *m*
　　　f　défaut *m* de structure
　　　r　дефект *m* структуры

S915　e　structural imperfection
　　　d　Strukturfehler, Strukturstörung *f*
　　　f　imperfection *f* de structure
　　　r　несовершенство *n* структуры

S916　e　structural isomer
　　　d　Strukturisomer *n*
　　　f　isomère *m* de constitution
　　　r　структурный изомер *m*

S917　e　structural isomerism
　　　d　Strukturisomerie *f*
　　　f　isomérie *f* de constitution
　　　r　структурная изомерия *f*

S918　e　structural phase transitions
　　　d　Strukturphasenübergänge *m pl*
　　　f　transitions *f pl* de phase structurales
　　　r　структурные фазовые
　　　　　переходы *m pl*

S919　e　structural transformation
　　　d　Strukturumwandlung *f*,
　　　　　Gefügeumwandlung *f*
　　　f　transformation *f* structurale
　　　r　структурное превращение *n*

S920　e　structural viscosity
　　　d　Strukturviskosität *f*
　　　f　viscosité *f* structurale
　　　r　структурная вязкость *f*

S921　e　structure amplitude
　　　d　Strukturamplitude *f*
　　　f　amplitude *f* de structure
　　　r　структурная амплитуда *f*

S922　e　structure factor
　　　d　Strukturfaktor *m*
　　　f　facteur *m* de structure
　　　r　структурный множитель *m*,
　　　　　структурный фактор *m*

S923　e　structure function
　　　d　Strukturfunktion *f*
　　　f　fonction *f* de structure
　　　r　структурная функция *f*

S924　e　Sturm-Liouville equation
　　　d　Sturm-Liouvillesche
　　　　　Differentialgleichung *f*
　　　f　équation *f* de Sturm-Liouville
　　　r　задача *f* Штурма - Лиувилля

S925　e　subatomic particle
　　　d　subatomares Teilchen *n*

　　　f　particule *f* subatomuqie
　　　r　субатомная частица *f*

S926　e　subcritical assembly
　　　d　unterkritische Anordnung *f*
　　　f　ensemble *m* sous-critique
　　　r　подкритическая сборка *f*

S927　e　subgroup
　　　d　Untergruppe *f*
　　　f　sous-groupe *m*
　　　r　подгруппа *f*

S928　e　subharmonic
　　　d　Subharmonische *f*,
　　　　　Unterharmonische *f*
　　　f　sous-harmonique *m*
　　　r　субгармоника *f*

S929　e　subharmonic cascade
　　　d　subharmonische Kaskade *f*
　　　f　cascade *f* sous-harmonique
　　　r　субгармонический каскад *m*

S930　e　sublattice
　　　d　Untergitter *n*
　　　f　sous-réseau *m*
　　　r　подрешётка *f*

S931　e　sublattice magnetization
　　　d　Untergittermagnetisierung *f*
　　　f　aimantation *f* du sous-réseau
　　　r　намагниченность *f* подрешётки

S932　e　sublayer
　　　d　Unterschicht *f*
　　　f　sous-couche *f*
　　　r　подслой *m*

S933　e　sublevel
　　　d　Unterniveau *n*, Subniveau *n*
　　　f　sous-niveau *m*
　　　r　подуровень *m*

S934　e　sublimation
　　　d　Sublimation *f*
　　　f　sublimation *f*
　　　r　возгонка *f*, сублимация *f*

S935　e　submersion
　　　d　Eintauchen *n*; Untertauchen *n*
　　　f　immersion *f*, submersion *f*
　　　r　погружение *n*

S936　e　submillimeter spectroscopy
　　　d　Submillimeterspektroskopie *f*
　　　f　spectroscopie *f* submillimétrique
　　　r　субмиллиметровая спектроскопия *f*

S937　e　submillimeter waves
　　　d　Submillimeterwellen *f pl*
　　　f　ondes *f pl* submillimétriques
　　　r　субмиллиметровые волны *f pl*

S938　e　submultiple units
　　　d　Teileinheiten *f pl*, Teile *m pl* der
　　　　　Einheiten

	f	unités f pl sous-multiples, sous-multiples m pl
	r	дольные единицы f pl
S939	e	subordinate series
	d	Nebenserie f
	f	série f secondaire
	r	побочная серия f
S940	e	subquark
	d	Unterquark n, Subquark n
	f	sous-quark m
	r	субкварк m
S941	e	subshell
	d	Unterschale f
	f	sous-couche f
	r	подоболочка f
S942	e	subsonic flight
	d	Unterschallflug m
	f	vol m subsonique
	r	полёт m с дозвуковой скоростью
S943	e	subsonic flow
	d	Unterschallströmung f
	f	écoulement m subsonique
	r	дозвуковое течение n, дозвуковой поток m
S944	e	subspace
	d	Unterraum m, Teilraum m
	f	sous-espace m
	r	подпространство n
S945	e	substance
	d	Stoff m; Werkstoff m; Substanz f; Material n
	f	substance f
	r	вещество n; материал m
S946	e	substitution
	d	Substitution f; Einsetzung f
	f	substitution f
	r	замещение n; подстановка f
S947	e	substitutional imperfection
	d	Substitutionsstörstelle f
	f	défaut m de substitution
	r	дефект m замещения
S948	e	substitutional solid solution
	d	Substitutionsmischkristall m
	f	solution f solide de substitution
	r	твёрдый раствор m замещения
S949	e	substitution of variables see change of variables
S950	e	substorm
	d	Untersturm m
	f	sous-tempête f
	r	суббуря f
S951	e	substrate
	d	Substrat n

	f	substrat m
	r	подложка f
S952	e	substructure
	d	Unterstruktur f, Substruktur f
	f	sous-structure f
	r	субструктура f
S953	e	subsystem
	d	Untersystem n
	f	sous-système m
	r	подсистема f
S954	e	subtractive color filter
	d	subtraktives Farbfilter n
	f	filtre m soustractif
	r	субтрактивный светофильтр m
S955	e	successive ionization
	d	sukzessive Ionisation f
	f	ionisation f successive
	r	последовательная ионизация f
S956	e	sudden commencement
	d	plötzlicher Anfang m
	f	commencement m brusque
	r	внезапное начало n (в геофизике)
S957	e	sudden cosmic noise absorption
	d	SCNA-Effekt m, plötzliche Verminderung f des kosmischen Störpegels
	f	absorption f brusque du bruit cosmique
	r	внезапное поглощение n космического радиоизлучения
S958	e	sudden disturbance
	d	plötzliche Störung f
	f	perturbation f brusque
	r	внезапное возмущение n
S959	e	sudden enhancement of atmospherics
	d	SEA-Effekt m, plötzliche Erhöhung f des atmosphärischen Störpegels
	f	renforcement m brusque des atmosphériques
	r	внезапное усиление n атмосфериков
S960	e	sudden field anomaly
	d	SFA-Effekt m, plötzliche Feldanomalie f
	f	anomalie f brusque du champ
	r	внезапная аномалия f поля
S961	e	sudden frequency deviation
	d	SFD-Effekt m, kurzzeitige Frequenzabweichung f
	f	déviation f brusque de la fréquence
	r	внезапная девиация f частоты
S962	e	sudden ionospheric disturbance
	d	SID-Effekt, plötzliche Ionosphärenstörung f
	f	perturbation f ionosphérique brusque

r внезапное ионосферное
возмущение *n*

S963 e **sudden perturbation method**
d Methode *f* der plötzlichen Störungen
f méthode *f* de perturbations brusques
r метод *m* внезапных возмущений

S964 e **sudden phase anomaly**
d SPA-Effekt, plötzliche
Phasenanomalie *f*
f anomalie *f* de phase à début brusque
r внезапное изменение *n* фазы

S965 e **sulphur, S**
d Schwefel *m*
f soufre *m*
r cepa *f*

S966 e **summation rule**
d Summenregel *f*
f règle *f* de sommes
r правило *n* сумм

S967 e **summation tones**
d Summationstöne *m pl*
f sons *m pl* résultants
r комбинационные тона *m pl*
суммарной частоты, суммовые
тона *m pl*

S968 e **sum rule** *see* **summation rule**

S969 e **Sun**
d Sonne *f*
f Soleil *m*
r Солнце *n*

S970 e **sunspot**
d Sonnenfleck *m*
f tache *f* solaire
r солнечное пятно *n*

S971 e **sunspot number**
d Sonnenfleckenzahl *f*
f nombre *m* des taches solaires
r число *n* солнечных пятен, число *n*
Вольфа

S972 e **supercalibration model**
d Supereichmodell *n*
f modèle *m* de supercalibrage
r суперкалибровочная модель *f*

S973 e **superconducting alloy**
d supraleitende Legierung *f*
f alliage *m* supraconducteur
r сверхпроводящий сплав *m*

S974 e **superconducting cable**
d Supraleitungskabel *n*, supraleitendes
Kabel *n*
f câble *m* supraconducteur
r сверхпроводящий кабель *m*

S975 e **superconducting ceramics**
d supraleitende Keramik *f*

f céramique *f* supraconductrice
r сверхпроводящая керамика *f*

S976 e **superconducting channel**
d Supraleitungskanal *m*, supraleitender
Kanal *m*
f canal *m* supraconducteur
r сверхпроводящий канал *m*

S977 e **superconducting coil**
d Supraleitungsspule *f*, supraleitende
Spule *f*
f bobine *f* supraconductrice
r сверхпроводящая катушка *f*,
сверхпроводящая обмотка *f*

S978 e **superconducting component**
d supraleitende Komponente *f*
f composante *f* supraconductive
r сверхпроводящая компонента *f*

S979 e **superconducting domain**
d Supraleitungsdomäne *f*, supraleitende
Domäne *f*
f domaine *m* supraconducteur
r сверхпроводящий домен *m*

S980 e **superconducting film**
d supraleitende Schicht *f*
f film *m* supraconducteur
r сверхпроводящая плёнка *f*

S981 e **superconducting magnet**
d supraleitender Magnet *m*
f aimant *m* supraconducteur
r сверхпроводящий магнит *m*

S982 e **superconducting magnetometer**
d supraleitendes Magnetometer *n*
f magnétomètre *m* supraconducteur
r сверхпроводящий магнетометр *m*

S983 e **superconducting quantum
interference device**
d Quanteninterferometer *n*, Squid *n*
f squid *m*
r сверхпроводящий квантовый
интерференционный датчик *m*,
сквид *m*

S984 e **superconducting quantum
interferometer** *see* **superconducting
quantum interference device**

S985 e **superconducting solenoid**
d supraleitendes Solenoid *n*
f solénoïde *m* supraconducteur
r сверхпроводящий соленоид *m*

S986 e **superconducting superlattice**
d supraleitendes Übergitter *n*
f superréseau *m* supraconducteur
r сверхпроводящая сверхрешётка *f*

S987 e **superconducting suspension**
d supraleitende Aufhängung *f*

	f	suspension *f* supraconductrice
	r	сверхпроводящий подвес *m*
S988	*e*	**superconducting transition**
	d	Supraleitungsübergang *m*
	f	transition *f* à l'état supraconducteur
	r	сверхпроводящий переход *m*, переход *m* в сверхпроводящее состояние
S989	*e*	**superconductivity**
	d	Supraleitfähigkeit *f*
	f	supraconductibilité *f*
	r	сверхпроводимость *f*
S990	*e*	**superconductor**
	d	Supraleiter *m*, supraleitender Stoff *m*
	f	supraconducteur *m*
	r	сверхпроводник *m*
S991	*e*	**supercooled liquid**
	d	unterkühlte Flüssigkeit *f*
	f	liquide *m* sous-réfrigéré
	r	переохлаждённая жидкость *f*
S992	*e*	**supercooling**
	d	Unterkühlung *f*
	f	surfusion *f*, sous-refroidissement *m*
	r	переохлаждение *n*
S993	*e*	**supercritical assembly**
	d	überkritische Anordnung *f*
	f	ensemble *m* surcritique
	r	надкритическая сборка *f*, сверхкритическая сборка *f*
S994	*e*	**superdense matter**
	d	superdichte Materie *f*
	f	matière *f* superdense
	r	сверхплотная материя *f*
S995	*e*	**superdense plasma**
	d	superdichtes Plasma *n*
	f	plasma *m* superdense
	r	сверхплотная плазма *f*
S996	*e*	**superelastic collision**
	d	superelastischer Stoß *m*, überelastischer Stoß *m*
	f	choc *m* superélastique, collision *f* superélastique
	r	сверхупругое столкновение *n*, сверхупругое соударение *n*
S997	*e*	**superfield**
	d	Superfeld *n*
	f	superchamp *m*
	r	суперполе *n*
S998	*e*	**superfluid**
	d	Supraflüssigkeit *f*
	f	liquide *m* superfluide
	r	сверхтекучая жидкость *f*
S999	*e*	**superfluid component**
	d	suprafluide Komponente *f*

	f	composante *f* superfluide
	r	сверхтекучая компонента *f*
S1000	*e*	**superfluid Fermi liquid**
	d	superfluide Fermi-Flüssigkeit *f*
	f	superfluide liquide *m* de Fermi
	r	сверхтекучая ферми-жидкость *f*
S1001	*e*	**superfluid 3He**
	d	superfluides Helium III *n*
	f	hélium *m* superfluide 3He
	r	сверхтекучий 3He *m*, сверхтекучий гелий-3 *m*
S1002	*e*	**superfluid 4He**
	d	superfluides Helium IV *n*
	f	hélium *m* superfluide 4He
	r	сверхтекучий 4He *m*, сверхтекучий гелий-4 *m*
S1003	*e*	**superfluidity**
	d	Superfluidität *f*, Suprafluidität *f*
	f	superfluidité *f*
	r	сверхтекучесть *f*
S1004	*e*	**superfluid state**
	d	superfluider Zustand *m*
	f	état *m* superfluide
	r	сверхтекучее состояние *n*
S1005	*e*	**superfluid transition**
	d	Superfluiditätsübergang *m*
	f	transition *f* à l'état superfluide
	r	переход *m* в сверхтекучее состояние
S1006	*e*	**supergage transformation**
	d	Supereichtransformation *f*
	f	transformation *f* de superjauge
	r	суперкалибровочное преобразование *n*
S1007	*e*	**super-Gaussian profile**
	d	super-Gaußsches Profil *n*
	f	profil *m* supergaussien
	r	супергауссов профиль *m*
S1008	*e*	**supergiant, supergiant star**
	d	Überriese *m*
	f	supergéante *f*
	r	сверхгигант *m*, звезда-сверхгигант *f*
S1009	*e*	**supergravity**
	d	Supergravitation *f*
	f	supergravitation *f*
	r	супергравитация *f*
S1010	*e*	**superheated vapor**
	d	überhitzter Dampf *m*
	f	vapeur *f* surchauffée
	r	перегретый пар *m*
S1011	*e*	**superheating**
	d	Überhitzung *f*
	f	surchauffage *m*, surchauffe *f*
	r	перегрев *m*
S1012	*e*	**superheterodyne**

    d Superheterodynempfänger *m*
    f superhétérodyne *f*
    r супергетеродин *m*

S1013 *e* **superintense magnetic fields**
    d superstarke Magnetfelder *n pl*
    f champs *m pl* magnétiques
       superintenses
    r сверхсильные магнитные поля *n pl*

S1014 *e* **superionic conductor**
    d Superionenleiter *m*
    f conducteur *m* supra-ionique, supra-
       ioniqie *m*
    r суперионный проводник *m*

S1015 *e* **superlattice**
    d Übergitter *n*, Überstrukturgitter *n*
    f superréseau *m*
    r сверхрешётка *f*

S1016 *e* **superlattice laser**
    d Supergitterlaser *m*
    f laser *m* à superréseau
    r лазер *m* на сверхрешётке

S1017 *e* **superluminal speed**
    d Überlichtgeschwindigkeit *f*
    f vitesse *f* dépassant celle de la lumière
    r сверхсветовая скорость *f*

S1018 *e* **superluminescence**
    d Superlumineszenz *f*
    f superluminescence *f*
    r сверхлюминесценция *f*,
       суперлюминесценция *f*

S1019 *e* **superluminescent amplifier**
    d Superlumineszenzverstärker *m*
    f amplificateur *m* à superluminescence
    r суперлюминесцентный усилитель *m*

S1020 *e* **supermultiplet**
    d Supermultiplett *n*
    f supermultiplet *m*
    r супермультиплет *m*

S1021 *e* **supernova, supernova star**
    d Supernova *f*
    f supernova *f*
    r сверхновая *f*, сверхновая звезда *f*

S1022 *e* **supernova explosion**
    d Supernovaausbruch *m*
    f explosion *f* de supernova
    r взрыв *m* сверхновой

S1023 *e* **supernova remnant**
    d Supernovaüberrest *m*
    f reste *m* de la supernova
    r остаток *m* вспышки сверхновой

S1024 *e* **superparamagnetism**
    d Superparamagnetismus *m*
    f superparamagnétisme *m*
    r суперпарамагнетизм *m*

S1025 *e* **superplasticity**
    d Superplastizität *f*
    f superplasticité *f*
    r сверхпластичность *f*

S1026 *e* **superposition of states**
    d Superposition *f* der Zustände
    f superposition *f* des états
    r суперпозиция *f* состояний

S1027 *e* **superposition of waves**
    d Wellensuperposition *f*,
       Wellenüberlagerung *f*
    f superposition *f* des ondes
    r суперпозиция *f* волн

S1028 *e* **superposition principle**
    d Superpositionsprinzip *n*
    f principe *m* de superposition
    r принцип *m* суперпозиции

S1029 *e* **superradiant fluorescence**
    d Superstrahlungsfluoreszenz *f*
    f fluorescence *f* superrayonnante
    r сверхизлучательная
       флуоресценция *f*

S1030 *e* **superradiant transition**
    d Superstrahlungsübergang *m*
    f transition *f* superradiante
    r сверхизлучательный переход *m*

S1031 *e* **superrefraction**
    d Superrefraktion *f*
    f superréfraction *f*
    r сверхрефракция *f*

S1032 *e* **supersaturated solution**
    d übersättigte Lösung *f*
    f solution *f* sursaturée
    r пересыщенный раствор *m*

S1033 *e* **supersaturated vapor**
    d übersättigter Dampf *m*
    f vapeur *f* sursaturée
    r пересыщенный пар *m*

S1034 *e* **supersonic flow**
    d Überschallströmung *f*,
       Überschallumströmung *f*
    f écoulement *m* supersonique
    r сверхзвуковое течение *n*,
       сверхзвуковое обтекание *n*

S1035 *e* **supersonic motion**
    d Überschallbewegung *f*
    f mouvement *m* supersonique
    r сверхзвуковое движение *n*,
       движение *n* со сверхзвуковой
       скоростью

S1036 *e* **supersonic speed**
    d Überschallgeschwindigkeit *f*
    f vitesse *f* supersonique
    r сверхзвуковая скорость *f*

S1037 *e* **superspace**

d Überraum *m*
f superespace *m*
r суперпространство *n*

S1038 e superstring
d Übersaite *f*
f supercorde *f*
r суперструна *f*

S1039 e superstructure
d Überstruktur *f*
f superstructure *f*
r сверхструктура *f*

S1040 e supersymmetrical model
d supersymmetrisches Modell *n*
f modèle *m* supersymétrique
r суперсимметричная модель *f*

S1041 e supersymmetry
d Supersymmetrie *f*
f supersymétrie *f*
r суперсимметрия *f*

S1042 e superunification
d Superunifikation *f*
f superunification *f*
r суперобъединение *n (в квантовой теории поля)*

S1043 e supply power
d Versorgungsleistung *f*
f puissance *f* d'alimentation
r мощность *f* питания

S1044 e support
d 1. Auflager *m*; Stütze *f* 2. Halterung *f*, Halter *m*
f support *m*
r 1. опора *f*, подставка *f* 2. держатель *m*, крепление *n*

S1045 e supraluminal object
d Überlichtobjekt *n*; Objekt *n* mit Überlichtgeschwindigkeit
f objet *m* à vitesse dépassant celle de la lumière
r сверхсветовой объект *m*; объект *m*, движущийся со сверхсветовой скоростью

S1046 e surfacant *see* surface active substance

S1047 e surface-acoustic-wave delay line
d SAW-Verzögerungsleitung *f*, Verzögerungsleitung *f* mit akustischen Oberflächenwellen
f ligne *f* à retard à ondes acoustiques de surface
r линия *f* задержки на поверхностных акустических волнах

S1048 e surface-acoustic-wave filter
d SAW-Filter *n*, akustisches Oberflächenwellenfilter *n*

f filtre *m* à ondes acoustiques de surface
r фильтр *m* на поверхностных акустических волнах, фильтр *m* на ПАВ

S1049 e surface acoustic waves
d akustische Oberflächenwellen *f pl*
f ondes *f pl* acoustiques de surface
r поверхностные акустические волны *f pl*, ПАВ

S1050 e surface active material
d oberflächenaktiver Stoff *m*
f matériau *m* tensio-actif
r поверхностно-активный материал *m*

S1051 e surface active substance
d oberflächenaktive Substanz *f*
f substance *f* tensio-active
r поверхностно-активное вещество *n*

S1052 e surface activity
d Oberflächenaktivität *f*
f activité *f* superficielle
r поверхностная активность *f*

S1053 e surface atom detection
d Oberflächendetektion *f* der Atome
f détection *f* des atomes sur la surface
r детектирование *n* атомов на поверхности

S1054 e surface boiling
d Oberflächensieden *n*
f ébullition *f* superficielle
r поверхностное кипение *n*

S1055 e surface breakdown
d Überschlag *m*; Oberflächendurchbruch *m*
f rupture *f* de surface
r поверхностный пробой *m*

S1056 e surface charge
d Oberflächenladung *f*
f charge *f* superficielle
r поверхностный заряд *m*

S1057 e surface charge density
d Ladungsoberflächendichte *f*
f densité *f* superficielle de charge
r поверхностная плотность *f* заряда

S1058 e surface concentration
d Oberflächenkonzentration *f*
f concentration *f* superficielle
r поверхностная концентрация *f*

S1059 e surface conductivity
d Oberflächenleitfähigkeit *f*
f conductivité *f* superficielle
r поверхностная электропроводность *f*

S1060 e surface curvature
d Oberflächenkrümmung *f*

f courbure f de surface
r кривизна f поверхности

S1061 e surface density
d Oberflächendichte f
f densité f superficielle
r поверхностная плотность f

S1062 e surface diffusion
d Oberflächendiffusion f
f diffusion f superficielle
r поверхностная диффузия f

S1063 e surface drag
d Oberflächenwiderstand m
f résistance f superficielle
r поверхностное сопротивление n

S1064 e surface energy
d Oberflächenenergie f
f énergie f superficielle
r поверхностная энергия f

S1065 e surface film
d Oberflächenschicht f
f film m de surface
r поверхностная плёнка f

S1066 e* surface finish quality
d Oberflächenbearbeitungsgüte f
f qualité f du fini de surface
r качество n обработки поверхности

S1067 e surface force
d Oberflächenkraft f
f force f superficielle
r поверхностная сила f

S1068 e surface hardening
d Oberflächenhärtung f
f trempe f superficielle
r поверхностная закалка f

S1069 e surface heating
d Oberflächenerwärmung f
f chauffage m superficiel
r поверхностный нагрев m

S1070 e surface impedance
d Oberflächenimpedanz f
f impédance f superficielle
r поверхностный импеданс m

S1071 e surface integral
d Oberflächenintegral n, Randintegral n
f intégrale f de surface
r поверхностный интеграл m,
интеграл m по поверхности

S1072 e surface ionization
d Oberflächenionisierung f,
Oberflächenionisation f
f ionisation f superficielle
r поверхностная ионизация f

S1073 e surface magnetism
d Oberflächenmagnetismus m

f magnétisme m superficiel
r поверхностный магнетизм m

S1074 e surface modification
d Oberflächenmodifikation f
f modification f de surface
r модификация f поверхности

S1075 e surface optical waves
d optische Oberflächenwellen f pl
f ondes f pl optiques de surface
r поверхностные оптические
волны f pl

S1076 e surface phenomena
d Oberflächenerscheinungen f pl,
Oberflächenphänomene m pl
f phénomènes m pl superficiels
r поверхностные явления n pl

S1077 e surface plasmon
d Oberflächenplasmon n
f plasmon m superficiel
r поверхностный плазмон m

S1078 e surface polariton
d Oberflächenpolariton n
f polariton m superficiel
r поверхностный поляритон m

S1079 e surface pressure
d Oberflächendruck m
f pression f superficielle
r поверхностное давление n

S1080 e surface resonance
d Oberflächenresonanz f
f résonance f superficielle
r поверхностный резонанс m

S1081 e surface scattering
d Oberflächenstreuung f
f diffusion f superficielle
r поверхностное рассеяние n

S1082 e surface states
d Oberflächenzustände m pl
f états m pl de surface
r поверхностные состояния n pl

S1083 e surface tension
d Oberflächenspannung f
f tension f superficielle
r поверхностное натяжение n

S1084 e surface tension coefficient
d Oberflächenspannungskoeffizient m
f coefficient m de tension de surface
r коэффициент m поверхностного
натяжения

S1085 e surface wave
d Oberflächenwelle f
f onde f de surface
r поверхностная волна f

S1086 e susceptance

	d	Suszeptanz *f*
	f	susceptance *f*
	r	реактивная проводимость *f*
S1087	*e*	**susceptibility**
	d	Suszeptibilität *f*
	f	susceptibilité *f*
	r	восприимчивость *f*
S1088	*e*	**suspension**
	d	1. Suspension *f* 2. Aufhängung *f*
	f	suspension *f*
	r	1. суспензия *f*, взвесь *f* 2. подвес *m*
S1089	*e*	**sweep**
	d	Abtastung *f*
	f	balayage *m*
	r	развёртка *f*
S1090	*e*	**sweeper** *see* **sweep generator**
S1091	*e*	**sweep generator**
	d	Wobbelfrequenzgenerator *m*, Wobbelgenerator *m*
	f	générateur *m* à balayage de fréquence
	r	свип-генератор *m*, генератор *m* качающейся частоты
S1092	*e*	**swelling**
	d	Schwellen *n*, Schwellung *f*, Anschwellen *n*
	f	gonflement *m*
	r	набухание *n*
S1093	*e*	**swept-frequency generator** *see* **sweep generator**
S1094	*e*	**switch**
	d	1. Schalter *m*; Taste *f* 2. Schalter *m*; Ausschalter *m* 3. Schalter *m*, Umschalter *m*
	f	1. disjoncteur *m* 2. interrupteur *m* 3. commutateur *m*
	r	1. ключ *m* 2. выключатель *m* 3. переключатель *m*
S1095	*e*	**symmetrical load** *see* **balanced load**
S1096	*e*	**symmetric bending**
	d	symmetrische Biegung *f*
	f	courbure *f* symétrique
	r	симметричный изгиб *m*
S1097	*e*	**symmetric configuration**
	d	symmetrische Konfiguration *f*
	f	configuration *f* symétrique
	r	симметричная конфигурация *f*
S1098	*e*	**symmetric molecule**
	d	symmetrisches Molekül *n*
	f	molécule *f* symétrique
	r	симметричная молекула *f*
S1099	*e*	**symmetric rotator**
	d	symmetrischer Rotator *m*
	f	rotateur *m* symétrique
	r	симметричный ротатор *m*

S1100	*e*	**symmetric top molecule**
	d	symmetrisches Kreiselmolekül *n*, symmetrischer Kreisel *m*
	f	molécule *f* du type toupie symétrique
	r	молекула *f* типа симметричного волчка
S1101	*e*	**symmetric wave function**
	d	symmetrische Wellenfunktion *f*
	f	fonction *f* d'onde symétrique
	r	симметричная волновая функция *f*
S1102	*e*	**symmetry**
	d	Symmetrie *f*
	f	symétrie *f*
	r	симметрия *f*
S1103	*e*	**symmetry breaking**
	d	Symmetriebrechung *f*
	f	violation *f* de symétrie
	r	нарушение *n* симметрии
S1104	*e*	**symmetry class**
	d	Symmetrieklasse *f*
	f	classe *f* de symétrie
	r	класс *m* симметрии
S1105	*e*	**symmetry groups**
	d	Symmetriegruppen *f pl*
	f	groupes *m pl* de symétrie
	r	группы *f pl* симметрии
S1106	*e*	**symmetry of wave function**
	d	Wellenfunktionssymmetrie *f*
	f	symétrie *f* de la fonction d'onde
	r	симметрия *f* волновой функции
S1107	*e*	**symmetry operation**
	d	Symmetrieoperation *f*, Deckoperation *f*
	f	opération *f* de symétrie
	r	операция *f* симметрии
S1108	*e*	**symmetry transformation**
	d	Symmetrietransformation *f*
	f	transformation *f* de symétrie
	r	преобразование *n* симметрии
S1109	*e*	**symmetry violation** *see* **symmetry breaking**
S1110	*e*	**synchrocyclotron**
	d	Synchrozyklotron *n*
	f	synchrocyclotron *m*
	r	синхроциклотрон *m*, фазотрон *m*
S1111	*e*	**synchronism**
	d	Synchronismus *m*, Gleichlauf *m*
	f	synchronisme *m*
	r	синхронизм *m*
S1112	*e*	**synchronization**
	d	Synchronisation *f*, Synchronisierung *f*
	f	synchronisation *f*
	r	синхронизация *f*
S1113	*e*	**synchronizing channel**
	d	Synchronisierkanal *m*, Synchronkanal *m*

f   canal *m* de synchronisation
r   канал *m* синхронизации

S1114 e   synchronizing pulse
d   Synchronisierimpuls *m*
f   impulsion *f* de synchronisation
r   синхронизирующий импульс *m*

S1115 e   synchronous detection
d   synchrone Demodulation *f*,
Synchrondemodulation *f*
f   détection *f* synchrone
r   синхронное детектирование *n*

S1116 e   synchronous detector
d   Synchrondemodulator *m*,
Synchrondetektor *m*
f   détecteur *m* synchrone
r   синхронный детектор *m*

S1117 e   synchrophasotron
d   Synchrophasotron *n*
f   synchrophasotron *m*
r   синхрофазотрон *m*

S1118 e   synchrotron
d   Synchrotron *n*
f   synchrotron *m*
r   синхротрон *m*

S1119 e   synchrotron oscillation
d   Synchrotronschwingungen *f pl*
f   oscillations *f pl* synchrotron
r   синхротронные колебания *n pl*

S1120 e   synchrotron radiation
d   Synchrotronstrahlung *f*
f   rayonnement *m* synchrotron
r   синхротронное излучение *n*,
магнитотормозное излучение *n*

S1121 e   synchrotron radiation source
d   Synchrotronstrahlungsquelle *f*
f   source *f* de rayonnement synchrotron
r   источник *m* синхротронного
излучения

S1122 e   synergetics
d   Synergetik *f*
f   synergétique *f*
r   синергетика *f*

S1123 e   synodic period
d   synodische Umlaufzeit *f*, synodischer
Umlauf *m*
f   période *f* synodique, révolution *f*
synodique
r   синодический период *m*, период *m*
обращения

S1124 e   synthesis
d   Synthese *f*
f   synthèse *f*
r   синтез *m*

S1125 e   synthesized aperture
d   synthetisierte Apertur *f*

f   ouverture *f* synthétisée
r   синтезированная апертура *f*

S1126 e   synthesized image
d   synthetisiertes Bild *n*
f   image *f* synthétisée
r   синтезированное изображение *n*

S1127 e   synthetic crystal
d   synthetischer Kristall *m*
f   cristal *m* synthétique
r   синтетический кристалл *m*

S1128 e   synthetic diamond
d   synthetischer Diamant *m*
f   diamant *m* artificiel
r   синтетический алмаз *m*

S1129 e   synthetic quartz
d   synthetischer Quarz *m*
f   quartz *m* synthétique
r   синтетический кварц *m*

S1130 e   system
d   System *n*
f   système *m*
r   1. система *f* 2. сингония *f*
(кристаллов)

S1131 e   systematic error
d   systematischer Fehler *m*
f   erreur *f* systématique
r   систематическая погрешность *f*

S1132 e   system of coordinates
d   Koordinatensystem *n*
f   système *m* de coordonnées
r   система *f* координат

S1133 e   system of units
d   Einheitensystem *n*
f   système *m* d'unités
r   система *f* единиц

S1134 e   Szilard-Chalmers reaction
d   Szilard-Chalmers-Effekt *m*
f   effet *m* de Szilard-Chalmers
r   эффект *m* Сциларда - Чалмерса

T

T1   e   tachyon
d   Tachyon *n*
f   tachyon *m*
r   тахион *m*

T2   e   tadpole
d   «Kaulquappe» *f*
f   «têtard» *m*
r   «головастик» *m* (тип всплеска
солнечного радиоизлучения)

T3	*e*	tag *see* label

T4	*e*	tail of comet
	d	Kometenschweif *m*
	f	queue *f* de la comète
	r	хвост *m* кометы

T5	*e*	Tamm-Dancoff method
	d	Tamm-Dancoff-Methode *f*
	f	méthode *f* de Tamm-Dancoff
	r	метод *m* Тамма - Данкова

T6	*e*	Tamm levels
	d	Tamm-Niveaus *n pl*
	f	niveaux *m pl* de Tamm
	r	уровни *m pl* Тамма

T7	*e*	Tamm states
	d	Tamm-Zustände *m pl*
	f	états *m pl* de Tamm
	r	таммовские состояния *n pl*

T8	*e*	tandem
	d	1. Tandem *n*
		2. Tandembeschleuniger *m*
	f	1. tandem *m* 2. accélérateur *m* tandem
	r	1. тандем *m* 2. перезарядный ускоритель *m*

T9	*e*	tangent
	d	1. Tangente *f* 2. Tangens *m*
	f	tangente *f*
	r	1. касательная *f* 2. тангенс *m*

T10	*e*	tangential acceleration
	d	Tangentialbeschleunigung *f*
	f	accélération *f* tangentielle
	r	касательное ускорение *n*, тангенциальное ускорение *n*

T11	*e*	tangential plane
	d	Tangentialebene *f*
	f	plan *m* tangentiel
	r	касательная плоскость *f*

T12	*e*	tangential stress
	d	Schubspannung *f*, Scherspannung *f*
	f	effort *m* tangentiel, tension *f* tangentielle
	r	касательное напряжение *n*, тангенциальное напряжение *n*

T13	*e*	tantalum, Ta
	d	Tantal *n*
	f	tantale *m*
	r	тантал *m*

T14	*e*	tape
	d	Band *n*; Streifen *m*
	f	bande *f*, ruban *m*
	r	лента *f*

T15	*e*	taper
	d	Kegel *m*
	f	cône *m*
	r	конус *m*; сужение *n*

T16	*e*	target
	d	Target *n*; Ziel *n*
	f	cible *f*
	r	мишень *f*; цель *f*

T17	*e*	target at rest *see* fixed target

T18	*e*	tautomerism
	d	Tautomerie *f*
	f	tautomérie *f*
	r	таутомерия *f*

T19	*e*	Taylor series
	d	Taylor-Serie *f*
	f	série *f* de Taylor
	r	ряд *m* Тейлора

T20	*e*	technetium, Tc
	d	Technetium *n*
	f	technétium *m*
	r	технеций *m*

T21	*e*	technicolor
	d	Technicolor *m*
	f	technicolor *m*
	r	техницвет *m*

T22	*e*	technicolor interaction
	d	Technicolor-Wechselwirkung *f*
	f	interaction *f* technicolor
	r	техницветное взаимодействие *n*

T23	*e*	technigluon
	d	Technigluon *n*
	f	technigluon *m*
	r	техниглюон *m*

T24	*e*	techniquark
	d	Techniquark *n*
	f	techniquark *m*
	r	техникварк *m*

T25	*e*	technique
	d	1. Verfahren *n*; Methode *f* 2. Technik *f*, Technologie *f*
	f	technique *f*
	r	1. метод *m*, способ *m* 2. технология *f*

T26	*e*	telemetry
	d	Fernmessung *f*; Telemetrie *f*
	f	télémesure *f*, télémétrie *f*
	r	телеметрия *f*

T27	*e*	telescope
	d	Fernrohr *n*; Teleskop *n*
	f	télescope *m*
	r	телескоп *m*; зрительная труба *f*

T28	*e*	television
	d	Fernsehen *n*
	f	télévision *f*
	r	телевидение *n*

T29	*e*	telluric currents
	d	tellurische Erdströme *pl*, induzierte Erdströme *pl*

	f	courants *pl* telluriques
	r	теллурические токи *pl*
T30	e	telluric lines
	d	tellurische Linien *f pl*, terrestrische Linien *f pl*
	f	raies *f pl* telluriques, lignes *f pl* telluriques
	r	теллурические линии *f pl*
T31	e	tellurium, Te
	d	Tellur *n*
	f	tellure *m*
	r	теллур *m*
T32	e	temperature
	d	Temperatur *f*
	f	température *f*
	r	температура *f*
T33	e	temperature coefficient of frequency
	d	Temperaturkoeffizient *m* der Frequenz
	f	coefficient *m* de température de la fréquence
	r	температурный коэффициент *m* частоты
T34	e	temperature coefficient of resistance
	d	Temperaturkoeffizient *m* des Widerstandes
	f	coefficient *m* de température de la résistance
	r	температурный коэффициент *m* сопротивления
T35	e	temperature compensation
	d	Temperaturkompensation *f*; Temperaturausgleich *m*; Temperaturkorrektur *f*
	f	compensation *f* thermique
	r	температурная компенсация *f*
T36	e	temperature dependence
	d	Temperaturabhängigkeit *f*
	f	dépendance *f* de température
	r	температурная зависимость *f*
T37	e	temperature difference
	d	Temperaturdifferenz *f*
	f	différence *f* de température
	r	разность *f* температур, температурный перепад *m*
T38	e	temperature gradient
	d	Temperaturgradient *m*, Temperaturgefälle *n*
	f	gradient *m* de température
	r	градиент *m* температуры, температурный градиент *m*
T39	e	temperature inversion
	d	Temperaturinversion *f*, Temperaturumkehr *f*
	f	inversion *f* de température
	r	температурная инверсия *f*
T40	e	temperature measurement
	d	Temperaturmessung *f*
	f	mesure *f* de température
	r	измерение *n* температуры
T41	e	temperature radiation
	d	Temperaturstrahlung *f*
	f	radiation *f* thermique, rayonnement *m* thermique
	r	температурное излучение *n*, тепловое излучение *n*
T42	e	temperature radiator
	d	Temperaturstrahler *m*, Wärmestrahler *m*
	f	radiateur *m* thermique
	r	тепловой излучатель *m*, температурный излучатель *m*
T43	e	temperature range
	d	Temperaturbereich *m*, Temperaturintervall *n*
	f	gamme *f* des températures
	r	интервал *m* температур
T44	e	temperature scale
	d	Temperaturskala *f*
	f	échelle *f* de température
	r	температурная шкала *f*
T45	e	temperature sensor
	d	Temperaturfühler *m*, Temperatursensor *m*
	f	capteur *m* de température, transmetteur *m* de température
	r	датчик *m* температуры
T46	e	temperature viscosity coefficient
	d	Temperatur-Viskositätskoeffizient *m*
	f	coefficient *m* thermique de viscosité
	r	температурный коэффициент *m* вязкости
T47	e	temperature waves
	d	Temperaturwellen *f pl*
	f	ondes *f pl* de température
	r	температурные волны *f pl*
T48	e	temporal coherence *see* time coherence
T49	e	temporal evolution
	d	Zeitevolution *f*, zeitliche Evolution *f*
	f	évolution *f* dans le temps
	r	эволюция *f* во времени, временная эволюция *f*
T50	e	tensile deformation
	d	Zugverformung *f*, Zugdehnung *f*
	f	déformation *f* de traction
	r	деформация *f* растяжения
T51	e	tensile fracture *see* tension fracture
T52	e	tensile strength
	d	Zugfestigkeitsgrenze *f*; Zugfestigkeit *f*
	f	résistance *f* à la traction

r предел *m* прочности на растяжение;
прочность *f* на растяжение

T53 *e* **tensile stress**
d Zugspannung *f*, Zugbeanspruchung *f*
f contrainte *f* de tension
r растягивающее напряжение *n*,
напряжение *n* при растяжении

T54 *e* **tension**
d Spannung *f*, Zugspannung *f*, Zug *m*
f tension *f*
r растяжение *n*, натяжение *n*;
напряжение *n*

T55 *e* **tension fracture**
d Dehnungsbruch *m*, Zugbruch *m*
f cassure *f* à la traction, rupture *f* à la traction
r разрыв *m* при растяжении

T56 *e* **tensometer**
d Tensometer *n*
f tensomètre *m*
r тензометр *m*

T57 *e* **tensor**
d Tensor *m*
f tenseur *m*
r тензор *m*

T58 *e* **tensor calculus**
d Tensorrechnung *f*
f calcul *m* tensoriel
r тензорное исчисление *n*

T59 *e* **tensoresistive effect**
d tensoelektrischer Effekt *m*,
Tensowiderstandseffekt *m*
f effet *m* tensorésistif
r тензорезистивный эффект *m*

T60 *e* **tensor field**
d Tensorfeld *n*
f champ *m* tenseur, champ *m* de tenseur
r тензорное поле *n*

T61 *e* **tephigram**
d Tephigramm *n*
f téphigramme *m*
r тефиграмма *f*

T62 *e* **terbium, Tb**
d Terbium *n*
f terbium *m*
r тербий *m*

T63 *e* **term**
d 1. Term *m*, Spektralterm *m*
2. Term *m*
f 1. terme *m* spectral 2. terme *m*
r 1. терм *m*, спектральный терм *m*
2. член *m*

T64 *e* **terminal**
d 1. Terminal *n* 2. Klemme *f*

f 1. terminal *m* 2. borne *f*
r 1. терминал *m* 2. зажим *m*

T65 *e* **terrestrial magnetism**
d Geomagnetismus *m*,
Erdmagnetismus *m*
f magnétisme *m* terrestre,
géomagnétisme *m*
r земной магнетизм *m*,
геомагнетизм *m*

T66 *e* **tesla, T**
d Tesla *n*
f tesla *m*
r тесла *m*, Тл

T67 *e* **teslameter**
d Teslameter *n*
f teslamètre *m*
r тесламетр *m*

T68 *e* **test**
d Prüfung *f*, Versuch *m*, Test *m*
f essai *m*
r испытание *n*, проверка *f*

T69 *e* **test charge**
d Probeladung *f*
f charge *f* de test
r пробный заряд *m*

T70 *e* **testing** *see* **test**

T71 *e* **test particle**
d Testteilchen *n*
f particule *f* témoin, particule *f* d'épreuve
r пробная частица *f*

T72 *e* **tetragonal system**
d tetragonales Kristallsystem *n*
f système *m* tétragonal
r тетрагональная сингония *f*;
тетрагональная система *f*

T73 *e* **tetrode**
d Tetrode *f*
f tétrode *f*
r тетрод *m*

T74 *e* **texture**
d Textur *f*
f texture *f*
r текстура *f*

T75 *e* **thallium, Tl**
d Thallium *n*
f thallium *m*
r таллий *m*

T76 *e* **theoretical curve**
d theoretische Kurve *f*
f courbe *f* théorique
r теоретическая кривая *f*

T77 *e* **theoretical physics**
d theoretische Physik *f*

	f	physique *f* théorique
	r	теоретическая физика *f*
T78	*e*	theoretical research
	d	theoretische Forschungen *f pl*
	f	recherche *f* théorique
	r	теоретические исследования *n pl*

T79   *e*   theory of elasticity
      d   Elastizitätstheorie *f*
      f   théorie *f* de l'élasticité
      r   теория *f* упругости

T80   *e*   theory of errors
      d   Fehlertheorie *f*
      f   calcul *m* des erreurs
      r   теория *f* ошибок

T81   *e*   theory of relativity
      d   Relativitätstheorie *f*
      f   théorie *f* de la relativité
      r   теория *f* относительности

T82   *e*   thermal analysis
      d   thermische Analyse *f*
      f   analyse *f* thermique, thermo-analyse *f*
      r   термический анализ *m*

T83   *e*   thermal balance *see* heat balance

T84   *e*   thermal boundary layer
      d   Temperaturgrenzschicht *f*, thermische Grenzschicht *f*
      f   couche *f* limite de température
      r   тепловой пограничный слой *m*

T85   *e*   thermal branching mechanism
      d   thermischer Verzweigungsmechanismus *m (Kettenreaktion)*
      f   mécanisme *m* de branchement thermique
      r   тепловой механизм *m* разветвления *(цепной реакции)*

T86   *e*   thermal breakdown
      d   Wärmedurchschlag *m*; Wärmedurchbruch *m*
      f   claquage *m* thermique
      r   тепловой пробой *m*

T87   *e*   thermal broadening
      d   thermische Verbreiterung *f*
      f   élargissement *m* thermique
      r   тепловое уширение *n*

T88   *e*   thermal capacitance *see* heat capacity

T89   *e*   thermal conductivity coefficient
      d   Wärmeleitzahl *f*
      f   coefficient *m* de conductibilité thermique, coefficient *m* de conductibilité calorique, coefficient *m* de conductibilité de chaleur
      r   коэффициент *m* теплопроводности

T90   *e*   thermal conductance *see* thermal conduction

T91   *e*   thermal conduction
      d   Wärmeleitung *f*
      f   conductibilité *f* thermique
      r   теплопроводность *f*

T92   *e*   thermal conduction of metals
      d   Wärmeleitung *f* der Metalle
      f   conductibilité *f* thermique des métaux
      r   теплопроводность *f* металлов

T93   *e*   thermal conductivity
      d   Wärmeleitfähigkeit *f*
      f   conductibilité *f* thermique spécifique
      r   удельная теплопроводность *f*

T94   *e*   thermal contact
      d   Wärmekontakt *m*, Thermokontakt *m*
      f   contact *m* thermique
      r   термический контакт *m*

T95   *e*   thermal convection
      d   Wärmekonvektion *f*
      f   convection *f* thermique
      r   тепловая конвекция *f*

T96   *e*   thermal crisis
      d   thermische Krise *f (im chemischen Laser)*
      f   crise *f* thermique *(au laser chimique)*
      r   тепловой кризис *m (в химическом лазере)*

T97   *e*   thermal defocusing
      d   thermische Defokussierung *f*
      f   défocalisation *f* thermique
      r   тепловая дефокусировка *f*

T98   *e*   thermal depolarization
      d   thermische Depolarisation *f*
      f   dépolarisation *f* thermique
      r   тепловая деполяризация *f*

T99   *e*   thermal detector
      d   Wärmedetektor *m*
      f   détecteur *m* thermique
      r   тепловой приёмник *m*

T100   *e*   thermal diffusion
      d   Thermodiffusion *f*
      f   diffusion *f* thermique
      r   термодиффузия *f*

T101   *e*   thermal diffusion coefficient
      d   Thermodiffusionskoeffizient *m*
      f   coefficient *m* de diffusion thermique
      r   коэффициент *m* термодиффузии

T102   *e*   thermal diffusivity
      d   Temperaturleitfähigkeit *f*
      f   diffusivité *f* thermique
      r   температуропроводность *f*

T103   *e*   thermal dilatation *see* thermal expansion

T104   *e*   thermal dissociation
      d   thermische Dissoziation *f*

f dissociation *f* thermique
r термическая диссоциация *f*,
тепловая диссоциация *f*

T105 *e* **thermal drift**
d Wärmedrift *f*
f dérive *f* thermique
r температурный дрейф *m*, тепловой
дрейф *m*

T106 *e* **thermal effect** *see* **heating effect**

T107 *e* **thermal efficiency**
d thermischer Wirkungsgrad *m*,
Wärmewirkungsgrad *m*
f rendement *m* thermique
r тепловой КПД *m*

T108 *e* **thermal electromotive force**
d Thermospannung *f*,
thermoelektromotorische Kraft *f*,
Thermo-EMK *f*
f force *f* thermo-électromotrice
r термоэдс *f*

T109 *e* **thermal electron**
d Glühelektron *n*, Thermoelektron *n*
f thermo-électron *m*
r термоэлектрон *m*

T110 *e* **thermal e.m.f.** *see* **thermal
electromotive force**

T111 *e* **thermal energy**
d Wärmeenergie *f*, thermische Energie *f*
f énergie *f* thermique
r тепловая энергия *f*

T112 *e* **thermal engine** *see* **heat engine**

T113 *e* **thermal equilibrium**
d thermisches Gleichgewicht *n*
f équilibre *m* thermique
r тепловое равновесие *n*

T114 *e* **thermal expansion**
d Wärmeausdehnung *f*
f dilatation *f* thermique, expansion *f*
thermique
r тепловое расширение *n*

T115 *e* **thermal expansion coefficient**
d Wärmeausdehnungskoeffizient *m*
f coefficient *m* de la dilatation
thermique
r коэффициент *m* теплового
расширения

T116 *e* **thermal explosion**
d Wärmeexplosion *f*
f explosion *f* thermique
r тепловой взрыв *m*

T117 *e* **thermal fatigue**
d thermische Ermüdung *f*
f fatigue *f* thermique
r термическая усталость *f*

T118 *e* **thermal flow**
d Wärmestrom *m*
f écoulement *m* thermique
r тепловой поток *m*

T119 *e* **thermal fluctuations**
d thermische Schwankungen *f pl*,
Wärmefluktuationen *f pl*
f fluctuations *f pl* thermiques
r тепловые флуктуации *f pl*

T120 *e* **thermal flux** *see* **thermal flow**

T121 *e* **thermal head**
d Wärmegefälle *n*
f chute *f* de la chaleur
r тепловой напор *m*

T122 *e* **thermal image**
d Wärmebild *n*, Infrarotbild *n*
f image *f* thermique
r тепловизионное изображение *n*

T123 *e* **thermal imager**
d Thermovisor *m*
f thermoviseur *m*
r тепловизор *m*

T124 *e* **thermal imagimg**
d Thermovision *f*
f thermovision *f*
r тепловидение *n*

T125 *e* **thermal inertia**
d Wärmeträgheit *f*, thermische
Trägheit *f*
f inertie *f* thermique, inertie *f*
calorifique
r тепловая инерция *f*

T126 *e* **thermal insulation**
d Wärmeisolierung *f*; Thermoisolation *f*
f isolement *m* thermique
r теплоизоляция *f*, термоизоляция *f*

T127 *e* **thermal ionization**
d thermische Ionisation *f*, thermische
Ionisierung *f*
f ionisation *f* thermique
r термическая ионизация *f*, тепловая
ионизация *f*

T128 *e* **thermalization length**
d Thermalisierungslänge *f*
f longueur *f* de thermalisation
r длина *f* термализации

T129 *e* **thermalization of neutrons**
d Thermalisierung *f* der Neutronen
f thermalisation *f* des neutrons
r термализация *f* нейтронов

T130 *e* **thermalized positrons**
d thermalisierte Positronen *n pl*
f positrons *m pl* thermalisés
r термализованные позитроны *m pl*

T131   *e*   thermal lag *see* thermal inertia

T132   *e*   **thermally insulated container**
      d   wärmeisolierter Container *m*
      f   conteneur *m* isothermique
      r   изотермический контейнер *m*

T133   *e*   **thermal motion**
      d   Wärmebewegung *f*
      f   mouvement *m* thermique
      r   тепловое движение *n*

T134   *e*   **thermal neutrons**
      d   thermische Neutronen *n pl*
      f   neutrons *m pl* thermiques
      r   тепловые нейтроны *m pl*

T135   *e*   **thermal neutron source**
      d   thermische Neutronenquelle *f*, Quelle
         f der thermischen Neutronen
      f   source *f* de neutrons thermiques
      r   источник *m* тепловых нейтронов

T136   *e*   **thermal noise**
      d   Wärmerauschen *n*
      f   bruit *m* thermique
      r   тепловой шум *m*

T137   *e*   **thermal pumping**
      d   thermisches Pumpen *n*
      f   pompage *m* thermique
      r   тепловая накачка *f*

T138   *e*   **thermal radiation**
      d   Wärmestrahlung *f*,
         Temperaturstrahlung *f*
      f   radiation *f* thermique, rayonnement *m*
         thermique
      r   тепловое излучение *n*,
         температурное излучение *n*

T139   *e*   **thermal radiator**
      d   Temperaturstrahler *m*,
         Wärmestrahler *m*
      f   radiateur *m* thermique
      r   тепловой излучатель *m*

T140   *e*   **thermal relaxation**
      d   thermische Relaxation *f*
      f   relaxation *f* thermique
      r   тепловая релаксация *f*

T141   *e*   **thermal resistance**
      d   thermischer Widerstand *m*,
         Wärmewiderstand *m*
      f   résistance *f* thermique
      r   термическое сопротивление *n*,
         термосопротивление *n*

T142   *e*   **thermal resistivity**
      d   spezifischer Wärmewiderstand *m*
      f   résistivité *f* thermique
      r   удельное термическое
         сопротивление *n*

T143   *e*   **thermal stress**
      d   Wärmespannung *f*, thermische
         Spannung *f*
      f   contrainte *f* thermique
      r   температурное напряжение *n*

T144   *e*   **thermal switch**
      d   Wärmeschalter *m*
      f   commutateur *m* thermique
      r   тепловой ключ *m*, тепловой
         затвор *m*

T145   *e*   **thermal treatment**
      d   Wärmebehandlung *f*
      f   traitement *m* thermique
      r   термическая обработка *f*

T146   *e*   **thermal vibrations**
      d   Wärmeschwingungen *f pl*
      f   oscillations *f pl* thermiques
      r   тепловые колебания *n pl*

T147   *e*   **thermal waves** *see* temperature
         waves

T148   *e*   **thermionic cathode**
      d   Glühkatode *f*
      f   cathode *f* thermo-ionique
      r   термоэлектрический катод *m*,
         термокатод *m*

T149   *e*   **thermionic emission**
      d   thermische Elektronenemission *f*,
         Glühemission *f*
      f   émission *f* thermo-ionique
      r   термоэлектронная эмиссия *f*

T150   *e*   **thermistor**
      d   Thermistor *m*
      f   thermistance *f*, thermistor *m*
      r   термистор *m*

T151   *e*   **thermocouple**
      d   Thermopaar *n*
      f   thermocouple *m*
      r   термопара *f*

T152   *e*   **thermocouple calorimeter**
      d   Kalorimeter *n* mit Thermoelementen
      f   calorimètre *m* à thermocouples
      r   термопарный калориметр *m*

T153   *e*   **thermodiffusion** *see* thermal
         diffusion

T154   *e*   **thermodynamic cycle**
      d   thermodynamischer Kreisprozeß *m*
      f   cycle *m* thermodynamique
      r   термодинамический цикл *m*

T155   *e*   **thermodynamic diagram**
      d   thermodynamisches Diagramm *n*
      f   diagramme *m* thermodynamique
      r   термодинамическая диаграмма *f*

T156   *e*   **thermodynamic equilibrium**
      d   thermodynamisches Gleichgewicht *n*
      f   équilibre *m* thermodynamique
      r   термодинамическое равновесие *n*

T157   e   **thermodynamic limit**
     d   thermodynamische Grenze *f*
     f   limite *f* thermodynamique
     r   термодинамический предел *m*

T158   e   **thermodynamic paradox**
     d   thermodynamisches Paradoxon *n*
     f   paradoxe *m* thermodynamique
     r   термодинамический парадокс *m*

T159   e   **thermodynamic parameter**
     d   thermodynamischer Parameter *m*
     f   paramètre *m* thermodynamique
     r   термодинамический параметр *m*

T160   e   **thermodynamic potential**
     d   thermodynamisches Potential *n*
     f   potentiel *m* thermodynamique
     r   термодинамический потенциал *m*

T161   e   **thermodynamic probability**
     d   thermodynamische Wahrscheinlichkeit *f*
     f   probabilité *f* thermodynamique
     r   термодинамическая вероятность *f*

T162   e   **thermodynamic process**
     d   thermodynamischer Prozeß *m*
     f   processus *m* thermodynamique
     r   термодинамический процесс *m*

T163   e   **thermodynamics**
     d   Thermodynamik *f*
     f   thermodynamique *f*
     r   термодинамика *f*

T164   e   **thermodynamic similarity**
     d   thermodynamische Ähnlichkeit *f*
     f   similitude *f* thermodynamique
     r   термодинамическое подобие *n*

T165   e   **thermodynamics of irreversible processes** *see* **irreversible thermodynamics**

T166   e   **thermodynamic state**
     d   thermodynamischer Zustand *m*
     f   état *m* thermodynamique
     r   термодинамическое состояние *n*

T167   e   **thermodynamic system**
     d   thermodynamisches System *n*
     f   système *m* thermodynamique
     r   термодинамическая система *f*

T168   e   **thermodynamic temperature**
     d   thermodynamische Temperatur *f*
     f   température *f* thermodynamique
     r   термодинамическая температура *f*

T169   e   **thermodynamic temperature scale**
     d   thermodynamische Temperaturskala *f*
     f   échelle *f* thermodynamique des températures, échelle *f* thermodynamique
     r   термодинамическая температурная шкала *f*

T170   e   **thermoelasticity**
     d   Thermoelastizität *f*
     f   thermo-élasticité *f*
     r   термоупругость *f*

T171   e   **thermoelastic stress**
     d   thermoelastische Spannung *f*
     f   tension *f* thermo-élastique
     r   термоупругое напряжение *n*

T172   e   **thermoelectric cooling**
     d   thermoelektrische Kühlung *f*
     f   refroidissement *m* thermo-électrique
     r   термоэлектрическое охлаждение *n*

T173   e   **thermoelectric effects**
     d   thermoelektrische Erscheinungen *f pl*, thermoelektrische Effekte *m pl*
     f   effets *m pl* thermo-électriques
     r   термоэлектрические явления *n pl*

T174   e   **thermoelectric generator**
     d   Thermogenerator *m*, thermoelektrischer Generator *m*
     f   générateur *m* thermo-électrique
     r   термоэлектрический генератор *m*

T175   e   **thermoelectric pyrometer**
     d   thermoelektrisches Pyrometer *n*
     f   pyromètre *m* thermo-électrique
     r   термоэлектрический пирометр *m*

T176   e   **thermoelectric refrigerator**
     d   thermoelektrische Kälteanlage *f*
     f   réfrigérateur *m* thermo-électrique
     r   термоэлектрический холодильник *m*

T177   e   **thermoelectron image**
     d   Glühelelektronenbild *n*, Thermoelektronenbild *n*
     f   image *f* à thermo-électrons.
     r   изображение *n* в термоэлектронах

T178   e   **thermogalvanomagnetic effects**
     d   thermogalvanomagnetische Erscheinungen *f pl*, thermogalvanomagnetische Effekte *m pl*
     f   effets *m pl* thermogalvanomagnétiques
     r   термогальваномагнитные явления *n pl*

T179   e   **thermogravimetric analysis**
     d   thermogravimetrische Analyse *f*
     f   analyse *f* thermogravimétrique
     r   термогравиметрический анализ *m*

T180   e   **thermoluminescence**
     d   Thermolumineszenz *f*
     f   thermoluminescence *f*
     r   термолюминесценция *f*

T181   e   **thermomagnetic effects**
     d   thermomagnetische Erscheinungen *f pl*, thermomagnetische Effekte *m pl*

f effets *m pl* thermomagnétiques
r термомагнитные явления *n pl*

T182 *e* **thermomagnetic insulation**
d thermomagnetische Isolation *f*
f isolement *m* thermomagnétique
r магнитная термоизоляция *f*

T183 *e* **thermomechanical effect**
d thermomechanischer Effekt *m*
f effet *m* thermomécanique
r термомеханический эффект *m*

T184 *e* **thermometer**
d Thermometer *n*
f thermomètre *m*
r термометр *m*

T185 *e* **thermometry**
d Thermometrie *f*
f thermométrie *f*
r термометрия *f*

T186 *e* **thermonuclear energy**
d Thermonuklearenergie *f*,
thermonukleare Energie *f*
f énergie *f* thermonucléaire
r термоядерная энергия *f*

T187 *e* **thermonuclear fusion**
d thermonukleare Kernfusion *f*
f fusion *f* thermonucléaire
r термоядерный синтез *m*

T188 *e* **thermonuclear plasma**
d thermonukleares Plasma *n*
f plasma *m* thermonucléaire
r термоядерная плазма *f*

T189 *e* **thermonuclear reaction**
d thermonukleare Reaktion *f*
f réaction *f* thermonucléaire
r термоядерная реакция *f*

T190 *e* **thermonuclear reactor**
d Fusionsreaktor *m*
f réacteur *m* thermonucléaire
r термоядерный реактор *m*

T191 *e* **thermonuclear target**
d thermonukleares Target *n*
f cible *f* thermonucléaire
r термоядерная мишень *f*

T192 *e* **thermoplastic material**
d Thermoplast *m*, thermoplastischer
Kunststoff *m*
f matière *f* thermoplastique
r термопластичный материал *m*

T193 *e* **thermoregulator**
d Temperaturregler *m*
f thermorégulateur *m*
r терморегулятор *m*

T194 *e* **thermosphere**
d Thermosphäre *f*

f thermosphère *f*
r термосфера *f*

T195 *e* **thermostat**
d Thermostat *m*
f thermostat *m*
r термостат *m*

T196 *e* **thermostated cell**
d thermostatierte Küvette *f*
f cellule *f* thermostatisée
r термостатированная кювета *f*

T197 *e* **thermostriction**
d Thermostriktion *f*
f thermostriction *f*
r термострикция *f*

T198 *e* **theta pinch**
d Theta-Pinch *m*
f pincement *m* orthogonal, striction *f*
orthogonal, thêta-pinch *m*
r тета-пинч *m*, ϑ-пинч *m*

T199 *e* **thick film**
d Dickschicht *f*, Dickfilm *m*
f film *m* épais
r толстая плёнка *f*

T200 *e* **thickness**
d Dicke *f*; Stärke *f*
f épaisseur *f*
r толщина *f*

T201 *e* **thickness gage**
d Dickenlehre *f*
f jauge *f* d'épaisseur
r толщиномер *m*

T202 *e* **thin film**
d Dünnschicht *f*, Dünnfilm *m*
f film *m* mince, couche *f* mince
r тонкая плёнка *f*

T203 *e* **thin-film electronics**
d Dünnschichtelektronik *f*,
Dünnfilmelektronik *f*
f électronique *f* à film mince,
électronique *f* à couche mince
r плёночная электроника *f*,
тонкоплёночная электроника *f*

T204 *e* **thin-film filter**
d Dünnfilmfilter *n*
f filtre *m* à film mince, filtre *m* à
couche mince
r тонкоплёночный фильтр *m*

T205 *e* **thin-film interferometer**
d Dünnschichtinterferometer *n*
f interféromètre *m* à film mince,
interféromètre *m* à couche mince
r тонкоплёночный интерферометр *m*

T206 *e* **thin-film laser**
d Dünnfilmlaser *m*, Dünnschichtlaser *m*
f laser *m* à couche mince
r тонкоплёночный лазер *m*

T207   *e*   thin lens
     d   dünne Linse *f*, kurze Linse *f*
     f   lentillè *f* mince
     r   тонкая линза *f*

T208   *e*   thin plate
     d   dünne Platte *f*
     f   plaque *f* mince
     r   тонкая пластинка *f*

T209   *e*   third law of thermodynamics
     d   dritter Hauptsatz *m* der
        Thermodynamik, Nernstscher
        Wärmesatz *m*
     f   troisième principe *m* de la
        thermodynamique
     r   третье начало *n* термодинамики

T210   *e*   third sound
     d   dritter Schall *m*
     f   troisième son *m*
     r   третий звук *m (в гелии)*

T211   *e*   thixotropy
     d   Thixotropie *f*
     f   thixotropie *f*
     r   тиксотропия *f*

T212   *e*   **Thomson scattering**
     d   Thomson-Streuung *f*, Thomsonsche
        Streuung *f*
     f   diffusion *f* de Thomson
     r   томсоновское рассеяние *n*

T213   *e*   thorium, Th
     d   Thorium *n*
     f   thorium *m*
     r   торий *m*

T214   *e*   three-body problem
     d   Dreikörperproblem *n*
     f   problème *m* des trois corps
     r   задача *f* трёх тел

T215   *e*   three-component sensor
     d   Dreikomponentengeber *m*,
        Dreikomponentensensor *m*
     f   capteur *m* à trois composantes
     r   трёхкомпонентный датчик *m*

T216   *e*   three-dimensional image, 3-D image
     d   räumliches Bild *n*,
        Dreidimensionalabbildung *f*
     f   image *f* à trois dimensions
     r   трёхмерное изображение *n*,
        объёмное изображение *n*,
        пространственное изображение *n*

T217   *e*   three-dimensional model
     d   dreidimensionales Modell *n*,
        räumliches Modell *n*
     f   modèle *m* à trois dimensions, modèle
        m spatial
     r   трёхмерная модель *f*,
        пространственная модель *f*

T218   *e*   three-dimensional space
     d   dreidimensionaler Raum *m*
     f   espace *m* à trois dimensions
     r   трёхмерное пространство *n*

T219   *e*   three-halves power law
     d   Drei-Halbe-Gesetz *n*, Langmuirsches
        Raumladungsgesetz *n*
     f   loi *f* de puissance 3/2
     r   закон *m* трёх вторых

T220   *e*   three-level laser
     d   Dreiniveaulaser *m*, Laser *m* mit drei
        Energieniveaus
     f   laser *m* à trois niveaux
     r   трёхуровневый лазер *m*

T221   *e*   three-level maser
     d   Dreiniveaumaser *m*
     f   maser *m* à trois niveaux
     r   трёхуровневый мазер *m*

T222   *e*   three-phase current
     d   Drehstrom *m*
     f   courant *m* triphasé
     r   трёхфазный ток *m*

T223   *e*   threshold
     d   Schwelle *f*
     f   seuil *m*
     r   порог *m*

T224   *e*   threshold intensity
     d   Schwellenintensität *f*
     f   intensité *f* de seuil
     r   пороговая интенсивность *f*

T225   *e*   threshold of hearing
     d   Hörschwelle *f*
     f   seuil *m* d'audibilité
     r   порог *m* слышимости

T226   *e*   threshold of pain
     d   obere Hörschwelle *f*,
        Schmerzschwelle *f*
     f   seuil *m* supérieur d'audibilité *(en
        acoustique)*
     r   порог *m* болевого ощущения *(в
        акустике)*

T227   *e*   threshold of power
     d   Grenzleistung *f*
     f   puissance *f* de seuil
     r   пороговая мощность *f*

T228   *e*   threshold of vision
     d   Sichtbarkeitsschwelle *f*
     f   seuil *m* de la visibilité
     r   порог *m* зрительного ощущения,
        порог *m* видимости

T229   *e*   threshold of visual perception *see*
        threshold of vision

T230   *e*   threshold voltage
     d   Schwellenspannung *f*

f tension *f* de seuil
r пороговое напряжение *n*

T231 *e* threshold wavelength
d obere Grenzwellenlänge *f*,
Grenzwellenlänge *f*
f longueur *f* d'onde de seuil
r пороговая длина *f* волны

T232 *e* throttling
d Drosseln *n*, Drosselung *f*
f étranglement *m*
r дросселирование *n*

T233 *e* thulium, Th
d Thulium *n*
f thulium *m*
r тулий *m*

T234 *e* thyratron
d Thyratron *n*
f thyratron *m*
r тиратрон *m*

T235 *e* thyristor
d Thyristor *m*
f thyristor *m*
r тиристор *m*

T236 *e* tidal motion
d Gezeitenbewegung *f*, Tidenbewegung *f*
f mouvement *m* dû aux marées
r приливное движение *n*

T237 *e* tide
d Flut *f*
f marée *f*
r прилив *m*

T238 *e* tilt *see* slope

T239 *e* timbre
d Klangfarbe *f*
f timbre *m*
r тембр *m*

T240 *e* time
d Zeit *f*
f temps *m*
r время *n*

T241 *e* time averaging
d Zeitmittelwertbildung *f*, zeitliches
Mitteln *n*
f moyennage *m* sur le temps
r усреднение *n* по времени

T242 *e* time base
d Zeitbasis *f*, Zeitachse *f*, Zeitlinie *f*
f base *f* de balayage
r развёртка *f* (в осциллографе)

T243 *e* time coherence
d Zeitkohärenz *f*, zeitliche Kohärenz *f*
f cohérence *f* temporelle
r временная когерентность *f*

T244 *e* time constant
d Zeitkonstante *f*
f constante *f* du temps
r постоянная *f* времени

T245 *e* time delay
d Zeitverzögerung *f*, zeitliche
Verzögerung *f*
f retard *m*, délai *m*
r временная задержка *f*;
запаздывание *n*

T246 *e* time dependence
d Zeitabhängigkeit *f*, zeitliche
Abhängigkeit *f*
f fonction *f* du temps
r зависимость *f* от времени,
временная зависимость *f*

T247 *e* time evolution *see* temporal
evolution

T248 *e* time interval
d Zeitintervall *n*
f intervalle *m m* de temps
r временной интервал *m*, интервал *m*
времени

T249 *e* time-interval measurement
d Zeitintervallmessung *f*
f mesure *f* des intervalles de temps
r измерение *n* интервалов времени

T250 *e* time inversion
d Zeitumkehr *f*
f inversion *f* de temps
r обращение *n* времени

T251 *e* time irreversibility
d Zeitirreversibilität *f*
f irréversibilité *f* du temps
r необратимость *f* времени

T252 *e* time lag, timelag *see* time delay

T253 *e* time-like interval
d zeitartiges Intervall *n*
f intervalle *m* du genre temps
r времениподобный интервал *m*

T254 *e* time measurement
d Zeitmessung *f*
f mesure *f* de temps
r измерение *n* времени

T255 *e* time-of-flight mass spectrometer
d Laufzeitmassenspektrometer *n*
f spectromètre *m* de masse à temps de
transit
r времяпролётный
масс-спектрометр *m*

T256 *e* time-of-flight spectrometer
d Laufzeitspektrometer *n*
f spectromètre *m* à temps de transit
r времяпролётный спектрометр *m*

T257　*e*　time resolution
　　　　d　Zeitauflösung *f*, zeitliches
　　　　　　Auflösungsvermögen *n*,
　　　　　　Zeitauflösungsvermögen *n*
　　　　f　pouvoir *m* de résolution dans le temps
　　　　r　временнóе разрешение *n*,
　　　　　　разрешающая способность *f* по
　　　　　　времени

T258　*e*　time-resolved spectroscopy
　　　　d　Zeitauflösungsspektroskopie *f*
　　　　f　spectroscopie *f* à pouvoir de résolution
　　　　　　dans le temps
　　　　r　спектроскопия *f* с временны́м
　　　　　　разрешением

T259　*e*　time reversal
　　　　d　Zeitumkehr *f*
　　　　f　inversion *f* de temps
　　　　r　обращение *n* времени

T260　*e*　time reversal invariance
　　　　d　T-Invarianz *f*
　　　　f　invariance *f* par rapport à l'inversion
　　　　　　de temps
　　　　r　инвариантность *f* относительно
　　　　　　обращения времени

T261　*e*　time variation
　　　　d　Zeitveränderlichkeit *f*, Zeitvariabilität *f*
　　　　f　variation *f* avec le temps
　　　　r　изменение *n* во времени

T262　*e*　timing
　　　　d　Zeitsteuerung *f*; Synchronisierung *f*
　　　　f　minutage *m*; synchronisation *f*
　　　　r　хронирование *n*; синхронизация *f*

T263　*e*　tin, Sn
　　　　d　Zinn *n*
　　　　f　étain *m*
　　　　r　олово

T264　*e*　T-invariance *see* time reversal
　　　　　　invariance

T265　*e*　titanium, Ti
　　　　d　Titan *n*
　　　　f　titane *m*
　　　　r　титан *m*

T266　*e*　tokamak
　　　　d　Tokamak *m*
　　　　f　tokamak *m*
　　　　r　токамак *m*

T267　*e*　tolerance dose
　　　　d　zulässige Dosis *f*, Toleranzdosis *f*,
　　　　　　zulässige Dosisleistung *f*, verträgliche
　　　　　　Dosisleistung *f*
　　　　f　dose *f* tolérée *(d'irradiation)*
　　　　r　допустимая доза *f* *(облучения)*

T268　*e*　tomographic image
　　　　d　Tomographenbild *n*

　　　　f　image *f* tomographique
　　　　r　томографическое изображение *n*

T269　*e*　tomography
　　　　d　Tomographie *f*
　　　　f　tomographie *f*
　　　　r　томография *f*

T270　*e*　tone
　　　　d　Ton *m*
　　　　f　son *m*, ton *m*
　　　　r　тон *m*

T271　*e*　tonne, t
　　　　d　Tonne *f*
　　　　f　tonne *f*
　　　　r　тонна *f*

T272　*e*　top
　　　　d　1. Kreisel *m* 2. Spitze *f*
　　　　f　1. rotateur *m*, toupie *f* 2. sommet *m*
　　　　r　1. волчок *m* 2. вершина *f*

T273　*e*　topological invariance
　　　　d　topologische Invarianz *f*
　　　　f　invariance *f* topologique
　　　　r　топологическая инвариантность *f*

T274　*e*　topological invariant
　　　　d　topologische Invariante *f*
　　　　f　invariant *m* topologique
　　　　r　топологический инвариант *m*

T275　*e*　topological structure
　　　　d　topologische Struktur *f*
　　　　f　structure *f* topologique
　　　　r　топологическая структура *f*

T276　*e*　topological transformation
　　　　d　topologische Transformation *f*
　　　　f　représentation *f* topologique
　　　　r　топологическое преобразование *n*

T277　*e*　topology
　　　　d　Topologie *f*
　　　　f　topologie *f*
　　　　r　топология *f*

T278　*e*　toponium
　　　　d　Toponium *n*
　　　　f　toponium *m*
　　　　r　топоний *m*

T279　*e*　top quark
　　　　d　t-Quark *n*
　　　　f　quark *m* t
　　　　r　верхний кварк *m*, t-кварк *m*

T280　*e*　torch discharge
　　　　d　Torch-Entladung *f*
　　　　f　décharge *f* en torche
　　　　r　факельный разряд *m*

T281　*e*　toroidal chamber
　　　　d　Toroidkammer *f*
　　　　f　chambre *f* toroïdale
　　　　r　тороидальная камера *f*

T282   *e*   **toroidal configuration**
     d   Toroidkonfiguration *f*
     f   configuration *f* toroïdale
     r   тороидальная конфигурация *f*

T283   *e*   **toroidal divertor**
     d   toroidaler Divertor *m*
     f   diverteur *m* toroïdal
     r   тороидальный дивертор *m*

T284   *e*   **toroidal magnetic field**
     d   toroidales magnetisches Feld *n*
     f   champ *m* toroïdal magnétique
     r   тороидальное магнитное поле *n*

T285   *e*   **toroidal pinch**
     d   toroidaler Pinch *m*, Toroidpinch *m*
     f   pincement *m* toroïdal, striction *f* toroïdale
     r   тороидальный пинч *m*

T286   *e*   **toroidal system**
     d   toroidales System *n*
     f   système *m* toroïdal
     r   тороидальная система *f*

T287   *e*   **torque**
     d   Drehmoment *n*, Moment *n* des Kräftepaares
     f   couple *m*, moment *m* du couple
     r   вращающий момент *m*; крутящий момент *m*

T288   *e*   **torque magnetometer**
     d   Torsionsmagnetometer *n*, Drehmagnetometer *n*
     f   magnétomètre *m* à torsion
     r   магнитный анизометр *m*

T289   *e*   **torr**
     d   Torr *n*
     f   torr *m*
     r   торр *m (единица давления)*

T290   *e*   **Torricellian vacuum**
     d   Torricellische Leere *f*
     f   vide *m* de Torricelli
     r   торричеллиева пустота *f*

T291   *e*   **torsion**
     d   Torsion *f*, Verdrehung *f*
     f   torsion *f*
     r   кручение *n*; скручивание *n*

T292   *e*   **torsional rigidity**
     d   Torsionssteifigkeit *f*, Verdrehungssteifigkeit *f*, Verdrehsteifigkeit *f*
     f   rigidité *f* de torsion
     r   крутильная жёсткость *f*

T293   *e*   **torsional strain**
     d   Torsionsverzerrung *f*, Torsionsdeformation *f*, Verdrehungsverformung *f*, Verdrehverformung *f*

     f   déformation *f* due à la torsion
     r   деформация *f* кручения

T294   *e*   **torsional vibrations**
     d   Torsionsschwingungen *f pl*
     f   vibrations *f pl* de torsion
     r   крутильные колебания *n pl*, торсионные колебания *n pl*

T295   *e*   **torsion balance**
     d   Torsionswaage *f*
     f   balance *f* de torsion
     r   крутильные весы *pl*

T296   *e*   **torsion modulus**
     d   Torsionsmodul *m*
     f   module *m* de torsion
     r   модуль *m* кручения

T297   *e*   **torsion pendulum**
     d   Torsionspendel *n*, Drehpendel *n*
     f   pendule *m* à torsion
     r   крутильный маятник *m*

T298   *e*   **total absorption**
     d   Gesamtabsorption *f*, Totalabsorption *f*
     f   absorption *f* totale
     r   полное поглощение *n*

T299   *e*   **total cross-section**
     d   Gesamtquerschnitt *m*
     f   section *f* totale
     r   полное сечение *n*

T300   *e*   **total cross-section for scattering**
     d   Streuungsgesamtquerschnitt *m*
     f   section *f* efficace totale de la diffusion
     r   полное сечение *n* рассеяния

T301   *e*   **total eclipse**
     d   totale Finsternis *f*, vollständige Verfinsterung *f*
     f   éclipse *f* totale
     r   полное затмение *n*

T302   *e*   **total intensity**
     d   Gesamtintensität *f*
     f   intensité *f* totale
     r   полная интенсивность *f*, интегральная интенсивность *f*

T303   *e*   **total internal reflection**
     d   innere Totalreflexion *f*
     f   réflexion *f* interne totale
     r   полное внутреннее отражение *n*

T304   *e*   **total quantum number** *see* **principal quantum number**

T305   *e*   **total radiator**
     d   schwarzer Strahler *m*
     f   radiateur *m* total
     r   полный излучатель *m*, чёрное тело *n*, абсолютно чёрное тело *n*

T306   *e*   **total reflection**
     d   Totalreflexion *f*, totale Reflexion *f*

f   réflexion f totale
r   полное отражение n

T307 e   **Townsend coefficient**
d   Townsend-Koeffizient m
f   coefficient m de Townsend
r   коэффициент m Таунсенда

T308 e   **Townsend discharge**
d   Townsend-Entladung f
f   décharge f Townsend, décharge f de
Townsend
r   разряд m Таунсенда,
таунсендовский разряд m

T309 e   **tracer**
d   Radioindikator m, Tracer m,
Leitisotop n, Isotopenindikator m
f   atome m marqué; indicateur m
atomique
r   меченый атом m; изотопный
индикатор m

T310 e   **tracer isotope**
d   Tracerisotop n, Leitisotop n
f   isotope m indicateur
r   изотоп-индикатор m

T311 e   **tracer method**
d   Indikatormethode f, Tracermethode f
f   méthode f des éléments traceurs,
méthode f des traceurs
r   метод m изотопных индикаторов,
метод m меченых атомов

T312 e   **track**
d   Spur f, Teilchenspur f
f   trace f
r   трек m (частицы)

T313 e   **track chamber**
d   Spurenkammer f
f   chambre f à trace
r   трековая камера f

T314 e   **track detector**
d   Spurdetektor m, Kernspurdetektor m
f   détecteur m à trace
r   трековый детектор m

T315 e   **track membrane**
d   Spurmembran f
f   membrane f à trace
r   трековая мембрана f, ядерный
фильтр m

T316 e   **trailing edge**
d   1. Hinterkante f, Abströmkante f 2.
Rückflanke f, Impulsrückflanke f
f   1. bord m de fuite 2. flanc m arrière
(d'impulsion)
r   1. задняя кромка f 2. срез m
(импульса)

T317 e   **trajectory**
d   Bahn f, Bahnkurve f, Bahnlinie f

f   trajectoire f
r   траектория f

T318 e   **trajectory perturbations**
d   Bahnstörungen f pl
f   perturbances f pl des trajectoires
r   возмущения n pl траекторий

T319 e   **transcrystalline fracture**
d   intrakristalliner Bruch m
f   cassure f intragranulaire, cassure f
intracristalline
r   внутризёренный излом m

T320 e   **transducer**
d   Meßumformer m
f   transducteur m de mesure; capteur m
r   измерительный преобразователь m;
датчик m

T321 e   **transfer**
d   Übertragung f
f   transfert
r   1. перенос m 2. передача f

T322 e   **transfer function**
d   Übertragungsfunktion f
f   fonction f de transfert
r   передаточная функция f

T323 e   **transform, transformation**
d   Transformation f
f   transformation f
r   преобразование n

T324 e   **transformation ratio**
d   Übersetzungsverhältnis n
f   rapport m de transformation
r   коэффициент m трансформации

T325 e   **transformer**
d   Transformator m, Trafo m
f   transformateur m
r   трансформатор m

T326 e   **transgranular fracture** see
transcrystalline fracture

T327 e   **transient** see **transient process**

T328 e   **transient motion** see **nonstationary
motion**

T329 e   **transient oscillation**
d   Übergangsschwingungen f pl
f   oscillations f pl transitoires
r   неустановившиеся колебания n pl,
переходные колебания n pl

T330 e   **transient process**
d   Übergangsvorgang m,
Übergangsprozeß f
f   processus m de transition
r   переходный процесс m;
установившийся процесс m

T331 e   **transient radiation** see **transition
radiation**

T332　e　transient response
　　　　d　Sprungcharakteristik f
　　　　f　caractéristique f transitoire
　　　　r　переходная характеристика f

T333　e　trans-isomer
　　　　d　trans-Form f, trans-Isomer n
　　　　f　isomère m trans
　　　　r　транс-изомер m

T334　e　transistor
　　　　d　Transistor m
　　　　f　transistor m
　　　　r　транзистор m

T335　e　transition
　　　　d　Übergang m
　　　　f　transition f
　　　　r　переход m

T336　e　transition identification
　　　　d　Übergangsidentifikation f
　　　　f　indentification f des transitions
　　　　r　идентификация f переходов

T337　e　transition intensity
　　　　d　Übergangsintensität f
　　　　f　intensité f de la transition
　　　　r　интенсивность f перехода

T338　e　transition metal
　　　　d　Übergangsmetall n
　　　　f　métal m de transition
　　　　r　переходный металл m

T339　e　transition operator
　　　　d　Übergangsoperator m
　　　　f　opérateur m de transition
　　　　r　оператор m перехода

T340　e　transition probability
　　　　d　Übergangswahrscheinlichkeit f
　　　　f　probabilité f de transition
　　　　r　вероятность f перехода

T341　e　transition radiation
　　　　d　Übergangsstrahlung f
　　　　f　rayonnement m de transition
　　　　r　переходное излучение n

T342　e　transition region
　　　　d　Übergangsgebiet n, Übergangszone f
　　　　f　zone f de transition
　　　　r　переходная область f, область f
　　　　　　перехода

T343　e　transition saturation
　　　　d　Übergangssättigung f
　　　　f　saturation f de la transition
　　　　r　насыщение n перехода

T344　e　transition state
　　　　d　Übergangszustand m
　　　　f　état m de transition
　　　　r　переходное состояние n

T345　e　transit time

　　　　d　Laufzeit f
　　　　f　temps m de vol
　　　　r　время n пролёта

T346　e　translation
　　　　d　1. Translation f, Schiebung f
　　　　　　2. Verschiebung f; Bewegung f
　　　　　　3. Translationsbewegung f
　　　　f　translation f
　　　　r　1. трансляция f; параллельный
　　　　　　перенос m 2. перемещение n
　　　　　　3. поступательное движение n

T347　e　translational invariance
　　　　d　Translationsinvarianz f
　　　　f　invariance f de translation
　　　　r　трансляционная инвариантность f

T348　e　translational motion
　　　　d　Translationsbewegung f
　　　　f　mouvement m de translation
　　　　r　1. переносное движение n
　　　　　　2. поступательное движение n

T349　e　translational symmetry
　　　　d　Translationssymmetrie f
　　　　f　symétrie f de translation
　　　　r　трансляционная симметрия f

T350　e　transmission
　　　　d　1. Durchlassung f, Transmission f
　　　　　　2. Fortleitung f 3. Übertragung f;
　　　　　　Senden n
　　　　f　transmission f
　　　　r　1. пропускание n (излучения)
　　　　　　2. распространение n 3. передача f

T351　e　transmission coefficient
　　　　d　Durchlaßkoeffizient m, Durchlaßgrad
　　　　　　m, Transmissionsgrad m
　　　　f　coefficient m de transmission
　　　　r　коэффициент m пропускания

T352　e　transmission curve
　　　　d　Durchlässigkeitskurve f
　　　　f　courbe f de transmission
　　　　r　кривая f пропускания

T353　e　transmission electron microscope
　　　　d　Durchstrahlungselektronenmikroskop
　　　　　　n, Transmissionselektronenmikroskop
　　　　　　n
　　　　f　microscope m électronique à
　　　　　　transmission
　　　　r　просвечивающий электронный
　　　　　　микроскоп m

T354　e　transmission factor see transmission
　　　　　　coefficient

T355　e　transmission line
　　　　d　Übertragungsleitung f
　　　　f　ligne f de transmission
　　　　r　линия f передачи

T356　e　transmittance see transmission
　　　　　　coefficient

T357   *e*   **transmitter**
     d   Sender *m*
     f   transmetteur *m*
     r   передатчик *m*

T358   *e*   **transmutation**
     d   Umwandlung *f*
     f   transmutation *f (des éléments)*
     r   превращение *n (элементов)*

T359   *e*   **transonic flight**
     d   transsonischer Flug *m*, schallnaher
       Flug *m*
     f   vol *m* à vitesse transsonique
     r   полёт *m* с околозвуковой скоростью

T360   *e*   **transonic flow**
     d   schallnahe Strömung *f*, transsonische
       Strömung *f*
     f   écoulement *m* transsonique
     r   околозвуковое течение *n*

T361   *e*   **transonic transition**
     d   Schalldurchgang *m*
     f   passage *m* transsonique
     r   переход *m* через звуковую скорость

T362   *e*   **transparency**
     d   Transparenz *f*
     f   transparence *f*
     r   1. прозрачность *f* 2. коэффициент
       m пропускания 3. транспарант *m*

T363   *e*   **transparent crystal**
     d   durchsichtiger Kristall *m*
     f   cristal *m* transparent
     r   прозрачный кристалл *m*

T364   *e*   **transparent dielectric**
     d   durchsichtiges Dielektrikum *n*
     f   diélectrique *m* transparent
     r   прозрачный диэлектрик *m*

T365   *e*   **transparent dye**
     d   durchlässiger Farbstoff *m*
     f   colorant *m* transparent
     r   прозрачный краситель *m*

T366   *e*   **transparent film**
     d   transparenter Film *m*
     f   film *m* transparent
     r   прозрачная плёнка *f*

T367   *e*   **transparent plasma**
     d   transparentes Plasma *n*
     f   plasma *m* transparent
     r   прозрачная плазма *f*

T368   *e*   **transport**
     d   Transport *m*
     f   transport *m*
     r   перенос *m*

T369   *e*   **transport coefficient**
     d   Transportfaktor *m*,
       Transportkoeffizient *m*
     f   coefficient *m* de transport
     r   коэффициент *m* переноса

T370   *e*   **transport cross-section**
     d   Transportwirkungsquerschnitt *m*,
       Wirkungsquerschnitt *m* des Transports
     f   section *f* efficace de transport
     r   сечение *n* переноса, транспортное
       сечение *n*

T371   *e*   **transport factor** *see* **kinetic coefficient**

T372   *e*   **transport phenomena**
     d   Transporterscheinungen *f pl*,
       Transportphänomene *m pl*
     f   phénomènes *m pl* de transfert,
       phénomènes *m pl* de transport
     r   явления *n pl* переноса

T373   *e*   **transport processes**
     d   Transportprozesse *m pl*
     f   processus *m pl* de transport
     r   процессы *m pl* переноса

T374   *e*   **transuranium element**
     d   Transuran *n*
     f   élément *m* transuranien
     r   трансурановый элемент *m*

T375   *e*   **transverse adiabatic invariant**
     d   transversale adiabatische Invariante *f*
     f   invariant *m* adiabatique transversal
     r   поперечный адиабатический
       инвариант *m*

T376   *e*   **transverse coherence**
     d   transversale Kohärenz *f*
     f   cohérence *f* transversale
     r   поперечная когерентность *f*

T377   *e*   **transverse diffusion**
     d   Transversaldiffusion *f*
     f   diffusion *f* transversale
     r   поперечная диффузия *f*

T378   *e*   **transverse electromagnetic wave**
     d   transversalelektromagnetische Welle *f*,
       TEM-Welle *f*
     f   onde *f* électromagnétique transversale
     r   поперечная электромагнитная волна
       f, TEM-волна *f*

T379   *e*   **transverse field**
     d   Transversalfeld *n*
     f   champ *m* transversal
     r   поперечное поле *n*

T380   *e*   **transverse mode**
     d   Transversalmode *f*, transversale
       Mode *f*
     f   mode *m* transversal
     r   поперечная мода *f*

T381   *e*   **transverse oscillation** *see* **transverse vibration**

T382 e transverse pumping
      d Transversalpumpen *n*
      f pompage *m* transversal
      r поперечная накачка *f*

T383 e transverse sound
      d transversaler Schall *m*,
         Transversalschall *m*
      f son *m* transversal
      r поперечный звук *m*

T384 e transverse vibration
      d transversale Schwingungen *f pl*
      f oscillations *f pl* transversales
      r поперечные колебания *n pl*

T385 e transverse wave
      d Transversalwelle *f*
      f onde *f* transversale
      r поперечная волна *f*

T386 e trap
      d Haftstelle *f*, Trap *m*
      f piège *m*
      r ловушка *f*

T387 e trap density
      d Haftstellendichte *f*
      f concentration *f* des pièges
      r концентрация *f* ловушек

T388 e trapped particle fraction
      d Anteil *m* der eingefangenen Teilchen
      f fraction *f* des particules captées
      r доля *f* захваченных частиц

T389 e trapped particles
      d eingefangene Teilchen *n pl*
      f particules *f pl* piégées
      r захваченные частицы *f pl*

T390 e trapped radiation
      d eingefangene Strahlung *f*
      f radiation *f* piégée
      r пленённое излучение *n*

T391 e trapping
      d Einfang *m*; Fangen *n*; Auffangen *n*
      f capture *f*, captage *m*
      r захват *m*; улавливание *n*

T392 e traveling ionospheric disturbance
      d ionosphärische Wanderstörung *f*
      f perturbation *f* ionosphérique mobile
      r перемещающееся ионосферное
         возмущение *n*

T393 e traveling wave
      d Wanderwelle *f*, fortschreitende Welle *f*
      f onde *f* progressive
      r бегущая волна *f*

T394 e traveling-wave aerial, traveling-wave
         antenna
      d Wanderwellenantenne *f*
      f antenne *f* à onde progressive
      r антенна *f* бегущей волны

T395 e traveling-wave factor
      d Wanderwellenkoeffizient *m*
      f taux *m* d'ondes progressives
      r коэффициент *m* бегущей волны,
         КБВ

T396 e traveling-wave tube
      d Wanderfeldröhre *f*
      f tube *m* à onde progressive
      r лампа *f* бегущей волны

T397 e travelling *see* traveling

T398 e trial-and-error method
      d Trial-and-error-Methode *f*,
         Probiermethode *f*
      f méthode *f* d'essai et d'erreur
      r метод *m* проб и ошибок

T399 e triangular pulse
      d Dreieckimpuls *m*
      f impulsion *f* triangulaire
      r треугольный импульс *m*, импульс *m*
         треугольной формы

T400 e triboelectricity
      d Reibungselektrizität *f*,
         Triboelektrizität *f*
      f tribo-électricité *f*
      r трибоэлектричество *n*

T401 e triboelectrization
      d Reibungselektrisierung *f*
      f électrisation *f* par frottement
      r электризация *f* трением

T402 e tribology
      d Tribologie *f*, Reibungslehre *f*
      f tribologie *f*
      r трибология *f (наука о трении)*

T403 e triboluminescence
      d Tribolumineszenz *f*,
         Reibungslumineszenz *f*
      f triboluminescence *f*
      r триболюминесценция *f*

T404 e trichromatic colorimetry
      d trichromatische Kolorimetrie *f*,
         Dreifarbenmessung *f*
      f colorimétrie *f* trichrome
      r трёхцветная колориметрия *f*

T405 e triclinic system
      d triklines Kristallsystem *n*, triklines
         System *n*
      f système *m* triclinique
      r триклинная сингония *f*, триклинная
         система *f*

T406 e trigatron
      d Trigatron *n*
      f trigatron *m*
      r тригатрон *m*

T407 e trigger
      d 1. Trigger *m* 2. Triggersignal *n*

	f	trigger *m*, basculeur *m*
	r	1. триггер *m* 2. запускающий сигнал *m*
T408	*e*	trigger pulse
	d	Triggerimpuls *m*, Auslöseimpuls *m*
	f	impulsion *f* de démarrage
	r	запускающий импульс *m*
T409	*e*	trigonal system
	d	trigonales Kristallsystem *n*
	f	système *m* trigonal
	r	тригональная сингония *f*, тригональная система *f*
T410	*e*	triode
	d	Triode *f*
	f	triode *f*
	r	триод *m*
T411	*e*	triple point
	d	Tripelpunkt *m*
	f	triple point *m*
	r	тройная точка *f*
T412	*e*	triplet
	d	Triplett *n*
	f	triplet *m*
	r	триплет *m*
T413	*e*	tritium, T
	d	Tritium *n*
	f	tritium *m*
	r	тритий *m*
T414	*e*	tritium target
	d	Tritiumtarget *n*
	f	cible *f* de tritium
	r	тритиевая мишень *f*
T415	*e*	triton
	d	Triton *n*
	f	triton *m*
	r	тритон *m*
T416	*e*	trochotron
	d	Trochotron *n*
	f	trochotron *m*
	r	трохотрон *m*
T417	*e*	tropical year
	d	tropisches Jahr *n*
	f	année *f* tropique
	r	тропический год *m*
T418	*e*	tropopause
	d	Tropopause *f*
	f	tropopause *f*
	r	тропопауза *f*
T419	*e*	troposphere
	d	Troposphäre *f*
	f	troposphère *f*
	r	тропосфера *f*
T420	*e*	tropospheric wave
	d	troposphärische Welle *f*, Troposphärenwelle *f*
	f	onde *f* troposphérique
	r	тропосферная волна *f*
T421	*e*	true absorption *see* proper absorption
T422	*e*	true neutral meson
	d	wahres Neutronmeson *n*
	f	méson *m* neutre vrai
	r	истинно нейтральный мезон *m*
T423	*e*	true neutral particle
	d	wahres Neutralteilchen *n*
	f	particule *f* neutre vraie
	r	абсолютно нейтральная частица *f*, истинно нейтральная частица *f*
T424	*e*	true quark
	d	wahres Quark *n*
	f	quark *m* vrai
	r	истинный кварк *m*
T425	*e*	tube
	d	Röhre *f*
	f	tube *m*
	r	1. трубка *f* 2. электронная лампа *f*
T426	*e*	tube of current
	d	Stromröhre *f*
	f	tube *m* de courant
	r	трубка *f* тока
T427	*e*	tunable laser
	d	durchstimmbarer Laser *m*
	f	laser *m* accordable
	r	перестраиваемый лазер *m*
T428	*e*	tunable magnetron
	d	durchstimmbares Magnetron *n*
	f	magnétron *m* accordable
	r	перестраиваемый магнетрон *m*
T429	*e*	tungsten, W
	d	Wolfram *n*
	f	tungstène *m*
	r	вольфрам *m*
T430	*e*	tuning
	d	Abstimmung *f*
	f	accord *m*
	r	настройка *f*
T431	*e*	tuning fork
	d	Stimmgabel *f*
	f	diapason *m*
	r	камертон *m*
T432	*e*	tuning indicator
	d	Abstimmanzeigeröhre *f*
	f	indicateur *m* de syntonisation, indicateur *m* d'accord
	r	индикатор *m* настройки
T433	*e*	tuning range
	d	Abstimmbereich *m*; Durchstimmbereich *m*
	f	étendue *f* d'accord, plage *f* d'accord
	r	диапазон *m* перестройки

T434   *e* tunnel current
     d Tunnelstrom *m*
     f courant *m* tunnel
     r туннельный ток *m*

T435   *e* tunnel diode
     d Tunneldiode *f*
     f diode *f* tunnel
     r туннельный диод *m*

T436   *e* tunnel effect
     d Tunneleffekt *m*
     f effet *m* tunnel
     r туннельный эффект *m*

T437   *e* tunnel electron microscope
     d Tunnelmikroskop *n*
     f microscope *m* tunnel
     r туннельный электронный
        микроскоп *m*

T438   *e* tunnel emission
     d Tunnelemission *f*
     f émission *f* tunnel
     r туннельная эмиссия *f*

T439   *e* tunneling
     d Tunneln *n*, Durchtunnelung *f*
     f effet *m* tunnel
     r туннелирование *n*

T440   *e* tunnel injection
     d Tunnelinjektion *f*
     f injection *f* par effet tunnel
     r туннельная инжекция *f*

T441   *e* tunnel microscope *see* tunnel
        electron microscope

T442   *e* tunnel transition
     d Tunnelübergang *m*
     f transition *f* tunnel
     r туннельный переход *m*

T443   *e* turbidity
     d Trübung *f*
     f turbidité *f*
     r мутность *f* *(среды)*

T444   *e* turbid medium
     d trübes Medium *n*
     f milieu *m* trouble
     r мутная среда *f*

T445   *e* turbine
     d Turbine *f*
     f turbine *f*
     r турбина *f*

T446   *e* turbulence
     d Turbulenz *f*
     f turbulence *f*
     r турбулентность *f*

T447   *e* turbulent boundary layer
     d turbulente Grenzschicht *f*
     f couche *f* limite turbulente
     r турбулентный пограничный слой *m*

T448   *e* turbulent diffusion
     d Turbulenzdiffusion *f*
     f diffusion *f* turbulente
     r турбулентная диффузия *f*

T449   *e* turbulent flow
     d turbulente Strömung *f*
     f écoulement *m* turbulent
     r турбулентное течение *n*

T450   *e* turbulent heating
     d turbulente Aufheizung *f*
     f chauffage *m* turbulent
     r турбулентный нагрев *m*

T451   *e* turbulent mixing
     d turbulente Durchmischung *f*,
        turbulente Mischung *f*,
        Turbulenzmischung *f*
     f mélange *m* turbulent
     r турбулентное перемешивание *n*

T452   *e* turbulent motion
     d turbulente Bewegung *f*,
        Turbulenzbewegung *f*
     f mouvement *m* turbulent
     r турбулентное движение *n*

T453   *e* turbulent plasma
     d turbulentes Plasma *n*
     f plasma *m* turbulent
     r турбулентная плазма *f*

T454   *e* turbulent plasma heating
     d turbulente Plasmaaufheizung *f*
     f chauffage *m* turbulent du plasma
     r турбулентный нагрев *m* плазмы

T455   *e* Turing machine
     d Turing-Maschine *f*
     f machine *f* de Turing
     r машина *f* Тьюринга

T456   *e* turn
     d 1. Windung *f* 2. Umdrehung *f*
     f 1. spire *f* 2. tour *m*
     r 1. виток *m* 2. оборот *m*

T457   *e* twin
     d Zwilling *m*, Zwillingskristall *m*
     f macle *f*, cristal *m* maclé
     r двойник *m* *(кристалла)*

T458   *e* twin boundary
     d Zwillingsgrenze *f*
     f joint *m* de macles
     r двойниковая граница *f*

T459   *e* twin calorimeter
     d Differentialkalorimeter *n*,
        Zwillingskalorimeter *n*
     f calorimètre *m* double
     r двойной калориметр *m*

T460   *e*   twinkling
      d   Funkeln *n*
      f   scintillation *f (des étoiles)*
      r   мерцание *(звёзд)*

T461   *e*   twinning
      d   Zwillingsbildung *f*, Verzwilligung *f*
      f   maclage *m*, hémitropie *f*
      r   двойникование *n*

T462   *e*   twinning plane
      d   Zwillingsebene *f*
      f   plan *m* double, plan *m* de macle
      r   плоскость *f* двойникования

T463   *e*   twin paradox
      d   Zwillingsparadoxon *n*
      f   paradoxe *m* de voyageurs de Langevin
      r   парадокс *m* близнецов, парадокс *m* часов

T464   *e*   twist, twisting
      d   Torsion *f*, Verdrehung *f*
      f   torsion *f*
      r   кручение *n*

T465   *e*   two-band model
      d   Zweibändermodell *n*
      f   modèle *m* à deux bandes
      r   двухзонная модель *f*

T466   *e*   two-base diode
      d   Doppelbasisdiode *f*
      f   diode *f* à deux bases
      r   двухбазовый диод *m*

T467   *e*   two-beam interference
      d   Zweistrahlinterferenz *f*
      f   interférence *f* à deux rayons
      r   двухлучевая интерференция *f*

T468   *e*   two-beam interferometer
      d   Zweistrahlinterferometer *n*
      f   interféromètre *m* à deux rayons
      r   двухлучевой интерферометр *m*

T469   *e*   two-body problem
      d   Zweikörperproblem *n*
      f   problème *m* des deux corps
      r   задача *f* двух тел

T470   *e*   two-component liquid
      d   Zweikomponentenflüssigkeit *f*
      f   liquide *m* à deux composantes
      r   двухкомпонентная жидкость *f*

T471   *e*   two-component plasma
      d   Zweikomponentenplasma *n*
      f   plasma *m* à deux composantes
      r   двухкомпонентная плазма *f*

T472   *e*   two-component plasma kinetics
      d   Kinetik *f* der Zweikomponentenplasma
      f   cinétique *f* du plasma à deux composantes
      r   кинетика *f* двухкомпонентной плазмы

T473   *e*   two-dimensional electron gas
      d   zweidimensionales Elektronengas *n*
      f   gaz *m* d'électrons bidimensionnel
      r   двумерный электронный газ *m*

T474   *e*   two-dimensional image, 2-D image
      d   zweidimensionales Bild *n*, Zweidimensionalabbildung *f*
      f   image *f* bidimensionnelle
      r   двумерное изображение *n*, плоское изображение *n*

T475   *e*   two-dimensional model
      d   zweidimensionales Modell *n*
      f   modèle *m* bidimensionnel
      r   двумерная модель *f*

T476   *e*   two-dimensional spectral classification
      d   zweidimensionale Spektralklassifikation *f*
      f   classification *f* spectrale bidimensionnelle
      r   двумерная спектральная классификация *f*

T477   *e*   two-element interferometer
      d   Zweielementeninterferometer *n*
      f   interféromètre *m* à deux éléments
      r   двухэлементный интерферометр *m*, суммирующий интерферометр *m*

T478   *e*   two-fluid model
      d   Zweiflüssigkeitenmodell *n (vom Helium)*
      f   modèle *m* à deux fluides *(d'hélium)*
      r   двухжидкостная модель *f (гелия)*

T479   *e*   two-level atom
      d   Zweiniveauatom *n*
      f   atome *m* à deux niveaux
      r   двухуровневый атом *m*

T480   *e*   two-level laser
      d   Zweiniveaulaser *m*
      f   laser *m* à deux niveaux
      r   двухуровневый лазер *m*

T481   *e*   two-level maser
      d   Zweiniveaumaser *m*
      f   maser *m* à deux niveaux
      r   двухуровневый мазер *m*

T482   *e*   two-level model
      d   Zweiniveaumodell *n*
      f   modèle *m* à deux niveaux
      r   двухуровневая модель *f*

T483   *e*   two-liquid hydrodynamics
      d   Zweiflüssigkeiten-Hydrodynamik *f (des Plasmas)*
      f   hydrodynamique *f* à deux liquides *(du plasma)*
      r   двухжидкостная гидродинамика *f (плазмы)*

T484 e two-magnon absorption
    d Zweimagnonenabsorption f
    f absorption f à deux magnons
    r двухмагнонное поглощение n

T485 e two-path interference see two-beam
      interference

T486 e two-phase flow
    d Zweiphasenströmung f
    f écoulement m à deux phases
    r двухфазное течение n

T487 e two-photon absorption
    d Zweiphotonenabsorption f
    f absorption f à deux photons
    r двухфотонное поглощение n

T488 e two-photon dissociation
    d Zweiphotonendissoziation f
    f dissociation f à deux photons
    r двухфотонная диссоциация f

T489 e two-photon radiation
    d Zweiphotonenstrahlung f
    f rayonnement m de deux photons
    r двухфотонное излучение n

T490 e two-photon transition
    d Zweiphotonenübergang m
    f transition f de deux photons
    r двухфотонный переход m

T491 e two-step ionization
    d Zweistufenionisation f
    f ionisation f à deux étapes
    r двухступенчатая ионизация f

T492 e Tyndall effect
    d Tyndall-Effekt m
    f effet m Tyndall
    r эффект m Тиндаля

U

U1 e UFO see unidentified flying object

U2 e ultimate density
    d Grenzdichte f
    f densité f limite
    r предельная плотность f

U3 e ultimate strength
    d Bruchfestigkeit f
    f résistance f limite
    r предел m прочности

U4 e ultimate tensile stress
    d Bruchspannung f
    f contrainte f de rupture
    r разрывное напряжение n,
      разрушающее напряжение n

U5 e ultra-cold neutrons
    d ultrakalte Neutronen n pl
    f neutrons m pl ultrafroids
    r ультрахолодные нейтроны m pl

U6 e ultrahigh pressure
    d Höchstdruck m
    f très haute pression f
    r сверхвысокое давление n

U7 e ultrahigh vacuum
    d Ultrahochvakuum n, Höchstvakuum n
    f ultravide m, ultra-haut vide m
    r сверхвысокий вакуум m

U8 e ultralong-distance propagation of
      radio waves
    d Überreichweite f der Radiowellen
    f propagation f hyperlointaine des
      ondes radioélectriques
    r сверхдальнее распространение n
      радиоволн

U9 e ultramicroscope
    d Ultramikroskop n
    f ultra-microscope m
    r ультрамикроскоп m

U10 e ultrashort pulse
    d Ultrakurzimpuls m
    f impulsion f ultra-courte
    r ультракороткий импульс m,
      сверхкороткий импульс m

U11 e ultrashort waves
    d Ultrakurzwellen f pl
    f ondes f pl ultra-courtes
    r ультракороткие волны f pl

U12 e ultrasonic absorption
    d Ultraschallabsorption f
    f absorption f ultrasonore
    r поглощение n ультразвука

U13 e ultrasonic amplification
    d Ultraschallverstärkung f
    f amplification f ultrasonore
    r усиление n ультразвука

U14 e ultrasonic attenuation
    d Ultraschalldämpfung f,
      Ultraschallabschwächung f
    f amortissement m ultrasonore
    r затухание n ультразвука

U15 e ultrasonic bubble chamber
    d Ultraschall-Blasenkammer f
    f chambre f à bulles ultrasonore
    r ультразвуковая пузырьковая
      камера f

U16 e ultrasonic cavitation
    d Ultraschallkavitation f
    f cavitation f à ultra-son
    r ультразвуковая кавитация f

U17 e ultrasonic cleaning

d   Ultraschallreinigung *f*
f   purification *f* par ultra-son
r   ультразвуковая очистка *f*

U18   e   ultrasonic cutting
d   Ultraschallschneiden *n*
f   coupe *f* par ultra-son
r   ультразвуковое резание *n*

U19   e   ultrasonic delay line
d   Ultraschallverzögerungsleitung *f*
f   ligne *f* à retard à ultra-son
r   ультразвуковая линия *f* задержки

U20   e   ultrasonic diagnostics
d   Ultraschalldiagnostik *f*
f   diagnostic *m* à ultra-son
r   ультразвуковая диагностика *f*

U21   e   ultrasonic dispersion
d   Ultraschalldispergierung *f*
f   dispersion *f* ultrasonique
r   ультразвуковое диспергирование *n*

U22   e   ultrasonic emulsification
d   Ultraschallemulgierung *f*
f   émulsification *f* ultrasonique
r   ультразвуковое эмульгирование *n*

U23   e   ultrasonic flaw detection
d   Ultraschallprüfung *f*,
    Ultraschalldefektoskopie *f*
f   détection *f* des défauts ultrasonique
r   ультразвуковая дефектоскопия *f*

U24   e   ultrasonic flaw detector
d   Ultraschallprüfgerät *n*,
    Ultraschalldefektoskop *n*
f   détecteur *m* des défauts ultrasonique
r   ультразвуковой дефектоскоп *m*

U25   e   ultrasonic light diffraction
d   Lichtbeugung *f* durch Ultraschall
f   diffraction *f* de la lumière par ultra-son
r   дифракция *f* света на ультразвуке;
    акустооптическая дифракция *f*

U26   e   ultrasonic light modulator
d   Ultraschall-Lichtmodulator *m*
f   modulateur *m* de lumière ultrasonique
r   ультразвуковой модулятор *m* света

U27   e   ultrasonic radiation
d   Ultraschallstrahlung *f*
f   rayonnement *m* ultrasonore
r   ультразвуковое излучение *n*

U28   e   ultrasonic radiator
d   Ultraschallstrahler *m*
f   radiateur *m* ultrasonore
r   излучатель *m* ультразвука,
    ультразвуковой излучатель *m*

U29   e   ultrasonics
d   Ultraschallehre *f*, Ultraschallakustik *f*

f   ultrasonique *f*, ultra-acoustique *f*
r   ультраакустика *f*; ультразвук *m*

U30   e   ultrasonic source *see* ultrasonic radiator

U31   e   ultrasonic sputtering
d   Ultraschallzerstäubung *f*
f   pulvérisation *f* par ultra-son
r   ультразвуковое распыление *n*

U32   e   ultrasonic surgery
d   Ultraschallchirurgie *f*
f   chirurgie *f* ultrasonique
r   ультразвуковая хирургия *f*

U33   e   ultrasonic testing *see* ultrasonic flaw detection

U34   e   ultrasonic therapy
d   Ultraschalltherapie *f*
f   thérapie *f* ultrasonique
r   ультразвуковая терапия *f*

U35   e   ultrasonic vibrations
d   Ultraschallschwingungen *f pl*
f   vibrations *f pl* ultrasonores
r   ультразвуковые колебания *n pl*

U36   e   ultrasonic waves
d   Ultraschallwellen *f pl*
f   ondes *f pl* ultra-sonores
r   ультразвуковые волны *f pl*

U37   e   ultrasound
d   Ultraschall *m*
f   ultra-son *m*
r   ультразвук *m*

U38   e   ultraviolet *see* ultraviolet radiation

U39   e   ultraviolet catastrophe
d   Ultraviolettkatastrophe *f*
f   catastrophe *f* ultraviolette
r   ультрафиолетовая катастрофа *f*

U40   e   ultraviolet divergence
d   Ultraviolettdivergenz *f*
f   divergence *f* ultraviolette
r   ультрафиолетовая расходимость *f*

U41   e   ultraviolet microscope
d   Ultraviolettmikroskop *n*
f   microscope *m* ultraviolet
r   ультрафиолетовый микроскоп *m*

U42   e   ultraviolet preionization
d   Ultraviolettvorionisation *f*
f   préionisation *f* ultraviolette
r   ультрафиолетовая предыонизация *f*

U43   e   ultraviolet radiation
d   Ultraviolettstrahlung *f*
f   rayonnement *m* ultraviolet, radiation *f* ultraviolette
r   ультрафиолетовое излучение *n*

U44   e   ultraviolet region

d Ultraviolettgebiet *n*, UV-Gebiet *n*
f région *f* ultraviolette
r ультрафиолетовая область *f* (спектра)

U45 e ultraviolet source
d Ultraviolettstrahler *m*
f source *f* d'ultraviolet
r источник *m* ультрафиолетового излучения

U46 e ultraviolet spectroscopy
d Ultraviolettspektroskopie *f*, UV-Spektroskopie *f*
f spectroscopie *f* ultraviolette
r ультрафиолетовая спектроскопия *f*

U47 e umklapp process
d Umklapp-Prozeß *m*
f processus *m* de renversement
r процесс *m* переброса, переброс *m*

U48 e uncertainty
d Unbestimmtheit *f*
f incertitude *f*, indétermination *f*
r неопределённость *f*

U49 e uncertainty principle
d Unbestimmtheitsprinzip *n*
f principe *m* d'incertitude
r принцип *m* неопределённости

U50 e uncertainty relation
d Unbestimmtheitsrelation *f*, Unschärferelation *f*
f relation *f* d'incertitude
r соотношение *n* неопределённостей

U51 e undersea sound channel
d unterseeischer Schallkanal *m*
f canal *m* sonore sous-marin
r подводный звуковой канал *m*

U52 e underwater acoustics
d Hydroakustik *f*, Unterwasserakustik *f*
f acoustique *f* sous-marine
r подводная акустика *f*

U53 e undisturbed plasma
d ruhiges Plasma *n*
f plasma *m* calmé
r невозмущённая плазма *f*

U54 e undulator
d Undulator *m*
f ondulateur *m*
r ондулятор *m*

U55 e undulatory radiation
d Undulatorstrahlung *f*
f rayonnement *m* ondulatoire, radiation *f* ondulatoire
r ондуляторное излучение *n*

U56 e unfavoured transition
d erschwerter Übergang *m*, nichtbegünstigter Übergang *m*

f transition *f* non favorisée
r затруднённый переход *m*

U57 e unforbidden transition
d nichtverbotener Übergang *m*
f transition *f* non défendue
r незапрещённый переход *m*

U58 e uniaxial crystal
d uniaxialer Kristall *m*, einachsiger Kristall *m*
f cristal *m* uniaxe, cristal *m* uniaxial
r одноосный кристалл *m*

U59 e unidentified flying object
d unidentifiziertes fliegendes Objekt *n*, UFO *n*
f objet *m* volant non identifié, OVNI
r неопознанный летающий объект *m*, НЛО

U60 e unification
d Unifikation *f*
f unification *f*
r объединение *n* (взаимодействий в физике высоких энергий)

U61 e unified field theory
d einheitliche Feldtheorie *f*
f théorie *f* des champs unifée
r единая теория *f* поля

U62 e uniform compression deformation
d Deformation *f* bei dreiachsiger Druckbeanspruchung
f déformation *f* de compression triaxiale, déformation *f* de compression volumétrique
r деформация *f* всестороннего сжатия

U63 e uniform dependence
d monotone Abhängigkeit *f*
f dépendance *f* uniforme
r монотонная зависимость *f*

U64 e uniform field *see* homogeneous field

U65 e uniformity
d 1. Uniformität *f*, Einheitlichkeit *f*, Homogenität *f* 2. Gleichförmigkeit *f*, Gleichmäßigkeit *f*
f uniformité *f*
r 1. однородность *f* 2. равномерность *f*

U66 e uniformly accelerated motion
d gleichförmig beschleunigte Bewegung *f*
f mouvement *m* uniformément accéléré
r равноускоренное движение *n*, равномерно ускоренное движение *n*

U67 e uniformly decelerated motion
d gleichmäßig verzögerte Bewegung *f*
f mouvement *m* uniformément retardé
r равнозамедленное движение *n*, равномерно замедленное движение *n*

U68 *e* **uniformly variable motion**
  d gleichformig veränderliche Bewegung *f*
  f mouvement *m* uniformément varié
  r равнопеременное движение *n*

U69 *e* **uniform motion**
  d gleichförmige Bewegung *f*
  f mouvement *m* uniforme
  r равномерное движение *n*

U70 *e* **unipolar induction**
  d Unipolarinduktion *f*
  f induction *f* unipolaire
  r униполярная индукция *f*

U71 *e* **uniqueness theorem**
  d Eindeutigkeitssatz *m*
  f théorème *m* d'unicité
  r теорема *f* единственности

U72 *e* **unit**
  d 1. Maßeinheit *f*, Einheit *f* 2. Aggregat
   n; Anlage *f* 3. Baueinheit *f*;
   Baustein *m*
  f unité *f*
  r 1. единица *f* измерения 2.
   установка *f* 3. блок *m*; узел *m*

U73 *e* **unitarity condition**
  d Unitaritätsbedingung *f*
  f condition *f* d'unitarité
  r условие *n* унитарности

U74 *e* **unitary limit**
  d unitäre Grenze *f*
  f limite *f* unitaire
  r унитарный предел *m*

U75 *e* **unitary symmetry**
  d unitäre Symmetrie *f*
  f symétrie *f* unitaire
  r унитарная симметрия *f*

U76 *e* **unit cell** *see* **lattice cell**

U77 *e* **unit cube**
  d Einheitswürfel *m*
  f cube *m* unitaire
  r элементарный куб *m*

U78 *e* **unit impulse**
  d Einheitsimpuls *m*, Dirac-Impuls *m*
  f impulsion *f* unitaire
  r единичный импульс *m*, дельта-
   функция *f* (*Дирака*)

U79 *e* **unit interval**
  d Einheitsintervall *n*
  f intervalle *m* unitaire
  r единичный интервал *m*

U80 *e* **unit vector**
  d Einheitsvektor *m*
  f vecteur *m* unitaire
  r единичный вектор *m*

U81 *e* **unit volume**
  d Volumeneinheit *f*, Volumeinheit *f*
  f unité *f* de volume
  r единичный объём *m*

U82 *e* **universal decimal classification**
  d Dezimalklassifkation *f*
  f classification *f* décimale universelle
  r универсальная десятичная
   классификация *f*, УДК

U83 *e* **universal time**
  d Weltzeit *f*
  f temps *m* universel
  r всемирное время *n*

U84 *e* **Universe**
  d Universum *n*
  f Univers *m*
  r Вселенная *f*

U85 *e* **Universe baryon asymmetry**
  d Baryonenasymmetrie *f* des Universums
  f asymétrie *f* baryonique de l'Univers
  r барионная асимметрия *f* Вселенной

U86 *e* **univibrator** *see* **single-shot**
   multivibrator

U87 *e* **unmatched load**
  d nichtangepaßte Belastung *f*
  f charge *f* non accordée
  r несогласованная нагрузка *f*

U88 *e* **unreflecting load** *see* **matched load**

U89 *e* **unresolved line**
  d nichtaufgelöste Linie *f*
  f raie *f* non résolue
  r неразрешённая линия *f*

U90 *e* **unsaturated absorption**
  d ungesättigte Absorption *f*
  f absorption *f* non saturée
  r ненасыщенное поглощение *n*

U91 *e* **unstable equilibrium**
  d instabiles Gleichgewicht *n*
  f équilibre *m* instable
  r неустойчивое равновесие *n*

U92 *e* **unstable isotope**
  d instabiles Isotop *n*
  f isotope *m* instable
  r неустойчивый изотоп *m*

U93 *e* **unsteady flow** *see* **nonstationary flow**

U94 *e* **unsteady motion** *see* **nonstationary**
   motion

U95 *e* **unsymmetrical bending**
  d unsymmetrische Biegung *f*
  f courbure *f* non symétrique
  r несимметричный изгиб *m*

U96 *e* **up conversion**
  d Konversion *f* mit der
   Frequenzerhöhung

 f conversion *f* à augmentation de la
  fréquence
 r преобразование *n* с повышением
  частоты

U97 e **up converter**
 d Aufwärtswandler *m*
 f convertisseur *m* à augmentation de la
  fréquence
 r преобразователь *m* с повышением
  частоты

U98 e **upper band**
 d obere Zone *f*
 f zone *f* supérieure
 r верхняя зона *f*

U99 e **upper ionosphere**
 d hohe Ionosphäre *f*
 f ionosphère *f* supérieure
 r верхняя ионосфера *f*

U100 e **upper limit**
 d Obergrenze *f*
 f limite *f* supérieure
 r верхний предел *m*

U101 e **upper quark, up quark**
 d u-Quark *n*
 f quark *m* u
 r верхний кварк *m*, u-кварк *m*

U102 e **upper sublevel**
 d oberes Unterniveau *n*
 f sous-niveau *m* supérieur
 r верхний подуровень *m*

U103 e **upper yield point**
 d obere Streckgrenze *f*, obere
  Fließgrenze *f*
 f limite *f* d'écoulement supérieure
 r верхний предел *m* текучести

U104 e **uranium, U**
 d Uran *n*
 f uranium *m*
 r уран *m*

U105 e **Uranus**
 d Uranus *m*
 f Uranus *m*
 r Уран *m*

U106 e **utilisation coefficient, utilisation
  factor**
 d Ausnutzungsfaktor *m*,
  Ausnutzungsgrad *m*
 f facteur *m* d'utilisation
 r коэффициент *m* использования

U107 e **utilisation of beam**
 d Strahlbündelausnutzung *f*
 f utilisation *f* du faisceau
 r использование *n* пучка (*в
  ускорителе*)

U108 e **UV radiation** *see* **ultraviolet
  radiation**

V

V1 e **vacancy**
 d Leerstelle *f*, Gitterlücke *f*
 f vacance *f*
 r вакансия *f*

V2 e **vacancy cluster**
 d Leerstellencluster *m*
 f cluster *m* de vacances, agglomération
  f de vacances
 r вакансионный кластер *m*

V3 e **vacancy creep**
 d Leerstellenkriechen *n*
 f fluage *m* de vacances
 r вакансионная ползучесть *f*

V4 e **vacancy migration**
 d Leerstellenwanderung *f*
 f migration *f* de vacances
 r миграция *f* вакансий

V5 e **vacansion**
 d Vakansion *n*
 f vacansion *m*
 r вакансион *m*

V6 e **vacant lattice site** *see* **vacancy**

V7 e **vacuum**
 d Vakuum *n*
 f vide *m*
 r вакуум *m*

V8 e **vacuum annealing**
 d Vakuumglühen *n*
 f recuit *m* dans le vide, recuit *m* sous
  vide, recuit *m* au vide
 r вакуумный отжиг *m*

V9 e **vacuum arc**
 d Vakuumbogen *m*,
  Vakuumlichtbogen *m*
 f arc *m* dans le vide
 r вакуумная дуга *f*

V10 e **vacuum average**
 d Vakuummittel *n*
 f moyenne *f* de vide
 r вакуумное среднее *n*

V11 e **vacuum breakdown**
 d Vakuumdurchschlag *m*
 f disruption *f* dans le vide
 r вакуумный пробой *m*

V12 e **vacuum chamber**
 d Vakuumkammer *f*
 f chambre *f* à vide
 r вакуумная камера *f*

V13 e **vacuum condensate**
 d Vakuumkondensat *n*
 f condensat *m* dans le vide
 r вакуумный конденсат *m*

V14 e vacuum degeneration
     d Vakuumentartung f
     f dégénération f du vide
     r вырождение n вакуума

V15 e vacuum deposition
     d Vakuumaufdampfung f
     f déposition f sous vide
     r вакуумное напыление n

V16 e vacuum deterioration
     d Vakuumfehler m
     f défaut m du vide
     r нарушение n вакуума

V17 e vacuum diode
     d Vakuumdiode f
     f diode f à vide
     r вакуумный диод m

V18 e vacuum discharge
     d Vakuumentladung f
     f décharge f dans le vide
     r разряд m в вакууме

V19 e vacuum evaporation method
     d Vakuumverdampfungsmethode f
     f méthode f d'évaporation à vide
     r метод m испарения в вакууме

V20 e vacuum flask see Dewar vessel

V21 e vacuum gage
     d Vakuummeter n, Vakuummeßgerät n
     f vacuomètre m
     r вакуумметр m

V22 e vacuum insulation
     d Vakuumisolation f
     f isolation f par le vide
     r вакуумная изоляция f

V23 e vacuum invariance
     d Vakuuminvarianz f
     f invariance f du vide
     r инвариантность f вакуума

V24 e vacuum materials
     d Vakuummaterialien n pl
     f matériaux m pl de vide
     r вакуумные материалы m pl

V25 e vacuum monochromator
     d Vakuummonochromator m
     f monochromateur m à vide
     r вакуумный монохроматор m

V26 e vacuum polarization
     d Vakuumpolarisation f, Polarisation f
        des Vakuums
     f polarisation f du vide
     r поляризация f вакуума

V27 e vacuum pump
     d Vakuumpumpe f
     f pompe f à vide
     r вакуумный насос m

V28 e vacuum spectroscopy
     d Vakuumspektroskopie f
     f spectroscopie f à vide
     r вакуумная спектроскопия f

V29 e vacuum system
     d Vakuumsystem n
     f système m à vide
     r вакуумная система f

V30 e vacuum ultraviolet
     d Vakuumultraviolett n, Vakuum-UV n
     f ultraviolet m à vide
     r вакуумный ультрафиолет m

V31 e vacuum ultraviolet spectroscopy
     d Vakuumultraviolettspektroskopie f
     f spectroscopie f d'ultraviolet à vide
     r спектроскопия f вакуумного
        ультрафиолета

V32 e valence see valency

V33 e valence angle
     d Valenzwinkel m, Bindungswinkel m
     f angle m de valence, angle m de
        liaison
     r валентный угол m

V34 e valence band
     d Valenzband n
     f bande f de valence
     r валентная зона f

V35 e valence bond
     d Valenzbindung f
     f liaison f de valence
     r валентная связь f

V36 e valence bond method
     d Valenzbindungsmethode f
     f méthode f des liaisons de valence
     r метод m валентных связей

V37 e valence electron
     d Valenzelektron n
     f électron m de valence
     r валентный электрон m

V38 e valence quark
     d Valenzquark n
     f quark m valent
     r валентный кварк m

V39 e valence state
     d Valenzzustand m
     f état m de valence
     r валентное состояние n

V40 e valence vibrations
     d Valenzschwingungen f pl
     f vibrations f pl de valence
     r валентные колебания n pl

V41 e valency
     d Valenz f, chemische Wertigkeit f

f valence f
r валентность f

V42 e **valley**
d Tal n
f vallée f
r долина f

V43 e **value**
d Wert m; Größe f
f valeur f
r значение n; величинаf

V44 e **valve**
d 1. Röhre f, Elektronenröhre f
2. Ventil n
f 1. tube m 2. valve f
r 1. электронная лампа f 2. вентиль
m; клапан m

V45 e **vanadium, V**
d Vanadin n, Vanadium n
f vanadium m
r ванадий m

V46 e **Van Allen belts** see **radiation belts**

V47 e **Van de Graaff accelerator**
d Van-de-Graaff-Beschleuniger m
f accélérateur m de Van de Graaff
r ускоритель m Ван-де-Граафа,
электростатический ускоритель m

V48 e **Van der Waals forces**
d Van-der-Waalssche Kräfte f pl
f forces f pl de Van der Waals
r Ван-дер-Ваальсовы силы f pl

V49 e **vapor**
d Dampf m
f vapeur f
r пар m

V50 e **vapor condensation**
d Dampfkondensation f
f condensation f de la vapeur
r конденсация f пара

V51 e **vaporization**
d Verdampfung f
f vaporisation f, évaporation f
r испарение n, парообразование n

V52 e **vaporization curve**
d Verdampfungskurve f
f courbe f de vaporisation
r кривая f парообразования

V53 e **vapor-liquid equilibrium**
d Dampf-Flüssigkeit-Gleichgewicht n
f équilibre m liquide-vapeur
r парожидкостное равновесие n,
равновесие n между паром и
жидкостью

V54 e **vapor pressure**
d Verdampfungsdruck m

f pression f de vapeur
r давление n пара

V55 e **vapour** see **vapor**

V56 e **VAr**
d Var n, Blindvoltampere n, Blindwatt n
f var m, voltampère m réactif
r вар m (единица реактивной
мощности в системе СИ)

V57 e **variable I**
d Variable f
f variable f
r переменная f

V58 e **variable II** see **variable star**

V59 e **variable inductance**
d veränderliche Induktivität f
f inductance f variable
r переменная индуктивность f

V60 e **variable mass mechanics**
d Mechanik f der Körper veränderlicher
Masse
f mécanique f des corps à masse
variable
r механика f тел переменной массы

V61 e **variable star**
d Veränderlicher m, veränderlicher
Stern m
f variable f, étoile f variable
r переменная f, переменная звезда f

V62 e **variance**
d 1. Varianz f, Dispersion f
2. Freiheitsgrad m
f 1. variance f 2. nombre m de degrés
de liberté
r 1. дисперсия f 2. число n степеней
свободы

V63 e **variational principles**
d Variationsprinzipien n pl
f principes m pl variationnels
r вариационные принципы m pl
(механики)

V64 e **variation method**
d Variationsmethode f
f méthode f des variations
r вариационный метод m

V65 e **variations**
d Variationen f pl
f variations f pl
r вариации f pl

V66 e **varicap**
d Kapazitätsdiode f, Varicap f
f varicap m
r варикап m

V67 e **varifocal lens**
d Objektiv n mit veränderlicher
Brennweite, Varioobjektiv n

	f	objectif *m* à focale variable
	r	трансфокатор *m*, объектив *m* с переменным фокусным расстоятнием
V68	*e*	variometer
	d	Variometer *n*
	f	variomètre *m*
	r	вариометр *m*
V69	*e*	varistor
	d	Varistor *m*, spannungsabhängiger Widerstand *m*
	f	varistance *f*
	r	варистор *m*
V70	*e*	vector
	d	Vektor *m*
	f	vecteur *m*
	r	вектор *m*
V71	*e*	vector analysis
	d	Vektoranalyse *f*
	f	analyse *f* vectorielle
	r	векторный анализ *m*
V72	*e*	vector boson
	d	Vektorboson *n*
	f	boson *m* vectoriel
	r	векторный бозон *m*
V73	*e*	vector component *see* component of a vector
V74	*e*	vector current
	d	Vektorstrom *m*
	f	courant *m* vectoriel
	r	векторный ток *m*
V75	*e*	vector diagram
	d	Vektordiagramm *n*
	f	diagramme *m* vectoriel
	r	векторная диаграмма *f*
V76	*e*	vector field
	d	Vektorfeld *n*
	f	champ *m* vectoriel
	r	векторное поле *n*
V77	*e*	vector flux
	d	Vektorfluß *m*
	f	flux *m* du vecteur
	r	поток *m* вектора
V78	*e*	vector gluon
	d	Vektorgluon *n*
	f	gluon *m* vectoriel
	r	векторный глюон *m*
V79	*e*	vector magnetometer
	d	Vektormagnetometer *n*
	f	magnétomètre *m* à vecteur
	r	векторный магнитометр *m*
V80	*e*	vector meson
	d	Vektormeson *n*, vektorielles Meson *n*

	f	méson *m* vectoriel
	r	векторный мезон *m*
V81	*e*	vector norm
	d	Vektornorm *f*
	f	norme *f* du vecteur
	r	норма *f* вектора
V82	*e*	vector of state
	d	Zustandsvektor *m*
	f	vecteur *m* d'état
	r	вектор *m* состояния
V83	*e*	vector particle
	d	Vektorteilchen *n*, vektorielles Teilchen *n*, Vekton *n*
	f	particule *f* vectorielle
	r	векторная частица *f*
V84	*e*	vector polygon
	d	Vektorpolygon *n*
	f	polygone *m* des vecteurs
	r	векторный многоугольник *m*
V85	*e*	vector potential
	d	Vektorpotential *n*
	f	potentiel-vecteur *m*
	r	векторный потенциал *m*
V86	*e*	vector product
	d	Vektorprodukt *n*
	f	produit *m* vectoriel
	r	векторное произведение *n*
V87	*e*	vector space
	d	Vektorraum *m*
	f	espace *m* vectoriel
	r	векторное пространство *n*
V88	*e*	velocimeter
	d	Geschwindigkeitsmesser *m*
	f	compteur *m* de vitesse
	r	измеритель *m* скорости
V89	*e*	velocity
	d	Geschwindigkeit *f*
	f	vitesse *f*
	r	скорость *f*
V90	*e*	velocity circulation
	d	Geschwindigkeitszirkulation *f*
	f	circulation *f* de la vitesse
	r	циркуляция *f* скорости
V91	*e*	velocity distribution
	d	Geschwindigkeitsverteilung *f*
	f	distribution *f* des vitesses
	r	распределение *n* по скоростям, распределение *n* скоростей
V92	*e*	velocity field
	d	Geschwindigkeitsfeld *n*
	f	champ *m* de vitesse
	r	поле *n* скоростей
V93	*e*	velocity head
	d	Staudruck *m*

	f	pression f dynamique
	r	скоростной напор m
V94	e	velocity measurement
	d	Geschwindigkeitsmessung f
	f	mesure f de la vitesse
	r	измерение n скорости
V95	e	velocity modulation
	d	Geschwindigkeitsmodulation f
	f	modulation f de la vitesse
	r	модуляция f скорости
V96	e	velocity of light
	d	Lichtgeschwindigkeit f
	f	vitesse f de la lumière
	r	скорость f света
V97	e	velocity of sound
	d	Schallgeschwindigkeit f
	f	vitesse f du son
	r	скорость f звука
V98	e	velocity potential
	d	Geschwindigkeitspotential n
	f	potentiel m des vitesses
	r	потенциал m скоростей
V99	e	velocity profile
	d	Geschwindigkeitsprofil n
	f	profil m des vitesses
	r	профиль m скоростей
V100	e	velocity range
	d	Geschwindigkeitsbereich m
	f	gamme f des vitesses
	r	интервал m скоростей, диапазон m скоростей
V101	e	velocity space
	d	Geschwindigkeitsraum m
	f	espace m des vitesses
	r	пространство n скоростей
V102	e	Venturi tube
	d	Venturi-Rohr n
	f	tube m Venturi, tube m de Venturi
	r	трубка f Вентури
V103	e	Venus
	d	Venus f
	f	Vénus f
	r	Венера f
V104	e	Verdet constant
	d	Verdetsche Konstante f, Verdet-Konstante f
	f	constante f de Verdet
	r	постоянная f Верде, удельное магнитное вращение n
V105	e	Verneuil method
	d	Verneuil-Verfahren n
	f	méthode f de Verneuil
	r	метод m Вернейля (выращивания кристаллов)

V106	e	vertex function
	d	Vertexfunktion f
	f	fonction f de sommet
	r	вершинная функция f
V107	e	vertical ionospheric sounding
	d	vertikale Ionosphärenecholotung f
	f	sondage m ionosphérique vertical
	r	вертикальное зондирование n ионосферы
V108	e	vertically polarized radiation
	d	vertikal polarisierte Strahlung f
	f	radiation f à polarisation verticale
	r	вертикально-поляризованное излучение n
V109	e	vertical transition
	d	Vertikalübergang m
	f	transition f verticale
	r	прямой переход m (между зонами)
V110	e	very-long-baseline interferometer
	d	Interferometer n mit sehr großer Basis
	f	interféromètre m à base très longue
	r	интерферометр m со сверхдлинной базой
V111	e	very long waves
	d	Längstwellen f pl
	f	ondes f pl très longues
	r	сверхдлинные волны f pl
V112	e	vibration
	d	1. Vibration f 2. s. vibrations
	f	1. vibration f 2. v. vibrations
	r	1. вибрация f 2. см. vibrations
V113	e	vibrational band
	d	Schwingungsbande f
	f	bande f de vibration
	r	колебательная полоса f
V114	e	vibrational energy
	d	Schwingungsenergie f
	f	énergie f de vibration
	r	колебательная энергия f
V115	e	vibrational level
	d	Schwingungsniveau n
	f	niveau m de vibration
	r	колебательный уровень m
V116	e	vibrational line
	d	Schwingungslinie f
	f	raie f de vibration
	r	колебательная линия f (спектра)
V117	e	vibrationally excited molecule
	d	schwingend-angeregtes Molekül n
	f	molécule f activée par vibration
	r	колебательно-возбуждённая молекула f
V118	e	vibrational motion
	d	schwingende Bewegung f, Schwingungsbewegung f

	f	mouvement m oscillatoire
	r	колебательное движение n
V119	e	**vibrational quantum**
	d	Schwingungsquant n
	f	quantum m oscillatoire
	r	колебательный квант m
V120	e	**vibrational quantum number**
	d	Schwingungsquantenzahl f
	f	nombre m quantique vibrationnel, nombre m quantique de vibration
	r	колебательное квантовое число n
V121	e	**vibrational-rotational band**
	d	Rotationsschwingungsbande f
	f	bande f de rotation-vibration
	r	колебательно-вращательная полоса f
V122	e	**vibrational-rotational interaction**
	d	Rotationsschwingungswechselwirkung f
	f	interaction f de rotation-vibration
	r	колебательно-вращательное взаимодействие n
V123	e	**vibrational-rotational sublevel**
	d	Rotationsschwingungsunterniveau n
	f	sous-niveau m de rotation-vibration
	r	колебательно-вращательный подуровень m
V124	e	**vibrational-rotational transition**
	d	Rotationsschwingungsübergang m
	f	transition f de rotation-vibration
	r	колебательно-вращательный переход m
V125	e	**vibrational spectrum**
	d	Schwingungsspektrum n
	f	spectre m de vibration
	r	колебательный спектр m
V126	e	**vibrational sublevel**
	d	Schwingungsunterniveau n
	f	sous-niveau m de vibration
	r	колебательный подуровень m
V127	e	**vibrational temperature**
	d	Schwingungstemperatur f
	f	température f de vibration
	r	колебательная температура f
V128	e	**vibrational velocity**
	d	Schwingungsgeschwindigkeit f
	f	vitesse f de vibration
	r	колебательная скорость f (частиц)
V129	e	**vibration damping** see **oscillation damping**
V130	e	**vibration frequency**
	d	Schwingungsfrequenz f, Schwingungszahl f
	f	fréquence f d'oscillations
	r	частота f колебаний
V131	e	**vibration of a string**
	d	Saitenschwingung f
	f	vibration f d'une corde
	r	колебания n pl струны
V132	e	**vibrations**
	d	Schwingungen f pl
	f	oscillations f pl
	r	колебания n pl
V133	e	**vibrator**
	d	Vibrator m
	f	vibrateur m
	r	вибратор m
V134	e	**vibron**
	d	Vibron n
	f	vibron m
	r	виброн m
V135	e	**vibronic excitation**
	d	vibronische Anregung f, Elektronenschwingungsanregung f
	f	excitation f vibronique
	r	вибронное возбуждение n
V136	e	**vibronic interaction**
	d	vibronische Wechselwirkung f
	f	interaction f vibronique
	r	вибронное взаимодействие n
V137	e	**vibronic spectra**
	d	vibronische Spektren n pl
	f	spectres m pl vibroniques
	r	вибронные спектры m pl
V138	e	**vicinal**
	d	Vizinalfläche f, Vizinalebene f
	f	face f vicinale
	r	вициналь f
V139	e	**Vickers hardness**
	d	Vickers-Härte f
	f	dureté f Vickers
	r	твёрдость f по Виккерсу
V140	e	**video pulse**
	d	Videoimpuls m
	f	impulsion f vidéo
	r	видеоимпульс m
V141	e	**vidicon**
	d	Vidikon n, Vidicon n
	f	vidicon m
	r	видикон m
V142	e	**viewfinder**
	d	Visiereinrichtung f, Sucher m, Bildsucher m
	f	viseur m
	r	визир m; видоискатель m
V143	e	**vignetting**
	d	Abschattung f, Vignettierung f
	f	vignettage m
	r	виньетирование n

V144   e   **Villari effect**
     d   Villari-Effekt *m*
     f   effet *m* Villari
     r   эффект *m* Виллари,
        магнитоупругий эффект *m*

V145   e   **violation**
     d   Verletzung *f*
     f   violation *f*
     r   нарушение *n (физического закона)*

V146   e   **virial coefficients**
     d   Virialkoeffizienten *m pl*
     f   coefficients *m pl* viriels
     r   вириальные коэффициенты *m pl*

V147   e   **virial expansion**
     d   Virialentwicklung *f*
     f   expansion *f* virielle
     r   вириальное разложение *n*

V148   e   **virial theorem**
     d   Virialsatz *m*, Virialgleichung *f*
     f   théorème *m* du viriel
     r   теорема *f* вириала

V149   e   **virtual cathode**
     d   virtuelle Katode *f*
     f   cathode *f* virtuelle
     r   виртуальный катод *m*

V150   e   **virtual displacement**
     d   virtuelle Verschiebung *f*
     f   déplacement *m* virtuel
     r   возможное перемещение *n*,
        виртуальное перемещение *n*

V151   e   **virtual image**
     d   virtuelles Bild *n*, scheinbares Bild *n*
     f   image *f* virtuelle
     r   мнимое изображение *n*

V152   e   **virtual level**
     d   virtuelles Niveau *n*
     f   niveau *m* virtuel
     r   виртуальный уровень *m*

V153   e   **virtual meson**
     d   virtuelles Meson *n*
     f   méson *m* virtuel
     r   виртуальный мезон *m*

V154   e   **virtual particles**
     d   virtuelle Teilchen *n pl*
     f   particules *f pl* virtuelles
     r   виртуальные частицы *f pl*

V155   e   **virtual state**
     d   virtueller Zustand *m*
     f   état *m* virtuel
     r   виртуальное состояние *n*

V156   e   **virtual transition**
     d   virtueller Übergang *m*
     f   transition *f* virtuelle
     r   виртуальный переход *m*

V157   e   **viscoelastic deformation**
     d   viskoelastische Deformation *f*
     f   déformation *f* viscoélastique
     r   вязкоупругая деформация *f*

V158   e   **viscoelasticity**
     d   Viskoelastizität *f*
     f   viscoélasticité *f*
     r   вязкоупругость *f*

V159   e   **viscoelastic liquid**
     d   viskoelastische Flüssigkeit *f*
     f   liquide *m* viscoélastique, fluide *m*
        viscoélastique
     r   вязкоупругая жидкость *f*,
        упруговязкая жидкость *f*

V160   e   **viscometer**
     d   Viskosimeter *n*
     f   viscosimètre *m*
     r   вискозиметр *m*

V161   e   **viscometry**
     d   Viskosimetrie *f*
     f   viscosimétrie *f*
     r   вискозиметрия *f*

V162   e   **viscosity**
     d   Viskosität *f*, Zähigkeit *f*
     f   viscosité *f*
     r   вязкость *f*

V163   e   **viscous damping**
     d   Reibungsdämpfung *f*
     f   amortissement *m* visqueux
     r   вязкостное демпфирование *n*,
        вязкое демпфирование *n*

V164   e   **viscous drag** *see* **viscous resistance**

V165   e   **viscous flow**
     d   zähe Strömung *f*, viskose Strömung *f*
     f   écoulement *m* visqueux
     r   вязкий поток *m*, вязкое течение *n*

V166   e   **viscous fluid** *see* **viscous liquid**

V167   e   **viscous liquid**
     d   viskose Flüssigkeit *f*, zähe Flüssigkeit
        f, reibungsbehaftete Flüssigkeit *f*
     f   liquide *m* visqueux, fluide *m* visqueux
     r   вязкая жидкость *f*

V168   e   **viscous resistance**
     d   Zähigkeitswiderstand *m*,
        Viskositätswiderstand *m*
     f   résistance *f* visqueuse, résistance *f* due
        à la viscosité
     r   вязкостное сопротивление *n*

V169   e   **visible image**
     d   sichtbares Bild *n*
     f   image *f* visible
     r   видимое изображение *n*

V170   e   **visible object**
     d   sichtbares Objekt *n*

f objet *m* visible
r видимый объект *m*

V171 *e* visible radiation
d sichtbare Strahlung *f*, Licht *n*
f rayonnement *m* visible, lumière *f*
r видимое излучение *n*, свет *m*

V172 *e* visible region
d sichtbares Spektralgebiet *n*, sichtbarer
Spektralbereich *m*
f région *f* visible
r видимая область *f* (спектра)

V173 *e* vision
d Sehen *n*; Vision *f*
f vision *f*
r зрение *n*

V174 *e* visual acuity
d Sehschärfe *f*
f acuité *f* visuelle
r острота *f* зрения

V175 *e* visual contrast
d Sehkontrast *m*
f contraste *m* visuel
r зрительный контраст *m*

V176 *e* visual image *see* visible image

V177 *e* visualization
d Sichtbarmachung *f*
f visualisation *f*
r визуализация *f*

V178 *e* visual method
d visuelle Methode *f*
f méthode *f* visuelle
r визуальный метод *m*

V179 *e* visual object *see* visible object

V180 *e* visual observations
d visuelle Beobachtungen *f pl*
f observations *f pl* visuelles
r зрительные наблюдения *n pl*,
визуальные наблюдения *n pl*

V181 *e* visual perception
d Gesichtswahrnehmung *f*, optische
Wahrnehmung *f*
f perception *f* visuelle
r зрительное восприятие *n*

V182 *e* visual photometer
d visuelles Photometer *n*
f photomètre *m* visuel
r визуальный фотометр *m*

V183 *e* visual source
d optische Quelle *f*
f source *f* lumineuse
r оптический источник *m* (в
астрономии)

V184 *e* Vlasov equations

d Wlassow-Gleichungen *f pl*, Vlasov-
Gleichungen *f pl*
f équations *f pl* de Vlasov
r уравнения *n pl* Власова

V185 *e* void
d Hohlraum *m*
f vide *m*, vacuité *f*; cavité *f*
r пустота *f*; полость *f*

V186 *e* volatile component
d flüchtige Komponente *f*
f composante *f* volatile
r летучая компонента *f*

V187 *e* volatility
d Flüchtigkeit *f*
f volatilité *f*
r летучесть *f*

V188 *e* volcanic eruption
d Vulkanausbruch *m*
f éruption *f* volcanique
r извержение *n* вулкана

V189 *e* volt, V
d Volt *n*
f volt *m*
r вольт *m*, В

V190 *e* voltage
d Spannung *f*, elektrische Spannung *f*
f tension *f*
r напряжение *n*; электрическое
напряжение *n*

V191 *e* voltage divider
d Spannungsteiler *m*
f diviseur *m* de tension
r делитель *m* напряжения

V192 *e* voltage division
d Spannungsteilung *f*
f division *f* de tension
r деление *n* напряжения

V193 *e* voltage fluctuations
d Spannungsschwankungen *f pl*
f fluctuations *f pl* de tension
r флуктуации *f pl* напряжения

V194 *e* voltage-reference diode
d Z-Diode *f*
f tube *m* stabilovolt
r стабилитрон *m*

V195 *e* voltage-reference tube
d Stabilisatorröhre *f*
f tube *m* régulateur de tension à vide
r электровакуумный стабилитрон *m*

V196 *e* voltage source
d Spannungsquelle *f*
f source *f* de tension
r источник *m* напряжения

V197 *e* voltage stabilization

	d	Spannungsstabilisation *f*
	f	stabilisation *f* de tension
	r	стабилизация *f* напряжения
V198	*e*	voltage standing-wave ratio
	d	Spannungsstehwellenverhältnis *n*
	f	taux *m* d'ondes stationnaires de tension, TOST
	r	коэффициент *m* стоячей волны по напряжению, КСВН
V199	*e*	voltage-tunable magnetron *see* mitron
V200	*e*	volt-ampere characteristic
	d	Strom-Spannungs-Kennlinie *f*, Strom-Spannungs-Charakteristik *f*
	f	caractéristique *f* intensité-tension
	r	вольт-амперная характеристика *f*, ВАХ
V201	*e*	Volterra equation
	d	Volterrasche Gleichung *f*
	f	équation *f* de Volterra
	r	уравнение *n* Вольтерры
V202	*e*	voltmeter
	d	Voltmeter *n*, Spannungsmesser *m*
	f	voltmètre *m*
	r	вольтметр *m*
V203	*e*	volume
	d	Volumen *n*, Volum *n*
	f	volume *m*
	r	объём *m*
V204	*e*	volume charge *see* space charge
V205	*e*	volume charge density
	d	Raumladungsdichte *f*
	f	densité *f* de charge volumique
	r	объёмная плотность *f* заряда
V206	*e*	volume deformation
	d	Volumendeformation *f*
	f	déformation *f* de volume
	r	объёмная деформация *f*
V207	*e*	volume elasticity *see* bulk elasticity
V208	*e*	volumetric analysis
	d	Maßanalyse *f*, Volumetrie *f*
	f	analyse *f* volumétrique
	r	объёмный анализ *m*
V209	*e*	volume velocity
	d	Schallfluß *m*, Schallenergiefluß *m*, Volumenschnelle *f*
	f	vitesse *f* volumique
	r	объёмная скорость *f*
V210	*e*	volume viscosity
	d	Volumenviskosität *f*, zweite Viskosität *f*
	f	viscosité *f* volumétrique
	r	вторая вязкость *f*, объёмная вязкость *f*
V211	*e*	vortex

	d	Wirbel *m*
	f	tourbillon *m*
	r	вихрь *m*
V212	*e*	vortex core
	d	Wirbelkern *m*
	f	noyau *m* tourbillonnaire
	r	ядро *n* вихря, сердцевина *f* вихря
V213	*e*	vortex field
	d	Wirbelfeld *n*
	f	champ *m* tourbillonnaire
	r	вихревое поле *n*
V214	*e*	vortex lattice
	d	Wirbelgitter *n*
	f	réseau *m* de tourbillon
	r	решётка *f* вихрей, решётка *f* квантованных вихрей, вихревая решётка *f*
V215	*e*	vortex motion
	d	Wirbelbewegung *f*
	f	mouvement *m* tourbillonnaire
	r	вихревое движение *n*
V216	*e*	vortex pair
	d	Wirbelpaar *n*
	f	paire *f* de tourbillons
	r	пара *f* вихрей
V217	*e*	vortex ring
	d	Wirbelring *m*
	f	anneau *m* tourbillonnaire, anneau *m* de tourbillon
	r	вихревое кольцо *n*
V218	*e*	vortex sheet
	d	Wirbelschicht *f*
	f	couche *f* tourbillonnaire
	r	вихревой слой *m*
V219	*e*	vortex street
	d	Wirbelstraße *f*
	f	piste *f* tourbillonnaire
	r	вихревая дорожка *f*
V220	*e*	vortex trail *see* vortex street
V221	*e*	vorticity
	d	Wirbelzustand *m*
	f	tourbillonnement *m*
	r	завихренность *f*; система *f* вихрей
V222	*e*	vorticity source
	d	Wirbelquelle *f*
	f	source *f* de tourbillonnement
	r	источник *m* вихреобразования

W

W1	*e*	wafer
	d	Wafer *m*
	f	tranche *f*

	r	полупроводниковая пластина *f*; подложка *f*
W2	*e*	**waist**
	d	Einschnürung *f*
	f	constriction *f*
	r	перетяжка *f (каустики)*
W3	*e*	**wake**
	d	Nachlauf *m*, Nachstrom *m*
	f	sillage *m*, sillage *m* arrière, sillage *m* dormant
	r	спутный след *m*, спутная струя *f*
W4	*e*	**wall**
	d	Wand *f*
	f	paroi *f*
	r	стенка *f*
W5	*e*	**Wannier-Mott exciton**
	d	Wannier-Mott-Exciton *n*
	f	exciton *m* de Wannier-Mott
	r	экситон *m* Ванье - Мотта
W6	*e*	**water**
	d	Wasser *n*
	f	eau *f*
	r	вода *f*
W7	*e*	**water-cooled and water-moderated reactor**
	d	Wasser-Wasser-Reaktor *m*, wassergekühlter wassermoderierter Reaktor *m*
	f	pile *f* modérée et refroidie par eau
	r	водо-водяной реактор *m*
W8	*e*	**water vapor**
	d	Wasserdampf *m*
	f	vapeur *f* d'eau
	r	водяной пар *m*
W9	*e*	**water waves**
	d	Wasserwellen *f pl*
	f	ondes *f pl* d'eau
	r	волны *f pl* на воде
W10	*e*	**watt, W**
	d	Watt *n*
	f	watt *m*
	r	ватт *m*, Вт
W11	*e*	**wattmeter**
	d	Wattmeter *n*, Leistungsmesser *m*
	f	wattmètre *m*
	r	ваттметр *m*
W12	*e*	**wave**
	d	Welle *f*
	f	onde *f*
	r	волна *f*
W13	*e*	**wave absorption**

	d	Wellenabsorption *f*
	f	absorption *f* d'ondes
	r	поглощение *n* волн
W14	*e*	**wave-corpuscle duality**
	d	Welle-Teilchen-Dualismus *m*
	f	dualité *f* onde-corpuscule
	r	корпускулярно-волновой дуализм *m*
W15	*e*	**wave damping**
	d	Wellendämpfung *f*
	f	amortissement *m* des ondes
	r	затухание *n* волн
W16	*e*	**wave diffraction**
	d	Wellenbeugung *f*
	f	diffraction *f* des ondes
	r	дифракция *f* волн
W17	*e*	**wave dispersion**
	d	Wellendispersion *f*
	f	dispersion *f* d'ondes
	r	дисперсия *f* волн
W18	*e*	**wave equation**
	d	Wellengleichung *f*
	f	équation *f* d'onde
	r	волновое уравнение *n*
W19	*e*	**wave front**
	d	Wellenfront *f*, Wellenfläche *f*
	f	front *m* d'onde
	r	фронт *m* волны, волновой фронт *m*
W20	*e*	**wave front compensation** *see* **wave front correction**
W21	*e*	**wave front correction**
	d	Wellenfrontkorrektion *f*
	f	correction *f* du front d'onde
	r	коррекция *f* волнового фронта
W22	*e*	**wave front corrector**
	d	Wellenfrontkorrektor *m*
	f	correcteur *m* du front d'onde
	r	корректор *m* волнового фронта
W23	*e*	**wave front curvature**
	d	Wellenfrontkrümmung *f*
	f	courbure *f* du front d'onde
	r	кривизна *f* волнового фронта
W24	*e*	**wave front reversal** *see* **phase conjugation**
W25	*e*	**wave front reversing mirror** *see* **phase-conjugate mirror**
W26	*e*	**wave function**
	d	Wellenfunktion *f*
	f	fonction *f* d'onde
	r	волновая функция *f*
W27	*e*	**wave function normalization**
	d	Wellenfunktionsnormierung *f*
	f	normalisation *f* de la fonction d'onde
	r	нормировка *f* волновой функции
W28	*e*	**waveguide**

    d Wellenleiter *m*
    f guide *m* d'ondes
    r волновод *m*

W29 *e* waveguide bend
    d Wellenleiterknie *n*; Hohlleiterkniestück
       n, Hohlleiterkrümmer *m*
    f courbure *f* du guide d'ondes
    r изгиб *m* волновода

W30 *e* waveguide channel
    d Wellenleiterkanal *m*
    f canal *m* du guide d'ondes
    r волноводный канал *m*

W31 *e* waveguide dispersion
    d Wellenleiterdispersion *f*;
       Hohlleiterdispersion *f*
    f dispersion *f* du guide d'ondes
    r волноводная дисперсия *f*

W32 *e* waveguide elbow *see* waveguide
       bend

W33 *e* waveguide laser
    d wellenleitergeführter Laser *m*
    f laser *m* à guide d'ondes
    r волноводный лазер *m*

W34 *e* waveguide mode
    d Hohlleitermode *f*
    f mode *m* du guide d'ondes
    r волноводная мода *f*

W35 *e* waveguide propagation
    d Wellenleiterausbreitung *f*
    f propagation *f* par guide d'ondes
    r волноводное распространение *n*
       (*радиоволн*)

W36 *e* waveguide radiator
    d Hohlleiterstrahler *m*
    f radiateur *m* à guide d'ondes
    r волноводный излучатель *m*

W37 *e* waveguide switch
    d Wellenleiterschalter *m*
    f commutateur *m* de guide d'ondes
    r волноводный переключатель *m*

W38 *e* waveguide window
    d Wellenleiterfenster *n*
    f fenêtre *f* de guide d'ondes
    r волноводное окно *n*

W39 *e* wave hierarchy
    d Wellenhierarchie *f*
    f hiérarchie *f* des ondes
    r иерархия *f* волн

W40 *e* wave impedance
    d Wellenwiderstand *m*, Wellenimpedanz
       f, Kennwiderstand *m*, Kennimpedanz *f*
    f impédance *f* d'ondes
    r волновой импеданс *m*,
       характеристический импеданс *m*

W41 *e* wave interaction
    d Wellenwechselwirkung *f*
    f interaction *f* d'ondes
    r взаимодействие *n* волн

W42 *e* wave interference
    d Welleninterferenz *f*
    f interférence *f* d'ondes
    r интерференция *f* волн

W43 *e* wavelength, wave length
    d Wellenlänge *f*
    f longueur *f* d'onde
    r длина *f* волны

W44 *e* wavelength range
    d Wellenbereich *m*,
       Wellenlängenbereich *m*; Wellenband *n*
    f gamme *f* de longueurs d'onde
    r диапазон *m* длин волн

W45 *e* wave mechanics
    d Wellenmechanik *f*
    f mécanique *f* ondulatoire
    r волновая механика *f*

W46 *e* wavemeter
    d Wellenmesser *m*; Frequenzmesser *m*
    f ondemètre *m*
    r волномер *m*; частотомер *m*

W47 *e* wave motion
    d Wellenbewegung *f*
    f mouvement *m* ondulatoire
    r волновое движение *n*

W48 *e* wave node
    d Knoten *m* der stehenden Welle,
       Wellenknoten *m*
    f nœud *m* d'onde stationnaire
    r узел *m* стоячей волны

W49 *e* wave normal
    d Wellennormale *f*,
       Wellenflächennormale *f*
    f normale *f* d'onde
    r волновая нормаль *f*

W50 *e* wave number
    d Wellenzahl *f*
    f nombre *m* d'onde
    r волновое число *n*

W51 *e* wave optics
    d Wellenoptik *f*
    f optique *f* d'ondes
    r волновая оптика *f*

W52 *e* wave packet
    d Wellenpaket *n*, Wellengruppe *f*
    f paquet *m* d'ondes
    r волновой пакет *m*

W53 *e* wave-particle interaction
    d Wellen-Teilchen-Wechselwirkung *f*
    f interaction *f* onde-particule
    r взаимодействие *n* частиц с волнами

W54   *e* **wave pattern**
     d Wellenbild *n*
     f image *f* d'onde
     r волновая картина *f*

W55   *e* **wave profile**
     d Wellenprofil *n*
     f profil *m* d'onde
     r профиль *m* волны

W56   *e* **wave reflection**
     d Wellenreflexion *f*
     f réflexion *f* d'onde
     r отражение *n* волн

W57   *e* **wave refraction**
     d Wellenbrechung *f*, Wellenrefraktion *f*
     f réfraction *f* d'ondes
     r преломление *n* волн; рефракция *f* волн

W58   *e* **wave resistance**
     d Wellenwiderstand *m*
     f résistance *f* d'onde
     r волновое сопротивление *n* (*в механике*)

W59   *e* **wave scattering**
     d Wellenstreuung *f*
     f diffusion *f* d'ondes
     r рассеяние *n* волн

W60   *e* **wave self-action**
     d Wellenselbstbeeinflussung *f*, Wellenselbsteinwirkung *f*
     f auto-action *f* d'ondes
     r самовоздействие *n* волн

W61   *e* **wave surface**
     d Wellenfläche *f*
     f surface *f* d'onde
     r волновая поверхность *f*

W62   *e* **wave transformation**
     d Wellentransformation *f*, Wellenumwandlung *f*
     f transformation *f* d'ondes
     r трансформация *f* волн; преобразование *n* волн

W63   *e* **wave vector**
     d Wellenvektor *m*
     f vecteur *m* d'onde
     r волновой вектор *m*

W64   *e* **wave zone**
     d Wellenzone *f*
     f zone *f* d'onde
     r волновая зона *f*

W65   *e* **weak coupling method**
     d Methode *f* der schwachen Kopplung
     f méthode *f* de couplage faible
     r метод *m* слабой связи

W66   *e* **weak ferromagnetism**
     d schwacher Ferromagnetismus *m*

     f ferromagnétisme *m* faible
     r слабый ферромагнетизм *m*

W67   *e* **weak field**
     d schwaches Feld *n*
     f champ *m* faible
     r слабое поле *n*

W68   *e* **weak focusing**
     d schwache Fokussierung *f*
     f focalisation *f* faible
     r слабая фокусировка *f*

W69   *e* **weak hypercharge**
     d schwache Hyperladung *f*
     f hypercharge *f* faible
     r слабый гиперзаряд *m*

W70   *e* **weak interaction**
     d schwache Wechselwirkung *f*
     f interaction *f* faible
     r слабое взаимодействие *n*

W71   *e* **weak interaction constant**
     d Konstante *f* der schwachen Wechselwirkung
     f constante *f* d'interaction faible
     r константа *f* слабого взаимодействия

W72   *e* **weak interaction quantum**
     d Quant *n* der schwachen Wechselwirkung
     f quantum *m* d'interaction faible
     r квант *m* слабого взаимодействия

W73   *e* **«weak» isospin**
     d «schwacher» Isospin *m*
     f isospin *m* «faible»
     r «слабый» изоспин *m*

W74   *e* **weak isotopic doublet**
     d schwaches Isodublett *n*, schwaches Isotopendublett *n*
     f doublet *m* isotopique faible
     r слабый изотопический дублет *m*

W75   *e* **weakly forbidden transition**
     d schwach verbotener Übergang *m*
     f transition *f* faiblement défendue
     r слабо запрещённый переход *m*

W76   *e* **weakly ionized plasma**
     d schwach ionisiertes Plasma *n*
     f plasma *m* faiblement ionisé
     r слабо ионизованная плазма *f*

W77   *e* **weakly nonideal plasma**
     d schwach nichtideales Plasma *n*
     f plasma *m* faiblement non idéal
     r слабо неидеальная плазма *f*

W78   *e* **weak transition**
     d schwacher Übergang *m*
     f transition *f* faible
     r слабый переход *m*

W79   *e* **wear cavitation** *see* **cavitation wear**

W80   *e*   wear resistance
     d   Verschleißfestigkeit *f*,
        Verschleißbeständigkeit *f*
     f   résistance *f* à l'usure
     r   износостойкость *f*

W81   *e*   wear-resistant coating
     d   verschleißfester Überzug *m*
     f   revêtement *m* résistant à l'usure
     r   износостойкое покрытие *n*

W82   *e*   wear-resistant material
     d   verschleißfester Stoff *m*
     f   matériau *m* résistant à l'usure
     r   износостойкий материал *m*

W83   *e*   wear strength *see* wear resistance

W84   *e*   weber, Wb
     d   Weber *n*
     f   weber *m*
     r   вебер *m*, Вб

W85   *e*   wedge
     d   Keil *m*
     f   coin *m*
     r   клин *m*

W86   *e*   wedge aerofoil
     d   keilförmiges Profil *n*
     f   profil *m* en coin
     r   клиновидный профиль *m* (крыла)

W87   *e*   weight
     d   Gewicht *n*
     f   poids *m*
     r   вес *m*

W88   *e*   weighted average
     d   gewichtetes Mittel *n*
     f   moyenne *f* pondérée
     r   взвешенное среднее *n*

W89   *e*   weight factor
     d   Gewichtsfaktor *m*, Wichtungsfaktor *m*
     f   facteur *m* de pondération
     r   весовой множитель *m*

W90   *e*   weighting
     d   Wichtung *f*
     f   pondération *f*
     r   взвешивание *n*

W91   *e*   weighting factor *see* weight factor

W92   *e*   Weinberg-Salam theory
     d   Weinberg-Salam-Theorie *f*
     f   théorie *f* de Weinberg-Salam
     r   теория *f* Вайнберга - Салама

W93   *e*   Weiss field
     d   Weisssches Molekularfeld *n*, inneres
        Weisssches Feld *n*
     f   champ *m* de Weiss, champ *m*
        moléculaire de Weiss
     r   поле *n* Вейса

W94   *e*   Weiss indices
     d   Weißsche Indizes *m pl*
     f   indices *m pl* de Weiss
     r   индексы *m pl* Вейса

W95   *e*   Weisskopf-Wigner approximation
     d   Weisskopf-Wigner-Approximation *f*,
        Weisskopf-Wigner-Näherung *f*
     f   approximation *f* de Weisskopf-Wigner
     r   аппроксимация *f* Вайскопфа -
        Вигнера

W96   *e*   Weizsäcker formula
     d   Weizsäcker-Formel *f*
     f   formule *f* de Weizsäcker
     r   формула *f* Вайцзеккера

W97   *e*   welding
     d   Schweißen *n*, Schweißung *f*
     f   soudage *m*
     r   сварка *f*

W98   *e*   Wentzel-Kramers-Brillouin method
     d   Wentzel-Kramers-Brillouin-Methode *f*,
        WKB-Methode *f*
     f   méthode *f* de Wentzel-Kramers-
        Brillouin
     r   метод *m* Венцеля - Крамерса -
        Бриллюэна, метод *m* ВКБ

W99   *e*   wetting
     d   Netzen *n*, Benetzen *n*, Benetzung *f*
     f   mouillage *m*
     r   смачивание *n*

W100   *e*   wet vapor
     d   Naßdampf *m*
     f   vapeur *f* humide
     r   влажный пар *m*

W101   *e*   Weyl equation
     d   Weylsche Gleichung *f*
     f   équation *f* de Weyl
     r   уравнение *n* Вейля

W102   *e*   Wheatstone bridge
     d   Wheatstone-Brücke *f*
     f   pont *m* de Wheatstone
     r   мост *m* Уитстона

W103   *e*   Wheeler-de Witt equation
     d   Wheeler-de Witt-Gleichung *f*
     f   équation *f* de Wheeler-de Witt
     r   уравнение *n* Уилера - де Витта

W104   *e*   whisker
     d   Whisker *m*, Haarkristall *m*,
        Fadenkristall *m*
     f   cristal *m* filamenteux
     r   нитевидный кристалл *m*

W105   *e*   whispering gallery
     d   Flüstergalerie *f*, Flüstergewölbe *n*
     f   voûte *f* acoustique, «whispering
        gallery» *m*
     r   шепчущая галерея *f*

W106 *e* whistler
    d Whistler *m*, atmosphärische
        Pfeifstörung *f*
    f siffleur *m*, atmosphérique *m* siffleur
    r свистящий атмосферик *m*,
        вистлер *m*

W107 *e* white dwarf
    d weißer Zwerg *m*
    f naine *f* blanche
    r белый карлик *m*

W108 *e* white hole
    d weißes Loch *n (im Universum)*
    f trou *m* blanc
    r белая дыра *f (во Вселенной)*

W109 *e* white light
    d weißes Licht *n*
    f lumière *f* blanche
    r белый свет *m*

W110 *e* white noise
    d weißes Rauschen *n*
    f bruit *m* blanc
    r белый шум *m*

W111 *e* white radiation
    d weiße Strahlung *f*
    f rayonnement *m* blanc
    r белое излучение *n*

W112 *e* Wick theorem
    d Wickscher Satz
    f théorème *m* de Wick
    r теорема *f* Вика

W113 *e* wide-angle lens
    d Weitwinkelobjektiv *n*
    f objectif *m* à grand angle de champ,
        grand-angulaire *m*
    r широкоугольный объектив *m*

W114 *e* Wideroe condition *see* betatron
       condition

W115 *e* width
    d Breite *f*
    f largeur *f*
    r ширина *f*

W116 *e* Wiedemann-Franz law
    d Wiedemann-Franzsches Gesetz *n*
    f loi *f* de Wiedemann-Franz
    r закон *m* Видемана - Франца

W117 *e* Wien bridge
    d Wien-Brücke *f*
    f pont *m* de Wien
    r мост *m* Вина

W118 *e* Wiener experiment
    d Wiener-Versuch *m*
    f expériment *m* de Wiener
    r опыт *m* Винера

W119 *e* Wiener-Hopf method
    d Wiener-Hopf-Verfahren *n*
    f méthode *f* de Wiener-Hopf
    r метод *m* Винера - Хопфа

W120 *e* Wien radiation law
    d Wiensches Gesetz *n*,
        thermodynamisches Gesetz *n* von
        Wien
    f loi *f* de Wien, loi *f* de Wien de la
        radiation
    r закон *m* излучения Вина

W121 *e* Wigner crystal
    d Wigner-Kristall *m*
    f cristal *m* de Wigner
    r вигнеровский кристалл *m*

W122 *e* Wigner functions
    d Wigner-Funktionen *f pl*
    f fonctions *f pl* de Wigner
    r функции *f pl* Вигнера

W123 *e* Wigner-Seitz cell
    d Wigner-Seitz-Zelle *f*
    f cellule *f* de Wigner-Seitz
    r ячейка *f* Вигнера - Зейтца

W124 *e* Wilson chamber
    d Wilson-Kammer *f*, Wilsonsche
        Nebelkammer *f*
    f chambre *f* de Wilson
    r камера *f* Вильсона

W125 *e* wind
    d Wind *m*
    f vent *m*
    r ветер *m*

W126 *e* wind-generated waves
    d Windwellen *f pl*
    f ondes *f pl* de vent
    r ветровые волны *f pl (на воде)*

W127 *e* winding
    d Wicklung *f*
    f enroulement *m*
    r обмотка *f*

W128 *e* window
    d Fenster *n*
    f fenêtre *f*
    r окно *n*

W129 *e* wind tunnel
    d Windkanal *m*
    f soufflerie *f*, tunnel *m* aérodynamique
    r аэродинамическая труба *f*

W130 *e* wing
    d Flügel *m*
    f aile *f*
    r крыло *n*

W131 *e* wing absorption
    d Flügelabsorption *f*
    f absorption *f* dans l'aile
    r поглощение *n* в крыле
       (спектральной линии)

W132 *e* wing of resonance curve
     d Resonanzkurvenflügel *m*
     f branche *f* de la courbe de résonance
     r крыло *n* резонансной кривой

W133 *e* wire chamber
     d Drahtelektroden-Funkenkammer *f*
     f chambre *f* à filament
     r проволочная камера *f*

W134 *e* withdrawal of the rod
     d Ausfahren *n* des Regelstabs
     f extraction *f* de la barre
     r извлечение *n* стержня *(из реактора)*

W135 *e* WKB approximation
     d WKB-Approximation *f*, WKB-Näherung *f*
     f approximation *f* W.K.B.
     r приближение *n* ВКБ, приближение *n* Венцеля - Крамера - Бриллюэна

W136 *e* **WKB method** *see* **Wentzel-Kramers-Brillouin method**

W137 *e* Wolf numbers
     d Wolfsche Zahlen *f pl*, Fleckenrelativzahlen *f pl*
     f nombres *m pl* de Wolf
     r числа *n pl* Вольфа, числа *n pl* солнечных пятен

W138 *e* wolframium, W
     d Wolfram *n*
     f tungstène *m*
     r вольфрам *m*

W139 *e* Wolf-Rayet stars
     d Wolf-Rayet-Sterne *m pl*
     f étoiles *f pl* de Wolf-Rayet
     r звёзды *f pl* Вольфа - Райе

W140 *e* Wollaston prism
     d Wollaston-Prisma *n*
     f prisme *m* de Wollaston
     r призма *f* Волластона

W141 *e* work
     d Arbeit *f*
     f travail *m*
     r работа *f*

W142 *e* world
     d Welt *f*
     f monde *m*
     r мир *m (в космологии)*

W143 *e* world interval
     d Weltintervall *n*
     f intervalle *m* mondial
     r мировой интервал *m*

W144 *e* world line
     d Weltlinie *f*
     f ligne *f* d'Univers
     r мировая линия *f*

W145 *e* wrench
     d Bewegungsschraube *f*, Kraftschraube *f*, Dyname *f*
     f torseur *m*
     r динамический винт *m*

W146 *e* Wulff surface
     d Wulffsche Fläche *f*
     f surface *f* de Wulff
     r поверхность *f* Вульфа

W147 *e* wurtzite structure
     d Wurtzitstruktur *f*
     f structure *f* de wurtzite
     r структура *f* вюрцита

X

X1 *e* xenon, Xe
     d Xenon *n*
     f xénon *m*
     r ксенон *m*

X2 *e* xi particle
     d Xi-Teilchen *n*
     f particule *f* xi
     r кси-частица *f*

X3 *e* X-ray absorption
     d Röntgenabsorption *f*
     f absorption *f* des rayons X
     r поглощение *n* рентгеновского излучения

X4 *e* X-ray absorption analysis
     d Röntgenabsorptionsspektralanalyse *f*
     f analyse *f* spectroscopique d'absorption par rayons X
     r абсорбционный рентгено-спектральный анализ *m*

X5 *e* X-ray absorption spectroscopy
     d Röntgenabsorptionsspektroskopie *f*
     f spectroscopie *f* d'absorption par rayons X
     r абсорбционная рентгеновская спектроскопия *f*

X6 *e* X-ray absorption spectrum
     d Röntgenabsorptionsspektrum *n*
     f spectre *m* d'absorption X, spectre *m* d'absorption des rayons X
     r рентгеновский спектр *m* поглощения

X7 *e* X-ray astronomy
     d Röntgenastronomie *f*
     f astronomie *f* aux rayons X
     r рентгеновская астрономия *f*

X8 *e* X-ray binary
     d Röntgen-Doppelsternsystem *n*

	f	binaire *m* à rayons X, système *m* stellaire binaire à rayons X
	r	рентгеновская двойная *f*, рентгеновская двойная звёздная система *f*

X9
e X-ray camera
d Röntgenkammer *f*
f chambre *f* à rayons X
r рентгеновская камера *f*

X10
e X-ray crystallographic analysis
d Röntgenstrukturanalyse *f*, Röntgenkristallstrukturanalyse *f*
f analyse *f* radiocristallographique
r рентгеноструктурный анализ *m*

X11
e X-ray crystallography
d Röntgenkristallstrukturanalyse *f*
f radiocristallographie *f*
r рентгеновская кристаллография *f*

X12
e X-ray diagnostics
d Röntgendiagnostik *f*
f diagnostic *m* à rayons X
r рентгеновская диагностика *f*

X13
e X-ray diffraction
d Röntgenbeugung *f*, Röntgendiffraktion *f*, Beugung *f* von Röntgenstrahlen
f diffraction *f* des rayons X
r дифракция *f* рентгеновских лучей, рентгеновская дифракция *f*

X14
e X-ray diffraction analysis *see* X-ray crystallographic analysis

X15
e X-ray diffraction method
d Röntgenbeugungsmethode *f*, Röntgendiffraktionsmethode *f*
f méthode *f* de diffraction des rayons X, méthode *f* de diffraction à rayons X
r рентгенодифракционный метод *m*, метод *m* рентгеноструктурного анализа

X16
e X-ray diffraction pattern
d Röntgendiagramm *n*, Röntgenbeugungsbild *n*
f diagramme *m* à rayons X
r рентгенограмма *f*

X17
e X-ray diffractometer
d Röntgendiffraktometer *n*, Röntgenbeugungsgerät *n*
f diffractomètre *m* à rayons X, radiodiffractomètre *m*
r рентгеновский дифрактометр *m*

X18
e X-ray diffractometry
d Röntgendiffraktometrie *f*
f diffractométrie *f* aux rayons X
r рентгеновская дифрактометрия *f*

X19
e X-ray emission

d Röntgenstrahlung *f*
f rayonnement *m* X
r рентгеновское излучение *n*

X22
e X-ray emission spectroscopy
d Röntgenemissionsspektroskopie *f*
f analyse *f* spectroscopique d'émission par rayons X
r эмиссионная рентгеновская спектроскопия *f*

X21
e X-ray emission spectrum
d Röntgenemissionsspektrum *n*
f spectre *m* d'émission X, spectre *m* d'émission des rayons X
r рентгеновский спектр *m* испускания

X22
e X-ray flare
d Röntgenausbruch *m*
f éruption *f* X
r рентгеновская солнечная вспышка *f*, рентгеновская вспышка *f*

X23
e X-ray flaw detection
d Röntgendefektoskopie *f*
f contrôle *m* radiographique, contrôle *m* aux rayons X
r рентгеновская дефектоскопия *f*

X24
e X-ray fluorescence
d Röntgenfluoreszenz *f*
f fluorescence *f* de rayons X
r рентгеновская флуоресценция *f*

X25
e X-ray fluorescence analysis
d Röntgenfluoreszenzanalyse *f*
f analyse *f* par fluorescence de rayons X
r рентгеновский флуоресцентный анализ *m*

X26
e X-ray goniometer
d Röntgengoniometer *n*
f radiogoniomètre *m* X
r рентгеновский гониометр *m*

X27
e X-ray hardness
d Röntgenhärte *f*
f dureté *f* de rayons X
r жёсткость *f* рентгеновского излучения

X28
e X-ray image
d Röntgenbild *n*
f image *f* radiographique
r изображение *n* в рентгеновских лучах

X29
e X-ray intensity
d Röntgenstrahlenintensität *f*
f intensité *f* du rayonnement X
r интенсивность *f* рентгеновского излучения

X30
e X-ray interference
d Röntgeninterferenz *f*, Röntgenstrahleninterferenz *f*

	f	interférence *f* des rayons X
	r	интерференция *f* рентгеновского излучения
X31	*e*	**X-ray interferometry**
	d	Röntgeninterferometrie *f*
	f	interférométrie *f* aux rayons X
	r	рентгеновская интерферометрия *f*
X32	*e*	**X-ray laboratory**
	d	Röntgenlaboratorium *n*, Röntgenlabor *n*
	f	laboratoire *m* à rayons X
	r	рентгеновская лаборатория *f*
X33	*e*	**X-ray laser**
	d	Röntgenlaser *m*, X-laser *m*
	f	laser *m* à rayons X
	r	рентгеновский лазер *m*
X34	*e*	**X-ray lens**
	d	Röntgenlinse *f*
	f	lentille *f* à rayons X
	r	рентгеновская линза *f*
X35	*e*	**X-ray lithography**
	d	Röntgenlithographie *f*
	f	lithographie *f* aux rayons X
	r	рентгеновская литография *f*, рентгенолитография *f*
X36	*e*	**X-ray microscope**
	d	Röntgenmikroskop *n*
	f	microscope *m* à rayons X
	r	рентгеновский микроскоп *m*
X37	*e*	**X-ray microscopy**
	d	Röntgenmikroskopie *f*
	f	microscopie *f* aux rayons X
	r	рентгеновская микроскопия *f*
X38	*e*	**X-ray mirror**
	d	Röntgenspiegel *m*
	f	miroir *m* à rayons X
	r	рентгеновское зеркало *n*
X39	*e*	**X-ray monochromator**
	d	Röntgenstrahlenmonochromator *m*
	f	monochromateur *m* de rayons X
	r	рентгеновский монохроматор *m*
X40	*e*	**X-ray optics**
	d	Röntgenoptik *f*
	f	optique *f* des rayons X
	r	рентгеновская оптика *f*
X41	*e*	**X-ray pulsar**
	d	Röntgenpulsar *m*
	f	pulsar *m* à rayons X
	r	рентгеновский пульсар *m*
X42	*e*	**X-ray quantum**
	d	Röntgenquant *n*, Röntgenstrahlungsquant *n*
	f	quantum *m* de rayonnement X
	r	рентгеновский квант *m*
X43	*e*	**X-ray radiography**
	d	Röntgenradiographie *f*
	f	radiographie *f* aux rayons X
	r	рентгенография *f*
X44	*e*	**X-rays**
	d	Röntgenstrahlen *m pl*; Röntgenstrahlung *f*
	f	rayonnement *m* X, rayons *m pl* X
	r	рентгеновское излучение *n*; рентгеновские лучи *pl*
X45	*e*	**X-ray scattering**
	d	Röntgenstreuung *f*, Röntgenstrahlenstreuung *f*
	f	diffusion *f* de rayons X, diffusion *f* X
	r	рассеяние *n* рентгеновских лучей
X46	*e*	**X-ray source**
	d	Röntgenstrahlenquelle *f*, Röntgenquelle *f*
	f	source *f* de rayons X, source *f* X
	r	рентгеновский источник *m*, источник *m* рентгеновского излучения
X47	*e*	**X-ray spectrometer**
	d	Röntgenspektrometer *n*
	f	spectromètre *m* à rayons X
	r	рентгеновский спектрометр *m*
X48	*e*	**X-ray spectroscopic analysis**
	d	Röntgenspektralanalyse *f*
	f	analyse *f* spectroscopique par rayons X
	r	рентгеноспектральный анализ *m*
X49	*e*	**X-ray spectroscopy**
	d	Röntgenspektroskopie *f*
	f	spectroscopie *f* aux rayons X
	r	рентгеновская спектроскопия *f*
X50	*e*	**X-ray spectrum**
	d	Röntgenspektrum *n*
	f	spectre *m* des rayons X
	r	рентгеновский спектр *m*
X51	*e*	**X-ray star**
	d	Röntgenstern *m*
	f	étoile *f* X
	r	рентгеновская звезда *f*
X52	*e*	**X-ray structural analysis**
	d	Röntgenstrukturanalyse *f*
	f	analyse *f* radiocristallographique
	r	рентгеноструктурный анализ *m*
X53	*e*	**X-ray telescope**
	d	Röntgenteleskop *n*
	f	télescope *m* à rayons X, lunette *f* à rayons X
	r	рентгеновский телескоп *m*
X54	*e*	**X-ray tomography**
	d	Röntgentomographie *f*

    f tomographie *f* aux rayons X
    r рентгеновская томография *f*

X55 *e* **X-ray topography**
    d Röntgentopographie *f*
    f topographie *f* aux rayons X
    r рентгеновская топография *f*

X56 *e* **X-ray tube**
    d Röntgenröhre *f*
    f tube *m* à rayons X
    r рентгеновская трубка *f*

Y

Y1 *e* **Yagi aerial, Yagi antenna**
    d Yagi-Antenne *f*
    f antenne *f* Yagi
    r директорная антенна *f*, антенна *f* типа «волновой канал»

Y2 *e* **YAG-laser**
    d YAG-Laser *m*, Yttrium-Aluminium-Granat-Laser *m*
    f laser *m* à grenat d'yttrium et d'aluminium
    r ИАГ-лазер *m*, лазер *m* на иттрий-алюминиевом гранате

Y3 *e* **Yang-Mills fields**
    d Yang-Mills-Felder *n pl*
    f champs *m pl* de Yang-Mills
    r поля *n pl* Янга - Миллса

Y4 *e* **year**
    d Jahr *n*
    f année *f*, an *m*
    r год *m*

Y5 *e* **yield point, yield stress**
    d Fließgrenze *f*
    f limite *f* d'écoulement
    r предел *m* текучести

Y6 *e* **YIG-laser**
    d YIG-Laser *m*
    f laser *m* YIG
    r ЖИГ-лазер *m*, лазер *m* на железо-иттриевом гранате

Y7 *e* **Young modulus**
    d Elastizitätsmodul *m*, E-Modul *m*, Youngscher Elastizitätsmodul *m*
    f module *m* d'élasticité, module *m* d'élasticité d'Young
    r модуль *m* Юнга

Y8 *e* **Y particle** *see* **ypsilon**

Y9 *e* **ypsilon, ypsilon particle**
    d Y-Teilchen *n*

    f particule *f* upsilon, particule *f* Y
    r ипсилон-частица *f*

Y10 *e* **yrast band**
    d Yrast-Band *n*
    f bande *f* yrast
    r ираст-полоса *f*

Y11 *e* **yrast level**
    d Yrast-Niveau *n*
    f niveau *m* yrast
    r ираст-уровень *m*

Y12 *e* **yrast line**
    d Yrast-Linie *f*
    f ligne *f* yrast
    r ираст-линия *f*

Y13 *e* **yrast trap**
    d Yrast-Trap *m*
    f piège *m* yrast
    r ираст-ловушка *f*

Y14 *e* **ytterbium, Yb**
    d Ytterbium *n*
    f ytterbium *m*
    r иттербий *m*

Y15 *e* **yttrium, Y**
    d Yttrium *n*
    f yttrium *m*
    r иттрий *m*

Y16 *e* **yttrium aluminium garnet**
    d Yttrium-Aluminium-Granat *m*
    f grenat *m* d'yttrium et d'aluminium
    r алюмо-иттриевый гранат *m*, иттрий-алюминиевый гранат *m*

Y17 *e* **yttrium iron garnet**
    d Yttrium-Eisen-Granat *m*
    f grenat *m* de fer et d'yttrium
    r железо-иттриевый гранат *m*, феррит-гранат *m* иттрия

Y18 *e* **Yukawa potential**
    d Yukawa-Potential *n*
    f potentiel *m* de Yukawa
    r потенциал *m* Юкавы

Z

Z1 *e* **Zeeman effect**
    d Zeeman-Effekt *m*
    f effet *m* Zeeman
    r эффект *m* Зеемана

Z2 *e* **Zeeman splitting**
    d Zeeman-Aufspaltung *f*
    f séparation *f* Zeeman, dédoublement *m* Zeeman
    r зеемановское расщепление *n*

Z3 e Zeeman splitting constant
    d Zeeman-Aufspaltungskonstante *f*
    f constante *f* de séparation Zeeman
    r константа *f* зеемановского
       расщепления

Z4 e Zeeman sublevel
    d Zeeman-Unterniveau *n*
    f sous-niveau *m* Zeeman
    r зеемановский подуровень *m*

Z5 e Zener diode
    d Z-Diode *f*
    f diode *f* Zener
    r стабилитрон *m*

Z6 e zenith
    d Zenit *m*
    f zénith *m*
    r зенит *m*

Z7 e zenith angle, zenith distance
    d Zenitdistanz *f*
    f distance *f* zénithale, coaltitude *f*
    r зенитный угол *m*, зенитное
       расстояние *n*

Z8 e Zernike polynomial
    d Zernikesches Polynom *n*, Zernikesches
       Orthogonalpolynom *n*
    f polynôme *m* de Zernike, polynôme *m*
       orthogonal de Zernike
    r многочлен *m* Цернике

Z9 e zero-gap semiconductor
    d energielückenloser Halbleiter *m*
    f semi-conducteur *m* à gap zéro
    r бесщелевой полупроводник *m*

Z10 e zero gravity
    d Schwerelosigkeit *f*
    f apesanteur *f*
    r невесомость *f*

Z11 e zero-point energy
    d Nullpunktsenergie *f*
    f énergie *f* au zéro absolu
    r нулевая энергия *f*

Z12 e zero-point oscillations
    d Nullpunktsschwingungen *f pl*
    f oscillations *f pl* au zéro absolu
    r нулевые колебания *n pl*

Z13 e zero sound
    d Nullpunktschall *m*
    f son *m* au zéro absolu
    r нулевой звук *m (в гелии)*

Z14 e Zhukovski profile
    d Joukowski-Profil *n*, Joukowski-
       Flügelprofil *n*

Z14 (cont.)
    f profil *m* Joukowski
    r профиль *m* Жуковского

Z15 e zinc, Zn
    d Zink *n*
    f zinc *m*
    r цинк *m*

Z16 e zirconium, Zr
    d Zirkonium *n*
    f zirconium *m*
    r цирконий *m*

Z17 e zodiacal light
    d Zodiakallicht *n*,
       Tierkreislicht *n*
    f lumière *f* zodiacale
    r зодиакальный свет *m*

Z18 e zone
    d 1. Zone *f*; Gebiet *n* 2. Band *n*,
       Energieband *n*
    f zone *f*
    r зона *f*; область *f*

Z19 e zone filling *see*
       zone occupation

Z20 e zone magnetism
    d Zonenmagnetismus *m*
    f magnétisme *m* de zone
    r зонный магнетизм *m*

Z21 e zone melting
    d Zonenschmelzen *n*;
       Zonenschmelzverfahren *n*
    f fusion *f* à zone; méthode *f* de la zone
       fondue
    r зонная плавка *f*; метод *m* зонной
       плавки

Z22 e zone occupation
    d Energiebandbesetzung *f*
    f remplissage *m* des zones
    r заполнение *n* зон

Z23 e zone plate
    d Zonenplatte *f*
    f plaque *f* zonale
    r зонная пластинка *f*, пластинка *f*
       Cope

Z24 e zoom lens *see* varifocal lens

Z25 e z-pinch
    d z-Pinch *m*
    f pincement *m* z
    r z-пинч *m*

Z26 e Zweig rule
    d Zweigsche Regel *f*
    f règle *f* de Zweig
    r правило *n* Цвейга

DEUTSCH

A

Abbau D194
~ von Polymeren P786
Abbe-Refraktometer A1
Abbesche Zahl C627
Abbesches Refraktometer A1
Abbild I23
Abbilden I36
Abbildung I23, M222, P550
~ in absorbierten Elektronen
   A30
~ in rückgestreuten Elektronen
   B11
Abbildungsfehler A2
Abbildungsfehlerkorrektur I26
Abbildungstheorie I34
Abbildungstiefe D179
Abbrand B378
Abbrennen D86
Abdruck R404
Aberration A2
~ des Fixsternlichts A3
Aberrationen des Auges E542
~ der Elektronenlinsen A4
Aberrationsfehler der optischen
   Systeme A5
Aberregung D78
Abfall D51, S343
abgebremste Neutronen M535
abgeleitete Einheit D184
abgelenkter Strahl D87
abgelenktes Strahlenbündel D87
abgelöste Strömung D199
abgeschirmte Kammer S235
~ Spule S236
abgeschlossene Menge C338
~ Schale C339
abgeschlossenes Intervall C335
~ System C340
Abhängigkeit D162, R339
Abklingen D9, D51
~ der Lumineszenz L417
abklingende Schwingungen D7
Abklingkonstante D10
Abklingkurve D53
Abklingzeit D57, D57
Abknickung K53
Abkühlen C698
Abkühlung C698, R324
Ablation A6
Ableitung D183, L233
ablenkende Spule D88
Ablenkplatten D89
Ablenkspannung D90

Ablenkspule D88
Ablenkung D91, D216
Ablenkungswinkel D92
Ablösung der Elektronen D200
Abmessung D346, D346
Abplattung O5
Abpumpen E428
Abrieb A8
Abrikosov-Gitter A11
abrupter Übergang S805
Abschalten D74
Abschattung V143
Abscheiden D174
Abscheidung D174
Abschirmkonstante S94
Abschirmung S93, S237
Abschirmungskonstante S94
Abschnitt S117
Abschrecken Q133
Abschwächer A651
Absolutbetrag A25
absolute Dielektrizitätskonstante
   A19
~ Einheiten A24
~ Feuchtigkeit A14
~ Größenklasse A21
~ Helligkeit A21
~ Instabilität A15
~ Labilität A15
~ Messung A17
~ Permeabilität A18
~ Temperatur A22
~ Zeit A23
absoluter Fehler A13
~ Nullpunkt A26
~ Strahler A20
~ Temperaturnullpunkt A26
absolutes Instabilitätskriterium
   A16
~ Labilitätskriterium A16
~ Vakuum P225
Absolutwert A25, M198
Absorbat A28
Absorbens A33
Absorber A34
absorbierender Stoff A33
absorbierte Dosis A29
~ Strahlung A32
absorbierter Stoff A28
absorbiertes Quant A31
Absorptiometer A37
Absorption A38
Absorptionsanalyse A39

Absorptionsapparat A34
Absorptionsbande A40
Absorptionsgrad A36
Absorptionsintensität A47
Absorptionskante A45
Absorptionskoeffizient A36
Absorptionskurve A44
Absorptionslänge A49
Absorptionslinie A50
Absorptionsmessung A52
Absorptionsmittel A33
Absorptionsquerschnitt A43
Absorptionsspektralanalyse A39
Absorptions-Spektralphotometrie
   A54
Absorptionsspektroskopie A55
Absorptionsspektrum A56
Absorptionssprung A48
Absorptionsverluste A51
Absorptionsvermögen A35, A57,
   A58
Absorptionswirkungsquerschnitt
   C872
Absorptionszahl A36
Absorptionszelle A41
Abstand D484, G50, I349
absteigender Knoten D186
Abstimmanzeigeröhre T432
abstimmbarer Laser F392
Abstimmbereich T433
Abstimmung T430
Abstoßung R407
Abstreifreaktion S903
Abströmkante T316
Abszisse A12
Abtaster S56
Abtastgerät S56
Abtastimpuls P920, S454
Abtastintervall S16
Abtastoptik S60
Abtastoszillograph S17
Abtastung S57, S1089
Abweichung D216, E406
Abzweigung B309
Achromat A92
achromatische Farbe A91
~ Linse A92
Achromatisierung eines
   Linsensystems A93
Achse A712
achsenentferntes Hologramm
   O30
Achsenfläche A718

Achtflach O21
Achtflächner O21
Actinium A162
Actinoid A163
Adaptation A190
adaptive Kompensation A191
~ Optik A193
adaptiver Spiegel A192
adaptives System A194
Adaptometer A195
Addition von Geschwindigkeiten
  C513
additive Quantenzahl A197
Additivität A198
Adhäsion A199
Adhäsionskontakt A200
Adiabate A201
adiabatische Änderung A204
~ Entmagnetisierung A206
~ Erwärmung A208
~ Falle A215
~ Fluktuationen A207
~ Hülle A214
~ Invariante A210
~ Invariantenmethode A211
~ Isolierung A209
~ Kernentmagnetisierung N343
~ Näherung A202
~ Störung A212
adiabatischer Prozeß A213
adiabatisches Isolieren A209
~ Kalorimeter A203
Admittanz A218
Adsorbat A220
Adsorbens A221
adsorbierender Stoff A221
adsorbierter Stoff A220
Adsorption A222
Adsorptionschromatographie
  A224
Adsorptionsgleichgewicht A225
Adsorptionsindikator A226
Adsorptionsisostere A227
Adsorptionsisotherme A228
Adsorptionskatalyse A223
Adsorptionskinetik A229
Adsorptionsmittel A221
Adsorptionspumpe A230
Adsorptiv A220
A/D-Umsetzer A365
Advektion A232
AE A567
Aerodynamik A249
aerodynamische Beiwerte A241
~ Eigenschaft A240
~ Erwärmung A243
~ Kraft A242
~ Messungen A245
aerodynamischer Neutralpunkt
  A239
~ Widerstand A248
aerodynamisches Moment A246
~ Rauschen A247

Aeroelastizität A252
Aerohydrodynamik F217
Aerologie A253
Aeronomie A254
Aerosol A255
Aerosolkoagulation A256
Aerostatik A257
affiner Raum A258
Affinität A259
Agglomerieren A267
Agglutination A268
Aggregat A269, S211, U72
Aggregation A270
Aggregatzustand S733
Aggregatzustandsänderung
  C182
Ahlidade A285
Ähnlichkeit S293
Ähnlichkeitskriterium S294
Ähnlichkeitstheorie S296
Airysches Integral A280
~ Regenbogenintegral A280
Akkommodation A79
~ des Auges A81
Akkommodationskoeffizient A80
Akkretion A83
Akkretionsscheibe A84
akkrezierender weißer Zwerg
  A82
Akkumulation A85
Akkumulator A86
Akkumulatorzelle C144
Aktinid A163
aktinisches Licht A159
Aktinität A161
Aktinium A162
Aktinoid A163
Aktinometer A164
Aktinometrie A165
Aktivator A175
aktive Güteschaltung A183
~ Katode A169
~ Modenkopplung A181
~ Substanz A185
~ Tage A177
~ Zone C719, R223
aktiver Dipol A178
~ Stoff A185
aktives Medium A179
aktivierte Katode A169
Aktivierung A171
Aktivierungsanalyse A172, R68
Aktivierungsenergie A173
Aktivierungsmethode A174
Aktivierungsmittel A175
Aktivität A187
Aktivitätsgebiet A184
Akustik A137
~ der bewegten Medien A138
akustische Abbildung A111
~ Bilderzeugung A112
~ Holographie A110
~ Impedanz A113

~ Interferenz A114
~ Kernresonanz N342
~ Koagulation A98
~ Leitfähigkeit A100
~ Linse A116
~ magnetische Kernresonanz
  A122
~ magnetische Resonanz A124
~ Messung A117
~ Messungen A117
~ Nichtlinearität A121
~ NMR A122
~ Oberflächenwellen S1049
~ Ortung S469
~ paramagnetische Resonanz
  A124
~ Relaxation A134
~ Schwingungen A141, S475
~ Strömung A108
~ Verzögerung A101
~ Verzögerungsleitung A102
~ Wellen A95
akustischer Dipol A104
~ Durchschlag A96
~ Entfernungsmesser S468
~ Impuls A128
~ Konzentrator A99
~ Quadrupol A129
~ Reflektor A133
~ Resonator A136
~ Spiegel A119
~ Strahler A130
~ Wellenleiter A143
~ Widerstand A135
~ Wind A145
akustisches Bild A111
~ Echolot A139
~ Filter A107
~ Gitter A109
~ Interferometer A115
~ Mikroskop A118
~ Oberflächenwellenfilter S1048
~ Rauschen A120
akustoelektrische Domäne A146
~ Wechselwirkung A148
akustoelektrischer Effekt A147
Akustoelektronik A149
Akustooptik A157
akustooptische Modulation A154
~ Qualität A156
~ Spektroskopie A158
~ Wechselwirkung A151
akustooptischer Ablenker A150
~ Deflektor A150
~ Effekt A153
~ Korrelator A152
~ Modulator A155
Akzeptor A73
Akzeptoratom A74
Akzeptorniveau A76
Akzeptorterm A76
Akzeptorverunreinigung A73
Akzeptorzentrum A75

Albedo A281
~ der kosmischen Strahlung C768
Alexandrit A282
Alfvénsche Wellen A283
Alfvén-Wellen A283
Algebra A284
Alkalimetall A287
All C786
Allfaserkomponenten A288
allgemeine Relativitätstheorie G107
Allobar A289
allotrope Kristallmodifikation A291
~ Modifikation A291
Allotropie A292
alpha-aktives Isotop A297
Alphaquelle A304
Alphaspektrometer A305
Alphaspektroskopie A306
alpha-stabiles Isotop A307
Alphastrahlen A303
alpha-strahlendes Isotop A297
Alphastrahlung A300, A301
Alphastrahlungsquelle A304
Alphateilchen A299
Alphateilchenemission A300
Alphaumwandlung A298
Alphazerfall A298
Alter des Universums A266
alternative Energiequellen A311
alternierende Phasierung S285
Altersbestimmung A263
~ mit Radionukliden I549
~ nach der Kohlenstoffmethode R95
Alterung A265
Aluminium A315
Alychne A316
AM A362
ambipolare Diffusion A320
ambipolarer Diffusionskoeffizient A321
AM-Demodulator A354
Americium A322
Amerizium A322
Amici-Prisma A323
Aminosäure A325
Ammoniakmaser A326
Ammoniumdihydrogenortho-phosphat A327
Ammoniumdihydrogenphosphat A327
amorphe Substanz A336
amorpher Cluster A329
~ Schwarm A329
~ Stoff A336
~ Zustand A335
amorphes Kondensat A330
~ Magnetikum A331
~ Material A332
~ Metall A333

~ Silicium A334
Ampere A337
Amperesches Gesetz A339
Ampermeter A324
Amperwindungen A340
Ampholyt A342
amphoteres Elektrolyt A342
Amplitude A351, M198, P178, R171
Amplitudenanalysator P996
Amplitudenbegrenzer A360
Amplitudencharakteristik A352
Amplitudendemodulator A354
Amplitudendetektierung A353
Amplitudendetektion A353
Amplitudendiskriminator A355
Amplitudenfrequenzcharakte-ristik F384
Amplitudenfrequenz-Kennlinie F384
Amplitudenhologramm A359
Amplitudenkennlinie A352
Amplitudenmodulation A362
amplitudenmodulierte Schwingungen A361
Amplitudenteilung A357
Amplitudenverzerrung A356
Amplitudenwert C838
amu A625
Analog-Digital-Umsetzer A365
Analogfilter A364
Analogie A366
Analysator A375
Analyse A367
Analysenwaage A368
Analysis A367
analytische Abhängigkeit A369
~ Fortsetzung A370
~ Funktion A371
~ Methode A373
analytisches Massenspektrometer A372
~ Signal A374
anamorphotische Linse A377
anamorphotischer Objektivvorsatz A376
Anamorphotvorsatz A376
Anastigmat A378
Anderson-Lokalisierung A379
Anemometer A383
Aneroidbarometer A384
Anfangsbedingungen I211
angepaßte Last M257
angepaßtes Filter M256
angeregter Zustand E465
angeregtes Atom E462
~ Ion E463
~ Molekül E464
angereichertes Isotop E338
~ Material E340
angewandte Forschung A506
~ Optik A504
~ Physik A505

Angriffslinie L272
Angström A393
Angström-Einheit A393
Anhalten A199
anharmonische Oszillation A410
anharmonischer Oszillator A411
anharmonisches Molekül A409
Anharmonizität A408
Anhäufung A85
Anion A412
anisotrope Strahlung A414
~ Streuung A417
~ Substanz A418
anisotroper Kristall A413
anisotropes Medium A415
~ Modell A416
Anisotropie A419
~ von elastischen Eigenschaften A421
~ von magnetischen Eigenschaften A422
Anisotropieenergie A420
Anker A528
Anlage U72
Anlagerung A645
~ von Elektronen A645
ANL-Laboratorium A525
Annäherung A509
Annahme A545
Annihilation A425
Annihilationsstrahlung A428
Annihilationsverluste A426
Anode A431, P702
Anodencharakteristik A432
Anodendetektierung A435
Anodendetektion A435
Anodendunkelraum A434
Anodenfall A437
Anodengebiet A439
Anodenglimmlicht A438
Anodenraum A439
Anodenspannung A440
Anodenstrom A433
anodische Behandlung A441
Anodisieren A441
anomale Brechung A446
~ Dispersion A443
~ Refraktion A446
~ Strahlung A445
~ Viskosität A447
anomaler Zeeman-Effekt A448
anomales magnetisches Moment A444
Anomalie A449
Anomalon A442
Anordnung A539
Anpassung A190
Anpassungsblende M258
Anpassungsgrad M259
Anregung E453, I213
Anregungsenergie E457
Anregungsimpuls E460
Anregungskanal E454

Anregungskinetik E458
Anregungskurve E456
Anregungsmethode E459
Anregungsquelle E461
Anregungsquerschnitt E455
Anreicherung E341
Anreicherungsschichtkontakt E339
Anschluß A645, J25
Anschwellen S1092
Ansprechen R454
Anstellwinkel A386
Anstiegskurve G286
Anstiegszeit R517
Anströmseite L162
Anströmwinkel A386
Anteil der eingefangenen Teilchen T388
Antenne A234
Antennengewinn A454
Antennengitter A235
Antennengruppe A235
Antennenrauschen A237
Antennenspeiseleitung A453
Antennentemperatur A238
Antennenverstärkung A454
Antennenwirklänge A452
Antennenzuleitung A453
anthropisches Prinzip A456
Antibaryon A457
Antiferroelektrikum A465
antiferroelektrischer Bezirk A467
~ Stoff A465
Antiferromagnetikum A466
antiferromagnetische Domäne A467
~ Ordnung A468
~ Resonanz A469
antiferromagnetischer Stoff A466
Antiferromagnetismus A470
Antikatode A458
Antikoinzidenzschaltung A459
Antikoinzidenzverfahren A461
Antikoinzidenzzähler A460
Antikommutator A462
Antimaterie A471
Antimon A472
Antineutrino A473
Antineutron A474
Antinukleon A476
antiparallele Injektion A477
Antiproton A479
Antiquark A480
Antireflexbelag A481
Anti-Stokes-Komponente A482
Anti-Stokes-Linie A483
antistokessche Komponente A482
~ Linie A483
Antisymmetrie A484
Antiteilchen A478

Antizyklon A464
Antwort R454
Antwortfunktion R455
Antwortzeit R456
Anwendung der Kernenergie für friedliche Zwecke P175
~ der Monte-Carlo-Methode M636
Anwendungsbereich F104
Anzahl Q26
~ der Freiheitsgrade N422
Anzeiger I124
Anziehung A652
Anziehungsbereich D529
Anzünden F142
AO A628
Äolsharfe A233
aperiodische Bewegung A487
~ Schwingungen A488, N276
aperiodischer Kreis A485
~ Prozeß N277
Aperiodizität A486
Apertur A489
Aperturblende A490
Aperturintegrator A492
Apertur-Synthese A495
Aperturverzerrungen A491
Aperturwinkel A395
Apex A496
Aplanat A499
aplanatische Linse A499
aplanatisches Objektiv A499
Apochromat A501
apochromatische Linse A501
apochromatisches Objektiv A501
Apodization A502
Apogäum A503
Apparat I242, S211
Apparatur E389
Approximation A509
Approximierung A509
Aquadag A510
Äquator E368
äquatoriale Fernrohrmontierung E370
~ Montierung E370
Äquatorialionosphäre E369
Äquipotentialfläche E393
Äquipotentialkreis E391
Äquipotentialkurve E392
Äquivalent E396
äquivalente Dosis E398
Äquivalenz E394
Äquivalenzprinzip E395
Aräometer A521, D150
Arbeit W141
Arbeitsvermögen P842
Archimedisches Gesetz A515
Argon A523
Argonlaser A524
Ar-Laser A524
Arm A526

Armco-Eisen A529
Armierung R338
Arsen A530
asphärische Optik A538
assoziative Ionisation A542
~ Recombination A543
Assoziativität A544
assoziierte Paarerzeugung A541
Astat A546
Asterismus A547
Asteroid A548, M502
Astigmatismus A549
~ des Auges A551
Astigmatismusberichtigung A550
Astigmatismuskorrektion A550
Astonscher Dunkelraum A552
Astrobiologie A553
Astrograph A556
Astrokamera A556
Astrokernphysik N344
Astroklima A554
Astrolabium A558
Astrometrie A559
Astronomie A568
astronomische Einheit A567
~ Instrumente A562
~ Kolorimetrie A561
~ Koordinaten C139
astronomischer Kalender A560
astronomisches Fernrohr A566
~ Observatorium A563
Astrophotometrie A564
Astrophysik A569
Astrospektrometrie A565
Asymmetrie A572
Asymmetriefehler C469
asymmetrisches Molekül A570
Asymptote A573
asymptotische Abhängigkeit A574
~ Entwicklung A575
~ Freiheit A576
~ Reihe A577
Äther E419
Ätherwind E420
Atmosphäre A578
Atmosphärenverschmutzung A277
atmosphärische Absorption A580
~ Beugung A584
~ Dämpfung A581
~ Diffusion A585
~ Dynamik A579
~ Gezeiten A598
~ Inhomogenität A588
~ Ionisation A587, I428
~ Konvektion A583
~ Optik A590
~ Pfeifstörung W106
~ Refraktion A595
~ Störungen A596
~ Strahlenbrechung A595

~ Strahlung A594
~ Streuung A597
~ Turbulenz A600
~ Zirkulation A582
atmosphärischer Druck A593
~ Wellenleiter A601
atmosphärisches Ozon A591
Atmospherics A596
Atom A603
~ auf dem Zwischengitterplatz I345
Atom- und Molekülspektroskopie A606
Atomabstand I277
atomare Absorption A605
~ Masseneinheit A625
~ Polarisierbarkeit A630
Atombau A639
Atombindung C819
Atombombe N345
Atomdetektierung A615
Atomdetektion A615
Atomformfaktor A618
Atomgewicht A642
Atom-g-Faktor A622
Atomgitterkristall A614
Atominterferometer A620
Atomion A621
Atomkern A626, N416
Atomkernenergie N357
Atomkristall A614, C820
Atommasse A624, A642
Atommaßstab A634
Atomniveaus A617
Atomnummer A627
Atomorbital A628
Atomphysik A629
Atompolarisation A631
Atompolarisierbarkeit A630
Atomradius A633
Atomrumpf A613
Atomsonde A632
Atomspektren A636
Atomspektroskopie A637
Atomstandard A638
Atomstöße A612
Atomstrahl A607
Atomstrahlfrequenzstandard A608
Atomstrahlquelle A609
Atomuhr A611
Atomzeit A640
Atomzeitstandard A641
Attachment A645
Attraktion A652
Attraktionsdomäne D529
Attraktor A653
Attraktorkrise C839
Ätzen E416
Ätzgraben E415
Ätzgruben E417
Ätzgrubenverfahren E418
Ätzung E416

Audiometer A659
Aufdampfen D174
Auffangen T391
Auffinden von Einzelatomen D203
~ von Einzelmolekülen D204
Aufflackern F173
Auffüllung von Zuständen O15
aufgelöste Linie R422
aufgelöster Stoff S425
aufgezeichnetes Bild R257
Aufhängung S1088
Auflager S1044
Auflösung D481, R421
Auflösungskammer D482
Auflösungsvermögen R423
Aufnahme P550
Aufnahmekammer C24
Aufsatz H66
Aufspaltung F150, S662
Aufspaltungsfaktor S663
aufsteigender Knoten A535
Auftragen D174
auftreffendes Teilchen P930
Auftrieb A244, B372, B373, E282, L202
Auftriebskraft B373
Aufwärtswandler U97
Auge E539
Augenabbildungsfehler E542
Augenblicksspannung I239
Augenblickswert I237
Augenoptik E540
Augenträgheit P265
Auger-Effekt A660
Auger-Elektronen A662
Auger-Elektronenabbildung A661
Auger-Elektronenbild A661
Auger-Spektroskopie A663
Aureole A665
Aurorabogen A669
Auroraionisation A670
Auroraionisierung A670
Auroralinie A672
Auroraspektrallinie A672
ausbleichbarer Farbstoff B225
Ausbleichen B224, B224
~ von Kristallen C894
Ausbreitungsrichtung D387
Ausbreitungsvektor P937
Ausbrennen des Wasserstoffs E476
Ausbruch B380
Ausdehnung E487, E519
Ausdehnungskoeffizient C361, E489
Ausdehnungskurve E490
Ausdehnungszahl E489
Außenschale O300
Außenschalenionisation O301
Außentriggerung E524
außeraxialer Strahl O29

äußere Atmosphäre E482
~ Kräfte E521
~ lichtelektrischer Effekt
~ Magnetosphäre O296
~ Planeten O297
~ Reibung E522
äußerer lichtelektrischer Effekt E523, P431, P434
~ Photoeffekt E523, P431, P434
~ photoelektrischer Effekt E523
~ Strahlungsgürtel O299
äußeres Problem O298
außerordentliche Welle E531
außerordentlicher Strahl E530
Außer-Phase-Bringen D164
Ausfahren des Regelstabs W134
Ausfall F14
Ausfällung P858
Ausführungskanal E527
Ausgangsklemmen O306
Ausgangskreis O303
Ausgangsleistung O304
Ausgangsspannung O307
Ausgangsstromkreis O303
Ausgangsteilchen P88
ausgedehnte Quelle E518
Ausgleich C496
Ausheilen von Defekten H69
Auslegung I334
Auslenken des Strahls B100
Auslenkspule D88
Auslenkvorrichtung D93
Auslöschung D197, E525
Auslöseimpuls I212, T408
Auslösung I213
Ausnutzungsfaktor U106
Ausnutzungsgrad U106
Ausrichtung A286
Ausrüstung E389
Ausschalter S1094
Ausscheidungshärtung A264, P859
Ausschleusungskanal E527
Ausstattung E389
Aussteuerungsgrad D180
Aussteuerungstiefe D180
Ausstrahlung E287, R22
Austausch E444, I282
Austauschentartung E446
Austauschinstabilität I283
Austauschintegral E448
Austauschkonstante E445
Austauschkräfte E447
Austauschmode E450
Austauschmodell E451
Austauschwechselwirkung E449
Austenit A677
Austenitkorn A678
Austritt E410
Austrittsöffnung E479
Austrittspupille E479
Austrittsrichtung E411

Austrittsspiegel E478
Auswahl S131
Auswahlregeln S132
Autoionisation A686
Autokatalyse A679
Autoklav A680
Autokollimation A681
Autokollimationsfernrohr A682
Autokorrelation A683
Autokorrelationsfunktion A684
automatische Abstimmung A687
~ Phasenstabilisierung P337
Autophasierung P337
Autoradiographie A688
avanciertes Potential A231
Avogadro-Konstante A699
Avogadro-Zahl A699
axiale Deformation A702
~ Eichung A703
~ Kanalierung A700
~ Verformung A702
axialer Quadrupol A706
~ Vektor A707
axiales Hologramm A704
Axialstrom A701
Axialstromdivergenz D516
axialsymmetrisches Feld A705
Axiom A708
axiomatische Methode A709
~ Quantenfeldtheorie A710
Axion A711
Axoid A718
Azbel-Kaner-Effekt A719
Azimut A720
azimutale Montierung A308
~ Quantenzahl A721, O228

B

Babinet-Prinzip B1
Bahn P164, T317
Bahnbewegung O227
Bahndrehimpuls O223
Bahndrehimpuls-Quantenzahl
    O228
Bahndurchmesser O230
Bahnebene O232
Bahnebenenneigung I90
Bahnenquantelung O233
Bahngeschwindigkeit O229
Bahnintegral P166
Bahnkurve T317
Bahnlänge P167
Bahnlinie T317
Bahnmoment O225
Bahnneigung I90
Bahnparameter O231
Bahnstörungen T318
Bahnumfang P167
Balance B20
Balken B88

Balkenbiegung B134
Ball B23
Ballistik B27
ballistische Kurve B24
ballistisches Galvanometer B25
~ Phonon B26
Ballon B29
Ballonastronomie B30
Balloninstabilität B31
Ballung B365
Balmer-Serie B33
Balmer-Sprung B32
Banach-Raum B34
Band B35, B35, T14, Z18
Band-Band-Übergänge I279
Bandbreite B44
Bandbreitenmessung B45
Bandenintensität B37
Bandenspektren B41
Bändermodell B39
Bänderstruktur B42
Bändertheorie B43
Bandfilter B40
Bandpaß B40
Bandunterkante B36
Bandverbiegung B136
Bar B46
Bardeen-Cooper-Schrieffer-
    Modell B47
Barium B51
Barkhausen-Effekt B52
Barkhausen-Kurz-Generator
    B53
Barn B54
Barnett-Effekt B55, M141
Barograph B56
Barometer B57
Barometerformel B58
Barometrie M301
barometrische Höhenformel B58
barometrischer Druck A593
barotropes Phänomen A60
barotropisches Phänomen A60
Barren B46
Barretter B62
Barriere B63
Baryon B70
Baryonenasymmetrie des
    Universums U85
~ des Weltalls B71
Baryonendekuplett B73
Baryonenladung B72
Baryonenzahl B72
Baryonium B75
Base B79
Basis B79, B82
Basisfläche B78
Batterie B83
Bauch der stehender Welle
    A475
Baueinheit U72
Bauform C578
Baugruppe A539

Baumkristall D149
Bauschinger-Effekt B84
Baustein U72
Baystörung M129
Beanspruchung L307, S855,
    S886
Beauty B128
Beauty-Meson B126
Beauty-Quark B127
Becquerel B129
Bedeckung O14
Bedeckungsveränderlicher E19
Bedeutung I59
Bedingung C558
Beeinflussung I187
Begrenzer L249, R461
Begrenzung R461
Behälter C635
Beharrung I167
Beharrungsvermögen I167, I176
Beimengung I71
Beiwert F8, I122
Bel B130
belasteter Gütewert L305
Belastung L303, L307
Beleuchtung I22, L225
Beleuchtungsstärke I21, I22
Beleuchtungsstärkemesser L445
Belichtung E516
Benetzen W99
Benetzung W99
beobachtbare Größe O8
Beobachtungen O9
Beobachtungsdaten O11
Berechnung C8
Bereich A520, B35, R171,
    R332
~ der elastischen Streuung E66
~ hoher Energien H187
Berkelium B142
Bernoullische
    Differentialgleichung B143
Bernsteinsche Mode B144
Berührungsspannung C633
Beryllium B145
Berylliumkeramik B146
Beschichtung F123
Beschickung L307
Beschießung B258
beschleunigendes Feld A62
Beschleuniger A69, C215
Beschleunigertarget A71
beschleunigte Bewegung A61
Beschleunigung A66
Beschleunigungsfeld A62
Beschleunigungskanal A70
Beschleunigungsmechanismus
    A67
Beschleunigungsmesser A72
Beschleunigungsrohr A64
Beschleunigungsspannung A65
Beschleunigungsspeicher-
    komplex A63

Biot-Savartsches Gesetz B207
Biprisma B208
bistabiles Interferometer B213
Bistabilität B212
Bit B214
Blanket B221
Bläschensieden B361, N406
Blase B352, B352
Blasenbildung B355
Blasendomäne B352
Blasenkammer B354
Blasenkavitation B353
Blasensieden B361, N406
Blasenverdampfung B361, N406
Blatt S230
Blauhimmelkatastrophe B235
Blei L160, P709
bleibende Formänderung I479
~ Verformung P699, R410
Bleichen B224
Blende A489, D239, L211, S849
Blendenöffnung A489
Blendenzahl F245
Blendung G168
Bleustein-Gulyaev-Wellen B226
Blindanteil I13
Blindbelastung R216
Blindlast R216
Blindleistung R217
Blindspannung R218
Blindstrom I14, R214
Blindvoltampere V56
Blindwatt V56
Blindwiderstand R205
Blitz L230
Blitzableiter L233, L235
Blitzeinschlag L236
Blitzentladung L234
Blitzkanal L232
Blitzlampe F178
Blitzlichtphotolyse F180
Blitzlichtphotolyse-Initiierung F181
Bloch-Kurve B227
Bloch-Linie B230
Blochsche Funktionen B228
~ Kurve B227
~ Linie B230
Blochsches Gesetz B229
~ Theorem B231
Bloch-Wand B232
Blockdiagramm B233
Blockierung L325
Blockschaltbild B233
Blockschema B233
Bodenwelle G275
Bogen A513
Bogenentladung A514
Bogenlampe A518
Bohrsche Bahn B244
Bohrscher Radius B245
Bohrsches Atommodell B242

~ Korrespondenzprinzip C752
~ Magneton B243
Bolid B251
Bolometer B252
bolometrische Helligkeit B254
~ Korrektion B253
Boltzmann-Konstante B255
Boltzmannsche Verteilung B256
Boltzmann-Statistik B257
Boltzmann-Verteilung B256
Bombenkalorimeter B259
Boolesche Algebra B269
Booster B270
Bootstrap B271
Bor B273
Borkarbid B274
Bornsche Näherung B272
Bose-Einstein-Kondensat B277
Bose-Einstein-Kondensation B278
Bose-Einstein-Statistik B280
Bose-Flüssigkeit B279
Bose-Gas B281
Bose-Kondensat B277
Bose-Kondensation B278
Bose-Teilchen B283
Boson B283
Bouguer-Lambert-Beer-Gesetz B286
Boyle-Mariottesches Gesetz B300
Boylesches Gesetz B300
b-Quark B285
Brachistochrone B301
Brachystochrone B301
Brackett-Serie B302
Bragg-Gleichung B305
Bragg-Reflexion B307
Braggsche Beugung B304
~ Gleichung B305
~ Reflexion B307
Braggscher Winkel B303
Bragg-Winkel B303
Brand B378
Bravais-Gitter B313
Brechkraft F250, O171
Brechung R314, R325
Brechungsindex R319
Brechungsindexdispersion D449
Brechungswinkel A391
Brechwert F250, O171
Brechzahl R319
Brechzahlbestimmung R322
Brechzahldispersion D449
Brechzahlmesser R321
Breitbandantenne B342
Breitbandstrahlung B344
Breitbandverstärker B343
Breite L130, W115
~ des Energieniveaus E323
Breit-Wigner-Formel B326
Bremsmittel M537
Bremsneutronen M535

Bremsstoff M537
Bremsstrahlung B327
Bremsung D580
Bremsvermögen S850
Brennebene F249
Brennelement F416
Brennen B378, B378, C477
Brennfläche F252
Brennfleck C112
Brennkammer C478
Brennpunkt F255
Brennstoffelement F415
Brennstoffladung R222
Brennweite F247
Brennwert C19
Brewster-Fenster B329
Brewsterscher Winkel B328
Brewstersches Gesetz B330
Brewster-Winkel P768
Bridgman-Methode B332
Briggscher Logarithmus D64
Brillenglas L175
Brillouinsche Zone B337
Brillouin-Streuung B336
Brillouin-Zone B337
Brinell-Härte B338
Brom B348
Bronze B349
Brownsche Bewegung B350
~ Molekularbewegung B350
Bruch F320, F320
Bruchfestigkeit B319, U3
Bruchfläche F320
Brüchigkeit F323
Bruchkriterium F321
Bruchmechanismus F322
Bruchspannung B320, U4
Bruchstück F324
Bruchverformung B318
Brücke B331
Brüten B322
Brüter B321
Brutfaktor B325
Brutgewinn B324
Brutmantel B221
Brutrate B325
Brutreaktor B321
Brutverhältnis B325
buchtähnliche magnetische Störung M129
Budkerscher Ring B357
Bugwelle B299
Buncher B366
Bündel B88, B368
Bündelerzeugung B103
Bündelung B367, F261
Bündelzerstreuer D40
Bündelzerstreuung D41
Bunsen-Brenner B370
Bunsen-Photometer B371
Bürette B374

E

~ Wellendruck E153
elektromagnetisches Feld E144
elektromechanischer
   Umwandlungsfaktor E155
Elektrometer E156
elektromotorische Kraft E157
Elektron E158
Elektronegativität E192
Elektron-Elektron-Streuung
   M606
Elektron-Elektron-
   Wechselwirkung E193
Elektronenablösung E186
Elektronenaffinität E160
Elektronenanlagerung E161
Elektronenbahn E226
Elektronenbeschleuniger E159
Elektronenbeugung E187
~ in Festkörpern D292
Elektronenbeugungsanalyse
   E188
Elektronenbeugungsaufnahme
   E189
Elektronenbeugungsbild E189
Elektronenbeugungsgerät E191
Elektronenbeugungsuntersu-
   chung E190
Elektronenbeweglichkeit E221
Elektronenbündel E163
Elektronendichte E181, E185
Elektronendurchtunnelung E247
Elektroneneinfang E176
~ durch den Kern C60
Elektronenemission E194
Elektronenenergieniveau E196
Elektronenenergieverteilung
   E195
Elektronenfalle E244
Elektronengas E198
Elektronenimpuls E222
Elektroneninjektion E212
Elektroneninjektor E213
Elektronenionisation E214
Elektronenkanalierung E177
Elektronenkanone E199, G297
Elektronenkollektivierung E180
Elektronenkonfiguration E184
Elektronenkonzentration E181,
   E185
Elektronenladung E178
Elektronenlawine E162
Elektronenleitung E182
Elektronenlinse E216
Elektronen-Löcher-Flüssigkeit
   E202
Elektronen-Löcher-Übergang
   E201
Elektronenlochtropfen
   E200
Elektronenmasse E217
Elektronenmeßgerät E205
Elektronenmikroskop E218
Elektronenoptik E225

elektronenoptische Aberration
   E223
Elektronenpaarbindung C819
Elektronenpaarung P11
Elektronenprojektor E231
Elektronenquelle E238
Elektronenradiographie E233
Elektronenradius E234
Elektronenröhre E246, V44
Elektronenschale E237
Elektronenschwingungsanregung
   V135
Elektronen-Schwingungs-
   spektren E210
Elektronensonde E230
Elektronenspektren E208
Elektronenspiegel E220
Elektronenspin E239
Elektronenspinresonanz E240
Elektronenstoß E211
Elektronenstoßionisation I415
Elektronenstrahl E163
Elektronenstrahlaufdampfen
   E164
Elektronenstrahlaufzeichnung
   E174
Elektronenstrahlbearbeitung
   E172
Elektronenstrahlerhitzung E167
Elektronenstrahlerwärmung
   E167
Elektronenstrahlerzeuger E199,
   G297
Elektronenstrahlgeräte E165
Elektronenstrahlinitiierung
   E168
Elektronenstrahlinterferenz
   E169
Elektronenstrahllithographie
   E170
Elektronenstrahloszillograph
   C108
Elektronenstrahlpumpen E173
Elektronenstrahlröhre C110,
   E175
Elektronenstrahlschmelzen
   E171
Elektronenstrahlung E232
Elektronenstrahlverdampfung
   E166
Elektronenstreuung E236
Elektronentemperatur E241
Elektronentheorie E242
Elektronenübergang E243
Elektronenvolt E249
Elektronenwanderung E219
Elektronen-Wärmekapazität
   E203
Elektronen-Wärmeleitfähigkeit
   E183, E204
Elektronen-Wärmeleitung E183,
   E204
Elektronenwolke E179

Elektronik E207
Elektron-Ion-Rekombination
   E215
elektronisches Relais E206
Elektron-Loch-Rekombination
   R247
Elektron-Phonon-
   Wechselwirkung E228
Elektron-Positron-Paar E229
Elektronvolt E249
Elektrooptik E256
elektrooptischer Deflektor E254
~ Effekt E251
~ Kerr-Effekt E251
~ Koeffizient E250
~ Kristall E253
~ Längseffekt P714
~ Modulator E255
~ Verschluß E252
Elektrophorese E257
Elektrophysik E258
Elektropositivität E259
elektroschwache
   Wechselwirkung E272
Elektroskop E260
Elektrostatik E270
elektrostatische Fokussierung
   E262
~ Induktion E265
~ Linse E267
elektrostatischer Generator
   E263
~ Quadrupol E269
elektrostatisches Bild E264
~ Feld E261
~ Meßinstrument E266
~ Potential E268
Elektrostriktion E271
Element E275
elementare Anregung E277
Elementarladung E276
Elementarlänge E278
Elementarteilchen E280, F431
Elementarteilchenphysik E279
Elementarzelle P885
Elementenaufbau E281
Elementenentstehung E281
Elementensynthese E281
Ellipsometer E283
Ellipsometrie E284
elliptische Polarisation E285
Emission E287
Emissionselektronik E288
Emissionsgrad E297
Emissionsintensität E289
Emissionslinie E290
Emissionsmaß E291
Emissionsmikroskop E292
Emissionsphotozelle P433
Emissionsspektroskopie E293
Emissionsspektrum E294
Emissionsvermögen E295
Emittanz E297

Emitter E299
Emitterelektrode E299
Emitterübergang E300
emittiertes Quant E298
EMK E157
E-Modul M555, Y7
Empfangsverstärkerröhre R231
Empfindlichkeit S200
Empfindung S198
empirische Abhängigkeit E301
empirisches Modell E302
Emulgator E304
Emulsion E305
Emulsionskammer E306
Enantiomer E307
Enantiomorphie E308
Endlagerung radioaktiver
   Abfälle B377
~ von radioaktiven Abfällen
   D462
endliche Bewegung F138
~ Deformation F135
endliches Intervall F137
Endlichkeit des Universums
   F139
Endstufe F130, O305
Energie E309
~ des elektromagnetischen
   Feldes E143
~ des magnetischen Feldes M53
Energieabgabe E331
Energieaustausch E318
Energieband B35, E311, Z18
Energiebandbesetzung Z22
Energiebanddeformation D98
Energiebändermodell B39
Energiebereich B35, E329,
   E330
Energiedegradation D117
Energiedichte E315
Energiedissipation D466
Energieerhaltung C612
Energieerhaltungssatz E313
Energiefluß E319
Energiefreisetzung E331
Energiegleichverteilung E388
Energiegleichverteilungssatz
   E387
Energie-Impuls-Tensor E327
Energieintervall E329, E330
Energiekanalierung E312
Energielücke E320
energielückenloser Halbleiter
   Z9
Energiemessung E325
Energieniveaus E322
~ des Atoms A617
Energieniveauschema E321
Energiequantelung E328
Energiequantisierung E328
Energiequelle E332
energiereiche Strahlung H202
Energiespeicher E310

Energiespektrum E333
Energietransport E335
Energieüberschuß E442
Energieumformung E314
Energieverlust E316, E324
Energieverteilung E317
~ im Spektrum D509
Energiewanderung E326
Energiezerstreuung E316
Energiezustände E334
Ensemble E342
entartete Mode D112
~ Schwingungen D113
~ Zone D109
entarteter Halbleiter D114
~ Heliumzwerg D111
~ Zustand D115
entartetes Gas D110
Entartung D103
~ des Energieniveaus D105
Entartungsgrad D107
Entartungstemperatur D108
Entfärbung B224
entferntes Objekt D487
Entfernung D484
Entfernungsmesser R172
Entfernungsmessung D485
Entfestigung L378
Entgasung D102
entgegengerichtete Injektion
   A477
Enthalpie E345, H79
Entionisierung D123
Entionisierungszeit D124
Entkopplung I520
Entkristallisation D72
Entladekammer E100
Entladekanal D399
Entladung D398
Entladungsinitiierung D402
Entladungskammer E100
Entladungskanal D399
Entladungslaser E102
Entladungszündung D401
Entleeren D173
Entleerung D166
entmagnetisierendes Feld D143
Entmagnetisierung D138
Entmagnetisierungsfaktor D141
Entmagnetisierungsfeld D143
Entmagnetisierungskurve D140
Entropie E347
~ des Weltalls E349
Entropiesatz S114
Entspannungskurve A424
Entstehung G108
Entweichungsgeschwindigkeit
   E412
Entwicklung D215, E439, E487
~ nach Eigenmoden E39
Entwicklungsmethode nach
   Eigenfunktionen E37
Entwicklungsmodell E440

Entzünden F142
Enveloppe E350
Eötvös E355
Eötvös-Drehwaage E356
Eötvös-Einheit E355
Eötvössche Drehwaage E356
Ephemeride E357
Ephemeridenzeit E358
Epidiaskop E360
Epiplanargerät P617
Epitaxialfilm E361
Epitaxialisolation E362
Epitaxiallaser E363
Epitaxial-Planargerät P617
Epitaxialverfahren E364
Epitaxie E365
Epitaxieisolation E362
Epitaxielaser E363
Epitaxieschicht E361
Epitaxieverfahren E364
Epizentrum E359
Erbium E399
Erdbeben E5
erdbebenaktive Zone S129
Erdbebenaktivität S127
Erdbebenwellen S128
Erdbeschleunigung A68, F345,
   G234
Erde E2, E3, G271
erdmagnetische Crochets M40
~ Variationen G127
erdmagnetischer Äquator M54
~ Sturm G125, M126
Erdmagnetismus G128, T65
Erdnähe P227
Erdschluß E2, G271
Erdströme E4
Erdung G272
Ereignis E437, O19
Ereignishorizont E438
Erg E403
Ergänzungsfarben C501
Ergodenhypothese E404
Ergodizität E405
Erhaltung der Baryonenzahl
   B77
~ des Drehimpulses C610
~ des Impulses C613
~ der Masse C614
~ des Vektorstroms C615
Erhaltungsmasse C619
Erhaltungssätze C609
Erhitzen H87
Erholungszeit R259
Erkennung I10, R235
erlaubte Linie A294
~ Zone P250
erlaubter Energiebereich A293
~ Übergang A295, P251
erlaubtes Band A293, P250
Ermüdung F33
Ermüdungsbruch F35
Ermüdungsdeformation F34

~ Kabel F90
Faserverbundstoff F88
Feeder F46
Fehler D79, E406, F185, I54
Fehlerfunktion E408
Fehlerintegral E409
Fehlerkurve E407
Fehlerquadratmethode M406
Fehlertheorie T80
fehlgeordneter Kristall D432
Fehlordnung D431, D435
Fehlstellenerzeugung D82
Fehlstellenwanderung D83
Feinmechanik F131
Feinmeßmikroskop M305
Feinstruktur F133
Feinstrukturkonstante F134
Feinwaage A368
Feld F95
Felddesorption F98
Feldeffekttransistor F111
Feldemission F99
Feldinvarianten F101
Feldionisation F102
Feldionisierung F102
Feldkomponenten F96
Feldkrümmung F97
Feld-Lagrange-Funktion F103
Feld-Lagrangian F103
Feldlinse C411
Feldplatte M179
Feldquantelung F107
Feldquantisierung F107
Feldstärke F109
Feldstärkelinie L273
Feldtheorie F110
Feldwaage M27
Femtosekunde F48
Femtosekundenimpuls F50
Femtosekundenlaser F49
Fenster W128
~ der Atmosphäre A599
Fermatsches Prinzip F51
Fermi-Alter F53
Fermi-Beschleunigung F52
Fermi-Dirac-Statistik F54
Fermi-Energie F55
Fermi-Fläche F61
Fermi-Flüssigkeit F58
Fermi-Gas F56
Fermi-Niveau F57
Fermi-Oberfläche F61
Fermion F59
Fermische Energie F55
Fermi-Teilchen F59
Fermium F62
Fernabtastung R392
ferne Infrarotstrahlung F26
ferner Gegenstand D487
fernes Infrarot F27
Fernfeldzone F25
Ferngeber R393
Fernglas B193

Fernmeldeleitung C486
Fernmessung R391, T26
Fernordnung L348
Fernrohr T27
Fernsehen T28
Fernsondierung R392
fernwirkende Komponente L346
Fernwirkung A167, L347
Ferrimagnetikum F63
ferrimagnetische Resonanz F64
ferrimagnetischer Stoff F63
Ferrimagnetismus F65
Ferrit F66
Ferritkernspule F68
Ferritring F69
Ferritzirkulator F67
Ferroelektrikum F72
ferroelektrische Hysteresis F75
ferroelektrischer Bezirk F74
~ Kristall F73
Ferroelektrizität F76
Ferrohydrodynamik F78
Ferromagnetikum F79
ferromagnetische Flüssigkeit
   F77
~ Resonanz F82
ferromagnetischer Bezirk F81
~ Kristall F80
~ Stoff F79
Ferromagnetismus F83
Ferrometer F84
feste Lösung S414
Festelektrolyt S411
fester Elektrolyt S411
~ Körper S409
festes Helium S412
~ Target F167
Festigkeit S884
Festigkeitsprüfung S885
Festkörper S409
Festkörperlaser S415
Festkörpermechanik M322
Festkörpermikroelektronik S416
Festkörperphysik S417
Festkörperplasma S418
Festlandsockel C640
Festlösung S414
Festspule F166
feststehende Spule F166
Feststoff S419
Feuchte M561
Feuchtigkeit M561
Feuer F140
Feuerball F141
Feuerkugel B251
Feynman-Diagramm D225, F85
Feynman-Diagrammindex I123
Feynman-Eichung F86
Feynman-Graph D225, F85
Feynman-Graphindex I123
F-Gebiet F359
Filamentkanal F115
Film F119

Filmkondensation F122
Filmsieden F120
Filmverdampfung F120
Filter F126
Filtration F129
Filtrierung F129
Finit-Element-Methode F136
Finsternis E15
Fizeauscher Interferenzversuch
   F168
~ Versuch F168
Fjodorow-Gruppen F43
Fläche A520
flache Haftstelle S215
Flächengeschwindigkeit S118
Flächeninhalt A520
flächenzentrierter Würfel F3
flächenzentriertes Gitter F5
Flachspiegel P624
Flackereffekt F196
Flackerphotometer F197
Flackerstern F176
Flamme F169
Flammenfortpflanzungsge-
   schwindigkeit B379
Flammenfront F170
Flammenphotometrie F171
Flammenspektrum F172
Flanke F410
Flattern F233
Flavor F184
Fleck S676
Fleckenrelativzahlen W137
Flexibilität F189
Flickereffekt F196
Fliehkraft C165
Fließen F204
Fließgrenze Y5
Flimmerphotometer F197
Flocculi F202
Flocken F202
Flotation F203
flüchtige Komponente V186
Flüchtigkeit F417, V187
Fluenz F215
Flügel W130
Flügelabsorption W131
Flughöhenmessung A313
Fluid F216
Fluidität F219
Fluidströmung F218
Fluktuationen F213
Fluktuon F214
Fluor F229
Fluoreszenz F222
Fluoreszenzanalyse F227
Fluoreszenzausbeute F223
Fluoreszenzlichtquelle F224
Fluoreszenzstrahlung F225
Fluorimeter F226
Fluorometer F226
Fluorometrie F228
Fluß C961, F204, F234

461

gebeugte Strahlung D274
gebeugter Strahl D273
Gebiet A520, R171, R332, Z18
~ der elastischen Streuung E66
~ der unelastischen Streuung I164
gebrochene Symmetrie B347
~ Welle R312
gebrochener Strahl R311
gebündelte Strahlung F258
gebündelter Strahl F259
Gebunden-Gebunden-Übergang B292
gebundene Bewegung F138, R462
~ Energie B295
~ Ladung B293
gebundener Wirbel B297
~ Zustand B296
gebundenes Elektron B294
gedämpfte Schwingungen D7
gefahrlose Konzentration S7
Gefälle I90, S343
gefalteter Hohlleiter C760
Gefrieren F356, R324
Gefrierpunkt F358
Gefrierpunkterniedrigung D176
Gefügefehler S914
Gefügeumwandlung S919
gegeneinandergeführte Strahlen C422
gegeneinanderlaufende Strahlen C422
Gegeninduktion M751
Gegeninduktivität M750
Gegenkopplung N48
Gegenrichtung B15
Gegenschein O79
gegenseitige Kohärenz M747
~ Kohärenzfunktion M748
~ Korrelation C865
Gegenseitigkeit R233
Gegenspannung B14
Gegenstandsraum O3
Gegentaktverstärker B21
Gehör H70
Gehörschärfe A188
Geiger-Müller-Zählrohr G92
Geiger-Nuttall-Regel G93
Geister G150
gekoppelte Kreise C810
~ Moden C811
~ Schwingungen C812
~ Systeme C813
gekreuzte Felder C866
gekrümmter Raum C980
Gel G94
geladene Komponente C205
geladener Strom C206
geladenes Kaon C211
~ K-Meson C211
~ Lepton C212
~ Meson C213

~ Teilchen C214
Gell-Mann-Matrizen G95
Gell-Mann-Nishijima-Formel G96
Gelöstes S425
gemeinsamer Faktor C483
gemischte Versetzung M517
gemischter Zustand M518
genaue Messung A89
Genauigkeit P861
Genauigkeitsklasse A87
Generalkonferenz für Maß und Gewicht G97
Generation G108
Generations-Rekombinations-Rauschen G110
Generationsschwelle O281
Generator G111, O282
Generatorröhre O270
Generierung G108
Generierungskanal G109
genetisch bedeutsame Dosis G112
Geoakustik G113
Geochronologie G114
Geodäsie G116
Geodätische G115
geodätische Linie G115
geographische Breite L130
~ Koordinaten G117
~ Länge L335
Geoid G118
geomagnetische Breite G121
~ Falle G126
~ Koordinaten G119
~ Länge G122
geomagnetischer Meridian G123
~ Pol G124
geomagnetisches Feld G120
Geomagnetismus G128, T65
Geometrie G139
geometrische Akustik G129
~ Anordnung G139
~ Gestaltung G139
~ Interferenz G138
~ Isomerie C308, G133
~ Kristallographie G131
~ Optik G134
~ Oszillationen G135
geometrischer Faktor G137
~ Ort L326
~ Querschnitt G130
geometrisches Isomer C307, G132
Geophon G140
Geophysik G141
geordnete Phase O236
geostationäre Bahn G142
Geothermie G145
geothermische Energie G143
geothermischer Gradient G144
gepulste Injektion P987
gepulster Laser P988

gequantelter Wirbel Q31
Gerade-gerade-Kern E435
gerader Stoß H67
Gerade-ungerade-Kern E436
geradlinige Bewegung L264, R266
Gerät D218, I242, S211
Gerätefehler I244
Geräteverzerrung I243
Geräusch N184
gerichtete Strahlung D384
Gerinnung C350
Germanium G146
Gesamtabsorption T298
Gesamtintensität I250, T302
Gesamtquerschnitt T299
gesättigte Lösung S21
gesättigter Dampf S22
geschichtete Atmosphäre S870
geschlitzte Meßleitung S347
geschlossene Konfiguration C331
~ Kurve C333
~ Linie C336
geschlossener Kreis C330, L357
~ Kreislauf C334
~ Stromkreis C330
geschlossenes Modell C337
Geschoßbewegung P931
Geschwindigkeit R185, S600, V89
~ der chemischen Reaktion C251
Geschwindigkeitsbereich V100
Geschwindigkeitsfeld V92
Geschwindigkeitsmesser V88
Geschwindigkeitsmessung V94
Geschwindigkeitsmodulation V95
Geschwindigkeitspotential V98
Geschwindigkeitsprofil V99
Geschwindigkeitsraum V101
Geschwindigkeitsverteilung V91
Geschwindigkeitszirkulation V90
Gesenkschmieden F284
Gesetz L150
~ des chemischen Gleichgewichts L152
~ der Partialdrücke D5
~ von Snellius S359
Gesichtsfeld F106
Gesichtsfeldblende F108
Gesichtswahrnehmung V181
Gesichtswinkel A392
gespeichertes Bild R257
Gestalt C578, S216
Gestaltanisotropie F288, S217
gestapelte optische Integration S703
gesteuerte Kernfusions-reaktionen C671
~ thermonukleare Fusion C670

gestörte Bewegung P269
~ Ionosphäre D512
~ Totalreflexion F414
gestörter Tag D511
gestörtes Gebiet D513
~ Problem P270
gestreute Neutronen S62
~ Strahlung S64
~ Welle S65
gestreutes Quant S63
getrennte Isotope S205
Getter G147
Getterpumpe G148
Gewicht W87
gewichtetes Mittel W88
Gewichtsfaktor W89
Gezeitenbewegung T236
g-Faktor G149
gg-Kern E435
Gibbs-Duhemsche Gleichung G158
Gibbs-Helmholtzsche Gleichungen G160
Gibbssche freie Energie G159
~ Gesamtheit G163
~ Phasenregel G162, P327
~ Verteilung G157
Gibbssches Paradoxon G161
~ thermodynamisches Potential G164
Gibbs-Verteilung C30, G157
Gießen C93
Gigant G156
Gilbert G165
Ginsburg-Landausche Theorie G166
Gitter G224, G265, L131
Gitterbaufehler L135, L139
Gitterbaustein L132
Gitterdefekt L135
Gitterdeformation L136
Gitterenergie L137
Gitterfehler L135
Gitterfehlordnung L139
Gitterfokussierung G268
Gitterfurche G270
Gittergeister G150
Gittergleichrichtung G267
Gitterinterferometer G228
Gitterkompressor G225
Gitterkonstante G226
Gitterkonstanten L134
Gitterleitfähigkeit L133
Gitterlücke V1
Gittermode L140
Gittermodulation G269
Gitterparameter C909
Gitterplatz A644, L142
Gitterschwingungen L143
Gitterstelle A644
Gitterstörstelle L135
Gitterstrich G270
Gitterunregelmäßigkeit L139

Gittervorspannung G266
Gitterwärmekapazität L138
Gitterwärmeleitfähigkeit L133
Glan-Thompson-Prisma G167
Glänzen G178
Glas G169
glasartiger Halbleiter G173
~ Zustand G174
Glasfaser G170
Glasfaseroptik F93
Glashalbleiter G173
Glashauseffekt G260
Glaslaser G171
Glasmetall M379
Glaszustand G174
glatte Kurve S358
Glauber-Korrektionen G175
gleichförmig beschleunigte Bewegung U66
~ veränderliche Bewegung U68
gleichförmige Bewegung U69
Gleichförmigkeit U65
Gleichgewicht B20, E371
Gleichgewichtsbahn E379
Gleichgewichtsbesetzung E382
Gleichgewichtsdichte E373
Gleichgewichtsionisation E378
Gleichgewichtskonfiguration E374
Gleichgewichtskonzentration E373
Gleichgewichtskurve E375
Gleichgewichtsladungsträger E372
Gleichgewichtsphase E380
Gleichgewichtsplasma E381
Gleichgewichtsprozeß E383
Gleichgewichtsstabilität S694
Gleichgewichtsträger E372
Gleichgewichtsverteilung E377
Gleichgewichtszustand E385
Gleichklang C620
Gleichlauf S1111
gleichmäßig verzögerte Bewegung U67
Gleichmäßigkeit U65
Gleichrichter R265
Gleichrichtung D202, R264
Gleichspannung D33
Gleichstrom D377
Gleichstrommagnetisierung D32
Gleichstromverstärker D31, D378
Gleichung von J. R. Mayer M294
Gleichverteilung der Energie E388
Gleichverteilungssatz E387
Gleitebene G177
Gleiten G176, S338
Gleitlinie S340
Gleitlinien L408
Gleitreibung S337

Gleitreibungszahl C359
Gleitspur S340
Gleitung S338
Gleitverschleiß A10
Glimmen G184
Glimmentladung G185
Glimmer M421
Glimmlampe G186
globale Dualität G179
~ Instabilität G180
Globalinvarianz G181
Globalsymmetrie G182
Glueball G187
Glühelektron T109
Glühelektronenbild T177
Glühemission T149
Glühen A423
Glühfaden F114
Glühkatode T148
Glühlampe I83
Gluino G188
Gluon G189
Gluonbag G190
Gluonsack G190
Gold G191
Goldberger-Treimansche Beziehung G192
Goldstone-Boson G193
Goldstone-Fermion G194
Goldstone-Moden G195
Goldstonesches Boson G193
Goniometer G196
Goniometrie G197
Grad D118
~ der Entartung D107
Gradation G198
Gradient G200
Gradientendrift G201
Gradientenfaser G199
Gradienteninvarianz G202
Gradiometer G203
Grafik G215
grafische Darstellung G217
Gramm G208
Grammatom G209
Grammolekül G210
Granat G51
Granulation G214
~ der Photosphäre P515
Granulierung G214
Graph G215
graphische Darstellung D224, P708
~ Integration G216
Graphit G218
Graphitkonstruktion G221
Graphitmoderator G220
graphitmoderierter Reaktor G219
Graphitreaktor G219
Graphitstapel G221
Graphitstruktur G221
Grashof-Zahl G222

H

I

~ der Frühphase des Weltalls E1
kosmologische Konstante C781
~ Nukleosynthese C783
~ Strahlung C784
kosmologischer Baryonenüberschuß C780
kosmologisches Modell C782
Kosmos C786
kovalente Bindung C819
kovalenter Kristall C820
~ Radius C821
Kovalenz C818
kovariante Ableitung C823
Kovarianz C822
Kovektor C824
kp K26
kp/s K27
Krabbennebel C830
Kraft F277
Kraftangriffslinie L272
Kraftarm A527
Kräfteaddition C512
Kräftepaar C809
Kräfteparallelogramm P40
Kräftepolygon P783
Kräftevieleck P783
Kräftezusammensetzung C512
Kraftfeld F282
Kraftimpuls I67
Kraftlinie L273
Kraftlinienfeld F282
Kraftmesser D636
Kraftmoment M610
Kraftschraube W145
Kragträger C35
Kramers-Kronigsche Relation K68
Kramers-Theorem K69
Kranzerscheinung A665
Krater C835
Kräuselwellen C55
Kreis C293, C296, L357
Kreisbahn C302
Kreisbeschleuniger C297
Kreisbewegung C301
Kreisdiagramm C294
Kreisel G307, T272
Kreiselhorizont A531
Kreiselkräfte G308
Kreiselmoment G311
Kreiselträgheit G309
kreisförmige Bewegung C301
~ Umlaufbahn C302
Kreislinie C293
Kreiswellenvektor P937
Kreiswellenzahlvektor P937
Kreiszylinderwelle C1010
Kreuzinterferometer C879
Kreuzkorrelation C865, M749
Kreuzmodulation C868
Kreuzrelaxation C870
Kriechen C837

Kristall C889
Kristallachse C924
Kristallachsenmessung C608
Kristallakustik C890
Kristallanisotropie C892
Kristallaser C905
Kristallbaufehler C899, C903
Kristallbeugung D278
Kristallbiegung C893
Kristallbildung C915
Kristallchemie C896
Kristalldefekt C903
Kristallebene C935
Kristallfeld C911
Kristallgefüge C937
Kristallgitter C906, L131
Kristallgitterbasis C907
Kristallgitterdynamik C908
Kristallgitterparameter C909
Kristallgittervibration C910
Kristallhabitus H1
Kristallhalterung C902
kristalliner Stoff C913
~ Zustand C912
Kristallisation C915
~ aus der Dampfphase C919
~ aus der Lösung C917
~ aus der Schmelze C916
Kristallisationsfrontkrümmung C920
Kristallisationsisotherme C921
Kristallisationskeim C147, N408
Kristallisationskinetik C922
Kristallisationswellen C923
Kristallisationszentrum C147
Kristallisieren C915
Kristallit C914
Kristallkeim F436, S125
Kristallklassen C897
Kristallkorn G205
Kristallkunde C927
Kristallographie C927
kristallographische Achse C924
~ Anisotropieenergie A420
~ Indizes C904
~ Richtung C925
kristallographischer Index C926
Kristalloid C928
Kristalloptik C929
Kristallphosphor C932
Kristall-Photoeffekt P407
Kristallphysik C933
Kristallrichtung C925
Kristallspektroskopie C936
Kristallstörstelle C899
Kristallstruktur C937
Kristallstrukturanalyse C891
Kristallstrukturbestimmung D207, S913
Kristallsymmetrie C938
Kristallsymmetriegruppen C939
Kristallsystem C940
Kristalltonabnehmer P568

Kristallunvollkommenheit C903
Kristallwachstum C901
Kristallwasser C941
Kristallzähler C898
Kristallzüchtung C901
~ nach dem Czochralski-Verfahren C1012
Kriterium C840
~ der konvektiven Instabilität C681
Kritikalität C850
kritische Anordnung C842
~ Beladung C843
~ Dämpfung C845
~ Dichte C846
~ Dynamik C847
~ Erscheinungen C855
~ Frequenz C848
~ Geschwindigkeit C862
~ Größe C859
~ Indizes C849
~ Leuchtkraft C851
~ magnetische Feldstärke C852
~ Masse C853
~ Mode C986
~ Opaleszenz C854
~ Phänomene C855
~ Stromstärke C844
~ Temperatur C861
kritischer Druck C857
~ Punkt C856
~ Radius C858
~ Zustand C850, C860
kritisches Volumen C863
Kritizität C850
Kroneker-Symbole K70
Kronig-Kramersche Beziehung K68
krummlinige Bewegung C982
~ Koordinaten C981
Krümmung B131, C978
Krümmungshalbmesser R147
Krümmungsradius R147
Kruskal-Bedingung K71
Kruskal-Schafranow-Bedingung K71
Kryoelektronik C882
Kryoflüssigkeit C885
kryogene Flüssigkeit C883
Kryogenik C884
Kryophysik C886, L403
Kryostat C887
Kryotron C888
Krypton K72
Kubikmeter C947
kubisch dichte Kugelpackung C944
~ dichteste Kugelpackung C944
kubische Gleichung C946
~ Nichtlinearität C948
~ Struktur C949
kubischer Ausdehnungskoeffizient C371

L

M

~ Cluster M34
~ Dipol M47
~ Durchbruch M28
~ Feldgradient M57
~ Fluß M66
~ Formfaktor M71
~ Inflektor M79
~ Kreis M32
~ Leitwert M36, P247
~ Meridian M92
~ Monopol D374, M95
~ Pol M105
~ Quadrupol M108
~ Rotationsdichroismus M33
~ Schirm M119
~ Spiegel M93
~ Stern M125
~ Sturm G125, M126
~ Werkstoff M90
~ Widerstand M114, R385
~ zirkularer Dichroismus M33
magnetisches Bild M76
~ Dielektrikum M45
~ Dipolmoment M48
~ Feld M55
~ Flußquant F242, M69
~ Führungsfeld G296
~ Kation M29
~ Kernmoment N371
~ Kernresonanzmagnetometer
  N373
~ Moment M94
~ Moment des Atoms A623
~ Neutronenmoment N136
~ Plasma M147
~ Potential M106
~ Quadrupolmoment M109
~ Untergitter M128
~ Variometer M137
magnetisierter Körper M146
magnetisiertes Gebiet M145
Magnetisierung M140
Magnetisierungskurve M142
Magnetisierungsvektor M144
Magnetisierungsverluste M88
Magnetisierungsverlustfaktor
  M89
Magnetismus M139
~ des Atomkerns N374
Magnetkompaßdeviation M44
Magnetkonfiguration M37
Magnetkreis M32
Magnetoakustik M150
magnetoakustische Resonanz
  M149
~ Wellen M151
magnetoakustischer Effekt
  M148
Magnetobremsstrahlung M152
Magnetochemie M154
Magnetodielektrikum M155
magnetoelastische Wechsel-
  wirkung M156

~ Wellen M157
magnetoelektrischer Effekt
  M158
Magnetograph M159
Magnetohydrodynamik M73,
  M163
magnetohydrodynamische
  Instabilität M161
~ Schwingungen M162
~ Wellen M164
magnetohydrodynamischer
  Generator M160, M419
magnetoionische Theorie M165
magnetokalorischer Effekt M153
magnetomechanische Effekte
  M166
magnetomechanisches
  Verhältnis M167
Magnetometer M168
magnetomotorische Kraft M169
Magneton M170
Magnetooptik M173
magnetooptischer Deflektor
  M171
~ Kerr-Effekt M172
Magnetopause M174
Magnetophononenresonanz
  M175
Magnetoplasma M147, M176
Magnetoplasmakompressor
  M177
Magnetorotation F21, M117
Magnetosphäre M182
Magnetosphärenschweif M185
magnetosphärische Konvektion
  M183
~ Störungen M184
Magnetostatik M187
magnetostatische Energie M186
~ Wellen M188
Magnetostriktion M189
Magnetostriktionswandler M190
Magnetothermo-EMK M191
magnetothermoelektrische
  Spannung M191
Magnetowiderstand M178
Magnetpulverfiguren M107
Magnetron M192
~ mit Kopplungsbügeln S867
Magnetronfunkenbildung M193
Magnetrontarget M194
Magnetschicht M65
Magnetspektrometer M124
Magnetspule M35
Magnetvariometer M137
Magnetverstärker M23
Magnetwerkstoff M90
Magnon M199
Magnus-Effekt M200
Magnus-Entwicklung M201
Majorana-Neutrino M204
Majorana-Neutrinomasse M205
Majorana-Teilchen M206

Majoritätsladungsträger M207
Majoritätsträger M207
Majoron M209
Makrogefüge M13
Makrokinetik M7
Makrokosmos M6
Makromolekül M8
makroskopische chemische
  Kinetik M10
~ Quanteneffekte M12
makroskopisches elektromagne-
  tisches Feld M11
Makrostruktur M13
Makroteilchen M9
Malusscher Satz M210
Mandelstam-Darstellung M211
Mangan M212
Manipulator M214
Manley-Rowe-Gleichungen
  M215
Mannigfaltigkeit M213
Manometer M216, P871
Mantel M217
manuelle Einstellung M218
Marke M224
markiertes Atom L2
Markierung L1, M224
Markierungsisotop I566
Markowsche Ketten M225
Markowscher Prozeß M226
Mars M227
Martensit M228
Martensitumwandlungen M229
Maschine E336
Maser M230
Masereffekt M231
Maserstrahlung M232
Maske M234
Maß M298
Maßanalyse V208
Masse E2, G271, M235
Masse-Energie-Äquivalenz
  M241
Masse-Energie-
  Äquivalenzprinzip P902
Masseerhaltung C614
Masse-Helligkeits-Beziehung
  M244
Maßeinheit U72
Masse-Leuchtkraft-Beziehung
  M244
masseloses Quark M243
Massenabsorptionskoeffizient
  M236
Massenabströmung M275
Massenanalysator M238
Massenanziehung G233
Massendefekt M240
Massenkraft M242
Massenmittelpunkt C151
Massenmittelpunktbewegung
  C152
Massenmittelpunktsystem C153

Massenoperator M247
Massenpunkt M263, M264
Massenpunktkinematik P133
Massenschwund M240
Massenseparator M248
Massenspektrograph M249
Massenspektrometer M250
Massenspektrometrie M251
Massenspektroskopie M252
Massenspektrum M253
Massenträgheit M314
Massentransport M254
Massenwiderstand I176
Massenwirkungsgesetz L154
Massenzahl M245
Maßstab S47
Maßstabgesetz S54
Maßstabinvarianz S50, S53
Maßstabsfaktor S49
Material M260, S945
Materialdispersion D456, M261
Materie M274
materielle Welt M265
Materieteilchen C733, M263
Materiewellen D39
mathematische Physik M267
mathematisches Pendel M266
~ Teilchen B49
Mathieusche Funktion M269
~ Gleichung M268
Matrix M270
Matrixdeformation M271
Matrixelement M272
Matrixspur S680
Matrizenmechanik M273
matte Oberfläche M277
Matthießensche Regel M276
maximale Arbeit M282
Maximalmodulprinzip M281
Maximon M278
Maximum M279, P176
Maximum-Likelihood-Methode
  M280
Maxwell M283
Maxwell-Boltzmann-Statistik
  C319
Maxwell-Boltzmann-Verteilung
  M284
Maxwell-Brücke M285
Maxwell-Helmholtzsches
  Farbendreieck M286
Maxwellsche Beziehungen M292
~ Brücke M285
~ Geschwindigkeitsverteilung
  M288
~ Gleichungen M289
~ Verteilung M288
Maxwellscher Dämon M287
~ Spannungstensor M291
Maxwellsches Dreieck M286
Maxwell-Verteilung M288
Mayer-Diagramme M293
Mayersche Beziehung M294

Mechanik M320
~ der festen Körper M322
~ der Flüssigkeiten und Gase
  F220
~ der Kontinua M321
~ der Körper veränderlicher
  Masse V60
~ der Massenpunkte P134
mechanische Beanspruchung
  M317
~ Bewegung M315
~ Bindungen M306
~ Deformation M307
~ Eigenschaften M316
~ Hysterese M313
~ Prüfung M318
~ Schwingungen M319
~ Spannung S886
~ Verformung M307
mechanischer Determinismus
  M308
~ Wirkungsgrad M309
mechanisches Gleichgewicht
  M310
~ Lichtäquivalent M312
~ Wärmeäquivalent M311
Mechanismus der
  Wärmeübertragung M323
mechanokalorischer Effekt
  M324
Mechanostriktion M325
Mediane M326
medizinische Physik M327
Meeresforschung O20
Meeresspiegel S100
Megaelektronvolt M331
Megahertz M332
Megawatt M333
Mehrdeutigkeit A319
mehrdimensionaler Raum M677
Mehrelementspiegel M679
mehrfach gekoppelter Kreis
  M723
~ geladenes Ion M722
~ zusammenhängendes Gebiet
  M724
Mehrfachbeschleuniger C992
Mehrfacheinheiten M713
Mehrfachinterferenz M704
Mehrfachionisation M708
Mehrfachprozeß M709
Mehrfachwechselwirkung M707
Mehrfachwegeeffekt M691
Mehrkammerklystron M706
Mehrkammermagnetron M672
Mehrkanaldiskriminator M673
Mehrkomponentenplasma M675
Mehrkomponentensystem M676
mehrkomponentiger Ordnungs-
  parameter M674
Mehrkörperproblem M220
Mehrphasenströmung M693
Mehrphononenprozeß M694

Mehrphotonen-Photoeffekt
  M700
Mehrphotonenabsorption M695
Mehrphotonenanregung M697
Mehrphotonendissoziation M696
Mehrphotonenionisation M698
Mehrphotonenisomerisation
  M699
Mehrphotonenprozeß M701
Mehrphotonenspektroskopie
  M702
Mehrphotonenübergang M703
Mehrquarkzustand M729
Mehrschichtfilm M680
Mehrstrahlinterferenz M704
Mehrstrahlinterferometer M705
Mehrstufenionisation M732
mehrstufige Ionisation M732
~ Rakete M733
Mehrteilchenerzeugung M688
Mehrteilchenwechselwirkung
  M221, M687
Mehrteilchenzustand M689
Mehrwegeausbreitung M691
mehrwertige Funktion M735
Meißner-Effekt M334
Mellin-Transformation M335
Mellinsche Transformation
  M335
Membran D239, M339
Mendelevium M340
Menge Q26
Mengenmeßgerät F209
Meniskus M341
Meniskusteleskop M342
Meridian M348
Merkur M344
Mermin-Wagner-Theorem M349
meromorphe Funktion M350
Mesastruktur M351
mesische Ladung M352
mesisches Atom M353
Mesoatom M353
Mesodynamik M354
Mesomolekül M355
mesomorpher Zustand M356
Mesomorphie M357
Meson M358
Mesonenatom M353
Mesonenchemie M359
Mesonenfabrik M360
Mesonenladung M352
mesonische Ladung M352
mesonisches Atom M353
Mesonium M364
Mesopause M365
Mesophase M366
Mesoskopik M367
Mesosphäre M368
Meßbrücke B331
Messer M401
Meßfehler M300
Meßgenauigkeit A88

mit bloßem Auge sichtbares
Objekt N3
Mitführungskoeffizient D581
Mitreißen D580
Mitron M516
Mitschleppen D580
Mitte C146
Mittel A696
Mittelenergiebereich I311
Mittelfrequenzen M328
Mitteln A697
Mittelpunkt C146
mittelschnelle Neutronen I313
Mittelung A697
Mittelwellen M329
Mittelwert A696
Mittelwertbildung A697
mittlere freie
Diffusionsweglänge D327
~ freie Weglänge M295
~ Frequenzen M328
~ Lebensdauer M296
~ quadratische Abweichung
S711
mittlerer quadratischer Wert
E32
MKSA-System M523
Mode M526
Modell M530
~ der elektroschwachen
Wechselwirkung E274
~ des expandierenden Weltalls
E485
~ der großen Unifikation G212
~ in natürlicher Größe F420
Modellierung S300
Mode-Locking M533
Moden höherer Ordnung H191
Modenauswahl M539
Modendispersion M525
modengekoppelter Laser M532
Modenkonkurrenz M527
Modenkonversion M528
Modenkonverter M529
Modenkopplung M533
Modenmischung M534
Modenselektion M539
Modenstruktur M540
Modensynchronisation M533
Modenumwandler M529
Modenumwandlung M528
Modenunterdrückung M541
Moderator M537
Moderator-Methode M538
Modifikation M542
Modifizierung M542
Modul M552, M553
Modulationsinstabilität M550
Modulationsgrad M549
Modulator C272, M551
Modulbauelement M552
Modulbaustein M552

modulierte Schwingungen M543
~ Spannung M545
~ Strahlung M544
Moiré M558
Moiréeffekt M559, M560
Moiréinterferenzmuster M559
Moirémuster M559, M560
Moiréstreifen M559
Mol G210, M567
Molalität M563
molare Konzentration M564
Molarität M564
Molekül M605
~ vom Typ des unsymmetri-
schen Kreisels A571
Molekularakustik M568
Molekularaustausch M597
Molekularaustauschmethode
M408
Molekularbewegung M590
Molekulardiffusion M577
Molekulardynamik M579
molekulare Dissoziation M578
~ Energieniveaus M580
~ Isomerie M586
~ Konzentration M573
~ Polarisierbarkeit M594
~ Strömung M583
~ Struktur M601
molekularer Kristall M576
molekulares Orbital M591
Molekularexciton M581
Molekularfeld M582
Molekularintegral M584
molekularkinetische
Vakuumpumpe M595
Molekularkonzentration M573
Molekularlaser M587
Molekularmaser M588
Molekularphysik M593
Molekularpolarisation M594
Molekularpumpe M595
Molekularrefraktion M596
Molekularstrahl M569
Molekularstrahlenbündel M569
Molekularstrahlepitaxie M570
Molekularstrahlquelle M571
Molekularströmung M583
Molekularstruktur M601
Molekularsubstitution M597
Moleküldissoziation M578
Molekülion M585
Molekülkonfiguration M574
Molekülkonformation M575
Molekülkristall M576
Molekülmasse M589
Molekülorbital M591
Molekülorbitalnäherung M592
Molekülphysik M593
Molekülrotation M598
Molekülschwingungen M604
Molekülspektroskopie M599
Molekülspektrum M600

Molekülsymmetrie M603
Møller-Streuung M606
Molrefraktion M596
Molybdän M607
Moment M608
~ des Atomkerns N378
~ höherer Ordnung H192
~ des Kräftepaares M609, T287
Momentangeschwindigkeit I238
Momentanpol I236
Momentanspannung I239
Momentanwert I237
Monat M637
Mond M638
Mondauto L441
Mondfahrzeug L441
Mondfinsternis L439
Mondlibration L195
Monitor der Strahlposition B112
Monitoring M620
Monochromasie M621
monochromatische Lichtquelle
M624
~ Strahlung M623
~ Wellen M625
monochromatisches Licht M622
Monochromator M626
monoklines System M627
Monomode-Faser M630
monomolekulare Schicht M629
Monopol M632
Monoschicht M629
monostabiler Multivibrator S320
monotone Abhängigkeit U63
~ Funktion M634
Montage A539, M661
Monte-Carlo-Methode M635,
M636
Montierung M661
Morin-Punkt M639
Morin-Übergang M640
Morphologie M641
Mosaikkristall M642
Mosaikstruktur M643
Mosaiktextur M643
Moseleysches Gesetz M644
Mößbauer-Effekt M645
Mößbauer-Faktor M646
Mößbauer-Linie M647
Mößbauer-Spektrometer M648
Mößbauer-Spektroskopie M649
Mößbauer-Spektrum M650
MOS-Struktur M388
Motor E336
Mott-Detektor M657
Mottsche Dielektrika M658
~ Streuung M659
Mottscher Übergang M660
Müller-Matrix M670
Müllersche Matrix M670
Multimode-Faser M681
Multimode-Laser M682
Multimodenbildung M683

Multimodenstrahlung M684
multiperiphere Wechselwirkung M692
Multiplett M712
Multiplexer M714
Multiplex-Holographie M715
Multiplikation M716
Multiplikationsfaktor F156, M718
multiplikative Quantenzahl M719
Multiplizität M720
Multipol M726
Multipolarität M725
Multipolmoment M727
Multipolordnung M725
Multipolstrahlung M728
Multistabilität M731
Multivibrator M736
Müon M738
Müonatom M739
Müonium M744
Müonneutrino M742
Musikakustik M746
Muster P168
Mutterteilchen P88
Myon M738
Myonatom M739
Myonen der kosmischen Strahlung C765
Myonenkatalyse M740
Myonenmolekül M741
Myonenzahl M743
myonisches Atom M739
Myonium M744
Myonkatalyse M740
Myonmolekül M741
Myonneutrino M742
Myonspinrelaxation M745
Myopie M752

N

Nablaoperator N1
Nachbarniveau N56
Nachbild A262
Nachbildung S300
Nachbildungskurve G286
Nacheilung L6, R465
Nachgiebigkeit C508
Nachhall R471
Nachhalldauer R473
Nachhallraum R472
Nachhallzeit R473
Nachlauf A250, W3
Nachleuchten A261, P264
~ des Leuchtstoffs P382
Nachrichtenkanal C485
Nachrichtenübertragungskanal C485
Nachstrom A250, W3

Nachthimmelleuchten A275
Nachweis D202
Nachwirkung A260
Nachwirkungseffekt A260
nackter Kern B48
nacktes Teilchen B49
Nadelkatode S618
Nadir N2
Nadirpunkt N2
nahe Infrarotstrahlung N32
naher Kosmos N36
Näherungsmethode A507
Näherungsverfahren A507
Näherungswert A508
nahes Infrarot N33
~ Infrarotgebiet N33
~ Ultraviolett N37
~ Ultraviolettgebiet N37
Nahfeld N29
Nahfeldmikroskop N30
Nahordnung S259
Nahwirkung S258
Nahwirkungsgebiet N31
Nahwirkungskraft S257
Nahzone N31
Nanobeugung N4
Nanodiffraktion N4
Nanolithographie N5
Nanosekundenimpuls N6
NASA N14
Naßdampf W100
Natrium S360
natürliche Häufigkeit N19
~ Isotopenhäufigkeit N19
~ Konvektion F340, N16
~ Spektrallinienbreite N15
natürlicher Logarithmus N21
natürliches Einheitensystem N23
~ Isotop N18
~ Licht N20
Navier-Stokessche Gleichung N24
Navigationssystem N25
Nebel F268, N38
Nebelkammer C343, E488
Nebenquantenzahl A721
Nebenschluß S271
Nebenserie S939
Nebensprechen C878
Neel-Punkt N39
Neel-Temperatur N39
Neel-Wand N40
Negativ N49
Negativbild N49
negative Absorption N41
~ Dispersion N46
~ Entropie N55
~ Krümmung N44
~ Ladung N42
~ Lumineszenz N51
~ Temperatur N54

negativer Differentialwiderstand N45
~ Kristall N43
~ Widerstand N53
negatives Ion N50
negativgeladenes Ion N50
Negentropie N55
Neigung D363, I90, S343
nematischer flüssiger Kristall N58
Neodym N62
Neodymglaslaser N63
Neodymlaser N27
neoklassische Diffusion N60
neoklassischer Transport N61
Neon N64
Neper N65
Neperscher Logarithmus N21
Nephelometer N66
Nephelometrie N67
Neptun N68
Neptunium N69
Nernst-Effekt N70
Nernst-Ettingshausen-Effekt N71
Nernstscher Wärmesatz N72, T209
Nervenimpuls N74
Nervenzelle N73
Nettoladung N75
Netzen W99
Netzwerk E91
Netzwerktheorie E78, N76
Neumann-Funktion N77
Neumann-Problem N79
Neumannsches Prinzip N78
~ Problem N79
Neumann-Seeliger-Paradoxon N80
Neuron N81
Neurtonenbeugungsdiagramm N120
Neutronendiffraktion N118
Neuschließen R251
neutrale Achse N82
~ Komponente N83
~ Zone D37
neutraler Strom N84
neutrales Kaon N89
~ K-Meson N89
~ Pion N91
~ Teilchen N90
~ Vektormeson N93
Neutralfilter N86
Neutralisation N88
Neutralkeil N94
Neutralstrom N84
Neutralstromschicht N85
Neutralteilcheneinschuß N87
Neutrino N95
Neutrinoastronomie N96
Neutrinoastrophysik N97
Neutrinooszillationen N98

O

Plasmainstabilität P670
Plasmakanal P644
Plasmakatode P643
Plasmakinetik P671
Plasmakonfiguration P649
Plasmakonvektion P653
Plasmalaser P673
Plasmaleitfähigkeit P648
Plasmalinse P674
Plasmamantel P675
Plasmaoptik P676
Plasmapause P678
Plasmaphysik P680
Plasma-Quasineutralität P683
Plasmaquelle P686
Plasmaresonanz P685
Plasmaschwingungen P677
Plasmasondierung P682
Plasmasphäre P687
Plasmaspritzen P688
Plasmastabilität P689
Plasmastrahl F114
Plasmastrahlentladung P642
Plasmastrahlung P684
Plasmatarget P690
Plasmatechnik P691
Plasmatechnologie P691
Plasmatrap P692
Plasmatron P693
Plasmaturbulenz P694
Plasmaverunreinigung P652
Plasmawelle P695
Plasmawellenleiter P696
plasmochemische Reaktion
    P645
Plasmoid P697
Plasmon P698
plastische Verformung P699
plastisches Fließen P700
Plastizität P701
Platin P705
Platinotron P704
Platte P702, S230
Plattenbiegung B135, P703
Platzwechsel I282
p-leitende Zone P865
Pleochroismus P707
plötzliche Erhöhung des
    atmosphärischen Störpegels
    S959
~ Feldanomalie S960
~ Ionosphärenstörung S962
~ Phasenanomalie S964
~ Störung S958
~ Verminderung des kosmischen
    Störpegels S957
plötzlicher Anfang S956
Pluto P710
Plutonium P711
p-n-Übergang E201, P712
Pockels-Effekt P714
Pockels-Zelle P713
Poincare-Gruppe P715

Poise P724
Poiseuillesche Gleichung P725
~ Rohrströmung P726
Poiseuillesches Gesetz P725
Poiseuille-Strömung P726
Poisson-Gleichung P728
Poissonsche Gleichung P728
~ Verteilung P727
Poissonsches Integral P729
Poisson-Verteilung P727
Poisson-Zahl P730
Pol P777
Polardiagramm P735
Polare P731
polares Molekül P772
Polarimeter P736
Polarimetrie P737
Polarionosphäre P738
Polarisation P744
~ der elektromagnetischen
    Strahlung P749
~ des Lichtes P750
~ des Mediums P751
~ des Vakuums V26
Polarisationsdrehung R561
Polarisationsebene P625
Polarisationsfilter P769
Polarisationskompensator P745
Polarisationsladung B293
Polarisationsmessungen P746
Polarisationsmikroskop P747
Polarisationsmikroskopie P748
Polarisationsprisma P770
Polarisationsvektor P755
Polarisationswinkel P768
Polarisator P767
Polarisierbarkeit P743
polarisierte Kerne P763
~ Lumineszenz P761
~ Neutronen P762
~ Strahlung P764
~ Welle P766
polarisierter Kristall P758
~ Strahl P756
polarisiertes Dielektrikum P759
~ Licht P760
~ Target P765
Polarisierung P744
Polariskop P739
Polarität P742
Polariton P740
Polaritonlumineszenz P741
Polarkoordinaten P734
Polarkreis P733
Polarlicht A666
Polarlichtionosphäre A671
Polarlichtoval A673
Polarlicht-Röntgenstrahlung
    A675
Polarlichtzonen A676
Polarogramm P773
Polarograph P774
Polarographie P775

Polaron P776
Polarradioreflexionen A674
Polhodie C169, P779
Polkappen P732
Polonium P780
Polschuh P778
Polung P742
Polyeder P784
Polygon P782
Polykristalle P781
Polykristallmethode P840
Polymerabbau P786
Polymere P788
Polymerisation P787
Polymerisierung P787
Polymerkristall P785
Polymorphie P789
Polymorphismus P789
Polynom P790
Polynomialverteilung P791
Polytrope P792
polytroper Prozeß P793
polytropische Zustandsänderung
    P793
Polytypie P794
Pomerantschuksches Theorem
    P796
Pomerantschuk-Theorem P796
Pomeron P797
ponderomotorische Kraft P799
~ Wirkung P798
Poren P803
Porigkeit P804
poröser Katalysator P805
Porosität P804
Positionsgeber P807
positiv bestimmte Form P815
~ geladenes Ion P814
Positivbild P813
positive Krümmung P811
~ Ladung P808
~ Richtung P812
~ Säule P809
positiver Kristall P810
positives Ion P814
Positron P817
Positronenkanalierung P818
Positronium P819
Potential P822
Potentialbarriere P823
Potentialbewegung P832
Potentialdifferenz P824
Potentialeichung P830
Potentialfeld P826
Potentialfläche P835
Potentialfunktion P829
Potentialgebirge P833
Potentialgradient P831
Potentialkräfte P828
Potentialmulde P837
Potentialschwelle P823
Potentialsenke P837
Potentialstreuung P834

Q

Quadrupollinse Q16
Quadrupolmoment Q17
Quadrupolstrahler Q19
Quadrupolstrahlung Q18
Quadrupolwechselwirkung Q15
Qualität Q22
qualitative Analyse Q20
~ Interpretation Q21
Qualitätsfaktor Q23
Quant Q34
~ der schwachen
    Wechselwirkung W72
Quantelung Q29
Quantenausbeute Q46, Q78
Quantenchemie Q35
Quantenchromodynamik Q36
Quantendefekt Q40
Quantendelokalisierung Q41
Quantendiffusion Q42
quantendimensioneller Effekt
    Q43
Quantendraht Q77
Quantendynamik Q44
Quanteneffekt Q45
Quantenelektrodynamik Q47
Quantenelektronik Q48
Quantenfeldtheorie Q49
Quantenflüssigkeit Q56
Quantenfrequenzstandard Q51
Quantengas Q52
Quanteninterferenz Q53
Quanteninterferometer Q54,
    S983
Quantenkinetik Q55
Quantenkohärenz Q38
Quantenkristall Q39
Quantenmagnetometer Q57
Quantenmechanik Q58
quantenmechanische Poisson-
    Klammern Q67
quantenmechanischer Übergang
    Q74
Quantenmetrologie Q59
Quantenmulde Q75
Quantenmuldenlaser Q76
Quantenoptik Q62
Quantenoszillationen Q63
Quantenoszillator Q64
Quantenphysik Q66
Quantenradiophysik Q68
Quantenstatistik Q70
Quantensystem Q71
Quantensystemstrahlung Q72
Quantentheorie Q73
Quantenübergang Q74
Quantenuhr Q37
Quantenwanne Q75
Quantenwannenlaser Q76
Quantenwirkungsgrad Q46
Quantenzahl Q60
Quantenzustand Q69
Quantisierung Q29
Quantisierungsrauschen Q30

Quantität Q26
quantitative Analyse Q24
~ Interpretation Q25
Quantometer Q32
Quantron Q33
Quark Q79
~ mit Farbquantenzahl C462
Quarkbag Q80
Quarkconfinement Q83
Quarkdiagramm Q84
Quarkdynamik Q85
Quark-Hadron-Dualität Q86
Quarkklassifikation Q81
Quarkkombinatorik Q82
Quarkmodell Q87
Quarkonium Q88
Quartett Q92
Quarz Q93
Quarzeicher C895
Quarzeichoszillator C895
Quarzfaser Q96
Quarzkeil Q97
Quarzkristall Q95
Quarzoszillator C930
Quarzuhr Q94
Quasag Q98
Quasage Q98
Quasar Q99, Q129
quasiabgeschlossenes
    Untersystem Q101
Quasideuteron Q104
quasielastische Kraft Q105
~ Streuung Q106
Quasienergie Q107
Quasi-Ergodenhypothese Q109
Quasi-Fermi-Niveau Q110
Quasigleichgewicht Q108
Quasiimpuls Q116
quasiklassische Näherung Q100
Quasikoordinaten Q102
Quasikristall Q103
quasilineare Plasmatheorie
    Q113
Quasiloch Q111
Quasimode Q114
Quasimolekül Q115
Quasineutralität Q117
Quasiniveau Q112
Quasioptik Q119
quasioptische Linie Q118
quasiperiodische Bewegung
    Q121
~ Schwingungen Q122
Quasipotential Q123
Quasiresonanz Q124
quasistationärer Prozeß Q127
~ Strom Q126
quasistatischer Prozeß Q125
quasistellare Galaxis Q98
~ Quelle Q130
~ Radioquelle Q99
quasistellares Objekt Q129
Quasiteilchen Q120

Quaternion Q131
Quecksilber M343
Quecksilberbarometer M345
Quecksilberdampflampe M346
Quecksilberthermometer M347
Quelle S477
~ der thermischen Neutronen
    T135
Quellenaktivität S478
Quellenelektrode S477
Quellenleistung S479
Quellenspannung E157
Quellenstärke S480
Quenchen von Bahnmomenten
    O226
Querbiegung L126
Querkohärenz L127
Querkraftmittelpunkt F191
Querschnitt C871
~ der nichtelastischen Streuung
    N213
Quetschzustände S687
Quintett Q139

R

Rabi-Frequenz R1
Rabi-Oszillationen R2
Racah-Koeffizienten R3
Rad R4
Radar R5
Radarastronomie R6
Radargerät R5
radiale Quantenzahl R8
Radialinjektion R7
Radialquantenzahl R8
Radiant R9
Radiator R67
radioaktive Abfälle R89
~ Asche R69
~ Kontamination R71
~ Niederschläge R75
~ Quelle R85
~ Strahlenquelle R85
~ Strahlung R83
~ Strahlungsquelle R85
~ Verseuchung C638, R71
~ Zerfallsfamilie R76
~ Zerfallskonstante D52, D418
~ Zerfallsreihe R84
radioaktiver Indikator R78
~ Staub R73
~ Stoff R87
~ Tracer R78
~ Zerfall R72
radioaktives Isotop R80, R114
~ Nuklid R82
Radioaktivität R90
Radioastronomie R92
Radiobiologie R93
Radiochemie R27, R98

Reaktionsgeschwindigkeitskon-
stante R211
Reaktionskanal R207
Reaktionskinematik R208
Reaktionskinetik K44, R209
Reaktionsquerschnitt N394
Reaktionsschwelle R212
Reaktionsstart I214
Reaktionsträgheit I176
reaktive Last R216
Reaktor N395, R220
Reaktorbehälter R226
Reaktorkanal R221
Reaktorkern R223
reales Gas R227
Realgas I53, R227
Realkristall I52
Reaumur-Skala R230
Rechner C538
rechnergestützte Tomographie
C537
Rechteckhohlleiter R263
Rechteckimpuls R262
Rechte-Hand-Regel R505
rechtes Quark R506
rechtwinklige Koordinaten R261
Reduktion R279
~ der Kräfte R280
reduzible Darstellung der
Transformationsgruppe R278
reduzibles Diagramm R277
reduzierte Koordinaten R272
~ Masse R274
~ Temperatur R276
~ Zustandsgleichung R273
reduzierter Impuls R275
Reduzierung R279
reelles Bild R228
Referenzdiode R282
Referenzstrahl R281
reflektierte Strahlung R289
~ Welle R291
reflektierter Strahl R290
Reflektor R292, R306
Reflektorspannung R308
Reflexion R293
Reflexionsbedingung von Bragg
B305
Reflexionselektronenmikroskop
R295
reflexionsfreier Raum A380
Reflexionsgrad R294, R305
Reflexionshologramm R298
Reflexionskoeffizient R294,
R305
Reflexionsmikroskop R295
Reflexionsordnung O240
Reflexionsprisma R302
Reflexionsschicht R304
Reflexionsspektrum R303
Reflexionsstrahlung R289
Reflexionsverlust R299
Reflexionswinkel A390

Reflexklystron R309
reflexmindernde Schicht A481
Reflexreflektor R470
Refraktion R314, R325
~ des Lichtes R316
Refraktionswinkel A391
Refraktometer R321
Refraktometrie R322
Refraktor R313
regellose Bewegung I477
Regellosigkeit D431
regelmäßige Reflexion S598
regelmäßiges Kristallsystem
C950
Regelung C668
Regelwiderstand R491
Regenbogenintegral von Airy
A280
Regeneration R326
Regenerativempfang R327
Regenerierung R326
Regge-Diagramm R328
Reggeon R329
Regge-Pol R330
Regge-Polenmethode R331
Regression R333
reguläre Bewegung R336
Regularisationsmethode R335
Rehbinder-Effekt R337
Reibung F400
reibungsbehaftete Flüssigkeit
V167
Reibungsdämpfung V163
Reibungselektrisierung F402,
T401
Reibungselektrizität F401, T400
Reibungskegel C573
Reibungskoeffizient C362
Reibungslehre T402
Reibungslumineszenz T403
Reibungspendel F413
Reibungsprobemaschine F407
Reibungsverluste F406
Reibungswinkel A387
Reibungszahl C362, F403
~ der Bewegung C359
Reichweite D484, R171
Reifbildungstemperatur F411
Reifpunkt F411
Reihe S207, S211
Reihenentwicklung E487
Reihenkreis S208
Reihenresonanz S210
Reihenschaltung S209
Reinstoff P1029
Rekombination R242
Rekombinationsbeiwert R244
Rekombinationskoeffizient R244
Rekombinationsleuchten R246
Rekombinationslumineszenz
R246
Rekombinationsquerschnitt
C876, R245

Rekombinationsstrahlung R248
Rekombinationsübergang R249
Rekombinationswellen R250
Rekombinationszentrum R243
rekonstruierende Quelle R254
rekonstruierender Strahl R253
rekonstruiertes Bild R252
Rekristallisation R260
Rekristallisationskinetik K50
Rekuperator R267
Rekurrenzerscheinungen R268
Relativbewegung R345
relative Änderung R340
~ Atommasse A624, A642
~ Bewegung R345
~ Deformation R342
~ Dispersion D454
~ Elementenhäufigkeit im
Kosmos C762
~ Konzentration R341
~ Linienintensität R344
~ Öffnung A493
~ Permeabilität R346
relatives Gleichgewicht R343
relativistisch invariante
Eichungen R347
relativistische Astrophysik R348
~ Bewegung R361
~ Dynamik R350
~ Effekte R351
~ Elektrodynamik R352
~ Geschwindigkeit R366
~ Invariante R355
~ Invarianz L363, R354
~ Kinematik R356
~ Kosmologie R349
~ Masse R357
~ Massenänderung R358
~ Mechanik R359
~ Thermodynamik R365
~ Verallgemeinerung R353
relativistischer Bereich R364
~ Impuls R360
relativistisches Plasma R363
~ Teilchen R362
Relativität R367
Relativitätsdynamik R350
Relativitätskinematik R356
Relativitätsmechanik R359
Relativitätsprinzip R368
Relativitätstheorie R367, R369,
T81
Relaxation D78, R370
Relaxationsgenerator R376
Relaxationskanal R371
Relaxationskurve R372
Relaxationslänge R374
Relaxationsschwingungen R375
Relaxationsübergänge R378
Relaxationsweglänge R374
Relaxationszeit R377
Reliktneutrino R381
Reliktquark R382

Sphäroid S613
Sphärolith S615
Sphärometer S614
sphärosymmetrische Strahlung S607
Spicula S616
Spiegel M505, R306
Spiegelantenne R307
Spiegelbild M507
Spiegelbildisomer E307, O139
Spiegelbildisomerie O140
Spiegelebene M512
Spiegelfalle M515
Spiegelisobar M508
Spiegelisomer M509
Spiegelkerne M511
Spiegelklystron R309
spiegelnde Reflexion S598
Spiegelsymmetrie M514
Spiegelteleskop R292
Spiegelung M513, S598
Spiegelverluste M510
Spiel C322
Spikulen S616
Spin S619
Spin-Bahn-Kopplungskonstante S638
Spin-Bahn-Wechselwirkung S639
Spindiffusion S621
Spindynamik S622
Spinecho S623
Spinell S624
Spin-Gitter-Relaxation S630
Spin-Gitter-Wechselwirkung S629
Spingläser S628
Spinkorrelation S620
spinloses Teilchen S631
Spinmagnetismus S632
Spinmatrix S633
Spinmoment S634
Spinor S635
Spinorbital S636
Spinor-Elektrodynamik S640
Spinorfeld S641
Spinorteilchen S642
Spin-Phonon-Wechselwirkung S644
Spinpolarisation S645
Spinquantenzahl S647
Spinquantisierung S646
Spinresonanz S648
Spin-Spin-Wechselwirkung S650
Spin-0-Teilchen S631
Spintemperatur S651
Spinthariskop S652
Spinübergang S653
Spinumkehr S625
Spinumkehrübergang S626
Spinumkehrung S625
Spinwelle S654

Spinwellen-Verzögerungsleitung S655
Spinwellenfunktion S636
Spirale H134, S657
Spiralgalaxie S658
Spiralität S660
Spiralnebel S658
Spiralstruktur H122
Spitze C983, P176, S617, T272
Spitzenkontakt P718
Spitzenleistung P177
Spitzenwert C838, P178
spontane Dissoziation S666
~ Emission S667
~ Lumineszenz S669
~ Magnetisierung S670
~ Polarisation S671
~ Polarisierung S671
~ Spaltung S668
~ Symmetriebrechung S665
Spontanemission S667
spontaner Übergang S675
spontanes Neuverbinden S673
~ Sieden S664
Spontanlumineszenz S669
Spontanmagnetisierung S670
Spontanspaltung S668
Sprachanalysator S599
Spreizdruck D420
Springbrunneneffekt F299
Sprödbruch B340
spröder Bruch B340
Sprödigkeit B341, F323
Sprühentladung S677
Sprung J24
Sprungcharakteristik T332
Spule C398
Spur T312
Spurdetektor T314
Spurenkammer T313
Spurion S679
Spurmembran T315
Sputtern S681
s-Quark S866
Squid S688, S983
SRS-Strahlung S689
SSWV C975
Stab B46, R524
Stäbchen R524
Stabdeformation R525
stabile Modifikation S701
stabiles Gleichgewicht S699
~ Isotop S700
Stabilisation S696
Stabilisator S697
Stabilisatorröhre V195
Stabilisierung S696
Stabilisierungskreisel G312
Stabilität S690
Stabilitätsbereich S695
Stabilitätsdiagramm S691
Stabilitätsgebiet S695
Stabilitätsreserve S692

Stabverdrehung R526
Stabvibrationen R527
Standard S707
Standardabweichung S711
Standardatmosphäre S708
Standardquelle R283, S715
Standardsignalgenerator S714
Standhöhenmesser L189
Stange R524
Stapelfehler S704
Stapelfehlordnung S704
stark nichtideales Plasma S910
Stark-Aufspaltung S727
Stärke D177, I262, S884, T200
starke Fokussierung S908
~ Wechselwirkung S909
Stark-Effekt S726
Stark-Effekt-Verbreiterung S725
starkes Feld S907
Stark-Teilniveau S728
Stark-Unterniveau S728
Stark-Verbreiterung S725
starre Drehung R510
~ Konstruktion R508
~ Rotation R510
starrer Körper R507
~ Rotator R511
Starrkonstruktion R508
Starrkörperbewegung M654
Startimpuls I212
Startmasse L146
Statik S742
stationäre Bewegung S746
~ Interferenz S744
~ Quelle S749
~ Schwingungen S747
~ Strömung S769
stationärer Prozeß S748
~ Strom S769, S772
~ Zustand S750
stationäres Modell S745
~ Sieden S743
~ Target F167
~ Universum S752
statische Belastung S740
~ Elektrizität S738
~ Ladung S737
statischer Druck S741
Statistik S768
statistische Gesamtheit S757
~ Interpretation S760
~ Mechanik S761
~ Optik S763
~ Physik S764
~ Radiophysik S765
~ Thermodynamik S766
~ Verteilung S756
statistischer Bootstrap S754
statistisches Gewicht S767
~ Gleichgewicht S758
~ Integral S759
~ Kriterium S755

~ Modell S762
Staub D610
staubfreier Raum C321
Staubwolke D611
Staudruck D624, H66, P873, V93
Staupunkt S706
Stefan-Boltzmann-Strahlungsgesetz S779
stehende Wellen S718
Stehwellen S718
Stehwellenmesser S716
Stehwellenverhältnis S717
steife Konstruktion R508
Steifheit S814
Steifigkeit S814
Steigung I90
Steigungswinkel P606
Steilheit S778
Stellarator S784
Stellardynamik S787
Stellungsisomerie P806
Steradiant S806
Stereobetatron S807
Stereochemie S808
stereographische Projektion S809
Stereoisomerie S810
Stereophonie S811
Stereoskopie S813
stereoskopisches Sehen S812
Stern S719
Sternaberration S780
Sternabstände S786
Sternaktivität S781
Sternassoziation S782
Sternatmosphäre S783
Sternbildung S723
Sterndynamik S787
Sternenbild S724
Sternenjahr S278
Sternentstehung S723
Sternentwicklung S788
Sternflimmern S799
Sterngröße S793
Sternhaufen S722
Sternhelligkeit B335, S785
Sterninneres S791
Sterninterferometer S790
Sternjahr S278
Sternkatalog S721
Sternnähe P226
Sternparallaxe S794
Sternphotometrie A564, S795
Sternpopulation S796
Sternrotation S798
Sternschnuppenfall M400
Sternspektren S800
Sternspektroskopie A565
Sternstrahlung S797
Sternsystem G25
Sternszintillieren S799
Sternverzeichnis S721

Sternwind S801
Sternzeit S277
stetige Abhängigkeit C647
~ Funktion C651
Stetigkeit C643
Steuergenerator M255
Steueroszillator M255
Steuerung C668
Stichprobe S15
Stichprobenprüfung P211
Stickstoff N176
stigmatische Abbildung S815
Stilb S816
stille Entladung S290
Stimmgabel T431
stimulierte Absorption S817
~ Brillouin-Streuung S819
~ Compton-Streuung S820
~ Desorption S821
~ Diffusion S822
~ Emission S823
~ Lichtstreuung S824
~ Lumineszenz S825
~ Raman-Streuung S829
~ Temperaturstreuung S830
~ Verstärkung S818
stimulierter Raman-Effekt S829
stimuliertes Quant S827
Stirling-Formel S833
Stirling-Prozeß S832
Stirlingsche Formel S833
Stirlingscher Kreisprozeß S832
stochastische Beschleunigung S834
~ Schwingungen S837
stochastischer Prozeß S838
Stochastisierung S840
Stochastizität S836
Stöchiometrie S843
stöchiometrischer Defekt S842
~ Faktor S841
~ Koeffizient S841
Stoff M260, M274, S945
Stoffmengenkonzentration M564
Stoffmodifikation durch Strahlen geladener Teilchen M262
Stokes S844
Stokessche Komponente S845
~ Linie S847
Stokesscher Parameter S848
Stokessches Gesetz S846
Störatom I72
störende Beeinflussung I292
~ Kraft P271
Störfestigkeit N188
Störion I78
Störkapazität S873
Störkraft P271
Störniveau I79
Störpegel N189
Störquelle I302
Störstelle D79, I71

Störstellenatom I72
Störstellenband I73
Störstellendichte D80, I76
Störstelleneinfang I74
Störstellengebiet I81
Störstellenhalbleiter E537
Störstellenkonzentration I76
Störstellenleitung I77
Storstellenniveau I79
Störstellenwanderung I80
Störstellenzentrum I75
Störung D510, I292, P267
Störungsmethode M410
Störungstheorie P268
Störwellenmethode D491
Störzentrum I75
Stoß C429, I41, S239
~ erster Art C440
~ zweiter Art C441
Stoßanregung S240
Stoßbeanspruchung I45
Stoßdiffusion C432
Stoßentladung P986
Stoßerregung S240
stoßfreie Dämpfung C436
~ Dissoziation C437
~ Stoßwellen C438
Stoßfrequenz C433
Stoßfront S241
Stoßimpuls I46
Stoßintegral C434
Stoßionisation C435, I44, I414
Stoßionisierung I44, I414
Stoßkoeffizient C368
Stoßparameter I47
Stoßparametermethode I48
Stoßpolare S244
Stoßquerschnitt C875
Stoßverbreiterung C430, I42
Stoßverlust C439
Stoßwahrscheinlichkeit C442
Stoßwelle S239, S247
Stoßwellen im stoßfreien Plasma C438
Stoßwellenfront S241
Stoßwellenrohr S246
Stoßwirkungsquerschnitt C431
Stoßzahl C368
Stoßzentrum C156
Strahl B88, J8, R189
Strahlantrieb J11
Strahlausblendung B97
Strahlauslenkvorrichtung B101
Strahlbegrenzung B97
Strahlbündelausnutzung U107
Strahldefokussierung B96
Strahldichte R10
Strahldivergenz A407, B98
Strahlejektion B100
Strahlenablenker B95
Strahlenakustik G129
Strahlenbelastung E517
Strahlenbrechung R325

U

verdeckte Masse H176
Verdet-Konstante V104
Verdetsche Konstante V104
Verdichter C531
Verdichtungskurve C524
Verdichtungsstoß C527, S239
verdrängte Flüssigkeit D457
Verdrehsteifigkeit T292
Verdrehung T291, T464
Verdrehungssteifigkeit T292
Verdrehungsverformung T293
Verdrehverformung T293
verdünntes Gas R182
Verdünnung D345
Verdunstungswärme H95
Vereinigung C351
Verfahren M403, P923, T25
Verfestigung H42
Verfinsterung E15
Verformung D97, S855
Verformungstensor S861
Vergleichslampe C491
Vergleichsquelle R283
Vergleichsspannung R285
Vergleichsstrahl R281
Vergleichstest C492
vergrößertes Bild M196
Vergrößerung E337, M195
Vergrößerungsglas M197
Vergütung A481
Verhältnis R188, R339
Verhältniszahl R188
verhinderte Totalreflexion F414
Verklebung A268
Verknüpfung C470
Verlängerung E286
Verletzung V145
~ der kombinierten Parität
   C475
Verlust L372
Verluste L372
Verlustfaktor D255
verlustfreies Dielektrikum L377
Verlustkegel L374
Verlustkegelinstabilität L375
Vermehrungsfaktor F156, M718
Vermeiden des
   Resonanzeinfangs R435
Vermischen M520
Verneuil-Verfahren V105
Vernichtung A425
~ von Elektron-Positron-Paaren
   A427
Vernichtungsoperator D195
Vernichtungsstrahlung A428
Verpuffung D86
Versagen F14
Verschiebung D458, M662,
   S238, T346
Verschiebungsgeber D460
Verschiebungsstrom D459, E84
Verschleiß A10
~ durch Auswaschung C130

Verschleißbeständigkeit W80
verschleißfester Stoff W82
~ Überzug W81
Verschleißfestigkeit W80
Verschluß S272
Verschlußblende S272
Verschmelzung C351
Verschmutzung C638
verschwommenes Bild D309
Versetzung D423, S238
Versetzungsdynamik D425
Versetzungseinsetzung D428
versetzungsfreier Einkristall
   D427
~ Kristall D426
Versetzungskeimbildung D428
Versetzungskonzentration D424
Versetzungsquelle D429
Versetzungswand D430
Verseuchung C638
Versorgungsleistung S1043
Verspätung L6
Verstärker A348
Verstärkerklystron A349
Verstärkerstufe A346
verstärkte Emission A347
Verstärkung A343, G12, R338
Verstärkungsfaktor A345, G12
Verstärkungsinkrement G13
Verstärkungskoeffizient A345,
   G12
Verstärkungssättigung G14
Verstärkungsstufe A346
Versteifung R338
Versuch E493, T68
Versuchsanlage P583
Versuchsbetrieb P583
Versuchsdaten E496
Versuchskanal E494
Versuchskurve E495
Vertauschung C487
Vertauschungsrelationen C488
verteilte Belastung D500
~ Induktivität D499
~ Ladung D497
~ Last D500
~ Quelle D503
verteilter Reflektor D502
verteiltes System D504
Verteilung D505
Verteilungschromatographie
   P148
Verteilungsfunktion D508, P149
Verteilungskoeffizient D506
Verteilungskurve D507
Vertexfunktion V106
vertikal polarisierte Strahlung
   V108
vertikale Ionosphärenecholotung
   V107
Vertikalübergang V109
verträgliche Dosisleistung T267
Vertrauensbereich C577

Verunreinigung C638, I71
~ der Luft A277
Verunreinigungskonzentration
   D80
Vervielfacher M721
Vervielfältigung M716
verzeichnetes Bild D490
Verzeichnung D492
verzerrtes Bild D490
Verzerrung D97, D492
~ von optischen Bildern D495
verzögerte Bewegung D58
~ Neutronen D129
~ Wirkung D128, R466
Verzögerung D60, D126, L6,
   R465
Verzögerungsfaktor D127
Verzögerungsleitung D131
~ mit akustischen
   Oberflächenwellen S1047
Verzögerungsspannung D59
Verzögerungssystem S351
Verzögerungszeit D132
Verzug D126
Verzugszeit D132
Verzweigung B310
Verzweigungsstelle B311
Verzwilligung T461
Vibration F233, V112
Vibrator V133
Vibron V134
vibronische Anregung V135
~ Spektren V137
~ Wechselwirkung V136
Vickers-Härte V139
Videoimpuls V140
Vidicon V141
Vidikon V141
Vieleck P782
Vielfachinterferometer M678
Vielfachionisierung M708
Vielfachprozeß M709
Vielfachstreuung M711
Vielflach P784
Vielflächner P784
Vielkammerklystron M706
Vielkanaldiskriminator M673
Vielkörperproblem M220
Vielmodenstrahlung M684
Vielstrahlinterferometer M705
Vielteilchendynamik M686
Vielteilchenkorrelator M685
vierdimensionale
   Geschwindigkeit F304
vierdimensionaler Drehimpuls
   F301
~ Vektor F303
vierdimensionales Intervall F300
~ Potential F302
Vierfermionenwechselwirkung
   F305
Vierniveaulaser F313
Viertelwellendrossel Q89

W

Winkelreflektor C724
Winkelspiegel C724
Winkelverteilungsisotropie A399
Winkelverteilung A398
Wirbel C960, E22, V211
Wirbelbewegung V215
Wirbelfeld V213
wirbelfreie Strömung I483
Wirbelfreiheit N280
Wirbelgitter V214
Wirbelkern V212
Wirbelpaar V216
Wirbelquelle V222
Wirbelring V217
Wirbelschicht V218
Wirbelstraße V219
Wirbelströme E23, F297
Wirbelzustand V221
Wirkbelastung R418
Wirklast R418
Wirkleistung A182
Wirkleitwert C559
wirkliches Bild R228
wirksame Antennenhöhe E29
~ Antennenlänge A452
~ Masse E30
wirksamer Wert E32
Wirksamkeit E34
Wirkspannung A186
Wirkstrom A176
Wirkung A166, E26
Wirkungsgrad E34
Wirkungsintegral A168
Wirkungslinie L272
Wirkungsquerschnitt des
    Einfangs C58
~ für Absorption C872
~ für Anregung E455
~ für Einfang C873
~ für elastische Streuung E65
~ für eine Kernreaktion N394
~ für Stoß C875
~ für Streuung C877
~ des Transports T370
Wirkwiderstand R415
Wirtschaftlichkeit der Licht-
    quelle L429
Wirtskristall H274
Wismut B211
wissenschaftliche Forschung
    S84
WKB-Approximation W135
WKB-Methode W98
WKB-Näherung Q100, W135
Wlassow-Gleichungen V184
Wobbelfrequenzgenerator
    S1091
Wobbelgenerator S1091
Wolfram T429, W138
Wolf-Rayet-Sterne W139
Wolfsche Zahlen W137
Wolke C342
Wollaston-Prisma W140

Wulffsche Fläche W146
Wurfbewegung P931
Würfel C943
Wurtzitstruktur W147

X

Xenon X1
Xi-Teilchen X2
X-laser X33

Y

Y-Teilchen Y9
YAG-Laser Y2
Yagi-Antenne Y1
Yang-Mills-Felder Y3
YIG-Laser Y6
Youngscher Elastizitätsmodul
    Y7
~ Modul M556
Yrast-Band Y10
Yrast-Linie Y12
Yrast-Niveau Y11
Yrast-Trap Y13
Ytterbium Y14
Yttrium Y15
Yttrium-Aluminium-Granat Y16
Yttrium-Aluminium-Granat-
    Laser Y2
Yttrium-Eisen-Granat Y17
Yukawa-Potential Y18

Z

Zacken S617
zähe Flüssigkeit V167
~ Strömung V165
Zähigkeit V162
Zähigkeitswiderstand V168
Zahl N421
~ der Freiheitsgrade N422
Zählen C802, C806
Zähler C803, C803
Zählerteleskop C805
Zählrate C807
Zählratenmesser C808
Zählrohr C803
Zählrohrteleskop C805
Zählwerk C803
Zäpfchen C575
Zäsium C5
Z-Diode V194, Z5
Zeeman-Aufspaltung Z2
Zeeman-Aufspaltungskonstante
    Z3
Zeeman-Effekt Z1

Zeeman-Unterniveau Z4
Zehnerlogarithmus D64
Zeichen S282
Zeiger A526
Zeit T240
Zeitabhängigkeit T246
Zeitachse T242
zeitartiges Intervall T253
Zeitauflösung T257
Zeitauflösungsspektroskopie
    T258
Zeitauflösungsvermögen T257
Zeitbasis T242
Zeitdauer D609
Zeitevolution T49
Zeitintervall T248
Zeitintervallmessung T249
Zeitirreversibilität T251
Zeitkohärenz T243
Zeitkonstante T244
zeitlich-räumliche Korrelation
    S503
zeitliche Abhängigkeit T246
~ Evolution T49
~ Kohärenz T243
~ Verzögerung T245
zeitliches Auflösungsvermögen
    T257
~ Mitteln T241
Zeitlinie T242
Zeitmessung C289, T254
Zeitmittelwertbildung T241
Zeitsteuerung T262
Zeitumkehr T250, T259
Zeitvariabilität T261
Zeitveränderlichkeit T261
Zeitverzögerung T245
Zelle C122, C144, C144
Zenit Z6
Zenitdistanz Z7
Zentimeter C160
Zentimeterwellen C161
zentraler Stoß H67
Zentralkräfte C162
Zentralstoß H67
zentralsymmetrischer Kristall
    C170
Zentrifugalbeschleunigung C164
Zentrifugalkraft C165
Zentrifuge C166
Zentripetalbeschleunigung C167
Zentripetalkraft C168
Zentroide C169
Zentrum C146
~ der parallelen Kräfte C155
Zer C176
Zerbrechlichkeit F323
Zerfall D51, D417
Zerfallsfamilie R76
Zerfallsinstabilität D54
Zerfallskinematik D55
Zerfallskonstante D52, D418
Zerfallskurve D53

Zerfallsrate D419
Zerfallsreihe R84
Zerfallszeit D57, D57
Zerhacker C272
Zerlegung R421
Zernikesches
  Orthogonalpolynom Z8
~ Polynom Z8
Zerstäubung A643
zerstörende Werkstoffprüfung
  D196
Zerstörung D194, F320
zerstörungsfreie Methode N210
~ Werkstoffprüfung N211
Zerstörungsprüfung D196
Zerstreuung D439, D465
Zerstreuungskreis D422
Zerstreuungslinse D519
Zertrümmerung F325
Ziehen D580
Ziel T16
Zimmertemperatur-Laser R532
Zink Z15
Zinn T263
Zirkonium Z16
zirkulare Polarisation C303,
  R564
zirkularer Dichroismus C298
Zirkularpolarisation C303,
  R564
Zirkulation C304
~ des Vektorfeldes C305
Zirkulator C306
Zodiakallicht Z17
Zoll I84
Zölostat C372
Zone A520, B35, R332, Z18
~ der radioaktiven Versuchung
  C637
Zonen der Polarlichter A676
Zonenmagnetismus B38, Z20
Zonenplatte Z23
Zonenschmelzen Z21
Zonenschmelzverfahren Z21
z-Pinch Z25
Züchten G284
Züchtung G284
zufällige Schwankungen R164
zufälliger Fehler R163
Zufallsabhängigkeit R162
Zufallsgröße R168
Zufallsimpuls R167
Zufallsprozeß S838
Zufallsschwingungen R166
Zufallssignaldemodulation R168
Zufallsvariable R168
Zufallsvariablendispersion R170
Zufallszählung A77
Zug T54
Zugbeanspruchung T53
Zugbruch T55
Zugdehnung T50
zugeordnete Legendre-

Funktionen A540
Zugfestigkeit T52
Zugfestigkeitsgrenze T52
Zugspannung T53, T54
Zugverformung T50
zulässige Dosis P248, T267
~ Dosisleistung T267
~ Strahlungsdosis P248
~ Überlastung P249
Zunahme A83
Zunahmekurve G286
Zündkriterium I17
Zündpotential I18
Zündspannung I18
Zündung F142, I16
Zurückbleiben L6
Zusammenballung B365
Zusammenbau A539
Zusammenbruch B314, C410
Zusammendrücken C522
Zusammenfließen C351
zusammengesetzer Zeeman-
  Effekt A448
Zusammenhang R339
Zusammenprall C429
Zusammensetzung C511
Zusammenstoß C429, I41
Zusammenstöße der Moleküle
  M572
~ von Atomen A612
zusammenstoßende Impulse
  C424
Zusammensturz C410
Zusammenziehung C663
Zustand S729
Zustandsänderung C182
Zustandsdiagramm C623, E376,
  P301
Zustandsdichte D158
Zustandsfunktion S730
Zustandsgleichung E366
~ der idealen Gase P218
Zustandsgrößen S734
Zustandsidentifikation S731
Zustandsinterferenz I299
Zustandsmatrix S732
Zustandsvektor S736, V82
Zustandswahrscheinlichkeit
  S735
Zuverlässigkeit R379
Zuverlässigkeitsprüfung R380
Zuwachs A83
Zwang C625
Zwangskräfte C626
Zwanzigflächner I5
zweiachsiger Kristall B176
zweiatomiges Molekül D242
zweiäugiges Sehen B194
Zweibändermodell T465
Zweideutigkeit A319
Zweidimensionalabbildung T474
zweidimensionale
  Spektralklassifikation T476

zweidimensionales Bild T474
~ Elektronengas T473
~ Modell T475
Zweielektronenrekombination
  D262
Zweielementeninterferometer
  T477
Zweiflüssigkeiten-
  Hydrodynamik T483
Zweiflüssigkeitenmodell T478
Zweifrequenzinterferometer
  D566
Zweig B309
Zweigsche Regel Z26
Zweikammerklystron D562
Zweikomponentenflüssigkeit
  T470
Zweikomponentenplasma T471
Zweikörperproblem T469
Zweikreisklystron D562
Zweimagnonenabsorption T484
Zweiniveauatom T479
Zweiniveaulaser T480
Zweiniveaumaser T481
Zweiniveaumodell T482
Zweiphasenströmung T486
Zweiphotonenabsorption T487
Zweiphotonendissoziation T488
Zweiphotonenstrahlung T489
Zweiphotonenübergang T490
Zweistrahlinterferenz T467
Zweistrahlinterferometer T468
Zweistrahloszilloskop D600
Zweistufenionisation T491
zweite kosmische
  Geschwindigkeit E412
~ Quantisierung S109
~ Viskosität V210
zweiteiliges Objektiv D577
zweiter Hauptsatz der Thermo-
  dynamik S114
~ Katodendunkelraum C864,
  F20
~ Schall S116
Zweiweggleichrichter F421
Zwerg D612
Zwilling T457
Zwillingsbildung T461
Zwillingsebene T462
Zwillingsgrenze T458
Zwillingskalorimeter D561,
  T459
Zwillingskristall T457
Zwillingsparadoxon T463
Zwischenbandtunnelung I280
Zwischenelektrodenkapazität
  I289
Zwischenfrequenz I312
Zwischengitteratom I345
Zwischengitterdefekt I346
Zwischengitterfehlstelle I346
Zwischengitterplatz I348
Zwischenkern C515

ZWISCHENMODENDISPERSION

FRANÇAIS

A

abaissement du point de
  congélation D176
abaque G215, N195
aberration A2
~ annuelle A429
~ chromatique C275
~ de la lumière A3
~ sphérique S602
~ stellaire S780
aberrations électrono-optiques
  E223
~ des lentilles électroniques A4
~ de l'œil E542
~ d'ouverture A491
~ des systèmes optiques A5
ablation A6
abondance O19
~ cosmique C762
~ isotopique I555
~ naturelle N19
abrasif A9
abrasion A8
abscisse A12
absorbance A27
absorbant A33
~ acoustique S440
~ du son S440
absorbat A28
absorbeur A34
~ acoustique A94
~ par résonance R425
absorptiomètre A37
absorption A38
~ dans l'aile W131
~ atmosphérique A580
~ atomique A605
~ brusque du bruit cosmique
  S957
~ continue C645
~ à deux magnons T484
~ à deux photons T487
~ diélectrique D248
~ interstellaire I338
~ de la lumière L205
~ de lumière photo-induite
  P454
~ multiphotonique M695
~ de n-photons N338
~ négative N41
~ de neutrons N102
~ non linéaire N233
~ non saturée U90
~ d'ondes W13

~ optique O81
~ optique non linéaire N252
~ par ozone O328
~ photo-électrique P416
~ à photon unique O54
~ des rayons X X3
~ par résonance R426
~ sélective S133
~ du son S441
~ stimulée S817
~ totale T298
~ ultrasonore U12
absorptivité A58
accélérateur A69
~ annulaire R513
~ circulaire C297
~ à courant d'intensité élevée
  H179
~ cyclique C992
~ d'électrons E159
~ de haut voltage H216
~ à induction I148
~ d'ions I382
~ linéaire L251
~ de particules A69
~ des particules chargées C215,
  P113
~ de plasma P641
~ de protons P955
~ de résonance R447
~ tandem T8
~ de Van de Graaff V47
accélération A66
~ angulaire A394
~ centrifuge C164
~ centripète C167, N315
~ collective C413
~ de Coriolis C721
~ de Fermi F52
~ normale N315
~ de particules P112
~ de la pesanteur A68, F345,
  G234
~ stochastique S834
~ tangentielle T10
accéléromètre A72
accepteur A73
accommodation A79
~ magnétique M19
~ de l'œil A81
accord T430
~ automatique A687
~ manuel M218

~ secondaire A286
accrétion A83
accrochage des fréquences
  L325
accumulateur A86
~ capacitif C42
~ d'énergie E310
~ inductif I155
accumulation A85
achromatisation des systèmes de
  lentilles A93
acide aminé A325
~ désoxyribonucléique D161
acier au carbone C68
acoustique A137
~ architecturale A517
~ géométrique G129
~ des milieux en mouvement
  A138
~ moléculaire M568
~ musicale M746
~ non linéaire N234
~ physiologique P544
~ sous-marine U52
acousto-électronique A149
acousto-optique A157
actinide A163
actinisme A161
actinité A161
actinium A162
actinomètre A164
actinométrie A165
action A166, E26
~ à distance A167
~ d'écran S93
~ pondéromotrice P798
~ protective P950
~ retardée D128, R466
~ tampon B358
actions biologiques de la
  radiation B203
activateur A175
~ de luminophore P379
~ optique O83
activation A171
activité A187
~ induite I130
~ optique O84
~ optique non linéaire N253
~ solaire S367
~ de la source S478
~ stellaire S781
~ superficielle S1052

acuimètre Q4
acuité auditive A188
~ visuelle A188, V174
adaptation A190
~ à la lumière L206
~ à l'obscurité D14
adapteur anamorphotique A376
adaptomètre A195
addition méttant en état
   amorphe A328
additivité A198
adhérence de l'électron E161
adhésion A199
adiabatique A201
admittance A218
ADN D161
adsorbant A221
adsorbat A220
adsorption A222
advection A232
aéro-élasticité A252
aérodynamique A249
aérologie A253
aéronomie A254
aérosol A255
aérostatique A257
affaiblissement A646, A646, D9
~ dans l'atmosphère A581
~ sonore S443
affaiblisseur A651
afficheur visuel D461
affinité A259
~ chimique C237
~ électronique E160
âge de Fermi F53
~ des neutrons N103
~ de l'Univers A266
agent de dispersion D437
~ d'échange thermique H103
~ émulsifiant E304
~ de transfert de la chaleur
   H103
agglomération A267
~ de vacances V2
agglutination A268
agitation moléculaire M590
agrandissement E337
agrégat A269
agrégation A270
aiguille A526
aile U130
~ de ligne de Rayleigh R196
aimant M18
~ désordonné D433
~ permanent P243
~ supraconducteur S981
~ de terre rare R179
aimantation M140
~ des domaines D528
~ rémanente R389
~ résiduelle R389
~ par rotation M141
~ de saturation S26

~ du sous-réseau S931
~ spontanée S670
~ vraie P80
air A272
aire A520
~ d'interaction I269
ajustage A217
ajustement A217
albédo A281
~ neutronique N104
~ des rayons cosmiques C768
aléa numérique R169
alexandrite A282
algèbre A284
~ de Boole B269
~ des courants C962
~ de Grassemann G223
~ de Lie L199
alidade A285
alignement A286
~ des spins nucléaires N402
alimentateur d'antenne A453
alliage A296
~ supraconducteur S973
alliages magnétiques M22
allobar A289
allongement E286
allotropie A292
allumage F142, I16
altimètre A312
altimétrie A313
altitude A314
aluminium A315
alychne A316
amas d'étoiles S722
~ galactique G16
~ de galaxies G16
~ globulaire G183
~ ouvert O61
ambiguïté A319
américium A322
amorçage I16
amorce F436
amortissement A646, D9, L372
~ apporté I229
~ critique C845
~ à friction F404
~ de Landau L29
~ non collisionnel C436
~ non linéaire de Landau N248
~ des ondes W15
~ des ondes radioélectriques
   R139
~ du signal S283
~ ultrasonore U14
~ visqueux V163
amortisseur D8, R461
ampère A337
ampère-tours A340
ampèremètre A324
ampholyte A342
amplificateur A348
~ cathodique C106

~ compensé B21
~ à courant continu D31, D378
~ à faible bruit L397
~ d'impulsions P979
~ à large bande B343
~ linéaire L252
~ magnétique M23
~ opérationnel O71
~ optique O85
~ paramagnétique quantique
   Q65
~ paramétrique P53
~ de Raman R151
~ à résistances R492
~ à résonance R427
~ à semi-conducteur S179
~ à superluminescence S1019
amplification A343
~ gazeuse G53
~ de la lumière L207
~ optique O124
~ paramétrique P52
~ stimulée S818
~ ultrasonore U13
amplitude A351, M198, R171
~ de diffusion S67
~ d'impulsion P980
~ normalisée N320
~ d'oscillations O272
~ de probabilité P908
~ de structure S921
an Y4
analogie A366
~ électro-acoustique E117
analyse A367
~ par activation A172, R68
~ de connexions N76
~ cristallographique C891
~ par diffraction D276
~ par diffraction électronique
   E188
~ par diffraction neutronique
   magnétique M96
~ de dimensions D347
~ dispersive D440
~ par fluorescence F227
~ par fluorescence de rayons X
   X25
~ de gaz G54
~ harmonique H50
~ par luminescence L423
~ de phases P281
~ qualitative Q20
~ quantitative Q24
~ par radioactivation R68
~ radiochimique R97
~ radiocristallographique X10,
   X52
~ de sédimentation S123
~ des sons S442
~ spectrale S544
~ spectrale absorptive A39
~ spectrophotométrique S582

~ spectroscopique d'absorption par rayons X X4
~ spectroscopique d'émission par rayons X X22
~ spectroscopique par rayons X X48
~ structurale S912
~ thermique T82
~ thermogravimétrique T179
~ vectorielle V71
~ volumétrique V208
analyseur A375
~ différentiel D266
~ de gaz G55
~ harmonique H49
~ de la hauteur d'impulsions P996
~ d'impulsions P996
~ de masse M238
~ des spectres S595
~ de voix S599
anastigmat A378
anastigmatique A378
anémomètre A383
~ à coquilles C955
~ à fil chaud H286
~ laser L55
angle A385
~ adapté à la phase A389
~ d'attaque A386
~ de Bragg B303
~ de Brewster B328, P768
~ de Cabibbo C1
~ critique C841
~ de déviation D92
~ de diffusion S68
~ de frottement A387
~ horaire H288
~ d'incidence A388
~ de liaison V33
~ de Mach M1
~ parallactique P33
~ de pertes L373
~ de pertes diélectriques D254
~ de phase P282
~ de polarisation P768
~ de réflexion A390
~ de réfraction A391
~ solide S410
~ de valence V33
~ visuel A392
angstrœm A393
anharmonicité A408
anion A412
anisotropie A419
~ cristalline C892
~ élastique A421, E50
~ de la forme F288, S217
~ induite I131
~ magnétique M24
~ optique O86
~ des propriétés élastiques A421

~ des propriétés magnétiques A422
anneau R512
~ d'autofocalisation S161
~ de Budker B357
~ de diffraction D302
~ en ferrite F69
~ de phase P326
~ de stockage S853
~ de tourbillon V217
~ tourbillonnaire V217
anneaux concentriques C546
~ d'interférence I301
~ de Newton N169
année Y4
année sidérale S278
~ tropique T417
année-lumière L246
annihilation A425
~ de paires électron-positron A427
anode A431, P702
anodisation A441
anomalie A449
~ brusque du champ S960
~ magnétique M25
~ de phase à début brusque S964
anomalies de la force de pesanteur G253
~ de gravité G253
~ de pesanteur G253
anomalon A442
antenne A234
~ à barreau diélectrique D249
~ à cadre F327, L358
~ en cadre L358
~ à cornet H271, H272
~ dipôle D365
~ à fente S345
~ hélicoïdale H120
~ à large bande B342
~ à lentille L176
~ en losange R494
~ omnidirectionnelle O43
~ à onde progressive T394
~ parabolique P18
~ à réflecteur R307
~ Yagi Y1
antibaryon A457
«antibunching» des photons P483
anticathode A458
anticommutateur A462
anticyclone A464
antiferroélectrique A465
antiferromagnétique A466
antiferromagnétisme A470
antimatière A471
antimoine A472
antineutrino A473
antineutron A474
antinœud A475

antinucléon A476
antiparticule A478
antipodes optiques O87
antiproton A479
antiquark A480
antisymétrie A484
apériodicité A486
apesanteur Z10
apex A496
aphélie A497
aplanat A499
aplanétique A499
aplatissement O5
apochromat A501
apochromatique A501
apodisation A502
apogée A503
appareil D218
~ à décharge gazeuse G60
~ de diffraction électronique E191
~ électrodynamique E128
~ de mesure M401
~ mesureur électrique E86
~ mesureur électrostatique E266
~ à pénombre H18
appareils à faisceau électronique E165
~ ioniques I405
appauvrissement D166
application M222
approximation A509
~ adiabatique A202
~ de Born B272
~ à électron unique O49
~ des impulsions I65
~ de Keldych K6
~ MO LCAO M565
~ de Padé P3
~ à particule unique O52
~ quasi classique Q100
~ de Weisskopf-Wigner W95
~ W.K.B. W135
aquadag A510
arc A513
~ auroral A669
~ à basse tension L405
~ au charbon C65
~ électrique E95
~ dans le vide V9
aréomètre A521
argent A522
argon A523
armature du condensateur C46
arme laser L121
~ à laser L121
~ nucléaire N405
armement R338
arsenic A530
aspérité A537
assemblage A539, A539
~ critique C842
association nucléonique N410

~ stellaire S782
associativité A544
assombrissement au bord solaire D17
astate A546
astérisme A547
astéroïde A548, M502
astigmatisme A549
~ de l'œil A551
astrobiologie A553
astroclimat A554
astrographe A556
astrolabe A558
astrométrie A559
astronef S509
astronomie A568
~ extraterrestre E533
~ infrarouge I195
~ neutrinique N96
~ de neutrino N96
~ radar R6
~ au rayonnement gamma G38
~ aux rayons X X7
~ stratosphérique B30
astrophotométrie A564
astrophysique A569
~ de neutrino N97
~ nucléaire N344
~ relativiste R348
astrospectroscopie A565
asymétrie A572
~ baryonique de l'Univers B71, U85
asymptote A573
atlas des couleurs C445
atmosphère A578
~ planétaire P632
~ solaire S369
~ standard S708
~ stellaire S783
~ stratifiée S870
atmosphérique siffleur W106
atmosphériques A596
atome A603
~ accepteur A74
~ deux fois ionisé D578
~ à deux niveaux T479
~ excité E462
~ fils D25
~ une fois ionisé S325
~ hadronique H6
~ d'impureté I72
~ interstitiel I345
~ ionisé I436
~ marqué L2, T309
~ mésique M353
~ mésonique M353
~ muonique M739
~ non excité N225
~ pi-mésonique P593
~ pionique P593
~ produit D25
~ de recul R237

~ de Rydberg R578
~ totalement ionisé F422
atomisation A643
attachement A645
~ d'électrons A645
attaque ionique I406
atténuateur A651
~ à piston P605
atténuation A646
~ dans l'espace libre F354
attracteur A653
~ étrange S862
attraction A652
audibilité A654
audiofréquences A656
audiomètre A659
auréole A665
aurore australe A667
~ boréale A668
~ polaire A666
austénite A677
auto-absorption S144
auto-accélération S145
auto-action S146
~ d'ondes W60
autocatalyse A679
autoclave A680
autocollimateur A682
autocollimation A681
autocontraction S152
autocorrélation A683
autodécharge S156
autodéfocalisation S153
autodiffusion S154
auto-énergie S157
auto-excitation S158
auto-inductance S164
auto-induction S165
auto-ionisation A686
autofocalisation S160
~ non stationnaire N305
automodulation S169
~ de phase P328
auto-oscillations S159
autophasage P337
autoprotection S172
autoradiographie A688
autorenversement S170
autosimilarité S174
avalanche A689
~ électronique E162
averse météorique M400
axe A712
~ d'aimantation facile A713, D386, E7
~ cristallographique C924
~ de déformation A716
~ hélicoïdal S95
~ d'inertie A714
~ neutre N82
~ optique O88, O211
~ principal de contrainte P889

~ principal de déformation P888
~ principal d'inertie P887
~ de rotation A715, R558
~ de symétrie A717
axiome A708
axion A711
azimut A720
azote liquide L291

B

bague R512
balance B20
~ d'Ampère C963
~ d'analyse A368
~ d'Eötvös E356
~ électrométrique C963
~ magnétique M27
~ de torsion T295
balayage S57, S1089
~ du faisceau B114, B120
~ de fréquence F390
balise B86
~ laser L57
balistique B27
ballon B29
banc optique O89
~ photométrique P470
bande B35, T14
~ d'absorption A40
~ de conduction C562
~ énergétique E311
~ de fréquences F363, F383
~ haute fréquence H195
~ d'impureté I73
~ inférieure L388
~ interdite F272
~ latérale S274
~ occupée F116, O17
~ passante P158
~ permise P250
~ pleine O17
~ de rotation R544
~ de rotation-vibration V121
~ spectrale S545
~ de valence V34
~ de vibration V113
~ vide E303
~ yrast Y10
bandes de recouvrement O315
bar B46
barn B54
barographe B56
baromètre B57
~ anéroïde A384
~ à mercure M345
barre B46, B382, R524
barretter B62
barrière B63
~ de Coulomb C792
~ de fission F153

~ de potentiel P823
~ de Schottky S80
~ du son S433
baryon B70
baryonium B75
baryum B51
basculement du spin S625
basculeur T407
base B79, B82
~ de balayage T242
~ de l'interféromètre I305
~ orthogonale O256
~ du réseau cristallin C907
basse température L399
basses fréquences L392
bâtonnet R524
battements B125
batterie B83
~ solaire S370
baume du Canada C26
beau méson B126
~ quark B127
beauté B128
becquerel B129
bel B130
berkélium B142
béryllium B145
bêtatron B167
biexciton B180
bifurcation B182
big bang B184
bilame B186
bilan B20
~ de la chaleur H73
~ de rayonnement R24
bille B23
binaire à rayons X X8
binormale B197
bioacoustique B198
biochimie B199
bioélectricité B200
bioluminescence B205
biophysique B206
biplaque de Savart S33
biprisme B208
~ de Fresnel F393
biréfringence B209, D573
~ induite I132
bismuth B211
bissectrice B210
bistabilité B212
~ optique O90
bit B214
blanchiment B224
~ du cristal C894
bleutage d'optique A481
blindage S93, S237
~ magnétique M120
blocage L325
bobine C398
~ blindée S236
~ de compensation C739
~ de correction C739

~ de déviation D88
~ fixe F166
~ de focalisation F262
~ d'inductance I146
~ d'induction I149
~ magnétique M35
~ mobile M664
~ à noyau de fer I467
~ à noyau en ferrite F68
~ quart d'onde Q89
~ supraconductrice S977
bobines de Helmholtz H135
bolide B251
bolomètre B252
~ à semi-conducteur S180
bombardement B258
~ ionique I389
bombe calorimétrique B259
~ nucléaire N345
booster B270
bootstrap B271
~ statistique S754
bord d'absorption A45
~ d'absorption optique O82
~ d'attaque L162
~ diffusé D308
~ de fuite T316
bore B273
borne T64
bornes d'entrée I227
~ de sortie O306
boson B283
~ de Goldstone G193
~ de Higgs H178
~ intermédiaire I310
~ jauge G4
~ vecteur intermédiaire I315
~ vectoriel V72
boucle L357
bouillonnement explosif E504
~ en film F120
~ hadronique H8
~ en pellicule F120
~ au sein de liquide B361
~ spontané S664
~ stationnaire S743
boule de feu F141
boussole d'inclinaison I91
bouton B383
b-quark B285
brachystochrone B301
branche B309
~ de la courbe de résonance
   W132
branchement B310
bras A526
~ de levier du couple A527
breeder B321
bremsstrahlung B327
brillance B333, B335
brisure de symétrie spontanée
   S665
brome B348

bronze B349
brouillard F268
broyage par chocs I43
bruit N184
~ acoustique A120
~ aérodynamique A247
~ d'antenne A237
~ blanc W110
~ de génération-recombinaison
   G110
~ de quantification Q30
~ thermique T136
brûlage B378
~ des trous H228
brûleur Bunsen B370
brume H65
bulle B352, C1009
~ de cavitation C125
«bunching» des photons P484
burette B374
burst B380
burster B381
bus B382

C

câble C2, C718
~ coaxial C354
~ de fibres optiques F90
~ à haute tension H217
~ supraconducteur S974
cache M234
cadence de comptage C807
cadmium C3
cadran D226
cadre F326, L357
cæsium C5
cage de Faraday F19
calcium C7
calcul C8, C9
~ combinatoire des quarks Q82
~ des erreurs T80
~ opérationnel O72
~ des probabilités P913
~ tensoriel T58
~ des variations C10
calendrier astronomique A560
calibrage C11
~ axial A703
~ du potentiel P830
calibrages à invariance
   relativiste R347
calibrateur piézo-électrique
   C895
californium C14
calorescence C16
calorie C18
calorifuge H88
calorifugeage H89, H100
calorimètre C20
~ adiabatique A203

~ double D561, T459
~ hadronique H9
~ d'ionisation I416
~ à liquide L282
~ à thermocouples T152
calorimétrie C21
~ à basse température L400
~ à haute température H212
calottes polaires P732
calutron C22
caméra C24
~ astrographique A556
~ électronique optique I25
~ à scintillation S86
camouflage aural A658
canal C184
~ accélérateur A70
~ chaud H277
~ de communication à fibres
  optiques F91
~ conducteur C566
~ de courant C965
~ de décharge D399
~ de diffusion élastique E52
~ de dissociation D474
~ d'éclair L232
~ d'étincelle S512
~ d'excitation E454
~ expérimental E494
~ d'extraction E527
~ de faisceau B89
~ des filaments F115
~ de formation du faisceau
  B115
~ de génération G109
~ du guide d'ondes W30
~ inélastique I159
~ d'ionisation I418
~ ionosphérique I448
~ neutronique N107
~ optique O94
~ plan P615
~ de plasma P644
~ de production P925
~ à protons P957
~ du réacteur R221
~ de la réaction R207
~ de réaction nucléaire N393
~ de relaxation R371
~ de résonance R430
~ de sécurité S9
~ sonore sous-marin U51
~ de streamer S878
~ supraconducteur S976
~ de synchronisation S1113
~ de transport du faisceau B121
canalisation axiale A700
~ des électrons E177
~ de l'énergie E312
~ d'ions I390
~ dans les monocristaux C185
~ des particules chargées C186
~ plane P616

~ des positrons P818
~ des protons P958
candela C28
canon électronique E199, G297
~ ionique I401
~ de Pierce P553
capacimètre C37
capacitance C36
capacité C36
~ de la couche d'arrêt B66
~ de diffusion D316
~ interélectrode I289
~ non linéaire N235
~ parasite S873
~ thermique H74
~ thermique électronique E203
~ thermique du réseau L138
~ thermique spécifique S534
capillaire C49
capsule C56
captage T391
~ de la charge C197
capteur P546, S204, T320
~ capacitif C41
~ de déplacement D460
~ à distance R393
~ à induction I154
~ piézo-électrique P573
~ de position P807
~ à semi-conducteur S192
~ de température T45
~ à trois composantes T215
capture I62, T391
~ électronique E176
~ de l'électron par un noyau
  C60
~ par gravitation G235
~ d'impureté I74
~ K K5
~ des neutrons N106
~ optique O92
~ des particules chargées C59,
  C223
~ des porteurs C82
~ radiative R59
~ de résonance R429
~ du trou H229
caractéristique C189
~ amplitude-amplitude A352
~ amplitude-fréquence F384
~ décroissante F16
~ intensité-tension V200
~ phase-fréquence P285
~ de plaque A432
~ transitoire T332
carat C61
carbonado C64
carbone C63
carbure de bore B274
carcinotron C69
carmatron C72
carré S682
cartouche de combustible F416

cascade C85
~ de bifurcations C89
~ nucléaire N346
~ des rayons cosmiques C769
~ sous-harmonique S929
cassure F320
~ du cordon de plasma P672
~ intracristalline T319
~ intragranulaire T319
~ à la traction T55
catalogue des étoiles S721
~ fondamental F428
catalyse C96
~ d'adsorption A223
~ à échange d'ions I399
~ hétérogène H155
~ homogène H257
~ muonique M740
catalyseur C97
~ poreux P805
cataphorèse C99
catastrophe C100
~ du ciel bleu B235
~ infrarouge I196
~ ultraviolette U39
cathode C101
~ activée A169
~ à chauffage direct D392
~ à chauffage indirect I127
~ à couche rapportée F121
~ creuse H237
~ froide C405
~ à oxyde O324
~ à plasma P643
~ de spike S618
~ thermo-électronique H276
~ thermo-ionique T148
~ virtuelle V149
cathodoluminescence C114
cathodoluminophore C116
cation C117
~ magnétique M29
catoptrique C118
causalité C120
caustique C121
cavitation C124
~ à bulles B353
~ à ultra-son U16
~ ultrasonique A97
cavité C132, V185
~ de cavitation C126
caviton C131
ceinture de protons P956
~ de radiation extérieure O299
~ de radiation intérieure I220
ceintures de radiation R25
cellule C122, C144
~ d'absorption A41
~ élémentaire P885
~ d'espace de phase P334
~ de Kerr K16
~ laser L60
~ magnétique M30

~ réversible R478
~ des variables C183
chaos C187
charge C196, L303
~ active R418
~ adaptée M257
~ baryonique B72
~ capacitive C40
~ de choc I45
~ compensée B22
~ concentrée L437
~ du condensateur C45
~ de couleur C449
~ creuse C953
~ critique C843
~ cyclique C994
~ distribuée D500
~ dynamique D622
~ effective E27
~ électrique E88, E96, Q27
~ d'électron E178
~ élémentaire E276
~ d'espace S482
~ d'essai P916
~ hadronique H10
~ inductive I153
~ induite I133
~ d'invariant I365
~ de l'ion I391
~ leptonique L183
~ libre F339
~ liée B293
~ localisée L318
~ magnétique M31
~ mésonique M352
~ mobile M663
~ négative N42
~ nette N75
~ du neutron N108
~ non accordée U87
~ du noyau N348
~ nucléaire N348
~ de nucléon N412
~ nulle N419
~ de polarisation B293
~ ponctuelle P717
~ positive P808
~ du réacteur R222
~ réactive R216
~ répartie D497, D500
~ résistive R418
~ spatiale S482
~ statique S737, S740
~ superficielle S1056
~ de test T69
chargement L307
~ du cœur C720
charme C232
charmonium C235
chauffage H87
~ adiabatique A208
~ par convection C678
~ direct D379

~ par faisceau électronique E167
~ à haute fréquence dans le conteneur froid H175
~ à haute fréquence du plasma R486
~ indirect I126
~ par induction I150
~ de Joule J19
~ laser du plasma L95
~ du plasma P666
~ par radiation R17
~ superficiel S1069
~ turbulent T450
~ turbulent du plasma T454
chemin P164
~ optique O166
~ de tourbillons de Karman K4
chercheur de fuites L164
cheval-vapeur H273
chicane B18
chimie C254
~ de coordination C710
~ des cristaux C896
~ de laser L61
~ mésonique M359
~ nucléaire N349
~ physique P527
~ quantique Q35
~ de radiation R27
chimiluminescence C252
chimisorption C253
chip C261
chiralité C264, E308
chirurgie laser L112
~ ultrasonique U32
chlore C269
choc I46, S239
~ de compression C527
~ de condensation C552
~ de deuxième espèce C441
~ électronique E211
~ de première espèce C440
~ superélastique S996
chromaticité C276
chromatographe C281
chromatographie C282
~ par adsorption A224
~ par échange d'ions I400
~ sur papier P16
~ de partage P148
~ en phase gazeuse G76
chrome C283
chromisation C284
chromodynamique C285
~ quantique Q36
chromosphère C286
~ solaire S371
chronographe C288
chronologie cosmique C778
~ isotopique I549
chronométrie C289
chute F15

~ anodique A437
~ cathodique C105
~ de la chaleur T121
~ de Lamb L16
~ libre F344
cible T16
~ d'accélérateur A71
~ de couche S233
~ de deutérium D213
~ à feuille F270
~ fixe F167
~ laser L114
~ à magnétron M194
~ nucléaire N404
~ de plasma P690
~ polarisée P765
~ sphérique S611
~ thermonucléaire T191
~ de tritium T414
cinématique K30
~ du corps B241
~ de désintégration D55
~ des fluides K33
~ des liquides K34
~ du milieu déformable D96
~ du point K32
~ du point matériel P133
~ de réaction R208
~ relativiste R356
~ du solide K35
cinescope K37
cinétique K43
~ d'adsorption A229
~ chimique C246
~ chimique macroscopique M10
~ de condensation C550
~ de cristallisation C922
~ de croissance G287
~ de désorption D193
~ de l'évaporation K45
~ d'excitation E458
~ des fluides K46
~ de non-équilibre N221
~ des phénomènes magnétiques K48
~ physique P530
~ du plasma P671
~ du plasma à deux composantes T472
~ de la population des niveaux K47
~ quantique Q55
~ du réacteur nucléaire K49
~ de réaction R209
~ des réactions chimiques K44
~ de la recristallisation K50
~ des transitions de phase P346
cinétostatique K52
C-invariance C292
circonférence C293
circuit C296, L357
~ à anticoïncidences A459
~ apériodique A485

~ de coïncidences C399
~ à connexion multiple M723
~ de différentiation D271
~ électrique E77, E91
~ d'entrée I223
~ équivalent E397
~ fermé C330
~ intégrateur I257
~ intégré I254
~ logique L332
~ magnétique M32
~ oscillant O284
~ parallèle P36
~ phantastron P277
~ résonnant R448
~ en série S208
~ de sortie O303
circuits couplés C810
circulateur C306
~ à ferrite F67
circulation C304
~ atmosphérique A582
~ du champ vecteur C305
~ de la vitesse V90
cisaillement S221
civilisations extraterrestres E534
claquage B314
~ en avalanche A690
~ électrique E76
~ thermique T86
classe d'éruption solaire F174
~ d'homologies H266
~ de luminosité L428
~ de précision A87
~ de symétrie S1104
classes cristallographiques C897
~ de cristaux C897
~ spectrales des étoiles S546
classification décimale
   universelle U82
~ des particules P116
~ périodique des éléments P233
~ des quarks Q81
~ spectrale S547
~ spectrale bidimensionnelle
   T476
clavier K21
clé K20
clean-room C321
climatisation A273
clivage C323
cloison de Bloch B232
cluster C345
~ amorphe A329
~ de fractales F318
~ magnétique M34
~ à nucléons N413
~ de vacances V2
coagulation C350
~ acoustique A98
~ des aérosols A256
~ des germes N417
coalescence C351

coaltitude Z7
cobalt C356
codage de l'information I192
coefficient d'absorption de
   masse M236
~ d'accommodation A80
~ d'adaptation M259
~ d'amortissement A647, D10
~ d'amortissement de Landau
   L30
~ d'amplification A345, G12
~ d'atténuation de la lumière
   L208
~ d'auto-induction S164
~ binomial B195
~ de bruit N185
~ cinétique K38
~ de condensation C549
~ de conductibilité calorique
   T89
~ de conductibilité de chaleur
   T89
~ de conductibilité thermique
   D333, T89
~ de conduction de chaleur
   H77
~ de conversion C690
~ de corrélation C744
~ de couplage C816
~ de couplage électromécanique
   E155
~ de diffusion D318, D333,
   S70
~ de diffusion ambipolaire A321
~ de diffusion thermique T101
~ de dilatation C361, E489
~ de dilatation linéaire C365
~ de dilatation thermique C369,
   T115
~ de dilatation volumétrique
   C371
~ de directivité D391
~ de distribution D506
~ d'élasticité C360
~ électro-optique E250
~ d'émission secondaire S105
~ d'entraînement D581
~ d'expansion E489
~ de Fourier F306
~ de frottement C362, F403
~ de frottement dynamique
   C359
~ de Hall H24
~ d'induction électromagnétique
   E149
~ d'interdiffusion I288
~ d'ionisation I419
~ de multiplication F156
~ de Peltier P193
~ de pertes D255
~ de pertes diélectriques D255
~ des pertes par hystérésis
   C363

~ de pertes magnétiques M89
~ de Poisson P730
~ de proportionnalité P944
~ de puissance P843
~ de qualité de la raie spectrale
   S558
~ de réaction F45
~ de recombinaison R244
~ de recombinaison radiative
   R64
~ de réflexion R294
~ de régénération B325
~ de résistance à la fatigue F38
~ de restitution C368
~ de retard D127
~ de sécurité S10
~ de séparation S206
~ stœchiométrique S841
~ de suppression du mode
   latéral S276
~ de température de la
   fréquence T33
~ de température de la
   résistance T34
~ de tension de surface S1084
~ thermique de viscosité T46
~ de Townsend T307
~ de transmission T351
~ de transport T369
~ de viscosité C370
coefficients aérodynamiques
   A241
~ d'Einstein E45
~ de Klebsch-Gordon K58
~ de Racah R3
~ viriels V146
cœlostat C372
coercibilité C375
coercimètre C373
cohérence C376
~ longitudinale L337
~ de la lumière C380
~ mutuelle M747
~ partielle P97
~ de phase-cohérence en phase
   P286
~ quantique Q38
~ spatiale S488
~ spatiale dans le temps S529
~ temporelle T243
~ transversale L127, T376
cohésion C397
coin W85
~ gris N94
~ neutre N94
~ optique O210, P478
~ photométrique P478
~ de quartz Q97
~ à quartz Q97
collapsus C410
~ gravitationnel G236
~ de Langmuir L36
collecteur C420

collectivisation des électrons
E180
collimateur C427
~ du faisceau B91
collimation C426
collinéarité C428
collision C429
~ centrale H67
~ frontale H67
~ de paire P6
~ de particules P117
~ superélastique S996
collisionneur C421
~ hadronique H4
collisions atomiques A612
~ élastiques E53
~ inélastiques I160
~ des molécules M572
~ phonon-phonon P372
colloïde C443
colonne de plasma P644
~ positive P809
colorant D613
~ blanchissable B225
~ saturable S20
~ transparent T365
colorimètre C455
colorimétrie C456, C457
~ astronomique A561
~ trichrome T404
coma C469
combinaison C470
~ linéaire L253
combustible nucléaire N363
combustion B378, C477
comète C479
commande C668
~ automatique de la fréquence
par la phase P314
commencement brusque S956
communication météorique
M398
~ optique O97
commutateur C489, S1094
~ de guide d'ondes W37
~ optique O199
~ thermique T144
commutation C487
~ active en Q A183
~ optique O200
~ passive en Q P160
comparateur C490
~ d'interférence I294
~ optique O98
~ de phase P287
compartiment cathodique C111
compatibilité C494
compensateur C497
~ interférométrique I306
~ optique O99
~ à polarisation P745
compensation C496
~ adaptive A191

~ de la charge d'espace S484
~ thermique T35
compétition de mode M527
complémentarité C499
complexe C505
complexons C507
composante antistokes A482
~ chargée C205
~ dure H41
~ de Fourier F307
~ à grand rayon d'action L346
~ d'une impulsion M614
~ à longue période L343
~ molle S361
~ neutre N83
~ réactive I13
~ de Stokes S845
~ supraconductive S978
~ superfluide S999
~ d'un vecteur C509
~ à vie courte S252
~ volatile V186
composants du champ F96
~ optiques purs A290
~ toute-fibre A288
composé C514
composés intermétalliques I316
~ lamellaires I281
composite C510
composition C511
~ en fibres F88
~ des forces C512
~ des vitesses C513
compresseur C531
~ optique O100
~ à plasma magnétique M177
~ à réseau G225
compressibilité C518
compression C522
~ des impulsions laser L99
~ non linéaire N236
comptage C806
compte C802, C806
compteur C803
~ à anticoïncidences A460
~ de Cherenkov C256
~ de coïncidences C400
~ à cristal C898
~ à étincelles S513
~ de Geiger-Müller G92
~ de particules P119
~ proportionnel P943
~ à scintillation S87
~ de vitesse V88
concentrateur C545
~ acoustique A99
~ des rayons solaires S372
concentration C542, D154
~ des contraintes S887
~ des défauts D80
~ des dislocations D424
~ de dopage D543
~ électronique E181, E185

~ d'équilibre E373
~ excessive E441
~ des impuretés I76
~ d'ions I393
~ locale L309
~ moléculaire M573
~ non équilibrée N216
~ des particules P118
~ des particules chargées C217
~ des pièges T387
~ des porteurs C76
~ des porteurs libres F337
~ relative R341
~ de la solution S427
~ du son S452
~ spécifique S531
~ superficielle S1058
~ sûre S7
~ des trous H230
condensat C547
~ amorphe A330
~ de Bose B277
~ de Bose-Einstein B277
~ dans le vide V13
condensateur C44, C557
condensation C548
~ de Bose B278
~ de Bose-Einstein B278
~ capillaire C50
~ coronale C730
~ d'excitons E468
~ en film F122
~ sous forme de gouttes D598
~ hétérogène H156
~ homogène H258
~ de la vapeur V50
condenseur C557
~ cardioïde C71
condition C558
~ bêtatron B168
~ de Bragg B305
~ de Lorentz L361
~ d'unitarité U73
conditions initiales I211
~ limites B288
~ aux limites approximatives de
Leontowitch L180
~ normales N327, S710
conductance C559
~ acoustique A100
conducteur C570
~ de la chaleur H78
~ supra-ionique S1014
conducteurs organiques O246
conductibilité électrique E80
~ du plasma P648
~ du réseau L133
~ spécifique S532
~ thermique H75, T91
~ thermique due au réseau
L133
~ thermique électronique E183,
E204

~ forcée F278
~ libre F340
~ magnétosphérique M183
~ naturelle F340, N16
~ du plasma P653
~ thermique T95
convergence C684
convergent C593
conversion C689
~ à augmentation de la fréquence U96
~ du combustible nucléaire N364
~ directe chaleur/électricité D376
~ d'énergie E314
~ de la fréquence F364
~ intermode I318
~ interne I321
~ des modes M528
~ de paire P7
~ paramétrique P54
convertisseur C693
~ analogique-digital A365
~ à augmentation de la fréquence U97
~ digital-analogique D339
~ à film F125
~ de fréquence optique O121
~ d'image électrono-optique E224, I24
~ inductif I156
~ des modes M529
~ optique O205
~ paramétrique P55
~ piézo-électrique P576
convolution C696
convolver C697
coordinance C709
coordonnée C706
coordonnées cartésiennes C84
~ célestes C139
~ de chromaticité C277
~ curvilignes C981
~ cylindriques C1007
~ d'espace de phase P335
~ généralisées G98, L7
~ géographiques G117
~ géomagnétiques G119
~ héliocentriques H125
~ du laboratoire L4
~ de Lagrange L7
~ non dimensionnelles D350
~ polaires P734
~ rectangulaires R261
~ réduites R272
~ sphériques S603
corde C273, C718, S897
cordes explosives E502
cordon de plasma P661
coronographe C729
corps B237
~ aimanté M146

~ cosmique C764
~ gris G262
~ isotrope I575
~ noir B216, F419
~ obtus B236
~ rigide R507
~ solide S409
corpuscule C733
correcteur C742
~ du front d'onde W22
~ de phase P295
~ de phase quadratique Q10
correction approximative R567
~ de l'astigmatisme A550
~ bolométrique B253
~ des distorsions atmosphériques C741
~ du front d'onde W21
~ d'image I26
corrections de Glauber G175
~ de rayonnement R28
corrélateur C750
~ acousto-optique A152
~ multiparticule M685
~ optique O106
~ spectral S548
corrélation C743
~ angulaire A396
~ espace-temps S503
~ des fluctuations F212
~ mutuelle C865, M749
~ des paires P8
~ par la phase P296
~ de spin S620
corrélomètre C751
corrosion C754
~ sous tension S888
cosinus C761
~ directeurs D385
cosmogonie C779
cosmologie C785
~ d'inflation I184
~ relativiste R349
~ de l'Univers primitif E1
cosmos C786
couche L158, S230, S231
~ antiréfléchissante A481
~ d'arrêt B65
~ bipolaire D563, E85
~ complète C339
~ de courant C972
~ de courant neutre N85
~ E E74
~ électronique E237
~ épuisée D167
~ d'épuisement D170
~ externe O300
~ F F188
~ intermédiaire magnétique M180
~ interne I221
~ d'inversion I375, R483
~ Kennelly-Heaviside K10

~ limite B289
~ limite de température T84
~ limite turbulente T447
~ mince T202
~ nucléaire N399
~ d'ozone O329
~ périphérique O300
~ pleine C339
~ remplie C339, F117
~ saturée C339, F117
~ tourbillonnaire V218
coude K53
coulage C93
couleur C444
~ achromatique A91
couleurs complémentaires C501
~ d'interférence I293
~ primaires P878
coulomb C791
coup accidentel A77
~ de foudre L236
coup-circuit à fusible F437
coupe laser L63
~ par ultra-son U18
couplage C815
~ capacitif C38
~ en cascade C86
~ inductif I151
~ en parallèle P37
couple C809, T287
~ de forces C809
coupleur C814
~ de diffraction D280
~ directif D381
~ directionnel D381
cœur C719
~ d'un atome A613
~ du réacteur R223
courant C961, S875
~ actif A176
~ alternatif A309
~ anodique A433
~ axial A701
~ chargé C206
~ de conduction C564
~ continu D377
~ de convection C674
~ critique C844
~ de déplacement D459
~ de déplacement électrique E84
~ de dérive D587
~ de diffusion D319, D322
~ électrique E97
~ de fuite L166
~ hadronique H5
~ induit I134
~ leptonique L182
~ neutre N84
~ d'obscurité D16
~ de Pedersen P184
~ photo-électrique P401
~ quasi stationnaire Q126

DÉFORMATION

~ inélastique I161
~ infinitésimale I181
~ irréversible I479
~ linéaire L255
~ longitudinale L338
~ de matrice M271
~ mécanique M307
~ nucléaire N351
~ plastique P699
~ relative R342
~ du réseau L136
~ résiduelle R410
~ réversible R480
~ de la spire de courant C977
~ d'une tige R525
~ de traction T50
~ viscoélastique V157
~ de volume V206
dégazage D102
dégazation D102
dégénération du vide V14
dégénérescence D103
~ par échange E446
~ des niveaux énergétiques D105
~ du vide D106
dégradation d'énergie D117
~ d'hologramme H241
~ des semi-conducteurs S182
degré D118
~ de cohérence D119
~ d'ionisation D121
~ de liberté D120
~ de turbulence S52
dégroupement D41
déionisation D123
délai L6, T245
délocalisation des défauts D81
~ quantique Q41
démagnétisation cyclique C993
~ nucléaire adiabatique N343
demi-largeur H14
demi-ombre P210
demi-plan H16
démodulateur D146
démodulation D145
démon de Maxwell M287
démultiplexeur D147
dendrite D148
densimétrie D151
densité D154
~ de charge C207
~ de la charge d'espace S485
~ de charge volumique V205
~ de courant C966
~ de courant de probabilité P909
~ critique C846
~ électronique E181, E185
~ d'énergie E315
~ d'énergie sonore S447
~ des états D158
~ du flux F235

~ de flux énergétique R16
~ de flux magnétique M78
~ du flux des particules P128
~ de flux rayonnant R16
~ de flux thermique H86
~ limite U2
~ de neutrons N115
~ nucléaire N353
~ optique D154, O109
~ photographique P441
~ de probabilité P910
~ de puissance spectrale P846
~ spectrale S549
~ superficielle S1061
~ superficielle de charge S1057
~ de la vapeur saturée D157
densitomètre D150, D152
densitométrie D153
dépendance D162
~ accidentelle R162
~ analytique A369
~ angulaire A397
~ asymptotique A574
~ continue C647
~ empirique E301
~ expérimentale E497
~ explicite E501
~ exponentielle E513
~ fonctionelle F426
~ fortuite R162
~ fréquentielle F365
~ implicite I58
~ lisse par morceaux P551
~ quadratique Q9
~ de température T36
~ uniforme U63
déphasage D164, P329
déphaseur P331
~ non réciproque N286
dépiégeage D165
déplacement D458, M662, O32
~ Doppler D550
~ électrique E83, E109
~ gravitationel G247
~ hélicoïdal S98
~ de Lamb L20
~ des niveaux L192
~ virtuel V150
déplétion de pompage P1014
dépolarisant D172
dépolarisation de lumière D171
~ de la luminescence L419
~ thermique T98
dépopulation D173
déposition D174
~ par faisceau électronique E164
~ des films F123
~ par laser L64
~ par pulvérisation S681
~ par pulvérisation du plasma P688
~ sous vide V15

dépôts radioactifs R75
dépression D175
dérive D585
~ des continents C639
~ électrique E104
~ de fréquence F371
~ de gradient G201
~ induite par la lumière L223
~ magnétique M52
~ des particules chargées C220
~ des porteurs C77
~ thermique T105
dérivée D183
~ covariante C823
désaccommodation D185
désactivateur D35
désactivation D34
désagrégation de cathode C113
désaimantation D138
~ adiabatique A206
désassemblage du réacteur R224
description D187
désensibilisateur D189
désensibilisation D188
désexcitation D74, D78
désintégration D51, D417, F325, S662
~ alpha A298
~ bêta B150
~ double bêta D559
~ hadronique H11
~ leptonique L184
~ du neutron N111
~ nucléaire N350
~ du phonon P361
~ du pion P594
~ radioactive R72
~ semi-leptonique S193
~ Stark S727
désordre D431, D435
désorption D192
~ du champ F98
~ par laser L65
~ photostimulée P519
~ stimulée S821
destructeur de luminescence K23, Q132
destruction B314, D194, F320
~ des polymères P786
desublimation D198
détachement d'électron E186
détecteur D146, D205
~ d'amplitude A354
~ de Cherenkov C257
~ des défauts F187
~ des défauts ultrasonique U24
~ à diamant D235
~ de lumière P404
~ de Mott M657
~ de neutrons N117
~ d'ondes stationnaires S716
~ de particules P122

~ magnétocalorique M153
~ Magnus M200
~ maser M231
~ mécanocalorique M324
~ Meissner M334
~ Mössbauer M645
~ Nernst N70
~ Nernst-Ettingshausen N71
~ normal de Zeeman N331
~ de Nottingham N335
~ optique de Kerr O142
~ optique de Stark O196
~ opto-acoustique O216
~ Overhauser O310
~ d'Ovshinsky O321
~ Paschen-Back P154
~ de peau S335
~ Peltier P194
~ Penning P205
~ photo-électrique P419
~ photo-électrique externe E523, P431
~ photo-électrique interne I325
~ photo-électrique nucléaire N381
~ photo-électrique à photons multiples M700
~ photo-émetteur P434
~ photodiélectrique P406
~ photodynamique P412
~ photomagnétique P466
~ photomagnéto-électrique P467
~ photopiézo-électrique P502
~ photovoltaïque P438, P526
~ piézo-électrique P563
~ piézo-optique P581
~ piézomagnétique P578
~ de pincement P588
~ Pockels P714
~ de premier ordre F145
~ pyro-électrique P1034
~ quantique Q45
~ Raman R152
~ Raman induit S829
~ Raman stimulé S829
~ Ramsauer R161
~ de rayonnement R35
~ Rehbinder R337
~ Righi-Leduc R504
~ Sabatier S1
~ Schottky S81
~ Seeback S124
~ de serre G260
~ Shubnikov-de Haas S270
~ Stark S726
~ stroboscopique S905
~ de Szilard-Chalmers S1134
~ tensorésistif T59
~ thermomécanique T183
~ tunnel T436, T439
~ tunnel d'électrons E247
~ tunnel interbande I280

~ Tyndall T492
~ Villari V144
~ Zeeman Z1
~ Zeeman anormal A448
effets électrocinétiques E136
~ galvanomagnétiques G33
~ gyromagnétiques G304
~ macroscopiques quantiques M12
~ magnétomécaniques M166
~ non linéaires N242
~ photo-acoustiques P386
~ photo-électromagnétiques P439
~ relativistes R351
~ thermo-électriques T173
~ thermogalvanomagnétiques T178
~ thermomagnétiques T181
efficacité lumineuse L429
~ lumineuse relative L430
efficience E34
effort S886
~ dynamique D631
~ de flexion B138
~ tangentiel T12
effusion E35
einsteinium E47
éjecteur E48
élargissement par collisions I42
~ Doppler D545
~ dû aux chocs C430
~ dû aux collisions C430
~ par effet Doppler D545
~ non uniforme N307
~ par pression P869
~ de raie L269
~ des raies spectrales B346
~ par résonance R428
~ Stark S725
~ thermique T87
élasticité E58
~ de volume B362
élastomère E69
électret E75
électricité E111
~ atmosphérique A586
~ statique S738
électrisation E116
~ par frottement F402, T401
électro-acoustique E118
électro-aimant E142
électro-optique E256
électrocardiographie E120
électrochimie E124
électrode E125
électrodynamique E129
~ classique C313
~ des milieux en mouvement E130
~ quantique Q47
~ relativiste R352
~ de spin S640

électro-encéphalographie E131
électrogiration E133
électrolyse E140
électrolyte E141
~ amphotérique A342
~ solide S411
électromètre E156
électron E158
~ Compton C533
~ de conduction C565
~ delta D135
~ libre F341
~ lié B294
~ pi P552
~ de valence V37
électron-volt E249
électronégativité E192
électronique E207
~ à couche mince T203
~ de courants d'intensité élevée H180
~ cryogénique C882
~ d'émission E288
~ à film mince T203
~ d'hyperfréquence M476
~ de micro-ondes M476
~ nucléaire N355
~ du plasma P657
~ de puissance H201
~ quantique Q48
~ des semi-conducteurs S187
électronogramme E189
électrons Auger A662
~ chauds H278
~ de conversion C691
~ découplés E413, R572
~ itinérants C414
~ de précipitation P856
électrophorèse E257
électrophysique E258
électropositivité E259
électroscope E260
électrostatique E270
électrostriction E271
élément E275
~ CCD C203
~ chauffant H82
~ galvanique E121
~ de matrice M272
~ non réciproque N285
~ porte G80
~ sensible S204
~ transuranien T374
éléments chimiques C241
élimination des défauts H69
ellipsoïde de conductivité C569
~ de Fresnel F395, R190
~ d'inertie I168
~ de Jacobi J2
ellipsomètre E283
ellipsométrie E284
émetteur E299
~ bêta B151

~ directif D390
~ de lumière L217
~ paramétrique P58
~ secondaire S111
émission E287
~ auto-induite S162
~ de champ F99
~ continue C654
~ coopérative C701
~ par effet de champ F99
~ électronique E194
~ électronique explosive E505
~ exo-électronique E481
~ forcée S823
~ induite I137, S823
~ interstellaire I340
~ ion-électron I396
~ ion-ion I412
~ ionique I398
~ laser L70
~ de lumière L216
~ maser M232
~ optique L216
~ paramétrique P57
~ des particules P125, P143
~ des particules alpha A300
~ photo-électrique P431
~ radioélectrique R126
~ Raman R153
~ secondaire S104
~ spontanée S667
~ stimulée S823
~ thermo-ionique T149
~ tunnel T438
émittance E297
~ énergétique R12
~ lumineuse L431, R12
empilement L307
~ compact C341
~ cubique compact C944
~ de graphite G221
~ serré C341
empreinte I116
émulsification ultrasonique U22
émulsion E305
~ nucléaire N356
~ photographique P443
énantiomère E307
énantiomorphisme E308
enceinte étanche C122
enclume de diamant D234
encorbellement C35
endoémetteur R125
énergétique nucléaire N386
énergie E309
~ acoustique A105
~ d'activation A173
~ d'anisotropie A420
~ cinétique K39
~ de corrélation C745
~ de dissociation D476
~ du domaine D527
~ électrique E105

~ électromagnétique E143
~ d'excitation E457
~ de Fermi F55
~ géothermique G143
~ d'interaction I271
~ interne I322
~ d'ionisation I423
~ de liaison B192, B261
~ libre F343, H136
~ libre de Gibbs G159
~ libre de Helmholtz H136
~ liée B295
~ lumineuse L432
~ magnétique M53
~ magnétostatique M186
~ nucléaire N357, N386
~ de phonon P365
~ potentielle P825
~ propre S157
~ rayonnante R13
~ au repos R457
~ en repos R457
~ du réseau L137
~ de résonance R434
~ de rotation R546
~ solaire S381
~ sonore A105, S446
~ superficielle S1064
~ thermique T111
~ thermonucléaire T186
~ de vibration V114
~ au zéro absolu Z11
engin E336
enregistrement par faisceau
   électronique E174
~ holographique H249
~ magnétique M112
~ optique O183, O186
enrichissement E341
enroulement W127
~ bifilaire B181
ensemble A539, E342, S211
~ accélérateur-accumulateur
   A63
~ canonique C31
~ fermé C338
~ microcanonique M429
~ sous-critique S926
~ statistique S757
~ statistique de Gibbs G163
~ surcritique S993
~ des valeurs R171
entaille N333
enthalpie E345, H79
entonnoir F434
entraînement de fréquence
   F374, F382
~ par les phonons P363
~ par les photons P485
~ de la réaction I214
entropie E347
~ négative N55
~ partielle P101

~ de l'Univers E349
enveloppe E350
~ adiabatique A214
~ des battements B123
~ fertile B221
~ du guide de lumière en fibre
   C309
eötvös E355
épaisseur D177, T200
~ optique O110
éphéméride E357
épicentre E359
épidiascope E360
épitaxie E365
~ à faisceau moléculaire M570
épuisement D166
~ de l'hydrogène E476
~ de l'onde de pompage D169
épuration des gaz G77
équateur E368
~ céleste C140
~ géomagnétique M54
~ magnétique M54
équation de Bernoulli B143
~ de Bethe-Salpeter B173
~ caractéristique C191
~ cinétique K40
~ de Clapeyron C310
~ de continuité C644
~ cubique C946
~ différentielle D268
~ différentielle de Bernoulli
   B143
~ de diffusion D321
~ de Dirac D371
~ de dispersion D442
~ de Drude D599
~ d'état E366
~ d'état réduite R273
~ de Fredholm F336
~ de Gibbs-Duhem G158
~ de Hamilton-Jacobi H36
~ intégrale I249
~ de Klein-Gordon K59
~ de Korteweg-de Vries K67
~ de Langmuir-Saha L40
~ de Laplace L44
~ des Londons L333
~ de Lorentz-Dirac L360
~ de Mathieu M268
~ de Mayer M294
~ de Navier-Stokes N24
~ non linéaire N243
~ d'onde W18
~ parabolique P20
~ de Pauli P170
~ de Percus-Yevick P214
~ de phase P304
~ de Pippard P601
~ de Poisson P728
~ de Richardson R499
~ de Schrödinger S82
~ de sinus Gordon S302

F

FOCALISATION

francium F329
frange F409
~ d'interférence F409
franges de diffraction D283
~ d'interférence I297
~ moirées M559
fréon F361
fréquence F362, R185
~ angulaire A400
~ des battements B124
~ de collisions C433
~ de combinaison C471
~ critique C848, C985
~ cyclotron C1000
~ cyclotronique C1000
~ de Debye D43
~ gyromagnétique G305
~ intermédiaire I312
~ de Langmuir L37
~ de Larmor L52
~ latérale S275
~ d'oscillations O275, V130
~ de plasma P664
~ propre N17
~ de Rabi R1
~ de répétition R403
~ de répétition des impulsions
   P1004
~ de résonance R437
~ de rotation Å400
~ spatiale S523
~ standard quantique Q51
fréquencemètre F376
fréquences acoustiques A656
~ audibles A656
~ d'ondes moyennes M328
friction F400
front F410
~ de choc S241
~ de flamme F170
~ de Mach M2
~ d'onde W19
~ d'onde de choc S241
~ de phase P310
frottement F400
~ externe E522
~ de glissement S337
~ interne I323
~ radiatif R61
~ de repos S739
~ de roulement R531
fugacité F417
fuite E410, L163
~ d'électrons E197
fullerenes F418
fusée à plusieurs étages M733
fusible F436
fusion F438, M336
~ par faisceau électronique
   E171
~ nucléaire N365
~ thermonucléaire T187

~ thermonucléaire contrôlée
   C670
~ thermonucléaire ionique I462
~ thermonucléaire par laser
   L118
~ thermonucléaire ménagée
   C670
~ à zone Z21

G

gadolinium G2
gain G12
~ d'antenne A454
~ de régénération B324
galaxie G25
~ quasi stellaire Q98
~ spirale S658
galaxies de Seifert S126
gallium G29
gallon G30
galvanoluminescence G32
galvanomètre G34
~ balistique B25
gamma G35
gammaradiographie G42
gamme R171
~ de basses fréquences L393
~ de fréquences F383
~ de fréquences acoustiques
   A657
~ haute fréquence H195
~ à hyperfréquence M482
~ de longueurs d'onde W44
~ des ondes courtes S263, S264
~ de pressions P877
~ des températures T43
~ des vitesses V100
gate G80
gauss G84
gaussmètre G87
gaz G52
~ de Bose B281
~ dégénéré D110
~ électronique E198
~ d'électrons bidimensionnel
   T473
~ de Fermi F56
~ idéal P217
~ inerte I166, N179
~ intergalactique I309
~ interstellaire I341
~ ionisé I437
~ noble I166
~ parfait I7, P217
~ de phonons P368
~ photonique P491
~ quantique Q52
~ raréfié R182
~ réel I53, R227
géante rouge R270

gel F356, F357, G94
gélatine bichromatée D246
généralisation relativiste
   R353
générateur G111
~ à balayage de fréquence
   S1091
~ de bruit N187
~ de bruits N187
~ en cascade C87
~ en dents de scie S35
~ électrostatique E263
~ de groupe G278
~ d'harmoniques H54
~ de Hartmann J9
~ d'impulsions I66, P995
~ magnétohydrodynamique
   M160, M419
~ MHD M160, M419
~ de neutrons N128
~ de plasma P665
~ R.C. R203
~ de signaux standard S714
~ thermo-électrique T174
génération G108, G108
~ d'harmoniques H53
~ paramétrique P62
géoacoustique C113
géochronologie G114
géodésie G116
géoïde G118
géomagnétisme G128, T65
géométrie G139
~ euclidienne E422
~ non euclidienne N224
géophone G140
géophysique G141
géothermie G145
gerbe S268
~ atmosphérique A279
~ en cascade C91
~ cosmique C773
~ des rayons cosmiques C773
germanium G146
germe N408, N416, S125
germination des dislocations
   D428
getter G147
ghosts S552
gilbert G165
glace I1
glissement G176, S338
~ facile E6
glueball G187
gluino G188
gluon G189
~ vectoriel V78
gonflement S1092
goniomètre G196
goniométrie G197
goutte D594
~ en chute libre D595
~ électron-trou E200

~ final F137
~ du genre espace S497
~ du genre temps T253
~ d'impulsions P1006
~ infini I178
~ mondial W143
~ quadridimensionnel F300
~ de temps T248
~ de temps de Planck P622
~ unitaire U79
invar I361
invariance I362
~ de la charge C225, C292
~ chirale C263
~ conforme C586
~ CP C825
~ CPT C826
~ d'échelle S50, S53
~ globale G181
~ de gradient G202
~ isotopique I559
~ de jauge G7
~ locale de jauge L313
~ de Lorentz L363
~ par rapport à l'inversion de temps T260
~ relativiste R354
~ de rénormalisation R399
~ topologique T273
~ de translation T347
~ du vide V23
invariant I364
~ adiabatique A210
~ adiabatique transversal T375
~ cinématique K29
~ isotopique I560
~ de jauge G8
~ longitudinal adiabatique L336
~ de Lorentz L364
~ relativiste R355
~ de Riemann R502
~ topologique T274
invariants du champ F101
~ du champ électromagnétique E145
inverseur de phase P312
inversion I373, R474
~ d'aimantation M143
~ combinée C473
~ de densité D155
~ d'espace S495
~ partielle P103
~ de population P801
~ des raies spectrales R475
~ de température T39
~ de temps T250, T259
inverteur I377
iode I380
ion I381
~ atomique A621
~ complexe C347
~ excité E463
~ implanté I56

~ d'impureté I78
~ moléculaire M585
~ monochargé S324
~ négatif N50
~ paramagnétique P45
~ plusieurs fois chargé M722
~ positif P814
~ de recul R239
~ de terre rare R178
ionisation I413
~ associative A542
~ de l'atmosphère A587
~ atmosphérique I428
~ aurorale A670
~ par avalanche A693
~ par champ électrique F102
~ par choc C435, I44
~ par choc électronique I415
~ par collision I414
~ de la couche périphérique O301
~ à deux étapes T491
~ dissociative D479
~ par électrons E214
~ des électrons internes I222
~ d'équilibre E378
~ par gradins S804
~ par impact I44
~ multiphotonique M698
~ multiple M708
~ à photon unique S317
~ à plusieurs étages M732
~ de résonance R450
~ sélective S137
~ successive S955
~ superficielle S1072
~ thermique T127
ioniseur I439
ionogramme I444
ionoluminescence I445
ionosonde I446
ionosphère I447
~ aurorale A671
~ calme Q137
~ équatoriale E369
~ inférieure L389
~ perturbée D512
~ polaire P738
~ supérieure U99
ions de précipitation P857
iridectomie laser L84
iridium I463
irradiance I469
irradiateur I472
irradiation I22, I470
irrégularité I476
~ atmosphérique A588
~ en échelle microscopique S355
~ en échelle réduite S355
~ de l'indice de réfraction R320
~ ionosphérique I452
~ à large échelle L50

irréversibilité I478
~ du temps T251
isallobare I485
isallotherme I486
isanémone I487
isanomale I488
isobare I492
~ nucléaire N367
~ reflétée M508
isochasme I497
isochore I498
isochrone I501
isochronisme I503
~ des oscillations I504
~ du pendule I505
isocinétique I517
isocline I509
isodense I510
isodose I511
isodoublet I537
isogone I515
isogroupe I516
isolant I246
~ acoustique S455
~ thermique H88
isolation I245, I520
~ adiabatique A209
~ calorifuge H89
~ magnétique M80
~ thermique H89
~ par le vide V22
isolement I245
~ électrique E87
~ épitaxial E362
~ thermique T126
~ thermomagnétique T182
isoligne I521
isom re I524
~ chimique C244
~ cis-trans C307, G132
~ de conformation C592
~ de constitution S916
~ fissile F159
~ de forme S218
~ géométrique C307, G132
~ nucléaire N368
~ optique E307, O139
~ reflété M509
~ de rotation C592
~ rotationnel C592, R547
~ trans T333
isomérie I525
~ chimique C245
~ cis-trans C308, G133
~ de conformation C591
~ de constitution S917
~ de fission F160
~ géométrique C308, G133
~ moléculaire M586
~ nucléaire N369
~ optique O140
~ de position P806

~ de rotation R548
isomérisation I526
~ multiphotonique M699
isométrie d'opérateurs O76
isomorphisme I527
~ hétérovalent H166
~ isovalent I579
isomultiplet I528, I538
isophase I529
isophote I530
isoplanatisme I531
isopycne I532
isoscalaire I533
isosingulet I534
isospin I536
~ «faible» W73
~ nucléaire N370
isostère I540
~ d'adsorption A227
isosymétrie I542
isotenseur I543
isotherme I544
~ d'adsorption A228
~ de cristallisation C921
isotone I547
isotope I548
~ alpha stable A307
~ bêta stable B166
~ déficient en neutrons
  N113
~ émetteur de rayons alpha
  A297
~ émetteur des rayons bêta
  B149
~ enrichi E338
~ à excès de neutrons N124
~ indicateur T310
~ instable U92
~ à longue période L344
~ lourd H105
~ naturel N18
~ pauvre en neutrons N130
~ radioactif R80, R114
~ riche en neutrons N150
~ stable S700
~ à vie courte S253
isotopes séparés S205
isotriplet I539, I568
isotropie I577
~ de distribution angulaire
  A399
~ de l'espace-temps S505
~ optique O141
~ de rayonnement R43
~ du rayonnement de relique
  R384
~ de la source radioactive R86
~ de l'Univers I578
isotropisation I576
~ des rayons cosmiques C771
isotypie I541
isovecteur I580
itération I582

J

jacobien J1
jansky J5
jauge G3, P915
~ bêta B152
~ de contrainte R416, S858
~ d'épaisseur T201
~ de Hamilton H31
~ à ionisation I425
~ de niveau L189
~ du vide à ionisation I434
jaugeage de Feynman F86
jet J8
~ coronal C732
~ de gaz G72
jeu C322, S211
joint de grains G206
~ de macles T458
jonction J25
~ asymétrique N306
~ émettrice E300
~ hétérogène H159
~ homogène H264
~ p-n E201, P712
~ semi-conducteur-métal S189
joule J17
jour D29
~ calme Q136
~ perturbé D511
~ solaire S378
jours actifs A177
jumeau Dauphinéen D26
jumelles B193
Jupiter J27

K

kelvin K7
kénotron K11
kerma K13
kg·m/s K27
kiloélectron-volt K24
kilogramme K25
kilogramme-force K26
kilogrammètre par seconde K27
kiloparsec K28
kinescope K37
kinoform K55
klystron K61
~ d'amplificateur A349
~ à deux cavités D562
~ de glissement D589
~ multicavité M706
~ à multicavités M706
~ optique O144
~ à réflexion R309
~ à temps de transit D589
~ à transit D589
kourtchatovium K73

krypton K72
kurtchatovium K73

L

label L1
laboratoire L3
~ ANL A525
~ chaud H281
~ Lawrence à Livermore L155
~ de métrologie S712
~ physique P531
~ à rayons X X32
~ de recherches R408
lacune énergétique E320
lagrangien L9
~ de champ F103
~ d'interaction I273
~ libre F346
laiton B312
lambert L17
lame bimétallique B186
~ de phase P323
~ quart d'onde Q91
laminarité L24
lampe L25
~ à arc A518
~ à décharge gazeuse D403
~ à décharge incandescente
  G186
~ à incandescence I83
~ à lumière du jour D30
~ de pompage P1022
~ tare C491
~ à vapeur de mercure M346
lampe-éclair F178
lanthane L43
lanthanides L42
laplacien L47
large distribution canonique
  L48
~ invariant cinématique L49
largeur W115
~ angulaire A407
~ de la bande B44
~ naturelle de la raie spectrale
  N15
~ neutronique N162
~ du niveau d'énergie E323
~ partielle P110
~ de la raie L277
laser L54
~ accordable F392, T427
~ annulaire R515
~ à argon A524
~ à arséniure de gallium G1
~ à auto-excitation F352
~ à autosynchronisation des
  modes S168
~ à centres F42
~ à centres de couleur C448

limbe L247
limitation R461
limite B287
~ de capture pour le cadmium C4
~ de convergence C685
~ du domaine D526, D532
~ d'écoulement Y5
~ d'écoulement supérieure U103
~ élastique E59
~ de fatigue F36
~ inférieure d'élasticité L391
~ de proportionnalité P945
~ de Roche R519
~ supérieure U100
~ thermodynamique T157
~ unitaire U74
limiteur L249, R461
~ d'amplitude A360
liner L274
liquéfaction en cascade C88
~ des gaz L280
liquide L281
~ de Bose B279
~ bouillant B248
~ de condensation C547
~ cryogénique C883
~ déplacé D457
~ à deux composantes T470
~ élastique E60
~ excitonique E471
~ de Fermi F58
~ à immersion I39
~ non newtonien N274
~ parfait P220
~ quantique Q56
~ de refroidissement C700
~ sous-réfrigéré S991
~ superfluide S998
~ viscoélastique V159
~ visqueux V167
lithium L300
lithographie L301
~ à faisceau électronique E170
~ à faisceau ionique I387
~ aux rayons X X35
litre L302
lobe L308
localisateur acoustique A139
localisation L317
~ d'Anderson A379
~ laser L104
~ laser de la Lune L440
~ à laser des satellites S19
~ sonore S469
localité L316
~ d'interaction I274
logarithme L327
~ de Brigg D64
~ de Coulomb C799
~ coulombien C799
~ décimal D64

~ naturel N21
loi L150
~ de l'action et de la réaction L151
~ d'action de masse L154
~ de l'attraction universelle de Newton N167
~ d'augmentation d'entropie E348
~ de Biot et Savart B207
~ de Bloch B229
~ de Bouguer-Lambert-Beer B286
~ de Boyle B300
~ de Boyle-Mariotte B300
~ de Brewster B330
~ de Charles C231
~ de la conservation de la charge C202
~ de la conservation de l'énergie E313
~ de la conservation du moment L153
~ de Coulomb C798
~ de Curie-Weiss C958
~ de Dalton D5
~ de Darcy D12
~ de dispersion D445
~ de Dulong et Petit D607
~ de l'équilibre chimique L152
~ d'équipartition E387
~ exponentielle E515, P844
~ de Gay-Lussac G91
~ généralisée G101
~ de Grüneisen G290
~ de Henry H140
~ de Hooke H268
~ d'induction de Faraday F23
~ de Joule J20, J21
~ de Kapitza K2
~ de Kepler K12
~ de Kirchhoff K56
~ de Lambert L18
~ de Lenz L179
~ linéaire L260
~ logarithmique L330
~ de Malus M210
~ de Moseley M644
~ d'Ohm O38
~ de Paschen P155
~ de Planck P621
~ de Poiseuille P725
~ de puissance 3/2 T219
~ de similitude S54
~ de Stefan-Boltzmann S779
~ de Stokes S846
~ de Wiedemann-Franz W116
~ de Wien W120
~ de Wien de la radiation W120
lois de conservation C609
~ de gaz parfait P218
~ de Newton N168

~ de rayonnement R44
longeur d'onde de De Broglie D38
longitude L335
~ géomagnétique G122
longue ligne L342
longueur L174
~ d'absorption A49
~ d'affaiblissement A650
~ de cohérence C378
~ de corrélation C748
~ de Debye D44
~ de diffusion D326, S76
~ efficace d'antenne A452
~ élémentaire E278
~ de focalisation F263
~ fondamentale F429
~ de liaison B265
~ de mélange M522
~ d'onde W43
~ d'onde de Compton C536
~ d'onde dans le guide d'ondes G292
~ d'onde dans l'espace libre F355
~ d'onde de seuil T231
~ d'oscillations O276
~ de parcours P167
~ du parcours libre des phonons P367
~ de Planck P619
~ de radiation R45
~ de relaxation R374
~ de thermalisation T128
~ de la voie P167
loupe L175, M197
lubrifiant G258
lubrification L407
lueur G184
~ anodique A438
~ de cathode C107
~ cathodique C107
lumen L409
lumen-seconde L410
lumière L204, V171
~ actinique A159
~ blanche W109
~ monochromatique M622
~ naturelle N20
~ partiellement polarisée P104
~ polarisée P760
~ zodiacale Z17
luminance L411
~ énergétique R10
~ visuelle B333, B335
luminescence L415
~ chaude H282
~ coopérative C702
~ électrique E137
~ métastable M395
~ négative N51
~ paramétrique P66
~ polarisée P761

~ à polariton P741
~ de recombinaison R246
~ de résonance R440
~ sensibilisée S202
~ spontanée S669
~ stimulée S825
luminophore L426, P378
luminosité L427
~ de l'air A275
~ critique C851
~ d'Eddington E21
~ stellaire S792
lunakhode L441
Lune M638
lunette R313
~ de Galilée G26
~ à rayons X X53
lutécium L442
lux L443
luxmètre L445
lyophilie L447
lyophobie L448
lyotropie L449

M

M. A. A362
M.F. F378
machine d'essai de friction F407
~ à expansion E491
~ de Turing T455
maclage T461
macle T457
~ Dauphinéenne D26
macrocausalité L316
macrocinétique M7
macrocosmos M6
macromolécule M8
macroparticule M9
macrostructure M13
magnésium M17
magnétique M18, N378
~ amorphe A331
~ de faible encombrement L384
~ supraconducteur S982
magnétisation par courant continu D32
magnétisme M139
~ des bandes B38
~ des microparticules M452
~ nucléaire N374
~ de spin S632
~ superficiel S1073
~ terrestre T65
~ de zone Z20
magnéto-acoustique M150
magnéto-optique M173
magnétochimie M154
magnétodiélectrique M155
magnétographe M159

~ solaire S389
magnétohydrodynamique M163
magnétomètre M168
~ à ferrosonde F237
~ de Hanle H40
~ à hélium H132
~ à protons P960
~ quantique Q57
~ à torsion T288
~ à vecteur V79
magnéton M170
~ de Bohr B243
~ nucléaire N375
magnétopause M174
magnétorésistance M178, M179
magnétosphère M182
~ externe O296
~ interne I218
~ de pulsar P976
magnétostatique M187
magnétostriction M189
magnétron M192
~ accordable T428
~ à cavités C133
~ à cavités multiples M672
~ coaxial C355
~ strappé S867
magnitude M198
~ bolométrique B254
~ stellaire S793
~ stellaire absolue A21
~ stellaire bolométrique B254
~ stellaire photographique P446
magnon M199
majoron M209
malléabilité F283
manganèse M212
manipulateur M214
manomètre M216, P871
~ capacitif C48
~ différentiel D269
~ à ionisation I425
~ piézo-électrique P570
~ de Pirani P603
manque de neutrons N112
manteau M217
~ de plasma P675
marée T237
marées atmosphériques A598
marge de stabilité S692
marquage laser L86
marque M224
~ isotopique I566
Mars M227
martensite M228
maser M230
~ à ammoniac A326
~ à deux niveaux T481
~ galactique G20
~ moléculaire M588
~ à résonance cyclotronique C1004
~ à trois niveaux T221

~ à trous chauds H279
masque M234
masse M235
~ atomique A624, A642
~ atomique relative A642
~ autre que nulle N313
~ cacheé H176
~ critique C853
~ effective E30
~ d'électron E217
~ gravitationnelle G232
~ inerte I173
~ de lancement L146
~ lourde G232
~ de Majorana du neutrino M205
~ moléculaire M589
~ obéissant à la loi de conservation C619
~ d'une particule M246
~ pesante G232
~ de Planck P620
~ réduite R274
~ relativiste R357
~ au repos M239
matériau M260
~ amorphe A332
~ anticorrosif A463
~ dur magnétique H43
~ élastique E61
~ élastico-plastique E71
~ enrichi E340
~ isolant E134
~ isotrope I570
~ magnétique M90
~ magnétiquement doux S363
~ résistant à la corrosion C758
~ résistant à l'usure W82
~ tensio-actif S1050
matériaux non linéaires N249
~ paramagnétiques P46
~ piézo-électriques P566
~ de vide V24
matériel photosensible L242
matière M274
~ condensée C553
~ de dopage D544
~ fissile F151
~ interplanétaire I331
~ interstellaire I343
~ invisible D19
~ luminescente L425
~ nucléaire N376
~ photochrome P394
~ photosensible P511
~ solide S419
~ superdense S994
~ thermoplastique T192
matrice M270
~ CCD C204
~ de cohérence C379
~ de densité D156
~ de diffusion S77

~ de Dirac D373
~ des états S732
~ de Müller M670
~ de photodétecteurs P405
~ de spin S633
~ de spin de Pauli P173, S633
matrices de Gell-Mann G95
~ hermitiennes H142
maximon M278
maximum M279, P176
~ d'activité solaire S390
~ de diffraction D287
~ primaire P892
~ principal M208
~ solaire S390
maxwell M283
mécanique M320
~ céleste C141
~ classique C315
~ des corps à masse variable V60
~ exacte F131
~ des fluides F220
~ matrice M273
~ des milieux continus M321
~ de Newton C315
~ newtonienne C315, N289
~ non linéaire N250
~ non relativiste N289
~ ondulatoire W45
~ du point matériel P134
~ quantique Q58
~ relativiste R359
~ des solides M322
~ statistique S761
mécanisme d'accélération A67
~ d'accélération bêtatron B170
~ d'accélération dissipatif D467
~ de branchement thermique T85
~ de claquage B315
~ de compensation A216
~ de conductibilité thermique H76
~ de rupture F322
~ de transmission de la chaleur M323
mécanostriction M325
méchanisme de Petschek P273
médecine laser L87
médiane M326
méga-électron-volt M331
mégahertz M332
mégawatt M333
mélange M520
~ des gaz G66
~ des modes M534
~ optique O157
~ paramétrique P67
~ paramétrique de quatre ondes P61
~ turbulent T451
mélangeur M519

membrane D239, M339
~ semi-perméable S195
~ à trace T315
mémoire S851
~ holographique H250
~ optique O155
~ de phase P317
mendélévium M340
ménisque M341
mercure M343
Mercure M344
méridien M348
~ céleste C142
~ géomagnétique G123
~ magnétique M92
mésodynamique M354
mésomorphie M357
méson M358
~ π P584
~ chargé C213
~ K K1, K62
~ K chargé C211
~ K neutre N89
~ lourd H107
~ neutre vrai T422
~ pi P584, P592
~ scalaire S42
~ vectoriel V80
~ vectoriel neutre N93
~ virtuel V153
mésonium M364
mésopause M365
mésophase M366
mésoscopique M367
mésosphère M368
mesurage M299
mesure M298, M299
~ absolue A17
~ de l'absorption A52
~ altimétrique A313
~ de la bande passante B45
~ de bruit N190
~ colorimétrique C456
~ de dispersion M303
~ de distance D485
~ à distance R391
~ de dose D558
~ de la dose de radiation M302
~ d'émission E291
~ de l'énergie E325
~ de fréquence F375
~ in situ I230
~ des intervalles de temps T249
~ de la période P236
~ précise A89, P860
~ de la pression atmosphérique M301
~ de probabilité P911
~ de température T40
~ de temps T254
~ de la vitesse V94
mesures acoustiques A117
~ aérodynamiques A245

~ angulaires A401
~ digitales D337
~ électriques E89
~ électriques des grandeurs non électriques E90
~ d'hyperfréquence M478
~ interférométriques I307
~ de longueur L262
~ magnétiques M91
~ optiques O154
~ photométriques P473
~ physiques P532
~ de polarisation P746
~ radioélectriques R107
~ à sonde P918
~ spectrales S560
mesureur des distorsions non linéaires D494
~ de vitesse de comptage C808
métacentre M369
métacouleur M371
métagalaxie M373
métal M374
~ alcalin A287
~ amorphe A333
~ ductile D605
~ liquide L290
~ de transition T338
métallisation M383
métallo-optique M387
métallocéramique M375
métallographie M384
métalloïde M385
métamagnétisme M391
métamérie M392
métamorphisme M393
métastabilité M394
métaux nobles N180
~ de terres rares R180
météore M397
météorite M399
méthode M403, P923
~ d'activation A174
~ d'allongement-recuit S856
~ analytique A373
~ à anticoïncidences A461
~ des approximations successives M412
~ approximative A507
~ des atomes marqués I561
~ augmentée des ondes planes A664
~ axiomatique A709
~ axiomatique formelle F286
~ de Bridgman B332
~ de caractéristiques M404
~ du champ autoconsistant S151
~ du col S6
~ collective C416
~ des combinaisons linéaires des orbitales atomiques M407
~ de contrôle non destructif N210

MÉTHODE

~ de couplage faible W65
~ de couplage fort S906
~ sans creuset C881
~ des cristaux tournants R538
~ Czochralski C1012
~ de Darwin-Fowler D21
~ de Debye-Scherrer D45
~ de Debye et Scherrer P840
~ de décoration D70
~ de différences finies M405
~ de diffraction D288
~ de diffraction des électrons de haute énergie H184
~ de diffraction des électrons de haute énergie par réflexion R297
~ de diffraction des électrons lents L386
~ de diffraction des rayons X X15
~ de diffraction à rayons X X15
~ de diffusion incohérente I102
~ de dilution isotopique I550
~ des éléments finis F136
~ des éléments traceurs T311
~ d'essai et d'erreur T398
~ d'essai à immersion I40
~ d'évaporation à vide V19
~ d'excitation E459
~ d'expansion aux fonctions propres E37
~ d'expansion aux modes propres E39
~ de factorisation F10
~ à fond noir D18
~ de Hartree-Fock H64, S151
~ de l'hodographe H225
~ des images I31
~ des invariants I366
~ d'invariants adiabatiques A211
~ d'itération I583
~ de Kirchhoff K57
~ de Laue L144
~ de Laue en retour B9
~ des liaisons de valence V36
~ de matrice de Jones J13
~ du maximum de vraisemblance M280
~ de modérateur M538
~ des moindres carrés M406
~ de Monte-Carlo M635
~ non paramétrique N275
~ des ombres S213
~ à ondes distordues D491
~ des orbitales moléculaires M592
~ du paramètre d'impact I48
~ perturbationnelle M410
~ de perturbations brusques S963
~ de piédestal P187

~ de la plus profonde descente S777
~ de la plus rapide descente M411
~ des points du col S6
~ des pôles de Regge R331
~ des poudres P840
~ du radiocarbone R96
~ de réflexions partielles P107
~ de régularisation R335
~ de remplacement moléculaire M408
~ de rétroréflexion B9
~ sol-gel S408
~ de sonde P919
~ de sonde optique O172
~ des stries S79
~ de Tamm-Dancoff T5
~ de théorie des groupes G280
~ des traceurs T311
~ de transformation rapide de Fourier F29
~ des variations V64
~ de Verneuil V105
~ visuelle V178
~ de Wentzel-Kramers-Brillouin W98
~ de Wiener-Hopf W119
~ de la zone fondue F201, Z21
mètre M401
~ carré S684
~ cube C947
métrique M413
~ de l'espace-temps S507
~ indéfinie I115
métrologie M418
~ quantique Q59
mica M421
micro-analyse M425
micro-analyseur M426
microbarographe M427
microcausalité L316, M431
microchamp M439
microchirurgie laser L88
microcible M469
microcosmos M485
microdensitomètre M434
microdiffraction M435
microdosimétrie M436
microdureté M440
micro-électronique M437
~ des corps solides S416
~ des semi-conducteurs S190
micro-explosion M438
microfissure M433
microflexion M428
micro-inclusion M442
micro-inhomogénéité M443
micro-instabilité M444
microlithographie M446
micromagnétisme M447
micromètre M448, M450

micron M450
micro-objectif M445
micro-ondes M483
microparticule M451
microphone M453
microphotographie M454
microphotomètre M455
micropincement M456
microplasma M457
microprocesseur M459
microprojection M460
micropulsation M461
microrelief M462
microscope M463
~ acoustique A118
~ à balayage S59
~ de champ proche N30
~ à contraste de phase P294
~ à effet de champ E292
~ électronique E218
~ électronique à réflexion R295
~ électronique à transmission T353
~ ionique I443
~ laser de projection L97
~ de mesure M305, M449
~ métallographique M386
~ optique O156
~ à photo-électrons P429
~ à photo-ions P460
~ polarisant P747
~ de projection P933
~ à projection P933
~ à rayons X X36
~ tunnel T437
~ ultraviolet U41
microscopie M464
~ à polarisation P748
~ aux rayons X X37
microséisme M465
microsonde M458
microspectrophotomètre M466
microstructure M468
microtension M467
microtron M470
micro-univers M485
microviscosité M472
mictomagnétisme M486
migration M488
~ des charges C226
~ de défauts D83
~ d'électrons E219
~ d'énergie E326
~ des excitons E472
~ des impuretés I80
~ des trous H234
~ de vacances V4
milieu actif A179
~ anisotropique A415
~ condensé C554
~ continu C652
~ dispersif D453
~ dissipatif D471

~ gyrotrope G315
~ hétérogène N227
~ homogène H260
~ inhomogène I210
~ isotropique I571
~ non linéaire N251
~ plan-stratifié P630
~ trouble T444
milieux optiquement épais O149
~ optiquement minces O151
millimètre M492
~ de colonne d'eau M494
~ d'eau M494
~ de mercure M493
minimum M497
~ d'activité solaire S391
~ de diffraction D289
~ solaire S391
minitron M498
minutage T262
minute M503
mirage M504
miroir M505
~ acoustique A119
~ adaptif A192
~ Brillouin à conjugaison des phases P288
~ collecteur C412
~ concave C540
~ à conjugaison des phases P289
~ convexe C694
~ dichroïque D244
~ diélectrique D257
~ électronique E220
~ flexible F190
~ laser L89
~ magnétique M93
~ parabolique P21
~ piézo-électrique P567
~ plan P624
~ à plusieurs éléments M679
~ à rayons X X38
~ secondaire S108
~ sélectif S138
~ semi-transparent S197
~ de sortie E478
~ sphérique S608
miroirs de Fresnel F398
mise en désordre D435
~ à feu F142
~ en phase alternée S285
~ à la terre E2, G271, G272
mitron M516
mobilité M524
~ des électrons E221
~ de Hall H26
~ des porteurs C81
~ des trous H235
mode M526
~ de Bernstein B144
~ de coupure C986
~ dégénéré D112

~ d'échange E450
~ fondamental F430
~ de guide d'ondes G293
~ du guide d'ondes W34
~ interdit F274
~ longitudinal L339
~ normal N324
~ phononique P370
~ pi P585
~ de réseau L140
~ transversal T380
modèle M530
~ anisotropique A416
~ atomique de Bohr B242
~ B.C.S. B47
~ des bandes B39
~ de Bardeen-Cooper-Schrieffer B47
~ bidimensionnel T475
~ classique C316
~ clos C337
~ «cluster» C349
~ à corde S898
~ cosmologique C782
~ à couches S232
~ des couches S232
~ à deux bandes T465
~ à deux fluides T478
~ à deux niveaux T482
~ d'échange E451
~ empirique E302
~ d'éruption solaire S384
~ évolutif E440
~ d'expansion E485
~ fermé C337
~ de Friedman F408
~ généralisé G102
~ de la goutte D596
~ de la goutte liquide L285
~ de grande unification G212
~ de Heisenberg H117
~ heuristique H167
~ homogène H261
~ à inflation I185
~ d'interaction électrofaible E274
~ d'Ising I491
~ isotrope I572
~ de Jaynes-Cummings J6
~ à large échelle L51
~ au naturel F420
~ du noyau à couches S232
~ optique O158
~ optique du noyau O158
~ ouvert O66
~ à particule unique O53
~ phénoménologique P356
~ planétaire P633
~ planétaire d'atome P633
~ des quarks Q87
~ de sac B19
~ spatial T217
~ stationnaire S745

~ statistique S762
~ de supercalibrage S972
~ supersymétrique S1040
~ de transition de phase P347
~ à trois dimensions T217
~ unidimensionnel O47
~ d'Univers expansif E485
modèles nucléaires N377
modérateur M537
~ en eau lourde H111
~ au graphite G220
modération des neutrons M536
modes de compétition C498
~ couplés C811
~ de Goldstone G195
~ d'ordre supérieur H191
~ orthogonaux O260
~ propres E40
modification M542
~ allotropique A291
~ de faisceau ionique I388
~ laser DNA D524
~ des matériaux par les faisceaux des particules chargées M262
~ stable S701
~ de surface S1074
modifications de glace I2
modulateur C272, M551
~ acousto-optique A155
~ électro-optique E255
~ de lumière L211, O159
~ de lumière espace-temps S506
~ de lumière ultrasonique U26
~ optique O159
~ de Q Q5
modulation M546
~ acousto-optique A154
~ d'amplitude A362
~ de brillance I265
~ par codes d'impulsions P985
~ croisée C868
~ de durée d'impulsions P992
~ de facteur Q Q7
~ du faisceau B109
~ en fréquence F378
~ à grille G269
~ d'impulsions P1000
~ d'impulsions en amplitude P983
~ par impulsions codées P985
~ d'impulsions en fréquence P994
~ d'impulsions en phase P1002
~ d'impulsions en position P1002
~ de lumière L228
~ de phase P319
~ de qualité Q7
~ de la vitesse V95
~ de la vitesse de groupe G283
module M198, M552, M553
~ de cisaillement M557

~ de dégénérescence D107
~ de fréquence F380
multipolarité M725
multipôle M726
multistabilité M731
~ optique O162
multivibrateur M736
muon M738
muonium M744
muons cosmiques C765
mur du son S433
~ sonique S433
myopie M752

N

nabla N1
nadir N2
naine D612
~ blanche W107
~ blanche à accrétion A82
~ à hélium dégénérée D111
~ rouge R269
nanodiffraction N4
nanolithographie N5
NASA N14
navigation dans l'espace S499
~ à inertie I172
~ spatiale S499
nébuleuse N38
~ du Crabe C830
~ gazeuse G67
~ planétaire P634
négatif N49
néguentropie N55
néodyme N62
néon N64
néper N65
néphélomètre N66
néphélométrie N67
Neptune N68
neptunium N69
neurone N81
neutralisation N88
~ de la charge C227
~ de la charge d'espace S486
neutrino N95
~ de Majorana M204
~ muonique M742
~ de relique R381
~ solaire S392
neutron N101
neutronisation N133
neutronogramme N120
neutrons différés D129
~ diffusés S62
~ de fission F161
~ froids C409
~ instantanés P936
~ instantanés de fission P936
~ intermédiaires I313

~ lents S350
~ modérés M535
~ polarisés P762
~ rapides F31
~ de résonance R441
~ thermiques T134
~ ultrafroids U5
newton N164
nickel N170
nilsbohrium N173
niobium N174
nit N175
nitrogène N176
niveau L186
~ accepteur A76
~ de bruit N189
~ donneur D538
~ d'énergie d'électrons E196
~ de Fermi F57
~ fondamental G273
~ d'impureté I79
~ de la mer S100
~ nucléaire N358
~ occupé O18
~ de résonance R438
~ rotationnel R549
~ de vibration V115
~ virtuel V152
~ voisin N56
~ yrast Y11
niveaux énergétiques E322
~ énergétiques moléculaires M580
~ d'énergie de l'atome A617
~ de Landau L32
~ superficiels magnétiques M131
~ supérieurs H189
~ de Tamm T6
nobélium N178
noircissement B218
nombre N421
~ atomique A627
~ d'Avogadro A699
~ baryonique B72
~ de coordination C711
~ de degrés de liberté N422, V62
~ entier I247
~ de Froude F412
~ de Grashof G222
~ de Hartmann H62
~ imaginaire I35
~ de Knudsen K64
~ de Loschmidt L371
~ de Mach M3
~ de masse M245
~ muonique M743
~ de Nusselt N425
~ d'onde W50
~ d'ouverture F245
~ de Péclet P180
~ de Prandtl P851

~ quantique Q60
~ quantique additif A197
~ quantique azimutal A721
~ quantique interne I326
~ quantique magnétique M110
~ quantique multiplicatif M719
~ quantique orbital O228
~ quantique principal P896
~ quantique radial R8
~ quantique de rotation R553
~ quantique de spin S647
~ quantique de vibration V120
~ quantique vibrationnel V120
~ de révolutions par seconde R484
~ de Reynolds R485
~ des taches solaires S971
nombres de Wolf W137
nomogramme N195
non-conservation N206
~ de la charge C228
~ de la parité P93
non-élasticité N382
nonet N223
non-linéarité N247
non-linéarité acoustique A121
~ cubique C948
~ non dissipative N212
~ optique O163
~ optique géante G151
non-localité N270
non-métal N272
non-monochromatisme N273
non-potentialité N280
non-prolifération des armes nucléaires N281
non-réciprocité N287
non-rénormalisabilité N293
non-sphéricité N299
non-uniformité N308
~ du champ magnétique M61
normale N314
~ d'onde W49
normalisation N319, N322
~ de la fonction d'onde W27
norme du vecteur V81
notation N332
nœud N182
~ ascendant A535
~ de courant C970
~ descendant D186
~ d'onde stationnaire W48
nova N336
noyau C719, K15, N416
~ atomique A626
~ cométaire C480
~ de la comète C480
~ composé C515
~ de condensation C551
~ convectif C673
~ déformé D101
~ fissile F152
~ de fissure C833

~ galactique G21
~ isobare I492
~ nu B48
~ pair-impair E436
~ pair-pair E435
~ de recul R241
~ tourbillonnaire V212
~ à vie courte S254
noyaux déficients en neutrons
  N114
~ à excès de neutrons N125
~ miroirs M511
~ à nombre magique M16
~ polarisés P763
nuage C342
~ de charge d'espace S483
~ de Cottrell C789
~ d'électricité C200
~ d'électrons C200, E179
~ de poussière D611
nucléation N407
nucléide N418
~ radioactif R82
nucléon N409
~ spectateur S542
nutation N426
~ optique O164

O

objectif L175, O2
~ catadioptrique C95
~ à deux lentilles D577
~ à focale variable V67
~ à grand angle de champ
  W113
objet distant D487
~ éloigné D487
~ ponctuel P722
~ quasi stellaire Q99, Q129
~ visible V170
~ visible à l'œil N3
~ à vitesse dépassant celle de la
  lumière S1045
~ volant non identifié U59
obliquité O7
observable O8
~ locale L319
observateur de référence S713
observations O9
~ visuelles V180
observatoire O10
~ astronomique A563
obstacle O12
obturateur B90, L211, S272
~ à cellule de Kerr O143
~ électro-optique E252
~ de laser L107
~ optique O190
~ optique passif P163
occlusion O13

occultation O14
occupation O16
océanographie physique P533
océanologie O20
octaèdre O21
octave O22
octet O23
octopôle O24
oculaire E541
ohm O34
ohmmètre O39
œil E539
omégatron O42
onde W12
~ acoustique A142
~ de choc S247
~ de choc de tête H68
~ de choc frontale B299
~ de cisaillement S229
~ de compression C529
~ conjuguée en phase P290
~ cylindrique C1010
~ à densité de charge C208
~ de détente B223
~ de détonation B223, D210
~ diffusée S65
~ élasto-plastique E72
~ électromagnétique
  transversale T378
~ entretenue C656
~ d'expansion E492
~ expansive B223
~ explosive E509
~ extraordinaire E531
~ de flexion F195
~ de guide d'ondes G294
~ idling I15
~ incidente I89
~ inverse B16
~ de Love L382
~ neutronique N161
~ d'objets O4
~ ordinaire O244
~ partielle P109
~ plane P637
~ de plasma P695
~ polarisée P766
~ progressive T393
~ radio ionosphérique S336
~ de référence R286
~ réfléchie R291
~ réfractée R312
~ de retour B16
~ de Riemann R503
~ riemannienne R503
~ sphérique S612
~ de spin S654
~ superficielle G275
~ de surface S1085
~ de tête B298
~ transversale T385
~ troposphérique T420
ondemètre W46

ondes acoustiques A95
~ acoustiques de surface S1049
~ d'Alfvén A283
~ atmosphériques A602
~ de Bleustein-Gulyaev B226
~ brogliennes D39
~ capillaires C55
~ centimétriques C161
~ de choc non collisionnelles
  C438
~ courtes S265
~ de cristallisation C923
~ décimétriques D65
~ de densité D160
~ de dérive D593
~ d'eau W9
~ élastiques E68
~ électromagnétiques E154
~ gravitationelles G249, G254
~ de gravité G254
~ de gravité internes I324
~ infrarouges I204
~ infrasonores I206
~ d'ionisation I435
~ de Lamb L21
~ de Langmuir L41
~ longitudinales L341
~ longues L354, L356
~ de lumière O209
~ lumineuses L245
~ magnéto-acoustiques M151
~ magnéto-élastiques M157
~ magnétohydrodynamiques
  M164
~ magnétostatiques M188
~ métriques M402
~ millimétriques M495
~ monochromatiques M625
~ moyennes M329
~ non linéaires N268
~ normales N330
~ optiques O209
~ optiques de surface S1075
~ de probabilité P914
~ radioélectriques R143
~ de Rayleigh R199
~ de recombinaison R250
~ séismiques S128
~ stationnaires S718
~ submillimétriques S937
~ de température T47
~ très longues V111
~ ultra-courtes U11
~ ultra-sonores U36
~ de vent W126
ondulateur U54
opacité O57
~ atmosphérique A589
opalescence O58
~ critique C854
opérateur O73
~ de création C836
~ création P926

~ partielle P105
~ piézo-électrique P569
~ du rayonnement
   électromagnétique P749
~ rémanente R390
~ rotatoire R564
~ rotatoire gauche C804
~ de spin S645
~ spontanée S671
~ du vide V26
polariscope P739
~ de Savart S33
polarisateur P767
polariseur P767
polarité P742
~ magnétique M104
polariton P740
~ superficiel S1078
polarogramme P773
polarographe P774
polarographie P775
polaron P776
pôle P777
~ géomagnétique G124
~ magnétique M105
~ de pion P595
~ de Regge R330
polhodie C169, P779
pollution de l'air A277
~ atmosphérique A277
~ d'environnement E352
~ du milieu ambiant E352
polonium P780
polycristaux P781
polyèdre P784
~ de coordination C712
polygone P782
~ des forces P783
~ funiculaire S899
~ des vecteurs V84
polymères P788
polymérisation P787
polymorphisme P789
polynôme P790
~ orthogonal de Zernike Z8
~ de Zernike Z8
polynômes hermitiens H144
~ de Legendre L173
~ orthogonaux O261
polytrope P792
polytypisme P794
pomeron P797
pompage P1013, P1015
~ par diode D360
~ par faisceau électronique
   E173
~ par lampe L26
~ par lampes-éclairs F179
~ par laser L100
~ nucléaire N388
~ optique O177
~ paramétrique P70
~ solaire S397

~ thermique T137
~ transversal T382
pompe P1013
~ d'adsorption A230
~ à chaleur H97
~ à diffusion D331
~ à getter G148
~ à huile O40
~ moléculaire M595
~ à vide V27
pondération W90
pont B331
~ déphaseur P330
~ double de Kelvin K8
~ de Maxwell M285
~ de Wheatstone W102
~ de Wien W117
population P800
~ d'équilibre E382
~ d'excès E443
~ inverse I368
~ du niveau L191
~ non équilibrée N220
~ stellaire S796
pores P803
porosité P804
portance E282, L202
~ aérodynamique A244
porte-à-faux C35
portée R171
~ de vision R174
porteur C75
~ majoritaire M207
porteurs de charge C199, C964
~ chauds H275
~ équilibrés E372
~ froids C404
~ libres F338
~ minoritaires M501
~ non équilibrés N215
portrait de phase P325
position interstitielle I348
positron P817
positronium P819
positrons thermalisés T130
posteffet élastique E49
postimage A262
postluminescence A261, P264
potassium P820
potentiel P822
~ avancé A231
~ chimique C249
~ cinétique K42
~ de déformation D99
~ de diffusion D330
~ électrique E92
~ électrochimique E123
~ électrostatique E268
~ flottant F200
~ de Gibbs G164
~ d'ionisation I429
~ magnétique M106
~ nucléaire N385

~ optique O170
~ quadridimensionnel F302
~ retardé R468
~ scalaire S45
~ thermodynamique T160
~ thermodynamique de Gibbs
   G164
~ des vitesses V98
~ de Yukawa Y18
potentiels bioélectriques B201
potentiel-vecteur V85
potentiomètre P838
pouce I84
poulie P974
poupée à diviser D522
poussière D610
~ interstellaire I339
~ radioactive R73
poutre B88
pouvoir absorbant A35, A57
~ amplificateur M195
~ d'arrêt S850
~ calorifique C19
~ convergent F250
~ émissif E295
~ grandissant M195
~ de résolution R423
~ de résolution dans le temps
   T257
~ tampon B358
p.p.s. C991
praséodyme P852
préaimantation B174
précession P853
~ de Larmor L53
~ nucléaire N387
~ planétaire P636
précipitation P855, P858, P858
~ de particules P141
précipitations P858
précision P861
~ de la mesure A88
prédissociation P863
préionisation P866
~ ultraviolette U42
prémagnétisation B174
premier principe de la
   thermodynamique F144
~ son F146
pression H66, P868
~ acoustique P876, S463
~ atmosphérique A593
~ barométrique A593
~ capillaire C54
~ de cavitation C129
~ du champ magnétique
   M63
~ de coinçage D420
~ critique C857
~ dynamique D624, V93
~ hydrostatique P873
~ du liquide F221
~ de lumière L237, P874

~ de l'onde électromagnétique E153
~ osmotique O293
~ partielle P106
~ du plasma P681
~ de radiation R50
~ de rayonnement P875, R50
~ sonore A126, S463
~ statique S741
~ superficielle S1079
~ de vapeur V54
~ de vapeur saturée S23
~ du vent solaire S404
preuve d'existence E477
principe anthropique A456
~ d'Archimède A515
~ de Babinet B1
~ du bilan détaillé P900
~ de Carathéodory C62
~ de Carnot C74
~ de complémentarité C500, P899
~ de correspondance C752
~ d'Alembert D3
~ de dualité D604, P901
~ d'équilibre détaillé D201
~ d'équivalence E395
~ d'équivalence masse-énergie P902
~ d'équivalence de masse et énergie P902
~ d'exclusion de Pauli E475, P171
~ de Fermat F51
~ de Franck et Condon F330
~ de Gauss G88
~ de Hamilton H37
~ des images I31
~ d'incertitude I120, U49
~ d'incertitude de Heisenberg H118
~ d'indétermination I120
~ de Le Chatelier L168
~ de maximum de module M281
~ de la moindre action P903
~ de Nernst N72
~ de Neumann N78
~ de Pascal P153
~ de Pauli P171
~ de Rayleigh-Jeans R194
~ de réciprocité R234
~ de la relativité R368
~ de relativité de Galilée G28
~ de superposition S1028
principes variationnels V63
prise de moyen A697
prisme P904
~ d'Amici A323
~ de Cornu C725
~ dispersant D438
~ de Glan-Thompson G167
~ neutronique N146
~ de Nicol N171

~ polariseur P770
~ de réflexion R302
~ de retournement E400
~ spectroscopique S590
~ de Wollaston W140
probabilité P907
~ de collision C442
~ d'état S735
~ de fission F162
~ thermodynamique T161
~ de transition T340
problème P922
~ des deux corps T469
~ de diffusion inverse I371
~ de Dirichlet D396
~ externe O298
~ de fonctions propres E38
~ idéalisé I9
~ incorrectement formulé I20
~ incorrectement posé I20
~ interne I219
~ inverse I369
~ aux limites B291
~ linéaire L266
~ de Neumann N79
~ non stationnaire N303
~ à une particule S316
~ perturbé P270
~ de plusieurs corps M220
~ des trois corps T214
~ de valeurs propres E42
procédé P923
~ adiabatique A213
~ réversible R481
processeur P924
~ optique O173
processus aléatoire S838
~ apériodique N277
~ en chaîne C180
~ cumulatif C952
~ à déroulement rapide H209
~ d'équilibre E383
~ d'inclusion I96
~ irréversible I480
~ isenthalpique I489
~ isentropique I490
~ isobarique I494
~ isochore I499
~ isotherme I546
~ de Markov M226
~ markovien M226
~ multiphononique M694
~ multiphotonique M701
~ multiple M709
~ non leptonique N232
~ non stationnaire N304
~ d'Oppenheimer-Phillips O77
~ photochimique P392
~ photophysique P501
~ profondément inélastique D75
~ quasi stationnaire Q127
~ quasi statique Q125
~ de renversement U47

~ stationnaire S748
~ stochastique S838
~ thermodynamique T162
~ de transition T330
~ de transport T373
production multiparticule M688
~ de particules P142
produit normal N326
~ scalaire S46
~ vectoriel V86
profil en coin W86
~ Doppler D549
~ de Gauss G89
~ Joukowski Z14
~ lorentzien L368
~ d'onde W55
~ de la raie spectrale S557
~ supergaussien S1007
~ des vitesses V99
profondeur D177
~ de champ D179
~ de foyer D179
~ de modulation D180
~ optique O110
~ d'oscillations O274
~ de pénétration D181, P202
projecteur P934
~ électronique E231
~ ionique I457
projection stéréographique S809
propagateur P938
~ à photons P494
propagation par guide d'ondes W35
~ hyperlointaine des ondes radioélectriques U8
~ d'ondes lumineuses O174
~ des ondes radioélectriques R142
~ du son S465
~ sur trajets multiples M691
~ transhorizon O318
propriété multimode M683
propriétés mécaniques M316
~ optiques O175
propulseur photonique P488
~ à plasma P658
propulsion P946
~ à réaction J11
protactinium P947
protection P948, S237, S237
~ biologique B204
~ contre la corrosion C757
~ d'environnement E353
~ du milieu ambiant E353
~ contre la radiation ionisante P949
~ radiochimique R26
protéine P951
protium P952
proto-étoiles P966
protogalaxie P953
proton P954

protoplanètes P965
protubérance P935
~ solaire S396
pseudo-scalaire P968
pseudo-tenseur P969
pseudo-vecteur P970
psychromètre P972
puissance O171, P842
~ acoustique A125
~ active A182
~ d'alimentation S1043
~ du bruit N191
~ de bruit N191
~ de crête P177
~ électrique E114
~ d'entrée I225
~ d'impulsion P1003
~ magnétothermoélectrique M191
~ de pompage P1023
~ de rayonnement R20
~ réactive R217
~ de rupture B319
~ de seuil T227
~ de sortie O304
~ de la source S479
puits S328
~ de potentiel P837
~ quantique Q75
pulsar P975
~ binaire B187
~ à rayons X X41
pulsation P977
pulvérisation cathodique C113
~ ionique I408, S681
~ par ultra-son U31
pupille d'entrée E346
~ de sortie E479
purification par ultra-son U17
pycnomètre P1031
pyramide de croissance G288
pyro-électricité P1035
pyro-électrique P1032
pyromètre P1036
~ bichromatique B177
~ en couleurs C461
~ optique O178, R52
~ photo-électrique P422
~ à radiation R52
~ thermo-électrique T175
pyrométrie P1037
~ optique O179

Q

Q-facteur F113
Q-mètre Q4
quadrant Q8
quadrature Q11
quadri-impulsion F301
quadripôle Q13

~ acoustique A129
~ axial A706
~ électrostatique E269
~ de focalisation F265
~ magnétique M108
quadruple Q12
qualité Q22
~ acousto-optique A156
~ du fini de surface S1066
quantification Q29
~ du champ F107
~ dimensionnelle S334
~ de Dirac D375
~ de l'énergie E328
~ de l'espace-temps S508
~ du flux F241
~ du flux magnétique M68
~ des fluxoïdes F240
~ d'une impulsion M617
~ des orbites O233
~ de la résistance de Hall H27
~ secondaire S109
~ spatiale S500
~ des spins S646
quantimètre Q32
quantisation dimensionnelle D348
quantité Q26
~ de chaleur Q28
~ d'électricité Q27
~ de mouvement M613
quantron Q33
quantum Q34
~ absorbé A31
~ diffusé S63
~ dur H46
~ émis E298
~ de flux F242
~ de flux magnétique F242, M69
~ gamma G36
~ induit I141, S827
~ d'interaction faible W72
~ de lumière P482
~ oscillatoire V119
~ de rayonnement R53
~ de rayonnement X X42
~ de rotation R552
~ stimulé S827
quark Q79
~ charmé C234
~ constituant C622
~ de couleur C462
~ de courant C971
~ droit R506
~ étrange S866
~ gauche L171
~ lourd H109
~ marin S101
~ sans masse M243
~ de relique R382
~ spectateur S543
~ t T279

~ u U101
~ valent V38
~ vrai T424
quarkonium Q88
quartet Q92
~ spectral S562
quartz Q93
~ piézo-électrique P582
~ synthétique S1129
quasage Q98
quasar Q99, Q129
quasi-coordonnées Q102
quasi-cristal Q103
quasi-deutéron Q104
quasi-énergie Q107
quasi-équilibre Q108
quasi-impulsion Q116
~ du phonon P374
quasi-mode Q114
quasi-molécule Q115
quasi-neutralité Q117
~ du plasma P683
quasi-niveau Q112
~ de Fermi Q110
quasi-optique Q119
quasi-particule Q120
quasi-potentiel Q123
quasi-résonance Q124
quasi-trou Q111
quaternion Q131
quatrième son F314
queue de la comète C481, T4
~ de magnétosphère M185
quintet Q139
~ spectral S563

R

racine carrée S685
rad R4
radar R5
~ laser L101
~ optique L198, O180
radian R9
radiance R10
radiateur R67
~ absolu A20
~ acoustique A130
~ bêta B151, B159
~ de Cherenkov C260
~ cohérent C392
~ dipolaire D369
~ à guide d'ondes W36
~ intégral F419
~ isotrope I574
~ à lentille L177
~ noir C502
~ omnidirectionnel O45
~ parfait P224
~ primaire P882
~ quadripolaire Q19

~ dans le vide V8
~ sous vide V8
~ au vide V8
recul R236
récupérateur R267
redressement R264
~ par couche d'arrêt B67
redresseur R265
~ à une alternance H22
~ diphasé F421
~ à oxyde de cuivre C715
~ au sélénium S143
réduction R279
~ des forces R280
réflecteur R292, R306
~ acoustique A133
~ en coin C724
~ distribué D502
~ réparti D502
réflexibilité R305
réflexion R293
~ acoustique S470
~ de Bragg B307
~ diffuse D312
~ interne I327
~ interne totale T303
~ de la lumière R300
~ d'onde W56
~ des ondes radioélectriques R301
~ régulière S598
~ spéculaire M513
~ totale T306
~ totale interne frustrée F414
réflexions aurores A674
réfracteur R313
réfraction R314, R325
~ anormale A446
~ atmosphérique A595
~ conique C599
~ côtière C352
~ de la lumière R316
~ moléculaire M596
~ nucléaire N396
~ d'ondes W57
~ des ondes radioélectriques R317
~ du son R318
~ spécifique S535
réfractomètre R321
~ d'Abbe A1
réfractométrie R322
réfrigérateur thermo-électrique T176
réfrigération R324
refroidissement C698, R324
~ par désaimantation adiabatique C699
~ des faisceaux B92
~ magnétique M39
~ optique O105
~ thermo-électrique T172
régénération R326, R405

~ des matériaux de fission B322
reggeon R329
région R332
~ active A184
~ anodique A439
~ à connexion multiple M724
~ de couche limite I291
~ D D584
~ de diffusion élastique E66
~ de diffusion inélastique I164
~ E E402
~ d'énergie E330
~ d'énergies intermédiaires I311
~ d'épuisement D170
~ F F359
~ de faibles énergies L387
~ focale F251
~ des hautes énergies H187
~ d'impureté I81
~ infrarouge I201
~ infrarouge lointaine F27
~ infrarouge proche N33
~ d'interaction I269
~ ionosphérique I453
~ n N339
~ p P865
~ perturbée D513
~ séismique S129
~ spectrale S565, S566
~ de stabilité S695
~ ultraviolette U44
~ ultraviolette proche N37
~ visible V172
réglage de foyer F261
règle d'Ampère C723
~ de Geiger-Nuttall G93
~ de la main droite R505
~ de la main gauche L170
~ de Matthiessen M276
~ des phases G162, P327
~ des phases de Gibbs G162
~ de sommes S966
~ de tire-bouchon C723
~ des trois doigts de la main gauche L170
~ de Zweig Z26
règles de sélection S132
régression R333
régularité F183
relais électronique E206
relation D162, R339
~ de Clapeyron C310
~ de Descartes-Snell S359
~ de Goldberger-Treiman G192
~ d'incertitude U50
~ d'incertitude de Heisenberg H119
~ de Kramers-Kronig K68
~ linéaire L256
~ masse-luminosité M244
~ non linéaire N237
~ période-luminosité P235
~ viscosité/température D163

relations de commutation C488
~ de dispersion D450
~ de Gibbs-Helmholtz G160
~ de Manley-Rowe M215
~ de Maxwell M292
~ d'Onsager O55
~ de paracommutation P25
~ de permutation P257
relativité R367
~ générale G107
relaxation D78, R370
~ acoustique A134
~ croisée C870
~ magnétique M113
~ nucléaire N397
~ paramagnétique P47
~ spin-muon M745
~ spin-réseau S630
~ des tensions S892
~ thermique T140
relief potentiel P833
rem R529
rémanence A260
remplacement moléculaire M597
remplissage des états O15
~ d'un niveau F118
~ des niveaux L190
~ partiel P102
~ des zones Z22
rendement E34
~ de luminescence L422
~ mécanique M309
~ de neutrons N163
~ quantique Q46, Q78
~ de réaction R213
~ thermique T107
rendu des couleurs C463
renforçateur d'image I29
renforcement R338
~ brusque des atmosphériques S959
rénormalisabilité R395
rénormalisation R397
renversement des raies du spectre R475
réorientation R401
~ du spin S627
répartition angulaire A398
~ canonique C30
~ de l'énergie par spectre D509
~ spectrale S550
repère M224
réplique R404
réponse R454
~ amplitude-amplitude A352
~ non linéaire N262
représentation M222
~ configurationnelle C579
~ conforme C587
~ graphique G217
~ impulsionnelle I69
~ irréductible I475, N288
~ de Mandelstam M211

~ solide de substitution S948
~ sursaturée S1032
~ tampon B359
solvant S429
solvatation S428
sommet T272
~ étroit N11
son S438, T270
~ harmonique O319
~ ionique I458
~ transversal T383
~ au zéro absolu Z13
sonage sous-marin S431
sonar S431
sondage S453
~ acoustique E14
~ à distance R392
~ Doppler D551
~ par fusées R522
~ ionosphérique I455
~ ionosphérique par diffusion en retour B13
~ ionosphérique vertical V107
~ laser L108
~ du plasma P682
sonde P915, S432, S438
~ acoustique A127
~ atomique A632
~ électrique double D564
~ électronique E230
~ de Langmuir L39
sonoluminescence S435
sonomètre S460
sons de combinaison C472
~ différentiels D264
~ résultants S967
sorption S436
sortie de fluorescence F223
soudage W97
~ laser L122
soufflerie W129
soufre S965
source S477
~ d'alimentation P847
~ de brouillages N192
~ de calibrage C13
~ cathodoluminescente C115
~ de chaleur H101
~ cohérente C394
~ cosmique C776
~ de courant C973
~ de courant d'intensité élevée H182
~ à décharge gazeuse G63
~ diffuse D314
~ de dislocations D429
~ d'électroluminescence E139
~ d'électrons E238
~ d'émission monochromatique M624
~ d'énergie E332
~ étalon S715
~ étendue D503, E518

~ d'étincelles S517
~ d'excitation E461
~ extragalactique E529
~ du faisceau atomique A609
~ de faisceau moléculaire M571
~ galactique G24
~ de haute voltage H220
~ à impulsions P990
~ incohérente I103
~ d'infrarouge I202
~ d'interférence I302
~ ionisante I431
~ d'ionisation I431
~ d'ions I460
~ d'isotopes I554
~ laser L109
~ de lumière L243
~ de lumière fluorescente F224
~ lumineuse V183
~ de neutron N153
~ de neutrons thermiques T135
~ optique O192
~ de photons P497
~ du plasma P686
~ de pompage P1027
~ ponctuelle D413, P723
~ quasi stellaire Q130
~ radioactive R85
~ de radionucléides ouverte B50
~ de rayonnement R55
~ de rayonnement ionisant I441
~ de rayonnement synchrotron S1121
~ des rayons alpha A304
~ de rayons bêta B159
~ des rayons cosmiques C774
~ de rayons gamma G45
~ de rayons X X46
~ des rayons X cosmiques C777
~ de reconstruction R254
~ de référence R283
~ renouvelable R394
~ scellée S99
~ sonore S472
~ spectrométrique S578
~ standard CIE C291
~ stationnaire S749
~ de sursauts de rayons gamma G41
~ de tension V196
~ de tourbillonnement V222
~ d'ultraviolet U45
~ X X46
sources d'énergie alternatives A311
sous-couche S932, S941
sous-espace S944
sous-groupe S927
sous-harmonique S928
sous-multiples S938
sous-niveau S933
~ inférieur L390
~ de rotation-vibration V123

~ de Stark S728
~ supérieur U102
~ de vibration V126
~ Zeeman Z4
sous-orage géomagnétique M129
~ magnétique M129
sous-quark S940
sous-refroidissement O308, S992
sous-réseau S930
~ magnétique M128
~ nucléaire N403
sous-structure S952
sous-système S953
~ rapide F32
sous-tempête S950
spectateur S541
spectre S593
~ d'absorption A56
~ d'absorption des rayons X X6
~ d'absorption X X6
~ acoustique S473
~ d'arc A519
~ bêta B162
~ de bruits N193
~ caractéristique C195
~ continu C655, C658
~ discret D414
~ d'émission E294
~ d'émission des rayons X X21
~ d'émission X X21
~ d'énergie E333
~ d'étincelle S518
~ de flamme F172
~ de fréquences F386
~ de masse M253
~ moléculaire M600
~ Mössbauer M650
~ optique O195
~ phononique P376
~ de phonons P376
~ de raies L276
~ Raman R160
~ de rayonnement R56
~ du rayonnement gamma G48
~ des rayons X X50
~ de réflexion R303
~ de rotation R554
~ rotationnel R554
~ solaire S400
~ sonore S473
~ de vibration V125
spectres atomiques A636
~ de bande B41
~ électroniques E208
~ électroniques vibrationnels E210
~ stellaires S800
~ vibroniques V137
spectrofluoromètre S572
spectrogramme S573
spectrographe S574

SPECTROGRAPHE

~ de masse M249
~ à prisme P906
~ à prismes P906
spectrohéliographe S576
spectromètre S577
~ alpha A305
~ bêta B160
~ de Fourier F310
~ gamma G46
~ magnétique M124
~ de masse M250
~ de masse analytique A372
~ de masse à temps de transit T255
~ Mössbauer M648
~ neutronique N154
~ optique O193
~ à paires P13
~ à rayons bêta B160
~ à rayons X X47
~ à réseau G229
~ de Rydberg R581
~ à temps de transit T256
spectrométrie S579
~ de masse M251
~ de masse à désorption par laser L66
~ de masse des ions secondaires S107
~ neutronique N155
~ photographique P449
spectrophotomètre S580
spectrophotométrie S583
~ d'absorption A54
spectropolarimètre S584
spectroradiomètre S585
spectroscope S586
spectroscopie S592
~ d'absorption A55
~ acoustique A140
~ acousto-optique A158
~ alpha A306
~ atomique A637
~ atomique et moléculaire A606
~ Auger A663
~ bêta B161
~ cohérente C395
~ cohérente anti-Stokes Raman C384
~ des cristaux C936
~ d'émission E293
~ excitonique E474
~ de Fourier F311
~ gamma G47
~ infrarouge I203
~ laser L111
~ laser intracavité I353
~ de masse M252
~ en micro-ondes M484
~ moléculaire M599
~ Mössbauer M649
~ multiphotonique M702
~ non linéaire N263

~ nucléaire N400
~ optique O194
~ opto-acoustique O217
~ photo-électrique P423
~ de photo-électrons P430
~ par photo-ionisation P459
~ à photo-ionisation laser L92
~ picoseconde P549
~ à pouvoir de résolution dans le temps T258
~ Raman R159
~ aux rayons X X49
~ submillimétrique S936
~ ultraviolette U46
~ d'ultraviolet à vide V31
~ à vide V28
sphère S601
~ céleste C143
sphéroïde S613
sphérolite S615
sphéromètre S614
spicules S616
spike S617
spin S619
~ de l'électron E239
~ isobarique I495
~ du neutron N156
~ nucléaire N401
spin-écho S623
spinelle S624
spineur S635
~ sphérique S610
spinthariscope S652
spirale H134, S657
~ de Cornu C726
spire T456
spot S676
~ cathodique C112
spurion S679
squelette de cristal D149
squid S688, S983
stabilisateur S697
stabilisation S696
~ de courant C974
~ de fréquence F388
~ de tension V197
stabilité S690
~ de couche limite S693
~ de durée réduite S261
~ dynamique D630
~ d'équilibre S694
~ de la fréquence F387
~ à long terme L351
~ du mouvement M655
~ d'oscillations O280
~ de phase P337
~ du plasma P689
standard S707
~ de fréquence F389
~ de fréquence de faisceau atomique A608
statique S742
statistique S768

~ de Boltzmann B257
~ de Bose B280
~ classique C319
~ de Fermi et Dirac F54
~ d'Ornstein-Uhlenbeck O253
~ de photons P498
~ physique P539
~ quantique Q70
stellarateur S784
stéradian S806
stéréo-isomérie S810
stéréobêtatron S807
stéréochimie S808
stéréophonie S811
stéréoscopie S813
stilb S816
stochasticité S836
stochastisation S840
stœchiométrie S843
stockage des déchets radioactifs B377
stokes S844
strates S868
stratification S869
stratopause S871
stratosphère S872
streamer S876
striction orthogonal T198
~ toroïdale T285
stroboscope S904
strontium S911
structure P168
~ de l'atome A639
~ atomique A639
~ atomique magnétique M26
~ en bande B42
~ compacte C341
~ cristalline C937
~ cubique C949
~ décélératrice S351
~ du diamant D238
~ fine F133
~ hélicoïdale H122
~ hétérophase H162
~ hexagonale compacte H169
~ incommensurable I106
~ magnétique M127
~ magnétique de domaines M51
~ magnétique hyperfine M74
~ mesa M351
~ mesa diffusée D307
~ métal-diélectrique-semi-conducteur M377
~ métal-oxyde-semi-conducteur M388
~ de modes M540
~ moléculaire M601
~ de molécule M601
~ mosaïque M643
~ du neutron N158
~ serrée C341
~ topologique T275
~ du type perowskite P259

~ thermo-élastique T171
tensomètre T56
téphigramme T61
terbium T62
terme T63
~ nucléaire N358
~ spectral T63
termes spectraux S571
terminal T64
terrasse continentale C640
terre E2, E3, G271
Terre E3
terres rares R181
tesla T66
teslamètre T67
«têtard» T2
tête H66
~ photométrique P471
tétrode T73
texture T74
~ magnétique M134
thallium T75
théorème d'Ampère A339
~ d'Archimède A515
~ de Bloch B231
~ de Clausius-C320
~ CPT C827
~ fondamental de Cauchy C119
~ de Gauss G90
~ de Kramers K69
~ de Liouville L279
~ de Mermin-Wagner M349
~ de Nernst N72
~ de Noether N183
~ d'Onsager O56
~ optique O203
~ de Pauli P174
~ de Peierls P189
~ de Pomerantchouk P796
~ de Poynting P848
~ d'unicité U71
~ du viriel V148
~ de Wick W112
théorie des bandes B43
~ du champ F110
~ du champ quantique non
   polynomiale N279
~ de champ quantique non
   rénormalisable N294
~ des champs quantique
   axiomatique A710
~ des champs unifée U61
~ cinétique des gaz K51
~ des circuits électriques E78
~ du corps solide de Debye
   D48
~ corpusculaire de la lumière
   C738
~ de l'élasticité T79
~ électronique E242
~ de Ginsburg-Landau G166
~ de l'image I34
~ de l'information I194

~ magnéto-ionique M165
~ de Mie M487
~ des perturbations P268
~ des perturbations
   rénormalisée R400
~ phénoménologique P357
~ des probabilités P913
~ des quanta du champ Q49
~ quantique Q73
~ quantique du champ non
   linéaire N261
~ quantique du champ non
   locale N271
~ quasi linéaire Q113
~ de la relativité R369, T81
~ de la relativité générale G107
~ rénormalisable R396
~ des réseaux N76
~ de la similitude S296
~ de Sommerfeld S430
~ spéciale de la relativité S530
~ de transitions de phase de
   Landau L33
~ de Weinberg-Salam W92
théories de jauge G10
thérapie bêta B163
~ laser L116
~ ultrasonique U34
thermalisation des neutrons
   T129
thermistance T150
thermistor T150
thermo-analyse T82
thermo-élasticité T170
thermo-électron T109
thermochimie laser L117
thermocouple T151
thermodynamique T163
~ des processus irréversibles
   I481
~ relativiste R365
~ statistique S766
thermoluminescence T180
thermomètre T184
~ à gaz G78
~ à liquide L286
~ à mercure M347
~ à résistance R417
thermométrie T185
thermorégulateur T193
thermosphère T194
thermostat T195
thermostriction T197
thermoviseur T123
thermovision T124
thêta-pinch T198
thixotropie T211
thorium T213
thulium T233
thyratron T234
thyristor T235
tige R524
«tiling» de Penrose P206

timbre T239
titane T265
tokamak T266
tomographie T269
~ aux rayons X X54
~ par voie d'ordinateur C537
ton T270
~ normal N328
tonne T271
topographie aux rayons X X55
topologie T277
toponium T278
torr T289
torseur W145
torsion T291, T464
~ de flexion B139
~ pure S299
~ simple S299
~ des tiges R526
TOS S717
T.O.S.C. C975
TOST V198
touche K20
toupie T272
tour T456
tourbillon C960, E22, V211
~ asservi B297
~ quantifié Q31
tourbillonnement V221
trace T312
~ d'une matrice S680
traceur isotopique I567
~ radioactif R78
traction D580
train d'impulsions P1008,
   P1011
traînage magnétique M20
traînée D580
~ aérodynamique A248
traitement des données D23
~ des données en temps réel
   R229
~ par faisceau électronique
   E172
~ laser L96
~ optique de l'information O108
~ thermique T145
trajectoire P164, T317
~ de Bohr B244
~ circulaire C302
~ d'une particule P146
~ de phase P321, P342
trajet optique O166
trame R184
tranche W1
transducteur magnétostrictif
   M190
~ de mesure T320
transfert T321
~ de la chaleur H102
~ de chaleur convectif C679
~ de la charge C230
~ d'énergie E335

~ de masse M254
~ néoclassique N61
~ non radiatif N283
~ parallèle P42
~ parallèle des données P38
~ de la quantité de mouvement M619
~ du rayonnement R58
~ thermique H85, H104
transformateur T325
~ de courant C976
transformation M222, T323
~ adiabatique A204
~ canonique C34
~ conforme C588
~ de Fourier F312
~ de Fourier inverse I367
~ de fréquence F391
~ de Hilbert H222
~ intégrale I253
~ irréversible I482
~ de jauge G11
~ de Laplace L46
~ linéaire L268
~ de Lorentz L370
~ de Mellin M335
~ non linéaire N266
~ d'ondes W62
~ ordre-désordre O235
~ polytropique P793
~ structurale S919
~ de superjauge S1006
~ de symétrie S1108
transformations de Galilée G27
~ martensitiques M229
~ de phases P344
transistor T334
~ à effet de champ F111
transition T335
~ de deux photons T490
~ diélectruqie - métal D256
~ électronique E243
~ à l'état supraconducteur S988
~ à l'état superfluide S1005
~ faible W78
~ faiblement défendue W75
~ fragile/ductile B339
~ par gradins S805
~ indirecte N311
~ interdite par parité P92
~ intrabande I351
~ laser L119
~ liée-liée B292
~ de Morin M640
~ de Mott M660
~ multiphotonique M703
~ non adiabatique N197
~ non défendue U57
~ non favorisée U56
~ non radiative N284
~ optique O207
~ de Peierls P190
~ de percolation P213

~ permise A295, P251
~ de phase P345
~ de phase «nématique-smectique» N59
~ de phase du deuxième ordre P349
~ de phase induite par laser L79
~ de phase induite par la lumière L224
~ de phase du premier ordre P348
~ photo-induite de Friedericksz P452
~ quantique Q74
~ quantique double D572
~ sans radiation R46
~ radiative R66
~ de recombinaison R249
~ de résonance R451
~ avec retournement de spin S626
~ réversible R482
~ de rotation R556
~ de rotation-vibration V124
~ rotatoinnelle R556
~ de spin S653
~ spontanée S675
~ stimulée S831
~ superradiante S1030
~ tunnel T442
~ verticale V109
~ virtuelle V156
transitions directes D395
~ indirectes I128
~ interbandes I279
~ d'intercombinaison I285
~ intervalées I350
~ de phase magnétiques M103
~ de phase non équilibrées N218
~ de phase d'orientation O251
~ de phase structurales S918
~ à relaxation R378
translation T346
transmetteur T357
~ de température T45
transmission T350
~ sélective S140
transmutation T358
transparence T362
~ auto-induite S163
~ de la barrière de potentiel B69
transport T368
~ de la chaleur H102
travail W141
~ maximum M282
tremblement J12
~ d'image I30
~ d'impulsion P999
~ de terre E5
trempe Q133

~ de concentration C543
~ au laser L77
~ superficielle S1068
très haute pression U6
triangle des couleurs C278
~ de couleurs de Maxwell M286
tribo-électricité F401, T400
tribologie T402
triboluminescence T403
trigatron T406
trigger T407
~ optique O208
triode T410
triple point T411
triplet T412
tritium T413
triton T415
trochotron T416
troisième principe de la thermodynamique N72, T209
~ son T210
tropopause T418
troposphère T419
trou H227, O65
~ blanc W108
~ coronal C731
~ noir B220
trous chauds H280
tube P600, T425, V44
~ d'accélération A64
~ amplificateur de réception R231
~ calorique H96
~ cathodique C110, E175
~ de choc S246
~ de courant F243, T426
~ à décharge gazeuse D404
~ de dérive D591
~ électronique E246
~ à onde progressive T396
~ à onde régressive B17
~ oscillateur O270
~ de Pitot P613
~ à rayons X X56
~ régulateur de tension à vide V195
~ stabilovolt V194
~ Venturi V102
~ de Venturi V102
tungstène T429, W138
tunnel aérodynamique W129
turbidité T443
turbine T445
~ à gaz G79
turbulence T446
~ atmosphérique A600
~ microscopique M471
~ du plasma P694
tuyau calorique H96
tuyère N337
~ de Laval L148

U

u.a. A567
ultra-acoustique U29
ultra-haut vide U7
ultra-hautes fréquences M477
ultra-microscope U9
ultra-son U37
ultrasonique U29
ultravide U7
ultraviolet à vide V30
u.m.a. A625
unification U60
uniformité U65
unité U72
~ Angström A393
~ astronomique A567
~ dérivée D184
~ logique optique O147
~ de masse atomique A625
~ rydberg R577
~ de volume U81
unités absolues A24
~ arbitraires A511
~ C.G.S. C178
~ multiples M713
~ photométriques P477
~ physiques P540
~ SI S332
~ sous-multiples S938
Univers U84
~ chaud H285
~ clos C337
~ de de-Sitter D191
~ expansif E486
~ en expansion E486
~ fermé C337
~ ouvert O66
~ stationnaire S752
univibrateur S320
uranium U104
Uranus U105
usine pilote P583
usure abrasive A10
~ par cavitation C130
~ par corrosion C759
~ corrosive C759
~ due à l'électro-érosion E132
~ par fatigue F40
utilisation du faisceau U107
~ pacifique de l'énergie
   atomique P175

V

vacance V1
vacansion V5
vacuité V185
vacuomètre V21
valence V41

valeur V43
~ absolue A25
~ adimensionnée D352
~ approximative A508
~ arbitraire A512
~ de crête C838, P178
~ effective E32
~ efficace R533
~ extrême E536
~ frontière B290
~ instantanée I237
~ moyenne A696
~ moyenne quadratique R533
~ non dimensionnelle D352
~ pH P276
~ propre E41
~ réelle A25
vallée V42
~ de la bande de conduction
   C563
valve V44
vanadium V45
vapeur V49
~ d'eau S774, W8
~ humide W100
~ saturée S22
~ surchauffée S1010
~ sursaturée S1033
vaporisation E430, V51
var V56
variable V57, V61
~ aléatoire R168
~ à éclipse E19
~ à flare F176
~ indépendante I119
~ du type UV Ceti F176
variance V62
~ de grandeur aléatoire R170
variateur de phase P331
variation annuelle A430
~ diurne D1
~ lumineuse L244
~ relativiste de la masse R358
~ avec le temps T261
variations V65
~ de courte période S255
~ diurnes D514
~ géomagnétiques G127
~ magnétiques M136
~ de rayons cosmiques C775
~ séculaires S120
varicap V66
variété M213
variomètre V68
~ magnétique M137
varistance V69
vase Dewar D220
vases communicants C484
vecteur V70
~ de l'aimantation M144
~ axial A707
~ de Burgers B376
~ d'état S736, V82

~ du genre espace S498
~ de glissement de Burgers
   B376
~ de Hertz H149
~ ket K19
~ de nombre d'onde circulaire
   P937
~ d'onde W63
~ d'onde circulaire P937
~ de polarisation P755
~ de Poynting P849
~ de propagation P937
~ propre E43
~ quadridimensionnel F303
~ unitaire U80
véhicule aérospatial S509
~ cosmique S509
vélocité de réaction chimique
   C251
vent U125
~ acoustique A145
~ d'éther E420
~ solaire S403
~ stellaire S801
Vénus V103
verre G169
~ métallique M379
~ optique O126
verres laser L74
~ de spin S628
verrouillage des modes M533
vibrateur V133
vibration V112
~ de cisaillement S228
~ d'une corde V131
~ infrasonore I205
~ longitudinale L340
~ moléculaire M604
~ des molécules M604
~ du réseau cristallin C910
vibrations V112
~ acoustiques S475
~ de flexion F194
~ du réseau L143
~ des tiges R527
~ de torsion T294
~ ultrasonores U35
~ de valence V40
vibron V134
vide V7, V185
~ parfait P225
~ de Torricelli T290
vidicon V141
vie L201
~ moyenne M296
vieillissement magnétique M21
vignettage V143
violation V145
~ de l'invariance I363
~ de la parité P95
~ de la parité combinée C475
~ de symétrie S1103
vis cinématique K31

W

X

Y

Z

РУССКИЙ

А

аксиальный вектор A707,
    P970
~ квадруполь A706
~ ток A701
аксиома A708
аксиоматическая квантовая
    теория поля A710
аксиоматический метод A709
аксион A711
аксоид A718
активатор A175
~ люминофора O83, P379
активационный анализ A172,
    R68
~ метод A174
активация A171
активированный катод A169
активная зона C719
~ зона реактора R223
~ модуляция добротности
    A183
~ мощность A182
~ нагрузка R418
~ область A184
~ проводимость C559
~ синхронизация мод A181
~ среда A179
активное вещество A185
~ зеркало A192
~ напряжение A186
~ сопротивление R415
активность A187
~ источника S478
активные дни A177
активный диполь A178
~ ток A176
актинид A163
актиний A162
актиничность A161
актиничный свет A159
актиноид A163
актинометр A164
актинометрия A165
акустика A137
~ движущихся сред A138
акустическая волна A142
~ голография A110
~ дифракционная решётка
    A109
~ задержка A101
~ кавитация A97
~ коагуляция A98
~ линза A116
~ линия задержки A102
~ мощность A125
~ нелинейность A121
~ проводимость A100
~ релаксация A134
~ спектроскопия A140
акустические волны A95
~ измерения A117
~ колебания A141, S475
акустический ветер A145

~ волновод A143
~ дальномер S468
~ детектор A103
~ диполь A104
~ зонд A127
~ излучатель A130
~ импеданс A113
~ импульс A128, S466
~ интерферометр A115
~ квадруполь A129
~ концентратор A99
~ локатор A139
~ микроскоп A118
~ парамагнитный резонанс
    A124
~ пробой A96
~ радиометр A131
~ резонатор A136
~ рефлектор A133
~ фильтр A107
~ шум A120
~ ядерный магнитный
    резонанс A122
акустическое зеркало A119
~ изображение A111
~ поле S450
~ сопротивление A135
~ течение A108
акустооптика A157
акустооптическая дифракция
    U25
~ модуляция A154
~ спектроскопия A158
акустооптический дефлектор
    A150
~ коррелятор A152
~ модулятор A155
~ эффект A153
акустооптическое
    взаимодействие A151
~ качество A156
акустоэлектрический домен
    A146
~ эффект A147
акустоэлектроника A149
акустоэлектронное
    взаимодействие A148
акцептор A73
акцепторная примесь A73
акцепторный уровень A76
~ центр A75
алгебра A284
~ Грассмана G223
~ Ли L199
~ логики B269
~ токов C962
александрит A282
алидада A285
алихна A316
аллобар A289
аллотропия A292
аллотропная модификация
    A291

алмаз D233
алмазная наковальня D234
алмазный детектор D235
~ индентор D236
альбедо A281
~ космических лучей C768
~ нейтронов N104
альвеновские волны A283
альтернативные источники
    энергии A311
альтиметр A312
альтиметрия A313
альфа-активный изотоп A297
альфа-излучение A301
альфа-лучи A301, A303
альфа-распад A298
альфа-спектрометр A305
альфа-спектроскопия A306
альфа-стабильный изотоп
    A307
альфа-частица A299
алюминий A315
алюмо-иттриевый гранат Y16
AM A362
амбиполярная диффузия
    A320
америций A322
аминокислота A325
аммиачный мазер A326
аморфизирующая добавка
    A328
аморфное вещество A336
~ состояние A335
аморфный кластер A329
~ конденсат A330
~ кремний A334
~ магнетик A331
~ материал A332
~ металл A333
ампер A337
ампер-весы C963
ампер-витки A340
амперметр A324
амплитуда A351, C838, M198,
    P178
~ вероятности P908
~ импульса P980
~ колебаний O272
~ рассеяния S67
амплитудная голограмма
    A359
~ модуляция A362
~ характеристика A352
амплитудное детектирование
    A353
амплитудно-импульсная
    модуляция P983
амплитудно-модулированные
    колебания A361
амплитудно-частотная
    характеристика F384
амплитудные искажения
    A356

амплитудный анализатор
импульсов P996
~ детектор A354
~ дискриминатор A355
~ ограничитель A360
амфотерный электролит A342
анализ A367
~ звука S442
~ размерностей D347
анализатор A375
~ гармоник H49
~ речи S599
~ спектра S595
аналитическая зависимость
A369
~ функция A371, H252
аналитические весы A368
аналитический масс-
спектрометр A372
~ метод A373
~ сигнал A374
аналитическое продолжение
A370
аналогия A366
аналоговый фильтр A364
аналого-цифровой
преобразователь A365
анаморфот A377
анаморфотная насадка A376
анастигмат A378
анастигматическая линза
A378
ангармонизм A408
ангармоническая молекула
A409
ангармонические колебания
A410
ангармонический осциллятор
A411
ангстрем A393
андерсоновская локализация
A379
анемометр A383
анизотропия A419
~ магнитных свойств A422
~ упругих свойств A421, E50
~ формы F288, S217
анизотропная модель
Вселенной A416
~ среда A415
анизотропное вещество A418
~ излучение A414
~ рассеяние A417
анизотропный кристалл A413
анион A412
аннигиляционное излучение
A428
аннигиляционные потери
A426
аннигиляция A425
~ электронно-позитронных
пар A427
анод A431, P702

анодирование A441
анодная область A439
~ характеристика A432
анодное детектирование A435
~ напряжение A440
~ падение A437
~ свечение A438
~ тёмное пространство A434
анодный ток A433
аномалии силы тяжести G253
аномалия A449
аномалон A442
аномальная вязкость A447
~ дисперсия A443
~ рефракция A446
аномальное излучение A445
аномальный магнитный
момент A444
~ эффект Зеемана A448
ансамбль E342
антенна A234
~ бегущей волны T394
~ типа «волновой канал» Y1
антенная решётка A235
антенный фидер A453
~ шум A237
антибарион A457
антивещество A471
антигруппировка фотонов
P483
антикатод A458
антикварк A480
антикоммутатор A462
антикоррозионный материал
A463
антиматерия A471
антинейтрино A473
антинейтрон A474
антинуклон A476
антипротон A479
антисегнетоэлектрик A465
антисимметрия A484
антистоксова компонента
A482
~ линия A483
антиферромагнетизм A470
антиферромагнетик A466
антиферромагнитное
упорядочение A468
антиферромагнитный домен
A467
~ резонанс A469
антициклон A464
античастица A478
антропный принцип A456
апекс A496
апериодические колебания
A488
апериодический контур A485
апериодическое движение
A487
апериодичность A486
апертура A489

апертурная диафрагма A490
апертурные искажения A491
апертурный интегратор A492
~ синтез A495
апланат A499
апланатическая линза A499
апогей A503
аподизация A502
апохромат A501
апохроматическая линза A501
аппаратура E389
аппроксимация A509
~ Вайскопфа - Вигнера W95
~ Паде P3
аргон A523
Аргоннская Национальная
лаборатория A525
аргоновый лазер A524
ареометр A521, D150
армирование R338
армко-железо A529
аромат F184
архимедова сила B372, B373
архитектурная акустика A517
асимметричная молекула
A570
асимметрия A572
асимптота A573
асимптотическая зависимость
A574
~ свобода A576
асимптотический ряд A577
асимптотическое разложение
A575
ассоциативная ионизация
A542
~ рекомбинация A543
ассоциативность A544
астат A546
астеризм A547
астероид A548, M502
астигматизм A549
~ глаза A551
астоново тёмное пространство
A552
астробиология A553
астрограф A556
астрографическая камера
A556
астроклимат A554
астролябия A558
астрометрия A559
астрономическая единица
A567
~ колориметрия A561
~ обсерватория A563
астрономические
инструменты A562
астрономический календарь
A560
~ телескоп A566
астрономия A568
астроспектроскопия A565

В

~ нагрев плазмы R486
~ разряд H197
высота A314, H114
~ звука P612
~ над уровнем моря H115
~ потенциального барьера B64
высотомер A312
выстраивание A286
~ ядерных спинов N402
высшие гармоники H188
~ уровни H189
высыпание P858
~ частиц P141
высыпающиеся ионы P857
~ электроны P856
выталкивающая сила B372, B373
вытесненная жидкость D457
выход люминесценции L422
~ нейтронов N163
~ реакции R213
~ флуоресценции F223
выходная мощность O304
выходное зеркало E478
~ напряжение O307
выходной зрачок E479
~ каскад O305
~ контур O303
выходные зажимы O306
вычет R414
вычисление C8
вычислительная машина C538
вязкая жидкость V167
вязкий поток V165
вязкое демпфирование V163
~ течение V165
вязкостное демпфирование V163
~ сопротивление V168
вязкость V162
вязкоупругая деформация V157
~ жидкость V159
вязкоупругость V158

Г

габитус H1
гадолиний G2
газ G52
газоанализатор G55
газовая динамика G65
~ постоянная G56
~ смесь G66
~ струя G72
~ туманность G67
~ турбина G79
~ фаза G68
~ хроматография G76

газовое усиление G53
газовый анализ G54
~ лазер G73
~ поток G71
~ разряд G57
~ термометр G78
газодинамика G65
газодинамический лазер G64
газообразное вещество G69
~ состояние вещества G68
газопоглотитель G147
газопроницаемость G74
газоразрядная камера G58
~ лампа D403, D404
~ плазма G62
~ трубка D404
газоразрядный источник G63
~ источник света G63
~ лазер G61
~ прибор G60
газоструйный излучатель H63, J9
газотрон G70
галактика G25
галактические космические лучи G17
галактический диск G18
~ источник G24
~ мазер G20
~ центр G15
галактическое гало G19
~ излучение G22
галлий G29
галлон G30
гало H29
галогены H30
гальванический элемент E121
гальванолюминесценция G32
гальваномагнитные явления G33
гальванометр G34
гамильтониан H32
гамильтонов формализм H33
гамильтонова калибровка H31
~ система H35
гамма G35
гамма-астрономия G38
гамма-всплески G40
гамма-дефектоскопия G42
гамма-излучение G44
гамма-квант G36
гамма-лазер G43
гамма-лучи G44
гамма-спектрометр G46
гамма-спектроскопия G47
гармоника H48
гармоническая функция H52
гармонические колебания H55, H56, S330
гармонический анализ H50
~ осциллятор H57
~ ряд H58
гармоническое движение H55

гартмановская диафрагма H60
гартмановское течение H61
гаситель Q132
гаусс G84
гауссов контур G89
гауссова система единиц G86
гашение Q133
Гб G165
гейзенберговская модель H117
гексагональная плотноупакованная структура H169
~ сингония H171
~ система H171
гексагональный кристалл H170
гексод H173
гектопаскаль H112
гелиевая вспышка H131
гелиевый детандер H130
~ криостат H129
~ магнитометр H132
гелий H128
гелий-неоновый лазер H133
геликоидальная структура H122
геликон H124
гелиограф H126
гелиостат H127
гелиоцентрические координаты H125
гель G94
Генеральная конференция по мерам и весам G97
генератор G111, O282
~ Баркгаузена - Курца B53
~ Ганна G301
~ гармоник H54
~ Гартмана H63, J9
~ группы G278
~ импульсов I66, P995
~ качающейся частоты S1091
~ озона O330
~ пилообразного напряжения S35
~ плазмы P665
~ стандартных сигналов S714
~ шума N187
RC-генератор R203
генераторная лампа O270
генерационно-рекомбинационный шум G110
генерация G108
~ гармоник H53
генерирование G108
генетически значимая доза G112
генри H139
геоакустика G113
географические координаты G117

геодезическая линия G115
геодезия G116
геоид G118
геомагнетизм G128, T65
геомагнитная буря G125
~ долгота G122
~ ловушка G126
~ широта G121
геомагнитное поле G120
геомагнитные вариации G127
~ координаты G119
геомагнитный меридиан G123
~ полюс G124
геометрическая акустика G129
~ изомерия C308, G133
~ интерференция G138
~ кристаллография G131
~ оптика G134
геометрические осцилляции G135
геометрический изомер C307, G132
~ фактор G137
геометрическое место L326
~ поперечное сечение G130
геометрия G139
~ Евклида E422
геостационарная орбита G142
геотермика G145
геотермическая энергия G143
геотермический градиент G144
геотермия G145
геофизика G141
геофон G140
геохронология G114
гептод H141
германий G146
герполодия H146
герц C991, H147
гетеровалентный изоморфизм H166
гетерогенная конденсация H156
~ система H158
гетерогенность H154
гетерогенный катализ H155
~ реактор H157
гетеродин H152
гетеродинирование света H153
гетеролазер H161
гетеропереход H159
гетерополярная связь H163, I402
гетероструктура H164
гетерофазная структура H162
гетерохромная фотометрия H151
геттер G147
геттерный насос G148
гибкое зеркало F190

гибкость F189
гигант G156
гигантская оптическая нелинейность G151
гигантские осцилляции G152
гигантский импульс G153
~ резонанс G155
гидродинамика плазмы P667
гидролокатор S431
гидролокация S431
гидростатический напор P873
гильберт G165
гильбертово пространство H221
λ-гиперон L14
гиратор G303
гиромагнитная частота C1000, G305
гиромагнитное отношение G306
гиромагнитные явления G304
гироскоп G307
гироскопические силы G308
гироскопический момент G311
гиростабилизатор G312
гиротрон G313
гиротропия G316
гиротропная среда G315
гиротропный кристалл G314
гистограмма H223
главная ось деформации P888
~ ось инерции P887
~ ось напряжения P889
~ серия P897
~ спектральная серия P897
главное зеркало P880
~ квантовое число P896
~ направление P890
~ напряжение P898
главные плоскости P895
главный максимум M208, P892
~ момент инерции P894
~ фокус P891
гладкая кривая S358
глаз E539
глауберовские поправки G175
глобальная дуальность G179
~ инвариантность G181
~ неустойчивость G180
~ симметрия G182
глубина D177
~ модуляции D180
~ осцилляций O274
~ проникновения D181, P202
~ резкости D179
глубокая ловушка D77
глубоко неупругий процесс D75
~ неупругое рассеяние D76
глюбол G187
глюино G188

глюон G189
глюонный мешок G190
Гн H139
год Y4
годичная аберрация A429
годичные вариации A430
годограф H224
годоскоп H226
«голая» частица B49
голдстоуновские моды G195
голдстоуновский бозон G193
~ фермион G194
«головастик» T2
головка H66
головная ударная волна B298, H68
голограмма H240
голографическая диагностика H243
~ запись H249
~ интерферограмма H246
~ интерферометрия H248
голографический интерферометр H247
голографическое запоминающее устройство H250
~ ЗУ H250
~ изображение H244
~ распознавание образов H245
голография H251
«голое» ядро B48
голоморфная функция H252
голономная система H253
гольмий H239
гомеополярная связь C819
гомогенная конденсация H258
~ система H263
гомогенный катализ H257
~ реактор H262
гомологический ряд H265
гомопереход H264
гомополярная связь H267
гомоцентрический пучок H254
гониометр G196
гониометрия G197
горелка Бунзена B370
горение B378, C477
горизонт H269
~ событий E438
горизонтально-поляризованное излучение H270
горячая Вселенная H285
~ лаборатория H281
~ люминесценция H282
~ плазма H213, H283
горячие дырки H280
~ носители H275
~ носители заряда H275
~ электроны H278

двояковыпуклая линза B179
двукратно ионизованный атом D578
двулучепреломление B209, D573
двумерная модель T475
~ спектральная классификация T476
двумерное изображение T474
двумерный электронный газ T473
двухатомная молекула D242
двухбазовый диод T466
двухжидкостная гидродинамика T483
~ модель T478
двухзонная модель T465
двухквантовый переход D572
двухкомпонентная жидкость T470
~ плазма T471
~ система B189
двухлинзовый объектив D577
двухлучевая интерференция T467
двухлучевой интерферометр T468
~ осциллограф D600
двухмагнонное поглощение T484
двухосный кристалл B176
двухполупериодный выпрямитель F421
двухрезонаторный клистрон D562
двухступенчатая ионизация T491
двухуровневая модель T482
двухуровневый атом T479
~ лазер T480
~ мазер T481
двухфазное течение T486
двухфотонная диссоциация T488
двухфотонное излучение T489
~ поглощение T487
двухфотонный переход T490
двухцветный пирометр B177
двухчастотный интерферометр D566
двухэлектронное возбуждение D565
двухэлементный интерферометр A196, T477
дебаевская длина D44
дебаевский радиус D44
дебаеграмма D46
дебай D42
дебанчер D40
де-бройлевская длина волны D38
девиатор D217

~ деформаций S857
~ напряжений S889
девиация D216
~ компаса M44
~ частоты F367
деградация голограммы H241
~ полупроводников S182
~ энергии D117
дезаккомодация D185
дезактиватор D35
дезактивационная камера D68
дезактивация D34
дезоксирибонуклеиновая кислота D161
деионизация D123
действие A166, E26, I187
~ излучения R35
~ на расстоянии A167
действительное изображение R228
действующая высота E29
~ диафрагма A490
~ длина антенны A452
действующее значение E32
~ напряжение E33
дейтериды D211
дейтериевая мишень D213
дейтерий D212
дейтрон D214
деканалирование D61
~ ионов I394
~ на дефектах D62
декартовы координаты C84
декатрон D125
декодер D67
декорирование D69
декремент D71
~ затухания D10
декристаллизация D72
деление D523, D523, F150
~ амплитуды A357
~ атомного ядра N361
~ напряжения V192
~ пучка B117
~ частоты F370
~ шкалы S48
делитель напряжения V191
~ пучка B99
~ частоты F369
делительная головка D522
~ изомерия F160
делокализация дефектов D81
делокализованный дефект D134
дельбрюковское рассеяние D133
дельта-лучи D137
дельта-функция D136, U78
~ Дирака D370
дельта-электрон D135
делящееся ядро F152
делящийся изомер F159

~ материал F151
демодулятор D146
демодуляция D145
демон Максвелла M287
демонтаж реактора R224
демпфер D8, R461
демпфирование D9
~ колебаний O273
демультиплексор D147
дендрит D148
дендритный кристалл D149
денсиметр A521, D150
денсиметрия D151
денситометр D152
денситометрия D153
день D29
депиннинг D165
деполяризатор D172
деполяризация люминесценции L419
~ света D171
держатель S1044
десенсибилизатор D189
десенсибилизация D188
десорбция D192
~ полем F98
деструктивная интерференция D197
деструкция D194
~ полимеров P786
десублимация D198
десятичный логарифм D64
детандер E491
детектирование D145, D202
~ атомов A615
~ атомов на поверхности S1053
~ гравитационных волн G248
~ единичных атомов D203
~ единичных молекул D204
~ нейтронов N116
~ огибающей E351
~ света L214, O111
~ случайных сигналов R168
детектор D146, D205
~ гамма-всплесков G39
~ излучения R31
~ Мотта M657
~ частиц P122
детерминант D206
детерминизм D208
детонационная волна D210
детонация D209
дефазировка D164
дефект D79, F185, I54
~ внедрения I346
~ замещения S947
~ кристалла C899
~ массы M240
~ решётки L135
~ структуры S914
~ упаковки S704
дефектон D84

~ иона I391
~ конденсатора C45
~ нейтрона N108
~ нуклона N412
~ электрона E178
~ ядра N348
зарядовая инвариантность C225
~ нейтрализация C227
~ чётность C229
зарядовое сопряжение C201
заряженная компонента C205
~ частица C214
заряженный К-мезон C211
~ каон C211
~ лептон C212
~ мезон C213
~ ток C206
заселение P800
~ уровня F118
заселённость O16, P800
затвердевание S413
затвор G80, S272
затмение E15
затменная переменная E19
~ переменная звезда E19
затравка F436, S125
затруднённый переход U56
затухание A646, D9, D51, L372
~ волн W15
~ в свободном пространстве F354
~ звука S443
~ колебаний O273
~ Ландау C436, L29
~ люминесценции L417
~ радиоволн R139
~ радиоволн в атмосфере A581
~ сигнала S283
~ ультразвука U14
затухающие колебания D7
затягивание частоты F382
захват T391
~ дырки H229
~ заряда C197
~ заряженных частиц C59, C223
~ нейтронов N106
~ носителей заряда C82
~ примеси I74
~ электрона E176
~ электрона ядром C60
К-захват K5
захватывание частоты F374, L325
захваченные частицы T389
захоронение радиоактивных отходов B377, D462
зацепление P591
защита P948, S92, S237
~ от ионизирующих

излучений P949
~ от коррозии C757
~ от облучения P949
защитное действие P950
Зв S280
звезда S719
звезда-гигант G156
звезда главной последовательности M203
звезда-карлик D612
звезда пробоя D6
звезда-сверхгигант S1008
звёздная аберрация S780
~ активность S781
~ ассоциация S782
~ атмосфера S783
~ величина S793
~ динамика S787
~ фотометрия S795
~ эволюция S788
звёздное время S277
~ излучение S797
~ население S796
~ скопление S722
звёздный ветер S801
~ год S278
~ дождь M400
~ интерферометр S790
~ каталог S721
звёздообразование S723
звёзды Вольфа - Райе U139
звук S438
звуковая волна A142
~ изоляция S456
~ энергия A105, S446
звуковидение A112
звуковое давление A126, S463
~ изображение A111
~ поле S450
звуковой барьер S433
~ ветер A145
~ импульс A128, S466
звуковые волны A95
~ колебания A141, S475
~ частоты A656
звукоизоляционный материал S455
звукоизоляция S456
звуколокация S469
звуколюминесценция S435
звукопоглотитель A94
звукопоглощающий материал S440
звукосниматель P546
зеемановский подуровень Z4
зеемановское расщепление Z2
землетрясение E5
земля E2, G271
Земля E3
земная волна G275
земной магнетизм G128, T65
земные токи E4
зенит Z6

зенитное расстояние Z7
зенитный угол Z7
зеркала Френеля F398
зеркало M505, R306
зеркальная антенна R307
~ магнитная ловушка M515
~ плоскость симметрии M512
~ симметрия M514
зеркальное изображение M507
~ отражение M513, S598
зеркально-линзовый объектив C95
зеркальные ядра M511
зеркальный изобар M508
~ изомер M509
~ телескоп R292
зернистая структура G207
зернистость G207, G213
зерно G205
зиверт S280
знак S282
знакопеременная фазировка S285
~ фокусировка S284
знакопостоянная фокусировка S288
значение S289, V43
значимость I59, S289
зодиакальный свет Z17
золото G191
золь S366
золь-гель-метод S408
зона A520, B35, R332, Z18
~ Бриллюэна B337
~ диффузии D332
~ пониженного давления D175
~ проводимости C562
~ радиоактивного заражения C637
~ Френеля F399
зонд P915, S432, S438
зондирование S453
~ ионосферы I455
~ плазмы P682
зондирующий импульс P920, S454
зондовая диагностика P917
зондовые измерения P918
зондовый метод P919
зонная модель B39
~ плавка Z21
~ пластинка Z23
~ структура B42
~ теория B43
зонный магнетизм B38, Z20
зрение V173
зрительная труба T27
зрительное восприятие V181
зрительные иллюзии O131
~ наблюдения V180
зрительный контраст V175

И

ИАГ-лазер Y2
игнитрон I19
игольчатая диаграмма
  направленности P197
игольчатый катод S618
идеализация I8
идеализированная задача I9
идеальная жидкость I6, P220
~ оптическая система P221
~ плазма P222
~ пластичность P223
идеальный газ I7, P217
~ диэлектрик P216
~ кристалл P215
идентификация I10, R235
~ переходов T336
~ состояний S731
~ частиц P130
идентичность I11
идиоморфизм I12
иерархия H177
~ волн W39
изаллобара I485
изаллотерма I486
изанемона I487
изаномала I488
избежание резонансного
  захвата R435
избирательное поглощение
  S133
избирательность S141
~ по частоте F385
~ резонатора R453
~ фильтра F127
избыток давления P870
~ цвета C452
~ энергии E442
избыточная концентрация
  E441
~ населённость E443
избыточный коэффициент
  воспроизводства B324
извержение вулкана V188
извлечение E526
~ стержня W134
изгиб B131
~ бруса B134
~ волновода W29
~ доменной границы D533
~ зоны B136
~ кристалла C893
~ пластинки B135
~ пластины P703
изгибающий момент B133
изгибная волна F195
~ деформация B132
~ жёсткость F193
изгибное кручение B139
изгибные колебания B140,
  F194

изинговская модель I491
излом F320, K53
~ плазменного шнура P672
~ по границам зёрен I286
~ по плоскости спайности
  C324
~ при сдвиге S223
~ при сжатии C525
излучаемая мощность R20
излучатель E299, R67
~ звука A130
~ Планка P224
~ света L217
~ ультразвука U28
излучательная рекомбинация
  R63
~ способность E295
излучательность E297, R12
излучательный переход R66
излучающая система R21
излучение E287, R22
~ атмосферы A594
~ Вавилова - Черенкова C259
~ звука S467
~ квантовой системы Q72
~ накачки P1025
~ нерелятивистских частиц
  N292
~ оптически толстой плазмы
  O150
~ оптически тонкой плазмы
  O152
~ плазмы P684
~ радиоволн R126
~ серого тела G263
~ фотосферы P517
~ частиц P143
~ чёрного тела B217, C135,
  E384
~ электрона E232
изменение блеска L244
~ во времени T261
~ направления на обратное
  R474
~ состояния C182
измерение D346, M299
~ in situ I230
~ атмосферного давления
  M301
~ в месте нахождения I230
~ времени T254
~ высоты A313
~ дальности D485
~ дозы излучения M302
~ интервалов времени T249
~ периода P236
~ поглощения A52
~ полосы пропускания B45
~ расстояния D485
~ скорости V94
~ температуры T40
~ частоты F375
~ шумов N190

~ энергии E325
измеритель добротности Q4
~ ёмкости C37
~ коэффициента стоячей
  волны S716
~ КСВ S716
~ магнитной индукции G87
~ нелинейных искажений
  D494
~ поглощающей способности
  A37
~ скорости V88
~ скорости счёта C808
измерительная линия S347
измерительный генератор
  S714
~ микроскоп M305, M449
~ мост B331
~ преобразователь T320
~ прибор G3, I242, M401
износостойкий материал W82
износостойкое покрытие W81
износостойкость W80
изобар I492
изобара I492
изобарический спин I495
изобарный процесс I494
изображение I23, P550
~ во вторичных электронах
  S106
~ в оже-электронах A661
~ в отражённых электронах
  B11
~ в поглощённых электронах
  A30
~ в рентгеновских лучах X28
~ в термоэлектронах T177
~ в фотоэлектронах P428
~ звезды S724
изовалентный изоморфизм
  I579
изовектор I580
изогона I515
изогруппа I516
изоденса I510
изодинама I512
изодоза I511
изокандела I496
изокинета I517
изоклина I509
изолиния I521
изолированная дислокация
  I518
~ система I519
изолюкс I523
изолятор I246
изоляция I245, I520
изомер I524
~ формы S218
изомеризация I526
изомерия I525
~ атомных ядер N369
~ молекул M586

индефинитная метрика I115
индивидуальный дозиметр P266
индий I129
индикатор I124
~ настройки T432
~ *ерегруйки* Ö~~~
~ положения пучка B111
индикатриса диффузии I125
~ рассеяния S74
индуктивная диафрагма I152
~ нагрузка I153
~ связь I151
индуктивность I145, I146, S164
индуктивный датчик I154
~ накопитель I155
~ преобразователь I156
индукционная катушка I149
индукционный нагрев I150
~ ускоритель I148
индукция I147
индуцированная дисперсия I135
индуцированное двулучепреломление I132
~ излучение I137, S823
~ поглощение S817
индуцированный заряд I133
~ квант I141, S827
~ ток I134
инертная масса I173
инертность I167, I176, S352
инертный газ I166, N179
инерциальная масса I173
~ навигация I172
~ система отсчёта I171
инерциальное движение I174
~ удержание I169
инерционность I167, R517, S352
~ зрительного восприятия P265
инерционные силы I170
инерция I167
~ вращения R536
~ гироскопа G309
инжектор I217
~ дырок H233
~ плазмы P669
~ пучка B106
~ таблеток P192
~ частиц P132
~ электронов E213
инжекционный лазер I216
инжекция I215
~ дырок H232
~ заряженных частиц C222
~ нейтральных частиц N87
~ неосновных носителей M500
~ носителей заряда C80
~ плазмы P668
~ пучка B105

~ таблеток P191
~ тока C967
~ частиц P131
~ электронов E212
инициирование I213
~ лазера L81
~ разряда D402
~ реакции I214
~ электрическим разрядом E101
~ электронным пучком E168
инициирующий импульс I212
инклинатор I91
инклюзивное сечение I95
инклюзивный процесс I96
инклюзия I94
инкремент I113
~ неустойчивости I235
~ усиления G13
инсоляция I231
инстантон I241
инструмент I242
инструментальные искажения I243
~ погрешности I244
интеграл I248
~ вероятности ошибок E409
~ движения I251
~ действия A168
~ перекрытия O313
~ по оптическому пути I252
~ по поверхности S1071
~ по траектории P166
~ Пуассона P729
~ рассеяния S75
~ столкновений C434
~ столкновений Ландау L27
~ Френеля F396
~ Фурье F308
~ Эйри A280
интегральная интенсивность I250, T302
~ микросхема C261, I254
~ оптика I256
~ плотность потока частиц P127
~ схема I254
интегральное преобразование I253
~ уравнение I249
интеграция I260
интегрирование I260
~ по замкнутому контуру C332
~ по контуру C661
интегрирующая ионизационная камера I258
~ цепь I257
интегрирующий фотометр I259
интенсивное излучение I261
интенсивность I262
~ деформации S860

~ звука S457
~ излучения E289, R42
~ испарения E433
~ испускания E289
~ источника S480
~ космического излучения C770
~ линии L271
~ люминесценции L420
~ накачки P1021
~ напряжений S891
~ непрерывного спектра C659
~ перехода T337
~ поглощения A47
~ полосы B37
~ пучка B108
~ радиоактивного излучения R79
~ рентгеновского излучения X29
~ света L226
~ спектральной линии I266, S556
интенсивные параметры I267
интервал I349, R171
~ времени T248
~ дискретизации S16
~ дуальности D603
~ между импульсами P1006
~ плотностей D159
~ скоростей V100
~ температур T43
~ энергий E329
интеркалированные соединения I281
интеркомбинационные линии I284
~ переходы I285
интерметаллические соединения I316
интерполирование I333
интерполяция I333
интерпретация I334
~ дифракционных картин I335
~ спектров I336
интерфейс I290
интерференционная картина I300
~ полоса F409
интерференционные кольца I301
~ полосы I297
~ фигуры I295
~ цвета I293
интерференционный компаратор I294
~ фильтр I296
интерференция I292
~ акустических волн A114
~ волн W42
~ вырожденных состояний D116

ИНТЕРФЕРЕНЦИЯ

~ поляризованных лучей Р757
~ радиоволн R141
~ рентгеновского излучения X30
~ света I298, O137
~ слабого и электромагнитного взаимодействий E273
~ состояний I299
~ электронных пучков E169
интерферограмма I300
интерферометр I304
~ Жамена J4
~ интенсивности I263
~ Майкельсона M423
~ Маха - Цендера M4
~ Рэлея R193
~ Саньяка S12
~ со сверхдлинной базой V110
~ с переключением фазы Р341
~ Фабри - Перо F2
интерферометрические измерения I307
интерферометрический компенсатор I306
интерферометрия I308
~ высокого разрешения H207
~ интенсивности I264
инфлектор I186
инфляционная космология I184
~ модель I185
инфляция I183
информатика I189
информационный канал I191
информация D22, I190
инфразвук I207
инфразвуковые волны I206
~ колебания I205
инфракрасная астрономия I195
~ катастрофа I196
~ многофотонная диссоциация I199
~ область спектра I201
~ расходимость I197
~ спектроскопия I203
инфракрасное излучение I200
инфракрасные волны I204
иод I380
ион I381
~ отдачи R239
ионизатор I439
ионизационная камера I417
~ кривая I422
~ неустойчивость I426
ионизационное равновесие I424
ионизационные волны I435
~ потери I427

ионизационный вакуумметр I434
~ калориметр I416
~ континуум I420
~ манометр I425
~ потенциал I429
ионизация I413
~ внешней оболочки O301
~ внутренней оболочки I222
~ полем F102
~ электронами E214
~ электронным ударом E214, I415
ионизированное состояние I432
ионизированный атом A621
~ газ I437
ионизирующее излучение I440
ионизованная молекула I438
ионизованное состояние I432
ионизованный атом I436
~ газ I437
ионная бомбардировка I389
~ имплантация I386
~ концентрация I393
~ проводимость I403
~ пушка I401
~ связь I402
~ температура I461
~ электропроводность I403
~ эмиссия I398
ионное легирование I411
~ распыление I408
~ травление I406
~ усиление G53
ионно-звуковая неустойчивость I383
ионно-звуковые колебания I384
ионно-ионная эмиссия I412
ионно-лучевая литография I387
~ модификация I388
ионно-электронная рекомбинация I397
~ эмиссия I396
ионные приборы I405
ионный заряд I391
~ звук I458
~ источник I460
~ кластер I392
~ кристалл I404
~ лазер I442
~ микроскоп I443
~ проектор I457
~ прожектор I401
~ пучок I385
~ радиус I407
~ термоядерный синтез I462
ионограмма I444
ионозонд I446
ионолюминесценция I445

ионообменная хроматография I400
ионообменный катализ I399
ионосфера I447
ионосферная волна S336
~ неоднородность I452
~ радиоволна S336
ионосферное динамо I451
ионосферные возмущения I450
~ данные I449
~ мерцания I454
ионосферный волновод I456
~ канал I448
ипсилон-частица Y9
ираст-линия Y12
ираст-ловушка Y13
ираст-полоса Y10
ираст-уровень Y11
иридий I463
ирисовая диафрагма I465
иррадиация I470
искажение A2, D97, D492
~ изображения I27
~ оптических изображений D495
искажения формы импульса P1009
искажённое изображение D490
искра S510
искрение в магнетроне M193
искривлённое пространство C980
искривлённость пространства S490
искровая камера S511
~ фотография S516
искровой источник S517
~ промежуток S515
~ разряд S510, S514
~ разрядник S515
~ спектр S518
~ счётчик S513
искусственная радиоактивность A533, I143
искусственный горизонт A531
~ интеллект A532
~ спутник A534
испарение E430, V51
«испарение» чёрных дыр E432
использование атомной энергии в мирных целях P175
~ пучка U107
испускание E287
~ альфа-частиц A300
~ фотонов P487
~ частиц P125, P143
~ частицы P143
испущенный квант E298
испытание T68

К

КОСМИЧЕСКИЕ

кюри C956
кюрий C959

Л

л L302
л.с. H273
лаборатория L3
лабораторная система
    координат L4
лабораторные испытания L5
лавина A689
лавинная ионизация A693
~ камера A691
лавинно-пролётный диод
    A694
лавинный пробой A690
~ разряд A692
лагранжев формализм L11
лагранжевы координаты L7
лагранжиан L9
~ взаимодействия I273
~ поля F103
лазер F352, F392, G154, L54,
    R532
~ на арсениде галлия G1
~ на гетеропереходе H161
~ на железо-иттриевом
    гранате Y6
~ на иттрий-алюминиевом
    гранате Y2
~ на квантовой яме Q76
~ на красителе D615
~ на красителях D615
~ на кристалле C905
~ на монокристалле S308
~ на неодимовом стекле N63
~ на оксиде углерода C402
~ на парах меди C716
~ на парах металлов M390
~ на сверхрешётке S1016
~ на свободных электронах
    F342
~ на стекле G171
~ на углекислом газе C403
~ на фосфатном стекле P377
~ на центрах F42
~ на центрах окраски C448
~, работающий в режиме
    гигантских импульсов G154
~, работающий в режиме
    свободной генерации F352
~, работающий при
    комнатной температуре
    R532
~ с дифракционной
    расходимостью пучка D286
~ с модулированной
    добротностью Q6
~ с распределённой обратной
    связью D498

~ с распределённым
    брэгговским отражателем
    D496
~ с самосинхронизацией мод
    S168
~ с синхронизацией мод M532
Ar-лазер A524
CO-лазер C402
CO_2-лазер C403
He-Ne-лазер H133
лазерная десорбционная масс-
    спектрометрия L66
~ десорбция L65
~ диагностика L68
~ закалка L77
~ интерферометрия L83
~ иридэктомия L84
~ искра L110
~ кювета L60
~ локация L104
~ локация искусственных
    спутников S19
~ локация Луны L440
~ маркировка L86
~ медицина L87
~ микрохирургия L88
~ мишень L114
~ модификация ДНК D524
~ накачка L100
~ обработка L96
~ офтальмология L90
~ плазма L94
~ резка L63
~ сварка L122
~ спектроскопия L111
~ терапия L116
~ термохимия L117
~ технология L115
~ фотоионизационная
    спектроскопия L92
~ фотохимия L91
~ химия L61
~ хирургия L112
лазерное гетеродинирование
    L78
~ детектирование L67
~ зеркало L89
~ зондирование L108
~ излучение L70
~ испарение L71
~ наведение L75
~ напыление L64, L71
~ оружие L121
~ осаждение L64
~ разделение изотопов L85
~ селективное детектирование
    L105
лазерно-индуцированный
    переход L79
лазерные стёкла L74
лазерный анемометр L55
~ гироскоп L76, O127
~ дальномер L103

~ диод L69
~ затвор L107
~ звукосниматель L93
~ импульс L98
~ интерферометр L82
~ источник L109
~ кристалл L62
~ локатор L101
~ луч L58
~ маяк L57
~ нагрев плазмы L95
~ отжиг L56
~ переход L119
~ проекционный микроскоп
    L97
~ пучок L58
~ термоядерный синтез L118
~ фокус L72
лайнер L274
ламберт L17
ламинарное течение L23
ламинарность L24
лампа L25
~ бегущей волны T396
~ дневного света D30
~ накаливания I83
~ накачки P1022
~ обратной волны B17, C69
~ сравнения C491
~ тлеющего разряда G186
лампа-вспышка F178
ламповая накачка L26
лантан L43
лантаниды L42
лантаноиды L42
лапласиан L47
ларморовская прецессия L53
~ частота L52
латунь B312
лауэграмма L145
Лб L17
левая поляризация C804
левитация L194
левый кварк L171
легирование D542
~ полупроводников S186
легированный кремний D541
~ кристалл D539
~ полупроводник D540
легирующее вещество D544
лёгкое скольжение E6
лёд I1
лемма Лоренца L365
ленгмюровская частота L37
ленгмюровские волны L41
~ колебания L38, P677
ленгмюровский зонд L39
~ коллапс L36
лента T14
лепесток L308
лептокварк L185
лептон L181
лептонный заряд L183

~ распад L184
~ ток L182
летучая компонента V186
летучесть F417, V187
либрация Луны L195
либрон L196
ливень S268
~ космических лучей C769, C773
Ливерморская лаборатория им. Лоуренса L155
ливневая камера S269
лиганды L203
лидар L198
лидер L161
ликвидус L298
лимб L247
линейная деформация L255
~ дислокация L270
~ зависимость L256
~ задача L266
~ комбинация L253
~ молекула L263
~ поляризация L265
~ система L267
линейное движение L264
~ детектирование L257
~ преобразование L268
~ расширение L259
линейно-поляризованное излучение L261
линейные дефекты L254
~ дифференциальные уравнения L258
~ измерения L262
линейный закон L260
~ усилитель L252
~ ускоритель L251
линейчатый спектр L276
линза L175
~ Френеля F397
линзовая антенна L176
линзовый волновод L178
~ излучатель L177
~ телескоп R313
линии Людерса - Чернова L408
~ скольжения L408
линия L250
~ генерации лазера L123
~ действия L272
~ задержки D131
~ задержки на поверхностных акустических волнах S1047
~ задержки на спиновых волнах S655
~ испускания E290
~ комбинационного рассеяния R156
~ передачи T355
~ плавления M337
~ поглощения A50
~ разрыва D407

~ Рэлея R195
~ связи C486, L278
~ скольжения S340
~ тока C969, S882
лиотропия L449
лиофильность L447
лиофобность L448
лист S230
литий L300
литография L301
литр L302
литьё C93
лк L443
лм L409
лм · с L410
лобовое столкновение H67
ЛОВ B17, C69
ловушка T386
логарифм L327
~ коэффициента поглощения A27
логарифмический декремент L328
~ декремент затухания L328
~ закон L330
~ инкремент L329
~ масштаб L331
логическая схема L332
логический элемент G80
локализация L317
локализованный заряд L318
локальная дуальность L311
~ ионная имплантация L315
~ калибровочная инвариантность L313
~ концентрация L309
~ наблюдаемая L319
~ симметрия L321
локальное взаимодействие L314
~ поле L312
~ термодинамическое равновесие L322
локальность L316, M431
~ взаимодействия I274
локальный оператор L320
ломкость F323
лоренц-инвариант L364
лоренц-инвариантность L363, R354
лоренцева линия L366
лоренцевский контур L368
лоуренсий L156
лошадиная сила H273
ЛПД A694
Луна M638
лунка I116
лунное затмение L439
луноход L441
лупа L175, M197
луч B88, R189
~ Педерсена P185
лучевая акустика G129

~ оптика G134
~ прочность O197
~ скорость R202
лучеиспускание R22
лучепреломление R325
лучистая экспозиция R14
~ энергия R13
лучистое равновесие R60
лучистость R10
лучистый поток R15
~ теплообмен R62
ЛЧМ-импульс C266
лэмбовский провал L16
~ сдвиг L20
люкс L443
Люксембург-Горьковский эффект C868, L444
люксметр L445
люмен L409
люмен-секунда L410
люминесцентный анализ L423
~ источник света F224
люминесцентное вещество L425
~ изображение L424
люминесценция L415
люминофор L426, P378
лютеций L442
лямбда-гиперон L14
лямбда-точка L15
лямбда-удвоение L13

М

магические ядра M16
магнетизм M139
~ микрочастиц M452
магнетик M18
магнетометр Ханле H40
магнетон M170
~ Бора B243
магнетосопротивление M178
магнетрон M192
~ со связками S867
магнетронная мишень M194
магний M17
магнит M18
магнитная аккомодация M19
~ анизотропия M24
~ аномалия M25
~ атомная структура M26
~ буря M126
~ восприимчивость M132
~ вязкость M138
~ гидродинамика M73, M163
~ дефектоскопия M98
~ дефокусировка M43
~ доменная структура M51
~ жёсткость M72
~ жидкость M86
~ запись M112

МАГНИТНАЯ

механический гистерезис M313
~ детерминизм M308
~ кпд M309
~ эквивалент света M312
~ эквивалент теплоты M311
механическое движение M315
~ напряжение M317
механокалорический эффект M324
механострикция M325
меченый атом L2, T309
мешок-нуклон N411
мигающий фотометр F197
миграция M488
~ вакансий V4
~ дефектов D83
~ дырок H234
~ зарядов C226
~ примесей I80
~ экситонов E472
~ электронов E219
~ энергии E326
микроанализ M425
микроанализатор M426
микробарограф M427
микровзрыв M438
микровключение M442
микроволновая диагностика M474
~ спектроскопия M484
~ электроника M476
микроволновое излучение M481
~ фоновое излучение M473
микроволновый диапазон M482
микроволны M483
микровязкость M472
микроденситометр M434
микродифракция M435
микродозиметрия M436
микрозонд M458
микроизгиб M428
микроканонический ансамбль M429
микроканоническое распределение M430
микролинза M445
микролитография M446
микромагнетизм M447
микрометр M448, M448, M450
микромир M485
микромишень M469
микрон M448, M450
микронапряжение M467
микронеоднородность M443
микронеустойчивость M444
микрообъектив M445
микропинч M456
микроплазма M457
микрополе M439

микропричинность L316, M431
микропроекция M460
микропроцессор M459
микропульсации M461
микрорельеф M462
микросейсм M465
микроскоп M463
~ ближнего поля N30
микроскопия M464
микроспектрофотометр M466
микроструктура M468
микротвёрдость M440
микротрещина M433
микротрон M470
микротурбулентность M471
микрофон M453
микрофотография M454
микрофотометр M455
микрочастица M451
микроэлектроника M437
миктомагнетизм M
миллеровские индексы M490
миллиметр M492
~ водяного столба M494
~ ртутного столба M493
миллиметровые волны M495
миллионная доля P151
минимум M497
~ солнечной активности S391
минитрон M498
минута M503
миопия M752
мир W142
мираж M504
мировая линия W144
мировой интервал W143
митрон M516
мишень T16
~ ускорителя A71
Мкс M283
Млечный путь M489
мм M492
мнимое изображение V151
~ число I35
многогранник P784
многозарядный ион M722
многозначная функция M735
многоканальный дискриминатор M673
многокварковое состояние M729
многокомпонентная плазма M675
~ система M676
многокомпонентный параметр порядка M674
многократная ионизация M708
многократное взаимодействие M707
~ рассеяние M711

многолучевая интерференция M704
многолучевое распространение M691
многолучевой интерферометр M705
многомерное пространство M677
многомодовое волокно M681
~ излучение M684
многомодовость M683
многомодовый лазер M682
многооборотная инжекция M734
многообразие M213
многорезонаторный клистрон M706
~ магнетрон C133, M672
многосвязная область M724
многосвязный контур M723
многослойная плёнка M680
многоступенчатая ионизация M732
~ ракета M733
многоугольник P782
~ сил P783
многофазное течение M693
многофононный процесс M694
многофотонная диссоциация M696
~ изомеризация M699
~ ионизация M698
~ спектроскопия M702
многофотонное возбуждение M697
~ поглощение M695
многофотонный переход M703
~ процесс M701
~ фотоэффект M700
многочастичная динамика M686
многочастичное взаимодействие M221, M687
~ состояние M689
многочастичный коррелятор M685
многочлен P790
~ Цернике Z8
многочлены Эрмита H144
многоэлементное зеркало M679
многоэлементный интерферометр M678
множественное рождение частиц M688
множественность M720
множественный процесс M709
множество S211
множитель F8
~ Ланде G149, L34
мода M526

~ Бернштейна B144
модели ядра N377
моделирование M531, S300
модель M530
~ анизотропной Вселенной A416
~ Бардина - Купера - Шриффера B47
~ БКШ B47
~ великого объединения G212
~ Гейзенберга H117
~ Джейниса - Каммингса J6
~ закрытой Вселенной C337
~ Изинга I491
~ мешка B19
~ однородной Вселенной H261
~ открытой Вселенной O66
~ раздувающейся Вселенной I185
~ расширяющейся Вселенной E485
~ солнечной вспышки S384
~ фазового перехода P347
~ Фридмана F408
~ электрослабого взаимодействия E274
модификации льда I2
модификация M542
~ материалов пучками заряженных частиц M262
~ поверхности S1074
модовая дисперсия M525
~ структура M540
модулированное излучение M544
~ напряжение M545
модулированные колебания M543
модуль A25, M198, M552, M553
~ всестороннего сжатия B363, M554
~ кручения T296
~ объёмного сжатия M554
~ объёмной упругости B363
~ продольной упругости M556
~ сдвига M557, S224
~ упругости E62, M555
~ Юнга M556, Y7
модулятор C272, M551
~ добротности Q5
~ света B90, L211, O159
модуляционная неустойчивость M550
модуляция M546
~ групповой скорости G283
~ добротности Q7
~ луча B109
~ пучка B109
~ света L228
~ скорости V95
~ яркости I265

моды высшего порядка H191
мозаичность M643
мозаичный кристалл M642
молекула M605
~ типа асимметричного волчка A571
~ типа симметричного волчка S1100
молекулярная акустика M568
~ динамика M579
~ диффузия M577
~ масса M589
~ орбиталь M591
~ рефракция M596
~ спектроскопия M599
~ физика M593
~ эпитаксия M570
молекулярное вращение M598
~ замещение M597
~ поле M582
~ течение M583
молекулярно-пучковая эпитаксия M570
молекулярные колебания M604
молекулярный генератор M588
~ интеграл M584
~ ион M585
~ кристалл M576
~ лазер M587
~ мазер M588
~ насос M595
~ пучок M569
~ спектр M600
~ экситон M581
молибден M607
молниеотвод L233, L235
молния L230
моль M567
мольность M564
моляльность M563
молярность M564
момент M608
~ высшего порядка H192
~ импульса A402, M612
~ инерции M611
~ количества движения A402, K41, M612
~ пары M609
~ силы M610
монитор положения пучка B112
мониторинг M620
моноклинная сингония M627
~ система M627
монокристалл M628, S304
монокристальный дифрактометр S305
монополь M632
~ Дирака D374
монослой M629
монотонная зависимость U63

~ функция M634
монохроматические волны M625
монохроматический источник M624
~ свет M622
монохроматическое излучение M623
монохроматичность M621
монохроматор M626
монтаж A539, M661
монтировка M661
МОП-структура M388
морской кварк S101
морфология M641
мост B331
~ Вина W117
~ Максвелла M285
~ Уитстона W102
моттовские диэлектрики M658
моттовское рассеяние M659
мощное излучение H202, I261
мощность P842
~ дозы D556
~ звука A125
~ излучения R20
~ импульса P1003
~ источника S479
~ кермы K14
~ накачки P1023
~ питания S1043
~ шума N191
муар M558
муаровая картина M560
муаровые интерференционные полосы M559
~ узоры M559, M560
музыкальная акустика M746
мультивибратор M736
мультипериферическое взаимодействие M692
мультиплексная голография M715
мультиплексор M714
мультиплет M712
мультипликативное квантовое число M719
мультипликативность M720
мультиполь M726
мультипольное излучение M728
мультипольность M725
мультипольный момент M727
мультистабильность M731
мутная среда T444
мутность T443
мышьяк A530
МэВ M331
мю-мезон M738
мюон M738
мюоний M744

неопознанный летающий объект U59
неопределённость A319, U48
неопределённый интеграл I114
неосновные носители M501
~ носители заряда M501
непараметрический метод N275
непер N65
неперенормируемая квантовая теория поля N294
неперенормируемость N293
непериодические колебания N276
непериодический процесс N277
непериодичность A486
неподвижная катушка F166
~ мишень F167
неполиномиальная квантовая теория поля N279
неполярные молекулы N278
непотенциальность N280
непрерывная зависимость C647
~ среда C652
~ функция C651
непрерывное излучение C654
~ поглощение C645
непрерывность C643
непрерывные колебания C653
непрерывный лазер C657
~ спектр C655, C658
неприводимая диаграмма I474
неприводимое представление I475, N288
непрозрачная плазма O59
непрозрачность O57
~ атмосферы A589
непрямой переход N311
непрямые переходы I128
Нептун N68
нептуний N69
неравенство I165
неравновесная концентрация N216
~ населённость N220
~ плазма N219
неравновесное состояние N222
~ течение N217
неравновесные носители N215
~ носители заряда N215
~ фазовые переходы N218
неравномерное движение I477, N309
неравномерность I476, N308
неразрешённая линия U89
неразрушающие испытания N211
неразрушающий контроль N211

~ метод N210
неразрывное течение C650
неразрывность C643
~ потока F206
нераспространение ядерного оружия N281
нерастворимость I232
нервная клетка N73
нервный импульс N74
нерегулярность I476
нерезонансное рассеяние N295
~ состояние O31
нерелятивистская механика N289
нерелятивистский импульс N290
нерелятивистское движение N291
неровность A537
несамостоятельный разряд N298
неселективный приёмник N297
несжимаемая жидкость I110
несжимаемость I108
несимметричное ядро D101
несимметричный изгиб U95
~ переход N306
несобственный интеграл I63
несовершенный кристалл I52
несовершенство I54
~ кристалла C903
~ кристаллической решётки L139
~ структуры S915
несовместимость I107
несогласованная нагрузка U87
несоизмеримость I104
несоразмерная структура I106
несоразмерность I104
несоразмерные фазы I105
несохранение N206
~ заряда C228
~ чётности P93
нестабильность I233
~ частоты F372
нестационарная задача N303
~ интерференция N301
~ самофокусировка N305
нестационарное движение N302
~ течение N300
нестационарный процесс N304
нестеснённое кручение S299
несущая C75
~ частота C75
несферичность N299
неупорядоченная система D434
неупорядоченный кристалл D432

неупругая деформация I161
неупругие столкновения I160
неупругий изгиб I158
~ канал I159
неупругое взаимодействие N214
~ рассеяние I163
неупругость A382
неустановившееся движение N302
~ течение N300
неустановившиеся колебания T329
неустановившийся процесс N304
неустойчивое равновесие U91
неустойчивость I233
~ плазмы P670
~ пучка B107
неустойчивый изотоп U92
нефелометр N66
нефелометрия N67
нецентральная сила N198
нечётное взаимодействие P94
нечётные состояния O27
неявная зависимость I58
нижний кварк B285, D579
~ подуровень L390
~ предел текучести L391
нижняя зона L388
~ ионосфера L389
низкая температура L399
низкие частоты L392
низковольтная дуга L405
низкоразмерный магнетик L384
низкотемпературная калориметрия L400
~ камера L401
~ плазма L404
низкотемпературный контейнер L402
низкочастотная область L396
низкочастотное излучение L395
низкочастотные колебания L394
низкочастотный диапазон L393
никель N170
нильпотентная группа N172
нильсборий N173
ниобий N174
нисходящий узел D186
нит N175
нитевидные кристаллы C942
нитевидный кристалл W104
нить F114
~ накала F114
НЛО U59
нобелий N178
новая N336
~ звезда N336

остаток R414
~ вспышки сверхновой S1023
остаточная деформация R410
~ магнитная индукция R388
~ намагниченность R389
~ поляризация R390
~ радиоактивность R409
остаточное напряжение R413
остаточный пробег R412
острота зрения A188, V174
~ слуха A188
осциллирующая частица O269
осциллистор O286
осциллограмма O287
осциллограф O289
осциллографическая трубка C110
осциллятор O282
осцилляции O271, O279
~ нейтрино N98
~ Раби R2
~ странности S864
ось A712
~ вращения A715, R558
~ деформации A716
~ инерции A714
~ лёгкого намагничивания A713, E7
~ симметрии A717
отбеливание B224
отверстие A489, O65
ответвитель C814
отдача R236
отжиг A423
отказ F14
откачка E428
отклик R454
отклонение D91, D216
~ частиц P120
отклонённый луч D87
~ пучок D87
отклоняющая катушка D88
отклоняющее напряжение D90
отклоняющие пластины D89
открытая конфигурация O62
~ ловушка O69
~ модель O66
~ система O68
открытый источник B50
~ радионуклидный источник B50
~ резонатор O67
отлипание электронов D200
относительная деформация R342
~ дисперсия D454
~ диэлектрическая проницаемость R346
~ интенсивность линии R344
~ концентрация R341

~ световая эффективность L430
относительное движение R345
~ изменение R340
~ отверстие A493
~ равновесие R343
~ относительность R367
отношение R188
~ сигнал/шум S286
отображение I23, M222
отпирающий импульс G82
отражатель B18, R306
отражательная голограмма R298
~ призма R302
~ способность R305
отражательный клистрон R309
~ электронный микроскоп R295
отражающее покрытие R304
отражение R293
~ волн W56
~ звука S470
~ радиоволн R301
~ света R300
отражённая волна R291
отражённое излучение R289
отражённый импульс R288
~ луч R290
отрезок S117
отрицательная дисперсия N46
~ дисторсия B61
~ кривизна N44
~ люминесценция N51
~ обратная связь N48
~ температура N54
отрицательное дифференциальное сопротивление N45
~ поглощение N41
~ сопротивление N53
отрицательный заряд N42
~ ион N50
~ кристалл N43
отрыв электрона E186
отрывное течение D199
отставание L6, R465
отсчёт C802
отталкивание R407
охлаждающая жидкость C700
охлаждение C698, R324
~ путём адиабатического размагничивания C699
~ пучков B92
охрана окружающей среды E353
очарование C232
очарованные частицы C233
очарованный кварк C234
очистка газов G77
ошибка E406
ощущение S198

П

П P724
Па P152
ПАВ S1049
падающая волна I89
~ капля D595
~ характеристика F16
падающее излучение I87
падающий луч I88
~ пучок I86
падение F15, I85
пайерлсовский диэлектрик P188
пакетная оптическая интеграция S703
палеомагнетизм P14
палладий P15
палочка R524
память S851
пар V49
пара вихрей V216
~ сил C809
~ частица - античастица P114
парабозе-статистика P24
парабола P17
параболическая антенна P18
~ скорость P22
параболическое зеркало P21
~ уравнение P20
параболоид P23
параводород P32
парагелий P89
парадокс P27
~ близнецов T463
~ возврата C327
~ времени C327
~ Гиббса G161
~ Неймана - Зеелигера N80
~ часов C327, T463
паразитная ёмкость S873
паракоммутационные соотношения P25
параксиальное изображение P86
параксиальный луч P87
~ пучок P85
параллакс P34
~ звезды S794
~ планеты P635
параллактическая монтировка E370
параллактический угол P33
параллелограмм сил P40
параллель P35
параллельная инжекция P39
~ передача P42
~ передача данных P38
параллельное соединение P37
параллельный контур P36
~ перенос T346
~ резонанс P41

ПОРОГОВАЯ

~ мощность T227
пороговое напряжение T230
порошковая рентгеновская
  камера P841
~ рентгенограмма D46
порошковое изображение
  P839
порошковые фигуры M107
порошковый метод P840
~ нейтронограф N145
поршневой аттенюатор P605
поры P803
порядковый номер A627
порядок O234
~ величины O239
~ интерференции O238
~ отражения O240
~ спектра O241
последействие A260
последовательная ионизация
  S955
последовательное соединение
  S209
последовательный контур
  S208
~ резонанс S210
послеизображение A262
послесвечение A261, P264
~ люминофора P382
постоянная C621
~ Авогадро A699
~ Больцмана B255
~ Верде V104
~ вращения R545
~ времени R456, T244
~ Лошмидта L371
~ намагниченность D32
~ Планка P618
~ распада D52, D418
~ Ридберга R579
~ тонкой структуры F134
~ Хаббла H290
~ экранирования S94
постоянное напряжение D33
постоянные Ламе L22
~ решётки L134
постоянный магнит P243
~ ток D377
поступательное движение
  P929, T346, T348
потемнение к краю
  солнечного диска D17
потенциал P822
~ зажигания I18
~ ионизации I429
~ скоростей V98
~ Юкавы Y18
потенциальная поверхность
  P835
~ температура P836
~ функция P829
~ энергия P825
~ яма P837

потенциальное движение
  P832
~ поле P826
~ рассеяние P834
~ течение I483, P827
потенциальные силы P828
потенциальный барьер P823
~ рельеф P833
потенциометр P838
потери L372
~ в железе I468
~ в сердечнике I468
~ на зеркале M510
~ на излучение R47
~ на отражение M510, R299
~ на поглощение A51
~ на трение F406
~ при столкновениях C439
~ энергии E324
потеря L372
поток C961, F204, F234, S875
~ вектора V77
~ жидкости F218
~ звуковой энергии S448
~ излучения R15
~ импульса M616
~ Кнудсена K63
~ количества импульса M616
~ нейтронов N126
~ несжимаемой среды I109
~ солнечного излучения S385
~ текучей среды F218
~ энергии E319
почернение B218
появление O19
пояс протонов P956
правила отбора S132
правило L150
~ Ампера C723
~ буравчика C723
~ левой руки L170
~ Ленца L179
~ Маттисена M276
~ правой руки R505
~ сумм S966
~ фаз G162, P327
~ фаз Гиббса G162
~ Цвейга Z26
правый кварк R506
празеодим P852
превращение T358
предварительная диссоциация
  P863
~ ионизация P866
предварительные данные
  P867
предел выносливости F36
~ пропорциональности P945
~ прочности U3
~ прочности на разрыв B319
~ прочности на растяжение
  B320, T52
~ прочности на сжатие C530

~ прочности при сдвиге S226
~ Роша R519
~ сходимости C685
~ текучести Y5
~ упругости E59
предельная плотность U2
предельный цикл L248
предметная волна O4
предметный пучок O1
предпочтительная ориентация
  P864
представление Манделстама
  M211
предшествующий импульс
  P862
преимущественная
  ориентация P864
«прелестный» кварк B127
«прелесть» B128
преломление R314
~ волн W57
~ радиоволн R317
~ света R316
преломлённая волна R312
преломлённый луч R311
преобразование C689, T323
~ волн W62
~ Гильберта H222
~ Лапласа L46
~ Лоренца L370
~ Меллина M335
~ мод M528
~ симметрии S1108
~ с повышением частоты U96
~ Фурье F312
~ частоты F364, F391
~ энергии E314
преобразования Галилея G27
преобразователь C693
~ изображения I24
~ мод M529
~ с повышением частоты U97
препятствие O12
прерыватель C272, S272
~ пучка B90
прецессия P853
~ Лармора L53
прецизионное измерение
  P860
приближение A509
~ Венцеля - Крамера -
  Бриллюэна W135
~ ВКБ W135
~ Келдыша K6
приближённое значение A508
приближённый метод A507
прибор D218
~ с зарядовой связью
  C203
приведение R279
~ сил R280
приведённая масса R274
~ температура R276

Р

С

САМОПРОИЗВОЛЬНОЕ

сегнетоэлектрический гистерезис F75
~ домен F74
~ кристалл F73
сегнетоэлектричество F76
седиментационный анализ S123
седиментация S122
седиментометрический анализ S123
седловая точка S5
сейсмическая зона S129
сейсмические волны S128
сейсмичность S127
сейсмология S130
сейфертовские галактики S126
секторная скорость S118
секунда S102
селективная диссоциация S135
~ ионизация S137
селективное детектирование S134
~ зеркало S138
~ извлечение S136
~ поглощение S133
~ пропускание S140
селективный излучатель S139
селекторный импульс G80
селекция S131
~ движущейся цели M668
~ мод M539
селен S142
селеновый выпрямитель S143
сенсибилизация S201
сенсибилизированная люминесценция S202
сенситометрия S203
сера S965
сердечник C719
сердцевина C719, K15
~ вихря V212
серебро A522
серия S207, S211
~ Бальмера B33
~ Брэкета B302
~ импульсов P1011
~ Лаймана L446
~ Пашена P156
~ Пфунда P275
~ Ридберга R580
серое излучение G263, G264
~ тело G262
сетка G265
сеточная модуляция G269
~ фокусировка G268
сеточное детектирование G267
~ смещение G266
сечение C871, S117
~ возбуждения E455
~ деления F155

~ захвата C58, C873
~ ионизации I421
~ неупругого рассеяния N213
~ перезарядки C874
~ переноса T370
~ поглощения A43, C872
~ пучка B94
~ рассеяния C877, S71
~ рекомбинации C876, R245
~ столкновения C431, C875
~ упругого рассеяния E65
~ ядерной реакции N394
сжатие C522, C663
~ лазерных импульсов L99
сжатые состояния S687
сжатый импульс C517
сжижение газов L280
сжимаемая жидкость C519
сжимаемость C518
сжимающее напряжение C528
СИ I330
сигнатура S287
СИД P451
сидерическое время S277
сила F277, S884
~ звука S457
~ излучения R18
~ Кориолиса C722
~ Лоренца L359
~ осциллятора O283
~ света L435
~ связи B263
~ тока C961
~ тяжести G252
силикаты S291
силовая линия L273
~ линия электрического поля E112
силовое поле F282
силы инерции I170
сильная фокусировка S908
сильно неидеальная плазма S910
сильное взаимодействие S909
~ поле S907
сильноточная электроника H180
сильноточный имплантер H181
~ источник H182
~ ускоритель H179
символ Леви - Чивиты L193
символы Кристоффеля C274
~ Кронекера K70
сименс S279
симметрическая нагрузка B22
симметричная волновая функция S1101
~ конфигурация S1097
~ молекула S1098
симметричный вибратор D365
~ изгиб S1096

~ ротатор S1099
симметрия S1102
~ волновой функции S1106
~ кристаллов C938
~ молекул M603
синглет S321
синглетное состояние S322
сингония C940, S1130
сингулярность S326
синергетика S1122
синодический период S1123
синтез S1124
~ голограмм H242
~ голограммы H242
синтезированная апертура S1125
синтезированное изображение S1126
синтетический алмаз S1128
~ кварц S1129
~ кристалл S1127
синусоида S301
синусоидальная кривая S301
синусоидальные колебания S330
синхронизация L325, P352, S1112, T262
~ мод M533
синхронизирующий импульс C328, S1114
синхронизм S1111
синхронное детектирование S1115
синхронный детектор S1116
синхротрон S1118
синхротронное излучение S1120
синхротронные колебания S1119
синхрофазотрон S1117
синхроциклотрон S1110
сирена S331
система S211, S1130
~ вихрей V221
~ вывода пучка B101
~ единиц S1133
~ единиц МКСА M523
~ Кассегрена C92
~ координат C708, S1132
~ Коперника C713
~ Лоренца L369
~ обозначений N332
~ отсчёта F326, F328
~ с распределёнными параметрами D501
~ с сосредоточенными параметрами L438
~ центра инерции C150
~ центра масс C153
систематическая погрешность S1131
скаляр S40
скалярная частица S43

СПОНТАННОЕ

~ излучение S667
~ кипение S664
~ нарушение симметрии S665
~ пересоединение S673
спонтанный переход S675
способ M403, T25
спутная струя W3
спутник S18
спутный след W3
сравнительные испытания C492
среднее время жизни M296
~ значение A696
~ по ансамблю E343
среднеквадратичное значение E32, R533
~ отклонение S711
средние волны M329
~ частоты M328
средний свободный пробег для диффузии D327
средняя длина свободного пробега M295
срез C984, T316
сродство A259
~ к электрону E160
срок службы L201
срыв S903
Ст S844
стабилизатор S697
стабилизация S696
~ напряжения V197
~ тока C974
~ частоты F388
стабилитрон V194, Z5
стабильность S690
~ фазы P337
~ частоты F387
стабильный изотоп S700
сталкивающиеся импульсы C424
стандарт S707
~ частоты F389
стандартная атмосфера S708
~ колориметрическая система S709
стандартное отклонение S711
стандартный источник S715
~ источник МКО C291
~ наблюдатель S713
старение A265
стартовая масса L146
статика S742
статистика S768
~ Бозе - Эйнштейна B280
~ Больцмана B257
~ Орнштейна - Уленбека O253
~ Ферми - Дирака F54
~ фотонов P498
статистическая интерпретация S760
~ механика S761

~ модель S762
~ оптика S763
~ радиофизика S765
~ термодинамика S766
~ физика S764
статистический ансамбль S757
~ ансамбль Гиббса G163
~ бутстрап S754
~ вес S767
~ интеграл S759
~ критерий S755
статистическое равновесие S758
~ распределение S756
статическая нагрузка S740
статический заряд S737
статическое давление S741
~ трение S739
~ электричество S738
стационарная Вселенная S752
~ интерференция S744
~ модель S745
стационарное движение S746
~ кипение S743
~ состояние S750
~ течение S769
стационарные колебания S747
стационарный источник S749
~ процесс S748
~ ток S772
стекло G169
стекловолокно G170
стеклообразное состояние G174
стеклообразные полупроводники G173
стеклянное волокно G170
стелларатор S784
стенка W4
~ Нееля N40
степенная зависимость P844
степенной закон P844
степень D118, P842
~ ионизации D121
~ когерентности D119
~ свободы D120
стерадиан S806
стереобетатрон S807
стереографическая проекция S809
стереоизомерия S810
стереоскопическое зрение S812
стереоскопия S813
стереофония S811
стереохимия S808
стержень B46, R524
стержневой молниеотвод L235
стехиометрический дефект S842
~ коэффициент S841
стехиометрия S843

стигматическое изображение S815
стильб S816
стимулированное излучение I137, S823
стимулированный квант I141, S827
сток D583, S328
стокс S844
стоксова компонента S845
~ линия S847
столкновение C429, I41
~ частиц P117
столкновения молекул M572
столкновительная диффузия C432
~ ионизация C435, I414
столкновительное уширение C430, S869
стохастизация S840
стохастические колебания S837
стохастический процесс S838
стохастическое ускорение S834
стохастичность S836
стоячие волны S718
странность S863
странные частицы S865
странный аттрактор S862
~ кварк S866
стратификация S869
стратопауза S871
стратосфера S872
страты S868
стрелка A526
стример S876
стримерная камера S877
стримерный канал S878
стробоскоп S904
стробоскопический осциллограф S17
~ эффект S905
строение атома A639
стронций S911
структура C511, P168
~ алмаза D238
~ вюрцита W147
~ кристалла C937
~ металл - диэлектрик - полупроводник M377
~ металл - оксид - полупроводник M388
~ молекул M601
~ молекулы M601
~ нейтрона N158
~ типа перовскита P259
структурная амплитуда S921
~ вязкость S920
~ изомерия S917
~ кристаллография S913
~ функция S923
~ функция фазы P339

Т

ТЕМПЕРАТУРНЫЙ

УСТРОЙСТВО

Ф

электрон-позитронная пара E229
электрон проводимости C565
электрон-фононное взаимодействие E228
электрон-электронное взаимодействие E193
электрооптика E256
электрооптический дефлектор E254
~ затвор E252
~ коэффициент E250
~ кристалл E253
~ модулятор E255
~ эффект E251
электроотрицательность E192
электроположительность E259
электропроводность E80
электроразрядная камера E100
электроразрядный лазер E102
электроскоп E260
электрослабое взаимодействие E272
электростатика E270
электростатическая индукция E265
~ линза E267
~ фокусировка E262
электростатический генератор E263
~ измерительный прибор E266
~ квадруполь E269
~ потенциал E268
~ ускоритель V47
электростатическое изображение E264
~ поле E261
электрострикция E271
электрофизика E258
электрофорез E257
электрохимический потенциал E123
~ эквивалент E122
электрохимия E124
электроэнцефалография E131
электроэрозионное изнашивание E132
элемент C144, E275
элементарная длина E278
~ ячейка L132
элементарное возбуждение E277
элементарные частицы E280, F431
элементарный заряд E276
~ куб U77
эллипсоид инерции I168
~ проводимости C569
~ Френеля F395, R190
~ Якоби J2
эллипсометр E283

эллипсометрия E284
эллиптическая поляризация E285
эмиссионная линия E290
~ рентгеновская спектроскопия X22
~ спектроскопия E293
~ электроника E288
эмиссионный микроскоп E292
~ спектр E294
эмиссия E287
эмиттанс E297
эмиттер E299
эмиттерный переход E300
эмпирическая зависимость E301
~ модель E302
эмульгатор E304
эмульсионная камера E306
эмульсия E305
энантиомер E307
энантиоморфизм E308
энергетическая зона E311
~ светимость R12
~ щель E320
~ экспозиция R14
~ яркость R10
энергетические состояния E334
~ уровни E322
~ уровни молекулы M580
энергетический интервал E329
~ спектр E333
энергия E309, P842
~ активации A173
~ анизотропии A420
~ взаимодействия I271
~ возбуждения E457
~ Гельмгольца H136
~ Гиббса G159
~ диссоциации D476
~ домена D527
~ излучения R13
~ ионизации I423
~ кристаллической решётки L137
~ покоя R457
~ связи B192, B261
~ Ферми F55
~ фонона P365
~ электромагнитного поля E143
энтальпия E345, H79
энтропия E347
~ Вселенной E349
эолова арфа A233
ЭОП E224, I24
эпидиаскоп E360
эпитаксиальная изоляция E362
эпитаксиальный лазер E363
~ метод E364

~ слой E361
эпитаксия E365
эпицентр E359
ЭПР E227
эрбий E399
эрг E403
эргодическая гипотеза E404
эргодичность E405
эрмитов оператор H143
эрмитовость H145
эрмитовы матрицы H142
эрстед O28
эталон E414, S707
~ Фабри - Перо F1
~ частоты F389
эталонный источник S715
этвеш E355
этикетка L1
эфемерида E357
эфемеридное время E358
эфир E419
эфирный ветер E420
эффект E26
~ Ааронова - Бома A271
~ Азбеля - Канера A719
~ Баркгаузена B52
~ Барнетта B55, M141
~ Баушингера B84
~ Вавилова - Черенкова C258
~ Виллари V144
~ Ганна G300
~ Гантмахера G49
~ де-Хааза - ван Альфена D122
~ Дембера D144, P407
~ Джозефсона J15
~ Джоуля - Томсона J23
~ Доплера D546
~ Зеебека S124
~ Зеемана Z1
~ Керра K17
~ Кикоина - Носкова K22, P467
~ Комптона C532
~ Кондо K65
~ Коттона C298
~ Коттона - Мутона C788
~ Магнуса M200
~ Маджи - Риги - Ледюка M15
~ Мейснера M334
~ Мёссбауэра M645
~ Нернста N70
~ Нернста - Эттингсгаузена N71
~ Ноттингема N335
~ Оверхаузера O310
~ Овшинского O321
~ Оже A660
~ Пашена - Бака P154
~ Пельтье P194
~ Пеннинга P205
~ первого порядка F145

NOTES

Aus unserem Verlagsprogramm

W. Greiner u.a. **Theoretische Physik**

Bd. 1 : Mechanik I • 6. Auflage 1992, 458 Seiten, geb., DM 48,- • ISBN 3-8171-1267-X

Bd. 2 : Mechanik II • 5. Auflage 1989, 480 Seiten, geb., DM 58,- • ISBN 3-8171-1136-3

Bd. 2 A : Hydrodynamik • 4. Auflage 1991, 414 Seiten, geb., DM 68,- • ISBN 3-8171-1204-1

Bd. 3 : Klassische Elektrodynamik • 5. Auflage 1990, 586 Seiten, geb., DM 68,- • ISBN 3-8171-1184-3

Bd. 3 A : Spezielle Relativitätstheorie • 3. Auflage 1992, 354 Seiten, geb., DM 58,- • ISBN 3-8171-1205-X

Bd. 4 : Quantenmechanik Teil 1 : Einführung • 5. Auflage 1992, 531 Seiten, geb., DM 58,- • ISBN 3-8171-1206-8

Bd. 4 A : Quantentheorie - Spezielle Kapitel • 3. Auflage 1993, 449 Seiten, geb., DM 68,- • ISBN 3-8171-1073-1

Bd. 5 : Quantenmechanik Teil 2 : Symmetrien • 3. Auflage 1990, 569 Seiten, geb., DM 78,- • ISBN 3-8171-1142-8

Bd. 6 : Relativistische Quantenmechanik - Wellengleichungen • 2 Auflage 1987, 568 Seiten, geb., DM 78,- • ISBN 3-8171-1022-7

Bd. 7 : Quantenelektrodynamik • 2. Auflage 1994, 548 Seiten, geb., DM 98,- • ISBN 3-8171-1426-5

Bd. 7 A : Feldquantisierung • 1993, 528 Seiten, geb., DM 78,- • ISBN 3-87144-975-X

Bd. 8 : Eichtheorie der schwachen Wechselwirkung • 2. Auflage 1994, 492 Seiten, geb., DM 98,- • ISBN 3-8171-1427-3

Bd. 9 : Thermodynamik und statistische Mechanik • 2. Auflage 1993, 578 Seiten, geb., DM 68,- • ISBN 3-8171-1262-9

Bd. 10 : Quantenchromodynamik • 1989, 464 Seiten, geb., DM 68,- • ISBN 3-87144-710-2

Ermäßigter Satzpreis statt DM 992,- nur DM 892,- • ISBN 3-8171-1430-3

L.D. Landau / E.M. Lifschitz, **Lehrbuch der Theoretischen Physik**

Band 1 : Mechanik
13. Auflage 1990, 231 Seiten, 56 Abbildungen, Ln., DM 38,- • ISBN 3-8171-1326-9

Band 2 : Klassische Feldtheorie
12. Auflage 1992, 480 Seiten, 25 Abbildungen, Ln., DM 58,- • ISBN 3-8171-1327-7

Band 3 : Quantenmechanik
9. Auflage 1992, 644 Seiten, 57 Abbildungen, 11 Tabellen, Ln., DM 58,- • ISBN 3-8171-1328-5

Band 4 : Quantenelektrodynamik
7. Auflage 1991, 614 Seiten, 25 Abbildungen, Ln., DM 88,- • ISBN 3-8171-1329-3

Band 5 : Statistische Physik, Teil 1
8. Auflage 1991, 517 Seiten, 78 Abbildungen, 3 Tabellen, Ln., DM 58,- • ISBN 3-8171-1330-7

Band 6 : Hydrodynamik
5. Auflage 1991, 683 Seiten, 136 Abbildungen, Ln., DM 78,- • ISBN 3-8171-1331-5

Band 7 : Elastizitätstheorie
7. Auflage 1991, 223 Seiten, 32 Abbildungen, Ln., DM 38,- • ISBN 3-8171-1332-3

Band 8 : Elektrodynamik der Kontinua
5. Auflage 1991, 565 Seiten, 65 Abbildungen, Ln., DM 78,- • ISBN 3-8171-1333-1

Band 9 : Statistische Physik, Teil 2
4. Auflage 1992, 390 Seiten, 18 Abbildungen, Ln., DM 58,- • ISBN 3-8171-1334-X

Band 10 : Physikalische Kinetik
2. Auflage 1992, 480 Seiten, 35 Abbildungen, Ln., DM 68,- • ISBN 3-8171-1335-8

Ermäßigter Satzpreis statt DM 620,- nur DM 580,- • ISBN 3-8171-1336-6

- Irrtümer und Preisänderungen vorbehalten -

Aus unserem Verlagsprogramm

Wörterbuch der Mathematik / Dictionary of Mathematics

von G. Eisenreich, R. Sube
Englisch-Deutsch-Französisch-Russisch.
2. Auflage 1982, 2 Bände, 1458 Seiten, 34.000 Fachbegriffe, Kunstleder, DM 320,-
ISBN 3-87144-445-6

Wörterbuch der Mathematik

von G. Eisenreich, R. Sube
Englisch - Deutsch (Studentenausgabe)
2. Auflage 1994, 466 Seiten, 34. 000 Fachbegriffe, kart., DM 59,80
ISBN 3-87144-939-3

M. Abramowitz, I.A. Stegun
Pocketbook of Mathematical Functions

1984, 468 Seiten, kart., DM 48,-
ISBN 3-87144-818-4

I.S. Gradstein, I.M. Ryshik
Summen-, Produkt- und Integraltafeln / Tables of Series, Products and Integrals

Übersetzt von Ludwig Boll
Deutscher und englischer Text nach der 5., von J. Geronimus und M. Zeitlin
bearbeiteten, russischen Auflage 1981, 2 Bände, 1.181 Seiten, Ln., DM 88,-
ISBN 3-87144-350-6

Fachlexikon ABC Mathematik

Ein alphabetisches Nachschlagewerk.
1978, 624 Seiten, etwa 700 Abbildungen, 6.000 Stichwörter, Lexikon-Format,
Leinen mit Schutzumschlag, DM 58,-
ISBN 3-87144-336-0

Fachlexikon ABC Physik

Ein alphabetisches Nachschlagewerk in 2 Bänden
2., überarbeitete Auflage 1989, 1.046 Seiten, etwa 11.000 Stichwörter, 1.600 Abbildungen im
Text, 48 teils farbige Tafeln, graphische Darstellungen und Literaturanhang,
Leinen mit Schutzumschlag, DM 128,-
ISBN 3-8171-1047-2
Halblederausgabe mit Goldprägung DM 148,-
ISBN 3-8171-1227-0

- Irrtümer und Preisänderungen vorbehalten -

H. Stöcker
Taschenbuch der Physik
2., völlig neu überarbeitete Auflage 1994, 874 Seiten, zahlr. Abbildungen, DM 32,-
ISBN 3-8171-1358-7
Ein Nachschlagewerk für Ingenieure und Naturwissenschaftler, die im physikalisch-technischen Sektor tätig sind. Eine Formelsammlung für Studierende dieser Fachrichtungen, die den relevanten Prüfungsstoff leicht auffinden möchten.

H. Stöcker u.a.
Taschenbuch mathematischer Formeln und moderner Verfahren
2., überarbeitete Auflage 1993, 814 Seiten, DM 29,80, ISBN 3-8171-1256-4
Alle Standardgebiete der Ingenieurmathematik, von der elementaren Basis bis hin zu fortgeschrittenen Methoden, werden mit Formeln, Sätzen, Hinweisen und erklärenden Beispielen übersichtlich dargeboten.

I.N. Bronstein, K.A. Semendjajew, G. Musiol, H. Mühlig
Taschenbuch der Mathematik
2. überarbeitete und erweiterte Auflage 1995, 1046 Seiten, DM 48,-, ISBN 3-8171-2002-8
Der neue zeitgerechte und praxisnahe „Bronstein" enthält einen Querschnitt der Mathematik, der sowohl für den Studenten als auch für den Ingenieur der Praxis, den Naturwissenschaftler und den Mathematiker für die tägliche Arbeit erforderlich ist.

I.N. Bronstein, K.A. Semendjajew
Handbook of Mathematics
English edition based on the 19.-22. German edition 1985, mainwork and supplement in one volume, 973 pages, DM 75,-, ISBN 3-87144-644-0

Y. Brytschkow, O. Maritschew, A. Prudnikow
Tabellen unbestimmter Integrale
1991, 200 Seiten, DM 28,-, ISBN 3-8171-1230-0

R. Kories, H. Schmidt-Walter
Taschenbuch der Elektrotechnik
2., überarbeitete und erweiterte Auflage 1995
733 Seiten, Stichwortverzeichnis deutsch / englisch, DM 36,-, ISBN 3-8171-1412-5
Ein kompaktes Nachschlagewerk für den Berufspraktiker. Jedes Kapitel ist für sich eine selbständige Einheit und enthält alle wichtigen Begriffe, Formeln, Regeln und Sätze sowie zahlreiche Beispiele und Anwendungen.

H. Rinne
Taschenbuch der Statistik
1995, 496 Seiten, zahlreiche Abbildungen und Tabellen, DM 29,80, ISBN 3-8171-1421-4
Nach Vorbild des "Bronstein" wird hier ein Nachschlagewerk für die Wirtschafts- und Sozialwissenschaften vorgelegt.

H. Lutz
Taschenbuch der Regelungstechnik
1995, 667 Seiten, zahlreiche Abbildungen, Plastik, ca. DM 34,-, ISBN 3-8171-1390-0